Organisational
Behaviour

4 EDITION

To Jennifer, Rachael, Scott and Jessica for their love and support–BM

To Ron, Gail, Irethra, Amy, Christopher, Elizabeth and Jamie for their love and support thoughout the busy times–TWM

Organisational
Behaviour

4 EDITION | STEPHEN P ROBBINS | BRUCE MILLETT | TERRY WATERS-MARSH

PEARSON
Prentice
Hall

Copyright © Pearson Education Australia (a division of Pearson Australia Group Pty Ltd)
2004

Pearson Education Australia
Unit 4, Level 2
14 Aquatic Drive
Frenchs Forest NSW 2086

www.pearsoned.com.au

Senior Acquisitions Editor: Alison Green
Development Editor: Lydia Pearce
Project Editor: Rebecca Pomponio
Editorial Coordinator: Natalie Crouch
Copy Editor: Robyn Flemming
Proofreader: Robyn Flemming
Cover and internal design by DesignBite
Cover photograph from Getty Images

Typeset by Midland Typesetters, Maryborough, Vic.

Printed in China

2 3 4 5 08 07 06 05 04

National Library of Australia
Cataloguing-in-Publication Data

Robbins, Stephen P., 1943- .
  Organisational behaviour.

  Includes index.
  For undergraduate business students.
  ISBN 1 74103 012 9.

  1. Organizational behavior - Australia. 2. Leadership -
  Australia. I. Millett, Bruce. II. Waters-Marsh, Terry.
  III. Title.

  658

An imprint of Pearson Education Australia (a division of Pearson Australia Group Pty Ltd)

Overview

PART 1 – INTRODUCTION 1

Ch 1   *What is Organisational Behaviour?* 2

PART 2 – THE INDIVIDUAL 37

Ch 2   *Foundations of Individual Behaviour* 38
Ch 3   *Values, Attitudes and Job Satisfaction* 66
Ch 4   *Personality and Emotions at Work* 98
Ch 5   *Perception and Individual Decision Making* 130
Ch 6   *Motivation Concepts* 162
Ch 7   *Motivation: From Concept to Applications* 202
            Part 2 Integrative Case Study A 235
            Part 2 Integrative Case Study B 237

PART 3 – THE GROUP 239

Ch 8   *Foundations of Group Behaviour* 240
Ch 9   *Understanding and Building Teams* 278
Ch 10   *Communication* 306
Ch 11   *Leadership Concepts and Theories* 336
Ch 12   *Contemporary Issues in Leadership* 360
Ch 13   *Power and Politics* 392
Ch 14   *Conflict and Negotiation* 424
            Part 3 Integrative Case Study A 454
            Part 3 Integrative Case Study B 456
            Part 3 Integrative Case Study C 460

PART 4 – THE ORGANISATION 463

Ch 15   *Foundations of Organisational Structure* 464
Ch 16   *Organisational Culture* 496
Ch 17   *Human Resource Policies and Practices* 530
Ch 18   *Organisational Change and Stress Management* 566
            Part 4 Integrative Case Study A 605
            Part 4 Integrative Case Study B 607

Contents

Preface   xv

PART 1 – INTRODUCTION   1

1. What is Organisational Behaviour?   2
What managers do   4
  Management functions   4
  Management roles   5
  Management skills   7
  Effective versus successful managerial activities   8
  A review of the manager's job   9
Enter organisational behaviour   9
  Replacing intuition with systematic study   9
Contributing disciplines to the OB field   10

MYTH OR SCIENCE? PRECONCEIVED NOTIONS VERSUS
SUBSTANTIVE EVIDENCE   11

  Psychology   11
  Sociology   12
  Social psychology   13
  Anthropology   13
  Political science   13
There are few absolutes in OB   13

THE REAL DEAL: THE NEW PEOPLE AT VIRGIN BLUE   14

Challenges and opportunities for OB   14
  Responding to globalisation   15
  Managing workforce diversity   15
  Improving quality and productivity   16

OB CONTROVERSIES: CREATING SUSTAINABLE ORGANISATIONS   18

  Responding to the labour shortage   19
  Improving customer service   19
  Improving people skills   20
  Empowering people   20
  Coping with 'temporariness'   21
  Stimulating innovation and change   21
  Helping employees balance work/life conflicts   22
  Improving ethical behaviour   22
Coming attractions: Developing an OB model   23
  An overview   23
  The dependent variables   23
  The independent variables   26
  Towards a contingency OB model   27
Summary and implications for managers   29

Point/Counterpoint: Successful organisations put
  people first   29
For discussion   30
Exercise 1a: Workforce diversity   31
Exercise 1b: What do you know about human
  behaviour?   32
CASE STUDY 1: Great Plains Software: Pursuing a
people-first strategy   33
Web workout   34
Notes   34

PART 2 – THE INDIVIDUAL   37

2. Foundations of Individual Behaviour   38
Biographical characteristics   40
  Age   40
  Gender   41

OB CONTROVERSIES: DO OLDER WORKERS WANT TO WORK?   41

  Marital status   43
  Seniority   43
Ability   43
  Intellectual abilities   44
  Physical abilities   45
  The ability–job fit   46
Learning   46
  A definition of learning   46
  Theories of learning   47

MYTH OR SCIENCE? 'YOU CAN'T TEACH AN OLD DOG NEW
TRICKS!'   49

  Shaping: A managerial tool   50

THE REAL DEAL: THE HIGH-TECH STOCK BUBBLE AND
REINFORCEMENT SCHEDULES   51

  Some specific organisational applications   55
Summary and implications for managers   57
Point/Counterpoint: All human behaviour is
  learned   58
For discussion   59
Exercise: Positive reinforcement versus punishment   59
CASE STUDY 2: Bonne Bell factory employees' average age 70   60
Web workout   61
KSS program: Developing effective disciplining skills   61
Notes   61

3. Values, Attitudes and Job Satisfaction **66**
Values 68
  Importance of values 68
  Sources of value systems 68
  Types of values 69
  Values, loyalty and ethical behaviour 71
OB CONTROVERSIES: CORPORATE VALUE STATEMENTS FOR SALE 72
  Values across cultures 73
Attitudes 76
  Types of attitudes 77
  Attitudes and consistency 78
  Cognitive dissonance theory 78
  Measuring the A–B relationship 79
  An application: Attitude surveys 80
  Attitudes and workforce diversity 82
Job satisfaction 82
THE REAL DEAL: CHANGING ATTITUDES 83
  Measuring job satisfaction 83
  How satisfied are people in their jobs? 84
  The effect of job satisfaction on employee performance 84
MYTH OR SCIENCE? 'HAPPY EMPLOYEES ARE PRODUCTIVE EMPLOYEES' 85
  Job satisfaction and OCB 87
  Job satisfaction and customer satisfaction 87
OB CONTROVERSIES: 'JAPANESE AND SINGAPOREAN WORKERS ARE HIGHLY SATISFIED' 88
Summary and implications for managers 89
Point/Counterpoint: Managers can create satisfied employees 89
For discussion 90
Exercise: Challenges in negotiating with Chinese executives 91
CASE STUDY 3: Maintaining job satisfaction when the ownership changes 92
Web workout 93
KSS program: Changing attitudes 93
Notes 93

4. Personality and Emotions at Work **98**
Personality 100
  What is personality? 100
  Personality determinants 100
  Personality traits 102
OB CONTROVERSIES: IS THE 'CROCODILE HUNTER' TYPICAL OF AUSTRALIAN MANAGERS? 104
  Major personality attributes influencing OB 105
  Personality and national culture 108

MYTH OR SCIENCE? 'DEEP DOWN, PEOPLE ARE ALL ALIKE' 109
  Achieving personality fit 110
Emotions 112
  What are emotions? 112
  Felt versus displayed emotions 113
  Emotion dimensions 114
  Can people be emotion*less*? 116
  Gender and emotions 116
  External constraints on emotions 116
  OB applications 117
THE REAL DEAL: THE INCREASING POPULARITY OF ANGER-MANAGEMENT CLASSES 120
Summary and implications for managers 121
Point/Counterpoint: Traits are powerful predictors of behaviour 121
For discussion 122
Exercise 4a: What is a 'team personality'? 123
Exercise 4b: Managing emotions at work 123
CASE STUDY 4: Roustabouts need understanding, too! 124
Web workout 124
KSS program: Reading emotions 125
Notes 125

5. Perception and Individual Decision Making **130**
What is perception, and why is it important? 132
Factors influencing perception 132
Person perception: Making judgments about others 133
  Attribution theory 133
  Frequently used shortcuts in judging others 135
  Specific applications in organisations 137
The link between perception and individual decision making 139
How should decisions be made? 140
  The rational decision-making process 140
  Improving creativity in decision making 141
OB CONTROVERSIES: MARRIAGE MAY DIM CREATIVITY 142
How are decisions actually made in organisations? 143
  Bounded rationality 143
  Intuition 144
  Problem identification 145
THE REAL DEAL: FIREFIGHTERS USE INTUITION TO MAKE THE RIGHT CHOICES 146
  Alternative development 146
  Making choices 147
  Individual differences: Decision-making styles 148

Organisational constraints 149
Cultural differences 151
What about ethics in decision making? 151
Three ethical decision criteria 151

MYTH OR SCIENCE? 'ETHICAL PEOPLE DON'T DO UNETHICAL THINGS' 152

Ethics and national culture 153
Summary and implications for managers 154
Point/Counterpoint: When hiring employees, emphasise the positive 155
For discussion 156
Exercise 5a: Biases in decision making 156
Exercise 5b: Five ethical decisions: What would you do? 157

CASE STUDY 5: John Neill at Unipart 158

Web workout 158
KSS program: Creative problem-solving skills 159
Notes 159

6. Motivation Concepts **162**
Defining motivation 164
Early theories of motivation 164
Hierarchy of needs theory 164
Theory X and Theory Y 165
Two-factor theory 166

MYTH OR SCIENCE? 'PEOPLE ARE INHERENTLY LAZY' 166

Contemporary theories of motivation 169
ERG theory 170
McClelland's theory of needs 170
Cognitive evaluation theory 172
Goal-setting theory 173

THE REAL DEAL: GETTING THE FEEDBACK WRONG DEMOTIVATES—AND COSTS! 175

Requisite task attributes theory 176
The job characteristics model 176
Social information processing theory 179
Reinforcement theory 179
Flow and intrinsic motivation theory 180
Equity theory 182
Expectancy theory 184
Don't forget ability and opportunity 186
Integrating contemporary theories of motivation 186

OB CONTROVERSIES: RECEIVE A KITA AND STAY MOTIVATED! 187

Caveat emptor: Motivation theories are culture-bound 189
Summary and implications for managers 191
Point/Counterpoint: Money motivates! 191
For discussion 193

Exercise: What do people want from their jobs? 193
CASE STUDY 6: What drives employees at Microsoft? 194
Web workout 195
Notes 195

7. Motivation: From Concept to Applications **202**
Management by objectives 204
What is MBO? 204
Linking MBO and goal-setting theory 205
MBO in practice 205
Employee recognition programs 206
What are employee recognition programs? 206
Linking recognition programs and reinforcement theory 206
Employee recognition programs in practice 206

THE REAL DEAL: EMPLOYER BRANDING: GETTING THE RECOGNITION RIGHT 207

Employee involvement programs 207
What is employee involvement? 208
Examples of employee involvement programs 208
Linking employee involvement programs and motivation theories 211
Employee involvement programs in practice 212
Variable-pay programs 212
What are variable-pay programs? 213
Linking variable-pay programs and expectancy theory 214
Variable-pay programs in practice 214

THE REAL DEAL: PAY FOR PERFORMANCE AT SIEBEL SYSTEMS 215

Skill-based pay plans 216
What are skill-based pay plans? 216
Linking skill-based pay plans to motivation theories 217
Skill-based pay in practice 217
Flexible benefits 217

OB CONTROVERSIES: ARE CEOs PAID TOO MUCH? 218

What are flexible benefits? 219
Linking flexible benefits and expectancy theory 219
Flexible benefits in practice 219
Comparable worth 220
What is comparable worth? 220
Comparable worth and equity theory 220
Comparable worth in practice 221
Job redesign 221
Job rotation 222
Job enlargement 222
Job enrichment 223
Special issues in motivation 224
Motivating professionals 224
Motivating contingent workers 225

Motivating the diversified workforce 225
Motivating low-skilled service employees 226
Motivating people doing highly repetitive tasks 226
Summary and implications for managers 227
Point/Counterpoint: The power of share options as a motivator 227
For discussion 228
Exercise: Goal-setting task 229
CASE STUDY 7: Radical approach pays dividends 230
Web workout 230
KSS program: Goal-setting skills 231
Notes 231
Part 2 Integrative case study A: A new broom sweeps clean 235
Part 2 Integrative case study B: What makes people want to come to work on Mondays? 237

PART 3 – THE GROUP 239

8. Foundations of Group Behaviour 240
Types of groups 242
Models of group development 242
Five-stage group-development model 243
The punctuated-equilibrium model 244
Towards explaining work group behaviour 245
External conditions imposed on the group 245
Group member attributes 247
Group structure 248
Group processes 258
Group tasks 259
THE REAL DEAL: LEGO ISN'T ONLY FOR KIDS 260
Group decision making 260
Groups versus the individual 260
Groupthink and groupshift 262
MYTH OR SCIENCE? 'TWO HEADS ARE BETTER THAN ONE' 263
Group decision-making techniques 265
OB CONTROVERSIES: VIRTUAL TEAMS AND THE LIMITS OF E-MAIL 268
Summary and implications for managers 269
Point/Counterpoint: All jobs should be designed around groups 270
For discussion 271
Exercise 8a: Assessing occupational status 271
Exercise 8b: Rating your group experience 272
CASE STUDY 8: Not easy to change a group 273
Web workout 273
Notes 274

9. Understanding and Building Teams 278
Why have teams become so popular? 280
How is a team different from a group? 280
Types of teams 281
Problem-solving teams 281
Self-managed work teams 282
Cross-functional teams 282
Virtual teams 283
Beware! Teams aren't always the answer 284
OB CONTROVERSIES: WORKING FOR A CAUSE, OR JUST MEETING THE CHALLENGE? 284
Creating effective teams 285
Work design 285
Composition 286
Context 288
Process 289
THE REAL DEAL: BUILDING A HIGH-CALIBRE TEAM 290
Turning individuals into team players 291
The challenge 291
MYTH OR SCIENCE? ARE SENIOR MANAGEMENT TEAMS REALLY TEAMS? 292
Shaping team players 293
Contemporary issues in managing teams 294
Teams and quality management 294
Teams and workforce diversity 295
Reinvigorating mature teams 296
Summary and implications for managers 297
Point/Counterpoint: Sports teams are good models for workplace teams 297
For discussion 298
Exercise: Building effective work teams 299
CASE STUDY 9: The dynamics of work teams 300
Web workout 300
KSS program: Creating effective teams 301
Notes 301

10. Communication 306
Functions of communication 308
The communication process 309
Direction of communication 309
Downward 309
Upward 310
Lateral 310
Interpersonal communication 310
Oral communication 310
Written communication 311
Non-verbal communication 311

MYTH OR SCIENCE? 'IT'S NOT WHAT YOU *SAY*, IT'S WHAT
YOU *DO*'   313
Organisational communication   313
    Formal small-group networks   313
    The grapevine   314
    Computer-aided communication   315
Choice of communication channel   318
Barriers to effective communication   319
    Filtering   319
    Selective perception   320
    Information overload   320
    Emotions   320
    Language   320
THE REAL DEAL: COMMUNICATION STRATEGIES AT BOSCH   321
    Communication apprehension   321
Current issues in communication   322
    Communication barriers between women and men   322
    Silence as communication   323
    'Politically correct' communication   323
    Cross-cultural communication   324
OB CONTROVERSIES: COMMUNICATION IN THE COCKPIT   326
Summary and implications for managers   329
Point/Counterpoint: Open-book management
improves the bottom line   329
For discussion   331
Exercise 10a: The impact of attentive listening skills   331
Exercise 10b: An absence of non-verbal
communication   332
CASE STUDY 10: Do we have a communication problem here?   333
Web workout   333
KSS program: Active listening skills   334
Notes   334

11. Leadership Concepts and Theories   336
What is leadership?   338
Trait theories   338
Behavioural theories   339
    Ohio State studies   340
OB CONTROVERSIES: EXECUTIVE LEADERS, THEIR PAY
AND THEIR PERFORMANCE   341
    University of Michigan studies   341
    The managerial grid   342
    Scandinavian studies   342
    Summary of behavioural theories   343
Contingency theories   343
    Fiedler model   344
    Hersey and Blanchard's situational theory   346
MYTH OR SCIENCE? 'IT'S EXPERIENCE THAT COUNTS!'   347

    Leader–member exchange theory   348
    Path–goal theory   349
    Leader-participation model   350
THE REAL DEAL: MAKING LEADERS OUT OF LAWYERS AND
ACCOUNTANTS   350
Summary and implications for managers   352
Point/Counterpoint: Leadership development is a
waste of money!   352
For discussion   354
Exercise 11a: The leader's in-group and out-group   354
Exercise 11b: Do leaders really matter?   354
CASE STUDY 11: Can a leader's means justify the ends?   355
Web workout   356
KSS program: Choosing the right leadership style   356
Notes   356

12. Contemporary Issues in Leadership   360
Trust: The foundation of leadership   362
    What is trust?   362
    Trust and leadership   363
    Three types of trust   364
Leaders as shapers of meaning   365
THE REAL DEAL: VARIOUS IMPACTS OF TRUST IN THE
WORKPLACE   366
    Framing issues   366
    Charismatic leadership   367
    Transformational leadership   369
OB CONTROVERSIES: THE DECLINE OF THE CHARISMATIC
LEADER   370
    Visionary leadership   371
Emotional intelligence and leadership
effectiveness   372
MYTH OR SCIENCE? 'MEN MAKE BETTER LEADERS THAN WOMEN'   373
Contemporary leadership roles   374
    Providing team leadership   374
    Mentoring   375
    Self-leadership   376
Moral leadership   377
On-line leadership: Some speculative thoughts   378
Challenges to the leadership construct   379
    Leadership as an attribution   380
    Substitutes and neutralisers to leadership   380
Finding and creating effective leaders   381
    Selection   381
    Training   382
Summary and implications for managers   383
Point/Counterpoint: Good leadership is
culturally-bound   383

For discussion 384
Exercise 12a: Practising to be charismatic 384
Exercise 12b: Affirmation of trust 385
CASE STUDY 12: When East comes to lead the West 386
Web workout 387
KSS program: Developing trust 388
Notes 388

13. Power and Politics 392
A definition of power 394
Contrasting leadership and power 394
Bases of power 394
   Formal power 394
   Personal power 395
Dependency: The key to power 396
   The general dependency postulate 396
   What creates dependency? 396
Power tactics 398
Power in groups: Coalitions 399
THE REAL DEAL: KYLIE'S INFLUENCE AT ERGON ENERGY 400
Sexual harassment: Unequal power in the
   workplace 401
Politics: Power in action 402
   Definition 402
   The reality of politics 403
OB CONTROVERSIES: EVEN JAQUES NASSER HAD A BOSS 404
   Factors contributing to political behaviour 405
MYTH OR SCIENCE? 'IT'S NOT *WHAT* YOU KNOW, IT'S *WHO*
YOU KNOW' 406
   How do people respond to organisational politics? 408
   Impression management 410
   The ethics of behaving politically 412
Summary and implications for managers 414
Point/Counterpoint: Creating 'special deals' for
   results 414
For discussion 415
Exercise 13a: Understanding power dynamics 416
Exercise 13b: Power orientation test 417
CASE STUDY 13: Damned if you do; damned if you don't 418
Web workout 419
KSS program: Building your power base 419
Notes 420

14. Conflict and Negotiation 424
A definition of conflict 426
Transitions in conflict thought 426
   The traditional view 427
   The human relations view 427

   The interactionist view 427
Functional versus dysfunctional conflict 427
OB CONTROVERSIES: AVOIDING THE CHRISTMAS PARTY BLUES 428
The conflict process 428
   Stage I: Potential opposition or incompatibility 428
MYTH OR SCIENCE? 'THE SOURCE OF MOST CONFLICTS IS
LACK OF COMMUNICATION' 431
   Stage II: Cognition and personalisation 431
   Stage III: Intentions 432
   Stage IV: Behaviour 433
   Stage V: Outcomes 434
THE REAL DEAL: CAN YOU SUFFER FROM AN ABSENCE
OF CONFLICT? 437
Negotiation 438
   Bargaining strategies 439
   The negotiation process 441
   Issues in negotiation 442
Summary and implications for managers 446
Point/Counterpoint: Conflict benefits organisations 447
For discussion 448
Exercise: A negotiation role play 448
CASE STUDY 14: Working at ThinkLink 450
Web workout 450
KSS program: Negotiating 451
Notes 451
Part 3 Integrative case study A: The merger of
   Synergis and Abacus 454
Part 3 Integrative case study B: Developing
   autonomous work teams at the Town of Kwinana 456
Part 3 Integrative case study C: Leadership and
   inclusivity at the Papua New Guinea, Port Moresby
   Port Authority 460

PART 4 – THE ORGANISATION 463

**15. Foundations of Organisational
   Structure** 464
What is organisational structure? 466
   Work specialisation 466
   Departmentalisation 468
   Chain of command 469
   Span of control 470
   Centralisation and decentralisation 471
MYTH OR SCIENCE? 'BUREAUCRACY IS DEAD' 472
   Formalisation 473
Common organisational designs 473
   The simple structure 473
   The bureaucracy 474
   The matrix structure 475

New design options 476
   The team structure 476
   The virtual organisation 477
   The boundaryless organisation 479

OB CONTROVERSIES: DOES STRUCTURE ENSURE ACCOUNTABILITY? 479

Why do structures differ? 481
   Strategy 481
   Organisation size 482
   Technology 483
   Environment 483

THE REAL DEAL: DEVELOPING A GLOBAL STRUCTURE 485

Organisational designs and employee
   behaviour 485
Summary and implications for managers 487
**Point/Counterpoint: Technology is reshaping
   organisations** 488
For discussion 489
**Exercise: What sort of structure do you like to
   work in?** 489

CASE STUDY 15: Working by the rules 491

Web workout 491
KSS program: Delegating authority/empowerment 492
Notes 492

16. Organisational Culture 496

Institutionalisation: A forerunner of culture 498
What is organisational culture? 498
   A definition 499
   Culture is a descriptive term 499
   Do organisations have uniform cultures? 499
   Strong versus weak cultures 501
   Culture versus formalisation 501
   Organisational culture versus national culture 501
Impact of major religions on culture 502
What do cultures do? 503
   Culture's functions 503
   Culture as a liability 504

MYTH OR SCIENCE? 'SUCCESS BREEDS SUCCESS' 505

Creating and sustaining culture 506
   How a culture begins 506
   Keeping a culture alive 506
   Summary: How cultures form 510

**OB CONTROVERSIES: ARE THE CULTURES OF GLOBAL
COMPANIES BECOMING THE SAME?** 511

How employees learn culture 511
   Stories 511
   Rituals 512

Material symbols 513
Language 513
Creating an ethical organisational culture 514

**THE REAL DEAL: ENRON AND THE CREATION OF AN
UNETHICAL CULTURE** 515

Creating a customer-responsive culture 515
   Key variables shaping customer-responsive cultures 516
   Managerial action 516
Spirituality and organisational culture 518
   What is workplace spirituality? 518
   Why spirituality now? 518
   Characteristics of a spiritual organisation 518
   Criticisms of spirituality 520
Summary and implications for managers 521
**Point/Counterpoint: Organisational cultures can't
   be changed** 521
For discussion 522
Exercise: Rate your classroom culture 523

CASE STUDY 16: Socially responsible—and profitable! 524

Web workout 525
KSS program: Reading an organisation's culture 525
Notes 525

17. Human Resource Policies and Practices 530

Human resources management 532
Selection practices 532
   Job analysis 533
   Selection devices 533

MYTH OR SCIENCE? 'IT'S FIRST IMPRESSIONS THAT COUNT' 534

Training and development programs 536

**OB CONTROVERSIES: IS IT UNETHICAL TO 'SHAPE' YOUR
RESUME?** 537

   Types of training 537
   Training methods 539
   Individualise formal training to fit the
      employee's learning style 540
Career development 540
Performance evaluation 541

THE REAL DEAL: FORCED RANKINGS GAIN IN POPULARITY 542

   Purposes of performance evaluation 542
   Performance evaluation and motivation 543
   What do we evaluate? 544
   Who should do the evaluating? 545
   Methods of performance evaluation 547
   Suggestions for improving performance
      evaluations 548
   Providing performance feedback 550
   What about team performance evaluations? 551

Employee relations interface 551
International human resource practices:
  Selected issues 553
    Selection 553
    Performance evaluation 553
Managing diversity in organisations 554
  Family-friendly workplaces 554
  Diversity training 557
Summary and implications for managers 558
Point/Counterpoint: It's time to abolish
  performance evaluations! 559
For discussion 560
Exercise: Evaluating performance and providing
  feedback 560

CASE STUDY 17: Is this any way to run a business? 561

Web workout 562
KSS program: Interviewing skills 562
Notes 562

18. Organisational Change and Stress
    Management 566
Forces for change 568
Managing planned change 569
Resistance to change 570
  Individual resistance 571
  Organisational resistance 572
  Overcoming resistance to change 573
  The politics of change 574
Approaches to managing organisational change 575
  Lewin's three-step model 575
  Action research 576

OB CONTROVERSIES: TREATING PEOPLE WITH RESPECT
AT QANTAS 577

  Organisational development 578
Contemporary change issues for today's
  managers 582
  Stimulating innovation 582
  Creating a learning organisation 583

THE REAL DEAL: SINGAPORE POLICE STRIVE TO BE A LEARNING
ORGANISATION 585
  Knowledge management 586
  Managing change: It is culture-bound 587
Work stress and its management 588
  What is stress? 589
  Understanding stress and its consequences 590
  Potential sources of stress 590
  Individual differences 592
  Consequences of stress 593
  Managing stress 595
Summary and implications for managers 597
Point/Counterpoint: Managing change is an
  episodic activity 597
For discussion 598
Exercise: Power and the changing environment 598

CASE STUDY 18: The Kingaroy Art & Card Company 600

Web workout 600
KSS program: Managing resistance to change 601
Notes 601
Part 4 Integrative case study A: Accenture practises
  what it preaches 605
Part 4 Integrative case study B: Instrumentation
  Pty Ltd 607

Appendix A Historical evolution of
  organisational behaviour 609

Appendix B Research in organisational
  behaviour 620

Appendix C Scoring Keys for Exercises 629

Skill-building Modules 631

Glossary 653

Index 661

Preface

Organisational behaviour (OB) is concerned with understanding the behaviour of people at work. Managers worldwide fully appreciate the significance of OB and how, as a field of study, it assists them in dealing with issues of job performance and job satisfaction. Since almost all of us are interested in human behaviour and expect to work at least part of our adult lives, OB has the potential to be a very interesting and relevant subject.

This book grew out of the need for a comprehensive introductory textbook about organisational behaviour in Australia and the Asia-Pacific region. Students, lecturers and tutors of OB told us they wanted a textbook using local examples from Australasian workplaces, yet still covering all the central aspects of OB theory which have developed over the past 100 years. The first, second and third editions of the text were released in 1994, 1998 and 2001 respectively. The text has become one of the top local management texts and we hope that the publication of the fourth edition of *Organisational Behaviour* will constitute another milestone in the teaching of OB in the Asia-Pacific region.

Stephen Robbins first published an OB text in America in 1979, and since that time, the Robbins book has been read by more than 900,000 students and used by students at more than a thousand colleges and universities worldwide. If there's such a thing as a 'global textbook,' the current edition and adaptations have probably earned that label. It's the number-one selling organizational behavior (OB) textbook in Australia, Hong Kong, Singapore, Thailand, the Philippines, Taiwan, South Korea, Malaysia, Indonesia, the United States, Canada, Mexico, Central America, South America, India, China, Sweden, Finland, Denmark, and Greece. There are also translations available in German, Chinese, Japanese, Korean, Thai, Spanish, Portuguese, and Indonesian; and this adaptation provides students with country-specific examples and content in the Asia-Pacific including Australia, New Zealand, Fiji, New Guinea, Singapore and Malaysia.

THE FOUNDATIONAL FEATURES OF THE BOOK

Although the field of OB has changed in the last 25 years and, with it, the contents of this textbook, a number of features have been retained from past editions. It is these features, in fact, that we think largely explain this book's success. These include the conversational writing style, the cutting-edge content, the extensive use of current examples, the three-level integrative model, the point/counterpoint dialogues, the end-of-chapter pedagogy, and the comprehensive supplement package. Let's elaborate on each of these points.

Writing style. This book is most often singled out for the writing style. Reviewers and users regularly tell us that it's 'conversational,' 'interesting,' 'student-friendly,' and 'very clear and understandable'. We believe the fourth edition maintains that tradition.

Cutting-edge content. This book was the first OB textbook to have a chapter on power and politics, a chapter on conflict, a chapter on organizational culture, and two chapters on motivation. The book continues to provide cutting-edge content that is often missing in other OB books.

Examples. Our teaching experience tells us that students may not remember a concept, but they'll remember an example. Moreover, a good example goes a long way in helping students to better understand a concept. So, as with the previous editions, you'll find this revision packed full of recent real-world examples drawn from a variety of organizations—business and not-for-profit, large and small, and local and international.

The three-level model of analysis. Since its first edition, this book has presented OB at three levels of analysis. It begins with individual behavior and then moves to group behavior. Finally, it adds the organization system to capture the full complexity of organizational behavior. Students seem to find this approach logical and straightforward.

'Point/Counterpoint' dialogues. These focused arguments allow students to see two sides of an OB controversy and to stimulate their critical thinking. Lecturers and tutors say they find these dialogues to be excellent devices for stimulating class discussion and getting students to think critically about OB issues in the workplace.

Pedagogy. This edition continues the tradition of providing the most complete assortment of in-text pedagogy available in any OB book. This includes review and critical-thinking questions, team exercises, ethical dilemma exercises, and case applications. As well, each chapter has a structure that makes it easy for students to follow. Chapter Outlines provide a list of contents for each chapter. Learning Objectives are provided at the outset of each chapter and linked to the text throughout in marginal annotations. There is also a running glossary of key terms and definitions in the margin adjacent to the point at which the term is first discussed at length.

Supplement package. This text provides the most comprehensive teaching and learning support package available. It is described in detail in the latter part of this Preface.

FEATURES ADDED IN THE PREVIOUS EDITION

A number of features that were added in the previous edition continue to receive positive comments from students, lecturers and tutors alike. These, too, have been retained. They include the integration of globalization, diversity, and ethics, and the 'Myth or Science?' boxes.

Integration of globalization, diversity, and ethics. The topics of globalization and cross-cultural differences, workforce diversity, and ethics are discussed throughout this book. Rather than presented in stand-alone chapters, they have been woven into the context of relevant issues. We have found that this integrative approach makes these issues more fully part of OB and reinforces their importance.

'Myth or Science?' boxes. This feature presents a commonly accepted 'fact' about human behavior, followed by confirming or disproving research evidence. Some examples include 'You Can't Teach an Old Dog New Tricks'; 'Happy Workers are Productive Workers'; and 'It's Not What You Know, It's Who You Know.' These boxes provide repeated evidence that common sense can often lead you astray in the attempt to understand human behavior, and that behavioral research offers a means for testing the validity of common-sense notions. These boxes are meant to help you to see how the field of OB, built on a large body of research evidence, can provide valuable insights toward understanding and explaining human behavior at work.

WHAT'S NEW IN THE 4TH EDITION?

Users of the previous edition will find that the most obvious changes in this revision are the inclusion of an additional chapter on leadership and the broadly expanded coverage of skills.

The additional chapter on leadership reflects the increasing awareness of the important role this concept plays in achieving effective organizational performance and the rapidly expanding body of leadership-related research findings.

By going from one chapter to two, we've been able to bring in new leadership-related material such as framing issues, mentoring, self-leadership, on-line leadership, and the GLOBE studies on cross-cultural leadership.

Previous editions had a box theme on 'Applying OB.' The expressed desire by students, lecturers and tutors for increased skill coverage led us to create the Skill-Building Modules in this edition. These modules have been integrated into the KSS Program. KSS refers to the three elements in building effective OB skills: Knowing the concepts, Self-awareness, and Skill applications. KSS proposes that the skill modules are best used when combined with text content and the Self-Assessment CD-ROM.

Specifically, students can build and improve their interpersonal and behavioral skills by reading a chapter, completing the relevant self-assessment(s), and then reading and practicing the appropriate skill module(s) in the back of the book.

A more careful review of this new edition will also reveal that Chapter 10 on communication has been reorganized and rewritten. This was undertaken to improve the flow of a widely encompassing and eclectic topic of study.

This book continues to lead the field in coverage of contemporary OB issues. New to this edition is material on Customer service, Work/life balance, Multiple intelligences, Evolutionary psychology and hardwired behavior, GLOBE measures of national cultural attributes, Motivation as flow, Thomas's intrinsic motivation model, Deviant workplace behavior, Silence as communication, Employee response to organizational politics, Creating ethical organizational cultures, Spirituality in organizations, Knowledge management, and Appreciative inquiry.

Of course, the entire book's research base has been revised and updated for this edition.

We are particularly enthusiastic about the new material on customer service and satisfaction. We all know the critical role that the customer plays in the success or failure of any organization—whether it's profit or nonprofit. Authors of OB textbooks, however, have tended to leave everything that has to do with the customer to our friends in marketing. That has been a mistake of omission. There is an increasing body of research demonstrating that customer satisfaction is linked to organizational performance and that employee attitudes and behavior are positively related to customer satisfaction. This edition shows why OB should be concerned with the customer, the role of displayed emotions in friendly and helpful service, how employee attitudes and behavior shape an organization's 'customer culture,' and what management can do to make an organization more customer-oriented.

SUPPLEMENTS

We have developed some supplementary material that is designed to complement the textbook.

Instructor's Resource Manual on CD

Instructor's Manual
Each chapter of the manual includes expanded outlines of the topics in each chapter, teaching tips to accompany the boxed text and exercises, and answers to all question material.
PowerPoint Slides
Over 250 full-colour sides have been developed to highlight the key concepts of the text.

Computerised test bank

The computerised test bank allows lecturers to create customised tests based on over 2,500 questions including multiple choice, true/false and essay questions. The program is easy to install and can be used for on-line testing. The computerised test bank has been prepared by Elliott Wood of Curtin University

Australian video

This video is a new supplement and has been specially commissioned and developed to support this textbook. The video comprises six segments and covers the topics of **Teams, Communication, Leadership, Conflict, Organisational Culture** and **Human Resources**. Each segment features five different managers from a variety of organisation types. The managers provide a practical point of view of these important OB topics. A theoretical perspective is provided by Emma Bowyer of UTS who introduces the segments and acted as content consultant.

Self-Assessment Library CD-Rom

This bonus CD is packaged with the book. The self-assessment library is a self-contained, interactive library of 49 behavioural questionnaires that help students discover things about themselves, their attitudes and their personal strengths and weaknesses. Suggested exercises to undertake are listed in the KSS segment at the end of every chapter.

Student Learning Guide and Workbook

The *Student Learning Guide and Workbook* is a saleable supplement which provides a variety of material to help students master the topics in the textbook. Each chapter of the study guide includes: chapter overview, fill-in the blanks, multiple choice questions, true/false questions, models and concepts questions, and additional questions on Point/Counterpoint activities. Answers for the multiple choice and true/false questions are provided at the end of the text. The Student study guide has been prepared by Jeff Wrathall of Monash University,

Companion website

A comprehensive website has been specifically developed for the new Australian edition.

The new Companion website provides students and academics with the following features:

- **Chapter specific current events** in organisational behaviour. Each current event story is written by an OB academic and addresses a topical and timely event. The current event is supported by review exercises, suggested group or tutorial activities and links to Internet resources.
- **Interactive study guide quizzes** that include on-line self-assessment and offer multiple choice questions and true/false questions for every chapter. The quiz answers are graded by our server and provide students with immediate feedback, including additional help and page references linked to the text.
- **Internet exercises** that introduce students to the Internet as a research tool to answer a variety of questions and apply what they have learned in each chapter.
- A powerful new **point-and-click syllabus** creation tool that can be used by lecturers for each section and course they teach. Students can view each course syllabus providing quick access to course information and assignments.
- **Teaching supplements** and suggested answers available to academics via a password.

The Companion website content is provided by Leslie Sonnenschein, of Griffith University. See this content-rich website at www.prenhall.com/robbins_au

ACKNOWLEDGMENTS

Textbooks are a team project and many people have contributed to our team. A number of colleagues have been kind enough to make suggestions for improvement, and review all or parts of this text. This is a better book because of insights and suggestions provided by:

Mr Bruce Acutt, Central Queensland University
Dr Yvonne Brunetto, Griffith University
Ms Melanie Bryant, Monash University
Ms Georgina Caillard, RMIT University
Dr Simon Down, University of Newcastle, UK
Professor Kevin Fagg, Central Queensland University
Dr Robert Lundy, University of New South Wales
Ms Bernadette Lynch, University of Southern Queensland
Ms Teresa Marchant, consultant
Dr Susan Mayson, Monash University
Mr Ken Parry, Griffith University
Dr Kylie Redfern, University of Technology, Sydney
Mr Gordon Ray, retired
Associate Professor Retha Wiesner, University of Southern Queensland
Ms Karen Windeknecht, Central Queensland University

We also acknowledge the contribution of Ron Cacioppe as an author on the previous editions of this text.

Regardless of how good the manuscript is, it's only a tall pile of paper until our friends at Pearson Education Australia swing into action. Pearson's crack team of editors, production personnel, designers, marketing specialists, artists and sales representatives turn that pile of paper into a bound textbook and see to it that it gets into faculty and students' hands. Our special thanks on this go to Alison Green, Lydia Pearce, Rebecca Pomponio, Pauline Stewart and Debbie Gray for their support and encouragement. We would also like to thank Robyn Flemming for her excellent work with the manuscript.

Finally, we want to acknowledge with gratitude the hundreds of academics teaching and researching in the OB discipline in Australia and New Zealand. These people demonstrate amazing commitment and dedication, often in the face of severe resource cutbacks and constraints, to teaching and research in OB in their respective countries. They are not afraid to take risks, to experiment and to share their successes and failures with others in the discipline. They are the true pioneers in the quest to define, refine and communicate the unique aspects of Australian and New Zealand OB for the benefit of our two societies.

One last point. We are always looking for suggestions on how to improve later editions of this book. If you have some ideas and would like to share them with us, drop us a line care of: Bruce Millett, Faculty of Business, University of Southern Queensland, Darling Heights Post Office, Toowoomba, Queensland, 4350, Australia (or e-mail to millett@usq.edu.au or Terry Waters-Marsh at T.Waters-Marsh@cqu.edu.au). We look forward to hearing from you.

Bruce Millett
Toowoomba, Queensland

Terry Waters-Marsh
Rockhampton, Queensland

Visual preface

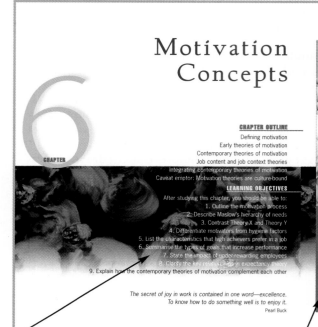

Chapter Learning Objectives To make your learning more efficient, each chapter opens with a list of learning objectives that describe what you should be able to do after studying the chapter. These objectives are designed to focus your attention on the major issues within each chapter.

Chapter Opening Story Each chapter opens with a case example about an individual or an organisation, which relates to the particular content in that chapter. The featured individuals, or organisations, come from a broad and varied spectrum and each example is selected specifically to help you link OB concepts to OB practice.

OB Controversies These boxes look at current issues in OB and put forward the differing points of view that surround the issue.

'Real Deal' boxes contain real world mini-cases which make OB issues relevant and enable you to apply the theory.

The **Learning Objective** is repeated in the margin where the relevant text appears in the chapter.

Key Terms These terms are highlighted in bold print when they first appear and are defined at the time in the adjoining margin. These same terms are also grouped together at the end of the book in the Glossary.

'Myth or science?' boxes present a commonly accepted 'fact' about human behaviour, followed by confirming or disproving research evidence. They help you see how the field of OB, built on a large body of research evidence can provide valuable insights towards understanding and explaining human behaviour at work.

[Page 146 excerpt — The Real Deal box]

146 | Part 2 The Individual

The Real Deal

Firefighters use intuition to make the right choice

Do fire commanders use the rational model to make life-and-death decisions? No. They rely on their intuition, built on years of experience. And intuition begins with recognition. The following illustrates how that recognition process works.

Recently a fire fighting commander and his crew encountered a fire at the back of a timber-framed house. The commander led his hose team into the building. Standing in the living room, they blasted water on to the smoke and flames that appeared to be consuming the kitchen. But the fire roared back and continued to burn. The men doused the fire again, and the flames briefly subsided. But then they flared up again with an even greater intensity. As the firefighters retreated and regrouped, the commander was gripped by an uneasy feeling. He quickly ordered everyone to leave. Just as the crew reached the street, the whole living-room floor caved in. Had the men stayed in the house, they would have plunged into a blazing basement.

Why did the commander give the order to leave? Because the fire's behaviour didn't match his expectations. Much of the fire was burning underneath the living-room floor, so it was unaffected by the firefighters' attack. Also, the rising heat made the room extremely hot—too hot for such a seemingly small fire. Another clue that this wasn't just a small kitchen fire was that the sounds it emitted were strangely quiet. Hot fires are loud. The commander was intuitively sensing that the floor was muffling the roar of the flames that were raging below.

Veteran firefighters have accumulated a storehouse of experiences and they subconsciously categorise fires according to how they should react to them. They look for cues or patterns in situations that direct them to take one action over another.

Experienced people whose jobs require quick decisions—firefighters, intensive-care nurses, jet-fighter pilots, SWAT team members—see a different world than novices in those same jobs. And what they see tells them what they should do. Ultimately, intuition is all about perception. The formal rules of decision making are almost incidental.

Source: Based on B. Breen, 'What's Your Intuition?', *Fast Company*, September 2000, pp. 290–300.

What occupational stereotypes do you hold about fire fighters? How do you think they were formed? What role do you think intuition plays in a fire fighter's mind when faced with difficult blazes to control?

ALTERNATIVE DEVELOPMENT

Because decision makers rarely seek an optimal solution, but rather a satisficing one, we should expect to find a minimal use of creativity in the search for alternatives. And that expectation is generally on target.

Efforts will be made to try to keep the search process simple. It will tend to be confined to the neighbourhood of the current alternative. More complex search behaviour, which includes the

---

[Page 147 excerpt — Chapter 5]

Chapter 5 Perception and Individual Decision Making | 147

Experience with a situation allows experts, such as master chess players, to use learned information, even subconsciously, to make quick decisions that we sometimes attribute to intuition.

development of creative alternatives, will be resorted to only when a simple search fails to uncover a satisfactory alternative.

Rather than formulating new and unique problem definitions and alternatives, with frequent journeys into unfamiliar territory, the evidence indicates that decision making is incremental rather than comprehensive. This means decision makers avoid the difficult task of considering all the important factors, weighing their relative merits and drawbacks, and calculating the value for each alternative. Instead, they make successive limited comparisons. This simplifies decision choices by comparing only the alternatives that differ in relatively small degrees from the choice currently in effect.

The picture that emerges is one of a decision maker who takes small steps towards his or her objective. Acknowledging the non-comprehensive nature of choice selection, decision makers make successive comparisons because decisions are never made forever and written in stone; rather, decisions are made and remade endlessly in small comparisons between narrow choices.

MAKING CHOICES

In order to avoid information overload, decision makers rely on **heuristics**, or judgmental short-cuts, in decision making. There are two common categories of heuristics—availability and representativeness. Each creates biases in judgment. Another bias that decision makers often have is the tendency to escalate commitment to a failing course of action.

Availability heuristic

Many more people suffer from fear of flying than fear of driving in a car. The reason is that many people think flying is more dangerous. It isn't, of course. With apologies ahead of time for this graphic example, if flying on a commercial airline was as dangerous as driving, the equivalent of two 747s filled to capacity would have to crash every week, killing all aboard, to match the risk of being killed in a car accident. But the media give a lot more attention to air accidents, so we tend to overstate the risk of flying and understate the risk of driving.

This illustrates an example of the **availability heuristic**, which is the tendency for people to base their judgments on information that is readily available to them. Events that evoke emotions, that are particularly vivid, or that have occurred more recently tend to be more available in our memory. As a result, we tend to be prone to overestimating unlikely events such as an airplane crash. The availability heuristic can also explain why managers, when doing annual performance appraisals, tend to give more weight to recent behaviours of an employee than those behaviours of six or nine months ago.

Representative heuristic

Literally thousands of Australian boys dream of playing Rugby League in the NRL. In reality, they have a far better chance of becoming medical doctors than they do of playing in the NRL, but these kids are suffering from a **representative heuristic**. They tend to assess the likelihood of an occurrence by trying to match it with a pre-existing category. They hear about a boy from their

LEARNING OBJECTIVE 8
Define heuristics and explain how they bias decisions

heuristics
Judgmental shortcuts in decision making.

availability heuristic
The tendency for people to base their judgments on information that is readily available to them.

representative heuristic
Assessing the likelihood of an occurrence by drawing analogies seeing identical situations in which they don't exist.

[Page 148 excerpt]

148 | Part 2 The Individual

Theory Y
The assumption that employees like work, are creative, seek responsibility and can exercise self-direction.

2. Since employees dislike work, they must be coerced, controlled or threatened with punishment to achieve goals.
3. Employees will avoid responsibilities and seek formal direction whenever possible.
4. Most workers place security above all other factors associated with work and will display little ambition.

In contrast to these negative views about the nature of human beings, McGregor listed the four positive assumptions that he called Theory Y:
1. Employees can view work as being as natural as rest or play.
2. People will exercise self-direction and self-control if they are committed to the objectives.
3. The average person can learn to accept, even seek, responsibility.
4. The ability to make innovative decisions is widely dispersed throughout the population and is not necessarily the sole province of those in management positions.

What are the motivational implications if you accept McGregor's analysis? The answer is best expressed in the framework presented by Maslow. Theory X assumes that lower-order needs dominate individuals. Theory Y assumes that higher-order needs dominate individuals. McGregor himself held to the belief that Theory Y assumptions were more valid than Theory X. Therefore, he proposed such ideas as participative decision-making, responsible and challenging jobs, and good group relations as approaches that would maximise an employee's job motivation.

Unfortunately, there is no evidence to confirm that either set of assumptions is valid or that accepting Theory Y assumptions and altering one's actions accordingly will lead to more motivated workers. As will become evident later in this chapter, either Theory X or Theory Y assumptions may be appropriate in a particular situation.

LEARNING OBJECTIVE 4
Differentiate motivators from hygiene factors

TWO-FACTOR THEORY

two-factor theory
Intrinsic factors are related to job satisfaction, while extrinsic factors are associated with dissatisfaction.

The **two-factor theory** (sometimes also called *motivation-hygiene theory*) was proposed by the psychologist Frederick Herzberg. In the belief that an individual's relation to work is basic and that one's attitude towards work can very well determine success or failure, Herzberg investigated the question, 'What do people want from their jobs?' He asked people to describe, in detail,

Myth or Science?

'People are inherently lazy'

This statement is false on two levels. *All* people are not inherently lazy; and 'laziness' is more a function of the situation than an inherent individual characteristic.

If this statement is meant to imply that *all* people are inherently lazy, the evidence strongly indicates the contrary. Many people today suffer from the opposite affliction—they are overly busy, overworked and suffer from overexertion. Whether externally motivated or internally driven, a good portion of the labour force is anything *but* lazy.

Managers frequently draw the conclusion that people are lazy from watching some of their employees, who may be lazy at work. But these same employees are often quite industrious in one or more activities *off* the job. People's need structures differ. As Figure 6.2 illustrates, evidence indicates that work needs differ by gender, age, income level, job type, and level in the organisation.

Unfortunately for employers, work often ranks low in its ability to satisfy individual needs. So, the same employee who shirks responsibility on the job may work obsessively on reconditioning an antique car, maintaining an award-winning garden, perfecting bowling skills, or selling Amway products on weekends. Very few people are perpetually lazy. They merely differ in terms of the activities they most enjoy doing. And because work isn't important to everyone, they may *appear* to be lazy.

Summary and Implications for Managers Each chapter concludes with a concise summary of the key themes in the chapter.

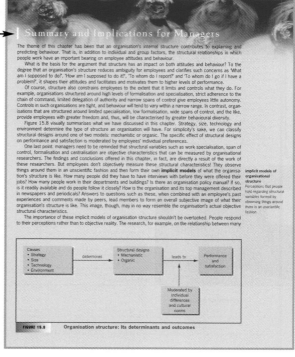

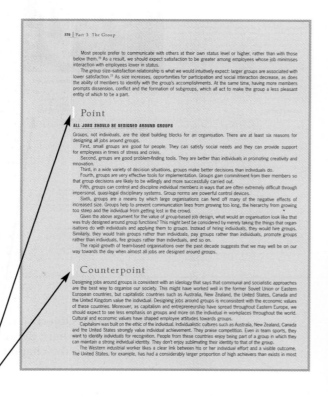

Point/Counterpoint dialogues These focused arguments allow you to see two sides of an OB controversy. These dialogues help to stimulate class discussion and encourage you to think critically about OB issues in the workplace.

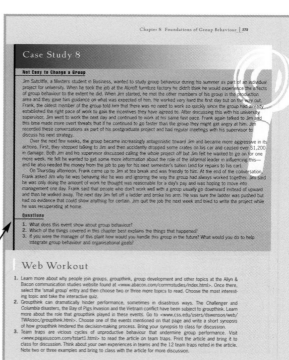

A **Case Study** at the end of every chapter gives you the opportunity to apply the knowledge gained in the chapter to hypothetical situations that could be encountered in organisations.

Web Workout This feature is designed to help you use the Internet in a critical way to aid your studies of OB.

KSS These features address the three elements of building effective OB skills— Knowing the concepts, Self awareness and Skill applications. Specifically you can build and improve your interpersonal and behavioural skills by reading a chapter, completing the relevant self-assessment(s), and then reading and practising the appropriate skills module(s) in the back of the book.

Integrative Cases appearing at the end of most parts.

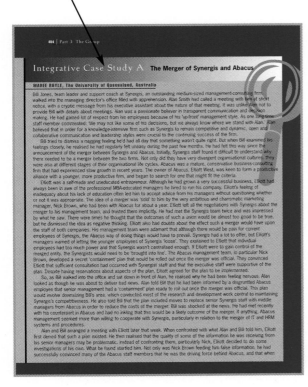

For Discussion questions promote interaction, self-study and critical thinking.

Exercises that give you an opportunity to apply the knowledge you've gained from that chapter. About half of the exercises are of the self-assessment variety. The other exercises are group-oriented and allow you to experience with some of your peers a number of OB concepts firsthand.

Chapter 12 Contemporary Issues in Leadership | 387

Web Workout

1. Who's hot and who's not? Find five companies whose CEOs have left (for reasons other than normal retirement) in the past 12 months. Assess their company's profit performance against the average for their industry group. A web search using terms such as CEO + turnover or resignation will yield a number of results. To find the share price performance, you can then use any of a number of on-line services such as <www.cnnfn.com>. What did this exercise tell you? Be prepared to discuss in class.
2. Do you trust your employer? How would your organisation know if you trusted it or not? Go to <http://management.about.com/library/weekly/aa022900.htm> to learn more about how an organisation can determine if its employees trust it. Be sure to link on and read the Seattle Times companion article. Write a few paragraphs addressing why you do or don't trust your organisation using the guidelines in the articles as a springboard for ideas. Bring your work to class for further discussion.
3. Trust no one? For some employees it is their new motto. Find out why at <http://careers.usatoday.com/service/usa/national/content/news/onthejob/2002-02-05-employee-trust>. Write a short reaction paper as to why you agree or don't agree with the article or parts of the article). Can you relate any of what is discussed to your own working career? If so, include that in your paper as well. What will be your strategy when selecting your next employer? Bring your paper to class for further discussion.
4. Write a short paper on the connection between charismatic leadership and impression management. Performing a search using the key words charismatic + leadership + impression + management will get you off to a good start. Try using the terms in different combinations to get additional links. Be prepared to discuss your findings in class.
5. Select one of the links at <www.css.edu/users/dswenson/web/Leadlink.htm>, which is a huge resource of on-line leadership resources. Once you have selected a topic, prepare a five-minute presentation to give to the class on that topic. Develop a handout, or print off selections from the website to distribute so that every member of the class will have their own 'leadership resource library' once the presentations are completed. Try to keep your handout to two pages or less.
6. A very royal vision! Visit <www.findarticles.com/cf_trvgnt/m0VOU/1997_March_17/47217411/p1/article.jhtml>. Read what CEO and chairman Richard Fain of Royal Caribbean Cruise Lines has to say about his company's vision. Analyse the case presented using the criteria for visionary leadership as discussed in the text. Bring your work to class for further discussion.

KSS Program

KNOW THE CONCEPTS   SELF-AWARENESS   SKILLS APPLICATIONS

Developing trust
After you have read this chapter, take Self-Assessment #29 ('Do Others See Me as Trusting?') on your enclosed CD-Rom and complete the skill-building module entitled 'Developing Trust' on page 641.

NOTES
1. This opening vignette is based on J. Steinhauer, 'In Crisis, Giuliani's Popularity Overflows City', New York Times, 20 September 2001, p. A1; C. Jones, 'Giuliani Exits as National Icon', USA Today, 28 December 2001, p. 3A; D. Barry, 'A Man Who Became More Than a Mayor', New York Times, 31 December 2001, p. A1; and E. Pooley, Mayor of the World', Time, 31 December 2001.
2. Based on E. D. Boon and J. G. Holmes, 'The Dynamics of Interpersonal Trust: Resolving Uncertainty in the Face of Risk', in R. A. Hinde and J. Groebel (eds), Cooperation and Prosocial Behaviour (Cambridge, UK: Cambridge University Press, 1991), p. 194; D. J. McAllister, 'Affect and Cognition-Based Trust as Foundations for Interpersonal Cooperation in Organizations', Academy of Management Journal, February 1995, p. 25; and D. M. Rousseau, S. B. Sitkie, R. S. Burt and C. Camerer, 'Not So Different After All: A Cross-Discipline View of Trust', Academy of Management Review, July 1998, pp. 393–404.
3. J. B. Rotter, 'Interpersonal Trust, Trustworthiness, and Gullibility', American Psychologist, January 1980, pp. 1–7.
4. J. D. Lewis and A. Weigert, 'Trust as a Social Reality', Social Forces, June 1985, p. 970.
5. J. K. Rempel, J. G. Holmes and M. P. Zanna, 'Trust in Close Relationships', Journal of Personality and Social Psychology, July 1985, p. 96.

Chapter 8 Foundations of Group Behaviour | 271

of the world. America breeds achievers, and achievers seek personal responsibility. They would be frustrated in job situations in which their contribution is commingled and homogenised with the contributions of others.

Western workers want to be hired, evaluated and rewarded on their individual achievements. They believe in an authority and status hierarchy. They accept a system in which there are bosses and subordinates. They aren't likely to accept a group's decision on such issues as their job assignments and wage increases. It's harder yet to imagine that they would be comfortable in a system in which the sole basis for their promotion or termination would be the performance of their group.

Source: Based on H. J. Leavitt, 'Suppose We Took Groups Seriously', in E. L. Cass and F. G. Zimmer (eds), Man and Work in Society (New York: Van Nostrand Reinhold, 1975), pp. 67–77.

For Discussion

1. Compare and contrast command, task, interest and friendship groups.
2. What might motivate you to join a group?
3. Describe the five-stage group-development model.
4. How could you use the punctuated-equilibrium model to better understand group behaviour?
5. What is the relationship between a work group and the organisation of which it is a part?
6. What are the implications of Zimbardo's prison experiment for OB?
7. Explain the implications from the Asch experiments.
8. How are status and norms related?
9. 'High cohesiveness in a group leads to higher group productivity.' Do you agree or disagree? Explain.
10. When do groups make better decisions than individuals?
11. How can a group's demography help you to predict turnover?
12. What is groupthink? What is its effect on decision-making quality?

Exercises

Exercise 8a
ASSESSING OCCUPATIONAL STATUS
Rank the following 20 occupations from most prestigious (1) to least prestigious (20):

Accountant
Air traffic controller
Barrister
Coach of a football team
Coach of a women's basketball team
Electrical engineer
Environmental scientist
Firefighter
Investment banker
Manager of an automobile production facility
Mayor of a large city
Minister of religion
Pharmacist
Plumber
Real estate salesperson
Sports agent
Surgeon
Teacher in a public school (primary/elementary)
Army colonel
Used car salesperson

Introduction
Part 1

CHAPTER 1   WHAT IS ORGANISATIONAL BEHAVIOUR?

What is Organisational Behaviour?

CHAPTER OUTLINE

What managers do
Enter organisational behaviour
Contributing disciplines to the OB field
There are few absolutes in OB
Challenges and opportunities for OB
Coming attractions: Developing an OB model

LEARNING OBJECTIVES

After studying this chapter, you should be able to:

1. Describe what managers do
2. Define organisational behaviour (OB)
3. Explain the value of the systematic study of OB
4. Identify the contributions made by the main behavioural science disciplines to OB
5. Explain the need for a contingency approach to the study of OB
6. List the main challenges and opportunities for managers to use OB concepts
7. Identify the three levels of analysis in this book's OB model
8. Describe why managers require a knowledge of OB

We must dream great dreams to create a future worth living in.

D. Dunphy

Michelle Smith appreciates the significance of sound people skills in the workplace.

Meet Michelle Smith. She has a business degree in human resources management with a minor in psychology from Queensland University of Technology in Brisbane and has spent the past 14 years working for the Queensland Water Board. For the past three-and-a-half of those years, Michelle has been a supervisor/team chief in an organisational change unit, overseeing between 13 and 18 people.

'My prior experience was as an HR manager, so I have a business background,' says Michelle. 'The people on my team are professionals—analysts, consultants, counsellors, and the like. My job, as a supervisor, is more "people-centred" than administrative. I have to understand the different needs of my people and the client-sections of the department. Some, for example, readily accept change. Some resist it when they can't see the benefits. Some people don't want to make decisions. Others enjoy jumping in and participating. I've had to learn to use different approaches to motivate these varied types of people. I've had to enhance my skills in communication. I've learned that communication is key in dealing with my employees and with the politics inside our organisation.'

Michelle Smith has learned what most managers learn very quickly: a large part of the success in any management job is developing good interpersonal, or people, skills. Managers need to be technically competent in their area of expertise. But technical knowledge isn't enough. Successful managers and entrepreneurs also need interpersonal skills in order to work with others.[1]

Where do managers acquire this knowledge? For many years most universities taught the practical aspects of management, through courses in law, accounting, finance, economics, statistical methods, operations management and the like. These courses did not teach managers the "how-to" of people management—the knowledge of human behaviour, people skills and interpersonal skills. Over the last decade or so most business schools changed their approaches to management education and now courses in human behaviour and interpersonal, or people, skills are the general rule.

Although practising managers have long understood the importance of interpersonal skills to managerial effectiveness, business schools were slower to get the message. Until the late 1980s, business school curricula focused almost singularly on the technical aspects of management, emphasising courses in economics, accounting, finance and quantitative techniques. Course work in human behaviour and people skills received minimal attention relative to the technical aspects of management. Over the past decade and a half, however, business faculty have come to realise the importance that an understanding of human behaviour plays in determining a manager's effectiveness, and required courses on people skills have been widely added to the curriculum.

Recognition of the importance of developing managers' interpersonal skills is closely tied to the need for organisations to get and keep high-performing employees. This becomes particularly crucial in a tight labour market.[2] Companies with reputations as a good place to work—such as Virgin Blue Airlines, Singapore Airlines, Bunnings, Fuji Xerox and Officeworks—have a big advantage. A national study of the workforce in the United States found that wages and salary benefits aren't the reason people like their jobs or stay with an employer. Far more important is the quality of the employees' jobs and the supportiveness of their work environments.[3] In Australia, a Morgan and Banks survey found that Australian workers rate their general experience of job satisfaction ahead of remuneration levels.[4] Like their American counterparts, they too look for a supportive and satisfying work environment. A recent survey of 148 large businesses in Asia and Australasia claims that lack of recognition and opportunities for development are the main reasons employees leave their jobs.[5] So, having managers with good interpersonal skills is likely to make the workplace more pleasant, which, in turn, makes it easier to hire and keep qualified people.

We have come to understand that technical skills are necessary, but insufficient, for succeeding in management. In today's increasingly competitive and demanding workplace, managers can't succeed on their technical skills alone. They also have to have good people skills. This book has been written to help both managers and potential managers develop those people skills.

What Managers Do

Let's begin by briefly defining the terms *manager* and the place where managers work—the *organisation*. Then let's look at the manager's job; specifically, what do managers do?

managers
Individuals who achieve goals through other people.

Managers get things done through other people. They make decisions, allocate resources and direct the activities of others to attain goals. Managers do their work in an **organisation**. This is a consciously coordinated social unit, composed of two or more people, that functions on a relatively continuous basis to achieve a common goal or set of goals. On the basis of this definition, manufacturing and service firms are organisations, and so are schools, hospitals, churches, military units, retail stores, police departments, and local, state and Commonwealth government agencies. The people who oversee the activities of others and who are responsible for attaining goals in these organisations are managers (although they are sometimes called *administrators*, especially in not-for-profit organisations).

organisation
A consciously coordinated social unit, composed of two or more people, that functions on a relatively continuous basis to achieve a common goal or set of goals.

MANAGEMENT FUNCTIONS

In the early part of the 20th century, a French industrialist by the name of Henri Fayol wrote that all managers perform five management functions: they plan, organise, command, coordinate and control.[6] Today, we have condensed these to four: planning, organising, leading and controlling.

- **Planning**: define goals, establish strategies, and develop plans to implement the strategies and achieve the goals.
- **Organising**: determine the tasks, who does them, how they are done, and responsibilities for decisions and follow-up.

- **Leading**: motivate employees, direct the activities of others, select the most effective communication channels, or resolve conflicts among group members.
- **Controlling**: monitor and compare performance with goals, and address performance shortfalls.

Since organisations exist to achieve goals, someone has to define those goals and the means by which they can be achieved. Management is that someone. The **planning** function encompasses defining an organisation's goals, establishing an overall strategy for achieving those goals, and developing a comprehensive hierarchy of plans to integrate and coordinate activities.

Managers are also responsible for designing an organisation's structure. We call this function **organising**. It includes the determination of what tasks are to be done, who is to do them, how the tasks are to be grouped, who reports to whom, and where decisions are to be made. Every organisation contains people, and it is management's job to direct and coordinate those people. This is the **leading** function. When managers motivate employees, direct the activities of others, select the most effective communication channels or resolve conflicts among members, they are engaging in leading.

The final function managers perform is **controlling**. To ensure that things are going as they should, management must monitor the organisation's performance. Actual performance must be compared with the previously set goals. If there are any significant deviations, it's management's job to get the organisation back on track. This monitoring, comparing and potential correcting is what is meant by the controlling function.

So, using the functional approach, the answer to the question, 'What do managers do?' is that they plan, organise, lead and control.

MANAGEMENT ROLES

In the late 1960s, a graduate student at Massachusetts Institute of Technology (MIT) in the United States, Henry Mintzberg, undertook a careful study of five executives to determine what these managers did on their jobs. On the basis of his observations of these managers, Mintzberg concluded that managers perform ten different, highly interrelated roles, or sets of behaviours attributable to their jobs.[7] As shown in Table 1.1, these ten roles can be grouped as being primarily concerned with interpersonal relationships, the transfer of information and decision making.

Interpersonal roles

All managers are required to perform duties that are ceremonial and symbolic in nature. When the chancellor of a university hands out diplomas at graduation or a factory supervisor gives a group of high school students a tour of the factory, he or she is acting in a *figurehead* role. All managers also have a *leadership* role. This role includes hiring, training, motivating and disciplining employees. The third role within the interpersonal grouping is the *liaison* role. Mintzberg described this activity as contacting outsiders who provide the manager with information. These may be individuals or groups inside or outside the organisation. The sales manager who obtains information from the company's quality-control manager has an internal liaison relationship. When that sales manager has contacts with other sales executives through a marketing trade association, he or she has an outside liaison relationship.

Informational roles

All managers, to some degree, collect information from organisations and institutions outside their own. Typically, they get information by reading newspapers and magazines and talking with other people to learn of changes in the public's tastes, what competitors may be planning, and the like. Mintzberg called this the *monitor* role. Managers also act as a conduit to transmit information to organisational members. This is the *disseminator* role. In addition, managers perform a *spokesperson* role when they represent the organisation to outsiders.

planning
A process that includes defining goals, establishing strategy, and developing plans to coordinate activities.

organising
Determining what tasks are to be done, who is to do them, how the tasks are to be grouped, who reports to whom, and where decisions are to be made.

leading
A function that includes motivating employees, directing others, selecting the most effective communication channels and resolving conflicts.

controlling
Monitoring activities to ensure they are being accomplished as planned and correcting any significant deviations.

TABLE 1.1	Mintzberg's managerial roles	
Role	**Description**	**Examples**
Interpersonal		
Figurehead	Symbolic head; required to perform a number of routine duties of a legal or social nature	Ceremonies, status requests, solicitations
Leader	Responsible for the motivation and direction of employees	Virtually all managerial activities involving employees
Liaison	Maintains a network of outside contacts who provide favours and information	Acknowledgment of mail, external board work
Informational		
Monitor	Receives wide variety of information; serves as nerve centre of internal and external information of the organisation	Handling all mail and contacts categorised as concerned primarily with receiving information
Disseminator	Transmits information received from outsiders or from other employees to members of the organisation	Forwarding mail into organisation for informational purposes; verbal contacts involving information flow to employees, such as review sessions
Spokesperson	Transmits information to outsiders on organisation's plans, policies, actions and results; serves as expert on organisation's industry	Board meetings; handling contacts involving transmission of information to outsiders
Decisional		
Entrepreneur	Searches organisation and its environment for opportunities and initiates projects to bring about change	Strategy and review sessions involving initiation or design of improvement projects
Disturbance handler	Responsible for corrective action when organisation faces important, unexpected disturbances	Strategy and review sessions involving disturbances and crises
Resource allocator	Making or approving significant organisational decisions	Scheduling; requests for authorisation; budgeting; the programming of employees' work
Negotiator	Responsible for representing the organisation at major negotiations	Contract negotiation

Source: Adapted from H. Mintzberg, *The Nature of Managerial Work.* Copyright © Reprinted by permission of Pearson Education, Inc., Upper Saddle River NJ.

Bunnings Warehouses are a network of large stores selling building supplies and materials across Australia. They pioneered the 'shed' concept in Australia with stores carrying over 40 000 products. In order to make the network successful, corporate and store managers alike must play Mintzberg's roles effectively.

Decisional roles

Finally, Mintzberg identified four roles that revolve around the making of choices. In the *entrepreneur* role, managers initiate and oversee new projects that will improve their organisation's performance. As *disturbance handlers*, managers take corrective action in response to unforeseen problems. As *resource allocators*, managers are responsible for allocating human, physical and monetary resources. Last, managers perform a *negotiator* role, in which they discuss issues and bargain with other units to gain advantages for their own unit.

MANAGEMENT SKILLS

Looking at what managers do from a different perspective is to look at the skills or competencies they need to achieve their goals. Robert Katz has identified three essential management skills: technical, human and conceptual.[8]

Technical skills

Technical skills encompass the ability to apply specialised knowledge or expertise. When you think of the skills held by professionals such as civil engineers or oral surgeons, you typically focus on their technical skills. Through extensive formal education, they have learned the special knowledge and practices of their field. Of course, professionals don't have a monopoly on technical skills, and not all technical skills have to be learned in TAFE colleges or formal training programs. All jobs require some specialised expertise, and many people develop their technical skills on the job.

technical skills
The ability to apply specialised knowledge or expertise.

human skills
The ability to work with, understand and motivate other people, both individually and in groups.

Human skills

The ability to work with, understand and motivate other people, both individually and in groups, describes **human skills**. Many people are technically proficient but interpersonally incompetent. They might be poor listeners, unable to understand the needs of others, or have difficulty managing conflicts. Since managers get things done through other people, they must have good human skills to communicate, motivate and delegate.

In our definition of organisations we include hospitals, churches, colleges and schools, though their 'managers' are more likely to go by the title 'administrator'. They perform all the management functions, and the concepts of organisational behaviour apply to them, their staffs, and their colleagues.

Conceptual skills

Managers must have the mental ability to analyse and diagnose complex situations. These tasks require **conceptual skills**. Decision making, for example, requires managers to recognise problems, identify alternatives that can correct them, evaluate those alternatives and select the best one. Managers can be technically and interpersonally competent, yet still fail because of an inability to rationally process and interpret information.

EFFECTIVE VERSUS SUCCESSFUL MANAGERIAL ACTIVITIES

Fred Luthans and his associates looked at the issue of what managers do from a somewhat different perspective.[9] They asked the question: 'Do managers who climb the promotions ladder most quickly in an organisation do the same activities and with the same emphasis as managers who do the best job?' You would tend to think that the managers who were the most effective in their jobs would also be the ones who were promoted fastest. But that's not what appears to happen.

Luthans and his associates studied more than 450 managers. What they found was that these managers all engaged in four managerial activities:

1. *Traditional management:* decision making, planning and controlling.
2. *Communication:* exchanging routine information and processing paperwork.
3. *Human resource management:* motivating, disciplining, managing conflict, staffing and training.
4. *Networking:* socialising, politicking and interacting with outsiders.

The 'average' manager in the study spent 32 per cent of their time in traditional management activities, 29 per cent communicating, 20 per cent in human resource management activities and 19 per cent networking. However, the amount of time and effort that different managers spent on those four activities varied a great deal. Specifically, as shown in Figure 1.1 managers who were *successful* (defined in terms of the speed of promotion within their organisation) had a very different emphasis than managers who were *effective* (defined in terms of the quantity and quality of their performance and the satisfaction and commitment of their employees). Among successful managers, networking made the largest relative contribution to success, and human resource management activities made the smallest relative contribution. Among effective managers, communication made the largest relative contribution and networking the smallest. A more recent study of Australian managers further confirms the importance of networking in relation to success.[10] Australian managers who actively networked received more promotions and enjoyed other rewards associated with career success.

This research adds important insights to our knowledge of what managers do. On average, managers spend approximately 20–30 per cent of their time on each of the four activities: tradi-

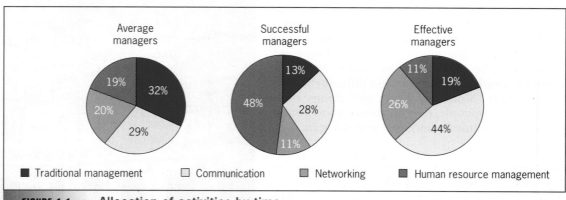

FIGURE 1.1   **Allocation of activities by time**

Source: Based on F. Luthans, R. M. Hodgetts and S. A. Rosenkrantz, *Real Managers* (Cambridge, MA: Ballinger, 1988).

tional management, communication, human resource management and networking. However, successful managers don't give the same emphasis to each of those activities as do effective managers. In fact, their emphases are almost the opposite. This finding challenges the historical assumption that promotions are based on performance, vividly illustrating the importance that social and political skills play in getting ahead in organisations.

A REVIEW OF THE MANAGER'S JOB

One common thread runs through the functions, roles, skills and activities approaches to management: each recognises the paramount importance of managing people. Regardless of whether it is called 'the leading function', 'interpersonal roles', 'human skills' or 'human resource management, communication and networking activities', it's clear that managers need to develop their people skills if they are going to be effective and successful.

Enter Organisational Behaviour

We have made the case for the importance of people skills. But neither this book, nor the discipline on which it is based, is called People Skills. The term that is widely used to describe the discipline is *organisational behaviour*.

Organisational behaviour (often abbreviated as **OB**) is a field of study that investigates the impact that individuals, groups and structure have on behaviour within organisations for the purpose of applying such knowledge towards improving an organisation's effectiveness. That's a lot of words, so let's break it down.

Organisational behaviour is a field of study. This statement means that it is a distinct area of expertise with a common body of knowledge. What does it study? It studies three determinants of behaviour in organisations: individuals, groups and structure. In addition, OB applies the knowledge gained about individuals, groups and the effect of structure on behaviour in order to make organisations work more effectively.

To sum up our definition, OB is concerned with the study of what people do in an organisation and how that behaviour affects the performance of the organisation. And because OB is concerned specifically with employment-related situations, you shouldn't be surprised to find that it emphasises behaviour as related to concerns such as jobs, work, absenteeism, employment turnover, productivity, human performance and management.

There is increasing agreement as to the components or topics that constitute the subject area of OB. Although there is still considerable debate as to the relative importance of each, there appears to be general agreement that OB includes the core topics of motivation, leader behaviour and power, interpersonal communication, group structure and processes, learning, attitude development and perception, emotions, change processes, conflict, work design and work stress, which are topics that will be explored in later chapters throughout this text.[11]

REPLACING INTUITION WITH SYSTEMATIC STUDY

Each of us is a student of behaviour. Since almost our birth, we have watched the actions of others and have attempted to interpret what we see. Whether or not you have explicitly thought about it before, you have been 'reading' people almost all your life. You watch what others do and try to explain to yourself why they have engaged in their behaviour. In addition, you have attempted to predict what they might do under different sets of conditions. Unfortunately, your casual or commonsense approach to reading others can often lead to erroneous predictions. However, you can improve your predictive ability by replacing your intuitive opinions with a more systematic approach.

The systematic approach used in this book will uncover important facts and relationships and will provide a base from which more-accurate predictions of behaviour can be made.

LEARNING OBJECTIVE

2

Define organisational behaviour (OB)

organisational behaviour (OB)
A field of study that investigates the impact that individuals, groups and structure have on behaviour within organisations, for the purpose of applying such knowledge towards improving an organisation's effectiveness.

LEARNING OBJECTIVE

3

Explain the value of the systematic study of OB

Underlying this systematic approach is the belief that behaviour isn't random. It stems from and is directed towards some end that the individual believes, rightly or wrongly, is in his or her best interest.

Behaviour generally is predictable if we know how the person perceived the situation and what is important to him or her. While people's behaviour may not appear to be rational to an outsider, there is reason to believe it usually is intended to be rational and they see it as rational. An observer often sees behaviour as non-rational because the observer doesn't have access to the same information or doesn't perceive the environment in the same way.[12]

Certainly there are differences between individuals. Placed in similar situations, all people don't act exactly alike. Move into another culture and the differences become even more obvious. However, there are certain fundamental consistencies underlying the behaviour of all individuals that can be identified and then modified to reflect individual differences.

These fundamental consistencies are very important. Why? Because they allow predictability. When you get into your car, you make some definite and usually highly accurate predictions about how other people will behave. In Australia, for example, you would predict that other drivers will stop at stop signs and red lights, drive on the left side of the road, pass on your right, and not cross the solid double line on bends and hilly roads. Notice that your predictions about the behaviour of people behind the wheels of their cars are almost always correct. Obviously, the rules of driving make predictions about driving behaviour fairly easy.

What may be less obvious is that there are rules (written and unwritten) in almost every setting. Therefore, it can be argued that it's possible to predict behaviour (undoubtedly, not always with 100 per cent accuracy) in supermarkets, classrooms, doctors' offices, elevators, and in most structured situations. For example, do you turn around and face the doors when you get into an elevator? Almost everyone does. But did you ever read that you're supposed to do this? Probably not! Just as we make predictions about motorists (for which there are definite rules of the road), we can make predictions about the behaviour of people in elevators (where there are few written rules). In a class of 60 students, if you wanted to ask a question of the lecturer, I predict that you would raise your hand. Why don't you clap, stand up, raise your leg, cough, or yell 'Hey, over here!'? The reason is that you have learned at a young age that raising your hand is appropriate behaviour at school. These examples support a major contention in this textbook: behaviour is generally predictable, and the *systematic study* of behaviour is a means to making reasonably accurate predictions.

systematic study
Looking at relationships, attempting to attribute causes and effects, and drawing conclusions based on scientific evidence.

When we use the phrase **systematic study**, we mean looking at relationships, attempting to attribute causes and effects, and basing our conclusions on scientific evidence—that is, on data gathered under controlled conditions and measured and interpreted in a reasonably rigorous manner. (See Appendix B for a basic review of research methods used in studies of organisational behaviour.)

intuition
A feeling not necessarily supported by research.

Systematic study replaces **intuition**, or those 'gut feelings' about 'why I do what I do' and 'what makes others tick'. Of course, a systematic approach doesn't mean that the things you have come to believe in an unsystematic way are necessarily incorrect. Some of the conclusions we make in this text, based on reasonably substantive research findings, will only support what you always knew was true. But you will also be exposed to research evidence that runs counter to what you may have thought was common sense One of the objectives of this text is to encourage you to move away from your intuitive views of behaviour towards a systematic analysis, in the belief that such analysis will improve your accuracy in explaining and predicting behaviour.

LEARNING OBJECTIVE

4

Identify the contributions made by the main behavioural science disciplines to OB

Contributing Disciplines to the OB Field

Organisational behaviour is an applied behavioural science that is built on contributions from a number of behavioural disciplines. The predominant areas are psychology, sociology, social psychology, anthropology and political science. As we shall learn, psychology's contributions

Myth *or* Science?

Preconceived notions versus substantive evidence

Assume you signed up to take an introductory course in calculus. On the first day of class your lecturer asks you to take out a piece of paper and answer the following question: 'Why is the sign of the second derivative negative when the first derivative is set equal to zero, if the function is concave from below?' It's unlikely you would be able to answer that question. Your reply to that lecturer would probably be something like, 'How am *I* supposed to know? That's why I'm taking this course!'

Now, change the scenario. You are in an introductory course in organisational behaviour. On the first day of class your lecturer asks you to write an answer to the following question: 'Why are employees not as motivated at work today as they were 30 years ago?'

You might feel a bit of reluctance, but I would guess you would begin writing. You would have no problem coming up with an explanation to this question of motivation.

The previous scenarios were meant to demonstrate one of the challenges of teaching a course in OB. You enter an OB course with a lot of *preconceived notions* that you accept as *facts*. You think you already know a lot about human behaviour.[13] Typically, that isn't true in calculus, physics, chemistry or even accounting. So, in contrast to many other disciples, OB not only introduces you to a comprehensive set of concepts and theories, it has to deal with a lot of commonly accepted 'facts' about human behaviour and organisations that you have acquired over the years. Some examples might include 'You can't teach an old dog new tricks'; 'happy workers are productive workers' and 'two heads are better than one'. But these 'facts' aren't necessarily true. So, one of the objectives of a course in organisational behaviour is to replace popularly held *notions*, often accepted without question, with science-based conclusions.

As you will see in this book, the field of OB is built on decades of research. This research provides a body of substantive evidence that is able to replace preconceived notions. Throughout this book, we have included boxes entitled 'Myth or Science?'. They call your attention to some of the more popular of these notions or myths about organisational behaviour. We use the boxes to show how OB research has disproved them or, in some cases, shown them to be true. We hope that you will find these boxes interesting. But more importantly, they should help to remind you that the study of human behaviour at work is a science and that you need to be vigilant about 'seat of the pants' explanations of work-related behaviours.

---

have been mainly at the individual or micro level of analysis, while the other four disciplines have contributed to our understanding of macro concepts such as group processes and organisation. Figure 1.2 is an overview of the major contributions to the study of organisational behaviour.

PSYCHOLOGY

Psychology is the science that seeks to measure, explain and sometimes change the behaviour of humans and other animals. Psychologists concern themselves with studying and attempting to understand individual behaviour. Those who have contributed and continue to add to the knowledge of OB are learning theorists, personality theorists, clinical psychologists and, most important, industrial and organisational psychologists.

Early industrial/organisational psychologists concerned themselves with the problems of fatigue, boredom and other factors relevant to working conditions that could impede efficient work performance. More recently, their contributions have been expanded to include learning, perception, personality, emotions, training, leadership effectiveness, needs and motivational forces, job satisfaction, decision-making processes, performance appraisals, attitude measurement, employee selection techniques, work design and job stress.

psychology
The science that seeks to measure, explain and sometimes change the behaviour of humans and other animals.

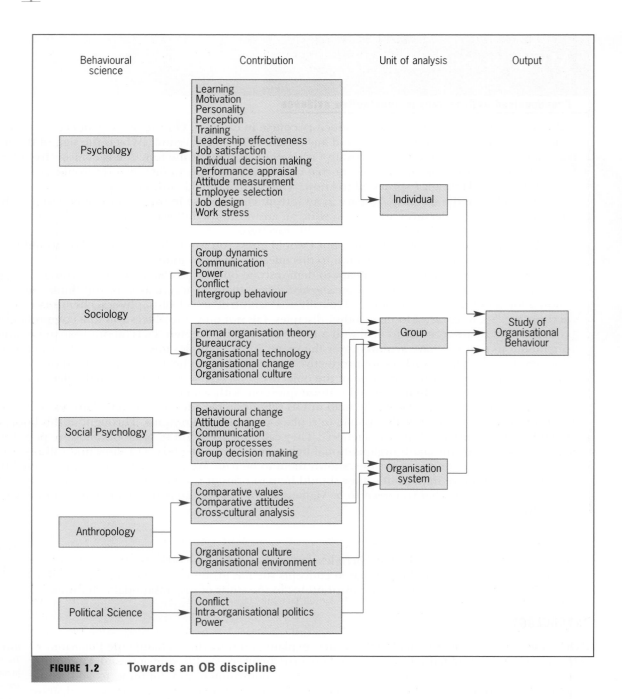

FIGURE 1.2   **Towards an OB discipline**

SOCIOLOGY

sociology
The study of people in relation to their fellow human beings.

While psychologists focus their attention on the individual, sociologists study the social system in which individuals fill their roles; that is, **sociology** studies people in relation to their fellow human beings. Specifically, sociologists have made their greatest contribution to OB through their study of group behaviour in organisations, particularly formal and complex organisations. Some of the areas within OB that have received valuable input from sociologists are group dynamics, design of work teams, organisational culture, formal organisation theory and structure, organisational technology, communications, power and conflict.

SOCIAL PSYCHOLOGY

Social psychology is an area within psychology, blending concepts from both psychology and sociology. It focuses on the influence of people on one another. One of the main areas receiving considerable investigation from social psychologists has been *change*—how to implement it and how to reduce barriers to its acceptance. In addition, we find social psychologists making significant contributions in the areas of measuring, understanding and changing attitudes; communication patterns; building trust; the ways in which group activities can satisfy individual needs; and group decision-making processes.

social psychology
An area within psychology that blends concepts from psychology and sociology and that focuses on the influence of people on one another.

ANTHROPOLOGY

Anthropology is the study of societies to learn about human beings and their activities. For example, anthropologists' work on cultures and environments has helped us to understand differences in fundamental values, attitudes and behaviour between people in different countries and within different organisations. Much of our current understanding of organisational culture, organisational environments and differences between national cultures is the result of the work of anthropologists or those using their methods.

anthropology
The study of societies to learn about human beings and their activities.

POLITICAL SCIENCE

Although frequently overlooked, the contributions of political scientists are significant to the understanding of behaviour in organisations. **Political science** studies the behaviour of individuals and groups within a political environment. Specific topics of concern here include the structuring of conflict, allocation of power, and how people manipulate power for individual self-interest.

political science
The study of the behaviour of individuals and groups within a political environment.

There are Few Absolutes in OB

There are few, if any, simple and universal principles that explain organisational behaviour. There are laws in the physical sciences—chemistry, astronomy, physics—that are consistent and apply in a wide range of situations. They allow scientists to generalise about the pull of gravity or to be confident about sending astronauts into space to repair satellites. But as one noted behavioural researcher aptly concluded, 'God gave all the easy problems to the physicists.' Human beings are complex. Because they are not alike, our ability to make simple, accurate and sweeping generalisations is limited. Two people often act very differently in the same situation, and the same person's behaviour changes in different situations. For example, not everyone is motivated by money, and you behave differently at a sporting match on Sunday than you did at a party the night before.

That doesn't mean, of course, that we can't offer reasonably accurate explanations of human behaviour or make valid predictions. However, it does mean that OB concepts must reflect situational, or contingency, conditions. We can say that x leads to y, but only under conditions specified in z (the **contingency variables**). The science of OB was developed by using general concepts and then altering their application to the particular situation. So, for example, OB scholars would avoid stating that effective leaders should always seek the ideas of their followers before making a decision. Rather, we shall find that in some situations a participative style is clearly superior, but, in other situations, an autocratic decision-making style is more effective.

contingency variables
Situational factors: variables that moderate the relationship between two or more other variables and improve the correlation.

The Real Deal

The new people at Virgin Blue

Ansett Airlines was established in 1931 and became an icon in the Australasian region. Its eventual collapse in 2002 put over 15,000 people out of work and raised questions about the way we manage a company and its people. Such a devastating corporate collapse emphasises the tremendous responsibly that managers have not only for the success or failure of a business, but for the people who also work for the business.

The collapse of Ansett has been a bonus for Virgin Blue, the new airline that was established in 2000 prior to the Olympic Games. At the outset, the Virgin Blue management team recognised the importance of getting the right staff on board and of developing a brand and a culture that, according to the HR director Bruce Highfield, reflects quality, a fun work environment, value for money to customers, and a desire to push the boundaries and challenge the establishment.

Brett Godfrey is Virgin Blue's chief executive officer and has worked in a number of other airlines.

He recognises the importance of organisational behaviour and was adamant that the company be built from the ground up, rather than taking on an existing airline. For Brett, culture is about how a company does business with its staff; and, once the culture has been established, its like the *Titanic*—it's difficult to change course. It's important that people's enthusiasm and commitment are sustained, and that's the challenge of management. Godfrey is proud of the high levels of employee engagement, despite the downturn in the global airline industry and the threat of terrorism and SARS.

Source: Craig Donaldson, 'Breaking in a New Culture: Virgin Blue's Story', *Human Resources*, 24 September 2003, pp. 10–12. Reproduced with permission.

High employee engagement helped Virgin Blue capture 30% of the Australian market despite poor market conditions.

In other words, the effectiveness of a particular leadership style is contingent on the situation in which it's used.

As you proceed through this book, you will encounter a wealth of research-based theories about how people behave in organisations. But don't expect to find a lot of straightforward cause-and-effect relationships. There aren't many! Organisational behaviour theories mirror the subject matter with which they deal. People are complex and complicated, and so too must be the theories developed to explain their actions.

LEARNING OBJECTIVE

6

List the main challenges and opportunities for managers to use OB concepts

Challenges and Opportunities for OB

Understanding organisational behaviour has never been more important for managers. A quick look at a few of the dramatic changes now taking place in organisations supports this claim. For

No company today can ignore the benefits diversity in race, gender, age and ethnicity can bring to the organisation. Not only do different perspectives assist problem solving but such diversity enriches the knowledge base of an organisation.

example, the typical employee is getting older; more and more women and members of minority groups are in the workplace; corporate downsizing and the heavy use of temporary employees are severing the bonds of loyalty that historically tied many employees to their employers; and global competition is requiring employees to become more flexible and to learn to cope with rapid change.

In short, there are a lot of challenges and opportunities today for managers to use OB concepts. In this section, we review some of the more critical issues confronting managers for which OB offers solutions—or at least some meaningful insights towards solutions.

RESPONDING TO GLOBALISATION

Organisations are no longer constrained by national borders. A British firm owns Burger King, and McDonald's sells hamburgers in 87 countries around the world. ExxonMobil, a so-called American company, receives almost 75 per cent of its revenues from sales outside the United States. New employees at Finland-based phone maker Nokia are increasingly being recruited from India, China and other developing countries—with non-Finns now outnumbering Finns at Nokia's renowned research centre in Helsinki. And all major automobile manufacturers now build cars outside their borders; for example, Honda builds cars in the United States; General Motors builds Daewoo vehicles in South Korea and Holdens in Australia; and both Mercedes and BMW build their cars in South Africa. These examples illustrate that the world has become a global village. In turn, managers have to become capable of working with people from different cultures.

Globalisation affects a manager's people skills in at least two ways. First, if you are a manager, you are increasingly likely to find yourself in a foreign assignment at some time in your working life. You may be recruited to an overseas location, or you may be transferred to your employer's operating division or subsidiary in another country. Once there, you will have to manage a workforce that is likely to be very different in needs, aspirations and attitudes from those you were used to back home. Second, even in your own country, you are going to find yourself working with managers, supervisors, peers, and other employees who were born and raised in many different cultures. What motivates you may not motivate them. Or your style of communication may be straightforward and open, but they may find this approach uncomfortable and threatening. To work effectively with these people, you will need to understand their culture, how it has shaped them and how to adapt your management style to their differences. As we discuss OB concepts throughout this book, we will frequently address how cultural differences might require managers to modify their practices.

MANAGING WORKFORCE DIVERSITY

One of the most important and broad-based challenges currently facing organisations is adapting to people who are different. The term we use for describing this challenge is *workforce diversity*. While globalisation focuses on differences between people *from* different countries, workforce diversity addresses differences among people *within* given countries.

workforce diversity
The concept that organisations are becoming more heterogeneous in terms of gender, race, ethnicity and inclusion of other diverse groups.

Workforce diversity means that organisations are becoming more heterogeneous in terms of gender, race and ethnicity—in other words, there are more differences than there are similarities among members of the organisation. But the term encompasses anyone who varies from the so-called norm. In addition to the more obvious groups—women, indigenous Australians, Asians—it also includes the physically or intellectually less-abled, gays and lesbians, and the elderly. Moreover, it's an increasingly important organisational issue in places such as Australia, the United States, Canada, South Africa, Japan, Malaysia, Singapore and Europe. Managers in Australia and Canada, for example, are having to adjust to large influxes of Asian employees. The 'new' South Africa is increasingly characterised by blacks holding important technical and managerial jobs, as well as the problems posed by there being 11 official national languages. Women, long confined to low-paying temporary jobs in Japan, Malaysia and Singapore, are moving into managerial positions. And the European Union cooperative trade arrangement, which opened up borders throughout much of Europe, has increased workforce diversity in organisations that operate in countries such as Germany, Poland, Portugal, Italy and France.

We used to take a melting-pot approach to differences in organisations, assuming that people who were different would somehow automatically want to assimilate. But we now recognise that employees don't set aside their cultural values and lifestyle preferences when they come to work. The challenge for organisations, therefore, is to make themselves more accommodating to diverse groups of people by addressing their different lifestyles, family needs and work styles. The melting-pot assumption is being replaced by one that recognises and values differences.[14]

Haven't organisations always included members of diverse groups? Yes, but they were a small percentage of the workforce and were, for the most part, ignored by large organisations. Moreover, it was assumed that these minorities would seek to blend in and assimilate. For example, the bulk of the pre-1980s workforce in Australia and the United States were white, predominantly European Anglo-Saxon males working full-time to support a non-employed wife and school-aged children. Since then, the workforce demographics have changed considerably.[15] The difference between the employment rates of men and women narrowed between 1980 and 2000. The employment rate for men dropped from 82 per cent to 77 per cent, while the rate for women rose from 47 per cent to 61 per cent. Women are receiving a greater proportion of all income. Between 1982 and 1999/2000, the share of income received by women rose from 33 per cent to 38 per cent, due mainly to the increase in the proportion of women working.[16] The proportion of minorities in the workforce has also increased.

Workforce diversity has important implications for management practice. Managers have to shift their philosophy from treating everyone alike, to recognising differences and responding to those differences in ways that ensure employee retention and greater productivity while, at the same time, not discriminating. This shift includes, for example, providing diversity training and revamping benefits programs to accommodate the different needs of different employees. Diversity, if positively managed, can increase creativity and innovation in organisations, as well as improve decision making by providing different perspectives on problems.[17] When diversity isn't managed properly, there is a potential for higher turnover, more-difficult communication and more interpersonal conflicts.

IMPROVING QUALITY AND PRODUCTIVITY

General Electric is a diversified services, technology and manufacturing company that introduced the Six Sigma production technique. This technique improves quality and productivity in the production process by removing any unwanted variations and defects. Ziggy Switkowski, the chief executive officer of Australia's largest telecommunications company, Telstra, has adopted the Six Sigma program in a bid to cut $100 million from the company's operating costs. BHP Billiton has been using the program for several years to manage its production costs in the context of fluctuating commodity prices.[18]

More and more managers are confronting the challenges that Telstra and BHP Billiton are facing. They are having to improve their organisation's productivity and the quality of the products and services they offer. Towards improving quality and productivity, they are implementing programs such as quality management and process reengineering—programs that require extensive employee involvement.

As Table 1.2 describes, **quality management (QM)** is driven by the constant attainment of customer satisfaction through the continuous improvement of all organisational processes.[19] It has implications for OB because it requires employees to rethink what they do and become more involved in workplace decisions.

In times of rapid and dramatic change, it's sometimes necessary to approach improving quality and productivity from the perspective of 'How would we do things around here if we were starting from scratch?' That, in essence, is the approach of **process reengineering**. It asks managers to reconsider how work would be done and their organisation structured if they were starting over.[20] The actions that companies using the Six Sigma program are taking illustrate process reengineering. Instead of merely making incremental changes in the basic production processes, they look for improvements in the whole production system. Every process is evaluated in terms of its contribution to the business goals. Inefficient processes are thrown out. Entire new systems can be introduced if considered necessary. Rather than try to make small improvements in a system that is too rigid and inflexible to meet changing customer needs, some companies completely revamp their business's production systems and the jobs of their employees. As a result of these changes, there can be a greater involvement by employees in terms of checking for quality, helping to establish productivity standards, and actively participating in introducing workflow innovations.

Today's managers understand that the success of any effort at improving quality and productivity must include their employees. These employees won't only be a major force in carrying out changes, but increasingly will actively participate in planning those changes. OB offers important insights into helping managers work through these changes.

quality management (QM)
The constant attainment of customer satisfaction through the continuous improvement of all organisational processes.

process reengineering
Reconsidering how work would be done and an organisation structured if it were starting over.

TABLE 1.2	**What is total quality management?**

1. *Intense focus on the customer:* The customer includes not only outsiders who buy the organisation's products or services, but also internal customers (such as shipping or accounts payable personnel) who interact with and serve others in the organisation.

2. *Concern for continual improvement:* TQM is a commitment to never being satisfied. 'Very good' isn't good enough. Quality can always be improved.

3. *Improvement in the quality of everything the organisation does:* TQM uses a very broad definition of quality. It relates not only to the final product, but also to how the organisation handles deliveries, how rapidly it responds to complaints, how politely the phones are answered, and the like.

4. *Accurate measurement:* TQM uses statistical techniques to measure every critical performance variable in the organisation's operations. These performance variables are then compared against standards or benchmarks to identify problems, and the problems are traced to their roots and the causes eliminated.

5. *Empowerment of employees:* TQM involves the people on the line in the improvement process. Teams are widely used in TQM programs as empowerment vehicles for finding and solving problems.

OB Controversies

Creating sustainable organisations

Whereas the last century was one of massive economic development and expansion, this century will be characterised as the period in which modern economies had to come to grips with finite resources and the devastating ecological and social impact of the wasteful practices of the previous century. Organisations will now have their part to play in developing new and sustainable approaches to their processes, consumption of resources, and the impact of every aspect of the organisation on the wider community.

Sustainability addresses four key goals: extending the socially useful life of individual organisations; augmenting the natural environment's capacity to recreate, regenerate and protect all living flora and fauna; increasing society's capability to resolve the major social issues; and improving the well-being of all the world's present and future citizens. Every organisation needs to play a part in these four goals.

A sustainable organisation as a concept isn't yet widely accepted, although the trend is positive in this direction. Indeed, Australian superannuation and managed investment funds now offer members the opportunity to invest in organisations committed to sustainability goals. Research has shown that organisations working to becoming sustainable organisations pass through six phases:
- rejection;
- non-responsiveness;
- compliance;
- efficiency;
- strategic proactivity; and
- the sustainable organisation.

The first two phases cover organisations that either reject outright the arguments for sustainability or focus solely on short-term profits to the exclusion of all other issues. Compliance organisations are those that seek to meet not only their legal obligations (pollution controls, workplace health and safety, and so on) but also attempt to meet community expectations for acting in a responsible, community-oriented manner. Fourth-phase organisations build on this view and seek ways of creating their products and services in a more efficient manner that is sustainable in the long term. Promoting recycling within the organisation, rethinking processes to find ways that don't pollute or damage the environment, and people-friendly workplaces are examples of efficient organisations.

Strategic proactivity, phase five, sees organisations place sustainability at the core of their business strategies. For example, Heinz Foods has a strategy for making Australia and New Zealand 'an environmental oasis for Heinz'—an environment relatively free of pollution and capable of producing fresh, contaminant-free food products. The final phase is the sustainable organisation. This organisation isn't only concerned with its own sustainability and survival, but is also active in the broader community, actively changing mindsets, attitudes, social issues and business practices. Fuji Xerox is one such organisation—it not only recycles all aspects of its manufactured products, but it goes further in remanufacturing, redesigning and reinventing its products to make them more environmentally friendly and sustainable (called eco-manufacturing). Fuji Xerox has proved that the sustainable organisation can be more profitable than the historical alternative organisations.

The sustainable organisation is a concept that is here to stay. Managers need to come to grips with its implications, and they need to understand how the effective management of organisational behaviour can play a significant role in sustaining organisations and communities well into the 21st century.

Source: This article is based on the pioneering works of Dexter Dunphy and his colleagues, as discussed in D. Dunphy, 'Corporate Sustainability: Challenge to Managerial Orthodoxies', the inaugural Leading Scholar paper, *Journal of the Australian and New Zealand Academy of Management*, vol. 8, no. 2, 2003, pp. 2–11.

RESPONDING TO THE LABOUR SHORTAGE

Economic ups and downs are difficult to predict. The world economy in the late 1990s, for example, was generally quite robust and labour markets were tight. Most employers found it difficult to find skilled employees to fill vacancies. Then, in 2002/03, most developed countries suffered an economic recession, in part fuelled by the war on terrorism. Layoffs and retrenchments were widespread, and the supply of skilled employees became much more plentiful in the short term. Judging from history, the past shortages of skilled labour will reappear in the not too distant future and the whole cycle will repeat itself. In contrast, demographic trends are much more predictable. And we are facing one that has direct implications for OB: barring some unforeseeable economic or political calamity—such as the recession in 2002/03—there will be a labour shortage for at least another ten to 15 years.[21] This shortage of skilled labour is already affecting Australia and New Zealand, and is also likely to be just as prevalent in most of Europe due to a greying population—13 per cent of Australia's population is over 65 years of age—and a declining birth rate—less than 21 per cent of households have members aged under 15 years.

The skilled labour shortage is a function of two factors—birth rates and labour participation rates. From the late 1960s to the late 1980s, employers benefited from the large number of baby-boomers (those born between 1946 and 1965) entering the workforce. Specifically, there are millions of baby-boomers in the workforce. But there are many fewer Gen-Xers to replace them when they retire. Some baby-boomers have already retired early. The problem will become severe in around 2006, when the major exodus of baby-boomers from the workplace will begin. Importantly, in spite of continued increases in immigration, new entrants to the workforce from foreign countries won't do much to correct the labour supply shortage.

The labour shortage problem is compounded by the fact that the latter part of the 20th century benefited from a huge increase in the number of women entering the workforce. That provided a new supply of talented and skilled employees. This source has now been tapped. Moreover, there is declining interest by older employees in staying in the labour force. In 1950, nearly 80 per cent of all 62-year-old men were still working. Today, only slightly more than half are still in the labour force. Improved pensions, expanded Social Security and health-care benefits, and a healthy share market have led many employees to retire early, especially those whose jobs were stressful or unchallenging. So, the combination of the smaller Generation X population, the already high participation rate of women in the workforce and early retirements will lead to a significantly smaller future labour pool from which employers can hire.

In times of labour shortage, good wages and benefits aren't going to be enough to get and keep skilled employees. Managers will need sophisticated recruitment and retention strategies. And OB can help managers to create these. In tight labour markets, managers who don't understand human behaviour and fail to treat their employees properly, risk having no one to manage!

IMPROVING CUSTOMER SERVICE

Recently, one of the authors of this book purchased a CD-R drive for his computer from Officeworks. A week later, while shopping at Officeworks for something else, he noticed that the price of the CD-R drive was quite a bit cheaper than when he had purchased one a week earlier. Slightly disappointed, he later happened to mention the drop in price to the sales assistant at the checkout. Much to his surprise, the sales assistant immediately refunded the difference—and in the process won the author's continued business and a customer for life.

Today, the majority of employees in developed countries work in service jobs. In Australia, 73 per cent work in service industries, while in the United States it's almost 80 per cent. In the United Kingdom, Germany and Japan, the percentages are 69, 68 and 65, respectively. Examples of these service jobs include technical support representatives, call-centre operators, fast-food counter employees, sales clerks, teachers, waiters or waitresses, nurses, automobile repair technicians, consultants, credit representatives, financial planners and flight attendants. The common

Empowered employees, whether they work individually or in teams like they do at Officeworks, need the tools and training to take responsibility for their work. Teams have a great deal of freedom to make decisions, while their managers act as advisers and coaches.

characteristic of these jobs is that they require substantial interaction with an organisation's customers. And since an organisation can't exist without customers—whether that organisation is Royal & SunAlliance, National Australia Bank, an electricity company, a law firm, a museum, a school or a government agency—management needs to ensure that employees do what it takes to please its customers. OB can help in that task.

An analysis of a Qantas Airways' passenger survey confirms the role that employees play in satisfying customers. Passengers were asked to rate their 'essential needs' in air travel. Almost every factor listed by passengers was directly influenced by the actions of Qantas's employees—from prompt baggage delivery, to courteous and efficient cabin crews, to assistance with connections, to quick and friendly airport check-ins.[22] Is it any wonder that John Travolta decked his private jet out in Qantas colours and acts as their global ambassador!

Except for OB researchers' interest in customer satisfaction through improvements in quality, the field of OB has generally ignored the customer. Focusing on the customer was thought to be the concern of people who study and practise marketing. But OB can contribute to improving an organisation's performance by showing managers how employee attitudes and behaviours are associated with customer satisfaction. Many an organisation has failed because its employees failed to please the customer. So, management needs to create a customer-responsive culture. And OB can provide considerable guidance in helping managers to create such cultures—cultures in which employees are friendly and courteous, accessible, knowledgeable, prompt in responding to customer needs, and willing to do what's necessary to please the customer.[23]

IMPROVING PEOPLE SKILLS

We opened this chapter by demonstrating how important people skills are to managerial effectiveness. We said, 'This book has been written to help both managers and potential managers develop those people skills.'

As you proceed through this book, we will present relevant concepts and theories that can help you to explain and predict the behaviour of people at work. In addition, you will gain insights into specific people skills that you can use on the job. For example, you will learn ways to design motivating jobs, techniques for improving your listening skills, and how to create more effective teams.

EMPOWERING PEOPLE

If you pick up any popular business periodical nowadays, you will read about the reshaping of the relationship between managers and those they are supposedly responsible for managing. You will find managers being called coaches, advisers, sponsors or facilitators. In some organisations, employees are now called associates. And there is a blurring between the roles of managers and employees. Decision making is being pushed down to the operating level, where employees are being given the freedom to make choices about schedules and procedures and to solve work-related problems.[24] In the 1980s, managers were encouraged to get their employees to participate in work-related decisions. Now, managers are going considerably further by allowing employees full control of their work. An increasing number of organisations are using self-managed teams, in which employees operate largely without bosses.

What's going on? What's going on is that managers are **empowering employees**. They are putting employees in charge of what they do. And, in so doing, managers are having to learn how to give up control, and employees are having to learn how to take responsibility for their work and make appropriate decisions. In later chapters, we will show how empowerment is changing leadership styles, power relationships, the way work is designed and the way organisations are structured.

empowering employees
Putting employees in charge of what they do.

COPING WITH 'TEMPORARINESS'

Managing used to be characterised by long periods of stability, interrupted occasionally by short periods of change. Managing today would be more accurately described as long periods of ongoing change, interrupted occasionally by short periods of stability. The world that most managers and employees face today is one of permanent temporariness. The actual jobs that employees perform are in a permanent state of change, so employees need to update their knowledge and skills continually in order to perform new job requirements. For example, production employees at companies such as General Motors-Holden, Ford and Toyota in Australia now need to know how to operate computerised production equipment. This wasn't part of their job descriptions 20 years ago. Work groups are also increasingly in a state of change. In the past, employees were assigned to a specific work group, and that assignment was relatively permanent. There was a considerable amount of security in working with the same people day in and day out. That predictability has been replaced by temporary work groups, teams that include members from different departments and whose members change all the time, the use of on-line employees telecommuting from other locations or even other countries, and the increased use of employee rotation to fill constantly changing work assignments. Finally, organisations themselves are in a state of change. They continually reorganise their various divisions, sell off poor-performing businesses, downsize operations, subcontract non-critical services and operations to other organisations, and replace permanent employees with temporary employees.

Today's managers and employees must learn to cope with temporariness. They have to learn to live with flexibility, spontaneity and unpredictability. The study of OB can provide important insights into helping you better understand a work world of continual change, how to overcome resistance to change, and how best to create an organisational culture that thrives on change.

STIMULATING INNOVATION AND CHANGE

Whatever happened to HIH, Ansett Airlines, Olympia and OneTel? All these giants went bust. Why have other giants, such as AMP, Telstra, Optus, Austar and Lucent Technologies implemented huge cost-cutting programs and eliminated thousands of jobs? The answer is simple—to avoid going bust.

Today's successful organisations must foster innovation and master the art of change or they will become candidates for extinction. Victory will go to the organisations that maintain their flexibility, continually improve their quality, and beat their competition to the marketplace with a constant stream of innovative products and services. Domino's single-handedly brought on the demise of thousands of small pizza parlours whose managers thought they could continue doing what they had been doing for years. Amazon.com is putting a lot of independent bookstores out of business in many countries, as it proves that books can successfully be sold from an Internet website. Rupert Murdoch's Fox Television successfully stole a major portion of the under-25 viewing audience from their larger network rivals through innovative programming such as *The Simpsons*.

An organisation's employees can be the impetus for innovation and change, or they can be a major stumbling block. The challenge for managers is to stimulate their employees' creativity and tolerance for change. The field of OB provides a wealth of ideas and techniques to aid in realising these goals.

HELPING EMPLOYEES BALANCE WORK/LIFE CONFLICTS

The typical employee in the 1960s or 1970s showed up at the workplace from Monday to Friday and did his or her job in eight- or nine-hour chunks of time. The workplace and hours were clearly specified. That's no longer true for a large segment of today's workforce. Employees are increasingly complaining that the line between work and non-work time has become blurred, creating personal conflicts and stress.[25]

A number of forces have contributed to blurring the lines between employees' work life and personal life. First, the creation of global organisations means their world never sleeps. At any time and on any day, for example, thousands of Malaysian, Singapore and Qantas airline flight crews are working somewhere. The need to consult with colleagues or customers eight or ten time zones away means that many employees of global firms are 'on call' 24 hours a day. Second, communication technology allows employees to do their work at home, in their cars, or on the beach in Thailand or on the Gold Coast in Queensland. This lets many people in technical and professional jobs do their work any time and from any place. Indeed, one of the authors of this book teaches his OB students over the Internet and has maintained contact with them even when he was in Asia, Europe and North America attending conferences. Third, organisations are asking employees to put in longer hours. For example, between 1977 and 1997, the average work week increased from 43 hours to 47 hours; and the number of people working 50 or more hours a week jumped from 24 per cent to 37 per cent. Finally, fewer families have only a single breadwinner. Today's married employee is typically part of a dual-career couple. This makes it increasingly difficult for married employees to find the time to fulfil commitments to home, spouse, children, parents and friends.

Employees are increasingly recognising that work is squeezing out personal lives, and they are not happy about it. For example, recent studies suggest that employees want jobs that give them flexibility in their work schedules so that they can better manage work/life conflicts.[26] In addition, the next generation of employees is likely to show similar concerns.[27] A majority of TAFE and university students say that attaining a balance between personal life and work is a primary career goal. They want 'a life' as well as a job. Organisations that don't help their people achieve work/life balance will find it increasingly hard to attract and retain the most capable and motivated employees. The increasing need will be for family-friendly organisations.

As you will see in later chapters, the field of OB offers a number of suggestions to guide managers in designing workplaces and jobs that can help employees deal with work/life conflicts.

IMPROVING ETHICAL BEHAVIOUR

In an organisational world characterised by retrenchments, expectations of increasing employee productivity and tough global competition in the marketplace, it's not altogether surprising that many employees feel pressured to cut corners, break rules and engage in other forms of questionable practices.

ethical dilemmas
Situations in which individuals are required to define right and wrong conduct.

Members of organisations are increasingly finding themselves facing **ethical dilemmas**, situations in which they are required to define right and wrong conduct. For example, should they 'blow the whistle' if they uncover illegal activities taking place in their company? Should they follow orders with which they don't personally agree? Do they give an inflated performance evaluation to an employee whom they like, knowing that such an evaluation could save that employee's job? Do they allow themselves to 'play politics' in the organisation if it will help their career advancement?

What constitutes good ethical behaviour has never been clearly defined. And, in recent years, the line differentiating right from wrong has become even more blurred. Employees see people all around them engaging in unethical practices—Australian Senators are charged for padding their travel accounts; successful executives use insider information for personal financial gain; some university administrators 'look the other way' when full-fee paying international students struggle to meet the standards; and even a President of the United States distorted the truth under oath and broke the law—but survived impeachment for doing so. They hear people, when caught, giving excuses such as 'everyone does it', or 'you have to seize every advantage nowadays' or 'I never thought I'd get caught'.

Managers and their organisations are responding to this problem from a number of directions.[28] They are writing and distributing codes of ethics to guide employees through ethical dilemmas. They are offering seminars, workshops and similar training programs to try to improve ethical behaviours. They are providing in-house advisers who can be contacted, in many cases anonymously, for assistance in dealing with ethical issues. And they are creating protection mechanisms for employees who reveal internal unethical practices.

Today's manager needs to create an ethically healthy climate for his or her employees, where they can do their work productively and confront a minimal degree of ambiguity regarding what constitutes right and wrong behaviours. In upcoming chapters, we will discuss the kinds of actions managers can take to create an ethically healthy climate and to help employees sort through ethically ambiguous situations. We will also present a number of exercises that will allow you to think through ethical issues and assess how you would handle them.

Coming Attractions: Developing an OB Model

We conclude this chapter by presenting a general model that defines the field of OB, stakes out its parameters, and identifies its primary dependent and independent variables. The end result will be a 'coming attraction' of the topics making up the remainder of this book.

AN OVERVIEW

A **model** is an abstraction of reality, a simplified representation of some real-world phenomenon. A mannequin in a retail store is a model. So, too, is the accountant's formula: Assets + Liabilities = Owners' Equity. Figure 1.3 presents the skeleton on which we will construct our OB model. It proposes that there are three levels of analysis in OB and that, as we move from the individual level to the organisation systems level, we add systematically to our understanding of behaviour in organisations. The three basic levels are analogous to building blocks; each level is constructed on the previous level. Group concepts grow out of the foundation laid in the individual section; we overlay structural constraints on the individual and group in order to arrive at organisational behaviour.

model
An abstraction of reality. A simplified representation of some real-world phenomenon.

THE DEPENDENT VARIABLES

Dependent variables are the key factors that you want to explain or predict and that are affected by some other factor. What are the primary dependent variables in OB? Scholars have historically tended to emphasise productivity, absenteeism, turnover and job satisfaction. More recently, a fifth variable—organisational citizenship—has been added to this list. Let's briefly review each of these variables to ensure that we understand what they mean and why they have achieved their level of distinction.

dependent variable
A response that is affected by an independent variable.

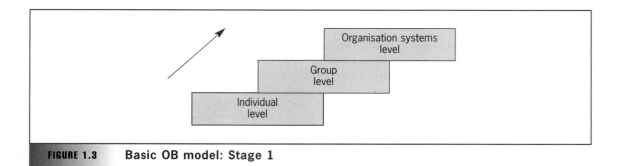

FIGURE 1.3 **Basic OB model: Stage 1**

Productivity

productivity
A performance measure that includes effectiveness and efficiency.

effectiveness
Achievement of goals.

efficiency
The ratio of effective output to the input required to achieve it.

An organisation is productive if it achieves its goals and does so by transferring inputs to outputs at the lowest cost. As such, **productivity** implies a concern for both **effectiveness** and **efficiency**.

A hospital, for example, is *effective* when it successfully meets the needs of its patients. It is *efficient* when it can do so at a low cost. If a hospital manages to achieve higher output from its present staff by reducing the average number of days a patient is confined to a bed or by increasing the number of staff–patient contacts per day, we say that the hospital has gained productive efficiency. A business firm is effective when it attains its sales or market share goals, but its productivity also depends on achieving those goals efficiently. Popular measures of organisational efficiency include return on investment, profit per dollar of sales and output per hour of labour.

We can also look at productivity from the perspective of the individual employee. Take the cases of Mike and Ted, who are both long-distance truck-drivers. If Mike is supposed to haul his fully loaded rig from Sydney to its destination in Perth in 75 hours or less, he is effective if he makes the trip within that time period. But measures of productivity must take into account the costs incurred in reaching the goal. That's where efficiency comes in. Let's assume that Mike made the Sydney to Perth run in 68 hours and averaged 5 kilometres per litre. Ted, on the other hand, made the trip in 68 hours also, but averaged 6.5 kilometres per litre of fuel (rigs and loads are identical). Both Mike and Ted were effective—they accomplished their goal—but Ted was more efficient than Mike because his rig consumed less fuel and, therefore, he achieved his goal at a lower cost.

Organisations in service industries need to include additionally 'attention to customer needs and requirements' in assessing their effectiveness. Why? Because in these types of businesses, there is a clear chain of cause-and-effect running from employee attitudes and behaviour to customer attitudes and behaviour to an organisation's revenues and profits. The US department store Sears, in fact, has carefully documented this chain.[29] The company's management found that a 5 per cent improvement in employee attitudes led to a 1.3 per cent increase in customer satisfaction, which in turn translated into a 0.5 per cent improvement in revenue growth. More specifically, Sears found that by training employees to improve the employee–customer interaction, it was able to improve customer satisfaction by 4 per cent over a 12-month period, which generated an estimated US$200 million in additional revenues.

In summary, one of OB's main concerns is productivity. We want to know what factors will influence the effectiveness and efficiency of individuals, of groups and of the overall organisation.

Absenteeism

absenteeism
The failure to report to work.

Absenteeism is the failure to report to work. Its annual cost has been estimated at over $8 billion for Australian organisations and $12 billion for Canadian firms.[30] In Germany, absences cost industrial firms more than 31 billion euros (approximately A$58 billion) each year.[31] At the job level, a one-day absence by a clerical employee can cost an employer several hundred dollars in reduced efficiency and increased supervisory workload. These figures indicate the importance to an organisation of keeping absenteeism low.

It's obviously difficult for an organisation to operate smoothly and to attain its objectives if employees fail to report to their jobs. The work flow is disrupted, and often important decisions must be delayed. In organisations that rely heavily on assembly-line production, absenteeism can be considerably more than a disruption; it can result in a drastic reduction in the quality of output, and, in some cases, it can bring about a complete shutdown of the production facility. But levels of absenteeism beyond the normal range in any organisation have a direct impact on that organisation's effectiveness and efficiency.

Are *all* absences bad? Probably not. Although most absences have a negative impact on the organisation, we can conceive of situations in which the organisation may benefit by an employee's voluntarily choosing not to come to work. For example, illness, fatigue or excess stress can significantly decrease an employee's productivity. In jobs in which an employee needs to be alert—surgeons and airline pilots are obvious examples—it may well be better for the organisation if the employee doesn't report to work rather than show up and perform poorly. The cost of an accident in such jobs could be prohibitive. Even in managerial jobs, where mistakes are less spectacular, performance may be improved when managers absent themselves from work rather than make a poor decision under stress. But these examples are clearly atypical. For the most part, we can assume that organisations benefit when employee absenteeism is low.

Turnover

Turnover is the voluntary and involuntary permanent withdrawal from an organisation. A high turnover rate results in increased recruiting, selection and training costs. What are those costs? They are higher than you might think. For example, in the United States the cost for a typical information-technology company to replace a programmer or systems analyst has been put at US$34,100; and the cost of a retail store to replace a lost sales clerk has been calculated at US$10,445.[32] In addition, a high rate of turnover can disrupt the efficient running of an organisation when knowledgeable and experienced personnel leave and replacements must be found and prepared to assume positions of responsibility.

turnover
The voluntary and involuntary permanent withdrawal from an organisation.

All organisations, of course, have some turnover. In fact, if the 'right' people are leaving the organisation—the marginal and submarginal employees—turnover can be positive. It may create the opportunity to replace an underperforming individual with someone who has higher skills or motivation, open up increased opportunities for promotions, and add new and fresh ideas to the organisation.[33] In today's changing world of work, reasonable levels of employee-initiated turnover facilitate organisational flexibility and employee independence, and they can lessen the need for management-initiated layoffs.

But turnover often involves the loss of people the organisation doesn't want to lose. For example, one study covering 900 employees who had resigned their jobs found that 92 per cent earned performance ratings of 'satisfactory' or better from their superiors.[34] So, when turnover is excessive, or when it involves valuable performers, it can be a disruptive factor, hindering the organisation's effectiveness and, from a management perspective, an indicator that there may be problems in the workplace.

Organisational citizenship

Organisational citizenship is discretionary behaviour that isn't part of an employee's formal job requirements, but that nevertheless promotes the effective functioning of the organisation.[35]

Successful organisations need employees who will do more than their usual job duties—who will provide performance that is *beyond* expectations. In today's dynamic workplace, where tasks are increasingly done in teams and where flexibility is critical, organisations need employees who will engage in 'good citizenship' behaviours such as making constructive statements about their work group and the organisation, helping others on their team, volunteering for extra job

organisational citizenship behaviour (OCB)
Discretionary behaviour that isn't part of an employee's formal job requirements, but that nevertheless promotes the effective functioning of the organisation.

activities, avoiding unnecessary conflicts, showing care for organisational property, respecting the spirit as well as the letter of rules and regulations, and gracefully tolerating the occasional work-related impositions and nuisances.

Organisations want and need employees who will do those things that aren't in any job description. And the evidence indicates that the organisations that have such employees out-perform those that don't.[36] As a result, OB is concerned with organisational citizenship behaviour (OCB) as a dependent variable.

Job satisfaction

job satisfaction
An individual's general attitude towards his or her job.

The final dependent variable we will look at is **job satisfaction**, which we define simply, at this point, as an individual's general attitude towards his or her job. (We expand considerably on that definition in later chapters.) Unlike the previous four variables, job satisfaction represents an attitude, rather than a behaviour. Why, then, has it become a primary dependent variable? For two reasons: its demonstrated relationship to performance factors and the value preferences held by many OB researchers.

The belief that satisfied employees are more productive than dissatisfied employees has been a basic tenet among managers for years. Although much evidence questions that assumed causal relationship, it can be argued that advanced societies should be concerned not only with the quantity of life—that is, concerns such as higher productivity and material acquisitions—but also with its quality. Those researchers with strong humanistic values argue that satisfaction is a legitimate objective of an organisation. Not only is satisfaction negatively related to absenteeism and turnover, but also, they argue, organisations have a responsibility to provide employees with jobs that are challenging and intrinsically rewarding. Therefore, although job satisfaction represents an attitude rather than a behaviour, OB researchers typically consider it an important dependent variable.

THE INDEPENDENT VARIABLES

independent variable
The presumed cause of some change in the dependent variable.

What are the main determinants of productivity, absenteeism, turnover, OCB and job satisfaction? Our answer to that question brings us to the **independent variables**. Consistent with our belief that organisational behaviour can best be understood when viewed essentially as a set of increasingly complex building blocks, the base, or first level, of our model lies in understanding individual behaviour.

Individual-level variables

It has been said that 'managers, unlike parents, must work with used, not new, human beings—human beings whom others have gotten to first'.[37] When individuals enter an organisation, they are a bit like used cars. Each is different. Some are 'low-mileage'—they have been treated carefully and have had only limited exposure to the realities of the elements. Others are 'well worn', having been driven over some rough roads. This metaphor indicates that people enter organisations with certain characteristics that will influence their behaviour at work. The more obvious of these are personal or biographical characteristics such as age, gender and marital status; personality characteristics; an inherent emotional framework; values and attitudes; and basic ability levels. These characteristics are essentially intact when an individual enters the workforce, and, for the most part, there is little management can do to alter them. Yet, they have a very real impact on employee behaviour. Therefore, each of these factors—biographical characteristics, ability, values, attitudes, personality and emotions—will be discussed as independent variables in Part 2.

There are four other individual-level variables that have been shown to affect employee behaviour: perception, individual decision making, learning and motivation. Those topics will also be introduced and discussed in Part 2.

Group-level variables

The behaviour of people in groups is more than the sum total of all the individuals acting in their own way. The complexity of our model is increased when we acknowledge that people's behaviour when they are in groups is different from their behaviour when they are alone. Therefore, the next step in the development of an understanding of OB is the study of group behaviour.

Chapter 8 lays the foundation for an understanding of the dynamics of group behaviour. That chapter discusses how individuals in groups are influenced by the patterns of behaviour they are expected to exhibit, what the group considers to be acceptable standards of behaviour, and the degree to which group members are attracted to each other. Chapter 9 translates our understanding of groups to the design of effective work teams. Chapters 10 to 14 demonstrate how communication patterns, leadership, power and politics, and levels of conflict affect group behaviour.

Organisation systems-level variables

Organisational behaviour reaches its highest level of sophistication when we add formal structure to our previous knowledge of individual and group behaviour. Just as groups are more than the sum of their individual members, so are organisations more than the sum of their member groups. The design of the formal organisation, work processes and jobs; the organisation's human resource policies and practices (that is, selection processes, training programs and performance evaluation methods); and the internal culture all have an impact on the dependent variables. These are discussed in detail in Part 3, Chapters 15 to 18.

TOWARDS A CONTINGENCY OB MODEL

Our final model is shown in Figure 1.4. It shows the five key dependent variables and a large number of independent variables, organised by level of analysis, that research indicates have varying effects on the former. As complicated as this model is, it still doesn't do justice to the complexity of the OB subject matter, but it should help to explain why the chapters in this book are arranged as they are and help you to explain and predict the behaviour of people at work.

For the most part, our model doesn't explicitly identify the vast number of contingency variables because of the tremendous complexity that would be involved in such a diagram. Rather, throughout this book we will introduce important contingency variables that will improve the explanatory linkage between the independent and dependent variables in our OB model.

Note that we have included the concepts of change and stress in Figure 1.4, acknowledging the dynamics of behaviour and the fact that work stress is an individual, group and organisational issue. Specifically, in the final chapter, we will discuss the change process, ways to manage organisational change, key change issues currently facing managers, consequences of work stress, and techniques for managing stress.

Also note that Figure 1.4 includes linkages between the three levels of analysis. For example, organisational structure is linked to leadership. This link is meant to convey that authority and leadership are related; management exerts its influence on group behaviour through leadership. Similarly, communication is the means by which individuals transmit information; thus, it is the link between individual and group behaviour.

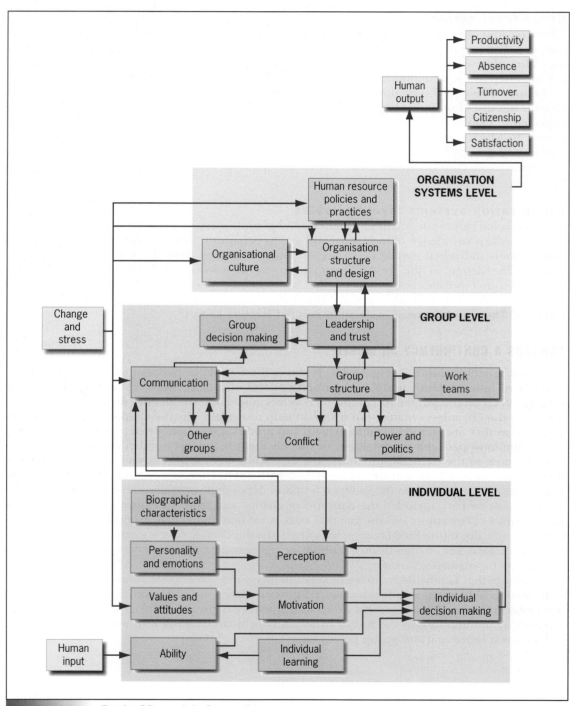

FIGURE 1.4   **Basic OB model: Stage II**

Summary and Implications for Managers

LEARNING OBJECTIVE

8

Describe why managers require a knowledge of OB

Managers need to develop their interpersonal or people skills if they are going to be effective in their jobs. Organisational behaviour (OB) is a field of study that investigates the impact that individuals, groups and structure have on behaviour within an organisation, and then it applies that knowledge to make organisations work more effectively. Specifically, OB focuses on how to improve productivity, reduce absenteeism and turnover, and increase employee citizenship and job satisfaction.

We all hold generalisations about the behaviour of people. Some of our generalisations may provide valid insights into human behaviour, but many are erroneous. Organisational behaviour uses systematic study to improve predictions of behaviour that would be made from intuition alone. But, because people are different, we need to look at OB in a contingency framework, using situational variables to moderate cause-and-effect relationships.

Organisational behaviour offers both challenges and opportunities for managers. It offers specific insights to improve a manager's people skills. It recognises differences and helps managers to see the value of workforce diversity and practices that may need to be changed when managing in different countries. It can improve quality and employee productivity by showing managers how to empower their people, design and implement change programs, and help employees balance work/life conflicts. It provides suggestions for helping managers meet chronic labour shortages. It can help managers to cope in a world of temporariness and to learn ways to stimulate innovation. Finally, OB can offer managers guidance in creating an ethically healthy work climate.

Point

SUCCESSFUL ORGANISATIONS PUT PEOPLE FIRST

Fuji Xerox does it. So does Bunnings, Microsoft, Virgin Blue, Officeworks, Johnson & Johnson and Starbucks. What is *it*? These companies pursue 'people-first' strategies.

There is an increasing amount of evidence that successful organisations put people first.* Why? Astute managers have come to learn that their organisation's employees are its only true competitive advantage. Competitors can match most organisations' products, processes, locations, distribution channels, and the like. What's far more difficult to emulate is a workforce made up of highly knowledgeable and motivated people. The characteristic that differentiates successful companies from their less successful counterparts in almost every industry is the quality of the people they are able to get and keep.

What kind of practices differentiate people-first organisations? We can list at least four: (1) They value cultural diversity. They actively seek a diverse workforce based on age, gender and race. (2) They are family-friendly. They help employees to balance work and personal responsibilities through programs such as flexible work schedules and on-site child-care facilities. (3) They invest in employee training. These organisations spend heavily to make sure employee skill levels are kept current. This not only ensures that employees can handle the latest technologies and processes for the organisation, but that employees will be marketable to other employers. (4) People-first organisations empower their employees. They push authority and responsibility down to the lowest levels.

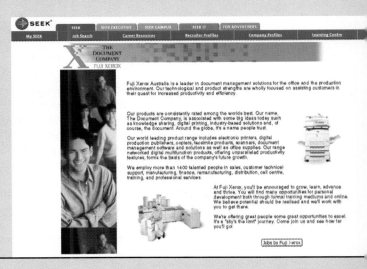

Fuji Xerox values its people and their diversity and is consistently rated among the best companies to work for. As a people-first organisation, Fuji Xerox sets a good example for other companies to follow.

Organisations that put people first have a more dedicated and committed workforce. This, in turn, converts into higher employee productivity and satisfaction. These employees are willing to put forth the extra effort—to do whatever is necessary to see that their jobs are done properly and completely. People-first strategies also lead to organisations being able to recruit smarter, more conscientious and more loyal employees.

Note: * See, for example, J. Pfeffer, *The Human Equation: Building Profits by Putting People First* (Boston: Harvard Business School Press, 1998); and P. Drucker, 'They're Not Employees, They're People', *Harvard Business Review*, February 2002, pp. 70–77.

Counterpoint

Putting 'people first' is easy to say. And it's currently politically correct. What manager, in his or her right mind, is going to admit publicly that employees take a back seat to cost cutting or profitability? It's important, however, not to confuse talk with action.

Putting people first isn't necessarily consistent with long-term competitiveness. Managers recognise this fact and are increasingly acting on it. Today's organisations are more typically pursuing a 'labour-cost-minimisation' strategy rather than a people-first strategy.

When you look beyond what managers say, you find that most business firms place profits over people. To stay competitive in a global economy, they look for cost-cutting measures. They reengineer processes and cut the size of their permanent workforce. They move jobs to countries with lower costs. And they substitute temporary employees for full-time permanent staff.

Organisations with problems typically look to staffing cuts as a first response. And organisations *without* problems are regularly reviewing their staffing needs to identify redundancies and overstaffing. Their goal is to keep themselves 'lean and mean'. In today's competitive environment, few organisations have the luxury to be able to provide employees with implied 'permanent employment' or to offer anything more than minimal job security.

For almost all organisations today, employees are a variable cost. Staffing levels are kept to a minimum, and employees are continually added or removed as needed.

Interestingly, the labour-cost-minimisation strategy appears to be spreading worldwide. It began in the United States in the early 1990s. Now it has become the model for companies in countries such as Japan, South Korea and Thailand, places that historically protected their employees in good times and bad. Many firms in these countries have abandoned their permanent-employment, people-first policies. Why? Because such policies are inconsistent with aggressive, low-cost, global competition.

Source: Points in this argument are based on N. Nicholson, 'How Hardwired is Human Behaviour?', *Harvard Business Review*, July–August 1998, pp. 135–47; and B. D. Pierce and R. White, 'The Evolution of Social Structure: Why Biology Matters', *Academy of Management Review*, October 1999, pp. 843–53.

For Discussion

1. How are OB concepts addressed in management functions, roles and skills?
2. Define organisational behaviour. Relate it to management.
3. What is an organisation? Is the family unit an organisation? Explain.
4. Identify and contrast the three general management roles.
5. What is a 'contingency approach' to OB?
6. Contrast psychology and sociology's contribution to OB.
7. 'Behaviour is generally predictable, so there is no need to formally study OB.' Why is that statement wrong?
8. What are the three levels of analysis in our OB model? Are they related? If so, how?
9. If job satisfaction isn't a behaviour, why is it considered an important dependent variable?
10. What are effectiveness and efficiency, and how are they related to organisational behaviour?
11. What do you think is the single most critical 'people' problem facing managers today? Give specific support for your position.

Exercises

Exercise 1a
WORKFORCE DIVERSITY

Purpose:
To learn about the different needs of a diverse workforce.

Time required:
Approximately 40 minutes.

Participants and roles:
Divide the class into six groups of approximately equal size. Each group is assigned one of the following roles:

- *Nancy* is 28 years old. She is a divorced mother of three children, aged three, five and seven. She is the department head. She earns $40,000 a year on her job and receives another $3,600 a year in child support from her ex-husband.
- *Ethel* is a 72-year-old widow. She works 25 hours a week to supplement her $8,000 annual pension. Including her hourly wage of $8.50, she earns $19,000 a year.
- *John* is a 34-year-old black male born in Trinidad who is now an Australian permanent resident. He is married and the father of two small children. John attends university at night and is within a year of earning his bachelor's degree. His salary is $27,000 a year. His wife is a solicitor and earns approximately $50,000 a year.
- *Lu* is a 26-year-old physically impaired male Asian Australian. He is single and has a master's degree in education. Lu is paralysed and confined to a wheelchair as a result of a car accident. He earns $32,000 a year.
- *Maria* is a single 22-year-old Samoan woman. Born and raised in Samoa, she came to Australia only three months ago. Maria's English needs considerable improvement. She earns $20,000 a year as a cleaner.
- *Mike* is a 16-year-old white male high school student who works ten hours a week after school and during holidays. He earns $10.20 an hour, or approximately $5,600 a year.

The members of each group are to assume the character consistent with their assigned role.

Background:
Our six participants work for a company that has recently installed a flexible benefits program. Instead of the traditional 'one benefit package fits all', the company is allocating an additional 25 per cent of each employee's annual pay to be used for discretionary benefits. Those benefits and their annual cost are listed below.

- Supplementary health care for employee:
  Plan A (no deductible and pays 90 per cent) = $3,000
  Plan B ($200 deductible and pays 80 per cent) = $2,000
  Plan C ($1,000 deductible and pays 70 per cent) = $500
- Supplementary health-care for dependants (same deductibles and percentages as above):
  Plan A = $2,000
  Plan B = $1,500
  Plan C = $500
- Supplementary dental plan = $500
- Life insurance:
  Plan A ($25,000 coverage) = $500
  Plan B ($50,000 coverage) = $1,000
  Plan C ($100,000 coverage) = $2,000
  Plan D ($250,000 coverage) = $3,000
- Mental health plan = $500
- Prepaid legal assistance = $300
- Leave = 2 per cent of annual pay for each week, up to six weeks a year
- Superannuation at retirement equal to approximately 50 per cent of final annual earnings = $1,500
- Four-day work week during the summer months (available only to full-time employees) = 4 per cent of annual pay

- Day-care services (after company contribution) = $2,000 for all of an employee's children, regardless of number
- Company-provided transportation to and from work = $750
- University fees reimbursement = $1,000
- Language class fees reimbursement = $500

The task:

1. Each group has 15 minutes to develop a flexible benefits package that consumes 25 per cent (and no more!) of their character's pay.
2. After completing step 1, each group appoints a spokesperson who describes to the entire class the benefits package they have arrived at for their character.
3. The entire class then discusses the results. How did the needs, concerns and problems of each participant influence the group's decision? What do the results suggest for trying to motivate a diverse workforce?

Note: Special thanks to Professor Penny Wright (San Diego State University) for her suggestions during the development of this exercise.

Exercise 1b
WHAT DO YOU KNOW ABOUT HUMAN BEHAVIOUR?

Much of what we 'know' about the world is based on intuition. We have opinions, biases, hunches and misinformation that we use both in making statements about others and in deciding what we do. The following 20 questions are designed to provide you with some feedback regarding what you 'know' about human behaviour. Read each statement and mark T (true) or F (false).

True or False

_____ 1. People who graduate in the upper third of their university course tend to make more money during their careers than do average students.

_____ 2. Exceptionally intelligent people tend to be physically weak and frail.

_____ 3. Most great athletes are of below-average intelligence.

_____ 4. All people in Australia are born equal in capacity for achievement.

_____ 5. On the average, women are slightly more intelligent than men.

_____ 6. People are definitely either introverted or extroverted.

_____ 7. After you learn something, you forget more of it in the next few hours than in the next several days.

_____ 8. In small doses, alcohol facilitates learning.

_____ 9. Women are more intuitive than men.

_____ 10. Smokers take more sick days per year than do non-smokers.

_____ 11. People 40 years old are more intelligent than people 20 years old.

_____ 12. If you have to reprimand someone for a misdeed, it's best to do so immediately after the mistake occurs.

_____ 13. People who do poorly in academic work are superior in mechanical ability.

_____ 14. High-achieving people are high risk takers.

_____ 15. Highly cohesive groups are also highly productive.

_____ 16. When people are frustrated, they frequently become aggressive.

_____ 17. Experiences as an infant tend to determine behaviour in later life.

_____ 18. Successful top managers have a greater need for money than for power.

_____ 19. Most people who work for the federal government are low risk takers.

_____ 20. Most managers are highly democratic in the way they supervise their people.

By studying OB, you will attempt to answer these questions based on the facts, rather than relying solely on intuition and workplace myths. OB is a systematic field of study that will assist you in applying knowledge about behaviour in organisations to workplace problems and issues.

Refer to Appendix C for scoring directions and key.

Source: Adapted from *Readings Organizational Behaviour PB*, 1st edition, by Altman S. © 1979. Reprinted with permission of South-Western, a division of Thomson Learning: <www.thomsonrights.com>. Fax 800 730 2215.

Case Study 1

Great Plains Software: Pursuing a People-first Strategy

Great Plains Software is a success story. Begun in 1983, today it employs 2,200 people, generates sales of US$195 million, and was recently bought by Microsoft for US$1 billion. Management attributes much of its success to the company's people-first strategy.

The company's CEO, Doug Burgum, says that the company's growth and success can be attributed to three guiding principles. First, make the company such a great place to work that people not only won't want to leave, they'll knock down the door to get in. Second, give employees ownership at every level. And third, let people grow—as professionals and as individuals.

What does Great Plains do to facilitate its people-first culture? Managers point to the company's structure and perks, and its commitment to helping employees develop their skills and leadership. Great Plains has a flat organisation structure with a minimal degree of hierarchy. Work is done mostly in teams, and there are no traditional status symbols such as executive parking spaces or corner office suites. Perks include share options for everyone, casual dress standards, an on-site child-care centre, and daily extracurricular classes in everything from aerobics to personal finance. But management is most proud of its commitment to the development of its people. The company offers a long list of training and educational opportunities to its employees. These are run on-site and designed to help employees build their skill level. Great Plains' premier training program is called 'Leadership is Everywhere'. It's designed to ensure that the company will have people who can assume new leadership roles in a continuously changing environment. The company reinforces classroom training by placing its employees in departmental teams. At the helm of these teams are 'team leaders', whose job is to help foster their charges' ideas and projects. They are also expected to provide one-on-one job coaching and career planning advice. Nearly all Great Plains employees are given the opportunity to become team leaders.

Burgum has more than just increased revenues to support his belief that his people-first strategy works. It has also succeeded in keeping employees contented. Turnover, for example, is a minuscule 5 per cent a year—far below the information-technology average of 18–25 per cent.

Questions

1. Putting people first has worked for Great Plains. If it's so effective, why do you think all firms haven't adopted these practices?
2. Do you think a people-first approach is more applicable to certain businesses or industries than others? If so, what might they be? Why?
3. What downside, if any, do you see in working at a company like Great Plains?
4. What downside, if any, do you see in managing at a company like Great Plains?
5. Some critics have argued, 'People-first policies don't lead to high profits. High profits allow people-first policies.' Do you agree? Explain your position.

Source: Adapted from S. Boehle, 'From Humble Roots', *Training*, October 2000, pp. 106–13.

Web Workout

Search engines are our navigational tool to explore the World Wide Web. Some commonly used search engines are:

- <www.goto.com>;
- <www.google.com>;
- <www.excite.com>;
- <www.lycos.com>;
- <www.hotbot.com>; and
- <www.looksmart.com>.

1. The OB issues that confront organisations are constantly changing. One possible emerging issue is Workplace Bullying. Go to <www.bullyonline.org/workbully/amibeing.htm> and then decide for yourself whether this issue is likely to become an OB challenge for organisations.
2. Visit the site <www.financeandprofitabilitybooks.com/Finance-and-Profitability-Books/Competing-in-the-Third-Wave.htm>. What implications does the concept of third-wave management have for leaders? For managers? For employees?
3. Go to <www.jezuk.co.uk/cgi-bin/view/jez/2001November> and scroll down to the posting dated 13 November 2001, which discusses the success or failure of managers. How might managers change to meet the new forces in the world today?
4. Many Australians move or are transferred to work in other countries. Working and living in other countries isn't without challenges. Go to <www.theage.com.au/articles/2003/07/02/1056825454566.html> and consider the challenges raised in this article. Are overseas work assignments good for everyone?
5. Read Tim Harcourt's address to the International Labour Organization at <www.cid.harvard.edu/cidtrade/Papers/Harcourt/DecentWork.pdf>. What benefits does he suggest outweigh the costs of organisations embracing a global market focus? Are they sufficient to counter the fears of many about the risks of globalisation?
6. The issue of temporary employment isn't confined solely to OB textbooks—it is a wider social issue. Indeed, it is a strong issue to the left side of the political spectrum, as the following site demonstrates: <www.wsws.org/articles/2003/jul2003/lab-j12.shtml>. How must managers balance the social and political views on temporary employees?
7. The site <http://cee.org.au/library/pdf/Managing%20Change/Managing%20Change_p09.pdf> puts forward the view that technology leads to change and that this change, in turn, leads to innovation and further change. How valid is this proposition in your view?
8. Achieving a balance between work and one's personal life, leading to a more committed and effective employee, is the premise of the site <www.eeo.gov.au/About_Equal_Opportunity/Key_Agenda_Items/Work_Life_Balance.asp>. Do you agree with this viewpoint?
9. Go to <www.pearsoned.com.au/52strategies> and take the 'Assess Your Work–Life Balance' on-line quiz. If you scored well, congratulations. If you didn't score well, how might you address the balance of work and personal needs in your life?

NOTES

1. See, for example, R. A. Baron and G. D. Markman, 'Beyond Social Capital: How Social Skills Can Enhance Entrepreneurs' Success', *Academy of Management Executive*, February 2000, pp. 106–16.
2. D. Foust, 'Wooing the Worker', *Business Week*, 22 May 2000, pp. 44–46.
3. *The 1997 National Study of the Changing Workforce* (New York: Families and Work Institute, 1997).
4. Georgina Curry. 'Most Value Pleasure over Pay Rate—Survey', *The Canberra Times*, 8 April 2001.
5. 'Staff Seek Paths', *Courier-Mail*, 29 January 2002.
6. H. Fayol, *Industrial and General Administration* (Paris: Dunod, 1916).
7. H. Mintzberg, *The Nature of Managerial Work* (Upper Saddle River, NJ: Prentice Hall, 1973).
8. R. L. Katz, 'Skills of an Effective Administrator', *Harvard Business Review*, September–October 1974, pp. 90–102.

9. F. Luthans, 'Successful vs. Effective Real Managers', *Academy of Management Executive*, May 1988, pp. 127–32; and F. Luthans, R. M. Hodgetts and S. A. Rosenkrantz, *Real Managers* (Cambridge, MA: Ballinger, 1988).

10. P. H. Langford, 'Importance of Relationship Management for the Career Success of Australian Managers', *Australian Journal of Psychology*, December 2000, pp. 163–69.

11. See, for example, J. E. Garcia and K. S. Keleman, 'What is Organizational Behavior Anyhow?', paper presented at the 16th Annual Organizational Behavior Teaching Conference, Columbia, MO, June 1989; and C. Heath and S. B. Sitkin, 'Big-B versus Big-O: What is *Organizational* about Organizational Behavior?', *Journal of Organizational Behavior*, February 2001, pp. 43–58.

12. E. E. Lawler, III and J. G. Rhode, *Information and Control in Organizations* (Pacific Palisades, CA: Goodyear, 1976), p. 22.

13. See F. D. Richard, C. F. Bond, Jr and J. J. Stokes-Zoota, ' "That is Completely Obvious . . . and Important": Lay Judgments of Social Psychological Findings', *Personality and Social Psychological Bulletin*, April 2001, pp. 497–505.

14. O. C. Richard, 'Racial Diversity, Business Strategy, and Firm Performance: A Resource-Based View', *Academy of Management Journal*, April 2000, pp. 164–77.

15. 'Bye-Bye, Ozzie and Harriet', *American Demographics*, December 2000, p. 59.

16. Australian Bureau of Statistics, <www.abs.gov.au/ausstats/abs@.nsf/0/FE25729C5B35DCE9CA256A620082F479?Open&Highlight=0, women,employment>, accessed 13 November 2003.

17. See, for example, E. E. Kossek and S. A. Lobel (eds), *Managing Diversity* (Cambridge, MA: Blackwell, 1996); 'Building a Competitive Workforce: Diversity—The Bottom Line', *Forbes*, 3 April 2000, pp. 181–94; and Richard, 'Racial Diversity, Business Strategy, and Firm Performance'.

18. David James, 'The Quality Equation', *Business Review Weekly*, 2–8 October 2003, pp. 64–65.

19. See, for example, W. J. Kolarik, *Creating Quality: Process Design for Results* (New York: McGraw Hill, 2000); and D. Bell, et al, *Managing Quality*, 2nd ed. (Woburn, MA: Butterworth-Heinemann, 2002).

20. See, for example, C. M. Khoong, *Reengineering in Action* (London: Imperial University Press, 1999); and J. A. Champy, *X-Engineering the Corporation* (New York: Warner Books, 2002).

21. This section is based on M. Bolch, 'The Coming Crunch', *Training*, April 2001, pp. 54–58; P. Nyhan, 'As Baby Boomers Retire, They'll Leave Big Gap in the Work Force, Chao Warns', *Seattle Post-Intelligencer*, 24 August 2001, p. C1; G. M. McEvoy and M. J. Blahna, 'Engagement or Disengagement? Older Workers and the Looming Labor Shortage', *Business Horizons*, September–October 2001, pp. 46–52; P. Francese, 'Looming Labor Shortages', *American Demographics*, November 2001, pp. 34–35; and D. Eisenberg, 'The Coming Job Boom', *Time*, 6 May 2002, pp. 40–44.

22. Cited in E. Naumann and D. W. Jackson, Jr, 'One More Time: How Do You Satisfy Customers?', *Business Horizons*, May–June 1999, p. 73.

23. See, for example, M. D. Hartline and O. C. Ferrell, 'The Management of Customer-Contact Service Employees: An Empirical Investigation', *Journal of Marketing*, October 1996, pp. 52–70; E. Naumann and D. W. Jackson, Jr, 'One More Time: How Do You Satisfy Customers?', pp. 71–76; W-C. Tsai, 'Determinants and Consequences of Employee Displayed Positive Emotions', *Journal of Management*, vol. 27, no. 4, 2001, pp. 497–512; and S. D. Pugh, 'Service with a Smile: Emotional Contagion in the Service Encounter', *Academy of Management Journal*, October 2001, pp. 1018–27.

24. J. Flaherty, 'Suggestions Rise from the Floors of U.S. Factories', *New York Times*, 18 April 2001, p. C1.

25. See, for example, P. Cappelli, J. Constantine and C. Chadwick, 'It Pays to Value Family: Work and Family Tradeoffs Reconsidered', *Industrial Relations*, April 2000, pp. 175–98; M. A. Verespej, 'Balancing Act', *Industry Week*, 15 May 2000, pp. 81–85; and R. C. Barnett and D. T. Hall, 'How to Use Reduced Hours to Win the War for Talent', *Organizational Dynamics*, vol. 29, no. 3, 2001, pp. 192–210.

26. M. Conlin, '9 to 5 Isn't Working Anymore', *Business Week*, 20 September 1999, p. 94; and 'The New World of Work: Flexibility is the Watchword', *Business Week*, 10 January 2000, p. 36.

27. S. Shellenbarger, 'What Job Candidates Really Want to Know: Will I Have a Life?', *Wall Street Journal*, 17 November 1999, p. B1; and 'U.S. Employers Polish Image to Woo a Demanding New Generation', *Manpower Argus*, February 2000, p. 2.

28. See, for example, G. R. Weaver, L. K. Trevino and P. L. Cochran, 'Corporate Ethics Practices in the Mid-1990's: An Empirical Study of the Fortune 1000', *Journal of Business Ethics*, February 1999, pp. 283–94.

29. A. J. Rucci, S. P. Kirn and R. T. Quinn, 'The Employee–Customer–Profit Chain at Sears', *Harvard Business Review*, January–February 1998, pp. 83–97.

30. S. R. Rhodes and R. M. Steers, *Managing Employee Absenteeism* (Reading, MA: Addison-Wesley, 1990). For a full review of the direct and indirect costs of absenteeism, see D. A. Harrison and J. J. Martocchio, 'Time for Absenteeism: A 20-Year Review of Origins, Offshoots, and Outcomes', *Journal of Management*, vol. 24, no. 3, 1998, pp. 305–50.

31. Cited in J. Schmid, ' "Sick" German Workers Get Corporate Medicine', *International Herald Tribune*, 28–29 September 1996, p. 1.

32. 'Employee Turnover Costs in the U.S.', *Manpower Argus*, January 2001, p. 5.

33. See, for example, D. R. Dalton and W. D. Todor, 'Functional Turnover: An Empirical Assessment', *Journal of Applied Psychology*, December

1981, pp. 716–21; G. M. McEvoy and W. F. Cascio, 'Do Good or Poor Performers Leave? A Meta-Analysis of the Relationship between Performance and Turnover', *Academy of Management Journal*, December 1987, pp. 744–62; S. Lorge, 'When Turnover Isn't So Bad', *Sales & Marketing Management*, September 1999, p. 13; and M. C. Sturman and C. O. Trevor, 'The Implications of Linking the Dynamic Performance and Turnover Literatures', *Journal of Applied Psychology*, August 2001, pp. 684–96.

34. Cited in 'You Often Lose the Ones You Love', *Industry Week*, 21 November 1988, p. 5.

35. D. W. Organ, *Organizational Citizenship Behavior: The Good Soldier Syndrome* (Lexington, MA: Lexington Books, 1988), p. 4. See also J. A. LePine, A. Erez and D. E. Johnson, 'The Nature and Dimensionality of Organizational Citizenship Behavior: A Critical Review and Meta-Analysis', *Journal of Applied Psychology*, February 2002, pp. 52–65.

36. P. M. Podsakoff, S. B. MacKenzie, J. B. Paine and D. G. Bachrach, 'Organizational Citizenship Behaviors: A Critical Review of the Theoretical and Empirical Literature and Suggestions for Future Research', *Journal of Management*, vol. 26, no. 3, 2000, pp. 543–48.

37. H. J. Leavitt, *Managerial Psychology*, rev. ed. (Chicago: University of Chicago Press, 1964), p. 3.

PHOTO CREDITS

The Individual
Part 2

CHAPTER 2   FOUNDATIONS OF INDIVIDUAL BEHAVIOUR
CHAPTER 3   VALUES, ATTITUDES AND JOB SATISFACTION
CHAPTER 4   PERSONALITY AND EMOTIONS AT WORK
CHAPTER 5   PERCEPTION AND INDIVIDUAL DECISION MAKING
CHAPTER 6   MOTIVATION CONCEPTS
CHAPTER 7   MOTIVATION: FROM CONCEPT TO APPLICATIONS

Foundations of Individual Behaviour

CHAPTER OUTLINE

Biographical characteristics
Ability
Learning

LEARNING OBJECTIVES

After studying this chapter, you should be able to:

1. Define the key biographical characteristics
2. Identify two types of ability
3. Shape the behaviour of others
4. Distinguish between the four schedules of reinforcement
5. Clarify the role of punishment in learning
6. Practise self-management

As a rule, the person who can do all things equally well is a very mediocre individual.

E. Hubbard

In accepting the award, Kirsty Dunphey is demonstrating the skill, competence and ability of a cohort of dynamic women not traditionally thought of as potential entrepreneurial or managerial material.

The Telstra National Business Women's Award was created in 1993 to recognise and reward women who quietly go about achieving extraordinary business success.[1] In the Young Business Woman of the Year category for 2002, perhaps no nominee was quite as extraordinary as the 23-year-old Tasmanian entrant, Kirsty Dunphey. Just two years before, at the age of 21, Kirsty became the youngest managing director of a real estate company in Australia, and within 18 months her firm had sold more than $20 million worth of real estate. When Kirsty won the Telstra Young Business Woman of the Year 2002 award, she was also one of three finalists for the Young Australian of the Year award presented by the Australia Day Council.

Together with her two co-directors, Kirsty works very hard to ensure that everything her company does is extraordinary. To ensure the future success of her business, Kirsty devotes a lot of attention to the rewards her staff receive for their extraordinary successes, a point not lost on the judges of the Telstra Young Business Woman of the Year 2002 award.

That we have such national awards for women is interesting, as it suggests there are differences in the role of women in organisations. In turn, this raises the question of how gender and other biographical characteristics such as age, marital status, seniority in the organisation and ability will affect the performance of individuals in the organisation. These important issues, and their impact on performance, are discussed in this chapter. We will also discuss how rewards shape behaviours such as attendance, customer service and performance. Knowing how and when those rewards should be administered to achieve the greatest impact on desired employee behaviours will also be looked at. First, however, we will look at how biographical characteristics and ability affect employee performance and satisfaction.

LEARNING OBJECTIVE

1

Define the key
biographical
characteristics

Biographical Characteristics

As discussed in Chapter 1, this textbook is essentially concerned with finding and analysing the variables that have an impact on employee productivity, absence, turnover and satisfaction. The list of those variables—as shown in Figure 1.4 of Chapter 1—is long and contains some complicated concepts. Many of the concepts—motivation, say, or power and politics, or organisational culture—are hard to assess. It might be valuable, then, to begin by looking at factors that are easily definable and readily available; data that can be obtained, for the most part, simply from information available in an employee's personnel file. What factors would these be? Obvious characteristics would be an employee's age, gender, marital status, and length of service with an organisation (seniority). Fortunately, there is a sizeable amount of research that has specifically analysed many of these **biographical characteristics**.

**biographical
characteristics**
Personal
characteristics—such as
age, gender and marital
status—that are objective
and easily obtained from
personnel records.

AGE

The relationship between age and job performance is likely to be an issue of increasing importance during the next decade. Why? There are at least three reasons. First, there is a widespread belief that job performance declines with increasing age. Regardless of whether it's true or not, a lot of people believe it and act on it. Second, as noted in Chapter 1, is the reality that the workforce is ageing. Employees aged 55 and older are currently the fastest-growing sector of the labour force.[2] Current estimates suggest the number of over-55s in Australia will rise by one-third to 1.4 million in the next decade; and worldwide, the International Labour Organization estimates that the number of persons over the age of 60 will rise 600 per cent, to 1.2 billion people, by the year 2025.[3] The third reason is government legislation that, for all intents and purposes, outlaws mandatory retirement. Most employees today no longer have to retire at the age of 65.

What is the perception of older employees? Evidence indicates that employers hold mixed feelings.[4] They see a number of positive qualities that older employees bring to their jobs: specifically, experience, judgment, a strong work ethic and commitment to quality. But older employees are also perceived as lacking flexibility and as being resistant to new technology. And in a time when organisations actively seek individuals who are adaptable and open to change, the negatives associated with age clearly hinder the initial hiring of older employees and increase the likelihood that they will be let go during cutbacks. Now let's take a look at the evidence. What effect does age actually have on turnover, absenteeism, productivity and satisfaction?

The older you get, the less likely you are to quit your job. That conclusion is based on studies of the age–turnover relationship.[5] Of course, this shouldn't be too surprising. As employees get older, they have fewer alternative job opportunities. In addition, older employees are less likely to resign than are younger employees because their long service and seniority tends to provide them with higher wage rates, longer paid holidays and more-attractive retirement benefits.

It's tempting to assume that age is also inversely related to absenteeism. After all, if older employees are less likely to quit, won't they also demonstrate higher stability by coming to work more regularly? Not necessarily. Most studies do show an inverse relationship, but close examination finds that the age–absence relationship is partially a function of whether the absence is avoidable or unavoidable.[6] In general, older employees have lower rates of avoidable absence than do younger employees. However, they have higher rates of unavoidable absence, probably due to the poorer health associated with ageing and the longer recovery period that older employees need when injured or ill. It is perhaps in recognition of this fact that many organisations now encourage or even provide flu vaccinations for employees, particularly older employees, every year.

How does age affect productivity? There is a widespread belief that productivity declines with age. It is often assumed that an individual's skills—particularly speed, agility, strength and coordination—decay over time and that prolonged job boredom and lack of intellectual stimulation all contribute to reduced productivity. The evidence, however, contradicts that belief and those assumptions. For example, during a three-year period, a large hardware chain staffed one of its stores solely with employees aged over 50 and compared its results with those of five stores with younger employees. The store staffed by the over-50 employees was significantly more productive (measured in terms of sales generated against labour costs) than two of the other stores and held its own with the other three.[7] Other reviews of the research find that age and job performance are unrelated.[8] Moreover, this finding seems to be true for almost all types of jobs, professional and non-professional. The natural conclusion is that the demands of most jobs, even those with heavy manual labour requirements, are not extreme enough for any declines in physical skills attributable to age to have an impact on productivity; or, if there is some decay due to age, it is offset by gains due to experience.[9]

Our final concern is the relationship between age and job satisfaction. On this issue, the evidence is mixed. Most studies indicate a positive association between age and satisfaction, at least up to age 60.[10] Other studies, however, have found a U-shaped relationship.[11] Several explanations could clear up these results, the most plausible being that these studies are intermixing professional and non-professional employees. When the two types are separated, satisfaction tends to continually increase among professionals as they age, whereas it falls among non-professionals during middle age and then rises again in the later years.

GENDER

Few issues initiate more debates, misconceptions and unsupported opinions than whether women perform as well on jobs as men do. In this section, we review the research on that issue.

The evidence suggests that the best place to begin is with the recognition that there are few, if any, important differences between men and women that will affect their job performance.

OB Controversies

Do older workers want to work?

Our discussion here has assumed that over-55s want to continue in the workforce and will find satisfaction in their work. As mentioned earlier in this chapter, although the number of employees over age 55 is expected to increase in Australia in the next ten years, recent research is suggesting that the percentage of over-55s currently in the Australian workforce is well down when compared with other similar economies.

It has recently come to light that less than 50 per cent of those aged between 55 and 64 years of age are still in the workforce in Australia, compared with over 70 per cent for Scandinavian countries. Why is the participation rate for this group in the Australian economy so low? Part of the reason may be the incentives to retire early. Many superannuation schemes encourage early retirement—that is, it is more lucrative to take early retirement than it is to remain in employment. Second, the 1980s and 1990s saw massive restructuring and downsizing of almost all sectors of the economy. This process had many casualties, as they no longer had the requisite skills needed in today's work environment. As such, many older employees were forced, rather than chose, to take early retirement. Perhaps the low participation rate of the 55 to 64 age-cohort is more a reflection on the lack of training for older employees than it is for other reasons. Finally, the low participation rate may be reflecting greater interest in non-work activities where individuals find greater satisfaction than they found in the workforce. Whatever the cause, it is unlikely that in the long term Australia as a society will be able to afford to have less than 50 per cent of this age-cohort out of the employment market.

Source: Based on S. Washington and J. Morris, 'Who'll Do the Work?', *Business Review Weekly*, 13 February 2003.

Many companies rely heavily on older employees to fill job vacancies. These companies find older employees to be highly productive and dependable employees. In turn these employees reward their employers with greater commitment and loyalty.

There are, for example, no consistent male–female differences in problem-solving ability, analytical skills, competitive drive, motivation, sociability or learning ability.[12] Psychological studies have found that women are more willing to conform to authority, and that men are more aggressive and more likely than women to have expectations of success, but those differences are minor and may be more a reflection of cultural forces than due to gender. Given the significant changes that have taken place in the past 30 years in terms of increasing female participation rates in the workforce and rethinking what constitutes male and female roles, you should operate on the assumption that there is no significant difference in job productivity between men and women. Similarly, there is no evidence indicating that an employee's gender affects job satisfaction.[13]

One issue that does seem to differ between genders, especially when the employee has preschool-age children, is preference for work schedules.[14] Working mothers are more likely to prefer part-time work, flexible work schedules and telecommuting in order to accommodate their family responsibilities.

But what about absence and turnover rates? Are women less stable employees than men? First, on the question of turnover, the evidence indicates no significant differences.[15] Women's quit rates are similar to those for men. The research on absence, however, consistently indicates that women have higher rates of absenteeism than men do.[16] The most logical explanation for this finding is that the research was conducted in North America, and North American culture has historically placed home and family responsibilities on the woman. When a child is ill or someone needs to stay home to wait for the plumber, it has been the woman who has traditionally taken time off from work. However, this research is undoubtedly time-bound.[17] The historical role of the woman in caring for children and as secondary breadwinner has definitely changed in the past generation, and a large proportion of men nowadays are as interested in day-care, and the problems associated with child-care in general, as are women.

This change in attitudes to and responsibility for child-care is also being reflected in the push for a national paid maternity leave scheme.[18] One of the causes of women leaving the workforce and of involuntary absences is the demands of pregnancy and child-care immediately after the child is born. Currently, only Australia and the United States, of all the 24 OECD countries, don't have such a mandatory national paid maternity leave scheme, and recent events suggest that it won't be long before Australia *does* have such a scheme. Paid maternity leave is not just for the immediate period of the birth, but extends up to anywhere from 12 to 18 months. This time period will depend on the health of both the mother and the child, economic pressures and goals of the family unit, and the availability of suitable child-care facilities. The benefits to organisations of paid maternity leave include reduced absenteeism and turnover for staff, retention of training investment and retention of key personnel. One could suggest that the differences in absenteeism between men and women are likely to become insignificant when such a national paid maternity leave scheme is finally introduced.

MARITAL STATUS

Research consistently indicates that married employees have fewer absences, undergo fewer job turnovers and are more satisfied with their jobs than are their unmarried co-workers.[19] Marriage imposes increased responsibilities that may make a steady job more valuable and important. But the question of causation is not clear. It may very well be that conscientious and satisfied employees are more likely to be married for reasons other than their marital status. Another offshoot of this issue is that research has not pursued statuses other than single or married. Does being divorced or widowed have an impact on an employee's performance and satisfaction? What about couples who live together without being married? These are questions in need of further investigation.

SENIORITY

The last biographical characteristic we will look at is length of service in the job, or seniority. With the exception of the issue of male–female differences, probably no issue is more subject to misconceptions and speculations than the impact of seniority on job performance.

Extensive reviews of the seniority–productivity relationship have been conducted.[20] If we define seniority as time on a particular job, we can say that the most recent evidence demonstrates a positive relationship between seniority and job productivity. So, seniority, expressed as work experience, appears to be a good predictor of employee productivity.

The research relating seniority to absence is quite straightforward. Studies consistently demonstrate seniority to be negatively related to absenteeism.[21] In fact, in terms of both frequencies of absence and total days lost at work, seniority is the single most important explanatory variable.[22] Seniority is also a potent variable in explaining turnover. The longer a person is in a job, the less likely they are to quit.[23] Moreover, consistent with research that suggests that past behaviour is the best predictor of future behaviour,[24] evidence indicates that seniority on an employee's previous job is a powerful predictor of that employee's future turnover.[25]

The evidence indicates that seniority and satisfaction are positively related.[26] In fact, when age and seniority are treated separately, seniority appears to be a more consistent and stable predictor of job satisfaction than is chronological age.

Ability

Contrary to what we were taught at school, we weren't all created equal. Most of us are to the left of the median on some normally distributed ability curve. Regardless of how motivated you are, it is unlikely that you can act as well as Nicole Kidman, run as fast as Cathy Freeman, write poetry as well as Henry Lawson, or sing as well as Kylie Minogue. Of course, just because we aren't all equal in abilities doesn't imply that some individuals are inherently inferior to others. What we are acknowledging is that everyone has strengths and weaknesses in terms of ability that make him or her relatively superior or inferior to others in performing certain tasks or activities.[27] From management's standpoint, the issue isn't whether people differ in terms of their abilities. They clearly do. The issue is knowing *how* people differ in abilities and using that knowledge to increase the likelihood that an employee will perform his or her job well.

What does ability mean? As we will use the term, **ability** refers to an individual's capacity to perform the various tasks in a job. It is a current assessment of what one can do. An individual's overall abilities are essentially made up of two sets of factors: intellectual and physical abilities.

INTELLECTUAL ABILITIES

Intellectual abilities are those needed to perform mental activities. Intelligence quotient (IQ) tests, for example, are designed to ascertain one's general intellectual abilities. So, too, are popular university admission tests such as the Tertiary Entrance Examination (TEE) and the graduate admission test in business (GMAT). The seven most frequently cited dimensions making up intellectual abilities are number aptitude, verbal comprehension, perceptual speed, inductive reasoning, deductive reasoning, spatial visualisation and memory.[28] Table 2.1 describes those dimensions.

Jobs differ in the demands they place on incumbents to use their intellectual abilities. Generally speaking, the more information-processing demands that exist in a job, the more general intelligence and verbal abilities will be necessary to perform the job successfully.[29] Of course, a high IQ isn't a prerequisite for all jobs. In fact, for many jobs—where employee behaviour is highly routine and there are few or no opportunities to exercise discretion—a high IQ may be unrelated to performance. On the other hand, a careful review of the evidence demonstrates that tests that assess verbal, numerical, spatial and perceptual abilities are valid predictors of job proficiency at all levels of jobs.[30] Therefore, tests that measure specific dimensions of intelligence have been found to be strong predictors of future job performance. This explains why computer

TABLE 2.1   Dimensions of intellectual ability

Dimension	Description	Job Example
Number aptitude	Ability to do speedy and accurate arithmetic	Accountant: Calculating the GST on a set of items
Verbal comprehension	Ability to understand what is read or heard and the relationship of words to each other	Factory manager: Following corporate policies
Perceptual speed	Ability to identify visual similarities and differences quickly and accurately	Fire investigator: Identifying clues to support a charge of arson
Inductive reasoning	Ability to identify a logical sequence in a problem and then solve the problem	Market researcher: Forecasting demand for a product in the next time period
Deductive reasoning	Ability to use logic and assess the implications of an argument	Supervisor: Choosing between two different suggestions offered by employees
Spatial visualisation	Ability to imagine how an object would look if its position in space were changed	Interior decorator: Redecorating an office
Memory	Ability to retain and recall past experiences	Salesperson: Remembering the names of customers

companies such as Microsoft and Apple emphasise assessing candidates' intelligence as a key element in their interview process.

The main dilemma faced by employers who use mental ability tests for selection, promotion, training and similar personnel decisions is that they may have a negative impact on racial and ethnic groups.[31] The evidence indicates that some minority groups score, on the average, as much as one standard deviation lower than whites on verbal, numerical and spatial ability tests.

In the past decade, researchers have begun to expand the meaning of intelligence beyond mental abilities. The most recent evidence suggests that intelligence can be better understood by breaking it down into four subparts: cognitive, social, emotional and cultural.[32] Cognitive intelligence encompasses the aptitudes that have long been tapped by traditional intelligence tests. Social intelligence is a person's ability to relate effectively to others. Emotional intelligence is the ability to identify, understand and manage emotions. And cultural intelligence is awareness of cross-cultural differences and the ability to function successfully in cross-cultural situations. Although this line of enquiry—towards **multiple intelligences**—is in its infancy, it does hold considerable promise.[33] For example, it may be able to help us explain why so-called smart people—those with high cognitive intelligence—don't necessarily adapt well to everyday life, work well with others, or succeed when placed in leadership roles. It may also explain why our national leaders are not necessarily highly intelligent—their strengths may lie in their social, emotional and cultural intelligence.

multiple intelligences
Intelligence contains four subparts: cognitive, social, emotional and cultural.

PHYSICAL ABILITIES

To the same degree that intellectual abilities play a larger role in complex jobs with demanding information-processing requirements, specific **physical abilities** gain importance for successfully doing less-skilled and more-standardised jobs. For example, jobs in which success demands stamina, manual dexterity, leg strength or similar talents require management to identify an employee's physical capabilities.

physical ability
The capacity to do tasks demanding stamina, dexterity, strength and similar characteristics.

Research on the requirements needed in hundreds of jobs has identified nine basic abilities involved in the performance of physical tasks.[34] These are described in Table 2.2. Individuals

TABLE 2.2	**Nine basic physical abilities**
Strength Factors	
1. *Dynamic strength*	Ability to exert muscular force repeatedly or continuously over time
2. *Trunk strength*	Ability to exert muscular strength using the trunk (particularly abdominal) muscles
3. *Static strength*	Ability to exert force against external objects
4. *Explosive strength*	Ability to expend a maximum of energy in one or a series of explosive acts
Flexibility Factors	
5. *Extent flexibility*	Ability to move the trunk and back muscles as far as possible
6. *Dynamic flexibility*	Ability to make rapid, repeated flexing movements
Other Factors	
7. *Body coordination*	Ability to coordinate the simultaneous actions of different parts of the body
8. *Balance*	Ability to maintain equilibrium despite forces pulling off balance
9. *Stamina*	Ability to continue maximum effort requiring prolonged effort over time

Source: Reprinted with permission of *HRMagazine*, published by the Society for Human Resource Management, Alexandria, VA, <www.shrm.com>.

differ in the extent to which they have each of these abilities. Not surprisingly, there is also little relationship between them: a high score on one is no assurance of a high score on others. High employee performance is likely to be achieved when management has ascertained the extent to which a job requires each of the nine abilities and then ensures that employees in that job have those abilities.

THE ABILITY–JOB FIT

Our concern is with explaining and predicting the behaviour of people at work. In this section, we have demonstrated that jobs make differing demands on people and that people differ in the abilities they possess. Therefore, employee performance is enhanced when there is a high ability–job fit.

The specific intellectual or physical abilities required for adequate job performance depend on the ability requirements of the job. So, for example, airline pilots need strong spatial–visualisation abilities; beach lifeguards need both strong spatial–visualisation abilities and body coordination; senior executives need verbal abilities; high-rise construction employees need balance; and journalists with weak reasoning abilities would likely have difficulty meeting minimum job-performance standards. Directing attention at only the employee's abilities or only the ability requirements of the job ignores the fact that employee performance depends on the interaction of the two.

What predictions can we make when the fit is poor? As alluded to previously, if employees lack the required abilities, they are likely to fail. If you are hired as a word processor and you cannot meet the job's basic keyboard typing requirements, your performance is going to be poor irrespective of your positive attitude or your high level of motivation. When the ability–job fit is out of sync because the employee has abilities that far exceed the requirements of the job, our predictions would be very different. Job performance is likely to be adequate, but there will be organisational inefficiencies and possible declines in employee satisfaction. Given that pay tends to reflect the highest skill level that employees possess, if an employee's abilities far exceed those necessary to do the job, management will be paying more than it needs to. Abilities significantly above those required can also reduce the employee's job satisfaction when the employee's desire to use his or her abilities is particularly strong and is frustrated by the limitations of the job.

Learning

All complex behaviour is learned. If we want to explain and predict behaviour, we need to understand how people learn. In this section, we define learning, present three popular learning theories, and describe how managers can facilitate employee learning.

A DEFINITION OF LEARNING

learning
Any relatively permanent change in behaviour that occurs as a result of experience.

What is **learning**? A psychologist's definition is considerably broader than the layperson's view that 'it's what we did when we went to school'. In actuality, each of us is continuously 'going to school'. Learning occurs all the time. Therefore, a generally accepted definition of learning is *any relatively permanent change in behaviour that occurs as a result of experience.*[35] Ironically, we can say that changes in behaviour indicate that learning has taken place and that learning is a change in behaviour.

Obviously, the foregoing definition suggests that we shall never see someone 'learning'. We can see changes taking place, but not the learning itself. The concept is theoretical and, hence, not directly observable:

> You have seen people in the process of learning, you have seen people who behave in a particular way as a result of learning and some of you (in fact, probably the majority of you) have 'learned'

at some time in your life. In other words, we infer that learning has taken place if an individual behaves, reacts, responds as a result of experience in a manner different from the way he formerly behaved.[36]

Our definition has several components that deserve clarification. First, learning involves change. Change may be good or bad from an organisational point of view. People can learn unfavourable behaviours—to hold prejudices or to restrict their output, for example—as well as favourable behaviours. Second, the change must be relatively permanent. Temporary changes may be only reflexive and may not represent learning. Therefore, the requirement that learning must be relatively permanent rules out behavioural changes caused by fatigue or temporary adaptations. Third, our definition is concerned with behaviour. Learning takes place when there is a change in actions. A change in an individual's thought processes or attitudes, if not accompanied by a change in behaviour, would not be learning. Finally, some form of experience is necessary for learning. Experience may be acquired directly through observation or practice, or it may be acquired indirectly, as through reading. The crucial test still remains: does this experience result in a relatively permanent change in behaviour? If the answer is 'yes', we can say that learning has taken place.

THEORIES OF LEARNING

How do we learn? Three theories have been offered to explain the process by which we acquire patterns of behaviour. These are classical conditioning, operant conditioning and social learning.

Classical conditioning

Classical conditioning grew out of experiments to teach dogs to salivate in response to the ringing of a bell, conducted at the turn of the 20th century by Russian physiologist Ivan Pavlov.[37] A simple surgical procedure allowed Pavlov to measure accurately the amount of saliva secreted by a dog. When Pavlov presented the dog with a piece of meat, the dog exhibited a noticeable increase in salivation. When Pavlov withheld the presentation of meat and merely rang a bell, the dog did not salivate. Then Pavlov proceeded to link the meat and the ringing of the bell. After repeatedly hearing the bell before getting the food, the dog began to salivate as soon as the bell rang. After a while, the dog would salivate merely at the sound of the bell, even if no food was offered. In effect, the dog had learned to respond—that is, to salivate—to the bell. Let's review this experiment to introduce the key concepts in classical conditioning.

The meat was an *unconditioned stimulus*; it invariably caused the dog to react in a specific way. The reaction that took place whenever the unconditioned stimulus occurred was called the *unconditioned response* (or the noticeable increase in salivation, in this case). The bell was an artificial stimulus, or what we call the *conditioned stimulus*. Although it was originally neutral, after the bell was paired with the meat (an unconditioned stimulus), it

classical conditioning
A type of conditioning in which an individual responds to some stimulus that wouldn't ordinarily produce such a response.

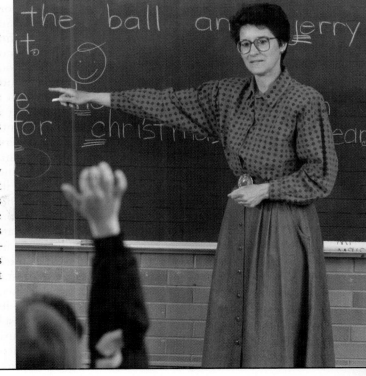

Learning occurs throughout life. Kerryn is becoming a teacher after changing careers. She not only learns on the job but also attends evening classes three times a week. 'This is the hardest thing I've ever done,' she says, 'but the sense of satisfaction is great.'

eventually produced a response when presented alone. The last key concept is the *conditioned response*. This describes the behaviour of the dog; it salivated in reaction to the bell alone.

Using these concepts, we can summarise classical conditioning. Essentially, learning a conditioned response involves building up an association between a conditioned stimulus and an unconditioned stimulus. When the stimuli, one compelling and the other one neutral, are paired, the neutral one becomes a conditioned stimulus and, hence, takes on the properties of the unconditioned stimulus.

Classical conditioning can be used to explain why Christmas carols often bring back pleasant memories of childhood; the songs are associated with the festive Christmas spirit and evoke fond memories and feelings of contentment. In an organisational setting, we can also see classical conditioning operating. For example, at one manufacturing facility, every time the top executives from the head office were scheduled to make a visit, the factory management would clean up the administrative offices and wash the windows. This went on for years. Eventually, employees would turn on their best behaviour and look prim and proper whenever the windows were cleaned—even in those occasional instances when the cleaning wasn't paired with the visit from the senior management. People had learned to associate the cleaning of the windows with a visit from the head office.

Classical conditioning is passive. Something happens and we react in a specific way. It is elicited in response to a specific, identifiable event. As such, it can explain simple reflexive behaviours. But most behaviour—particularly the complex behaviour of individuals in organisations—is emitted, rather than elicited. It is voluntary, rather than reflexive. For example, employees choose to arrive at work on time, ask their boss for help with problems or 'slacken off' when no one is watching. The learning of those behaviours is better understood by looking at operant conditioning.

Operant conditioning

operant conditioning
A type of conditioning in which desired voluntary behaviour leads to a reward or prevents a punishment.

Operant conditioning argues that behaviour is a function of its consequences. People learn to behave to get something they want or to avoid something they don't want. Operant behaviour means voluntary or learned behaviour, in contrast to reflexive or unlearned behaviour. The tendency to repeat such behaviour is influenced by the reinforcement or lack of reinforcement brought about by the consequences of the behaviour. Therefore, reinforcement strengthens a behaviour and increases the likelihood that it will be repeated.

What Pavlov did for classical conditioning, the Harvard psychologist B. F. Skinner did for operant conditioning.[38] Building on earlier work in the field, Skinner's research extensively expanded our knowledge of operant conditioning. Even his staunchest critics, who represent a sizeable group, admit that his operant concepts work.

Behaviour is assumed to be determined from without—that is, learned—rather than from within—reflexive, or unlearned. Skinner argued that creating pleasing consequences to follow specific forms of behaviour would increase the frequency of that behaviour. People will most likely engage in desired behaviours if they are positively reinforced for doing so. Rewards are most effective if they immediately follow the desired response. In addition, behaviour that is not rewarded, or is punished, is less likely to be repeated.

One can see illustrations of operant conditioning everywhere. For example, any situation in which it is either explicitly stated or implicitly suggested that reinforcements are contingent on some action on your part involves the use of operant learning. Your lecturer says that if you want a high grade in the course, you must supply correct answers on the test. A commissioned salesperson wanting to earn a sizeable income finds that doing so is contingent on generating high sales in her territory. Of course, the linkage can also work to teach the individual to engage in behaviours that work against the best interests of the organisation. Assume that your boss tells you that if you will work overtime during the next three-week busy season, you will be compensated for it at the next performance appraisal. However, when performance appraisal time comes, you find that you are given no positive reinforcement for your overtime work. The next time your boss asks you to work overtime, what will you do? You'll probably decline! Your behaviour can be explained by operant conditioning: if a behaviour fails to be positively reinforced, the probability that the behaviour will be repeated declines.

Social learning

Individuals can also learn by observing what happens to other people and just by being told about something, as well as by direct experiences. So, for example, much of what we have learned comes from watching role models—parents, teachers, peers, film and television performers, bosses, and so forth. This view that we can learn through both observation and direct experience has been called **social-learning theory**.[39]

social-learning theory
People can learn through observation and direct experience.

Although social-learning theory is an extension of operant conditioning—that is, it assumes that behaviour is a function of consequences—it also acknowledges the existence of observational learning and the importance of perception in learning. People respond to how they perceive and define consequences, not to the objective consequences themselves.

The influence of models is central to the social-learning viewpoint. Four processes have been found to determine the influence that a model will have on an individual. As we will show later in this chapter, the inclusion of the following processes when management sets up employee-training programs will significantly improve the likelihood that the programs will be successful:

1. *Attentional processes.* People learn from a model only when they recognise and pay attention to its critical features. We tend to be most influenced by models that are attractive, repeatedly available, important to us, or similar to us in our estimation.
2. *Retention processes.* A model's influence will depend on how well the individual remembers the model's action after the model is no longer readily available.
3. *Motor reproduction processes.* After a person has seen a new behaviour by observing the model, the watching must be converted to doing. This process then demonstrates that the individual can perform the modelled activities.
4. *Reinforcement processes.* Individuals will be motivated to exhibit the modelled behaviour if positive incentives or rewards are provided. Behaviours that are positively reinforced will be given more attention, learned better and performed more often.

Myth *or* Science?

'You can't teach an old dog new tricks!'

This statement is false. It reflects the widely held stereotype that older employees have difficulties in adapting to new methods and techniques. Studies consistently demonstrate that older employees are *perceived* as being relatively inflexible, resistant to change and less trainable than their younger counterparts, particularly with respect to information technology skills.[40] But these perceptions are wrong.

The evidence indicates that older employees (typically defined as people aged 50 and over) want to learn and are just as capable of learning as any other employee group. Older employees do seem to be somewhat less efficient in acquiring complex or demanding skills. That is, they may take longer to train. But once trained, they perform at levels comparable to those of younger employees.[41]

The ability to acquire the skills, knowledge or behaviour necessary to perform a job at a given level—that is, trainability—has been the subject of much research. And the evidence indicates that there are differences between people in their trainability. A number of individual-difference factors (such as ability, motivational level and personality) have been found to significantly influence learning and training outcomes.[42] However, age has not been found to influence these outcomes.

LEARNING OBJECTIVE

3

Shape the
behaviour of others

shaping behaviour
Systematically reinforcing
each successive step that
moves an individual
closer to the desired
response.

SHAPING: A MANAGERIAL TOOL

Because learning takes place on the job as well as prior to it, managers will be concerned with how they can teach employees to behave in ways that most benefit the organisation. When we attempt to mould individuals by guiding their learning in graduated steps, we are **shaping behaviour**.

Consider the situation in which an employee's behaviour is significantly different from that sought by management. If management rewarded the individual only when he or she showed desirable responses, there might be very little reinforcement taking place. In such a case, shaping offers a logical approach towards achieving the desired behaviour.

We *shape* behaviour by systematically reinforcing each successive step that moves the individual closer to the desired response. If an employee who has chronically been a half-hour late for work comes in only 20 minutes late, we can reinforce that improvement. Reinforcement would increase as responses more closely approximated the desired behaviour.

Methods of shaping behaviour

There are four ways in which to shape behaviour: through positive reinforcement, negative reinforcement, punishment and extinction.

Following a response with something pleasant is called *positive reinforcement*. This would describe, for example, the boss who praises an employee for a job well done. Following a response by the termination or withdrawal of something unpleasant is called *negative reinforcement*. If your lecturer asks a question and you don't know the answer, looking through your lecture notes is likely to preclude your being called on. This is a negative reinforcement because you have learned that looking busily through your notes prevents the lecturer from calling on you. *Punishment* is causing an unpleasant condition in an attempt to eliminate an undesirable behaviour. Giving an employee a two-day suspension from work without pay for showing up drunk is an example of punishment. Eliminating any reinforcement that is maintaining a behaviour is called *extinction*. When the behaviour isn't reinforced, it tends to be gradually extinguished. Lecturers and tutors who wish to discourage students from asking questions in class can eliminate this behaviour in their students by ignoring those who raise their hands to ask questions. Hand-raising will become extinct when it is invariably met with an absence of reinforcement.

Both positive and negative reinforcement result in learning. They strengthen a response and increase the probability of repetition. In the preceding illustrations, praise strengthens and increases the behaviour of doing a good job because praise is desired. The behaviour of 'looking busy' is similarly strengthened and increased by its terminating the undesirable consequence of being called on by the lecturer. However, both punishment and extinction weaken behaviour and tend to decrease its subsequent frequency.

Reinforcement, whether it is positive or negative, has an impressive record as a shaping tool. Our interest, therefore, is in reinforcement rather than in punishment or extinction. A review of research findings on the impact of reinforcement upon behaviour in organisations concluded that

1. Some type of reinforcement is necessary to produce a change in behaviour.
2. Some types of rewards are more effective than others for use in organisations.
3. The speed with which learning takes place and the permanence of its effects will be determined by the timing of reinforcement.[43]

Point 3 is extremely important and deserves considerable elaboration.

LEARNING OBJECTIVE

4

Distinguish between
the four schedules
of reinforcement

**continuous
reinforcement**
A desired behaviour is
reinforced each time it is
demonstrated.

Schedules of reinforcement

The two main types of reinforcement schedules are *continuous* and *intermittent*. A **continuous reinforcement** schedule reinforces the desired behaviour each and every time it is demonstrated. Take, for example, the case of someone who has historically had trouble arriving at work on time. Every time he isn't late, his manager might compliment him on his desirable behaviour. In an intermittent schedule, on the other hand, not every instance of the desirable behaviour is reinforced, but reinforcement is given often enough to make the behaviour worth repeating. This latter schedule can be compared to the workings of a poker machine, which people will continue to play even when they know that it is adjusted to give a considerable return to the pub, club or casino. The intermittent payoffs occur just often enough to reinforce the behaviour of slipping in coins and pressing the button. Evidence indicates that the intermittent, or varied, form of reinforcement tends to promote more resistance to extinction than does the continuous form.[44]

An **intermittent reinforcement** can be of a ratio or interval type. *Ratio schedules* depend on how many responses the subject makes. The individual is reinforced after giving a certain number of specific types of behaviour. *Interval schedules* depend on how much time has passed since the previous reinforcement. With interval schedules, the individual is reinforced on the first appropriate behaviour after a particular time has elapsed. A reinforcement can also be classified as fixed or variable.

When rewards are spaced at uniform time intervals, the reinforcement schedule is of the **fixed-interval** type. The critical variable is time, and it is held constant. This is the predominant schedule for most salaried employees in Australia. When you get your pay deposited into your bank account on a weekly, fortnightly, monthly or other predetermined time basis, you are rewarded on a fixed-interval reinforcement schedule.

intermittent reinforcement
A desired behaviour is reinforced often enough to make the behaviour worth repeating, but not every time it is demonstrated.

fixed-interval schedule
Rewards are spaced at uniform time intervals.

The Real Deal

The high-tech stock bubble and reinforcement schedules

The Nasdaq share index, which is heavily laden with the shares of high-tech and Internet-related companies, soared to over 5,000 in March 2000. In 1998 and 1999, this index had been rising at better than 80 per cent per year. In spite of stratospheric price–earnings ratios (many of the fastest-rising shares, in fact, had no earnings and were losing tens of millions of dollars a month), most share market analysts continued to recommend that investors buy shares in companies such as Cisco Systems, Oracle, Pets.com and Amazon.com because of the analysts' belief that the price of these shares would go a whole lot higher. They were wrong (in the summer of 2002, the Nasdaq index was below 1,400), but millions of investors bought into the analysts' irrational exuberance.

With the rally in technology stocks in the late 1990s came a change in the way that many people looked at their investment portfolios. Instead of passively handing their money over to a traditional sharebroker and pursuing a long-term strategy, many people became aggressive traders. They opened up on-line brokerage accounts and relied on real-time quotes and CNBC to provide them with a day-long supply of market news and share recommendations. They actively bought and sold shares, in some cases selling a share within minutes of buying it if they could lock in a quick profit.

In retrospect, the explosive run-up in the Nasdaq index was an example of the power of intermittent reinforcement schedules. Many of the investors who bid up Internet shares were happy to admit they knew nothing about business or technology or valuation theories. Like a poker-machine addict at Crown Casino, they just wanted in on the game. Ironically, for many traders during 1998 and 1999, trading in technology shares actually looked more like continuous reinforcement than intermittent. Everything they bought went up in price. A large number of investors who stood on the sidelines, chastising the foolishness of buying 'Internet dreams', eventually began to consider themselves fools for not playing the game. Why stand on the sidelines, watching everyone else make money, when they could play, too? By spring 2000, millions of historically conservative investors had been sucked into the high-tech bubble and ended up losing a large part of their savings and retirement portfolios.

Source: Based on *Wall Street Journal* editorial, 7 March 2001, p. A23.

variable-interval
schedule
Rewards are initiated
after a fixed or constant
number of responses.

fixed-ratio schedule
Rewards are initiated
after a fixed or constant
number of responses.

variable-ratio schedule
The reward varies relative
to the behaviour of the
individual.

If rewards are distributed in time so that reinforcements are unpredictable, the schedule is of the **variable-interval** type. When a tutor advises her class that short multiple-choice quizzes will be given during the term (the exact number of which is unknown to the students) and the quizzes will account for 20 per cent of the course grade, she is using a variable-interval schedule. Similarly, a series of randomly timed unannounced visits to a company office by the corporate audit staff is an example of a variable-interval schedule.

In a **fixed-ratio** schedule, after a fixed or constant number of responses are given, a reward is initiated. For example, a piece-rate incentive plan is a fixed-ratio schedule; the employee receives a reward based on the number of work pieces generated. If the piece rate for a zipper installer in a dressmaking factory is $5 a dozen, the reinforcement (money, in this case) is fixed to the number of zippers sewn into garments. After every dozen is sewn in, the installer has earned another $5.

When the reward varies relative to the behaviour of the individual, he or she is said to be reinforced on a **variable-ratio** schedule. Salespeople on commission are examples of individuals on such a reinforcement schedule. On some occasions, they may make a sale after only two calls on a potential customer. On other occasions, they might need to make 20 or more calls to secure a sale. The reward, then, is variable in relation to the number of successful calls the salesperson makes. Table 2.3 summarises the schedules of reinforcement.

Reinforcement schedules and behaviour

Continuous reinforcement schedules can lead to early satiation, and under this schedule behaviour tends to weaken rapidly when reinforcers are withheld. However, continuous reinforcers are appropriate for newly emitted, unstable or low-frequency responses. In contrast, intermittent reinforcers preclude early satiation because they don't follow every response. They are appropriate for stable or high-frequency responses.

In general, variable schedules tend to lead to higher performance than fixed schedules (see Figure 2.1). For example, as noted previously, most employees in organisations are paid on

TABLE 2.3	**Schedules of reinforcement**		
Reinforcement Schedule	Nature of Reinforcement	Effect on Behaviour	Example
Continuous	Reward given after each desired behaviour	Fast learning of new behaviour but rapid extinction	Compliments
Fixed-interval	Reward given at fixed time intervals	Average and irregular performance with rapid extinction	Weekly pay cheques
Variable-interval	Reward given at variable times	Moderately high and stable performance with slow extinction	Pop quizzes
Fixed-ratio	Reward given at fixed amounts of output	High and stable performance attained quickly but also with rapid extinction	Piece-rate pay
Variable-ratio	Reward given at variable amounts of output	Very high performance with slow extinction	Commissioned sales

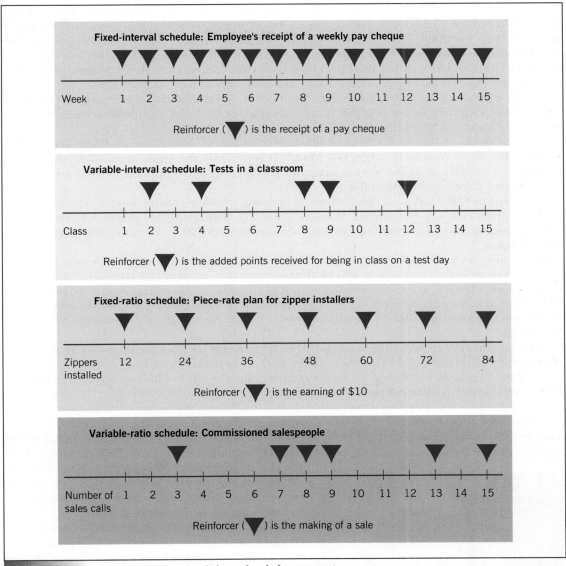

FIGURE 2.1   **Intermittent schedules of reinforcement**

fixed-interval schedules. But such a schedule doesn't clearly link performance and rewards. The reward is given for time spent on the job, rather than for a specific response (performance). In contrast, variable-interval schedules generate high rates of response and more stable and consistent behaviour because of a high correlation between performance and reward and because of the uncertainty involved—the employee tends to be more alert because there is a surprise factor.

Behaviour modification
There is a now-classic study that took place a number of years ago in the United States with freight packers at Emery Air Freight (now part of the global FedEx company).[45] Emery's management wanted packers to use freight containers for shipments whenever possible because of specific

economic savings. When packers were asked about the percentage of shipments contained, the standard reply was 90 per cent. An analysis by Emery found, however, that the actual container utilisation rate was only 45 per cent. In order to encourage employees to use containers, management established a program of feedback and positive reinforcements. Each packer was instructed to keep a checklist of his or her daily packings, both containerised and non-containerised. At the end of each day, the packer calculated his or her container utilisation rate. Almost unbelievably, container utilisation jumped to more than 90 per cent on the first day of the program and held at that level. Emery reported that this simple program of feedback and positive reinforcements saved the company US$2 million over a three-year period.

This program at Emery Air Freight illustrates the use of behaviour modification, or what has become more popularly called **OB Mod**.[46] It represents the application of reinforcement concepts to individuals in the work setting and is becoming very common in local government councils and shires around Australia.

The typical OB Mod program follows a five-step problem-solving model: (1) identifying critical behaviours; (2) developing baseline data; (3) identifying behavioural consequences; (4) developing and implementing an intervention strategy; and (5) evaluating performance improvement.[47]

Everything an employee does on his or her job isn't equally important in terms of performance outcomes. The first step in OB Mod, therefore, is to identify the critical behaviours that make a significant impact on the employee's job performance. These are those 5–10 per cent of behaviours that may account for up to 70–80 per cent of each employee's performance. Using containers whenever possible by freight packers at Emery Air Freight is an example of a critical behaviour.

The second step requires the manager to develop some baseline performance data. This is obtained by determining the number of times the identified behaviour is occurring under present conditions. In our freight packing example at Emery, this would have revealed that 45 per cent of all shipments were containerised.

The third step is to perform a functional analysis to identify the behavioural contingencies or consequences of performance. This tells the manager the antecedent cues that emit the behaviour and the consequences that are currently maintaining it. At Emery Air Freight, social norms and the greater difficulty in packing containers were the antecedent cues. This encouraged the practice of packing items separately. Moreover, the consequences for continuing the behaviour, prior to the OB Mod intervention, were social acceptance and escaping more demanding work.

Once the functional analysis is complete, the manager is ready to develop and implement an intervention strategy to strengthen desirable performance behaviours and weaken undesirable behaviours. The appropriate strategy will entail changing some elements of the performance–reward linkage—structure, processes, technology, groups or the task—with the goal of making high-level performance more rewarding. In the Emery example, the work technology was altered to require

OB Mod
The application of reinforcement concepts to individuals in the work setting.

This office employee handles a number of tasks—answering phones, filing, copying, keyboarding—but only a few behaviours will account for about 70 to 80 per cent of her performance. Determining what those critical behaviours are is the first step in designing an OB Mod program to reinforce desired behaviours.

the keeping of a checklist. The checklist plus the calculation, at the end of the day, of a container utilisation rate acted to reinforce the desirable behaviour of using containers.

The final step in OB Mod is to evaluate performance improvement. In the Emery intervention, the immediate improvement in the container utilisation rate demonstrated that behavioural change took place. That it rose to 90 per cent and held at that level further indicates that learning took place. That is, the employees underwent a relatively permanent change in behaviour.

OB Mod has been used by a number of organisations to improve employee productivity, to reduce errors, absenteeism, lateness and accident rates, and to improve friendliness towards customers.[48] For example, a clothing manufacturer saved $60,000 in one year from fewer absences. A packing firm improved productivity 16 per cent, cut errors by 40 per cent and reduced accidents by more than 43 per cent—resulting in savings of over $1 million. A bank successfully used OB Mod to increase the friendliness of its tellers, which led to a demonstrable improvement in customer satisfaction.

SOME SPECIFIC ORGANISATIONAL APPLICATIONS

We have alluded to a number of situations in which learning theory could be helpful to managers. In this section, we will briefly look at four specific applications: substituting well pay for sick pay, disciplining problem employees, developing effective employee training programs, and applying learning theory to self-management.

Well pay versus sick pay
Most organisations provide their salaried employees with paid sick leave as part of the employee's benefit program. But, ironically, organisations with paid sick leave programs experience almost twice the absenteeism of organisations without such programs.[49] The reality is that sick leave programs reinforce the wrong behaviour—absence from work. When employees receive ten paid sick days a year, it's the unusual employee who isn't sure to use them all up, regardless of whether he or she is sick. Organisations should reward *attendance*, not *absence*.

As a case in point, one oil company based in Sydney implemented a well-pay program that paid a bonus to employees working at the refinery who had no absence for any given four-week period and then paid for sick leave only after the first eight hours of absence.[50] Evaluation of the well-pay program found that it produced increased savings to the organisation, reduced absenteeism, increased productivity and improved employee satisfaction.

Forbes magazine in the United States used the same approach to cut its health-care costs.[51] It rewarded employees who stayed healthy and didn't file medical claims by paying them the difference between $500 and their medical claims, then doubling the amount. So, if someone submitted no claims in a given year, he or she would receive $1,000 ($500 × 2). By rewarding employees for good health, *Forbes* cut its major medical and dental insurance claims by over 30 per cent

Employee discipline
Every manager will, at some time, have to deal with an employee who stands around gossiping and chatting, arrives consistently late for work, steals company property, takes illegal drugs on the job, or engages in similar problem behaviours. Managers will respond with disciplinary actions such as oral reprimands, written warnings and temporary suspensions. But our knowledge about punishment's effect on behaviour indicates that the use of discipline carries costs. It may provide only a short-term solution and result in serious side effects.

Disciplining employees for undesirable behaviours tells them only what *not* to do. It doesn't tell them what alternative behaviours are preferred. The result is that this form of punishment frequently leads to only short-term suppression of the undesirable behaviour, rather than its elimination. Continued use of punishment, rather than positive reinforcement, also tends to produce a fear of the manager. As the punishing agent, the manager becomes associated in employees'

LEARNING OBJECTIVE 5
Clarify the role of punishment in learning

minds with adverse consequences. Employees respond by 'hiding' from their boss. Hence, the use of punishment can undermine manager–employee relations.

Discipline does have a place in organisations. In practice, it tends to be popular because of its ability to produce fast results in the short run. Moreover, managers are reinforced for using discipline, because it produces an immediate change in the employee's behaviour.

Developing training programs

Most organisations have some type of systematic training program. More specifically, Australian companies spent in excess of $4.7 billion in one recent year on formal training for employees, with companies employing over 100 employees spending the most—an average of 3.2 per cent of total annual salary expenditure.[52] Can these organisations draw from our discussion of learning in order to improve the effectiveness of their training programs? Certainly.

Social-learning theory offers such a guide. It tells us that training should offer a model to grab the trainee's attention; provide motivational properties; help the trainee to file away what he or she has learned for later use; provide opportunities to practise new behaviours; offer positive rewards for accomplishments; and, if the training has taken place off the job, allow the trainee some opportunity to transfer what he or she has learned to the job.[53]

Self-management

Organisational applications of learning concepts are not restricted to managing the behaviour of others. These concepts can also be used to allow individuals to manage their own behaviour and, in so doing, reduce the need for managerial control. This is called **self-management**.[54]

Self-management requires an individual to deliberately manipulate stimuli, internal processes and responses to achieve personal behavioural outcomes. The basic processes involve observing one's own behaviour, comparing the behaviour with a standard, and rewarding oneself if the behaviour meets the standard.

So, how might self-management be applied? Here's an illustration. A group of state government blue-collar employees received eight hours of training in which they were taught self-management skills.[55] They were then shown how the skills could be used for improving job attendance. They were instructed on how to set specific goals for job attendance, in both the short and intermediate term. They learned how to write a behavioural contract with themselves and to identify self-chosen reinforcers. Finally, they learned the importance of self-monitoring their attendance behaviour and administering incentives when they achieved their goals. The net result for these participants was a significant improvement in job attendance.

LEARNING OBJECTIVE

6

Practise self-management

self-management
Learning techniques that allow individuals to manage their own behaviour so that less external management control is necessary.

Summary and Implications for Managers

This chapter looked at three individual variables—biographical characteristics, ability and learning. Let's now try to summarise what we found and consider their importance for the manager who is trying to understand organisational behaviour.

Biographical characteristics

Biographical characteristics are readily available to managers. For the most part, they include data that are contained in almost every employee's personnel file. The most important conclusions that we can draw after our review of the evidence are that age seems to have no relationship to productivity; older employees and those with more and longer seniority are less likely to resign; and married employees have fewer absences, less turnover and report higher job satisfaction than do unmarried employees. But what value can this information have for managers? The obvious answer is that it can help in making choices among job applicants.

Ability

Ability directly influences an employee's level of performance and satisfaction through the ability–job fit. Given management's desire to get a compatible fit, what can be done?

First, an effective selection process will improve the fit. A job analysis will provide information about jobs currently being done and the abilities that individuals need in order to perform the jobs adequately. Applicants can then be tested, interviewed and evaluated on the degree to which they possess the necessary abilities.

Second, promotion and transfer decisions affecting individuals already in the organisation's employ should reflect the abilities of candidates. As with new employees, care should be taken to assess critical abilities that incumbents will need in the job and to match those requirements with the organisation's human resources.

Third, the fit can be improved by fine-tuning the job to better match an incumbent's abilities. Often, modifications can be made in the job that, while not having a significant impact on the job's basic activities, better adapt it to the specific talents of a given employee. Examples would be to change some of the equipment used or to reorganise tasks within a group of employees.

A final alternative is to provide training for employees. This is applicable to both new employees and job incumbents. Training can keep the abilities of incumbents current or provide new skills as times and conditions change.

Learning

Any observable change in behaviour is prima facie evidence that learning has taken place. What we want to do, of course, is to ascertain if learning concepts provide us with any insights that would allow us to explain and predict behaviour.

Positive reinforcement is a powerful tool for modifying behaviour. By identifying and rewarding performance-enhancing behaviours, management increases the likelihood that they will be repeated.

Our knowledge about learning further suggests that reinforcement is a more effective tool than punishment. Although punishment eliminates undesired behaviour more quickly than negative reinforcement does, punished behaviour tends to be only temporarily suppressed rather than permanently changed. And punishment may produce unpleasant side effects such as lower morale and higher absenteeism or turnover. In addition, the recipients of punishment tend to become resentful of the punisher. Managers, therefore, are advised to use reinforcement rather than punishment.

Finally, managers should expect that employees will look to them as models. Managers who are constantly late to work, or take two hours for lunch, or help themselves to company office supplies for personal use should expect employees to read the message they are sending and model their behaviour accordingly.

Point

ALL HUMAN BEHAVIOUR IS LEARNED

Human beings are essentially blank slates that are shaped by their environment. B. F. Skinner, in fact, summarised his belief in the power of the environment to shape behaviour when he said, 'Give me a child at birth and I can make him into anything you want.'

We have numerous societal mechanisms that exist because of this belief in the power of learned behaviour. Let's identify some of them:

- *Role of parenting*. We place a great deal of importance on the role of mothers and fathers in the raising of children. We believe, for example, that children raised without fathers will be hindered by their lack of a male role model. And parents who have continual run-ins with the law risk having government authorities take their children from them. The latter action is typically taken because society believes that irresponsible parents don't provide the proper learning environment for their children.
- *Importance of education*. Most advanced societies invest heavily in the education of their young. They typically provide ten or more years of free education. And in countries such as Australia, going on to higher education after finishing high school has become the norm rather than the exception. This investment in education is undertaken because it is seen as a way for young people to learn knowledge and skills.
- *Job training*. For individuals who don't go on to higher education, most will pursue job-training programs to develop specific work-related skills. They will take courses to become proficient as auto mechanics, dental assistants, and the like. Similarly, people who seek to become skilled trades employees will pursue apprenticeships as carpenters, electricians or plumbers. In addition, business firms invest billions of dollars each year in training and education to keep current employees' skills up to date.
- *Manipulating of rewards*. Complex compensation programs are designed by organisations to reward employees fairly for their work performance. But these programs are also designed with the intention to motivate employees. They are designed to encourage employees to engage in behaviours that management desires and to extinguish behaviours that management wants to discourage. Salary levels, for example, typically reward employee loyalty, encourage the learning of new skills, and motivate individuals to assume greater responsibilities in the organisation.

The above mechanisms all exist and flourish because organisations and society believe that people can learn and change their behaviour.

Counterpoint

While people can learn and can be influenced by their environment, far too little attention has been paid to the role that evolution has played in shaping human behaviour. Evolutionary psychology tells us that human beings are basically hardwired at birth. We start our lives with ingrained traits, honed and adapted over millions of years, that shape and limit our behaviour.

All living creatures are 'designed' by specific combinations of genes. As a result of natural selection, genes that produce faulty design features are eliminated. Characteristics that help a species survive tend to endure and get passed on to future generations. In the case of human beings, many of the characteristics that helped our early *Homo sapiens* ancestors survive live on today and influence the way we behave. Here are a few examples:

- *Emotions*. Stone Age people, at the mercy of wild predators and natural disasters, learned to trust their instincts. Those with the best instincts survived. Today, emotions remain the first screen to all information we receive. We know we're supposed to act rationally, but our emotions can never be fully suppressed.
- *Risk avoidance*. Ancient hunter-gatherers who survived weren't big risk takers. They were cautious. Today, when we're comfortable with the status quo, we typically see any change as risky and, thus, tend to resist it.
- *Stereotyping*. To prosper in a clan society, Early Man had to become expert at making judicious alliances. He had to quickly 'size-up' who he could trust and who he couldn't. Those who could do this quickly were more likely to survive. Today, like our ancestors, we naturally stereotype people based on very small pieces of evidence, mainly their looks and a few readily apparent behaviours.

- *Male competitiveness.* Males in early human societies frequently had to engage in games or battles in which there were clear winners and losers. Winners attained high status, were viewed as more attractive mates, and were more likely to reproduce. The ingrained male desire to do public battle and display virility and competence persists today.

Evolutionary psychology challenges the notion that people are free to change their behaviour if trained or motivated. It doesn't say that we can't engage in learning or exercise free will. What it does say is that nature predisposes us to act and interact in particular ways in particular circumstances. As a result, we find that people in organisational settings often behave in ways that don't appear to be beneficial to themselves or their employers.

Sources: Points in this argument are based on N. Nicholson, 'How Hardwired is Human Behavior?', *Harvard Business Review*, July–August 1998, pp. 135–47; and B. D. Pierce and R. White, 'The Evolution of Social Structure: Why Biology Matters', *Academy of Management Review*, October 1999, pp. 843–53.

For Discussion

1. Which biographical characteristics best predict productivity? Absenteeism? Turnover? Satisfaction?
2. Assess the validity of using intelligence scores for selecting new employees.
3. 'All organisations would benefit from hiring the smartest people they can get.' Do you agree or disagree with this statement? Support your answer.
4. What do you think is more likely to lead to success on a job—a good *ability–job* fit or *personality–organisation* fit? Explain.
5. Describe the specific steps you would take to ensure that an individual has the appropriate abilities to do a given job satisfactorily.
6. Contrast classical conditioning, operant conditioning and social learning.
7. Describe the four types of intermittent reinforcers.
8. What have you learned about 'learning' that could help you to explain the behaviour of students in a classroom if: (a) The lecturer gives only one test—a final examination at the end of the course? (b) The lecturer gives four exams during the year, all of which are announced on the first day of class? (c) The student's grade is based on the results of numerous exams, none of which are announced by the lecturer ahead of time?
9. What are the five steps in behaviour modification?
10. If you had to take disciplinary action against an employee, how, specifically, would you do it?
11. In addition to past work history and an employee's job performance, what other mitigating factors do you think a manager should use in applying discipline? And doesn't the mere attempt to use mitigating circumstances turn disciplinary action into a political process?
12. Describe the four processes in successful social learning.

Exercise

POSITIVE REINFORCEMENT VERSUS PUNISHMENT

Exercise overview (Steps 1–4)
This ten-step exercise takes approximately 20 minutes.

1. Two volunteers are selected to receive reinforcement or punishment from the class while performing a particular task. The volunteers leave the room.
2. The lecturer identifies an object for the student volunteers to locate when they return to the room. (The object should be unobstructed but clearly visible to the class. Examples that have worked well include a small triangular piece of paper that was left behind when a notice was torn off a classroom bulletin board, a smudge on the chalkboard, and a chip in the plaster of a classroom wall.)
3. The lecturer specifies the actions that will be in effect when the volunteers return to the room. For punishment, students should hiss or boo when the first volunteer is moving away from the object. For positive reinforcement, they should cheer and applaud when the second volunteer is getting closer to the object.

4. The lecturer should assign a student to keep a record of the time it takes each of the volunteers to locate the object.

Volunteer 1 (Steps 5 and 6)

5. Volunteer 1 is brought back into the room and is told, 'Your task is to locate and touch a particular object in the room and the class has agreed to help you. You cannot use words or ask questions. Begin.'
6. Volunteer 1 continues to look for the object until it is found, while the class engages in the punishing behaviour.

Volunteer 2 (Steps 7 and 8)

7. Volunteer 2 is brought back into the room and is told, 'Your task is to locate and touch a particular object in the room and the class has agreed to help you. You cannot use words or ask questions. Begin.'
8. Volunteer 2 continues to look for the object until it is found, while the class assists by giving positive reinforcement.

Class review (Steps 9 and 10)

9. The timekeeper will present the results on how long it took each volunteer to find the object.
10. The class will discuss: What was the difference in behaviour of the two volunteers? What are the implications of this exercise for shaping behaviour in organisations?

Source: Adapted from an exercise developed by Dr Larry Michaelson of the University of Oklahoma. Reproduced with permission.

Case Study 2

Bonne Bell Factory Employees' Average Age 70

The morning shift at the Bonne Bell plant—composed of 86 assembly-line employees—packed and boxed 10,800 tubes of lipstick. Anything over 10,000 is considered good. But in addition to meeting their production goals, what's unique on this assembly line is that the average age of these employees is 70. The oldest just turned 90.

This seniors-only production department was launched in 1997, not as some grand social experiment, but as a practical business decision. The company needed employees, labour markets were tight, and seniors were available. The company's president, who himself was 76, suggested the idea. His executives in charge of manufacturing and packaging were sceptical. They thought older employees would be too slow and costly or be misfits in a high-tech world. They worried that seniors would complain they couldn't do the work or that they needed breaks or weren't feeling well. The company's president refused to accept these stereotypes. Although he didn't know of any other company that had a senior department, he said, 'Let's try it and see if it works.'

And work it did. Retirees now account for close to 20 per cent of Bonne Bell's workforce of 500. The group handles work that once was outsourced, saving the company more than $1 million in its first four years and effectively silencing the sceptics. Shipment goals are set and met. Turnover is almost nil. And the company has a sizeable waiting list of seniors who are interested in taking jobs when they become available. Seniors have proven to be an ideal source for new employees.

Not only have seniors proven to be productive and loyal, they also help keep costs down. Since most receive Social Security, they don't rely on their jobs to fully support themselves. They don't need $15- or $20-an-hour jobs to make ends meet. They seem more than happy to accept pay rates that start at $7.50 an hour and move to $8 after a year. In addition, the company saves by providing these employees with no health benefits. Most of these employees are covered by a spouse's medical plan or Medicare and say they don't need extra coverage.

Questions

1. How do the facts in this case align with research on age in the chapter?
2. Is this factory engaging in reverse age-discrimination?
3. Do you think these older employees would perform as well if they were integrated into a department with younger employees? Support your position.
4. Do you think the success that Bonne Bell has had with hiring older employees is transferable to other companies? Would it work in Australia? Why or why not?

Source: Based on C. Ansberry, 'Averaging Age 70, Staff in This Cosmetics Plant Retires Old Stereotypes', *Wall Street Journal*, 5 February 2001, p. A1.

Web Workout

1. Age, gender and marital status all have some bearing on employee performance. If you were a business looking to locate a new operation, how would the information contained at <www.sesahs.nsw.gov.au/inter-multicult/POPprofile/Age,%20Gender,%20and%20Geographical%20Distribution%20pt1.htm> assist you in making your decisions?

2. Read the article at <www.pamij.com/7_4/v7n4_perryer.pdf>. What conclusions can you draw about the role of age and gender in the realm of ethical beliefs? Do you agree with the author's conclusions? What implications would there be for organisational performance from this study?

3. Go to <www.iamps.org/paper-pdf/love-zambelli-report.pdf> and scroll down to pages 5–6. Reported here is a study of attitudes of Armed Forces personnel in Australia. How is length of service and job satisfaction related, according to the findings of the study? Is this consistent with the theory on seniority and job satisfaction discussed in this chapter?

4. Jobs differ in the demands they place on employees. Have a read of the article at <www.careerone.com.au/resources/story/0,8523,2055809-22549,00.html>. Is intellectual ability the sole determinant of success, or are other facets of the individual also important?

5. Measuring a job applicant's intellectual ability for their potential job performance isn't an easy task. What is being offered by the New Zealand company Employers Assistance at <www.employersassist.co.nz/ea/NZ/Prod/rec/Assess/Tests.htm> to help potential employers make judgments on job applicants? How reliable do you feel a five-minute or a 12-minute test would be?

6. Operant conditioning has emerged as a vital tool in the management of health and safety issues in the workplace. Visit the site <www.nsms.us/pages/rolesupervisor.html> and read how operant conditioning has helped to improve employee safety. Why is operant conditioning, rather than classical conditioning, more suitable for this important area of organisational activity?

7. At the site <www.performancexpress.org/0208/mainframe0208.html>, locate and read the article by Aimee Boyd called 'Does Technology Work?'. This paper presents some interesting perspectives on social-learning theory. How might some of those insights have implications for managers in other organisations and industries?

8. Washing one's hands is a crucial activity for medical staff in any hospital. Read how OB Mod was used to increase the compliance with professional standards in this regard at <www.mja.com.au/public/issues/apr1/tibballs/tibball.html>.

KSS Program

KNOW THE CONCEPTS   SELF-AWARENESS   SKILLS APPLICATIONS

Developing effective disciplining skills

After you have read this chapter, take Self-Assessment #26 (How Good Am I at Giving Feedback?) on your enclosed CD-Rom and complete the skill-building module entitled 'Effective Disciplining' on page 631.

NOTES

1. Based on <www.morrisonrealestateonline.com/kristy.html> and <www.telstra.com.au/newsroom/release.cfm?ReleaseID=23681>.

2. M. Bolch, 'The Changing Face of the Workforce', *Training*, December 2000, pp. 73–78.

3. J. Morris, 'The Declining Years', *Business Review Weekly*, 20 March 2003; Australian Bureau of Statistics, 2000, *Population Projections 1999 to 2101*, Cat. No. 3222.0, Canberra, AGPS.

4. 'American Business and Older Workers: A Road Map to the 21st Century', a report prepared for the American Association of Retired Persons by DYG Inc., 1995; 'Valuing Older Workers: A Study of Costs and Productivity', a report prepared for the American Association of Retired Persons by ICF Inc., 1995; and W. C. K. Chiu, A. W. Chan, E. Snape and T. Redman, 'Age Stereotypes and Discriminatory Attitudes towards Older Workers: An East–West Comparison', *Human Relations*, May 2001, pp. 629–61.

5. S. R. Rhodes, 'Age-Related Differences in Work Attitudes and Behavior: A Review and Conceptual Analysis', *Psychological Bulletin*, March 1983, pp. 328–67; J. L. Cotton and J. M. Tuttle, 'Employee Turnover: A Meta-Analysis and Review with Implications for Research', *Academy*

of Management Review, January 1986, pp. 55–70; and D. R. Davies, G. Matthews and C. S. K. Wong, 'Ageing and Work', in C. L. Cooper and I. T. Robertson (eds), *International Review of Industrial and Organizational Psychology*, vol. 6 (Chichester, England: Wiley, 1991), pp. 183–87.

6. Rhodes, 'Age-Related Differences in Work Attitudes and Behavior', pp. 347–49; R. D. Hackett, 'Age, Tenure, and Employee Absenteeism', *Human Relations*, July 1990, pp. 601–19; and Davies, Matthews and Wong, 'Ageing and Work', pp. 183–87.

7. Cited in K. Labich, 'The New Unemployed', *Fortune*, 8 March 1993, p. 43.

8. See G. M. McEvoy and W. F. Cascio, 'Cumulative Evidence of the Relationship between Employee Age and Job Performance', *Journal of Applied Psychology*, February 1989, pp. 11–17; and F. L. Schmidt and J. E. Hunter, 'The Validity and Utility of Selection Methods in Personnel Psychology: Practical and Theoretical Implications of 85 Years of Research Findings', *Psychological Bulletin*, September 1998, pp. 262–74.

9. See, for example, F. J. Landy, et al, *Alternatives to Chronological Age in Determining Standards of Suitability for Public Safety Jobs* (University Park, PA: Center for Applied Behavioral Sciences, Pennsylvania State University, 1992).

10. A. L. Kalleberg and K. A. Loscocco, 'Aging, Values, and Rewards: Explaining Age Differences in Job Satisfaction', *American Sociological Review*, February 1983, pp. 78–90; R. Lee and E. R. Wilbur, 'Age, Education, Job Tenure, Salary, Job Characteristics, and Job Satisfaction: A Multivariate Analysis', *Human Relations*, August 1985, pp. 781–91; and Davies, Matthews and Wong, 'Ageing and Work', pp. 176–83.

11. K. M. Kacmar and G. R. Ferris, 'Theoretical and Methodological Considerations in the Age–Job Satisfaction Relationship', *Journal of Applied Psychology*, April 1989, pp. 201–07; G. Zeitz, 'Age and Work Satisfaction in a Government Agency: A Situational Perspective', *Human Relations*, May 1990, pp. 419–38; and G. Koretz, 'Yes, Workers Are Grumpier', *Business Week*, 13 November 2000, p. 42.

12. See, for example, A. H. Eagly and L. L. Carli, 'Sex Researchers and Sex-Typed Communications as Determinants of Sex Differences in Influenceability: A Meta-Analysis of Social Influence Studies', *Psychological Bulletin*, August 1981, pp. 1–20; J. S. Hyde, 'How Large Are Cognitive Gender Differences?', *American Psychologist*, October 1981, pp. 892–901; and P. Chance, 'Biology, Destiny, and All That', *Across the Board*, July–August 1988, pp. 19–23.

13. R. P. Quinn, G. L. Staines and M. R. McCullough, *Job Satisfaction: Is There a Trend?* Document 2900-00195 (Washington, DC: Government Printing Office, 1974).

14. See, for example, B. Kantrowitz, P. Wingert and K. Robins, 'Advocating a "Mommy Track"', *Newsweek*, 13 March 1989, p. 45; and S. Shellenbarger, 'More Job Seekers Put Family Needs First', *Wall Street Journal*, 15 November 1991, p. B1.

15. R. W. Griffeth, P. W. Hom and S. Gaertner, 'A Meta-Analysis of Antecedents and Correlates of Employee Turnover: Update, Moderator Tests, and Research Implications for the Next Millennium', *Journal of Management*, vol. 26, no. 3, 2000, pp. 463–88.

16. See, for example, J. P. Leigh, 'Sex Differences in Absenteeism', *Industrial Relations*, Fall 1983, pp. 349–61; K. D. Scott and E. L. McClellan, 'Gender Differences in Absenteeism', *Public Personnel Management*, Summer 1990, pp. 229–53; and A. VandenHeuvel and M. Wooden, 'Do Explanations of Absenteeism Differ for Men and Women?', *Human Relations*, November 1995, pp. 1309–29.

17. See, for example, M. Tait, M. Y. Padgett and T. T. Baldwin, 'Job and Life Satisfaction: A Reevaluation of the Strength of the Relationship and Gender Effects as a Function of the Date of the Study', *Journal of Applied Psychology*, June 1989, pp. 502–07; and M. B. Grover, 'Daddy Stress', *Forbes*, 6 September 1999, pp. 202–08.

18. This paragraph is based on G. McColl, 'Motherhood Statement', *Business Review Weekly*, 20 February 2003.

19. K. R. Garrison and P. M. Muchinsky, 'Attitudinal and Biographical Predictors of Incidental Absenteeism', *Journal of Vocational Behavior*, April 1977, pp. 221–30; C. J. Watson, 'An Evaluation and Some Aspects of the Steers and Rhodes Model of Employee Attendance', *Journal of Applied Psychology*, June 1981, pp. 385–89; R. T. Keller, 'Predicting Absenteeism from Prior Absenteeism, Attitudinal Factors, and Nonattitudinal Factors', *Journal of Applied Psychology*, August 1983, pp. 536–40; J. M. Federico, P. Federico and G. W. Lundquist, 'Predicting Women's Turnover as a Function of Extent of Met Salary Expectations and Biodemographic Data', *Personnel Psychology*, Winter 1976, pp. 559–66; R. Marsh and H. Mannari, 'Organizational Commitment and Turnover: A Predictive Study', *Administrative Science Quarterly*, March 1977, pp. 57–75; and D. R. Austrom, T. Baldwin and G. J. Macy, 'The Single Worker: An Empirical Exploration of Attitudes, Behavior, and Well-Being', *Canadian Journal of Administrative Sciences*, December 1988, pp. 22–29.

20. M. E. Gordon and W. J. Fitzgibbons, 'Empirical Test of the Validity of Seniority as a Factor in Staffing Decisions', *Journal of Applied Psychology*, June 1982, pp. 311–19; M. E. Gordon and W. A. Johnson, 'Seniority: A Review of Its Legal and Scientific Standing', *Personnel Psychology*, Summer 1982, pp. 255–80; M. A. McDaniel, F. L. Schmidt and J. E. Hunter, 'Job Experience Correlates of Job Performance', *Journal of Applied Psychology*, May 1988, pp. 327–30; and M. A. Quinones, J. K. Ford and M. S. Teachout, 'The Relationship between Work Experience and Job Performance: A Conceptual and Meta-Analytic Review', *Personnel Psychology*, Winter 1995, pp. 887–910.

21. Garrison and Muchinsky, 'Attitudinal and Biographical Predictors of Incidental Absenteeism'; N. Nicholson, C. A. Brown and J. K. Chadwick-Jones, 'Absence from Work and Personal Characteristics', *Journal of Applied Psychology*, June 1977, pp. 319–27; and R. T. Keller, 'Predicting Absenteeism from Prior Absenteeism, Attitudinal Factors, and Nonattitudinal Factors', *Journal of Applied Psychology*, August 1983, pp. 536–40.

22. P. O. Popp and J. A. Belohlav, 'Absenteeism in a Low Status Work Environment', *Academy of Management Journal*, September 1982, p. 681.

23. Griffeth, Hom and Gaertner, 'A Meta-Analysis of Antecedents and Correlates of Employee Turnover'.

24. R. D. Gatewood and H. S. Field, *Human Resource Selection* (Chicago: Dryden Press, 1987).

25. J. A. Breaugh and D. L. Dossett, 'The Effectiveness of Biodata for Predicting Turnover', paper presented at the National Academy of Management Conference, New Orleans, August 1987.

26. A. G. Bedeian, G. R. Ferris and K. M. Kacmar, 'Age, Tenure, and Job Satisfaction: A Tale of Two Perspectives', *Journal of Vocational Behavior*, February 1992, pp. 33–48.

27. K. R. Murphy (ed.), *Individual Differences and Behavior in Organizations* (San Francisco: Jossey-Bass, 1996).

28. M. D. Dunnette, 'Aptitudes, Abilities, and Skills', in M. D. Dunnette (ed.), *Handbook of Industrial and Organizational Psychology* (Chicago: Rand McNally, 1976), pp. 478–83.

29. D. Lubinski and R. V. Dawis, 'Aptitudes, Skills, and Proficiencies', in M. D. Dunnette and L. M. Hough (eds), *Handbook of Industrial & Organizational Psychology*, 2nd ed., vol. 3 (Palo Alto, CA: Consulting Psychologists Press, 1992), pp. 30–33.

30. See, for example, J. E. Hunter and R. F. Hunter, 'Validity and Utility of Alternative Predictors of Job Performance', *Psychological Bulletin*, January 1984, pp. 72–98; J. E. Hunter, 'Cognitive Ability, Cognitive Aptitudes, Job Knowledge, and Job Performance', *Journal of Vocational Behavior*, December 1986, pp. 340–62; W. M. Coward and P. R. Sackett, 'Linearity of Ability–Performance Relationships: A Reconfirmation', *Journal of Applied Psychology*, June 1990, pp. 297–300; M. J. Ree, J. A. Earles and M. S. Teachout, 'Predicting Job Performance: Not Much More Than *g*', *Journal of Applied Psychology*, August 1994, pp. 518–24; and Schmidt and Hunter, 'The Validity and Utility of Selection Methods in Personnel Psychology'.

31. P. Bobko, P. L. Roth and D. Potosky, 'Derivation and Implications of a Meta-Analytic Matrix Incorporating Cognitive Ability, Alternative Predictors, and Job Performance', *Personnel Psychology*, Autumn 1999, pp. 561–89.

32. This section is based on R. E. Riggio, S. E. Murphy and F. J. Pirozzolo (eds), *Multiple Intelligences and Leadership* (Mahwah, NJ: Lawrence Erlbaum, 2002).

33. H. Gardner, *Intelligence Reframed: Multiple Intelligence for the 21st Century* (New York: Basic Books, 1999).

34. E. A. Fleishman, 'Evaluating Physical Abilities Required by Jobs', *Personnel Administrator*, June 1979, pp. 82–92.

35. See, for example, H. M. Weiss, 'Learning Theory and Industrial and Organizational Psychology', in M. D. Dunnette and L.M. Hough (eds), *Handbook of Industrial & Organizational Psychology*, 2nd ed., vol. 1 (Palo Alto: Consulting Psychologists Press, 1990), pp. 172–73.

36. W. McGehee, 'Are We Using What We Know about Training? Learning Theory and Training', *Personnel Psychology*, Spring 1958, p. 2.

37. I. P. Pavlov, *The Work of the Digestive Glands*, trans. W. H. Thompson (London: Charles Griffin, 1902). See also the special issue of *American Psychologist* (September 1997, pp. 933–72) commemorating Pavlov's work.

38. B. F. Skinner, *Contingencies of Reinforcement* (East Norwalk, CT: Appleton-Century-Crofts, 1971).

39. A. Bandura, *Social Learning Theory* (Upper Saddle River, NJ: Prentice Hall, 1977).

40. See literature review in Davies, Matthews and Wong, 'Ageing and Work', in C.L. Cooper and I.T. Robertson (eds.), *International Review of Industrial and Organizational Psychology*, vol. 6 (Chichester, England: Wiley, 1991), pp. 159–60.

41. Ibid, p. 165.

42. M. E. Gordon and S. L. Cohen, 'Training Behavior as a Predictor of Trainability', *Personnel Psychology*, Summer 1973, pp. 261–72; and I. Robertson and S. Downs, 'Learning and the Prediction of Performance: Development of Trainability Testing in the United Kingdom', *Journal of Applied Psychology*, February 1979, pp. 42–50.

43. T. W. Costello and S. S. Zalkind, *Psychology in Administration* (Englewood Cliffs, NJ: Prentice Hall, 1963), p. 193.

44. F. Luthans and R. Kreitner, *Organizational Behavior Modification and Beyond*, 2nd ed. (Glenview, IL: Scott, Foresman, 1985); and A. D. Stajkovic and F. Luthans, 'A Meta-Analysis of the Effects of Organizational Behavior Modification on Task Performance, 1975–95', *Academy of Management Journal*, October 1997, pp. 1122–49.

45. 'At Emery Air Freight: Positive Reinforcement Boosts Performance', *Organizational Dynamics*, Winter 1973, pp. 41–50.

46. F. Luthans and R. Kreitner, *Organizational Behavior Modification and Beyond: An Operant and Social Learning Approach* (Glenview, IL: Scott, Foresman, 1985); and Stajkovic and Luthans, 'A Meta-Analysis of the Effects of Organizational Behavior Modification on Task Performance, 1975–95'.

47. Stajkovic and Luthans, 'A Meta-Analysis of the Effects of Organizational Behavior Modification on Task Performance', p. 1123.

48. See, for example, L. W. Frederiksen, *Handbook of Organizational Behavior Management* (New York: Wiley, 1982); B. Sulzer-Azarof, B. Loafman, R. J. Merante and A.C. Hlavacek, 'Improving Occupational Safety in a Large Industrial Plant: A Systematic Replication', *Journal of Organizational Behavior Management*, vol. 11, no. 1, 1990, pp. 99–120; J. C. Landau, 'The Impact of a Change in an Attendance Control System on Absenteeism and Tardiness', *Journal of Organizational Behavior Management*, vol. 13, no. 2, 1993, pp. 51–70; C. S. Brown and B. Sulzer-Azaroff, 'An Assessment of the Relationship between Customer Satisfaction and Service Friendliness', *Journal of*

Organizational Behavior Management, vol. 14, no. 2, 1994, pp. 55–75; and F. Luthans and A. D. Stajkovic, 'Reinforce for Performance: The Need to Go Beyond Pay and Even Rewards', *Academy of Management Executive,* May 1999, pp. 49–57.

49. D. Willings, 'The Absentee Worker', *Personnel and Training Management,* December 1968, pp. 10–12.

50. B. H. Harvey, J. F. Rogers and J. A. Schultz, 'Sick Pay vs. Well Pay: An Analysis of the Impact of Rewarding Employees for Being on the Job', *Public Personnel Management Journal,* Summer 1983, pp. 218–24.

51. M. S. Forbes, Jr, 'There is a Better Way', *Forbes,* 26 April 1993, p. 23.

52. Australian Bureau of Statistics, 1997, *Employer Training Expenditure Australia: July to September 1996,* Cat. No. 6353.0, Canberra, AGPS.

53. See, for example, S. J. Simon and J. M. Werner, 'Computer Training Through Behavior Modeling, Self-Paced, and Instructional Approaches: A Field Experiment', *Journal of Applied Psychology,* December 1996, pp. 648–59; and D. Stamps, 'Learning is Social. Training is Irrelevant?', *Training,* February 1997, pp. 34–42.

54. See, for example, S. E. Markham and I. S. Markham, 'Self-Management and Self-Leadership Reexamined: A Levels-of-Analysis Perspective', *Leadership Quarterly,* Fall 1995, pp. 343–60; and C. A. Frayne and J. M. Geringer, 'Self-Management Training for Improving Job Performance: A Field Experiment Involving Salespeople', *Journal of Applied Psychology,* June 2000, pp. 361–72.

55. G. P. Latham and C. A. Frayne, 'Self-Management Training for Increasing Job Attendance: A Follow-up and a Replication', *Journal of Applied Psychology,* June 1989, pp. 411–16.

3

Values, Attitudes and Job Satisfaction

CHAPTER OUTLINE

Values
Attitudes
Job satisfaction

LEARNING OBJECTIVES

After studying this chapter, you should be able to:

1. Contrast terminal and instrumental values
2. List the dominant values in today's workforce
3. Identify the five value dimensions of national culture
4. Contrast the three components of an attitude
5. Summarise the relationship between attitudes and behaviour
6. Identify the role consistency plays in attitudes
7. State the relationship between job satisfaction and behaviour
8. Identify four employee responses to dissatisfaction

*How can I know what I think
'til I see what I say?*
E. M. Forster

Predicting the future is no easy task as Marg Savage and her team can attest—get it wrong and Marg is out of a job!

Marg Savage has an interesting job. The 30-year-old Microsoft employee heads up a group that is trying to figure out what the Generation Nexters—those people born after 1980 (see endnote)—thinks and wants.[1] She hopes to use this information to help Microsoft better understand its future employees and customers. After all, this is the first generation that never knew a world without computers and the Internet—something in which Microsoft has a crucial commercial interest. Savage is using a number of approaches to tap into the values of Generation Nexters. For example, on one recent July morning, she invited ten of the company's 500-plus summer interns to talk about their lives and dreams over coffee in a Seattle restaurant. A question was posed: 'What's most important to you in your ideal job?' At first, the interns' replies were predictable: good people, a balance between work and life, flexible hours. Then the interns became more passionate. They talked about integrity, teamwork and moral support, responsibility, and freedom to pursue their visions. When one pounded the table and yelled, 'I don't ever, *ever* want to lose the kid-like view that I can change the world!' the rest of the interns cheered. This comment had hit a button. But Marge wasn't really surprised. Her research, and that of others who are studying the Generation Nexters, confirms that these young people want to work for a company that understands their generation, provides a work climate that supports their needs, and where they can have a significant influence in shaping society. More specifically, and good news for Microsoft, Generation Nexters see technology and the Internet as a major force for changing the world. In this chapter, we look at values, how they've changed from generation to generation, and what these changes mean for managing people of different ages. We'll also review research on the topic of attitudes, demonstrate the link between attitudes and behaviour, and look at factors that shape employees' satisfaction with their jobs.

Values

Is capital punishment right or wrong? If a person likes power, is that good or bad? The answers to these questions are value-laden. Some might argue, for example, that capital punishment is right because it is an appropriate retribution for crimes such as murder and treason. However, others might argue, just as strongly, that no government has the right to order the taking of anyone's life.

Values represent basic convictions that 'a specific mode of conduct or end-state of existence is personally or socially preferable to an opposite or converse mode of conduct or end-state of existence'.[2] They contain a judgmental element in that they carry an individual's ideas as to what is right, good or desirable. Values have both content and intensity attributes. The content attribute says that a mode of conduct or end-state of existence is *important*. The intensity attribute specifies *how important* it is. When we rank an individual's values in terms of their intensity, we obtain that person's **value system**. All of us have a hierarchy of values that forms our value system. This system is identified by the relative importance we assign to values such as freedom, pleasure, self-respect, honesty, obedience and equality.

Are values fluid and flexible? Generally speaking, no. Values tend to be relatively stable and enduring.[3] A significant portion of the values we hold is established in our early years—from parents, teachers, friends and others. As children, we are told that certain behaviours or outcomes are always desirable or always undesirable. There were few grey areas. You were told, for example, that you should be honest and responsible. You were never taught to be just a little bit honest or a little bit responsible. It is this absolute or 'black-or-white' learning of values that more or less ensures their stability and endurance. The process of questioning our values, of course, may result in a change. We may decide that these underlying convictions are no longer acceptable. More often, our questioning merely acts to reinforce the values we hold.

values
Basic convictions that a specific mode of conduct or end-state of existence is personally or socially preferable to an opposite or converse mode of conduct or end-state of existence.

value system
A hierarchy based on a ranking of an individual's values in terms of their intensity.

IMPORTANCE OF VALUES

Values are important to the study of organisational behaviour because they lay the foundation for the understanding of attitudes and motivation and because they influence our perceptions. Individuals enter an organisation with preconceived notions of what 'ought' and what 'ought not' to be. Of course, these notions are not value free. On the contrary, they contain interpretations of right and wrong. Furthermore, they imply that certain behaviours or outcomes are preferred over others. As a result, values cloud objectivity and rationality.

Values generally influence attitudes and behaviour.[4] Suppose that you enter an organisation with the view that allocating pay on the basis of performance is right, while allocating pay on the basis of seniority is wrong or inferior. How are you going to react if you find that the organisation you have just joined rewards seniority and not performance? You're likely to be disappointed— and this can lead to job dissatisfaction and the decision not to exert a high level of effort since 'it's probably not going to lead to more money, anyway'. Would your attitudes and behaviour be different if your values aligned with the organisation's pay policies? Most likely.

SOURCES OF VALUE SYSTEMS

When we were children, why did many of our mothers tell us 'you should always eat everything on your plate'? Why is it that, at least historically in our society, achievement has been considered good and being lazy has been considered bad? The answer is that, in our culture, certain values have developed over time and are continuously reinforced. Achievement, peace, cooperation, equity, fairness and the right to have your say are societal values that are considered desirable to most people in Australia and New Zealand.[5] These values aren't fixed, but when they change, they do so very slowly.

The values we hold are essentially established in our early childhood years—from parents, relatives, teachers, friends, television and other influences. Your early idea of what is right and wrong was probably formulated from the views expressed by your parents. Think back to your early views on such topics as education, sex, religion and politics. For the most part, they were the same as those expressed by your parents. As you grew up and were exposed to other value systems, you might have altered some of your values. For example, in high school, if you wanted to be a member of a peer group whose values included the conviction that 'every person should listen to loud music', there is a good probability that you changed your value system to align with members of the group, even if it meant rejecting your parents' value that 'music should only be listened to at a moderate volume or it will damage your ears'.

TYPES OF VALUES

Can we classify values? The answer is: yes. In this section, we review two approaches to developing value typologies.

Rokeach Value Survey

Milton Rokeach created the Rokeach Value Survey (RVS).[6] The RVS consists of two sets of values, with each set containing 18 individual value items. One set, called **terminal values**, refers to desirable end-states of existence. These are the goals that a person would like to achieve during his or her lifetime. The other set, called **instrumental values**, refers to preferable modes of behaviour, or means of achieving the terminal values. Table 3.1 gives common examples for each of these sets.

Several studies confirm that the RVS values vary among groups.[7] People in the same occupations or categories (for example, corporate managers, union members, parents, students) tend

LEARNING OBJECTIVE

1

Contrast terminal and instrumental values

terminal values
Desirable end-states of existence; the goals that a person would like to achieve during his or her lifetime.

instrumental values
Preferable modes of behaviour or means of achieving one's terminal values.

TABLE 3.1	Terminal and instrumental values in the Rokeach Value Survey
Terminal Values	**Instrumental Values**
A comfortable life (a prosperous life)	Ambitious (hard-working, aspiring)
An exciting life (a stimulating, active life)	Broadminded (open-minded)
A sense of accomplishment (lasting contribution)	Capable (competent, effective)
A world of peace (free of war and conflict)	Cheerful (lighthearted, joyful)
A world of beauty (beauty of nature and the arts)	Clean (neat, tidy)
Equality (brotherhood, equal opportunity for all)	Courageous (standing up for beliefs)
Family security (taking care of loved ones)	Forgiving (willing to pardon others)
Freedom (independence, free choice)	Helpful (working for the welfare of others)
Happiness (contentedness)	Honest (sincere, truthful)
Inner harmony (freedom from inner conflict)	Imaginative (daring, creative)
Mature love (sexual and spiritual intimacy)	Independent (self-reliant, self-sufficient)
National security (protection from attack)	Intellectual (intelligent, reflective)
Pleasure (an enjoyable, leisurely life)	Logical (consistent, rational)
Salvation (saved, eternal life)	Loving (affectionate, tender)
Self-respect (self-esteem)	Obedient (dutiful, respectful)
Social recognition (respect, admiration)	Polite (courteous, well-mannered)
True friendship (close companionship)	Responsible (dependable, reliable)
Wisdom (a mature understanding of life)	Self-controlled (restrained, self-disciplined)

Source: Reprinted with the permission of The Free Press, a Division of Simon & Schuster, Inc., from *The Nature of Human Values* by Milton Rokeach. Copyright © 1973 by The Free Press. All rights reserved.

to hold similar values. For example, one study compared corporate executives, members of the steelworkers' union and members of a community activist group. Although a good deal of overlap was found among the three groups,[8] there were also some very significant differences (see Table 3.2). The activists had value preferences that were quite different from those of the other two groups. They ranked 'equality' as their most important terminal value; executives and union members ranked this value 12 and 13, respectively. Activists ranked 'helpful' as their second-highest instrumental value. The other two groups both ranked it 14. These differences are important, because executives, union members and activists all have a vested interest in what corporations do. 'When corporations and critical stakeholder groups such as these [other] two come together in negotiations or contend with one another over economic and social policies, they are likely to begin with these built-in differences in personal value preferences . . . Reaching agreement on any specific issue or policy where these personal values are importantly implicated might prove to be quite difficult.'[9] Being aware of these differences and having an understanding of different value systems can help managers to predict behaviour better and therefore manage situations where different value systems occur.

LEARNING OBJECTIVE

2

List the dominant values in today's workforce

Contemporary work cohorts

We have integrated several recent analyses of work values into four groups that attempt to capture the unique values of different cohorts or generations in the workforce.[10] (No assumption is made that this framework would apply universally across all cultures.[11]) Table 3.3 proposes that employees can be segmented by the era in which they entered the workforce. Because most people start work between the ages of 18 and 23, the eras also correlate closely with the chronological age of employees.

Employees who grew up influenced by the Great Depression, the Second World War, the Andrews Sisters, the Cold War, Korea and the Berlin blockage entered the workforce through the 1950s and early 1960s believing in hard work, the status quo and authority figures. We call them *veterans*. Once hired, veterans tended to be loyal to their employer. In terms of the terminal values on the RVS, these employees are likely to place the greatest importance on a comfortable life and family security.

Baby-boomers entered the workforce from the mid-1960s through to the mid-1980s. This cohort were influenced heavily by the civil rights movement, women's lib, the Beatles, the Vietnam War, the anti-war movement and baby-boom competition. They brought with them a large measure of the 'hippie ethic' and distrust of authority. But they place a great deal of emphasis on achievement and material success. They are pragmatists who believe that ends can justify means. Baby-

---

TABLE 3.2   Mean value rankings of executives, union members and activists (top five only)

Executives		Union Members		Activists	
Terminal	**Instrumental**	**Terminal**	**Instrumental**	**Terminal**	**Instrumental**
1. Self-respect	1. Honest	1. Family security	1. Responsible	1. Equality	1. Honest
2. Family security	2. Responsible	2. Freedom	2. Honest	2. A world at peace	2. Helpful
3. Freedom	3. Capable	3. Happiness	3. Courageous	3. Family security	3. Courageous
4. A sense of accomplishment	4. Ambitious	4. Self-respect	4. Independent	4. Self-respect	4. Responsible
5. Happiness	5. Independent	5. Mature love	5. Capable	5. Freedom	5. Capable

Source: Based on W. C. Frederick and J. Weber, 'The Values of Corporate Managers and Their Critics: An Empirical Description and Normative Implications', in W. C. Frederick and L. E. Preston (eds), *Business Ethics: Research Issues and Empirical Studies* (Greenwich, CT: JAI Press, 1990), pp. 123–44.

TABLE 3.3	Dominant work values in today's workforce		
Cohort	Approximate Period Born	Current Age	Dominant Work Values
Veterans	1920s to early 1940s	60+	Hardworking, conservative, conforming; loyalty to the organisation
Baby-boomers	1945–1960	40–60	Success, achievement, ambition, dislike of authority; loyalty to career
Gen-Xers	1960–1980	25–40	Work/life balance, team-oriented, dislike of rules; loyalty to relationships
Nexters	1980 to present	Under 25	Confident, financial success, self-reliant but team-oriented; loyalty to both self and relationships

Source: Based on <www.businessweek.com/1999/99_07/b3616001.htm>; <www.committment.com/getalong.html>; and <www.gentrends.com/Articles/Instore2000/Millennials%20Nexters%20Strangers.pdf>.

boomers see the organisations that employ them merely as vehicles for their careers. Terminal values such as a sense of accomplishment and social recognition rank high with them.

Gen-Xers' lives have been shaped by globalisation, two-career parents, MTV, AIDS and computers. They value flexibility, life options and the achievement of job satisfaction. Family and relationships are very important to this cohort. They also enjoy team-oriented work. Money is important as an indicator of career performance, but Gen-Xers are willing to trade off salary increases, titles, security and promotions for increased leisure time and expanded lifestyle options. In search of balance in their lives, Gen-Xers are less willing to make personal sacrifices for the sake of their employer than previous generations were. On the RVS, they rate high on true friendship, happiness and pleasure.

The most recent entrants to the workforce, the *Nexters*, grew up during prosperous times. Defining events in their development and growth include diversity and multiculturalism, violence at home, school and in the media, single-parent families are more the norm, terrorism, 24-hour news, and TV talk shows on every possible topic. They tend to have high expectations, believe in themselves, and are confident about their ability to succeed. They seem to be on a never-ending search for the ideal job, see nothing wrong with constant job-hopping, and continually look for meaning in their work. Nexters are at ease with diversity and are the first generation to take technology for granted. They have lived most of their lives with CD players, VCRs, cellular phones and the Internet. This generation is very money-oriented and desirous of the things that money can buy. They seek financial success. Like Xers, they enjoy teamwork but they are also highly self-reliant and value civic duty and achievement. They tend to emphasise terminal values such as freedom and a comfortable life.

An understanding that individuals' values differ but tend to reflect the societal values of the period in which they grew up can be a valuable aid in explaining and predicting behaviour. Employees in their sixties, for example, are more likely to accept authority than their fellow employees who are ten or 15 years younger. And workers in their thirties are more likely than their parents to resist having to work weekends and are more prone to leave a job in mid-career to pursue another that provides more leisure time.

VALUES, LOYALTY AND ETHICAL BEHAVIOUR

Has there been a decline in business ethics? While the issue is debatable, a lot of people think ethical standards began to erode in the late 1970s.[12] If there has been a decline in ethical

OB Controversies

Corporate value statements for sale

A recent employee attitude survey asked workers about the company's statement of values that included quality, integrity, respect for the individual and profitability. Even though nearly all the employees were aware of the value statement, only 60 per cent of them actually believed that the company meant it. Only 45 per cent of employees at the company believed that the company lived its creed when it came to 'soft' values such as integrity and respect. A study at another company compared what top executives said with its published values. It turned out that the leaders talked about hard values, such as profitability, all the time, discussing soft values far less often. Values and trust are interdependent, and trust is a two-way street: employer trusting employee, employee trusting employer. People don't buy corporate values, according to Thomas Stewart; they make their own. Over time, he believes, self-interest distorts corporate values.

T. J. Larkin, an Australian expert on organisational communication, feels strongly that senior managers should stop all this discussion and communication about values. He goes even further and says that if an organisation and senior managers are spending a lot of time telling their staff about values, it's a pretty good sign that fraud is likely—they are probably not living up to the values they talk about. He points to one study that shows that 43 per cent of employees believe that management cheats and lies, and that it's the frontline staff who are most cynical about corporate values. It's behaviour that indicates values, not value statements, and there are many examples where companies adopt 'Trust, Teamwork and Tomorrow'-type values and then downsize, outsource and, in some cases, have private investigators watch employees during and after work!

A number of organisations are attempting to introduce 'value-driven' change. The idea is first to define the values you want to operate your organisation by—usually values that will lead to a successful business. Then you define objectives and behaviours you want from your staff—you are then on the road to success.

Well, many staff will play the 'value game', because it's good. They will list all the nice values humans and organisations should live by. They will then sit back and watch if management conducts the organisation by them or if the 'numbers' drive the business!

Source: Based on articles by T. Stewart, 'Why Value Statements Don't Work', *Fortune*, 10 June 1996, pp. 137–38; and T. Larkin and S. Larkin, 'Reaching and Changing Frontline Employees', *Harvard Business Review*, May–June 1996, pp. 95–104.

standards, perhaps we should look to our work cohorts' values model (see Table 3.3) for a possible explanation. After all, managers consistently report that the action of their bosses is the most important factor influencing ethical and unethical behaviour in their organisations.[13] Given this fact, the values of those in middle and upper management should have a significant bearing on the entire ethical climate within an organisation.

Through the mid-1970s, veterans, whose loyalties were to their employers, dominated the managerial ranks. When faced with ethical dilemmas, their decisions were made in terms of what was best for their organisation. Beginning in the mid-to-late 1970s, baby-boomers began to rise into the upper levels of management. By the early 1990s, a large portion of middle and top management positions in business organisations were held by baby-boomers.

The loyalty of baby-boomers is to their careers. Their focus is inward and their primary concern is with looking out for 'Number One'. Recent large multi-million-dollar CEO payouts add weight to this view. Such self-centred values would be consistent with a decline in ethical standards. Could this help to explain the alleged decline in business ethics beginning in the late 1970s?

The potential good news in this analysis is that Gen-Xers are now in the process of moving into middle-management slots and soon will be rising into top management. Since their loyalty is to relationships, they are more likely to consider the ethical implications of their actions on others around them. The result? We might look forward to an uplifting of ethical standards in business over the next decade or two merely as a result of changing values within the managerial ranks.

VALUES ACROSS CULTURES

In Chapter 1, we described the new global village and said 'managers have to become capable of working with people from different cultures'. Because values differ across cultures, an understanding of these differences should be helpful in explaining and predicting behaviour of employees from different countries.

Hofstede's framework for assessing cultures

One of the most widely referenced approaches for analysing variations among cultures has been developed by Geert Hofstede.[14] He surveyed more than 116,000 IBM employees in 40 countries about their work-related values. He found that managers and employees vary on five value dimensions of national culture. They are listed and defined as follows:

- **Power distance**. The degree to which people in a country accept that power in institutions and organisations is distributed unequally. Ranges from relatively equal (low power distance) to extremely unequal (high power distance).
- **Individualism** versus **collectivism**. Individualism is the degree to which people in a country prefer to act as individuals rather than as members of groups. Collectivism is the equivalent of low individualism.
- **Quantity of life** versus **quality of life**. Quantity of life is the degree to which values such as assertiveness, the acquisition of money and material goods, and competition prevail. Quality of life is the degree to which people value relationships, and show sensitivity and concern for the welfare of others.[15]
- **Uncertainty avoidance**. The degree to which people in a country prefer structured over unstructured situations. In countries that score high on uncertainty avoidance, people have an increased level of anxiety, which manifests itself in greater nervousness, stress and aggressiveness.
- **Long-term** versus **short-term orientation**. People in cultures with long-term orientations look to the future and value thrift and persistence. A short-term orientation values the past and present, and emphasises respect for tradition and fulfilling social obligations.

What did Hofstede's research conclude? A few highlights are shown in Table 3.4. China and West Africa scored high on power distance; the United States and the Netherlands scored low. Most Asian countries were more collectivist than individualistic; the United States ranked highest among all countries on individualism. Germany and Hong Kong rated high on quantity of life; Russia and the Netherlands rated low. On uncertainty avoidance, France and Russia were high; Hong Kong and the United States were low. And China and Hong Kong had a long-term orientation, whereas France and the United States had a short-term orientation.

The GLOBE framework for assessing cultures

Hofstede's cultural dimensions have become the basic framework for differentiating among national cultures. This is in spite of the fact that the data on which it's based comes from a single company and is nearly 30 years old. Since these data were originally gathered, a lot has happened on the world scene. Some of the most obvious include the fall of the Soviet Union, the merging of East and West Germany, the end of apartheid in South Africa and the rise of China as a global power. All this suggests the need for an updated assessment of cultural dimensions. The GLOBE study provides such an update.[16]

Begun in 1993, the Global Leadership and Organizational Behavior Effectiveness (GLOBE) research program is an ongoing cross-cultural investigation of leadership and national culture. Using data from 825 organisations in 62 countries, the GLOBE team identified nine dimensions

LEARNING OBJECTIVE

3

Identify the five value dimensions of national culture

power distance
A national culture attribute describing the extent to which a society accepts that power in institutions and organisations is distributed unequally.

individualism
A national culture attribute describing the degree to which people prefer to act as individuals rather than as a member of groups.

collectivism
A national culture attribute that describes a tight social framework in which people expect others in groups of which they are a part to look after them and protect them (*see also* **culture**).

quantity of life
A national culture attribute describing the extent to which societal values are characterised by assertiveness and materialism.

quality of life
A national culture attribute that emphasises relationships and concern for others.

uncertainty avoidance
A national culture attribute describing the extent to which a society feels threatened by uncertain and ambiguous situations and tries to avoid them.

long-term orientation
A national culture attribute that emphasises the future, thrift and persistence.

short-term orientation
A national culture attribute that emphasises the past and present, respect for tradition and fulfilling social obligation.

TABLE 3.4	**Examples of cultural dimensions**				
Country	Power Distance	Individualism*	Quantity of Life**	Uncertainty Avoidance	Long-term Orientation***
China	High	Low	Moderate	Moderate	High
France	High	High	Moderate	High	Low
Germany	Low	High	High	Moderate	Moderate
Hong Kong	High	Low	High	Low	High
Indonesia	High	Low	Moderate	Low	Low
Japan	Moderate	Moderate	High	Moderate	Moderate
Netherlands	Low	High	Low	Moderate	Moderate
Russia	High	Moderate	Low	High	Low
United States	Low	High	High	Low	Low
West Africa	High	Low	Moderate	Moderate	Low
Australia	Low	High	High	Low	Low

*A low score is synonymous with collectivism. **A low score is synonymous with high quality of life. ***A low score is synonymous with a short-term orientation.

Source: Adapted from G. Hofstede, 'Cultural Constraints in Management Theories', *Academy of Management Executive*, February 1993, p. 91. Copyright © 1993 by Academy of Management. Reprinted by permission of Academy of Management in the format Textbook via the Copyright Clearance Center.

on which national cultures differ. (See Table 3.5 for examples of country ratings on each of the dimensions.)

- *Assertiveness.* The extent to which a society encourages people to be tough, confrontational, assertive and competitive versus modest and tender. This is essentially equivalent to Hofstede's quantity-of-life dimension.
- *Future orientation.* The extent to which a society encourages and rewards future-oriented behaviours such as planning, investing in the future and delaying gratification. This is essentially equivalent to Hofstede's long-term/short-term orientation.
- *Gender differentiation.* The extent to which a society maximises gender role differences.
- *Uncertainty avoidance.* As identified by Hofstede, the GLOBE team defined this term as a society's reliance on social norms and procedures to alleviate the unpredictability of future events.
- *Power distance.* As did Hofstede, the GLOBE team defined this as the degree to which members of a society expect power to be unequally shared.
- *Individualism/collectivism.* Again, this term was defined, as was Hofstede's, as the degree to which individuals are encouraged by societal institutions to be integrated into groups within organisations and society.

France is one country high on power distance, individualism and uncertainty avoidance while it is rated moderate for quantity of life and has a short-term orientation. This contrasts with its neighbour Germany which is low on power distance, high on individualism and quantity of life, and moderate on the other two dimensions.

TABLE 3.5   **GLOBE highlights**

Dimension	Countries Rating Low	Countries Rating Moderate	Countries Rating High
Assertiveness	Sweden New Zealand Switzerland	Egypt Ireland Philippines	Spain US Greece
Future orientation	Russia Argentina Poland	Slovenia Egypt Ireland	Denmark Canada Netherlands
Gender differentiation	Sweden Denmark Slovenia	Italy Brazil Argentina	South Korea Egypt Morocco
Uncertainty avoidance	Russia Hungary Bolivia	Israel US Mexico	Austria Denmark Germany
Power distance	Denmark Netherlands South Africa	England France Brazil	Russia Spain Thailand
Individualism/collectivism*	Denmark Singapore Japan	Hong Kong US Egypt	Greece Hungary Germany
In-group collectivism	Denmark Sweden New Zealand	Japan Israel Qatar	Egypt China Morocco
Performance orientation	Russia Argentina Greece	Sweden Israel Spain	US Taiwan New Zealand
Humane orientation	Germany Spain France	Hong Kong Sweden Taiwan	Indonesia Egypt Malaysia

*A low score is synonymous with collectivism.

Source: M. Javidan and R. J. House, 'Cultural Acumen for the Global Manager: Lessons from Project GLOBE', *Organizational Dynamics*, Spring 2001, pp. 289–305. Reprinted with permission of Elsevier.

- *In-group collectivism.* In contrast to focusing on societal institutions, this dimension encompasses the extent to which members of a society take pride in membership in small groups, such as their family and circle of close friends, and the organisations in which they are employed.
- *Performance orientation.* This refers to the degree to which a society encourages and rewards group members for performance improvement and excellence.
- *Humane orientation.* This is defined as the degree to which a society encourages and rewards individuals for being fair, altruistic, generous, caring and kind to others. This closely approximates Hofstede's quality-of-life dimension.

A comparison of the GLOBE dimensions against those identified by Hofstede suggests that the former has extended Hofstede's work rather than replaced it. The GLOBE study confirms that Hofstede's five dimensions are still valid. However, it has added some additional dimensions and provides us with an updated measure of where countries rate on each dimension. For example, while the United States led the world in individualism in the 1970s, today it scores in the mid-ranks of countries. We can expect future cross-cultural studies of human behaviour and organisational practices to increasingly use the GLOBE dimensions to assess differences between countries.

Implications for OB

Most of the concepts that currently make up the body of knowledge we call *organisational behaviour* have been developed by Americans using American subjects within domestic contexts. A comprehensive study, for example, of more than 11,000 articles published in 24 management and organisational behaviour journals over a ten-year period revealed that approximately 80 per cent of the studies were done in the United States and had been conducted by Americans.[17] Follow-up studies continue to confirm the lack of cross-cultural considerations in management and OB research,[18] although the past half-dozen years has seen some improvement. What this means is that (1) not all OB theories and concepts are universally applicable to managing people around the world, especially in countries where work values are considerably different from those in the United States; and (2) you should take into consideration cultural values when trying to understand the behaviour of people in different countries. To help you with this second point, we'll regularly consider the generalisability of theories and concepts presented in this book to different cultures.

LEARNING OBJECTIVE 4

Contrast the three components of an attitude

Attitudes

attitudes
Evaluative statements or judgments concerning objects, people or events (*see also* **attitude surveys**).

cognitive component of an attitude
The opinion or belief segment of an attitude.

affective component of an attitude
The emotional or feeling segment of an attitude.

behavioural component of an attitude
An intention to behave in a certain way towards someone or something.

Attitudes are evaluative statements—either favourable or unfavourable—concerning objects, people or events. They reflect how one feels about something. When I say, 'I like my job', I am expressing my attitude about work.

Attitudes are not the same as values, but the two are interrelated. You can see this by looking at the three components of an attitude: cognition, affect and behaviour.[19]

The belief that 'discrimination is wrong' is a value statement. Such an opinion is the **cognitive component of an attitude**. It sets the stage for the more critical part of an attitude—its **affective component**. Affect is the emotional or feeling segment of an attitude and is reflected in the statement, 'I don't like Jon because he discriminates against Aborigines and other minorities.' Finally, and we'll discuss this issue at considerable length later in this section, affect can lead to behavioural outcomes. The **behavioural component of an attitude** refers to an intention to behave in a certain way towards someone or something. So, to continue our example, I might choose to avoid Jon because of my feeling about him.

Viewing attitudes as made up of three components—cognition, affect and behaviour—is helpful in understanding their complexity and the potential relationship between attitudes and behaviour. But for clarity's sake, keep in mind that the term *attitude* essentially refers to the affect part of the three components.

Also keep in mind that, in contrast to values, your attitudes are less stable. Advertising messages, for example, attempt to alter your attitudes towards a certain product or service: if the people at BP can get you to hold a favourable feeling towards their petroleum products, that attitude may lead to a desirable behaviour (for them)—your purchase of BP products. One of the ways advertisers attempt to alter attitudes is by the use of colour. BP uses green as the dominant colour in its marketing to give the impression of environmental awareness—despite petroleum products being a very large contributor to greenhouse gases, global warming and the destruction of the ozone layer.

In organisations, attitudes are important because they affect job behaviour. If employees believe, for example, that supervisors, auditors, managers, and time-and-motion engineers are all in a conspiracy to make employees work harder for the same or less money, then it makes sense to try to understand how these attitudes were formed, their relationship to actual job behaviour and how they might be changed.

LEARNING OBJECTIVE

5

Summarise the relationship between attitudes and behaviour

TYPES OF ATTITUDES

A person can have thousands of attitudes, but OB focuses our attention on a very limited number of work-related attitudes. These work-related attitudes tap positive or negative evaluations that employees hold about aspects of their work environment. Most of the research in OB has been concerned with three attitudes: job satisfaction, job involvement and organisational commitment.[20]

Job satisaction

The term *job satisfaction* refers to an individual's general attitude towards his or her job. A person with a high level of job satisfaction holds positive attitudes about the job, while a person who is dissatisfied with his or her job holds negative attitudes about the job. When people speak of employee attitudes, more often than not they mean job satisfaction. In fact, the two are frequently used interchangeably. Because of the high importance OB researchers have given to job satisfaction, we'll review this attitude in considerable detail later in this chapter.

Job involvement

The term **job involvement** is a more recent addition to the OB literature.[21] While there isn't complete agreement over what the term means, a workable definition states that job involvement measures the degree to which a person identifies psychologically with his or her job and considers his or her perceived performance level important to self-worth.[22] Employees with a high level of job involvement strongly identify with and really care about the kind of work they do.

High levels of job involvement have been found to be related to fewer absences and lower resignation rates.[23] However, it seems to more consistently predict turnover than absenteeism, accounting for as much as 16 per cent of the variance in the former.[24]

job involvement
The degree to which a person identifies with his or her job, actively participates in it, and considers his or her performance important to self-worth.

Organisational commitment

The third job attitude we will discuss is **organisational commitment**, which is defined as a state in which an employee identifies with a particular organisation and its goals, and wishes to maintain membership in the organisation.[25] So, high job involvement means identifying with one's specific job, while high organisational commitment means identifying with one's employing organisation.

As with job involvement, the research evidence demonstrates negative relationships between organisational commitment and both absenteeism and turnover.[26] In fact, studies demonstrate that an individual's level of organisational commitment is a better indicator of turnover than the far more frequently used job satisfaction predictor, explaining as much as 34 per cent of the variance.[27] Organisational commitment is probably a better predictor because it is a more global and enduring response to the organisation as a whole than is job satisfaction.[28] An employee may be dissatisfied with their particular job and consider it a temporary condition, yet not be dissatisfied with the organisation as a whole. But when dissatisfaction spreads to the organisation itself, individuals are more likely to consider resigning.

The above evidence, most of which was produced more than two decades ago, needs to be qualified to reflect the changing employee–employer relationship. The unwritten loyalty contract that existed 20 years ago between employees and employers has been seriously damaged; and the notion of an employee staying with a single organisation for most of his or her career has become increasingly obsolete. As such, 'measures of employee–firm attachment, such as commitment, are problematic for new employment relations'.[29] This suggests that *organisational* commitment is

organisational commitment
The degree to which an employee identifies with a particular organisation and its goals, and wishes to maintain membership in the organisation.

probably less important as a work-related attitude than it once was. In its place, we might expect something akin to *occupational* commitment to become a more relevant variable because it better reflects today's fluid workforce.[30]

LEARNING OBJECTIVE

6

Identify the role consistency plays in attitudes

ATTITUDES AND CONSISTENCY

Did you ever notice how people change what they say so that it doesn't contradict what they do? Perhaps a friend of yours has consistently argued that the quality of locally-produced cars isn't up to that of the imports and that he would never own anything but an imported vehicle. However, when his father gives him a late-model Australian-made car, suddenly they're not so bad. Or, when standing for election to Parliament, a new potential candidate believes that public service is a good chance to achieve social goals and plays a very important role. If she fails to get elected, however, she may say, 'I recognise that political office isn't all it's cracked up to be, anyway!'

Research has generally concluded that people seek consistency among their attitudes and between their attitudes and their behaviour.[31] This means that individuals seek to reconcile divergent attitudes and to align their attitudes and behaviour so that they appear rational and consistent. When there is an inconsistency, forces are initiated to return the individual to an equilibrium state in which attitudes and behaviour are again consistent. This can be done by altering either the attitudes or the behaviour, or by developing a rationalisation for the discrepancy. Bank personnel provide an example.[32] How, you might wonder, do these people cope with the ongoing barrage of negative media reports and being lampooned by comedians? They can deny that the banks are acting in a greedy manner and that any claims of unfair fees, charges or actions are not true. They can brainwash themselves by continually articulating the benefits of the major banks to society. They can acknowledge the negative consequences of high fees and charges and closures of rural banks, but rationalise that shareholders demand these measures. They can accept the social responsibility arguments and begin actively working to reduce fees and charges, or at least to reduce their cost to the more vulnerable members of society, such as those on pensions or social welfare. Or they can quit their job because the dissonance is too great.

COGNITIVE DISSONANCE THEORY

Can we also assume from this consistency principle that an individual's behaviour can always be predicted if we know his or her attitude on a subject? If Mr Jones views the company's pay level as too low, will a substantial increase in his pay change his behaviour—that is, make him work harder? The answer to this question is, unfortunately, more complex than merely a 'yes' or 'no'.

cognitive dissonance
Any incompatibility between two or more attitudes or between behaviour and attitudes.

In the late 1950s, Leon Festinger proposed the theory of **cognitive dissonance**.[33] This theory sought to explain the linkage between attitudes and behaviour. *Dissonance* means an inconsistency. *Cognitive dissonance* refers to any incompatibility that an individual might perceive between two or more of his or her attitudes, or between his or her behaviour and attitudes. Festinger argued that any form of inconsistency is uncomfortable and that individuals will attempt to reduce the dissonance and, hence, the discomfort. Therefore, individuals will seek a stable state, in which there is a minimum of dissonance.

Of course, no individual can completely avoid dissonance. You know that cheating on your income tax is wrong, but you 'fudge' the numbers a bit every year, and hope you're not audited. Or you tell your children to brush their teeth after every meal, but *you* don't. So, how do people cope? Festinger would propose that the desire to reduce dissonance would be determined by the *importance* of the elements creating the dissonance, the degree of *influence* the individual believes he or she has over the elements, and the rewards that may be involved in dissonance.

If the elements creating the dissonance are relatively unimportant, the pressure to correct this imbalance will be low. However, say that a corporate manager—Mrs Wong—believes strongly that no company should pollute the air or water. Unfortunately, Mrs Wong, because of the requirements of her job, is placed in the position of having to make decisions that would trade off her company's profitability against her attitudes on pollution. She knows that dumping the company's raw sewage into the local river (which we shall assume is legal in this case) is in the best economic interest of her firm. What will she do? Clearly, Mrs Wong is experiencing a high degree of cognitive dissonance. Because of the importance of the elements in this example, we cannot expect Mrs Wong to ignore the inconsistency. There are several paths she can follow to deal with her dilemma. She can change her behaviour (stop polluting the river). Or she can reduce dissonance by concluding that the dissonant behaviour isn't so important after all. ('I've got to make a living, and in my role as a corporate decision maker, I often have to place the good of my company above that of the environment or society.') A third alternative would be for Mrs Wong to change her attitude. ('There is nothing wrong with polluting the river.') Still another choice would be to seek out more consonant elements to outweigh the dissonant ones. ('The benefits to society from manufacturing our products more than offset the cost to society of the resulting water pollution.')

The degree of influence that individuals believe they have over the elements will have an impact on how they will react to the dissonance. If they perceive the dissonance to be an uncontrollable result—something over which they have no choice—they are less likely to be receptive to attitude change. If, for example, the dissonance-producing behaviour is required as a result of the boss's directive, the pressure to reduce dissonance would be less than if the behaviour was performed voluntarily. While dissonance exists, it can be rationalised and justified.

Rewards also influence the degree to which individuals are motivated to reduce dissonance. High rewards accompanying high dissonance tend to reduce the tension inherent in the dissonance. The rewards act to reduce dissonance by increasing the consistency side of the individual's balance sheet.

These moderating factors suggest that just because individuals experience dissonance, they won't necessarily move directly towards consistency—that is, towards reduction of this dissonance. If the issues underlying the dissonance are of minimal importance, if an individual perceives that the dissonance is externally imposed and is substantially uncontrollable by him or her, or if rewards are significant enough to offset the dissonance, the individual won't be under great tension to reduce the dissonance.

What are the organisational implications of the theory of cognitive dissonance? It can help to predict the propensity to engage in attitude and behavioural change. For example, if individuals are required by the demands of their job to say or do things that contradict their personal attitude, they will tend to modify their attitude in order to make it compatible with the cognition of what they have said or done. In addition, the greater the dissonance—after it has been moderated by importance, choice and reward factors—the greater the pressures to reduce it.

MEASURING THE A–B RELATIONSHIP

We have maintained throughout this chapter that attitudes affect behaviour. Early research on attitudes assumed that they were causally related to behaviour—that is, the attitudes that people hold determine what they do. Common sense, too, suggests a relationship. Is it not logical that people watch television programs that they say they like, or that employees try to avoid assignments they find distasteful?

However, in the late 1960s, this assumed relationship between attitudes (A) and behaviour (B), expressed as the A–B relationship, was challenged by a review of the research.[34] Based on an evaluation of a number of studies that investigated the A–B relationship, the reviewer concluded that attitudes were unrelated to behaviour or, at best, only slightly related.[35] More recent research has demonstrated that attitudes significantly predict future behaviour and confirmed Festinger's original belief that taking moderating variables into account can enhance the relationship.[36]

LEARNING OBJECTIVE

7

State the relationship between job satisfaction and behaviour

Moderating variables

The most powerful moderators have been found to be the *importance* of the attitude, its *specificity*, its *accessibility*, whether there exist *social pressures*, and whether a person has *direct experience* with the attitude.[37]

Important attitudes are ones that reflect fundamental values, self-interest, or identification with individuals or groups that a person values. Attitudes that individuals consider important tend to show a strong relationship to behaviour.

The more specific the attitude and the more specific the behaviour, the stronger the link between the two. For example, asking someone specifically about her intention to stay with the organisation for the next six months is likely to better predict turnover for that person than if you asked her how satisfied she was with her pay.

Attitudes that are easily remembered are more likely to predict behaviour than attitudes that are not accessible in memory. Interestingly, you are more likely to remember attitudes that are frequently expressed. So, the more you talk about your attitude on a subject, the more you are likely to remember it, and the more likely it is to shape your behaviour.

Discrepancies between attitudes and behaviour are more likely to occur when social pressures to behave in certain ways hold exceptional power. This tends to characterise behaviour in organisations. This may explain why an employee who holds strong anti-union attitudes attends pro-union organising meetings; or why executives of tobacco companies, who are not smokers themselves and who tend to believe the research linking smoking and cancer, don't actively discourage others from smoking in their offices.

Finally, the attitude–behaviour relationship is likely to be much stronger if an attitude refers to something with which the individual has direct personal experience. Asking university students with no significant work experience how they would respond to working for an authoritarian supervisor is far less likely to predict actual behaviour than asking that same question of employees who have worked for such an individual.

Self-perception theory

self-perception theory
Attitudes are used after the fact to make sense out of an action that has already occurred.

Although most A–B studies yield positive results, researchers have achieved still higher correlations by pursuing another direction—looking at whether or not behaviour influences attitudes. This view, called **self-perception theory**, has generated some encouraging findings. Let's briefly review the theory.[38]

When asked about an attitude towards some object, individuals recall their behaviour relevant to that object and then infer their attitude from their past behaviour. So, if an employee were asked about her feelings about being a training specialist at Marriott, she would likely think, 'I've had this same job with Marriott as a trainer for ten years. Nobody forced me to stay on this job. So I must like it!' Self-perception theory, therefore, argues that attitudes are used, after the fact, to make sense out of an action that has already occurred, rather than as devices that precede and guide action. And contrary to cognitive dissonance theory, attitudes are just casual verbal statements. When people are asked about their attitudes, and they don't have strong convictions or feelings, self-perception theory says they tend to create plausible answers.

Self-perception theory has been well supported.[39] While the traditional attitude–behaviour relationship is generally positive, the behaviour–attitude relationship is stronger. This is particularly true when attitudes are vague and ambiguous. When you have had few experiences regarding an attitude issue or given little previous thought to it, you'll tend to infer your attitudes from your behaviour. However, when your attitudes have been established for a while and are well defined, those attitudes are likely to guide your behaviour.

AN APPLICATION: ATTITUDE SURVEYS

The preceding review indicates that a knowledge of employee attitudes can be helpful to managers in attempting to predict employee behaviour. But how does management get informa-

Consistent with self-perception theory, volunteer work can be a powerful force in shaping attitudes towards community service among employees. It also benefits organisations with more focused and competent staff upon their return to the company.

tion about employee attitudes? The most popular method is through the use of **attitude surveys**.[40]

Table 3.6 illustrates what an attitude survey might look like. Typically, attitude surveys present the employee with a set of statements or questions. Ideally, the items are tailored to obtain the specific information that management desires. An attitude score is achieved by summing up responses to individual questionnaire items. These scores can then be averaged for work groups, departments, divisions or the organisation as a whole.

Results from attitude surveys can frequently surprise management. For example, managers at the Heavy-Duty Division of Springfield Remanufacturing thought everything was great.[41] Because employees were actively involved in division decisions and profitability was the highest within the entire company, management assumed that morale was high. To confirm their beliefs, they conducted a short attitude survey. Employees were asked if they agreed or disagreed with the following statements: (1) At work, your opinions count; (2) those of you who want to be a leader in this company have the opportunity to become one; and (3) in the past six months, someone has talked to you about your personal development. In the survey, 43 per cent disagreed with the first statement, 48 per cent with the second, and 62 per cent with the third. Management was astounded. How could this be? The division had been holding shop floor meetings to review the numbers every week for more than 12 years. And most of the managers

attitude surveys
Eliciting responses from employees through questionnaires about how they feel about their jobs, work groups, supervisors and the organisation.

TABLE 3.6	Sample attitude survey
Answer each of the following statements using the following rating scale:	
5 = Strongly agree 4 = Agree 3 = Undecided 2 = Disagree 1 = Strongly disagree	

Statement	Rating
1. This company is a good place to work.	_____
2. I can get ahead in this company if I make the effort.	_____
3. This company's wage rates are competitive with those of other companies.	_____
4. Employee promotion decisions are handled fairly.	_____
5. I understand the various fringe benefits the company offers.	_____
6. My job makes the best use of my abilities.	_____
7. My workload is challenging.	_____
8. I have trust in my boss.	_____
9. I feel free to tell my boss what I think.	_____
10. I know what my boss expects of me.	_____

had come up through the ranks. Management responded by creating a committee made up of representatives from every department in the division and all three shifts. The committee quickly found that there were lots of little things the division was doing that were alienating employees. Out of this committee came a large number of suggestions, which, after implementation, significantly improved employees' perception of their decision-making influence and their career opportunities in the division.

Using attitude surveys on a regular basis provides managers with valuable feedback on how employees perceive their working conditions. Policies and practices that management views as objective and fair may be seen as inequitable by employees in general or by certain groups of employees. If distorted perceptions lead to negative attitudes about the job and organisation, it's important for management to know about it. Why? Because employee behaviours are based on perceptions, not reality. Remember, the employee who quits because she believes she is underpaid—when, in fact, management has objective data to support that her salary is highly competitive—is just as gone as if she had actually been underpaid. The use of regular attitude surveys can alert management to potential problems and employees' intentions early so that action can be taken to prevent repercussions.[42]

ATTITUDES AND WORKFORCE DIVERSITY

Managers are increasingly concerned with changing employee attitudes to reflect shifting perspectives on racial, gender and other diversity issues. A comment to a fellow employee of the opposite sex, which 20 years ago might have been taken as a compliment, can today become a career-limiting episode. As such, organisations are investing in training to help reshape the attitudes of employees.

The majority of large public and private employers and a substantial proportion of medium-sized and smaller ones sponsor some sort of diversity training.[43] Some examples: Avis Australia, a car-rental business, has regular diversity training seminars for all its employees. Australian universities now require all staff to attend diversity training to satisfy not only legal requirements from the Commonwealth government, but also to guard against litigation for discrimination. Sydney Water requires all staff to undertake diversity training, and managers have annual performance targets in diversity awareness.

What do these diversity programs look like and how do they address attitude change?[44] They almost all include a self-evaluation phase. People are pressed to examine themselves and to confront ethnic and cultural stereotypes they might hold. Then participants typically take part in group discussions or panels with representatives from diverse groups. So, for example, a Hmong man might describe his extended family's life in Laos and explain why they fled communism there and settled in Melbourne; or a lesbian might describe how she discovered her sexual identity, and the reaction of her friends and family when she came out.

Additional activities designed to change attitudes include arranging for people to do volunteer work in community or social service centres in order to meet face to face with individuals and groups from diverse backgrounds, and using exercises that let participants feel what it's like to be different. For example, when participants see the film *Eye of the Beholder*, in which people are segregated and stereotyped according to their eye colour, participants see what it's like to be judged by something over which they have no control.

Job Satisfaction

We have already discussed *job satisfaction* briefly—earlier in this chapter as well as in Chapter 1. In this section, we want to dissect the concept more carefully. How do we measure job satisfaction? How satisfied are employees in their jobs? What's the effect of job satisfaction on employee productivity, absenteeism and turnover rates?

The Real Deal

Changing attitudes

There are a lot of people who believe you can't change another person's attitude, so why bother! Others say that you can change another person's attitude by rational argument and facts. Most people are reasonable, according to this view; with a good dose of reason and facts, most people will change their opinion.

Can you change unfavourable employee attitudes? The answer is: sometimes! It depends on who you are, the strength of the employee's attitude, the magnitude of the change, and the technique you choose to try to change the attitude.

Employees are most likely to respond to change efforts made by someone who is liked, credible and convincing. If people like you, they are more apt to identify with you and adopt your message. Credibility implies trust, expertise and objectivity. So, you're more likely to change an employee's attitude if that employee sees you as believable, knowledgeable and unbiased in your presentation. Finally, successful attitude change is enhanced when you present your arguments clearly and persuasively.

It's easier to change an employee's attitude if he or she isn't strongly committed to it. Conversely, the stronger the belief about the attitude, the harder it is to change it. In addition, attitudes that have been expressed publicly are more difficult to change, because it requires admitting that one has made a mistake.

It's easier to change attitudes when that change isn't very significant. To get an employee to accept a new attitude that varies greatly from his or her current position requires more effort. It may also threaten other deeply held attitudes and create increased dissonance.

All attitude-change techniques aren't equally effective across situations. Oral persuasion techniques are most effective when you use a positive, tactful tone; present strong evidence to support your position; tailor your argument to the listener; use logic; and support your evidence by appealing to the employee's fears, frustration and other emotions. But people are more likely to embrace change when they can experience it. The use of training sessions in which employees share and personalise experiences and practise new behaviours can be powerful stimulants for change. Consistent with self-perception theory, changes in behaviour can lead to changes in attitudes.

Sources: Based on A. Bednar and W. H. Levie, *Instructional Message Design: Principles from the Behavioural and Cognitive Sciences*, 2nd ed. (Upper Saddle River, NJ: Educational Technology Publications, 1993); and R. E. Perry, D. T. Wegener and L. R. Fabrigar, 'Attitudes and Attitude Change', *Annual Review of Psychology*, vol. 48, February 1997, pp. 609–47.

MEASURING JOB SATISFACTION

We have previously defined job satisfaction as an individual's general attitude towards his or her job. This definition is clearly a very broad one.[45] Yet, this is inherent in the concept. Remember, a person's job is more than just the obvious activities of shuffling papers, writing programming code, waiting on customers or driving a truck. Jobs require interaction with other employees and managers, following organisational rules and policies, meeting performance standards, living with working conditions that are often less than ideal, and the like.[46] This means that an employee's assessment of how satisfied or dissatisfied he or she is with his or her job is a complex summation of a number of discrete job elements. How, then, do we measure the concept?

The two most widely used approaches are a *single global rating* and a *summation score* made up of a number of job facets. The single global rating method is nothing more than asking individuals to respond to one question, such as 'All things considered, how satisfied are you with your job?' Respondents then reply by circling a number between one and five that corresponds to answers from 'highly satisfied' to 'highly dissatisfied'. The other approach—a summation of job facets—is more sophisticated. It identifies key elements in a job and asks for the employee's feelings about each. Typical factors that would be included are the nature of the work, supervision, present pay, promotion opportunities, and relations with co-workers.[47] These factors are rated on a standardised scale and then added up to create an overall job satisfaction score.

Is one of the foregoing approaches superior to the other? Intuitively, it would seem that summing up responses to a number of job factors would achieve a more accurate evaluation of job satisfaction. The research, however, doesn't support this intuition.[48] This is one of those rare instances in which simplicity seems to work as well as complexity. Comparisons of one-question global ratings with the more lengthy summation-of-job-factors method indicate that the former is essentially as valid as the latter. The best explanation for this outcome is that the concept of job satisfaction is inherently so broad that the single question captures its essence.

HOW SATISFIED ARE PEOPLE IN THEIR JOBS?

Are Australian employees satisfied with their jobs? The answer seems to be that, generally, most people are satisfied. Studies generally indicate that from 70 to 80 per cent of employees report that they are satisfied.[49] Moreover, these results are generally applicable to other developed OECD countries. For example, comparable studies among workers in Canada, Mexico and Europe indicate more positive than negative results.[50] In spite of the generally positive results, recent trends are not encouraging. The evidence indicates a marked decline in job satisfaction since the early 1990s. A Conference Board study found that 58.6 per cent of Americans were satisfied with their jobs in 1995. By the year 2000, that figure was down to 50.7 per cent.[51] This intuitively seems surprising, since those five years were ones of economic expansion, increased incomes and a strong labour market. Apparently, economic prosperity doesn't necessarily translate into higher job satisfaction. And even though all income groups in the Conference Board study indicated lower job satisfaction in 2000 than in 1995, money did seem to buy some happiness. Job satisfaction increased directly with pay for every income category in both 1995 and 2000. Similar results would seem likely here in Australia.

What factors might explain this recent drop in job satisfaction? Experts suggest it might be due to employers' efforts at trying to increase productivity through heavier employee workloads and tighter deadlines. Another contributing factor may be a feeling, increasingly reported by workers, that they have less control over their work.[52] But does the fact that job satisfaction increases with pay mean that money can buy happiness? Not necessarily. While it's possible that higher pay alone translates into higher job satisfaction, an alternative explanation is that higher pay is reflecting different types of jobs.[53] Higher-paying jobs generally require higher skills, give incumbents greater responsibilities, are more stimulating and provide more challenges, and allow workers more control. So, it may be that the reports of higher satisfaction among better-paid workers reflect the greater challenge and freedom they have in their jobs, rather than the pay itself.

THE EFFECT OF JOB SATISFACTION ON EMPLOYEE PERFORMANCE

Managers' interest in job satisfaction tends to centre on its effect on employee performance. Researchers have recognised this interest, so we find a large number of studies that have been designed to assess the impact of job satisfaction on employee productivity, absenteeism and turnover. Let's look at the current state of our knowledge.

Satisfaction and productivity

As the 'Myth or Science?' box concludes, happy employees aren't necessarily productive employees. At the individual level, the evidence suggests the reverse to be more accurate—that productivity is likely to lead to satisfaction.

Interestingly, if we move from the individual level to that of the organisation, there is renewed support for the original satisfaction–performance relationship.[54] When satisfaction and produc-

Myth *or* Science?

'Happy employees are productive employees'

This statement is generally false. The myth that 'happy employees are productive employees' developed in the 1930s and 1940s, largely as a result of findings drawn by researchers conducting the Hawthorne studies at Western Electric. Based on those conclusions, managers began efforts to make their employees happier by engaging in practices such as laissez-faire leadership, improving working conditions, expanding health and family benefits such as insurance and reimbursement of university tuition fees, providing company picnics and other informal get-togethers, and offering counselling services for employees.

But these paternalistic practices were based on questionable findings. Reviews of the research indicate that, if there is a positive relationship between happiness (that is, satisfaction) and productivity, the correlation is in the low-to-moderate range—somewhere between +.17 and +.30. This means that no more than 3–9 per cent of the variance in output can be accounted for by employee satisfaction.[55]

Based on the evidence, a more accurate conclusion is actually the reverse—productive employees are likely to be happy employees. That is, productivity leads to satisfaction, rather than the other way around.[56] If you do a good job, you intrinsically feel good about it. In addition, assuming that the organisation rewards productivity, your higher productivity should increase verbal recognition, your pay level and probabilities for promotion. These rewards, in turn, increase your level of satisfaction with the job.

tivity data are gathered for the organisation as a whole, rather than at the individual level, we find that organisations with more satisfied employees tend to be more effective than organisations with fewer satisfied employees. It may well be that the reason we haven't gotten strong support for the satisfaction-causes-productivity thesis is that studies have focused on individuals, rather than on the organisation, and that individual-level measures of productivity don't take into consideration all the interactions and complexities in the work process. So, while we might not be able to say that a happy *employee* is more productive, it might be true that happy *organisations* are more productive.

Satisfaction and absenteeism

We find a consistent negative relationship between satisfaction and absenteeism, but the correlation is moderate—usually less than +.40.[57] While it certainly makes sense that dissatisfied employees are more likely to miss work, other factors have an impact on the relationship and reduce the correlation coefficient. For example, remember our discussion of sick pay versus well pay in Chapter 2? Organisations that provide liberal sick leave benefits are encouraging all their employees—including those who are highly satisfied—to take days off. Assuming that you have a reasonable number of varied interests, you can find work satisfying and yet still take days off work to enjoy a three-day weekend or watch the World Series Cricket on television, if those days come free with no penalties.

An excellent illustration of how satisfaction directly leads to attendance, when there is a minimum impact from other factors, is a study done at a large national retail chain.[58] Satisfaction data were available on employees at the organisation's two headquarters in different states. In addition, it is important to note that the organisation's policy was not to permit employees to be absent from work for avoidable reasons without penalty. The occurrence of a freak storm in one city created the opportunity to compare employee attendance at the two offices when the weather was fine in the other city. The interesting dimension in this study is that the storm gave the first city employees a built-in excuse not to come to work. The storm crippled the city's transportation, and individuals knew they could miss work this day with no penalty. This natural experiment permitted the comparison of attendance records for satisfied and dissatisfied employees at two locations—one where you were expected to be at work (with normal pressures for attendance) and the other where you were free to choose with no penalty involved. If satisfaction leads to attendance, when there is an absence of outside factors, the more satisfied employees should have come to work in the first city, while dissatisfied employees should have stayed home. The study found that on this particular day, absenteeism rates in the second city were just as high for satisfied groups of employees as for dissatisfied groups. But in the first city, the employees with high satisfaction scores had much higher attendance than did those with lower satisfaction levels. These findings are exactly what we would have expected if satisfaction is negatively correlated with absenteeism.

Satisfaction and turnover

Satisfaction is also negatively related to turnover, but the correlation is stronger than what we found for absenteeism.[59] Yet, again, other factors such as labour-market conditions, expectations about alternative job opportunities, and length of tenure with the organisation are important constraints on the actual decision to leave one's current job.[60]

Evidence indicates that an important moderator of the satisfaction–turnover relationship is the employee's level of performance.[61] Specifically, level of satisfaction is less important in predicting turnover for superior performers. Why? The organisation typically makes considerable efforts to keep these people. They get pay increases, praise, recognition, increased promotional opportunities, and so forth. Just the opposite tends to apply to poor performers. Few attempts are made by the organisation to retain them. There may even be subtle pressures to encourage them to quit. We would expect, therefore, that job satisfaction is more important in influencing poor performers to stay than superior performers. Regardless of level of satisfaction, the latter are more likely to remain with the organisation because the receipt of recognition, praise and other rewards gives them more reasons for staying.

How employees can express dissatisfaction

Employee dissatisfaction can be expressed in a number of ways.[62] For example, rather than quit, employees can complain, be insubordinate, steal organisational property, or shirk a part of their work responsibilities. Figure 3.1 offers four responses that differ from one another along two dimensions: constructive/destructive and active/passive, which are defined as follows:[63]

- **Exit**: Behaviour directed towards leaving the organisation, including looking for a new position as well as resigning.
- **Voice**: Actively and constructively attempting to improve conditions, including suggesting improvements, discussing problems with superiors, and some forms of union activity.
- **Loyalty**: Passively but optimistically waiting for conditions to improve, including speaking up for the organisation in the face of external criticism and trusting the organisation and its management to 'do the right thing'.
- **Neglect**: Passively allowing conditions to worsen, including chronic absenteeism or lateness, reduced effort and increased error rate.

Exit and neglect behaviours encompass our performance variables—productivity, absenteeism and turnover. But this model expands employee response to include voice and loyalty—constructive behaviours that allow individuals to tolerate unpleasant situations or to revive satisfactory working conditions. It helps us to understand situations, such as those sometimes found among unionised employees, for whom low job satisfaction is coupled with low turnover.[64] Union members often express dissatisfaction through the grievance procedure or through formal contract negotiations. These voice mechanisms allow union members to continue in their jobs while convincing themselves that they are acting to improve the situation.

LEARNING OBJECTIVE

8

Identify four employee responses to dissatisfaction

exit
Dissatisfaction expressed through behaviour directed towards leaving the organisation.

voice
Dissatisfaction expressed through active and constructive attempts to improve conditions.

loyalty
Dissatisfaction expressed by passively waiting for conditions to improve.

neglect
Dissatisfaction expressed through allowing conditions to worsen.

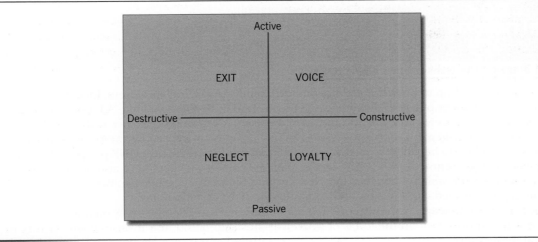

FIGURE 3.1   **Responses to job dissatisfaction**

Source: C. Rusbult and D. Lowery, 'When Bureaucrats Get the Blues', *Journal of Applied Social Psychology*, vol. 15, no. 1, 1985, p. 83. Copyright © V. H. Winston & Son, Inc., 360 South Ocean Boulevard, Palm Beach, FL 33480. All rights reserved.

JOB SATISFACTION AND OCB

It seems logical to assume that job satisfaction should be a major determinant of an employee's organisational citizenship behaviour (OCB).[65] Satisfied employees would seem more likely to talk positively about the organisation, help others, and go beyond the normal expectations in their job. Moreover, satisfied employees might be more prone to go beyond the call of duty because they want to reciprocate their positive experiences. Consistent with this thinking, early discussions of OCB assumed that it was closely linked with satisfaction.[66] More recent evidence, however, suggests that satisfaction influences OCB, but through perceptions of fairness.

There is a modest overall relationship between job satisfaction and OCB.[67] But satisfaction is unrelated to OCB when fairness is controlled for.[68] What does this mean? Basically, job satisfaction comes down to conceptions of fair outcomes, treatment and procedures.[69] If you don't feel like your supervisor, the organisation's procedures or pay policies are fair, your job satisfaction is likely to suffer significantly. However, when you perceive organisational processes and outcomes to be fair, trust is developed. And when you trust your employer, you're more willing to voluntarily engage in behaviours that go beyond your formal job requirements.

JOB SATISFACTION AND CUSTOMER SATISFACTION

As we noted in Chapter 1, employees in service jobs often interact with customers. Since the management of service organisations should be concerned with pleasing those customers, it is reasonable to ask: is employee satisfaction related to positive customer outcomes? For frontline employees who have regular contact with customers, the answer is 'yes'.

The evidence indicates that satisfied employees increase customer satisfaction and loyalty.[70] Why? In service organisations, customer retention is highly dependent on how frontline employees deal with customers. Satisfied employees are more likely to be friendly, upbeat and responsive—which customers appreciate. And because satisfied employees are less prone to turnover, customers are more likely to encounter familiar faces and receive experienced service. These qualities build customer satisfaction and loyalty. In addition, the relationship seems to apply in reverse—dissatisfied customers can increase an employee's job dissatisfaction. Employees who

OB Controversies

'Japanese and Singaporean workers are highly satisfied'

In the 1980s, Japan was held up to be the model nation, with highly productive employees, lifelong employment, and management practices that got everyone involved in decision making. A lot of Australian and New Zealand organisations felt that that was the way they also needed to go, and they rushed to implement total quality management so that they could be like Japanese organisations. More recently, Singapore has been held up to be a highly productive, small nation with the highest GNP per person in the world. The Singaporean government, work ethic and intelligent business practices were also recognised as forming another model from which Australian and New Zealand businesses could learn. But were the workers in Japan and Singapore satisfied in their work and committed to their organisations?

International Survey Research recently conducted an employee satisfaction survey on a worldwide basis, which provided information on the levels of worker dissatisfaction and how it varies from country to country. Overall, results showed that the Swiss are the most satisfied employees. Workers in Denmark and Austria also ranked in the top three. The United States falls in the middle range. Germany and Sweden, two of the countries celebrated for an enlightened approach to work, were also in the middle range.

Japanese workers are the least satisfied of any workers in the world, with Singapore and Hong Kong workers also showing their strong discontent. While not widely known, Japanese workers have shown consistently high levels of job dissatisfaction over the last 30 years. Because of the Japanese culture, they may not openly express it in the workplace, but when given a chance to indicate how they feel in anonymous surveys, it's apparent that the Japanese worker has been unhappy for a long time. While Japan was at the top of the productivity charts, no one seemed to think that worker dissatisfaction was important. Now that Japanese national productivity is declining, the experts say that maybe one of the key reasons is their unhappy workforce.

Another job satisfaction survey conducted in Britain showed that male workers in their thirties who are well-educated and who work long hours, and workers in large establishments, have lower levels of job satisfaction than other groups in Britain. We are starting to get a picture of job satisfaction around the world, but we still need to find out where Australia and New Zealand fit into the picture and whether we want to sacrifice job satisfaction for productivity.

Source: Based on articles by M. Mandel, 'Satisfaction at Work', *Business Week*, 24 June 1996, p. 28; J. Bodil, 'Global Happiness Ratings', *Management Review*, July 1996, p. 53; and A. Clark, 'Job Satisfaction in Britain', *British Journal of Industrial Relations*, June 1996, pp. 189–217.

have regular contact with customers report that rude, thoughtless or unreasonably demanding customers adversely affect the employees' job satisfaction.[71]

A number of companies are acting on this evidence. Service-oriented businesses such as airlines, retail stores, banks, and now even universities, have become almost obsessive about pleasing their clients. Towards that end, they also focus on building employee satisfaction—recognising that employee satisfaction will go a long way towards contributing to their goal of having happy customers. These firms seek to hire upbeat and friendly employees, they train employees in the importance of customer service, they reward customer service, they provide positive employee work climates, and they regularly track employee satisfaction through attitude surveys.

Summary and Implications for Managers

Why is it important to know an individual's values? Although they don't have a direct impact on behaviour, values strongly influence a person's attitudes. So, knowledge of an individual's value system can provide insight into his or her attitudes.

Given that people's values differ, managers can use the Rokeach Value Survey to assess potential employees and determine if their values align with the dominant values of the organisation. An employee's performance and satisfaction are likely to be higher if their values fit well with the organisation. For example, the person who places high importance on imagination, independence and freedom is likely to be poorly matched with an organisation that seeks conformity from its employees. Managers are more likely to appreciate, evaluate positively and allocate rewards to employees who 'fit in', and employees are more likely to be satisfied if they perceive that they do fit. This argues for management to strive during the selection of new employees to find job candidates who not only have the ability, experience and motivation to perform, but also a value system that is compatible with the organisation's core values.

Managers should be interested in their employees' attitudes, because attitudes give warnings of potential problems and because they influence behaviour. Satisfied and committed employees, for example, have lower rates of turnover and absenteeism. Given that managers want to keep resignations and absences down—especially among their more productive employees—they will want to do the things that will generate positive job attitudes and promote job satisfaction.

Managers should also be aware that employees will try to reduce cognitive dissonance. More important, dissonance can be managed. If employees are required to engage in activities that appear inconsistent to them or that are at odds with their attitudes, the pressures to reduce the resulting dissonance are lessened when the employee perceives that the dissonance is externally imposed and is beyond his or her control, or if the rewards are significant enough to offset the dissonance.

Point

MANAGERS CAN CREATE SATISFIED EMPLOYEES

A review of the evidence has identified four factors conducive to high levels of employee job satisfaction: mentally challenging work, equitable rewards, supportive working conditions and supportive colleagues. Importantly, each of these factors is controllable by management.

Mentally challenging work. People prefer jobs that give them opportunities to use their skills and abilities and offer a variety of tasks, freedom and feedback on how well they are doing. These characteristics make work mentally challenging.

Equitable rewards. Employees want pay systems and promotion policies that they perceive as being just, unambiguous and in line with their expectations. When pay is seen as fair based on job demands, individual skill level and community pay standards, satisfaction is likely to result. Similarly, employees seek fair promotion policies and practices. Promotions provide opportunities for personal growth, more responsibilities and increased social status. Individuals who perceive that promotion decisions are made in a fair and just manner, therefore, are likely to experience satisfaction from their jobs.

Supportive working conditions. Employees are concerned with their work environment for both personal comfort and facilitating doing a good job. Studies demonstrate that employees prefer physical surroundings that are not dangerous or uncomfortable. In addition, most employees prefer working relatively close to home, in clean and relatively modern facilities, and with adequate tools and equipment.

Supportive colleagues. People get more out of work than merely money or tangible achievements. For most employees, work also fills the need for social interaction. Not surprisingly, therefore, having friendly and supportive fellow employees leads to increased job satisfaction. The behaviour of one's supervisor or manager is also a major determinant of satisfaction. Studies generally find that employee satisfaction is increased when the immediate supervisor is understanding and friendly, offers praise for good performance, listens to employees' opinions and shows a personal interest in them.

Counterpoint

The notion that managers and organisations can control the level of employee job satisfaction is inherently attractive. It fits nicely with the view that managers directly influence organisational processes and outcomes. Unfortunately, there is a growing body of evidence that challenges the notion that managers control the factors that influence employee job satisfaction. The most recent findings indicate that employee job satisfaction is largely genetically determined.

Whether a person is happy or not is essentially determined by his or her gene structure. Approximately 80 per cent of people's differences in happiness, or subjective well-being, have been found to be attributable to their different genes.

Analysis of satisfaction data for a selected sample of individuals over a 50-year period found that individual results were consistently stable over time, even when these people changed employers and occupations. This and other research suggests that an individual's disposition towards life—positive or negative—is established by their genetic make-up, holds over time, and carries over into their disposition towards work.

Given these findings, there is probably little that most managers can do to influence employee satisfaction. In spite of the fact that managers and organisations go to extensive lengths to try to improve employee job satisfaction through actions such as manipulating job characteristics, working conditions and rewards, these actions are likely to have little effect. The only place where managers will have any significant influence will be through their control of the selection process. If managers want satisfied employees, they need to make sure their selection process screens out the negative, maladjusted, trouble-making fault finders who derive little satisfaction in anything about their jobs.

Sources: E. A. Locke, 'The Nature and Causes of Job Satisfaction', in M. D. Dunnette (ed.), *Handbook of Industrial and Organizational Psychology* (Chicago: Rand McNally), 1976, pp. 1319–28; R. D. Arvey, B. McCall, T. J. Bouchard, Jr and P. Taubman, 'Genetic Influences on Job Satisfaction and Work Values', *Personality and Individual Differences*, July 1994, pp. 21–33; D. Lykken and A. Tellegen, 'Happiness is a Stochastic Phenomenon', *Psychological Science*, May 1996, pp. 186–89; and T. A. Judge, E. A. Locke, C. C. Durham and A. N. Kluger, 'Dispositional Effects on Job and Life Satisfaction: The Role of Core Evaluations', *Journal of Applied Psychology*, February 1998, pp. 17–34.

For Discussion

1. 'Thirty-five years ago, young employees we hired were ambitious, conscientious, hardworking and honest. Today's young workers don't have the same values.' Do you agree or disagree with this manager's comments? Support your position.
2. Contrast the veteran, baby-boomers, Gen-Xers and Generation Nexters classifications with the terminal values identified in the Rokeach Value Survey.
3. Contrast the cognitive and affective components of an attitude.
4. What is cognitive dissonance and how is it related to attitudes?
5. What is self-perception theory? How does it increase our ability to predict behaviour?
6. What contingency factors can improve the statistical relationship between attitudes and behaviour?
7. Discuss the advantages and disadvantages of using regular attitude surveys to monitor employee job satisfaction.
8. When employees are asked whether they would again choose the same work or whether they would want their children to follow in their footsteps, typically less than half answer in the affirmative. What, if anything, do you think this implies about employee job satisfaction?
9. What explains the recent declines in employee job satisfaction?
10. 'Managers should do everything they can to enhance the job satisfaction of their employees.' Do you agree or disagree? Support your position.
11. What is the relationship between job satisfaction and absenteeism? Turnover? Which is the stronger relationship?
12. How can managers get employees to more readily accept working with colleagues who are different from them?

13. Contrast exit, voice, loyalty and neglect as employee responses to job dissatisfaction.
14. Are happy workers productive workers?

Exercise

CHALLENGES IN NEGOTIATING WITH CHINESE EXECUTIVES

Form into teams of three to five members each. All your team's members work for a company in the western suburbs of Melbourne that manufactures bathroom fixtures such as sinks, toilets and bathtubs. Your company's senior management has decided to make a serious effort to expand sales of its fixtures into the Chinese market. And to begin the process, your team has been chosen to make a ten-day trip to Beijing and Shanghai to meet with purchasing executives at half-a-dozen Chinese residential and commercial real estate construction developers.

Your team will be leaving for its trip in a week. You will have a translator in both cities, but your team wants to do whatever it can to make a good impression on the Chinese executives they will be meeting. Unfortunately, the members of your team have a relatively limited knowledge of Chinese culture. To help with the trip, one of your team members has found a brochure that summarises some of the unique characteristics of the Chinese and that might prove valuable in opening negotiations. The highlights of that brochure included:

- China is a group-oriented society and any negotiations must cover the interests of many different parties.
- Emphasis is placed on trust and mutual connections.
- The Chinese are interested in long-term benefits.
- The Chinese seem to have a compelling need to dwell on the subject of friendship.
- Initial business meetings are devoted to pleasantries—such as serving tea and chit-chat.
- So as not to lose face, the Chinese prefer to negotiate through an intermediary.
- The Chinese expect reciprocal invitations—if a banquet is given in the honour of your team, they expect you to give a banquet for their team.
- The Chinese are sensitive about foreigners' comments on Chinese politics.
- The Chinese are punctual and expect others will arrive promptly on time for each meeting.
- The Chinese are well aware of Australians' reputation for abruptness and impatience. They will often take their time in decision making to gain an advantage in negotiations.
- The Chinese do not like to be touched or slapped on the back, or even to shake hands. A slight bow and a brief shake of the hands are more appropriate.
- The Chinese generally believe that foreign businesspeople will be highly qualified technically in their specific area of expertise.
- Chinese posture becomes rigid whenever they feel their goals are being compromised.
- Very often, several visits are necessary to consummate any business transaction.
- Foreigners should not focus on the individual Chinese person, but rather on the group of individuals who are working towards a particular goal.
- Telephone calls and fax machines are a vital part of doing business in China, but the Chinese believe that important business should be conducted face-to-face.
- In negotiations with the Chinese, nothing should be considered final until it has been actually realised.

Your team has 30 minutes to rough out a strategy for meeting with the Chinese purchasing executives. Be as specific as possible. When finished, be prepared to present your strategy to the entire class.

Source: This exercise is adapted from information in R. Harris and R. T. Moran, *Managing Cultural Differences*, 4th ed. (Houston, TX: Gulf Publishing, 1996), pp. 252–57.

Case Study 3

Maintaining Job Satisfaction When the Ownership Changes

Vivienne Sommerville was as surprised as everyone else when she heard the news. She was the HR manager for the Petroleum Division of Western Mining and everyone assumed that she knew it was going to happen and didn't tell them. The Petroleum Division was an important business of Western Mining. It wasn't a 'core business' yet, but its vision statement said it aimed to be one of the five key businesses by the year 2008. This meant they would have to increase their business quite substantially within four years. The corporate headquarters supported this and Vivienne had been working hard over the last two years to help build teamwork and trust between management and the 120 engineers, geologists, accountants and other staff. It seemed some progress was being made; people's attitudes seemed to have improved, they had developed a code of ethics, each section had developed its own vision statement and business plans, the whole division now placed a high priority on safety, and they were even working on a common set of values that would guide the way they worked. Vivienne had organised outdoor team-building programs, team reviews and planning sessions. Staff and the managers were starting to respond well to creating a positive culture of teamwork. Stephen Keenihan, the general manager of the Petroleum Division, was great to work with. He went along with many of Vivienne's ideas and supported them 100 per cent—even sometimes when he wasn't sure they would work. Many of the managers now had more concern about the welfare of their staff and practised more skills in listening and asking staff for their input into decisions.

On the Tuesday morning of the announcement, things changed radically. Some people cracked jokes, many didn't comment at all, others just went about their day as if they didn't hear that the Petroleum Division was being sold on the open market. What made it even more difficult was that the process would probably take over eight months while Western Mining looked for a buyer, and that after the sale no staff member could be guaranteed they would still have a job.

Vivienne's job was quite different now. She knew that she had to help keep the morale, job satisfaction and commitment of the staff up for the next eight months. It was a real dilemma to be in. On one hand, she needed to help arrange career counselling so that people could be prepared if the new company were to ask people to leave. On the other hand, she needed to keep up people's commitment to their project teams so that they wouldn't wind up selling a company that had oil and gas equipment and assets but few good professionals left who were highly motivated.

This sudden decision to sell the Petroleum Division stirred up a lot of different reactions within people. For many, it struck at their key life values (for example, 'How important is this job to me?' 'What do I do next?' 'They were totally unfair for selling it without consulting us first!') and affected how committed they would be to the company and their job for the next eight months. For others, the announcement didn't seem to matter at all, while still others were confused and didn't quite know what to do.

Vivienne had initially thought she should find another job, either in Western Mining or in another company. There wasn't a high likelihood that the new company would want to keep the previous HR manager on—they would probably want to bring in their own person. But after thinking it over, she decided to stay and see things through. It was probably one of the biggest challenges she could face—to help Stephen Keenihan, the managers of the Petroleum Division and the 120 staff manage this change. Also, deep down she knew she was really concerned about these people and was committed to their welfare. The team spirit she had helped to build over the last two years was vital to pulling through the rough times ahead, and she didn't want to walk away from them now.

Questions

1. Design an employee attitude survey that Vivienne might use to guide her in tapping into the employees' attitudes after the announcement.
2. What predictions, if any, could you make about job satisfaction at Petroleum Division? How might job satisfaction affect work outcomes during this period of uncertainty?
3. How might the decision to sell the division affect the attitudes of the Petroleum Division employees? What, if anything, could Vivienne and the other managers do to shape those attitudes positively?

Web Workout

1. Visit the site <www.committment.com/getalong.html>. Advice is given here on the differing values of the different generational cohorts. What conclusions can you draw with respect to the values and attitudes of each generational cohort? If you were a manager, how might you prevent conflict between Generation-Xers and Nexters?

2. <www.airpower.maxwell.af.mil/airchronicles/apj/apj01/sum01/iversen.doc> provides an interesting perspective on how the American Air Force is being forced to change its training programs and processes to accommodate the Generation-Xers. What further changes are they likely to have to make to accommodate the Generation Nexters who will follow the current intakes of pilots? What is likely to happen to all the military forces if they don't change their recruitment and training techniques for military personnel?

3. Increasingly, we are seeing doctors and nurses in our medical profession who have trained in different countries and cultures. The implications of cross-cultural differences in health-care have been found to be significant, according to a recent study found at <www.xculture.org/new/news/detail.cfm?NID=53&list=53%2C52%2C48%2C46%2C44>. How might medical authorities address these serious health-care issues?

4. Retaining military personnel is becoming a crucial issue to many armed forces around the world. The site <www.iamps.org/paper-pdf/love-zambelli-report.pdf> presents a synopsis of studies that look at how attitude surveys have assisted military officials to design rewards and incentives to retain key personnel as well as attract new recruits. What are the techniques and strategies developed from these attitude studies to reduce turnover and recruitment failures?

5. Organisational commitment is an attitude that relates to the degree whereby an individual identifies with an organisation, its goals and outcomes. It is an important attitude in any organisation, but perhaps most especially in volunteer organisations where job satisfaction and commitment comes from non-monetary rewards and outcomes. This is recognised by many volunteer organisations, such as the one at <wgacomau.webhostcontrol.com/volunteers.htm>. What strategies does Women's Golf Australia adopt to create and increase the organisational commitment of volunteers in the sport?

6. Attitude surveys are gaining in popularity in Australia. Visit <www.loc-gov-focus.aus.net/1996/sept/SASurv.htm> and consider how the attitude survey assisted the managers of the Brimbank City Council.

7. How do Australians feel about their jobs? Aon Consulting examined this question in its study entitled 'Australia@Work 2002'. Go to the site <www.aon.com.au/australiaatwork/index.asp> and enter your details to obtain a free electronic download of their report. What are the implications of the declining levels of commitment and expectations of employees of their employers? How loyal are most employees?

8. Visit the site <www.uncg.edu/iss/kirkman.htm>. Organisational citizenship behaviour has been found to be an important issue in America, but this article suggests this is not the case in all other countries. Why might it not be significant in the People's Republic of China?

KSS Program

KNOW THE CONCEPTS   SELF-AWARENESS   SKILLS APPLICATIONS

Changing attitudes
After you have read this chapter, take Self-Assessment #11 (How Satisfied Am I with My Job?) on your enclosed CD-Rom and complete the skill-building module entitled 'Changing Attitudes' on page 633.

NOTES
1. C . Y. Chen, 'Chasing the Net Generation', *Fortune*, 4 September 2000, pp. 295–98. Generation Nexters are also known as Generation Y, Generation Why, the Internet Generation, Millennials and the 'Click-n-go' Generation. Even before we have consensus of the label for this generation, we are already seeing those born post-1994 being labelled by marketers as the Pokemon Generation! See, for further discussion, <www.gentrends.com/Articles/Instore2000/Millennials%20Nexters%20Strangers.pdf>.
2. M. Rokeach, *The Nature of Human Values* (New York: Free Press, 1973), p. 5.
3. M. Rokeach and S. J. Ball-Rokeach, 'Stability and Change in American Value Priorities, 1968–1981', *American Psychologist*, May 1989,

pp. 775–84; and B. M. Meglino and E. C. Ravlin, 'Individual Values in Organizations: Concepts, Controversies, and Research', *Journal of Management*, vol. 24, no. 3, 1998, p. 355.

4. See, for example, Meglino and Ravlin, 'Individual Values in Organizations', pp. 351–89.

5. This common set of values doesn't extend to all members of our society, particularly so in the case of the peoples who lived in Australia and New Zealand before British occupation. We need to be aware that a set of values held by the majority should not be the basis for arguing for their application to all people—this is a form of cultural imperialism.

6. Rokeach, *The Nature of Human Values*, p. 6.

7. J. M. Munson and B. Z. Posner, 'The Factorial Validity of a Modified Rokeach Value Survey for Four Diverse Samples', *Educational and Psychological Measurement*, Winter 1980, pp. 1073–79; and W. C. Frederick and J. Weber, 'The Values of Corporate Managers and Their Critics: An Empirical Description and Normative Implications', in W. C. Frederick and L. E. Preston (eds), *Business Ethics: Research Issues and Empirical Studies* (Greenwich, CT: JAI Press, 1990), pp. 123–44.

8. Frederick and Weber, 'The Values of Corporate Managers and Their Critics'.

9. Ibid, p. 132.

10. See, for example, R. Zemke, C. Raines and B. Filipczak, *Generations at Work: Managing the Clash of Veterans, Boomers, Xers, and Nexters in Your Workplace* (New York: AMACOM, 1999); C. Penttila, 'Generational Gyrations', *Entrepreneur*, April 2001, pp. 102–05; R. Zemke, 'Here Come the Millennials', *Training*, July 2001, pp. 44–49; J. Pruitt, 'The Generational Blur', *Training*, January 2002, p. 64; and P. Paul, 'Global Generation Gap', *American Demographics*, March 2002, pp. 18–19.

11. As noted to one of your authors by R. Volkema and R. L. Neal, Jr, of American University, this model may also be limited in its application to minority populations and recent immigrants to North America.

12. R. E. Hattwick, Y. Kathawala, M. Monipullil and L. Wall, 'On the Alleged Decline in Business Ethics', *Journal of Behavioral Economics*, Summer 1989, pp. 129–43.

13. B. Z. Posner and W. H. Schmidt, 'Values and the American Manager: An Update Updated', *California Management Review*, Spring 1992, p. 86.

14. G. Hofstede, *Culture's Consequences: International Differences in Work Related Values* (Beverly Hills, CA: Sage, 1980); G. Hofstede, *Cultures and Organizations: Software of the Mind* (London: McGraw-Hill, 1991); G. Hofstede, 'Cultural Constraints in Management Theories', *Academy of Management Executive*, February 1993, pp. 81–94; G. Hofstede and M. F. Peterson, 'National Values and Organizational Practices', in N. M. Ashkanasy, C. M. Wilderom and M. F. Peterson (eds), *Handbook of Organizational Culture and Climate* (Thousand Oaks, CA: Sage, 2000), pp. 401–16. For criticism of this research, see B. McSweeney, 'Hofstede's Model of National Cultural Differences and Their Consequences: A Triumph of Faith—a Failure of Analysis', *Human Relations*, January 2002, pp. 89–118.

15. Hofstede called this dimension masculinity versus femininity, but we have changed his terms because of their strong sexist connotation.

16. M. Javidan and R. J. House, 'Cultural Acumen for the Global Manager: Lessons from Project GLOBE', *Organizational Dynamics*, Spring 2001, pp. 289–305.

17. N. J. Adler, 'Cross-Cultural Management Research: The Ostrich and the Trend', *Academy of Management Review*, April 1983, pp. 226–32.

18. L. Godkin, C. E. Braye and C. L. Caunch, 'U.S.-Based Cross Cultural Management Research in the Eighties', *Journal of Business and Economic Perspectives*, vol. 15, 1989, pp. 37–45; and T. K. Peng, M. F. Peterson and Y. Shyi, 'Quantitative Methods in Cross-National Management Research: Trends and Equivalence Issues', *Journal of Organizational Behavior*, vol. 12, 1991, pp. 87–107.

19. S. J. Breckler, 'Empirical Validation of Affect, Behavior, and Cognition as Distinct Components of Attitude', *Journal of Personality and Social Psychology*, May 1984, pp. 1191–205; and S. L. Crites, Jr, L. R. Fabrigar and R. E. Petty, 'Measuring the Affective and Cognitive Properties of Attitudes: Conceptual and Methodological Issues', *Personality and Social Psychology Bulletin*, December 1994, pp. 619–34.

20. P. P. Brooke, Jr, D. W. Russell and J. L. Price, 'Discriminant Validation of Measures of Job Satisfaction, Job Involvement, and Organizational Commitment', *Journal of Applied Psychology*, May 1988, pp. 139–45; and R. T. Keller, 'Job Involvement and Organizational Commitment as Longitudinal Predictors of Job Performance: A Study of Scientists and Engineers', *Journal of Applied Psychology*, August 1997, pp. 539–45.

21. See, for example, S. Rabinowitz and D. T. Hall, 'Organizational Research in Job Involvement', *Psychological Bulletin*, March 1977, pp. 265–88; G. J. Blau, 'A Multiple Study Investigation of the Dimensionality of Job Involvement', *Journal of Vocational Behavior*, August 1985, pp. 19–36; and N. A. Jans, 'Organizational Factors and Work Involvement', *Organizational Behavior and Human Decision Processes*, June 1985, pp. 382–96.

22. Based on G. J. Blau and K. R. Boal, 'Conceptualizing How Job Involvement and Organizational Commitment Affect Turnover and Absenteeism', *Academy of Management Review*, April 1987, p. 290.

23. G. J. Blau, 'Job Involvement and Organizational Commitment as Interactive Predictors of Tardiness and Absenteeism', *Journal of Management*, Winter 1986, pp. 577–84; and K. Boal and R. Cidambi, 'Attitudinal Correlates of Turnover and Absenteeism: A Meta Analysis', paper presented at the meeting of the American Psychological Association, Toronto, Canada, 1984.

24. G. Farris, 'A Predictive Study of Turnover', *Personnel Psychology*, Summer 1971, pp. 311–28.

25. Blau and Boal, 'Conceptualizing', p. 290.

26. See, for example, W. Hom, R. Katerberg and C. L. Hulin, 'Comparative Examination of Three Approaches to the Prediction of Turnover', *Journal of Applied Psychology*, June 1979, pp. 280–90; H. Angle and J. Perry, 'Organizational Commitment: Individual and Organizational Influence', *Work and Occupations*, May 1983, pp. 123–46; and J. L. Pierce and R. B. Dunham, 'Organizational Commitment: Pre-Employment Propensity and Initial Work Experiences', *Journal of Management*, Spring 1987, pp. 163–78.

27. Hom, Katerberg and Hulin, 'Comparative Examination'; and R. T. Mowday, L. W. Porter and R. M. Steers, *Employee Organization Linkages: The Psychology of Commitment, Absenteeism, and Turnover* (New York: Academic Press, 1982).

28. L. W. Porter, R. M. Steers, R. T. Mowday and V. Boulian, 'Organizational Commitment, Job Satisfaction, and Turnover among Psychiatric Technicians', *Journal of Applied Psychology*, October 1974, pp. 603–09.

29. D. M. Rousseau, 'Organizational Behavior in the New Organizational Era', in J. T. Spence, J. M. Darley and D. J. Foss (eds), *Annual Review of Psychology*, vol. 48 (Palo Alto, CA: Annual Reviews, Inc., 1997), p. 523.

30. Ibid.

31. See, for example, A. J. Elliot and G. Devine, 'On the Motivational Nature of Cognitive Dissonance: Dissonance as Psychological Discomfort', *Journal of Personality and Social Psychology*, September 1994, pp. 382–94.

32. See R. Rosenblatt, 'How Do Tobacco Executives Live with Themselves?', *The New York Times Magazine*, 20 March 1994, pp. 34–41; and J. A. Byrne, 'Philip Morris: Inside America's Most Reviled Company', *U.S. News & World Report*, 29 November 1999, pp. 176–92.

33. L. Festinger, *A Theory of Cognitive Dissonance* (Stanford, CA: Stanford University Press, 1957).

34. A. W. Wicker, 'Attitude versus Action: The Relationship of Verbal and Overt Behavioral Responses to Attitude Objects', *Journal of Social Issues*, Autumn 1969, pp. 41–78.

35. Ibid, p. 65.

36. See S. J. Kraus, 'Attitudes and the Prediction of Behavior: A Meta-Analysis of the Empirical Literature', *Personality and Social Psychology Bulletin*, January 1995, pp. 58–75; I. Ajzen, 'The Directive Influence of Attitudes on Behavior', in M. Gollwitzer and J. A. Bargh (eds), *The Psychology of Action: Linking Cognition and Motivation to Behavior* (New York: Guilford, 1996), pp. 385–403; and I. Ajzen, 'Nature and Operation of Attitudes', in S. T. Fiske, D. L. Schacter and C. Zahn-Waxler (eds), *Annual Review of Psychology*, vol. 52 (Palo Alto, CA: Annual Reviews, Inc., 2001), pp. 27–58.

37. Ibid.

38. D. J. Bem, 'Self-Perception Theory', in L. Berkowitz (ed.), *Advances in Experimental Social Psychology*, vol. 6 (New York: Academic Press, 1972), pp. 1–62.

39. See C. A. Kiesler, R. E. Nisbett and M. Zanna, 'On Inferring One's Belief from One's Behavior', *Journal of Personality and Social Psychology*, April 1969, pp. 321–27; S. E. Taylor, 'On Inferring One's Attitudes from One's Behavior: Some Delimiting Conditions', *Journal of Personality and Social Psychology*, January 1975, pp. 126–31; and A. M. Tybout and C. A. Scott, 'Availability of Well-Defined Internal Knowledge and the Attitude Formation Process: Information Aggregation Versus Self-Perception', *Journal of Personality and Social Psychology*, March 1983, pp. 474–91.

40. See, for example, B. Fishel, 'A New Perspective: How to Get the Real Story from Attitude Surveys', *Training*, February 1998, pp. 91–94.

41. J. Stack, 'Measuring Morale', *INC.*, January 1997, pp. 29–30.

42. See S. Shellenbarger, 'Companies Are Finding It Really Pays to Be Nice to Employees', *Wall Street Journal*, 22 July 1998, p. B1.

43. See Society for Human Resource Management, 'Impact of Diversity on the Bottom Line', <www.fortune.com/sections>, 31 August 2001, pp. 5–12; and M. Bendick, Jr, M. L. Egan and S. M. Lofhjelm, 'Workforce Diversity Training: From Anti-Discrimination Compliance to Organizational Development', *Human Resource Planning*, vol. 24, no. 2, 2001, pp. 10–25.

44. This section is based on A. Rossett and T. Bickham, 'Diversity Training: Hope, Faith and Cynicism', *Training*, January 1994, pp. 40–46.

45. For problems with the concept of job satisfaction, see R. Hodson, 'Workplace Behaviors', *Work and Occupations*, August 1991, pp. 271–90; and H. M. Weiss and R. Cropanzano, 'Affective Events Theory: A Theoretical Discussion of the Structure, Causes and Consequences of Affective Experiences at Work', in B. M. Staw and L. L. Cummings (eds), *Research in Organizational Behavior*, vol. 18 (Greenwich, CT: JAI Press, 1996), pp. 1–3.

46. The Wyatt Company's 1989 national WorkAmerica study identified 12 dimensions of satisfaction: work organisation, working conditions, communications, job performance and performance review, co-workers, supervision, company management, pay, benefits, career development and training, job content and satisfaction, and company image and change.

47. See E. Spector, *Job Satisfaction: Application, Assessment, Causes, and Consequences* (Thousand Oaks, CA: Sage, 1997), p. 3.

48. J. Wanous, A. E. Reichers and M. J. Hudy, 'Overall Job Satisfaction: How Good Are Single-Item Measures?', *Journal of Applied Psychology*, April 1997, pp. 247–52.

49. L. K. Savery, 'Men and Women in the Workplace: Evidence of Occupational Differences', *Leadership and Organizational Development*

Journal, vol. 11, no. 2, 1990, pp. 13–16; E. Graham, 'Work May Be a Rat Race, but It's Not a Daily Grind', *Wall Street Journal*, 19 September 1997, p. R1; and J. L. Seglin, 'Americans @ Work', *INC.*, June 1998, pp. 91–94.

50. L. Grant, 'Unhappy in Japan', *Fortune*, 13 January 1997, p. 142; 'Survey Finds Satisfied Workers in Canada', *Manpower Argus*, January 1997, p. 6; and T. Mudd, 'Europeans Generally Happy in the Workplace', *Industry Week*, 4 October 1999, pp. 11–12.

51. Conference Board study of job satisfaction, <www.consumerresearchcenter.org>; October 2000.

52. Ibid; and R. Gardyn, 'Happiness Grows on Trees', *American Demographics*, May 2001, pp. 18–21.

53. Gardyn, 'Happiness Grows on Trees'.

54. C. Ostroff, 'The Relationship between Satisfaction, Attitudes, and Performance: An Organizational Level Analysis', *Journal of Applied Psychology*, December 1992, pp. 963–74; and A. M. Ryan, M. J. Schmit and R. Johnson, 'Attitudes and Effectiveness: Examining Relations at an Organizational Level', *Personnel Psychology*, Winter 1996, pp. 853–82.

55. M. T. Iaffaldano and M. Muchinsky, 'Job Satisfaction and Job Performance: A Meta-Analysis', *Psychological Bulletin*, March 1985, pp. 251–73; and T. A. Judge, C. J. Thoresen, J. E. Bono and G. K. Patton, 'The Job Satisfaction–Job Performance Relationship: A Qualitative and Quantitative Review', *Psychological Bulletin*, May 2001, pp. 376–407.

56. C. N. Greene, 'The Satisfaction–Performance Controversy', *Business Horizons*, February 1972, pp. 31–41; E. E. Lawler III, *Motivation in Organizations* (Monterey, CA: Brooks/Cole, 1973); and M. M. Petty, G. W. McGee and J. W. Cavender, 'A Meta-Analysis of the Relationship Between Individual Job Satisfaction and Individual Performance', *Academy of Management Review*, October 1984, pp. 712–21.

57. E. A. Locke, 'The Nature and Causes of Job Satisfaction', in M. D. Dunnette (ed.), *Handbook of Industrial and Organizational Psychology* (Chicago: Rand McNally, 1976), p. 1331; S. L. McShane, 'Job Satisfaction and Absenteeism: A Meta-Analytic Re-Examination', *Canadian Journal of Administrative Science*, June 1984, pp. 61–77; R. D. Hackett and R. M. Guion, 'A Reevaluation of the Absenteeism–Job Satisfaction Relationship', *Organizational Behavior and Human Decision Processes*, June 1985, pp. 340–81; K. D. Scott and G. S. Taylor, 'An Examination of Conflicting Findings on the Relationship between Job Satisfaction and Absenteeism: A Meta-Analysis', *Academy of Management Journal*, September 1985, pp. 599–612; R. D. Hackett, 'Work Attitudes and Employee Absenteeism: A Synthesis of the Literature', paper presented at 1988 National Academy of Management Conference, Anaheim, CA, August 1988; and R. Steel and J. R. Rentsch, 'Influence of Cumulation Strategies on the Long-Range Prediction of Absenteeism', *Academy of Management Journal*, December 1995, pp. 1616–34.

58. F. J. Smith, 'Work Attitudes as Predictors of Attendance on a Specific Day', *Journal of Applied Psychology*, February 1977, pp. 16–19.

59. W. Hom and R. W. Griffeth, *Employee Turnover* (Cincinnati, OH: Southwestern, 1995); and R. W. Griffeth, P. W. Hom and S. Gaertner, 'A Meta-Analysis of Antecedents and Correlates of Employee Turnover: Update, Moderator Tests, and Research Implications for the Next Millennium', *Journal of Management*, vol. 26, no. 3, 2000, p. 479.

60. See, for example, C. L. Hulin, M. Roznowski and D. Hachiya, 'Alternative Opportunities and Withdrawal Decisions: Empirical and Theoretical Discrepancies and an Integration', *Psychological Bulletin*, July 1985, pp. 233–50; and J. M. Carsten and P. E. Spector, 'Unemployment, Job Satisfaction, and Employee Turnover: A Meta-Analytic Test of the Muchinsky Model', *Journal of Applied Psychology*, August 1987, pp. 374–81.

61. D. G. Spencer and R. M. Steers, 'Performance as a Moderator of the Job Satisfaction–Turnover Relationship', *Journal of Applied Psychology*, August 1981, pp. 511–14.

62. S. M. Puffer, 'Prosocial Behavior, Noncompliant Behavior, and Work Performance among Commission Salespeople', *Journal of Applied Psychology*, November 1987, pp. 615–21; J. Hogan and R. Hogan, 'How to Measure Employee Reliability', *Journal of Applied Psychology*, May 1989, pp. 273–79; and C. D. Fisher and E. A. Locke, 'The New Look in Job Satisfaction Research and Theory', in C. J. Cranny, P. C. Smith and E. F. Stone (eds), *Job Satisfaction* (New York: Lexington Books, 1992), pp. 165–94.

63. See D. Farrell, 'Exit, Voice, Loyalty, and Neglect as Responses to Job Dissatisfaction: A Multidimensional Scaling Study', *Academy of Management Journal*, December 1983, pp. 596–606; C. E. Rusbult, D. Farrell, G. Rogers and A. G. Mainous, III, 'Impact of Exchange Variables on Exit, Voice, Loyalty, and Neglect: An Integrative Model of Responses to Declining Job Satisfaction', *Academy of Management Journal*, September 1988, pp. 599–627; M. J. Withey and W. H. Cooper, 'Predicting Exit, Voice, Loyalty, and Neglect', *Administrative Science Quarterly*, December 1989, pp. 521–39; and J. Zhou and J. M. George, 'When Job Dissatisfaction Leads to Creativity: Encouraging the Expression of Voice', *Academy of Management Journal*, August 2001, pp. 682–96.

64. R. B. Freeman, 'Job Satisfaction as an Economic Variable', *American Economic Review*, January 1978, pp. 135–41.

65. Spector, *Job Satisfaction*, pp. 57–58.

66. See T. S. Bateman and D. W. Organ, 'Job Satisfaction and the Good Soldier: The Relationship between Affect and Employee "Citizenship"', *Academy of Management Journal*, December 1983, pp. 587–95; C. A. Smith, D. W. Organ and J. Near, 'Organizational Citizenship Behavior: Its Nature and Antecedents', *Journal of Applied Psychology*, October 1983, pp. 653–63; A. P. Brief, *Attitudes in and around Organizations* (Thousand Oaks, CA: Sage, 1998), pp. 44–45; and M. Podsakoff, S. B. MacKenzie, J. B. Paine and D. G. Bachrach, 'Organizational Citizenship Behaviors: A Critical Review of the Theoretical and Empirical Literature and Suggestions for Future Research', *Journal of Management*, vol. 26, no. 3, 2000, pp. 513–63.

67. D. W. Organ and K. Ryan, 'A Meta-Analytic Review of Attitudinal and Dispositional Predictors of Organizational Citizenship Behavior', *Personnel Psychology*, Winter 1995, p. 791; and J. A. LePine, A. Erez and D. E. Johnson, 'The Nature and Dimensionality of Organizational Citizenship Behavior: A Critical Review and Meta-Analysis', *Journal of Applied Psychology*, February 2002, pp. 52–65.

68. J. Fahr, P. M. Podsakoff and D. W. Organ, 'Accounting for Organizational Citizenship Behavior: Leader Fairness and Task Scope Versus Satisfaction', *Journal of Management*, December 1990, pp. 705–22; R. H. Moorman, 'Relationship between Organization Justice and Organizational Citizenship Behaviors: Do Fairness Perceptions Influence Employee Citizenship?', *Journal of Applied Psychology*, December 1991, pp. 845–55; and M. A. Konovsky and D. W. Organ, 'Dispositional and Contextual Determinants of Organizational Citizenship Behavior', *Journal of Organizational Behavior*, May 1996, pp. 253–66.

69. D. W. Organ, 'Personality and Organizational Citizenship Behavior', *Journal of Management*, Summer 1994, p. 466.

70. See, for example, B. Schneider and D. E. Bowen, 'Employee and Customer Perceptions of Service in Banks: Replication and Extension', *Journal of Applied Psychology*, August 1985, pp. 423–33; W. W. Tornow and J. W. Wiley, 'Service Quality and Management Practices: A Look at Employee Attitudes, Customer Satisfaction, and Bottom-line Consequences', *Human Resource Planning*, vol. 4, no. 2, 1991, pp. 105–16; E. Naumann and D. W. Jackson, Jr, 'One More Time: How Do You Satisfy Customers?', *Business Horizons*, May–June 1999, pp. 71–76; D. J. Koys, 'The Effects of Employee Satisfaction, Organizational Citizenship Behavior, and Turnover on Organizational Effectiveness: A Unit-Level, Longitudinal Study', *Personnel Psychology*, Spring 2001, pp. 101–14; and J. Griffith, 'Do Satisfied Employees Satisfy Customers? Support-Services Staff Morale and Satisfaction among Public School Administrators, Students, and Parents', *Journal of Applied Social Psychology*, August 2001, pp. 1627–58.

71. M. J. Bitner, B. H. Booms and L. A. Mohr, 'Critical Service Encounters: The Employee's Viewpoint', *Journal of Marketing*, October 1994, pp. 95–106.

PHOTO CREDITS

Personality and Emotions at Work

CHAPTER OUTLINE
Personality
Emotions

LEARNING OBJECTIVES

After studying this chapter, you should be able to:

1. Explain the factors that determine an individual's personality
2. Describe the MBTI personality framework
3. Identify the key traits in the Big Five personality model
4. Explain the impact of job typology on the personality/job performance relationship
5. Differentiate emotions from moods
6. Contrast *felt* versus *displayed* emotions
7. Understand how to read emotions
8. Explain gender differences in emotions
9. Describe external constraints on emotions
10. Apply concepts on emotions to OB issues

*'Be yourself' is the worst advice
you can give some people.*
T. Masson

While not high profile like his rival Bill Gates—Charles Wang has nonetheless created a huge empire with very different approaches, values and attitudes.

The terms often used to describe Charles B. Wang aren't very complimentary. He has frequently been described as a mercenary brute, ruthless, authoritarian, defiant, volatile, blunt, tactless and isolated.[1] So, who is Charles Wang and what makes him so tough and aggressive?

Wang emigrated to New York City from Shanghai in 1952, when he was eight years old. He attended Queens College in New York and obtained a degree in mathematics. In 1976 he founded a company called Computer Associates. Today, Computer Associates is the third-largest software company in the United States, behind Microsoft and Oracle, and Wang is its chairman. The highly successful company has made Wang a billionaire. But if you want insights into Wang's personality and behaviour, you need to understand the experiences that shaped them.

Unlike Microsoft co-founder and fellow billionaire Bill Gates, Wang didn't grow up rich. Wang's view of the world as tough and ruthless was forged by the harshness of his early immigrant experience. 'I know what it is to go hungry,' Wang says. '[Bill Gates] doesn't.'

Wang was always keenly aware that he was a Chinese immigrant in New York City. When he, his parents and brothers settled in Queens in the early 1950s, the borough wasn't the multiethnic mosaic that it is today. The Wang boys were the only Chinese kids at grade school and on their Little League baseball teams. Incidents of blatant racism were rare, but the family abandoned its first attempt at exchanging their walk-up apartment for a house after neighbours-to-be circulated an anti-Chinese petition. Growing up being different made Wang highly sensitive to slights. In fact, in Computer Associates' early years, Wang would become irate if anyone disrespected his company. Even today, revenge still seems to matter to Wang. Managers who resign are treated as traitors. Anyone who isn't Wang's friend, and therefore Computer Associates' friend, seems automatically to be his enemy.

Today, Wang, his wife and three children live a secluded life on a large estate near Oyster Bay on Long Island. Unlike other software moguls such as Bill Gates and Oracle's Lawrence Ellison, who are outgoing and play to the media, Wang has recreated (in a very luxurious fashion!) the isolation he experienced in his formative years in New York City. That may have been nearly 50 years ago, but Wang hasn't forgotten. The isolated and angry man of today has been largely forged by his early family experiences. Charles Wang isn't unique—there are millions of people like him all around the world. *All* our behaviour is somewhat shaped by our personalities and our emotions. In the first half of this chapter, we review the research on personality and its relationship to behaviour. In the latter half, we look at how emotions shape many of our work-related behaviours.

Personality

Why are some people quiet and passive, while others are loud and aggressive? Are certain personality types better adapted for certain job types? Before we can answer these questions, we need to address a more basic one: what is personality?

WHAT IS PERSONALITY?

When we talk of personality, we don't mean that a person has charm, a positive attitude towards life, a smiling face, or is a finalist for 'Best and Fairest' in this year's football competition. When psychologists talk of personality, they mean a dynamic concept describing the growth and development of a person's whole psychological system. Rather than looking at parts of the person, personality looks at some aggregate whole that is greater than the sum of the parts.

Gordon Allport produced the most frequently used definition of personality more than 65 years ago. He said personality is 'the dynamic organisation within the individual of those psychophysical systems that determine his unique adjustments to his environment'.[2] For our purposes, you should think of **personality** as the sum total of ways in which an individual reacts to and interacts with others. It is most often described in terms of measurable traits that a person exhibits.

personality
The sum total of ways in which an individual reacts and interacts with others.

PERSONALITY DETERMINANTS

LEARNING OBJECTIVE

1

Explain the factors that determine an individual's personality

An early debate in personality research centred on whether an individual's personality was the result of their heredity or of their environment. Was the personality predetermined at birth, or was it the result of the individual's interaction with their environment? Clearly, there is no simple black-and-white answer. Personality appears to be a result of both influences. In addition, today we recognise a third factor—the situation. Thus, an adult's personality is now generally considered to be made up of both hereditary and environmental factors, moderated by situational conditions.

Heredity

Heredity refers to those factors that were determined at conception. Physical stature, facial attractiveness, gender, temperament, muscle composition and reflexes, energy level and biological rhythms are characteristics that are generally considered to be either completely or substantially influenced by who your parents are: that is, by their biological, physiological and inherent psychological make-up. The heredity approach argues that the ultimate explanation of an individual's personality is the molecular structure of the genes, located in the chromosomes.

Three different streams of research lend some credibility to the argument that heredity plays an important part in determining an individual's personality. The first looks at the genetic underpinnings of human behaviour and temperament among young children. The second addresses the study of twins who were separated at birth. The third examines the consistency in job satisfaction over time and across situations.

Recent studies of young children lend strong support to the power of heredity.[3] Evidence demonstrates that traits such as shyness, fear and distress are most likely caused by inherited genetic characteristics. This finding suggests that some personality traits may be built into the same genetic code that affects factors such as height and hair colour.

Researchers have studied more than 100 sets of identical twins that were separated at birth and raised separately.[4] If heredity played little or no part in determining personality, you would expect to find few similarities between the separated twins. But the researchers found a lot in common. For almost every behavioural trait, a significant part of the variation between the twins turned out to be associated with genetic factors. For example, one set of twins who had been separated for 39 years and raised 70 kilometres apart were found to drive the same model and colour car, chain-smoked the same brand of cigarette, owned dogs with the same name, and regularly holidayed within three blocks of each other in a beach community 2,400 kilometres away. Researchers have found that genetics accounts for about 50 per cent of the personality differences and more than 30 per cent of the variation in occupational and leisure interests.

Further support for the importance of heredity can be found in studies of individual job satisfaction, which we discussed in the previous chapter. Individual job satisfaction is found to be remarkably stable over time. This result is consistent with what you would expect if satisfaction is determined by something inherent in the person, rather than by external environmental factors.

If personality characteristics were *completely* dictated by heredity, they would be fixed at birth and no amount of experience could alter them. If you were relaxed and easygoing as a child, for example, that would be the result of your genes, and it wouldn't be possible for you to change those characteristics. But personality characteristics aren't completely dictated by heredity.

Environment

Among the factors that exert pressures on our personality formation are the culture in which we are raised; our early conditioning; the norms among our family, friends and social groups; and other influences that we experience. These environmental factors play a substantial role in shaping our personalities.

For example, culture establishes the norms, attitudes and values that are passed along from one generation to the next and create consistencies over time. An ideology that is intensely fostered in one culture may have only moderate influence in another. For example, Australians have had the themes of industriousness, success, competition, independence, mateship and a strong work ethic constantly instilled in them through the media, the school system, family and friends. Australians, as a result, tend to be more ambitious and aggressive when compared to individuals raised in cultures that have emphasised getting along with others, cooperation, and the priority of family over work and career.

Careful consideration of the arguments favouring either heredity or environment as the primary determinant of personality leaves us with the conclusion that *both* are important. Heredity sets the parameters or outer limits, but an individual's full potential will be determined by how well he or she adjusts to the demands and requirements of the environment.

Situation

A third factor, the situation, influences the effects of heredity and environment on personality. An individual's personality, although generally stable and consistent, does change in different situations. The different demands of different situations call forth different aspects of one's personality. So, we shouldn't look at personality patterns in isolation.[5]

It seems only logical to suppose that situations will influence an individual's personality, but a neat classification scheme that would tell us the impact of various types of situations has so far eluded us. However, we do know that certain situations are more relevant than others in influencing personality.

What is of interest taxonomically is that situations seem to differ substantially in the constraints they impose on behaviour. Some situations—for example, club membership or an employment interview—constrain many behaviours; other situations—for example, a picnic in a public park—constrain relatively few.[6]

Furthermore, although certain generalisations can be made about personality, there are significant individual differences. As we shall see, the study of individual differences has come to receive greater emphasis in personality research, which originally sought out more general, universal patterns.

Early training and the culture in which we are raised are important environmental factors that shape our personalities. Other influences are family norms and memberships in social groups.

PERSONALITY TRAITS

The early work in the structure of personality revolved around attempts to identify and label enduring characteristics that describe an individual's behaviour. Popular characteristics include shy, aggressive, submissive, lazy, ambitious, loyal and timid. Those characteristics, when they are exhibited in a large number of situations, are called **personality traits**.[7] The more consistent the characteristic and the more frequently it occurs in diverse situations, the more important that trait is in describing the individual.

personality traits
Enduring characteristics that describe an individual's behaviour.

Early search for primary traits

Efforts to isolate traits have been hindered because there are so many of them. In one study, 17,953 individual traits were identified.[8] Obviously, it's virtually impossible to predict behaviour when such a large number of traits must be taken into account. As a result, attention has been directed towards reducing these thousands to a more manageable number.

One researcher isolated 171 traits, but concluded that they were superficial and lacking in descriptive power.[9] What he sought was a reduced set of traits that would identify underlying patterns. The result was the identification of 16 personality factors, which he called the *source*, or *primary*, *traits*. They are shown in Table 4.1. These 16 traits have been found to be generally steady

TABLE 4.1	Sixteen primary traits	
1. Reserved	vs.	Outgoing
2. Less intelligent	vs.	More intelligent
3. Affected by feelings	vs.	Emotionally stable
4. Submissive	vs.	Dominant
5. Serious	vs.	Happy-go-lucky
6. Expedient	vs.	Conscientious
7. Timid	vs.	Venturesome
8. Tough-minded	vs.	Sensitive
9. Trusting	vs.	Suspicious
10. Practical	vs.	Imaginative
11. Forthright	vs.	Shrewd
12. Self-assured	vs.	Apprehensive
13. Conservative	vs.	Experimenting
14. Group-dependent	vs.	Self-sufficient
15. Uncontrolled	vs.	Controlled
16. Relaxed	vs.	Tense

and constant sources of behaviour, allowing prediction of an individual's behaviour in specific situations by weighing the characteristics for their situational relevance.

The Myers–Briggs Type Indicator

One of the most widely used personality frameworks is called the **Myers–Briggs Type Indicator (MBTI)**.[10] It is essentially a 100-question personality test that asks people how they usually feel or act in particular situations.

On the basis of the answers individuals give to the test, they are classified as extroverted (E) or introverted (I), sensing (S) or intuitive (N), thinking (T) or feeling (F), and perceiving (P) or judging (J). These classifications are then combined into 16 personality types. (These types are different from the 16 primary traits in Table 4.1.) To illustrate, let's take several examples. INTJs are *visionaries*. They usually have original minds and great drive for their own ideas and purposes. They are characterised as sceptical, critical, independent, determined and often stubborn. ESTJs are *organisers*. They are realistic, logical, analytical and decisive, and have a natural head for business or mechanics. They like to organise and run activities. The ENTP type is a *conceptualiser*. He or she is innovative, individualistic, versatile and attracted to entrepreneurial ideas. This person tends to be resourceful in solving challenging problems but may neglect routine assignments. A recent book that profiled 13 contemporary businesspeople who created very successful and large multinational companies found that all 13 are intuitive thinkers (NTs).[11] This result is particularly interesting because intuitive thinkers represent only about 5 per cent of the population.

Many tens of thousands of people a year take the MBTI in Australia and New Zealand. Organisations using the MBTI include hospitals, IT firms, banks, emergency services (fire, police, ambulance), finance companies, local councils, educational institutions and even the Australian Defence Forces. Results from all these MBTI tests reveals that, in general, managers in education and HRM, along with politicians, tend to have higher intuition scores, while managers in the armed forces, police and financial management tend to have lower scores in intuition.[12]

Ironically, there is no hard evidence that the MBTI is a valid measure of personality. But lack of evidence doesn't seem to deter its use in a wide range of organisations.

The Big Five model

MBTI may lack valid supporting evidence, but that can't be said for the five-factor model of personality—more typically called the 'Big Five'.[13] In recent years, an impressive body of research supports that five basic dimensions underlie all others and encompass most of the significant variation in human personality. The Big Five factors are:

- **Extroversion**. This dimension captures one's comfort level with relationships. Extroverts tend to be gregarious, assertive and sociable. Introverts tend to be reserved, timid and quiet.
- **Agreeableness**. This dimension refers to an individual's propensity to defer to others. Highly agreeable people are cooperative, warm and trusting. People who score low on agreeableness are cold, disagreeable and antagonistic.
- **Conscientiousness**. This dimension is a measure of reliability. A highly conscientious person is responsible, organised, dependable and persistent. Those who score low on this dimension are easily distracted, disorganised and unreliable.
- **Emotional stability**. This dimension taps a person's ability to withstand stress. People with positive emotional stability tend to be calm, self-confident and secure. Those with high negative scores tend to be nervous, anxious, depressed and insecure.
- **Openness to experience**. The final dimension addresses one's range of interests and fascination with novelty. Extremely open people are creative, curious and artistically sensitive. Those at the other end of the openness category are conventional and find comfort in the familiar.

In addition to providing a unifying personality framework, research on the Big Five also has found important relationships between these personality dimensions and job performance.[14]

LEARNING OBJECTIVE

2

Describe the MBTI personality framework

Myers-Briggs Type Indicator (MBTI)
A personality test that taps four characteristics and classifies people into one of 16 personality types.

extroversion
A personality dimension describing someone who is sociable, gregarious and assertive.

agreeableness
A personality dimension that describes someone who is good-natured, cooperative and trusting.

LEARNING OBJECTIVE

3

Identify the key traits in the Big Five personality model

conscientiousness
A personality dimension that describes someone who is responsible, dependable, persistent and organised.

emotional stability
A personality dimension that characterises someone as calm, self-confident and secure (positive) versus nervous, depressed and insecure (negative).

openness to experience
A personality dimension that characterises someone in terms of imaginativeness, artistic ability, sensitivity and intellectualism.

OB Controversies

Is the 'crocodile hunter' typical of Australian managers?

Steve Irwin, the 'crocodile hunter', is one of the most well-known Australian characters around the world. Famous for his daredevil antics with Australian wildlife, he is seen to typify the Australian as having a down-to-earth, straight-forward, honest and no frills image, coupled with a very wry sense of humour. This image is often carried across to images of Australian managers. Yet, how close is this image to reality?

In one study, 475 managers from marketing, HR and engineering were tested using the 16 Personality Factors Inventory (16 PF—see Table 4.1) and the results compared with British and American managers. These results showed the Australian managers to be less intelligent, less extroverted, more dominating, more forthright and more self-assured than their American and British counterparts. This led to the managers being more flexible, more willing to help those in need, more adaptable and less stressed than their overseas counterparts.

Another study examined the differences in value systems of managers from Australia, the United States, Korea, Japan and India. As would be expected, the Australian managers were far more like the American managers than the Asian managers. Despite being more similar, Australian managers were found to have higher levels of humanistic orientation (helping others); had a higher degree of moralistic orientation (were more ethical); and placed far less emphasis on material and personal success than did the American managers surveyed.

Finally, in a third study of Australian managers with the MBTI, evidence emerged for most managers being practical, concrete and having specific ways of looking at the world (sensing-thinking). They preferred to make decisions using logic and facts rather than intuitively and through empathy or human values. Australian managers liked to have control over events, things around them and their environment, preferring to live in an organised and scheduled way.

Are Australian managers really like the 'crocodile hunter'? The evidence would seem to suggest otherwise. Crikey!

Sources: B. Barry and P. Dowling, *Towards an Australian Management Style? A Study of the Personality Characteristics and Management Style of Australian Managers* (Melbourne: The Australian Institute of Management, 1984); G. England, 'Managers and Their Value Systems; A Five-Country Comparative Study', *Columbia Journal of World Business*, vol. 13, no. 2, 1978, pp. 35–44; and R. Cacioppe and B. Findlayson, 'The Personality Characteristics of Australian Managers and Differences Between Public and Private Managers', monograph, Curtin University, Perth, Western Australia, 1986.

LEARNING OBJECTIVE

4

Explain the impact of job typology on the personality/job performance relationship

A broad spectrum of occupations was looked at: professionals (including engineers, architects, accountants, lawyers), police, managers, sales people, and semiskilled and skilled employees. Job performance was defined in terms of performance ratings, training proficiency (performance during training programs), and personnel data such as salary level. The results showed that conscientiousness predicted job performance for all occupational groups. 'The preponderance of evidence shows that individuals who are dependable, reliable, careful, thorough, able to plan, organised, hardworking, persistent, and achievement-oriented tend to have higher job performance in most if not all occupations.'[15] In addition, employees who score higher in conscientiousness develop higher levels of job knowledge, probably because highly conscientious people exert greater levels of effort on their jobs. The higher levels of job knowledge then contribute to higher levels of job performance. Consistent with these findings, evidence also finds a relatively strong and consistent relationship between conscientiousness and organisational citizenship behaviour (OCB).[16] This, however, seems to be the only personality dimension that predicts OCB.

For the other personality dimensions, predictability depended on both the performance criterion and the occupational group. For example, extroversion predicted performance in managerial and sales positions. This finding makes sense because those occupations involve high social interaction. Similarly, openness to experience was found to be important in predicting training proficiency, which, too, seems logical. What wasn't so clear was why positive emotional stability wasn't related to job performance. Intuitively, it would seem that people who are calm and secure would do better on almost all jobs than people who are anxious and insecure. The answer might be that only people who score fairly high on emotional stability retain their jobs. So, the range among those people studied, all of whom were employed, would tend to be quite small.

MAJOR PERSONALITY ATTRIBUTES INFLUENCING OB

In this section, we want to more carefully evaluate specific personality attributes that have been found to be powerful predictors of behaviour in organisations. The first is related to where one perceives the locus of control to be in one's life. The others are Machiavellianism, self-esteem, self-monitoring, propensity for risk taking and Type A personality. In this section, we shall briefly introduce these attributes and summarise what we know about their ability to explain and predict employee behaviour.

Locus of control

Some people believe that they are masters of their own fate. Other people see themselves as pawns of fate, believing that what happens to them in their lives is due to luck or chance. The first type, those who believe that they control their destinies, have been labelled **internals**, whereas the latter, who see their lives as being controlled by outside forces, have been called **externals**.[17] A person's perception of the source of his or her fate is termed **locus of control**.

A large amount of research comparing internals with externals has consistently shown that individuals who rate high in externality are less satisfied with their jobs, have higher absenteeism rates, are more alienated from the work setting, and are less involved in their jobs than are internals.[18] Externals are also less likely to initially get a job. Why? In contrast to externals, internals exhibit more motivation and willingness to take action in their initial interviews, which has been shown to relate to significantly more second interviews.[19]

Why are externals more dissatisfied? The answer is probably that they perceive themselves as having little control over the organisational outcomes that are important to them. Internals, facing the same situation, attribute organisational outcomes to their own actions. If the situation is unattractive, they believe that they have no one else to blame but themselves. Also, the dissatisfied internal is more likely to quit a dissatisfying job.

The impact of locus of control on absence is an interesting one. Internals believe that health is substantially under their own control through proper habits, so they take more responsibility for their health and have better health habits. Consequently, their incidences of sickness and, hence, of absenteeism, are lower.[20]

We shouldn't expect any clear relationship between locus of control and turnover, because there are opposing forces at work. 'On the one hand, internals tend to take action and thus might be expected to quit jobs more readily. On the other hand, they tend to be more successful on the job and more satisfied, factors associated with less individual turnover.'[21]

The overall evidence indicates that internals generally perform better on their jobs, but that conclusion should be moderated to reflect differences in jobs. Internals search more actively for information before making a decision, are more motivated to achieve, and make a greater attempt to control their environment. Externals, however, are more compliant and willing to follow directions. Therefore, internals do well on sophisticated tasks—which include most managerial and professional jobs—that require complex information processing and learning. In addition, internals are more suited to jobs that require initiative and independence of action. Almost all successful sales people, for example, are internals. Why? Because it's pretty difficult to succeed in sales if you don't believe you can effectively influence outcomes. In contrast, externals should do well on jobs that are well structured and routine and in which success depends heavily on complying with the direction of others.

internals
Individuals who believe that they control what happens to them.

externals
Individuals who believe that what happens to them is controlled by outside forces such as luck or chance.

locus of control
The degree to which people believe they are masters of their own fate.

Machiavellianism

The personality characteristic of **Machiavellianism** (Mach) is named after Niccolo Machiavelli, who wrote in the 16th century on how to gain and use power. An individual high in Machiavellianism is pragmatic, maintains emotional distance and believes that ends can justify means. 'If it works, use it' is consistent with a high-Mach perspective.

A considerable amount of research has been directed towards relating high- and low-Mach personalities to certain behavioural outcomes.[22] High Machs manipulate more, win more, are persuaded less, and persuade others more than do low Machs.[23] Yet, these high-Mach outcomes are moderated by situational factors. It has been found that high Machs flourish (1) when they interact face to face with others, rather than indirectly; (2) when the situation has a minimum number of rules and regulations, thus allowing latitude for improvisation; and (3) when emotional involvement with details irrelevant to winning distracts low Machs.[24]

Should we conclude that high Machs make good employees? That answer depends on the type of job and whether you consider ethical implications in evaluating performance. In jobs that require bargaining skills (such as labour negotiation) or that offer substantial rewards for winning (as in commissioned sales), high Machs will be productive. But if ends can't justify the means, if there are absolute standards of behaviour, or if the three situational factors noted in the preceding paragraph are not in evidence, our ability to predict a high Mach's performance will be severely curtailed.

Self-esteem

People differ in the degree to which they like or dislike themselves. This trait is called **self-esteem**.[25] The research on self-esteem (SE) offers some interesting insights into organisational behaviour. For example, self-esteem is directly related to expectations for success. High SEs believe that they possess the ability they need to succeed at work.

Individuals with high self-esteem will take more risks in job selection and are more likely to choose unconventional jobs than people with low self-esteem.

The most generalisable finding on self-esteem is that low SEs are more susceptible to external influence than are high SEs. Low SEs are dependent on the receipt of positive evaluations from others. As a result, they are more likely to seek approval from others and more prone to conform to the beliefs and behaviours of those they respect than are high SEs. In managerial positions, low SEs will tend to be concerned with pleasing others and, therefore, are less likely to take unpopular stands than are high SEs.

Not surprisingly, self-esteem has also been found to be related to job satisfaction. A number of studies confirm that high SEs are more satisfied with their jobs than are low SEs.

Self-monitoring

A personality trait that has recently received increased attention is called **self-monitoring**.[26] It refers to an individual's ability to adjust his or her behaviour to external, situational factors.

Individuals high in self-monitoring do show considerable adaptability in adjusting their behaviour to external situational factors. They are highly sensitive to external cues and can behave differently in different situations. High self-monitors are capable of presenting striking contradictions between their public persona and their private self. Low self-monitors can't disguise themselves in that way. They tend to display their true dispositions and attitudes in every situation; hence, there is high behavioural consistency between who they are and what they do.

The research on self-monitoring is in its infancy, so predictions must be guarded. However, preliminary evidence suggests that high self-monitors tend to pay closer attention to the behaviour of others and are more capable of conforming than are low self-monitors.[27] In addition, high self-monitoring managers tend to be more mobile in their careers, receive more promotions (both internal and cross-organisational), and are more likely to occupy central positions in an organisation.[28] We might also hypothesise that high self-monitors will be more successful in managerial positions in which individuals are required to play multiple, and even contradicting,

Rupert Murdoch personifies the risk-taking personality. He thrives in business situations that most others would find perilous and stressful.

roles and in political office. The high self-monitor is capable of putting on different 'faces' for different audiences.

Risk taking

Rupert Murdoch stands out for his willingness to take risks. He started with almost nothing in 1952 with the low-circulation *The Adelaide News*. By the early 1980s, he had made a fortune after buying *The Times* in London, *The New York Post*, *The News of The World* and the Sydney *Sun* newspapers and turning them into very profitable concerns. Then, trying to capitalise on his previous successes, Murdoch overextended himself by moving into cable TV and buying the 20th Century Fox movie empire. The company nearly collapsed under the weight of debt in 1991. But by taking risks, the year 2000 saw his News Corporation company with assets of A\$36 billion and revenues of A\$14 billion. Never fearful of taking chances, Murdoch subsequently leveraged the News Corporation assets on several European cable TV ventures in his attempt to create a global pay-TV network. He failed and in 2002 the company posted a A\$12 billion loss. Perhaps the greatest irony was that News Corp.'s share price actually rose on the news of the size of the loss—no doubt helped by the release on the same day of news of the losses by his main rival in Europe, Vivendi, which amounted to A\$23 billion![29]

People differ in their willingness to take chances. This propensity to assume or avoid risk has been shown to have an impact on how long it takes managers to make a decision and how much information they require before making their choice. For example, 79 managers worked on simulated personnel exercises that required them to make hiring decisions.[30] High risk-taking managers made more rapid decisions and used less information in making their choices than did the low risk-taking managers. Interestingly, the decision accuracy was the same for both groups.

In general, managers in large organisations tend to be risk averse, especially in contrast to growth-oriented entrepreneurs who actively manage small businesses.[31] For the work population as a whole, there are also differences in risk propensity.[32] As a result, it makes sense to recognise these differences and even to consider aligning risk-taking propensity with specific job demands. For example, a high risk-taking propensity may lead to more effective performance for a share trader in a brokerage firm because that type of job demands rapid decision making. On the other hand, a willingness to take risks might prove a major obstacle to an accountant who performs auditing activities. Someone with a low risk-taking propensity might better fill the latter job.

Type A personality

Do you know people who are excessively competitive and always seem to be experiencing a sense of time urgency? If you do, it's a good bet that those people have a **Type A personality**. A person with a Type A personality is 'aggressively involved in a chronic, incessant struggle to achieve more

Type A personality
Aggressive involvement in a chronic, incessant struggle to achieve more and more in less and less time and, if necessary, against the opposing efforts of other things or other people.

and more in less and less time, and, if required to do so, against the opposing efforts of other things or other persons'.[33] In Western cultures, such characteristics tend to be highly prized and positively associated with ambition and the successful acquisition of material goods.

In contrast to the Type A personality is the Type B, who is exactly opposite (see Table 4.2). Type B's are 'rarely harried by the desire to obtain a wildly increasing number of things or participate in an endless growing series of events in an ever-decreasing amount of time'.[34]

Type A's operate under moderate to high levels of stress. They subject themselves to more or less continuous time pressure, creating for themselves a life of deadlines. These characteristics result in some rather specific behavioural outcomes. For example, Type A's are fast workers, because they emphasise quantity over quality. In managerial positions, Type A's demonstrate their competitiveness by working long hours and, not infrequently, making poor decisions because they make them too fast. Type A's are also rarely creative. Because of their concern with quantity and speed, they rely on past experiences when faced with problems. They will not allocate the time necessary to develop unique solutions to new problems. They rarely vary in their responses to specific challenges in their milieu; hence, their behaviour is easier to predict than that of Type B's.

Do Type A's differ from Type B's in their ability to get hired? The answer appears to be 'yes'.[35] Type A's do better in job interviews because they are more likely to be judged as having desirable traits such as high drive, competence, aggressiveness and success motivation. Are Type A's or Type B's more successful in organisations? Despite the Type A's hard work, the Type B's are the ones who appear to make it to the top. Great sales people are usually Type A's; senior executives are usually Type B's. Why? The answer lies in the tendency of Type A's to trade off quality of effort for quantity. Promotions in corporate and professional organisations 'usually go to those who are wise rather than to those who are merely hasty, to those who are tactful rather than to those who are hostile, and to those who are creative rather than to those who are merely agile in competitive strife'.[36]

PERSONALITY AND NATIONAL CULTURE

Do personality frameworks, such as the 'Big Five' model, transfer across cultures? Are dimensions such as locus of control and the Type A personality relevant in all cultures? Let's try to answer these questions.

The five personality factors identified in the 'Big Five' model appear in almost all cross-cultural studies.[37] This includes a wide variety of diverse cultures—such as China, Israel, Germany, Japan, Spain, Nigeria, Norway, Pakistan, the United States and Australia. Differences tend to

TABLE 4.2	Type A personality versus Type B personality	
Type A's	**Type B's**
1. are always moving, walking and eating rapidly;	1. never suffer from a sense of time urgency with its accompanying impatience;
2. feel impatient with the rate at which most events take place;	2. feel no need to display or discuss either their achievements or accomplishments unless such exposure is demanded by the situation;
3. strive to think or do two or more things at once;	3. play for fun and relaxation, rather than to exhibit their superiority at any cost;
4. cannot cope with leisure time;	4. can relax without guilt.
5. are obsessed with numbers, measuring their success in terms of how many or how much of everything they acquire.	

surface by the emphasis on dimensions. Chinese, for example, use the category of conscientiousness more often and use the category of agreeableness less often than do Australians. But there is a surprisingly high amount of agreement, especially among individuals from developed countries. As a case in point, a comprehensive review of studies covering people from the 15-nation European Union found that conscientiousness was a valid predictor of performance across jobs and occupational groups.[38] This is exactly what US studies have found.

There are no common personality types for a given country. You can, for example, find high and low risk takers in almost any culture. Yet, a country's culture influences the dominant personality characteristics of its population. We can see this by looking at locus of control and the Type A personality.

There is evidence that cultures differ in terms of people's relationship to their environment.[39] In some cultures, such as those in Australia and Canada, people believe that they can dominate their environment. People in other societies, such as Middle Eastern countries, believe that life is essentially preordained. Note the close parallel to internal and external locus of control.[40] We should expect, therefore, a larger proportion of internals in the Australian and Canadian workforce than in the Saudi Arabian or Iranian workforce.

The prevalence of Type A personalities will be somewhat influenced by the culture in which a person grows up. There are Type A's in every country, but there will be more in capitalistic countries, where achievement and material success are highly valued. For example, it is estimated that about 50 per cent of the North American population, the home of capitalism, is Type A.[41] This percentage shouldn't be too surprising. The Americans and Canadians both have a high emphasis on time management and efficiency. Both have cultures that stress accomplishments and acquisition of money and material goods. On the other hand, in cultures such as Sweden and France, where materialism is less revered, we would predict a smaller proportion of Type A personalities.

Myth *or* Science?

'Deep down, people are all alike'

This statement is essentially false. Only in the broadest sense can we say that 'people are all alike'. For example, it's true that people all have values, attitudes, likes and dislikes, feelings, goals and similar general attributes. But individual differences are far more illuminating. People differ in intelligence, personality, abilities, ambition, motivations, emotional display, values, verbal expression, priorities, expectations, and the like. If we want to understand, explain or predict human behaviour accurately, we need to focus on individual differences. Your ability to predict behaviour will be severely limited if you constantly assume that all people are alike or that everyone is like you.

As an illustration, consider the task of selecting among job applicants. Managers regularly use information about a candidate's personality (in addition to experience, knowledge, skill level and intellectual abilities) to help make their hiring decisions. Recognising that jobs differ in terms of demands and requirements, managers interview and test applicants to (1) categorise them by specific traits, (2) assess job tasks in terms of the type of personality best suited for effectively completing those tasks, and (3) match applicants and job tasks to find an appropriate fit. So, by using an individual-difference variable—in this case, personality—managers improve the likelihood of identifying and hiring high-performing employees.

Source: Based on P. L. Ackerman and L. G. Humphreys, 'Individual Differences Theory in Industrial and Organizational Psychology', in M. D. Dunnette and L. M. Hough (eds), *Handbook of Industrial & Organizational Psychology*, 2nd ed., vol. 1 (Palo Alto, CA: Consulting Psychologists, 1990), pp. 223–82.

ACHIEVING PERSONALITY FIT

Twenty years ago, organisations were concerned with personality primarily because they wanted to match individuals to specific jobs. That concern still exists. But, in recent years, interest has expanded to include the individual–organisation fit. Why? Because managers today are less interested in an applicant's ability to perform a *specific* job than with his or her *flexibility* to meet changing situations.

The person–job fit

In the discussion of personality attributes, our conclusions were often qualified to recognise that the requirements of the job moderated the relationship between possession of the personality characteristic and job performance. This concern with matching the job requirements with personality characteristics is best articulated in John Holland's **personality-job fit theory**.[42] The theory is based on the notion of fit between an individual's personality characteristics and his or her occupational environment. Holland presents six personality types and proposes that satisfaction and the propensity to leave a job depend on the degree to which individuals successfully match their personalities to an occupational environment.

Each one of the six personality types has a congruent occupational environment. Table 4.3 describes the six types and their personality characteristics and gives examples of congruent occupations.

Holland has developed a Vocational Preference Inventory questionnaire that contains 160 occupational titles. Respondents indicate which of these occupations they like or dislike, and their answers are used to form personality profiles. Using this procedure, research strongly

personality–job fit theory
Identifies six personality types and proposes that the fit between personality type and occupational environment determines satisfaction and turnover.

TABLE 4.3	Holland's typology of personality and congruent occupations	
Type	**Personality Characteristics**	**Congruent Occupations**
Realistic: Prefers physical activities that require skill, strength and coordination	Shy, genuine, persistent, stable, conforming, practical	Mechanic, drill-press operator, assembly-line worker, farmer
Investigative: Prefers activities that involve thinking, organising and understanding	Analytical, original, curious, independent	Biologist, economist, mathematician, news reporter
Social: Prefers activities that involve helping and developing others	Sociable, friendly, cooperative, understanding	Social worker, teacher, counsellor, clinical psychologist
Conventional: Prefers rule-regulated, orderly and unambiguous activities	Conforming, efficient, practical, unimaginative, inflexible	Accountant, corporate manager, bank teller, file clerk
Enterprising: Prefers verbal activities in which there are opportunities to influence others and attain power	Self-confident, ambitious, energetic, domineering	Lawyer, real estate agent, public relations specialist, small business manager
Artistic: Prefers ambiguous and unsystematic activities that allow creative expression	Imaginative, disorderly, idealistic, emotional, impractical	Painter, musician, writer, interior decorator

supports the hexagonal diagram shown in Figure 4.1.[43] This figure shows that the closer two fields or orientations are in the hexagon, the more compatible they are. Adjacent categories are quite similar, whereas those diagonally opposite are highly dissimilar.

What does all this mean? The theory argues that satisfaction is highest and turnover lowest when personality and occupation are in agreement. Social individuals should be in social jobs (for example, teacher, counsellor), conventional people in conventional jobs (for example, accountant, bank teller), and so forth. A realistic person in a realistic job (for example, mechanic, farmer) is in a more congruent situation than is a realistic person in an investigative job (for example, biologist, economist). A realistic person in a social job is in the most incongruent situation possible. The key points of this model are: (1) there do appear to be intrinsic differences in personality among individuals; (2) there are different types of jobs; and (3) people in job environments congruent with their personality types should be more satisfied and less likely to voluntarily resign than should people in incongruent jobs.

The person–organisation fit

As previously noted, attention in recent years has expanded to include matching people to *organisations* as well as *jobs*. To the degree that an organisation faces a dynamic and changing environment and requires employees who are able to readily change tasks and move fluidly between teams, it's probably more important that employees' personalities fit with the overall organisation's culture than with the characteristics of any specific job.

The person–organisation fit essentially argues that people leave jobs that are not compatible with their personalities.[44] Using the 'Big Five' terminology, for example, we could expect that people high on extroversion fit better with aggressive and team-oriented cultures; that people high on agreeableness will match up better with a supportive organisational climate than with one that focuses on aggressiveness; and that people high on openness to experience fit better into

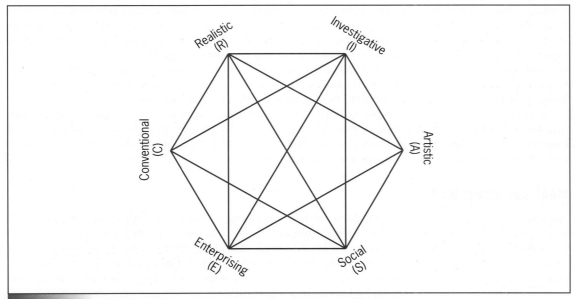

| FIGURE 4.1 | Relationship among occupational personality type |

Source: J. L. Holland, *Making Vocational Choices: A Theory of Vocational Personalities and Work Environments,* 3rd ed, © 1973, 1985, 1992, 1997 by the Psychological Assessment Resources Inc. Reproduced by special permission of the Publisher, Psychological Association Resources Inc., 16204 North Florida Avenue, Lutz, FL 33549. All rights reserved.

organisations that emphasise innovation rather than standardisation.[45] Following these guidelines at the time of hiring should lead to selecting new employees who fit better with the organisation's culture, which, in turn, should result in higher employee satisfaction and reduced turnover.

Emotions

On 9 August 1987, Julian Knight, a 19-year old former Australian Army officer cadet, walked into Hoddle Street, Melbourne. Armed with a Ruger assault rifle, a Mossberg pump-action shotgun and an M-14 semi-automatic military rifle, he then proceeded to kill and wound innocent bystanders and those who tried to assist the injured. Why? He was purportedly angry over his impending court case (he had stabbed his company sergeant major several months earlier and subsequently been dismissed from the army), his inability to readjust to civilian life, the break-up with his girlfriend, and the gear-box in his car having seized up earlier in the day—all of this anger was compounded by excessive alcohol consumption that day.[46] For Knight, anger over victimisation and bastardisation while an army officer cadet at Duntroon Military College had led to him stabbing his superior NCO and started a tragic sequence of violence that ended with seven people dead and 19 wounded, including two police officers.

Going on a shooting rampage is an extreme example, but it does dramatically illustrate the theme of this section—emotions are a critical factor in employee behaviour. In Knight's case, his mistreatment at the military college, and the impact this had on his emotional well-being, had very real consequences that no organisation can ignore.

Given the obvious role that emotions play in our everyday life, it might surprise you to learn that, until very recently, the topic of emotions had been given little or no attention within the field of OB.[47] How could this be? We can offer two possible explanations. The first is the *myth of rationality*.[48] Since the late 19th century and the rise of scientific management, organisations have been specifically designed with the objective of trying to control emotions. A well-run organisation was one that successfully eliminated frustration, fear, anger, love, hate, joy, grief and similar feelings. Such emotions were the antithesis of rationality. So, while researchers and managers knew that emotions were an inseparable part of everyday life, they tried to create organisations that were emotion-free. That, of course, wasn't possible. The second factor that acted to keep emotions out of OB was the belief that *emotions of any kind were disruptive*.[49] When emotions were considered, the discussion focused on strong negative emotions—especially anger—that interfered with an employee's ability to do his or her job effectively. Emotions were rarely viewed as being constructive or able to stimulate performance-enhancing behaviours.

Certainly, some emotions, particularly when exhibited at the wrong time, can reduce employee performance. But this doesn't change the reality that employees bring an emotional component with them to work every day and that no study of OB could be comprehensive without considering the role of emotions in workplace behaviour.

affect
A broad range of feelings that people experience.

emotions
Intense feelings that are directed at someone or something.

moods
Feelings that tend to be less intense than emotions and that lack a contextual stimulus.

WHAT ARE EMOTIONS?

Although we don't want to get tied down with too many definitions, before we can proceed with our analysis, we need to clarify three terms that are closely intertwined: *affect, emotions* and *moods*.

Affect is a generic term that covers a broad range of feelings that people experience. It's an umbrella concept that encompasses both emotions and moods.[50] **Emotions** are intense feelings that are directed at someone or something.[51] Finally, **moods** are feelings that tend to be less intense than emotions and which lack a contextual stimulus.[52]

Emotions are reactions to an object, not a trait. They are object-specific. You show your emotions when you are 'happy about something, angry at someone, afraid of something'.[53] Moods, on the other hand, aren't directed at an object. Emotions can turn into moods when you lose focus on the contextual object. So, when a work colleague criticises you for the way you spoke to a client, you might become angry with him. That is, you show emotion (anger) towards a specific object (your colleague). But later in the day, you might find yourself just generally dispirited. You can't attribute this feeling to any single event—you're just not your normal, upbeat self. This affect state describes a mood.

A related affect-term that is gaining increasing importance in organisational behaviour is *emotional labour*. Every employee expends physical and mental labour when they put their bodies and cognitive capabilities, respectively, into their job. But most jobs also require **emotional labour**. This is when an employee expresses organisationally desired emotions during interpersonal transactions.[54] The concept of emotional labour originally developed in relation to service jobs. Airline flight attendants, for example, are expected to be cheerful, funeral counsellors sombre, and doctors emotionally neutral. But today, the concept of emotional labour seems relevant to almost every job. You are expected, for example, to be courteous and not hostile in interactions with fellow employees. And leaders are expected to draw on emotional labour to 'motivate the troops'. Almost every great speech, for example, contains a strong emotional component that stirs feelings in others. As we proceed in this section, you will see that it's because of the increasing importance of emotional labour as a key component of effective job performance that an understanding of emotion has gained heightened relevance within the field of OB.

> **emotional labour**
> A situation in which an employee expresses organisationally desired emotions during interpersonal transactions.

FELT VERSUS DISPLAYED EMOTIONS

Emotional labour creates dilemmas for employees when their job requires them to exhibit emotions that are incongruous with their actual feelings. Not surprisingly, this is a frequent occurrence. There are people with whom you have to work with whom you find it very difficult to be friendly. Maybe you consider their personality abrasive. Maybe you know they have said negative things about you behind your back. Regardless, your job requires you to interact with these people on a regular basis. So, you're forced to feign friendliness. Or maybe you're a sales clerk in a retail store. Management expects you to smile and be friendly with customers, but there are days when you just don't feel like smiling and being friendly.

It can help you to better understand emotions if you separate them into *felt* versus *displayed* emotions.[55] **Felt emotions** are an individual's actual emotions. In contrast, **displayed emotions** are those that are organisationally required and considered appropriate in a given job. They are not innate; they are learned. 'The ritual look of delight on the face of the first runner-up as the new beauty pageant winner is announced is a product of the display rule that losers should mask their sadness with an expression of joy for the winner.'[56] Similarly, most of us know that we're expected to act sad at funerals regardless of whether we consider the person's death to be a loss, and to pretend to be happy at weddings even if we don't feel like celebrating.[57] Effective managers have learned to be serious when giving an employee a negative performance evaluation

> **LEARNING OBJECTIVE**
> **6**
> Contrast *felt* versus *displayed* emotions

> **felt emotions**
> An individual's actual emotions.

> **displayed emotions**
> Emotions that are organisationally required and considered appropriate in a given job.

Flight attendants at many airlines are selected largely for their ability to exhibit positive emotions and an upbeat personality. A major portion of an airline customer's impression of the airline's overall service is formed by interaction with booking clerks and flight attendants.

and to cover up their anger when they have been passed over for promotion. And the sales person who hasn't learned to smile and appear friendly, regardless of his or her true feelings at the moment, isn't typically going to last long in most sales jobs.

The key point here is that felt and displayed emotions are often different. In fact, many people have problems working with others simply because they naively assume that the emotions they see others display are what those others actually feel. This is particularly true in organisations where role demands and situations often require people to exhibit emotional behaviours that mask their true feelings. In addition, jobs today increasingly require employees to interact with customers. And customers aren't always easy to deal with. They often complain, behave rudely, speak sarcastically and make unrealistic demands. In such instances, an employee's felt emotions may need to be disguised. Employees who aren't able to project a friendly and helpful demeanour in such situations are likely to alienate customers and are unlikely to be effective in their jobs.

EMOTION DIMENSIONS

How many emotions are there? In what ways do they vary? We will answer these questions in this section.

Variety

There are dozens of emotions. They include anger, contempt, enthusiasm, envy, fear, frustration, happiness, hate, hope, jealousy, joy, love, pride, surprise and sadness. One way to classify them is by whether they are positive or negative.[58] Positive emotions—such as happiness and hope—express a favourable evaluation or feeling. Negative emotions—such as anger or hate—express the opposite. And keep in mind that emotions can't be neutral. Being neutral is non-emotional.[59] Importantly, negative emotions seem to have a greater effect on individuals. People reflect on and think about events that induce strong negative emotions five times as long as they do about events that induce strong positive ones.[60] So, we should expect people to recall negative experiences more readily than positive ones.

There have been numerous efforts to limit and define the dozens of emotions into a fundamental or basic set of emotions.[61] Research has identified six universal emotions: anger, fear, sadness, happiness, disgust and surprise.[62]

LEARNING OBJECTIVE

7

Understand how to read emotions

One factor that has strongly shaped what is and isn't listed in this basic set is the manner in which they were identified. Researchers tended to look for universally identified facial expressions and then convert them into categories (see Figure 4.2). Emotions that couldn't be readily identified by others through facial expressions, or that were considered a subset of one of the basic six, weren't selected.

Figure 4.3 illustrates that the six emotions can be conceptualised as existing along a continuum.[63] The closer any two emotions are to each other on this continuum, the more people are likely to confuse them. For example, happiness and surprise are frequently mistaken for each other, while happiness and disgust are rarely confused. In addition, as we will elaborate later in this section, cultural factors can also influence interpretations.

Do these six basic emotions surface in the workplace? Absolutely. 'I get *angry* after receiving a poor performance appraisal.' 'I *fear* that I could be laid off as a result of a company cutback.' 'I'm *sad* about one of my peers leaving to take a new job in another city.' 'I'm *happy* after being selected as employee-of-the-month.' 'I'm *disgusted* with the way my supervisor treats the women on our team.' 'And I'm *surprised* to find out that management plans a complete restructuring of the company's retirement program.'

Intensity

People give different responses to identical emotion-provoking stimuli. In some cases, this can be attributed to the individual's personality; other times, it's a result of the job requirements.

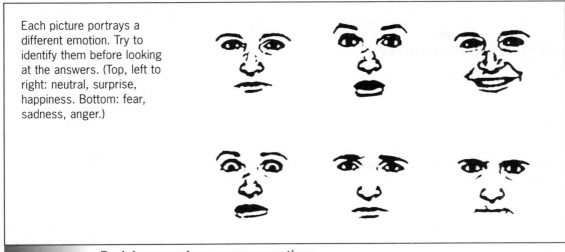

Each picture portrays a different emotion. Try to identify them before looking at the answers. (Top, left to right: neutral, surprise, happiness. Bottom: fear, sadness, anger.)

FIGURE 4.2   Facial expressions convey emotions

FIGURE 4.3   Emotion continuum

Source: Based on R. D. Woodworth, *Experimental Psychology* (New York: Holt, 1938).

People vary in their inherent ability to express intensity. You undoubtedly know individuals who almost never show their feelings. They rarely get angry. They are very calm and never show rage. In contrast, you probably also know people who seem to be on an emotional roller coaster. When they're happy, they're ecstatic. When they're sad, they're deeply depressed. And two people can be in the exact same situation, but with one showing excitement and joy, the other remaining calm and collected.

Jobs make different intensity demands in terms of emotional labour. For example, air force pilots, Emergency Room doctors and courtroom judges are expected to be calm and controlled, even in stressful situations. Conversely, the effectiveness of television evangelists, sports announcers calling the sporting events, and lawyers defending or prosecuting a case can depend on their ability to alter their displayed emotional intensity as the need arises.

Frequency and duration

How often does an emotion need to be exhibited, and for how long?

Sue Wolfson is basically a quiet and reserved person. She loves her job as a financial planner. She doesn't enjoy, however, having to give speeches in order to increase her visibility and to promote her programs. But she still has to give speeches occasionally. 'If I had to speak to large audiences every day, I'd quit this business,' she says. 'I think this works for me because I can fake excitement and enthusiasm for an hour, a couple of times a month.'

Emotional labour that requires high frequency or long durations is more demanding and requires more exertion by employees. So, whether an employee can successfully meet the emotional demands of a given job depends not only on what emotions need to be displayed and their intensity, but also on how frequently and for how long the effort has to be made.

CAN PEOPLE BE EMOTION*LESS*?

Some people seem outwardly calm or apathetic in situations in which others are clearly emotionally charged. Are the former without feeling? Can people be emotion*less*?

Some people have severe difficulty in expressing their emotions and understanding the emotions of others. Psychologists call this *alexithymia* (which is Greek for 'lack of emotion').[64] People who suffer from alexithymia rarely cry and are often seen by others as bland and cold. Their own feelings make them uncomfortable, and they are not able to discriminate among their different emotions. In addition, they are often at a complete loss to understand what others around them feel.

Does this inability to express emotions and read others mean that people who suffer from alexithymia are poor work performers? Not necessarily. Consistent with our discussion on matching personality types with appropriate jobs, people who lack emotion need to be in jobs that require little or no emotional labour. These people are not well suited to sales and managerial positions. But they might very well be effective performers, for example, in a job writing program code or in any work that is confined exclusively to computer interaction.

LEARNING OBJECTIVE

8

Explain gender differences in emotions

GENDER AND EMOTIONS

It is widely assumed that women are more 'in touch' with their feelings than men—that they react more emotionally and are better able to read emotions in others. Is there any truth to these assumptions?

The evidence does confirm differences between men and women when it comes to emotional reactions and ability to read others. In contrasting the genders, women show greater emotional expression than men;[65] they experience emotions more intensely; and they display more frequent expressions of both positive and negative emotions, except anger.[66] In contrast to men, women also report more comfort in expressing emotions. Finally, women are better at reading non-verbal and paralinguistic cues than are men.[67]

What explains these differences? Three possible answers have been suggested. One explanation is the different ways men and women have been socialised.[68] Men are taught to be tough and brave; and showing emotion is inconsistent with this image. Women, on the other hand, are socialised to be nurturing. This may account for the perception that women are generally warmer and friendlier than men. For example, women are expected to express more positive emotions on the job (shown by smiling) than men, and they do.[69] A second explanation is that women may have more innate ability to read others and present their emotions than do men.[70] Third, women may have a greater need for social approval and, thus, a higher propensity to show positive emotions such as happiness.

LEARNING OBJECTIVE

9

Describe external constraints on emotions

EXTERNAL CONSTRAINTS ON EMOTIONS

An emotion that is acceptable on the athletic playing field may be totally unacceptable when exhibited at the workplace. Similarly, what is appropriate in one country is often inappropriate in another. These facts illustrate the role that external constraints play in shaping displayed emotions.

Every organisation defines boundaries that identify what emotions are acceptable and the degree to which they can be expressed. The same applies in different cultures. In this section, we look at organisational and cultural influences on emotions.

Organisational influences

If you can't smile and appear happy, you are unlikely to have much of a career working at an amusement park. And a manual produced by McDonald's states that its counter personnel 'must display traits such as sincerity, enthusiasm, confidence, and a sense of humour'.[71]

There is no single emotional 'set' sought by all organisations. However, at least in Australia, the evidence indicates that there is a bias against negative and intense emotions. Expressions of negative emotions such as fear, anxiety and anger tend to be unacceptable except under fairly specific conditions.[72] For example, one such condition might be a high-status member of a group conveying impatience with a low-status member.[73] Moreover, expressions of intense emotion, whether negative or positive, tend to be typically unacceptable because they are seen as undermining routine task performance.[74] Again, there are exceptional conditions in which this isn't true—for example, a brief grieving over the sudden death of a company's CEO or the celebration of a record year of profits. But for the most part, consistent with the myth of rationality, well-managed organisations are expected to be essentially emotion-free.

Cultural influences

Cultural norms in countries such as Australia, New Zealand, Canada and the United States dictate that employees in service organisations should smile and act friendly when interacting with customers.[75] But this norm doesn't apply worldwide. In Israel, smiling by supermarket cashiers is seen as a sign of inexperience, so cashiers are encouraged to look sombre.[76] In Moslem cultures, smiling is frequently taken as a sign of sexual attraction or flirting, so women are socialised not to smile at men.[77] And the American retail giant Wal-Mart has found that its emphasis on employee friendliness, which has won them a loyal following among North American shoppers, doesn't work in Germany. Accustomed to a culture where 'the customer traditionally comes last', serious German shoppers have been turned off by Wal-Mart's friendly store greeters who welcome you into the store and the very helpful sales personnel.[78]

The above examples illustrate the need to consider cultural factors as influencing what is or isn't considered as emotionally appropriate.[79] What's acceptable in one culture may seem extremely unusual or even dysfunctional in another. And cultures differ in terms of the interpretation they give to emotions.

There tends to be high agreement on what emotions mean *within* cultures, but not between them. For example, one study asked Americans to match facial expressions with the six basic emotions.[80] The range of agreement was between 86 per cent and 98 per cent. When a group of Japanese subjects were given the same task, they only correctly labelled surprise (with 97 per cent agreement). On the other five emotions, their accuracy ranged from only 27 per cent to 70 per cent. In addition, studies indicate that some cultures lack words for standard emotions such as *anxiety*, *depression* or *guilt*. Tahitians, as a case in point, don't have a word directly equivalent to *sadness*. When Tahitians are sad, their peers typically attribute their state to a physical illness.[81]

OB APPLICATIONS

We conclude our discussion of emotions by considering their application to several topics in OB. In this section, we assess how an understanding of emotions can improve our ability to explain and predict the selection process in organisations, decision making, motivation, leadership, interpersonal conflict and deviant workplace behaviours.

OB applications of personality theory include personality assessment tools such as tests that attempt to improve hiring and reduce turnover by screening job applicants for particular personality traits such as patience, empathy, argumentativeness, persistence, open-mindedness and humour. This is particularly pertinent to the retail industry where good customer service is vital.

Ability and selection

People who know their own emotions and are good at reading others' emotions may be more effective in their jobs. That, in essence, is the theme underlying recent research on *emotional intelligence.*[82]

emotional intelligence (EI)
An assortment of non-cognitive skills, capabilities and competencies that influence a person's ability to succeed in coping with environmental demands and pressures.

Emotional intelligence (EI) refers to an assortment of non-cognitive skills, capabilities and competencies that influence a person's ability to succeed in coping with environmental demands and pressures. It is composed of five dimensions:

- *Self-awareness:* being aware of what you're feeling.
- *Self-management:* the ability to manage one's own emotions and impulses.
- *Self-motivation:* the ability to persist in the face of setbacks and failures.
- *Empathy:* the ability to sense how others are feeling.
- *Social skills:* the ability to handle the emotions of others.

Several studies suggest that EI may play an important role in job performance. For example, one study looked at the characteristics of IT engineers who were rated as stars by their peers. The researchers concluded that stars were better at relating to others. That is, it was EI, not intelligence levels, that characterised high performers. A study of US Air Force recruiters generated similar findings. Top-performing recruiters exhibited high levels of EI. Using these findings, the armed forces revamped their selection criteria for recruiters. A follow-up investigation found that future employees hired that had high EI scores were 2.6 times more successful than those who had low EI scores. By using EI in selection, the Air Force was able to cut turnover among new recruits in one year by more than 90 per cent and save nearly US$3 million in hiring and training costs. Another illuminating study looked at the successes and failures of 11 American presidents—from Franklin Roosevelt to Bill Clinton. They were evaluated on six qualities—communication, organisation, political skill, vision, cognitive style and emotional intelligence. It was found that the key quality that differentiated the successful (Roosevelt, Kennedy and Reagan) from the unsuccessful (Johnson, Carter and Nixon) was emotional intelligence.

The implications from the initial evidence on EI is that employers should consider it as a factor in selection, especially in jobs that demand a high degree of social interaction.

Decision making

As you will see in the next chapter, traditional approaches to the study of decision making in organisations have emphasised rationality. They have downplayed, or even ignored, the role of anxiety, fear, frustration, happiness, envy and similar emotions. Yet, it's naive to assume that decision choices aren't influenced by one's feelings at a particular moment.[83] Given the same objective data, we should expect that people may make different choices when they are angry and stressed out than when they are calm and collected.

Negative emotions can result in a limited search for new alternatives and a less vigilant use of information. On the other hand, positive emotions can increase problem-solving skills and facilitate the integration of information.[84]

You can improve your understanding of decision making by considering 'the heart' as well as 'the head'. People use emotions as well as rational and intuitive processes in making decisions. Failure to incorporate emotions into the study of decision processes will result in an incomplete (and often inaccurate) view of the process.

Motivation

We will discuss motivation thoroughly in later chapters—at this point, we want merely to introduce the idea that, like decision making, the dominant approaches to the study of motivation reflect an overrationalised view of individuals.[85]

Motivation theories basically propose that individuals 'are motivated to the extent that their behaviour is expected to lead to desired outcomes. The image is that of rational exchange: the employee essentially trades effort for pay, security, promotions, and so forth.'[86] But people aren't cold, unfeeling machines. Their perceptions and calculations of situations are filled with emotional content that significantly influences how much effort they exert. Moreover, when you see people who are highly motivated in their jobs, they are emotionally committed. People who are engaged in their work 'become physically, cognitively, *and* emotionally immersed in the experience of activity, in the pursuit of a goal'.[87]

Are all people emotionally engaged in their work? No. But many are. And if we focus only on rational calculations of inducements and contributions, we fail to be able to explain behaviours such as the individual who forgets to have dinner and works late into the night, lost in the thrill of her work.[88]

Leadership

The ability to lead others is a fundamental quality sought by organisations. We will discuss the topic of leadership, in depth, in Part 3. Here, however, we briefly introduce how emotions can be an integral part of leadership.

Effective leaders almost all rely on the expression of feelings to help convey their messages.[89] In fact, the expression of emotions in speeches is often the critical element that results in individuals accepting or rejecting a leader's message. 'When leaders feel excited, enthusiastic, and active, they may be more likely to energize their subordinates and convey a sense of efficacy, competence, optimism, and enjoyment.'[90] Politicians, as a case in point, have learned to show enthusiasm when talking about their chances for winning an election, even when polls suggest otherwise.

Corporate executives know that emotional content is critical if employees are to buy into their vision of their company's future and accept change. When new visions are offered, especially when they contain distant or vague goals, change is often difficult to accept. So, when effective leaders want to implement significant changes, they rely on 'the evocation, framing, and mobilisation of *emotions*'.[91] By arousing emotions and linking them to an appealing vision, leaders increase the likelihood that managers and employees alike will accept and support change.

Interpersonal conflict

Few issues are more intertwined with emotions than the topic of interpersonal conflict. Whenever conflicts arise, you can be fairly certain that emotions are also surfacing. A manager's success in trying to resolve conflicts, in fact, is often largely attributable to his or her ability to identify the emotional elements in the conflict and to get the conflicting parties to work through their emotions. And the manager who ignores the emotional elements in conflicts, focusing singularly on rational and task-focused concerns, is unlikely to be very effective in resolving those conflicts.

Deviant workplace behaviours

Negative emotions can lead to a number of deviant workplace behaviours.

Anyone who has spent much time in an organisation realises that people often engage in voluntary actions that violate established norms and which threaten the organisation, its members, or both. These actions are called **employee deviance**.[92] These deviant behaviours can be violent or non-violent and fall into categories such as production (that is, leaving early, intentionally working slowly); property (theft, sabotage); political (that is, gossiping, blaming fellow employees or supervisors); and personal aggression (that is, sexual harassment, verbal abuse, threatening behaviour).[93] Many of these deviant behaviours can be traced to negative emotions.

employee deviance
Voluntary actions that violate established norms and that threaten the organisation, its members, or both.

For example, envy is an emotion that occurs when you resent someone for having something that you don't, and which you strongly desire—such as a better work assignment, larger office or higher salary.[94] It can lead to malicious or deviant behaviours. Envy, for example, has been found to be associated with hostility, 'backstabbing' and other forms of political behaviour, negatively distorting others' successes, and positively distorting one's own accomplishments.[95]

The Real Deal

The increasing popularity of anger-management classes

Anger-management classes have become a trendy solution for dealing with people who have difficulty controlling their tempers. Magistrates and judges, for example, are ordering thousands of criminals to undertake anger-management courses each year. Men who menace their wives or girlfriends are finding that a frequent legal solution is for them to attend anger-management classes. Hotheaded sports celebrities have been required by their coaches or clubs to take these classes to help them cool their tempers while on the playing field. And companies are increasingly sending short-tempered employees to these classes to help them manage their negative emotions.

Courses in anger management tend to be similar in content. Participants share their stories that have led them to the course, then they are told to think about the consequences of what they do when they get worked up. They are taught how to look at the big picture, how not to let small things bother them, how to be a good listener, how to accept someone else's opinion without going out of control, and the like.

Mental-health professionals say that anger-management classes can be beneficial. They say that making mature decisions is a skill that can be taught. But it requires committed students over a long period. Unfortunately, many people who suffer from anger problems aren't willing to admit they have a problem and are even less willing to put in the effort—one expert says her clients typically need about a year to overcome their anger issues—to try to control it. But studies of anger-management programs find little to support their effectiveness. This may be due to several factors. It may reflect a lack of commitment by participants. It may be that many people in these programs actually need other kinds of therapy. Anger management is designed to deal with spontaneous rage, yet many of the individuals taking these courses are just cold, calculating people. Or it may well be that it's not possible to change a basic personality that includes the tendency to exhibit spontaneous rage when angered or frustrated.

Source: Based on J. Cloud, 'Classroom for Hotheads', *Time*, 10 April 2000, pp. 53–54.

Summary and Implications for Managers

Personality

A review of the personality literature offers general guidelines that can lead to effective job performance. As such, it can improve hiring, transfer and promotion decisions. Because personality characteristics create the parameters for people's behaviour, they give us a framework for predicting behaviour. For example, individuals who are shy, introverted and uncomfortable in social situations would probably be ill-suited as salespeople. Individuals who are submissive and conforming might not be effective as advertising 'idea' people.

Can we predict which people will be high performers in sales, research or assembly-line work on the basis of their personality characteristics alone? The answer is 'no'. Personality assessment should be used in conjunction with other information such as skills, abilities and experience.[96] But knowledge of an individual's personality can aid in reducing mismatches, which, in turn, can lead to reduced turnover and higher job satisfaction.

We can look at certain personality characteristics that tend to be related to job success, test for those traits, and use the data to make selection more effective. A person who accepts rules, conformity and dependence, for example, is likely to feel more comfortable in, say, a structured assembly-line job, as an admittance clerk in a hospital or as an administrator in a large public agency than as a researcher or an employee whose job requires a high degree of creativity.

Emotions

Can managers control the emotions of their colleagues and employees? No. Emotions are a natural part of an individual's make-up. Where managers err is if they ignore the emotional elements in organisational behaviour and assess individual behaviour as if it were completely rational. As one consultant aptly put it, 'You can't divorce emotions from the workplace because you can't divorce emotions from people.'[97] Managers who understand the role of emotions will significantly improve their ability to explain and predict individual behaviour.

Do emotions affect job performance? Yes. They can *hinder* performance, especially negative emotions. That's probably why organisations, for the most part, try to extract emotions out of the workplace. But emotions can also *enhance* performance. How? Two ways.[98] First, emotions can increase arousal levels, thus acting as motivators to higher performance. Second, emotional labour recognises that feelings can be part of a job's required behaviour. So, for example, the ability to effectively manage emotions in leadership, sales and customer-interface positions may be critical to success in those positions.

What differentiates functional from dysfunctional emotions at work? While there is no precise answer to this, it's been suggested that the critical moderating variable is the complexity of the individual's task.[99] The more complex a task, the lower the level of arousal that can be tolerated without interfering with performance. While a certain minimal level of arousal is probably necessary for good performance, very high levels interfere with the ability to function, especially if the job requires calculative and detailed cognitive processes. Given that the trend is towards jobs becoming more complex, you can see why organisations are likely to go to considerable efforts to discourage the overt display of emotions—especially intense ones—in the workplace.

Point

TRAITS ARE POWERFUL PREDICTORS OF BEHAVIOUR

The essence of trait approaches in OB is that employees possess stable personality characteristics that significantly influence their attitudes towards, and behavioural reactions to, organisational settings. People with particular traits tend to be relatively consistent in their attitudes and behaviour over time and across situations.[a]

Of course, trait theorists recognise that all traits are not equally powerful. They tend to put them into one of three categories. *Cardinal traits* are those so strong and generalised that they influence every act a person performs. *Primary traits* are generally consistent influences on behaviour, but they may not show up in all situations. Finally, *secondary traits* are attributes that do not form a vital part of the personality but come into play only in particular situations. For the most part, trait theories have focused on the power of primary traits to predict employee behaviour.

Trait theorists do a fairly good job of meeting the average person's face-validity test. Think of friends, relatives and acquaintances you have known for a number of years. Do they have traits that have remained essentially stable over time? Most of us would answer that question in the affirmative. If cousin Anne was shy and nervous when we last saw her ten years ago, we would be surprised to find her outgoing and relaxed now.

Managers seem to have a strong belief in the power of traits to predict behaviour. If managers believed that situations determined behaviour, they would hire people almost at random and structure the situation properly. But the employee selection process in most organisations places a great deal of emphasis on how applicants perform in interviews and on tests. Assume you are an interviewer and ask yourself: What am I looking for in job candidates? If you answered with terms such as *conscientious*, *hardworking*, *persistent*, *confident* and *dependable*, you're a trait theorist.

Counterpoint

Few people would dispute that there are some stable individual attributes that affect reactions to the workplace. But trait theorists go beyond that generality and argue that individual behaviour consistencies are widespread and account for much of the differences in behaviour among people.[b]

There are two important problems with using traits to explain a large proportion of behaviour in organisations. First, organisational settings are strong situations that have a large impact on employee behaviour. Second, individuals are highly adaptive and personality traits change in response to organisational situations.

It has been well known for some time that the effects of traits are likely to be strongest in relatively weak situations and weakest in relatively strong situations. Organisational settings tend to be strong situations, because they have rules and other formal regulations that define acceptable behaviour and punish deviant behaviour; and they have informal norms that dictate appropriate behaviours. These formal and informal constraints minimise the effects of personality traits.

By arguing that employees possess stable traits that lead to cross-situational consistencies in behaviours, trait theorists are implying that individuals don't really adapt to different situations. But there is a growing body of evidence that an individual's traits are changed by the organisations that that individual participates in. If the individual's personality changes as a result of exposure to organisational settings, in what sense can that individual be said to have traits that persistently and consistently affect his or her reactions to those very settings? Moreover, people typically belong to multiple organisations that often include very different kinds of members. And they adapt to those different situations. Instead of being the prisoners of a rigid and stable personality framework as trait theorists propose, people regularly adjust their behaviour to reflect the requirements of various situations.

Sources: [a]Some of the points in this argument are from R. J. House, S. A. Shane and D. M. Herold, 'Rumors of the Death of Dispositional Research Are Vastly Exaggerated', *Academy of Management Review*, January 1996, pp. 203–24. [b]Based on A. Davis-Blake and J. Pfeffer, 'Just a Mirage: The Search for Dispositional Effects in Organisational Research', *Academy of Management Review*, July 1989, pp. 385–400.

For Discussion

1. 'Heredity determines personality.' (a) Build an argument to support this statement. (b) Build an argument against this statement.
2. What behavioural predictions might you make if you knew that an employee had (a) an external locus of control? (b) a low Mach score? (c) low self-esteem? (d) a Type A personality?
3. What is the Myers–Briggs Type Indicator?
4. Describe the factors in the 'Big Five' model. Which factor shows the greatest value in predicting behaviour? Why does it?
5. One day your boss comes in and he is nervous, edgy and argumentative. The next day, he is calm and relaxed. Does this behaviour suggest that personality traits are not consistent from day to day?

6. Do people from the same country have a common personality type? Explain.
7. Why might managers today pay more attention to the person–organisation fit than the person–job fit?
8. What is *emotional labour*, and why is it important in understanding OB?
9. How does national culture influence expressed emotions?
10. What is *emotional intelligence*, and why is it important?
11. Give some examples of situations in which the overt expression of emotions might enhance job performance.

Exercises

Exercise 4a

WHAT IS A 'TEAM PERSONALITY'?

It's the unusual organisation today that isn't using work teams. But not everybody is a good team player. This prompts the questions: What individual personality characteristics enhance a team's performance? And what characteristics might hinder team performance?

Break into groups of five or six. Based on the research presented in this chapter, each group should: (a) identify personality characteristics they think are associated with high-performance teams and justify their choices; (b) identify personality characteristics they think hinder high-performance teams and justify their choices; and (c) resolve whether it is better to have teams composed of individuals with similar or dissimilar traits.

Each group should select an individual who will present his or her group's findings to the class.

Exercise 4b

MANAGING EMOTIONS AT WORK

Our understanding of emotions at work has increased rapidly in the past decade. We are now at the point at which we are capable of managing, or close to being able to manage, the emotions of employees. For example, companies that want to create open and friendly workplaces are using the selection process to 'select out' job applicants who aren't outgoing and enthusiastic and are providing training to teach employees how to smile and appear cheerful. Some organisations are going further in attempting to create 'emotionally humanistic' work environments by not only shaping the emotions that workers evoke in their daily contacts with customers, but also by selecting employee applicants with high emotional intelligence, controlling the emotional atmosphere of teams and work groups, and similar emotion-management practices.

Groucho Marx once joked, 'The secret of success in show business is honesty and sincerity. Once you learn how to fake that, you've got it made.' In many service organisations today, Groucho's remark is being applied. For example, telephone-sales staff in a number of insurance companies are trained to invoke positive feelings from customers—to make it easy for them to say 'yes'. Employees are taught to avoid using words with negative connotations and to replace them with upbeat and confidence-building words such as 'certainly', 'rest assured', 'immediate' and 'great'. Moreover, employees are taught to convey these 'scripts' in a way that seems natural and spontaneous. To ensure that these 'authentic' positive feelings are consistently evoked, the phone calls of these sales people are often monitored.

Organisations such as McDonald's, Dreamworld and Seaworld select and train employees to be upbeat and friendly. They allow employees no choices. Moreover, these organisations export their emotional expectations to everywhere in the world in which they operate. When the Big Mac hamburgers come to town, the typical grimace of the Muscovite or shyness of the Finnish employee are subject to a similar genre of smile-training.

1. Is asking people to feign specific job-related emotions unethical if it conflicts with their basic personality?
2. Is exporting standardised emotional 'rule books' to alien cultures unethical? What do you think?

Source: Exercise 4b is based on S. Fineman, 'Managing Emotions at Work: Some Political Reflections', paper presented at a symposium at the Academy of Management Conference, Washington, DC, August 2001.

Case Study 4

Roustabouts Need Understanding, Too!

If you were to walk around one of Transocean Sedco Forex's offshore oil-rigs, you would see something that might puzzle you. Most of the employees have three stickers on their hard hats. One says, 'Start to Understand Me.' The other two are coloured dots. What's this all about? The coloured dots are there to tell fellow employees about the personality under the hat. The company believes that employees are better able to understand each other and get along if they know the personalities of the people with whom they have to work.

Transocean has hired an outside consulting firm to provide personality assessment to its 8,300 workers worldwide. For example, employees are presented with 28 sets of four words. Employees pick a word that describes them best and a word that describes them least. A typical set might be fussy, obedient, firm and playful. Employees then are shown how to score their test and find out their two dominant colours. For example, reds are 'driven, strong-willed and decisive'. Yellows are 'emotional, talkative and have a fondness for people'. Greens are 'cautious and serious'. And blues 'dislike change' and can be 'a little wishy-washy'. Rig workers wear their dots on their hats, while land-based employees post theirs outside their office doors. No one is forced to display their colours, and some think the program may be too intrusive. Tim Callais, a Transocean consultant for operational rig safety, says those who question the program's credibility are 'probably blue people'.

A number of employees seem to find the dots helpful. Thom Keeton, a 'red–green' rig manager, keeps a colour chart under the glass covering his desk for quick reference. Tom Watkins, a senior rig hand on a drilling ship who is also a 'red–green', thinks the colours correctly reflect his personality—blunt, to the point, and not liking to talk much. David Gray, a 'blue–yellow', says the coloured dots help him deal with high-strung 'red–greens' now that he's figured out that he just has to get to the point more quickly.

This program isn't being applied only at Transocean. Similar personality-based coding systems are being put into place with a number of blue-collar employees. Assembly-line employees in America are using the system, as are police officers, electricians, construction employees, and carpenters and plumbers.

Questions

1. Why would oil-rig workers buy into a program like this?
2. How valid do you think colour-coded personality ratings are?
3. Do you think having employees 'wear their personalities on their hats' is an intrusion into the employee's personal liberties? Is it unethical?
4. Transocean's CEO supports the program but says, 'I can be whatever colour I want to be.' Do you agree with him? Explain.

Source: Based on C. Cummins, 'Workers Wear Feelings on Their Hard Hats and Show True Colors', *Wall Street Journal*, 7 November 2000, p. A1.

Web Workout

1. Visit the following website: <www.knowyourtype.com/intro.html>. Analyse the discussion about the 16 types and eight preferences. How robust do you feel the MBTI is? How would you assess its reliability and validity?
2. What role did the researchers find was played by locus of control in the study on entrepreneurs in small towns at the site <www.sbaer.uca.edu/Research/2000/ASBE/00asbe188.htm>? What generalisations might we draw from this study about locus of control?
3. Read the article on emotional labour and tears at work at <www.justlabour.yorku.ca/soares_justlabour.PDF>. To what extent do tears of sadness express emotional labour overload, or do they indicate other factors as well? What might those factors be?

4. On the site <www.abc.net.au/catalyst/stories/s581804.htm>, there is a discussion among a number of experts in the area of emotional intelligence. How do they counter the argument about the lack of reliability and validity in measures of emotional intelligence?

5. In the company advertisement at <www.v-mgroup.com/workshops/index.asp?PCID=234>, how realistic are the claims made about the role of EI in organisations? Is there a risk that such claims can harm the development of emotional intelligence as a factor in organisational behaviour? What do you think?

KSS Program

KNOW THE CONCEPTS   SELF-AWARENESS   SKILLS APPLICATIONS

Reading emotions

After you have read this chapter, take Self-Assessment #20 (What's My Emotional Intelligence Score?) on your enclosed CD-Rom and complete the skill-building module entitled 'Reading Emotions' on page 634.

NOTES

1. Based on A. Bianco, 'Software's Tough Guy', *Business Week*, 6 March 2000, pp. 133–44; and <www.askmen.com/men/business>, 1 October 2001.

2. G. W. Allport, *Personality: A Psychological Interpretation* (New York: Holt, Rinehart & Winston, 1937), p. 48.

3. Reported in R. L. Hotz, 'Genetics, Not Parenting, Key to Temperament, Studies Say', *Los Angeles Times,* 20 February 1994, p. A1.

4. See R. D. Arvey and T. J. Bouchard, Jr, 'Genetics, Twins, and Organizational Behavior', in B. M. Staw and L. L. Cummings, *Research in Organizational Behavior*, vol. 16 (Greenwich, CT: JAI Press, 1994), pp. 65–66; D. Lykken and A. Tellegen, 'Happiness is a Stochastic Phenomenon', *Psychological Science*, May 1996, pp. 186–89; and W. Wright, *Born That Way: Genes, Behavior, Personality* (New York: Knopf, 1998).

5. R. C. Carson, 'Personality', in M. R. Rosenzweig and L. W. Porter (eds), *Annual Review of Psychology*, vol. 40 (Palo Alto, CA: Annual Reviews, 1989), pp. 228–29.

6. W. Mischel, 'The Interaction of Person and Situation', in D. Magnusson and N. S. Endler (eds), *Personality at the Crossroads: Current Issues in Interactional Psychology* (Hillsdale, NJ: Erlbaum, 1977), pp. 166–207.

7. See A. H. Buss, 'Personality as Traits', *American Psychologist*, November 1989, pp. 1378–88; R. R. McCrae, 'Trait Psychology and the Revival of Personality and Culture Studies', *American Behavioral Scientist*, September 2000, pp. 10–31; and L. R. James and M. D. Mazerolle, *Personality in Work Organizations* (Thousand Oaks, CA: Sage, 2002).

8. G. W. Allport and H. S. Odbert, 'Trait Names, A Psycholexical Study', *Psychological Monographs*, no. 47, 1936.

9. R. B. Cattell, 'Personality Pinned Down', *Psychology Today*, July 1973, pp. 40–46.

10. See R. R. McCrae and T. Costa, Jr, 'Reinterpreting the Myers–Briggs Type Indicator from the Perspective of the Five Factor Model of Personality', *Journal of Personality*, March 1989, pp. 17–40; and N. L. Quenk, *Essentials of Myers-Briggs Type Indicator Assessment* (New York: Wiley, 2000).

11. G. N. Landrum, *Profiles of Genius* (New York: Prometheus, 1993).

12. W. Agor, 'Intuition as a Brain Skill in Management', *Public Personnel Management,* vol. 14, no. 1, Spring 1985.

13. See, for example, J. M. Digman, 'Personality Structure: Emergence of the Five-Factor Model', in M. R. Rosenzweig and L. W. Porter (eds), *Annual Review of Psychology*, vol. 41 (Palo Alto, CA: Annual Reviews, 1990), pp. 417–40; R. R. McCrae, 'Special Issue: The Five-Factor Model: Issues and Applications', *Journal of Personality*, June 1992; P. H. Raymark, M. J. Schmit and R. M. Guion, 'Identifying Potentially Useful Personality Constructs for Employee Selection', *Personnel Psychology*, Autumn 1997, pp. 723–36; and D. B. Smith, P. J. Hanges and M. W. Dickson, 'Personnel Selection and the Five-Factor Model: Reexamining the Effects of Applicant's Frame of Reference', *Journal of Applied Psychology*, April 2001, pp. 304–15.

14. See, for example, M. R. Barrick and M. K. Mount, 'The Big Five Personality Dimensions and Job Performance: A Meta-Analysis', *Personnel Psychology*, vol. 44, 1991, pp. 1–26; R. P. Tett, D. N. Jackson and M. Rothstein, 'Personality Measures as Predictors of Job Performance: A Meta-Analytic Review', *Personnel Psychology*, Winter 1991, pp. 703–42; O. Behling, 'Employee Selection: Will Intelligence and Conscientiousness Do the Job?', *Academy of Management Executive*, February 1998, pp. 77–86; A. J. Vinchur, J. S. Schippmann, F. S. Switzer, III and P. L. Roth, 'A Meta-Analytic Review of Predictors of Job Performance for Salespeople', *Journal of Applied Psychology*, August 1998, pp. 586–97; G. M. Hurtz and J. J. Donovan, 'Personality and Job Performance: The Big Five Revisited', *Journal of Applied Psychology*, December 2000, pp. 869–79; and T. A. Judge and J. E. Bono, 'Relationship of Core Self-Evaluations Traits—Self-Esteem,

Generalized Self-Efficacy, Locus of Control, and Emotional Stability—With Job Satisfaction and Job Performance: A Meta-Analysis', *Journal of Applied Psychology*, February 2001, pp. 80–92.

15. M. K. Mount, M. R. Barrick and J. P. Strauss, 'Validity of Observer Ratings of the Big Five Personality Factors', *Journal of Applied Psychology*, April 1994, p. 272. Additionally confirmed by Hurtz and Donovan, 'Personality and Job Performance: The Big Five Revisited'.

16. D. W. Organ, 'Personality and Organizational Citizenship Behavior', *Journal of Management*, Summer 1994, pp. 465–78; D. W. Organ and K. Ryan, 'A Meta-Analytic Review of Attitudinal and Dispositional Predictors of Organizational Citizenship Behavior', *Personnel Psychology*, Winter 1995, pp. 775–802; M. A. Konovsky and D. W. Organ, 'Dispositional and Contextual Determinants of Organizational Citizenship Behavior', *Journal of Organizational Behavior*, May 1996, pp. 253–66; and P. M. Podsakoff, S. B. MacKenzie, J. B. Paine and D. G. Bachrach, 'Organizational Citizenship Behaviors: A Critical Review of the Theoretical and Empirical Literature and Suggestions for Future Research', *Journal of Management*, vol. 6, no. 3, 2000, pp. 513–63.

17. J. B. Rotter, 'Generalized Expectancies for Internal versus External Control of Reinforcement', *Psychological Monographs*, vol. 80, no. 609, 1966.

18. See P. E. Spector, 'Behavior in Organizations as a Function of Employee's Locus of Control', *Psychological Bulletin*, May 1982, pp. 482–97; and G. J. Blau, 'Locus of Control as a Potential Moderator of the Turnover Process', *Journal of Occupational Psychology*, Fall 1987, pp. 21–29.

19. K. W. Cook, C. A. Vance and P. E. Spector, 'The Relation of Candidate Personality with Selection-Interview Outcomes', *Journal of Applied Social Psychology*, April 2000, pp. 867–85.

20. R. T. Keller, 'Predicting Absenteeism from Prior Absenteeism, Attitudinal Factors, and Nonattitudinal Factors', *Journal of Applied Psychology*, August 1983, pp. 536–40.

21. Spector, 'Behavior in Organizations as a Function of Employee's Locus of Control', p. 493.

22. R. G. Vleeming, 'Machiavellianism: A Preliminary Review', *Psychological Reports*, February 1979, pp. 295–310.

23. R. Christie and F. L. Geis, *Studies in Machiavellianism* (New York: Academic Press, 1970), p. 312; and N. V. Ramanaiah, A. Byravan and F. R. J. Detwiler, 'Revised Neo Personality Inventory Profiles of Machiavellian and Non-Machiavellian People', *Psychological Reports*, October 1994, pp. 937–38.

24. Christie and Geis, *Studies in Machiavellianism*.

25. See J. Brockner, *Self-Esteem at Work* (Lexington, MA: Lexington Books, 1988); and N. Branden, *Self-Esteem at Work* (San Francisco: Jossey-Bass, 1998).

26. See M. Snyder, *Public Appearances/Private Realities: The Psychology of Self-Monitoring* (New York: W. H. Freeman, 1987); and D. V. Day, D. J. Schleicher, A. L. Unckless and N. J. Hiller, 'Self-Monitoring Personality at Work: A Meta-Analytic Investigation of Construct Validity', *Journal of Applied Psychology*, April 2002, pp. 390–401.

27. M. Snyder, *Public Appearances/Private Realities*.

28. M. Kilduff and D. V. Day, 'Do Chameleons Get Ahead? The Effects of Self-Monitoring on Managerial Careers', *Academy of Management Journal*, August 1994, pp. 1047–60; and A. Mehra, M. Kilduff and D. J. Brass, 'The Social Networks of High and Low Self-Monitors: Implications for Workplace Performance', *Administrative Science Quarterly*, March 2001, pp. 121–46.

29. A. Patrick, 'Murdoch Promises the News Will Improve', *Business Review Weekly*, vol. 24, no. 33, 22 August 2002.

30. R. N. Taylor and M. D. Dunnette, 'Influence of Dogmatism, Risk-Taking Propensity, and Intelligence on Decision-Making Strategies for a Sample of Industrial Managers', *Journal of Applied Psychology*, August 1974, pp. 420–23.

31. I. L. Janis and L. Mann, *Decision Making: A Psychological Analysis of Conflict, Choice, and Commitment* (New York: Free Press, 1977); and W. H. Stewart, Jr and L. Roth, 'Risk Propensity Differences between Entrepreneurs and Managers: A Meta-Analytic Review', *Journal of Applied Psychology*, February 2001, pp. 145–53.

32. N. Kogan and M. A. Wallach, 'Group Risk Taking as a Function of Members' Anxiety and Defensiveness', *Journal of Personality*, March 1967, pp. 50–63.

33. M. Friedman and R. H. Rosenman, *Type A Behavior and Your Heart* (New York: Alfred A. Knopf, 1974), p. 84 (emphasis in original).

34. Ibid, pp. 84–85.

35. Cook, Vance and Spector, 'The Relation of Candidate Personality with Selection-Interview Outcomes'.

36. Friedman and Rosenman, *Type A Behavior and Your Heart*, p. 86.

37. See, for example, G. W. M. Ip and M. H. Bond, 'Culture, Values, and the Spontaneous Self-Concept', *Asian Journal of Psychology*, vol. 1, 1995, pp. 30–36; J. E. Williams, J. L. Saiz, D. L. FormyDuval, M. L. Munick, E. E. Fogle, A. Adom, A. Haque, F. Neto and J. Yu, 'Cross-Cultural Variation in the Importance of Psychological Characteristics: A Seven-Country Study', *International Journal of Psychology*, October 1995, pp. 529–50; V. Benet and N. G. Waller, 'The Big Seven Factor Model of Personality Description: Evidence for Its Cross-Cultural Generalizability in a Spanish Sample', *Journal of Personality and Social Psychology*, October 1995, pp. 701–18; R. R. McCrae and P. T. Costa, Jr, 'Personality Trait Structure as a Human Universal', *American Psychologist*, vol. 52, no. 5, May 1997, pp. 509–16; and M. J. Schmit, J. A. Kihm and C. Robie, 'Development of a Global Measure of Personality', *Personnel Psychology*, Spring 2000, pp. 153–93.

38. J. F. Salgado, 'The Five Factor Model of Personality and Job Performance in the European Community', *Journal of Applied Psychology*, February 1997, pp. 30–43.

39. F. Kluckhohn and F. L. Strodtbeck, *Variations in Value Orientations* (Evanston, IL: Row Peterson, 1961).

40. P. B. Smith, F. Trompenaars and S. Dugan, 'The Rotter Locus of Control Scale in 43 Countries: A Test of Cultural Relativity', *International Journal of Psychology*, June 1995, pp. 377–400.

41. Friedman and Rosenman, *Type A Behavior and Your Heart*, p. 86.

42. J. L. Holland, *Making Vocational Choices: A Theory of Vocational Personalities and Work Environments* (Odessa, FL: Psychological Assessment Resources, 1997).

43. See, for example, A. R. Spokane, 'A Review of Research on Person–Environment Congruence in Holland's Theory of Careers', *Journal of Vocational Behavior*, June 1985, pp. 306–43; J. L. Holland and G. D. Gottfredson, 'Studies of the Hexagonal Model: An Evaluation (or, The Perils of Stalking the Perfect Hexagon)', *Journal of Vocational Behavior*, April 1992, pp. 158–70; T. J. Tracey and J. Rounds, 'Evaluating Holland's and Gati's Vocational-Interest Models: A Structural Meta-Analysis', *Psychological Bulletin*, March 1993, pp. 229–46; and F. De Fruyt and I. Mervielde, 'RIASEC Types and Big Five Traits as Predictors of Employment Status and Nature of Employment', *Personnel Psychology*, Autumn 1999, pp. 701–27.

44. See B. Schneider, 'The People Make the Place', *Personnel Psychology*, Autumn 1987, pp. 437–53; D. E. Bowen, G. E. Ledford, Jr and B. R. Nathan, 'Hiring for the Organization, Not the Job', *Academy of Management Executive*, November 1991, pp. 35–51; B. Schneider, H. W. Goldstein and D. B. Smith, 'The ASA Framework: An Update', *Personnel Psychology*, Winter 1995, pp. 747–73; A. L. Kristof, 'Person–Organization Fit: An Integrative Review of Its Conceptualizations, Measurement, and Implications', *Personnel Psychology*, Spring 1996, pp. 1–49; and B. Schneider, D. B. Smith, S. Taylor and J. Fleenor, 'Personality and Organizations: A Test of the Homogeneity of Personality Hypothesis', *Journal of Applied Psychology*, June 1998, pp. 462–70.

45. Based on T. A. Judge and D. M. Cable, 'Applicant Personality, Organizational Culture, and Organization Attraction', *Personnel Psychology*, Summer 1997, pp. 359–94.

46. See <http://massmurder.zyns.com/julian_knight_doc_00.htm>. Accessed 24 February 2004.

47. See, for example, C. D. Fisher and N. M. Ashkanasy, 'The Emerging Role of Emotions in Work Life: An Introduction', *Journal of Organizational Behavior*, Special Issue 2000, pp. 123–29; and N. M. Ashkanasy, C. E. J. Hartel and W. J. Zerbe (eds), *Emotions in the Workplace: Research, Theory, and Practice* (Westport, CT: Quorum Books, 2000).

48. See, for example, L. L. Putnam and D. K. Mumby, 'Organizations, Emotion and the Myth of Rationality', in S. Fineman (ed.), *Emotion in Organizations* (Thousand Oaks, CA: Sage, 1993), pp. 36–57; and J. Martin, K. Knopoff and C. Beckman, 'An Alternative to Bureaucratic Impersonality and Emotional Labor: Bounded Emotionality at the Body Shop', *Administrative Science Quarterly*, June 1998, pp. 429–69.

49. B. E. Ashforth and R. H. Humphrey, 'Emotion in the Workplace: A Reappraisal', *Human Relations*, February 1995, pp. 97–125.

50. J. M. George, 'Trait and State Affect', in K. R. Murphy (ed.), *Individual Differences and Behavior in Organizations* (San Francisco: Jossey-Bass, 1996), p. 145.

51. See N. H. Frijda, 'Moods, Emotion Episodes and Emotions', in M. Lewis and J. M. Haviland (eds), *Handbook of Emotions* (New York: Guildford Press, 1993), pp. 381–403.

52. H. M. Weiss and R. Cropanzano, 'Affective Events Theory', in B. M. Staw and L. L. Cummings, *Research in Organizational Behavior*, vol. 18 (Greenwich, CT: JAI Press, 1996), pp. 17–19.

53. Frijda, 'Moods, Emotion Episodes and Emotions', p. 381.

54. See J. A. Morris and D. C. Feldman, 'Managing Emotions in the Workplace', *Journal of Managerial Issues*, vol. 9, no. 3, 1997, pp. 257–74; and S. M. Kruml and D. Geddes, 'Catching Fire without Burning Out: Is There an Ideal Way to Perform Emotional Labor?', in Ashkansay, Hartel and Zerbe, *Emotions in the Workplace*, pp. 177–88.

55. A. R. Hochschild, 'Emotion Work, Feeling Rules, and Social Structure', *American Journal of Sociology*, November 1979, pp. 551–75; and S. Mann, *Hiding What We Feel, Faking What We Don't* (Shaftesbury, Dorset, UK: Element, 1999).

56. B. M. DePaulo, 'Nonverbal Behavior and Self-Presentation', *Psychological Bulletin*, March 1992, pp. 203–43.

57. C. S. Hunt, 'Although I Might Be Laughing Loud and Hearty, Deep Inside I'm Blue: Individual Perceptions Regarding Feeling and Displaying Emotions at Work', paper presented at the Academy of Management Conference, Cincinnati, August 1996, p. 3.

58. D. Watson, L. A. Clark and A. Tellegen, 'Development and Validation of Brief Measures of Positive and Negative Affect: The PANAS Scales', *Journal of Personality and Social Psychology*, vol. 54, no. 6, June 1988, pp. 1063–70.

59. A. Ben-Ze'ev, *The Subtlety of Emotions* (Cambridge, MA: MIT Press, 2000), p. 94.

60. Cited in ibid, p. 99.

61. See, for example, P. Shaver, J. Schwartz, D. Kirson and C. O'Connor, 'Emotion Knowledge: Further Exploration of a Prototype Approach', *Journal of Personality and Social Psychology*, June 1987, pp. 1061–86; P. Ekman, 'An Argument for Basic Emotions', *Cognition and Emotion*, May–July 1992, pp. 169–200; C. E. Izard, 'Basic Emotions, Relations among Emotions, and Emotion–Cognition Relations',

Psychological Bulletin, November 1992, pp. 561–65; and R. Plutchik, *The Psychology and Biology of Emotion* (New York: HarperCollins, 1994).

62. Weiss and Cropanzano, 'Affective Events Theory', pp. 20–22.

63. Cited in R. D. Woodworth, *Experimental Psychology* (New York: Holt, 1938).

64. See, for example, J. K. Salminen, S. Saarijanvi, E. Aairela and T. Tamminen, 'Alexithymia: State or Trait? One-Year Follow-up Study of General Hospital Psychiatric Consultation Outpatients', *Journal of Psychosomatic Research*, July 1994, pp. 681–85; and M. F. R. Kets de Vries, 'Organizational Sleepwalkers: Emotional Distress at Midlife', *Human Relations*, November 1999, pp. 1377–401.

65. K. Deaux, 'Sex Differences', in M. R. Rosenzweig and L. W. Porter (eds), *Annual Review of Psychology*, vol. 26 (Palo Alto, CA: Annual Reviews, 1985), pp. 48–82; M. LaFrance and M. Banaji, 'Toward a Reconsideration of the Gender–Emotion Relationship', in M. Clark (ed.), *Review of Personality and Social Psychology*, vol. 14 (Newbury Park, CA: Sage, 1992), pp. 178–97; and A. M. Kring and A. H. Gordon, 'Sex Differences in Emotion: Expression, Experience, and Physiology', *Journal of Personality and Social Psychology*, March 1998, pp. 686–703.

66. L. R. Brody and J. A. Hall, 'Gender and Emotion', in M. Lewis and J. M. Haviland (eds), *Handbook of Emotions* (New York: Guilford Press, 1993), pp. 447–60; and M. Grossman and W. Wood, 'Sex Differences in Intensity of Emotional Experience: A Social Role Interpretation', *Journal of Personality and Social Psychology*, November 1992, pp. 1010–22.

67. J. A. Hall, *Nonverbal Sex Differences: Communication Accuracy and Expressive Style* (Baltimore, MD: Johns Hopkins Press, 1984).

68. N. James, 'Emotional Labor: Skill and Work in the Social Regulations of Feelings', *Sociological Review*, February 1989, pp. 15–42; A. Hochschild, *The Second Shift* (New York: Viking, 1989); and F. M. Deutsch, 'Status, Sex, and Smiling: The Effect of Role on Smiling in Men and Women', *Personality and Social Psychology Bulletin*, September 1990, pp. 531–40.

69. A. Rafaeli, 'When Clerks Meet Customers: A Test of Variables Related to Emotional Expression on the Job', *Journal of Applied Psychology*, June 1989, pp. 385–93; and LaFrance and Banaji, 'Toward a Reconsideration of the Gender–Emotion Relationship'.

70. L. W. Hoffman, 'Early Childhood Experiences and Women's Achievement Motives', *Journal of Social Issues*, vol. 28, no. 2, 1972, pp. 129–55.

71. M. Boas and S. Chain, *Big Mac: The Unauthorized Story of McDonald's* (New York: Dutton, 1976), p. 84.

72. Ashforth and Humphrey, 'Emotion in the Workplace', p. 104.

73. G. L. Flett, K. R. Blankstein, P. Pliner and C. Bator, 'Impression-Management and Self-Deception Components of Appraised Emotional Experience', *British Journal of Social Psychology*, January 1988, pp. 67–77.

74. Ashforth and Humphrey, 'Emotion in the Workplace', p. 104.

75. A. Rafaeli and R. I. Sutton, 'The Expression of Emotion in Organizational Life', in L. L. Cummings and B. M. Staw, *Research in Organizational Behavior*, vol. 11 (Greenwich, CT: JAI Press, 1989), p. 8.

76. A. Rafaeli, 'When Cashiers Meet Customers: An Analysis of Supermarket Cashiers', *Academy of Management Journal*, June 1989, pp. 245–73.

77. Ibid.

78. D. Rubin, 'Grumpy German Shoppers Distrust the Wal-Mart Style', *Seattle Times*, 30 December 2001, p. A15.

79. B. Mesquita and N. H. Frijda, 'Cultural Variations in Emotions: A Review', *Psychological Bulletin*, September 1992, pp. 179–204; and B. Mesquita, 'Emotions in Collectivist and Individualist Contexts', *Journal of Personality and Social Psychology*, January 2001, pp. 68–74.

80. Described in S. Emmons, 'Emotions at Face Value', *Los Angeles Times*, 9 January 1998, p. E1.

81. R. I. Levy, *Tahitians: Mind and Experience in the Society Islands* (Chicago: University of Chicago Press, 1973).

82. This section is based on Daniel Goleman, *Emotional Intelligence* (New York: Bantam, 1995); J. D. Mayer and G. Geher, 'Emotional Intelligence and the Identification of Emotion', *Intelligence*, March–April 1996, pp. 89–113; R. K. Cooper, 'Applying Emotional Intelligence in the Workplace', *Training & Development*, December 1997, pp. 31–38; 'HR Pulse: Emotional Intelligence', *HRMagazine*, January 1998, p. 19; M. Davies, L. Stankov and R. D. Roberts, 'Emotional Intelligence: In Search of an Elusive Construct', *Journal of Personality and Social Psychology*, October 1998, pp. 989–1015; D. Goleman, *Working with Emotional Intelligence* (New York: Bantam, 1999); R. Bar-On and J. D. A. Parker (eds), *The Handbook of Emotional Intelligence: Theory, Development, Assessment, and Application at Home, School, and in the Workplace* (San Francisco: Jossey-Bass, 2000); T. Schwartz, 'How Do You Feel?', *Fast Company*, June 2000, pp. 297–313; and F I. Greenstein, *The Presidential Difference* (Princeton, NJ: Princeton University Press, 2001).

83. S. Fineman, 'Emotional Arenas Revisited', in S. Fineman (ed.), *Emotion in Organizations*, 2nd ed. (Thousand Oaks, CA: Sage, 2000), p. 11.

84. See, for example, K. Fiedler, 'Emotional Mood, Cognitive Style, and Behavioral Regulation', in K. Fiedler and J. Forgas (eds), *Affect, Cognition, and Social Behavior* (Toronto: Hogrefe International, 1988), pp. 100–19; M. Luce, J. Bettman and J. W. Payne, 'Choice Processing in Difficult Decisions', *Journal of Experimental Psychology: Learning, Memory, and Cognition*, vol. 23, 1997, pp. 384–405; and A. M. Isen, 'Positive Affect and Decision Making', in M. Lewis and J. M. Haviland-Jones (eds), *Handbook of Emotions*, 2nd ed. (New York: Guilford, 2000), pp. 261–77.

85. Ashforth and Humphrey, 'Emotion in the Workplace', p. 109; and M. G. Seo, 'The Role of Emotion in Motivation', paper presented at the Annual Academy of Management Conference, Toronto, Canada, August 2000.
86. Ashforth and Humphrey, 'Emotion in the Workplace', p. 109.
87. Ibid, p. 110.
88. Ibid.
89. K. M. Lewis, 'When Leaders Display Emotion: How Followers Respond to Negative Emotional Expression of Male and Female Leaders', *Journal of Organizational Behavior*, March 2000, pp. 221–34; and J. M. George, 'Emotions and Leadership: The Role of Emotional Intelligence', *Human Relations*, August 2000, pp. 1027–55.
90. George, 'Trait and State Affect', p. 162.
91. Ashforth and Humphrey, 'Emotion in the Workplace', p. 116.
92. See S. L. Robinson and R. J. Bennett, 'A Typology of Deviant Workplace Behaviors: A Multidimensional Scaling Study', *Academy of Management Journal*, April 1995, p. 556; and R. J. Bennett and S. L. Robinson, 'Development of a Measure of Workplace Deviance', *Journal of Applied Psychology*, June 2000, pp. 349–60.
93. R. W. Griffin, A. O'Leary-Kelly and J. M. Collins (eds), *Dysfunctional Behavior in Organizations* (Parts A & B), vol. 23 (Stamford, CT: JAI Press, 1998).
94. A. G. Bedeian, 'Workplace Envy', *Organizational Dynamics*, Spring 1995, p. 50; and Ben-Ze'ev, *The Subtlety of Emotions*, pp. 281–326.
95. Ibid, p. 54.
96. R. Hogan, J. Hogan and B. W. Roberts, 'Personality Measurement and Employment Decisions', *American Psychologist*, May 1996, p. 475.
97. S. Nelton, 'Emotions in the Workplace', *Nation's Business*, February 1996, p. 25.
98. Weiss and Cropanzano, 'Affective Events Theory', p. 55.
99. See the Yerkes–Dodson law cited in D. O. Hebb, 'Drives and the CNS (Conceptual Nervous System)', *Psychological Review*, July 1955, pp. 243–54.

PHOTO CREDITS

Perception and Individual Decision Making

CHAPTER OUTLINE

What is perception, and why is it important?
Factors influencing perception
Person perception: Making judgments about others
The link between perception and individual decision making
How should decisions be made?
How are decisions actually made in organisations?
What about ethics in decision making?

LEARNING OBJECTIVES

After studying this chapter, you should be able to:

1. Explain how two people can see the same thing and interpret it differently
2. List the three determinants of attribution
3. Describe how shortcuts can assist in or distort our judgment of others
4. Explain how perception affects the decision-making process
5. Outline the six steps in the rational decision-making model
6. Describe the actions of the bounded rational decision maker
7. Identify the conditions in which individuals are most likely to use intuition in decision making
8. Define heuristics and explain how they bias decisions
9. Describe four styles of decision making
10. Contrast the three ethical decision criteria

*We don't see things as they are,
we see things as we are.*

A. Nin

As a politician, John Howard is required to make difficult decisions.

John Howard, the Australian prime minister at the time, was faced with a difficult decision in 2002 and 2003. He had been asked by the American president George W. Bush and the British prime minister Tony Blair to support a 'coalition of the willing' to force the Iraqi president Saddam Hussein to give up his cache of weapons of mass destruction. This was a serious decision for any Australian prime minister to make and the subsequent events suggested he didn't have all the relevant information in making that decision.[1]

What was known at the time of the decision will remain a hotly debated issue for a long time to come. However, what is known is that some of the information was flawed and some of it was greatly exaggerated. The reports of Iraq having obtained weapons-grade uranium from rebels in Africa have been proved to be false. This revelation didn't affect John Howard's stated conviction to use military means to rid Iraq of these deadly weapons and to depose Saddam Hussein. Other reports were hotly debated as being greatly exaggerated to 'please' the readers of the reports, namely Bush, Blair and Howard. It was suggested the three leaders were already predisposed to a certain view and the report-writers were writing what they believed was expected from them.

The decision-making process used by John Howard also reveals the reality that serious and important decisions are rarely, if ever, made on the spur of the moment. The intense diplomatic manoeuvres began in 2002, nearly 12 years after Saddam Hussein had agreed to end his weapons of mass destruction program. Despite intense media speculation, numerous press statements and interviews, the prime minister publicly declared that the final decision to engage Australian troops to resolve the issue was still not taken as late as March 2003. This was significant because, at that point in time, a large contingent of Australian forces had already been sent to the area in anticipation of military action. Howard's reluctance to finalise the decision was due in part to the growing opposition to a possible war throughout Australia.

Analysis of the decision-making process employed by the prime minister also reveals the role that perceptions played in the process. All the leaders of the 'coalition of the willing' expressed negative viewpoints on the character and intentions of the Iraqi leader—some based on fact, but many based on supposition, conjecture and, most importantly, personal bias and perceptions. Hussein was portrayed as evil, while Bush, Blair and Howard were trying to occupy the 'good guys' perception, at least in the minds of the people and in the court of world opinion. Not everyone accepted this perception of the role these leaders tried to assume. To some, Howard was perceived as being a decisive, strong leader; to others he was the doormat for Bush and Blair, manipulated into risking Australian lives in a war with Iraq.

Making decisions is also a critical element of organisational life, and as the John Howard example illustrates, those decisions can follow a long and carefully formulated rational process, a process in which perceptions play an important role. In this chapter, we will also describe how decisions in organisations are made. But first, we discuss perceptual processes and show how they are linked to individual decision making.

LEARNING OBJECTIVE

1

Explain how two people can see the same thing and interpret it differently

perception
A process by which individuals organise and interpret their sensory impressions in order to give meaning to their environment.

What is Perception, and Why is it Important?

Perception is a process by which individuals organise and interpret their sensory impressions in order to give meaning to their environment. However, what one perceives can be substantially different from objective reality. It need not be, but there is often disagreement. For example, it is possible that all employees in a firm may view it as a great place to work—favourable working conditions, interesting job assignments, good pay, an understanding and responsible management—but, as most of us know, it's very unusual to find such agreement.

In New Zealand, for example, some writers argue that a large number of employees view the workplace as a rest place. The workplace is there to recover from the long and frantic weekend hours spent doing home renovations, sports and other strenuous activities—a view probably not too dissimilar to many employees in Australia.[2]

Why is perception important in the study of OB? Simply because people's behaviour is based on their perception of what reality is, not on reality itself. *The world as it is perceived is the world that is behaviourally important.*

Factors Influencing Perception

How do we explain that individuals may look at the same thing, yet perceive it differently? A number of factors operate to shape and sometimes distort perception. These factors can reside in the *perceiver*, in the object or *target* being perceived, or in the context of the *situation* in which the perception is made (see Figure 5.1).

When an individual looks at a target and attempts to interpret what he or she sees, that interpretation is heavily influenced by the personal characteristics of the individual perceiver. Personal characteristics that affect perception include a person's attitudes (whether positive or negative),

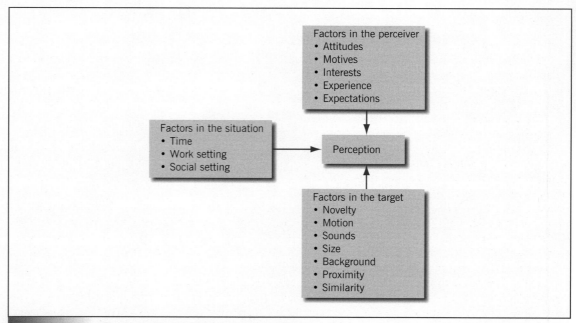

FIGURE 5.1   **Factors that influence perception**

personality (introvert versus extrovert), unsatisfied needs and motives (such as hunger, security, protection, and so on), interests, past experiences, and expectations. For example, if you expect police officers to be authoritative, young people to be unambitious, or individuals holding public office to be unscrupulous, you may perceive them as such regardless of their actual traits. Similarly, if you haven't eaten for 24 hours, things you do see will remind you of food or will resemble food.[3]

Characteristics of the target being observed can affect what is perceived. Loud people are more likely to be noticed in a group than quiet ones. So, too, are extremely attractive or unattractive individuals. Because targets aren't looked at in isolation, the relationship of a target to its background also influences perception, as does our tendency to group close things and similar things together. This is because what we see is dependent on how we separate a figure from its general background. For example, women, Asians, Aborigines or members of any other group that has clearly distinguishable characteristics in terms of features or colour are often perceived as alike in other, unrelated characteristics as well.

The context in which we see objects or events is also important. The time at which an object or event is seen can influence attention, as can location, light, heat or any number of situational factors. You may not notice a 22-year-old female in an evening gown and heavy make-up at an awards night. Yet that same woman so attired for your Monday morning OB lecture would certainly catch your attention (and that of the rest of the class!). Neither the perceiver nor the target changed between the awards night and Monday morning, but the *situation* is different.

Person Perception: Making Judgments About Others

Now we turn to the most relevant application of perception concepts to OB. This is the issue of *person perception*.

ATTRIBUTION THEORY

Our perceptions of people differ from our perceptions of inanimate objects such as desks, machines or buildings, because we make inferences about the actions of people that we don't make about inanimate objects. Non-living objects are subject to the laws of nature, but they have no beliefs, motives or intentions. But people do—the result is that when we observe people, we attempt to develop explanations of why they behave in certain ways. Our perception and judgment of a person's actions, therefore, will be significantly influenced by the assumptions we make about that person's internal state.

Knowing what people's perceptions are of other people can assist organisations that rely on interpersonal interaction with consumers. In one recent Australian study, patients who were being fitted with contact lenses were studied to determine their perceptions of the optometrist.[4] It was hypothesised that these perceptions would affect the patient's compliance with the optometrist's instructions on eye and contact lens care. The study found that, although the information-giving skills of the optometrist were most important in determining patients' perceptions, other interpersonal skills such as empathy, warmth and supportiveness were almost as important.[5] Armed with this knowledge, health-care professionals can adjust their approach to their patients to ensure greater compliance with care requirements.

Attribution theory has been proposed to develop explanations of the ways in which we judge people differently, depending on what meaning we attribute to a given behaviour.[6] Basically, the theory suggests that when we observe an individual's behaviour, we attempt to determine whether it was internally or externally caused. That determination, however, depends largely on three factors: (1) distinctiveness, (2) consensus, and (3) consistency. First, let's clarify the differences

LEARNING OBJECTIVE

2

List the three determinants of attribution

attribution theory
When individuals observe behaviour, they attempt to determine whether it is internally or externally caused.

between internal and external causation and then we will elaborate on each of the three determining factors.

Internally caused behaviours are those that are believed to be under the personal control of the individual. *Externally* caused behaviour is seen as resulting from outside causes; that is, the person is seen as having been forced into the behaviour by the situation. If one of your employees is late for work, you might attribute their lateness to their partying into the wee hours of the morning and then sleeping through the ringing of their alarm clock. This would be an internal attribution. But if you attribute their arriving late to an automobile accident that tied up traffic on the road that this employee regularly uses, then you would be making an external attribution.

Distinctiveness refers to whether an individual displays different behaviours in different situations. Is the employee who arrives late today also the source of complaints by fellow employees for being a 'slacker'? What we want to know is whether this behaviour is unusual. If it is, the observer is likely to give the behaviour an external attribution. If this action isn't unusual, it will probably be judged as internal.

If everyone who is faced with a similar situation responds in the same way, we can say the behaviour shows *consensus*. The behaviour of the employee discussed above would meet this criterion if all employees who took the same route to work were also late. From an attribution perspective, if consensus were high, you would be expected to give an external attribution to the employee's tardiness, whereas if other employees who took the same route made it to work on time, your conclusion as to causation would be internal.

Finally, an observer looks for *consistency* in a person's actions. Does the person respond the same way over time? Coming in ten minutes late for work isn't perceived in the same way for the employee for whom it is an unusual case (she hasn't been late for several months) as it is for the employee for whom it is part of a routine pattern (she is regularly late two or three times a week). The more consistent the behaviour, the more the observer is inclined to attribute it to internal causes.

Figure 5.2 summarises the key elements in attribution theory. It would tell us, for example, that if your employee—Kim Randolph—generally performs at about the same level on other related tasks as she does on her current task (low distinctiveness), if other employees frequently perform differently—better or worse—than Kim does on that current task (low consensus), and

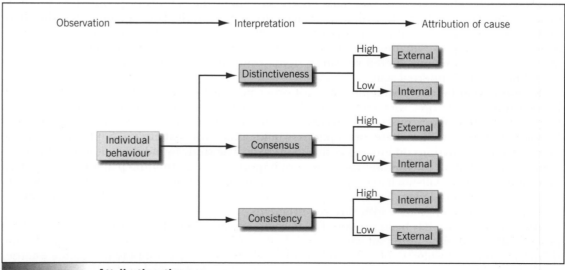

FIGURE 5.2   **Attribution theory**

if Kim's performance on this current task is consistent over time (high consistency), you or anyone else who is judging Kim's work is likely to hold her primarily responsible for her task performance (internal attribution).

One of the more interesting findings from attribution theory is that there are errors or biases that distort attributions. For example, there is substantial evidence that when we make judgments about the behaviour of other people, we have a tendency to underestimate the influence of external factors and overestimate the influence of internal or personal factors.[7] This is called the **fundamental attribution error** and can explain why a sales manager is prone to attribute the poor performance of her sales agents to laziness rather than to the innovative product line introduced by a competitor. There is also a tendency for individuals to attribute their own successes to internal factors such as ability or effort, while putting the blame for failure on external factors such as bad luck or unproductive fellow employees. This is called the **self-serving bias**.[8] During the high-tech stock market rally between 1996 and early 2000, investors were quick to brag about their expertise and take credit for their investing smarts. However, when that market imploded in the spring of 2000 and eventually declined more than 70 per cent, most of those same investors were looking for external sources to blame—the investment analysts who kept hyping technology shares because they had a vested interest in pumping up their prices, their brokers being too aggressive, the Reserve Bank for not cutting interest rates fast enough, and the like.

Are these errors or biases that distort attributions universal across different cultures? We can't answer that question definitively, but there is some preliminary evidence that indicates cultural differences.[9] For example, a study of Korean managers found that, contrary to the self-serving bias, they tended to accept responsibility for group failure 'because I was not a capable leader' instead of attributing it to group members.[10] Attribution theory was developed largely based on experiments with Americans and Western Europeans. But the Korean study suggests caution in making attribution theory predictions in non-Western societies, especially in countries with strong collectivist traditions.

FREQUENTLY USED SHORTCUTS IN JUDGING OTHERS

We use a number of shortcuts when we judge others. Perceiving and interpreting what others do is burdensome. As a result, individuals develop techniques for making the task more manageable. These techniques are frequently valuable—they allow us to make accurate perceptions rapidly and provide valid data for making predictions. However, they aren't foolproof. They can and do get us into trouble. An understanding of these shortcuts can be helpful in recognising when they can result in significant distortions.

Selective perception

Any characteristic that makes a person, object or event stand out will increase the probability that it will be perceived. Why? Because it is impossible for us to assimilate everything we see—only certain stimuli can be taken in. This tendency explains why, as we noted earlier, you are more likely to notice cars like your own or why some people may be reprimanded by their boss for doing

fundamental attribution error
The tendency to underestimate the influence of external factors and overestimate the influence of internal factors when making judgments about the behaviour of others.

self-serving bias
The tendency for individuals to attribute their own successes to internal factors while putting the blame for failures on external factors.

LEARNING OBJECTIVE
3
Describe how shortcuts can assist in or distort our judgment of others

Many share traders credited the gains they made in high-tech stocks between 1996 and early 2000 to their personal skills. But they blamed external sources for the losses they incurred when the prices of high-tech stocks took a nosedive.

something that, when done by another employee, goes unnoticed. Since we can't observe everything going on about us, we engage in **selective perception**. A classic example shows how vested interests can significantly influence which problems we see.

Dearborn and Simon performed a perceptual study in which 23 business executives read a comprehensive case describing the organisation and activities of a steel company.[11] Of the 23 executives, six were in the sales area, five in production, four in accounting, and eight in miscellaneous functions. Each manager was asked to write down the most important problem they found in the case. Eighty-three per cent of the sales executives rated sales important; only 29 per cent of the others did so. This, along with other results of the study, led the researchers to conclude that the participants perceived aspects of a situation that were specifically related to the activities and goals of the unit to which they were attached. A group's perception of organisational activities is selectively altered to align with the vested interests they represent. In other words, when the stimuli are ambiguous, as in the steel company case, perception tends to be influenced more by an individual's base of interpretation (that is, attitudes, interests and background) than by the stimulus itself.

But how does selectivity work as a shortcut in judging other people? Since we cannot assimilate all that we observe, we take in bits and pieces. But those bits and pieces aren't chosen randomly; rather, they are selectively chosen according to our interests, background, experience and attitudes. Selective perception allows us to 'speed-read' others, but not without the risk of drawing an inaccurate picture. Because we see what we want to see, we can draw unwarranted conclusions from an ambiguous situation.

Halo effect

When we draw a general impression about an individual on the basis of a single characteristic, such as intelligence, sociability or appearance, a **halo effect** is operating.[12] This phenomenon frequently occurs when students appraise their classroom lecturer. Students may give prominence to a single trait such as enthusiasm and allow their entire evaluation to be tainted by how they judge the lecturer on that one trait. Thus, a lecturer may be quiet, assured, knowledgeable and highly qualified, but if his style lacks eagerness, those students would probably give him a low rating.

The reality of the halo effect was confirmed in a classic study in which subjects were given a list of traits such as intelligent, skilful, practical, industrious, determined and warm, and were asked to evaluate the person to whom those traits applied.[13] When those traits were used, the person was judged to be wise, humorous, popular and imaginative. When the same list was modified—cold was substituted for warm—a completely different set of perceptions was obtained. Clearly, the subjects were allowing a single trait to influence their overall impression of the person being judged.

The propensity for the halo effect to operate isn't random. Research suggests that it is likely to be most extreme when the traits to be perceived are ambiguous in behavioural terms, when the traits have moral overtones, and when the perceiver is judging traits with which he or she has had limited experience.[14]

Contrast effects

There is an old adage among entertainers who perform in variety shows: never follow an act that has kids or animals in it. Why? The common belief is that audiences love children and animals so much that you'll look bad in comparison. This example demonstrates how **contrast effects** can distort perceptions. We don't evaluate a person in isolation. Our reaction to one person is influenced by other persons we have recently encountered.

An illustration of how contrast effects operate is an interview situation in which one sees a pool of job applicants. Distortions in any given candidate's evaluation can occur as a result of their place in the interview schedule. A candidate is likely to receive a more favourable evaluation if preceded by mediocre applicants and a less favourable evaluation if preceded by strong applicants.

selective perception
People selectively interpret what they see on the basis of their interests, background, experience and attitudes.

halo effect
Drawing a general impression about an individual on the basis of a single characteristic.

contrast effects
Evaluation of a person's characteristics that are affected by comparisons with other people recently encountered who rank higher or lower on the same characteristics.

Projection

It's easy to judge others if we assume that they are similar to us. For example, if you want challenge and responsibility in your job, you assume that others want the same. Or, you are honest and trustworthy, so you take it for granted that other people are equally honest and trustworthy. This tendency to attribute one's own characteristics to other people—which is called **projection**—can distort perceptions made about others.

People who engage in projection tend to perceive others according to what they themselves are like, rather than according to what the person being observed is really like. When managers engage in projection, they compromise their ability to respond to individual differences. They tend to see people as more homogeneous than they really are.

projection
Attributing one's own characteristics to other people.

Stereotyping

When we judge someone on the basis of our perception of the group to which he or she belongs, we are using the shortcut called **stereotyping**.[15] F. Scott Fitzgerald engaged in stereotyping in his reported conversation with Ernest Hemingway when he said, 'The very rich are different from you and me.' Hemingway's reply, 'Yes, they have more money', indicated that he refused to generalise characteristics about people on the basis of their wealth.

stereotyping
Judging someone on the basis of one's perception of the group to which that person belongs.

Generalisation, of course, isn't without advantages. It's a means of simplifying a complex world, and it permits us to maintain consistency. It's less difficult to deal with an unmanageable number of stimuli if we use stereotypes. As an example, assume you are a sales manager looking to fill a sales position in your territory. You want to hire someone who is ambitious and hardworking and who can deal well with adversity. You have had success in the past by hiring individuals who participate in sports. So, you focus your search by looking for candidates who play sport. In so doing, you have cut down considerably on your search time. Furthermore, to the extent that sports people are ambitious, hardworking and able to deal with adversity, the use of this stereotype can improve your decision making. The problem, of course, is when we inaccurately stereotype.[16] All sports men and women are *not necessarily* ambitious, hardworking or good at dealing with adversity.

In organisations, we frequently hear comments that represent stereotypes based on gender, age, race, ethnicity and even weight[17]: 'women won't relocate for a promotion'; 'men aren't interested in child-care'; 'older employees can't learn new skills'; 'Asian immigrants are hardworking and conscientious'; 'overweight people lack discipline'. From a perceptual standpoint, if people expect to see these stereotypes, that is what they will perceive, whether or not they are accurate.

Sex-role stereotypes can be all-pervasive in our culture. Some years ago, Katies, a women's fashion retailer chain, ran an advertisement to advertise their post-Christmas sales. In the ad, they portrayed offices and reception areas as being deserted while the voice-over warned employers to expect their female employees to abandon their jobs while the sale was on. The reaction from women was swift and decisive—Katies was forced to withdraw the advertisement after only one day. The makers of the ad were guilty of sex-role stereotypes—portraying women as irresponsible and likely to abandon their employment for the sake of a clothing sale. This is clearly not true, but it does reflect how widespread sex-role stereotyping is today. This is especially true for female managers—studies in Australia and New Zealand consistently show the reality of negative stereotypes about the ability of women to manage effectively.

Obviously, one of the problems of stereotypes is that they are widespread, despite the fact that they may not contain a shred of truth or that they may be irrelevant. Their being widespread may mean only that many people are making the same inaccurate perception on the basis of a false premise about a group.

SPECIFIC APPLICATIONS IN ORGANISATIONS

People in organisations are always judging each other. Managers must appraise their employees' performances. We evaluate how much effort our fellow employees are putting into their jobs.

When a new person joins a work team, he or she is immediately 'sized up' by the other team members. In many cases, these judgments have important consequences for the organisation. Let's look briefly at a few of the more obvious applications.

Employment interview

A major input into who is hired and who is rejected in any organisation is the employment interview. It's fair to say that few people are hired without an interview. But the evidence indicates that interviewers make perceptual judgments that are often inaccurate. In addition, agreement among interviewers is often poor; that is, different interviewers see different things in the same candidate and thus arrive at different conclusions about the applicant.

Interviewers generally draw early impressions that become very quickly entrenched. If negative information is exposed early in the interview, it tends to be more heavily weighted than if that same information comes out later.[18] Studies indicate that most interviewers' decisions change very little after the first four or five minutes of the interview. As a result, information elicited early in the interview carries greater weight than does information elicited later, and a 'good applicant' is probably characterised more by the absence of unfavourable characteristics than by the presence of favourable characteristics.

Importantly, who *you* think is a good candidate and who *we* think is one may differ markedly. Because interviews usually have so little consistent structure and interviewers vary in terms of what they are looking for in a candidate, judgments about the same candidate can vary widely. If the employment interview is an important input into the hiring decision—and it usually is—you should recognise that perceptual factors influence who is hired and, eventually, the quality of an organisation's labour force.

Performance expectations

There is an impressive amount of evidence which demonstrates that people will attempt to validate their perceptions of reality, even when those perceptions are faulty.[19] This characteristic is particularly relevant when we consider performance expectations on the job.

self-fulfilling prophecy
A situation in which one person inaccurately perceives a second person and the resulting expectations cause the second person to behave in ways consistent with the original perception.

The terms **self-fulfilling prophecy**, or *Pygmalion effect*, have evolved to characterise the fact that people's expectations determine their behaviour. In other words, if a manager expects big things from his or her people, they are not likely to let him or her down. Similarly, if a manager expects people to perform minimally, they will tend to behave so as to meet those low expectations. The result, then, is that the expectations become reality.

An interesting illustration of the self-fulfilling prophecy is a study undertaken with 105 soldiers in the Israeli Defence Forces who were taking a 15-week combat command course.[20] The four course lecturers were told that one-third of the specific incoming trainees had high potential, one-third had normal potential, and the potential of the rest was unknown. In reality, the trainees were randomly placed into those categories by the researchers. The results confirmed the existence of a self-fulfilling prophecy. The trainees whom lecturers were told had high potential scored significantly higher on objective achievement tests, exhibited more positive attitudes, and held their leaders in higher regard than did the other two groups. The lecturers of the supposedly high-potential trainees got better results from them because the lecturers expected it.

Performance evaluation

Although the impact of performance evaluations on behaviour will be discussed more fully later in this book, it should be pointed out here that an employee's performance appraisal is very much dependent on the perceptual process.[21] An employee's future is closely tied to their appraisal—promotions, pay increases and continuation of employment are among the most obvious outcomes. The performance appraisal represents an assessment of an employee's work. Although the appraisal can be objective (for example, a salesperson is appraised on how many dollars of sales she generates in her territory), many jobs are evaluated in subjective terms. Subjective measures are easier to implement, they provide managers with greater discretion, and many jobs don't readily lend themselves to objective measures. Subjective measures are, by definition, judgmental. The evaluator forms a general impression of an employee's work. To the degree that managers use subjective measures in appraising employees, what the evaluator perceives to be good or bad employee characteristics or behaviours will significantly influence the outcome of the appraisal.

Employee effort

An individual's future in an organisation is usually not dependent on performance alone. In many organisations, the level of an employee's effort is given high importance. Just as teachers frequently consider how hard you try in a course as well as how you perform on examinations, so, often, do managers. An assessment of an individual's effort is a subjective judgment susceptible to perceptual distortions and bias.

The Link between Perception and Individual Decision Making

Individuals in organisations make **decisions**. That is, they make choices from among two or more alternatives. Top managers, for example, determine their organisation's goals, what products or services to offer, how best to finance operations or where to locate a new manufacturing plant. Middle- and lower-level managers determine production schedules, select new employees and decide how pay increases are to be allocated. Of course, making decisions isn't the sole province of managers. Non-managerial employees also make decisions that affect their jobs and the organisations for which they work. The more obvious of these decisions might include whether or not to come to work on any given day, how much effort to put forth once at work, and whether or not to comply with a request made by the boss. In addition, an increasing number of organisations in recent years have been empowering their non-managerial employees with job-related decision-making authority that historically was reserved for managers alone. Individual decision making, therefore, is an important part of organisational behaviour. But how individuals in organisations make decisions and the quality of their final choices are largely influenced by their perceptions.

Decision making occurs as a reaction to a **problem**.[22] That is, there is a discrepancy between some current state of affairs and some desired state, requiring the consideration of alternative courses of action. So, if your car breaks down and you rely on it to get to work, you have a problem that requires a decision on your part. Unfortunately, most problems don't come neatly packaged with a label 'problem' clearly displayed on them. One person's *problem* is another person's *satisfactory state of affairs*. One manager may view her division's 2 per cent decline in quarterly sales to be a serious problem requiring immediate action on her part. In contrast, her counterpart in another division of the same company, who also had a 2 per cent sales decrease, may consider that percentage quite acceptable. So, the awareness that a problem exists and that a decision needs to be made is a perceptual issue.

Moreover, every decision requires the interpretation and evaluation of information. Data are typically received from multiple sources and they need to be screened, processed and interpreted. Which data, for example, are relevant to the decision and which are not? The perceptions of the decision maker will answer that question. Alternatives will be developed, and the strengths and weaknesses of each will need to be evaluated. Again, because alternatives don't come with 'red flags' identifying them as such or with their strengths and weaknesses clearly marked, the individual decision maker's perceptual process will have a large bearing on the final outcome.

decisions
The choices made from among two or more alternatives.

LEARNING OBJECTIVE
4
Explain how perception affects the decision-making process

problem
A discrepancy between some current state of affairs and some desired state.

How Should Decisions be Made?

Let's begin by describing how individuals should behave in order to maximise or optimise a certain outcome. We call this the *rational decision-making process.*

THE RATIONAL DECISION-MAKING PROCESS

rational
Making consistent, value-maximising choices within specified constraints.

The optimising decision maker is **rational**. That is, he or she makes consistent, value-maximising choices within specified constraints.[23] These choices are made following a six-step **rational decision-making model**.[24] Moreover, specific assumptions underlie this model.

rational decision-making model
A decision-making model that describes how individuals should behave in order to maximise some outcome.

The rational model

The six steps in the rational decision-making model are listed in Table 5.1.

The model begins by *defining the problem.* As noted previously, a problem exists when there is a discrepancy between an existing and a desired state of affairs.[25] If you calculate your monthly expenses and find you're spending $50 more than you allocated in your budget, you have defined a problem. Many poor decisions can be traced to the decision maker overlooking a problem or defining the wrong problem.

Once a decision maker has defined the problem, he or she needs to *identify the decision criteria* that will be important in solving the problem. In this step, the decision maker determines what is relevant in making the decision. This step brings the decision maker's interests, values and similar personal preferences into the process. Identifying criteria is important, because what one person thinks is relevant another person may not. Also, keep in mind that any factors not identified in this step are considered irrelevant to the decision maker.

The criteria identified are rarely all equal in importance. So, the third step requires the decision maker to *weight the previously identified criteria* in order to give them the correct priority in the decision.

The fourth step requires the decision maker to *generate possible alternatives* that could succeed in resolving the problem. No attempt is made in this step to appraise these alternatives, only to list them.

Once the alternatives have been generated, the decision maker must critically analyse and evaluate each one. This is done by *rating each alternative on each criterion.* The strengths and weaknesses of each alternative become evident as they are compared with the criteria and weights established in the second and third steps.

The final step in this model requires *calculating the optimal decision.* This is done by evaluating each alternative against the weighted criteria and selecting the alternative with the highest total score.

TABLE 5.1	**Steps in the rational decision-making model**

1. Define the problem.
2. Identify the decision criteria.
3. Allocate weights to the criteria.
4. Develop the alternatives.
5. Evaluate the alternatives.
6. Select the best alternative.

Assumptions of the model
The rational decision-making model we just described contains a number of assumptions.[26] Table 5.2 outlines those assumptions.

IMPROVING CREATIVITY IN DECISION MAKING

The rational decision maker needs **creativity**—that is, the ability to produce novel and useful ideas.[27] These are ideas that are different from what has been done before but that are also appropriate to the problem or opportunity presented. Why is creativity important to decision making? It allows the decision maker to more fully appraise and understand the problem, including seeing problems others can't see. However, creativity's most obvious value is in helping the decision maker to identify all viable alternatives.

creativity
The ability to produce novel and useful ideas.

Creative potential
Most people have creative potential that they can use when confronted with a decision-making problem. But to unleash that potential, they have to get out of the psychological ruts many of us get into and learn how to think about a problem in divergent ways.

We can start with the obvious. People differ in their inherent creativity. Einstein, Edison, Picasso and Mozart were individuals of exceptional creativity. Not surprisingly, exceptional creativity is scarce. A study of the lifetime creativity of 461 men and women found that less than 1 per cent were exceptionally creative.[28] But 10 per cent were highly creative and about 60 per cent were somewhat creative. This suggests that most of us have creative potential; we just need to learn how to unleash it.

Three-component model of creativity
Given that most people have the capacity to be at least moderately creative, what can individuals and organisations do to stimulate employee creativity? The best answer to this question lies in the **three-component model of creativity**.[29] Based on an extensive body of research, this model proposes that individual creativity essentially requires expertise, creative-thinking skills and intrinsic task motivation (see Figure 5.3). Studies confirm that the higher the level of each of these three components, the higher the creativity.

Expertise is the foundation for all creative work. Picasso's understanding of art and Einstein's knowledge of physics were necessary conditions for them to be able to make creative contributions

three-component model of creativity
Proposition that individual creativity requires expertise, creative-thinking skills and intrinsic task motivation.

TABLE 5.2	Assumptions of the rational decision-making model

1. *Problem clarity.* The problem is clear and unambiguous. The decision maker is assumed to have complete information regarding the decision situation.
2. *Known options.* It is assumed the decision maker can identify all the relevant criteria and can list all the viable alternatives. Furthermore, the decision maker is aware of all the possible consequences of each alternative.
3. *Clear preferences.* Rationality assumes that the criteria and alternatives can be ranked and weighted to reflect their importance.
4. *Constant preferences.* It's assumed that the specific decision criteria are constant and that the weights assigned to them are stable over time.
5. *No time or cost constraints.* The rational decision maker can obtain full information about criteria and alternatives because it's assumed that there are no time or cost constraints.
6. *Maximum payoff.* The rational decision maker will choose the alternative that yields the highest perceived value.

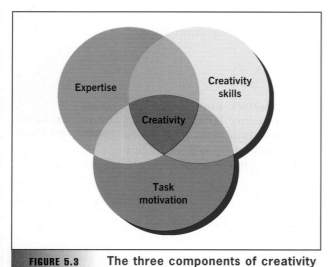

FIGURE 5.3   **The three components of creativity**

Source: T. M. Amabile, 'Motivating Creativity in Organizations', *California Management Review*, Vol 40, No 1, 1997, p. 43. Copyright © by The Regents of the University of California. Reprinted with permission.

to their fields. And you wouldn't expect someone with a minimal knowledge of programming to be very creative as a software engineer. The potential for creativity is enhanced when individuals have abilities, knowledge, proficiencies and similar expertise in their field of endeavour.

The second component is *creative-thinking skills*. This encompasses personality characteristics associated with creativity, the ability to use analogies, as well as the talent to see the familiar in a different light. For example, the following individual traits have been found to be associated with the development of creative ideas: intelligence, independence, self-confidence, risk taking, an internal locus of control, tolerance for ambiguity, and perseverance in the face of frustration.[30] The effective use of analogies allows decision makers to apply an idea from one context to another. One of the most famous examples in which analogy resulted in a creative breakthrough was Alexander Graham Bell's observation that it might be possible to take concepts that operate in the ear and apply them to his 'talking box'. He noticed that a delicate, thin membrane operates the bones in the ear. He wondered why, then, a thicker and strong piece of membrane shouldn't be able to move a piece of steel. Out of that analogy, the telephone was conceived. Of course, some people have developed their skill at being able to see problems in a new way. They are able to make the strange familiar and the familiar strange.[31] For example, most of us think of hens laying eggs. But how many of us have considered that a hen is only an egg's way of making another egg?

The final component in our model is *intrinsic task motivation*. This is the desire to work on something because it's interesting, involving, exciting, satisfying or personally challenging. This

OB Controversies

Marriage may dim creativity

Recently a New Zealand researcher, Dr Satoshi Kanazawa, a psychologist at the University of Canterbury, studied the biographies of 280 great scientists, noting their age at the time when they carried out their greatest work. Dr Kanazawa found that nearly two-thirds of these great scientists had made their greatest contribution before they were 30 years old. Furthermore, within five years of marriage, at least one-quarter of all these scientists made no further contribution to the field of scientific discovery. The study, replicated in other fields of endeavour, suggests that creativity is diminished by age and marital status. One possible explanation is the effects of testosterone—the hormone found in greatest concentrations in young males of many species. In young males, the high levels of testosterone are hypothesised to spur them to impress possible female partners and are manifest in the area of greatest talent for these individuals. Once the search for a partner is finished and/or advancing age sees a reduction in testosterone levels, the drive to be creative appears to decline sharply. While further studies are needed to test these hypotheses and replicate Dr Kanazawa's research, it does suggest that creativity is negatively correlated with age and marital status.

Source: S. Kanazawa, 'Why Productivity Fades with Age: The Crime–Genius Connection', *Journal of Research in Personality*, vol. 37, no. 4, August 2003, pp. 257–72. Copyright © 2003, with permission from Elsevier.

Intrinsic task motivation is what makes work personally challenging and inspires creativity and strong positive feelings about the job, even when there are mundane and boring aspects to the job. Good carpenters focus on pride in their work.

motivational component is what turns creativity *potential* into *actual* creative ideas. It determines the extent to which individuals fully engage their expertise and creative skills. So, creative people often love their work, to the point of seeming obsessed. Importantly, an individual's work environment can have a significant effect on intrinsic motivation. Work-environment stimulants that have been found to foster creativity include a culture that encourages the flow of ideas, fair and constructive judgment of ideas, and rewards, and recognises creative work; sufficient financial, material and information resources; freedom to decide what work is to be done and how to do it; a supervisor who communicates effectively, shows confidence in others and supports the work group; and work-group members who support and trust each other.[32]

How are Decisions Actually Made in Organisations?

Are decision makers in organisations rational? Do they carefully assess problems, identify all relevant criteria, use their creativity to identify all viable alternatives, and painstakingly evaluate every alternative to find an optimal choice? For novice decision makers with little experience, decision makers faced with simple problems that have few alternative courses of action, or when the cost of searching out and evaluating alternatives is low, the rational model provides a fairly accurate description of the decision process.[33] But such situations are the exception. Most decisions in the real world don't follow the rational model. For example, people are usually content to find an acceptable or reasonable solution to their problem, rather than an optimal one. As such, decision makers generally make limited use of their creativity. Choices tend to be confined to the neighbourhood of the problem symptom and to the neighbourhood of the current alternative. As one expert in decision making put it: 'Most significant decisions are made by judgment, rather than by a defined prescriptive model.'[34]

The following reviews a large body of evidence to provide you with a more accurate description of how most decisions in organisations are actually made.[35]

BOUNDED RATIONALITY

When you considered which university to attend, did you look at *every* viable alternative? Did you carefully identify *all* the criteria that were important in your decision? Did you evaluate *each* alternative against the criteria in order to find the optimal university? We expect that the answers to these questions are probably 'no'. Well, don't feel bad. Few people made their university choice this way. Instead of optimising, you probably satisfied.

When faced with a complex problem, most people respond by reducing the problem to a level at which it can be readily understood. This is because the limited information-processing capability of human beings makes it impossible to assimilate and understand all the information

LEARNING OBJECTIVE

6

Describe the actions of the bounded rational decision maker

necessary to optimise. So, people *satisfice*; that is, they seek solutions that are satisfactory and sufficient.

Because the capacity of the human mind for formulating and solving complex problems is far too small to meet the requirements for full rationality, individuals operate within the confines of **bounded rationality**. They construct simplified models that extract the essential features from problems without capturing all their complexity.[36] Individuals can then behave rationally within the limits of the simple model.

bounded rationality
Individuals make decisions by constructing simplified models that extract the essential features from problems without capturing all their complexity.

How does bounded rationality work for the typical individual? Once a problem is identified, the search for criteria and alternatives begins. But the list of criteria is likely to be far from exhaustive. The decision maker will identify a limited list made up of the more conspicuous choices. These are the choices that are easy to find and that tend to be highly visible. In most cases, they will represent familiar criteria and previously tried-and-true solutions. Once this limited set of alternatives is identified, the decision maker will begin reviewing it. But the review won't be comprehensive—not all the alternatives will be carefully evaluated. Instead, the decision maker will begin with alternatives that differ only in a relatively small degree from the choice currently in effect. Following along familiar and well-worn paths, the decision maker proceeds to review alternatives only until he or she identifies an alternative that is 'good enough'—one that meets an acceptable level of performance. The first alternative that meets the 'good enough' criterion ends the search. So the final solution represents a satisficing choice rather than an optimal one.

One of the more interesting aspects of bounded rationality is that the order in which alternatives are considered is critical in determining which alternative is selected. Remember, in the fully rational decision-making model, all alternatives are eventually listed in a hierarchy of preferred order. Because all alternatives are considered, the initial order in which they are evaluated is irrelevant. Every potential solution would get a full and complete evaluation. But this isn't the case with bounded rationality. Assuming that a problem has more than one potential solution, the satisficing choice will be the first *acceptable* one the decision maker encounters. Since decision makers use simple and limited models, they typically begin by identifying alternatives that are obvious, ones with which they are familiar, and those not too far from the status quo. The solutions that depart least from the status quo and meet the decision criteria are those most likely to be selected. A unique and creative alternative may present an optimising solution to the problem; however, it's unlikely to be chosen, because an acceptable solution will be identified well before the decision maker is required to search very far beyond the status quo.

INTUITION

Tom Jackson has just committed his company to spend in excess of $40 million to build a new factory in Gladstone, Queensland, to manufacture electronic components for satellite communication equipment. The CEO of his organisation, Tom had before him a comprehensive analysis of five possible factory locations developed by a site-location consulting firm he had hired. This report ranked the Gladstone location third among the five alternatives. After carefully reading the report and its conclusions, Tom decided against the consultant's recommendation. When asked to explain his decision, Tom said, 'I looked the report over very carefully. But in spite of its recommendation, I felt that the numbers didn't tell the whole story. Intuitively, I just sensed that Gladstone would prove to be the best bet over the long run.'

Intuitive decision making, like that used by Tom Jackson, has recently come out of the closet and into some respectability. Experts no longer automatically assume that using intuition to make decisions is irrational or ineffective.[37] There is growing recognition that rational analysis has been overemphasised and that, in certain instances, relying on intuition can improve decision making.

What do we mean by intuitive decision making? There are a number of ways to conceptualise intuition.[38] For example, some consider it a form of extrasensory power or sixth sense, and some believe it is a personality trait with which a limited number of people are born. For our purposes, we define **intuitive decision making** as an unconscious process created out of distilled experience. It doesn't necessarily operate independently of rational analysis; rather, the two complement each other.

intuitive decision making
An unconscious process created out of distilled experience.

Research on chess playing provides an excellent example of how intuition works.[39] Novice chess players and grand masters were shown an actual, but unfamiliar, chess game with about 25 pieces on the board. After five or ten seconds, the pieces were removed and each was asked to reconstruct the pieces by position. On average, the grand master could put 23 or 24 pieces in their correct squares, while the novice was able to replace only six. Then the exercise was changed. This time the pieces were placed randomly on the board. Again, the novice got only about six correct, but so did the grand master! The second exercise demonstrated that the grand master didn't have any better memory than the novice. What he did have was the ability, based on the experience of having played thousands of chess games, to recognise patterns and clusters of pieces that occur on chessboards in the course of games. Studies further show that chess professionals can play 50 or more games simultaneously, in which decisions often must be made in only seconds, and exhibit only a moderately lower level of skill than when playing one game under tournament conditions, where decisions take half an hour or longer. The expert's experience allows him or her to recognise the pattern in a situation and draw on previously learned information associated with that pattern to arrive at a decision choice quickly. The result is that the intuitive decision maker can decide rapidly based on what appears to be very limited information.

When are people most likely to use intuitive decision making? Eight conditions have been identified: (1) when a high level of uncertainty exists; (2) when there is little precedent to draw on; (3) when variables are less scientifically predictable; (4) when 'facts' are limited; (5) when facts don't clearly point the way; (6) when analytical data are of little use; (7) when there are several plausible alternative solutions from which to choose, with good arguments for each; and (8) when time is limited and there is pressure to come up with the right decision.[40]

LEARNING OBJECTIVE

7

Identify the conditions in which individuals are most likely to use intuition in decision making

Although intuitive decision making has gained in respectability, don't expect people—especially in Anglo-Saxon cultures in which rational analysis is the approved way of making decisions—to acknowledge they are using it. People with strong intuitive abilities don't usually tell their colleagues how they reached their conclusions. Since rational analysis is considered more socially desirable, intuitive ability is often disguised or hidden. As one top executive commented, 'Sometimes one must dress up a gut decision in "data clothes" to make it acceptable or palatable, but this fine-tuning is usually after the fact of the decision.'[41]

PROBLEM IDENTIFICATION

As suggested earlier, problems don't come with flashing neon lights to identify themselves. And one person's *problem* is another person's *acceptable status quo*. So, how do decision makers identify and select problems?

Problems that are visible tend to have a higher probability of being selected than ones that are important.[42] Why? We can offer at least two reasons. First, visible problems are more likely to catch a decision maker's attention. This explains why politicians are more likely to talk about the 'crime problem' than the 'illiteracy problem'. Second, remember we are concerned with decision making in organisations. Decision makers want to appear competent and 'on top of problems'. This motivates them to focus attention on problems that are visible to others.

Don't ignore the decision maker's self-interest. If a decision maker faces a conflict between selecting a problem that is important to the organisation and one that is important to the decision maker, self-interest tends to win out.[43] This also ties in with the issue of visibility. It's usually in a decision maker's best interest to attack high-profile problems. It conveys to others that things are under control. Moreover, when the decision maker's performance is later reviewed, the evaluator is more likely to give a high rating to someone who has been aggressively attacking visible problems than to someone whose actions have been less obvious.

The Real Deal

Firefighters use intuition to make the right choices

Do fire commanders use the rational model to make life-and-death decisions? No. They rely on their intuition, built on years of experience. And intuition begins with recognition. The following illustrates how that recognition process works.

Recently a fire fighting commander and his crew encountered a fire at the back of a timber-framed house. The commander led his hose team into the building. Standing in the living room, they blasted water on to the smoke and flames that appeared to be consuming the kitchen. But the fire roared back and continued to burn. The men doused the fire again, and the flames briefly subsided. But then they flared up again with an even greater intensity. As the firefighters retreated and regrouped, the commander was gripped by an uneasy feeling. He quickly ordered everyone to leave. Just as the crew reached the street, the whole living-room floor caved in. Had the men stayed in the house, they would have plunged into a blazing basement.

Why did the commander give the order to leave? Because the fire's behaviour didn't match his expectations. Much of the fire was burning underneath the living-room floor, so it was unaffected by the firefighters' attack. Also, the rising heat made the room extremely hot—too hot for such a seemingly small fire. Another clue that this wasn't just a small kitchen fire was that the sounds it emitted were strangely quiet. Hot fires are loud. The commander was intuitively sensing that the floor was muffling

the roar of the flames that were raging below.

Veteran firefighters have accumulated a storehouse of experiences and they subconsciously categorise fires according to how they should react to them. They look for cues or patterns in situations that direct them to take one action over another.

Experienced people whose jobs require quick decisions—firefighters, intensive-care nurses, jet-fighter pilots, SWAT team members—see a different world than novices in those same jobs do. And what they see tells them what they should do. Ultimately, intuition is all about perception. The formal rules of decision making are almost incidental.

Source: Based on B. Breen, 'What's Your Intuition?', *Fast Company*, September 2000, pp. 290–300.

What occupational stereotypes do you hold about fire fighters? How do you think they were formed? What role do you think intuition plays in a fire fighter's mind when faced with difficult blazes to control?

ALTERNATIVE DEVELOPMENT

Because decision makers rarely seek an optimal solution, but rather a satisficing one, we should expect to find a minimal use of creativity in the search for alternatives. And that expectation is generally on target.

Efforts will be made to try to keep the search process simple. It will tend to be confined to the neighbourhood of the current alternative. More complex search behaviour, which includes the

Experience with a situation allows experts, such as master chess players, to use learned information, even subconsciously, to make quick decisions that we sometimes attribute to intuition.

development of creative alternatives, will be resorted to only when a simple search fails to uncover a satisfactory alternative.

Rather than formulating new and unique problem definitions and alternatives, with frequent journeys into unfamiliar territory, the evidence indicates that decision making is incremental rather than comprehensive.[44] This means decision makers avoid the difficult task of considering all the important factors, weighing their relative merits and drawbacks, and calculating the value for each alternative. Instead, they make successive limited comparisons. This simplifies decision choices by comparing only the alternatives that differ in relatively small degrees from the choice currently in effect.

The picture that emerges is one of a decision maker who takes small steps towards his or her objective. Acknowledging the non-comprehensive nature of choice selection, decision makers make successive comparisons because decisions are never made forever and written in stone; rather, decisions are made and remade endlessly in small comparisons between narrow choices.

MAKING CHOICES

In order to avoid information overload, decision makers rely on **heuristics**, or judgmental shortcuts, in decision making.[45] There are two common categories of heuristics—availability and representativeness. Each creates biases in judgment. Another bias that decision makers often have is the tendency to escalate commitment to a failing course of action.

Availability heuristic

Many more people suffer from fear of flying than fear of driving in a car. The reason is that many people think flying is more dangerous. It isn't, of course. With apologies ahead of time for this graphic example, if flying on a commercial airline was as dangerous as driving, the equivalent of two 747s filled to capacity would have to crash every week, killing all aboard, to match the risk of being killed in a car accident. But the media give a lot more attention to air accidents, so we tend to overstate the risk of flying and understate the risk of driving.

This illustrates an example of the **availability heuristic**, which is the tendency for people to base their judgments on information that is readily available to them. Events that evoke emotions, that are particularly vivid, or that have occurred more recently tend to be more available in our memory. As a result, we tend to be prone to overestimating unlikely events such as an airplane crash. The availability heuristic can also explain why managers, when doing annual performance appraisals, tend to give more weight to recent behaviours of an employee than those behaviours of six or nine months ago.

Representative heuristic

Literally thousands of Australian boys dream of playing Rugby League in the NRL. In reality, they have a far better chance of becoming medical doctors than they do of playing in the NRL, but these kids are suffering from a **representative heuristic**. They tend to assess the likelihood of an occurrence by trying to match it with a pre-existing category. They hear about a boy from their

LEARNING OBJECTIVE

8

Define heuristics and explain how they bias decisions

heuristics
Judgmental shortcuts in decision making.

availability heuristic
The tendency for people to base their judgments on information that is readily available to them.

representative heuristic
Assessing the likelihood of an occurrence by drawing analogies seeing identical situations in which they don't exist.

school ten years ago who went on to play professional league football. Or they watch NRL announcers interviewing players on television and think that those players are very like them. We all are guilty of using this heuristic at times. Managers, for example, frequently predict the performance of a new product by relating it to a previous product's success. Or if three graduates from the same university were hired and turned out to be poor performers, managers may predict that a current job applicant from the same university won't be a good employee.

Escalation of commitment

escalation of commitment
An increased commitment to a previous decision in spite of negative information.

Another bias that creeps into decisions in practice is a tendency to escalate commitment when a decision stream represents a series of decisions.[46] **Escalation of commitment** refers to staying with a decision even when there is clear evidence that it is wrong. For example, a friend of ours had been dating a woman for about four years. Although he admitted that things weren't going too well in the relationship, he informed us that he was going to marry the woman. A bit surprised by his decision, we asked him why. He responded: 'I have a lot invested in the relationship!'

It has been well documented that individuals escalate commitment to a failing course of action when they view themselves as responsible for the failure. That is, they 'throw good money after bad' to demonstrate that their initial decision wasn't wrong and to avoid having to admit they made a mistake. Escalation of commitment is also congruent with evidence that people try to appear consistent in what they say and do. Increasing commitment to previous actions conveys consistency.

Escalation of commitment has obvious implications for managerial decisions. Many an organisation has suffered large losses because a manager was determined to prove that his or her original decision was right by continuing to commit resources to what was a lost cause from the beginning. In addition, consistency is a characteristic often associated with effective leaders. So managers, in an effort to appear effective, may be motivated to be consistent, when switching to another course of action may be preferable. In actuality, effective managers are those who are able to differentiate between situations in which persistence will pay off and situations in which it will not.

INDIVIDUAL DIFFERENCES: DECISION-MAKING STYLES

Put Kwan and Sean into the same decision situation and Kwan almost always seems to take longer to come to a solution. Kwan's final choices aren't necessarily always better than Sean's; he just takes more time to process the information. In addition, if there is an obvious risk dimension in the decision, Sean seems to consistently prefer a riskier option than does Kwan. What this illustrates is that all of us bring our individual style to the decisions we make.

Research on decision styles has identified four different individual approaches to making decisions.[47] This model was designed to be used by managers and aspiring managers, but its general framework can be used with any individual decision maker.

LEARNING OBJECTIVE

9

Describe four styles of decision making

The basic foundation of the model is the recognition that people differ along two dimensions. The first is their way of *thinking*. Some people are logical and rational. They process information serially. In contrast, some people are intuitive and creative. They perceive things as a whole. Note that these differences are above and beyond general human limitations such as those we described regarding bounded rationality. The other dimension addresses a person's *tolerance for ambiguity*. Some people have a high need to structure information in ways that minimise ambiguity, while others are able to process many thoughts at the same time. When these two dimensions are diagrammed, they form four styles of decision making (see Figure 5.4). These are: directive, analytic, conceptual and behavioural.

People using the *directive* style have a low tolerance for ambiguity and seek rationality. They are efficient and logical, but their efficiency concerns result in decisions made with minimal information and with few alternatives assessed. Directive types make decisions fast and they focus on the short run.

The *analytic* type has a much greater tolerance for ambiguity than do directive decision makers. This leads to the desire for more information and consideration of more alternatives than is true for directives. Analytic managers would be best characterised as careful decision makers with the ability to adapt to or cope with novel and unexpected situations.

Individuals with a *conceptual* style tend to use data from multiple sources and consider many alternatives. Their focus is long range, and they are very good at finding creative solutions to problems.

The final category—the *behavioural* style—characterises decision makers who have a strong concern for the people in the organisation and their development. They are concerned with the well-being of their subordinates and are receptive to suggestions from others. They tend to focus on the short term and to downplay the use of data in their decision making. This type of manager tries to avoid conflict and seeks acceptance.

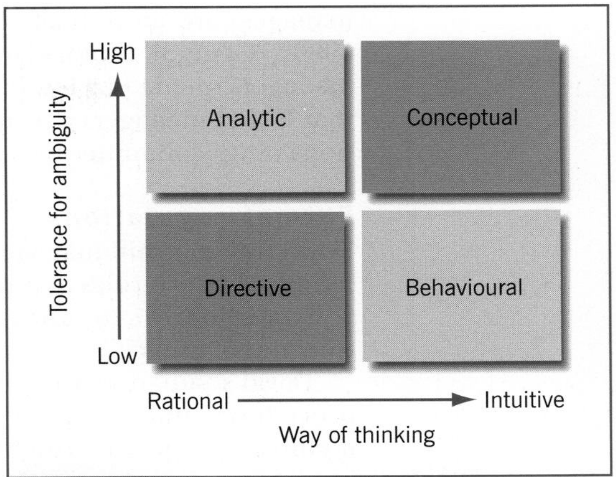

Although these four categories are distinct, most managers have characteristics that fall into more than one. It's probably best to think in terms of a manager's dominant style and his or her backup styles. Some managers rely almost exclusively on their dominant style; however, more flexible managers can make shifts, depending on the situation.

Australian business students, lower-level managers and top executives tend to score highest in the analytic style. That's not surprising given the emphasis that formal education, particularly business education, gives to developing rational thinking. For example, courses in accounting, statistics and finance all stress rational analysis. In contrast, evidence indicates that managers in China and Japan tend to rely more on directive and behavioural styles, respectively.[48] This may be explained by the Chinese emphasis on maintaining social order and the strong sense among Japanese of collectivism in the workplace.

In addition to providing a framework for looking at individual differences, focusing on decision styles can be useful for helping you to understand how two equally intelligent people, with access to the same information, can differ in the ways they approach decisions and the final choices they make. It can also help you to understand how individuals from different cultures might approach a decision problem.

FIGURE 5.4   Decision-style model

Source: A. J. Rowe and J. D. Boulgarides, *Managerial Decision Making* (Upper Saddle River, NJ: Prentice Hall, 1992), p. 29. © Alan J. Rowe, 1992.

ORGANISATIONAL CONSTRAINTS

The organisation itself constrains decision makers. Managers, for example, shape their decisions to reflect the organisation's performance evaluation and reward system, to comply with the organisation's formal regulations, and to meet organisationally imposed time constraints. Previous organisational decisions also act as precedents to constrain current decisions.

Performance evaluation
Managers are strongly influenced in their decision making by the criteria by which they are evaluated. If a division manager believes that the manufacturing facilities under her responsibility are operating best when she hears nothing negative, we shouldn't be surprised to find her factory managers spending a good part of their time ensuring that negative information doesn't reach the division manager. Similarly, if a university faculty dean believes that a lecturer should never fail more than 10 per cent of her students—to fail more reflects on the lecturer's ability to teach—we should expect that lecturers who want to receive favourable evaluations would decide not to fail too many students.

Reward systems
The organisation's reward system influences decision makers by suggesting to them what choices are preferable in terms of personal payoff. For example, if the organisation rewards risk aversion,

managers are more likely to make conservative decisions. From the 1950s through to the mid-1980s, General Motors-Holden (GM-H) consistently gave out promotions and bonuses to managers who kept a low profile, avoided controversy and were good team players. The result was that GM-H managers became very adept at dodging tough issues and passing controversial decisions on to committees.

Formal regulations

David Jones, a shift manager at a fast-food restaurant in Sydney, describes constraints he faces on his job: 'I've got rules and regulations covering almost every decision I make—from how to make a pizza or burger to how often I need to clean the restrooms. My job doesn't come with much freedom of choice.'

David's situation isn't unique. All but the smallest of organisations create rules, policies, procedures and other formalised regulations in order to standardise the behaviour of their members. By pre-determining decisions, organisations are able to get individuals to achieve high levels of performance without paying for the years of experience that would be necessary in the absence of regulations. And, of course, in so doing, they limit the decision maker's choices.

System-imposed time constraints

Organisations impose deadlines on decisions. For example, department budgets need to be completed by next Friday. Or the report on new-product development has to be ready for the executive committee to review by the first of the month. A host of decisions must be made quickly in order to stay ahead of the competition and keep customers satisfied. And almost all important decisions come with explicit deadlines. These conditions create time pressures on decision makers and often make it difficult, if not impossible, to gather all the information they might like to have before making a final choice.

Historical precedents

Decisions aren't made in a vacuum. They have a context. In fact, individual decisions are more accurately characterised as points in a stream of decisions.

Decisions made in the past are ghosts that continually haunt current choices. For example, commitments made in the past constrain current options. To use a social situation as an example, the decision you might make after meeting 'Mr or Ms Right' is more complicated if you're already married than if you're single. Prior commitments—in this case, having chosen to get married previously—constrain your options. Government budget decisions also offer an illustration of our point. It's common knowledge that the largest determining factor of the size of any given year's budget is last year's budget.[49] Choices made today, therefore, are largely a result of choices made over a number of years.

David Jones, has very little opportunity for making decisions—everything from how the food is prepared to cleanliness standards are rigidly determined by the company. Such rigid constraints guarantee quality compliance but reduce individual motivation.

CULTURAL DIFFERENCES

The rational model makes no acknowledgment of cultural differences. But Arabs, for example, don't necessarily make decisions the same way that Australians do. Therefore, we need to recognise that the cultural background of the decision maker can have significant influence on his or her selection of problems, depth of analysis, the importance placed on logic and rationality, or whether organisational decisions should be made autocratically by an individual manager or collectively in groups.[50]

Cultures, for example, differ in terms of time orientation, the importance of rationality, their belief in the ability of people to solve problems, and their preference for collective decision making. Differences in time orientation help us to understand why managers in Egypt will make decisions at a much slower and more deliberate pace than their Australian counterparts. Whereas rationality is valued in Australia, that's not true everywhere in the world. An Australian manager might make an important decision intuitively, but he or she knows that it's important to appear to proceed in a rational fashion. This is because rationality is highly valued in the West. In countries such as Iran, where rationality isn't deified, efforts to appear rational aren't necessary. Certainly from a Western perspective, Saddam Hussein's handling of the Western powers prior to the 2003 war certainly seemed to defy all rational logic!

Some cultures emphasise solving problems, while others focus on accepting situations as they are. Australia and New Zealand fall in the former category, while Thailand and Indonesia are examples of cultures that fall into the latter category. Because problem-solving managers believe they can and should change situations to their benefit, Australian managers might identify a problem long before their Thai or Indonesian counterparts would choose to recognise it as such.

Decision making by Japanese managers is much more group-oriented than in Australia. The Japanese value conformity and cooperation. So, before Japanese CEOs make an important decision, they collect a large amount of information, which is then used in consensus-forming group decisions.

What About Ethics in Decision Making?

No contemporary discussion of decision making would be complete without inclusion of ethics, because ethical considerations should be an important criterion in organisational decision making. In this final section, we present three different ways to frame decisions ethically and look at how ethical standards vary across national cultures.

THREE ETHICAL DECISION CRITERIA

An individual can use three different criteria in making ethical choices.[51] The first is the *utilitarian* criterion, in which decisions are made solely on the basis of their outcomes or consequences. The goal of **utilitarianism** is to provide the greatest good for the greatest number. This view tends to dominate business decision making. It is consistent with goals such as efficiency, productivity and high profits. By maximising profits, for example, a business executive at a national Australian bank can argue that he is securing the greatest good for the greatest number—as he hands out dismissal notices to 35 per cent of his employees.

Another ethical criterion is to focus on *rights*. This calls on individuals to make decisions consistent with fundamental liberties and privileges as set forth in documents such as the Constitution. An emphasis on rights in decision making means respecting and protecting the basic rights of individuals, such as the right to privacy, to free speech and to due process. For example, use of this criterion would protect **whistle blowers**—individuals who report unethical or illegal practices by their employer to outsiders—when they reveal unethical practices by their organisation to the press or government agencies on the grounds of their right to free speech.

utilitarianism
Decisions are made to provide the greatest good for the greatest number.

whistle blowers
Individuals who report unethical practices by their employer to outsiders.

A third criterion is to focus on *justice*. This requires individuals to impose and enforce rules fairly and impartially so that there is an equitable distribution of benefits and costs. Union members typically favour this view. It justifies paying people the same wage for a given job, regardless of performance differences, and using seniority as the primary determination in making layoff decisions.

Each of these three criteria has advantages and liabilities. A focus on utilitarianism promotes efficiency and productivity, but it can result in ignoring the rights of some individuals, particularly those with minority representation in the organisation. The use of rights as a criterion protects individuals from injury and is consistent with freedom and privacy, but it can create an overly legalistic work environment that hinders productivity and efficiency. A focus on justice protects the interests of the under-represented and less powerful, but it can encourage a sense of entitlement that reduces risk taking, innovation and productivity.

Decision makers, particularly in for-profit organisations, tend to feel safe and comfortable when they use utilitarianism. A lot of questionable actions can be justified when framed as being in the best interests of 'the organisation' and shareholders. But many critics of business decision makers argue that this perspective needs to change.[52] Increased concern in society about individual rights and social justice suggests the need for managers to develop ethical standards based on non-utilitarian criteria. This presents a solid challenge to today's managers, because making decisions using criteria such as individual rights and social justice involves far more ambiguities than using utilitarian criteria such as effects on efficiency and profits. This helps to explain why managers are increasingly criticised for their actions. Raising prices, selling products with questionable effects on consumer health, closing down inefficient plants, laying off large numbers of employees, moving production overseas to cut costs, and similar decisions can be justified in utilitarian terms. But that may no longer be the single criterion by which good decisions should be judged.

Myth *or* Science?

'Ethical people don't do unethical things'

This statement is mostly true. People with high ethical standards are less likely to engage in unethical practices, even in organisations or situations in which there are strong pressures to conform.

The essential issue that this statement addresses is whether ethical behaviour is more a function of the individual or the situational context. The evidence indicates that people with high ethical principles will follow them in spite of what others do or the dictates of organisational norms.[53] But when an individual's ethical and moral development are not of the highest level, he or she is more likely to be influenced by strong cultures. This is true even when those cultures encourage questionable practices.

Because ethical people essentially avoid unethical practices, managers should be encouraged to screen job candidates (through testing and background investigations) to determine their ethical standards. By seeking out people with integrity and strong ethical principles, the organisation increases the likelihood that employees will act ethically. Of course, unethical practices can be further minimised by providing individuals with a supportive work climate.[54] This would include clear job descriptions, a written code of ethics, positive management role models, the evaluating and rewarding of means as well as ends, and a culture that encourages individuals to openly challenge questionable practices.

ETHICS AND NATIONAL CULTURE

What is seen as an ethical decision in India may not be seen as such in Australia. The reason is that there are no global ethical standards.[55] Contrasts between Asia and the West provide an illustration.[56] Because bribery is commonplace in some Asian countries such as China, an Australian working in Asia might face the dilemma, 'Should I pay a bribe to secure business if it is an accepted part of that country's culture?' Or how about this for a shock? A manager of a large multinational company operating in China caught an employee stealing. Following company policy, she fired him and turned him over to the local authorities. Later, she was horrified to learn that the employee had been summarily executed by firing squad.[57]

Although ethical standards may seem ambiguous in the West, criteria defining right and wrong are actually much clearer in the West than in Asia. Few issues are black and white there; most are grey. The need for global organisations to establish ethical principles for decision makers in countries such as India and China, and modifying them to reflect cultural norms, may be critical if high standards are to be upheld and consistent practices achieved.

Summary and Implications for Managers

Perception

Individuals behave in a given manner based not on the way their external environment actually is but, rather, on what they see or believe it to be. It is the employee's perception of a situation that becomes the basis for his or her behaviour. Whether or not a job is actually interesting or challenging is irrelevant. Whether or not a manager successfully plans and organises the work of his or her employees and actually helps them to structure their work more efficiently and effectively is far less important than how employees perceive the manager's efforts. Similarly, issues such as fair pay for work performed, the validity of performance appraisals, and the adequacy of working conditions are not judged by employees in a way that ensures common perceptions; nor can we be assured that individuals will interpret conditions about their jobs in a favourable light. Therefore, to be able to influence productivity, it's necessary to assess how employees perceive their jobs.

Absenteeism, turnover and job satisfaction are also reactions to the individual's perceptions. Dissatisfaction with working conditions, or the belief that there is a lack of promotion opportunities in the organisation, are judgments based on attempts to make some meaning out of one's job. The employee's conclusion that a job is good or bad is an interpretation. Managers must spend time understanding how each individual interprets reality and, when there is a significant difference between what is seen and what exists, try to eliminate the distortions. Failure to deal with the differences when individuals perceive the job in negative terms will result in increased absenteeism and turnover and lower job satisfaction.

Individual decision making

Individuals think and reason before they act. It is because of this that an understanding of how people make decisions can be helpful for explaining and predicting their behaviour.

Under some decision situations, people follow the rational decision-making model. But for most people, and most non-routine decisions, this is probably more the exception than the rule. Few important decisions are simple or unambiguous enough for the rational model's assumptions to apply. So we find individuals looking for solutions that satisfice rather than optimise, injecting biases and prejudices into the decision process, and relying on intuition.

Given the evidence we've described on how decisions are actually made in organisations, what can managers do to improve their decision making? We offer five suggestions.

First, analyse the situation. Adjust your decision-making style to the national culture you are operating in and to the criteria your organisation evaluates and rewards. For example, if you are in a country that doesn't value rationality, don't feel compelled to follow the rational decision-making model or even to try to make your decisions appear rational. Similarly, organisations differ in terms of the importance they place on risk, the use of groups, and the like. Adjust your decision style to ensure that it's compatible with the organisation's culture.

Second, be aware of biases. We all bring biases to the decisions we make. If you understand the biases influencing your judgment, you can begin to change the way you make decisions to reduce those biases.

Third, combine rational analysis with intuition. These are not conflicting approaches to decision making. By using both, you can actually improve your decision-making effectiveness. As you gain managerial experience, you should feel increasingly confident in imposing your intuitive processes on top of your rational analysis.

Fourth, don't assume that your specific decision style is appropriate for every job. Just as organisations differ, so too do jobs within organisations. And your effectiveness as a decision maker will increase if you match your decision style to the requirements of the job. For example, if your decision-making style is directive, you'll be more effective working with people whose jobs require quick action. This style might match well with managing stockbrokers. An analytic style, on the other hand, might be more effective in managing accountants, market researchers or financial analysts.

Finally, try to enhance your creativity. Overtly look for novel solutions to problems, attempt to see problems in new ways, and use analogies. In addition, try to remove work and organisational barriers that might impede your creativity.

Point

WHEN HIRING EMPLOYEES, EMPHASISE THE POSITIVE

Hiring new employees requires managers to become salespeople. They have to emphasise the positive, even if it means failing to mention the negative aspects in the job. While there is a real risk of setting unrealistic expectations about the organisation and about the specific job, that's a risk managers have to take. As in dealing with any sales person, it is the job applicant's responsibility to follow the dictum *caveat emptor*—let the buyer beware!

Why should managers emphasise the positive when discussing a job with a prospective candidate? They have no choice. First, there is a dwindling supply of qualified applicants for many job vacancies; and second, this approach is necessary to meet the competition.

Downsizing and company layoffs have received a lot of attention in recent years. What has often been overlooked in this process is the growing shortage of qualified applicants for literally millions of jobs. Through the foreseeable future, managers will find it increasingly difficult to get qualified people who can fill jobs such as legal secretary, nurse, accountant, maintenance mechanic, computer-repair specialist, software programmer, social worker, physical therapist, environmental engineer and telecommunications specialist. But managers will also find it harder to get qualified people to fill entry-level, minimum-wage jobs. There may be no shortage of physical bodies, but finding individuals who can read, write, perform basic mathematical calculations and have the proper work habits to effectively perform these jobs isn't so easy. There is a growing gap between the skills employees have and the skills employers require. So, managers need to *sell* jobs to the limited pool of applicants. And this means presenting the job and the organisation in the most favourable light possible.

Another reason management is forced to emphasise the positive with job candidates is that this is what the competition is doing. Other employers also face a limited applicant pool. As a result, to get people to join their organisations, they are forced to put a positive 'spin' on their descriptions of their organisations and the jobs they seek to fill. In this competitive environment, any employer who presents jobs realistically to applicants— that is, openly provides the negative aspects of a job along with the positive—risks losing many of the most desirable candidates.

Counterpoint

Regardless of labour-market conditions, managers who treat the recruiting and hiring of candidates as if the applicants must be sold on the job and exposed to only positive aspects set themselves up to have a workforce that is dissatisfied and prone to high turnover.[a]

Every applicant acquires, during the selection process, a set of expectations about the organisation and about the specific job he or she hopes to be offered. When the information an applicant receives is excessively inflated, a number of things happen that have potentially negative effects on the organisation. First, mismatched applicants who will probably become dissatisfied with the job and soon quit are less likely to select themselves out of the search process. Second, the absence of negative information builds unrealistic expectations. And these unrealistic expectations often lead to premature resignations. Third, new hires are prone to become disillusioned and less committed to the organisation when they come face-to-face with the negatives in the job. Employees who feel they were tricked or misled during the hiring process are unlikely to be satisfied employees.

To increase job satisfaction among employees and reduce turnover, applicants should be given a realistic job preview—provided both unfavourable and favourable information—before an offer is made. For example, in addition to positive comments, the candidate might be told that there are limited opportunities to talk with fellow employees during work hours, or that erratic fluctuations in workloads create considerable stress on employees during rush periods.

Research indicates that applicants who have been given a realistic job preview hold lower and more realistic expectations about the job they will be doing and are better prepared for coping with the job and its frustrating elements. The result is fewer unexpected resignations by new employees. Remember that retaining qualified people is as critical as hiring them in the first place. Presenting only the positive aspects of a job to a recruit may initially entice him or her to join the organisation, but it may be a marriage that both parties will quickly regret.

Sources: [a] Information in this argument comes from J. M. Phillips, 'Effects of Realistic Job Previews on Multiple Organizational Outcomes: A Meta-Analysis', *Academy of Management Journal*, December 1998, pp. 673–90; and J. A. Breaugh and M. Starke, 'Research on Employee Recruitment: So Many Studies, So Many Remaining Questions', *Journal of Management*, vol. 26, no. 3, 2000, pp. 415–17.

For Discussion

1. Define *perception*. How might the differences in the experiences of students and lecturers affect their perceptions of students' written work and class comments?
2. What is attribution theory? If an employee does an unsatisfactory job on an assigned project, explain the attribution process that this person's manager will use to form judgments about this employee's job performance.
3. How are our perceptions of our own actions different from our perceptions of the actions of others?
4. How does selectivity affect perception? Give an example of how selectivity can create perceptual distortion.
5. What is stereotyping? Give an example of how stereotyping can create perceptual distortion.
6. Give some positive results of using shortcuts when judging others.
7. What is the rational decision-making model? Under what conditions is it applicable?
8. 'For the most part, individual decision making in organisations is an irrational process.' Do you agree or disagree? Discuss.
9. Describe organisational factors that might constrain decision makers.
10. What role does intuition play in effective decision making? When is it likely to be most effective?
11. Are unethical decisions more a function of the individual decision maker or the decision maker's work environment? Explain.

Exercises

Exercise 5a
BIASES IN DECISION MAKING

Step 1: Answer each of the following problems.
1. The following ten companies were ranked by *Business Review Weekly* magazine to be among the 100 largest Australian-based firms according to sales volume for 2001:
   Group A: Harvey Norman, Woolworths, PBL (Publishing & Broadcasting Limited), Westfield Holdings, Foster's Group
   Group B: Cochlear, Mayne, National Australia Bank, Brambles Industries, Telstra
   Which group of five organisations listed (A or B) had the larger total sales volume? By what percentage (10 per cent, 50 per cent, 100 per cent or ? per cent) do you think the higher group's sales exceeded the lower group's?
2. The best student in an introductory MBA class this past semester at Queensland University of Technology writes poetry and is rather shy and small in stature. What was the student's undergraduate major: Chinese studies or psychology?
3. Which of the following causes more deaths in Australia each year:
   (a) Stomach cancer?
   (b) Motor vehicle accidents?
4. Which would you choose:
   (a) A sure gain of $240?
   (b) A 25 per cent chance of winning $100,000 and a 75 per cent chance of winning nothing?

5. Which would you choose:
   (a) A sure loss of $750?
   (b) A 75 per cent chance of losing $1,000 and a 25 per cent chance of losing nothing.
6. Which would you choose:
   (a) A sure loss of $3,000?
   (b) An 80 per cent chance of losing $4,000 and a 20 per cent chance of losing nothing?

Step 2: Form groups of three to five people. Compare your answers. Explain why you chose the answers that you did.

Step 3: Your lecturer will give you the correct answers to the first three problems.

Now discuss the accuracy of your decisions, the biases evident in the decisions you reached, and how you might improve your decision making to make it more accurate.

Source: These problems are based on examples provided in M. H. Bazerman, *Judgment in Managerial Decision Making*, 3rd ed. (New York: Wiley, 1994).

Exercise 5b
FIVE ETHICAL DECISIONS: WHAT WOULD YOU DO?

Assume you are a middle manager in a large Australian company with about a thousand employees. How would you respond to each of the following situations?

1. You are negotiating a contract with a potentially very large customer whose representative has hinted that you could almost certainly be assured of getting his business if you gave him and his wife an all-expenses-paid two-week holiday in Hong Kong. You know the representative's employer wouldn't approve of such a 'payoff', but you have the discretion to authorise such expenditure. What would you do?
2. You have the opportunity to steal $100,000 from your company with absolute certainty that you wouldn't be detected or caught. Would you do it?
3. Your company policy on reimbursement for meals while travelling on company business is that you will be repaid for your out-of-pocket costs, not to exceed $60 a day. You don't need receipts for these expenses—the company will take your word. When travelling, you tend to eat at fast-food places and rarely spend in excess of $15 a day. Most of your peers put in reimbursement requests in the range of $45 to $50 a day regardless of what their actual expenses are. How much would you request for your meal reimbursements?
4. Another executive, who is part of a small planning team in which you're a member, frequently has the smell of alcohol on his breath. You have noticed that his work hasn't been up to standard lately and is hurting your team's performance. This executive happens to be the son-in-law of the company's owner and is held in very high regard by the owner. What would you do?
5. You have discovered that one of your closest friends at work has stolen a large sum of money from the company. Would you: (a) Do nothing? (b) Go directly to an executive to report the incident before talking about it with the offender? (c) Confront the individual before taking action? (d) Make contact with the individual with the goal of persuading that person to return the money?

Case Study 5

John Neill at Unipart

Whereas most part suppliers for the United Kingdom's automobile industry are struggling, one company is doing just fine—Unipart. This 2.3 billion euro company has done well largely because of the decisions made by its CEO, John Neill.

In 1974, at the youthful age of 29, John Neill was made managing director of the Unipart division of British Leyland (BL). He immediately began to ruffle the feathers of conservative BL executives by developing innovative marketing campaigns and focusing company attention on the parts business (in contrast to its cars and trucks). He increased the division's marketing budget sixfold, created a retail shop program, altered the packaging, and began promoting the division's parts on television. His 'parts first' pitch didn't go down well with his bosses, who saw it as an attack on the viability of BL itself. But it was too late for BL's top management to do much about it. Neill had created a viable business, while the rest of the company (which later became part of the Rover Group) laboured along, losing market share every year.

Almost from the beginning, Neill envisioned making Unipart independent from BL. In 1987, he did just that. He negotiated an 89.5 million euro management buy-out of Unipart from BL. He then immediately began taking actions that would allow Unipart to stand on its own two feet. 'We knew the future would be worse,' Neill recalls, 'because today's market share was smaller than yesterday's. So the parts business would go down unless we did something dramatically different.' That 'something' was to move away from providing original parts for Rover. Instead, Unipart would commit to creating a strong consumer brand built around replacement parts. Today, Unipart has become a highly recognisable consumer brand in the United Kingdom. It has also diversified into a range of other businesses. Producing and selling automotive parts is still the company's main activity, but it also runs a successful warehouse and a logistics business, and has created an Internet trading platform.

In 1987, when Unipart became independent, sales to Rover represented 90 per cent of its business. It's now down to 3 per cent. No longer are Unipart's fortunes tied singularly to Rover. In fact, one of Unipart's most profitable current businesses is running Jaguar's entire parts operation on a for-fee basis.

Despite Neill's success since the buy-out, Unipart faces tough times ahead. The UK auto industry suffers from massive over-capacity. Intensive downward pricing pressure on suppliers is likely to eat away at Unipart's profits. In response, Neill has expanded Unipart's logistic business by paying 292 million euros for automotive parts distributor, Partco. This acquisition makes Unipart the biggest automotive parts distributor in the United Kingdom. Neill is also diversifying beyond Unipart's automotive parts roots, especially on the e-commerce front.

Questions

1. John Neill isn't smart—he's just damned lucky. Do you agree or disagree? Explain.
2. Did intuition play a role in Neill's decisions? Discuss.
3. Contrast the main strategic decisions at Unipart and British Leyland.
4. Do you think John Neill would have been equally successful if, back in 1987, he had been made head of BL? Explain.

Source: Based on T. Rubython and A. Sibillin, 'The Reality Man', *EuroBusiness*, October 2000, pp. 76–78.

| Web Workout

1. <www.p-p.com.au/toolsofthetrade.asp> is a website for an organisation that relies on changing perceptions. What perceptions are they getting paid to change?
2. What role does self-serving bias play in teachers' attributions in the study undertaken at six schools in New South Wales in the research study reported at <http://education.curtin.edu.au/iier/iier10/mccormick.html>? How might managers alter this self-serving bias in a productive manner?

3. Read the various cases and decisions at <www.tved.net.au/ten_new/subscribers/snd_vic/back_papers/a0004vi2.htm>. One feature most have in common is differences in perceptions. How have these differences in perceptions led to decisions that came to be challenged in the courts? What practical steps could be taken by organisations to reduce the risk of litigation and poor decision making?

4. What factors influence intuitive decision making? How important is it the higher one goes in the organisational ladder? See if the following site answers these questions: <www.google.com.au/search?q=cache:jsaYyG5Ua-sJ:www.thehindubusinessline.com/businessline/mentor/stories/2003082500431100.htm+Australia+%22Intuitive+decision+making%22+-agency+-jobs&hl=en&ie=UTF-8>.

5. Discuss the cross-cultural challenges with respect to ethics and decision making raised in the article at <http://hsb.baylor.edu/ramsower/ais.ac.96/papers/cohen.htm>.

KSS Program

KNOW THE CONCEPTS   SELF-AWARENESS   SKILLS APPLICATIONS

Creative problem-solving skills

After you have read this chapter, take Self-Assessment #8 (How Creative Am I?) on your enclosed CD-Rom and complete the skill-building module entitled 'Creative Problem Solving' on page 635.

NOTES

1. Based on Anon, 'Australia on the Verge of War Decision', *The Age*, 14 March 2003 (<www.theage.com.au/articles/2003/03/14/1047583698969.html>); H. Williams, 'Howard under Fire over Iraq', *CNN.com/WORLD*, 17 July 2003 (<www.cnn.com/2003/WORLD/asiapcf/07/17/sprj.irq.australia.wmd/>); and J. Howard, 'The Prime Minister's Statement to the Parliament on Iraq, May 14 2003' (<www.pm.gov.au/iraq/index.cfm>).

2. P. Toulson and M. Smith, 'The Study of Beliefs About Work and Their Contribution to Personnel Practices', paper presented to the Institute of Personnel Management (New Zealand) conference, November 1989; and V. J. Twinn, 'The Kiwi and the Work Ethic', *New Zealand Journal of Industrial Relations*, vol. 2, 1977, pp. 97–100.

3. D. C. McClelland and J. W. Atkinson, 'The Projective Expression of Needs; The Effect of Different Intensities of the Hunger Drive on Perception', *Journal of Psychology*, vol. 25, 1948, pp. 205–22.

4. B. M. Thompson, G. N. Hearn and M. J. Collins, 'Patient Perceptions of Health Professional Interpersonal Skills', *Australian Psychologist*, vol. 27, no. 2, pp. 91–95.

5. Ibid, p. 93.

6. H. H. Kelley, 'Attribution in Social Interaction', in E. Jones, et al (eds), *Attribution: Perceiving the Causes of Behavior* (Morristown, NJ: General Learning Press, 1972).

7. See L. Ross, 'The Intuitive Psychologist and His Shortcomings', in L. Berkowitz (ed.), *Advances in Experimental Social Psychology*, vol. 10 (Orlando, FL: Academic Press, 1977), pp. 174–220; and A. G. Miller and T. Lawson, 'The Effect of an Informational Option on the Fundamental Attribution Error', *Personality and Social Psychology Bulletin*, June 1989, pp. 194–204.

8. See, for example, G. Johns, 'A Multi-Level Theory of Self-Serving Behavior in and by Organizations', in R. I. Sutton and B. M. Staw (eds), *Research in Organizational Behavior*, vol. 21 (Stamford, CT: JAI Press, 1999), pp. 1–38; and N. Epley and D. Dunning, 'Feeling "Holier Than Thou": Are Self-Serving Assessments Produced by Errors in Self- or Social Prediction?', *Journal of Personality and Social Psychology*, December 2000, pp. 861–75.

9. See, for example, G. R. Semin, 'A Gloss on Attribution Theory', *British Journal of Social and Clinical Psychology*, November 1980, pp. 291–30; and M. W. Morris and K. Peng, 'Culture and Cause: American and Chinese Attributions for Social and Physical Events', *Journal of Personality and Social Psychology*, December 1994, pp. 949–71.

10. S. Nam, 'Cultural and Managerial Attributions for Group Performance', unpublished doctoral dissertation; University of Oregon. Cited in R. M. Steers, S. J. Bischoff and L. H. Higgins, 'Cross-Cultural Management Research', *Journal of Management Inquiry*, December 1992, pp. 325–26.

11. D. C. Dearborn and H. A. Simon, 'Selective Perception: A Note on the Departmental Identification of Executives', *Sociometry*, June 1958, pp. 140–44. Some of the conclusions in this classic study have recently been challenged in J. Walsh, 'Selectivity and Selective Perception: An Investigation of Managers' Belief Structures and Information Processing', *Academy of Management Journal*, December 1988, pp. 873–96; M. J. Waller, G. Huber and W. H. Glick, 'Functional Background as a Determinant of Executives' Selective Perception', *Academy*

of Management Journal, August 1995, pp. 943–74; and J. M. Beyer, P. Chattopadhyay, E. George, W. H. Glick, D. T. Ogilvie and D. Pugliese, 'The Selective Perception of Managers Revisited', *Academy of Management Journal*, June 1997, pp. 716–37.

12. See K. R. Murphy and R. L. Anhalt, 'Is Halo a Property of the Rater, the Ratees, or the Specific Behavior Observed?', *Journal of Applied Psychology*, June 1992, pp. 494–500; and K. R. Murphy, R. A. Jako and R. L. Anhalt, 'Nature and Consequences of Halo Error: A Critical Analysis', *Journal of Applied Psychology*, April 1993, pp. 218–25.

13. S. E. Asch, 'Forming Impressions of Personality', *Journal of Abnormal and Social Psychology*, July 1946, pp. 258–90.

14. J. S. Bruner and R. Tagiuri, 'The Perception of People', in E. Lindzey (ed.), *Handbook of Social Psychology* (Reading, MA: Addison-Wesley, 1954), p. 641.

15. J. L. Hilton and W. von Hippel, 'Stereotypes', in J. T. Spence, J. M. Darley and D. J. Foss (eds), *Annual Review of Psychology*, vol. 47 (Palo Alto, CA: Annual Reviews Inc., 1996), pp. 237–71.

16. See, for example, C. M. Judd and B. Park, 'Definition and Assessment of Accuracy in Social Stereotypes', *Psychological Review*, January 1993, pp. 109–28.

17. See, for example, S. T. Fiske, D. N. Beroff, E. Borgida, K. Deaux and M. E. Heilman, 'Use of Sex Stereotyping Research in Price Waterhouse vs. Hopkins', *American Psychologist*, October 1991, pp. 1049–60; G. N. Powell, 'The Good Manager: Business Students' Stereotypes of Japanese Managers versus Stereotypes of American Managers', *Group & Organizational Management*, March 1992, pp. 44–56; and W. C. K. Chiu, A. W. Chan, E. Snape and T. Redman, 'Age Stereotypes and Discriminatory Attitudes Towards Older Workers: An East–West Comparison', *Human Relations*, May 2001, pp. 629–61.

18. See, for example, E. C. Webster, *Decision Making in the Employment Interview* (Montreal: McGill University, Industrial Relations Center, 1964).

19. See, for example, D. Eden, *Pygmalion in Management* (Lexington, MA: Lexington, 1990); D. Eden, 'Leadership and Expectations: Pygmalion Effects and Other Self-Fulfilling Prophecies', *Leadership Quarterly*, Winter 1992, pp. 271–305; D. B. McNatt, 'Ancient Pygmalion Joins Contemporary Management: A Meta-Analysis of the Result', *Journal of Applied Psychology*, April 2000, pp. 314–22; and O. B. Davidson and D. Eden, 'Remedial Self-Fulfilling Prophecy: Two Field Experiments to Prevent Golem Effects Among Disadvantaged Women', *Journal of Applied Psychology*, June 2000, pp. 386–98.

20. D. Eden and A. B. Shani, 'Pygmalion Goes to Boot Camp: Expectancy, Leadership, and Trainee Performance', *Journal of Applied Psychology*, April 1982, pp. 194–99.

21. See, for example, R. D. Bretz, Jr, G. T. Milkovich and W. Read, 'The Current State of Performance Appraisal Research and Practice: Concerns, Directions, and Implications', *Journal of Management*, June 1992, pp. 323–24; and P. M. Swiercz, M. L. Icenogle, N. B. Bryan and R. W. Renn, 'Do Perceptions of Performance Appraisal Fairness Predict Employee Attitudes and Performance?', in D. P. Moore (ed.), *Proceedings of the Academy of Management* (Atlanta, GA: Academy of Management, 1993), pp. 304–08.

22. R. Sanders, *The Executive Decisionmaking Process: Identifying Problems and Assessing Outcomes* (Westport, CT: Quorum, 1999).

23. See H. A. Simon, 'Rationality in Psychology and Economics', *Journal of Business*, October 1986, pp. 209–24; and A. Langley, 'In Search of Rationality: The Purposes Behind the Use of Formal Analysis in Organizations', *Administrative Science Quarterly*, December 1989, pp. 598–631.

24. For a review of the rational model, see E. F. Harrison, *The Managerial Decision-Making Process*, 5th ed. (Boston: Houghton Mifflin, 1999), pp. 75–102.

25. W. Pounds, 'The Process of Problem Finding', *Industrial Management Review*, Fall 1969, pp. 1–19.

26. J. G. March, *A Primer on Decision Making* (New York: Free Press, 1994), pp. 2–7.

27. T. M. Amabile, 'A Model of Creativity and Innovation in Organizations', in B. M. Staw and L. L. Cummings (eds), *Research in Organizational Behavior*, vol. 10 (Greenwich, CT: JAI Press, 1988), p. 126; and T. M. Amabile, 'Motivating Creativity in Organizations', *California Management Review*, Fall 1997, p. 40.

28. Cited in C. G. Morris, *Psychology: An Introduction*, 9th ed. (Upper Saddle River, NJ: Prentice Hall, 1996), p. 344.

29. This section is based on Amabile, 'Motivating Creativity in Organizations', pp. 42–52.

30. R. W. Woodman, J. E. Sawyer and R. W. Griffin, 'Toward a Theory of Organizational Creativity', *Academy of Management Review*, April 1993, p. 298.

31. W. J. J. Gordon, *Synectics* (New York: Harper & Row, 1961).

32. See T. M. Amabile, *KEYS: Assessing the Climate for Creativity* (Greensboro, NC: Center for Creative Leadership, 1995).

33. D. L. Rados, 'Selection and Evaluation of Alternatives in Repetitive Decision Making', *Administrative Science Quarterly*, June 1972, pp. 196–206; and G. Klein, *Sources of Power: How People Make Decisions* (Cambridge, MA: MIT Press, 1998).

34. M. Bazerman, *Judgment in Managerial Decision Making*, 3rd ed. (New York: Wiley, 1994), p. 5.

35. See, for example, L. R. Beach, *The Psychology of Decision Making* (Thousand Oaks, CA: Sage, 1997).

36. See H. A. Simon, *Administrative Behavior*, 4th ed. (New York: Free Press, 1997); and M. Augier, 'Simon Says: Bounded Rationality Matters', *Journal of Management Inquiry*, September 2001, pp. 268–75.

37. W. H. Agor (ed.), *Intuition in Organizations* (Newbury Park, CA: Sage Publications, 1989); O. Behling and N. L. Eckel, 'Making Sense out of Intuition', *Academy of Management Executive*, February 1991, pp. 46–47; L. A. Burke and M. K. Miller, 'Taking the Mystery out of Intuitive Decision Making', *Academy of Management Executive*, November 1999, pp. 91–99; and N. Khatri and H. A. Ng, 'The Role of Intuition in Strategic Decision Making', *Human Relations*, January 2000, pp. 57–86.

38. Behling and Eckel, 'Making Sense out of Intuition', pp. 46–54.

39. As described in H. A. Simon, 'Making Management Decisions: The Role of Intuition and Emotion', *Academy of Management Executive*, February 1987, pp. 59–60.

40. Agor, *Intuition in Organizations*, p. 9.

41. Ibid, p. 15.

42. See, for example, M. D. Cohen, J. G. March and J. P. Olsen, 'A Garbage Can Model of Organizational Choice', *Administrative Science Quarterly*, March 1972, pp. 1–25.

43. See J. G. Thompson, *Organizations in Action* (New York: McGraw-Hill, 1967), p. 123.

44. C. E. Lindholm, 'The Science of "Muddling Through"', *Public Administration Review*, Spring 1959, pp. 79–88.

45. A. Tversky and K. Kahneman, 'Judgment under Uncertainty: Heuristics and Biases', *Science*, September 1974, pp. 1124–31; and J. S. Hammond, R. L. Keeney and H. Raiffa, 'The Hidden Traps in Decision Making', *Harvard Business Review*, September–October 1998, pp. 47–58.

46. See B. M. Staw, 'The Escalation of Commitment to a Course of Action', *Academy of Management Review*, October 1981, pp. 577–87; and H. Moon, 'Looking Forward and Looking Back: Integrating Completion and Sunk-Cost Effects within an Escalation-of-Commitment Progress Decision', *Journal of Applied Psychology*, February 2001, pp. 104–13.

47. A. J. Rowe and J. D. Boulgarides, *Managerial Decision Making* (Englewood Cliffs, NJ: Prentice Hall, 1992).

48. M. G. Martinsons, 'Comparing the Decision Styles of American and Asian Business Leaders', paper presented at the 61st annual meeting of the Academy of Management, Washington, DC, August 2001.

49. A. Wildavsky, *The Politics of the Budgetary Process* (Boston: Little Brown, 1964).

50. N. J. Adler, *International Dimensions of Organizational Behavior*, 4th ed. (Cincinnati, OH: Southwestern, 2002), pp. 182–89.

51. G. F. Cavanagh, D. J. Moberg and M. Valasquez, 'The Ethics of Organizational Politics', *Academy of Management Journal*, June 1981, pp. 363–74.

52. See, for example, T. Machan (ed.), *Commerce and Morality* (Totowa, NJ: Rowman and Littlefield, 1988).

53. L. Kohlberg, 'Stage and Sequence: The Cognitive-Developmental Approach to Socialization', in D. A. Goslin (ed.), *Handbook of Socialization Theory and Research* (Chicago: Rand McNally, 1969), pp. 347–480.

54. See, for example, B. Victor and J. B. Cullen, 'The Organizational Bases of Ethical Work Climates', *Administrative Science Quarterly*, March 1988, pp. 101–25; and J. C. Wimbush, 'The Effect of Cognitive Moral Development and Supervisory Influence on Subordinates' Ethical Behavior', *Journal of Business Ethics*, February 1999, pp. 383–95.

55. T. Jackson, 'Cultural Values and Management Ethics: A 10-Nation Study', *Human Relations*, October 2001, pp. 1267–302.

56. W. Chow Hou, 'To Bribe or Not to Bribe?', *Asia, Inc.*, October 1996, p. 104.

57. P. Digh, 'Shades of Gray in the Global Marketplace', *HRMagazine*, April 1997, p. 91.

PHOTO CREDITS

6 CHAPTER

Motivation Concepts

CHAPTER OUTLINE

Defining motivation
Early theories of motivation
Contemporary theories of motivation
Job content and job context theories
Integrating contemporary theories of motivation
Caveat emptor: Motivation theories are culture-bound

LEARNING OBJECTIVES

After studying this chapter, you should be able to:

1. Outline the motivation process
2. Describe Maslow's hierarchy of needs
3. Contrast Theory X and Theory Y
4. Differentiate motivators from hygiene factors
5. List the characteristics that high achievers prefer in a job
6. Summarise the types of goals that increase performance
7. State the impact of under-rewarding employees
8. Clarify the key relationships in expectancy theory
9. Explain how the contemporary theories of motivation complement each other

The secret of joy in work is contained in one word—excellence.
To know how to do something well is to enjoy it.

Pearl Buck

Taking a very hands-on approach has ensured Tim has never been happier.

Recently, 40-year-old Tim Pethick left his $600,000 CEO position with BTLookSmart to start up a natural fruit juice business in New South Wales from scratch.[1] His friends told him he was mad, and his parents were very worried that he had 'thrown his life away'. How could he give up a lucrative job with status, lots of world travel and security, and replace it with the uncertainty of his own business, the Nudie Fruit Juice Company? 'I wanted to do something real, something tangible,' was his reply. Faced with his material needs already covered, a pregnant wife expecting their first child and a desire for a more satisfying way of life where he wasn't away from home 80 per cent of the year, Tim found the change both exciting and very rewarding. And, asked if he would return to his former career if the fruit juice business failed, he said he would never return to the normal career path he left behind at BTLookSmart.[2] So, the simplistic view that money motivates may not be so true after all!

Motivation is one of the most frequently researched topics in OB.[3] In spite of the fact that managers continue to search for innovative ways to motivate their employees and that a significant proportion of today's employees seem to be unmotivated, we actually know a great deal about how to improve employee motivation. In this chapter and the following one, we will review the basics of motivation, assess a number of motivation theories, provide an integrative model that shows how the best of these theories fit together, and offer some guidelines for designing effective motivation programs.

Defining Motivation

What is motivation? Maybe the place to begin is to say what motivation *isn't*. Many people incorrectly view motivation as a personal trait—that is, some have it and others don't. In practice, inexperienced managers often label employees who seem to lack motivation as lazy. Such a label assumes that an individual is always lazy or is lacking in motivation. Our knowledge of motivation tells us that this just isn't true. What we know is that motivation is the result of the interaction of the individual and the situation. Certainly, individuals differ in their basic motivational drive. But the same student who finds it difficult to read a textbook for more than 20 minutes may devour the latest *Harry Potter* book in one weekend. For this student, the change in motivation is driven by the situation. So, as we analyse the concept of motivation, keep in mind that the level of motivation varies both between individuals and within individuals at different times.

motivation
The processes that account for an individual's intensity, direction and persistence of effort towards attaining a goal.

We will define **motivation** as the processes that account for an individual's intensity, direction and persistence of effort towards attaining a goal.[4] While general motivation is concerned with effort towards *any* goal, we will narrow the focus to *organisational* goals in order to reflect our singular interest in work-related behaviour.

The three key elements in our definition are intensity, direction and persistence. *Intensity* is concerned with how hard a person tries. This is the element most of us focus on when we talk about motivation. However, high intensity is unlikely to lead to favourable job-performance outcomes unless the effort is channelled in a *direction* that benefits the organisation. Therefore, we have to consider the quality of effort as well as its intensity. Effort that is directed towards, and consistent with, the organisation's goals is the kind of effort that we should be seeking. Finally, motivation has a *persistence* dimension. This is a measure of how long a person can maintain their effort. Motivated individuals stay with a task long enough to achieve their goal.

Early Theories of Motivation

The 1950s were a fruitful period in the development of motivation concepts. Three specific theories were formulated during this period, which although heavily attacked and now questionable in terms of validity, are probably still the best-known explanations for employee motivation. These are the hierarchy of needs theory, Theories X and Y, and the two-factor theory. As you will see later in this chapter, we have since developed more valid explanations of motivation, but you should know these early theories for at least two reasons: (1) they represent a foundation from which contemporary theories have grown; and (2) practising managers still regularly use these theories and their terminology in explaining employee motivation.

HIERARCHY OF NEEDS THEORY

hierarchy of needs theory
There is a hierarchy of five needs—physiological, safety, social, esteem and self-actualisation; as each need is substantially satisfied, the next need becomes dominant.

It's probably safe to say that the most well-known theory of motivation is Abraham Maslow's **hierarchy of needs**.[5] Maslow hypothesised that within every human being there exists a hierarchy of five needs. These needs are:

1. *Physiological:* Includes hunger, thirst, shelter, sex and other bodily needs.
2. *Safety:* Includes security and protection from physical and emotional harm.
3. *Social:* Includes affection, belongingness, acceptance and friendship.
4. *Esteem:* Includes internal esteem factors such as self-respect, autonomy and achievement; and external esteem factors such as status, recognition and attention.
5. *Self-actualisation:* The drive to become what one is capable of becoming; includes growth, achieving one's potential and self-fulfilment.

self-actualisation
The drive to become what one is capable of becoming.

As each of these needs becomes substantially satisfied, the next need becomes dominant. In terms of Figure 6.1, the individual moves up the steps of the hierarchy. From the standpoint of

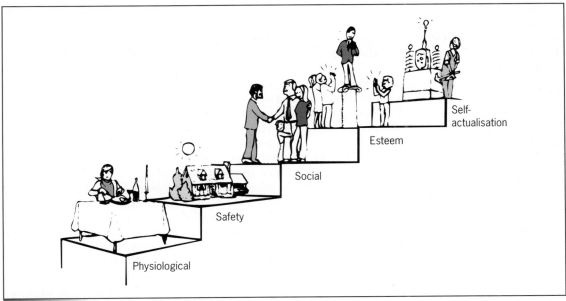

FIGURE 6.1   **Maslow's hierarchy of needs**

motivation, the theory would say that although no need is ever fully gratified, a substantially satisfied need no longer motivates. So, if you want to motivate someone, according to Maslow, you need to understand what level of the hierarchy that person is currently on and focus on satisfying the needs at or above that level.

Maslow separated the five needs into higher and lower orders. Physiological and safety needs were described as **lower-order needs** and social, esteem and self-actualisation as **higher-order needs**. The differentiation between the two orders was made on the premise that higher-order needs are satisfied internally (within the person), whereas lower-order needs are predominantly satisfied externally (by things such as pay, union contracts and tenure).

Maslow's need theory has received wide recognition, particularly among practising managers. This can be attributed to the theory's intuitive logic and ease of understanding. Unfortunately, however, research does not generally validate the theory. Maslow provided no empirical substantiation, and several studies that sought to validate the theory found no support for it.[6]

Old theories, especially ones that are intuitively logical, don't disappear easily. Although the need hierarchy theory and its terminology have remained popular with practising managers, it has minimal empirical support for its predictions.[7] More specifically, there is little evidence that need structures are organised along the dimensions proposed by Maslow, that unsatisfied needs motivate, or that a satisfied need activates movement to a new need level.[8]

THEORY X AND THEORY Y

Douglas McGregor proposed two distinct views of human beings: one basically negative, labelled **Theory X**, and the other basically positive, labelled **Theory Y**.[9] After viewing the way in which managers dealt with employees, McGregor concluded that a manager's view of the nature of human beings is based on a certain grouping of assumptions and that he or she tends to mould his or her behaviour towards employees according to these assumptions.

Under Theory X, the four assumptions held by managers are:

1. Employees inherently dislike work and, whenever possible, will attempt to avoid it.

lower-order needs
Needs that are satisfied externally; physiological and safety needs.

higher-order needs
Needs that are satisfied internally; social, esteem and self-actualisation needs.

LEARNING OBJECTIVE
3
Contrast Theory X and Theory Y

Theory X
The assumption that employees dislike work, are lazy, dislike responsibility and must be coerced to perform.

Theory Y
The assumption that employees like work, are creative, seek responsibility and can exercise self-direction.

2. Since employees dislike work, they must be coerced, controlled or threatened with punishment to achieve goals.
3. Employees will avoid responsibilities and seek formal direction whenever possible.
4. Most workers place security above all other factors associated with work and will display little ambition.

In contrast to these negative views about the nature of human beings, McGregor listed the four positive assumptions that he called Theory Y:

1. Employees can view work as being as natural as rest or play.
2. People will exercise self-direction and self-control if they are committed to the objectives.
3. The average person can learn to accept, even seek, responsibility.
4. The ability to make innovative decisions is widely dispersed throughout the population and is not necessarily the sole province of those in management positions.

What are the motivational implications if you accept McGregor's analysis? The answer is best expressed in the framework presented by Maslow. Theory X assumes that lower-order needs dominate individuals. Theory Y assumes that higher-order needs dominate individuals. McGregor himself held to the belief that Theory Y assumptions were more valid than Theory X. Therefore, he proposed such ideas as participative decision-making, responsible and challenging jobs, and good group relations as approaches that would maximise an employee's job motivation.

Unfortunately, there is no evidence to confirm that either set of assumptions is valid or that accepting Theory Y assumptions and altering one's actions accordingly will lead to more motivated workers. As will become evident later in this chapter, either Theory X or Theory Y assumptions may be appropriate in a particular situation.

LEARNING OBJECTIVE

4

Differentiate motivators from hygiene factors

two-factor theory
Intrinsic factors are related to job satisfaction, while extrinsic factors are associated with dissatisfaction.

TWO-FACTOR THEORY

The **two-factor theory** (sometimes also called *motivation-hygiene theory*) was proposed by the psychologist Frederick Herzberg.[10] In the belief that an individual's relation to work is basic and that one's attitude towards work can very well determine success or failure, Herzberg investigated the question, 'What do people want from their jobs?' He asked people to describe, in detail,

Myth *or* Science?

'People are inherently lazy'

This statement is false on two levels. *All* people are not inherently lazy; and 'laziness' is more a function of the situation than an inherent individual characteristic.

If this statement is meant to imply that *all* people are inherently lazy, the evidence strongly indicates the contrary.[11] Many people today suffer from the opposite affliction—they are overly busy, overworked and suffer from overexertion. Whether externally motivated or internally driven, a good portion of the labour force is anything *but* lazy.

Managers frequently draw the conclusion that people are lazy from watching some of their employees, who may be lazy at work. But these same employees are often quite industrious in one or more activities *off* the job. People's need structures differ.[12] As Figure 6.2 illustrates, evidence indicates that work needs differ by gender, age, income level, job type, and level in the organisation.

Unfortunately for employers, work often ranks low in its ability to satisfy individual needs. So, the same employee who shirks responsibility on the job may work obsessively on reconditioning an antique car, maintaining an award-winning garden, perfecting bowling skills, or selling Amway products on weekends. Very few people are perpetually lazy. They merely differ in terms of the activities they most enjoy doing. And because work isn't important to everyone, they may *appear* to be lazy.

	All Employees	Sex		Age				Income Level				Job Type				Organisation Level		
		Men	Women	Under 30	31–40	41–50	Over 50	Under US$25,000	US$25,001–US$40,000	US$40,001–US$50,000	Over US$50,000	Blue-collar Unskilled	Blue-collar Skilled	White-collar Unskilled	White-collar Skilled	Lower Non-supervisory	Middle Non-supervisory	Higher Non-supervisory
Interesting work	1	1	2	4	2	3	1	5	2	1	1	2	1	1	2	3	1	1
Full appreciation of work done	2	2	1	5	3	2	2	4	3	3	2	1	6	3	1	4	2	2
Feeling of being in on things	3	3	3	6	4	1	3	6	1	2	4	5	2	5	4	5	3	3
Job security	4	5	4	2	1	4	7	2	4	4	3	4	3	7	5	2	4	6
Good wages	5	4	5	1	5	5	8	1	5	6	8	3	4	6	6	1	6	8
Promotion and growth in organisation	6	6	6	3	6	8	9	3	6	5	7	6	5	4	3	6	5	5
Good working conditions	7	7	10	7	7	7	4	8	7	7	6	9	7	2	7	7	7	4
Personal loyalty to employees	8	8	8	9	9	6	5	7	8	8	5	8	9	9	8	8	8	7
Tactful discipline	9	9	9	8	10	9	10	10	9	9	10	7	10	10	9	9	9	10
Sympathetic help with personal problems	10	10	7	10	8	10	6	9	10	10	9	10	8	8	10	10	10	9

FIGURE 6.2 **What workers want, ranked by subgroups***

* Ranked from 1 (highest) to 10 (lowest).

Source: Courtesy of Prof. K. A. Kovach, George Mason University. Results are from a study of 1,000 employees conducted in 1995.

situations in which they felt exceptionally *good* or *bad* about their jobs. These responses were then tabulated and categorised.

From the categorised responses, Herzberg concluded that the replies people gave when they felt good about their jobs were significantly different from the replies given when they felt bad. As seen in Figure 6.3, certain characteristics tend to be consistently related to job satisfaction and others to job dissatisfaction. Intrinsic factors, such as advancement, recognition, responsibility and achievement, seem to be related to job satisfaction. Respondents who felt good about their work tended to attribute these factors to themselves. On the other hand, dissatisfied respondents tended to cite extrinsic factors, such as supervision, pay, company policies and working conditions.

The data suggest, said Herzberg, that the opposite of satisfaction isn't dissatisfaction, as was traditionally believed. Removing dissatisfying characteristics from a job doesn't necessarily make the job satisfying. As illustrated in Figure 6.4, Herzberg proposed that his findings indicated the existence of a dual continuum: The opposite of 'Satisfaction' is 'No Satisfaction', and the opposite of 'Dissatisfaction' is 'No Dissatisfaction'.

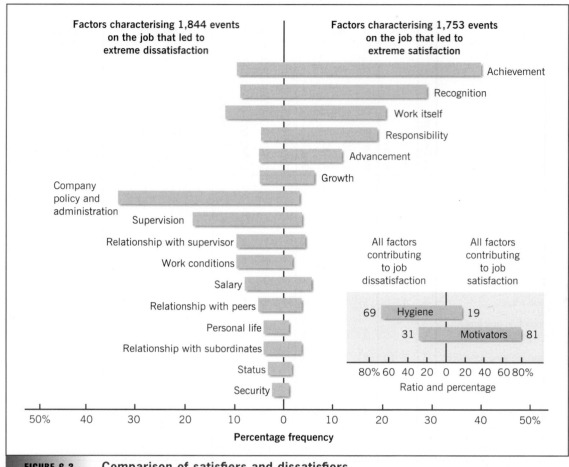

Factors characterising 1,844 events on the job that led to extreme dissatisfaction

Factors characterising 1,753 events on the job that led to extreme satisfaction

Achievement
Recognition
Work itself
Responsibility
Advancement
Growth

Company policy and administration
Supervision
Relationship with supervisor
Work conditions
Salary
Relationship with peers
Personal life
Relationship with subordinates
Status
Security

All factors contributing to job dissatisfaction

All factors contributing to job satisfaction

69 Hygiene 19
31 Motivators 81

80% 60 40 20 0 20 40 60 80%
Ratio and percentage

50% 40 30 20 10 0 10 20 30 40 50%
Percentage frequency

FIGURE 6.3 **Comparison of satisfiers and dissatisfiers**

Source: Reprinted by permission of *Harvard Business Review*. Frederick Herzberg, 'One More Time: How Do You Motivate Employees?', *Harvard Business Review*, January 2003. Copyright © 2003 by the Harvard Business School Publishing Corporation. All rights reserved.

According to Herzberg, the factors leading to job satisfaction are separate and distinct from those that lead to job dissatisfaction. Therefore, managers who seek to eliminate factors that can create job dissatisfaction may bring about peace but not necessarily motivation. They will be placating their workforce rather than motivating them. As a result, conditions surrounding the job such as quality of supervision, pay, company policies, physical working conditions, relations with others and job security were characterised by Herzberg as **hygiene factors**. When they are adequate, people won't be dissatisfied; neither will they be satisfied. If we want to motivate people on their jobs, Herzberg suggested emphasising factors associated with the work itself or outcomes directly derived from it, such as promotional opportunities, opportunities for personal growth, recognition, responsibility and achievement. These are the characteristics that people find intrinsically rewarding.

The two-factor theory isn't without detractors.[13] The criticisms of the theory include the following:

1. The procedure that Herzberg used is limited by its methodology. When things are going well, people tend to take credit themselves. Contrarily, they blame failure on the extrinsic environment—internal/external attributions.

hygiene factors
Factors—such as company policy and administration, supervision and salary—that, when adequate in a job, placate workers. When these factors are adequate, people won't be dissatisfied.

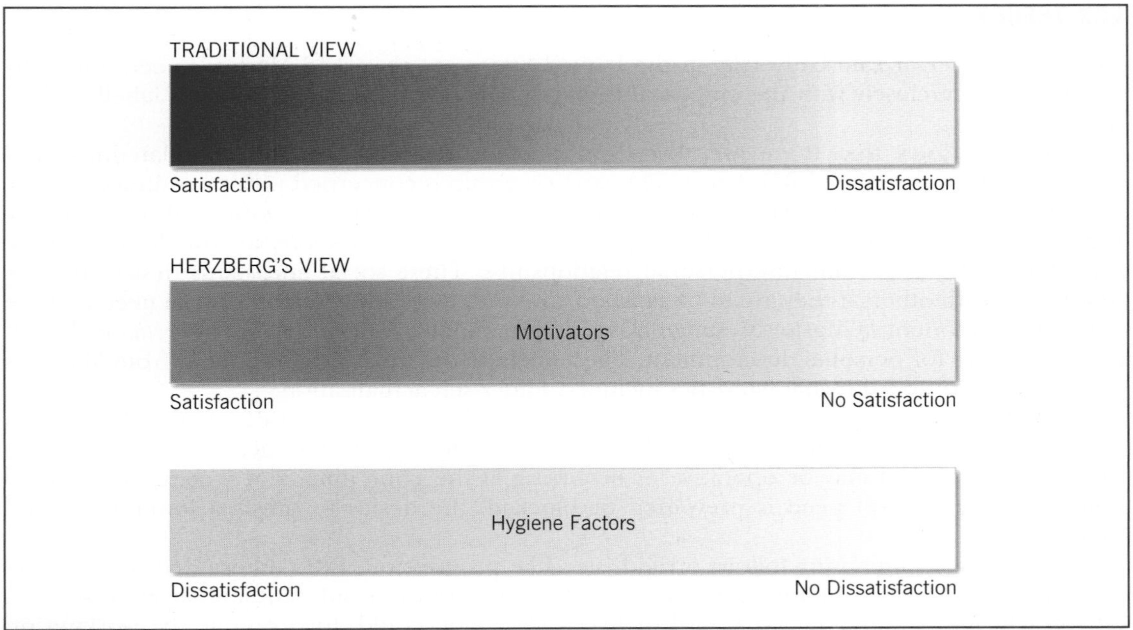

TRADITIONAL VIEW

Satisfaction   Dissatisfaction

HERZBERG'S VIEW

Motivators

Satisfaction   No Satisfaction

Hygiene Factors

Dissatisfaction   No Dissatisfaction

FIGURE 6.4   Contrasting views on satisfaction–dissatisfaction

2. The reliability of Herzberg's methodology is questioned. Raters have to make interpretations, so they may contaminate the findings by interpreting one response in one manner while treating a similar response differently.
3. No overall measure of satisfaction was utilised. A person may dislike part of his or her job, yet still think the job is acceptable.
4. The theory is inconsistent with previous research. The two-factor theory ignores situational variables.
5. Herzberg assumed a relationship between satisfaction and productivity, but the research methodology he used looked only at satisfaction, not at productivity. To make such research relevant, one must assume a strong relationship between satisfaction and productivity.

Regardless of criticisms, Herzberg's theory has been widely read and few managers are unfamiliar with his recommendations. The popularity over the past 35 years of vertically expanding jobs to allow workers greater responsibility in planning and controlling their work can probably be attributed largely to Herzberg's findings and recommendations.

Contemporary Theories of Motivation

The previous theories are well known but, unfortunately, have not held up well under close examination. However, all is not lost. There are a number of contemporary theories that have one thing in common—each has a reasonable degree of valid supporting documentation. Of course, this doesn't mean that the theories we are about to introduce are either unquestionably right or the only 'acceptable' theories of motivation. We instead call them 'contemporary theories', not because they necessarily were developed recently, but because they represent the current state of the art in explaining employee motivation.

ERG THEORY

ERG theory
There are three groups of
core needs: existence,
relatedness and growth.

Clayton Alderfer of Yale University in the United States has reworked Maslow's need hierarchy to align it more closely with the empirical research. His revised need hierarchy is labelled **ERG theory**.[14]

Alderfer argues that there are three groups of core needs—existence, relatedness and growth—hence, the label: ERG theory. The *existence* group is concerned with providing our basic material existence requirements. They include the items that Maslow considered to be physiological and safety needs. The second group of needs are those of *relatedness*—the desire we have for maintaining important interpersonal relationships. These social and status desires require interaction with others if they are to be satisfied, and they align with Maslow's social need and the external component of Maslow's esteem classification. Finally, Alderfer isolates *growth* needs—an intrinsic desire for personal development. These include the intrinsic component from Maslow's esteem category and the characteristics included under self-actualisation.

Aside from substituting three needs for five, how does Alderfer's ERG theory differ from Maslow's? In contrast to the hierarchy of needs theory, the ERG theory demonstrates that first, more than one need may be operative or occurring at the same time, and second, if the fulfilment of a higher-level need is prevented or blocked, the desire to satisfy a lower-level need increases.

Maslow's need hierarchy follows a rigid, step-like progression. ERG theory does not assume that there exists a rigid hierarchy in which a lower need must be substantially satisfied before a person can move up to the next level of needs. A person could, for example, be working on growth even though existence or relatedness needs are unsatisfied; or all three need categories could be operating at the same time. An example might be a postgraduate student who sacrifices higher income, leisure pursuits, and time with family and friends to complete their course of study.

ERG theory also contains a frustration–regression dimension. Maslow, you will recall, argued that an individual would stay at a certain need level until that need was satisfied. ERG theory counters by noting that when a higher-order need level is frustrated, the individual's desire to increase a lower-level need takes place. Inability to satisfy a need for social interaction, for example, might increase the desire for more money or better working conditions. So, frustration can lead to a regression to, and intensification of, a lower need.

In summary, ERG theory argues, like Maslow's theory, that satisfied lower-order needs lead to the desire to satisfy higher-order needs; but multiple needs can be operating as motivators at the same time, and frustration in attempting to satisfy a higher-level need can result in regression to a lower-level need.

ERG theory is more consistent with our knowledge of individual differences among people. Variables such as education, family background and cultural environment can alter the importance or driving force that a group of needs holds for a particular individual. The evidence demonstrating that people in other cultures rank the need categories differently—for example, natives of Spain and Japan place social needs before their physiological requirements[15]—would be consistent with ERG theory. Several studies have supported ERG theory,[16] but there is also evidence that it doesn't work in all organisations.[17] Overall, however, ERG theory represents a more valid version of the need hierarchy.

LEARNING OBJECTIVE

5

List the
characteristics that
high achievers
prefer in a job

McCLELLAND'S THEORY OF NEEDS

You have one ball and there are five targets set up in front of you. Each one is progressively further away and, hence, more difficult to hit. Target A is a cinch. It sits almost within arm's reach of you. If you hit it, you get $2. Target B is a bit further out, but about 80 per cent of the people who try can hit it—it pays $4. Target C pays $8, and about half the people who try can hit it. Very few people can hit Target D, but the payoff is $16 if you do. Finally, Target E pays $32, but it's almost impossible to achieve. Which target would you try for? If you selected C, you are likely to be a high achiever. Why? Read on.

McClelland's theory of needs was developed by David McClelland and his associates.[18] The theory focuses on three needs: achievement, power and affiliation. They are defined as follows:

- **Need for achievement**: The drive to excel, to achieve in relation to a set of standards, to strive to succeed.
- **Need for power**: The need to make others behave in a way that they wouldn't have behaved otherwise.
- **Need for affiliation**: The desire for friendly and close interpersonal relationships.

Some people have a compelling drive to succeed. They are striving for personal achievement, rather than the rewards of success per se. They have a desire to do something better or more efficiently than it has been done before. This drive is the achievement need (*nAch*). From research into the achievement need, McClelland found that high achievers differentiate themselves from others by their desire to do things better.[19] They seek situations in which they can attain personal responsibility for finding solutions to problems, in which they can receive rapid feedback on their performance so they can determine easily whether they are improving or not, and in which they can set moderately challenging goals. High achievers aren't gamblers; they dislike succeeding by chance. They prefer the challenge of working at a problem and accepting the personal responsibility for success or failure rather than leaving the outcome to chance or the actions of others. Importantly, they avoid what they perceive to be very easy or very difficult tasks. They prefer tasks of intermediate difficulty.

High achievers perform best when they perceive their probability of success as being 0.5—that is, when they estimate that they have a 50–50 chance of success. They dislike gambling with high odds because they get no achievement satisfaction from success due to luck alone. Similarly, they dislike low odds (high probability of success) because then there is no challenge to their skills. They like to set goals that require stretching themselves outside of their 'comfort zones'.

The need for power (*nPow*) is the desire to have impact, to be influential and to control others. Individuals high in nPow enjoy being 'in charge', strive for influence over others, prefer to be placed into competitive and status-oriented situations, and tend to be more concerned with prestige and gaining influence over others than with effective performance.

The third need isolated by McClelland is affiliation (*nAff*). This need has received the least attention from researchers. Individuals with a high affiliation motive strive for friendship, prefer cooperative situations rather than competitive ones, and desire relationships that involve a high degree of mutual understanding.

How do you find out if someone is, for example, a high achiever? There are questionnaires that tap this motive,[20] but most research uses a projective test in which subjects respond to pictures.[21] Each picture is briefly shown to the subject and then he or she writes a story based on the picture. As an example, the picture may show a male sitting at a desk in a pensive position, looking at a photograph of a woman and two children that rests at the corner of the desk. The

Employees with high affiliation needs are happiest and more motivated to come to work when they find friendships and understanding among their fellow employees and customers. In this regard, the coffee shop has become an important feature of the workplace.

McClelland's theory of needs
Achievement, power and affiliation are three important needs that help to explain motivation.

need for achievement
The drive to excel, to achieve in relation to a set of standards, to strive to succeed.

need for power
The need to make others behave in a way that they would not have behaved otherwise.

need for affiliation
The desire for friendly and close interpersonal relationships.

subject will then be asked to write a story describing what is going on, what preceded this situation, what will happen in the future, and the like. The stories become, in effect, projective tests that measure unconscious motives. Each story is scored and a subject's rating on each of the three motives is obtained.

Relying on an extensive amount of research, some reasonably well-supported predictions can be made based on the relationship between achievement need and job performance. Although less research has been done on power and affiliation needs, there are consistent findings here, too.

First, as shown in Figure 6.5, individuals with a high need to achieve prefer job situations with personal responsibility, feedback and an intermediate degree of risk. When these characteristics are prevalent, high achievers will be strongly motivated. The evidence consistently demonstrates, for example, that high achievers are successful in entrepreneurial activities such as running their own businesses and managing a self-contained unit within a large organisation.[22]

Second, a high need to achieve doesn't necessarily lead to being a good manager, especially in large organisations. People with a high achievement need are interested in how well they do personally and not in influencing others to do well. High-nAch salespeople don't necessarily make good sales managers, and the good general manager in a large organisation doesn't typically have a high need to achieve.[23]

Third, the needs for affiliation and power tend to be closely related to managerial success. The best managers are high in their need for power and low in their need for affiliation.[24] In fact, a high power motive may be a requirement for managerial effectiveness.[25] Of course, what the cause is and what the effect is are arguable. It has been suggested that a high power need may occur simply as a function of one's level in a hierarchical organisation.[26] The latter argument proposes that the higher the level an individual rises to in the organisation, the greater is the incumbent's power motive. As a result, powerful positions would be the stimulus to a high power motive.

Finally, employees have been successfully trained to stimulate their achievement need. Trainers have been effective in teaching individuals to think in terms of accomplishments, winning and success, and then helping them to learn how to *act* in a high achievement way by preferring situations in which they have personal responsibility, feedback and moderate risks. So, if the job calls for a high achiever, management can select a person with a high nAch or develop its own candidate through achievement training.[27]

COGNITIVE EVALUATION THEORY

cognitive evaluation theory
Allocating extrinsic rewards for behaviour that had been previously intrinsically rewarding tends to decrease the overall level of motivation.

In the late 1960s, one researcher proposed that the introduction of extrinsic rewards, such as pay, for work effort that had been previously intrinsically rewarding due to the pleasure associated with the content of the work would itself tend to decrease the overall level of motivation.[28] This proposal—which has come to be called the **cognitive evaluation theory**—has been extensively researched, and a large number of studies have been supportive.[29] As we will show, the main implications for this theory relate to the way in which people are paid in organisations.

Historically, motivation theorists generally assumed that intrinsic motivations such as achievement, responsibility and competence were independent of extrinsic motivators such as high pay, promotions, good supervisor relations and pleasant working conditions. That is, the stimulation of one wouldn't affect the other. But the cognitive evaluation theory suggests otherwise. It argues that when extrinsic rewards are used by organisations as payoffs for superior performance, the intrinsic rewards, which are derived from individuals doing what they like, are reduced. In other words, when extrinsic rewards are given to someone for performing an interesting task, it causes intrinsic interest in the task itself to decline.

FIGURE 6.5   Matching achievers and jobs

Achievers prefer jobs that offer → Personal responsibility

→ Feedback

→ Moderate risks

Why would such an outcome occur? The popular explanation is that the individual experiences a loss of control over his or her own behaviour so that the previous intrinsic motivation diminishes. Furthermore, the elimination of extrinsic rewards can produce a shift—from an external to an internal explanation—in an individual's perception of causation of why he or she works on a task. If you are reading a novel a week because your English teacher requires you to, you can attribute your reading behaviour to an external source. However, after the course is over, if you find yourself continuing to read a novel a week, your natural inclination is to say, 'I must enjoy reading novels, because I'm still reading one a week.'

If the cognitive evaluation theory is valid, it should have major implications for managerial practices. It has been a truism among compensation specialists for years that if pay or other extrinsic rewards are to be effective motivators, they should be made contingent on an individual's performance. But, cognitive evaluation theorists would argue that this will only tend to decrease the internal satisfaction that the individual receives from doing the job. We have substituted an external stimulus for an internal stimulus. In fact, if cognitive evaluation theory is correct, it would make sense to make an individual's pay non-contingent on performance in order to avoid decreasing intrinsic motivation.

We noted earlier that the cognitive evaluation theory has been supported in a number of studies. Yet, it has also met with attacks, specifically on the methodology used in these studies[30] and in the interpretation of the findings.[31] But where does this theory stand today? Can we say that when organisations use extrinsic motivators such as pay and promotions to stimulate workers' performance, they do so at the expense of reducing intrinsic interest and motivation in the work being done? The answer is not a simple 'yes' or 'no'.

Although further research is needed to clarify some of the current ambiguity, the evidence does lead us to conclude that the interdependence of extrinsic and intrinsic rewards is a real phenomenon.[32] However, its impact on employee motivation at work, in contrast to motivation in general, may be considerably less than originally thought. First, many of the studies testing the theory were done with students, not paid organisational employees. The researchers would observe what happens to a student's behaviour when a reward that had been allocated is stopped. This is interesting, but it doesn't represent the typical work situation. In the real world, when extrinsic rewards are stopped, it usually means the individual is no longer part of the organisation. Second, evidence indicates that very high intrinsic motivation levels are strongly resistant to the detrimental impacts of extrinsic rewards.[33] Even when a job is inherently interesting, there still exists a powerful norm for extrinsic payment or reward of some sort.[34] At the other extreme, on dull tasks extrinsic rewards appear to increase intrinsic motivation.[35] Therefore, the theory may have limited applicability to work organisations because most low-level jobs aren't inherently satisfying enough to foster high intrinsic interest and many managerial and professional positions offer intrinsic rewards. Cognitive evaluation theory may be relevant to that set of organisational jobs that falls in between—those that are neither extremely dull nor extremely interesting.

GOAL-SETTING THEORY

Imagine for a moment the coach of the local high school cross-country team giving her squad these last words before they approached the starting line for the state championship race: 'Each one of you is physically ready. Now, get out there and do your best. No one can ever ask more of you than that.'

You've heard the phrase a number of times yourself: 'Just do your best. That's all anyone can ask for.' But what does 'do your best' mean? Do we ever know if we have achieved that vague goal? Would the cross-country runners have recorded faster times if their coach had given each of them a specific goal to shoot for? Might you have done better in your high school English class if your parents had said, 'You should strive for 85 per cent or higher on all your work in English', rather than telling you to 'do your best'? The research on **goal-setting theory** addresses these issues, and

LEARNING OBJECTIVE

6

Summarise the types of goals that increase performance

goal-setting theory
The theory that specific and difficult goals, with feedback, lead to higher performance.

the findings, as you will see, are impressive in terms of the effect that goal specificity, challenge and feedback have on performance.

In the late 1960s, Edwin Locke proposed that intentions to work towards a goal are a major source of work motivation.[36] That is, goals tell an employee what needs to be done and how much effort will need to be expended.[37] The evidence strongly supports the value of goals. More to the point, we can say that specific goals increase performance; that difficult goals, when accepted, result in higher performance than do easy goals; and that feedback leads to higher performance than does non-feedback.[38]

Specific hard goals produce a higher level of output than does the generalised goal of 'do your best'. The specificity of the goal itself acts as an internal stimulus. For example, when a truck-driver commits to making six round-trip hauls between Brisbane and Sydney each week, this intention gives him a specific objective to try to attain. We can say that, all things being equal, the trucker with a specific goal will outperform his or her counterpart operating with no goals or the generalised goal of 'do your best'.

If factors such as ability and acceptance of the goals are held constant, we can also state that the more difficult the goal, the higher the level of performance. However, it's logical to assume that easier goals are more likely to be accepted. But once an employee accepts a hard task, he or she will exert a high level of effort until it is achieved, lowered or abandoned.

People will do better when they get feedback on how well they are progressing towards their goals because feedback helps to identify discrepancies between what they have done and what they want to do; that is, feedback acts to guide behaviour. But all feedback isn't equally persuasive. Self-generated feedback—for which the employee is able to monitor his or her own progress—has been shown to be a more powerful motivator than externally generated feedback.[39]

If employees have the opportunity to participate in the setting of their own goals, will they try harder? The evidence is mixed regarding the superiority of participative over-assigned goals.[40] In some cases, participatively set goals elicited superior performance, while in other cases, individuals performed best when assigned goals by their boss. But a major advantage of participation may be in increasing acceptance of the goal itself as a desirable one towards which to work.[41] As we noted, resistance is greater when goals are difficult. If people participate in goal setting, they are more likely to accept even a difficult goal than if they are arbitrarily assigned it by their boss. The reason is that individuals are more committed to choices in which they have a part. Thus, although participative goals may have no superiority over assigned goals when acceptance is taken as a given, participation does increase the probability that more difficult goals will be agreed to and acted on.

Are there any contingencies in goal-setting theory, or can we take it as a universal truth that difficult and specific goals will always lead to higher performance? In addition to feedback, four other factors have been found to influence the goals–performance relationship. These are goal commitment, adequate self-efficacy, task characteristics and national culture. Goal-setting theory presupposes that an individual is committed to the goal—that is, is determined not to lower or abandon the goal. This is most likely to occur when goals are made public, when the individual has an internal locus of control, and when the goals are self-set rather than assigned.[42] **Self-efficacy** refers to an individual's belief that he or she is capable of performing a task.[43] The higher your self-efficacy, the more confidence you have in your ability to succeed in a task. So, in difficult situations, we find that people with low self-efficacy are more likely to lessen their effort or give up altogether, while those with high self-efficacy will try harder to master the challenge.[44] In addition, individuals high in self-efficacy seem to respond to negative feedback with increased effort and motivation, whereas those low in self-efficacy are likely to lessen their effort when given negative feedback.[45]

Research indicates that individual goal setting doesn't work equally well on all tasks. The evidence suggests that goals seem to have a more substantial effect on performance when tasks are simple rather than complex, well-learned rather than novel, and independent rather than interdependent.[46] On interdependent tasks, group goals are preferable. Finally, goal-setting

self-efficacy
The individual's belief that he or she is capable of performing a task.

The Real Deal

Getting the feedback wrong demotivates—and costs!

In June 2002, Rio Tinto agreed to pay $25 million to 190 former employees of Coal and Allied in Australia's largest unfair-dismissal case. At the core of the case was the use of a performance review system in the company in which employees had no opportunity to challenge unfavourable reviews from their supervisors and were subsequently dismissed. The net effect of these unfavourable reviews and lack of corrective measures to challenge the errors in the review angered and demotivated employees, hastening their subsequent dismissals from the company. While it is possible that some companies use performance reviews as a pretext to downsize their operations without paying costly redundancy provisions, most HR experts agree it is more usually due to poor management skills, lack of training, lack of time and/or resources to perform the reviews properly, and poor communication and people skills. When an incompetent manager reviews an employee's performance, the resulting outcome will usually be lower employee motivation and reduced performance—a Catch-22 situation, as the purpose of performance reviews is to raise motivation through feedback and increase employee productivity. All organisations that are serious about fair treatment of employees need to closely scrutinise their performance review programs to ensure adequate training of managers in evaluating and communicating effectively an employee's performance. Failures, as the Rio Tinto case demonstrates, are just too costly for all concerned!

Source: Based on N. Way, 'Non-Performing Reviews', *Business Review Weekly*, 3 April 2003.

theory is culture bound. It's well-adapted to countries such as Australia, New Zealand, the United States and Canada because its key components align reasonably well with those cultures. It assumes that employees will be reasonably independent (not too high a score on power distance), that managers and employees will seek challenging goals (low in uncertainty avoidance), and that performance is considered important by both (high in quantity of life). So, don't expect goal setting to necessarily lead to higher employee performance in countries such as China or Indonesia, where the opposite conditions exist.

Our overall conclusion is that intentions—as articulated in terms of hard and specific goals—are a potent motivating force. Under the proper conditions, they can lead to higher performance. However, there is no evidence that such goals are associated with increased job satisfaction.[47]

Talking on the phone all day can quickly become boring and unproductive unless employees have set goals to aim for and are recognised for reaching them.

REQUISITE TASK ATTRIBUTES THEORY

The task characteristics approach began with the pioneering work of Turner and Lawrence in the mid-1960s.[48] They developed a research study to assess the effect of different kinds of jobs on employee satisfaction and absenteeism. They defined job complexity in terms of six task characteristics:

- variety;
- autonomy;
- responsibility;
- knowledge and skill;
- required social interaction; and
- optional social interaction.

The higher a job scored on these characteristics, according to Turner and Lawrence, the more complex it was.

Their findings confirmed their absenteeism prediction. Employees in high-complexity tasks had better attendance records. But they found no general correlation between task complexity and satisfaction—until they broke their data down by the background of employees. When individual differences in the form of urban background versus rural background were taken into account, employees from urban settings were shown to be more satisfied with low-complexity jobs. Employees with rural backgrounds reported higher satisfaction in high-complexity jobs. Turner and Lawrence concluded that employees in larger communities had a greater variety of non-work interests and thus were less involved and motivated by their work. In contrast, employees from smaller towns had fewer non-work interests and were more receptive to the complex tasks of their jobs.

requisite task attributes theory
Identifies six characteristics of job complexity and the influence of the degree of job complexity on performance, satisfaction and absenteeism.

Turner and Lawrence's **requisite task attributes theory** was important for at least three reasons. First, they demonstrated that employees did respond differently to different types of jobs. Second, they provided a preliminary set of task attributes by which jobs could be assessed. And third, they focused attention on the need to consider the influence of individual differences on employees' reactions to jobs.

THE JOB CHARACTERISTICS MODEL

job characteristics model
Identifies five job characteristics and their relationship to personal and work outcomes.

Turner and Lawrence's theory laid the foundation for what is, today, one of the major frameworks for defining task characteristics that are important to employee motivation—that is, Hackman and Oldham's **job characteristics model (JCM)**.[49] According to the JCM, any job can be described in terms of five core job dimensions, defined as follows:

- *Skill variety:* The degree to which the job requires a variety of activities so that the employee can use a number of different skills and talents.
- *Task identity:* The degree to which the job requires completion of a whole and identifiable piece of work.
- *Task significance:* The degree to which the job has a substantial effect on the lives or work of other people.
- *Autonomy:* The degree to which the job provides substantial freedom, independence and discretion to the employee in scheduling the work and in determining the procedures to be used in carrying it out.
- *Feedback:* The degree to which carrying out the work activities required by the job results in the employee receiving direct and clear information about the effectiveness of their performance.

Table 6.1 offers examples of job activities that rate high and low for each characteristic.

Figure 6.6 presents the model. Notice how the first three dimensions—skill variety, task identity and task significance—combine to create purposeful work. If these three characteristics exist in a job, we can predict that the incumbent will view the job as being important, valuable and worthwhile. Notice, too, that jobs that possess autonomy give the job holder a feeling of

TABLE 6.1	Examples of high and low job characteristics

Skill variety

High variety	The owner-operator of a garage who does electrical repairs, rebuilds engines, does body work and interacts with customers
Low variety	A body shop worker who sprays paint eight hours a day.

Task identity

High identity	A cabinetmaker who designs a piece of furniture, selects the wood, builds the object and finishes it to perfection.
Low identity	A worker in a furniture factory who operates a lathe solely to make table legs.

Task significance

High significance	Nursing the sick in a hospital intensive care unit.
Low significance	Sweeping hospital floors.

Autonomy

High autonomy	A telephone installer who schedules their own work for the day, makes visits without supervision, and decides on the most effective techniques for a particular installation.
Low autonomy	A telephone operator who must handle calls as they come according to a routine, highly specified procedure.

Feedback

High feedback	An electronics factory worker who assembles a radio and then tests it to determine if it operates properly.
Low feedback	An electronics factory worker who assembles a radio and then routes it to a quality control inspector who tests it for proper operation and makes needed adjustments.

Source: G. Johns, *Organizational Behavior: Understanding and Managing Life at Work*, 4th ed. Reprinted by permission of Pearson Education Inc., Upper Saddle River: NJ.

personal responsibility for the results and that, if a job provides feedback, the employee will know how effectively they are performing. From a motivational standpoint, the model says that internal rewards are gained by an employee when they learn (knowledge of results) that they personally (experienced responsibility) have performed well on a task that they care about (experienced purpose).[50] The more that these three psychological states are present, the greater will be the employee's motivation, performance and satisfaction, and the lower their absenteeism and likelihood of leaving the organisation. As Figure 6.6 shows, the links between the job dimensions and the outcomes are moderated or adjusted by the strength of the employee's growth need—that is, by the employee's desire for self-esteem and self-actualisation. This means that employees with a high growth need are more likely to experience the psychological states when their jobs are enriched than are their counterparts with a low growth need. Moreover, they will respond more positively to the psychological states, when they are present, than will low growth need employees.

The core dimensions can be combined into a single predictive index, called the **motivating potential score (MPS)**. Its calculation is shown in Figure 6.7.

Jobs that are high on motivating potential must be high on at least one of the three factors that lead to experienced purpose, and they must be high on both autonomy and feedback. If jobs score high on motivating potential, the model predicts that motivation, performance and satisfaction will be positively affected, while the likelihood of absence and turnover is reduced.

motivating potential score (MPS)
A predictive index suggesting the motivation potential in a job.

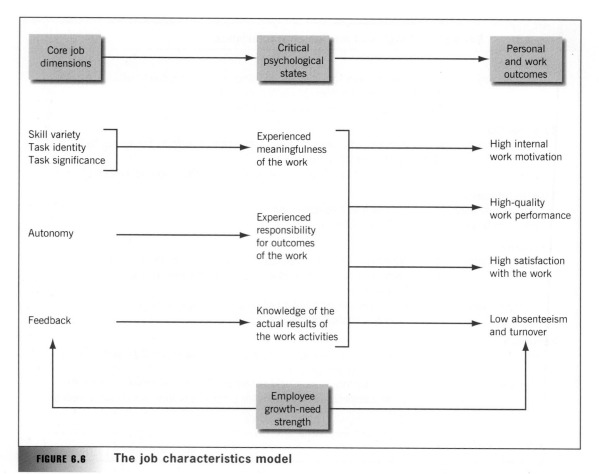

FIGURE 6.6   **The job characteristics model**

Source: J. R. Hackman, 'Work Design', in J. R. Hackman and J. L. Suttle (eds), *Improving Life at Work* (Glenview, IL: Scott, Foresman, 1977), p. 129. Reproduced with permission.

$$\text{Motivating potential score (MPS)} = \left[\frac{\text{Skill variety} + \text{Task identity} + \text{Task significance}}{3} \right] \times \text{Feedback} \times \text{Autonomy}$$

FIGURE 6.7   **Calculating a motivating potential score**

The job characteristics model has been well researched. Most of the evidence supports the general framework of the theory—that is, there is a multiple set of job characteristics and these characteristics affect behavioural outcomes.[51] But there is still considerable debate about the five specific core dimensions in the JCM, the multiplicative properties of the MPS and whether other moderating variables may not be as good as or better than strength of growth need.

There is some question if task identity adds to the model's predictive ability,[52] and there is evidence suggesting that skill variety may be redundant with autonomy.[53] Further, many studies have found that by adding all the variables in the MPS, rather than adding some and multiplying by others, the MPS becomes a better predictor of work outcomes.[54] Finally, while the strength of an employee's growth needs has been found to be a purposeful moderating variable in many studies,[55] other variables—such as the presence or absence of social cues, perceived equity with comparison groups, and propensity to assimilate work experience—have also been found to moderate the job characteristics–outcome relationship. Given the current state of research on moderating variables, we should be cautious in unequivocally accepting growth need strength as originally included in the JCM.

Where does this leave us? Given the current state of evidence, we can make the following statements with relative confidence:

1. People who work on jobs with high-core job dimensions are generally more motivated, satisfied and productive than are those who do not.
2. Job dimensions operate through the psychological states in influencing personal and work outcome variables, rather than influencing them directly.[56]

SOCIAL INFORMATION PROCESSING THEORY

At the beginning of this section on job content and context theories, do you remember Amy Summerville complaining about her former job on the core roller assembly line? Would it surprise you to know that one of Amy's best friends, Elizabeth Wright, is still working at the core roller assembly line, doing the same job that Amy did, and that Elizabeth thinks her job is really good? Probably not! Why? Because, consistent with our discussion of perception previously in this book, we recognise that people can look at the same job and evaluate it differently. The fact that people respond to their jobs *as they perceive them*, rather than to the *objective* jobs, is the central idea in our third theory focusing on the job. It is called the **social information processing (SIP) model**.[57]

The SIP model argues that employees adopt attitudes and behaviours in response to the social cues provided by other people with whom they have contact. These others can be colleagues, supervisors, friends, family members or customers. For example, Gary Ling got a summer job working in a New Zealand sawmill. Since jobs were scarce and this one paid particularly well, Gary arrived on his first day of work highly motivated. Two weeks later, however, his motivation was quite low. What happened was that his colleagues consistently spoke poorly of their jobs. They said the work was boring, that having to clock on and off proved that management didn't trust them and that supervisors never listened to their opinions. The objective characteristics of Gary's job hadn't changed in the two-week period; rather, Gary had reconstructed reality based on messages he had received from other employees.

A number of studies confirm the validity of the SIP model.[58] For example, it has been shown that employee motivation and satisfaction can be manipulated by such subtle actions as a colleague or manager commenting on the existence or absence of job features such as difficulty, challenge and autonomy. So, managers should give as much (or more) attention to employees' perceptions of their jobs as to the actual characteristics of those jobs. They might spend more time telling employees how interesting and important their jobs are. Managers should also recognise that newly hired employees, and people transferred or promoted to a new position, are more likely to be receptive to social information than are those with greater seniority.

social information processing (SIP) model Employees adopt attitudes and behaviours in response to the social cues provided by others with whom they have contact.

REINFORCEMENT THEORY

A counterpoint to goal-setting theory is **reinforcement theory**. The former is a cognitive approach, proposing that an individual's purposes direct his or her action. In reinforcement theory, we have a behaviouristic approach, which argues that reinforcement conditions behaviour. The two are clearly at odds philosophically. Reinforcement theorists see behaviour as being environmentally caused. You need not be concerned, they would argue, with internal cognitive

reinforcement theory Behaviour is a function of its consequences.

events; what controls behaviour are reinforcers—any consequence that, when immediately following a response, increases the probability that the behaviour will be repeated.

Reinforcement theory ignores the inner state of the individual and concentrates solely on what happens to a person when he or she takes some action. Because it does not concern itself with what initiates behaviour, it is not, strictly speaking, a theory of motivation. But it does provide a powerful means of analysis of what controls behaviour, and it is for this reason that it is typically considered in discussions of motivation.[59]

We discussed the reinforcement process in detail earlier in this book. We showed how using reinforcers to condition behaviour gives us considerable insight into how people learn. Yet, we cannot ignore the fact that reinforcement has a wide following as a motivational device. In its pure form, however, reinforcement theory ignores feelings, attitudes, expectations, and other cognitive variables that are known to impact behaviour. In fact, some researchers look at the same experiments that reinforcement theorists use to support their position and interpret the findings in a cognitive framework.[60]

Reinforcement is undoubtedly an important influence on behaviour, but few scholars are prepared to argue that it is the only influence. The behaviours you engage in at work and the amount of effort you allocate to each task are affected by the consequences that follow from your behaviour. If you are consistently reprimanded for out-producing your colleagues, you will likely reduce your productivity. But your lower productivity may also be explained in terms of goals, inequity or expectancies.

FLOW AND INTRINSIC MOTIVATION THEORY

Can you think of times in your life when you have been so deeply involved in something that nothing else seems to matter? The task consumes you totally and you lose track of time. Most people can. It's likely to occur when you are doing a favourite activity: running, skiing, dancing, reading a novel, playing a computer game, listening to music, cooking an elegant meal. Athletes commonly refer to it as being 'in the zone'. But as we will show, it can also occur at work. Motivation researchers call this state of absolute concentration: *flow*.[61]

The flow experience

A key element of the flow experience is that its motivation is unrelated to end goals. The activity people are pursuing when they achieve the timeless feeling of flow comes from the process of the activity itself, rather than from trying to reach a goal. So, when a person experiences flow, he or she is completely intrinsically motivated.

Do people typically feel happy when they are experiencing flow? The answer, which might surprise you, is 'no'. They are too consumed in deep concentration. But when the flow task is completed, and the person looks back on what has happened, he or she is flooded with feelings of gratitude for the experience. It's then that the satisfaction received from the experience is realised. And it's the desire to repeat the experience that creates continued motivation.

Are there conditions that are likely to produce flow? Yes. When people have described flow experiences, they talked about common characteristics in the tasks they were doing. The tasks were challenging and required using a high level of skills. They were goal-directed and had feedback on how well they were performing. The tasks demanded total concentration and creativity. And the tasks were so consuming that people had no attention left over to think about anything irrelevant or to worry about problems. Note again, though, that although the task was goal-directed, it wasn't the goal that provided the motivation. It was the task.

One of the most surprising research findings related to flow is that it's not associated with leisure. People, in fact, rarely report the flow experience when they are doing leisure activities such as watching television or relaxing. Another surprise is that it's more likely to be experienced at work than at home.

If you ask people if they would like to work less, the answer is almost always 'yes'. People link

The 'buzz' experience arises more often at work than during leisure and is sometimes called being 'in the zone'. It is characterised by intense concentration and motivation that centres on the process more than on the goal. Chef Maggie Beer experiences 'the buzz' as she prepares a meal.

leisure with happiness. They think if they had more free time, they would be happier. Studies of thousands of people suggest that people are generally wrong in this belief. When people spend time at home, for example, they often lack a clear purpose, don't know how well they are doing, get distracted, and feel that their skills are under-used. They frequently describe themselves as bored. But work has many of the properties that stimulate flow. It usually has clear goals. It provides people with feedback on how well they are doing—either from the work process itself or through a boss's evaluation. People's skills are typically matched to their jobs, which provides challenge. And jobs usually encourage concentration and prevent distractions.

A model of intrinsic motivation

A clearer understanding of flow has been offered in Ken Thomas's model of intrinsic motivation.[62] This extension of the flow concept identifies the key elements that create intrinsic motivation.

Thomas describes employees as intrinsically motivated when they genuinely care about their work, look for better ways to do it, and are energised and fulfilled by doing it well. As with flow, the rewards an employee gets from intrinsic motivation come from the work itself, rather than from external factors such as increases in pay or compliments from the boss.

Thomas's model proposes that intrinsic motivation is achieved when people experience feelings of choice, competence, meaningfulness and progress. He defines these components as follows:

- *Choice* is the opportunity to be able to select task activities that make sense to you and to perform them in ways that seem appropriate.
- *Competence* is the accomplishment you feel in skilfully performing task activities you have chosen.
- *Meaningfulness* is the opportunity to pursue a worthy task purpose; a purpose that matters in the larger scheme of things.
- *Progress* is feeling that you are making significant advancement in achieving the task's purpose.

Thomas reports a number of studies demonstrating that these four components of intrinsic motivation are significantly related to improved job satisfaction and increased performance as rated by supervisors.[63] However, almost all the studies reported by Thomas were done with professional and managerial employees. Whether these four components will predict intrinsic motivation with, for example, rank-and-file blue-collar workers is currently unclear.

Note how Thomas's four intrinsic-motivation components link with the concept of flow. When a task is *meaningful*, people find themselves resenting the time they have to spend on other, less meaningful tasks. They are totally absorbed in the intrinsic task, thinking about it all the time. We should even expect them to borrow time from other activities in order to devote more time to something that's meaningful. When a task provides a flow experience, a person typically is free to *choose* to work on that task in contrast to others. *Competence* also stimulates the flow experience.

We tend to be 'most engaged in a task when we are performing activities most competently—having all our attention on meeting the challenge of the activities we are performing'.[64] Finally, *progress* enhances feelings that our time and efforts are paying off. You feel enthusiastic about the task and are eager to keep investing your time and effort in it.

EQUITY THEORY

Tzu Fang graduated last year from Central Queensland University with a degree in accounting. After interviews with a number of organisations on her CQU campus in Sydney, she accepted a position with one of the nation's largest public accounting firms and was assigned to their Melbourne office. Tzu was very pleased with the offer she received: challenging work with a prestigious firm, an excellent opportunity to gain valuable experience, and the highest salary any accounting graduate at Central Queensland University was offered last year—$47,550 per annum. But Tzu was the top student in her class; she was ambitious and articulate, and fully expected to receive a commensurate salary.

Twelve months have passed since Tzu joined her employer. The work has proved to be as challenging and satisfying as she had hoped. Her employer is extremely pleased with her performance; in fact, she recently received a $2,000 per annum raise. However, Tzu's motivational level has dropped dramatically in the past few weeks. Why? Her employer has just hired a fresh university graduate from Melbourne University, who lacks the one-year experience Tzu has gained, for $49,600 per annum—$50 more than Tzu now makes! It would be an understatement to describe Tzu in any other terms than irate. Tzu is even talking about looking for another job.

Tzu's situation illustrates the role that equity plays in motivation. Employees make comparisons of their job inputs (that is, effort, experience, education, competence) and outcomes (that is, salary levels, raises, recognition) relative to those of others. We perceive what we get from a job situation (outcomes) in relation to what we put into it (inputs), and then we compare our outcome–input ratio with the outcome–input ratio of relevant others. This is shown in Table 6.2. If we perceive our ratio to be equal to that of the relevant others with whom we compare ourselves, a state of equity is said to exist. We perceive our situation as fair—that justice prevails. When we see the ratio as unequal, we experience equity tension. When we see ourselves as under-rewarded, the tension creates anger; when over-rewarded, the tension creates guilt. J. Stacy Adams has proposed that this negative tension state provides the motivation to do something to correct it.[65]

The referent that an employee selects adds to the complexity of **equity theory**. Evidence indicates that the referent chosen is an important variable in equity theory.[66] There are four referent comparisons that an employee can use:

equity theory
Individuals compare their job inputs and outcomes with those of others and then respond to eliminate any inequities.

TABLE 6.2	Equity theory	
Ratio Comparisons*		**Perception**
$\dfrac{O}{I_A} < \dfrac{O}{I_B}$		Inequity due to being under-rewarded
$\dfrac{O}{I_A} = \dfrac{O}{I_B}$		Equity
$\dfrac{O}{I_A} > \dfrac{O}{I_B}$		Inequity due to being over-rewarded

*Where $\dfrac{O}{I_A}$ represents the employee and $\dfrac{O}{I_B}$ represents relevant others.

1. *Self-inside:* An employee's experiences in a different position inside his or her current organisation.
2. *Self-outside:* An employee's experiences in a situation or position outside his or her current organisation.
3. *Other-inside:* Another individual or group of individuals inside the employee's organisation.
4. *Other-outside:* Another individual or group of individuals outside the employee's organisation.

Employees might compare themselves to friends, neighbours, fellow employees, or colleagues in other organisations, or compare their present job with past jobs they themselves have had. Which referent an employee chooses will be influenced by the information the employee holds about referents, as well as by the attractiveness of the referent. This has led to focusing on four moderating variables—gender, length of tenure, level in the organisation, and amount of education or professionalism.[67] Research shows that both men and women prefer same-sex comparisons. The research also demonstrates that women are typically paid less than men in comparable jobs and have lower pay expectations than men for the same work. So, a woman who uses another woman as a referent tends to calculate a lower comparative standard. This leads us to conclude that employees in jobs that are not sex segregated will make more cross-sex comparisons than those in jobs that are either male- or female-dominated. This also suggests that if women are tolerant of lower pay, it may be due to the comparative standard they use.

Employees with short tenure in their current organisations tend to have little information about others inside the organisation, so they rely on their own personal experiences. On the other hand, employees with long tenure rely more heavily on co-workers for comparison. Upper-level employees, those in the professional ranks, and those with higher amounts of education tend to be more cosmopolitan and have better information about people in other organisations. Therefore, these types of employees will make more other-outside comparisons.

Based on equity theory, when employees perceive an inequity, they can be predicted to make one of six choices:[68]

1. They change their inputs (for example, don't exert as much effort).
2. They change their outcomes (for example, individuals paid on a piece-rate basis can increase their pay by producing a higher quantity of units of lower quality).
3. They distort perceptions of self (for example, 'I used to think I worked at a moderate pace, but now I realise that I work a lot harder than everyone else.').
4. They distort perceptions of others (for example, 'Mike's job isn't as desirable as I previously thought it was.').
5. They choose a different referent (for example, 'I may not make as much as my brother-in-law, but I'm doing a lot better than my Dad did when he was my age.').
6. They leave the field (for example, quit the job).

The theory establishes the following propositions relating to inequitable pay:

A. *Given payment by time, over-rewarded employees will produce more than will equitably paid employees.* Hourly and salaried employees will generate high quantity or quality of production in order to increase the input side of the ratio and bring about equity.
B. *Given payment by quantity of production, over-rewarded employees will produce fewer, but higher-quality, units than will equitably paid employees.* Individuals paid on a piece-rate basis will increase their effort to achieve equity, which can result in greater quality or quantity. However, increases in quantity will only increase inequity, since every unit produced results in further over-payment. Therefore, effort is directed towards increasing quality rather than increasing quantity.
C. *Given payment by time, under-rewarded employees will produce less or a poorer quality of output.* Effort will be decreased, which will bring about lower productivity or poorer-quality output than equitably paid subjects.
D. *Given payment by quantity of production, under-rewarded employees will produce a large number of low-quality units in comparison with equitably paid employees.* Employees on piece-rate pay plans can bring about equity, because trading off quality of output for quantity will result in an increase in rewards with little or no increase in contributions.

LEARNING OBJECTIVE

7

State the impact of under-rewarding employees

These propositions have generally been supported, with a few minor qualifications.[69] First, inequities created by over-payment don't seem to have a very significant impact on behaviour in most work situations. Apparently, people have a great deal more tolerance of over-payment inequities than of under-payment inequities, or are better able to rationalise them. Second, not all people are equity sensitive.[70] For example, there is a small part of the working population who actually prefer that their outcome–input ratio be less than the referent comparison. Predictions from equity theory aren't likely to be very accurate with these 'benevolent types'.

It's also important to note that while most research on equity theory has focused on pay, employees seem to look for equity in the distribution of other organisational rewards. For example, it has been shown that the use of high-status job titles as well as large and lavishly furnished offices may function as outcomes for some employees in their equity equation.[71]

Finally, recent research has been directed at expanding what is meant by equity or fairness.[72] Historically, equity theory focused on **distributive justice** or the perceived fairness of the *amount and allocation* of rewards among individuals. But equity should also consider **procedural justice**— the perceived fairness of the *process* used to determine the distribution of rewards. The evidence indicates that distributive justice has a greater influence on employee satisfaction than procedural justice, while procedural justice tends to affect an employee's organisational commitment, trust in his or her boss, and intention to quit.[73] As a result, managers should consider openly sharing information on how allocation decisions are made, following consistent and unbiased procedures, and engaging in similar practices to increase the perception of procedural justice. By increasing the perception of procedural fairness, employees are likely to view their bosses and the organisation as positive even if they are dissatisfied with pay, promotions and other personal outcomes. Moreover, as noted earlier in this book, organisational citizenship behaviour (OCB) is significantly influenced by perceptions of fairness. Specifically, evidence indicates that although distributive justice issues such as pay are important, perceptions of procedural justice are particularly relevant to OCB.[74] So, another plus from employees' perceptions of fair treatment is that they will be more satisfied and reciprocate by volunteering for extra job activities, helping others, and engaging in similar positive behaviours.

In conclusion, equity theory demonstrates that, for most employees, motivation is influenced significantly by relative rewards as well as by absolute rewards, but some key issues are still unclear.[75] For example, how do employees handle conflicting equity signals, such as when unions point to other employee groups who are substantially *better off*, while management argues how much things have *improved*? How do employees define inputs and outcomes? How do they combine and weigh their inputs and outcomes to arrive at totals? When and how do the factors change over time? Yet, regardless of these problems, equity theory continues to offer us some important insights into employee motivation.

EXPECTANCY THEORY

Currently, one of the most widely accepted explanations of motivation is Victor Vroom's **expectancy theory**.[76] Although it has its critics,[77] most of the evidence is supportive of the theory.[78]

Expectancy theory argues that the strength of a tendency to act in a certain way depends on the strength of an expectation that the act will be followed by a given outcome, and on the attractiveness of that outcome to the individual. In more practical terms, expectancy theory says that an employee will be motivated to exert a high level of effort when he or she believes that effort will lead to a good performance appraisal; that a good appraisal will lead to organisational rewards such as a bonus, a salary increase or a promotion; and that the rewards will satisfy the employee's personal goals. The theory, therefore, focuses on three relationships (see Figure 6.8).

1. *Effort–performance relationship:* The probability perceived by the individual that exerting a given amount of effort would lead to performance.
2. *Performance–reward relationship:* The degree to which the individual believes that performing at a particular level will lead to the attainment of a desired outcome.

distributive justice
Perceived fairness of the amount and allocation of rewards among individuals.

procedural justice
Perceived fairness of the process used to determine the distribution of rewards.

LEARNING OBJECTIVE 8
Clarify the key relationships in expectancy theory

expectancy theory
The strength of a tendency to act in a certain way depends on the strength of an expectation that the act will be followed by a given outcome and on the attractiveness of that outcome to the individual.

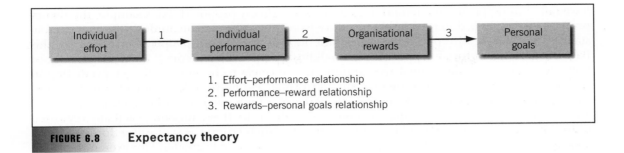

FIGURE 6.8   **Expectancy theory**

3. *Rewards–personal goals relationship:* The degree to which organisational rewards satisfy an individual's personal goals or needs, and the attractiveness of those potential rewards for the individual.[79]

Expectancy theory helps to explain why a lot of employees aren't motivated on their jobs and only do the minimum necessary to get by. This is evident when we look at the theory's three relationships in a little more detail. We present them below as questions employees need to answer in the affirmative if their motivation is to be maximised.

First, *if I give a maximum effort, will it be recognised in my performance appraisal?* For a lot of employees, the answer is 'no'. Why? Their skill level may be deficient, which means that no matter how hard they try, they are not likely to be a high performer. The organisation's performance appraisal system may be designed to assess non-performance factors such as loyalty, initiative or courage, which means more effort won't necessarily result in a higher evaluation. Still another possibility is that the employee, rightly or wrongly, perceives that her boss doesn't like her. As a result, she expects to get a poor appraisal regardless of her level of effort. These examples suggest that one possible source of low employee motivation is the belief by the employee that no matter how hard she works, the likelihood of getting a good performance appraisal is low.

Second, *if I get a good performance appraisal, will it lead to organisational rewards?* Many employees see the performance–reward relationship in their job as weak. The reason, as we elaborate on in the next chapter, is that organisations reward a lot of things besides just performance. For example, when pay is allocated to employees based on factors such as seniority, being cooperative, or for 'kissing up' to the boss, employees are likely to see the performance–reward relationship as being weak and demotivating.

Finally, *if I'm rewarded, are the rewards ones that I find personally attractive?* The employee works hard in hope of getting a promotion, but gets a pay rise instead. Or the employee wants a more interesting and challenging job, but receives only a few words of praise. Or the employee puts in extra effort to be relocated to the company's Paris office, but instead is transferred to Singapore. These examples illustrate the importance of the rewards being tailored to individual employee needs. Unfortunately, many managers are limited in the rewards they can distribute, which makes it difficult to individualise rewards. Moreover, some managers incorrectly assume that all employees want the same thing, thus overlooking the motivational effects of differentiating rewards. In either case, employee motivation is sub-maximised.

In summary, the key to expectancy theory is the understanding of an individual's goals and the linkage between effort and performance, between performance and rewards, and, finally, between the rewards and individual goal satisfaction. As a contingency model, expectancy theory recognises that there is no universal principle for explaining everyone's motivations. In addition, just because we understand what needs a person seeks to satisfy doesn't ensure that the individual perceives high performance as necessarily leading to the satisfaction of these needs.

Does expectancy theory work? Attempts to validate the theory have been complicated by methodological, criterion and measurement problems. As a result, many published studies that purport to support or negate the theory must be viewed with caution. Importantly, most studies have failed to replicate the methodology as it was originally proposed. For example, the theory proposes to explain different levels of effort from the same person under different circumstances, but almost all replication studies have looked at different people. Correcting for this flaw has greatly improved support for the validity of expectancy theory.[80] Some critics suggest that the theory has only limited use, arguing that it tends to be more valid for predicting in situations in which effort–performance and performance–reward linkages are clearly perceived by the individual.[81] Because few individuals perceive a high correlation between performance and rewards in their jobs, the theory tends to be idealistic. If organisations actually rewarded individuals for performance rather than according to such criteria as seniority, effort, skill level and job difficulty, then the theory's validity might be considerably greater. However, rather than invalidating expectancy theory, this criticism can be used in support of the theory, because it explains why a significant segment of the workforce exerts low levels of effort in carrying out job responsibilities.

DON'T FORGET ABILITY AND OPPORTUNITY

Robyn and Chris both graduated from university a couple of years ago with their diplomas in primary education. They each took jobs as primary teachers, but in different school districts. Robyn immediately confronted a number of obstacles on the job: a large class (42 students), a small and dingy classroom, and inadequate supplies. Chris's situation couldn't have been more different. He had only 15 students in his class, plus a teacher's-aide for 15 hours each week, a modern and well-lighted classroom, a well-stocked supply cabinet, 16 Pentium 4 computers for the students to use, and a highly supportive school principal. Not surprisingly, at the end of their first school year, Chris had been considerably more effective as a teacher than had Robyn.

The preceding episode illustrates an obvious, but often overlooked, fact. Success on a job is facilitated or hindered by the existence or absence of support resources.

A popular, although arguably simplistic, way of thinking about employee performance is as a function (f) of the interaction of ability (A) and motivation (M); that is, performance = $f(A \times M)$. If either is inadequate, performance will be negatively affected. This helps to explain, for example, the hard-working athlete or student with modest abilities who consistently outperforms his or her more gifted, but lazy, rival. So, as we noted earlier in this book, an individual's intelligence and skills (subsumed under the label *ability*) must be considered in addition to motivation if we are to be able to accurately explain and predict employee performance. But a piece of the puzzle is still missing. We need to add **opportunity to perform** (O) to our equation performance = $f(A \times M \times O)$.[82] Even though an individual may be willing and able, there may be obstacles that constrain performance. This is shown in Figure 6.9.

opportunity to perform High levels of performance are partially a function of an absence of obstacles that constrain the employee.

When you attempt to assess why an employee may not be performing to the level that you believe he or she is capable of, take a look at the work environment to see if it's supportive. Does the employee have adequate tools, equipment, materials and supplies? Does the employee have favourable working conditions, helpful co-workers, supportive work rules and procedures, sufficient information to make job-related decisions, adequate time to do a good job, and the like? If not, performance will suffer.

Integrating Contemporary Theories of Motivation

We have looked at a lot of motivation theories in this chapter. The fact that a number of these theories have been supported only complicates the matter. How simple it would have been if, after presenting several theories, only one was found to be valid? But, these theories are not all in competition with one another. Because one is valid doesn't automatically make the others

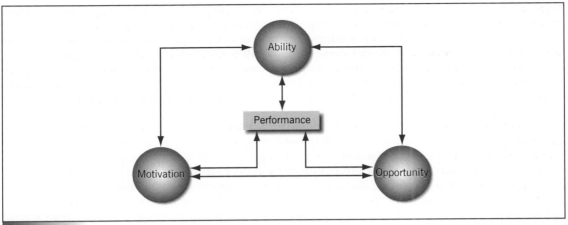

FIGURE 6.9   **Performance dimensions**

Source: Adapted from M. Blumberg and C. D. Pringle, 'The Missing Opportunity in Organizational Research: Some Implications for a Theory of Work Performance', *Academy of Management Review*, October 1982, p. 565.

OB Controversies

Receive a KITA and stay motivated!

No, KITA is not a new computer game—it is what Herzberg called a 'Kick in the A…' This is a guaranteed way to get results. But since Herzberg's description of this tactic, which is attributed to the old style of management, we have been told that staff can be motivated by a new style of management. In his research on the way CEOs in Australia manage change, Hugh Kingsley reported that many CEOs have set about developing a new culture that is market-oriented, customer-oriented and quality-focused. To do this, Kingsley suggests many CEOs have adopted a new style of management based on employee participation, involvement and empowerment.

Kingsley identified a paradox in what he observed during his research. CEOs don't dispute that people are the organisation's greatest asset, as they hold the key to gaining and maintaining competitive advantage over competitors. Yet, employees 'are being devalued by organisational change' (p. 28), the same organisational change usually instigated by the CEOs. There have been disappointing results from the changes to a new organisational culture and a new style of management. One consequence that stands out in Kingsley's report is the carnage experienced during restructuring and rightsizing caused primarily by global changes. While the CEOs have concentrated on the technical and financial aspects of the changes, employees have become frustrated and burnt out, causing valuable human resources to be wasted. Organisations now have employees full of fear and anxiety caused by the lack of job security and the constant fear of further retrenchments.

In Maslow's terms, when people's basic needs are threatened, they are hardly likely to be fully committed, feel empowered and enthusiastically involved under the guise of participation and involvement in the changes. Is asking people to do far more with much less, and under considerably more pressure, a new form of motivation using KITA?

Source: Based on F. Herzberg, 'One More Time: How Do You Motivate Employees?', *Harvard Business Review,* vol. 46, no. 1, January–February 1968, pp. 53–62; and H. Kingsley, 'A New Paradigm for CEOs', *HRMonthly,* July 1999, pp. 28–29.

invalid. In fact, many of the theories presented in this chapter are complementary. The challenge is now to tie these theories together to help you understand their interrelationships.[83]

Figure 6.10 presents a model that integrates much of what we know about motivation. Its basic foundation is the expectancy model shown in Figure 6.8. Let's work through Figure 6.10.

We begin by explicitly recognising that opportunities can aid or hinder individual effort. The individual effort box also has another arrow leading into it. This arrow flows out of the person's goals. Consistent with goal-setting theory, this goal–effort loop is meant to remind us that goals direct behaviour.

Expectancy theory predicts that an employee will exert a high level of effort if he or she perceives that there is a strong relationship between effort and performance, performance and rewards, and rewards and satisfaction of personal goals. Each of these relationships, in turn, is influenced by certain factors. For effort to lead to good performance, the individual must have the requisite ability to perform, and the performance appraisal system that measures the individual's performance must be perceived as being fair and objective. The performance–reward relationship will be strong if the individual perceives that it is performance (rather than seniority, personal favourites or other criteria) that is rewarded. If cognitive evaluation theory were fully valid in the actual workplace, we would predict here that basing rewards on performance should decrease the individual's intrinsic motivation. The final link in expectancy theory is the

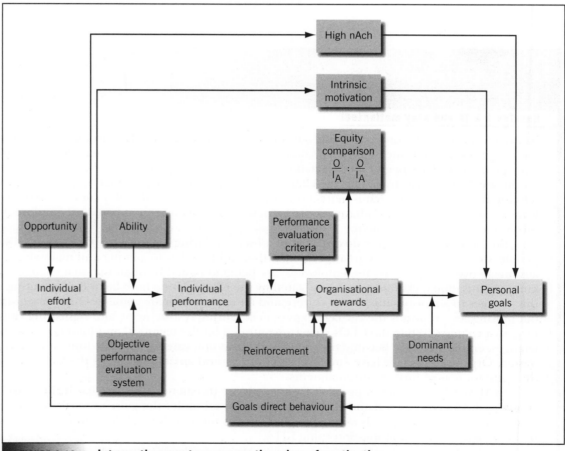

FIGURE 6.10   **Integrating contemporary theories of motivation**

rewards–goals relationship. ERG theory would come into play at this point. Motivation would be high to the degree that the rewards an individual received, for his or her high performance, satisfied the dominant needs consistent with his or her individual goals.

A closer look at Figure 6.10 will also reveal that the model considers the achievement need, intrinsic motivation, and reinforcement and equity theories. The high achiever isn't motivated by the organisation's assessment of his or her performance or organisational rewards; hence, the jump from effort to personal goals for those with a high nAch. Remember, high achievers are internally driven as long as the jobs they are doing provide them with personal responsibility, feedback and moderate risks. They are not concerned with the effort–performance, performance–rewards or rewards–goal linkages. Similarly, if tasks create intrinsic motivation as a result of providing choice, competence, meaningfulness and progress, then individual effort should be internally driven towards goals.

Reinforcement theory enters our model by recognising that the organisation's rewards reinforce the individual's performance. If management has designed a reward system that is seen by employees as 'paying off' for good performance, the rewards will reinforce and encourage continued good performance. Rewards also play the key part in equity theory. Individuals will compare the rewards (outcomes) they receive from the inputs they make with the outcome–input ratio of relevant others $(O/I_A : O/I_B)$, and inequities may influence the effort expended.

Caveat Emptor: Motivation Theories are Culture-bound

In our discussion of goal setting, we said that care needs to be taken in applying this theory because it assumes cultural characteristics that are not universal. This is true for many of the theories presented in this chapter. Most current motivation theories were developed in the United States by Americans and about Americans.[84] Maybe the most blatant pro-American characteristic inherent in these theories is the strong emphasis on what we defined earlier in this book as individualism and quality of life. For example, both goal-setting and expectancy theories emphasise goal accomplishment, as well as rational and individual thought. Let's take a look at several motivation theories and consider their cross-cultural transferability.

Maslow's need hierarchy argues that people start at the physiological level and then move progressively up the hierarchy in this order: physiological, safety, social, esteem and self-actualisation. This hierarchy, if it has any application at all, aligns with Western cultures. In countries such as Japan, Greece and Mexico, where uncertainty avoidance characteristics are strong, security needs would be on top of the need hierarchy. Countries that score high on quality-of-life characteristics—Denmark, Sweden, Norway, the Netherlands and Finland—would have social needs on top.[85] We would predict, for example, that group work would motivate employees more when the country's culture scores high on the quality criterion.

Another motivation concept that clearly has a North American bias is the achievement need. The view that a high achievement need acts as an internal motivator presupposes two cultural characteristics—a willingness to accept a moderate degree of risk (which excludes countries with strong uncertainty avoidance characteristics) and a concern with performance (which applies almost singularly to countries with strong quality-of-life characteristics). This combination is found in Anglo-American countries such as the United States, Canada, Australia, New Zealand and the United Kingdom.[86] On the other hand, these characteristics are relatively absent in countries such as Chile and Portugal.

Equity theory has gained a relatively strong following in the United States. That's not surprising, since US-style reward systems are based on the assumption that workers are highly sensitive to equity in reward allocations. And in the United States, equity is meant to be closely tying pay to performance. However, recent evidence suggests that in collectivist cultures, especially in the former socialist economies of Central and Eastern Europe, employees expect rewards to reflect their individual needs as well as their performance.[87] Moreover, consistent with a legacy of communism and centrally planned economies, employees exhibited an entitlement attitude— that is, they expected outcomes to be *greater* than their inputs.[88] These findings suggest that US-style pay practices may need modification, especially in Russia and the former communist countries, in order to be perceived as fair by employees.

But don't assume there are *no* cross-cultural consistencies. For example, the desire for interesting work seems important to almost all employees, regardless of their national culture. In a study of seven countries, employees in Belgium, Britain, Israel and the United States ranked 'interesting work' number one among 11 work goals. And this factor was ranked either second or third in Japan, the Netherlands and Germany.[89] Similarly, in a study comparing job-preference outcomes among graduate students in the United States, Canada, Australia and Singapore, growth, achievement and responsibility were rated the top three and had identical rankings.[90] Both of these studies suggest some universality to the importance of intrinsic factors in the two-factor theory.

The theories we have discussed in this chapter address different outcome variables. Some, for example, are directed at explaining turnover, while others emphasise productivity. The theories also differ in their predictive strength. In this section, we (1) review the most established motivation theories to determine their relevance in explaining our dependent variables, and (2) assess the predictive power of each.[91]

Need theories

We introduced four theories that focused on needs. These were Maslow's hierarchy, two-factor, ERG and McClelland's needs theories. The strongest of these is probably the last, particularly regarding the relationship between achievement and productivity. If the other three have any value at all, that value relates to explaining and predicting job satisfaction.

Goal-setting theory

There is little dispute that clear and difficult goals lead to higher levels of employee productivity. This evidence leads us to conclude that goal-setting theory provides one of the more powerful explanations of this dependent variable. The theory, however, doesn't address absenteeism, turnover or satisfaction.

Reinforcement theory

This theory has an impressive record for predicting factors such as quality and quantity of work, persistence of effort, absenteeism, tardiness and accident rates. It doesn't offer much insight into employee satisfaction or the decision to quit.

Equity theory

Equity theory deals with all four dependent variables. However, it is strongest when predicting absence and turnover behaviours and weak when predicting differences in employee productivity.

Expectancy theory

Our final theory focused on performance variables. It has proved to offer a relatively powerful explanation of employee productivity, absenteeism and turnover. But expectancy theory assumes that employees have few constraints on their decision discretion. It makes many of the same assumptions that the rational model makes about individual decision making. (See the discussion of decision making earlier in this book.) This acts to restrict its applicability.

For major decisions, such as accepting or resigning from a job, expectancy theory works well because people don't rush into decisions of this nature. They are more prone to take the time to carefully consider the costs and benefits of all the alternatives. However, expectancy theory isn't a very good explanation for more typical types of work behaviour, especially for individuals in lower-level jobs, because such jobs come with considerable limitations imposed by work methods, supervisors and company policies. We would conclude, therefore, that expectancy theory's power in explaining employee productivity increases when the jobs being performed are more complex and higher in the organisation (where discretion is greater).

Point

MONEY MOTIVATES!

Behavioural scientists tend to downplay money as a motivator. They prefer to emphasise the importance of challenging jobs, goals, participative decision-making, feedback, cohesive work teams and other non-monetary factors. We argue otherwise here—that is, money is *the* critical incentive to work motivation.

Money is important to employees because it's a medium of exchange. People may not work *only* for money, but take the money away and how many people would come to work? A study of nearly 2,500 employees found that although these people disagreed over what was their number-one motivator, they unanimously chose money as their number two.[a]

As equity theory suggests, money has symbolic value in addition to its exchange value. We use pay as the primary outcome against which we compare our inputs to determine if we are being treated equitably. That an organisation pays one executive $80,000 a year and another $95,000 means more than the latter's earning $15,000 a year more. It's a message, from the organisation to both employees, of how much it values the contribution of each.

In addition to equity theory, both reinforcement and expectancy theories attest to the value of money as a motivator.[b] In the former, if pay is contingent on performance, it will encourage workers to generate high levels of effort. Consistent with expectancy theory, money will motivate to the extent that it is seen as being able to satisfy an individual's personal goals and is perceived as being dependent on performance criteria.

However, maybe the best case for money is a review of studies that looked at four methods of motivating employee performance: money, goal setting, participative decision making, and redesigning jobs to give workers more challenge and responsibility. The average improvement from money was consistently higher than with any of the other methods.[c]

Sources: [a] S. Caudron, 'Motivation? Money's Only No. 2', *Industry Week*, 15 November 1993, p. 33.

[b] T. R. Mitchell and A. E. Mickel, 'The Meaning of Money: An Individual-Difference Perspective', *Academy of Management Review*, July 1999, p. 570.

[c] E. A. Locke et al, 'The Relative Effectiveness of Four Methods of Motivating Employee Performance', in K. D. Duncan, M. M. Gruenberg and D. Wallis (eds), *Changes in Working Life* (London: Wiley, 1980), pp. 363–83.

Counterpoint

Money can motivate *some* people under *some* conditions, so the issue isn't really whether or not money can motivate. The answer to that is: 'It can!' The more relevant question is: Does money motivate most employees in the workforce today? The answer to this question, we'll argue, is 'no'.

For money to motivate an individual's performance, certain conditions must be met. First, money must be important to the individual. But money isn't important to everybody. High achievers, for example, are intrinsically motivated. Money would have little impact on these people.

Second, money must be perceived by the individual as being a direct reward for performance. Unfortunately, performance and pay are poorly linked in most organisations. Pay increases are far more often determined by non-performance factors such as experience, community pay standards or company profitability.

Third, the marginal amount of money offered for the performance must be perceived by the individual as being significant. Research indicates that merit raises must be at least 7 per cent of base pay for employees to perceive them as motivating. Unfortunately, recent data indicates average merit increases are only in the 3.9 to 4.4 per cent range.[d]

Finally, management must have the discretion to reward high performers with more money. But unions and organisational compensation policies constrain managerial discretion. Where unions exist, that discretion is almost zero. In non-unionised environments, traditional limited compensation grades create severe restrictions on pay increases. For example, in one organisation, a Systems Analyst IV's pay grade ranges from $4,775 to $5,500 a month. No matter how good a job that analyst does, her boss cannot pay her more than $5,500 a month. Similarly, no matter how poorly she performs, she won't earn less than $4,775. So, money might be theoretically capable of motivating employee performance, but most managers aren't given enough flexibility to do much about it.

Sources: [d] A. Mitra, N. Gupta and G. D. Jenkins, Jr, 'The Case of the Invisible Merit Raise: How People See Their Pay Raises', *Compensation & Benefits Review*, May–June 1995, pp. 71–76; and Hewitt Associates Salary Survey, 2000.

For Discussion

1. Does motivation come from within a person or is it a result of the situation? Explain.
2. What are the implications of Theories X and Y for motivation practices?
3. Compare and contrast Maslow's hierarchy of needs theory with (a) Alderfer's ERG theory, and (b) Herzberg's two-factor theory.
4. Describe the three needs isolated by McClelland. How are they related to worker behaviour?
5. Explain cognitive evaluation theory. How applicable is it to management practice?
6. What is the role of self-efficacy in goal setting?
7. Contrast distributive and procedural justice. What implications might they have for designing pay systems in different countries?
8. Identify the variables in expectancy theory.
9. Explain the formula: Performance = $f(A \times M \times O)$ and give an example.
10. What consistencies among motivation concepts, if any, apply cross-culturally?
11. 'The cognitive evaluation theory is contradictory to reinforcement and expectancy theories.' Do you agree or disagree? Explain.
12. 'Managers should be able, through proper selection and job design, to have every employee experience flow in his or her job.' Do you agree or disagree? Discuss.
13. Analyse the application of Maslow's and Herzberg's theories to an Indonesian or South Pacific island nation where more than a quarter of the population is unemployed.
14. Can an individual be too motivated, so that his or her performance declines as a result of excessive effort? Discuss.
15. Identify three activities you really enjoy (for example, playing tennis, reading a novel, going shopping). Next, identify three activities you really dislike (for example, going to the dentist, cleaning the house, staying on a restricted-kilojoule diet). Using the expectancy model, analyse each of your answers to assess why some activities stimulate your effort, while others don't.

Exercise

WHAT DO PEOPLE WANT FROM THEIR JOBS?

Each class member begins by completing the following questionnaire:
Rate the following 12 job factors according to how important each is to you.
Place a number on a scale of 1 to 5 on the line before each factor.

Very important		Somewhat important		Not important
5	4	3	2	1

_____ 1. An interesting job
_____ 2. A good boss
_____ 3. Recognition and appreciation for the work I do
_____ 4. The opportunity for advancement
_____ 5. A satisfying personal life
_____ 6. A prestigious or status job
_____ 7. Job responsibility
_____ 8. Good working conditions
_____ 9. Sensible company rules, regulations, procedures and policies
_____ 10. The opportunity to grow through learning new things
_____ 11. A job I can do well and succeed at
_____ 12. Job security

This questionnaire taps the dimensions in Herzberg's two-factor theory. To determine if hygiene or motivating factors are important to you, place the numbers 1–5 that represent your answers below.

Hygiene factors score	Motivational factors score
2. _____	1. _____
5. _____	3. _____
6. _____	4. _____
8. _____	7. _____
9. _____	10. _____
12. _____	11. _____
Total points _____	Total points _____

Add up each column. Did you select hygiene or motivating factors as being most important to you?

Now break into groups of five or six and compare your questionnaire results. (a) How similar are your scores? (b) How close did your group's results come to those found by Herzberg? (c) What motivational implications did your group arrive at based on your analysis?

Source: This exercise is based on R. N. Lussier, *Human Relations in Organizations: A Skill Building Approach*, 2nd ed. (Homewood, IL: Irwin, 1993). Reprinted with permission.

Case Study 6

What Drives Employees at Microsoft?

The reality of software development in a huge company such as Microsoft—it employs more than 39,000 people—is that a substantial portion of your work involves days of boredom punctuated by hours of tedium. You basically spend your time in an isolated office writing code and sitting in meetings during which you participate in looking for and evaluating hundreds of bugs and potential bugs. Yet, Microsoft has no problem in finding and retaining software programmers. Their programmers work horrendously long hours and obsess on the goal of shipping product.

From the day new employees begin work at Microsoft, they know they are special and that their employer is special. New hires all have one thing in common—they are smart. The company prides itself on putting all recruits through a gruelling 'interview loop', during which they confront a barrage of brain-teasers by future colleagues to see how well they think. Only the best and the brightest survive to become employees. The company does this because 'Microsofties' truly believe that their company is special. For example, it has a high tolerance for nonconformity. Would you believe that one software tester comes to work every day dressed in extravagant Victorian outfits? But the underlying theme that unites Microsofties is the belief that the firm has a manifest destiny to change the world. The least consequential decision by a programmer can have an outsized importance when it can affect a new release that might be used by 50 million people.

Microsoft employees are famous for putting in long hours. One program manager said, 'In my first five years, I was the Microsoft stereotype. I lived on caffeine and vending-machine hamburgers and free beer and 20-hour workdays. I had no life. I considered everything outside the building as a necessary evil.' More recently, things have changed. There are still a number of people who put in 80-hour weeks, but 60- and 70-hour weeks are more typical and some even are doing their jobs in only 40 hours.

No discussion of employee life at Microsoft would be complete without mentioning the company's lucrative stock option program. Microsoft created more millionaire employees, faster, than any company in American history—more than 10,000 by the late 1990s. While the company is certainly more than a place to get rich, executives still realise that money matters. One former manager claims that the human resources department actually kept a running chart of employee satisfaction versus the company's share price. 'When the stock was up, human resources could turn off the ventilation and everybody would say they were happy. When the stock was down, we could give people massages and they would tell us that the massages were too hard.' In the go-go 1990s, when the value of Microsoft shares was doubling every few months and yearly stock splits were predictable, employees not only got to participate in Microsoft's manifest destiny, they could get rich in the process. By the spring of 2002, with the world in a recession, stock prices down, and the growth for Microsoft products slowing, it wasn't so clear what was driving its employees to continue the company's dominance of the software industry.

Questions

1. If you were a programmer, would you want to work at Microsoft? Why or why not?
2. How many activities in this case can you tie into specific motivation theories? List the activities, the motivation theories and how they apply.
3. As Microsoft continues to get larger and its growth rate flattens, do you think management will have to modify any of its motivation practices? Elaborate.

Source: Based on M. Gimein, 'Smart Is Not Enough!', *Fortune*, 8 January 2001, pp. 124–36.

Web Workout

1. TeleTech is a global company. Visit <www.teletech.com/teletech.asp?cid=237> and look at the sort of services it provides in Australia and the Asian region. What sort of motivational challenges would this company face?
2. Motivating employees in the information technology sector has unique challenges. Some of these challenges are addressed at <www.zdnet.com.au/itmanager/management/story/0,2000029576,20265070,00.htm>. Try to identify the motivation theories that Bob Weinstein discusses in the various solutions proposed at this page.
3. <www.optimalthinking.com/employee-motivation.html> is an advertisement for a company offering speakers to advise companies on employee motivation. Why do you think companies such as Optimal.com appear to be so successful?
4. How can encouragement of employees to have time off from their jobs to undertake voluntary community projects actually benefit the employer? Have a look at <www.cavill.com.au/Heartshare/3staff-motivation.html> and see if you can find the motivation elements of this program.
5. Visit <www.becnorthernbeaches.com.au/03_sub/03_Employing%20Staff.htm>. What motivational theory(ies) are being presented on this website?

NOTES

1. E. Ross, 'A Brilliant New Career', *Business Review Weekly*, 3 July 2003, p. 79.
2. Ibid.
3. C. A. O'Reilly III, 'Organizational Behavior: Where We've Been, Where We're Going', in M. R. Rosenzweig and L. W. Porter (eds), *Annual Review of Psychology*, vol. 42 (Palo Alto, CA: Annual Reviews, Inc., 1991), p. 431. See also M. L. Ambrose and C. T. Kulik, 'Old Friends, New Faces: Motivation Research in the 1990s', *Journal of Management*, vol. 25, no. 3, 1999, pp. 231–92.
4. See, for example, T. R. Mitchell, 'Matching Motivational Strategies with Organizational Contexts', in L. L. Cummings and B. M. Staw (eds), *Research in Organizational Behavior*, vol. 19 (Greenwich, CT: JAI Press, 1997), pp. 60–62.
5. A. Maslow, *Motivation and Personality* (New York: Harper & Row, 1954).
6. See, for example, E. E. Lawler III and J. L. Suttle, 'A Causal Correlation Test of the Need Hierarchy Concept', *Organizational Behavior and Human Performance*, April 1972, pp. 265–87; D. T. Hall and K. E. Nougaim, 'An Examination of Maslow's Need Hierarchy in an Organizational Setting', *Organizational Behavior and Human Performance*, February 1968, pp. 12–35; and J. Rauschenberger, N. Schmitt and J. E. Hunter, 'A Test of the Need Hierarchy Concept by a Markov Model of Change in Need Strength', *Administrative Science Quarterly*, December 1980, pp. 654–70.
7. A. K. Korman, J. H. Greenhaus and I. J. Badin, 'Personnel Attitudes and Motivation', in M. R. Rosenzweig and L. W. Porter (eds), *Annual Review of Psychology* (Palo Alto, CA: Annual Reviews, Inc., 1977), pp. 178–79.
8. M. A. Wahba and L. G. Bridwell, 'Maslow Reconsidered: A Review of Research on the Need Hierarchy Theory', *Organizational Behavior and Human Performance*, April 1976, pp. 212–40.
9. D. McGregor, *The Human Side of Enterprise* (New York: McGraw-Hill, 1960). For an updated analysis of Theory X and Theory Y constructs, see R. J. Summers and S. F. Cronshaw, 'A Study of McGregor's Theory X, Theory Y and the Influence of Theory X, Theory Y Assumptions

on Causal Attributions for Instances of Worker Poor Performance', in S. L. McShane (ed.), *Organizational Behavior, ASAC 1988 Conference Proceedings*, vol. 9, Part 5 (Halifax, Nova Scotia: 1988), pp. 115–23.

10. F. Herzberg, B. Mausner and B. Snyderman, *The Motivation to Work* (New York: Wiley, 1959).

11. See, for example, E. E. Lawler III, *Motivation in Work Organizations* (Belmont, CA: Brooks/Cole, 1973); B. Weiner, *Human Motivation* (New York: Holt, Rinehart and Winston, 1980); and K. W. Thomas, *Intrinsic Motivation at Work* (San Francisco: Berrett-Koehler, 2000).

12. See, for example, K. A. Kovach, 'What Motivates Employees? Workers and Supervisors Give Different Answers', *Business Horizons*, September–October 1987, p. 61. This research was updated in 1995 and reported in a paper by K. A. Kovach, 'Employee Motivation: Addressing a Crucial Factor in Your Organization's Performance' (Fairfax, VA: George Mason University).

13. R. J. House and L. A. Wigdor, 'Herzberg's Dual-Factor Theory of Job Satisfaction and Motivations: A Review of the Evidence and Criticism', *Personnel Psychology*, Winter 1967, pp. 369–89; D. P. Schwab and L. L. Cummings, 'Theories of Performance and Satisfaction: A Review', *Industrial Relations*, October 1970, pp. 403–30; R. J. Caston and R. Braito, 'A Specification Issue in Job Satisfaction Research', *Sociological Perspectives*, April 1985, pp. 175–97; and J. Phillipchuk and J. Whittaker, 'An Inquiry into the Continuing Relevance of Herzberg's Motivation Theory', *Engineering Management Journal*, vol. 8, 1996, pp. 15–20.

14. C. P. Alderfer, 'An Empirical Test of a New Theory of Human Needs', *Organizational Behavior and Human Performance*, May 1969, pp. 142–75.

15. M. Haire, E. E. Ghiselli and L. W. Porter, 'Cultural Patterns in the Role of the Manager', *Industrial Relations*, February 1963, pp. 95–117.

16. C. P. Schneider and C. P. Alderfer, 'Three Studies of Measures of Need Satisfaction in Organizations', *Administrative Science Quarterly*, December 1973, pp. 489–505; and I. Borg and M. Braun, 'Work Values in East and West Germany: Different Weights, But Identical Structures', *Journal of Organizational Behavior*, vol. 17, special issue, 1996, pp. 541–55.

17. J. P. Wanous and A. Zwany, 'A Cross-Sectional Test of Need Hierarchy Theory', *Organizational Behavior and Human Performance*, May 1977, pp. 78–97.

18. D. C. McClelland, *The Achieving Society* (New York: Van Nostrand Reinhold, 1961); J. W. Atkinson and J. O. Raynor, *Motivation and Achievement* (Washington, DC: Winston, 1974); D. C. McClelland, *Power: The Inner Experience* (New York: Irvington, 1975); and M. J. Stahl, *Managerial and Technical Motivation: Assessing Needs for Achievement, Power, and Affiliation* (New York: Praeger, 1986).

19. McClelland, *The Achieving Society*.

20. See, for example, A. Mehrabian, 'Measures of Achieving Tendency', *Educational and Psychological Measurement*, Summer 1969, pp. 445–51; H. J. M. Hermans, 'A Questionnaire Measure of Achievement Motivation', *Journal of Applied Psychology*, August 1970, pp. 353–63; and J. M. Smith, 'A Quick Measure of Achievement Motivation', *British Journal of Social and Clinical Psychology*, June 1973, pp. 137–43.

21. See W. D. Spangler, 'Validity of Questionnaire and TAT Measures of Need for Achievement: Two Meta-Analyses', *Psychological Bulletin*, July 1992, pp. 140–54.

22. D. C. McClelland and D. G. Winter, *Motivating Economic Achievement* (New York: Free Press, 1969); and J. B. Miner, N. R. Smith and J. S. Bracker, 'Role of Entrepreneurial Task Motivation in the Growth of Technologically Innovative Firms: Interpretations from Follow-up Data', *Journal of Applied Psychology*, October 1994, pp. 627–30.

23. McClelland, *Power*; D. C. McClelland and D. H. Burnham, 'Power Is the Great Motivator', *Harvard Business Review*, March–April 1976, pp. 100–10; and R. E. Boyatzis, 'The Need for Close Relationships and the Manager's Job', in D. A. Kolb, I. M. Rubin and J. M. McIntyre, *Organizational Psychology: Readings on Human Behavior in Organizations*, 4th ed. (Upper Saddle River, NJ: Prentice Hall, 1984), pp. 81–86.

24. D. G. Winter, 'The Motivational Dimensions of Leadership: Power, Achievement, and Affiliation', in R. E. Riggio, S. E. Murphy and F. J. Pirozzolo (eds), *Multiple Intelligences and Leadership* (Mahwah, NJ: Lawrence Erlbaum, 2002), pp. 119–38.

25. J. B. Miner, *Studies in Management Education* (New York: Springer, 1965).

26. D. Kipnis, 'The Powerholder', in J. T. Tedeschi (ed.), *Perspectives in Social Power* (Chicago: Aldine, 1974), pp. 82–123.

27. D. McClelland, 'Toward a Theory of Motive Acquisition', *American Psychologist*, May 1965, pp. 321–33; and D. Miron and D. C. McClelland, 'The Impact of Achievement Motivation Training on Small Businesses', *California Management Review*, Summer 1979, pp. 13–28.

28. R. de Charms, *Personal Causation: The Internal Affective Determinants of Behavior* (New York: Academic Press, 1968).

29. E. L. Deci, *Intrinsic Motivation* (New York: Plenum, 1975); J. Cameron and W. D. Pierce, 'Reinforcement, Reward, and Intrinsic Motivation: A Meta-Analysis', *Review of Educational Research*, Fall 1994, pp. 363–423; and S. Tang and V. C. Hall, 'The Overjustification Effect: A Meta-Analysis', *Applied Cognitive Psychology*, October 1995, pp. 365–404.

30. W. E. Scott, 'The Effects of Extrinsic Rewards on "Intrinsic Motivation": A Critique', *Organizational Behavior and Human Performance*, February 1976, pp. 117–19; B. J. Calder and B. M. Staw, 'Interaction of Intrinsic and Extrinsic Motivation: Some Methodological Notes', *Journal of Personality and Social Psychology*, January 1975, pp. 76–80; and K. B. Boal and L. L. Cummings, 'Cognitive Evaluation Theory: An Experimental Test of Processes and Outcomes', *Organizational Behavior and Human Performance*, December 1981, pp. 289–310.

31. G. R. Salancik, 'Interaction Effects of Performance and Money on Self-Perception of Intrinsic Motivation', *Organizational Behavior and Human*

Performance, June 1975, pp. 339–51; and F. Luthans, M. Martinko and T. Kess, 'An Analysis of the Impact of Contingency Monetary Rewards on Intrinsic Motivation', *Proceedings of the Nineteenth Annual Midwest Academy of Management* (St Louis, MO: 1976), pp. 209–21.

32. J. B. Miner, *Theories of Organizational Behavior* (Hinsdale, IL: Dryden Press, 1980), p. 157.

33. H. J. Arnold, 'Effects of Performance Feedback and Extrinsic Reward upon High Intrinsic Motivation', *Organizational Behavior and Human Performance*, December 1976, pp. 275–88.

34. B. M. Staw, 'Motivation in Organizations: Toward Synthesis and Redirection', in B. M. Staw and G. R. Salancik (eds), *New Directions in Organizational Behavior* (Chicago: St Clair, 1977), p. 76.

35. B. J. Calder and B. M. Staw, 'Self-Perception of Intrinsic and Extrinsic Motivation', *Journal of Personality and Social Psychology*, April 1975, pp. 599–605.

36. E. A. Locke, 'Toward a Theory of Task Motivation and Incentives', *Organizational Behavior and Human Performance*, May 1968, pp. 157–89.

37. P. C. Earley, P. Wojnaroski and W. Prest, 'Task Planning and Energy Expended: Exploration of How Goals Influence Performance', *Journal of Applied Psychology*, February 1987, pp. 107–14.

38. G. P. Latham and G. A. Yukl, 'A Review of Research on the Application of Goal Setting in Organizations', *Academy of Management Journal*, December 1975, pp. 824–45; E. A. Locke, K. N. Shaw, L. M. Saari and G. P. Latham, 'Goal Setting and Task Performance', *Psychological Bulletin*, January 1981, pp. 125–52; A. J. Mento, R. P. Steel and R. J. Karren, 'A Meta-Analytic Study of the Effects of Goal Setting on Task Performance: 1966–1984', *Organizational Behavior and Human Decision Processes*, February 1987, pp. 52–83; M. E. Tubbs, 'Goal Setting: A Meta-Analytic Examination of the Empirical Evidence', *Journal of Applied Psychology*, August 1986, pp. 474–83; E. A. Locke and G. P. Latham, *A Theory of Goal Setting and Task Performance* (Upper Saddle River, NJ: Prentice Hall, 1990); J. C. Wofford, V. L. Goodwin and S. Premack, 'Meta-Analysis of the Antecedents of Personal Goal Level and of the Antecedents and Consequences of Goal Commitment', *Journal of Management*, vol. 18, no. 3, 1992, pp. 595–615; and E. A. Locke, 'Motivation through Conscious Goal Setting', *Applied and Preventive Psychology*, vol. 5, 1996, pp. 117–24.

39. J. M. Ivancevich and J. T. McMahon, 'The Effects of Goal Setting, External Feedback, and Self-Generated Feedback on Outcome Variables: A Field Experiment', *Academy of Management Journal*, June 1982, pp. 359–72; and Locke, 'Motivation through Conscious Goal Setting'.

40. See, for example, G. P. Latham, M. Erez and E. A. Locke, 'Resolving Scientific Disputes by the Joint Design of Crucial Experiments by the Antagonists: Application to the Erez-Latham Dispute Regarding Participation in Goal Setting', *Journal of Applied Psychology*, November 1988, pp. 753–72; T. D. Ludwig and E. S. Geller, 'Assigned versus Participative Goal Setting and Response Generalization: Managing Injury Control among Professional Pizza Deliverers', *Journal of Applied Psychology*, April 1997, pp. 253–61; and S. G. Harkins and M. D. Lowe, 'The Effects of Self-Set Goals on Task Performance', *Journal of Applied Social Psychology*, January 2000, pp. 1–40.

41. M. Erez, P. C. Earley and C. L. Hulin, 'The Impact of Participation on Goal Acceptance and Performance: A Two-Step Model', *Academy of Management Journal*, March 1985, pp. 50–66.

42. J. R. Hollenbeck, C. R. Williams and H. J. Klein, 'An Empirical Examination of the Antecedents of Commitment to Difficult Goals', *Journal of Applied Psychology*, February 1989, pp. 18–23. See also J. C. Wofford, V. L. Goodwin and S. Premack, 'Meta-Analysis of the Antecedents of Personal Goal Level and of the Antecedents and Consequences of Goal Commitment', *Journal of Management*, September 1992, pp. 595–615; and M. E. Tubbs, 'Commitment as a Moderator of the Goal–Performance Relation: A Case for Clearer Construct Definition', *Journal of Applied Psychology*, February 1993, pp. 86–97.

43. A. Bandura, *Self-Efficacy: The Exercise of Control* (New York: Freeman, 1997).

44. E. A. Locke, E. Frederick, C. Lee and P. Bobko, 'Effect of Self-Efficacy, Goals, and Task Strategies on Task Performance', *Journal of Applied Psychology*, May 1984, pp. 241–51; M. E. Gist and T. R. Mitchell, 'Self-Efficacy: A Theoretical Analysis of Its Determinants and Malleability', *Academy of Management Review*, April 1992, pp. 183–211; and A. D. Stajkovic and F. Luthans, 'Self-Efficacy and Work-Related Performance: A Meta-Analysis', *Psychological Bulletin*, September 1998, pp. 240–61.

45. A. Bandura and D. Cervone, 'Differential Engagement in Self-Reactive Influences in Cognitively-Based Motivation', *Organizational Behavior and Human Decision Processes*, August 1986, pp. 92–113.

46. See R. E. Wood, A. J. Mento and E. A. Locke, 'Task Complexity as a Moderator of Goal Effects: A Meta Analysis', *Journal of Applied Psychology*, August 1987, pp. 416–25; R. Kanfer and P. L. Ackerman, 'Motivation and Cognitive Abilities: An Integrative/Aptitude-Treatment Interaction Approach to Skill Acquisition', *Journal of Applied Psychology (monograph)*, vol. 74, 1989, pp. 657–90; T. R. Mitchell and W. S. Silver, 'Individual and Group Goals When Workers Are Interdependent: Effects on Task Strategies and Performance', *Journal of Applied Psychology*, April 1990, pp. 185–93; and A. M. O'Leary-Kelly, J. J. Martocchio and D. D. Frink, 'A Review of the Influence of Group Goals on Group Performance', *Academy of Management Journal*, October 1994, pp. 1285–301.

47. See J. C. Anderson and C. A. O'Reilly, 'Effects of an Organizational Control System on Managerial Satisfaction and Performance', *Human Relations*, June 1981, pp. 491–501; and J. P. Meyer, B. Schacht-Cole and I. R. Gellatly, 'An Examination of the Cognitive Mechanisms by Which Assigned Goals Affect Task Performance and Reactions to Performance', *Journal of Applied Social Psychology*, vol. 18, no. 5, 1988, pp. 390–408.

48. A. N. Turner and P. R. Lawrence, *Industrial Jobs and the Worker* (Boston: Harvard University Press, 1965).

49. J. R. Hackman and G. R. Oldham, 'Motivation Through the Design of Work: Test of a Theory', *Organizational Behavior and Human Performance*, August 1976, pp. 250–79.

50. J. R. Hackman, 'Work Design', in J. R. Hackman and J. L. Suttle (eds), *Improving Life at Work* (Santa Monica, CA: Goodyear, 1977), p. 129.

51. See 'Job Characteristics Theory of Work Redesign', in J. B. Miner, *Theories of Organizational Behavior* (Hinsdale, IL: Dryden Press, 1980), pp. 231–66; B. T. Loher, R. A. Noe, N. L. Moeller and M. P. Fitzgerald, 'A Meta-Analysis of the Relation of Job Characteristics to Job Satisfaction', *Journal of Applied Psychology*, May 1985, pp. 280–89; W. H. Glick, G. D. Jenkins, Jr, and N. Gupta, 'Method versus Substance: How Strong are Underlying Relationships between Job Characteristics and Attitudinal Outcomes?', *Academy of Management Journal*, September 1986, pp. 441–64; Y. Fried and G. R. Ferns, 'The Validity of the Job Characteristics Model: A Review and Meta-Analysis', *Personnel Psychology*, Summer 1987, pp. 287–322; and S. J. Zaccaro and E. F. Stone, 'Incremental Validity of an Empirically Based Measure of Job Characteristics', *Journal of Applied Psychology*, May 1988, pp. 245–52.

52. See R. B. Dunham, 'Measurement and Dimensionality of Job Characteristics', *Journal of Applied Psychology*, August 1976, pp. 404–09; J. L. Pierce and R. B. Dunham, 'Task Design: A Literature Review', *Academy of Management Review*, January 1976, pp. 83–97; and D. M. Rousseau, 'Technological Differences in Job Characteristics, Employee Satisfaction, and Motivation: A Synthesis of Job Design Research and Sociotechnical Systems Theory', *Organizational Behavior and Human Performance*, October 1977, pp. 18–42.

53. Ibid; and Y. Fried and G. R. Ferris, 'The Dimensionality of Job Characteristics: Some Neglected Issues', *Journal of Applied Psychology*, August 1986, pp. 419–26.

54. See, for example, Fried and Ferns, 'The Dimensionality of Job Characteristics'; and M. G. Evans and D. A. Ondrack, 'The Motivational Potential of Jobs: Is a Multiplicative Model Really Necessary?', in S. L. McShane (ed.), *Organizational Behavior, ASAC Conference Proceedings*, vol. 9, part 5 (Halifax, Nova Scotia: 1988), pp. 31–39.

55. See P. E. Spector, 'Higher-Order Need Strength as a Moderator of the Job Scope–Employee Outcome Relationship: A Meta-Analysis', *Journal of Occupational Psychology*, June 1985, pp. 119–27; G. B. Graen, T. A. Scandura and M. R. Graen, 'A Field Experimental Test of the Moderating Effects of Growth Need Strength on Productivity', *Journal of Applied Psychology*, August 1986, pp. 484–91; and Fried and Ferns, 'The Validity of the Job Characteristics Model'.

56. C. A. O'Reilly and D. E Caldwell, 'Informational Influence as a Determinant of Perceived Task Characteristics and Job Satisfaction', *Journal of Applied Psychology*, April 1979, pp. 157–65; R. V. Montagno, 'The Effects of Comparison Others and Prior Experience on Responses to Task Design', *Academy of Management Journal*, June 1985, pp. 491–98; P. C. Bottger and K. H. Chew, 'The Job Characteristics Model and Growth Satisfaction: Main Effects of Assimilation of Work Experience and Context Satisfaction', *Human Relations*, June 1986, pp. 575–94; and Hackman, 'Work Design', pp. 132–33.

57. G. R. Salancik and J. Pfeffer, 'A Social Information Processing Approach to Job Attitudes and Task Design', *Administrative Science Quarterly*, June 1978, pp. 224–53; J. G. Thomas and R. W. Griffin, 'The Power of Social Information in the Workplace', *Organizational Dynamics*, Autumn 1989, pp. 63–75; and M. D. Zalesny and J. K. Ford, 'Extending the Social Information Processing Perspective: New Links to Attitudes, Behaviors, and Perceptions', *Organizational Behavior and Human Decision Processes*, December 1990, pp. 205–46.

58. See J. Thomas and R. W. Griffin, 'The Social Information Processing Model of Task Design: A Review of the Literature', *Academy of Management Journal*, October 1983, pp. 672–82; and Zalesny and Ford, 'Extending the Social Processing Information Perspective'.

59. J. L. Komaki, T. Coombs and S. Schepman, 'Motivational Implications of Reinforcement Theory', in R. M. Steers, L. W. Porter and G. Bigley (eds), *Motivation and Work Behavior*, 6th ed. (New York: McGraw-Hill, 1996), pp. 87–107.

60. E. A. Locke, 'Latham vs. Komaki: A Tale of Two Paradigms', *Journal of Applied Psychology*, February 1980, pp. 16–23.

61. M. Csikszentmihalyi, *Flow: The Psychology of Optimal Experience* (New York: HarperCollins, 1990); M. Csikszentmihalyi, *Finding Flow* (New York: Basic Books, 1997); and C. Mainemelis, 'When the Muse Takes It All: A Model for the Experience of Timelessness in Organizations', *Academy of Management Review*, October 2001, pp. 548–65.

62. This section is based on Thomas, *Intrinsic Motivation at Work*; and K. W. Thomas, 'Intrinsic Motivation and How It Works', *Training*, October 2000, pp. 130–35.

63. As reported in K. W. Thomas and W. G. Tymon, Jr, 'Bridging the Motivation Gap in Total Quality', *Quality Management Journal*, vol. 4, no. 2, 1997, p. 89.

64. Thomas, *Intrinsic Motivation at Work*, p. 79.

65. J. S. Adams, 'Inequity in Social Exchanges', in L. Berkowitz (ed.), *Advances in Experimental Social Psychology* (New York: Academic Press, 1965), pp. 267–300.

66. P. S. Goodman, 'An Examination of Referents Used in the Evaluation of Pay', *Organizational Behavior and Human Performance*, October 1974, pp. 170–95; S. Ronen, 'Equity Perception in Multiple Comparisons: A Field Study', *Human Relations*, April 1986, pp. 333–46; R. W. Scholl, E. A. Cooper and J. F. McKenna, 'Referent Selection in Determining Equity Perception: Differential Effects on Behavioral and

Attitudinal Outcomes', *Personnel Psychology*, Spring 1987, pp. 113–27; and T. P. Summers and A. S. DeNisi, 'In Search of Adams' Other: Re-examination of Referents Used in the Evaluation of Pay', *Human Relations*, June 1990, pp. 497–511.

67. C. T. Kulik and M. L. Ambrose, 'Personal and Situational Determinants of Referent Choice', *Academy of Management Review*, April 1992, pp. 212–37.

68. See, for example, E. Walster, G. W. Walster and W. G. Scott, *Equity: Theory and Research* (Boston: Allyn & Bacon, 1978); and J. Greenberg, 'Cognitive Reevaluation of Outcomes in Response to Underpayment Inequity', *Academy of Management Journal*, March 1989, pp. 174–84.

69. P. S. Goodman and A. Friedman, 'An Examination of Adams' Theory of Inequity', *Administrative Science Quarterly*, September 1971, pp. 271–88; R. P. Vecchio, 'An Individual-Differences Interpretation of the Conflicting Predictions Generated by Equity Theory and Expectancy Theory', *Journal of Applied Psychology*, August 1981, pp. 470–81; J. Greenberg, 'Approaching Equity and Avoiding Inequity in Groups and Organizations', in J. Greenberg and R. L. Cohen (eds), *Equity and Justice in Social Behavior* (New York: Academic Press, 1982), pp. 389–435; R. T. Mowday, 'Equity Theory Predictions of Behavior in Organizations', in R. Steers, L. W. Porter and G. Bigley (eds), *Motivation and Work Behavior*, 6th ed. (New York: McGraw-Hill, 1996), pp. 111–31; S. Werner and N. P. Mero, 'Fair or Foul? The Effects of External, Internal, and Employee Equity on Changes in Performance of Major League Baseball Players', *Human Relations*, October 1999, pp. 1291–312; and R. W. Griffeth and S. Gaertner, 'A Role for Equity Theory in the Turnover Process: An Empirical Test', *Journal of Applied Social Psychology*, May 2001, pp. 1017–37.

70. See, for example, K. S. Sauley and A. G. Bedeian, 'Equity Sensitivity: Construction of a Measure and Examination of Its Psychometric Properties', *Journal of Management*, vol. 26, no. 5, pp. 885–910; and M. N. Bing and S. M. Burroughs, 'The Predictive and Interactive Effects of Equity Sensitivity in Teamwork-Oriented Organizations', *Journal of Organizational Behavior*, May 2001, pp. 271–90.

71. J. Greenberg and S. Ornstein, 'High Status Job Title as Compensation for Underpayment: A Test of Equity Theory', *Journal of Applied Psychology*, May 1983, pp. 285–97; and J. Greenberg, 'Equity and Workplace Status: A Field Experiment', *Journal of Applied Psychology*, November 1988, pp. 606–13.

72. See, for example, J. Greenberg, *The Quest for Justice on the Job* (Thousand Oaks, CA: Sage, 1996); R. Cropanzano and J. Greenberg, 'Progress in Organizational Justice: Tunneling through the Maze', in C. L. Cooper and I. T. Robertson (eds), *International Review of Industrial and Organizational Psychology*, vol. 12 (New York: Wiley, 1997); and J. A. Colquitt, D. E. Conlon, M. J. Wesson, C .O. L. H. Porter and K. Y. Ng, 'Justice at the Millennium: A Meta-Analytic Review of the 25 Years of Organizational Justice Research', *Journal of Applied Psychology*, June 2001, pp. 425–45.

73. See, for example, R. C. Dailey and D. J. Kirk, 'Distributive and Procedural Justice as Antecedents of Job Dissatisfaction and Intent to Turnover', *Human Relations*, March 1992, pp. 305–16; D. B. McFarlin and P. D. Sweeney, 'Distributive and Procedural Justice as Predictors of Satisfaction with Personal and Organizational Outcomes', *Academy of Management Journal*, August 1992, pp. 626–37; and M. A. Konovsky, 'Understanding Procedural Justice and Its Impact on Business Organizations', *Journal of Management*, vol. 26, no. 3, 2000, pp. 489–511.

74. R. H. Moorman, 'Relationship Between Justice and Organizational Citizenship Behaviors: Do Fairness Perceptions Influence Employee Citizenship?', *Journal of Applied Psychology*, December 1991, pp. 845–55.

75. P. S. Goodman, 'Social Comparison Process in Organizations', in B. M. Staw and G. R. Salancik (eds), *New Directions in Organizational Behavior* (Chicago: St. Clair, 1977), pp. 97–132; and J. Greenberg, 'A Taxonomy of Organizational Justice Theories', *Academy of Management Review*, January 1987, pp. 9–22.

76. V. H. Vroom, *Work and Motivation* (New York: John Wiley, 1964).

77. See, for example, H. G. Heneman III and D. P. Schwab, 'Evaluation of Research on Expectancy Theory Prediction of Employee Performance', *Psychological Bulletin*, July 1972, pp. 1–9; T. R. Mitchell, 'Expectancy Models of Job Satisfaction, Occupational Preference and Effort: A Theoretical, Methodological and Empirical Appraisal', *Psychological Bulletin*, November 1974, pp. 1053–77; and L. Reinharth and M. A. Wahba, 'Expectancy Theory as a Predictor of Work Motivation, Effort Expenditure, and Job Performance', *Academy of Management Journal*, September 1975, pp. 502–37.

78. See, for example, L. W. Porter and E. E. Lawler III, *Managerial Attitudes and Performance* (Homewood, IL: Irwin, 1968); D. F. Parker and L. Dyer, 'Expectancy Theory as a Within-Person Behavioral Choice Model: An Empirical Test of Some Conceptual and Methodological Refinements', *Organizational Behavior and Human Performance*, October 1976, pp. 97–117; H. J. Arnold, 'A Test of the Multiplicative Hypothesis of Expectancy-Valence Theories of Work Motivation', *Academy of Management Journal*, April 1981, pp. 128–41; and W. Van Eerde and H. Thierry, 'Vroom's Expectancy Models and Work-Related Criteria: A Meta-Analysis', *Journal of Applied Psychology*, October 1996, pp. 575–86.

79. Vroom refers to these three variables as expectancy, instrumentality and valence, respectively.

80. P. M. Muchinsky, 'A Comparison of Within- and Across-Subjects Analyses of the Expectancy-Valence Model for Predicting Effort', *Academy of Management Journal*, March 1977, pp. 154–58.

81. R. J. House, H. J. Shapiro and M. A. Wahba, 'Expectancy Theory as a Predictor of Work Behavior and Attitudes: A Re-evaluation of Empirical Evidence', *Decision Sciences*, January 1974, pp. 481–506.

82. L. H. Peters, E. J. O'Connor and C. J. Rudolf, 'The Behavioral and Affective Consequences of Performance-Relevant Situational Variables', *Organizational Behavior and Human Performance*, February 1980, pp. 79–96; M. Blumberg and C. D. Pringle, 'The Missing Opportunity in Organizational Research: Some Implications for a Theory of Work Performance', *Academy of Management Review*, October 1982, pp. 560–69; D. A. Waldman and W. D. Spangler, 'Putting Together the Pieces: A Closer Look at the Determinants of Job Performance', *Human Performance*, vol. 2, 1989, pp. 29–59; and J. Hall, 'Americans Know How to Be Productive If Managers Will Let Them', *Organizational Dynamics*, Winter 1994, pp. 33–46.

83. For other examples of models that seek to integrate motivation theories, see H. J. Klein, 'An Integrated Control Theory Model of Work Motivation', *Academy of Management Review*, April 1989, pp. 150–72; E. A. Locke, 'The Motivation Sequence, the Motivation Hub, and the Motivation Core', *Organizational Behavior and Human Decision Processes*, December 1991, pp. 288–99; and T. R. Mitchell, 'Matching Motivational Strategies with Organizational Contexts', in *Research in Organizational Behavior*.

84. N. J. Adler, *International Dimensions of Organizational Behavior*, 4th ed. (Cincinnati, OH: Southwestern, 2002), p. 174.

85. G. Hofstede, 'Motivation, Leadership, and Organization: Do American Theories Apply Abroad?', *Organizational Dynamics*, Summer 1980, p. 55.

86. Ibid.

87. J. K. Giacobbe-Miller, D. J. Miller and V. I. Victorov, 'A Comparison of Russian and U.S. Pay Allocation Decisions, Distributive Justice Judgments, and Productivity under Different Payment Conditions', *Personnel Psychology*, Spring 1998, pp. 137–63.

88. S. L. Mueller and L. D. Clarke, 'Political-Economic Context and Sensitivity to Equity: Differences between the United States and the Transition Economies of Central and Eastern Europe', *Academy of Management Journal*, June 1998, pp. 319–29.

89. I. Harpaz, 'The Importance of Work Goals: An International Perspective', *Journal of International Business Studies*, First Quarter 1990, pp. 75–93.

90. G. E. Popp, H. J. Davis and T. T. Herbert, 'An International Study of Intrinsic Motivation Composition', *Management International Review*, January 1986, pp. 28–35.

91. This section is based on F. J. Landy and W. S. Becker, 'Motivation Theory Reconsidered', in L. L. Cummings and B. M. Staw (eds), *Research in Organizational Behavior*, vol. 9 (Greenwich, CT: JAI Press, 1987), pp. 24–35.

PHOTO CREDITS

181 Reproduced with permission of Maggie Beer.

7

Motivation: From Concept to Applications

CHAPTER OUTLINE

Management by objectives
Employee recognition programs
Employee involvement programs
Variable-pay programs
Skill-based pay plans
Flexible benefits
Comparable worth
Job redesign
Special issues in motivation

LEARNING OBJECTIVES

After studying this chapter, you should be able to:
1. Identify the four ingredients common to MBO programs
2. Explain why managers might want to use employee involvement programs
3. Contrast participative management with employee involvement
4. Define quality circles
5. Explain how share ownership can increase employee motivation
6. Contrast gain sharing and profit sharing
7. Describe the link between skill-based pay plans and motivation theories
8. Explain how flexible benefits turn benefits into motivators
9. Describe the role of comparable worth
10. Explain the basis and potential benefits of job redesign and enrichment
11. Contrast the challenges of motivating professional employees versus low-skilled employees

Having money does not ensure happiness. People with ten million dollars are no happier than people with nine million dollars!

Hobart Brown

Making a painted-hand mural has serious motivation benefits by helping to gain group identity and commitment—and can be a lot of fun too!

People come to work for many different reasons—money, security, sense of worth, to learn and so on. But, at a growing number of workplaces, people are coming to work to have fun—yes, fun! At Customer Care Solutions (CCS), having fun at work is a serious business strategy. As Colin Chodos, the managing director of CCS, states, 'Everything we do from a fun and humour perspective has a very serious business strategy to it.'[1]

Fun activities are planned according to the business goal they are designed to support—some will emphasise collaboration and teamwork, while others will emphasise individual achievements and rewards. One popular fun activity that is used when two departments or sections aren't working well together is to play 'Changing Rooms', modelled on the TV program of the same name. In this activity, each team goes into the work area of the other group and remodels their work area. Working to a small budget, the exercise increases communication and teamwork, and the players have a lot of fun doing it. At the end of the exercise, the company is the big winner—employees are happier, more excited about their work and, most of all, more productive.

Companies such as Flight Centre and Virgin Blue are also using fun as a serious business strategy—and winning awards for being rated the best places to work as a result! Will other features of the workplace and the job also provide sources of motivation that organisations can harness to improve employee and executive performances? In this chapter, we want to focus on how to apply motivation concepts. We want to link theories to practices such as employee involvement. For it's one thing to be able to reproduce motivation theories. It's often another to see how, as a manager, you could use them.

In the following pages, we review a number of motivation techniques and programs that have gained varying degrees of acceptance in practice. And for each of the techniques and programs we review, we specifically address how they build on one or more of the motivation theories covered in the previous chapter.

Management by Objectives

Goal-setting theory has an impressive base of research support. But, as a manager, how do you make goal setting operational? The best answer to that question is: install a management by objectives (MBO) program. Many companies, local councils and state governments have an MBO-type program.[2] Managers attribute this program with unlocking the organisation's employees' potential, helping the organisation to higher performance, growth and output.

WHAT IS MBO?

management by objectives (MBO)
A program that encompasses specific goals, participatively set, for an explicit time period, with feedback on goal progress.

Management by objectives (MBO) emphasises participatively set goals that are tangible, verifiable and measurable. It's not a new idea. In fact, it was originally proposed 50 years ago as a means of using goals to motivate people, rather than to control them.[3] Today, no introduction to basic management concepts would be complete without a discussion of MBO.

MBO's appeal undoubtedly lies in its emphasis on converting overall organisational objectives into specific objectives for organisational units and individual members. MBO operationalises the concept of objectives by devising a process by which objectives cascade down through the organisation. As depicted in Figure 7.1, the organisation's overall objectives are translated into specific objectives for each succeeding level (that is, divisional, departmental, individual) in the organisation. But because lower-unit managers jointly participate in setting their own goals, MBO works from the 'bottom up' as well as from the 'top down'. The result is a hierarchy that links objectives at one level to those at the next level. And for the individual employee, MBO provides specific personal performance objectives.

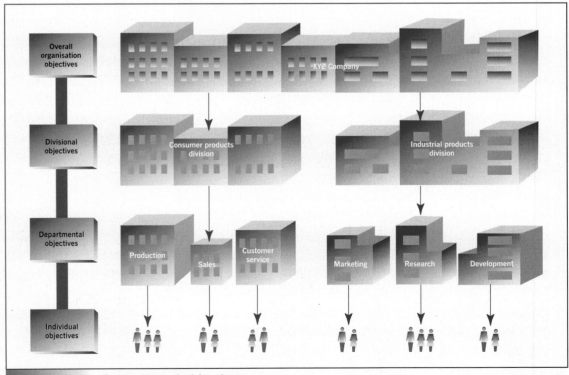

FIGURE 7.1   **Cascading of objectives**

There are four ingredients common to MBO programs. These are goal specificity, participative decision making, an explicit time period, and performance feedback.[4]

The objectives in MBO should be concise statements of expected accomplishments. It's not adequate, for example, merely to state a desire to cut costs, improve service or increase quality. Such desires have to be converted into tangible objectives that can be measured and evaluated. To cut departmental costs *by 7 per cent*, to improve service by ensuring that all telephone orders are processed *within 24 hours of receipt*, to grade and return student assignments *within ten working days*, or to increase quality *by keeping returns to less than 1 per cent of sales* are examples of specific objectives.

The objectives in MBO are not unilaterally set by the boss and then assigned to employees. MBO replaces imposed goals with participatively determined goals. Managers and employees jointly choose the goals and agree on how they will be measured.

Each objective has a specific time period in which it is to be completed. Typically, the time period is three months, six months or a year. So, managers and employees have specific objectives and stipulated time periods in which to accomplish them.

The final ingredient in an MBO program is feedback on performance. MBO seeks to give continuous feedback on progress towards goals. Ideally, this is accomplished by giving ongoing feedback to individuals so that they can monitor and correct their own actions. This is supplemented by periodic managerial evaluations, when progress is reviewed.

LEARNING OBJECTIVE
1
Identify the four ingredients common to MBO programs

LINKING MBO AND GOAL-SETTING THEORY

Goal-setting theory demonstrates that hard goals result in a higher level of individual performance than do easy goals, that specific hard goals result in higher levels of performance than do no goals at all or the generalised goal of 'do your best', and that feedback on one's performance leads to higher performance. Compare these findings with MBO.

MBO directly advocates specific goals and feedback. MBO implies, rather than explicitly states, that goals must be perceived as feasible. Consistent with goal setting, MBO would be most effective when the goals are difficult enough to require the person to do some stretching.

The only area of possible disagreement between MBO and goal-setting theory relates to the issue of participation—MBO strongly advocates it, while goal-setting theory demonstrates that assigning goals to subordinates frequently works just as well. The major benefit to using participation, however, is that it appears to induce individuals to establish more difficult goals.

MBO IN PRACTICE

How widely used is MBO? Reviews of studies that have sought to answer this question suggest that it's a popular technique. You will find MBO programs in many business, health-care, educational, government and non-profit organisations.[5]

MBO's popularity shouldn't be construed to mean that it always works. There are a number of documented cases in which MBO has been implemented but failed to meet management's expectations.[6] A close look at these cases, however, indicates that the problems rarely lie with MBO's basic components. Rather, the culprits tend to be factors such as unrealistic expectations regarding results, lack of commitment by top management, and an inability or unwillingness by management to allocate rewards based on goal accomplishment. Failures can also arise out of cultural incompatibilities, as noted in the previous chapter. For instance, Fujitsu recently scrapped its MBO-type program because management found it didn't fit well with the Japanese culture's emphasis on long-term goals and minimising risk.

Employee Recognition Programs

Laura Jackson makes only $11.50 an hour working at her fast-food job in Brisbane, and the job isn't very challenging or interesting. Yet, Laura talks enthusiastically about her job, her boss and the company that employs her. 'What I like is the fact that Guy [her supervisor] appreciates the effort I make. He compliments me regularly in front of the other people on my shift, and I've been chosen "Employee of the Month" twice in the past six months. Did you see my picture on that plaque on the wall?'

Organisations are increasingly recognising what Laura Jackson is acknowledging: recognition can be a potent motivator.

WHAT ARE EMPLOYEE RECOGNITION PROGRAMS?

Employee recognition programs consist of personal attention, and expressing interest, approval and appreciation for a job well done.[7] They can take numerous forms. For example, Nichols Foods Ltd, a British bottler of soft drinks and cordial syrups, has a comprehensive recognition program.[8] The central hallway in its production area is lined with 'bragging boards', where the accomplishments of various individuals and teams are regularly updated. Monthly awards are presented to people who have been nominated by peers for extraordinary effort on the job. And monthly award winners are eligible for further recognition at an annual off-site meeting for all employees. In contrast, most managers use a far more informal approach. As a case in point, Julia Stewart, president of Applebee's restaurants, frequently leaves sealed notes on the chairs of employees after everyone has gone home.[9] These notes explain how critical Stewart thinks the person's work is or how much she appreciates the completion of a recent project. Stewart also relies heavily on voice mail messages left after office hours to tell employees how appreciative she is for a job well done.

LINKING RECOGNITION PROGRAMS AND REINFORCEMENT THEORY

A few years back, 1,500 employees were surveyed in a variety of work settings to find out what they considered to be the most powerful workplace motivator. Their response? Recognition, recognition and more recognition![10]

Consistent with reinforcement theory, rewarding a behaviour with recognition immediately following that behaviour is likely to encourage its repetition. Recognition can take many forms. You can personally congratulate an employee in private for a good job. You can send a handwritten note or an e-mail message acknowledging something positive that the employee has done. For employees with a strong need for social acceptance, you can publicly recognise their accomplishments. And to enhance group cohesiveness and motivation, you can celebrate team successes. You can use meetings to recognise the contributions and achievements of successful work teams, or throw a team pizza party to celebrate a team's accomplishments.

EMPLOYEE RECOGNITION PROGRAMS IN PRACTICE

In today's highly competitive global economy, most organisations are under severe cost pressures. That makes recognition programs particularly attractive. In contrast to most other motivators, recognising an employee's superior performance often costs little or no money.[11] Maybe that's why a recent Conference Board study found that 85 per cent of companies surveyed

Source: S. Adams, *Share the Wales*, p. 66.
Copyright © United Feature Syndicate Inc.

The Real Deal

Employer branding: Getting the recognition right

In Australia, it goes almost without saying that the banks are very low on the popularity scales of most people. One bank which recognised this reality and uses it to its advantage is the St George Bank, based in Sydney. In media advertisements, it portrayed a small group of people at a dinner party. When one person responded to the question as to his work with the reply, 'I work for a bank', there is a sudden horror-struck silence—until he says he works for St George—whereupon everyone laughs in a relaxed and contented way. What the advertisement is signalling is the value of the employees to the company. It also establishes a form of employer branding—in this case, that employee value and recognition is more than just a cliché or slogan. It is part of the organisation's strategy and cultural values and relies very heavily on employee recognition. In the case of Lion Nathan, they did a lot of homework on the corporate values and culture before launching into employer branding. They must be doing it right, because in a survey of employees of over 160 companies in Australia, Lion Nathan ranked fourth as the best place to work.

Source: Based on S. Lloyd, 'Branding From the Inside Out', *Business Review Weekly,* 14 March 2002.

reported that they use recognition programs to reward and motivate employees—with a new emphasis on job performance rather than the historical criterion of career milestones (that is, 20 years of service).[12]

One of the most well-known and widely used recognition devices is the use of suggestion systems. Employees offer suggestions for improving processes or cutting costs and are recognised with small cash awards. The Japanese have been especially effective at making suggestion systems work. For example, a typical high-performing Japanese factory in the automotive components business generates 47 suggestions per employee a year and pays the equivalent of around US$35 per suggestion. In contrast, a comparable Western factory generates about one suggestion per employee per year, but pays out US$90 per suggestion.[13]

Employee Involvement Programs

At the BIC Corporation plant in Connecticut, in the United States, which makes pens, razors and cigarette lighters, production employees meet every week to review offerings from the employee suggestion box. Whenever a group voices its support for a proposal, it is immediately passed on to the appropriate supervisor, who has ten days to put the change in place.[14] At General Electric's aircraft-engine

At Lion Nathan Brewery, self-managed teams share responsibility for their own production, wastage, continuous improvement, quality assurance, training and a range of safety measures. In turn, greater control over their work provides employees with greater pride and commitment in what they do.

assembly facility in North Carolina, the plant's 170 employees essentially manage themselves. Jet engines are produced by nine teams of people and they are given just one basic directive: the day that their next engine must be loaded on to a truck. All other decisions are made within the teams. The Donnelly Corporation, a major supplier of glass products to motor vehicle manufacturers, uses committees of elected representatives to make all key decisions affecting Donnelly employees.[15] The laws of Germany, France, Denmark, Sweden and Austria require companies to have elected representatives from their employee groups as members of their boards of directors.

The common theme throughout the preceding examples is that they all illustrate employee involvement programs. In this section, we clarify what we mean by employee involvement, describe some of the various forms that it takes, consider the motivational implications of these programs, and show some applications.

WHAT IS EMPLOYEE INVOLVEMENT?

LEARNING OBJECTIVE

2

Explain why managers might want to use employee involvement programs

Employee involvement has become a convenient catch-all term to cover a variety of techniques.[16] For example, it encompasses popular ideas such as employee participation or participative management, workplace democracy, empowerment and employee ownership. Our position is, although each of these ideas has some unique characteristics, they all have a common core—that of employee involvement.

employee involvement program
A participative process that uses the entire capacity of employees and is designed to encourage increased commitment to the organisation's success.

What, specifically, do we mean by **employee involvement**? We define it as a participative process that uses the entire capacity of employees and is designed to encourage increased commitment to the organisation's success.[17] The underlying logic is that by involving workers in the decisions that affect them and by increasing their autonomy and control over their work lives, employees will become more motivated, more committed to the organisation, more productive, and more satisfied with their jobs.[18]

Does this mean that participation and employee involvement are synonyms for each other? No. Participation is a more limited term. It's a subset within the larger framework of employee involvement. All of the employee involvement programs we describe include some form of employee participation, but the term *participation*, per se, is too narrow and too limiting.

EXAMPLES OF EMPLOYEE INVOLVEMENT PROGRAMS

LEARNING OBJECTIVE

3

Contrast participative management with employee involvement

In this section, we review four forms of employee involvement: participative management, representative participation, quality circles, and employee share ownership plans.

Participative management

participative management
A process in which subordinates share a significant degree of decision-making power with their immediate superiors.

The distinct characteristic common to all **participative management** programs is the use of joint decision making. That is, subordinates actually share a significant degree of decision-making power with their immediate superiors.

Participative management has, at times, been promoted as a panacea for poor morale and low productivity. Some authors have even proposed that participative management is an ethical imperative.[19] But participative management isn't appropriate for every organisation or every work unit. For it to work, the issues in which employees get involved must be relevant to their interests so that they will be motivated, employees must have the competence and knowledge to make a useful contribution, and there must be trust and confidence between all the parties involved.[20]

Why would management want to share its decision-making power with subordinates? There are a number of good reasons. As jobs have become more complex, managers often don't know everything their employees do. Thus, participation allows those who know the most to contribute. The result can be better decisions. The interdependence in tasks that employees often perform today also requires consultation with people in other departments and work units. This increases the need for teams, committees and group meetings to resolve issues that affect them jointly.

Participation additionally increases commitment to decisions. People are less likely to undermine a decision at the time of its implementation if they shared in making that decision. Finally, participation provides intrinsic rewards for employees. It can make their jobs more interesting and more meaningful.

Dozens of studies have been conducted on the participation–performance relationship. The findings, however, are mixed.[21] When the research is reviewed carefully, it appears that participation typically has only a modest influence on variables such as employee productivity, motivation and job satisfaction. Of course, this doesn't mean that the use of participative management can't be beneficial under the right conditions. What it says, however, is that the use of participation is no sure means for improving employee performance.

Representative participation

Almost every country in Western Europe has some type of legislation requiring companies to practise **representative participation**. That is, rather than participate directly in decisions, workers are represented by a small group of employees who actually participate. Representative participation has been called 'the most widely legislated form of employee involvement around the world'.[22]

The goal of representative participation is to redistribute power within an organisation, putting labour on a more equal footing with the interests of management and shareholders.

The two most common forms which representative participation takes are works councils and board representatives.[23] **Works councils** link employees with management. They are groups of nominated or elected employees who must be consulted when management makes decisions involving personnel. For example, in the Netherlands, if a Dutch company is taken over by another firm, the former's works council must be informed at an early stage, and if the council objects, it has 30 days to seek a court injunction to stop the takeover.[24] **Board representatives** are employees who sit on a company's board of directors and represent the interests of the firm's employees. In some countries, large companies may be legally required to make sure that employee representatives have the same number of board seats as shareholder representatives.

The overall influence of representative participation on working employees seems to be minimal.[25] For example, the evidence suggests that works councils are dominated by management and have little impact on employees or the organisation. And while this form of employee involvement might increase the motivation and satisfaction of the individuals who are doing the representing, there is little evidence that this trickles down to the operating employees whom they represent. Overall, 'the greatest value of representative participation is symbolic. If one is interested in changing employee attitudes or in improving organisational performance, representative participation would be a poor choice.'[26]

Quality circles

The quality circle concept is frequently mentioned as one of the techniques that Japanese firms use that has allowed them to make high-quality products at low costs. Originally begun in the United States and exported to Japan in the 1950s, the quality circle became quite popular in North America, Australia and Europe during the 1980s.[27]

What is a **quality circle**? It is a work group of eight to ten employees and supervisors who have a shared area of responsibility. They meet regularly—typically once a week, on company time and on company premises—to discuss their quality problems, investigate causes of the problems, recommend solutions and take corrective actions. They take over the responsibility for solving quality problems, and they generate and evaluate their own feedback. But management typically retains control over the final decision regarding implementation of recommended solutions. Of course, it is not presumed that employees inherently have this ability to analyse and solve quality problems. Therefore, part of the quality circle concept includes teaching participating employees group communication skills, various quality strategies, and measurement and problem analysis techniques. Figure 7.2 describes a typical quality circle process.

---

representative participation
Workers participate in organisational decision making through a small group of representative employees.

works councils
Groups of nominated or elected employees who must be consulted when management makes decisions involving personnel.

board representative
A form of representative participation; employees sit on a company's board of directors and represent the interests of the firm's employees.

LEARNING OBJECTIVE

4

Define quality circles

quality circle
A work group of employees who meet regularly to discuss their quality problems, investigate causes, recommend solutions and take corrective actions.

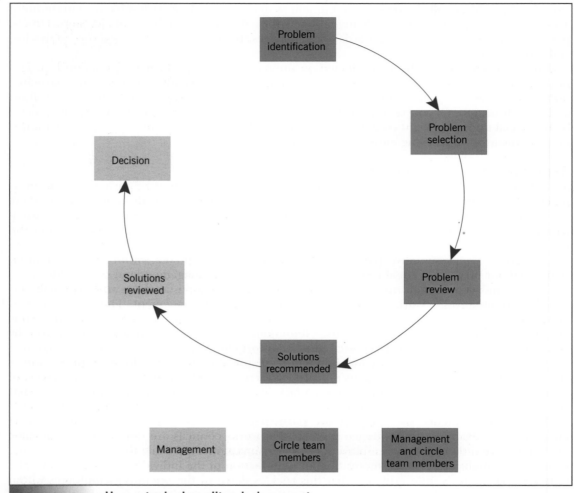

FIGURE 7.2   How a typical quality circle operates

Do quality circles improve employee productivity and satisfaction? A review of the evidence indicates that they are much more likely to positively affect productivity. They tend to show little or no effect on employee satisfaction; and although many studies report positive results from quality circles on productivity, these results are by no means guaranteed.[28] The failure of many quality circle programs to produce measurable benefits has also led to a large number of them being discontinued.

One business writer has gone as far as to say that although quality circles were the management fad of the 1980s, they have 'become a flop'.[29] He offers two possible explanations for their disappointing results. First is the little bit of time that actually deals with employee involvement. 'At most, these programs operate for 1 hour per week, with the remaining 39 hours unchanged. Why should changes in 2.5 percent of a person's job have a major impact?'[30] Second, the ease of implementing quality circles often worked against them. They were seen as a simple device that could be added on to the organisation with few changes required outside the program itself. In many cases, the only significant involvement by management was funding the program. So, quality circles became an easy way for management to get on the employee involvement

When Telstra first listed on the Australian Stock Exchange, over 92 per cent of its employees took up options to buy parcels of Telstra shares, demonstrating how popular such plans are.

bandwagon. And, unfortunately, the lack of planning and commitment of top management often contributed to the failure of quality circles.

Share-ownership plans

The final employee involvement approach we will discuss is employee **share-ownership** schemes or plans.[31]

Employee share ownership can mean any number of things, from employees owning some shares in the company at which they work, to the individuals working in the company owning and personally operating the firm. Employee share-ownership plans are company-established benefit plans in which employees acquire shares as part of their remuneration benefits. United Airlines is 100 per cent owned by its employees, Polaroid is 20 per cent owned by its employees, and over 70 per cent of Avis shares are owned by its employees.[32] When Telstra first listed on the Australian Stock Exchange, over 92 per cent of its employees took up options to buy parcels of Telstra shares, demonstrating how popular such plans are.

In the typical share-ownership scheme or plan, an employee share-ownership trust is created. Companies contribute either shares or cash to buy shares for the trust and allocate the shares to employees. While employees hold shares in their company, they usually cannot take physical possession of their shares or sell them as long as they are still employed at the company.

The overseas research on share ownership by employees indicates that it increases employee satisfaction.[33] But its impact on performance is less clear. For example, one study compared 45 companies with share-ownership schemes against 238 companies that didn't have such plans.[34] The companies with share-ownership plans outperformed the firms that didn't, both in terms of employment and sales growth. Another study found that organisations with share-ownership schemes had total shareholder returns that averaged 6.9 percentage points higher over the four years after the share-ownership plan was set up than market returns of similar companies without employee share-ownership plans.[35] But other studies have shown disappointing results, especially in Australia where it is estimated that fewer than 3 per cent of companies have employee share-ownership plans.[36] The main obstacles cited for the lack of employee share-ownership plans in Australia were union opposition, employee concerns over declines in share values, and a tax system that acted as an expensive barrier to such schemes.[37]

Employee share ownership has the potential to increase both employee job satisfaction and work motivation. But for this potential to be realised, employees need to psychologically experience ownership. That is, in addition to merely having a financial stake in the company, employees need to be kept regularly informed on the status of the business and also have the opportunity to exercise influence over the business. The evidence consistently indicates that it takes ownership and a participative style of management to achieve significant improvements in an organisation's performance. Just ask Andrew Dunoon, the founder of the Melbourne catering firm Elizabeth Andrews—he found sharing the company profits with employees so successful in motivating employees he is now setting up a share-ownership plan so that employees can get more incentive from their jobs.[38]

LINKING EMPLOYEE INVOLVEMENT PROGRAMS AND MOTIVATION THEORIES

Employee involvement draws on a number of the motivation theories discussed in the previous chapter. For example, Theory Y is consistent with participative management, while Theory X

LEARNING OBJECTIVE

5

Explain how share ownership can increase employee motivation

share ownership
Company-established benefit plans in which employees acquire shares in the company as part of their benefits.

aligns with the more traditional autocratic style of managing people. In terms of two-factor theory, employee involvement programs could provide employees with intrinsic motivation by increasing opportunities for growth, responsibility and involvement in the work itself. Similarly, the opportunity to make and implement decisions, and then seeing them work out, can help to satisfy an employee's needs for responsibility, achievement, recognition, growth and enhanced self-esteem. So, employee involvement is compatible with ERG theory and efforts to stimulate the achievement need. And extensive employee involvement programs clearly have the potential to increase employee intrinsic motivation in work tasks and create a flow experience.

EMPLOYEE INVOLVEMENT PROGRAMS IN PRACTICE

Germany, France, Holland and the Scandinavian countries have firmly established the principle of industrial democracy in Europe; and other nations, including Japan and Israel, have traditionally practised some form of representative participation for decades. Participative management and representative participation were much slower to gain ground in Australian organisations. But nowadays, employee involvement programs that stress participation have become the norm.

A study comparing the acceptance of employee involvement programs in four countries, including the United States and India, confirmed the importance of modifying practices to reflect national culture.[39] Specifically, while American employees readily accepted these programs, managers in India who tried to empower their employees were rated low by those employees; and the use of empowerment also negatively affected employee satisfaction. These reactions are consistent with India's high power–distance culture, which accepts and expects differences in authority.

What about quality circles? How popular are they in practice? The names of companies that have used quality circles reads like a *Who's Who* of business: Hewlett-Packard, MIM, Texas Instruments, BHP, FujiXerox, Eastman Kodak, Procter & Gamble, Mitsubishi, General Motors-Holden, Ford Australia and IBM.[40] But, as we noted, the success of quality circles has been far from overwhelming. They were popular in the 1980s, largely because they were easy to implement. In more recent years, many organisations have dropped their quality circles and replaced them with more comprehensive team-based structures (which we discuss in a later chapter of this book).

What about share-ownership schemes? They have grown from just a handful in the mid-1970s to around 11,500 now, covering approximately 10 million employees in the United States but only 3 per cent of private companies in Australia.[41] Many large, well-known global companies have implemented share-ownership plans, but most tend to be small, private firms. And that is likely to increase, as the growth in employment over the last ten years has been in mostly small businesses and because both sides of politics in Australia now recognise the motivating potential of such schemes and are working to increase their number.[42]

Variable-pay Programs

'Why should I put any extra effort into this job?' asked Anne Garcia, a Year 4 primary-school teacher in Mackay, Queensland. 'I can excel or I can do the bare minimum. It makes no difference. I still get paid the same. Why do anything above the minimum to get by?'

Schoolteachers have voiced comments similar to Anne's for decades, because pay increases were tied to seniority and awards. Recently, however, a number of school boards have begun revamping their compensation systems to motivate people like Anne to strive for excellence in their jobs.[43] Teachers in several schools are having their pay tied to the performance of the students in their classrooms. In some instances, teachers whose students improve on standardised tests can earn an extra increase in salary.

A number of organisations—business firms, as well as school boards and other government agencies—are moving away from paying people based solely on credentials or length of service towards variable-pay programs.

WHAT ARE VARIABLE-PAY PROGRAMS?

Piece-rate plans, wage incentives, profit sharing, bonuses and gain sharing are all forms of **variable-pay programs**. What differentiates these forms of compensation from more traditional programs is that, instead of paying a person only for time on the job or seniority, a portion of an employee's pay is based on some individual and/or organisational measure of performance. Unlike more traditional base-pay programs, variable pay isn't an annuity. There is no guarantee that, just because you made $60,000 last year, you'll make the same amount this year. With variable pay, earnings fluctuate up and down with the measure of performance.[44]

It is precisely the fluctuation in variable pay that has made these programs attractive to management. It turns part of an organisation's fixed labour costs into a variable cost, thus reducing expenses when performance declines. So, when the economy entered a downturn in 2001, companies with variable pay were able to reduce their labour costs much faster than companies that had maintained non-performance-based compensation systems.[45] In addition, by tying pay to performance, earnings recognise contribution, rather than being a form of entitlement. Low performers find, over time, that their pay stagnates, while high performers enjoy pay increases commensurate with their contribution.

Four of the more widely used variable-pay programs are piece-rate wages, bonuses, profit sharing and gain sharing.

Piece-rate wages have been around for nearly a century. They have long been popular as a means for compensating production workers. In **piece-rate pay plans**, workers are paid a fixed sum for each unit of production completed. When an employee gets no base salary and is paid only for what he or she produces, this is a pure piece-rate plan. People who work sports stadiums selling meat pies, ice creams and soft drinks frequently are paid this way. They might get to keep $0.50 for every drink they sell. If they sell 200 drinks during a game, they make $100. If they sell only 40 drinks, their take is only $20. The harder they work and the more items they sell, the more they earn. Many organisations use a modified piece-rate plan, in which employees earn a base hourly wage plus a piece-rate differential. So, a medical records transcriber might be paid $7 an hour plus 20 cents per page. Such modified plans provide a floor under an employee's earnings, while still offering a productivity incentive. However, it is worth reiterating what was raised in an earlier chapter of this book—that is, if employees are paid on a per item that is produced basis, production will increase, but quality may decrease as a result.

Bonuses can be paid exclusively to executives or to all employees. For example, annual bonuses in the millions of dollars are not uncommon in Australian companies. A big part of Colonial First State's former CEO Chris Cuffe's $33 million payout was accrued bonuses.[46] Increasingly, bonus plans are taking on a larger focus within organisations to include lower-ranking employees.[47] Many companies now routinely reward production employees with bonuses in the thousands of dollars when company profits improve. The bonuses may not always be in cash, either—marginal tax rates in Australia of nearly 50 per cent make non-cash bonuses such as paid accounts, school fees, second cars and travel more attractive to managers and employees alike.

Profit-sharing plans are organisation-wide programs that distribute compensation based on some established formula designed around a company's profitability. These can be direct cash outlays or, particularly in the case of top managers, allocated as share options. When you read about executives such as Sanford Weill, the CEO at Citigroup, earning over US$200 million in one year, almost all of this comes from cashing in share options previously granted based on company profit performance.

The variable-pay program that has gotten the most attention in recent years is undoubtedly **gain sharing**.[48] This is a formula-based group incentive plan. Improvements in group productivity—from one period to another—determine the total amount of money that is to be allocated. The division of productivity savings can be split between the company and employees in any number of ways, but 50–50 is pretty typical.

Isn't gain sharing the same thing as profit sharing? They are similar but not the same thing.

variable-pay programs
A portion of an employee's pay is based on some individual and/or organisational measure of performance.

piece-rate pay plans
Workers are paid a fixed sum for each unit of production completed.

LEARNING OBJECTIVE

6

Contrast gain sharing and profit sharing

profit-sharing plans
Organisation-wide programs that distribute compensation based on some established formula designed around a company's profitability.

gain sharing
An incentive plan in which improvements in group productivity determine the total amount of money that is allocated.

By focusing on productivity gains rather than on profits, gain sharing rewards specific behaviours that are less influenced by external factors. Employees in a gain-sharing plan can receive incentive awards even when the organisation isn't profitable.

A study by Equity Strategies indicated the popularity of executive share and share option plans. The company, a share-plan consultancy, examined the annual reports of 122 of the top 150 largest public companies in a search for executive share plans. Of these 122 companies, 52 had introduced, amended or renewed share option plans and 15 had introduced, amended or revised share plans.[49] Seventy-eight per cent of these plans contain performance requirements or hurdles. A spokesperson for Equity Strategies made the point that annual cash bonuses tend to reward executives for meeting short-term goals. Bonuses are often designed to encourage executives to reach individual or team targets. By contrast, shares and share options tend to reward executives for meeting longer-term, organisation-wide performance goals, such as return on shareholder funds. Share and share option plans usually have performance targets spanning three to five years.

Do variable-pay programs work? Do they increase motivation and productivity? The answer is a qualified 'yes'. For example, studies generally support that organisations with profit-sharing plans have higher levels of profitability than those without them.[50] Similarly, gain sharing has been found to improve productivity in a majority of cases and often has a positive impact on employee attitudes.[51] One management study of 83 companies that used gain sharing found, on average, that grievances dropped 83 per cent, absences fell 84 per cent and lost-time accidents decreased by 69 per cent.[52] The downside of variable pay, from an employee's perspective, is its unpredictability. With a straight base salary, employees know what they will be earning. Adding in merit and cost-of-living increases, they can make fairly accurate predictions about what they will be making next year and the year after that. They can finance cars and homes based on reasonably solid assumptions. That's more difficult to do with variable pay. Your group's performance might slip this year, or a recession might undermine your company's profits. Depending on how your variable pay is determined, these can cut your income. Moreover, people begin to take repeated annual performance bonuses for granted. A 15 or 20 per cent bonus, received three years in a row, begins to become expected in the fourth year. If it doesn't materialise, management will find itself with some disgruntled employees on its hands.

LINKING VARIABLE-PAY PROGRAMS AND EXPECTANCY THEORY

Variable pay is probably most compatible with expectancy theory predictions. Specifically, individuals should perceive a strong relationship between their performance and the rewards they receive if motivation is to be maximised. If rewards are allocated completely on non-performance factors—such as seniority or job title—then employees are likely to reduce their effort.

The evidence supports the importance of this linkage, especially for operative employees working under piece-rate systems. For example, one study of 400 manufacturing firms found that companies with wage incentive plans achieved 43 to 64 per cent greater productivity than those without such plans.[53]

Group and organisation-wide incentives reinforce and encourage employees to sublimate personal goals for the best interests of their department or the organisation. Group-based performance incentives are also a natural extension for organisations that are trying to build a strong team ethic. By linking rewards to team performance, employees are encouraged to make extra efforts to help their team succeed.

VARIABLE-PAY PROGRAMS IN PRACTICE

Variable pay is a concept that is rapidly replacing the annual cost-of-living raise. One reason, as cited earlier, is its motivational power—but don't ignore the cost implications. Bonuses, gain sharing, and other variable-based reward programs avoid the fixed expense of permanent salary boosts. Variable pay, for example, allowed the management of many companies in 2001 and 2002 to cushion profits (or cut losses) during times of economic recession.

Pay for performance has been 'in' for compensating managers for more than a decade. The new trend has been expanding this practice to non-managerial employees. IBM, Pizza Hut and John Deere Machinery are just a few examples of companies using variable pay with rank-and-file employees.[54] Today, 78 per cent of American companies have some form of variable-pay plan for non-executives; up from 47 per cent in 1990.[55] However, Australian companies have been comparatively slow in adopting such practices, preferring instead to offer salary-based remuneration based on knowledge- or skill-based pay with incentives linked to the performance of individuals.[56]

Variable pay also seems to be gaining in global popularity. For example, a survey found that 21.8 per cent of Japanese companies are now using such pay systems. The rate was less than 10 per cent in the 1980s.[57]

Gain sharing's popularity seems to be narrowly focused among large, unionised manufacturing companies.[58] Among firms that haven't introduced performance-based compensation programs, common concerns tend to surface.[59] Managers fret over what should constitute performance and how it should be measured. They have to overcome the historical attachment to cost-of-living adjustments and the belief that they have an obligation to keep all employees' pay in step with inflation. Other barriers include salary scales keyed to what the competition is paying, traditional compensation systems that rely heavily on specific pay grades and relatively narrow pay ranges, and performance appraisal practices that produce inflated evaluations and expectations of full rewards. Of course, from the employees' standpoint, the major concern is a potential drop in earnings. Pay for performance means employees have to share in the risks, as well as the rewards, of their employer's business.

The Real Deal

Pay for performance at Siebel Systems

Executives at Siebel Systems, the sales-automation software firm headquartered in San Mateo, California, understand how rewards shape behaviour. So, they have scrapped their traditional system of rewarding their sales people solely on the basis of how well they achieve their sales targets. They have replaced it with a new motivation system that broadens the definition of sales performance to include building long-term customer satisfaction.

Siebel considers building long-term customer relationships to be its top priority. Says the company's vice president of technical services, Steve Mankoff: '[If reps] close a contract with a customer, continue to follow up with that customer, and make sure that customer is successful, chances are that customer will come back for more. In any given quarter, 45 to 60 per cent of our business is from repeat customers.'

So, now nearly 40 per cent of each sales person's incentive compensation is based on their customers' reported satisfaction with service and implementation of the products they have purchased. To determine how well its sales people are doing, Siebel regularly surveys customers on the responsiveness of its sales organisation, the sales consultant's ability to integrate a customer's requirements with Siebel's software solutions, the rep's knowledge of the products, and of the customer's project, and ease of purchasing and contracting.

By broadening pay for performance from just generating sales to also including customer satisfaction, Siebel is getting its sales force to focus on the needs of its customers. 'It works,' says Mankoff. 'Our loyalty rate among customers is in the 96 to 99 per cent range.'

Source: E. Zimmerman, 'Quota Busters', *Sales & Marketing Management*, January 2001, pp. 59–63. Copyright © 2001 VNU Business Media, Inc. Reprinted with permission.

Skill-based Pay Plans

Organisations hire people for their skills, then typically put them in jobs and pay them based on their job title or rank. For example, the director of operations earns $180,000 a year, the regional operations managers make $125,000, and plant operations managers get $85,000. But if organisations hire people because of their competencies, why don't they pay them for those same competencies? Some organisations do.[60] For example, production and maintenance workers at JLG Industries earn an extra 30 cents an hour for each new skill they acquire within a specific family of job activities. Employees at American Steel & Wire can boost their annual salaries by up to $12,480 by acquiring as many as ten skills. And Frito-Lay Corporation ties its compensation for frontline operations managers to developing their skills in leadership, workforce development and functional excellence. Amcor, Multiplex Constructions and Brown Brothers are just some of the Australian companies that also use skill-based pay arrangements.

WHAT ARE SKILL-BASED PAY PLANS?

skill-based pay plans
Pay levels are based on how many skills employees have or how many jobs they can do.

Skill-based pay is an alternative to job-based pay. Rather than having an individual's job title define his or her pay category, **skill-based pay** (also sometimes called *competency-based* or *knowledge-based pay*) sets pay levels on the basis of how many skills employees have or how many jobs they can do.[61]

What's the appeal of skill-based pay plans? From management's perspective: flexibility. Filling staffing needs is easier when employee skills are interchangeable. This is particularly true today, as many organisations cut the size of their workforce. Downsized organisations require more generalists and fewer specialists. Whereas skill-based pay encourages employees to acquire a broader range of skills, there are also other benefits. It facilitates communication across the organisation because people gain a better understanding of others' jobs. It lessens dysfunctional 'protection of territory' behaviour. Where skill-based pay exists, you are less likely to hear the phrase, 'It's not my job!' In addition, skill-based pay helps to meet the needs of ambitious employees who confront minimal advancement opportunities. These people can increase their earnings and knowledge without a promotion in job title. Finally, skill-based pay appears to lead to performance improvements. A broad-based survey of Fortune 1000 firms found that 60 per cent of those with skill-based pay plans rated their plans as successful or very successful in increasing organisational performance, while only 6 per cent considered them unsuccessful or very unsuccessful.[62]

What about the downside of skill-based pay? People can 'top out'—learning all the skills the program calls for them to learn. This can frustrate employees after they have become challenged by an environment of learning, growth and continual pay rises. Skills can become obsolete. When this happens, what should management do? Cut employee pay, or continue to pay for skills that are no longer relevant? (The former Power Brewing Company at Yatala in Queensland, now owned by Carlton United Brewery, addressed this issue by assigning a 'use-by' date on all skills—this helped to ensure skills were being reassessed and updated continually.) There is also the problem created by paying people for acquiring skills for which there may be no immediate need. This happened at IDS Financial Services.[63] The company found itself paying people more money even though there was little immediate use for their new skills. IDS eventually dropped its skill-based pay plan and replaced it with one that equally balances individual contribution and gains in work-team productivity. Finally, skill-based plans don't address the level of performance. They deal only with the issue of whether or not someone can perform the skill. For some skills, such as checking quality or leading a team, level of performance may be equivocal. However, it's possible to assess how well employees perform each of the skills and to combine that with a skill-based plan that is not an inherent part of skill-based pay.

LINKING SKILL-BASED PAY PLANS TO MOTIVATION THEORIES

Skill-based pay plans are consistent with several motivation theories. Because they encourage employees to learn, expand their skills and grow, they are consistent with ERG theory. Among employees whose lower-order needs are substantially satisfied, the opportunity to experience growth can be a motivator.

Paying people to expand their skill levels is also consistent with research on the achievement need. High achievers have a compelling drive to do things better or more efficiently. By learning new skills or improving the skills they already hold, high achievers will find their jobs more challenging.

There is also a link between reinforcement theory and skill-based pay. Skill-based pay encourages employees to develop their flexibility, to continue to learn, to cross-train, to be generalists rather than specialists, and to work cooperatively with others in the organisation. To the degree that management wants employees to demonstrate such behaviours, skill-based pay should act as a reinforcer.

In addition, skill-based pay may have equity implications. When employees make their input–outcome comparisons, skills may provide a fairer input criterion for determining pay than factors such as seniority or education. To the degree that employees perceive skills as the critical variable in job performance, the use of skill-based pay may increase the perception of equity and help to optimise employee motivation.

LEARNING OBJECTIVE

7

Describe the link between skill-based pay plans and motivation theories

SKILL-BASED PAY IN PRACTICE

A number of studies have investigated the use and effectiveness of skill-based pay. The overall conclusion, based on these studies, is that skill-based pay is expanding and that it generally leads to higher employee performance, satisfaction, and perceptions of fairness in pay systems.[64]

Research has also identified some interesting trends. The increased use of skills as a basis for pay appears particularly strong among organisations facing aggressive foreign competition and companies with shorter product life cycles and speed-to-market concerns.[65] Also, skill-based pay is moving from the shop floor to the white-collar workforce, and sometimes as far as the executive suite.[66]

Skilled-based pay appears to be an idea whose time has come. As one expert noted, 'Slowly, but surely, we're becoming a skill-based society where your market value is tied to what you can do and what your skill set is. In this new world where skills and knowledge are what really counts, it doesn't make sense to treat people as job holders. It makes sense to treat them as people with specific skills and to pay them for those skills.'[67]

Flexible Benefits

Todd Evans and Allison Murphy both work for Coca-Cola Amatil (CCA), but they have very different needs in terms of employee benefits. Todd is married, with three young children and a wife who is at home full-time. Allison, too, is married, but her husband has a high-paying job with the federal government and they have no children. Todd is concerned about having access to a good corporate health insurance plan and enough life insurance to support his family if he weren't around. In contrast, Allison's husband already has her medical needs covered on his corporate health insurance plan, and life insurance is a low priority for both her and her husband. Allison is more interested in extra holiday time and long-term financial benefits such as a tax-deferred savings plan.

A standardised benefit package for all employees at Coca-Cola Amatil (CCA) would be unlikely to meet the optimal needs of both Todd and Allison. They could, however, optimise their needs if CCA offered flexible benefits.

OB Controversies

Are CEOs paid too much?

Critics have described the astronomical pay packages given to Australian CEOs as 'rampant greed' and question whether the skills and competencies of CEOs warrant the pay packages that they are getting. They note, for example, that during the last 15 years, after-tax return on shareholder funds fell 50 per cent, and during this same period employees' pay rose only 28 per cent. Yet, CEO salaries and benefits rose nearly 1,000 per cent! In the year 2002, the average CEO of a major Australian corporation made over 100 times as much as the average Australian employee. If the average production employee's pay had increased at the same rate as CEO salaries during this period, employee pay would be closer to $180,000 today, rather than less than $50,000.

High levels of executive compensation seem to be widespread in the many Western OECD countries. In the United States in 2000, for example, John Chambers of Cisco Systems took home [the Australian dollar equivalent of] $157.3 million; General Electric's Jack Welch was paid $122.6 million; and Coca-Cola's Douglas Daft earned $91.7 million. In Australia, CEOs of Australia's top four banks each earn in excess of $15 million per annum. Eight-figure CEO salaries are increasingly common in the top 100 Australian companies, with the average being over $2 million. These figures were for salary, benefits and exercised share options only. They do *not* include potentially hundreds of millions more from appreciated value of unexercised share options or many more millions of dollars for early termination of their contracts. (Brian Gilbertson left BHP Billiton after only six months with over $30 million in his pocket.) In 2002, ten former Australian CEOs left their companies, taking a combined total of $170 million in contract payouts!

How do you explain these astronomical pay packages? Some say this represents a classic economic response to a situation in which the demand is great for high-quality top executive talent and the supply is low. Ira Kay, a compensation consultant, says: 'It's not fair to compare [executives] with hourly-paid employees. Their market is the global market for executives.' Other arguments in favour of paying executives $2 million a year or more are: the need to compensate people for the tremendous responsibilities and stress that go with such jobs; the motivating potential that seven- and eight-figure annual incomes provide to senior executives and those who might aspire to be; the need to keep the best and the brightest in the corporate world, rather than being enticed into investment banking or venture capital firms; and the influence that senior executives have on a company's bottom line.

Contrary to the global argument, executive pay is considerably higher in the United States than in most other countries. In 1998, the most recent year for which data are available, American CEOs of industrial companies with annual revenues of [in Australian dollars] $250 million to $500 million made, on average, $1,072,400. Comparable figures for Britain, France, Canada, Australia and Japan were, respectively, $645,540, $520,389, $498,118, $475,000 and $420,855. All evidence suggests that this gap between American CEOs and those from other countries has only grown since these data were calculated.

Critics of executive pay practices in the main OECD countries argue that CEOs choose board members whom they can count on to support ever-increasing pay (including lucrative bonus and share option plans) for top management. If board members fail to 'play along', they risk losing their positions, their fees, and the prestige and power inherent in board membership.

Is high compensation of executives a problem? If so, does the blame for the problem lie with CEOs or with the shareholders and boards that knowingly allow the practice? Are CEOs greedy? Are these CEOs acting unethically? What do you think?

Sources: N. Way and A. Heathcote, '20 Highest Paid CEOs', *Business Review Weekly*, 20 February 2003; Towers, Perrin, *Worldwide Total Rewards 1998* (April 1998), p. 21; J. Greenfield, 'Study Finds Inequities in CEO Pay, Worker Pay, Profits', *The Working Stiff Journal*, October 1999; L. Lavelle, 'Executive Pay', *Business Week*, 16 April 2001, pp. 76–80; and R. C. Longworth, 'CEO Pay 531 Times That of Workers; Study: Gap Grows Despite Downturn', *Chicago Tribune*, 28 August 2001.

WHAT ARE FLEXIBLE BENEFITS?

Flexible benefits allow employees to pick benefits that most meet their needs. The idea is to allow each employee to choose a benefit package that is individually tailored to his or her own needs and situation. It replaces the traditional 'one-benefit-plan-fits-all' programs that dominated organisations for more than 50 years.[68]

The average organisation provides fringe benefits worth approximately 40 per cent of an employee's salary. Traditional benefit programs were designed for the typical employee of the 1950s—a male with a wife and two children at home. Less than 10 per cent of employees now fit this stereotype. While 25 per cent of today's employees are single, a third are part of two-income families with no children. As such, these traditional programs don't tend to meet the needs of today's more diverse workforce. Flexible benefits, however, *do* meet these diverse needs. They can be uniquely tailored to reflect differences in employee needs based on age, marital status, spouse's benefit status, number and age of dependants, and the like.

The three most popular types of benefit plans are modular plans, core-plus options and flexible spending accounts.[69] *Modular plans* are predesigned packages of benefits, with each module put together to meet the needs of a specific group of employees. So, a module designed for single employees with no dependants might include only essential benefits. Another, designed for single parents, might have additional life insurance, disability insurance and expanded health insurance coverage. *Core-plus plans* consist of a core of essential benefits and a menu-like selection of other benefit options from which employees can select and add to the core. Typically, each employee is given 'benefit credits', which allow the 'purchase' of additional benefits that uniquely meet his or her needs. *Flexible spending plans* allow employees to set aside up to the dollar amount offered in the plan to pay for particular services. It's a convenient way, for example, for employees to pay for health-care and extra superannuation payments. Flexible spending accounts can increase employee take-home pay because employees don't have to pay taxes on the dollars they spend out of these accounts, called salary sacrifice in Australia.

LINKING FLEXIBLE BENEFITS AND EXPECTANCY THEORY

Giving all employees the same benefits assumes that all employees have the same needs. Of course, we know this assumption is false. Thus, flexible benefits turn the benefits' expenditure into a motivator.

Consistent with expectancy theory's thesis that organisational rewards should be linked to each individual employee's goals, flexible benefits individualise rewards by allowing each employee to choose the compensation package that best satisfies his or her current needs. The fact that flexible benefits can turn the traditional homogeneous benefit program into a motivator was demonstrated at one company when 80 per cent of the organisation's employees changed their fixed benefit packages when a flexible plan was put into effect.[70]

FLEXIBLE BENEFITS IN PRACTICE

Approximately 13 per cent of large- and medium-sized companies in the United States have flexible benefit plans in place. This includes TRW Systems, Educational Testing Services, DaimlerChrysler and Verizon.[71] In the future, we can probably expect this percentage to increase to reflect the expanding diversity among employees.

The idea of flexible benefits is also gaining ground in Australia. Westpac Banking Corporation, for example, has developed a program to encourage women employees to return to work after maternity leave. Westpac had found that less than 4 per cent of women returned to work with the bank after maternity leave, even though a majority of women had expressed willingness to do so. The program included the appointment of a coordinator to facilitate the return of women after maternity leave and the adoption of flexible work practices. Many other

flexible benefits
Employees tailor their benefit program to meet their personal needs by picking and choosing from a menu of benefit options.

LEARNING OBJECTIVE 8
Explain how flexible benefits turn benefits into motivators

companies are adopting family-friendly flexible benefit practices in order to attract and retain the best employees.

Now, let's look at the benefits and drawbacks. For employees, flexibility is attractive because they can tailor their benefits and levels of coverage to their own needs. The main drawback, from the employee's standpoint, is, for example, that the costs of corporate health-care plans often go up as employees drop out in favour of other flexible benefits, so fewer total flexible benefits can be 'purchased' in the salary package. From the organisation's standpoint, the good news is that flexible benefits often produce savings. Many organisations use the introduction of flexible benefits to offset demands for salary increases. Moreover, once in place, costly increases in things like health insurance premiums often have to be substantially absorbed by the employee. The bad news for the organisation is that these plans are more cumbersome for management to oversee, and administering the programs is often expensive.

LEARNING OBJECTIVE

9

Describe the role of comparable worth

Comparable Worth

Is it fair that two employees do equally demanding jobs requiring the same amount of education and training, and have similar responsibilities, yet one receives significantly less pay than the other? Probably not. But such situations aren't that uncommon, with women usually earning the lesser amounts. What is the source of this inequity? Some economists would argue that it merely reflects the market forces of supply and demand. Another interpretation—and one gaining an increasing audience—is that these differences are the result of gender-based wage discrimination.

It's not unusual for jobs in industries or careers dominated by women (such as infants and primary schoolteacher, nurse, librarian) to pay less than jobs in industries or careers dominated by men (such as truck driver, timber cutter, chef), even though they are of equal or greater comparable value. This inequity has stimulated considerable interest in the concept of *comparable worth*.

WHAT IS COMPARABLE WORTH?

comparable worth
A doctrine that holds that jobs equal in value to an organisation should be equally compensated, whether or not the work content of those jobs is similar.

Comparable worth is a doctrine that holds that jobs equal in value to an organisation should be equally compensated, whether or not the work content of those jobs is similar.[72] That is, if the positions of secretary and draftsman (historically viewed as women's and men's jobs, respectively) require similar skills and make comparable demands on employees, they should pay the same, regardless of external market factors. Specifically, proponents of comparable worth argue that jobs should be evaluated and scored on four criteria—skill, effort, responsibility and work conditions. The criteria should be weighted and given points, with the points then used to value and compare jobs.

Comparable worth is a controversial idea. It is assumed that totally dissimilar jobs can be accurately compared, that job classes can be identified and objectively rated, and that pay rates based on supply and demand factors in the job market are frequently inequitable and discriminatory.

COMPARABLE WORTH AND EQUITY THEORY

The idea of comparable worth relies on the notion of 'equal pay for equal work' to include jobs that are dissimilar but of comparable value. As such, it is a direct application of equity theory.

As long as women in traditionally lower-paid, female-dominated jobs compare themselves solely to other women in female-dominated jobs, they are unlikely to perceive gender-based wage inequities. But when other referents are chosen, inequities often become quickly evident. This is because 'women's' jobs have been historically devalued. Take the following case. You went to a university for six years, earned a bachelor of arts and a graduate diploma in library science, and for four years you have taken on increased responsibilities as a reference librarian for a public library in the city of Newcastle, in New South Wales. Your current pay is $3,460 a month. Your younger brother also works for the Newcastle City Council, but as a driver of a road repair truck. He is a high school leaver with no university education and has also held his job for four years. He makes $3,625 a month. You compare your pay with your brother's and conclude that you are being underpaid.

To the degree that job classes reflect historical gender discrimination and create pay inequities, comparable worth provides a potential remedy. For those in these discriminated job classes (usually but not restricted to women), the application of the comparable worth concept should reduce inequities and increase work motivation.

COMPARABLE WORTH IN PRACTICE

In Australia, women earn, on average, about 65 cents for each dollar that men earn. Part of this difference can be explained in market terms.[73] For example, in one study the average number of years of professional job preparation is 4.2 for men and 0.4 for women. Men also have, on average, 12.6 years of job seniority compared to only 2.4 for women.[74] Yet, even after objective differences are accounted for, such as years of job seniority lost due to the issue of women taking leave from work to have and raise a family, a good portion of the variance remains. It is this variance that comparable worth is addressing.

The comparable worth issue has received most attention in jobs in the public sector. The state government of Ontario, Canada, passed the *Pay Equity Act* in 1987, which defines men and women's job classes, establishes criteria by which they are to be valued and mandates pay based on comparable worth.[75] A number of Canadian business and government employees have received substantial pay rises as a result of this legislation.

Businesses in industrialised nations are concerned about the influence of comparative worth legislation and will probably lobby hard against comparable worth. They are worried that pay increases will make their products and services uncompetitive. Those in favour of comparable worth will counter with statistics showing that cultural forces and societal pay systems have created gender-based discrimination in certain job classes and argue that only legislation can provide a near-term solution to the problem. At one point, the legislation introduced in Canada looked as though it would sweep through New Zealand and Australia. A change in government in New Zealand in 1990 led to the demise of the Pay Equity Commission, and in Australia the election of the Coalition under John Howard during a recession has led to the equal pay for equal value issue becoming dormant.[76]

Job Redesign

When you think about how mass-produced vehicles are made, what images come to mind? Do you think of cars moving along an assembly line, with employees bolting on bumper bars and hooking on doors? That may be the way most cars are mass-produced, but not at Volvo's manufacturing plant in Uddevalla, Sweden.[77]

Uddevalla produces the Volvo 940 luxury model using teams. Each team is made up of eight to ten employees. The teams work in one area and each team assembles about three cars per shift. Each team is largely self-managed, handling scheduling, quality control, hiring and other duties normally performed by supervisors. The teams, in fact, have no first-line supervisors. Each team appoints a spokesperson, which reports to one of six plant managers, who, in turn, reports to the president of the entire complex.

Volvo's management believes the team concept provides several positive benefits for employees. It can reduce the tedium of the conventional assembly line where work cycles are only one or two minutes long, it encourages employees to increase their range of skills, and it gives employees more control over their jobs. At Uddevalla, work team members are trained to handle all assembly jobs, so they work an average of three hours before having to repeat the same task.

job design
The way that tasks are combined to form complete jobs.

Job design is concerned with the way in which tasks are combined to form complete jobs. Job redesign focuses on changing jobs. The Volvo example illustrates how management can increase motivation by redesigning the job around self-managed work teams. In this section, we will also look at three other approaches for improving motivation through job redesign.

JOB ROTATION

job rotation
The periodic shifting of an employee from one task to another.

One way to deal with the routines of work is to use **job rotation**. When an activity is no longer challenging, the employee is rotated to another job, at the same level, that has similar skill requirements. From time to time, various managers at the Surfers Paradise Marriott Resort are rotated to give them an appreciation of managing an area of responsibility that is technically different from their general experiences. In this case, job rotation is a very useful technique for career development and for providing valuable experience for managers with leadership potential. Bank West rotates many of its bank officers and staff to different branches so that they gain experience in various locations and develop different skills. This also adds to the interest of the job.

The strength of job rotation is that it reduces boredom by diversifying the employee's activities. Of course, it can also have indirect benefits for the organisation, since employees with a wider range of skills give management more flexibility in scheduling work, adapting to changes and filling vacancies. On the other hand, job rotation has its drawbacks. Training costs are increased, and productivity is reduced by moving an employee into a new position just when their efficiency at the previous job was creating organisational economies. Job rotation also creates disruptions. Members of the work group have to adjust to the new employee. The supervisor may also have to spend more time answering questions and monitoring the work of the recently rotated employee. Finally, job rotation can demotivate intelligent and ambitious trainees who seek specific responsibilities in their chosen speciality.

JOB ENLARGEMENT

job enlargement
The horizontal expansion of jobs.

In the 1950s, the idea of expanding jobs horizontally, called **job enlargement**, grew in popularity. Increasing the number and variety of tasks that an employee performed resulted in jobs with more diversity. Instead of only sorting the incoming mail by department, for example, a mail sorter's job could be enlarged to include physically delivering the mail to the various departments or running outgoing letters through the franking machine.

Efforts at job enlargement met with less than enthusiastic results. As one employee who experienced such a redesign of his job remarked, 'Before, I had one boring job. Now, through enlargement, I have three!' However, there have been some successful applications of job enlargement. The Australian Bureau of Statistics (ABS) expanded jobs as a result of the federal government's drive to reduce the number of job bands or categories. In some cases, staff wound up with a number of smaller jobs which were more boring than their previous work, but in the majority of cases officers in the ABS had an expanded and wider range of job responsibilities.

Providing opportunities for increased variety and number of tasks has a tangible benefit with greater employee motivation and performance. This is crucial in service industries where your employees interact directly with the clients.

So, while job enlargement tries to overcome the problem of the lack of diversity in over-specialised jobs, it sometimes does little to instil challenge or purpose in an employee's activities. Job enrichment was introduced to deal with the shortcomings of enlargement.

JOB ENRICHMENT

Job enrichment refers to the vertical expansion of jobs. It increases the degree to which the employee controls the planning, execution and evaluation of their work. An enriched job organises tasks so as to allow the employee to do a complete activity, increases the employee's freedom and independence, increases responsibility, and provides feedback so that an employee will be able to assess and correct their own performance.

> **job enrichment**
> The increase of responsibility and higher-order skills required of jobs.

How does management enrich an employee's job? The following five suggestions, based on the job characteristics model discussed in an earlier chapter of this book, specify the types of changes in jobs that are most likely to improve their motivating potential (see Figure 7.3).

1. *Combine tasks:* Managers should seek to take existing and fractionalised tasks and put them back together to form a new and larger module of work. This increases skill variety and task identity.
2. *Create natural work units:* The creation of natural work units means that the tasks an employee does form an identifiable and purposeful whole. This increases employee 'ownership' of the work and improves the likelihood that employees will view their work as purposeful and important, rather than as irrelevant and boring. This increases task identity and autonomy.
3. *Establish client relationships:* The client is the user of the product or service that the employee works on. Wherever possible, managers should try to establish direct relationships between the employees and their clients. This increases skill variety, autonomy and feedback for the employee.
4. *Expand jobs vertically:* Vertical expansion gives employees responsibilities and control that were formerly reserved for management. It seeks to partially close the gap between the 'doing' and the 'controlling' aspects of the job, and it increases employee autonomy.
5. *Open feedback channels:* By increasing feedback, employees learn how well they are performing their jobs and whether their performance is improving, deteriorating or remaining at a constant level. Ideally, this feedback about performance should be received directly as the employee does the job, rather than from management on an occasional basis.[78]

> **LEARNING OBJECTIVE**
> **10**
> Explain the basis and potential benefits of job redesign and enrichment

Citibank used the previous suggestions to design a job enrichment program for its bank office employees who processed all the bank's financial transactions.[79] These jobs had been split up so that each employee performed a single, routine task over and over again. Employees had become dissatisfied with these mundane jobs and this dissatisfaction showed in their work. Severe backlogs had developed and error rates were unacceptably high. Citibank's management redesigned the work around customer types. Tasks were combined and individual employees were given complete

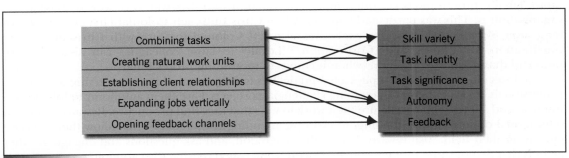

FIGURE 7.3 **Guidelines for enriching a job**

Source: From J. R. Hackman and J. L. Suttle, *Improving Life at Work.* Copyright © 1977 by Scott, Foresman & Co., Glenview, IL. Reprinted by permission.

processing and customer-service responsibility for a small group of customers in a defined product area. In the newly designed jobs, employees dealt directly with customers and handled entire transactions from the time they came into the bank until they left. As might be predicted, this enrichment program improved the quality of work, as well as employee motivation and satisfaction.

The enterprise agreement between management and employees at BHP's Brisbane rolling mill includes elements of multiskilling, job redesign and performance compensation. The BHP mill was initially started as a non-union site, but the mill manager was willing to try a new approach with an enterprise agreement when he was approached by the Federated Ironworkers Union (now the FIMME). The intention of the agreement was to provide fulfilling and challenging jobs that would lead to greater flexibility and productivity in the workplace.[80]

Special Issues in Motivation

Various groups provide specific challenges in terms of motivation. In this section, we look at some of the unique problems faced in trying to motivate professional employees, contingent workers, the diverse workforce, low-skilled service workers, and people doing highly repetitive tasks.

MOTIVATING PROFESSIONALS

In contrast to a generation ago, the typical employee today is more likely to be a highly trained professional with a university degree than a semi-skilled blue-collar employee. These professionals receive a great deal of intrinsic satisfaction from their work. They tend to be well paid. So what, if any, special concerns should you be aware of when trying to motivate a team of researchers at CSIRO, a software designer at Microsoft, or a group of CPAs at PricewaterhouseCoopers?

Professionals are typically different from non-professionals.[81] They have a strong and long-term commitment to their field of expertise. Their loyalty is more often to their profession than to their employer. To keep current in their field, they need to update their knowledge regularly, and their commitment to their profession means they rarely define their work week in terms of 8 to 5 and five days a week.

What motivates professionals? Money and promotions typically are low on their priority list. Why? They tend to be well paid and they enjoy what they do. In contrast, job challenge tends to be ranked high. They like to tackle problems and find solutions. Their chief reward in their job is the work itself. Professionals also value support and acknowledgment. They want others to think what they are working on is important. Although this may be true for all employees, because professionals tend to be more focused on their work as their central life interest, non-professionals typically have other interests outside of work that can compensate for needs not met on the job. Professionals place a high level of importance on having skill-development opportunities. Finally, professionals are often more interested in who they will work with than what the organisation is. This was particularly obvious when Chris Cuffe left Colonial First State and, not long after, several of his former executives also left Colonial to work with Chris in his new organisation, CPH Investment Corporation.[82] Loyalty to close colleagues can also be more powerful than money or positions when it comes to motivating professionals.

The foregoing description implies a few guidelines to keep in mind if you are trying to motivate professionals. Provide them with ongoing challenging projects. Give them autonomy to follow their interests and allow them to structure their work in ways that they find productive. Reward them with educational opportunities—training, workshops, attending conferences—that allow them to keep current in their field. Also reward them with recognition, and ask questions and engage in other actions that demonstrate to them you are sincerely interested in what they are doing.

An increasing number of companies are creating alternative career paths for their professional/technical people, allowing employees to earn more money and status, without assuming managerial responsibilities. At Merck & Co., IBM and AT&T, the best scientists, engineers and researchers gain titles such as 'fellow' and 'senior scientist'. Their pay and prestige are comparable to those of managers but without the corresponding authority or responsibility.

MOTIVATING CONTINGENT WORKERS

We noted in Chapter 1 that one of the more comprehensive changes taking place in organisations is the increasing use of temporary or contingent employees. As downsizing has eliminated millions of 'permanent' jobs, an increasing number of new openings are for 'non-permanent' employees. For example, approximately 2.3 million Australians, or over 35 per cent of those with jobs, consider themselves to be part of the contingent workforce.[83] These include part-timers, on-call employees, short-term hires, temps, day labourers, independent contractors and leased employees. The common denominator among these contingent employees is that they don't have the security or stability that permanent employees have. As such, they don't identify with the organisation or display the commitment that other employees do. Temporary employees also are typically provided with little or no health-care, superannuation or similar benefits.[84]

There is no simple solution for motivating contingent employees. For those who prefer the freedom of their temporary status—many students, working mothers, seniors and professionals who don't want the demands of a permanent job—the lack of stability may not be an issue. Interestingly, this seems to be considerably more people than originally thought. Recent estimates indicate that 35 to 40 per cent of contingent workers have chosen this status voluntarily.[85] The challenge, however, is in dealing with temporary employees who are in this status involuntarily.

What will motivate involuntarily contingent employees? An obvious answer is the opportunity for permanent status. In cases in which permanent employees are selected from the pool of temporaries, temporaries will often work hard in hopes of becoming permanent. A less obvious answer is the opportunity for training. The ability of a contingent employee to find a new job is largely dependent on his or her skills. If the employee sees that the job he or she is doing for you can help to develop saleable skills, then motivation is increased. From an equity standpoint, you should also consider the repercussions of mixing permanent and contingent employees where pay differentials are significant.[86] For example, when temps work alongside permanent employees who earn more, and get benefits too, for doing the same job, the performance of temps is likely to suffer (and similarly, if in some instances, the temporary staff can actually earn more than permanent staff, it can demotivate the permanent staff). Separating such employees or converting all employees to a variable-pay or skill-based pay plan might help to lessen this problem.

MOTIVATING THE DIVERSIFIED WORKFORCE

Not everyone is motivated by money. Not everyone wants a challenging job. The needs of women, singles, immigrants, the physically disabled, senior citizens, and others from diverse groups are not the same as a married white Australian male with three dependants. A couple of examples can make this point clearer. Employees who are attending TAFE or university typically place a high value on flexible work schedules. Such individuals may be attracted to organisations

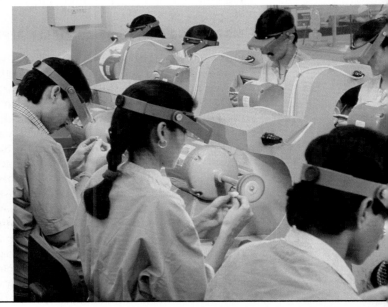

Even though they are all performing the same tasks, the motivation to work of each person in the photo is likely to be very different. The challenge is to find out all the different motivators and try to provide them.

that offer flexible work hours, job sharing or temporary assignments. Similarly, a father may prefer to work the midnight to 8 am shift in order to spend time with his children during the day when his wife is at work.

If you are going to maximise your employees' motivation, you have got to understand and respond to this diversity. How? The key words to guide you should be *flexibility* and *communication* to identify their needs in the first instance and to address these needs. Be ready to design work schedules, compensation plans, benefits, physical work settings, and the like to reflect your employees' varied needs. This might include offering child- and elder-care, flexible work hours, and job sharing for employees with family responsibilities. It also might include offering flexible leave policies for immigrants who want occasionally to make extensive return trips to their home-lands, or creating work teams for employees who come from countries with a strong collectivist orientation, or allowing employees who are studying part-time to vary their work schedules from semester to semester.

MOTIVATING LOW-SKILLED SERVICE EMPLOYEES

One of the most challenging motivation problems in industries such as retailing and fast food is: how do you motivate individuals who are making very low wages and have limited job scope and who have little opportunity to significantly increase their pay in either their current jobs or through promotions? These jobs are typically filled with people who have limited education and skills, and whose pay levels are little above minimum wage.

Traditional approaches for motivating these people have focused on providing more flexible work schedules and filling these jobs with teenagers and retirees whose financial needs are less. This has met with less than enthusiastic results. For example, turnover rates of 200 per cent or more are not uncommon for businesses such as McDonald's. Taco Bell has tried to make some of its service jobs more interesting and challenging, but with limited results.[87] It has experimented with incentive pay and share options for cashiers and cooks. These employees also have been given broader responsibility for inventory, scheduling and hiring. But over a four-year period, this experiment has only reduced annual turnover from 223 per cent to 160 per cent.

What choices are left? Unless pay and benefits are significantly increased, high turnover probably has to be expected in these jobs. This can be somewhat offset by widening the recruiting net, making these jobs more appealing, and raising pay levels.

MOTIVATING PEOPLE DOING HIGHLY REPETITIVE TASKS

Our final category considers employees who do standardised and repetitive jobs. For example, working on an assembly line or transcribing court reports are jobs that employees often find boring and even stressful.

Motivating individuals in these jobs can be made easier through careful selection. People vary in their tolerance for ambiguity. Many individuals prefer jobs that have a minimal amount of discretion and variety. Such individuals are obviously a better match to standardised jobs than individuals with strong needs for growth and autonomy. Standardised jobs should also be the first considered for automation. This helps to explain management's motivation to install ATMs at banks, self-service soft drink machines in fast-food restaurants, and customer-operated check-in kiosks at airports.

Many standardised jobs, especially in the manufacturing sector, pay well. This makes it relatively easy to fill vacancies. While high pay can ease recruitment problems and reduce turnover, it doesn't necessarily lead to highly motivated employees. And realistically, there are jobs that don't readily lend themselves to being made more challenging and interesting or to being redesigned. Some tasks, for example, are just far more efficiently done on assembly lines than in teams. This leaves limited options. You may not be able to do much more than try to make a bad situation tolerable by creating a pleasant work climate. This might include providing clean and attractive work surroundings, ample work breaks, the opportunity to socialise with colleagues during these breaks, and empathetic supervisors.

Summary and Implications for Managers

We have presented a number of motivation theories and applications in this and the previous chapter. While it's always dangerous to synthesise a large number of complex ideas into a few simple guidelines, the following suggestions summarise the essence of what we know about motivating employees in organisations.

Recognise individual differences

Employees have different needs. Don't treat them all alike. Moreover, spend the time necessary to understand what's important to each employee. This will allow you to individualise goals, level of involvement, and rewards to align with individual needs. Flexibility is needed too—especially as the needs of employees will be varied and often different.

Use goals and feedback

Employees should have hard, specific goals, as well as feedback on how well they are faring in pursuit of those goals.

Allow employees to participate in decisions that affect them

Employees can contribute to a number of decisions that affect them: setting work goals, choosing their own benefits packages, solving productivity and quality problems, and the like. This can increase employee productivity, commitment to work goals, motivation and job satisfaction.

Link rewards to performance

Rewards should be contingent on performance. Importantly, employees must perceive a clear linkage. Regardless of how closely rewards are actually correlated to performance criteria, if individuals perceive this relationship to be low, the results will be low performance, a decrease in job satisfaction, and an increase in turnover and absenteeism.

Check the system for equity

Rewards should also be perceived by employees as equating with the inputs they bring to the job. At a simplistic level, this should mean that experience, skills, abilities, effort, and other obvious inputs should explain differences in performance and, hence, pay, job assignments and other obvious rewards.

Point

THE POWER OF SHARE OPTIONS AS A MOTIVATOR

Share options are being used in the United States as incentives for booksellers at Borders, clerks at Wal-Mart, box packers at Pfizer, chemical-plant operators at Monsanto, baggage handlers at Delta Air Lines, and part-time espresso servers at Starbucks.[a]

Approximately 10 million US employees currently receive share options, roughly a ten-fold jump since 1992. One study found that 39 per cent of large US companies now have share option plans that cover all or a majority of employees—from the CEO down to operatives. And while plans vary, most are allocated as a percentage of annual income and allow employees to buy their employer's shares at a price below the fair market value.

Proponents of broad-based shares offer a long list of reasons to explain these plans' popularity: They help to create a company-wide 'ownership' culture by focusing employees' attention on the employers' financial performance; create a pay-for-performance climate; foster pride of ownership; raise morale; encourage retention of employees; help to attract new employees; and motivate frontline employees who interact with customers.

Starbucks' experience provides insights into the power of share options as a motivator. Their program began in 1991. Each employee was awarded share options worth 12 per cent of his or her annual base pay. Every October since then, high profits have allowed Starbucks to raise the grant to 14 per cent of base pay. An employee making $20,000 a year in 1991 could have recently cashed in their 1991 options alone for more than $70,000.

Starbucks' management believes share options allow employees to share both the ownership of the company and the rewards of financial success. And management contends that it's working. The company's CEO says, 'People started coming up with innovative ideas about how to cut costs, to increase sales, to create value. Most important, they could speak to our customers from the heart, as partners in the business.'

Sources: [a] This is based on 'Starbucks' Secret Weapon', *Fortune*, 29 September 1997, p. 268; 'Stock Options for the Ranks', *Business Week*, 7 September 1998, p. 22; and E. Ackerman, 'Optionnaires, Beware!', *U.S. News & World Report*, 6 March 2000, pp. 36–38.

Counterpoint

Broad-based share options sound terrific in theory. Motivation increases because employees see themselves as owners, rather than merely employees. And these options create the opportunity for moderately paid employees to accumulate substantial savings. What's wrong with the theory? Several things. [b]

First is the fact that share options tend to be disproportionately allocated to managers. Because share options are typically distributed as a percentage of base pay, managers get more of them because they make more money. Senior executives also tend to get additional share options based on company profitability or share performance. This is how someone like Gerald Levin, when he was CEO of AOL Time Warner, could make US$152 million in one year alone from his share options. Such huge payoffs make the few thousand dollars a low-level AOL Time Warner employee gets from her share options seem like 'chicken feed'. This comparison is just as likely to anger or frustrate non-managerial employees as it is to motivate them.

Second, share options are poor motivators because they offer a weak link between employee effort and rewards. How much impact can the average employee really have on the company's share price? Very little! The decline in the price of high-tech stocks in 2000 and 2001 made a majority of share options at these firms worthless, yet this was a time when many employees of these high-tech firms were working harder than ever to try to keep their companies (and jobs) alive.

Finally, share options are great when a company is growing rapidly or during bull markets in shares. Starbucks' plan proved very profitable for employees between 1991 and 2000 because the company grew rapidly. But all companies aren't growing, nor do share markets go up forever. Share options issued to employees at companies such as Cisco Systems, Amazon.com, Oracle and eToys in the mid-1990s were essentially worthless in the spring of 2001. When high-tech share companies imploded, so did thousands of employees' dreams of wealth and early retirement. Share options may actually become demotivators when employees realise that they are like a lottery, with very few big winners.

Sources: [b] This is based on K. Capell, 'Options for Everyone', *Business Week*, 22 July 1996, pp. 80–84; P. Coy, 'The Drawbacks of Stock-Option Fever', *Business Week*, 13 December 1999, p. 204; and D. Henry and M. Conlin, 'Too Much of a Good Incentive?', *Business Week*, 4 March 2002, pp. 38–39.

For Discussion

1. Relate goal-setting theory to the MBO process. How are they similar? Different?
2. Identify five different criteria by which organisations can compensate employees. Based on your knowledge and experience, do you think performance is the criterion most used in practice? Discuss.
3. Explain the roles of employees and management in quality circles.
4. What are the pluses of variable-pay programs from an employee's viewpoint? From management's viewpoint?
5. Contrast job-based and skill-based pay.
6. 'Recognition may be motivational for the moment, but it doesn't have any staying power. It's an empty reinforcer. Why? Because when you go to the supermarket, they don't take recognition as a form of payment!' Do you agree or disagree? Discuss.

7. What motivates professional employees?
8. What motivates contingent employees?
9. Is it possible to motivate low-skilled service workers? Discuss.
10. What can you do, as a manager, to increase the likelihood that your employees will exert a high level of effort?
11. 'Performance can't be measured, so any effort to link pay with performance is a fantasy. Differences in performance are often caused by the system, which means the organisation ends up rewarding the circumstances. It's the same thing as rewarding the weather forecaster for a pleasant day.' Do you agree or disagree with this statement? Support your position.
12. This book argues for recognising individual differences. It also suggests paying attention to members of diversity groups. Is this contradictory? Discuss.

Exercise

GOAL-SETTING TASK

Purpose: This exercise will help you to learn how to write tangible, verifiable, measurable and relevant goals as might evolve from an MBO program.

Time: Approximately 20 to 30 minutes.

Instructions:
1. Break into groups of three to five.
2. Spend a few minutes discussing your class instructor's job. What does he or she do? What defines good performance? What behaviours will lead to good performance?
3. Each group is to develop a list of five goals that, although not established participatively with your instructor, you believe might be developed in an MBO program at your university. Try to select goals that seem most critical to the effective performance of your instructor's job.
4. Each group will select a leader who will share his or her group's goals with the entire class. For each group's goals, class discussion should focus on their: (a) specificity, (b) ease of measurement, (c) importance, and (d) motivational properties.

Case Study 7

Radical Approach Pays Dividends

In 1983, when Ricardo Semler's father handed him control of the family's small Brazilian company, Semco, a maker of industrial machinery, the business was on the verge of bankruptcy. While only 22 years old and short on experience, Semler recognised he had to take some drastic steps if he was to save the company. Ironically, his youth and naiveté may have worked to his advantage. He wasn't bogged down with traditional notions of how a business was supposed to be run.

What Semler proceeded to do was downright radical for the time. He fired most of the company's top managers, cut out almost the firm's entire bureaucratic overhead, and eliminated nearly all job titles. In place of a hierarchical structure, he basically turned the company over to his employees. He allowed people to interview and select their own co-workers. He told employees to set their own salaries and work schedules. He opened up the company's books and encouraged workers to learn how to read the firm's financial statements. And he allowed workers to choose their managers by vote, to evaluate them regularly, and to post the evaluations on bulletin boards for everyone to see. Today, although Semler owns the company, he likes to boast that he hasn't made a decision in ten years and hasn't had his own office in 14 years. The job of CEO at Semco is transitory—with half-a-dozen senior managers trading the title every six months.

Semler's radical approach has been an overwhelming success. In the 20 years since he took over, sales have grown at a 24 per cent annual rate. Since 1996 alone, profits have tripled and employment has gone from 350 to 2,500. The annual turnover of employees averages less than 1 per cent—against an industry average closer to 20 per cent. When Semler is asked what he attributes Semco's success to, he quickly responds that he has taken top management out of managing the company. He has used employee involvement to stimulate motivation and to create a place where people want to come to work in the morning. 'It's hard to attract people away from us,' says Semler. 'If you can set your own vacation, go to the beach on a Wednesday if you want and take part in decision making about the company budget, why would you do a nine-to-five job for 20 per cent more?'

Questions

1. Why has such a radical approach been so successful?
2. What are the advantages and disadvantages for employees of having so much access to decision making and information?
3. What are the ethical implications, if any, of employees in a company choosing who the new employees will be?
4. Discuss the motivational potential of allowing employees control over the decisions and practices of the company.

Sources: This case is based on G. Dyer, 'A Renaissance Maverick', *Financial Times*, 18 October 2001, pp. 10–11; and G. Colvin, 'The Anti-Control Freak', *Fortune*, 26 November 2001, p. 60.

Web Workout

1. Go to <www.cqu.edu.au/ppmanual/staff/prpd/prpdacademic.prn.pdf> and examine the policy document there. What application of employee motivation is being applied here?
2. What do all the companies described at <www.incentivecentral.org/pages/employee.html> have in common? How successful has the Sydney Monorail been in implementing an employee recognition plan?
3. Discuss how TXU is using employee involvement to achieve broader community outcomes, as well as improved employee performance. (See their site at <www.txucorp.com/comminv/comminv/au/employ_inv.asp>.)
4. The International Labour Organisation (ILO) has concerns about the use of skill-based pay plans. After looking at their site, discuss their criticisms in light of the benefits advocated in this chapter (<www.ilo.org/public/english/dialogue/actemp/papers/1998/srspaysy.htm#C5>).
5. In Australia, there is an association that deals with the issue of employee share-ownership plans. Visit their site, <www.aeoa.org.au/pdf/NS01.pdf>, and critically assess just what are the motivational merits advocated by the association in its submission to the Nelson Committee Report.

KSS Program

KNOW THE CONCEPTS   SELF-AWARENESS   SKILLS APPLICATIONS

Goal-setting skills

After you have read Chapter 6 and this chapter, take Self-Assessment #22 (How Good Am I at Personal Planning?) on your enclosed CD-Rom and complete the skill-building module entitled 'Setting Goals' on page 637.

NOTES

1. Based on G. McColl, 'Workers' Playtime', *Business Review Weekly*, 24 April 2003, p. 88.
2. E. O. Welles, 'Great Expectations', *INC.*, March 2001, pp. 68–73.
3. P. F. Drucker, *The Practice of Management* (New York: Harper & Row, 1954).
4. See, for example, S. J. Carroll and H. L. Tosi, *Management by Objectives: Applications and Research* (New York: Macmillan, 1973); and R. Rodgers and J. E. Hunter, 'Impact of Management by Objectives on Organizational Productivity', *Journal of Applied Psychology*, April 1991, pp. 322–36.
5. See, for example, R. C. Ford, F. S. MacLaughlin and J. Nixdorf, 'Ten Questions about MBO', *California Management Review*, winter 1980, p. 89; T. J. Collamore, 'Making MBO Work in the Public Sector', *Bureaucrat*, Fall 1989, pp. 37–40; G. Dabbs, 'Nonprofit Businesses in the 1990s: Models for Success', *Business Horizons*, September–October 1991, pp. 68–71; R. Rodgers and J. E. Hunter, 'A Foundation of Good Management Practice in Government: Management by Objectives', *Public Administration Review*, January–February 1992, pp. 27–39; T. H. Poister and G. Streib, 'MBO in Municipal Government: Variations on a Traditional Management Tool', *Public Administration Review*, January/February 1995, pp. 48–56; and C. Garvey, 'Goalsharing Scores', *HRMagazine*, April 2000, pp. 99–106.
6. See, for example, C. H. Ford, 'MBO: An Idea Whose Time Has Gone?', *Business Horizons*, December 1979, p. 49; R. Rodgers and J. E. Hunter, 'Impact of Management by Objectives on Organizational Productivity', *Journal of Applied Psychology*, April 1991, pp. 322–36; R. Rodgers, J. E. Hunter and D. L. Rogers, 'Influence of Top Management Commitment on Management Program Success', *Journal of Applied Psychology*, February 1993, pp. 151–55; and M. Tanikawa, 'Fujitsu Decides to Backtrack on Performance-Based Pay', *New York Times*, 22 March 2001, p. W1.
7. F. Luthans and A. D. Stajkovic, 'Provide Recognition for Performance Improvement', in E. A. Locke (ed.), *Principles of Organizational Behaviour* (Oxford: Blackwell, 2000), pp. 166–80.
8. D. Drickhamer, 'Best Plant Winners: Nichols Foods Ltd.', *Industry Week*, 1 October 2001, pp. 17–19.
9. M. Littman, 'Best Bosses Tell All', *Working Woman*, October 2000, p. 54.
10. Cited in S. Caudron, 'The Top 20 Ways to Motivate Employees', *Industry Week*, 3 April 1995, pp. 15–16. See also B. Nelson, 'Try Praise', *INC.*, September 1996, p. 115.
11. A. D. Stajkovic and F. Luthans, 'Differential Effects of Incentive Motivators on Work Performance', *Academy of Management Journal*, June 2001, p. 587.
12. B. Leonard, 'Performance is the Key to Reforming Reward Programs', *HRMagazine*, May 2000, p. 20.
13. Cited in *Asian Business*, December 1994, p. 3.
14. Several of these examples come from C. Fishman, 'Engines of Democracy', *Fast Company*, October 1999, pp. 174–202; and J. Flaherty, 'Suggestions Rise From the Floors of U.S. Factories', *New York Times*, 18 April 2001, p. C1.
15. R. Levering and M. Moskowitz, 'The Ten Best Companies to Work for in America', *Business and Society Review*, Spring 1993, p. 29.
16. J. L. Cotton, *Employee Involvement* (Newbury Park, CA: Sage, 1993), pp. 3, 14.
17. Ibid, p. 3.
18. See, for example, the increasing body of literature on empowerment, such as R. C. Ford and M. D. Fottler, 'Empowerment: A Matter of Degree', *The Academy of Management Executive*, August 1995, pp. 21–31; K. Blanchard, J. P. Carlos and W. A. Randolph, *The 3 Keys to Empowerment: Release the Power within People for Astonishing Results* (San Francisco: Berrett-Koehler, 1999); W. A. Randolph, 'Re-Thinking Empowerment: Why is it So Hard to Achieve?', *Organizational Dynamics*, vol. 29, no. 2, 2000, pp. 94–107; and D. P. Ashmos, D. Duchon, R. R. McDaniel, Jr and J. W. Huonker, 'What a Mess! Participation as a Simple Managerial Rule to "Complexify" Organizations', *Journal of Management Studies*, March 2002, pp. 189–206.
19. See M. Sashkin, 'Participative Management is an Ethical Imperative', *Organizational Dynamics*, Spring 1984, pp. 5–22; and D. Collins, 'The Ethical Superiority and Inevitability of Participatory Management as an Organizational System', *Organization Science*, September–October 1997, pp. 489–507.
20. F. Heller, E. Pusic, G. Strauss and B. Wilpert, *Organizational Participation: Myth and Reality* (Oxford: Oxford University Press, 1998).

21. K. L. Miller and P. R. Monge, 'Participation, Satisfaction, and Productivity: A Meta-Analytic Review', *Academy of Management Journal*, December 1986, pp. 727–53; J. A. Wagner III and R. Z. Gooding, 'Shared Influence and Organizational Behavior: A Meta-Analysis of Situational Variables Expected to Moderate Participation–Outcome Relationships', *Academy of Management Journal*, September 1987, pp. 524–41; J. A. Wagner III, 'Participation's Effects on Performance and Satisfaction: A Reconsideration of Research Evidence', *Academy of Management Review*, April 1994, pp. 312–30; C. Doucouliagos, 'Worker Participation and Productivity in Labour-Managed and Participatory Capitalist Firms: A Meta-Analysis', *Industrial and Labor Relations Review*, October 1995, pp. 58–77; J. A. Wagner III, C. R. Leana, E. A. Locke and D. M. Schweiger, 'Cognitive and Motivational Frameworks in U.S. Research on Participation: A Meta-Analysis of Primary Effects', *Journal of Organizational Behavior*, vol. 18, 1997, pp. 49–65; J. S. Black and H. B. Gregersen, 'Participative Decision-Making: An Integration of Multiple Dimensions', *Human Relations*, July 1997, pp. 859–78; and E. A. Locke, M. Alavi and J. A. Wagner III, 'Participation in Decision Making: An Information Exchange Perspective', in G. R. Ferris (ed.), *Research in Personnel and Human Resource Management,* vol. 15 (Greenwich, CT: JAI Press, 1997), pp. 293–331.
22. Cotton, *Employee Involvement*, p. 114.
23. See, for example, M. Poole, 'Industrial Democracy: A Comparative Analysis', *Industrial Relations*, Fall 1979, pp. 262–72; IDE International Research Group, *European Industrial Relations* (Oxford: Clarendon, 1981); E. M. Kassalow, 'Employee Representation on U.S., German Boards', *Monthly Labor Review*, September 1989, pp. 39–42; T. H. Hammer, S. C. Currall and R. N. Stern, 'Worker Representation on Boards of Directors: A Study of Competing Roles', *Industrial and Labor Relations Review*, winter 1991, pp. 661–80; and P. Kunst and J. Soeters, 'Works Council Membership and Career Opportunities', *Organization Studies*, vol. 12, no. 1, 1991, pp. 75–93.
24. J. D. Kleyn and S. Perrick, 'Netherlands', *International Financial Law Review*, February 1990, pp. 51–56.
25. Cotton, *Employee Involvement*, pp. 129–30, 139–40.
26. Ibid, p. 140.
27. See, for example, G. W. Meyer and R. G. Stott, 'Quality Circles: Panacea or Pandora's Box?', *Organizational Dynamics*, Spring 1985, pp. 34–50; E. E. Lawler III and S. A. Mohrman, 'Quality Circles: After the Honeymoon', *Organizational Dynamics*, Spring 1987, pp. 42–54; T. R. Miller, 'The Quality Circle Phenomenon: A Review and Appraisal', *SAM Advanced Management Journal*, Winter 1989, pp. 4–7; K. Buch and R. Spangler, 'The Effects of Quality Circles on Performance and Promotions', *Human Relations*, June 1990, pp. 573–82; P. R. Liverpool, 'Employee Participation in Decision-Making: An Analysis of the Perceptions of Members and Nonmembers of Quality Circles', *Journal of Business and Psychology*, Summer 1990, pp. 411–22, and E. E. Adams, Jr, 'Quality Circle Performance', *Journal of Management*, March 1991, pp. 25–39.
28. Cotton, *Employee Involvement*, p. 76.
29. Ibid, p. 78.
30. Ibid, p. 87.
31. See K. M. Young (ed.), *The Expanding Role of ESOPs in Public Companies* (New York: Quorum, 1990); J. L. Pierce and C. A. Furo, 'Employee Ownership: Implications for Management', *Organizational Dynamics*, Winter 1990, pp. 32–43; A. A. Buchko, 'The Effects of Employee Ownership on Employee Attitudes: An Integrated Causal Model and Path Analysis', *Journal of Management Studies*, July 1993, pp. 633–56; and J. McDonald, 'The Boom in Employee Ownership', *INC.*, August 2000, pp. 106–12.
32. 'The Employee Ownership 100', <www.nceo.org>; December 2001.
33. Buchko, 'The Effects of Employee Ownership on Employee Attitudes'.
34. C. M. Rosen and M. Quarrey, 'How Well is Employee Ownership Working?', *Harvard Business Review*, September–October 1987, pp. 126–32.
35. Cited in 'ESOP Benefits Are No Fables', *Business Week*, 6 September 1999, p. 26.
36. W. N. Davidson and D. L. Worrell, 'ESOP's Fables: The Influence of Employee Stock Ownership Plans on Corporate Stock Prices and Subsequent Operating Performance', *Human Resource Planning*, January 1994, pp. 69–85.
37. J. Walker, 'New Push for Share Plans', *Business Review Weekly*, 7 August 2003, p. 66; Pierce and Furo, 'Employee Ownership'.
38. See data in D. Stamps, 'A Piece of the Action', *Training*, March 1996, p. 66; Walker, 'New Push for Share Plans'.
39. C. Robert, T. M. Probst, J. J. Martocchio, R. Drasgow, and J. J. Lawler, 'Empowerment and Continuous Improvement in the United States, Mexico, Poland, and India: Predicting Fit on the Basis of the Dimensions of Power Distance and Individualism', *Journal of Applied Psychology*, October 2000, pp. 643–58.
40. Pierce and Furo, 'Employee Ownership', p. 32; and S. Kaufman, 'ESOPs' Appeal on the Increase', *Nation's Business*, June 1997, p. 43.
41. M. Arndt, 'From Milestone to Millstone?', *Business Week*, 20 March 2000, pp. 120–22.
42. C. Farrell, 'Now, More Can Join the ESOP Game', *Business Week*, 25 May 1998, pp. ENT20–22; Walker, 'New Push for Share Plans'.
43. 'Denver Teachers Accept Plan Linking Pay to Performance', *New York Times*, 12 September 1999, p. Y25; and T. Henry, 'States to Tie Teacher Pay to Results', *USA Today*, 30 September 1999, p. 1A.
44. Based on J. R. Schuster and P. K. Zingheim, 'The New Variable Pay: Key Design Issues', *Compensation & Benefits Review*, March–April

1993, p. 28; and K. S. Abosch, 'Variable Pay: Do We Have the Basics in Place?', *Compensation & Benefits Review*, July–August 1998, pp. 12–22.

45. B. Wysocki, Jr, 'Chilling Reality Awaits Even the Employed', *Wall Street Journal*, 5 November 2001, p. A1.

46. N. Way, J. Thomson, J. Stensholt and A. Heathcote, 'Performance Anxiety', *Business Review Weekly*, 1 May 2003; M. Laurence, 'Make the Bonus Work Harder', *Business Review Weekly*, 13 March 2003.

47. R. Balu, 'Bonuses Aren't Just for the Bosses', *Fast Company*, December 2000, pp. 74–76; and M. Conlin, 'A Little Less in the Envelope This Week', *Business Week*, 18 February 2002, pp. 64–66.

48. See, for example, S. E. Gross and D. Duncan, 'Case Study: Gainsharing Plans Spurs Record Productivity and Payouts at AmeriSteel', *Compensation and Benefits Review*, November–December 1998, pp. 46–50; J. B. Arthur and G. S. Jelf, 'The Effects of Gainsharing on Grievance Rates and Absenteeism', *Journal of Labor Research*, vol. 20, 1999, pp. 133–45; and L. R. Gomez-Mejia, T. M. Welbourne and R. M. Wiseman, 'The Role of Risk Sharing and Risk Taking Under Gainsharing', *Academy of Management Review*, July 2000, pp. 492–507.

49. M. Laurence, 'Employee Shares and Option Plans are Coming up to Harvest Time', *Business Review Weekly*, 22 June 1998, pp. 102–04.

50. C. G. Hanson and W. D. Bell, *Profit Sharing and Profitability: How Profit Sharing Promotes Business Success* (London: Kogan Page, 1987); and M. Magnan and S. St-Onge, 'Profit-Sharing and Firm Performance: A Comparative and Longitudinal Analysis', paper presented at the 58th annual meeting of the Academy of Management, San Diego, August 1998.

51. T. M. Welbourne and L. R. Gomez-Mejia, 'Gainsharing: A Critical Review and a Future Research Agenda', *Journal of Management*, vol. 21, no. 3, 1995, pp. 559–609.

52. See Cotton, *Employee Involvement*, pp. 89–113; and W. Imberman, 'Boosting Plant Performance with Gainsharing', *Business Horizons*, November–December 1992, p. 79.

53. M. Fein, 'Work Measurement and Wage Incentives', *Industrial Engineering*, September 1973, pp. 49–51. For an updated review of the effect of pay on performance, see G. D. Jenkins, Jr, N. Gupta, A. Mitra and J. D. Shaw, 'Are Financial Incentives Related to Performance? A Meta-Analytic Review of Empirical Research', *Journal of Applied Psychology*, October 1998, pp. 777–87.

54. W. Zellner, 'Trickle-Down is Trickling Down at Work', *Business Week*, 18 March 1996, p. 34; and 'Linking Pay to Performance is Becoming a Norm in the Workplace', *Wall Street Journal*, 6 April 1999, p. A1.

55. G. Koretz, 'Pay Perks Cloud the Crystal Ball', *Business Week*, 10 September 2001, p. 34; and 'As Bonuses Evaporate, a Reluctant Consumer', *New York Times*, 10 December 2001, p. C5.

56. B. Philips, 'People Power', *Business Review Weekly*, 30 April 1999, p. 21.

57. 'More Than 20 Percent of Japanese Firms Use Pay Systems Based on Performance', *Manpower Argus*, May 1998, p. 7.

58. 'U.S. Wage and Productivity Growth Attainable Through Gainsharing', Employment Policy Foundation, <www.epf.org>; 10 May 2000.

59. See, for example, R. Ganzel, 'What's Wrong with Pay for Performance?', *Training*, December 1998, pp. 34–40.

60. See 'Skilled-Based Pay Boosts Worker Productivity and Morale', *Wall Street Journal*, 23 June 1992, p. A1; L. Wiener, 'No New Skills? No Raise', *U.S. News & World Report*, 26 October 1992, p. 78; and M. A. Verespej, 'New Responsibilities? New Pay!', *Industry Week*, 15 August 1994, p. 14; and 'Skill-Based Pay Program', <www.bmpoc.org>; 29 June 2001.

61. G. E. Ledford, Jr, 'Paying for the Skills, Knowledge, and Competencies of Knowledge Workers', *Compensation & Benefits Review*, July–August 1995, pp. 55–62; and B. Murray and B. Gerhart, 'An Empirical Analysis of a Skill-Based Pay Program and Plant Performance Outcomes', *Academy of Management Journal*, February 1998, pp. 68–78.

62. E. E. Lawler III, G. E. Ledford, Jr and L. Chang, 'Who Uses Skill-Based Pay, and Why', *Compensation & Benefits Review*, March–April 1993, p. 22.

63. 'Tensions of a New Pay Plan', *New York Times*, 17 May 1992, p. F5.

64. E. E. Lawler III, S. A. Mohrman and G. E. Ledford, Jr, *Creating High Performance Organizations: Practices and Results in the Fortune 1000* (San Francisco: Jossey-Bass, 1995); C. Lee, K. S. Law and P. Bobko, 'The Importance of Justice Perceptions on Pay Effectiveness: A Two-Year Study of a Skilled-Based Pay Plan', *Journal of Management*, vol. 25, no. 6, 1999, pp. 851–73; A. Podolske, 'Seven-Year Update on Skill-Based Pay Plans', <www.ioma.com>; July 1999.

65. Lawler, Ledford and Chang, 'Who Uses Skill-Based Pay, and Why'.

66. M. Rowland, 'It's What You Can Do That Counts', *New York Times*, 6 June 1993, p. F17.

67. Ibid.

68. See, for example, M. W. Barringer and G. T. Milkovich, 'A Theoretical Exploration of the Adoption and Design of Flexible Benefit Plans: A Case of Human Resource Innovation', *Academy of Management Review*, April 1998, pp. 305–24; J. A. Fraser, 'Stretching Your Benefits Dollar', *INC.*, March 2000, pp. 123–26; and J. J. Meyer, 'The Future of Flexible Benefit Plans', *Employee Benefits Journal*, June 2000, pp. 3–7.

69. D. A. DeCenzo and S. P. Robbins, *Human Resource Management*, 7th ed. (New York: Wiley, 2002), pp. 346–48.

70. E. E. Lawler III, 'Reward Systems', in J. R. Hackman and J. L. Suttle (eds), *Improving Life at Work* (Santa Monica, CA: Goodyear, 1977), p. 182.

71. L. Alderman and S. Kim, 'Get the Most from Your Company Benefits', *Money*, January 1996, pp. 102–06.

72. D. Grider and M. Shurden, 'The Gathering Storm of Comparable Worth', *Business Horizons*, July–August 1987, pp. 81–86.

73. D. Lander and G. O'Neil, 'Pay Equity Applies: Apples, Oranges and a Can of Worms', *Asia Pacific Human Resource Management*, vol. 29, no. 1, Autumn 1991, pp. 16–28.

74. Cited in T. J. Patten, *Fair Play* (San Francisco: Jossey-Bass, 1988), p. 31.

75. Cited in K. A. Kavach and P. E. Millspaugh, 'Comparable Worth: Canada Legislation Pay Equity', *Academy of Management Executive*, May 1990, p. 97.

76. M. Bennet, 'Future Directions in Remuneration Management', *Asia Pacific Human Resource Management*, Winter 1991, pp. 59–66.

77. J. Kapstein, 'Volvo's Radical New Plant: "The Death of the Assembly Line"?', *Business Week*, 28 August 1989, pp. 92–93.

78. J. R. Hackman, 'Work Design', in Hackman and Suttle, *Improving Life at Work*, pp. 132–33.

79. R. W. Walters, 'The Citibank Project: Improving Productivity Through Work Design', in D. L. Kirkpatrick (ed.), *How to Manage Change Effectively* (San Francisco: Jossey-Bass, 1985), pp. 195–208.

80. T. Thomas, 'Every Man is a Manager at BHP's Queensland Mill', *Business Review Weekly*, 31 January 1992, pp. 56–57.

81. See, for example, M. Alpert, 'The Care and Feeding of Engineers', *Fortune*, 21 September 1992, pp. 86–95.

82. See, for example, L. Morrow, 'The Temping of America', *Time*, 29 March 1993, pp. 40–47; B. Geber, 'The Flexible Work Force', *Training*, December 1993, pp. 23–30; M. Barrier, 'Now You Hire Them, Now You Don't', *Nation's Business*, January 1994, pp. 30–31; and J. Fierman, 'The Contingency Work Force', *Fortune*, 24 January 1994, pp. 30–36.

83. M. Smith, 'Casualisation: What is the Debate We Should be Having?', *Workers Online*, Issue No. 85, 23 February 2001.

84. Ibid.

85. See, for example, C. Meyer, 'What Makes Workers Tick?', *INC.*, December 1997, pp. 74–81; N. Munk, 'The New Organization Man', *Fortune*, 16 March 1998, pp. 62–74; D. Levy, 'Net Elite: 'It's Not About Money', *USA Today*, 22 February 1999, p. B1; and M. W. Walsh, 'Money Isn't Everything', *New York Times*, 30 January 2001, p. E10.

86. E. Ross, 'Poacher's Picnic', *Business Review Weekly*, 13 March 2003.

87. R. Denniss, 'Measuring Unemployment in the 21st Century: New Measures for Overwork and Underemployment', <www.tai.org.au/Publications_Files/DP_Files/DP36SUM.PDF>.

Integrative Case Study A A New Broom Sweeps Clean

DR GLENICE J. WOOD, University of Ballarat, Australia

Christine Nixon was appointed to the role of Chief Commissioner of Police by the Victorian government in 2001. The appointment was a milestone, as she is the first female officer in Australia to achieve the role of Chief Commissioner of Police.

Although she has been in the police force for 30 years, Christine Nixon's route to the top hasn't always been smooth. She was initially rejected as an applicant into the NSW force because of not meeting the minimum height requirements. More public was her falling out with a very senior officer, when she refused to sack staff under her control. From these experiences she learned that policies relating to policing could be unjust and pedantic, and that the power of senior officers was absolute. She has personally felt the brunt of that political power when she was sidelined to a posting in Wollongong, effectively blocking her career path.

Such experiences may stand her in good stead when it comes to dealing with the morale problem she inherited when she took over the role of Chief Commissioner. Nixon was surprised by the unhappiness exhibited by police officers, which became evident during her meetings with people after she commenced in the job. She also learned of the morale problem through e-mails, which she encourages people to send to her, covering a range of issues from their personal lives to police matters. In summing up the situation, Christine Nixon believes that members of the police force didn't feel they were being supported by management, and the issues that had been troubling them for three to four years hadn't been resolved.

Her vision for change encompasses a major crime squad reform, and she is committed to the development of a new command team. When she first took over the job, Christine Nixon set up internal working parties to deal with a range of police matters. Over 500 recommendations for change were generated, and of these, 95 per cent will be adopted. She also plans to significantly change the discipline system she has inherited, and is keen to see an external police authority appointed by the government to ensure that an independent process is achieved. 'People involved in the system may not like the outcome but they should believe they have been dealt with fairly' (Silvester, John, 'The Force is With Her', *The Age*, 20 April 2002, Insight, p. 3).

Christine Nixon continues to work towards crime squad reform after some initial setbacks caused by an industrial law agreement. Her concerns relate to corrupt relationships that some detectives appear to have formed with criminal elements. Her goal is to turn the crime squad into a 'high quality area that is filled with people who are trustworthy' through 'catching police who are corrupt but not persecuting those who make mistakes' (Silvester, p. 3).

Christine Nixon would like to have the power to dismiss police who are unsatisfactory in the role. In addition, she has four areas of focus she wishes to embrace during her term. These include stolen vehicles, burglaries, the road toll, and domestic violence and sexual assault; all issues that Christine Nixon believes fundamentally affect people's lives.

Her personal leadership style is distinctive, and may go some way to explaining the improvements that have been noted in Victoria's police force over the past two years (Silvester, p. 3). She appears to manage by a strong sense of social justice and personal integrity. One example of this was her decision to march in the Gay and Lesbian Pride March in St Kilda, Melbourne, in uniform. This sent a message to observers and police members alike that entrenched bias wasn't going to be tolerated, and that Christine Nixon had the integrity and courage to stand by what she sees as fair and appropriate behaviour. She prefers a consultative style of communication, although she is adamant that some issues should remain non-negotiable, such as instigating a process of alcohol and drug testing for police officers. Her view is that addicted police shouldn't be able to continue in operational work in the force.

One of her great skills appears to be that of making people feel comfortable and at ease when dealing with her. Her desire to interact in the community has her agreeing to talk to groups several days a week. She travels by road constantly to meet with her officers, and has opened up a two-way communication process through e-mail, which she responds to regularly. One example of her willingness to engage in meaningful dialogue was a correspondence that involved her personally addressing, and quashing, a rumour that had been circulating through the Victorian Police Force, intimating that she was likely to return to New South Wales before her term had expired. Her reply underscored the fact that she had given her commitment to a full term in the role, and that she had every intention of fulfilling that commitment. In addition to improving communications, she has made other changes that have met with the approval of the police force, including allowing beards to be worn, doing away with rigid rules that applied to uniforms, and championing flexible recruiting.

It would appear that Christine Nixon is well on track to achieving her vision of a corruption-free Victorian Police Force. Morale is now reported to be improving (with police resignations dropping from 60 per month to 12), and much of this has been attributed to Nixon's management style, and her understanding of natural justice and fairness. However, she is equally able to make tough decisions, such as refusing to roll over contracts of senior personnel in incumbent positions. It would appear that Christine Nixon has bi-partisan political support, as well as the respect of her officers and the community at large … a difficult balancing act!

Activities for discussion, analysis and further research

1. What values and attitudes (in terms of the three components of an attitude) are evident in Christine Nixon's approach to her role?
2. With reference to the various learning theories covered in the preceding chapters, which learning theories best describe how members of the Victorian Police Force are learning to adapt to the changes in culture of their organisation?
3. In terms of personality theory, describe how Christine Nixon may rate on the 'Big 5' personality traits and on an emotional intelligence scale. What other personality traits does she exhibit that are relevant to her work behaviour?
4. How would you describe Christine Nixon's job satisfaction in the role of Commissioner of the Victorian Police Force? Outline four factors that are likely to have enhanced her job satisfaction, as well as that of police officers generally.
5. Do you feel that the organisational commitment of the members of the Victorian Police Force has improved since 2001, when Christine Nixon took over her role? Explain your view.
6. In terms of individual decision making, which ethical decision criteria do you believe Christine Nixon draws on?
7. Explain what impact Christine Nixon's leadership style may have on increasing the motivation of members of the Victorian Police Force.

Integrative Case Study B What Makes People Want to Come to Work on Mondays?

ALLISON JAMES, Australian Maritime College

A friend and I were invited to stay in Bangkok with an ex-colleague. We went to many of the usual tourist destinations. The Temple of the Golden Buddha and the tale behind it is memorable. The temple itself, both inside and out, is modest; however, the presence of a solid-gold Buddha is remarkable.

Our guide told us this tale:

In the 1950s, monks had to relocate a clay, ten-and-a-half-foot-tall Buddha from their temple. In the move, the idol began to crack. It also began to rain. They covered the Buddha to protect it from the rain. Later, a monk using a torch checked on the Buddha. He noticed a 'gleam'. He fetched a chisel and hammer and began to chip away at the clay. The 'gleam' grew bigger. When the clay was removed, beneath was the solid-gold Buddha.

How long did it take him to chip away at the 'bland' clay exterior before he realised the stunning, solid-gold Buddha was hidden underneath?

Some employees are like the clay Buddha, with a shell of hardness or blandness, yet underneath is the golden spirit, the real self. Much like the monk, a manager's task may be to motivate and assist employees to uncover their true self. How long do you have to work at it? How long and how hard do you 'chip away'? One of the most challenging aspects of being a manager is motivating your staff. Highly motivated employees and colleagues are organisational assets.

Motivation manifests itself through output, absenteeism, effort, loyalty, turnover and achievement. You have no doubt observed that some of your colleagues appear to be highly motivated. Just what is it that makes them this way? Just what is it that makes some people demonstrate a burning desire to achieve and accept increased responsibility, while others remain passive or accept mediocre performance? What really motivates employees? Money? Status? Power? Self-fulfilment? When we ask such questions, we are exploring motivation, the 'force' that energises and gives direction to behaviour. We are starting to see what is underneath the clay exterior.

We operate as part of a global workforce of vastly different skills and one that is culturally diverse. An inclusive style of management seems to be a developing theme—a collegial style that takes into consideration all stakeholders and builds competitive advantage. What unique motivation challenges face the inclusive manager?

Ricardo Semler, of Semco, has successfully learned to uncover the gold. We can glean many ideas from his well-known philosophy that take us into the 21st century. By creating an 'unusual workplace' in the 1990s with an unconventional management style, Semler supervised one of South America's fastest-growing companies with people waiting to be employed. Semco manufactures a variety of products, including pumps that can empty an oil-tanker in a night, dishwashers, cooling units, mixers that blend everything from rocket fuel to bubble gum, and biscuit factories; however, it isn't what Semco produces that has management experts waiting months to tour the plants—it's the way the people of Semco make it. Semler creates an environment in which others make decisions; he believes that success means not having to make decisions himself. Semler states: 'I never leave a number where I can be reached when I'm away and I don't call in. I want everyone at Semco to be self-sufficient.' (Semler, R, *Maverick: the success story behind the world's most unusual workplace*, 1993, London: Arrow Books, p. 31.)

The factory employees sometimes set their own production quotas. They help to redesign the products they make and work on the marketing strategy. Their bosses can run their units with extraordinary freedom, determining business strategy without interference from the top brass. They even set their own salaries, with no strings. Everyone will know what they are, since all financial information is openly discussed.

Semler describes Semco's factories as 'messy ... with ... machines ... set at odd angles and in unexpected places'. Why might this layout actually be a motivator, even though it is in apparent conflict with both ergonomic efficiency and Taylorist theory?

The last sentence of Ricardo Semler's book says it all. What we need to do is:

... to forget socialism, capitalism, just-in-time deliveries, salary surveys, and the rest of it, and to concentrate on building organisations that accomplish that most difficult of all challenges: to make people look forward to coming to work in the morning.

Semler decided he needed people to *want* to come to work on Mondays—and set about creating an environment that achieved this. Semco takes workplace democracy to previously unimagined frontiers. Semco creates an environment in which decisions previously made by managers are made by employees, where shopfloor employees sometimes set their own productivity targets and monitor the results. It is acknowledged as a place where people want to work, with a waiting list of thousands hoping to join.

Some of Semler's ideas may not be for every industry. However, the basic approach is valid for every industry and organisation, in the sense that it involves thinking outside of current norms and breaking with commonplace traditions. It is about finding ways to 'energise', motivate or find the gold underneath employees' 'clay'.

If we, as managers, were to decide that our job—the challenge—is to create an environment where employees were actually pleased to come to work in the morning, then we would have an interesting approach to motivation and understanding people. We have noted, in this part, that to get the most out of people, you must first understand them as *individuals*.

Activities for discussion, analysis and further research

Select any organisation or department/section that you are familiar with where motivation could be improved. This could be a current or previous employer, a company you do regular business with or one that interests you. If you cannot think of one, then pick an area in your university.[1] Assume you are charged with the task of improving motivation and morale:

1. What individual characteristics affect behaviours of staff?
2. Explain why an understanding of the individual and perception is important to motivation.
3. What values affect productivity and satisfaction? Where possible, explain through examples.
4. What basic motivation concepts are particularly relevant?
5. Take Semler's challenge and recommend innovative ways to make the workplace interesting and enjoyable—to uncover the gold.

---

[1] This activity can be run as a team exercise if students are familiar with a particular organisation. Students could practise brainstorming and/or the Nominal Group Technique. Teams could present their answers and vie for the most innovative responses, particularly for questions 4 and 5.

The Group
Part 3

CHAPTER 8   FOUNDATIONS OF GROUP BEHAVIOUR

CHAPTER 9   UNDERSTANDING AND BUILDING TEAMS

CHAPTER 10   COMMUNICATION

CHAPTER 11   LEADERSHIP CONCEPTS AND THEORIES

CHAPTER 12   CONTEMPORARY ISSUES IN LEADERSHIP

CHAPTER 13   POWER AND POLITICS

CHAPTER 14   CONFLICT AND NEGOTIATION

Foundations of Group Behaviour

CHAPTER OUTLINE

Types of groups
Models of group development
Towards explaining work group behaviour
Group decision making

LEARNING OBJECTIVES

After studying this chapter, you should be able to:

1. Differentiate between formal and informal groups
2. Compare two models of group development
3. Identify the key factors in explaining group behaviour
4. Explain how role requirements change in different situations
5. Describe how norms exert influence on an individual's behaviour
6. Define social loafing and describe its effect on group performance
7. Identify the benefits and disadvantages of cohesive groups
8. List the strengths and weaknesses of group decision making
9. Contrast the effectiveness of interacting, brainstorming, nominal group technique and electronic meeting groups

Madness is the exception in individuals but the rule in groups.
Friedrich Nietzsche

E-mail has become a significant factor in the way groups interact in the workplace.

Many of us like to think that status isn't as important as it was a generation or two ago. We can point to government legislation concerning discrimination and equal employment opportunity, open office designs, casual work dress, increase in general educational levels in the workforce and employee empowerment as examples of forces that have made organisations more egalitarian. The reality is that we continue to live in an essentially class-structured society. Despite all attempts to make it more egalitarian, we have made little progress towards a classless society. Even the smallest group will develop roles, rights and rituals to differentiate its members. We are even finding that New Economy organisations adapt mechanisms to create status differences. Take e-mail, for example. Here is a communication tool that its proponents claim democratises organisations. It allows people to communicate up and down hierarchical lines, unimpeded by gatekeepers and protocols. It allows, for example, people low in the organisation to directly communicate with higher-ups without going through traditional authority channels. But, do you know what? Status differences have crept into the e-mail process. A recent study of some 30,000 e-mail messages at a New Economy firm that didn't use job titles, was organised around teams and prided itself on democratic decision making provides interesting insights.[1]

In spite of e-mail's egalitarian intentions, employees in this company had found ways to use it and still create social distinctions. For example, high-status employees tended to send short, curt messages, in part to minimise contact with lower-status workers but also to convey comfort with their own authority. In contrast, mid-status employees tended to produce long, argumentative messages loaded with jargon or over-explained answers to simple questions. And low-status employees' e-mails would contain non-work-related elements such as forwarded jokes or happy-face 'emoticons'. In addition, the study found that senior managers would take the longest to reply, and had the poorest spelling and the worst grammar—which all conveyed that they have better things to do with their time.

The creation of status differences is just one of a number of naturally occurring actions in groups. Along with concepts such as roles and norms, an understanding of status can help you better explain and predict the behaviour of people in groups. The objectives of this and the following chapter are to provide you with a foundation for understanding how groups work and to show you how to create effective teams. Let's begin by defining groups and explaining why people join them.

LEARNING OBJECTIVE

1

Differentiate between formal and informal groups

Types of Groups

A **group** is defined as two or more individuals, interacting and interdependent, who have come together to achieve particular objectives. Groups can be either formal or informal. By **formal groups**, we mean those defined by the organisation's structure, with designated work assignments establishing tasks. In formal groups, the behaviours that one should engage in are stipulated by and directed towards organisational goals. The six members making up an airline flight crew are an example of a formal group. In contrast, **informal groups** are alliances that are neither formally structured nor organisationally determined. These groups are natural formations in the work environment that appear in response to the need for social contact. Three employees from different departments who regularly eat lunch together are an example of an informal group.

group(s)
Two or more individuals, interacting and interdependent, who have come together to achieve particular objectives (*see also* **work group**).

formal group
A designated work group defined by the organisation's structure.

informal group
A group that is neither formally structured nor organisationally determined; appears in response to the need for social contact.

command group
A group composed of the individuals who report directly to a given manager.

task group
Those working together to complete a job task.

interest group
Those working together to attain a specific objective with which each is concerned.

friendship group
Those brought together because they share one or more common characteristics.

It's possible to subclassify groups as command, task, interest or friendship groups.[2] Command and task groups are dictated by the formal organisation, whereas interest and friendship groups are informal alliances.

A **command group** is determined by the organisation chart. It is composed of the individuals who report directly to a given manager. A high school principal and her 18 teachers form a command group, as do the director of company audits and his five audit inspectors.

Task groups, also organisationally determined, represent those working together to complete a job task. However, a task group's boundaries are not limited to its immediate hierarchical superior. It can cross command relationships. For example, if a university student is accused of a campus crime, it may require communication and coordination among the dean of the faculty, the registrar, the director of security and the student's legal adviser. Such a formation would constitute a task group. It should be noted that all command groups are also task groups, but because task groups can cut across the organisation, the reverse need not be true.

People who may or may not be aligned into common command or task groups may affiliate to attain a specific objective with which each is concerned. This is an **interest group**. Employees who band together to have their holiday schedules altered, to support a peer who has been fired, or to seek improved working conditions represent the formation of a united body to further their common interest.

Groups often develop because the individual members have one or more common characteristics. We call these formations **friendship groups**. Social alliances, which frequently extend outside the work situation, can be based on similar age or ethnic heritage, support for AFL football, or the holding of similar political views, to name just a few such characteristics.

Informal groups provide a very important service by satisfying their members' social needs. Because of interactions that result from the close proximity of workstations or task interactions, we find workers often do things together—such as play golf, commute to work, eat lunch, and chat during coffee breaks. We must recognise that these types of interactions among individuals, even though informal, deeply affect their behaviour and performance.

There is no single reason why individuals join groups. Because most people belong to a number of groups, it's obvious that different groups provide different benefits to their members. Table 8.1 summarises the most popular reasons people have for joining groups.

LEARNING OBJECTIVE

2

Compare two models of group development

Models of Group Development

Groups generally pass through a standardised sequence in their evolution. We call this sequence the five-stage model of group development. Recent studies, however, indicate that temporary groups with task-specific deadlines follow a very different pattern. We call this pattern the punctuated-equilibrium model. In this section, we describe both of these models of group development.

TABLE 8.1	Why do people join groups?

Security. By joining a group, individuals can reduce the insecurity of 'standing alone'. People feel stronger, have fewer self-doubts, and are more resistant to threats when they are part of a group.

Status. Inclusion in a group that is viewed as important by others provides recognition and status for its members.

Self-esteem. Groups can provide people with feelings of self-worth. That is, in addition to conveying status to those outside the group, membership can also give increased feelings of worth to the group members themselves.

Affiliation. Groups can fulfil social needs. People enjoy the regular interaction that comes with group membership. For many people, these on-the-job interactions are their primary source for fulfilling their needs for affiliation.

Power. What cannot be achieved individually often becomes possible through group action. There is power in numbers.

Goal achievement. There are times when it takes more than one person to accomplish a particular task—there is a need to pool talents, knowledge or power in order to complete a job. In such instances, management will rely on the use of a formal group.

FIVE-STAGE GROUP-DEVELOPMENT MODEL

As shown in Figure 8.1, the **five-stage group-development model** characterises groups as proceeding through five distinct stages: forming, storming, norming, performing and adjourning.[3]

The first stage, **forming**, is characterised by a great deal of uncertainty about the group's purpose, structure and leadership. Members are 'testing the waters' to determine what types of behaviour are acceptable. This stage is complete when members have begun to think of themselves as part of a group.

The **storming** stage is one of intragroup conflict. Members accept the existence of the group, but there is resistance to the control the group imposes on individuality. There is sometimes conflict over who will control the group. When this stage is complete, there will be a relatively clear hierarchy of leadership within the group.

The third stage is one in which close relationships develop and the group demonstrates cohesiveness. There is now a strong sense of group identity and 'mateship'. This **norming** stage is complete when the group structure solidifies and the group has assimilated a common set of expectations of what defines correct member behaviour.

The fourth stage is **performing**. The group relationships and structures are set and accepted. Group energy has moved from getting to know and understand each other, to performing the task at hand. For permanent work groups, performing is the last stage in their development.

five-stage group-development model
Groups go through five distinct stages: forming, storming, norming, performing and adjourning.

forming stage
The first stage in group development, characterised by much uncertainty.

storming stage
The second stage in group development, characterised by intragroup conflict.

norming stage
The third stage in group development, characterised by close relationships and cohesiveness.

performing stage
The fourth stage in group development, when the group is fully functional.

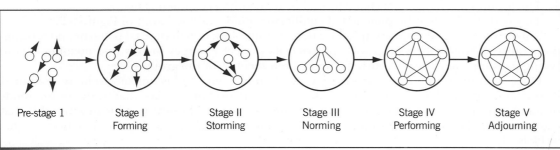

| Pre-stage 1 | Stage I Forming | Stage II Storming | Stage III Norming | Stage IV Performing | Stage V Adjourning |

FIGURE 8.1	Stages of group development

adjourning stage
The final stage in group
development for
temporary groups,
characterised by concern
with wrapping up
activities rather than task
performance.

However, for temporary committees, task forces, teams and work groups that have completed their task, the **adjourning** stage occurs. In this stage, the group prepares for its disbandment. High task performance is no longer the group's top priority. Instead, attention is directed towards finalising activities. As the group approaches the terminal phase, members break off their bonds of affection and stop interacting with each other. Members have to complete the business of the group, communicate (or not) about the performance of the group and its members, and deal with saying goodbye. This can be a regressive phase of group development diametrically opposed to the progressive phase seen in the initial stages. Responses of group members vary in this stage. Some feel pride in what the group has accomplished. Others may be negative and critical of the way the organisation has treated the group, and others may be sad over the loss of friendship gained during the life of the work group.

Groups don't necessarily become more effective as they progress through the first four stages. Under some conditions, high levels of conflict are conducive to high group performance. So, we might find situations where groups in Stage II outperform those in Stage III or IV. Similarly, groups don't always proceed clearly from one stage to the next. Sometimes, in fact, several stages go on simultaneously, as when groups are storming and performing at the same time. Groups even occasionally regress to previous stages. Therefore, even the strongest proponents of this model don't assume that all groups precisely follow its five-stage process or that Stage IV is always the most preferable.

Another problem with the five-stage model, in terms of understanding work-related behaviour, is that it ignores organisational context.[4] For example, a study of a cockpit crew in an airliner found that, within ten minutes, three strangers assigned to fly together for the first time had become a high-performing group. What allowed for this speedy group development was the strong organisational context surrounding the tasks of the cockpit crew. This context provided the rules, task definitions, information and resources needed for the group to perform. They didn't need to develop plans, assign roles, determine and allocate resources, resolve conflicts and set norms the way the five-stage model predicts. Since much group behaviour in organisations takes place within a strong organisational context, it would appear that the five-stage development model may have limited applicability in our quest to understand work groups.

THE PUNCTUATED-EQUILIBRIUM MODEL

Temporary groups with deadlines don't seem to follow the previous model. Studies indicate that they have their own unique sequencing of actions (or inaction):
1. Their first meeting sets the group's direction.
2. This first phase of group activity is one of inertia.
3. A transition takes place at the end of this first phase, which occurs exactly when the group has used up half its allotted time.
4. A transition initiates major changes.
5. A second phase of inertia follows the transition.
6. The group's last meeting is characterised by markedly accelerated activity.[5]

This pattern is called the **punctuated-equilibrium model** and is shown in Figure 8.2.

The first meeting sets the group's direction. A framework of behavioural patterns and assumptions through which the group will approach its project emerges in this first meeting. These lasting patterns can appear as early as the first few seconds of the group's life.

**punctuated-equilibrium
model**
Temporary groups go
through transitions
between inertia and
activity.

Once set, the group's direction becomes 'written in stone' and is unlikely to be re-examined throughout the first half of the group's life. This is a period of inertia—that is, the group tends to stand still or become locked into a fixed course of action. Even if it gains new insights that challenge initial patterns and assumptions, the group is incapable of acting on these new insights in Phase 1.

One of the more interesting discoveries made in these studies was that each group experienced its transition at the same point in its calendar—precisely halfway between its first meeting

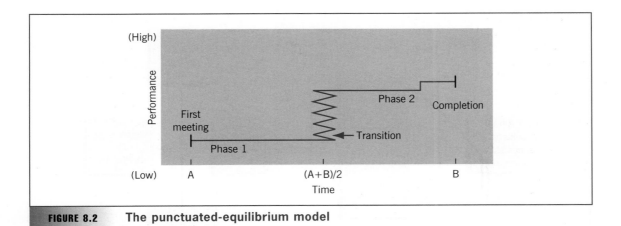

FIGURE 8.2   **The punctuated-equilibrium model**

and its official deadline—despite the fact that some groups spent as little as an hour on their project, while others spent six months. It was as if the groups universally experienced a midlife crisis at this point. The midpoint appears to work like an alarm clock, heightening members' awareness that their time is limited and that they need to 'get moving'.

This transition ends Phase 1 and is characterised by a concentrated burst of changes, dropping of old patterns and adoption of new perspectives. The transition sets a revised direction for Phase 2.

Phase 2 is a new equilibrium or period of inertia. In this phase, the group executes plans created during the transition period.

The group's last meeting is characterised by a final burst of activity to finish its work.

In summary, the punctuated-equilibrium model characterises groups as exhibiting long periods of inertia interspersed with brief revolutionary changes triggered primarily by their members' awareness of time and deadlines. Keep in mind, however, that this model doesn't apply to all groups. It's essentially limited to temporary task groups who are working under a time-constrained completion deadline.[6]

Towards Explaining Work Group Behaviour

Why are some group efforts more successful than others? The answer to that question is complex, but it includes variables such as the ability of the group's members, the size of the group, the level of conflict, and the internal pressures on members to conform to the group's norms. Figure 8.3 presents the main components that determine group performance and satisfaction for its members.[7] The following discussions are based on this model.

EXTERNAL CONDITIONS IMPOSED ON THE GROUP

We can begin to understand the behaviour of a work group when we view it as a subset of a larger organisational system.[8] Work groups don't exist in isolation. A research team in Dow's plastic products division, for example, must live within the rules and policies dictated by the global chemical company's divisional and corporate headquarters. While academics at the University of Sydney think they have a high degree of autonomy in their work, they still must conform to the policy guidelines of the university. So, every work group is influenced by conditions imposed from outside it. These external conditions include the organisation's overall strategy, culture, authority structures, formal regulations, resources, employee selection process, performance evaluation and reward systems, and physical work setting.

LEARNING OBJECTIVE

3

Identify the key factors in explaining group behaviour

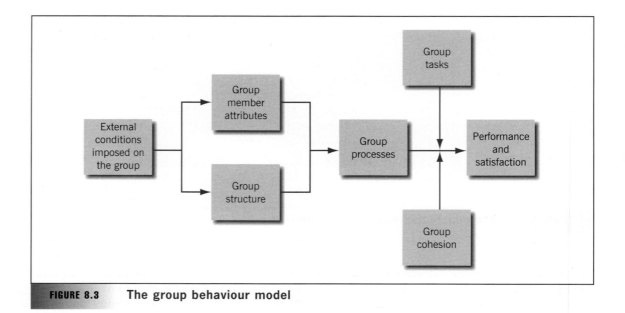

FIGURE 8.3   **The group behaviour model**

An organisation has a strategy that defines what business it is in or wants to be in, and the kind of organisation it wants to be. It is set by top management, often in collaboration with lower-level managers. A strategy outlines the organisation's goals and the means for attaining these goals. It might, for example, direct the organisation towards reducing costs, improving quality, expanding market share or shrinking the size of its overall operations. The strategy that an organisation is pursuing, at any given time, influences the power of various work groups, which, in turn, determines the resources that the organisation's top management is willing to allocate to it for performing its tasks. For example, a major government department had to cut back on its employees and total budget. The training group, in turn, had to operate with fewer people and less money. This resulted in increased stress and frustration in the training group and more conflict with other groups, because they couldn't deliver the quantity and quality of training other departments were expecting.

Every organisation has an unwritten culture that defines for employees acceptable and unacceptable behaviours. After a few months, most employees understand their organisation's culture. They know things such as what is appropriate dress for work, which rules are rigidly enforced, what kinds of unusual behaviours are likely to get them into trouble and which are likely to be overlooked, the importance of honesty and integrity, and which management goals really do count and which don't. While most groups have their own subculture with modified or unique standards, there is usually a dominant organisational culture that conveys to all employees those values the organisation considers most important. Members of work groups have to conform to the standards implied in the organisation's dominant culture if they are to remain in good standing.

Some organisations are large and profitable, with an abundance of resources. Their employees, for example, will have modern, high-quality tools and equipment to do their jobs. Other organisations aren't as fortunate. When organisations have limited resources, so do their work groups. What a group actually accomplishes is, to a large degree, determined by the money, time, raw materials and equipment that are allocated to the group by the organisation.

Organisations have authority structures that define who reports to whom, who makes decisions, and what decisions individuals or groups are empowered to make. This structure typically determines where a given work group is placed in the organisation's hierarchy, the formal leader of the group and the formal relationships between groups. While a group might have an informal leader, the formally designated manager—appointed by the organisation—has authority that others in the group don't have.

Organisations create rules, procedures, policies and other forms of regulations to standardise employee behaviour. Because McDonald's has standard operating procedures for taking orders, cooking hamburgers and making thick shakes, the discretion of work group members to do things differently is severely limited. The more formal the regulations that the organisation imposes on all its employees, the more the behaviour of work group members will be consistent and predictable.

Members of any work group are, first, members of the organisation of which the group is a part. Members of a cost-reduction task force at Boeing first had to be hired as employees of the company. So, the criteria that an organisation uses in its selection decisions determine the kinds of people that are to be in its work groups.

Does the organisation provide employees with performance objectives that are challenging and specific? Does the organisation reward accomplishment of individual or group objectives? Since work groups are part of the larger organisational system, group members' behaviour is influenced by how the organisation evaluates performance and what behaviours are rewarded.[9]

Finally, the physical work setting that is imposed on the group by external factors has an important bearing on work group behaviour.[10] Architects, industrial engineers and office designers make decisions about the size and physical layout of an employee's work space, the arrangement of equipment, illumination levels, and the need for acoustics to cut down on noise distractions. These create both barriers and opportunities for work group interaction. It's a lot easier for employees to talk or 'bludge' if their workstations are close together with no physical barriers between them and their supervisor is in an enclosed office 50 metres away. Even the colour of the walls and equipment may have an effect on the mood of the work group.

GROUP MEMBER ATTRIBUTES

A group's potential level of performance is, to a large extent, dependent on the attributes that its members individually bring to the group. In this section, we look at two general resources that have received the greatest amount of attention: knowledge, skills and abilities; and personality characteristics.

Knowledge, skills and abilities

Part of a group's performance can be predicted by assessing the intellectual abilities of its individual members related to the type of tasks they do. Sometimes a mediocre sporting team of players beats another highly talented team because of excellent coaching, determination and precision teamwork. But such cases make the news precisely because they represent an aberration. Group performance isn't merely the summation of its individual members' abilities. However, these abilities set the possibilities for what members can do and how effectively they perform in a group.

A review of the evidence has found that interpersonal skills consistently emerge as important for high performance by work groups.[11] These include conflict management and resolution, collaborative problem solving, and communication. For example, members need to be able to recognise the type and source of conflict confronting the group and to implement an appropriate conflict-resolution strategy; identify situations requiring participative group problem solving and utilise the proper degree and type of participation; and listen non-evaluatively and use active listening techniques appropriately.

Personality characteristics

There has been a great deal of research on the relationship between personality traits and group attitudes and behaviour. The general conclusion is that attributes that tend to have a positive

Different office layouts can influence the group dynamics in an organisation. Many organisations have conference rooms which they can use for multiple purposes such as meetings, project coordination, video conferencing or brainstorming.

connotation in our culture tend to be positively related to group productivity, morale and cohesiveness. These include traits such as sociability, self-reliance and independence. In contrast, negatively evaluated characteristics such as authoritarianism, dominance and unconventionality tend to be negatively related to the dependent variables.[12] These personality traits affect group performance by strongly influencing how the individual interacts with other group members.

The magnitude of the effect of any *single* characteristic is small, but all *together* the consequences for group behaviour are of major significance. We can conclude, therefore, that personality characteristics of group members play an important part in determining group behaviour.

GROUP STRUCTURE

Work groups are not an unorganised mob. They have a structure that shapes the behaviour of members and makes it possible to explain and predict a large portion of individual behaviour within the group, as well as the performance of the group itself. What are some of these structural variables? They include formal leadership, roles, norms, status, group size and composition of the group.

Formal leadership

Almost every work group has a formal leader. She or he is typically identified by titles such as 'department manager', 'supervisor', 'foreperson', 'project leader', 'task force head' or 'committee chair'. This leader can play an important part in the group's success, and this is covered in more depth in later chapters.

Roles

Shakespeare once described the world as a stage where all of us are merely players, each with our part to play. In the same way, all members of a group are actors, each with a role to play. By **role**, we mean a set of responsibilities and tasks each person is expected to perform as part of their position held in the group. The understanding of roles would be easier if each of us chose one role and carried it out regularly and consistently. Unfortunately, we are required to play a number of diverse roles, both on and off the job. Thus, one of the tasks in understanding behaviour is grasping the role, or complex set of roles, that a person is currently playing.

For example, Bill Chitlow is a manager of engineering for BHP, the major Australian steel producer, and is located in Perth, Western Australia. He has a number of roles that he fulfils in that job—a member of middle management, part of the electrical engineering group and a member of a quality improvement team. Off the job, Bill finds himself in more roles: husband,

LEARNING OBJECTIVE

4

Explain how role requirements change in different situations

role(s)
A set of expected behaviour patterns attributed to someone occupying a given position in a social unit.

father, Catholic, tennis player, member of the golf club and president of the Parent–Teacher Association. Many of these roles are compatible, while some create conflicts. For example, his religious beliefs are sometimes incompatible with the AIDS policy his company has adopted. A recent offer of promotion requires Bill to relocate, yet his family very much wants to stay in Perth. Can the role demands of his job be reconciled with the role demands of husband and father?

The issue should be clear. Like Bill Chitlow, we are all required to play a number of roles, and our behaviour varies with the role we are playing. Bill's behaviour when he attends church on Sunday morning is different from his behaviour when he chairs a meeting about the introduction of some cost-saving measures at work the next day. So, different groups impose different role requirements on individuals.

Role identity

There are certain attitudes and actual behaviours consistent with a role and they create the **role identity**. People have the ability to shift roles rapidly when they recognise that the situation and its demands clearly require major changes. For example, when union stewards were promoted to supervisory positions, it was found that their attitudes changed from pro-union to pro-management within a few months of their promotion. When these promotions had to be rescinded later because of economic difficulties in the organisation, it was found that the demoted supervisors had once again adopted their pro-union attitudes.[13]

> **role identity**
> Certain attitudes and behaviours consistent with a role.

Role perception

Often we act in a situation based on how we believe we are *supposed* to behave. This is called a **role perception**. Where do we obtain these perceptions? We obtain them from stimuli all around us—friends, books, peers, television and managers. Apprentice programs exist in many trades and professions to allow beginners to watch an 'expert' so that they can learn to act as they are supposed to. And when we start a new job, we often watch and ask questions of employees with longer experience in the job, to determine what's expected of us; we form our role perception at this time.

> **role perception**
> An individual's view of how he or she is supposed to act in a given situation.

Role expectations

Role expectations are defined as how others believe you should act in a given situation. How you behave is determined largely by the role defined in the context in which you are acting. The role of a foreign ambassador is viewed as having propriety and dignity, whereas a football coach is seen as omnipotent, aggressive and inspiring to his players. When role expectations are concentrated into generalised categories, we have role stereotypes.

In the workplace, it can be helpful to look at the topic of role expectations through the perspective of the **psychological contract**. There is an unwritten and often implied agreement that exists between employees and their employer. This psychological contract sets out mutual expectations—what management expects from employees, and vice versa.[14] In effect, this contract defines the behavioural expectations that go with every role. Management is expected to treat employees justly, provide acceptable working conditions, clearly communicate what is a fair day's work and give feedback on how well the employee is doing. Employees are expected to respond by demonstrating a good attitude, following directions and showing loyalty to the organisation.

What happens when role expectations as implied in the psychological contract aren't met? If management is derelict in keeping up its part of the bargain, we can expect negative repercussions on employee performance and satisfaction. When employees fail to live up to expectations, the result is usually some form of disciplinary action up to, and including, being dismissed.

> **role expectations**
> How others believe a person should act in a given situation.

> **psychological contract**
> An unwritten agreement that sets out what management expects from the employee, and vice versa.

> **role conflict**
> A situation in which an individual is confronted by divergent role expectations.

Role conflict

When an individual is confronted by divergent role expectations, the result is **role conflict**. It exists when an individual finds that compliance with one role requirement may make more difficult the compliance with another.[15] At the extreme, it would include situations in which two or more role expectations are mutually contradictory.

Our previous discussion of the different roles of Bill Chitlow included several role conflicts—for example, Bill's attempt to reconcile the expectations placed on him as a husband and father and as a manager with BHP. The former emphasises stability and concern for his wife and family to remain in Perth. BHP, on the other hand, expects its employees to be responsive to the needs and requirements of the organisation. Although it might be in Bill's financial and career interests to accept a relocation, the conflict comes down to choosing between family and career role expectations.

How strongly do our roles affect our behaviour? Many people believe that they adopt a work role or home role, but that they are basically the same and their personality isn't changed very much by the role they are in. Role experiments carried out by Philip Zimbardo at Stanford University in California challenge this view.[16] He created a 'prison' in the basement of the Stanford psychology building; hired, at US$15 a day, 24 emotionally stable, physically healthy, law-abiding students who scored 'normal average' on extensive personality tests; randomly assigned them the role of either 'guard' or 'prisoner'; and established some basic rules. The experimenters then stood back to see what would happen.

At the start of the planned two-week simulation, there were no measurable differences between those students assigned to be guards and those chosen to be prisoners. Additionally, the guards received no special training in how to be prison guards. They were told only to 'maintain law and order' in the prison and not to take any nonsense from the prisoners: physical violence was forbidden. To simulate further the realities of prison life, the prisoners were allowed visits from relatives and friends, but while the mock guards worked eight-hour shifts, the mock prisoners were kept in their cells around the clock and were allowed out only for meals, exercise, toilet privileges, head-count line-ups and work details.

It took little time for the prisoners to accept the authority positions of the guards and for the mock guards to adjust to their authority roles. After the guards crushed a rebellion attempt on the second day, the prisoners became increasingly passive. Whatever the guards 'dished out', the prisoners took. The prisoners actually began to believe and act as if they were, as the guards constantly reminded them, inferior and powerless. And every guard, at some time during the simulation, engaged in abusive, authoritative behaviour. For example, one guard said, 'I was surprised at myself . . . I made them call each other names and clean the toilets out with their bare hands. I practically considered the prisoners cattle and I kept thinking: "I have to watch out for them in case they try something."'

The simulation actually proved *too* successful in demonstrating how quickly individuals learn new roles. The researchers had to stop the experiment after only six days because of the pathological reactions that the participants were demonstrating. And remember, these were individuals chosen precisely for their normalcy and emotional stability!

What should you conclude from this prison simulation? The participants in this study had, like the rest of us, learned stereotyped concepts of guard and prisoner roles from the mass media and their own personal experiences in power and powerlessness relationships gained at home (parent–child), in school (teacher–student) and in other situations. This, then, allowed them easily and rapidly to assume roles that were very different from their inherent personalities. In this case, we saw that people with no previous personality pathology or training in their roles could execute extreme forms of behaviour consistent with the roles they were playing.

Norms

Did you ever notice that golfers don't speak while their partners are putting on the green, or that employees don't criticise their bosses in public? Why? The answer is: 'Norms!'

All groups have established **norms**—that is, acceptable standards of behaviour that are shared by the group's members. Norms tell members what they ought and ought not to do under certain circumstances. From an individual's standpoint, they tell what is expected of you in certain

LEARNING OBJECTIVE

5

Describe how norms exert influence on an individual's behaviour

norms
Acceptable standards of behaviour within a group that are shared by the group's members.

situations. When agreed to and accepted by the group, norms act as a means of influencing the behaviour of group members with a minimum of external controls. Norms differ among groups, communities and societies, but they all have them.[17]

Common types of norms

A work group's norms are like an individual's fingerprints—each is unique. Yet, there are some common types of norms that appear in most work groups.[18]

Probably the most common types of norms deal with *performance-related processes*. Work groups typically provide their members with explicit cues on how hard they should work, how to get the job done, their level of output and appropriate communication channels.[19] These norms are extremely powerful in affecting an individual employee's performance—they are capable of significantly modifying a performance prediction that was based solely on the employee's ability and level of personal motivation.

A second category of norms encompasses *appearance factors*. This includes things such as appropriate dress, loyalty to the work group or organisation, when to look busy and when it's acceptable to 'bludge'. Some organisations have formal dress codes. However, even in their absence, norms frequently develop to dictate the kind of clothing that should be worn to work. Presenting the appearance of loyalty is important in many work groups. For example, it's considered inappropriate and disloyal for professionals and executives in an organisation to be openly looking for another job. This concern to demonstrate loyalty is often the reason why ambitious hopefuls for top management positions willingly take home work at night, come in on weekends, and accept transfers to locations they would otherwise prefer not to live in.

Another type of norm concerns *social arrangements*. These norms come from informal work groups and primarily regulate social interactions within the group. These norms influence friendships on and off the job, who group members eat lunch with, and social activities.

A final category of norms relates to *allocation of resources*. These norms can originate in the group or in the organisation and cover things such as pay, assignment of difficult jobs, and allocation of new tools and equipment. In some departments, it may be the more senior professionals and managers who get the best equipment, while the newer or junior employees may be the last to get their own personal computers. These resource allocation norms can have a direct impact on employee satisfaction and an indirect effect on group performance.

Conformity

As a member of a group, you want to feel that you belong and are an important part of the group. Because of your desire for acceptance, you are susceptible to **conforming** to the group's norms. There is considerable evidence that groups can place strong pressure on individual members to change their attitudes and behaviours to conform to the group's standard.[20]

Do individuals conform to the pressures of all the groups to which they belong? Obviously not, because people belong to many groups and their norms vary. In some cases, they may even have contradictory norms. So, what do people do? They conform to the important groups to which they belong or hope to belong. The important groups are called **reference groups** and are characterised as the ones where people define themselves as members, or would like to be members, and they feel that the group members are significant to them.[21] The implication, then, is that all groups don't impose equal conformity pressures on their members.

The impact that group pressures for conformity can have on an individual member's judgment and attitudes was demonstrated in the classic studies by Solomon Asch.[22] Asch made up groups of seven or eight people who sat in a classroom and were asked to compare two cards held by the experimenter. One card had one line, the other had three lines of varying length. As shown in Figure 8.4, one of the lines of the three-line card was identical to the line on the one-line card. Also, as shown in the figure, the difference in line length was quite obvious; under ordinary conditions, subjects made fewer than 1 per cent errors. The object was to announce aloud which of the three lines matched the single line. But what happens if the members in the

conforming
Adjusting one's behaviour to align with the norms of the group.

reference groups
Important groups to which individuals belong or hope to belong and with whose norms individuals are likely to conform.

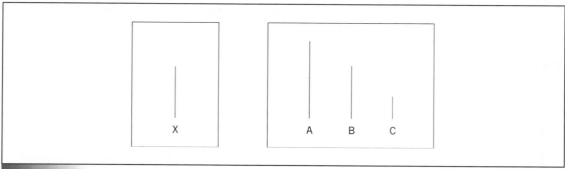

FIGURE 8.4   Examples of cards used in the Asch studies

group begin to give incorrect answers? Will the pressures to conform result in an unsuspecting subject (USS) altering their answer to align with the others? Asch arranged the group so that only the USS was unaware that the experiment was 'fixed'. The seating was prearranged: the USS was placed so as to be the last to announce their decision.

The experiment began with several sets of matching exercises. All the subjects gave the right answers. On the third set, however, the first subject would give an obviously wrong answer—for example, saying 'C' in Figure 8.4. The next subject gave the same wrong answer, and so did the others until it got to the unknowing subject. She or he knew 'B' was the same as 'X', yet everyone had said 'C'. The decision confronting the USS is: Do I state a perception publicly that differs markedly from the pre-announced position of the others? Or do I give an answer that I strongly believe is incorrect in order to have my response agree with the other subjects in the group?

The results obtained by Asch demonstrated that over many experiments and many trials, 75 per cent of the subjects gave at least one answer that conformed—that is, that they knew was wrong but that was consistent with the replies of other group members—and the average for conformers was 37 per cent. What meaning can we draw from these results? They suggest that there are group norms that press us towards conformity. That is, we desire to be one of the group and avoid being visibly different.

The above conclusions are based on research that was conducted 50 years ago. Has time altered their validity? And should we consider these findings generalisable across cultures? The evidence indicates that there have been changes in the level of conformity over time; and Asch's findings are culture-bound.[23] Specifically, levels of conformity have steadily declined since Asch's studies in the early 1950s. In addition, conformity to social norms is higher in collectivist cultures than in individualistic cultures. Nevertheless, even in highly individualistic countries such as Australia, you should consider conformity to norms still to be a powerful force in groups.

Deviant workplace behaviour

Roger Yeo is frustrated by a co-worker who constantly spreads malicious and unsubstantiated rumours about him. Debra Hundley is tired of a member of her work team who, when confronted with a problem, takes out his frustration by yelling and screaming at her and other work team members. And Susan Lomu recently quit her job as a dental hygienist after being constantly sexually harassed by her employer.

What do these three episodes have in common? They represent employees being exposed to acts of **deviant workplace behaviour**.[24] This term covers a full range of antisocial actions by organisational members that intentionally violate established norms and that result in negative consequences for the organisation, its members, or both. Figure 8.5 provides a typology of deviant workplace behaviours with examples of each.

deviant workplace behaviour
Antisocial actions by organisational members that intentionally violate established norms and that result in negative consequences for the organisation, its members, or both.

Category	Examples
Production	Leaving early Intentionally working slowly Wasting resources
Property	Sabotage Lying about hours worked Stealing from the organisation
Political	Showing favouritism Gossiping and spreading rumours Blaming co-workers
Personal aggression	Sexual harassment Verbal abuse Stealing from co-workers

FIGURE 8.5   Typology of deviant workplace behaviours

Source: Adapted from S. L. Robinson and R. J. Bennett, 'A Typology of Deviant Workplace Behaviors: A Multidimensional Scaling Study', *Academy of Management Journal*, April 1995, p. 565. Copyright © 1995 by Academy of Management. Reproduced with permission in the format Textbook via Copyright Clearance Centre.

Few organisations will admit to creating or condoning conditions that encourage and maintain deviant norms. Yet, they exist. Employees report, for example, an increase in rudeness and disregard towards others by bosses and co-workers in recent years. And nearly half of employees who have suffered this incivility report that it has led them to think about changing jobs, with 12 per cent actually quitting because of it.[25]

As with norms in general, individual employees' antisocial actions are shaped by the group context within which they work. Evidence demonstrates that the antisocial behaviour exhibited by a work group is a significant predictor of an individual's antisocial behaviour at work.[26] In other words, deviant workplace behaviour is likely to flourish where it's supported by group norms. What this means for managers is that when deviant workplace norms surface, employee cooperation, commitment and motivation is likely to suffer. This, in turn, can lead to reduced employee productivity and job satisfaction, and increased turnover.

Status

While teaching a university course on adolescence, the lecturer asked the class to list things that contributed to status when they were in high school. The list was long and included being an athlete or a school representative, and being able to skip classes without getting caught. Then the lecturer asked the students to list things that *didn't* contribute to status. Again, it was easy for the students to create a long list: getting high marks, having your mother drive you to school, and so forth. Finally, the students were asked to develop a third list—those things that didn't matter one way or the other. There was a long silence. At last, one student in the back row volunteered, 'In high school, *nothing* didn't matter.'[27]

Status is a socially defined position or rank given to groups or group members by others and it permeates society far beyond the walls of high school. It would not be extravagant to rephrase the preceding quotation to read, 'In the status hierarchy of life, *nothing* doesn't matter.' Despite all attempts to make it more egalitarian, we have made little progress towards a classless society. Even the smallest group will develop roles, rights and rituals to differentiate its members. Status is an important factor in understanding human behaviour because it is a significant motivator and has major behavioural consequences when individuals perceive a disparity between what they believe their status to be and what others perceive it to be.

status
A socially defined position or rank given to groups or group members by others.

Status and norms

Status has been shown to have some interesting effects on the power of norms and pressures to conform. For example, high-status members of groups often are given more freedom to deviate from norms than are other group members.[28] High-status people also are better able to resist conformity pressures than their lower-status peers. An individual who is highly valued by a group but who doesn't much need or care about the social rewards the group provides is particularly able to pay minimal attention to conformity norms.[29]

The previous findings explain why many star athletes, celebrities, top-performing sales people and outstanding academics seem oblivious to appearance or social norms that constrain their peers. As high-status individuals, they are given a wider range of discretion. But this is true only as long as the high-status person's activities aren't severely detrimental to group goal achievement.[30]

Status equity

It is important for group members to believe that the status hierarchy is equitable. When inequity is perceived, it creates disequilibrium that results in various types of corrective behaviour.[31]

The concept of equity presented in a previous chapter applies to status. People expect rewards to be in line with the costs incurred in acting a role. If Dana and Anne are the two leading contenders for the head nurse position in a hospital, and it's clear that Dana has more seniority and is better prepared for assuming the promotion, Anne will view the selection of Dana to be equitable. However, if Anne is chosen because she is the daughter-in-law of the hospital director, then Dana and other employees may believe an injustice has occurred.

The trappings that go with formal positions are also important elements in maintaining equity. When we believe that there is an inequity between the perceived ranking of an employee and the status furniture and equipment that the employee is given by the organisation, we experience *status incongruence*. Examples of incongruence occur when the more desirable office location is held by a lower-ranking employee and a company car is provided to section managers but not the senior executives. Incongruence has been a longstanding problem in the insurance industry, where top sales agents often earn two to five times more than senior corporate executives. The result is that it's hard for insurance companies to entice agents into management positions. The main point here is that employees expect the things an individual has and receives to be congruent with the individual's status.

Groups generally agree within themselves on status criteria and, hence, there is usually high congruence in group rankings of members. However, individuals can find themselves in a conflict situation when they move between groups whose status criteria are different, or when they form groups whose members have heterogeneous backgrounds. Business executives may use income, total wealth or size of the organisations they run as determinants of status. Blue-collar employees may use years of seniority, job assignments or success in horse-race betting. In groups made up of different people, or when different groups are amalgamated or merged, status differences may initiate conflict as the group attempts to reconcile and align the differing hierarchies.

Status and culture

Before we leave the topic of status, we should briefly address the issue of cross-culture transferability. Do cultural differences affect status? The answer is a resounding 'Yes!'[32]

Cultural differences have a strong effect on status. The importance of status does vary between cultures. The French, for example, are highly status-conscious. Additionally, countries differ on the criteria that create status. For example, status for Latin Americans and Asians tends to be derived from family position and formal roles held in organisations. In contrast, while status is still important in countries such as Australia and the United States, it tends to be less 'in your face'. And it tends to be bestowed more on accomplishments than on titles and family trees.

The message here is to make sure you understand who and what holds status when interacting with people from a culture different from your own. An Australian manager who doesn't understand that office size is no measure of a Japanese executive's position, or who fails to grasp the importance that the British place on family background and social class, is likely to unintentionally offend his or her Japanese or British counterpart and, in doing so, lessen his or her interpersonal effectiveness.

Size

Does the size of a group affect the group's overall behaviour? The answer is 'yes', but the effect depends on what dependent variable you look at.[33] The evidence indicates, for example, that smaller groups are quicker at completing tasks than are larger ones. However, if the group is engaged in problem solving, large groups consistently attain better marks than their smaller counterparts. Translating these results into specific numbers is a bit more difficult, but we can offer some guidelines. Large groups—with a dozen or more members—are good for gaining diverse input. So, if the goal of the group is fact finding, larger groups should be more effective. On the other hand, smaller groups are better at doing something productive with that input. Groups of approximately seven members, therefore, tend to be more effective for taking action.

One of the most important findings related to the size of a group has been labelled social loafing. **Social loafing** is the tendency for individuals to expend less effort when working collectively than when working individually.[34] It directly challenges the logic that the productivity of the whole should at least equal the sum of the productivity of each person in the group.

A common stereotype about groups is that the sense of team spirit spurs individual effort and enhances the group's overall productivity. One study compared the results of individual and group performance on a rope-pulling task.[35] It was expected that the group's effort would be equal to the sum of the efforts of individuals within the group. That is, three people pulling together should exert three times as much pull on the rope as one person, and eight people should exert eight times as much pull. The results, however, didn't confirm these expectations. Groups of three people exerted a force only two-and-a-half times the average individual performance. Groups of eight collectively achieved less than four times the solo rate.

Replications of the original research have generally supported these findings that increases in group size are inversely related to individual performance.[36] More may be better in that total productivity of a group of four is greater than that of one or two people, but the individual productivity of each group member declines as the size of the group increases.

What causes this social loafing effect? It may be the result of a belief that others in the group aren't pulling their weight. If you see others as lazy or inept, you can re-establish equity by reducing your effort. Another explanation is the dispersion of responsibility. Because the results of the group can't be attributed to any single person, the relationship between an individual's input and the group's output is clouded. In such situations, individuals may become 'free riders' and coast on the group's efforts. In other words, there will be a reduction in efficiency where individuals think that their contribution can't be measured.

The implications for group work are significant. Where managers use collective work situations to enhance morale and teamwork, they must also provide a means by which individual efforts can be identified. If this isn't done, management must weigh the potential losses in productivity against any possible gains in employee satisfaction.[37] However, this conclusion has a Western bias. It is consistent with individualistic cultures, such as Australia, New Zealand and the United States, that are dominated by self-interest. It's not consistent with collectivist societies where individuals are motivated by in-group goals. For example, in studies comparing employees from the United States with employees from the People's Republic of China and Israel (both collectivist societies), the Chinese and Israelis showed no propensity to engage in social loafing. In fact, the Chinese and Israelis actually performed better in a group than when working alone.[38]

LEARNING OBJECTIVE

6

Define social loafing and describe its effect on group performance

social loafing
The tendency for individuals to expend less effort when working collectively than when working individually.

The research on group size leads us to two additional conclusions:

1. Groups with an odd number of members tend to be preferred to those with an even number.
2. Groups made up of five or seven members do an efficient job of exercising the best elements of both small and large groups.[39]

Working with an odd number of members eliminates the possibility of ties when votes are taken. Groups made up of five or seven members are large enough to form a majority and allow for diverse input. Yet, they are small enough to avoid the negative outcomes often associated with large groups, such as domination by a few members, development of subgroups, inhibited participation by some members, and excessive time taken to reach a decision. Research also shows that use of electronic brainstorming can reduce social loafing and increase productivity by 63 per cent.[40]

Composition

Most group activities require a variety of skills and knowledge. Given this requirement, it would be reasonable to conclude that heterogeneous groups—those composed of dissimilar individuals—would be more likely to have diverse abilities and information and should be more effective. Research studies substantiate this conclusion, especially on cognitive, creativity-demanding tasks.[41]

When a group is diverse in terms of personality, gender, age, education, functional specialisation and experience, there is an increased probability that the group will possess the needed characteristics to complete its tasks effectively.[42] The group may be more conflict-laden and less expedient as varied positions are introduced and assimilated, but the evidence generally supports the conclusion that heterogeneous groups perform more effectively than do those that are homogeneous. Essentially, diversity promotes conflict, which stimulates creativity, which leads to improved decision making.

But what about diversity created by racial or national differences? The evidence indicates that these elements of diversity interfere with group processes, at least in the short term.[43] Cultural diversity seems to be an asset for tasks that call for a variety of viewpoints. But culturally heterogeneous groups have more difficulty in learning to work with each other and in solving problems. The good news is that these difficulties seem to dissipate with time. Although newly formed culturally diverse groups underperform newly formed culturally homogeneous groups, the differences disappear after about three months. The reason is that it takes diverse groups a while to learn how to work through disagreements and different approaches to solving problems.

Another side of diversity relates to the way we deal with diversity in groups, both in terms of composition and the general work environment. Cognitive processing theory illustrates how diversity leads to these outcomes by describing the way people process most information through automatic use of scripts and schemas that assist them to understand situations and organise actions. When individuals are unable to fit a new situation into an existing schema, they have to increase their awareness and either modify their existing schema or generate a new one. A moderate diversity results in a stimulation of new ideas, but if diversity increases to a level that leads to the individuals within the group feeling uncomfortable, then communication suffers, conflict occurs and individuals choose to leave the group.[44]

group demography
The degree to which members of a group share a common demographic attribute, such as age, sex, race, educational level or length of service in the organisation, and the impact of this attribute on turnover.

An offshoot of the composition issue has recently received a great deal of attention by group researchers. This is the degree to which members of a group share a common demographic attribute, such as age, sex, race, educational level or length of service in the organisation, and the impact of this attribute on turnover. We call this variable **group demography**.

We discussed individual biographical factors in an earlier chapter. Here we consider the same type of factors, but in a group context. That is, it's not whether a person is male or female or has been employed with the organisation for a year rather than ten years that concerns us now, but rather the individual's attribute in relationship to the attributes of others with whom he or she works. Let's work through the logic of group demography, review the evidence and then consider the implications.

Groups and organisations are composed of **cohorts**, which we define as individuals who hold a common attribute. For example, everyone born in 1960 is of the same age. This means they also have shared common experiences. People born in 1970 have experienced the information revolution, but not the Korean conflict. People born in 1945 shared the Vietnam War, but not the Great Depression. Women in many organisations today who were born before 1945 matured prior to the women's liberation movement and have had substantially different experiences from women born after 1960. Group demography, therefore, suggests that attributes such as age or the date that someone joins a specific work group or organisation should help us to predict turnover. Essentially, the logic goes like this: turnover will be greater among those with dissimilar experiences, because communication is more difficult. Conflict and power struggles are more likely and more severe when they occur. The increased conflict makes group membership less attractive, so employees are more likely to quit. Similarly, the losers in a power struggle are more apt to leave voluntarily or to be forced out.

Several studies have sought to test this thesis, and the evidence is quite encouraging.[45] For example, in departments or separate work groups in which a large portion of members entered at the same time, there is considerably more turnover among those outside this cohort. Also, when there are large gaps between cohorts, turnover is higher. People who enter a group or an organisation together, or at approximately the same time, are more likely to associate with one another, have a similar perspective on the group or organisation, and thus be more likely to stay. On the other hand, discontinuities or bulges in the group's date-of-entry distribution are likely to result in a higher turnover rate within that group.

The implication of this line of inquiry is that the composition of a group may be an important predictor of turnover. Differences per se may not predict turnover. But large differences within a single group will lead to turnover. If everyone is moderately dissimilar from everyone else in a group, the feelings of being an outsider are reduced. So, it is the degree of dispersion on an attribute, rather than the level, that matters most.

It appears that variance within a group about variables other than date of entry, such as social background, gender and levels of education, might similarly create discontinuities or bulges in the distribution that will encourage some members to leave. To extend this idea further, the fact that a group member is a woman may mean little in predicting turnover. In fact, if the work group is made up of nine women and one man, we would be more likely to predict that the lone man would leave. In the executive ranks of organisations, where women are the minority, we would predict that this minority status would increase the likelihood that managers who are women would either quit or suffer reduced promotion opportunities.[46]

Cohesiveness

Groups differ in their **cohesiveness**—that is, the degree to which members are attracted to each other and are motivated to stay in the group.[47] For example, some work groups are cohesive because the members have spent a great deal of time together, or the group's small size facilitates high interaction, or the group has experienced external threats that have brought members close together. Cohesiveness is important because it has been found to be related to the group's productivity.[48]

Studies consistently show that the relationship of cohesiveness and productivity depends on the performance-related norms established by the group. If performance-related norms are high (for example, high output, quality work, cooperation with individuals outside the group), a cohesive group will be more productive than will a less cohesive group. But if cohesiveness is high and performance norms are low, productivity will be low. If cohesiveness is low and performance norms are high, productivity increases, but less than in the high-cohesiveness/high-norms situation. When cohesiveness and performance-related norms are both low, productivity will tend to fall into the low-to-moderate range. These conclusions are summarised in Figure 8.6.

What can you do to encourage group cohesiveness? You might try one or more of the following suggestions: (1) Make the group smaller. (2) Encourage agreement with group goals.

cohorts
Individuals who, as part of a group, hold a common attribute.

LEARNING OBJECTIVE
7
Identify the benefits and disadvantages of cohesive groups

cohesiveness
Degree to which group members are attracted to each other and are motivated to stay in the group.

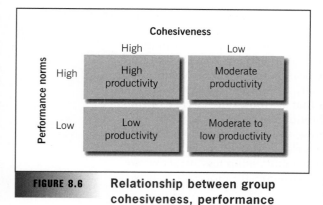

Performance norms

Cohesiveness

	High	Low
High	High productivity	Moderate productivity
Low	Low productivity	Moderate to low productivity

FIGURE 8.6 **Relationship between group cohesiveness, performance norms and productivity**

(3) Increase the time members spend together. (4) Increase the status of the group and the perceived difficulty of attaining membership in the group. (5) Stimulate competition with other groups. (6) Give rewards to the group rather than to individual members. (7) Physically isolate the group.[49]

GROUP PROCESSES

The next component of our group behaviour model considers the processes that go on within a work group—the communication patterns used by members for information exchanges, group decision processes, leader behaviour, power dynamics, conflict interactions, and the like. The following chapters elaborate on many of these processes.

Why are processes important to understanding work group behaviour? One way to answer this question is to return to the topic of social loafing. We found out that 1 + 1 + 1 doesn't necessarily add up to 3. In group tasks where each member's contribution isn't clearly identified, there is a tendency for individuals to decrease their effort. Social loafing, in other words, illustrates a process loss as a result of using groups. But group processes can also produce results. That is, groups can create outputs greater than the sum of their inputs. The development of creative alternatives by a diverse group would be one such instance. Figure 8.7 illustrates how group processes can have an impact on a group's actual effectiveness.[50]

synergy
An action of two or more substances that results in an effect that is different from the individual summation of the substances.

Synergy is a term used in biology that refers to an action of two or more substances that results in an effect that is different from the individual summation of the substances. We can use the concept to better understand group processes.

Social loafing, for example, represents *negative* synergy: the whole is less than the sum of the parts. Research teams, on the other hand, are often used in research laboratories because they can use the diverse skills of various individuals to produce more significant research as a group than could be generated by all of the researchers working independently. That is, they produce *positive* synergy: their process gains exceed their process losses.

Another line of research that helps us to better understand group processes is the social facilitation effect.[51] Have you ever noticed that performing a task in front of others can have a positive or negative effect on your performance? For example, you privately practise a complex springboard dive at your home pool for weeks. Then you do the dive in front of a group of friends and you do it better than ever. Or you practise a speech in private and finally get it down perfect, but you 'bomb' when you have to give the speech in public.

social facilitation effect
The tendency for performance to improve or decline in response to the presence of others.

The **social facilitation effect** refers to this tendency for performance to improve or decline in response to the presence of others. While this effect is not entirely a group phenomenon—people can work in the presence of others and not be members of a group—the group situation is more likely to provide the conditions for social facilitation to occur. The research on social facilitation tells us that the performance of simple, routine tasks tends to be speeded up and made more accurate by the presence of others. When the work is more complex, requiring closer

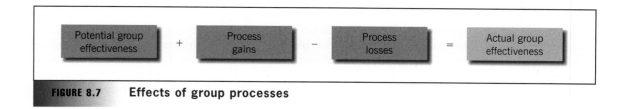

Potential group effectiveness + Process gains − Process losses = Actual group effectiveness

FIGURE 8.7 **Effects of group processes**

attention, the presence of others is likely to have a negative effect on performance.[52] So, what are the implications of this research in terms of managing process gains and losses? The implications relate to learning and training. People seem to perform better on a task in the presence of others if that task is very well learned, but perform less well if it is not well learned. So, process gains will be maximised by training people for simple tasks in groups, and training people for complex tasks in individual private practice sessions.

GROUP TASKS

Imagine, for a moment, that there are two groups at a major oil company. The job of the first is to consider possible sites for a new refinery. The decision is going to affect people in many areas of the company—production, engineering, marketing, distribution, personnel, purchasing, real estate development, and the like—so key people from each of these areas will need to provide input into the decision. The job of the second group is to coordinate the building of the refinery after the site has been selected, the design finalised and the financial arrangements completed. Research on group effectiveness tells us that management would be well advised to use a larger group for the first task than for the second.[53] The reason is that large groups facilitate pooling of information. The addition of a diverse perspective to a problem-solving committee typically results in a process gain. But when a group's task is coordinating and implementing a decision, the process loss created by each additional member's presence is likely to be greater than the process gain made. So, the size–performance relationship is moderated by the group's task requirements.

Recent research in Australia has challenged the idea that team decision making is more effective than individual decisions. The research has shown that individual job satisfaction can be lowered in some groups and that political tactics will take on increased emphasis in groups that don't have strong leadership.[54]

The preceding conclusions can be extended: the impact of group processes on the group's performance and member satisfaction is also moderated by the tasks that the group is doing. The evidence indicates that the complexity and interdependence of tasks influence the group's effectiveness.[55]

Tasks can be generalised as either simple or complex. Complex tasks tend to be novel or non-routine. Simple ones are routine and standardised. We would hypothesise that the more complex the task, the more the group will benefit from discussion among members on alternative work methods. If the task is simple, group members don't need to discuss such alternatives. They can rely on standardised operating procedures for doing the job. Similarly, if there is a high degree of interdependence among the tasks that group members must perform, they will need to inter-act more. Effective communication and minimal levels of conflict should therefore be relevant to group performance when tasks are interdependent.

These conclusions are consistent with what we know about information-processing capacity and uncertainty.[56] Tasks that have higher uncertainty—those that are complex and interdependent—require more information processing. This, in turn, places more importance on group processes. So, just because a group is characterised by poor communication, weak leadership, high levels of conflict, and the like, it doesn't necessarily mean that it will be low-performing. If the group's tasks are simple and require little interdependence among members, the group may still be effective.

The Real Deal

LEGO isn't only for kids

Robert Rasmussen is president of Executive Discovery, a company that has developed an unusual technique for getting people to work together and generate innovative ideas. LEGO Serious Play is a management communication technique that can be used in group sessions. LEGO Serious Play aims to explore the relationships and connections between people and their worlds. The technique is based on participants building landscape models with LEGO bricks and then assigning meaning to their creations by telling a story about them and playing out various possible scenarios. This process is said to deepen understanding, sharpen insight and socially bond together the members of the group, who have fun playing and engaging with each other through this technique.

According to Executive Discovery, LEGO Serious Play is an efficient, practical and effective process that can work for everyone within an organisation. The company maintains that participants come away with skills to communicate more effectively, to engage their imagination more readily, and to approach their work with increased confidence, commitment and insight.

LEGO Serious Play may be used to get a team of senior executives together to come up with a new corporate strategy. In such a scenario, a working group could be asked to build a model that describes where the company is going, and every member would be able to talk about the model and make changes to it.

Colin Tan is a human resource manager for Maxtor Corporation, in Singapore. Maxtor is one of the world's largest suppliers of hard-disk-drive storage products and solutions. Tan was able to explain his work and his company to 30 other executives through his LEGO creation, which clearly showed a person standing on a platform that had two pieces sticking out on the side. The pieces represented semiconductors.

Robert Rasmussen is a little critical of group facilitators talking to groups of executives using PowerPoint slides and then expecting them to change their behaviour back in the workplace. He believes that his technique engages people as individuals and in groups. As he points out, 'The hands are directly connected to the brain, and when the hands are working, the brain is also engaged . . . People talk more, they think more, and they remember better after the meeting is over.' He relies on his understanding of group dynamics to get results.

Sources: Kenneth Lim, 'The Building Blocks of Business — Using LEGO', *Business Times Singapore*, 21 July 2003; and <www.seriousplay.com/what.html>, accessed 1 August 2003.

Group Decision Making

There is an inherent belief that two heads are better than one. This is the basic premise of our jury system and the reason why many decisions in organisations are made by councils, boards, teams or committees. There are permanent executive committees that meet on a regular basis, special task forces created to analyse unique problems, temporary project teams used to develop new products, and 'quality teams' made up of representatives from management and workers which meet to identify and solve production problems, to name a few of the more obvious examples.

GROUPS VERSUS THE INDIVIDUAL

Decision-making groups may be widely used in organisations, but does this imply that group decisions are preferable to those made by an individual? The answer to this question depends on a number of factors. Let's begin by looking at the strengths and weaknesses of groups.[57]

Strengths and weaknesses of group decision making

Individual and group decisions each have their own sets of strengths. Neither is ideal for all situations. Table 8.2 identifies the main advantages that groups offer over individuals in the making of decisions, as well as the weaknesses of group decision making.

Effectiveness and efficiency

Whether groups are more effective than individuals depends on the criteria you use for defining effectiveness. In regard to *accuracy*, group decisions will tend to be more accurate. The evidence indicates that, on the average, groups make better-quality decisions than do individuals.[58] However, if decision effectiveness is defined by speed, individuals are superior. If creativity is important, groups tend to be more effective than individuals. And if effectiveness means the degree of acceptance the final solution achieves, the success again goes to the group.[59]

LEARNING OBJECTIVE

8

List the strengths and weaknesses of group decision making

TABLE 8.2	**Strengths and weaknesses of group decision making**

Strengths	Weaknesses
• *More complete information and knowledge.* By aggregating the resources of several individuals, we bring more input into the decision process.	• *Time-consuming.* It takes time to assemble a group. The interaction that takes place once the group is in place is frequently inefficient. The result is that groups take longer to reach a solution than would be the case if an individual were making the decision. This can limit management's ability to act quickly and decisively when necessary.
• *Increased diversity of views.* In addition to more input, groups can bring heterogeneity to the decision process. This opens up the opportunity for more approaches and alternatives to be considered.	• *Pressures to conform.* There are social pressures in groups. The desire by group members to be accepted and considered as an asset to the group can result in squashing any overt disagreement, thus encouraging conformity among viewpoints.
• *Increased acceptance of a solution.* Many decisions fail after the final choice has been made, because people don't accept the solution. However, if employees who will be affected by a decision and who will be instrumental in implementing it are able to participate in the decision itself, they will be more likely to accept it and encourage others to accept it. This translates into more support for the decision and higher satisfaction among those employees required to implement it.	• *Domination by the few.* Group discussion can be dominated by one or a few members. If this dominant coalition is composed of low- and medium-ability members, the group's overall effectiveness will suffer.
• *Increased legitimacy.* Western capitalistic societies value democratic methods. The group decision-making process is consistent with democratic ideals and therefore may be perceived as being more legitimate than decisions made by an individual. When an individual decision maker fails to consult with other employees before making a decision, the decision maker's complete power can create the perception that the decision was made autocratically and arbitrarily.	• *Ambiguous responsibility.* Group members share responsibility, but who is actually accountable for the final outcome? In an individual decision, it is clear who is responsible. In a group decision, the responsibility of any single member is reduced.

The management team at the Marriott work closely together to decide on the profile of staff to be recruited. The Marriott Hotel has a five-star reputation to protect and its managers work together to ensure their staff are providing five-star service expected by guests.

GOLD COAST · AUSTRALIA
SURFERS PARADISE **Marriott** RESORT

But effectiveness can't be considered without also assessing efficiency. In efficiency, groups almost always are a poor second to the individual decision maker. With few exceptions, group decision making consumes more work hours than if an individual were to tackle the same problem alone. The exceptions tend to be those instances where, to achieve comparable quantities of diverse input, the single decision maker must spend a great deal of time reviewing files and talking to people. Because groups can include members from diverse areas, the time spent searching for information can be reduced. However, as we noted, these advantages in efficiency tend to be the exception. Groups are generally less efficient than individuals. In deciding whether to use groups, then, consideration should be given to assessing whether increases in effectiveness are more than enough to offset the losses in efficiency.

Summary

Groups offer an excellent vehicle for performing many of the steps in the decision-making process. They are a source of both breadth and depth of input for information gathering. If the group is composed of individuals with diverse backgrounds, the alternatives generated should be more extensive and the analysis more critical. When the final solution is agreed upon, there are more people in a group decision to support and implement it. These pluses, however, can be more than offset by the time consumed by group decisions, the internal conflicts they create and the pressures they generate towards conformity.

GROUPTHINK AND GROUPSHIFT

groupthink
Phenomenon in which the norm for consensus overrides the realistic appraisal of alternative courses of action.

groupshift
A change in decision risk between the group's decision and the individual decision that members within the group would make; can be either towards conservatism or greater risk.

Two by-products of group decision making have received a considerable amount of attention by researchers in OB. As we will show, these two phenomena have the potential to affect the group's ability to appraise alternatives objectively and arrive at quality decision solutions.

The first phenomenon, called **groupthink**, is related to norms. It describes situations in which group pressures for conformity deter the group from critically evaluating unusual, minority or unpopular views. Groupthink is a disease that attacks many groups and can dramatically hinder their performance. The second phenomenon we review is called **groupshift**. It indicates that in discussing a given set of alternatives and arriving at a solution, group members tend to exaggerate the initial positions that they hold. In some situations, caution dominates and there is a conservative shift. More often, however, the evidence indicates that groups tend towards a risky shift. Let's look at each of these phenomena in more detail.

Myth *or* Science?

'Two heads are better than one'

This statement is mostly true if 'better' means that two people will come up with more original and workable answers to a problem than one person working alone.

The evidence generally confirms the superiority of groups over individuals in terms of decision-making quality. Groups usually produce more and better solutions to problems than do individuals working alone. And the choices groups make will be more accurate and creative. Why is this? Groups bring more complete information and knowledge to a decision, so they generate more ideas. In addition, the give-and-take that typically takes place in group decision processes provides diversity of opinion and increases the likelihood that weak alternatives will be identified and abandoned.

Research indicates that certain conditions favour groups over individuals. These conditions include the following: (1) Diversity among members—the benefits of 'two heads' require that they differ in relevant skills and abilities. (2) The group members must be able to communicate their ideas freely and openly. This requires an absence of hostility and intimidation. (3) The task being undertaken is complex. Relative to individuals, groups do better on complex, rather than simple, tasks.

Sources: See G. W. Hill, 'Group versus Individual Performance', and L. K. Michaelsen, W. E. Watson and R. H. Black, 'A Realistic Test of Individual versus Group Consensus Decision Making', in J. H. Davis, *Group Performance* (Reading, MA: Addison-Wesley, 1969); J. P. Wanous and M. A. Youtz, 'Solution Diversity and the Quality of Group Decisions', *Academy of Management Journal*, March 1986, pp. 149–59; and R. Libby, K. T. Trotman and I. Zimmer, 'Member Variation, Recognition of Expertise, and Group Performance', *Journal of Applied Psychology*, February 1987, pp. 81–87.

Groupthink

The Australian Department of Defence has been undergoing considerable change in recent years. It has been restructuring its organisation so that military personnel and civilians are integrated and more efficient in their work. As part of the change program, each branch of the department was required to do a complete review of its mission and function, the resources it required and the number of staff it had.

A consultant was brought in to work with the Operations Branch, which was made up of all military staff, from a colonel to privates. A group of eight officers and non-commissioned officers were to attend the workshop. The consultant began the workshop by saying he wanted everyone to look at the branch as a new entity and to recreate it without any assumptions or preconceived ideas. The first person to speak was a major, who said that he had compiled a working paper (as requested by the colonel) that described everything the workshop was aiming to accomplish; he suggested that the discussion just focus on his suggestions instead of 'reinventing' the wheel. The major then asked the sergeant and the privates what they thought. They agreed with the major. The consultant accepted their viewpoint but resisted following the major's suggestion and asked everyone to start over and redefine their mission. Slowly, with a lot of hard work, debate and patience, the consultant was able to help the group redefine its mission and drop two of its functions by agreeing that these could be better served by other parts of the army, thus reducing its numbers by one colonel and two orderlies.

The consultant and the group were feeling a sense of something worthwhile having been achieved for the day, when the brigadier general walked into the room and asked how the group was doing. The consultant explained the changes the group would like to make and asked the brigadier for his opinion. The brigadier said the changes suggested weren't really appropriate, because he needed a colonel's position in the division and the functions that were dropped by the group needed to be kept if the colonel was in the branch. When the consultant asked the group what they thought, everyone agreed with the brigadier. The workshop ended in the next ten minutes with all of the suggestions being dropped and the major's original working paper being accepted just as it was. As the military personnel walked out of the room the major said to the consultant, 'I told you this workshop would be a waste of time!'

Have you ever felt like speaking up in a meeting, classroom or informal group, but decided against it? One reason may have been shyness. On the other hand, you may have been a victim of groupthink, the phenomenon that occurs when group members become so enamoured of seeking concurrence that the norm for consensus overrides the realistic evaluation of alternative courses of action and the full expression of deviant, minority or unpopular views. It describes a deterioration in an individual's mental efficiency, reality testing and moral judgment, as a result of group pressures.[60]

We have all seen the symptoms of the groupthink phenomenon:

- Group members rationalise any resistance to the assumptions they have made. No matter how strongly the evidence might contradict their basic assumptions, members behave so as to reinforce those assumptions continually.
- Members apply direct pressures on those who momentarily express doubts about any of the group's shared views or who question the validity of arguments supporting the alternative favoured by the majority.
- Those members who have doubts or hold differing viewpoints seek to avoid deviating from what appears to be group consensus by keeping silent about misgivings and even minimising to themselves the importance of their doubts.
- There appears to be an illusion of unanimity. If someone doesn't speak, it is assumed that they are in full accord. In other words, abstention becomes viewed as a 'yes' vote.[61]

The groupthink phenomenon arose out of some classic studies of historic American foreign policy decisions. The symptoms of groupthink were found to prevail on a number of occasions when government policy-making groups failed: unpreparedness for the Japanese bombing of Pearl Harbor in 1941, the US invasion of North Korea, the Bay of Pigs fiasco where US-backed forces invaded Cuba and the escalation of the Vietnam conflict. More recently, the *Challenger* and *Columbia* space shuttle disasters, in 1986 and 2003, respectively, and the failure of the main mirror on the *Hubble* telescope, have been linked to decision processes at NASA in which groupthink symptoms were evident.[62]

The Australian government's handling of the Norwegian freighter *Tampa*, which rescued 433 boat people in August 2001 and its reaction to the 'people overboard' incident some months later, was seen to display the symptoms of groupthink by various people involved in the decision-making processes.[63] These incidents occurred during the government's campaign against illegal boat people.

Groupthink appears to be closely aligned with the conclusions Asch drew in his experiments with a lone dissenter. Individuals who hold a position that is different from that of the dominant majority are under pressure to suppress, withhold or modify their true feelings and beliefs. As members of a group, we find it more pleasant to be in agreement—to be a positive part of the group—than to be a disruptive force, even if disruption is necessary to improve the effectiveness of the group's decisions.

Does groupthink attack all groups? No. It seems to occur most often when there is a clear group identity, where members hold a positive image of their group that they want to protect, and when the group perceives a collective threat to this positive image.[64] So, groupthink is not a dissenter-suppression mechanism as much as it's a means for a group to protect its positive image. In the cases of the *Challenger, Columbia* and *Hubble* fiascos, it was NASA's attempt to confirm its identity as 'the elite organization that could do no wrong'.[65]

What can managers do to minimise groupthink?[66] One thing is to monitor group size. People grow more intimidated and hesitant as group size increases and, although there is no magic number that will eliminate groupthink, individuals are likely to feel less personal responsibility when groups get larger than about ten people. Managers should also encourage group leaders to play an impartial role. Leaders should actively seek input from all members and avoid expressing their own opinions, especially in the early stages of deliberation. Another thing is to appoint one group member to play the role of devil's advocate. This member's role is to overtly challenge the majority position and offer divergent perspectives. Still another suggestion is to use exercises that stimulate active discussion of diverse alternatives without threatening the group and intensifying identity protection. One such exercise is to have group members talk about the dangers or risks involved in a decision and delaying discussion of any potential gains. By requiring members to focus first on the negatives of a decision alternative, the group is less likely to stifle dissenting views and more likely to gain an objective evaluation.

Groupshift

In comparing group decisions with the individual decisions of members within the group, evidence suggests that there are differences.[67] In some cases, the group decisions are more conservative than the individual decisions. More often, the shift is towards greater risk.[68]

What appears to happen in groups is that the discussion leads to a significant shift in the positions of members towards a more extreme position. This is often in the direction towards which they were already leaning before the discussion. So, conservative types become more cautious and the more aggressive types take on more risk. The group discussion tends to *exaggerate* the initial position of the group.

The groupshift can be viewed as actually a special case of groupthink. The decision of the group reflects the dominant decision-making norm that develops during the group's discussion. Whether the shift in the group's decision is towards greater caution or more risk depends on the dominant pre-discussion norm.

The greater occurrence of the shift towards risk has generated several explanations for the phenomenon.[69] It has been argued, for example, that the discussion creates familiarisation among the members. As they become more comfortable with each other, they also become more bold and daring. Another argument is that our society values risk, that we admire individuals who are willing to take risks, and that group discussion motivates members to show that they are at least as willing as their peers to take risks. The most plausible explanation of the shift towards risk, however, seems to be that the group diffuses responsibility. Group decisions free any single member from accountability for the group's final choice. Greater risk can be taken because, even if the decision fails, no one member can be held wholly responsible.

So, how should you use the findings on groupshift? You should recognise that group decisions exaggerate the initial position of the individual members, that the shift has been shown more often to be towards greater risk, and that whether a group will shift towards greater risk or caution is a function of the members' pre-discussion inclinations.

GROUP DECISION-MAKING TECHNIQUES

The most common form of group decision making takes place in face-to-face **interacting groups**. In these groups, members meet face-to-face and rely on both verbal and non-verbal interaction to communicate with each other. But as our discussion of groupthink demonstrates, interacting groups often censor themselves and pressure individual members towards conformity of opinion. Brainstorming, nominal group technique and electronic meetings have been proposed as ways to reduce many of the problems inherent in the traditional interacting group.

Brainstorming is meant to overcome pressures for conformity in the interacting group that retard the development of creative alternatives.[70] It does this by using an idea-generation process that specifically encourages any and all alternatives, while withholding any criticism of those alternatives.

In a typical brainstorming session, a small group of people sit around a table. The group leader states the problem in a clear manner so that it's understood by all members. Members then 'free-wheel' as many alternatives as they can in a given length of time. No criticism is allowed, and

LEARNING OBJECTIVE

9

Contrast the effectiveness of interacting, brainstorming, nominal group technique and electronic meeting groups

interacting groups
Typical groups, in which members interact with each other face-to-face.

brainstorming
An idea-generation process that specifically encourages any and all alternatives, while withholding any criticism of those alternatives.

The sight of staff sitting around a table can give the impression that they are engaged in constructive problem-solving. However, what is not revealed in such a scenario is the effectiveness of the group decision-making technique being used.

all the alternatives are recorded for later discussion and analysis. One idea is used to stimulate other members, and judgments of even the most bizarre suggestions are withheld. This encourages group members to 'think the unusual'. Brainstorming, however, is merely a process for generating ideas. The next three techniques go further by offering methods of actually arriving at a preferred solution.[71]

The **nominal group technique** restricts discussion or interpersonal communication during the decision-making process; hence the term *nominal*.

nominal group technique
A group decision-making method in which individual members meet face-to-face to pool their judgments in a systematic but independent fashion.

Group members are all physically present, as in a traditional committee meeting, but members operate independently. Specifically, a problem is presented and then the following steps take place:

1. Members meet as a group, but before any discussion takes place, each member independently writes down their ideas on the problem.
2. This silent period is followed by each member presenting one idea to the group. Each member takes a turn, going around the table, presenting a single idea until all ideas have been presented and recorded (typically on a flip chart or whiteboard). No discussion takes place until all ideas have been recorded.
3. The group now discusses the ideas for clarity and evaluates them. Some ideas may be combined or dropped.
4. Each group member silently and independently rank-orders the ideas. The final decision is determined by the idea with the highest aggregate ranking.

The chief advantage of the nominal group technique is that it permits the group to meet formally but doesn't restrict independent thinking, as does the interacting group.

The most recent approach to group decision making blends the nominal group technique with sophisticated computer technology.[72] It's called computer-assisted group or **electronic meeting**.

electronic meeting
A meeting in which members interact on computers, allowing for anonymity of comments and aggregation of votes.

Once the technology is in place, the concept is simple. Up to 50 people sit around a horseshoe-shaped table, empty except for a series of computer terminals. Issues are presented to participants and they type their responses on to their computer screen. Individual comments, as well as aggregate votes, are displayed on a projection screen.

The main advantages of electronic meetings are anonymity, honesty and speed. Participants can anonymously type any message they want and it flashes on the screen for all to see at the push of a participant's board key. It also allows people to be brutally honest without penalty. And it's quick, because chit-chat is eliminated, discussions don't digress and many participants can 'talk' at once. The future of group meetings undoubtedly will include extensive use of this technology.

Each of these four group decision techniques has its own set of strengths and weaknesses. The choice of one technique over another will depend on what criteria you want to emphasise and the cost–benefit trade-off. For example, as Table 8.3 indicates, the interacting group is good for building group cohesiveness, brainstorming keeps social pressures to a minimum, the nominal group technique is an inexpensive means for generating a large number of ideas, and electronic meetings process ideas quickly.

TABLE 8.3	**Evaluating group effectiveness**			
		Type of Group		
Effectiveness Criteria	**Interacting**	**Brainstorming**	**Nominal**	**Electronic**
Number of ideas	Low	Moderate	High	High
Quality of ideas	Low	Moderate	High	High
Social pressure	High	Low	Moderate	Low
Money costs	Low	Low	Low	High
Speed	Moderate	Moderate	Moderate	High
Task orientation	Low	High	High	High
Potential for interpersonal conflict	High	Low	Moderate	Low
Feelings of accomplishment	High to low	High	High	High
Commitment to solution	High	Not applicable	Moderate	Moderate
Development of group cohesiveness	High	High	Moderate	Low

Source: Based on J. K. Murnighan, 'Group Decision Making: What Strategies Should You Use?', *Management Review*, February 1981, p. 61.

OB Controversies

Virtual teams and the limits of e-mail

Demand for corporate governance workshops has increased significantly for Deborah Smithers, the national leader of KPMG's board and corporate governance advisory service. The pressure for greater accountability for boards of directors has been a boom for those who can provide the right sort of educational programs. Smithers' division of five staff members works effectively as a virtual team given that they are split between offices in Melbourne and Sydney.

What is interesting about the rise of virtual teams is the changing nature of the dynamics in these groups. What can be controversial is the faceless aspect of group interaction.

The use of virtual teams is increasing with the mobility of staff and the usage of the Internet these days. The Australian Taxation Office has started providing training to staff in virtual team management. John Browne, chief executive of British Petroleum Company (BP), describes his corporation as flat and lean, with US$70 billion in revenues, 53,000 employees and approximately 90 business units around the world. He sees the value in sharing knowledge among the business units through what he deems as BP's virtual team network. From his virtual workstation, Browne recently had productive discussions with his executive team in Singapore and Johannesburg.

E-mail has become a central vehicle for interactions among members of virtual teams operating across diverse geographical locations. E-mail is fine for some communications but it has its limitations. And, unfortunately, many people are using it to convey messages that are best expressed in other ways.

Relationships can suffer when people use e-mail as a substitute for face-to-face interaction between members of a work group. For example, one writer tells of communicating with an editor by e-mail about an article he had written. The relationship turned sour because each was taking the other's comments as far more critical than intended. 'We had to get off-line and apologise,' says the writer.

One expert says, 'There's a tremendous over-reliance on e-mail, which is leading to a lot of confusion, misunderstanding, anger and frustration.' The 'over-reliance' factor is due to the popularity of the technology. The negative responses to e-mail are due to its inherent limitations and misuse. These include:

- *Low feedback.* Conversation is a give-and-take exchange, but e-mail allows one to 'talk' at length without any response.
- *Reduced social cues.* When we talk, we can hear the tone of a joke that might come across as stern on a computer screen. And emoticons can hint that something is meant lightly but can't replace voice or visual cues.
- *Excess attention.* E-mail allows people to create carefully worded messages that can be interpreted as more formal than verbal messages. The same words expressed off-handedly in a verbal conversation often take on greater meaning and importance when read in an e-mail.
- *Wordiness.* E-mail allows the writer to go on forever, often confusing the receiver as to what's important and what isn't. In face-to-face contact, senders get verbal and non-verbal cues—interruptions, quizzical looks, glassy eyes—indicating the message is getting too long.

While technology can help, managers need to be aware of the broader impacts of technology on groups. Managers need to understand more than just the communication issues. They need to understand all aspects of group dynamics. And we can see from this chapter that there are many different aspects to work groups and managing teams. They need to understand how the dynamics of the new virtual teams impact team performance.

Sources: Based on Kath Walters, *Business Review Weekly*, 11 July 2002, p. 77; <http://choo.fis.utoronto.ca/dla98/KC.BP.html>; and J. Kornblum, 'E-Mail's Limits Create Confusion, Hurt Feelings', *USA Today*, 5 February 2002, p. 6D.

Summary and Implications for Managers

We have covered a lot in this chapter. Since we organised our discussion around the group behaviour model in Figure 8.3, let's use this model to summarise our findings regarding performance and satisfaction.

Performance

Any predictions about a group's performance must begin by recognising that work groups are part of a larger organisation and that factors such as the organisation's strategy, authority structure, selection procedures and reward system can provide a favourable or unfavourable climate for the group to operate within. For example, if an organisation is characterised by distrust between management and employees, it's more likely that work groups in that organisation will develop norms to restrict effort and output than will work groups within an organisation where trust is high. So, don't look at any group in isolation. Rather, begin by assessing the degree of support that external conditions provide to the group. It's obviously a lot easier for any work group to be productive when the overall organisation, of which it is a part, is growing and has both top management's support and abundant resources. Similarly, a group is more likely to be productive when its members have the requisite skills to do the group's tasks and the personality characteristics that facilitate working well together.

A number of structural factors show a relationship to performance. Among the more prominent are role perception, norms, size of the group, status inequities and its demographic make-up, the group's task, and cohesiveness.

There is a positive relationship between role perception and an employee's performance evaluation.[73] The degree of congruence that exists between an employee and her or his boss in the perception of the employee's job influences the degree to which that employee will be judged as an effective performer by the boss. To the extent that the employee's role perception fulfils the boss's role expectation, the employee will receive a higher performance evaluation.

Norms control group member behaviour by establishing standards of right and wrong. If we know the norms of a given group, it can help us to explain the behaviours of its members. Where norms support high output, we can expect individual performance to be markedly higher than where group norms aim to restrict output. Similarly, norms that support antisocial behaviour increase the likelihood that individuals will engage in deviant workplace activities.

Status inequities create frustration and can adversely influence productivity and the willingness to remain with an organisation. Among those individuals who are equity-sensitive, incongruence is likely to lead to reduced motivation and an increased search for ways to bring about fairness (such as by taking another job). The effect of size on a group's performance depends upon the type of task in which the group is engaged. Larger groups are more effective at fact-finding activities.

Smaller groups are more effective at action-taking tasks. Our knowledge of social loafing suggests that, if management uses larger groups, efforts should be made to provide measures of each person's performance within the group.

We found the group's demographic composition to be a key determinant of individual turnover. Specifically, the evidence indicates that group members who share a common age or date of entry into the work group, for example, are less prone to resign.

We also found that cohesiveness can play an important function in influencing a group's level of productivity. Whether or not it does depends on the group's performance-related norms.

The primary contingency variable moderating the relationship between group processes and performance is the group's task. The more complex and interdependent the tasks, the more likely it is that inefficient processes will lead to reduced group performance.

Satisfaction

As with the role perception–performance relationship, high congruence between a boss's and an employee's perception of the employee's job shows a significant association with high employee satisfaction.[74] Similarly, role conflict is associated with job-induced tension and job dissatisfaction.[75]

Most people prefer to communicate with others at their own status level or higher, rather than with those below them.[76] As a result, we should expect satisfaction to be greater among employees whose job minimises interaction with employees lower in status.

The group size–satisfaction relationship is what we would intuitively expect: larger groups are associated with lower satisfaction.[77] As size increases, opportunities for participation and social interaction decrease, as does the ability of members to identify with the group's accomplishments. At the same time, having more members prompts dissension, conflict and the formation of subgroups, which all act to make the group a less pleasant entity of which to be a part.

Point

ALL JOBS SHOULD BE DESIGNED AROUND GROUPS

Groups, not individuals, are the ideal building blocks for an organisation. There are at least six reasons for designing all jobs around groups.

First, small groups are good for people. They can satisfy social needs and they can provide support for employees in times of stress and crisis.

Second, groups are good problem-finding tools. They are better than individuals in promoting creativity and innovation.

Third, in a wide variety of decision situations, groups make better decisions than individuals do.

Fourth, groups are very effective tools for implementation. Groups gain commitment from their members so that group decisions are likely to be willingly and more successfully carried out.

Fifth, groups can control and discipline individual members in ways that are often extremely difficult through impersonal, quasi-legal disciplinary systems. Group norms are powerful control devices.

Sixth, groups are a means by which large organisations can fend off many of the negative effects of increased size. Groups help to prevent communication lines from growing too long, the hierarchy from growing too steep and the individual from getting lost in the crowd.

Given the above argument for the value of group-based job design, what would an organisation look like that was truly designed around group functions? This might best be considered by merely taking the things that organisations do with individuals and applying them to groups. Instead of hiring individuals, they would hire groups. Similarly, they would train groups rather than individuals, pay groups rather than individuals, promote groups rather than individuals, fire groups rather than individuals, and so on.

The rapid growth of team-based organisations over the past decade suggests that we may well be on our way towards the day when almost all jobs are designed around groups.

Counterpoint

Designing jobs around groups is consistent with an ideology that says that communal and socialistic approaches are the best way to organise our society. This might have worked well in the former Soviet Union or Eastern European countries, but capitalistic countries such as Australia, New Zealand, the United States, Canada and the United Kingdom value the individual. Designing jobs around groups is inconsistent with the economic values of these countries. Moreover, as capitalism and entrepreneurship have spread throughout Eastern Europe, we should expect to see less emphasis on groups and more on the individual in workplaces throughout the world. Cultural and economic values have shaped employee attitudes towards groups.

Capitalism was built on the ethic of the individual. Individualistic cultures such as Australia, New Zealand, Canada and the United States strongly value individual achievement. They praise competition. Even in team sports, they want to identify individuals for recognition. People from these countries enjoy being part of a group in which they can maintain a strong individual identity. They don't enjoy sublimating their identity to that of the group.

The Western industrial worker likes a clear link between his or her individual effort and a visible outcome. The United States, for example, has had a considerably larger proportion of high achievers than exists in most of the world. America breeds achievers, and achievers seek personal responsibility. They would be frustrated in job situations in which their contribution is commingled and homogenised with the contributions of others.

Western workers want to be hired, evaluated and rewarded on their individual achievements. They believe in an authority and status hierarchy. They accept a system in which there are bosses and subordinates. They aren't likely to accept a group's decision on such issues as their job assignments and wage increases. It's harder yet to imagine that they would be comfortable in a system in which the sole basis for their promotion or termination would be the performance of their group.

Source: Based on H. J. Leavitt, 'Suppose We Took Groups Seriously', in E. L. Cass and F. G. Zimmer (eds), *Man and Work in Society* (New York: Van Nostrand Reinhold, 1975), pp. 67–77.

For Discussion

1. Compare and contrast command, task, interest and friendship groups.
2. What might motivate you to join a group?
3. Describe the five-stage group-development model.
4. How could you use the punctuated-equilibrium model to better understand group behaviour?
5. What is the relationship between a work group and the organisation of which it is a part?
6. What are the implications of Zimbardo's prison experiment for OB?
7. Explain the implications from the Asch experiments.
8. How are status and norms related?
9. 'High cohesiveness in a group leads to higher group productivity.' Do you agree or disagree? Explain.
10. When do groups make better decisions than individuals?
11. How can a group's demography help you to predict turnover?
12. What is groupthink? What is its effect on decision-making quality?

Exercises

Exercise 8a
ASSESSING OCCUPATIONAL STATUS

Rank the following 20 occupations from most prestigious (1) to least prestigious (20):

Accountant
Air traffic controller
Barrister
Coach of a football team
Coach of a women's basketball team
Electrical engineer
Environmental scientist
Firefighter
Investment banker
Manager of an automobile production facility
Mayor of a large city
Minister of religion
Pharmacist
Plumber
Real estate salesperson
Sports agent
Surgeon
Teacher in a public school (primary/elementary)
Army colonel
Used car salesperson

Now form into groups of three to five students each. Answer the following questions:
(a) How closely did your top five choices (1–5) match?
(b) How closely did your bottom five choices (16–20) match?
(c) What occupations were generally easiest to rate? Which were most difficult? Why?
(d) What does this exercise tell you about criteria for assessing status?
(e) What does this exercise tell you about stereotypes?

Exercise 8b
RATING YOUR GROUP EXPERIENCE

Most of us have had experience in writing a report, doing an assignment or working on a project in a group in a course or in the workplace. These can be very fulfilling or very frustrating experiences.

Think back to your most recent experience of working in a group. Imagine yourself at a critical stage in the completion of that group assignment. Using your mind-set at this point, answer the following 20 questions. This questionnaire measures your feelings about that work group.

Add your scores for items 4, 6, 7, 8, 9, 10, 14, 17, 19 and 20. Obtain a corrected score by subtracting the score for each of the remaining questions from 10. For example, if you marked 3 for item 1, you would obtain a corrected score of 7 (10–3). Add the corrected scores together with the total obtained on the ten items scored directly.

Now form groups of three to five members.

1. Compare your scores. Were your group experiences generally positive or negative?
2. Assess the degree to which you felt any different about your group at the end of the project compared with how you felt at the halfway point. If your feelings changed, explain why.
3. Discuss the degree to which your feelings about the group may have influenced your group's grade.
4. Discuss to what degree you think the grade your team got on the paper influenced your subsequent feelings about the group.

	Agree							Disagree	
1. I want to remain a member of this group.	1	2	3	4	5	6	7	8	9
2. I like my group.	1	2	3	4	5	6	7	8	9
3. I look forward to coming to the group.	1	2	3	4	5	6	7	8	9
4. I don't care what happens in this group.	1	2	3	4	5	6	7	8	9
5. I feel involved in what is happening in my group.	1	2	3	4	5	6	7	8	9
6. If I could drop out of the group now, I would.	1	2	3	4	5	6	7	8	9
7. I dread coming to this group.	1	2	3	4	5	6	7	8	9
8. I wish it were possible for the group to end now.	1	2	3	4	5	6	7	8	9
9. I am dissatisfied with the group.	1	2	3	4	5	6	7	8	9
10. If it were possible to move to another group at this time, I would.	1	2	3	4	5	6	7	8	9
11. I feel included in the group.	1	2	3	4	5	6	7	8	9
12. In spite of individual differences, a feeling of unity exists in my group.	1	2	3	4	5	6	7	8	9
13. Compared with other groups I know of, I feel my group is better than most.	1	2	3	4	5	6	7	8	9
14. I don't feel a part of the group's activities.	1	2	3	4	5	6	7	8	9
15. I feel it would make a difference to the group if I were not here.	1	2	3	4	5	6	7	8	9
16. If I were told my group would not meet today, I would feel bad.	1	2	3	4	5	6	7	8	9
17. I feel distant from the group.	1	2	3	4	5	6	7	8	9
18. It makes a difference to me how this group turns out.	1	2	3	4	5	6	7	8	9
19. I feel my absence would not matter to the group.	1	2	3	4	5	6	7	8	9
20. I would not feel bad if I had to miss a meeting of this group.	1	2	3	4	5	6	7	8	9

Source: Reproduced from N. J. Evans and P. A. Jarvis, 'The Group Attitude Scale: A Measure of Attraction to Group', *Small Group Behavior*, May 1986, pp. 203–16. Reprinted by permission of Sage Publications, Inc.

Case Study 8

Not Easy to Change a Group

Jim Sutcliffe, a Masters student in Business, wanted to study group behaviour during his summer as part of an individual project for university. When he took the job at the Alcroft furniture factory he didn't think he would experience the effects of group behaviour to the extent he did. When Jim started, he met the other members of his group in the production area and they gave him guidance on what was expected of him. He worked very hard the first day but on the way out, Frank, the oldest member of the group told him that there was no need to work so quickly since the group had already established the right pace of work to gain the incentives they have agreed to. After discussing this with his university supervisor, Jim went to work the next day and continued to work at his same fast pace. Frank again talked to Jim and this time made more overt threats that if he continued to go faster than the group they might get angry at him. Jim recorded these conversations as part of his postgraduate project and had regular meetings with his supervisor to discuss his next strategy.

Over the next few weeks, the group became increasingly antagonistic toward Jim and became more aggressive in its actions. First, they stopped talking to Jim and then accidently dropped some crates on his car and caused over $1,200 in damage. Both Jim and his supervisor discussed calling the whole project off but Jim felt he wanted to go on for one more week. He felt he wanted to get some more information about the role of the informal leader in influencing this—and he also needed the money from the job to pay for his next semester's tuition (and for repairs to his car).

On Thursday afternoon, Frank came up to Jim at tea break and was friendly to him. At the end of the conversation, Frank asked Jim why he was behaving like he was and ignoring the way the group had always worked together. Jim said he was only doing the amount of work he thought was reasonable for a day's pay and was hoping to move into management one day. Frank said that people who don't work well with a group usually go downward instead of upward and then he walked away. The next day Jim fell off a ladder and broke his arm. He was sure the ladder was pushed but had no evidence that could show anything for certain. Jim quit the job the next week and tried to write the project while he was recuperating at home.

Questions

1. What does this event show about group behaviour?
2. Which of the things covered in this chapter best explains the things that happened?
3. If you were the manager of this plant how would you handle this group in the future? What would you do to help integrate group behaviour and organisational goals?

Web Workout

1. Learn more about why people join groups, groupthink, group development and other topics at the Allyn & Bacon communication studies website found at <www.abacon.com/commstudies/index.html>. Once there, select the 'small group' entry and then choose two or three more topics to read. Choose the most interesting topic and take the interactive quiz.

2. Groupthink can dramatically hinder performance, sometimes in disastrous ways. The *Challenger* and *Columbia* disasters, the Bay of Pigs Invasion and the Vietnam conflict have been subject to groupthink. Learn more about the role that groupthink played in these events. Go to <www.css.edu/users/dswenson/web/TWAssoc/groupthink.html>. Choose one of the events mentioned on that page and write a short synopsis of how groupthink hindered the decision-making process. Bring your synopsis to class for discussion.

3. Team traps are vicious cycles of unproductive behaviour that undermine group performance. Visit <www.pegasuscom.com/tstart1.html> to read the article on team traps. Print the article and bring it to class for discussion. Think about your own experiences in teams and the 12 team traps noted in the article. Note two or three examples and bring to class with the article for more discussion.

4. Brainstorming is a group technique to encourage the development of creative alternatives. Now that we know what it is, how do we do it? What would you do if you were called upon to lead a brainstorming session? Visit this UK website for an overview on how to conduct a brainstorming session: <www.brainstorming.co.uk/tutorials/preparingforbrainstorming.html>. You might also be interested in visiting the home page of this same site found at <www.brainstorming.co.uk/contents.html>, where you will find lots of creativity, exercises, puzzles, free training, articles and more. Make a list of the five most important things you must do to prepare for a brainstorming session and bring it to class.

5. What is the link between social loafing and group cohesiveness? Does one enhance or detract from the other? Write a two-page paper on the topic. Conduct a web page search with these two terms. A place to start is <www.geocities.com/Athens/Forum/1650/htmlgroups16.html>.

6. Peer pressure can be a positive thing; it is really just a way to communicate group norms. To learn more about how to use positive peer pressure to prevent binge drinking on campus, visit <www.csmonitor.com/durable/1997/10/27/feat/learning.2.html>.

NOTES

1. This section is based on B. Headlam, 'How to E-Mail Like a C.E.O.', *New York Times Magazine*, 8 April 2001, pp. 7–8.

2. L. R. Sayles, 'Work Group Behavior and the Larger Organization', in C. Arensburg, et al (eds), *Research in Industrial Relations* (New York: Harper & Row, 1957), pp. 131–45.

3. B. W. Tuckman, 'Developmental Sequences in Small Groups', *Psychological Bulletin*, June 1965, pp. 384–99; B. W. Tuckman and M. C. Jenson, 'Stages of Small-group Development Revised', *Group and Organizational Studies*, December 1977, pp. 419–27; and M. F. Maples, 'Group Development: Extending Tuckman's Theory', *Journal for Specialists in Group Work*, Fall 1988, pp. 17–23.3A.

4. R. C. Ginnett, 'The Airline Cockpit Crew', in J. R. Hackman (ed.), *Groups That Work (and Those That Don't)* (San Francisco: Jossey-Bass, 1990).

5. C. J. G. Gersick, 'Time and Transition in Work Teams: Toward a New Model of Group Development', *Academy of Management Journal*, March 1988, pp. 9–41; C. J. G. Gersick, 'Marking Time: Predictable Transitions in Task Groups', *Academy of Management Journal*, June 1989, pp. 274–309; and M. J. Waller, J. M. Conte, C. B. Gibson and M. A. Carpenter, 'The Effect of Individual Perceptions of Deadlines on Team Performance', *Academy of Management Review*, October 2001, pp. 586–600.

6. A. Seers and S. Woodruff, 'Temporal Pacing in Task Forces: Group Development or Deadline Pressure?', *Journal of Management*, vol. 23, no. 2, 1997, pp. 169–87.

7. This model is based on the work of P. S. Goodman, E. Ravlin and M. Schminke, 'Understanding Groups in Organizations', in L. L. Cummings and B. M. Staw (eds), *Research in Organizational Behavior*, vol. 9 (Greenwich, CT: JAI Press, 1987), pp. 124–28; J. R. Hackman, 'The Design of Work Teams', in J. W. Lorsch (ed.), *Handbook of Organizational Behavior* (Englewood Cliffs, NJ: Prentice Hall, 1987), pp. 315–42; G. R. Bushe and A. L. Johnson, 'Contextual and Internal Variables Affecting Task Group Outcomes in Organizations', *Group and Organization Studies*, December 1989, pp. 462–82; M. A. Campion, G. J. Medsker and A. C. Higgs, 'Relations Between Work Group Characteristics and Effectiveness: Implications for Designing Effective Work Groups', *Personnel Psychology*, Winter 1993, pp. 823–50; D. E. Hyatt and T. M. Ruddy, 'An Examination of the Relationship Between Work Group Characteristics and Performance: Once More into the Breach', *Personnel Psychology*, Autumn 1997, pp. 553–85; and P. E. Tesluk and J. E. Mathieu, 'Overcoming Roadblocks to Effectiveness: Incorporating Management of Performance Barriers into Models of Work Group Effectiveness', *Journal of Applied Psychology*, April 1999, pp. 200–17.

8. F. Friedlander, 'The Ecology of Work Groups', in Lorsch (ed.), *Handbook of Organizational Behavior*, pp. 301–14; P. B. Paulus and D. Nagar, 'Environmental Influences on Groups', in P. Paulus (ed.), *Psychology of Group Influence*, 2nd ed. (Hillsdale, NJ: Erlbaum, 1989); and E. Sundstrom and I. Altman, 'Physical Environments and Work-Group Effectiveness', in L. L. Cummings and B. M. Staw (eds), *Research in Organizational Behavior*, vol. 11 (Greenwich, CT: JAI Press, 1989), pp. 175–209.

9. Hackman, 'The Design of Work Teams', pp. 325–26; and D. Dunphy and B. Hackman, 'Performance Appraisal as a Strategic Intervention', *Human Resource Management Australia*, vol. 26, no. 2, 1988, pp. 23–34.

10. See, for example, R. A. Baron, 'The Physical Environment of Work Settings: Effects on Task Performance, Interpersonal Relations, and Job Satisfaction', in B. M. Staw and L. L. Cummings (eds), *Research in Organizational Behavior*, vol. 16 (Greenwich, CT: JAI Press, 1994), pp. 1–46; and M. Rich, 'Shut Up So We Can Do Our Jobs!', *Wall Street Journal*, 29 August 2001, p. B1.

11. M. J. Stevens and M. A. Campion, 'The Knowledge, Skill, and Ability Requirements for Teamwork: Implications for Human Resource Management', *Journal of Management*, Summer 1994, pp. 503–30.

12. M. E. Shaw, *Contemporary Topics in Social Psychology* (Morristown, NJ: General Learning Press, 1976); and D. C. Kinlaw, *Developing Superior Work Teams: Building Quality and the Competitive Edge* (San Diego, CA: Lexington, 1991).

13. S. Lieberman, 'The Effects of Change in Roles on the Attitudes of Role Occupants', *Human Relations*, November 1956, pp. 385–402.

14. See D. M. Rousseau, *Psychological Contracts in Organizations: Understanding Written and Unwritten Agreements* (Thousand Oaks, CA: Sage, 1995); and D. Rousseau and R. Schalk (eds), *Psychological Contracts in Employment: Cross-Cultural Perspectives* (San Francisco: Jossey-Bass, 2000).

15. See M. F. Peterson, et al, 'Role Conflict, Ambiguity, and Overload: A 21-Nation Study', *Academy of Management Journal*, April 1995, pp. 429–52.

16. P. G. Zimbardo, C. Haney, W. C. Banks and D. Jaffe, 'The Mind Is a Formidable Jailer: A Pirandellian Prison', *The New York Times*, 8 April 1973, pp. 38–60; and C. Haney and P. G. Zimbardo, 'Social Roles and Role-Playing: Observations from the Stanford Prison Study', *Behavioral and Social Science Teacher*, January 1973, pp. 25–45.

17. For a review of the research on group norms, see J. R. Hackman, 'Group Influences on Individuals in Organizations', in M. D. Dunnette and L. M. Hough (eds), *Handbook of Industrial & Organizational Psychology*, 2nd ed., vol. 3 (Palo Alto, CA: Consulting Psychologists Press, 1992), pp. 235–50.

18. Adapted from Goodman, Ravlin and Schminke, 'Understanding Groups in Organizations', p. 159.

19. See, for example, G. Blau, 'Influence of Group Lateness on Individual Lateness: A Cross-Level Examination', *Academy of Management Journal*, October 1995, pp. 1483–96.

20. C. A. Kiesler and S. B. Kiesler, *Conformity* (Reading, MA: Addison-Wesley, 1969).

21. Ibid, p. 27.

22. S. E. Asch, 'Effects of Group Pressure upon the Modification and Distortion of Judgments', in H. Guetzkow (ed.), *Groups, Leadership and Men* (Pittsburgh, PA: Carnegie Press, 1951), pp. 177–90; and S. E. Asch, 'Studies of Independence and Conformity: A Minority of One Against a Unanimous Majority', *Psychological Monographs: General and Applied*, vol. 70, no. 9, 1956, pp. 1–70.

23. R. Bond and P. B. Smith, 'Culture and Conformity: A Meta-Analysis of Studies Using Asch's (1952, 1956) Line Judgment Task', *Psychological Bulletin*, January 1996, pp. 111–37.

24. See S. L. Robinson and R. J. Bennett, 'A Typology of Deviant Workplace Behaviors: A Multidimensional Scaling Study', *Academy of Management Journal*, April 1995, pp. 555–72; S. L. Robinson and J. Greenberg, 'Employees Behaving Badly: Dimensions, Determinants, and Dilemmas in the Study of Workplace Deviance', in D. M. Rousseau and C. Cooper (eds), *Trends in Organizational Behavior*, vol. 5 (New York: Wiley, 1998); S. L. Robinson and A. M. O'Leary-Kelly, 'Monkey See, Monkey Do: The Influence of Work Groups on the Antisocial Behavior of Employees', *Academy of Management Journal*, December 1998, pp. 658–72; and C. M. Pearson, L. M. Andersson and C. L. Porath, 'Assessing and Attacking Workplace Incivility', *Organizational Dynamics*, vol. 29, no. 2, 2000, pp. 123–37.

25. Pearson, Andersson and Porath, 'Assessing and Attacking Workplace Civility', p. 130.

26. Robinson and O'Leary-Kelly, 'Monkey See, Monkey Do'.

27. R. Keyes, *Is There Life After High School?* (New York: Warner Books, 1976).

28. Cited in Hackman, 'Group Influences on Individuals in Organizations', p. 236.

29. O. J. Harvey and C. Consalvi, 'Status and Conformity to Pressures in Informal Groups', *Journal of Abnormal and Social Psychology*, Spring 1960, pp. 182–87.

30. J. A. Wiggins, F. Dill and R. D. Schwartz, 'On "Status-Liability"', *Sociometry*, April–May 1965, pp. 197–209.

31. J. Greenberg, 'Equity and Workplace Status: A Field Experiment', *Journal of Applied Psychology*, November 1988, pp. 606–13.

32. This section is based on P. R. Harris and R. T. Moran, *Managing Cultural Differences*, 4th ed. (Houston: Gulf Publishing, 1996).

33. J. Thomas and C. F. Fink, 'Effects of Group Size', *Psychological Bulletin*, July 1963, pp. 371–84; A. P. Hare, *Handbook of Small Group Research* (New York: The Free Press, 1976); and M. E. Shaw, *Group Dynamics: The Psychology of Small Group Behavior*, 3rd ed. (New York: McGraw-Hill, 1981).

34. See D. R. Comer, 'A Model of Social Loafing in Real Work Groups', *Human Relations*, June 1995, pp. 647–67.

35. W. Moede, 'Die Richtlinien der Leistungs-Psychologie', *Industrielle Psychotechnik*, vol. 4, 1927, pp. 193–207. See also D. A. Kravitz and B. Martin, 'Ringlemann Rediscovered: The Original Article', *Journal of Personality and Social Psychology*, May 1986, pp. 936–41.

36. See, for example, J. A. Shepperd, 'Productivity Loss in Performance Groups: A Motivation Analysis', *Psychological Bulletin*, January 1993, pp. 67–81; and S. J. Karau and K. D. Williams, 'Social Loafing: A Meta-Analytic Review and Theoretical Integration', *Journal of Personality and Social Psychology*, October 1993, pp. 681–706.

37. S. G. Harkins and K. Szymanski, 'Social Loafing and Group Evaluation', *Journal of Personality and Social Psychology*, December 1989, pp. 934–41.

38. See P. C. Earley, 'Social Loafing and Collectivism: A Comparison of the United States and the People's Republic of China', *Administrative Science Quarterly*, December 1989, pp. 565–81; and P. C. Earley, 'East Meets West Meets Mideast: Further Explorations of Collectivistic and Individualistic Work Groups', *Academy of Management Journal*, April 1993, pp. 319–48.

39. Thomas and Fink, 'Effects of Group Size'; Hare, *Handbook of Small Group Research*; Shaw, *Group Dynamics*; and P. Yetton and P. Bottgert, 'The Relationships among Group Size, Member Ability, Social Decision Schemes, and Performance', *Organizational Behavior and Human Performance*, October 1983, pp. 145–59.

40. M. M. Shepherd, R. O. Briggs, B. A. Reinig, J. Yen and J. F. Nunamaker, 'Invoking Social Comparisons to Improve Electronic Brainstorming: Beyond Anonymity', *Journal of Management Information*, Winter 1995/96, pp. 155–70.

41. See, for example, R. A. Guzzo and G. P. Shea, 'Group Performance and Intergroup Relations in Organizations', in M. D. Dunnette and L. M. Hough (eds), *Handbook of Industrial & Organizational Psychology*, 2nd ed., vol. 3 (Palo Alto, CA: Consulting Psychologists Press, 1992), pp. 288–90; S. E. Jackson, K. E. May and K. Whitney, 'Understanding the Dynamics of Diversity in Decision-Making Teams', in R. A. Guzzo and E. Salas (eds), *Team Effectiveness and Decision Making in Organizations* (San Francisco: Jossey-Bass, 1995), pp. 204–61; K. Y. Williams and C. A. O'Reilly III, 'Demography and Diversity in Organizations: A Review of 40 Years of Research', in B. M. Staw and L. L. Cummings (eds), *Research in Organizational Behavior*, vol. 20 (Greenwich, CT: JAI Press, 1998), pp. 77–140; and F. Linnehan and A. M. Konrad, 'Diluting Diversity: Implications for Intergroup Inequality in Organizations', *Journal of Management Inquiry*, December 1999, pp. 399–414.

42. Shaw, *Contemporary Topics*, p. 356.

43. W. E. Watson, K. Kumar and L. K. Michaelsen, 'Cultural Diversity's Impact on Interaction Process and Performance: Comparing Homogeneous and Diverse Task Groups', *Academy of Management Journal*, June 1993, pp. 590–602; and P. C. Earley and E. Mosakowski, 'Creating Hybrid Team Cultures: An Empirical Test of Transnational Team Functioning', *Academy of Management Journal*, February 2000, pp. 26–49.

44. J. Austin, 'A Cognitive Framework for Understanding Demographic Influences in Groups', *International Journal of Organizational Analysis*, vol. 5, no. 4, October 1997, pp. 342–59.

45. W. G. Wagner, J. Pfeffer and C. A. O'Reilly III, 'Organizational Demography and Turnover in Top-Management Groups', *Administrative Science Quarterly*, March 1984, pp. 74–92; J. Pfeffer and C. A. O'Reilly III, 'Hospital Demography and Turnover among Nurses', *Industrial Relations*, Spring 1987, pp. 158–73; C. A. O'Reilly III, D. F. Caldwell and W. P. Barnett, 'Work Group Demography, Social Integration, and Turnover', *Administrative Science Quarterly*, March 1989, pp. 21–37; S. E. Jackson, J. F. Brett, V. I. Sessa, D. M. Cooper, J. A. Julin and K. Peyronnin, 'Some Differences Make a Difference: Individual Dissimilarity and Group Heterogeneity as Correlates of Recruitment, Promotions, and Turnover', *Journal of Applied Psychology*, August 1991, pp. 675–89; M. F. Wiersema and A. Bird, 'Organizational Demography in Japanese Firms: Group Heterogeneity, Individual Dissimilarity, and Top Management Team Turnover', *Academy of Management Journal*, October 1993, pp. 996–1025; F. J. Milliken and L. L. Martins, 'Searching for Common Threads: Understanding the Multiple Effects of Diversity in Organizational Groups', *Academy of Management Review*, April 1996, pp. 402–33; and B. Lawrence, 'The Black Box of Organizational Demography', *Organizational Science*, February 1997, pp. 1–22.

46. P. Tharenou and D. Conroy, 'Opportunities for, and Barriers to, Managerial Role Attainment: A Comparison of Male and Female Managers', in G. Palmer (ed.), *Australian Personnel Management: A Reader* (Melbourne: Macmillan, 1988), pp. 179–221.

47. For some of the controversy surrounding the definition of cohesion, see J. Keyton and J. Springston, 'Redefining Cohesiveness in Groups', *Small Group Research*, May 1990, pp. 234–54.

48. C. R. Evans and K. L. Dion, 'Group Cohesion and Performance: A Meta-Analysis', *Small Group Research*, May 1991, pp. 175–86; B. Mullen and C. Cooper, 'The Relation between Group Cohesiveness and Performance: An Integration', *Psychological Bulletin*, March 1994, pp. 210–27; and P. M. Podsakoff, S. B. MacKenzie and M. Ahearne, 'Moderating Effects of Goal Acceptance on the Relationship Between Group Cohesiveness and Productivity', *Journal of Applied Psychology*, December 1997, pp. 974–83.

49. Based on J. L. Gibson, J. M. Ivancevich and J. H. Donnelly, Jr, *Organizations*, 8th ed. (Burr Ridge, IL: Irwin, 1994), p. 323.

50. I. D. Steiner, *Group Process and Productivity* (New York: Academic Press, 1972).

51. R. B. Zajonc, 'Social Facilitation', *Science*, March 1965, pp. 269–74.

52. C. F. Bond, Jr and L. J. Titus, 'Social Facilitation: A Meta-Analysis of 241 Studies', *Psychological Bulletin*, September 1983, pp. 265–92.

53. V. F. Nieva, E. A. Fleishman and A. Rieck, 'Team Dimensions: Their Identity, Their Measurement, and Their Relationships', Final Technical Report for Contract No. DAHC 19-C-0001, Washington, DC, Advanced Research Resources Organizations, 1978.

54. L. English, 'The Tyranny of Teamness', *Australian Accountant*, November 1988, pp. 14–16.

55. See, for example, J. R. Hackman and C. G. Morris, 'Group Tasks, Group Interaction Process and Group Performance Effectiveness: A Review and Proposed Integration', in L. Berkowitz (ed.), *Advances in Experimental Social Psychology* (New York: Academic Press, 1975), pp. 45–99; R. Saavedra, P. C. Earley and L. Van Dyne, 'Complex Interdependence in Task-Performing Groups', *Journal of Applied Psychology*, February 1993, pp. 61–72; and K. A. Jehn, G. B. Northcraft and M. A. Neale, 'Why Differences Make a Difference: A Field Study of Diversity, Conflict, and Performance in Workgroups', *Administrative Science Quarterly*, December 1999, pp. 741–63.

56. J. Galbraith, *Organizational Design* (Reading, MA: Addison-Wesley, 1977).

57. See N. R. F. Maier, 'Assets and Liabilities in Group Problem Solving: The Need for an Integrative Function', *Psychological Review*, April 1967, pp. 239–49; G. W. Hill, 'Group versus Individual Performance: Are Two Heads Better Than One?', *Psychological Bulletin*, May 1982, pp. 517–39; and A. E. Schwartz and J. Levin, 'Better Group Decision Making', *Supervisory Management*, June 1990, p. 4.

58. See, for example, R. A. Cooke and J. A. Kernaghan, 'Estimating the Difference between Group versus Individual Performance on Problem-solving Tasks', *Group and Organization Studies*, September 1987, pp. 319–42; and L. K. Michaelsen, W. E. Watson and R. H. Black, 'A Realistic Test of Individual versus Group Consensus Decision Making', *Journal of Applied Psychology*, October 1989, pp. 834–39.

59. See, for example, W. C. Swap and Associates, *Group Decision Making* (Newbury Park, CA: Sage, 1984).

60. I. L. Janis, *Groupthink* (Boston: Houghton Mifflin, 1982); W. Park, 'A Review of Research on Groupthink', *Journal of Behavioral Decision Making*, July 1990, pp. 229–45; C. P. Neck and G. Moorhead, 'Groupthink Remodeled: The Importance of Leadership, Time Pressure, and Methodical Decision-Making Procedures', *Human Relations*, May 1995, pp. 537–58; and J. N. Choi and M. U. Kim, 'The Organizational Application of Groupthink and Its Limits in Organizations', *Journal of Applied Psychology*, April 1999, pp. 297–306.

61. Janis, *Groupthink*.

62. G. Moorhead, R. Ference and C. P. Neck, 'Group Decision Fiascos Continue: Space Shuttle *Challenger* and a Revised Groupthink Framework', *Human Relations*, May 1991, pp. 539–50; and E. J. Chisson, *The Hubble Wars* (New York: HarperPerennial, 1994).

63. David Marr and Marian Wilkinson, *Dark Victory* (Sydney: Allen & Unwin, 2003).

64. M. E. Turner and A. R. Pratkanis, 'Mitigating Groupthink by Stimulating Constructive Conflict', in C. De Dreu and E. Van de Vliert (eds), *Using Conflict in Organizations* (London: Sage, 1997), pp. 53–71.

65. Ibid, p. 68.

66. See N. R. F. Maier, *Principles of Human Relations* (New York: Wiley, 1952); I. L. Janis, *Groupthink: Psychological Studies of Policy Decisions and Fiascoes*, 2nd ed. (Boston: Houghton Mifflin, 1982); C. R. Leana, 'A Partial Test of Janis' Groupthink Model: Effects of Group Cohesiveness and Leader Behavior on Defective Decision Making', *Journal of Management*, Spring 1985, pp. 5–17; and L. Thompson, *Making the Team: A Guide for Managers* (Upper Saddle River, NJ: Prentice Hall, 2000), pp. 116–18.

67. See D. J. Isenberg, 'Group Polarization: A Critical Review and Meta-Analysis', *Journal of Personality and Social Psychology*, December 1986, pp. 1141–51; J. L. Hale and F. J. Boster, 'Comparing Effect Coded Models of Choice Shifts', *Communication Research Reports*, April 1988, pp. 180–86; and P. W. Paese, M. Bieser and M. E. Tubbs, 'Framing Effects and Choice Shifts in Group Decision Making', *Organizational Behavior and Human Decision Processes*, October 1993, pp. 149–65.

68. See, for example, N. Kogan and M. A. Wallach, 'Risk Taking as a Function of the Situation, the Person, and the Group', in *New Directions in Psychology*, vol. 3 (New York: Holt, Rinehart and Winston, 1967); and M. A. Wallach, N. Kogan and D. J. Bem, 'Group Influence on Individual Risk Taking', *Journal of Abnormal and Social Psychology*, vol. 65, 1962, pp. 75–86.

69. R. D. Clark III, 'Group-induced Shift Toward Risk: A Critical Appraisal', *Psychological Bulletin*, October 1971, pp. 251–70.

70. A. F. Osborn, *Applied Imagination: Principles and Procedures of Creative Thinking*, 3rd ed. (New York: Scribner, 1963). See also T. Rickards, 'Brainstorming Revisited: A Question of Context', *International Journal of Management Reviews*, March 1999, pp. 91–110.

71. See A. L. Delbecq, A. H. Van deVen and D. H. Gustafson, *Group Techniques for Program Planning: A Guide to Nominal and Delphi Processes* (Glenview, IL: Scott, Foresman, 1975); and P. B. Paulus and H.-C. Yang, 'Idea Generation in Groups: A Basis for Creativity in Organizations', *Organizational Behavior and Human Decision Processing*, May 2000, pp. 76–87.

72. See, for example, R. B. Gallupe and W. H. Cooper, 'Brainstorming Electronically', *Sloan Management Review*, Fall 1993, pp. 27–36; A. B. Hollingshead and J. E. McGrath, 'Computer-Assisted Groups: A Critical Review of the Empirical Research', in Guzzo and Salas (eds), *Team Effectiveness and Decision Making in Organizations*, pp. 46–78; and M. Stepanek, 'Using the Net for Brainstorming', *Business Week e.biz*, 13 December 1999, pp. EB55–57.

73. T. P. Verney, 'Role Perception Congruence, Performance, and Satisfaction', in D. J. Vredenburgh and R. S. Schuler (eds), *Effective Management: Research and Application*, Proceedings of the 20th Annual Eastern Academy of Management, Pittsburgh, Pennsylvania, May 1983, pp. 24–27.

74. Ibid.

75. M. Van Sell, A. P. Brief and R. S. Schuler, 'Role Conflict and Role Ambiguity: Integration of the Literature and Directions for Future Research', *Human Relations*, January 1981, pp. 43–71; and A. G. Bedeian and A. A. Armenakis, 'A Path-analysis Study of the Consequences of Role Conflict and Ambiguity', *Academy of Management Journal*, June 1981, pp. 417–24.

76. Shaw, *Group Dynamics*.

77. B. Mullen, C. Symons, L. Hu and E. Salas, 'Group Size, Leadership Behavior, and Subordinate Satisfaction', *Journal of General Psychology*, April 1989, pp. 155–70.

PHOTO CREDITS

Understanding and Building Teams

CHAPTER 9

CHAPTER OUTLINE

Why have teams become so popular?
How is a team different from a group?
Types of teams
Beware! Teams aren't always the answer
Creating effective teams
Turning individuals into team players
Contemporary issues in managing teams

LEARNING OBJECTIVES

After studying this chapter, you should be able to:
1. Explain the growing popularity of teams in organisations
2. Contrast teams with groups
3. Identify four types of teams
4. Describe conditions when teams are preferred over individuals
5. Specify the characteristics of effective teams
6. Explain how organisations can create team players
7. Describe the advantages and disadvantages of diversity for work teams
8. Explain how management can keep teams from becoming stagnant and rigid

*Is it true that everyone's responsibility is,
in reality, nobody's responsibility?*
Anonymous

Jacquie McDonald is an instructional designer at USQ. She works closely with academics in a team environment.

Jacquie McDonald works for the Distance Education Centre (DEC) at the University of Southern Queensland (USQ). Staff in the Faculty of Business in the university refer to Jacquie as an ID; an instructional designer who provides advice to academic staff on the pedagogical aspects of the design and delivery of course materials to off-campus students. The faculty has a large number of students enrolled off campus who receive their course materials through the mail in the form of printed booklets. Recently, the faculty has started to deliver materials to students in some courses on a CD-Rom. Jacquie's role is to work with academic staff in the faculty and assist them in coming to grips with the new digital technologies. CD-Rom and Web-based delivery platforms such as WebCT and Blackboard allow staff to do much more to enhance the student's learning experience than the old print-based packages. But staff need to develop new skills and knowledge about how to enhance the learning process using such technologies. Jacquie has to rely on her team management skills to achieve the outcomes expected by the faculty. She considers her team to be a community of practice (COP); a term used to identify teams whose members volunteer to regularly engage in sharing and learning, based on common interests. In this case, the common interest is to learn how to utilise the new technologies to deliver an enhanced learning experience for students.

A vital aspect of leading a team of professionals is facilitating their ability to share critical knowledge, and this is Jacquie's challenge. Alastair Rylatt, a leading Australian management consultant, points to the problems of withholding knowledge. Alastair recently asked a stockbroker from Sydney about sharing knowledge with his colleagues. The stockbroker thought that sharing knowledge was a noble idea but that it would also mean professional suicide, as knowledge is power; if nothing was secret, what was his worth to his organisation?[1] Encouraging teams to share their knowledge unlocks the potential that organisations have invested in their people. Jacquie is working in a team environment to share and build knowledge within the context of a faculty-based community of practice.

Jacquie is one of many professionals in organisations today who are consciously embracing the concept of teamwork. As a management consultant, Alastair is committed to demonstrating to organisations the power of teams in the management of knowledge. Teams are increasingly becoming the primary means for organising work in contemporary business firms.

LEARNING OBJECTIVE

1

Explain the growing popularity of teams in organisations

Why Have Teams Become so Popular?

Twenty-five years ago, when organisations such as the Australian Taxation Office, Volvo and General Foods introduced teams into their production processes, it made news, because no one else was doing it. Today, it's just the opposite. It's the organisation that *doesn't* use teams that has become newsworthy. Currently, 80 per cent of Fortune 500 companies in the United States have half or more of their employees on teams. And 68 per cent of small US manufacturers are using teams in their production areas.[2]

How do we explain the current popularity of teams? The evidence suggests that teams typically outperform individuals when the tasks being done require multiple skills, judgment and experience.[3] As organisations have restructured themselves to compete more effectively and efficiently, they have turned to teams as a way to make better use of employee talents. Management has found that teams are more flexible and responsive to changing events than are traditional departments or other forms of permanent groupings. Teams have the capability to quickly assemble, deploy, refocus and disband.

But don't overlook the motivational properties of teams. Consistent with our discussion in a previous chapter of the role of employee involvement as a motivator, teams facilitate employee participation in operating decisions. For example, some assembly-line workers at John Deere, the farm machinery manufacturer, are part of sales teams that call on customers.[4] These workers know the products better than any traditional sales person; and by travelling and speaking with farmers, these hourly workers develop new skills and become more involved in their jobs. So, another explanation for the popularity of teams is that they are an effective means for management to democratise their organisations and increase employee motivation.

LEARNING OBJECTIVE

2

Contrast teams with groups

How is a Team Different from a Group?

Groups and teams are not the same thing. In this section, we want to define and clarify the difference between a work group and a work team.[5]

In the previous chapter, we defined a *group* as two or more individuals, interacting and interdependent, who have come together to achieve particular objectives. A **work group** is a group that interacts primarily to share information and to make decisions to help each member perform within his or her area of responsibility.

Work groups have no need or opportunity to engage in collective work that requires joint effort. So, their performance is merely the summation of each group member's individual contribution. There is no positive synergy that would create an overall level of performance that is greater than the sum of the inputs.

A **work team** generates positive synergy through coordinated effort. Their individual efforts result in a level of performance that is greater than the sum of those individual inputs. Figure 9.1 highlights the differences between work groups and work teams.

These definitions help to clarify why so many organisations have recently restructured work processes around teams. Management is looking for that positive synergy that will allow their organisations to increase performance. The extensive use of teams creates the *potential* for an organisation to generate greater outputs with no increase in inputs. Notice, however, we said 'potential'. There is nothing inherently magical in the creation of teams that ensures the achievement of this positive synergy. Merely calling a *group* a *team* doesn't automatically increase its performance. As we show later in this chapter, effective teams have certain common characteristics. If management hopes to gain increases in organisational performance through the use of teams, it will need to ensure that its teams possess these characteristics.

work group
A group that interacts primarily to share information and to make decisions to help each group member perform within his or her area of responsibility (*see also* **group[s]**).

work team
A group whose individual efforts result in a performance that is greater than the sum of the individual inputs.

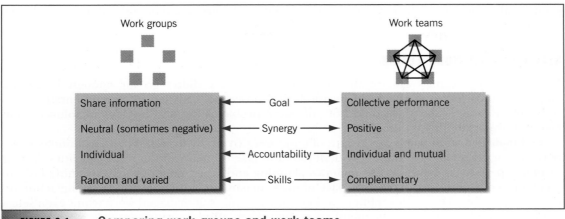

FIGURE 9.1   **Comparing work groups and work teams**

Types of Teams

Teams can do a variety of things. They can make products, provide services, negotiate deals, coordinate projects, offer advice and make decisions.[6] In this section, we will describe the four most common types of teams you are likely to find in an organisation: *problem-solving teams, self-managed teams, cross-functional teams* and *virtual teams* (see Figure 9.2).

PROBLEM-SOLVING TEAMS

If we look back 20 years or so, teams were just beginning to grow in popularity, and most of those teams took a similar form. These were typically composed of from five to 12 employees from the same department or section who met for a few hours each week to discuss ways of improving quality, efficiency and the work environment.[7] We call these **problem-solving teams**.

In problem-solving teams, members share ideas or offer suggestions on how work processes and methods can be improved. Rarely, however, are these teams given the authority to unilaterally implement any of their suggested actions.

One of the most widely practised applications of problem-solving teams during the 1980s was quality circles.[8] As described in a previous chapter, these are work teams of from eight to ten employees and supervisors who have a shared area of responsibility and meet regularly to discuss

problem-solving teams
Groups of from five to
12 employees from the
same department who
meet for a few hours
each week to discuss
ways of improving quality,
efficiency and the work
environment.

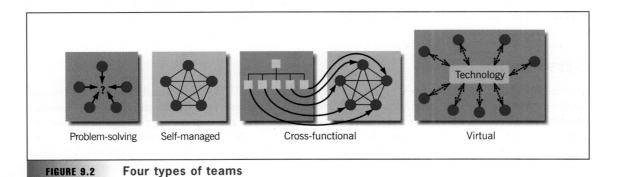

FIGURE 9.2   **Four types of teams**

their quality problems, investigate causes of the problems, recommend solutions and take corrective actions.

SELF-MANAGED WORK TEAMS

Problem-solving teams were on the right track, but they didn't go far enough in getting employees involved in work-related decisions and processes. This led to experimentation with truly autonomous teams that could not only solve problems but also implement solutions and take full responsibility for outcomes.

self-managed work teams
Groups of from ten to 15 people who take on responsibilities of their former supervisors.

Self-managed work teams are groups of employees (typically from ten to 15 in number) who perform highly related or interdependent jobs and take on many of the responsibilities of their former supervisors.[9] Typically, this includes planning and scheduling of work, assigning tasks to members, collective control over the pace of work, making operating decisions, taking action on problems, and working with suppliers and customers. Fully self-managed work teams even select their own members and have the members evaluate each others' performance. As a result, supervisory positions take on decreased importance and may even be eliminated.

A factory at Eaton Corp's Aeroquip Global Hose Division provides an example of how self-managed teams are being used in industry.[10] This factory makes hydraulic hose that is used in trucks, tractors and other heavy equipment. In 1994, to improve quality and productivity, Eaton-Aeroquip's management threw out the assembly line and organised the factory's 285 workers into more than 50 self-managed teams. Workers were suddenly free to participate in decisions that were previously reserved solely for management—for example, the teams set their own schedules, selected new members, negotiated with suppliers, made calls on customers, and disciplined members who created problems. And the results? Between 1993 and 1999, response time to customer concerns improved 99 per cent; productivity and manufacturing output both increased by more than 50 per cent; and accident rates more than halved.

Xerox, General Motors, PepsiCo, Hewlett-Packard and M&M/Mars are just a few familiar names that have implemented self-managed work teams.[11] Business periodicals have run many articles describing successful applications of self-managed teams. But a word of caution needs to be offered. Some organisations have been disappointed with the results from self-managed teams. For example, they don't seem to work well during organisational downsizing. Employees often view cooperating with the team concept as an exercise in assisting one's own executioner.[12] The overall research on the effectiveness of self-managed work teams hasn't been uniformly positive.[13] Moreover, although individuals on these teams do tend to report higher levels of job satisfaction, they also sometimes have higher absenteeism and turnover rates. Inconsistency in findings suggests that the effectiveness of self-managed teams is situationally dependent.[14] In addition to downsizing, factors such as the strength and make-up of team norms, the type of tasks the team undertakes, and the reward structure can significantly influence how well the team performs. Finally, care needs to be taken when introducing self-managed teams globally. For example, evidence suggests that these types of teams have not fared well in Thailand, largely due to that culture's low tolerance of ambiguity and uncertainty and employees' strong respect for hierarchical authority.

CROSS-FUNCTIONAL TEAMS

Custom Research, a market-research firm, had been historically organised around functional departments, but senior management concluded that these functional departments weren't meeting the changing needs of the firm's clients. So, management reorganised Custom Research's 100 employees into account teams.[15] The idea behind the teams was to have every aspect of a client's work handled within one team, rather than by separate departments. The goal was to improve communication and tracking of work, which would lead to increased productivity and more satisfied clients.

Custom Research's reorganisation illustrates the use of **cross-functional teams**. These are teams made up of employees from about the same hierarchical level, but from different work areas, who come together to accomplish a task.

Many organisations have used horizontal, boundary-spanning groups for decades. For example, IBM created a large task force in the 1960s—made up of employees from across departments in the company—to develop its highly successful System 360. And a *task force* is really nothing other than a temporary cross-functional team. Similarly, *committees* composed of members from across departmental lines are another example of cross-functional teams. But the popularity of cross-discipline work teams exploded in the late 1980s. For example, all the major automobile manufacturers—including Toyota, Honda, Nissan, BMW, GM, Ford and DaimlerChrysler—currently use this form of team to coordinate complex projects. Harley-Davidson relies on specific cross-functional teams to manage each line of its motorcycles. These teams include Harley employees from design, manufacturing and purchasing, as well as representatives from key outside suppliers.[16] And IBM still makes use of temporary cross-functional teams. Between November 1999 and June 2000, for example, IBM's senior management pulled together 21 employees from among its 100,000 information technology staff to come up with recommendations on how the company could speed up projects and bring products to market faster.[17] The 21 members were selected because they had one common characteristic—they had all successfully led fast-moving projects. The Speed Team, as they came to be known, spent eight months sharing experiences, examining differences between fast-moving projects and slow ones, and eventually generated recommendations on how to speed up IBM projects.

Cross-functional teams are an effective means for allowing people from diverse areas within an organisation (or even between organisations) to exchange information, develop new ideas and solve problems, and coordinate complex projects. Of course, cross-functional teams are no picnic to manage. Their early stages of development are often very time-consuming as members learn to work with diversity and complexity. It takes time to build trust and teamwork, especially among people from different backgrounds, with different experiences and perspectives.

cross-functional teams
Employees from about the same hierarchical level, but from different work areas, who come together to accomplish a task.

VIRTUAL TEAMS

The previous types of teams do their work face-to-face. **Virtual teams** use computer technology to tie together physically dispersed members in order to achieve a common goal.[18] They allow people to collaborate on-line—using communication links such as wide-area networks, video conferencing or e-mail—whether they are only a room away or continents apart.

Virtual teams can do all the things that other teams do—share information, make decisions, complete tasks. And they can include members from the same organisation or link an organisation's members with employees from other organisations (that is, suppliers and joint partners). They can convene for a few days to solve a problem, a few months to complete a project, or exist permanently.[19]

The three primary factors that differentiate virtual teams from face-to-face teams are: (1) the absence of paraverbal (tone of voice, inflection, voice volume) and non-verbal (eye movement, facial expression, hand gestures and other body language) cues; (2) limited social context; and (3) the ability to overcome time and space constraints. In face-to-face conversation, people use paraverbal and non-verbal cues. These help to clarify communication by providing increased meaning, but they aren't available in on-line interactions. Virtual teams often suffer from less social rapport and less direct interaction among members. They aren't able to duplicate the normal give-and-take of face-to-face discussion. Especially when members haven't personally met, virtual teams tend to be more task-oriented and exchange less social–emotional information. Not surprisingly, virtual team members report less satisfaction with the group interaction process than do face-to-face teams. Finally, virtual teams are able to do their work even if members are thousands of kilometres apart and separated by a dozen or more time zones. It allows people to work together who might otherwise never be able to collaborate. For example, Robyn Flemming,

virtual teams
Teams that use computer technology to tie together physically dispersed members in order to achieve a common goal.

a freelance editor living in Australia, is a member of a virtual team that edits a website for a dot.com company in Bermuda. The six team members are spread around the world in different time zones (Bermuda, Australia, Hong Kong and the UK), so as to be able to provide their client with a round-the-clock editing service.

Companies such as Hewlett-Packard, Boeing, Ford, VeriFone and Royal Dutch/Shell have become heavy users of virtual teams. VeriFone, for example, is a maker of computerised swipe machines that read credit card information. Yet, the use of virtual teams allows its 3,000 employees, who are located all around the globe, to work together on design projects, marketing plans and making sales presentations. Moreover, VeriFone has found that virtual teams provide strong recruiting inducements.[20] Alfresco Design is a Brisbane-based company that helps organisations make the transition to virtual team structures and reap the benefits of reduced real estate expenses, increased productivity and access to global markets.[21]

LEARNING OBJECTIVE

4

Describe conditions when teams are preferred over individuals

Beware! Teams Aren't Always the Answer

Teamwork takes more time and often more resources than individual work. Teams, for example, have increased communication demands, conflicts to be managed, and meetings to be run. So, the benefits of using teams have to exceed the costs. And that's not always the case. In the excitement to enjoy the benefits of teams, some managers have introduced them into situations where

OB Controversies

Working for a cause, or just meeting the challenge?

Graham Hubbard identified what he believed was the 'First XI' companies in Australia. The companies included Woolworths, Telstra, Qantas, the Salvation Army, Westfield, Rio Tinto, National Australia Bank, Lend Lease, Harvey Norman, Macquarie Bank and Brambles. The term 'First XI' comes from the sport of cricket and indicates the top 11 players.

The top 11 companies have effective leadership and effective teams. But an interesting and controversial finding in Hubbard's study relates to whether teams and individuals are working for a cause or just meeting the challenge. Hubbard explains: 'A key difference between US and Australian employees is that US employees respond well to a large challenge, while Australian employees tend to retreat from such challenges. Instead, they want to feel that their organisation has a "cause" worth working for, so that "work" isn't just a job. People in Australian organisations want to be supported, nurtured and enrolled in the cause by the leadership. They don't want to be told to "go get it" in terms of seeking to achieve a difficult challenge. This may explain why overseas managers, particularly Americans, struggle to apply their management principles successfully here.'

Hubbard's statement suggests that team development in the Australian context should include a 'cause' as a rallying point and that leadership is the significant factor for getting team members to achieve. In an era of downsizing, excessive remuneration packages for senior executives and increasing mobility among Australian employees, it is becoming more difficult to rally people to an organisational cause. Instead, leaders need to align the motivational dynamics in teams with the challenges presented to the teams. As a sporting nation, Australians are used to rising to the challenge and take pride in their achievements. The controversy is that the distinction between challenges and causes is blurred when it comes to focusing and engaging teams. It could be claimed that people become passionate about their work, rather than their organisations.

Source: Graham Hubbard, 'A Recipe for the Right People: The Corporate First XI Approach', *Human Resources*, February 2003, pp. 20–21. Reproduced with permission.

the work is better done by individuals. So, before you rush to implement teams, you should carefully assess whether the work requires or will benefit from a collective effort.

How do you know if the work of your group would be better done in teams? It has been suggested that three tests be applied to see if a team fits the situation.[22] First, can the work be done better by more than one person? A good indicator is the complexity of the work and the need for different perspectives. Simple tasks that don't require diverse input are probably better left to individuals. Second, does the work create a common purpose or set of goals for the people in the group that is more than the aggregate of individual goals? For example, many new-car dealer service departments have introduced teams that link customer service personnel, mechanics, parts specialists and sales representatives. Such teams can better manage collective responsibility for ensuring that customer needs are properly met. The final test to assess whether teams fit the situation is: are the members of the group interdependent? Teams make sense when there is interdependence between tasks; when the success of the whole depends on the success of each one; *and* the success of each one depends on the success of the others. Soccer, for example, is an obvious *team* sport. Success requires a great deal of coordination between interdependent players. Conversely, except possibly for relays, swimming teams aren't really teams. They are groups of individuals, performing individually, whose total performance is merely the aggregate summation of their individual performances.

Creating Effective Teams

LEARNING OBJECTIVE

5

Specify the characteristics of effective teams

There is no shortage of efforts at trying to identify factors related to team effectiveness.[23] However, recent studies have taken what was once a 'veritable laundry list of characteristics'[24] and organised them into a relatively focused model.[25] Figure 9.3 summarises what we currently know about what makes teams effective. As you will see, it builds on many of the group concepts introduced in the previous chapter.

The following discussion is based on the model in Figure 9.3. Keep in mind two caveats before we proceed. First, teams differ in form and structure. Since the model we present attempts to generalise across all varieties of teams, you need to be careful not to rigidly apply the model's predictions to all teams.[26] The model should be used as a guide, not as an inflexible prescription. Second, the model assumes that it has already been determined that teamwork is preferable over individual work. Creating 'effective' teams in situations in which individuals can do the job better is equivalent to solving the wrong problem perfectly.

The key components making up effective teams can be subsumed into four general categories. The first category is *work design*. The second relates to the team's *composition*. Third is the resources and other *contextual* influences that make teams effective. Finally, *process* variables reflect those things that go on in the team that influence effectiveness.

What does *team effectiveness* mean in this model? Typically, this has included objective measures of the team's productivity, managers' ratings of the team's performance, and aggregate measures of member satisfaction.

WORK DESIGN

Effective teams need to work together and take collective responsibility to complete significant tasks. They must be more than a 'team-in-name-only'.[27] The work-design category includes variables such as freedom and autonomy, the opportunity to use different skills and talents, the ability to complete a whole and identifiable task or product, and working on a task or project that has a substantial impact on others. The evidence indicates that these characteristics enhance member motivation and increase team effectiveness.[28] These work-design characteristics motivate because they increase members' sense of responsibility and ownership over the work, and because they make the work more interesting to perform.[29]

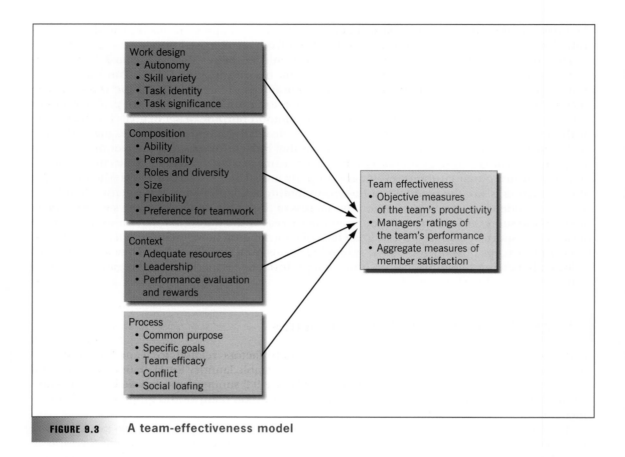

FIGURE 9.3   **A team-effectiveness model**

COMPOSITION

This category includes variables that relate to how teams should be staffed. In this section, we will address the ability and personality of team members, allocating roles and diversity, size of the team, member flexibility, and members' preference for teamwork.

Abilities of members

To perform effectively, a team requires three different types of skills. First, it needs people with *technical expertise*. Second, it needs people with the *problem-solving and decision-making skills* to be able to identify problems, generate alternatives, evaluate those alternatives and make competent choices. Finally, teams need people with good listening, feedback, conflict resolution and other *interpersonal skills*.[30]

No team can achieve its performance potential without developing all three types of skills. The right mix is crucial. Too much of one at the expense of others will result in lower team performance. But teams don't need to have all the complementary skills in place at their beginning. It's not uncommon for one or more members to take responsibility to learn the skills in which the group is deficient, thereby allowing the team to reach its full potential.

Personality

We demonstrated in a previous chapter that personality has a significant influence on individual employee behaviour. This can also be extended to team behaviour. Many of the dimensions identified in the 'Big Five' personality model have been shown to be relevant to team effectiveness. Specifically, teams that rate higher in mean levels of extroversion, agreeableness, conscientiousness and emotional stability tend to receive higher managerial ratings for team performance.[31]

Very interestingly, the evidence indicates that the variance in personality characteristics may be more important than the mean.[32] So, for example, while higher mean levels of conscientiousness on a team is desirable, mixing both conscientious and not-so-conscientious members tends to lower performance. 'This may be because, in such teams, members who are highly conscientious not only must perform their own tasks but also must perform or re-do the tasks of low-conscientious members. It may also be because such diversity leads to feelings of contribution inequity.'[33] Another interesting finding related to personality is that 'one bad apple can spoil the barrel'. A single team member who lacks a minimal level of, say, agreeableness, can negatively affect the whole team's performance. So, including just one person who is low on agreeableness, conscientiousness or extroversion can result in strained internal processes and decreased overall performance.[34]

Allocating roles and diversity

Teams have different needs, and people should be selected for a team to ensure that there is diversity and that all the various roles are filled.

We can identify nine potential team roles (see Figure 9.4). Successful work teams have people to fill all these roles and have selected people to play in these roles based on their skills and preferences.[35] (On many teams, individuals will play multiple roles.) Managers need to understand the individual strengths that each person can bring to a team, select members with their strengths in mind, and allocate work assignments that fit with members' preferred styles. By matching individual preferences with team role demands, managers increase the likelihood that the team members will work well together and ultimately be successful and productive.

Size of teams

The president of AOL Technologies says the secret to a great team is: 'Think small. Ideally, your team should have seven to nine people.'[36] His advice is supported by evidence.[37] Generally speaking, the most effective teams have fewer than ten members. And experts suggest using the smallest number of people who can do the task. Unfortunately, there is a pervasive tendency for managers to err on the side of making teams too large. While a minimum of four or five may be necessary to develop diversity of views and skills, managers seem to seriously underestimate how coordination problems can geometrically increase as team members are added. When teams have excess members, cohesiveness and mutual accountability declines, social loafing increases, and more and more people do less talking relative to others. So, in designing effective teams, managers should try to keep them to fewer than ten people. If a natural working unit is larger and you want a team effort, consider breaking the group down into subteams.

Effective teams need to possess different kinds of skills, including interpersonal skills such as listening and feedback. Such diversity in the abilities of team members helps consulting firms such as Gary Palmer and associates, to provide their clients with sound advice.

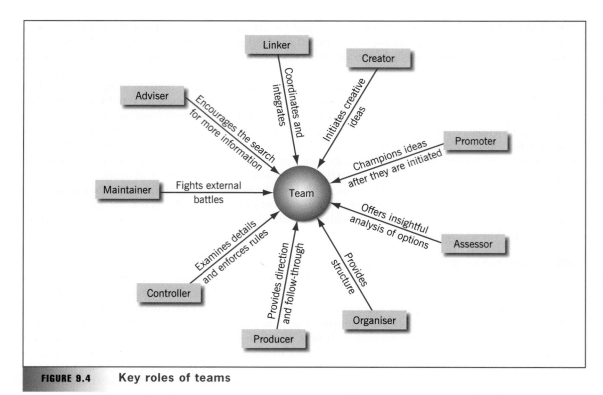

FIGURE 9.4   **Key roles of teams**

Source: Based on C. Margerison and D. McCann, *Team Management: Practical New Approaches* (London: Mercury Books, 1990).

Member flexibility

Teams made up of flexible individuals have members who can complete each others' tasks. This is an obvious plus to a team, because it greatly improves its adaptability and makes it less reliant on any single member.[38] So, selecting members who themselves value flexibility, then cross-training them to be able to do each others' jobs, should lead to higher team performance over time.

Member preferences

Not every employee is a team player. Given the option, many employees will select themselves *out* of team participation. When people who would prefer to work alone are required to team-up, there is a direct threat to the team's morale and to individual member satisfaction.[39] This suggests that, when selecting team members, individual preferences should be considered, as well as abilities, personalities and skills. High-performing teams are likely to be composed of people who prefer working as part of a group.

CONTEXT

The four contextual factors that appear to be most significantly related to team performance are the presence of adequate resources, effective leadership, a climate of trust, and a performance evaluation and reward system that reflects team contributions.

Adequate resources

In our work-group model in the previous chapter, we acknowledged that a work group is part of a larger organisation system. As such, all work teams rely on resources outside the group to sustain it. And a scarcity of resources directly reduces the ability of the team to perform its job effectively. As one set of researchers concluded, after looking at 13 factors potentially related to group performance, 'perhaps one of the most important characteristics of an effective work group is the support the group receives from the organization'.[40] This support includes timely information, technology, adequate staffing, encouragement and administrative assistance. Teams must receive the necessary support from management and the larger organisation if they are going to succeed in achieving their goals.

Leadership and structure

Team members must agree on who is to do what and ensure that all members contribute equally in sharing the workload. In addition, the team needs to determine how schedules will be set, what skills need to be developed, how the group will resolve conflicts, and how it will make and modify decisions. Agreeing on the specifics of work and how they fit together to integrate individual skills requires team leadership and structure. This, incidentally, can be provided directly by management or by the team members themselves as they fulfil promoter, organiser, producer, maintainer and linker roles (refer back to Figure 9.4).

Leadership, of course, isn't always needed. For example, the evidence indicates that self-managed work teams often perform better than teams with formally appointed leaders.[41] And leaders can obstruct high performance when they interfere with self-managing teams.[42] On self-managed teams, team members absorb many of the duties typically assumed by managers.

On traditionally managed teams, we find that two factors seem to be important in influencing team performance—the leader's expectations, and his or her mood. Leaders who expect good things from their team are more likely to get them. For example, military platoons under leaders who held high expectations performed significantly better in training than control platoons.[43] In addition, studies have found that leaders who exhibit a positive mood get better team performance and lower turnover.[44]

Climate of trust

Members of effective teams trust each other. And they also exhibit trust in their leaders.[45] Interpersonal trust among team members facilitates cooperation, reduces the need to monitor each others' behaviour, and bonds members around the belief that others on the team won't take advantage of them. Team members, for example, are more likely to take risks and expose vulnerabilities when they believe they can trust others on their team. Similarly, as we will show in a coming chapter, trust is the foundation of leadership. Trust in leadership is important in that it allows the team to be willing to accept and commit to their leader's goals and decisions.

Performance evaluation and reward systems

How do you get team members to be both individually and jointly accountable? The traditional, individually oriented evaluation and reward system must be modified to reflect team performance.[46]

Individual performance evaluations, fixed hourly wages, individual incentives, and the like are not consistent with the development of high-performance teams. So, in addition to evaluating and rewarding employees for their individual contributions, management should consider group-based appraisals, profit sharing, gain sharing, small-group incentives, and other system modifications that will reinforce team effort and commitment.

PROCESS

The final category related to team effectiveness is process variables. These variables include member commitment to a common purpose, establishment of specific team goals, team efficacy, a managed level of conflict, and minimising social loafing.

The Real Deal

Building a high-calibre team

Deloitte Touche Tohmatsu is considered to be the number two accounting and management consulting firm in the world and number one in Australia. But being number one didn't mean that it didn't experience some difficulties. Several years ago, the human resources (HR) team was having difficulties. The members of the team weren't collaborating effectively. They were perceived to be not adding value to the Australian operations and as being somewhat out of touch with the business. Moreover, morale was low.

Then, in 2000, Peter May arrived from one of the other big accounting firms, PricewaterhouseCoopers, and took over the HR team. In the early 1990s, he had studied philosophy, theology and history as a student priest with the Australian Jesuits. In his new role as partner and National Director, People and Knowledge, he focused on rebuilding the HR team. From his experience, he knows that a highly motivated team that is aligned to the core business of the organisation is absolutely essential to any HR director who wants to demonstrate that HR adds value.

May created one team nationally from the four existing groups based on Melbourne, Sydney, and national and business units. This move was about building a strong focus on the business, and a focus on achievement. Recently, Craig Donaldson from *Human Resources* magazine, interviewed Peter May about his approach to building an effective team and received this response: 'My approach to building a high-calibre team is about really understanding what they are about as people. This helps you build a team that cares deeply about the business, wants to understand the business, and also wants to be highly responsive to it as well. If those people can join you on that journey, add a lot of value and have a lot of fun, then that's great.' Peter May won the Mercer Award for Best HR Director for 2002.

Source: Craig Donaldson, 'Getting the House in Order: Directing HR at Deloitte', *Human Resources*, January 2003, pp. 10–12. Reproduced with permission.

A common purpose

Effective teams have a common and meaningful purpose that provides direction, momentum and commitment for members.[47] This purpose is a vision. It is broader than specific goals.

Members of successful teams put a tremendous amount of time and effort into discussing, shaping and agreeing on a purpose that belongs to them both collectively and individually. This common purpose, when accepted by the team, becomes the equivalent of what celestial navigation is to a ship captain—it provides direction and guidance under any and all conditions.

Specific goals

Successful teams translate their common purpose into specific, measurable and realistic performance goals. Just as we demonstrated in a previous chapter how goals lead individuals to higher performance, goals also energise teams. These specific goals facilitate clear communication. They also help teams to maintain their focus on getting results.

Also, consistent with the research on individual goals, team goals should be challenging. Difficult goals have been found to raise team performance on those criteria for which they are set. So, for example, goals for quantity tend to raise quantity, goals for speed tend to raise speed, goals for accuracy raise accuracy, and so on.[48]

Team efficacy

Effective teams have confidence in themselves. They believe that they can succeed. We call this *team efficacy*.[49]

Success breeds success. Teams that have been successful raise their beliefs about future success, which, in turn, motivates them to work harder.

What, if anything, can management do to increase team efficacy? Two possible options are helping the team to achieve small successes and skill training. Small successes build team confidence. As a team develops an increasingly stronger performance record, it also increases the collective belief that future efforts will lead to success. In addition, managers should consider providing training to improve members' technical and interpersonal skills. The greater the abilities of team members, the greater the likelihood that the team will develop confidence and the capability to deliver on that confidence.

Conflict levels

Conflict on a team isn't necessarily bad. As we will elaborate in a coming chapter, teams that are completely void of conflict are likely to become apathetic and stagnant. So, conflict can actually improve team effectiveness.[50] But, not all types of conflict. Relationship conflicts—those based on interpersonal incompatibilities, tension, and animosity towards others—are almost always dysfunctional. However, on teams performing non-routine activities, disagreement among members about task content (called task conflicts) is not detrimental. In fact, it is often beneficial, because it lessens the likelihood of groupthink. Task conflicts stimulate discussion, promote critical assessment of problems and options, and can lead to better team decisions. So, effective teams will be characterised by an appropriate level of conflict.

Social loafing

We learned in the previous chapter that individuals can hide inside a group. They can engage in social loafing and coast on the group's effort because their individual contributions can't be identified. Effective teams undermine this tendency by holding themselves accountable at both the individual and team level.

Successful teams make members individually and jointly accountable for the team's purpose, goals and approach.[51] They are clear on what they are individually responsible for and what they are jointly responsible for.

LEARNING OBJECTIVE

6

Explain how organisations can create team players

| Turning Individuals into Team Players

To this point, we have made a strong case for the value and growing popularity of teams. But many people aren't inherently team players. They are loners, or people who want to be recognised for their individual achievements. There are also many organisations that have historically nurtured individual accomplishments. They have created competitive work environments in which only the strong survive. If these organisations adopt teams, what do they do about the selfish, 'I've-got-to-look-out-for-me' employees that they have created? Finally, as we discussed in a previous chapter, countries differ in terms of how they rate on individualism and collectivism. Teams fit well with countries that score high on collectivism.[52] But what if an organisation wants to introduce teams into a work population that is made up largely of individuals born and raised in a highly individualistic society? As one writer so aptly put it, in describing the role of teams in the United States: 'Americans don't grow up learning how to function in teams. In school we never receive a team report card or learn the names of the team of sailors who traveled with Columbus to America.'[53] This limitation would obviously be just as true of Australians, New Zealanders, Canadians, British, and others from highly individualistic societies.

THE CHALLENGE

The previous points are meant to dramatise that one substantial barrier to using work teams is individual resistance. An employee's success is no longer defined in terms of individual performance. To perform well as team members, individuals must be able to communicate openly and honestly, to confront differences and resolve conflicts, and to sublimate personal goals for the

Myth *or* Science?

Are senior management teams really teams?

Senior management teams have become the focus of interest in recent times because of the strong impact they have on the rest of the organisation. No matter how good the teamwork is in a company, if the senior management team isn't working well it can have negative consequences for the whole team. Members of senior management teams are more likely than other teams to place a greater emphasis on change and innovation, but are more likely to be lower on people and analytical skills.[54]

Interviews with 23 CEOs of major American and European companies identified five main problems:

- inadequate capabilities of a single executive;
- a common team-wide shortcoming;
- harmful internal rivalries;
- groupthink; and
- fragmentation.

Fragmentation is the most critical problem, because senior executives are pursuing their own agenda with a minimum of collaboration or exchange. Fragmented executive teams can be acceptable when the organisation is successful or stable. When there is a major environmental shift, however, the fragmented team is slow, acts in a piecemeal fashion and is maladaptive.

In a study involving over 2,500 senior managers in eight countries, more than 50 per cent of the managers indicated that their top management team wasn't sensitive to issues that warranted attention. Issues affecting the long term, the structure of the organisation, and relationships between departments/functions were not getting attention in all the countries studied. This shows that process issues were most often being ignored by senior management groups. The results also showed that managers reported that the top teams who paid greater attention to internal issues and had a shared vision reported greater job satisfaction than did other teams. Managers in this study also indicated that increased profitability, better internal relations and better performance would result if internal issues were dealt with and agreement on vision was shared. Another study showed that smaller executive teams led to greater openness and more positive cognitive conflict (willingness to have different judgments and ideas).[55]

Other studies have shown that there is no direct relationship between success and the length of tenure of members in top-level teams, although it has been shown that firms that went bankrupt had significantly shorter firm tenure in their executive teams.[56] Having a wide range of ages on a senior management team was shown to be related to higher turnover.[57] Having different functional backgrounds on the top management team helps to improve the strategic planning process, but different levels of educational background appear to increase turnover. The number of members of a top team may also have an effect. More members means that more senior managers are committed to and working towards the corporate objective. It also requires more coordination cost and time, and possibly leads to more conflict and turnover.

CEOs must therefore find ways to mould the senior management group into a well-functioning and cohesive team. The strong personality, status and experience of senior managers, as well as the limitations on their time, require different team-building strategies.[58] An important skill for the senior management team members is to know when to operate as a team and when to be independent directors of their own divisional teams. For example, putting together a strategic plan and then achieving corporate objectives requires a high level of cohesion and teamwork from the senior management team. Achieving the division objectives may require some autonomy and independent creativity from a senior manager and therefore doesn't require 'team player' behaviour. Balancing the commitment to the senior management team and the corporate objectives with the individual division objectives is a major challenge for every organisation.

good of the team. For many employees, this is a difficult—sometimes impossible—task. The challenge of creating team players will be greatest when (1) the national culture is highly individualistic and (2) the teams are being introduced into an established organisation that has historically valued individual achievement. This describes, for example, what faced managers at AT&T, Ford and Motorola. These firms prospered by hiring and rewarding corporate stars, and they bred a competitive climate that encouraged individual achievement and recognition. Employees in these types of firms can be jolted by this sudden shift to the importance of team play.[59] A veteran employee of a large company, who had done well working alone, described the experience of joining a team: 'I'm learning my lesson. I just had my first negative performance appraisal in 20 years.'[60]

On the other hand, the challenge for management is less demanding when teams are introduced where employees have strong collectivist values—such as in Japan or Thailand, or in new organisations that use teams as their initial form for structuring work. Saturn Corp., for example, is an American organisation owned by General Motors. The company was designed around teams from its inception. Everyone at Saturn was hired with the knowledge that they would be working in teams. The ability to be a good team player was a basic hiring qualification that had to be met by all new employees.

SHAPING TEAM PLAYERS

The following summarises the primary options managers have for trying to turn individuals into team players.

Selection

Some people already possess the interpersonal skills to be effective team players. When hiring team members, in addition to the technical skills required to fill the job, care should be taken to ensure that candidates can fulfil their team roles as well as technical requirements.[61]

Many job candidates don't have team skills. This is especially true for those socialised around individual contributions. When faced with such candidates, managers basically have three options. The candidates can undergo training to 'make them into team players'. If this isn't possible or doesn't work, the other two options are to transfer the individual to another unit within the organisation, without teams (if this possibility exists); or don't hire the candidate. In established organisations that decide to redesign jobs around teams, it should be expected that some employees will resist being team players and may be untrainable. Unfortunately, such people typically become casualties of the team approach.

Training

On a more optimistic note, a large proportion of people raised on the importance of individual accomplishments can be trained to become team players. Training specialists conduct exercises that allow employees to experience the satisfaction

When the New Zealand All Blacks and the Australian Wallabies meet on the rugby field, there is a lot at stake and little room for error. Every rugby fan appreciates the enormous amount of training that players are involved in to develop their individual and team skills.

that teamwork can provide. They also typically offer workshops to help employees improve their problem-solving, communication, negotiation, conflict-management and coaching skills. Employees also learn the five-stage group development model described in the previous chapter. At Bell Atlantic, a telecommunications company, for example, trainers focus on how a team goes through various stages before it finally gels. And employees are reminded of the importance of patience—because teams take longer to make decisions than if employees were acting alone.[62]

Emerson Electric's Specialty Motor Division, for example, has achieved remarkable success in getting its 650-member workforce not only to accept, but to welcome, team training.[63] Outside consultants were brought in to give workers practical skills for working in teams. After less than a year, employees have enthusiastically accepted the value of teamwork.

Rewards

The reward system needs to be reworked to encourage cooperative efforts rather than competitive ones.[64] For example, in the United States, Hallmark Cards, Inc., added an annual bonus based on achievement of team goals to its basic individual-incentive system.[65]

Promotions, pay raises and other forms of recognition should be given to individuals for how effective they are as a collaborative team member. This doesn't mean individual contributions are ignored; rather, they are balanced with selfless contributions to the team. Examples of behaviours that should be rewarded include training new colleagues, sharing information with teammates, helping to resolve team conflicts, and mastering new skills that the team needs but in which it is deficient.

Lastly, don't forget the intrinsic rewards that employees can receive from teamwork. Teams provide camaraderie. It's exciting and satisfying to be an integral part of a successful team. The opportunity to engage in personal development and to help teammates grow can be a very satisfying and rewarding experience for employees.

Contemporary Issues in Managing Teams

In this section, we address three issues related to managing teams: (1) How do teams facilitate the adoption of quality management? (2) What are the implications of workforce diversity on team performance? and (3) How does management re-energise stagnant teams?

TEAMS AND QUALITY MANAGEMENT

One of the central characteristics of quality management (QM) is the use of teams. But why are teams an essential part of QM?

The essence of QM is process improvement, and employee involvement is the linchpin of process improvement. In other words, QM requires management to give employees the encouragement to share ideas and act on what they suggest. As one author put it, 'None of the various [quality management] processes and techniques will catch on and be applied except in work teams. All such techniques and processes require high levels of communication and contact, response and adaptation, and coordination and sequencing. They require, in short, the environment that can be supplied only by superior work teams.'[66]

Teams provide the natural vehicle for employees to share ideas and implement improvements. As stated by Gil Mosard, a QM specialist at Boeing: 'When your measurement system tells you your process is out of control, you need teamwork for structured problem solving. Not everyone needs to know how to do all kinds of fancy control charts for performance tracking, but everybody does need to know where their process stands so they can judge if it is improving.'[67] Examples from Ford Motor Co. and Amana Refrigeration, Inc., illustrate how teams are being used in QM programs.[68]

Ford began its QM efforts in the early 1980s with teams as the primary organising mechanism. 'Because this business is so complex, you can't make an impact on it without a team approach,' noted one Ford manager. In designing its quality problem-solving teams, Ford's management identified five goals. The teams should (1) be small enough to be efficient and effective; (2) be properly trained in the skills their members will need; (3) be allocated enough time to work on the problems they plan to address; (4) be given the authority to resolve the problems and implement corrective action; and (5) each have a designated 'champion' whose job it is to help the team get around roadblocks that arise.

At Amana, cross-functional task forces made up of people from different levels within the company are used to deal with quality problems that cut across departmental lines. The various task forces each have a unique area of problem-solving responsibility. For example, one handles in-plant products, another deals with items that arise outside the production facility, and still another focuses its attention specifically on supplier problems. Amana claims that the use of these teams has improved vertical and horizontal communication within the company and substantially reduced both the number of units that don't meet company specifications and the number of service problems in the field.

LEARNING OBJECTIVE

7

Describe the advantages and disadvantages of diversity for work teams

TEAMS AND WORKFORCE DIVERSITY

Managing diversity on teams is a balancing act (see Table 9.1). Diversity typically provides fresh perspectives on issues, but it makes it more difficult to unify the team and reach agreements.

The strongest case for diversity on work teams is when these teams are engaged in problem-solving and decision-making tasks.[69] Heterogeneous teams bring multiple perspectives to the discussion, thus increasing the likelihood that the team will identify creative or unique solutions. In addition, the lack of a common perspective usually means diverse teams spend more time discussing issues, which decreases the chances that a weak alternative will be chosen. However, keep in mind that the positive contribution that diversity makes to decision-making teams undoubtedly declines over time. As we pointed out in the previous chapter, diverse groups have more difficulty working together and solving problems, *but this dissipates with time*. Expect the value-added component of diverse teams to increase as members become more familiar with each other and the team becomes more cohesive.

Studies tell us that members of cohesive teams have greater satisfaction, lower absenteeism and lower attrition from the group.[70] Yet, cohesiveness is likely to be lower on diverse teams.[71] So, here is a potential negative of diversity: it is detrimental to group cohesiveness. But again, referring to the previous chapter, we found that the relationship between cohesiveness and group productivity was moderated by performance-related norms. We suggest that if the norms of the team are supportive of diversity, then a team can maximise the value of heterogeneity while, at the same time, achieving the benefits of high cohesiveness.[72] This makes a strong case for team members to participate in diversity training.

TABLE 9.1 Advantages and disadvantages of diversity	
Advantages	**Disadvantages**
Multiple perspectives	Ambiguity
Greater openness to new ideas	Complexity
Multiple interpretations	Confusion
Increased creativity	Miscommunication
Increased flexibility	Difficulty in reaching a single agreement
Increased problem-solving skills	Difficulty in agreeing on specific actions

Source: Adapted from *International Dimensions of Organizational Behavior*, 4th ed., by N. J. Adler. Copyright © 2002 (p. 109). Reprinted with permission of South-Western College Publishing, a division of Thomson Learning <www.thomsonrights.com>, fax 800 730-2215.

REINVIGORATING MATURE TEAMS

Just because a team is performing well at a given point in time is no assurance that it will continue to do so.[73] Effective teams can become stagnant. Initial enthusiasm can give way to apathy. Time can diminish the positive value from diverse perspectives as cohesiveness increases.

In terms of the five-stage development model introduced in the previous chapter, teams don't automatically stay at the 'performing stage'. Familiarity breeds apathy. Success can lead to complacency. And maturity brings less openness to novel ideas and innovation.

Mature teams are particularly prone to suffer from groupthink. Members begin to believe they can read everyone's mind, so they assume they know what everyone is thinking. As a result, team members become reluctant to express their thoughts and less likely to challenge each other.

Another source of problems for mature teams is that their early successes are often due to having taken on easy tasks. It's normal for new teams to begin by taking on issues and problems that they can handle most easily. But, as time passes, the easy problems become solved and the team has to begin to confront more difficult issues. At this point, the team has typically developed entrenched processes and routines, and members are reluctant to change the 'perfect' system they have already worked out. The results can often be disastrous. Internal team processes no longer work smoothly. Communication bogs down. Conflicts increase, because problems are less likely to have obvious solutions. And team performance can drop dramatically.

What can be done to reinvigorate mature teams? We offer four suggestions: (1) *Prepare members to deal with the problems of maturity*. Remind team members that they are not unique—all successful teams have to confront maturity issues. They shouldn't feel let down or lose their confidence in the team concept when the initial euphoria subsides and conflicts surface. (2) *Offer refresher training*. When teams get into ruts, it may help to provide them with refresher training in communication, conflict resolution, team processes and similar skills. This can help members to regain confidence and trust in one another. (3) *Offer advanced training*. The skills that worked with easy problems may be insufficient for more difficult ones. So, mature teams can often benefit from advanced training to help members develop stronger problem-solving, interpersonal and technical skills. (4) *Encourage teams to treat their development as a constant learning experience*. Like quality management, teams should approach their own development as part of a search for continuous improvement. Teams should look for ways to improve, to confront member fears and frustrations, and to use conflict as a learning opportunity.

Summary and Implications for Managers

Few trends have influenced employee jobs as much as the massive movement to introduce teams into the workplace. The shift from working alone to working on teams requires employees to cooperate with others, share information, confront differences, and sublimate personal interests for the greater good of the team.

Effective teams have been found to have common characteristics. The work that members do should provide freedom and autonomy, the opportunity to use different skills and talents, the ability to complete a whole and identifiable task or product, and work that has a substantial impact on others. The teams require individuals with technical expertise, as well as problem-solving, decision-making and interpersonal skills; and high scores on the personality characteristics of extroversion, agreeableness, conscientiousness and emotional stability. Effective teams tend to be small—with fewer than ten people. They have members who fill role demands, are flexible, and who prefer to be part of a group. They also have adequate resources, effective leadership, a climate of trust, and a performance evaluation and reward system that reflects team contributions. Finally, effective teams have members committed to a common purpose, specific team goals, members who believe in the team's capabilities, a manageable level of conflict and a minimal degree of social loafing.

Because individualistic organisations and societies attract and reward individual accomplishments, it is more difficult to create team players in these environments. To make the conversion, management should try to select individuals with the interpersonal skills to be effective team players, provide training to develop teamwork skills, and reward individuals for cooperative efforts.

Once teams are mature and performing effectively, management's job isn't over. Mature teams can become stagnant and complacent. Managers need to support mature teams with advice, guidance and training if these teams are to continue to improve.

Point

SPORTS TEAMS ARE GOOD MODELS FOR WORKPLACE TEAMS

Studies from different football codes, basketball, hockey, athletics and baseball have found a number of elements that successful sports teams have that can be extrapolated to successful work teams.

Successful teams integrate cooperation and competition. Effective team coaches get athletes to help one another, but also push one another to perform at their best. Sports teams with the best win–loss record had coaches who promoted a strong spirit of cooperation and a high level of healthy competition among their players.

Successful teams score early wins. Early successes build teammates' faith in themselves and their capacity as a team. For example, research on hockey teams of relatively equal ability found that 72 per cent of the time the team that was ahead at the end of the first period went on to win the game. So, managers should provide teams with early tasks that are simple and provide 'easy wins'.

Successful teams avoid losing streaks. Losing can become a self-fulfilling prophecy. A couple of failures can lead to a downward spiral if a team becomes demoralised and believes it is helpless to end its losing streak. Managers need to instil confidence in team members that they can turn things around when they encounter setbacks.

Practice makes perfect. Successful sports teams execute on game day but learn from their mistakes in practice. Practice should be used to try new things and fail. A wise manager carves out time and space in which work teams can experiment and learn.

Successful teams use half-time breaks. The best coaches in basketball and football use half-time during a game to reassess what is working and what isn't. Managers of work teams should similarly build in assessments at the approximate halfway point in a team project to evaluate what it can do to improve.

Winning teams have a stable membership. Stability improves performance. For example, studies of professional basketball teams have found that the more stable a team's membership, the more likely the team is to win. The more time teammates have together, the more able they are to anticipate one another's moves and the clearer they are about one another's roles.

Successful teams debrief after failures and successes. The best sports teams study the game video. Similarly, work teams need to take time to routinely reflect on, and learn from, both their successes and failures.

Counterpoint

There are flaws in using sports as a model for developing effective work teams. Here are just four caveats.

- *All sport teams aren't alike.* In cricket, for example, there is little interaction among teammates. Rarely are more than two or three players directly involved in a play. The performance of the team is largely the sum of the performance of its individual players. In contrast, basketball has much more interdependence among players. Geographic distribution is dense. Usually all players are involved in every play, team members have to be able to switch from offence to defence at a moment's notice, and there is continuous movement by all, not just the player with the ball. The performance of the team is more than the sum of its individual players. So, when using sports teams as a model for work teams, you have to make sure you are making the correct comparison.
- *Work teams are more varied and complex.* In an athletic competition, the design of the task, the design of the team, and the team's context vary relatively little from team to team. But these variables can vary tremendously between work teams. As a result, coaching plays a much more significant part in a sports team's performance than for a work team. Performance of work teams is more a function of getting the team's structural and design variables right. So, in contrast to sports, managers of work teams should focus more on getting the team set up for success than on coaching.
- *Some employees can't relate to sports metaphors.* Not everyone on work teams is conversant in sports. Women, for example, often are not as interested in sports as men and aren't as savvy about sports terminology. And team members from different cultures may not know the sports metaphors you are using. Most Malaysians and Singaporeans, for example, are unfamiliar with the rules and terminology of Australian Rules football.
- *Work team outcomes aren't easily defined in terms of wins and losses.* Sports teams typically measure success in terms of wins and losses. Such measures of success are rarely as clear for work teams. When managers try to define success in wins and losses, it tends to infer that the workplace is ethically no more complex than the playing field, which is rarely true.

Source: Both of these arguments are based on N. Katz, 'Sports Teams as a Model for Workplace Teams: Lessons and Liabilities', *Academy of Management Executive*, August 2001, pp. 56–67.

For Discussion

1. Contrast self-managed and cross-functional teams.
2. Contrast virtual and face-to-face teams.
3. List and describe nine team roles.
4. How do effective teams minimise social loafing?
5. How do effective teams minimise groupthink?
6. List and describe the process variables associated with effective team performance.
7. Under what conditions will the challenge of creating team players be greatest?
8. What role do teams play in quality management?
9. Contrast the pros and cons of having diverse teams.
10. How can management invigorate stagnant teams?
11. Don't teams create conflict? Isn't conflict bad? Why, then, would management support the concept of teams?
12. What problems might surface in teams at each stage in the five-stage group development model?
13. Would you prefer to work alone or as part of a team? Why? How do you think your answer compares with others in your class?

Exercise

BUILDING EFFECTIVE WORK TEAMS

Objective: This exercise is designed to allow class members to (a) experience working together as a team on a specific task and (b) analyse this experience.

Time: Teams will have 90 minutes to engage in Steps 2 and 3 below. Another 45–60 minutes will be used in class to critique and evaluate the exercise.

Procedure:

1. Class members are assigned to teams of about six people.
2. Each team is required to:
   (a) Determine a team name.
   (b) Compose a team song.
3. Each team is to try to find the following items on its scavenger hunt:
   (a) A picture of a team
   (b) A newspaper article about a group or team
   (c) A piece of apparel with the university name or logo
   (d) A set of chopsticks
   (e) A ball of wool
   (f) A piece of stationery from a university department
   (g) A bottle of Liquid Paper
   (h) A floppy disk
   (i) A cup from McDonald's
   (j) A dog leash
   (k) An electricity account
   (l) A calendar from last year
   (m) A book by Tom Clancy
   (n) An ad brochure for a Ford product
   (o) A test tube
   (p) A packet of chewing gum
   (q) A cob of corn
   (r) A Britney Spears tape or CD
4. After 90 minutes, all teams are to be back in the classroom. (A penalty, determined by the lecturer, will be imposed on late teams.) The team with the most items on the list will be declared the winner. The class and lecturer will determine whether or not the items meet the requirements of the exercise.
5. Debriefing of the exercise will begin by having each team engage in self-evaluation. Specifically, it should answer the following:
   (a) What was the team's strategy?
   (b) What roles did individual members perform?
   (c) How effective was the team?
   (d) What could the team have done to be more effective?
6. Full class discussion will focus on issues such as:
   (a) What differentiated the more effective teams from the less effective teams?
   (b) What did you learn from this experience that is relevant to the design of effective teams?

Source: Adapted from M. R. Manning and P. J. Schmidt, 'Building Effective Work Teams: A Quick Exercise Based on a Scavenger Hunt', *Journal of Management Education*, August 1995, pp. 392–98. Copyright © 1995. Reprinted by permission of Sage Publications, Inc.

Case Study 9

The Dynamics of Work Teams

There were a lot of changes being made at State Bank. New technology was being implemented, the organisation had downsized from 2,300 staff to 1,550 in the last eight months, and there was now talk of a merger. While the bank was reasonably profitable, some benchmark studies showed that for a bank with this amount of assets and this number of staff, the State Bank should make another 2.4 per cent profit on total revenue. Jim Watako, the director of operations, was told by the CEO to consider ways to improve productivity and reduce costs. Jim had recently run across the idea of self-managed teams and wanted to try it out in the bank to see if it would work. From his understanding of self-managed teams, he was attracted to the idea that by insisting on less direct supervision by work group managers and giving more discretion to the group, he would achieve greater productivity. Jim could envisage that potential synergies could be gained if some of his work groups could act more like teams where staff could play a greater role in how the groups managed their affairs.

Jim was waiting for Barbara Ormston and Kim Chang to arrive in his office in the next few minutes. Barbara was head of the Information Technology section, and Kim was a branch manager of a rapidly growing branch in a fairly well-off suburb.

Barbara's section had 65 people, including systems analysers, system programmers, data input operators, technical support people and computer operators, as well as secretarial staff. She had five groups, each with about 12 people plus one supervisor. Jim has heard that the department runs well, except for the technical support people who seem to be pretty independent and don't have a great regard for Barbara, who is in her early thirties, young, female and with no computer hardware experience. The technicians are all male, and their average age is over 35.

Kim's branch seems to be going well. Its revenue is in the top 5 per cent of all branches, but its costs are also higher than 85 per cent of the other branches. Jim is sure that this branch could operate more efficiently and save costs. He also thinks the idea of testing the self-managed work group approach at this branch would be well-received, since Kim and his staff have been more responsive to change than other branches. Kim has 35 staff in three groups: counter staff, administration and customer relations (who look after customers with accounts above $100,000).

Jim has already informed the board and received approval to introduce self-managed teams in two departments in the bank, and with the help of his senior management team he has picked these two departments. Jim has also received approval to give each section an additional $15,000 for the next six months to help implement the change.

Questions

1. Based on a knowledge of group dynamics and behaviour, what are the factors Jim, Kim and Barbara will need to consider in setting up self-managed work teams?
2. What type of approach should Jim, Kim and Barbara adopt in introducing self-managed work teams, and what problems will they need to consider?

Web Workout

1. Moving from a traditional hierarchical structure to teams requires thought and planning. How teams will be applied within the organisation and their goals can be one of the most challenging aspects of the process. Go to the website <www.teamtechnology.co.uk/tt/t-articl/tb-basic.htm> to learn more about team building.
2. What is the difference between a self-managed team and a self-directed team? The following website <www.mapnp.org/library/grp_skll/slf_drct/slf_drct.htm> has a series of links on team topics where you can find answers to the above questions and many other questions. Write a short reaction paper on one of the topics from this site.

3. Virtual teams require tools to support their effectiveness. For example, how do they hold meetings? We often assume the technology is there (for example, the telephone), but most technology supports only one-on-one communication. When a meeting is held on the phone, there must be technology to support all members being on the line at once. Learn more about virtual team tools at <www.objs.com/survey/groupware.htm>. Write five facts you learned about groupware and collaboration support, and bring to class for further discussion.

4. When teams experience conflict, effectiveness can diminish. There are team skills that can be learned and applied to get a team through a difficult period and possibly make them stronger and more effective as a result. For a learning module on developing skills to confront team conflict, go to <www.vta.spcomm. uiuc.edu/TCT/tct-ov.html>. Write a one-page summary paper on what you learned.

5. For a brief overview of the characteristics of effective teams, go to <www.stanford.edu/class/e140/ e140a/effective.html>. After reviewing this list, think of a team or group you have worked with in the past. Don't name names, but take each characteristic listed and apply your experience to it. For example, characteristic number one is, 'There is a clear unity of purpose.' Did your group have that unity? Why or why not? How did you know—was there a mission statement (or lack of one); were there goals (or no goals), etc? Bring your completed analysis to class for group discussion.

6. What can be learned from a WebMonkey? Eight ways to find and keep web team players. Go to <http://hotwired.lycos.com/webmonkey/98/22/index0a_page3.html>. How do WebMonkey's recommendations compare to what we have learned in class? Write a paragraph or two as to why you agree or disagree with these recommendations and what you would change if necessary. Bring to class for further discussion.

KSS Program

KNOW THE CONCEPTS   SELF-AWARENESS   SKILLS APPLICATIONS

Creating effective teams
After you have read Chapter 8 and this chapter, take Self-Assessment #30 (How Good Am I at Building and Leading a Team?) on your enclosed CD-Rom and complete the skill-building module entitled 'Creating Effective Teams' on page 638.

NOTES

1. Alastair Rylatt, *Winning the Knowledge Game* (Sydney: McGraw-Hill Australia, 2003), p. 132.

2. Cited in C. Joinson, 'Teams at Work', *HRMagazine*, May 1999, p. 30; and P. Strozniak, 'Teams at Work', *Industry Week*, 18 September 2000, p. 47.

3. See, for example, S. A. Mohrman, S. G. Cohen and A. M. Mohrman, Jr, *Designing Team-Based Organizations* (San Francisco: Jossey-Bass, 1995); P. MacMillan, *The Performance Factor: Unlocking the Secrets of Teamwork* (Nashville, TN: Broadman & Holman, 2001); and E. Salas, C. A. Bowers and E. Edens (eds), *Improving Teamwork in Organizations: Applications of Resource Management Training* (Mahwah, NJ: Lawrence Erlbaum, 2002).

4. K. Kelly, 'The New Soul of John Deere', *Business Week*, 31 January 1994, pp. 64–66.

5. This section is based on J. R. Katzenbach and D. K. Smith, *The Wisdom of Teams* (Cambridge, MA: Harvard University Press, 1993), pp. 21, 45 and 85; and D. C. Kinlaw, *Developing Superior Work Teams* (Lexington, MA: Lexington Books, 1991), pp. 3–21.

6. See, for example, E. Sunstrom, K. DeMeuse and D. Futrell, 'Work Teams: Applications and Effectiveness', *American Psychologist*, February 1990, pp. 120–33.

7. J. H. Shonk, *Team-Based Organizations* (Homewood, IL: Business One Irwin, 1992); and M. A. Verespej, 'When Workers Get New Roles', *Industry Week*, 3 February 1992, p. 11.

8. M. L. Marks, P. H. Mirvis, E. J. Hackett and J. F. Grady, Jr, 'Employee Participation in a Quality Circle Program: Impact on Quality of Work Life, Productivity, and Absenteeism', *Journal of Applied Psychology*, February 1986, pp. 61–69; T. R. Miller, 'The Quality Circle Phenomenon: A Review and Appraisal', *SAM Advanced Management Journal*, Winter 1989, pp. 4–7; and E. E. Adams, Jr, 'Quality Circle Performance', *Journal of Management*, March 1991, pp. 25–39.

9. See, for example, S. G. Cohen, G. E. Ledford, Jr and G. M. Spreitzer, 'A Predictive Model of Self-Managing Work Team Effectiveness', *Human Relations*, May 1996, pp. 643–76; D. E. Yeats and C. Hyten, *High-Performing Self-Managed Work Teams: A Comparison of Theory to*

Practice (Thousand Oaks, CA: Sage, 1998); and C. E. Nicholls, H. W. Lane and M. Brehm Brechu, 'Taking Self-Managed Teams to Mexico', *Academy of Management Executive*, August 1999, pp. 15–27.

10. W. Royal, 'Team-Centered Success', *Industry Week*, 18 October 1999, pp. 56–58.

11. 'Teams', *Training*, October 1996, p. 69; and Joinson, 'Teams at Work', p. 30.

12. R. Zemke, 'Rethinking the Rush to Team Up', *Training*, November 1993, pp. 55–61.

13. See, for example, T. D. Wall, N. J. Kemp, P. R. Jackson and C. W. Clegg, 'Outcomes of Autonomous Workgroups: A Long-Term Field Experiment', *Academy of Management Journal*, June 1986, pp. 280–304; and J. L. Cordery, W. S. Mueller and L. M. Smith, 'Attitudinal and Behavioral Effects of Autonomous Group Working: A Longitudinal Field Study', *Academy of Management Journal*, June 1991, pp. 464–76.

14. J. R. Barker, 'Tightening the Iron Cage: Concertive Control in Self-Managing Teams', *Administrative Science Quarterly*, September 1993, pp. 408–37; S. G. Cohen and G. E. Ledford, Jr, 'The Effectiveness of Self-Managing Teams: A Field Experiment', *Human Relations*, January 1994, pp. 13–43; and C. Smith and D. Comer, 'Self-Organization in Small Groups: A Study of Group Effectiveness Within Non-Equilibrium Conditions', *Human Relations*, May 1994, pp. 553–81.

15. R. Maynard, 'A Client-Centered Firm's Lessons in Teamwork', *Nation's Business*, March 1997, p. 32.

16. M. Brunelli, 'How Harley-Davidson Uses Cross-Functional Teams', *Purchasing Online*, 4 November 1999; <www.manufacturing.net/magazine/purchasing/archives/1999>.

17. S. Kirsner, 'Faster Company', *Fast Company*, May 2000, pp. 162–72.

18. See, for example, A. M. Townsend, S. M. DeMarie and A. R. Hendrickson, 'Virtual Teams: Technology and the Workplace of the Future', *Academy of Management Executive*, August 1998, pp. 17–29; D. Duarte and N. T. Snyder, *Mastering Virtual Teams: Strategies, Tools, and Techniques* (San Francisco: Jossey-Bass, 1999); M. L. Maznevski and K. M. Chudoba, 'Bridging Space over Time: Global Virtual Team Dynamics and Effectiveness', *Organization Science*, September–October 2000, pp. 473–92; and J. Katzenbach and D. Smith, 'Virtual Teaming', *Forbes*, 21 May 2001, pp. 48–51.

19. K. Kiser, 'Working on World Time', *Training*, March 1999, p. 30.

20. Ibid.

21. <www.alfresco.com.au/services/virtual_teams_collaboration.html>.

22. A. B. Drexler and R. Forrester, 'Teamwork—Not Necessarily the Answer', *HRMagazine*, January 1998, pp. 55–58.

23. See, for example, D. L. Gladstein, 'Groups in Context: A Model of Task Group Effectiveness', *Administrative Science Quarterly*, December 1984, pp. 499–517; J. R. Hackman, 'The Design of Work Teams', in J. W. Lorsch (ed.), *Handbook of Organizational Behavior* (Englewood Cliffs, NJ: Prentice Hall, 1987), pp. 315–42; M. A. Campion, G. J. Medsker and C. A. Higgs, 'Relations between Work Group Characteristics and Effectiveness: Implications for Designing Effective Work Groups', *Personnel Psychology*, Winter 1993, pp. 823–50; and R. A. Guzzo and M. W. Dickson, 'Teams in Organizations: Recent Research on Performance and Effectiveness', in J. T. Spence, J. M. Darley and D. J. Foss, *Annual Review of Psychology*, vol. 47, pp. 307–38.

24. D. E. Hyatt and T. M. Ruddy, 'An Examination of the Relationship between Work Group Characteristics and Performance: Once More into the Breech', *Personnel Psychology*, Autumn 1997, p. 555.

25. This model is based on M. A. Campion, E. M. Papper and G. J. Medsker, 'Relations between Work Team Characteristics and Effectiveness: A Replication and Extension', *Personnel Psychology*, Summer 1996, pp. 429–52; Hyatt and Ruddy, 'An Examination of the Relationship between Work Group Characteristics and Performance', pp. 553–85; S. G. Cohen and D. E. Bailey, 'What Makes Teams Work: Group Effectiveness Research from the Shop Floor to the Executive Suite', *Journal of Management*, vol. 23, no. 3, 1997, pp. 239–90; G. A. Neuman and J. Wright, 'Team Effectiveness: Beyond Skills and Cognitive Ability', *Journal of Applied Psychology*, June 1999, pp. 376–89; L. Thompson, *Making the Team* (Upper Saddle River, NJ: Prentice Hall, 2000), pp. 18–33.

26. See M. Mattson, T. V. Mumford and G. S. Sintay, 'Taking Teams to Task: A Normative Model for Designing or Recalibrating Work Teams', paper presented at the National Academy of Management Conference; Chicago, August 1999; and G. L. Stewart and M. R. Barrick, 'Team Structure and Performance: Assessing the Mediating Role of Intrateam Process and the Moderating Role of Task Type', *Academy of Management Journal*, April 2000, pp. 135–48.

27. R. Wageman, 'Critical Success Factors for Creating Superb Self-Managing Teams', *Organizational Dynamics*, Summer 1997, p. 55.

28. Campion, Papper and Medsker, 'Relations between Work Team Characteristics and Effectiveness', p. 430; and B. L. Kirkman and B. Rosen, 'Powering Up Teams', *Organizational Dynamics*, Winter 2000, pp. 48–66.

29. Campion, Papper and Medsker, 'Relations between Work Team Characteristics and Effectiveness', p. 430.

30. For a more detailed breakdown on team skills, see M. J. Stevens and M. A. Campion, 'The Knowledge, Skill, and Ability Requirements for Teamwork: Implications for Human Resource Management', *Journal of Management*, Summer 1994, pp. 503–30.

31. M. R. Barrick, G. L. Stewart, M. J. Neubert and M. K. Mount, 'Relating Member Ability and Personality to Work-Team Processes and Team Effectiveness', *Journal of Applied Psychology*, June 1998, pp. 377–91; and G. A. Neuman and J. Wright, 'Team Effectiveness: Beyond Skills and Cognitive Ability', *Journal of Applied Psychology*, June 1999, pp. 376–89.

32. Barrick, Stewart, Neubert and Mount, 'Relating Member Ability and Personality to Work-Team Processes and Team Effectiveness'.

33. Ibid, p. 388.

34. Ibid.

35. C. Margerison and D. McCann, *Team Management: Practical New Approaches* (London: Mercury Books, 1990).

36. J. Katzenbach, 'What Makes Teams Work?', *Fast Company*, November 2000, p. 110.

37. The evidence in this section is described in Thompson, *Making the Team*, pp. 65–67.

38. E. Sundstrom, K. P. Meuse and D. Futrell, 'Work Teams: Applications and Effectiveness', *American Psychologist*, February 1990, pp. 120–33.

39. Hyatt and Ruddy, 'An Examination of the Relationship between Work Group Characteristics and Performance'; and J. D. Shaw, M. K. Duffy and E. M. Stark, 'Interdependence and Preference for Group Work: Main and Congruence Effects on the Satisfaction and Performance of Group Members', *Journal of Management*, vol. 26, no. 2, 2000, pp. 259–79.

40. Hyatt and Ruddy, 'An Examination of the Relationship between Work Group Characteristics and Performance', p. 577. See also J. W. Bishop, K. D. Scott and S. M. Burroughs, 'Support, Commitment, and Employee Outcomes in a Team Environment', *Journal of Management*, vol. 26, no. 6, 2000, pp. 1113–32.

41. R. I. Beekun, 'Assessing the Effectiveness of Sociotechnical Interventions: Antidote or Fad?', *Human Relations*, August 1989, pp. 877–97.

42. Cohen, Ledford and Spreitzer, 'A Predictive Model of Self-Managing Work Team Effectiveness'.

43. D. Eden, 'Pygmalion without Interpersonal Contrast Effects: Whole Groups Gain from Raising Manager Expectations', *Journal of Applied Psychology*, August 1990, pp. 394–98.

44. J. M. George and K. Bettenhausen, 'Understanding Prosocial Behavior, Sales, Performance, and Turnover: A Group-Level Analysis in a Service Context', *Journal of Applied Psychology*, October 1990, pp. 698–709; and J. M. George, 'Leader Positive Mood and Group Performance: The Case of Customer Service', *Journal of Applied Social Psychology*, December 1995, pp. 778–94.

45. K. T. Dirks, 'Trust in Leadership and Team Performance: Evidence from NCAA Basketball', *Journal of Applied Psychology*, December 2000, pp. 1004–12; and M. Williams, 'In Whom We Trust: Group Membership as an Affective Context for Trust Development', *Academy of Management Review*, July 2001, pp. 377–96.

46. See S. T. Johnson, 'Work Teams: What's Ahead in Work Design and Rewards Management', *Compensation & Benefits Review*, March–April 1993, pp. 35–41; and L. N. McClurg, 'Team Rewards: How Far Have We Come?', *Human Resource Management*, Spring 2001, pp. 73–86.

47. K. Hess, *Creating the High-Performance Team* (New York: Wiley, 1987); Katzenbach and Smith, *The Wisdom of Teams*, pp. 43–64; and K. D. Scott and A. Townsend, 'Teams: Why Some Succeed and Others Fail', *HRMagazine*, August 1994, pp. 62–67.

48. E. Weldon and L. R. Weingart, 'Group Goals and Group Performance', *British Journal of Social Psychology*, Spring 1993, pp. 307–34.

49. R. A. Guzzo, P. R. Yost, R. J. Campbell and G. P. Shea, 'Potency in Groups: Articulating a Construct', *British Journal of Social Psychology*, March 1993, pp. 87–106; S. J. Zaccaro, V. Blair, C. Peterson and M. Zazanis, 'Collective Efficacy', in J. E. Maddux (ed.), *Self-Efficacy, Adaptation and Adjustment: Theory, Research and Application* (New York: Plenum, 1995), pp. 308–30; and D. L. Feltz and C. D. Lirgg, 'Perceived Team and Player Efficacy in Hockey', *Journal of Applied Psychology*, August 1998, pp. 557–64.

50. K. A. Jehn, 'A Qualitative Analysis of Conflict Types and Dimensions in Organizational Groups', *Administrative Science Quarterly*, September 1997, pp. 530–57.

51. Hess, *Creating the High-Performance Team*.

52. See, for example, B. L. Kirkman and D. L. Shapiro, 'The Impact of Cultural Values on Employee Resistance to Teams: Toward a Model of Globalized Self-Managing Work Team Effectiveness', *Academy of Management Review*, July 1997, pp. 730–57; and B. L. Kirkman, C. B. Gibson and D. L. Shapiro, ' "Exporting" Teams: Enhancing the Implementation and Effectiveness of Work Teams in Global Affiliates', *Organizational Dynamics*, vol. 30, no. 1, 2001, pp. 12–29.

53. D. Harrington-Mackin, *The Team Building Tool Kit* (New York: AMACOM, 1994), p. 53.

54. R. Lessem and Y. Baruch, 'Testing the SMT and Belbin Inventories on Top Team Management', *The Leadership and Organization Development Journal*, vol. 21, no. 2, 2000, pp. 75–83.

55. A. Amason and H. Sapienza, 'The Effects of Top Management Team Size and Interaction Norms on Cognitive and Affective Conflict', *Journal of Management*, July–August 1997, vol. 23, no. 4, pp. 495–517.

56. C. Schwenk, 'Management Tenure and Explanations for Success and Failure', *OMEGA International Journal of Management Science*, vol. 2, no. 4, pp. 449–56.

57. M. Wiersema and K. Bantel, 'Top Management Team Demography and Corporate Strategic Change', *Academy of Management Journal*, vol. 35, no. 1, pp. 91–21.

58. Based on A. D. Hambrick, 'Fragmentation and the Other Problems CEOs have with their Top Management Teams', *California Management Review*, Spring 1995, pp. 110–27; and B. A. Kakabadse, J. McMahon and A. Myers, 'Correlates of Internal and External Leadership of Top Management Teams', *Leadership & Organization Development Journal*, vol. 16, no. 7, 1995, pp. 10–17.

59. T. D. Schellhardt, 'To Be a Star among Equals, Be a Team Player', *Wall Street Journal*, 20 April 1994, p. B1.

60. Ibid.

61. See, for example, J. Prieto, 'The Team Perspective in Selection and Assessment', in H. Schuler, J. L. Farr and M. Smith (eds), *Personnel Selection and Assessment: Industrial and Organizational Perspectives* (Hillsdale, NJ: Erlbaum, 1994); R. Klimoski and R. G. Jones, 'Staffing for Effective Group Decision Making: Key Issues in Matching People and Teams', in R. A. Guzzo and E. Salas (eds), *Team Effectiveness and Decision Making in Organizations* (San Francisco: Jossey-Bass, 1995), pp. 307–26; and C. Hymowitz, 'How to Avoid Hiring the Prima Donnas Who Hate Teamwork', *Wall Street Journal*, 15 February 2000, p. B1.

62. Schellhardt, 'To Be a Star among Equals, Be a Team Player'.

63. 'Teaming Up for Success', *Training*, January 1994, p. S41.

64. J. S. DeMatteo, L. T. Eby and E. Sundstrom, 'Team-Based Rewards: Current Empirical Evidence and Directions for Future Research', in B. M. Staw and L. L. Cummings (eds), *Research in Organizational Behavior*, vol. 20 (Greenwich, CT: JAI Press, 1998), pp. 141–83.

66. B. Geber, 'The Bugaboo of Team Pay', *Training*, August 1995, pp. 27, 34.

66. Kinlaw, *Developing Superior Work Teams*, p. 43.

67. B. Krone, 'Total Quality Management: An American Odyssey', *The Bureaucrat*, Fall 1990, p. 37.

68. *Profiles in Quality: Blueprints for Action from 50 Leading Companies* (Boston: Allyn & Bacon, 1991), pp. 71–72, 76–77.

69. See the review of the literature in S. E. Jackson, V. K. Stone and E. B. Alvarez, 'Socialization Amidst Diversity: The Impact of Demographics on Work Team Oldtimers and Newcomers', in L. L. Cummings and B. M. Staw (eds), *Research in Organizational Behavior*, vol. 15 (Greenwich, CT: JAI Press, 1993), p. 64.

70. R. M. Stogdill, 'Group Productivity, Drive, and Cohesiveness', *Organizational Behavior and Human Performance*, February 1972, pp. 36–43. See also M. Mayo, J. C. Pastor and J. R. Meindl, 'The Effects of Group Heterogeneity on the Self-Perceived Efficacy of Group Leaders', *Leadership Quarterly*, Summer 1996, pp. 265–84.

71. J. E. McGrath, *Groups: Interaction and Performance* (Englewood Cliffs, NJ: Prentice Hall, 1984).

72. This idea is proposed in Jackson, Stone and Alvarez, 'Socialization Amidst Diversity', p. 68.

73. This section is based on M. Kaeter, 'Repotting Mature Work Teams', *Training*, April 1994 (Supplement), pp. 4–6.

PHOTO CREDITS

279 Image reproduced with permission of Liza Mattiazz.

Communication

10

CHAPTER OUTLINE

Functions of communication
The communication process
Direction of communication
Interpersonal communication
Organisational communication
Choice of communication channel
Barriers to effective communication
Current issues in communication

LEARNING OBJECTIVES

After studying this chapter, you should be able to:
1. Describe the communication process
2. Contrast the advantages and disadvantages of oral versus written communication
3. Compare the effectiveness of the chain, wheel and all-channel networks
4. Identify the factors affecting the use of the grapevine
5. Discuss how computer-aided technology is changing organisational communication
6. Explain the importance of channel richness to improving communication effectiveness
7. Identify common barriers to effective communication
8. Contrast the meaning of talk for men versus women
9. Describe the potential problems in cross-cultural communication

*I didn't say that I didn't say it. I said that I didn't say that I said it.
I want to make that very clear.*
G. Romney

Communication skills are vital to the relationship between police officers and the community.

Communication is an important facet of managing any organisation, and this is particularly apparent for various government agencies such as ambulance, police and fire services. Such organisations generally have communication centres for handling critical emergency calls and directing operational responses to these calls. For example, the Townsville Police Communications Centre is Queensland's busiest police communication centre outside of Brisbane, handling thousands of emergency phone calls every week. It is the control point for all radio and telephone communications for the Townsville police region, which includes Collinsville, Palm Island, Pentland, Ingham, the Burdekin and Townsville city.

Such communication centres are vital to serving local communities. There are many examples that demonstrate the importance of effective communication in dealing with emergency situations.

In a big city such as Kuala Lumpur, the emergency services communications centre has to deal with a much larger population than Townsville and hence has to deal with more complexities, such as problems of access to telephones, mapping, house numbering and signage when responding to calls. It is reported that in approximately 20 per cent of cases of emergency calls being made in Kuala Lumpur, the ambulance is unable to locate the patient.[1] Of course, communication errors in emergency service call centres can have embarrassing results as well.

A New Zealand woman was angry and embarrassed after a communications mistake led to the armed offenders squad storming her house in Dunedin. This followed a phone call received by St John Ambulance where the caller referred to gun wounds and asked if police would need to be called. Unfortunately, two calls were made to the ambulance centre within five minutes of each other and the wrong message went to the police. Consequently, the woman's street was cordoned off and her family were hauled out of the house and made to sit in a police car. Her husband had to put his hands on his head while guns were pointed at him. Apparently a guest at the woman's home accidentally dialled the ambulance centre when trying to call a taxi.[2]

The handling of emergency calls is critical to the performance of the various police and emergency service agencies. Effective communication is central to these operations, as they are to all organisations. But, for some organisations, communication effectiveness can be a matter of life or death. In this chapter, we will show (obviously not in as dramatic a fashion) that good communication is essential to any group's or organisation's effectiveness.

Research indicates that poor communication is probably the most frequently cited source of interpersonal conflict.[3] Because individuals spend nearly 70 per cent of their waking hours communicating—writing, reading, speaking, listening—it seems reasonable to conclude that one of the most inhibiting forces to successful group performance is a lack of effective communication.

No group can exist without communication: the transference of meaning among its members. It is only through transmitting meaning from one person to another that information and ideas can be conveyed. Communication, however, is more than merely imparting meaning. It must also be understood. In a group in which one member speaks only German and the others don't know German, the individual speaking German won't be fully understood. Therefore, **communication** must include both the *transference and the understanding of meaning.*

communication
The transference and understanding of meaning.

An idea, no matter how great, is useless until it is transmitted and understood by others. Perfect communication, if there were such a thing, would exist when a thought or an idea was transmitted so that the mental picture perceived by the receiver was exactly the same as that envisioned by the sender. Although elementary in theory, perfect communication is never achieved in practice, for reasons we shall expand on later in the chapter.

Before making too many generalisations concerning communication and problems in communicating effectively, we need to review briefly the functions that communication performs and describe the communication process.

Functions of Communication

Communication serves four main functions within a group or organisation: control, motivation, emotional expression and information.[4]

Communication acts to *control* member behaviour in several ways. Organisations have authority hierarchies and formal guidelines that employees are required to follow. When employees, for example, are required to first communicate any job-related grievance to their immediate boss, to follow their job description, or to comply with company policies, communication is performing a control function. But informal communication also controls behaviour. When work groups tease or harass a member who produces too much (and makes the rest of the group look bad), they are informally communicating with, and controlling, the member's behaviour.

Communication fosters *motivation* by clarifying to employees what is to be done, how well they are doing, and what can be done to improve performance if it is below acceptable standards. We saw this operating in our review of goal-setting and reinforcement theories in a previous chapter. The formation of specific goals, feedback on progress towards the goals, and reinforcement of desired behaviour all stimulate motivation and require communication.

For many employees, their work group is a primary source for social interaction. The communication that takes place within the group is a fundamental mechanism by which members show their frustrations and feelings of satisfaction. Communication, therefore, provides a release for the *emotional expression* of feelings and for fulfilment of social needs.

The final function that communication performs relates to its role in facilitating decision making. It provides the *information* that individuals and groups need to make decisions by transmitting the data to identify and evaluate alternative choices.

No one of these four functions should be seen as being more important than the others. For groups to perform effectively, they need to maintain some form of control over members, stimulate members to perform, provide a means for emotional expression and make decision choices. You can assume that almost every communication interaction that takes place in a group or organisation performs one or more of these four functions.

The Communication Process

Before communication can take place, a purpose, expressed as a message to be conveyed, is needed. It passes between a source (the sender) and a receiver. The message is encoded (converted to a symbolic form) and passed by way of some medium (channel) to the receiver, who retranslates (decodes) the message initiated by the sender. The result is a transference of meaning from one person to another.[5]

Figure 10.1 depicts this **communication process**. This model is made up of seven parts: (1) the communication source, (2) encoding, (3) the message, (4) the channel, (5) decoding, (6) the receiver, and (7) feedback.

The *source* initiates a message by encoding a thought. The *message* is the actual physical product from the source *encoding*. When we speak, the speech is the message. When we write, the writing is the message. When we gesture, the movements of our arms and the expressions on our faces are the message. The *channel* is the medium through which the message travels. It is selected by the source, who must determine whether to use a formal or informal channel. Formal channels are established by the organisation and transmit messages that are related to the professional activities of members. They traditionally follow the authority chain within the organisation. Other forms of messages, such as personal or social, follow the informal channels in the organisation. The *receiver* is the object to whom the message is directed. But before the message can be received, the symbols in it must be translated into a form that can be understood by the receiver. This step is the *decoding* of the message. The final link in the communication process is a feedback loop. *Feedback* is the check on how successful we have been in transferring our messages as originally intended. It determines whether understanding has been achieved.

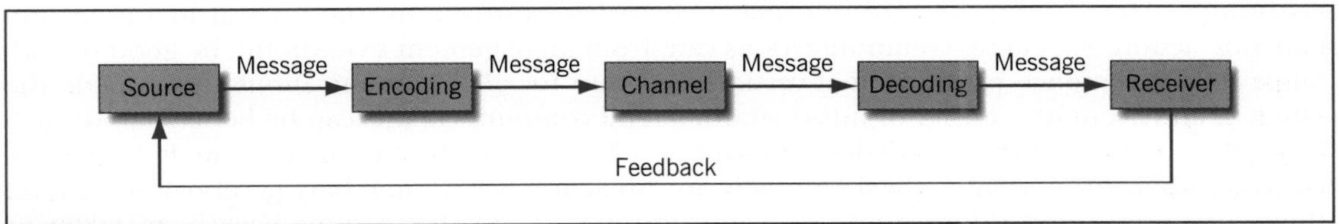

LEARNING OBJECTIVE 1
Describe the communication process

communication process
The steps between a source and a receiver that result in the transference and understanding of meaning.

FIGURE 10.1 **The communication process model**

Direction of Communication

Communication can flow vertically or laterally. The vertical dimension can be further divided into downward and upward directions.[6]

DOWNWARD

Communication that flows from one level of a group or organisation to a lower level is a downward communication. When we think of managers communicating with employees, the downward pattern is the one we are usually thinking of. It is used by group leaders and managers to assign goals, provide job instructions, inform employees of policies and procedures, point out problems that need attention and to offer feedback about performance. But downward communication doesn't have to be oral or face-to-face contact. When management sends letters to employees' homes to advise them of the organisation's new sick leave policy, it is using downward communication. So is an e-mail from a team leader to the members of her team, reminding them of an upcoming deadline.

UPWARD

Upward communication flows to a higher level in the group or organisation. It is used to provide feedback to higher-ups, inform them of progress towards goals and to relay current problems. Upward communication keeps managers aware of how employees feel about their jobs, co-workers and the organisation in general. Managers also rely on upward communication for ideas on how things can be improved.

Some organisational examples of upward communication are performance reports prepared by lower management for review by middle and top management, suggestion boxes, employee attitude surveys, grievance procedures, superior–subordinate discussions, and informal 'gripe' sessions in which employees have the opportunity to identify and discuss problems with their boss or representatives of higher management. For example, the Marriott Hotels group prides itself on its balanced scorecard approach to communicating performance results to all employees. Each of its hotels collects, and regularly displays to employees, information on occupancy rates and customer satisfaction. In addition, every employee is surveyed annually on all aspects of their hotel. This information is used as part of the performance reviews of the hotel managers.

LATERAL

When communication takes place among members of the same work group, among members of work groups at the same level, among managers at the same level, or among any horizontally equivalent personnel, we describe it as lateral communications.

Why would there be a need for horizontal communications if a group or organisation's vertical communications are effective? The answer is that horizontal communications are often necessary to save time and facilitate coordination. In some cases, these lateral relationships are formally sanctioned. More often, they are informally created to short-circuit the vertical hierarchy and expedite action. So, lateral communications can, from management's viewpoint, be good or bad. Since strict adherence to the formal vertical structure for all communications can impede the efficient and accurate transfer of information, lateral communications can be beneficial. In such cases, they occur with the knowledge and support of superiors. But they can create dysfunctional conflicts when the formal vertical channels are breached, when members go above or around their superiors to get things done, or when bosses find out that actions have been taken or decisions made without their knowledge.

LEARNING OBJECTIVE

2

Contrast the advantages and disadvantages of oral versus written communication

Interpersonal Communication

How do group members transfer meaning between and among each other? There are three basic methods. People essentially rely on oral, written and non-verbal communication.

ORAL COMMUNICATION

The chief means of conveying messages is oral communication. Speeches, formal one-on-one and group discussions, and the informal rumour mill or grapevine are popular forms of oral communication.

The advantages of oral communication are speed and feedback. A verbal message can be conveyed and a response received in a minimal amount of time. If the receiver is unsure of the message, rapid feedback allows for early detection by the sender and, hence, allows for early correction.

The main disadvantage of oral communication surfaces in organisations or whenever the message has to be passed through a number of people. The more people a message must pass through, the greater the potential distortion. If you ever played the game 'Telephone' at a party, you know the problem. Each person interprets the message in their own way. The message's content, when it reaches its destination, is often very different from that of the original. In an organisation where decisions and other communiqués are verbally passed up and down the authority hierarchy, there are considerable opportunities for messages to become distorted.

WRITTEN COMMUNICATION

Written communications include memos, letters, electronic mail, fax transmissions, organisational periodicals, notices placed on bulletin boards, or any other device that is transmitted via written words or symbols.

Why would a sender choose to use written communications? They are tangible and verifiable. Typically, both the sender and receiver have a record of the communication. The message can be stored for an indefinite period. If there are questions concerning the content of the message, it is physically available for later reference. This feature is particularly important for complex and lengthy communications. The marketing plan for a new product, for example, is likely to contain a number of tasks spread out over several months. By putting it in writing, those who have to initiate the plan can readily refer to it over the life of the plan. A final benefit of written communication comes from the process itself. You are usually more careful with the written word than the oral word. You are forced to think more thoroughly about what you want to convey in a written message than in a spoken one. Thus, written communications are more likely to be well thought out, logical and clear.

Of course, written messages have their drawbacks. They are time consuming. You could convey far more information to a university lecturer in a one-hour oral exam than in a one-hour written exam. In fact, you could probably say the same thing in ten to 15 minutes that it would take you an hour to write. So, although writing may be more precise, it also consumes a great deal of time. The other main disadvantage is feedback, or lack of it. Oral communication allows the receiver to respond rapidly to what he thinks he hears. Written communication, however, doesn't have a built-in feedback mechanism. The result is that the mailing of a memo is no assurance that it has been received, and, if received, there is no guarantee the recipient will interpret it as the sender intended. The latter point is also relevant in oral communiqués, except it is easy in such cases merely to ask the receiver to summarise what you have said. An accurate summary presents feedback evidence that the message has been received and understood.

NON-VERBAL COMMUNICATION

Every time we verbally give a message to someone, we also impart a non-verbal message. In some instances, the non-verbal component may stand alone. For example, in a singles bar, a glance, a stare, a smile, a frown, and a provocative body movement all convey meaning. As such, no discussion of communication would be complete without consideration of *non-verbal communication*—which includes body movements, the intonations or emphasis we give to words, facial expressions, and the physical distance between the sender and receiver.

It can be argued that every *body movement* has a meaning and no movement is accidental. For example, through body language we say: 'Help me, I'm lonely'; 'Take me, I'm available'; 'Leave me alone, I'm depressed.' And rarely do we send our messages consciously. We act out our state of being with non-verbal body language. We lift one eyebrow for disbelief. We rub our noses for puzzlement. We clasp our arms to isolate ourselves or to protect ourselves. We shrug our shoulders for indifference, wink one eye for intimacy, tap our fingers for impatience, slap our forehead for forgetfulness.[7]

The two most important messages that body language conveys are: (1) the extent to which an individual likes another and is interested in their views; and (2) the relative perceived status between a sender and a receiver.[8] For example, we are more likely to position ourselves closer to people we like and to touch them more often. Similarly, if you feel that you are higher in status than another, you are more likely to display body movements—such as crossed legs or a slouched seating position—that reflect a casual and relaxed manner.

Body language adds to, and often complicates, verbal communication. A body position or movement doesn't by itself have a precise or universal meaning, but when it is linked with spoken language, it gives fuller meaning to a sender's message.

If you read the verbatim minutes of a meeting, you wouldn't grasp the impact of what was said in the same way that you would if you had been there or saw the meeting on video. Why? There is no record of non-verbal communication, and the emphasis given to words or phrases is missing. The tone of speech (for example, friendly, angry/aggressive, and so on) used by participants in a meeting is also an important non-verbal cue to aid understanding and interpretation of the message by the receiver. Table 10.1 illustrates how *intonations* can change the meaning of a message.

Facial expressions also convey meaning. A snarling face says something different from a smile. Facial expressions, along with intonations, can show arrogance, aggressiveness, fear, shyness, and other characteristics that would never be communicated if you read a transcript of what had been said.

The way individuals space themselves in terms of *physical distance* also has meaning. What is considered proper spacing is largely dependent on cultural norms. For example, what is considered a businesslike distance in some European countries would be viewed as intimate in many parts of Australasia. If someone stands closer to you than is considered appropriate, it may indicate aggressiveness or sexual interest; if further away than usual, it may mean disinterest or displeasure with what is being said.

It is important for the receiver to be alert to these non-verbal aspects of communication. You should look for non-verbal cues, as well as listen to the literal meaning of a sender's words. You should particularly be aware of contradictions between the messages. Your boss may say she is free to talk to you about a pressing budget problem, but you may see non-verbal signals suggesting that this isn't the time to discuss the subject. Regardless of what is being said, an individual who frequently glances at her wristwatch is giving the message that she would prefer to terminate the conversation. We misinform others when we express one message verbally, such as trust, but non-verbally communicate a contradictory message that reads, 'I don't have confidence in you.'

TABLE 10.1   Intonations: It's the way you say it

Change your tone and you change your meaning

Placement of the emphasis	What it means
Why don't I take **you** to dinner tonight?	I was going to take someone else.
Why don't **I** take you to dinner tonight?	Instead of the guy you were going with
Why **don't** I take you to dinner tonight?	I'm trying to find a reason why I shouldn't take you.
Why don't I take you to dinner tonight?	Do you have a problem with me?
Why don't I **take** you to dinner tonight?	Instead of going on your own.
Why don't I take you to **dinner** tonight?	Instead of lunch tomorrow.
Why don't I take you to dinner **tonight**?	Not tomorrow night.

Source: Based on M. Kiely, 'When "No" Means "Yes"', *Marketing*, October 1993, pp. 7–9. Reproduced in A. Huczynski and D. Buchanan, *Organizational Behavior*, 4th ed. (Essex, England: Pearson Education, 2001), p. 194.

Myth *or* Science?

'It's not what you *say*, it's what you *do*'

This statement is mostly true. Actions DO speak louder than words.[9] When faced with inconsistencies between words and actions, people tend to give greater credence to actions. It's behaviour that counts. The implication of this is that managers and leaders are role models. Employees will imitate their behaviours and attitudes. They will, for example, watch what their boss does and then imitate or adapt what they do. This conclusion doesn't mean that words fall on deaf ears. Words can influence others.[10] But, when words and actions diverge, people focus most on what they see in terms of behaviour.

There is an obvious exception to the previous conclusion. An increasing number of leaders (and their associates) have developed the skill of shaping words and putting the proper 'spin' on situations so that others focus on the leader's words rather than the behaviour. Successful politicians seem particularly adept at this skill. Why people believe these spins when faced with conflicting behavioural evidence isn't clear. Do we want to believe that our leaders wouldn't lie to us? Do we want to believe what politicians say, especially when we hold them in high regard? Do we give high-status people, for whom we have previously given our vote, the benefit of the doubt when confronted with their negative behaviour? Additional research is necessary to clarify these questions.

Organisational Communication

In this section, we move from interpersonal communication to organisational communication. Our focus here will be on formal networks, the grapevine, and computer-aided mechanisms used by organisations to facilitate communication.

LEARNING OBJECTIVE

3

Compare the effectiveness of the chain, wheel and all-channel networks

FORMAL SMALL-GROUP NETWORKS

Formal organisational networks can be very complicated. They can, for example, include hundreds of people and six or more hierarchical levels. To simplify our discussion, we have condensed these networks into three common small groups of five people each (see Figure 10.2).

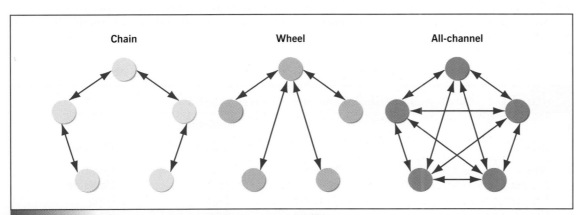

FIGURE 10.2 **Three common small-group networks**

These three networks are the chain, wheel and all-channel. Although these three networks have been extremely simplified, they do allow us to describe the unique qualities of each.

The *chain* rigidly follows the formal chain of command. This network approximates the communication channels you might find in a rigid three-level organisation. The *wheel* relies on a central figure to act as the conduit for the entire group's communication. It simulates the communication network you would find on a team with a strong leader. The *all-channel* network permits all group members to actively communicate with each other. The all-channel network is most often characterised in practice by self-managed teams, in which all group members are free to contribute and no one person takes on a leadership role.

As Table 10.2 demonstrates, the effectiveness of each network depends on the dependent variable you are concerned about. For example, the structure of the wheel facilitates the emergence of a leader, the all-channel network is best if you are concerned with having high member satisfaction, and the chain is best if accuracy is most important. Table 10.2 leads us to the conclusion that no single network will be best for all occasions.

THE GRAPEVINE

LEARNING OBJECTIVE 4

Identify the factors affecting the use of the grapevine

grapevine
The organisation's informal communication network.

The formal system isn't the only communication network in a group or organisation. There is also an informal one, which is called the **grapevine**.[11] And although the grapevine may be informal, this doesn't mean it's not an important source of information. For example, a survey found that 75 per cent of employees hear about matters first through rumours on the grapevine.[12]

The grapevine has three main characteristics.[13] First, it isn't controlled by management. Second, it is perceived by most employees as being more believable and reliable than formal communiqués issued by top management. And third, it is largely used to serve the self-interests of the people within it.

One of the most famous studies of the grapevine investigated the communication pattern among 67 managerial personnel in a small manufacturing firm.[14] The basic approach used was to learn from each communication recipient how they first received a given piece of information and then trace it back to its source. It was found that, while the grapevine was an important source of information, only 10 per cent of the executives acted as liaison individuals—that is, passed the information on to more than one other person. For example, when one executive decided to resign to enter the insurance business, 81 per cent of the executives knew about it, but only 11 per cent transmitted this information to others.

Two other conclusions from this study are also worth noting. Information on events of general interest tended to flow between the main functional groups (production, sales) rather than within them. Also, no evidence surfaced to suggest that any one group consistently acted as liaisons; rather, different types of information passed through different liaison persons.

An attempt to replicate this study among employees in a small state government office also found that only 10 per cent act as liaison individuals.[15] This finding is interesting, because the

TABLE 10.2	Small-group networks and effectiveness criteria		
	Networks		
Criteria	Chain	Wheel	All-channel
Speed	Moderate	Fast	Fast
Accuracy	High	High	Moderate
Emergence of a leader	Moderate	High	None
Member satisfaction	Moderate	Low	High

The grapevine is so pervasive as a means of communication in organisations that websites to confirm or deny popular rumours now exist. Websites about urban legends are becoming popular. An urban legend is usually a captivating story that many people have chosen to believe despite the lack of supporting evidence to substantiate it.

replication contained a wider spectrum of employees, including operative as well as managerial personnel. But the flow of information in the government office took place within, rather than between, functional groups. It was proposed that this discrepancy might be due to comparing an executive-only sample against one that also included operative workers. Managers, for example, might feel greater pressure to stay informed and thus cultivate others outside their immediate functional group. Also, in contrast to the findings of the original study, the replication found that a consistent group of individuals acted as liaisons by transmitting information in the government office.

Is the information that flows along the grapevine accurate? The evidence indicates that about 75 per cent of what is carried is accurate.[16] But what conditions foster an active grapevine? What gets the rumour mill rolling?

It is frequently assumed that rumours start because they make titillating gossip. This is rarely the case. Rumours emerge as a response to situations that are *important* to us, when there is *ambiguity* and under conditions that arouse *anxiety*.[17] The fact that work situations frequently contain these three elements explains why rumours flourish in organisations. The secrecy and competition that typically prevail in large organisations—around issues such as the appointment of new bosses, the relocation of offices, downsizing decisions, and the realignment of work assignments—create conditions that encourage and sustain rumours on the grapevine. A rumour will persist either until the wants and expectations creating the uncertainty underlying the rumour are fulfilled or until the anxiety is reduced.

What can we conclude from the preceding discussion? Certainly, the grapevine is an important part of any group or organisation's communication network and is well worth understanding.[18] It identifies for managers the confusing issues that employees consider important and that create anxiety. It acts, therefore, as both a filter and a feedback mechanism, picking up the issues that employees consider relevant. For employees, the grapevine is particularly valuable for translating formal communications into their group's own jargon. Maybe more important, again from a managerial perspective, it seems possible to analyse grapevine information and to predict its flow, given that only a small set of individuals (approximately 10 per cent) actively pass on information to more than one other person. By assessing which liaison individuals will consider a given piece of information to be relevant, we can improve our ability to explain and predict the pattern of the grapevine.

Can management entirely eliminate rumours? No. What management should do, however, is minimise the negative consequences of rumours by limiting their range and impact. Table 10.3 offers a few suggestions for minimising those negative consequences.

COMPUTER-AIDED COMMUNICATION

Communication in today's organisations is enhanced and enriched by computer-aided technologies. These include electronic mail, intranet and extranet links, and videoconferencing.

LEARNING OBJECTIVE

5

Discuss how computer-aided technology is changing organisational communication

TABLE 10.3	Suggestions for reducing the negative consequences of rumours

1. Announce timetables for making important decisions.
2. Explain decisions and behaviours that may appear inconsistent or secretive.
3. Emphasise the downside, as well as the upside, of current decisions and future plans.
4. Openly discuss worst-case possibilities—it is almost never as anxiety-provoking as the unspoken fantasy.

Source: Adapted from L. Hirschhorn, 'Managing Rumors', in L. Hirschhorn (ed.), *Cutting Back* (San Francisco: Jossey-Bass, 1983), pp. 54–56. With permission of Larry Hirschhorn, Principal, Center for Applied Research.

Electronic mail, for example, has dramatically reduced the number of memos, letters and phone calls that employees historically used to communicate among themselves and with suppliers, customers or other outside stakeholders.

Computer-aided communication has implications for all sorts of communities. A recent survey revealed that the Internet was proving important for breaking down communication barriers that geographic isolation often created. The average individual in rural Queensland accessed the Internet 56 times during a three-month period in 2002, compared with 42 times for capital city dwellers, and was also logged on for longer, spending an average of 29 hours on the Internet compared to the metropolitan average of 24 hours. These figures indicate that rural communities are able to overcome the communication barriers often associated with living in the bush.[19]

E-mail

Electronic mail (or e-mail) uses the Internet to transmit and receive computer-generated text and documents. Its growth has been spectacular. Most white-collar employees now regularly use e-mail, and organisations are recognising the value of e-mail for all workers. Ford Motor Co., for example, recently made a computer, modem, printer and e-mail account available for US$5 a month to all of its more than 300,000 employees worldwide.[20]

As a communication tool, e-mail has a long list of benefits. E-mail messages can be quickly written, edited and stored. They can be distributed to one person or thousands with a click of a mouse. They can be read, in their entirety, at the convenience of the recipient. And the cost of sending formal e-mail messages to employees is a fraction of what it would cost to print, duplicate and distribute a comparable letter or brochure.

E-mail, of course, isn't without its drawbacks. At the top of the list is information overload. It's not unusual for employees to get a hundred or more e-mails a day. Reading, absorbing and responding to such an inflow can literally consume an employee's entire day. In fact, recent research by Suzan Burton and Paul Nesbit of Sydney's Macquarie Graduate School of Management revealed that managers' time is being drained by increasing e-mail.[21] In essence, e-mail's ease of use has become its biggest negative. Employees are finding it increasingly difficult to distinguish important e-mails from junk mail and irrelevant messages—so much so, that the Australian government has recently launched an investigation into the growing problem of junk e-mails due to the fact that the number has increased six-fold within two years from 2000.[22] Another drawback of e-mails is that they lack emotional content. The non-verbal cues in a face-to-face message or the tone of voice from a phone call convey important information that doesn't come across in an e-mail, although efforts have been made to create emotional icons (see Table 10.4). Finally, e-mail tends to be cold and impersonal. As such, it's not the ideal means to convey information such as layoffs, factory closings, or other messages that might evoke emotional responses and require empathy or social support.

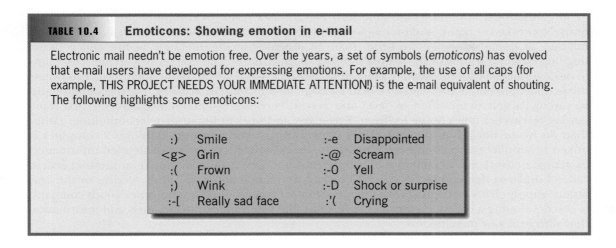

TABLE 10.4   Emoticons: Showing emotion in e-mail

Electronic mail needn't be emotion free. Over the years, a set of symbols (*emoticons*) has evolved that e-mail users have developed for expressing emotions. For example, the use of all caps (for example, THIS PROJECT NEEDS YOUR IMMEDIATE ATTENTION!) is the e-mail equivalent of shouting. The following highlights some emoticons:

:)	Smile	:-e	Disappointed
<g>	Grin	:-@	Scream
:(	Frown	:-O	Yell
;)	Wink	:-D	Shock or surprise
:-[	Really sad face	:'(	Crying

Intranet and extranet links

Intranets are private, organisation-wide information networks that look and act like a website but to which only people in an organisation have access. Intranets are rapidly becoming the preferred means for employees within companies to communicate with each other. IBM, as a case in point, recently brought together 52,000 of its employees on-line for what it called WorldJam.[23] Using the company's intranet, IBMers everywhere swapped ideas on everything from how to retain employees to how to work faster without undermining quality.

In addition, organisations are creating *extranet* links that connect internal employees with selected suppliers, customers and strategic partners. For example, an extranet allows General Motors employees to send electronic messages and documents to its steel and rubber suppliers, as well as to communicate with its dealers. Similarly, Woolworths Limited has implemented its Project Refresh strategy. The Australian retail and wholesale group has instituted a new centralised buying program. The new vendor extranet has improved the communication links with suppliers and is central to monitoring the inventory status of its products at all Woolworths stores.

Videoconferencing

Videoconferencing is an extension of intranet or extranet systems. It permits employees in an organisation to have meetings with people at different locations. Live audio and video images of members allow them to see, hear and talk with each other. Videoconferencing technology, in effect, allows employees to conduct interactive meetings without the necessity of all physically being in the same location.

In the late 1990s, videoconferencing was basically conducted from special rooms equipped with television cameras, located at company facilities. More recently, cameras and microphones are being attached to individual computers, allowing people to participate in videoconferences without leaving their desks. As the cost of this technology drops in price, videoconferencing is likely to be increasingly seen as an alternative to expensive and time-consuming travel.

Summary

Computer-aided communications are reshaping the way we communicate in organisations. Specifically, it is no longer necessary for employees to be at their work station or desk to be 'available'. Pagers, mobile phones and personal communicators allow employees to be reached when they are in a meeting, during a lunch break, while visiting a customer across town, or during a golf game on Saturday morning. The line between an employee's work and non-work life is no longer distinct. In the electronic age, all employees can theoretically be 'on call' 24 hours a day, seven days a week.

Organisational boundaries become less relevant as a result of computer-aided communications. Networked computers allow employees to jump vertical levels within the organisation, work full-time at home or someplace other than an organisationally operated facility, and conduct ongoing communications with people in other organisations. The market researcher who wants to discuss an issue with the head of marketing (who is three levels up in the hierarchy) can bypass the people in-between and send an e-mail message directly. And in so doing, the traditional status hierarchy, largely determined by level and access, becomes essentially negated. Or that same market researcher may choose to live in Byron Bay and work at home via telecommuting, rather than do his or her job in the company's Darwin office. And when an employee's computer is linked to suppliers' and customers' computers, the advantages to such an extended information exchange network are tremendous. As a case in point, Levi Strauss designed an intranet system called Eureka so that employees can get crucial information about products, services or the Levi Strauss supply chain through HTML links. Procter & Gamble, another consumer goods company, is also developing a corporate intranet to improve the communication channels and information flow with its major stakeholders.

LEARNING OBJECTIVE

6

Explain the importance of channel richness to improving communication effectiveness

Choice of Communication Channel

Neal L. Patterson, CEO at medical-software maker Cerner Corp., likes e-mail. Maybe too much so. Some time ago, upset with his staff's work ethic, he sent a seething e-mail to his firm's 400 managers.[24] Here are some of that e-mail's highlights:

> Hell will freeze over before this CEO implements ANOTHER EMPLOYEE benefit in this Culture. . . . We are getting less than 40 hours of work from a large number of our . . . City-based employees. The parking lot is sparsely used at 8 A.M.; likewise at 5 P.M. As managers—you either do not know what your EMPLOYEES are doing; or YOU do not CARE. . . . You have a problem and you will fix it or I will replace you. . . . What you are doing, as managers, with this company makes me SICK.

Patterson's e-mail additionally suggested that managers schedule meetings at 7am, 6pm and Saturday mornings; promised a staff reduction of 5 per cent and institution of a time-clock system; and stated Patterson's intention to charge unapproved absences to employees' holiday time.

Within hours of this e-mail being sent, copies of it had made its way on to a Yahoo! website. And within three days, Cerner's share price had plummeted 22 per cent. Although one can argue about whether such harsh criticism should be communicated at all, one thing is certainly clear: Patterson erred by selecting the wrong channel for his message. Such an emotional and sensitive message would likely have been better received in a face-to-face meeting.

Why do people choose one channel of communication over another—for example, a phone call instead of a face-to-face talk? Is there any general insight we might be able to provide regarding choice of communication channel? The answer to the latter question is a qualified 'yes'. A model of media richness has been developed to explain channel selection among managers.[25]

Research has found that channels differ in their capacity to convey information. Some are rich in that they have the ability to (1) handle multiple cues simultaneously, (2) facilitate rapid feedback, and (3) be very personal. Others are lean in that they score low on these three factors. As Figure 10.3 illustrates, face-to-face conversation scores highest in terms of **channel richness** because it provides for the maximum amount of information to be transmitted during a communication episode. That is, it offers multiple information cues (words, postures, facial expressions, gestures, intonations), immediate feedback (both verbal and non-verbal), and the personal touch of 'being there'. Impersonal written media such as formal reports and bulletins rate lowest in richness.

The choice of one channel over another depends on whether the message is routine or non-routine. The former types of messages tend to be straightforward and have a minimum of ambiguity. The latter are likely to be complicated and have the potential for misunderstanding.

channel richness The amount of information that can be transmitted during a communication episode.

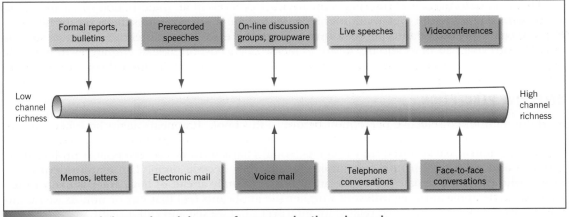

FIGURE 10.3   **Information richness of communication channels**

Sources: Based on R. H. Lengel and D. L. Daft, 'The Selection of Communication Media as an Executive Skill', *Academy of Management Executive*, August 1988, pp. 225–32; and R. L. Daft and R. H. Lengel, 'Organizational Information Requirements, Media Richness, and Structural Design', *Managerial Science*, May 1996, pp. 554–72. Reproduced from R. L. Daft and R. A. Noe, *Organizational Behavior* (Fort Worth, TX: Harcourt, 2001), p. 311.

Managers can communicate routine messages efficiently through channels that are lower in richness. However, they can communicate non-routine messages effectively only by selecting rich channels. Referring back to our opening example at Cerner Corp., it appears that Neal Patterson's problem was using a channel relatively low in richness (e-mail) to convey a message that, because of its non-routine nature and complexity, should have been conveyed using a rich communication medium.

Evidence indicates that high-performing managers tend to be more media-sensitive than low-performing managers.[26] That is, they are better able to match appropriate media richness with the ambiguity involved in the communication.

The media richness model is consistent with organisational trends and practices during the past decade. It is not just coincidence that more and more senior managers have been using meetings to facilitate communication and regularly leaving the isolated sanctuary of their executive offices to manage by walking around. These executives are relying on richer channels of communication to transmit the more ambiguous messages they need to convey. The past decade has been characterised by organisations closing facilities, imposing large layoffs, restructuring, merging, consolidating, and introducing new products and services at an accelerated pace—all non-routine messages high in ambiguity and requiring the use of channels that can convey a large amount of information. It is not surprising, therefore, to see the most effective managers expanding their use of rich channels.

Barriers to Effective Communication

A number of barriers can retard or distort effective communication. In this section, we highlight the more important of these barriers.

FILTERING

Filtering refers to a sender's purposely manipulating information so that it will be seen more favourably by the receiver. For example, when a manager tells his boss what he feels his boss wants to hear, he is filtering information.

LEARNING OBJECTIVE

7

Identify common barriers to effective communication

filtering
A sender's manipulation of information so that it will be seen more favourably by the receiver.

The main determinant of filtering is the number of levels in an organisation's structure. The more vertical levels in the organisation's hierarchy, the more opportunities there are for filtering. But you can expect some filtering to occur wherever there are status differences. Factors such as fear of conveying bad news and the desire to please one's boss often lead employees to tell their superiors what they think those superiors want to hear, thus distorting upward communications.

SELECTIVE PERCEPTION

We have mentioned selective perception before in this book. It appears again here because the receivers in the communication process selectively see and hear based on their needs, motivations, experience, background and other personal characteristics. Receivers also project their interests and expectations into communications as they decode them. The employment interviewer who expects a female job applicant to put her family ahead of her career is likely to see that in female applicants, regardless of whether the applicants feel that way or not. As we said in a previous chapter, we don't see reality; we interpret what we see and call it reality.

INFORMATION OVERLOAD

information overload
A condition in which information inflow exceeds an individual's processing capacity.

Individuals have a finite capacity for processing data. As noted in our previous discussion of e-mail, when the information we have to work with exceeds our processing capacity, the result is **information overload**. And with e-mails, phone calls, faxes, meetings, and the need to keep current in one's field, more and more managers and professionals are complaining that they are suffering overload.

What happens when individuals have more information than they can sort out and use? They tend to select out, ignore, pass over or forget information. Or they may put off further processing until the overload situation is over. Regardless, the result is lost information and less effective communication.

EMOTIONS

How the receiver feels at the time of receipt of a communication will influence how they interpret it. The same message received when you are angry or distraught is often interpreted differently from when you are happy. Extreme emotions such as jubilation or depression are most likely to hinder effective communication. In such instances, we are most prone to disregard our rational and objective thinking processes and substitute emotional judgments.

LANGUAGE

Words mean different things to different people. Age, education and cultural background are three of the more obvious variables that influence the language a person uses and the definitions they give to words.

In an organisation, employees usually come from diverse backgrounds. Further, the grouping of employees into departments creates specialists who develop their own jargon, or technical language. In large organisations, members are also frequently widely dispersed geographically—even operating in different countries—and individuals in each locale will use terms and phrases that are unique to their area. The existence of vertical levels can also cause language problems. For example, differences in meaning with regard to words such as *incentives* and *quotas* have been found at different levels in management. Top managers often speak about the need for incentives and quotas, yet these terms imply manipulation and create resentment among many lower managers.

The point is that, although we probably speak a common language—English—our use of that language is far from uniform. If we knew how each of us modified the language, communication

The Real Deal

Communication strategies at Bosch

Bosch is a multinational company that has its origins in Stuttgart where, in 1886, Robert Bosch started a small electrical engineering workshop. While the company is famous for supplying component parts to the automotive industry, it is also known for many other products in communications and industrial technology, power tools, security solutions and household appliances. In 1922, August Hoette opened the first Bosch agency in Melbourne, and since 1958, the Bosch organisation has expanded into Singapore, Malaysia, Thailand, the Philippines, Vietnam, Myanmar and Indonesia.

The Australian operation contributes approximately 1 per cent of Bosch's total annual revenue of $64 billion. However, Bosch Australia, like Bosch South East Asia, is an integral part of a global business network covering 37 countries. It not only supplies Australian industry with automotive parts, but also successfully exports products to other markets. The challenges for management at the Melbourne factory are many. One such challenge is making English one of the workers' new essential skills.

Over many years, Melbourne's industrial complex has benefited by the thousands of migrants who arrived in Australia looking for work and a new home. Initially, the migrants were Germans and other northern Europeans, followed by Italians, Greeks and other southern Europeans. More recently, these were followed by migrants from central and eastern Europe in the 1980s, and in the 1990s by Vietnamese and Cambodians. For many of them, English was their second language.

For Bosch Australia, a multicultural workplace is an essential part of its culture, with up to 63 different nationalities on the shop floor. Communication is a big factor in any organisation, but it becomes even more significant when a company actively promotes diversity in its workforce and has confidence in their ability to work in teams with an increasing level of sophistication in the systems and technology used in the manufacturing processes.

Effective communication in the workplace is based on proficiency in the common language—in this case, English. Some of the issues have to do with the receiver; as one employee pointed out, a lack of understanding of English can create difficulties in understanding management. The sender can also be at fault; it was also highlighted by employees that the use of the English language by some Australian managers can also create confusion. The Australian accent takes time to come to grips with.

Bosch Australia uses the services of AMES Consulting to develop an English course that suits the needs of its employees and the business. While the training issues are dealt with by a formal consultation process, Bosch actively seeks to involve the informal leaders among the ethnic groups. These employees can often help in overcoming communication barriers.

Source: Nicholas Way, 'Bosch Minds Its Language', *Business Review Weekly*, 27 March 2003, pp. 70–73. With permission.

difficulties would be minimised. The problem is that members in an organisation usually don't know how those with whom they interact have modified the language. Senders tend to assume that the words and terms they use mean the same to the receiver as they do to them. This assumption is often incorrect.

COMMUNICATION APPREHENSION

Another main barrier to effective communication is that some people—an estimated 5–20 per cent of the population[27]—suffer from debilitating **communication apprehension** or anxiety. Although lots of people dread speaking in front of a group, communication apprehension is a more serious problem because it affects a whole category of communication techniques. People who suffer from it experience undue tension and anxiety in oral communication, written communication, or both.[28] For example, oral apprehensives may find it extremely difficult to talk

communication apprehension
Undue tension and anxiety about oral communication, written communication, or both.

with others face-to-face or become extremely anxious when they have to use the telephone. As a result, they may rely on memos or faxes to convey messages, when a phone call would be not only faster but also more appropriate.

Studies demonstrate that oral-communication apprehensives avoid situations that require them to engage in oral communication.[29] We should expect to find some self-selection in jobs so that such individuals don't take positions, such as that of teacher, for which oral communication is a dominant requirement.[30] But almost all jobs require some oral communication. And of greater concern is the evidence that high-oral-communication apprehensives distort the communication demands of their jobs in order to minimise the need for communication.[31] So, we need to be aware that there is a set of people in organisations who severely limit their oral communication and rationalise this practice by telling themselves that more communication isn't necessary for them to do their job effectively.

Current Issues in Communication

In this section, we discuss four current issues related to communication in organisations: Why do men and women often have difficulty communicating with each other? What role does silence play in communication? What are the implications of the 'politically correct' movement on communications in organisations? And how can individuals improve their cross-cultural communications?

LEARNING OBJECTIVE

8

Contrast the meaning of talk for men versus women

COMMUNICATION BARRIERS BETWEEN WOMEN AND MEN

Research by Deborah Tannen provides us with some important insights into the differences between men and women in terms of their conversational styles.[32] In particular, she has been able to explain why gender often creates oral communication barriers.

The essence of Tannen's research is that men use talk to emphasise status, whereas women use it to create connection. Her conclusion, of course, doesn't apply to *every* man or *every* woman. As she puts it, her generalisation means that 'a larger percentage of women or men *as a group* talk in a particular way, or individual women and men *are more likely* to talk one way or the other'.[33]

Tannen states that communication is a continual balancing act, juggling the conflicting needs for intimacy and independence. Intimacy emphasises closeness and commonalities. Independence emphasises separateness and differences. But here's the kick: women speak and hear a language of connection and intimacy; men speak and hear a language of status, power and independence. So, for many men, conversations are primarily a means to preserve independence and maintain status in a hierarchical social order. For many women, conversations are negotiations for closeness in which people try to seek and give confirmation and support. A few examples will illustrate Tannen's thesis:

- Men frequently complain that women talk on and on about their problems. Women criticise men for not listening. What's happening is that when men hear of a problem, they frequently assert their desire for independence and control by offering solutions. Many women, on the other hand, view talking about a problem as a means to promote closeness. The women present the problem to gain support and connection, not to get the man's advice. Mutual understanding is symmetrical. But giving advice is asymmetrical—it sets up the advice giver as more knowledgeable, more reasonable and more in control. This contributes to distancing men and women in their efforts to communicate.
- Men are often more direct than women in conversation. A man might say, 'I think you're wrong on that point.' A woman might say, 'Have you looked at the marketing department's research report on that point?' (the implication being that the report will show the error). Men frequently see female indirectness as 'covert' or 'sneaky', but women aren't as concerned as men with the status and one-upmanship that directness often creates.

- Women tend to be less boastful than men. They often downplay their authority or accomplishments to avoid appearing as braggarts and to take the other person's feelings into account. However, men can frequently misinterpret this and incorrectly conclude that a woman is less confident and competent than she really is.
- Finally, men often criticise women for seeming to apologise all the time. Men tend to see the phrase 'I'm sorry' as a weakness, because they interpret the phrase to mean the woman is accepting blame, when he knows she's not to blame. The woman also knows she's not to blame. The problem is that women frequently use 'I'm sorry' to express regret and restore balance to a conversation: 'I know you must feel bad about this; I do, too.' For many women, 'I'm sorry' is an expression of understanding and caring about the other person's feelings, rather than an apology.

SILENCE AS COMMUNICATION

Sherlock Holmes once solved a murder mystery based not on what happened but on what *didn't* happen. Holmes remarked to his assistant, Dr Watson, about 'the curious incident of the dog in the nighttime'. Watson, surprised, responds: 'But the dog did nothing in the nighttime.' To which Holmes replied, 'That was the curious incident.' Holmes concluded that the crime had to have been committed by someone with whom the watchdog was familiar, because it didn't bark.

The dog that didn't bark in the night is often used as a metaphor for an event that is significant by reason of its absence. That story is also an excellent illustration of the importance of silence in communication.

Silence—defined here as an absence of speech or noise—has been generally ignored as a form of communication in OB because it represents *in*action or non-behavior. But it's not necessarily inaction. Nor is silence, as many believe, a failure to communicate. It can, in fact, be a powerful form of communication.[34] It can mean that someone is thinking or contemplating a response to a question. It can mean that a person is anxious and fearful of speaking. It can signal agreement, dissent, frustration or anger.

In terms of OB, we can see several links between silence and work-related behaviour. For example, silence is a critical element of groupthink, in which it implies agreement with the majority. It can be a way for employees to express dissatisfaction, as when they 'suffer in silence'. It can be a sign that someone is upset, as when a typically talkative person suddenly says nothing— 'What's the matter with him? Is he all right?' It's a powerful tool used by managers to signal disfavour by shunning or ignoring employees with 'silent insults'. And, of course, it's a crucial element of group decision making, allowing individuals to think over and contemplate what others have said.

Failing to pay close attention to the silent portion of a conversation can result in missing a vital part of the message. Astute communicators watch for gaps, pauses and hesitations. They hear and interpret silence. They treat pauses, for example, as analogous to a flashing yellow light at an intersection—they pay attention to what comes next. Is the person thinking, deciding how to frame an answer? Is the person suffering from communication apprehension? Sometimes the real message in a communication is buried in the silence.

'POLITICALLY CORRECT' COMMUNICATION

What words do you use to describe a colleague who is wheelchair-bound? What terms do you use in addressing a female customer? How do you communicate with a brand-new client who isn't like you? Your answers can mean the difference between losing a client, an employee, a lawsuit, a harassment claim or a job.[35]

Most of us are acutely aware of how our vocabulary has been modified to reflect political correctness. For example, most of us have cleansed the words *handicapped, blind* and *elderly* from

Research indicates that men and women use talk differently. Women use language to create connection. Men, in contrast, use language to emphasise status and power. Managers need to be sensitive to the gender differences embedded in conversations.

our vocabulary—and replaced them with terms like *physically challenged*, *visually impaired* and *senior*. The *Los Angeles Times*, for example, allows its journalists to use the term *old age* but cautions that the onset of old age varies from 'person to person', so a group of 75-year-olds aren't necessarily all old.[36]

We must be sensitive to others' feelings. Certain words can and do stereotype, intimidate and insult individuals. In an increasingly diverse workforce, we must be sensitive to how words might offend others. But there is a downside to political correctness. It is complicating our vocabulary and making it more difficult for people to communicate. To illustrate, you probably know what these four terms mean: *death*, *garbage*, *quotas* and *women*. But each of these words also has been found to offend one or more groups. They have been replaced with terms such as *negative patient outcome*, *post-consumer waste materials*, *educational equity* and *people of gender*. The problem is that this latter group of terms is much less likely to convey a uniform message than the words they replaced. *You* know what *death* means; *I* know what *death* means; but can you be sure that 'negative patient outcome' will be consistently defined as synonymous with death? No. For example, the phrase could also mean a longer stay than expected in the hospital, or notification that your health insurance won't cover all your hospital bill.

Some critics, for humour's sake, enjoy carrying political correctness to the extreme. Even those of us with thinning scalps, who aren't too thrilled at being labelled 'bald', have to smirk when we are referred to as 'folliclely challenged'. But our concern here is with how politically correct language is contributing a new barrier to effective communication.

Words are the primary means by which people communicate. When we eliminate words from use because they are politically incorrect, we reduce our options for conveying messages in the clearest and most accurate form. For the most part, the larger the vocabulary used by a sender and a receiver, the greater the opportunity to accurately transmit messages. By removing certain words from our vocabulary, we make it harder to communicate accurately. When we further replace these words with new terms whose meanings are less well understood, we have reduced the likelihood that our messages will be received as we had intended them.

We must be sensitive to how our choice of words might offend others. But we also have to be careful not to sanitise our language to the point at which it clearly restricts clarity of communication. There is no simple solution to this dilemma. However, you should be aware of the trade-offs and the need to find a proper balance.

LEARNING OBJECTIVE

9

Describe the potential problems in cross-cultural communication

CROSS-CULTURAL COMMUNICATION

Effective communication is difficult under the best of conditions. Cross-cultural factors clearly create the potential for increased communication problems. This is illustrated in Figure 10.4. A gesture that is well understood and acceptable in one culture can be meaningless or lewd in another.[37]

The A-OK Sign

In Australia and the United States, this is just a friendly sign for 'All right!' or 'Good going'. In Islamic countries, it is equivalent to what generations of high school students know as 'flipping the bird'.

The 'Hook'em Horns' Sign

This sign is a good luck gesture in Brazil and Venezuela. In parts of Africa, it is a curse. In Italy, it is signalling to another that 'your spouse is being unfaithful'.

'V' for Victory Sign

In many parts of the world, this means 'victory' or 'peace'. In Australia, if the palm and fingers face inward, it means 'Up yours!' especially if executed with an upward jerk of the fingers.

Finger-beckoning Sign

This sign means 'come here' in the United States. In Malaysia, it is used only for calling animals. In Indonesia and Australia, it is used for beckoning 'ladies of the night'.

FIGURE 10.4   **Hand gestures mean different things in different countries**

Source: 'What's A-OK in the U.S.A. Is Lewd and Worthless Beyond', *New York Times*, 18 August 1996, p. E7. From Roger E. Axtell, *GESTURES: The Do's and Taboos of Body Language Around the World*. Copyright © 1991. Reprinted by permission of John Wiley & Sons, Inc.

Cultural barriers

One author has identified four specific problems related to language difficulties in cross-cultural communications.[38]

First, there are *barriers caused by semantics*. As we have noted previously, words mean different things to different people. This is particularly true for people from different national cultures. Some words, for example, don't translate between cultures. Understanding the word *sisu* will help you in communicating with people from Finland, but this word is untranslatable into English. It means something akin to 'guts' or 'dogged persistence'. Similarly, the new capitalists in Russia may have difficulty communicating with their British or Canadian counterparts, because English terms such as *efficiency, free market* and *regulation* are not directly translatable into Russian.

Second, there are *barriers caused by word connotations*. Words imply different things in different languages. Negotiations between Australian and Japanese executives, for example, are made more difficult because the Japanese word *hai* translates as 'yes', but its connotation may be 'yes, I'm listening', rather than 'yes, I agree'.

Third are *barriers caused by tone differences*. In some cultures, language is formal, while in others it's informal. In some cultures, the tone changes depending on the context: people speak differently at home, in social situations and at work. Using a personal, informal style in a situation in which a more formal style is expected can be embarrassing and off-putting.

Fourth, there are *barriers caused by differences among perceptions*. People who speak different languages actually view the world in different ways. Eskimos perceive snow differently because they have many words for it. Thais perceive 'no' differently than do Australians, because the former have no such word in their vocabulary.

Cultural context

A better understanding of these cultural barriers and their implications for communicating across cultures can be achieved by considering the concepts of high- and low-context cultures.[39]

OB Controversies

Communication in the cockpit

A Singapore Airline's Boeing 747-400 jet bound for Los Angeles from Taiwan crashed on 31 October 2000, killing 83 people. The plane was reported to have mistakenly turned on to a runway at Taipei's Chiang Kai-shek airport that was closed for repairs as it prepared for take-off on a stormy, windy night. The jumbo jet exploded when it ploughed into construction equipment. Taiwan authorities blamed pilot error for the tragedy.

Dr Graham Braithwaite, an aircraft safety expert at the University of New South Wales, commented that 'pilot error' is a complex issue and is generally not the cause, but rather a symptom, of a whole number of factors involved in a disaster. In relation to future disasters, he referred to a prediction by the Boeing company that by 2010, or 2015 at the latest, there will be one wide-bodied aircraft crashing every week. Such a prediction heightens the concern for more effective communications in the cockpit and between the cockpit and the control tower staff.

One of the controversial issues in any airline disaster concerning 'pilot error' relates to the conversations that take place in the cockpit prior to any crash. The misunderstanding of a few words may literally mean the difference between life and death. A number of aviation disasters have been largely attributed to problems in communication. Consider the following:

- History's worst aviation disaster occurred in 1977 at foggy Tenerife, in the Canary Islands. The captain of a KLM flight thought the air traffic controller had cleared him to take off. But the controller intended only to give departure instructions. Although the language spoken between the Dutch KLM captain and the Spanish controller was English, confusion was created by heavy accents and improper terminology. The KLM Boeing 747 hit a Pan Am 747 at full throttle on the runway, killing 583 people.
- In 1993, Chinese pilots flying a US-built MD-80 tried to land in heavy fog at Urumqi, in northwest China. They were baffled by an audio alarm from the jet's ground proximity warning system. Just before impact, the cockpit recorder picked up one crew member saying to the other in Chinese: 'What does "pull up" mean?' The plane hit power lines and crashed, killing 12.
- In September 1997, a Garuda Airlines jetliner crashed into a jungle, around 30 kilometres south of Medan Airport on the island of Sumatra. All 234 aboard were killed. The cause of this disaster was the pilot and the air traffic controller confusing the words 'left' and 'right' as the plane approached the airport under poor visibility conditions.

These examples tragically illustrate how miscommunication can have deadly consequences. The controversy arises from who is to blame. There is no doubt that communication plays an important role in avoiding disasters and that the focus for aviation communications in the future should be to avoid the predictions of the Boeing company by learning from past mistakes.

Sources: Based on S. Cushing, *Fatal Words: Communication Clashes and Aircraft Crashes* (Chicago: University of Chicago Press, 1997); <www.singapore-window.org/sw02/021015af.htm>; <www.wsws.org/articles/2000/nov2000/air-07n.shtml>; 'Pilot Communication Risks Flight Safety', <www.abc.net.au>, 21 March 2001.

Cultures tend to differ in the importance of context in influencing the meaning that individuals take from what is actually said or written, in light of who the other person is. Countries such as China, Korea, Japan and Vietnam are **high-context cultures**. They rely heavily on non-verbal and subtle situational cues when communicating with others. What is *not* said may be more significant than what *is* said. A person's official status, place in society and reputation carry considerable weight in communications. In contrast, people from Europe reflect their **low-context cultures**. They rely essentially on words to convey meaning. Body language or formal titles are secondary to spoken and written words (see Figure 10.5).

What do these contextual differences mean in terms of communication? Actually, quite a lot. Communication in high-context cultures implies considerably more trust by both parties. What may appear, to an outsider, as casual and insignificant conversations is important because it reflects the desire to build a relationship and create trust. Oral agreements imply strong commitments in high-context cultures. And who you are—your age, seniority, rank in the organisation—is highly valued and heavily influences your credibility. But in low-context cultures, enforceable contracts will tend to be in writing, precisely worded and highly legalistic. Similarly, low-context cultures value directness. Managers are expected to be explicit and precise in conveying intended meaning. It is quite different in high-context cultures, in which managers tend to 'make suggestions' rather than give orders.

high-context cultures
Cultures that rely heavily on non-verbal and subtle situational cues in communication.

low-context cultures
Cultures that rely heavily on words to convey meaning in communication.

A cultural guide

When communicating with people from a different culture, what can you do to reduce misperceptions, misinterpretations and misevaluations? You can begin by trying to assess the cultural context. You are likely to have fewer difficulties if these people come from a similar cultural context to you. In addition, the following four rules can be helpful:[40]

1. *Assume differences until similarity is proven.* Most of us assume that others are more similar to us than they actually are. But people from different countries often are very different from us. So, you are far less likely to make an error if you assume that others are different from you, rather than assuming similarity until difference is proven.
2. *Emphasise description rather than interpretation or evaluation.* Interpreting or evaluating what someone has said or done, in contrast to description, is based more on the observer's culture

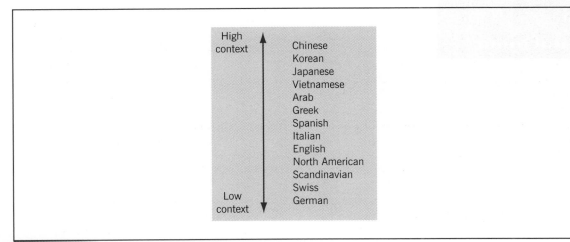

FIGURE 10.5 **High-context versus low-context cultures**

Source: Based on the work of E. T. Hall. From R. E. Duleck, J. S. Fielden and J. S. Hall, 'International Communications: An Executive Primer', *Business Horizons*, January–February 1991, p. 21.

Cultural differences in communication can hinder even the best-intentioned efforts. To assist employees posted abroad as they make their way in a new culture, the Australian government operates a website that provides practical information to Australians living and working abroad.

and background than on the observed situation. As a result, delay judgment until you have had sufficient time to observe and interpret the situation from the differing perspectives of all the cultures involved.

3. *Practise empathy.* Before sending a message, put yourself in the recipient's shoes. What are their values, experiences and frames of reference? What do you know about their education, upbringing and background that can give you added insight? Try to see the other person as they really are.

4. *Treat your interpretations as a working hypothesis.* Once you have developed an explanation for a new situation or think you empathise with someone from a foreign culture, treat your interpretation as a hypothesis that needs further testing, rather than as a certainty. Carefully assess the feedback provided by recipients to see if it confirms your hypothesis. For important decisions or communiqués, you can also check with other foreign and home-country colleagues to make sure that your interpretations are on target.

Summary and Implications for Managers

A careful review of this chapter finds a common theme regarding the relationship between communication and employee satisfaction: the less the uncertainty, the greater the satisfaction. Distortions, ambiguities and incongruities all increase uncertainty and, hence, they have a negative impact on satisfaction.[41]

The less distortion that occurs in communication, the more that goals, feedback and other management messages to employees will be received as they were intended.[42] This, in turn, should reduce ambiguities and clarify the group's task. Extensive use of vertical, lateral and informal channels will increase communication flow, reduce uncertainty, and improve group performance and satisfaction. We should also expect incongruities between verbal and non-verbal communiqués to increase uncertainty and reduce satisfaction.

Findings in the chapter further suggest that the goal of perfect communication is unattainable. Yet, there is evidence that demonstrates a positive relationship between effective communication (which includes factors such as perceived trust, perceived accuracy, desire for interaction, top-management receptiveness, and upward information requirements) and worker productivity.[43] Choosing the correct channel, being an effective listener and using feedback may, therefore, make for more effective communication. But the human factor generates distortions that can never be fully eliminated. The communication process represents an exchange of messages, but the outcome is meanings that may or may not approximate those that the sender intended. Whatever the sender's expectations, the decoded message in the mind of the receiver represents their reality. And it is this 'reality' that will determine performance, along with the individual's level of motivation and their degree of satisfaction. The issue of motivation is critical, so we should briefly review how communication is central in determining an individual's degree of motivation.

You will remember from expectancy theory that the degree of effort an individual exerts depends on their perception of the effort–performance, performance–reward and reward–goal satisfaction links. If individuals aren't given the data necessary to make the perceived probability of these links high, motivation will suffer. If rewards aren't made clear, if the criteria for determining and measuring performance are ambiguous, or if individuals aren't relatively certain that their effort will lead to satisfactory performance, then effort will be reduced. So, communication plays a significant role in determining the level of employee motivation.

A final implication from the communication literature relates to predicting turnover. The use of realistic job previews acts as a communication device for clarifying role expectations. Employees who have been exposed to a realistic job preview have more accurate information about that job. Comparisons of turnover rates between organisations that use the realistic job preview versus either no preview or presentation of only positive job information show that those not using the realistic preview have, on average, almost 29 per cent higher turnover.[44] This makes a strong case for managers to convey honest and accurate information about a job to applicants during the recruiting and selection process.

Point

OPEN-BOOK MANAGEMENT IMPROVES THE BOTTOM LINE

Open-book management (OBM) seeks to get every employee to think and behave like an owner.[a] It throws out the notion that bosses run things and employees do what they are told. In the open-book approach, employees are given the information that historically was kept strictly within the management ranks.

There are three key elements to any OBM program. First, management opens the company's books and shares detailed financial and operating information with employees. If employees don't know how the company makes money, how can they be expected to make the firm more successful? Second, employees need to be taught to understand the company's financial statements. This means management must provide employees with a 'basic course' in how to read and interpret statements of financial performance, of financial position and of cash flows. And third, management needs to show employees how their work influences financial results. Showing employees the impact of their jobs on the bottom line makes financial statement analysis relevant.

Who is using OBM? A growing list of Australian firms are using open-book management, including Mt Isa Mines, Purkis Partners near Gosford in New South Wales, Brisbane-based firm Ashley and Munro, Textor, Fusion

Design Consultants and accounting firm Darcy Kennedy in Dubbo, New South Wales. Textor is a textile technologies company that invites all staff to attend and participate in monthly profit and loss meetings and to take personal responsibility for raising productivity or minimising costs in specific areas of the business. The company believes that ethical and cooperative behaviour leads to industrial harmony and a workforce that believes in the company and its products.[b]

Why should it work? Access to detailed financial information and the ability to understand that information makes employees think like owners. And this leads to them making decisions that are best for the organisation, not just for themselves.

Does it work? Most firms that have introduced OBM offer evidence that it has significantly helped the business. For example, the American company Springfield Remanufacturing was losing US$61,000 on sales of US$16 million. Management attributes much of the company's current success—profits of US$6 million a year on sales of US$100 million—to OBM. Similarly, Allstate's Business Insurance Group used OBM to boost return on equity from 2.9 per cent to 16.5 per cent in just three years. Accounting firm Darcy Kennedy improved its productivity by restructuring the firm and the roles of partners and professionals.[c] One of the key elements was an open-book style of management. Warrick McLean, a non-accountant, was appointed practice manager at the start of the restructuring in 1997. He helped to bring a climate of openness by undertaking performance reviews on the partners, insisting that performance information applies to everyone in the organisation. He previously worked in a university and believes that dealing with partners wasn't too difficult after working with academics. Senior partner, Michael Kennedy, says that staff have access to all the firm's books and are able to work on their own productivity. Damien Mair, of Australia's Fusion Design Consultants, states that his company's OBM model is based on weekly profit updates leading to improved employee motivation and greater commitment to the organisation.[d]

Sources: [a] Based on J. Case, 'The Open-book Revolution', *INC.*, June 1995, pp. 26–50; J. P. Schuster, J. Carpenter and M. P. Kane, *The Power of Open-book Management* (New York: John Wiley, 1996); and R. Aggarwal and B. J. Simkins, 'Open Book Management—Optimizing Human Capital', *Business Horizons*, September–October 2001, pp. 5–13.

[b] <www.textortextiles.com/corporate.html>.

[c] Tony Thomas, 'Restructuring: Country Firm's Winning New Ways', *Business Review Weekly*, 22 October 1999, pp. 122–24.

[d] M. Kaplan, 'Opening the Books', *Australasian Business Intelligence*, 6 May 2003.

Counterpoint

The owners of Optics 1 Inc., an optical-engineering company with 23 employees and sales of less than US$10 million a year, implemented an OBM program. After a short time, the program was discontinued. Said one of the co-owners, 'Employees used the information against me. When we made a profit, they demanded bigger bonuses and new computers. When I used profits to finance a new product line, everybody said, "That's nice, but what's in it for me?". . . If your employees misinterpret financial information, it's more damaging than their not having access at all. I gave them general and administrative rates. Next thing I knew, they were backing out everyone's salaries, and I'd hear, "You're paying that guy $86,000? I contribute more."'

As this example illustrates, part of the downside to OBM is that employees may misuse or misinterpret the information they are given.[e] Another potential problem is the leaking of confidential information to competitors. In the hands of the competition, detailed information about the company's operations and financial position may undermine a firm's competitive advantage.

Matrix Builders and Project Managers, a private Brisbane construction company, has committed to an open-book policy in terms of each construction project and is introducing profit sharing for its staff.[f] The firm believes that its management approach has led to a more productive work climate. However, while this has created greater involvement and participation by staff, it can have a downside. The firm intends to engage lifestyle consultants to ensure that employees balance their work and home commitments. According to Peter Burt, joint owner and managing director, 'The most difficult thing is getting some staff to go home . . . We find people working here from very early in the morning into the night and then on weekends. When you get people spending 60 to 80 hours a week at the workplace, it's not healthy. The work is fairly stressful to start with, and if you exacerbate that with very long working hours there is a risk that the work problems go home—and, before you know it, there are home problems coming to work.'

When OBM succeeds, two factors seem to exist. First, the organisation or unit in which it is implemented tends to be small. It's a lot easier to introduce OBM in a small, start-up company than in a large, geographically dispersed company that has operated for years with closed books and little employee involvement. Second, there needs to be a mutually trusting relationship between management and workers. In organisational cultures in which management doesn't trust employees to act selflessly, or in which managers and accountants have been trained to keep information under lock and key, OBM isn't likely to work. Nor will it succeed when employees believe that any new change program is only likely to further manipulate or exploit them for management's advantage.

Sources: [e] Based on S. L. Gruner, 'Why Open the Books?', *INC.*, November 1996, p. 95; and T. R. V. Davis, 'Open-book Management: Its Promise and Pitfalls', *Organizational Dynamics*, Winter 1997, pp. 7–20.

[f] M. Massey, 'Builders Try to Get Work and Leisure Matrix Right', *Business Review Weekly*, 19 October 1998, pp. 120–21.

For Discussion

1. Describe the functions that communication provides within a group or organisation. Give an example of each.
2. 'Ineffective communication is the fault of the sender.' Do you agree or disagree? Discuss.
3. Contrast encoding and decoding.
4. Contrast downward with upward communication.
5. What is non-verbal communication? Does it aid or hinder verbal communication?
6. Why do you think so many people are poor listeners?
7. What conditions stimulate the emergence of rumours?
8. How might managers use the grapevine for their benefit?
9. What can you do to improve the likelihood that your communiqués will be received and understood as you intend?
10. What are the advantages and disadvantages of e-mail?
11. What can managers do to improve their skills at providing performance feedback?
12. What does the phrase 'sometimes the real message in a communication is buried in the silence' mean?
13. Describe how political correctness can hinder effective communication.
14. Contrast high- and low-context cultures.

Exercises

Exercise 10a
THE IMPACT OF ATTENTIVE LISTENING SKILLS

The objective of this exercise is to show the importance of listening skills to interpersonal success.

Form groups by counting off by sixes. There should be a minimum of three students and a maximum of seven students per group.

Each group has 30 minutes to address the following four questions. The groups should begin by brainstorming answers and then narrowing their selection to the three most significant answers. Appoint one member of the group to transcribe the answers on the board and another to tell the class why the group selected these answers.
1. How do you know when a person is listening to you?
2. Describe a situation in which you exhibited outstanding listening behaviour. How did it influence the speaker's subsequent communication behaviours?

3. How do you know when a person is ignoring you?
4. Describe a situation in which you ignored someone. What impact did it have on that person's subsequent communication behaviours?

Source: Adapted from T. Clark, 'Sharing the Importance of Attentive Listening Skills', *Journal of Management Education*, April 1999, pp. 216–23.

Exercise 10b
AN ABSENCE OF NON-VERBAL COMMUNICATION

This exercise helps you to see the value of non-verbal communication to small-group interaction.
1. The class should be organised into an even number of groups, each of five or six people. Next, pair up each of the groups with one other. The two groups will work together, one acting as a decision-making group and the other as observers.
2. The decision-making group should rank the following 14 crimes in terms of their severity, from most severe (1) to least severe (14). Complete this task in 20 minutes. During the ranking procedure, the decision-making group may communicate only verbally. They may *not* use gestures, any facial or body movements, or any other non-verbal communication. It may help to have members of the decision-making group sit on their hands to remind them of their restrictions.
   Crimes
   ___ Person kills victim by recklessly driving a car while drunk.
   ___ Person runs a narcotics ring.
   ___ Person plants bomb in public building; explosion kills one person.
   ___ Wife stabs husband to death.
   ___ Man rapes woman, who dies from injuries.
   ___ Politician takes $10,000 company bribe to support company.
   ___ Man tries to entice minor into car for immoral purposes.
   ___ Person runs prostitution ring.
   ___ Husband stabs wife to death.
   ___ Person smuggles ecstasy tablets into country for resale.
   ___ Person shoots victim fatally during robbery.
   ___ Person commits arson—$500,000 damage.
   ___ Person breaks into home and steals $1,000.
   ___ Person kidnaps a victim.
3. After watching the decision making, the observers should answer the following questions:
   (a) How effective was communication?
   (b) What barriers to communication existed?
   (c) What purpose does non-verbal communication serve?
4. Convene the entire class and again answer the three questions posed in (3).

Sources: Based on J. Powers, 'The Blind Decision-makers', *Exchange: The Organizational Behavior Teaching Journal*, January 1975, pp. 32–33; and C. Taylor, 'Crimes, Death, and Stress: Three New Consensus Tasks', *Organizational Behavior Teaching Review*, vol. 12, no. 2, 1987–88, pp. 115–17.

Case Study 10

Do We Have a Communication Problem Here?

'I don't want to hear your excuses. Just get those planes in the air,' Graham Taylor was screaming at his gate manager. As head of Great Southern Airlines' operations at Sydney International Airport, Taylor has been consistently frustrated by the attitude displayed by his local employees. Transferred from Perth to Sydney only three months ago, Taylor was having difficulty adjusting to the style of work in one of Australia's busiest airports. 'Am I critical of these people? You bet I am! They don't listen when I talk. They think things are just fine and fight every change I suggest. And they have no appreciation for the importance of keeping on schedule.'

If Taylor is critical of his staff, it's mutual. They universally dislike him. Here are a few anonymous comments made about their boss: 'He's totally insensitive to our needs.' 'He thinks if he yells and screams, that things will improve. We don't see it that way.' 'I've been working here for four years. Before he came here, this was a good place to work. Not anymore. I'm constantly in fear of being abused. I feel stressed all the time, even at home. My husband has started commenting on it a lot.'

Taylor was brought in specifically to tighten up this major operation for Great Southern Airlines. High on his list of goals is improving the on-time record, increasing productivity and improving customer service. When Taylor was asked if he thought he had any problems with his staff, he replied, 'Yep. We just can't seem to communicate.'

Questions

1. Does Graham Taylor have a communication problem? Explain.
2. What suggestions, if any, would you make to Graham to help him improve his managerial effectiveness?
3. What does this case tell you about the significance of managing communications in organisations?

Web Workout

1. You can become a better listener. The website <www.coping.org/communi/listen.htm> has a number of tips and exercises to get you to think about your listening skills. Print the page and complete the exercises under 'Practice listening for feelings' and bring it to class. Also jot down brief responses to one or two of the role-plays listed on the page. If there is time, we will complete some of them in class.
2. Listening requires more than a physical presence—it requires a mental presence, too! Learn more about how to develop your skills as an empathetic listener at <http://crs.uvm.edu/gopher/nerl/personal/comm/e.html>. Write a short journal entry describing how you plan to further develop one technique listed in the article.
3. Are there do's and don'ts for e-mail? Learn more by doing a search on 'netiquette', which are the courtesy guidelines of e-mail. Print one of the better pages and bring to class along with an e-mail you have sent or received recently. Delete the names of the parties in the e-mail. In class, we will edit these e-mails for breeches of netiquette guidelines.
4. Organisational communication has been drastically changed by the introduction of modern technologies just in the last ten years. However, it doesn't just happen. There must be support personnel and products to assist users with communication via technology. Go to <www.databasesystemscorp.com/psccproducts.htm> to explore one vendor's products and services to support organisational communication. Write a short journal entry about what you learned from this website.
5. Learn more about effective cross-cultural communication. Go to the website <www.nwrel.org/cnorse/booklets/ccc/>. The first four chapters are particularly interesting. Write a paragraph or two about what you learned from this page.

6. Open-book management has worked for many companies. To learn more, go to *Inc.* magazine's website and key in 'open book management' using the search feature. A number of articles are available for review. Additionally, the following websites have more information. Write a one-page 'summary' of what you have learned.
  - <www.nceo.org/library/obm_poolcovers.html>; and
  - <www.nceo.org/library/obm_nceostudy.html>.

7. What is an intranet and how does it work? Chances are, if you haven't been on one here at university or at work, you will be in the future. Go to <www.netxs.com.pk/intranet/index.htm> for a comprehensive look at intranets and organisations that have put them to work to increase organisational effectiveness through communication.

KSS Program

KNOW THE CONCEPTS   SELF-AWARENESS   SKILLS APPLICATIONS

Active listening skills
After you have read this chapter, take Self-Assessment #25 (How Good Are My Listening Skills?) on your enclosed CD-Rom and complete the skill-building module entitled 'Active Listening' on page 639.

NOTES

1. <www.skyaid.org/Skyaid%20Org/Medical/kuala_lumpur_ems.htm>.
2. Anonymous, 'Woman Sees Red at Mix-up over Police Callout', *New Zealand Herald*, 30 May 2003, p. 3.
3. See, for example, K. W. Thomas and W. H. Schmidt, 'A Survey of Managerial Interests with Respect to Conflict', *Academy of Management Journal*, June 1976, p. 317.
4. W. G. Scott and T. R. Mitchell, *Organization Theory: A Structural and Behavioral Analysis* (Homewood, IL: Richard D. Irwin, 1976).
5. D. K. Berlo, *The Process of Communication* (New York: Holt, Rinehart & Winston, 1960), pp. 30–32.
6. R. L. Simpson, 'Vertical and Horizontal Communication in Formal Organizations', *Administrative Science Quarterly*, September 1959, pp. 188–96; B. Harriman, 'Up and Down the Communications Ladder', *Harvard Business Review*, September–October 1974, pp. 143–51; and A. G. Walker and J. W. Smither, 'A Five-Year Study of Upward Feedback: What Managers Do With Their Results Matter', *Personnel Psychology*, Summer 1999, pp. 393–424.
7. J. Fast, *Body Language* (Philadelphia: M. Evan, 1970), p. 7.
8. A. Mehrabian, *Nonverbal Communication* (Chicago: Aldine-Atherton, 1972).
9. A. Bandura, *Social Learning Theory* (Englewood Cliffs, NJ: Prentice Hall, 1977).
10. An example is assigned goals. See E. A. Locke and G. P. Latham, *A Theory of Goal Setting and Task Performance* (Upper Saddle River, NJ: Prentice Hall, 1990).
11. See, for example, N. B. Kurland and L. H. Pelled, 'Passing the Word: Toward a Model of Gossip and Power in the Workplace', *Academy of Management Review*, April 2000, pp. 428–38; and N. Nicholson, 'The New Word on Gossip', *Psychology Today*, June 2001, pp. 41–45.
12. Cited in 'Heard It Through the Grapevine', *Forbes*, 10 February 1997, p. 22.
13. See, for example, J. W. Newstrom, R. E. Monczka and W. E. Reif, 'Perceptions of the Grapevine: Its Value and Influence', *Journal of Business Communication*, Spring 1974, pp. 12–20; and S. J. Modic, 'Grapevine Rated Most Believable', *Industry Week*, 15 May 1989, p. 14.
14. K. Davis, 'Management Communication and the Grapevine', *Harvard Business Review*, September–October 1953, pp. 43–49.
15. H. Sutton and L. W. Porter, 'A Study of the Grapevine in a Governmental Organization', *Personnel Psychology*, Summer 1968, pp. 223–30.
16. K. Davis, cited in R. Rowan, 'Where Did That Rumor Come From?', *Fortune*, 13 August 1979, p. 134.
17. R. L. Rosnow and G. A. Fine, *Rumor and Gossip: The Social Psychology of Hearsay* (New York: Elsevier, 1976).
18. See, for example, J. G. March and G. Sevon, 'Gossip, Information and Decision Making', in J. G. March (ed.), *Decisions and Organizations* (Oxford: Blackwell, 1988), pp. 429–42; M. Noon and R. Delbridge, 'News from Behind My Hand: Gossip in Organizations', *Organization Studies*, vol. 14, no. 1, 1993, pp. 23–36; and N. DiFonzo, P. Bordia and R. L. Rosnow, 'Reining in Rumors', *Organizational Dynamics*, Summer 1994, pp. 47–62.
19. Anonymous, 'Internet Fever Hits Rural Queensland', *Innisfail Advocate*, 17 June 2003, p. 11.
20. 'Ford to Offer Employees Home PCs for $5 a Month', <www.ifnormationweek.com>, 3 February 2000.
21. Matthew Bayley, 'Staff Hit by Email Fatigue', *Sunday Telegraph*, 10 March 2002.

22. Ibid.

23. G. Anders, 'Inside Job', *Fast Company*, September 2001, p. 178.

24. T. M. Burton and R. E. Silverman, 'Lots of Empty Spaces in Cerner Parking Lot Get CEO Riled Up', *Wall Street Journal*, 30 March 2001, p. B3; and E. Wong, 'A Stinging Office Memo Boomerangs', *New York Times*, 5 April 2001, p. C1.

25. See R. L. Daft and R. H. Lengel, 'Information Richness: A New Approach to Managerial Behavior and Organization Design', in B. M. Staw and L. L. Cummings (eds.), *Research in Organizational Behavior*, vol. 6 (Greenwich, CT: JAI Press, 1984), pp. 191–233; R. L. Daft and R. H. Lengel, 'Organizational Information Requirements, Media Richness, and Structural Design', *Managerial Science*, May 1986, pp. 554–72; R. E. Rice, 'Task Analyzability, Use of New Media, and Effectiveness', *Organization Science*, November 1992, pp. 475–500; S. G. Straus and J. E. McGrath, 'Does the Medium Matter? The Interaction of Task Type and Technology on Group Performance and Member Reaction', *Journal of Applied Psychology*, February 1994, pp. 87–97; and L. K. Trevino, J. Webster and E. W. Stein, 'Making Connections: Complementary Influences on Communication Media Choices, Attitudes, and Use', *Organization Science*, March–April 2000, pp. 163–82.

26. R. L. Daft, R. H. Lengel and L. K. Trevino, 'Message Equivocality, Media Selection, and Manager Performance: Implications for Information Systems', *MIS Quarterly*, September 1987, pp. 355–68.

27. J. C. McCroskey, J. A. Daly and G. Sorenson, 'Personality Correlates of Communication Apprehension', *Human Communication Research*, Spring 1976, pp. 376–80.

28. B. H. Spitzberg and M. L. Hecht, 'A Competent Model of Relational Competence', *Human Communication Research*, Summer 1984, pp. 575–99.

29. See, for example, L. Stafford and J. A. Daly, 'Conversational Memory: The Effects of Instructional Set and Recall Mode on Memory for Natural Conversations', *Human Communication Research*, Spring 1984, pp. 379–402.

30. J. A. Daly and J. C. McCrosky, 'Occupational Choice and Desirability as a Function of Communication Apprehension', paper presented at the annual meeting of the International Communication Association, Chicago, 1975.

31. J. A. Daly and M. D. Miller, 'The Empirical Development of an Instrument of Writing Apprehension', *Research in the Teaching of English*, Winter 1975, pp. 242–49.

32. See D. Tannen, *You Just Don't Understand: Women and Men in Conversation* (New York: Ballentine Books, 1991); and D. Tannen, *Talking from 9 to 5* (New York: William Morrow, 1995).

33. Tannen, *Talking from 9 to 5*, p. 15.

34. This section is largely based on C. G. Pinder and K. P. Harlos, 'Silent Organizational Behavior', paper presented at the Western Academy of Management Conference, March 2000; and P. Mornell, "The Sounds of Silence', *INC.*, February 2001, pp. 117–18.

35. M. L. LaGanga, 'Are There Words That Neither Offend Nor Bore?', *Los Angeles Times*, 18 May 1994, p. II–27; and J. Leo, 'Language in the Dumps', *U.S. News & World Report*, 27 July 1998, p. 16.

36. Cited in J. Leo, 'Falling for Sensitivity', *U.S. News & World Report*, 13 December 1993, p. 27.

37. R. E. Axtell, *Gestures: The Do's and Taboos of Body Language Around the World* (New York: Wiley, 1991).

38. See M. Munter, 'Cross-Cultural Communication for Managers', *Business Horizons*, May–June 1993, pp. 75–76.

39. See E. T. Hall, *Beyond Culture* (Garden City, NY: Anchor Press/Doubleday, 1976); E. T. Hall, 'How Cultures Collide', *Psychology Today*, July 1976, pp. 67–74; E. T. Hall and M. R. Hall, *Understanding Cultural Differences* (Yarmouth, ME: Intercultural Press, 1990); and R. E. Dulek, J. S. Fielden and J. S. Hill, 'International Communication: An Executive Primer', *Business Horizons*, January–February 1991, pp. 20–25.

40. N. Adler, *International Dimensions of Organizational Behavior*, 4th ed. (Cincinnati, OH: Southwestern, 2002), p. 94.

41. See, for example. R. S. Schuler, 'A Role Perception Transactional Process Model for Organizational Communication–Outcome Relationships', *Organizational Behavior and Human Performance*, April 1979, pp. 268–91.

42. J. P. Walsh, S. J. Ashford and T. E. Hill, 'Feedback Obstruction: The Influence of the Information Environment on Employee Turnover Intentions', *Human Relations*, January 1985, pp. 23–46.

43. S. A. Hellweg and S. L. Phillips, 'Communication and Productivity in Organizations: A State-of-the-Art Review', in *Proceedings of the 40th Annual Academy of Management Conference*, Detroit, 1980, pp. 188–92.

44. R. R. Reilly, B. Brown, M. R. Blood and C. Z. Malatesta, 'The Effects of Realistic Previews: A Study and Discussion of the Literature', *Personnel Psychology*, Winter 1981, pp. 823–34.

PHOTO CREDITS
307 Image reproduced with the permission of the NSW Police Force.

11

Leadership Concepts and Theories

CHAPTER OUTLINE

What is leadership?
Trait theories
Behavioural theories
Contingency theories

LEARNING OBJECTIVES

After studying this chapter, you should be able to:
1. Contrast leadership and management
2. Summarise the conclusions of trait theories
3. Identify the limitations of behavioural theories
4. Describe Fiedler's contingency model
5. Explain Hersey and Blanchard's situational theory
6. Summarise leader–member exchange theory
7. Describe the path–goal theory
8. Identify the situational variables in the leader-participation model

Lead, follow, or get out of the way!
Anonymous

Outstanding leadership by Jo Hogan has helped to develop Mecca Cosmetica into a successful business.

Can one person make a difference to an organisation's performance? There are many examples that suggest leaders *can* make a difference. Let's look at the achievements of Jo Horgan (founder and managing director of Mecca Cosmetica) and Andrea Jung (chairman and CEO of Avon).[1] As a senior marketing manager for the global cosmetics company L'Oreal, Jo Horgan saw an opportunity to start her own business and consequently opened her first Mecca Cosmetica store in Melbourne in 1997. Since then, the business has grown to eight stores in Australia, with 100 employees. Jo's vision is to provide customised service in purpose-built stores for imported cosmetic products that virtually sell themselves. Jo has realised her vision through a focus on staff and education and a determination to stay close to the customer's desires. She has achieved recognition for her company as one of the top five cosmetic retailers in the world and, as a leader, she recognises that effective staffing is 80 per cent of the leadership challenge.

Andrea Jung is another success story in cosmetics. She joined Avon in 1994 to create a global brand. She did this by integrating and standardising the company's logo, packaging and ads to create a uniform image; and by pushing for the current corporate slogan, 'The company for women.' She was appointed chairman and CEO in 1999.

The company that Jung took over was in deep trouble. The day of the 'Avon Lady' seemed to have passed. Fewer women were signing on as Avon reps, and sales were sagging. But after only four weeks in her new job, Jung had a turnaround plan worked out. Avon would launch an entirely new line of businesses, develop blockbuster products and begin selling Avon products in retail stores—something it had never done in its long history. She added 46 per cent to Avon's research and development budget to get blockbusters to the market faster. She also reduced the number of Avon suppliers from 300 to 75, saving the company $60 million a year. Maybe most importantly, Jung has breathed new life into the ranks of the 'Avon Ladies'. After two years on the job, Jung's leadership has truly made a difference in Avon's performance. Sales growth climbed from 1.5 per cent a year to 6 per cent; operating profits grew from 4 per cent to 7 per cent; and the company's shares were up 70 per cent.

As Jo Horgan and Andrea Jung have demonstrated, leaders can make a difference. In this chapter, we will look at three basic approaches to determining what makes an effective leader and what differentiates leaders from non-leaders. First, we will present trait theories. They dominated the study of leadership up to the late 1940s. Then we will discuss behavioural theories, which were popular until the late 1960s. Finally, we will introduce contingency theories, currently the dominant approach to the field of leadership. But let's first clarify what we mean by the term *leadership*.

What is Leadership?

Leadership and *management* are two terms that are often confused. What's the difference between them?

John Kotter of the Harvard Business School argues that management is about coping with complexity.[2] Good management brings about order and consistency by drawing up formal plans, designing rigid organisation structures and monitoring results against the plans. Leadership, in contrast, is about coping with change. Leaders establish direction by developing a vision of the future; then they align people by communicating this vision and inspiring them to overcome hurdles.

Robert House of the Wharton School at the University of Pennsylvania basically concurs when he says that managers use the authority inherent in their designated formal rank to obtain compliance from organisational members.[3] Management consists of implementing the vision and strategy provided by leaders, coordinating and staffing the organisation, and handling day-to-day problems.

Although Kotter and House provide separate definitions of the two terms, both researchers and practising managers frequently make no such distinctions. So, we need to present leadership in a way that can capture how it is used in theory and practice.

leadership
The ability to influence
a group towards the
achievement of goals.

We define **leadership** as the ability to influence a group towards the achievement of goals. The source of this influence may be formal, such as that provided by the possession of managerial rank in an organisation. Since management positions come with some degree of formally designated authority, a person may assume a leadership role simply because of the position they hold in the organisation. But not all leaders are managers; nor, for that matter, are all managers identified as leaders. Just because an organisation provides its managers with certain formal rights is no assurance that they will be able to lead effectively. We find that non-sanctioned leadership— that is, the ability to influence that arises outside the formal structure of the organisation—is often as important or more important than formal influence. In other words, leaders can emerge from within a group, as well as by formal appointment to lead a group.

You should note that our definition makes no specific mention of a vision, even though both Kotter and House use the term in their efforts to differentiate leadership and management. This omission is purposeful. While most contemporary discussions of the leadership concept include articulating a common *vision*,[4] almost all work on leadership conducted prior to the 1980s made no reference to this concept. So, in order for our definition to encompass both historical and contemporary approaches to leadership, we make no explicit reference to vision.

One last comment before we move on: organisations need strong leadership and strong management for optimal effectiveness. In today's dynamic world, we need leaders to challenge the status quo, to create visions of the future, and to inspire organisational members to want to achieve the visions. We also need managers to formulate detailed plans, create efficient organisational structures and oversee day-to-day operations.

Trait Theories

trait theories of leadership
Theories that consider
personal qualities and
characteristics that
differentiate leaders from
non-leaders.

When Margaret Thatcher was prime minister of Great Britain, she was regularly singled out for her leadership. She was described in terms such as *confident, iron-willed, determined* and *decisive.* These terms are traits and, whether Thatcher's advocates and critics recognised it at the time, when they described her in such terms they became trait-theorist supporters. Similarly, the former Malaysian prime minister, Mahathir Mohamad, has been described as a strong, domineering personality in Southeast Asian politics.

The media has long been a believer in **trait theories of leadership**—differentiating leaders from non-leaders by focusing on personal qualities and characteristics. The media identify people such as Margaret Thatcher, South Africa's Nelson Mandela, Virgin Group CEO Sir Richard Branson, former Singaporean prime minister Lee Kuan Yew and Woolworths' CEO, Roger Corbett, as leaders, and use terms such as *charismatic, enthusiastic* and *courageous* to describe them. Well, the media isn't alone. The search for personality, social, physical or intellectual attributes that would describe leaders and differentiate them from non-leaders goes back to the 1930s.

Research efforts at isolating leadership traits resulted in a number of dead ends. For example, a review of 20 different studies identified nearly 80 leadership traits, but only five of these traits were common to four or more of the investigations.[5] If the search was intended to identify a set of traits that would *always* differentiate leaders from followers, and effective leaders from ineffective leaders, the search failed. Perhaps it was a bit optimistic to believe that there could be consistent and unique traits that would apply universally to all effective leaders, no matter whether they were in charge of Mitsubishi Motor Corporation, the Catholic Church, Maddog Surfboards Australia, the Chinese national soccer team or Sydney University.

If, however, the search was intended to identify traits that were consistently associated with leadership, the results can be interpreted in a more impressive light. For example, six traits on which leaders tend to differ from non-leaders are ambition and energy, the desire to lead, honesty and integrity, self-confidence, intelligence and job-relevant knowledge.[6] In addition, more recent research provides strong evidence that people who are high self-monitors—that is, are highly flexible in adjusting their behaviour in different situations—are much more likely to emerge as leaders in groups than are low self-monitors.[7] Overall, the cumulative findings from more than half a century of research lead us to conclude that some traits increase the likelihood of success as a leader, but none of the traits *guarantee* success.[8]

But the trait approach has at least four limitations. First, there are no universal traits that predict leadership in all situations. Rather, traits appear to predict leadership in *selective* situations.[9] Second, traits predict behaviour more in 'weak' situations than in 'strong' situations.[10] Strong situations are those in which there are strong behavioural norms, strong incentives for specific types of behaviours, and clear expectations as to what behaviours are rewarded and punished. Such strong situations create less opportunity for leaders to express their inherent dispositional tendencies. Since highly formalised organisations and those with strong cultures fit the description of strong situations, the power of traits to predict leadership in many organisations is probably limited. Third, the evidence is unclear in separating cause from effect. For example, does self-confidence create leadership, or does success as a leader build self-confidence? Finally, traits do a better job at predicting the appearance of leadership than in actually distinguishing between *effective* and *ineffective* leaders.[11] The fact that an individual exhibits the traits, and that others consider that person to be a leader, doesn't necessarily mean that the leader is successful at getting their group to achieve its goals.

These limitations have led researchers to look in other directions. Although there has been a resurgent interest in traits during the past 20 years, a major movement away from traits began as early as the 1940s. Leadership research from the late 1940s through to the late 1960s emphasised the preferred behavioural styles that leaders demonstrated.

LEARNING OBJECTIVE 2

Summarise the conclusions of trait theories

Behavioural Theories

The inability to strike 'gold' in the trait 'mines' led researchers to look at the behaviours exhibited by specific leaders. They wondered if there was something unique in the way that effective leaders behave. For example, in the United States, Titan International CEO Morry Taylor and Siebel Systems' CEO Tom Siebel both have been very successful in leading their companies through difficult times.[12] And they both rely on a common leadership style—tough-talking, intense, autocratic. Does this suggest that autocratic behaviour is a preferred style for all leaders? In this section, we look at four different **behavioural theories of leadership** in order to answer that

behavioural theories of leadership
Theories proposing that specific behaviours differentiate leaders from non-leaders.

Virgin Group CEO, Sir Richard Branson, is one of many business leaders who have been described in the press in terms of such traits as *charismatic*, *enthusiastic* and *courageous*. Sir Richard uses his public persona to advantage to portray a passion and excitement about all his business endeavours.

question. First, however, let's consider the practical implications of the behavioural approach.

If the behavioural approach to leadership were successful, it would have implications quite different from those of the trait approach. If trait research had been successful, it would have provided a basis for *selecting* the 'right' persons to assume formal positions in groups and organisations requiring leadership. In contrast, if behavioural studies were to turn up critical behavioural determinants of leadership, we could *train* people to be leaders. The difference between trait and behavioural theories, in terms of application, lies in their underlying assumptions. If trait theories were valid, then leaders are born, rather than made. On the other hand, if there were specific behaviours that identified leaders, then we could teach leadership—we could design programs that implanted these behavioural patterns in individuals who desired to be effective leaders. This was surely a more exciting avenue, for it meant that the supply of leaders could be expanded. If training worked, we could have an infinite supply of effective leaders.

OHIO STATE STUDIES

The most comprehensive and replicated of the behavioural theories resulted from research that began at Ohio State University, in the United States, in the late 1940s.[13] These researchers sought to identify independent dimensions of leader behaviour. Beginning with over a thousand dimensions, they eventually narrowed the list to two categories that substantially accounted for most of the leadership behaviour described by employees. They called these two dimensions *initiating structure* and *consideration*.

initiating structure
The extent to which a leader is likely to define and structure his or her role and those of subordinates in the search for goal attainment.

Initiating structure refers to the extent to which a leader is likely to define and structure their role and those of employees in the search for goal attainment. It includes behaviour that attempts to organise work, work relationships and goals. The leader characterised as high in initiating structure could be described as someone who 'assigns group members to particular tasks', 'expects workers to maintain definite standards of performance' and 'emphasises the meeting of deadlines'. Morry Taylor and Tom Siebel exhibit high initiating structure behaviour.

consideration
The extent to which a leader is likely to have job relationships characterised by mutual trust, respect for subordinates' ideas and regard for their feelings.

Consideration is described as the extent to which a person is likely to have job relationships that are characterised by mutual trust, respect for employees' ideas and regard for their feelings. They show concern for followers' comfort, well-being, status and satisfaction. A leader high in consideration could be described as one who helps employees with personal problems, is friendly and approachable, and treats all employees as equals. AOL is known by many in the Asia-Pacific region. AOL is the world's largest Internet company, with over 35 million members around the globe. CEO, Richard Parsons, rates high on consideration behaviour. His leadership style is very people-oriented, emphasising cooperation and consensus-building.[14]

Extensive research, based on these definitions, found that leaders high in initiating structure and consideration (a 'high–high' leader) tended to achieve high employee performance and satisfaction more frequently than those who rated low on consideration, initiating structure, or both. However, the 'high–high' style didn't always result in positive consequences. For example,

OB Controversies

Executive leaders, their pay and their performance

Leadership has been researched extensively in the last 50 years, and thousands of articles have been written about the significance of effective leadership to the performance of an organisation. In order to establish a link with performance, researchers have looked at the attributes of successful leaders, their charismatic qualities, their motivations, styles and approaches, as well as the attributes of their followers. But the research has shed little light on one of the great current controversies in executive leadership—as a moderating variable, does the amount of executive pay have a direct influence on a company's performance?

Dick Warburton is chairman of the large Australian retail chain, David Jones, as well as of Caltex Australia. He believes that executive salaries are too high. This is a theme that has regularly featured in recent *Business Review Weekly* and other business magazine articles. A common response is that competitive market forces determine the level of remuneration paid to executives who compete for the top leadership jobs around the world. But do exorbitant salaries provide the formula for executives to sustain high company performance?

According to Nicholas Way and Andrew Heathcote, multi-million-dollar payouts and generous salary increases are generating a massive backlash from various stakeholders at a time of falling share prices. There is much anger towards what investors see as executive greed. Since the late 1990s, and at a time of strong economic growth, the chief executives of many companies have destroyed value, rather than created it. Commonwealth Bank of Australia CEO David Murray told shareholders in 2003 that a key executive had walked away with a $32.75 million payout, which was an Australian record. This was despite a 48 per cent decrease in profit, to $622 million in 2002, and a $426 million write-down on its wealth management business. Prior to that, BHP Billiton paid $30 million to Brian Gilbertson after just six months in the top position.

Human resource managers have no difficulty bringing in the consultants to review jobs and salary and wage structures for their employees. The consultants rely on their research to justify the remuneration levels for various job designations. Why does the research not inform companies about their top leadership positions when it comes to rewards for performance? As Stuart Wilson points out, why aren't chief executives required to buy shares in their company? At least this would reflect an aspect of the relationship between wealth and performance a little better. Stuart is chief executive of the Australian Shareholders' Association.

Sources: Nicholas Way and Andrew Heathcote, '20 Highest-paid CEOs', *Business Review Weekly*, 20 February 2003, pp. 44–50; and John Stensholt, 'What is Fair Pay?', *Business Review Weekly*, 29 August 2002, pp. 66–68. With permission.

leader behaviour characterised as high on initiating structure led to greater rates of grievances, absenteeism and turnover, and lower levels of job satisfaction for workers performing routine tasks. Other studies found that high consideration was negatively related to performance ratings of the leader by their superior. In conclusion, the Ohio State studies suggested that the 'high–high' style generally resulted in positive outcomes, but enough exceptions were found to indicate that situational factors needed to be integrated into the theory.

UNIVERSITY OF MICHIGAN STUDIES

Leadership studies undertaken at the University of Michigan's Survey Research Center, at about the same time as those being done at Ohio State, had similar research objectives: to locate behavioural characteristics of leaders that appeared to be related to measures of performance effectiveness.

The Michigan group also came up with two dimensions of leadership behaviour that they labelled **employee-oriented** and **production-oriented**.[15] Leaders who were employee-oriented were described as emphasising interpersonal relations; they took a personal interest in the needs of their employees and accepted individual differences among members. The production-oriented leaders, in contrast, tended to emphasise the technical or task aspects of the job—their main concern was in accomplishing their group's tasks, and the group members were a means to that end.

The conclusions arrived at by the Michigan researchers strongly favoured the leaders who were employee-oriented in their behaviour. Employee-oriented leaders were associated with higher group productivity and higher job satisfaction. Production-oriented leaders tended to be associated with low group productivity and lower job satisfaction.

THE MANAGERIAL GRID

A graphic portrayal of a two-dimensional view of leadership style was developed by Blake and Mouton.[16] They proposed a **managerial grid** (sometimes also now called the *leadership grid*) based on the styles of 'concern for people' and 'concern for production', which essentially represent the Ohio State dimensions of consideration and initiating structure, or the Michigan dimensions of employee-oriented and production-oriented.

The grid, depicted in Figure 11.1 has nine possible positions along each axis, creating 81 different positions in which the leader's style may fall. The grid doesn't show results produced but, rather, the dominating factors in a leader's thinking in regard to getting results.

Based on the findings of Blake and Mouton, managers were found to perform best under a 9,9 style, as contrasted, for example, with a 9,1 (authority-type) or 1,9 (laissez-faire-type) style.[17] Unfortunately, the grid offers a better framework for conceptualising leadership style than for presenting any tangible new information in clarifying the leadership quandary, because there is little substantive evidence to support the conclusion that a 9,9 style is most effective in all situations.[18]

SCANDINAVIAN STUDIES

The three behavioural approaches we have just reviewed were essentially developed between the late 1940s and early 1960s. These approaches evolved during a time when the world was a far more stable and predictable place. In the belief that these studies fail to capture the more dynamic realities of today, researchers in Finland and Sweden have been reassessing whether there are only two dimensions that capture the essence of leadership behaviour.[19] Their basic premise is that in a changing world, effective leaders would exhibit **development-oriented** behaviour. These are leaders who value experimentation, seek new ideas, and generate and implement change.

For example, these Scandinavian researchers reviewed the original Ohio State data. They found that the Ohio State people included development items such as 'pushes new ways of doing things', 'originates new approaches to problems' and 'encourages members to start new activities'. But these items, at the time, didn't explain much towards effective leadership. It could be, the Scandinavian researchers proposed, that this was because developing new ideas and implementing change were not critical in those days. In today's dynamic environment, this may no longer be true. So, the Scandinavian researchers have been conducting new studies looking to see if there is a third dimension—development orientation—that is related to leader effectiveness.

employee-oriented leader
Emphasising interpersonal relations; taking a personal interest in the needs of employees and accepting individual differences among members.

production-oriented leader
One who emphasises technical or task aspects of the job.

managerial grid
A nine-by-nine matrix outlining 81 different leadership styles.

development-oriented leader
One who values experimentation, seeks new ideas, and generates and implements change.

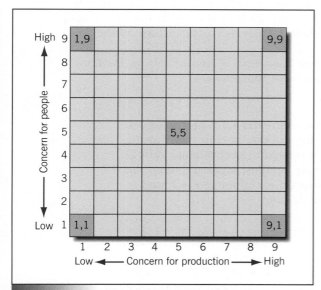

FIGURE 11.1 **The managerial grid**

The early evidence is positive. Using samples of leaders in Finland and Sweden, the researchers have found strong support for development-oriented leader behaviour as a separate and independent dimension. That is, the previous behavioural approaches that focused in on only two behaviours may not appropriately capture leadership in the 21st century. Moreover, while initial conclusions need to be guarded without more confirming evidence, it also appears that leaders who demonstrate development-oriented behaviour have more satisfied employees and are seen as more competent by those employees.

SUMMARY OF BEHAVIOURAL THEORIES

LEARNING OBJECTIVE

3

Identify the limitations of behavioural theories

The behavioural theories have had modest success in identifying consistent relationships between leadership behaviour and group performance. What seems to be missing is consideration of the situational factors that influence success or failure. For example, it seems unlikely that Germaine Greer would have been a great feminist and anarchist leader at the turn of the 20th century; yet, she had a great influence over social affairs in Australia in the 1960s and 1970s. Would Anita Roddick, founder of The Body Shop, have emerged as an influential activist on globalisation if she had been born in 1842 rather than 1942, or been raised in Fiji rather than Sussex, in England? It seems quite unlikely, yet the behavioural approaches we have described couldn't clarify these situational factors.

Contingency Theories

Linda Wachner had a reputation as being a very tough boss. And for a number of years, this style worked. In 1987, Wachner became CEO of Warnaco, a struggling US$425 million-a-year apparel company in the United States. Over a 14-year period, she transformed Warnaco into a US$2.2 billion company whose products ranged from Calvin Klein jeans to Speedo swimsuits. In spite of an abrasive style that included frequently humiliating employees in front of their peers, and which led to rapid turnover among top managers, Wachner's style worked for most of the 1990s and she was recognised for her success as a businesswoman. But times change and Wachner didn't.[20] Beginning in 1998, the company's business began to unravel, hurt by a reduction in demand for its products and a fast-eroding market share. Wachner's headstrong approach and brash tactics, which had driven off many competent executives, was now alienating creditors and licensers as well as employees. In June 2001, Warnaco was forced to file for bankruptcy protection. Five months later, the restructuring committee of Warnaco's board of directors fired Wachner.

Linda Wachner's rise and fall illustrates what became increasingly clear to those studying the leadership phenomenon decades earlier: predicting leadership success is more complex than isolating a few traits or preferable behaviours. In Wachner's case, what worked in 1990 didn't work in 2000. The failure by researchers to obtain consistent results led to a focus on situational influences. The relationship between leadership style and effectiveness suggested that under condition *a*, style *x* would be appropriate, whereas style *y* would be more suitable for condition *b*, and style *z* for condition *c*. But what were the conditions *a*, *b*, *c*, and so forth? It was one thing to say that leadership effectiveness was dependent on the situation, and another to be able to isolate those situational conditions.

Several approaches to isolating key situational variables have proven more successful than others and, as a result, have gained wider recognition. We shall consider five of these: the Fiedler model, Hersey and Blanchard's situational theory, leader–member exchange theory, and the path–goal and leader-participation models.

FIEDLER MODEL

LEARNING OBJECTIVE
4
Describe Fiedler's contingency model

The first comprehensive contingency model for leadership was developed by Fred Fiedler.[21] The **Fiedler contingency model** proposes that effective group performance depends on the proper match between the leader's style and the degree to which the situation gives control to the leader.

Fiedler contingency model
The theory that effective groups depend on a proper match between a leader's style of interacting with subordinates and the degree to which the situation gives control and influence to the leader.

Identifying leadership style

Fiedler believes a key factor in leadership success is the individual's basic leadership style. So, he begins by trying to find out what that basic style is. Fiedler created the **least preferred co-worker (LPC) questionnaire** for this purpose; it purports to measure whether a person is task- or relationship-oriented. The LPC questionnaire contains sets of 16 contrasting adjectives (such as pleasant–unpleasant, efficient–inefficient, open–guarded, supportive–hostile). It asks respondents to think of all the co-workers they have ever had and to describe the one person they *least enjoyed* working with by rating them on a scale of 1 to 8 for each of the 16 sets of contrasting adjectives. Fiedler believes that based on the respondents' answers to this LPC questionnaire, he can determine their basic leadership style. If the least preferred co-worker is described in relatively positive terms (a high LPC score), then the respondent is primarily interested in good personal relations with this co-worker. That is, if you essentially describe the person you are least able to work with in favourable terms, Fiedler would label you *relationship-oriented*. In contrast, if the least preferred co-worker is seen in relatively unfavourable terms (a low LPC score), the respondent is primarily interested in productivity and thus would be labelled *task-oriented*. About 16 per cent of respondents score in the middle range.[22] Such individuals cannot be classified as either relationship-oriented or task-oriented, and thus fall outside the theory's predictions. The rest of our discussion, therefore, relates to the 84 per cent who score in either the high or low range of the LPC.

least preferred co-worker (LPC) questionnaire
An instrument that purports to measure whether a person is task- or relationship-oriented.

Fiedler assumes that an individual's leadership style is fixed. As we will show below, this is important because it means that if a situation requires a task-oriented leader and the person in that leadership position is relationship-oriented, either the situation has to be modified or the leader replaced if optimal effectiveness is to be achieved.

Defining the situation

After an individual's basic leadership style has been assessed through the LPC, it is necessary to match the leader with the situation. Fiedler has identified three contingency dimensions which, he argues, define the key situational factors that determine leadership effectiveness. These are leader–member relations, task structure and position power. They are defined as follows:

leader–member relations
The degree of confidence, trust and respect subordinates have in their leader.

1. *Leader–member relations:* The degree of confidence, trust and respect members have in their leader.
2. *Task structure:* The degree to which the job assignments are procedurised (that is, structured or unstructured).
3. *Position power:* The degree of influence a leader has over power variables such as hiring, firing, discipline, promotions and salary increases.

task structure
The degree to which the job assignments are procedurised.

The next step in the Fiedler model is to evaluate the situation in terms of these three contingency variables. Leader–member relations are either good or poor, task structure is either high or low, and position power is either strong or weak.

Fiedler states the better the leader–member relations, the more highly structured the job, and the stronger the position power, the more control the leader has. For example, a very favourable situation (in which the leader would have a great deal of control) might involve a payroll manager who is well respected and whose employees have confidence in her (good leader–member relations), for which the activities to be done—such as wage calculation, cheque writing, report filing—are specific and clear (high task structure), and the job provides considerable freedom for her to reward and punish her employees (strong position power). On the other hand, an unfavourable situation might be the disliked chairperson of a voluntary church fund-raising

position power
Influence derived from one's formal structural position in the organisation; includes power to hire, fire, discipline, promote and give salary increases.

Research evidence suggests that the emphasis which military units place on leadership training and experienced-based promotions is well founded. Battle conditions are highly stressful. As cognitive resource theory demonstrates, experience (achieved through training and on-the-job practice) is important to success under high-stress conditions.

team. In this job, the leader has very little control. Altogether, by mixing the three contingency variables, there are potentially eight different situations or categories in which leaders could find themselves.

Matching leaders and situations

With knowledge of an individual's LPC and an assessment of the three contingency variables, the Fiedler model proposes matching them up to achieve maximum leadership effectiveness.[23] Based on his research, Fiedler concluded that task-oriented leaders tend to perform better in situations that were very favourable to them and in situations that were very unfavourable (see Figure 11.2). So, Fiedler would predict that when faced with a category I, II, III, VII or VIII situation, task-oriented leaders perform better. Relationship-oriented leaders, however, perform better in moderately favourable situations—categories IV to VI. In recent years, Fiedler has condensed these eight situations down to three.[24] He now says that task-oriented leaders perform best in situations of high and low control, while relationship-oriented leaders perform best in moderate control situations.

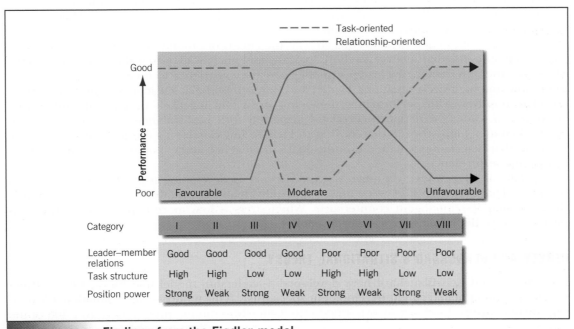

FIGURE 11.2   **Findings from the Fiedler model**

Given Fiedler's findings, how would you apply them? You would seek to match leaders and situations. Individuals' LPC scores would determine the type of situation for which they were best suited. That 'situation' would be defined by evaluating the three contingency factors of leader–member relations, task structure and position power. But remember that Fiedler views an individual's leadership style as being fixed. Therefore, there are really only two ways in which to improve leader effectiveness.

First, you can change the leader to fit the situation—as in a softball game, a coach can put a right-handed pitcher or a left-handed pitcher into the game, depending on the situational characteristics of the hitter. So, for example, if a group situation rates as highly unfavourable but is currently led by a relationship-oriented coach, the group's performance could be improved by replacing that coach with one who is task-oriented. The second alternative would be to change the situation to fit the leader. That could be done by restructuring tasks or increasing or decreasing the power that the leader has to control factors such as salary increases, promotions and disciplinary actions.

Evaluation

As a whole, reviews of the major studies that tested the overall validity of the Fiedler model lead to a generally positive conclusion. That is, there is considerable evidence to support at least substantial parts of the model.[25] If predictions from the model use only three categories rather than the original eight, there is ample evidence to support Fiedler's conclusions.[26] But there are problems with the LPC and the practical use of the model that need to be addressed. For example, the logic underlying the LPC is not well understood and studies have shown that respondents' LPC scores aren't stable.[27] Also, the contingency variables are complex and difficult for practitioners to assess. It's often difficult in practice to determine how good the leader–member relations are, how structured the task is, and how much position power the leader has.[28]

Cognitive resource theory

More recently, Fiedler and an associate, Joe Garcia, reconceptualised the former's original theory.[29] Specifically, they focused on the role of stress as a form of situational unfavourableness and how a leader's intelligence and experience influence their reaction to stress. They call this reconceptualisation **cognitive resource theory**.

The essence of the new theory is that stress is the enemy of rationality. It's difficult for leaders (or anyone else, for that matter) to think logically and analytically when they are under stress. Moreover, the importance of a leader's intelligence and experience to their effectiveness differs under low- and high-stress situations. Fiedler and Garcia found that a leader's intellectual abilities correlate positively with performance under low stress but negatively under high stress. And, conversely, a leader's experience correlates negatively with performance under low stress but positively under high stress. So, according to Fiedler and Garcia, it's the level of stress in the situation that determines whether an individual's intelligence and experience will contribute to leadership performance.

In spite of its newness, cognitive resource theory is developing a solid body of research support.[30] That is, in high-stress situations, bright individuals perform worse in the leadership role than do their less intelligent counterparts. When stress is low, more experienced individuals perform worse than do less experienced people.

HERSEY AND BLANCHARD'S SITUATIONAL THEORY

Paul Hersey and Ken Blanchard have developed a leadership model that has gained a strong following among management development specialists.[31] This model—called **situational leadership theory (SLT)**—has been incorporated into leadership training programs at over 400 of the Fortune 500 companies in the United States; and over one million managers a year from a wide variety of organisations are being taught its basic elements.[32]

cognitive resource theory
A theory of leadership that states that stress unfavourably affects a situation and that intelligence and experience can lessen the influence of stress on the leader.

LEARNING OBJECTIVE

5

Explain Hersey and Blanchard's situational theory

situational leadership theory (SLT)
A contingency theory that focuses on followers' readiness.

Myth *or* Science?

'It's experience that counts!'

The belief in the value of experience as a predictor of leadership effectiveness is very strong and widespread. Unfortunately, experience alone is generally a poor predictor of leadership.[33]

Organisations carefully screen outside candidates for senior management positions on the basis of their experience. Similarly, organisations usually require several years of experience at one managerial level before a person can be considered for promotions. For that matter, have you ever filled out an employment application that *didn't* ask about previous experience or job history? Clearly, management believes that experience counts. But the evidence doesn't support this view. Studies of military officers, research and development teams, shop supervisors, post office administrators and school principals tell us that experienced managers tend to be no more effective than managers with little experience.

One flaw in the 'experience counts' logic is the assumption that length of time on a job is actually a measure of experience. This says nothing about the quality of experience. The fact that one person has 20 years' experience while another has two years' doesn't necessarily mean that the former has had ten times as many meaningful experiences. Too often, 20 years of experience is nothing more than one year of experience repeated 20 times! In even the most complex jobs, real learning typically ends after about two years. By then, almost all new and unique situations have been experienced. So, one problem with trying to link experience with leadership effectiveness is not paying attention to the quality and diversity of the experience.

A second problem is that there is variability between situations that influence the transferability or relevance of experience. Situations in which experience is obtained is rarely comparable to new situations. Jobs differ, support resources differ, organisational cultures differ, follower characteristics differ, and so on. So, another reason that leadership experience isn't strongly related to leadership performance is undoubtedly due to variability of situations.

Situational leadership is a contingency theory that focuses on the followers. Successful leadership is achieved by selecting the right leadership style, which Hersey and Blanchard argue is contingent on the level of the followers' readiness. Before we proceed, we should clarify two points: Why focus on the followers? and What do they mean by the term *readiness*?

The emphasis on the followers in leadership effectiveness reflects the reality that it is the followers who accept or reject the leader. Regardless of what the leader does, effectiveness depends on the actions of their followers. This is an important dimension that has been overlooked or underemphasised in most leadership theories. The term *readiness*, as defined by Hersey and Blanchard, refers to the extent to which people have the ability and willingness to accomplish a specific task.

SLT essentially views the leader–follower relationship as analogous to that between a parent and a child. Just as a parent needs to relinquish control as a child becomes more mature and responsible, so too should leaders. Hersey and Blanchard identify four specific leader behaviours—from highly directive to highly laissez-faire. The most effective behaviour depends on a follower's ability and motivation. So, SLT says if a follower is *unable* and *unwilling* to do a task, the leader needs to give clear and specific directions; if the follower is *unable* and *willing*, the leader needs to display high task orientation to compensate for the follower's lack of ability and high relationship orientation to get the follower to 'buy into' the leader's desires; if the follower is *able* and *unwilling*, the leader needs to use a supportive and participative style; and if the employee is both *able* and *willing*, the leader doesn't need to do much. SLT has an intuitive appeal. It acknowledges the importance of followers and builds on the logic that leaders can compensate for ability and motivational limitations in their followers. Yet, research efforts to test and support the theory have generally been disappointing.[34] Why? Possible explanations include internal ambiguities and inconsistencies in the model itself, as well as problems with research methodology in tests of the theory. So, in spite of its intuitive appeal and wide popularity, at least at this time, any enthusiastic endorsement has to be cautioned against.

LEADER–MEMBER EXCHANGE THEORY

For the most part, the leadership theories we have covered to this point have largely assumed that leaders treat all their followers in the same manner. That is, they assume that leaders use a fairly homogeneous style with all of the people in their work unit. But think about your experiences in groups. Did you notice that leaders often act very differently towards different people? Did the leader tend to have favourites who made up their 'in-group'? If you answered 'yes' to both these questions, you are acknowledging the foundation of leader–member exchange theory.[35]

leader–member exchange (LMX) theory
Leaders create in-groups and out-groups, and subordinates with in-group status will have higher performance ratings, less turnover and greater job satisfaction.

The **leader–member exchange (LMX) theory** argues that because of time pressures, leaders establish a special relationship with a small group of their followers. These individuals make up the in-group—they are trusted, get a disproportionate amount of the leader's attention and are more likely to receive special privileges. Other followers fall into the out-group. They get less of the leader's time, fewer of the preferred rewards that the leader controls, and have leader–follower relations based on formal authority interactions.

The theory proposes that early in the history of the interaction between a leader and a given follower, the leader implicitly categorises the follower as an 'in' or an 'out' and that relationship is relatively stable over time.[36] Just precisely how the leader chooses who falls into each category is unclear, but there is evidence that leaders tend to choose in-group members because they have attitude and personality characteristics that are similar to the leader's or a higher level of competence than out-group members[37] (see Figure 11.3). A key point to note here is that even though it is the leader who is doing the choosing, it is the follower's characteristics that are driving the leader's categorising decision.

Research to test LMX theory has been generally supportive. More specifically, the theory and research surrounding it provide substantive evidence that leaders do differentiate among followers; that these disparities are far from random; and that followers with in-group status will have higher performance ratings, lower turnover intentions, greater satisfaction with their superior, and higher overall satisfaction than will the out-group.[38] These positive findings for in-group members shouldn't be totally surprising given our knowledge of the self-fulfilling prophecy

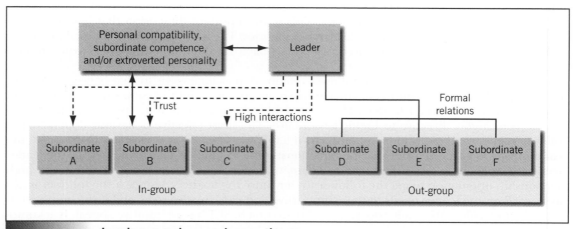

FIGURE 11.3 **Leader–member exchange theory**

mentioned in a previous chapter. Leaders invest their resources with those they expect to perform best. And 'knowing' that in-group members are the most competent, leaders treat them as such and unwittingly fulfil their prophecy.[39]

PATH–GOAL THEORY

Currently, one of the most respected approaches to leadership is the path–goal theory. Developed by Robert House, path–goal theory is a contingency model of leadership that extracts key elements from the Ohio State leadership research on initiating structure and consideration and the expectancy theory of motivation.[40]

The essence of the **path–goal theory** is that it is the leader's job to assist followers in attaining their goals and to provide the necessary direction and/or support to ensure that their goals are compatible with the overall objectives of the group or organisation. The term *path–goal* is derived from the belief that effective leaders clarify the path to help their followers get from where they are to the achievement of their work goals and to make the journey along the path easier by reducing roadblocks.

House identified four leadership behaviours. The *directive leader* lets followers know what is expected of them, schedules work to be done, and gives specific guidance as to how to accomplish tasks. The *supportive leader* is friendly and shows concern for the needs of followers. The *participative leader* consults with followers and uses their suggestions before making a decision. The *achievement-oriented leader* sets challenging goals and expects followers to perform at their highest level. In contrast to Fiedler, House assumes that leaders are flexible and that the same leader can display any or all of these behaviours depending on the situation.

As Figure 11.4 illustrates, path–goal theory proposes two classes of situational or contingency variables that moderate the leadership behaviour–outcome relationship—those in the environment that are outside the control of the employee (task structure, the formal authority system and the work group) and those that are part of the personal characteristics of the employee (locus of control, experience and perceived ability). Environmental factors determine the type of leader behaviour required as a complement if follower outcomes are to be maximised, while personal characteristics of the employee determine how the environment and leader behaviour are interpreted. So, the theory proposes that leader behaviour will be ineffective when it is redundant with

LEARNING OBJECTIVE

7

Describe the path–goal theory

path–goal theory
The theory that it is the leader's job to assist followers in attaining their goals and to provide the necessary direction and/or support to ensure that their goals are compatible with the overall objectives of the group or organisation.

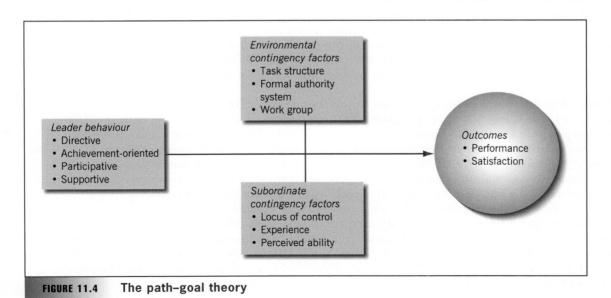

FIGURE 11.4   **The path–goal theory**

sources of environmental structure or incongruent with employee characteristics. For example, the following are illustrations of predictions based on path–goal theory:

- Directive leadership leads to greater satisfaction when tasks are ambiguous or stressful than when they are highly structured and well laid out.
- Supportive leadership results in high employee performance and satisfaction when employees are performing structured tasks.
- Directive leadership is likely to be perceived as redundant among employees with high perceived ability or with considerable experience.
- Employees with an internal locus of control will be more satisfied with a participative style.
- Achievement-oriented leadership will increase employees' expectancies that effort will lead to high performance when tasks are ambiguously structured.

The research evidence generally supports the logic underlying the path–goal theory.[41] That is, employee performance and satisfaction are likely to be positively influenced when the leader compensates for things lacking in either the employee or the work setting. However, the leader who spends time explaining tasks when those tasks are already clear or when the employee has the ability and experience to handle them without interference is likely to be ineffective because the employee will see such directive behaviour as redundant or even insulting.

LEARNING OBJECTIVE

8

Identify the situational variables in the leader-participation model

leader-participation model
A leadership theory that provides a set of rules to determine the form and amount of participative decision making in different situations.

LEADER-PARTICIPATION MODEL

Victor Vroom and Phillip Yetton developed a **leader-participation model** that related leadership behaviour and participation in decision making.[42] Recognising that task structures have varying demands for routine and non-routine activities, these researchers argued that leader behaviour must adjust to reflect the task structure. Vroom and Yetton's model was normative—it provided a

The Real Deal

Making leaders out of lawyers and accountants

As they have successfully expanded their businesses, many accounting and law firms have recognised that the old model of practice was deficient. Young recruits would hone their technical skills, build their client base and seek admission as a partner to the firm. Firms would represent a federation of semi-independent professionals. Now, there is a recognition that strong leadership skills need to be developed among these professionals to deal with sophisticated clients and complex deals in teams based on diverse skills and roles.

People skills and leadership capability are now a core requirement. Minter Ellison is a law firm with offices in Hong Kong, Shanghai, Bangkok and throughout Australasia. It has recently developed a leadership program for 48 of its partners and senior associates. The international accounting firm of Deloitte Touche Tohmatsu has sent eight partners of its Australian executive team to Chicago for a course on 'reinventing leadership'. One of Australia's leading law firms, Clayton Utz, has its new graduate recruits complete a national two-week orientation program. Senior associates are undertaking a future leaders program, and a number of partners are receiving one-on-one executive coaching.

Avril Henry, the national director of human resources for Clayton Utz, indicates the importance of its orientation program for emphasising teamwork, communication, ethics, respect and stress management. The cooking class is also a popular component of the program for developing teamwork. The firm's staff are predominantly from Generations X and Y (born after 1965) and look for challenging work, developmental opportunities, constructive feedback and leadership. Leadership development is becoming a reality in professionals traditionally focused on their technical prowess.

Source: Lucinda Schmidt, 'The New Professionals', *Business Review Weekly*, 26 June 2003, pp. 70–72. With permission.

sequential set of rules that should be followed in determining the form and amount of participation in decision making, as determined by different types of situations. The model was a decision tree incorporating seven contingencies (whose relevance could be identified by making 'yes' or 'no' choices) and five alternative leadership styles.

More recent work by Vroom and Arthur Jago has resulted in a revision of this model.[43] The new model retains the same five alternative leadership styles—from the leader's making the decision completely by themselves, to sharing the problem with the group and developing a consensus decision—but adds a set of problem types and expands the contingency variables to 12. The 12 contingency variables are listed in Table 11.1.

Research testing both the original and revised leader-participation models has been encouraging.[44] Criticism has tended to focus on variables that have been omitted and on the model's overall complexity.[45] Other contingency theories demonstrate that stress, intelligence and experience are important situational variables. Yet, the leader-participation model fails to include them. But more importantly, at least from a practical point of view, is the fact that the model is far too complicated for the typical manager to use on a regular basis. While Vroom and Jago have developed a computer program to guide managers through all the decision branches in the revised model, it is not very realistic to expect practising managers to consider 12 contingency variables, eight problem types and five leadership styles in trying to select the appropriate decision process for a specific problem.

We obviously haven't done justice in this discussion to the model's sophistication. So, what can you gain from this brief review? Certainly, we have provided additional insights into relevant contingency variables. Vroom and his associates have provided us with some specific, empirically-supported contingency variables that you should consider when choosing your leadership style.

TABLE 11.1	Contingency variables in the revised leader-participation model
1.	Importance of the decision
2.	Importance of obtaining follower commitment to the decision
3.	Whether the leader has sufficient information to make a good decision
4.	How well structured the problem is
5.	Whether an autocratic decision would receive follower commitment
6.	Whether followers 'buy into' the organisation's goals
7.	Whether there is likely to be conflict among followers over solution alternatives
8.	Whether followers have the necessary information to make a good decision
9.	Time constraints on the leader that may limit follower involvement
10.	Whether costs to bring geographically dispersed members together is justified
11.	Importance to the leader of minimising the time it takes to make the decision
12.	Importance of using participation as a tool for developing follower decision skills

Summary and Implications for Managers

Leadership plays a central part in understanding group behaviour, for it is the leader who usually provides the direction towards goal attainment. Therefore, a more accurate predictive capability should be valuable in improving group performance.

The original search for a set of universal leadership traits failed. At best, we can say that individuals who are ambitious, have high energy, a desire to lead, self-confidence and intelligence, who hold job-relevant knowledge, are perceived as honest and trustworthy, and who are flexible are more likely to succeed as leaders than are individuals without these traits.

The main contribution of the behavioural approach was to narrow leadership into task-oriented and people-oriented styles. But no one style was found to be effective in all situations.

A major breakthrough in our understanding of leadership came when we recognised the need to develop contingency theories that included situational factors. At present, the evidence indicates that relevant situational variables would include the task structure of the job, level of situational stress, level of group support, the leader's intelligence and experience, and follower characteristics such as personality, experience, ability and motivation.

Leadership is an evolving concept, and there is no doubt about its significance to organisations. There is no one secret to success, but an awareness of different theories and approaches is important to understanding what is involved in successful leadership situations.

Point

LEADERSHIP DEVELOPMENT IS A WASTE OF MONEY!

Organisations spend billions of dollars on leadership training every year. They send managers to a wide range of leadership training activities—formal MBA programs, leadership seminars, weekend retreats and even Outward Bound adventures. They appoint mentors and establish 'fast tracks' and development centres for high-potential individuals so that they can gain the right knowledge and experience.

After 50 years of management courses and MBA programs, there is little evidence that these programs have led to an improvement in management and leadership skills. More specifically, there is no evidence to suggest that managers who attend these programs make fewer mistakes in the way they handle staff or manage the business than do other managers. Often managers come back from the new 'management wonder course' and try to institute the latest fad—quality management, 'principle-centred leadership', business reengineering, Investment in Excellence, empowerment, self-managing teams, and so on—without fully understanding whether it is right for the organisation at this time. Staff quietly attend the latest training program and pretend that they are instituting the change—until the next new idea comes along.[a]

When the cost of all of this is added up, there seems to be little evidence that the benefits of leadership development justify the costs. The main economic benefits have been to the 'management gurus', Tom Peters, Stephen Covey and the 10,000 other experts who profess to have the secrets of successful leadership. If they really have found the secret, why are so many organisations downsizing or having trouble surviving, and why do so many employees describe their leaders as ineffective and untrustworthy? Not only do these management gurus proclaim they have found 'the answer', but a year later they come out with another book or video proclaiming a *new* 'answer', better than and different from the previous one.

The experts can't even agree what leadership is, so how can they teach it? They aren't sure whether it's a trait, a behaviour, a role, a style or an ability in different situations. Some experts argue that leadership is more in the eyes of the follower—so we should be training for followership, not leadership! Others suggest that leaders are the people who get credit for successes and take the blame for failures, but they actually have little control over organisational outcomes. We are attributing leadership to people who don't actually have it. When we look at successful business and government leaders, how many of them have attended university or leadership training programs? It seems these successful leaders—Kerry Stokes (executive chairman of the Channel 7 TV Network), Anita Roddick (founder of The Body Shop) and Nelson Mandela (former president of South Africa)—

have a combination of intelligence, a burning passion and an ability to be in the right place at the right time. Courses can't teach this—they only study people who have made it.

Beyond the time and expense for these courses, there is another cost. Staff expect their managers to be better leaders when they return from these programs—and when they don't see any improvement, they become even more cynical and disillusioned.

A lot of noise is made about leadership and the need for it to move organisations into the future, but managers know that leadership occurs only through experience and hard work, so they only invest a minimum amount in something they aren't sure delivers the value added. We do seem to be able to teach individuals about leadership. And if leadership is about personality traits to some degree, a number of managers may not have the right personality to lead. And there is no evidence that training can substantially alter a person's traits or style. Unfortunately, findings indicate we aren't so good at teaching people to lead. What we have learned as a result of all the research on leadership is that it's a lot more complex and involves many more variables than we imagined. Too many to be able to teach anyone effectively. Leadership is more of an art than a science, so why try to pretend that we can teach it the way we do dentistry, physics or computing science?

Sources: [a] Based on R. A. Barker, 'How Can We Train Leaders If We Do Not Know What Leadership Is?', *Human Relations*, April 1997, pp. 343–62; and R. J. House and R. N. Aditya, 'The Social Scientific Study of Leadership: Quo Vadis?', *Journal of Management*, vol. 23, no. 3, 1997, pp. 460–61.

Counterpoint

Leadership training exists and is a multi-billion-dollar business because it works. Would companies such as General Electric, IBM and Australia Post spend tens of millions of dollars each year on leadership development if they didn't feel they were getting a reasonable return? A review of leadership literature, in fact, led two academics to conclude that the research shows 'a consistent effect for leadership explaining 20 to 45 per cent of the variance in relevant organisational outcomes'. Peter Drucker, the well-known management writer, feels that there aren't enough born leaders, so leadership must be learned and this consists of a few simple but vital skills. Others believe it's possible for managers to learn and practise leadership traits and, as they become more proficient, they will gain confidence and skills in leadership. The University of Tampa Center for Leadership, in Florida, offers extensive leadership development activities based on concepts they describe as 'new science', deriving from quantum mechanics, self-organising systems and chaos theory. The theories and concepts help managers to question their own actions and consider the alternatives available.[b]

It is useful to study leadership, because being exposed to the ideas helps managers to recognise the types of mistakes that have been made and to see the skills and behaviours that have resulted in the success of great leaders. Learning about leadership, however, doesn't guarantee that leadership will occur.

The US Military Academy at West Point was built on the premise that it could build military and national leaders for the United States. Its record in producing military leaders and presidents of the United States is quite impressive. The Academy goes to great lengths, however, to ensure that the people who enter it already have excellent leadership potential. The job of West Point, therefore, is to develop the potential. The Royal Military College at Duntroon follows a similar approach for Australian defence personnel.

Part of the problem may be that too many programs are advertised as leadership development programs when all they really do is teach basic skills in management and human relations. Also, people learn in different ways, but many teaching methods don't recognise this and use lectures and academic 'experts' to teach by topics. Some programs are poorly matched to people's learning style and the specific leadership competencies each manager needs. Effective programs in leadership development don't aim to teach everyone leadership skills; they aim to develop leadership skills in people who are already leaders. That's quite a different matter— and one that is much more possible and manageable. We need to invest more money in research to find out which leadership programs are most effective and why. Maybe leadership can't be learned but only developed in people who already have the essentials of leadership!

Sources: [b] Based on D. V. Day and R. G. Lord, 'Executive Leadership and Organizational Performance: Suggestions for a New Theory and Methodology', *Journal of Management*, Fall 1988; P. Drucker, 'Not Enough Generals Were Killed!', *Forbes*, 8 April 1996, ASAP supplement, p. 104;

M. L. Guarriello, 'The Management of Leadership', *Hospital Material Management Quarterly*, February 1996, pp. 17–20; and S. A. Stumpf, 'Applying New Science Theories in Leadership Development Activities', *Journal of Management Development*, vol. 14, no. 5, 1995, pp. 39–49.

For Discussion

1. Trace the development of leadership research.
2. Describe the strengths and weaknesses in the trait approach to leadership.
3. Review trait theories in the context of the 'nature vs. nurture' debate.
4. What is initiating structure? Consideration?
5. What is the managerial grid? Contrast its approach to leadership with the approaches of the Ohio State and Michigan groups.
6. What was the contribution of the Scandinavian studies to the behavioural theories?
7. What are Fiedler's three contingency variables?
8. If you were a manager, how would you assess a situation in terms of Fiedler's three contingency variables?
9. Develop an example where you operationalise the Fiedler model.
10. What contribution does cognitive resource theory make to leadership?
11. What are the implications of LMX theory for leadership practice?
12. What are the contingency variables in path–goal theory?
13. Develop an example where you operationalise path–goal theory.
14. What are the implications if leaders are inflexible in adjusting their style?

Exercises

Exercise 11a
THE LEADER'S IN-GROUP AND OUT-GROUP

Consider either a school group, a work group, a social group or a team you are part of. Classify members of the group as either in-group or out-group members according to who has the formal and informal power, who goes to who for help, and which people have the most influence. List their names or initials below.

In-group	Out-group

What are the differences in behaviour, style and amount of contact that you notice between the in-group members and the out-group members? Why does this occur? What are the advantages and disadvantages of the way in which the group functions as a result of this?

Exercise 11b
DO LEADERS REALLY MATTER?

Divide the class into groups of two. One group member will argue, 'Leaders are the primary determinant of an organisation's success or failure.' The other group member will argue, 'Leaders don't really matter because most of the things that affect an organisation's success or failure are outside a leader's control.' Take ten minutes to develop your arguments; then you have ten minutes to conduct your debate.

After the debates, form into teams of six. Three from each of these groups should have taken the 'pro' argument on leadership and three should have taken the 'con' side. The teams have 15 minutes to reconcile their arguments and to develop a unified position. When the 15 minutes are up, each team should be prepared to make a brief presentation to the class, summarising their unified position.

Case Study 11

Can a Leader's Means Justify the Ends?

Jack Welch is almost a household name in business circles due mainly to the books written about his time with the multinational giant General Electric (GE). By any objective measure, Jack Welch's 20-year reign as CEO of GE would have to be called an overwhelming success. When Welch took over the head job at GE, the company had a market value of US$13 billion. When he retired in 2001, the company was worth US$400 billion. Its profits in 2000 of US$12.7 billion were more than eight times the US$1.5 billion it earned in 1980. Welch's performance paid off for shareholders. Including dividends, the value of GE shares rose an average of 21.3 per cent a year since he took over. This is compared with about 14.3 per cent for the S&P 500 during the same period.

How did Welch achieve such success? On a strategic level, he redefined GE's objectives for every business in which it operated. He said GE would either be No. 1 or No. 2 in all businesses or get out of them. He dropped those with low growth prospects, such as small appliances and TVs, while expanding fast-growth businesses such as financial services and broadcasting. During his tenure as CEO, Welch oversaw 933 acquisitions and the sale of 408 businesses. He was obsessed with improving efficiency, cutting costs and improving performance. To achieve these ends, Welch completely remoulded GE in his style—impatient, aggressive and competitive.

In the 1980s, as Welch began his remaking of GE, he picked up the nickname of 'Neutron Jack'—a playoff of the neutron bomb, which kills people but leaves buildings standing. Welch cut more than 100,000 jobs—a fourth of GE's workforce—through mass layoffs, divestitures, forced retirements, and relocating US jobs to overseas locations with cheaper labour. He pressured his managers and the employees who remained to drive themselves to meet ever-more-demanding efficiency standards. He was blatantly impatient when things didn't move very rapidly. For example, a former technical worker at a GE plant that makes industrial drives says his unit set aggressive goals every year. 'We would meet and beat those goals, but it was never good enough. It was always, "We could have done more." We felt the philosophy at General Electric was that they could replace us in a heartbeat.' To reinforce the competitive environment, Welch established a comprehensive performance evaluation and ranking system for managers. Outstanding managers were highly rewarded, while those at the bottom of the annual rankings were routinely fired.

Welch's demanding goals and penchant for closing down poor-performing units upended the lives of thousands of employees and severely strained the bonds between the company and many of the communities in which it operated. There were also a number of scandals that surfaced under Welch's watch at GE. These ranged from the company's 1985 admission that it had submitted time cards for too much overtime on government contracts, to the 1994 bond-trading scandal at its former Kidder Peabody & Co. investment-banking unit.

Welch's style was a blend of restlessness, bluntness, sarcasm, emotional volatility and teasing humour. As one former GE vice chairman said about Welch, 'Even when he has fun, he's driving himself. He won't give up till he has won, whatever he does.' Welch regularly put in days of 12 hours or more, but he expected the same kind of dedication from his employees. When he got angry, he could lash out with personal attacks that sometimes left shamed managers hurt and speechless.

Questions

1. Describe Jack Welch's leadership style using (a) the Ohio State dimensions, (b) the managerial grid, and (c) LMX theory.
2. Assess Jack Welch's leadership effectiveness as assessed by (a) shareholders, (b) GE managers, (c) GE employees, and (d) communities where GE operations are located.
3. Would you describe Jack Welch as a successful leader at GE? Explain.
4. How would you rate the ethics of Jack Welch's leadership?
5. Would you have wanted to work for Jack Welch? Why or why not?

Source: Based on M. Murray, 'Why Jack Welch's Brand of Leadership Matters', *Wall Street Journal*, 5 September 2001, p. B1.

Web Workout

1. Learn about your personal leadership characteristics by taking the following assessment instrument at <www.nwlink.com/~donclark/leader/survlead.html>. The survey is designed to provide you with feedback about your level of preference or comfort with leadership characteristics and skills. Note what your strengths are and areas for development.

2. Point to <www.nwlink.com/~donclark/leader/leader.html>. This site provides free access to extensive materials on group leadership. Once at the site, scroll down through the topics and choose one that interests you. Write a two-page paper on the topic. (Feel free to do additional searches if you need more information.) Bring the paper to class for your lecturer.

3. Find five companies whose CEOs have left (for reasons other than normal retirement) in the past 12 months. Assess their company's profit performance against the average for their industry group. Using terms such as *CEO + turnover* or *resignation* will yield a number of results, such as this article <www.idg.net/federator/IDGSearch.jsp>, announcing the resignation of Grant Saviers, the CEO and chairman of Adaptec. To find the share price performance, you can then use any of a number of on-line services such as <www.cnnfn.com>. What did this exercise tell you? Write a short paper on what you learned.

4. If leadership is a skill that can be learned, then it presupposes that one can make mistakes. What are mistakes that new leaders make, and how can they be remedied? Go to <www.ed.gov/databases/ERIC_Digests/ed422604.html> and read the research article discussing the mistakes of school administrators/leaders. Write a journal entry about a mistake you have observed a leader make and describe how it could have been corrected.

5. Do women's leadership styles differ from men's? Go to the following website to read more: <www.ed.gov/databases/ERIC_Digests/ed400025.html>. Do another search with *women* or *females + leadership*. Write a journal entry on what you learned.

6. Leading can be a difficult task. It is hard to know what other leaders are thinking, what is important to them, and how they do it day in and day out. Visit the US Coast Guard's website and read how leaders do their job every day from their own essays. Point to <www.uscg.mil/hq/g-w/g-wt/g-wtl/essays/index.htm>. Select two essays and print. Apply a leadership theory to the writer's thoughts. Bring it to class for a group discussion.

7. Leaders face challenges every day. Visit <www.css.edu/users/dswenson/web/lead9.html> to learn more about the nine dilemmas leaders face. Write a short reaction paper to the article. Have you found yourself facing one (or more) of these dilemmas in a leadership position you have held? Do you agree with the author? How should a manager deal with these issues?

KSS Program

KNOW THE CONCEPTS   SELF-AWARENESS   SKILLS APPLICATIONS

Choosing the right leadership style

After you have read this chapter, take Self-Assessment #27 (What's My Leadership Style?) on your enclosed CD-Rom and complete the skill-building module entitled 'Choosing an Effective Leadership Style' on page 640.

NOTES

1. Based on Emily Ross, 'Rising Stars', *Business Review Weekly*, 27 February 2003, pp. 56–65; and K. Brooker, 'It Took a Lady to Save Avon', *Fortune*, 15 October 2001, pp. 203–08.

2. J. P. Kotter, 'What Leaders Really Do', *Harvard Business Review*, May–June 1990, pp. 103–11; and J. P. Kotter, *A Force for Change: How Leadership Differs from Management* (New York: Free Press, 1990).

3. R. J. House and R. N. Aditya, 'The Social Scientific Study of Leadership: Quo Vadis?', *Journal of Management*, vol. 23, no. 3, 1997, p. 445.

4. See, for example, W. B. Snavely, 'Organizational Leadership: An Alternative View and Implications for Managerial Education', paper presented at the Midwest Academy of Management Conference, Toledo, OH, April 2001.

5. J. G. Geier, 'A Trait Approach to the Study of Leadership in Small Groups', *Journal of Communication*, December 1967, pp. 316–23.

6. S. A. Kirkpatrick and E. A. Locke, 'Leadership: Do Traits Matter?', *Academy of Management Executive*, May 1991, pp. 48–60.

7. G. H. Dobbins. W. S. Long, E. J. Dedrick and T. C. Clemons, 'The Role of Self-Monitoring and Gender on Leader Emergence: A Laboratory and Field Study', *Journal of Management*, September 1990, pp. 609–18; and S. J. Zaccaro, R. J. Foti and D. A. Kenny, 'Self-Monitoring and Trait-Based Variance in Leadership: An Investigation of Leader Flexibility across Multiple Group Situations', *Journal of Applied Psychology*, April 1991, pp. 308–15.

8. G. Yukl and D. D. Van Fleet, 'Theory and Research on Leadership in Organizations', in M. D. Dunnette and L. M. Hough (eds), *Handbook of Industrial & Organizational Psychology*, 2nd ed., vol. 3 (Palo Alto, CA: Consulting Psychologists Press, 1992), p. 150.

9. B. Schneider, 'Interactional Psychology and Organizational Behavior', in L. L. Cummings and B. M. Staw (eds), *Research in Organizational Behavior*, vol. 5 (Greenwich, CT: JAI Press, 1983), pp. 1–31.

10. See W. Mischel, 'Toward a Cognitive Social Learning Reconceptualization of Personality', *Psychological Review*, July 1973, pp. 252–83; and M. R. Barrick and M. K. Mount, 'Autonomy as a Moderator of the Relationship between the Big Five Personality Dimensions and Job Performance', *Journal of Applied Psychology*, February 1993, pp. 111–18.

11. R. G. Lord, C. L. DeVader and G. M. Alliger, 'A Meta-Analysis of the Relation between Personality Traits and Leadership Perceptions: An Application of Validity Generalization Procedures', *Journal of Applied Psychology*, August 1986, pp. 402–10; and J. A. Smith and R. J. Foti, 'A Pattern Approach to the Study of Leader Emergence', *Leadership Quarterly*, Summer 1998, pp. 147–60.

12. See C. Palmeri, 'The Grizz Gets Grizzly', *Forbes*, 16 November 1998, p. 196; and M. Warner, 'Confessions of a Control Freak', *Fortune*, 4 September 2000, pp. 130–40.

13. R. M. Stogdill and A. E. Coons (eds), *Leader Behavior: Its Description and Measurement*, Research Monograph no. 88 (Columbus, OH: Ohio State University, Bureau of Business Research, 1951). This research is updated in C. A. Schriesheim, C. C. Cogliser and L. L. Neider, 'Is It "Trustworthy"? A Multiple-Levels-of-Analysis Reexamination of an Ohio State Leadership Study, with Implications for Future Research', *Leadership Quarterly*, Summer 1995, pp. 111–45.

14. H. Yen, 'Richard Parsons, AOL Time Warner's New CEO, Known as Consensus-Builder', <www.tbo.com>, 6 December 2001.

15. R. Kahn and D. Katz, 'Leadership Practices in Relation to Productivity and Morale', in D. Cartwright and A. Zander (eds), *Group Dynamics: Research and Theory*, 2nd ed. (Elmsford, NY: Row, Paterson, 1960).

16. R. R. Blake and J. S. Mouton, *The Managerial Grid* (Houston: Gulf, 1964).

17. See, for example, R. R. Blake and J. S. Mouton, 'A Comparative Analysis of Situationalism and 9,9 Management by Principle', *Organizational Dynamics*, Spring 1982, pp. 20–43.

18. See, for example, L. L. Larson, J. G. Hunt and R. N. Osborn, 'The Great Hi-Hi Leader Behavior Myth: A Lesson from Occam's Razor', *Academy of Management Journal*, December 1976, pp. 628–41; and P. C. Nystrom, 'Managers and the Hi-Hi Leader Myth', *Academy of Management Journal*, June 1978, pp. 325–31.

19. See G. Ekvall and J. Arvonen, 'Change-Centered Leadership: An Extension of the Two-Dimensional Model', *Scandinavian Journal of Management*, vol. 7, no. 1, 1991, pp. 17–26; M. Lindell and G. Rosenqvist, 'Is There a Third Management Style?', *The Finnish Journal of Business Economics*, vol. 3, 1992, pp. 171–98; and M. Lindell and G. Rosenqvist, 'Management Behavior Dimensions and Development Orientation', *Leadership Quarterly*, Winter 1992, pp. 355–77.

20. M. McDonald, 'Lingerie's Iron Maiden Is Undone', *U.S. News & World Report*, 25 June 2001, p. 37; and A. D'Innocenzio, 'Wachner Ousted as CEO, Chairman at Warnaco', *The Detroit News*, 17 November 2001, p. D1.

21. F. E. Fiedler, *A Theory of Leadership Effectiveness* (New York: McGraw-Hill, 1967).

22. S. Shiflett, 'Is There a Problem with the LPC Score in LEADER MATCH?', *Personnel Psychology*, Winter 1981, pp. 765–69.

23. F. E. Fiedler, M. M. Chemers and L. Mahar, *Improving Leadership Effectiveness: The Leader Match Concept* (New York: John Wiley, 1977).

24. Cited in House and Aditya, 'The Social Scientific Study of Leadership', p. 422.

25. L. H. Peters, D. D. Hartke and J. T. Pohlmann, 'Fiedler's Contingency Theory of Leadership: An Application of the Meta-Analysis Procedures of Schmidt and Hunter', *Psychological Bulletin*, March 1985, pp. 274–85; C. A. Schriesheim, B. J. Tepper and L. A. Tetrault, 'Least Preferred Co-Worker Score, Situational Control, and Leadership Effectiveness: A Meta-Analysis of Contingency Model Performance Predictions', *Journal of Applied Psychology*, August 1994, pp. 561–73; and R. Ayman, M. M. Chemers and F. Fiedler, 'The Contingency Model of Leadership Effectiveness: Its Levels of Analysis', *Leadership Quarterly*, Summer 1995, pp. 147–67.

26. House and Aditya, 'The Social Scientific Study of Leadership', p. 422.

27. See, for example, R. W. Rice, 'Psychometric Properties of the Esteem for the Least Preferred Coworker (LPC) Scale', *Academy of Management Review*, January 1978, pp. 106–18; C. A. Schriesheim, B. D. Bannister and W. H. Money, 'Psychometric Properties of the LPC Scale: An Extension of Rice's Review', *Academy of Management Review*, April 1979, pp. 287–90; and J. K. Kennedy, J. M. Houston, M. A. Korgaard and D. D. Gallo, 'Construct Space of the Least Preferred Co-Worker (LPC) Scale', *Educational & Psychological Measurement*, Fall 1987, pp. 807–14.

28. See E. H. Schein, *Organizational Psychology*, 3rd ed. (Upper Saddle River, NJ: Prentice Hall, 1980), pp. 116–17; and B. Kabanoff, 'A Critique of Leader Match and Its Implications for Leadership Research', *Personnel Psychology*, Winter 1981, pp. 749–64.

29. F. E. Fiedler and J. E. Garcia, *New Approaches to Effective Leadership: Cognitive Resources and Organizational Performance* (New York: Wiley, 1987).

30. See F. W. Gibson, F. E. Fiedler and K. M. Barrett, 'Stress, Babble, and the Utilization of the Leader's Intellectual Abilities', *Leadership Quarterly*, Summer 1993, pp. 189–208; F. E. Fiedler, 'Cognitive Resources and Leadership Performance', *Applied Psychology—An International Review*, January 1995, pp. 5–28; and F. E. Fiedler, 'The Curious Role of Cognitive Resources in Leadership', in R. E. Riggio, S. E. Murphy and F. J. Pirozzolo (eds), *Multiple Intelligences and Leadership* (Mahwah, NJ: Lawrence Erlbaum, 2002), pp. 91–104.

31. P. Hersey and K. H. Blanchard, 'So You Want to Know Your Leadership Style?', *Training and Development Journal*, February 1974, pp. 1–15; and P. Hersey, K. H. Blanchard and D. E. Johnson, *Management of Organizational Behavior: Leading Human Resources*, 8th ed. (Upper Saddle River, NJ: Prentice Hall, 2001).

32. Cited in C. F. Fernandez and R. P. Vecchio, 'Situational Leadership Theory Revisited: A Test of an Across-Jobs Perspective', *Leadership Quarterly*, vol. 8, no. 1, 1997, p. 67.

33. F. E. Fiedler, 'Leadership Experience and Leadership Performance: Another Hypothesis Shot to Hell', *Organizational Behavior and Human Performance*, January 1970, pp. 1–14; F. E. Fiedler, 'Time-Based Measures of Leadership Experience and Organizational Performance: A Review of Research and a Preliminary Model', *Leadership Quarterly*, Spring 1992, pp. 5–23; and M. A. Quinones, J. K. Ford and M. S. Teachout, 'The Relationship between Work Experience and Job Performance: A Conceptual and Meta-Analytic Review', *Personnel Psychology*, Winter 1995, pp. 887–910.

34. See, for example, ibid, pp. 67–84; and C. L. Graeff, 'Evolution of Situational Leadership Theory: A Critical Review', *Leadership Quarterly*, vol. 8, no. 2, 1997, pp. 153–70.

35. R. M. Dienesch and R. C. Liden, 'Leader–Member Exchange Model of Leadership: A Critique and Further Development', *Academy of Management Review*, July 1986, pp. 618–34; G. B. Graen and M. Uhl-Bien, 'Relationship-Based Approach to Leadership: Development of Leader–Member Exchange (LMX) Theory of Leadership Over 25 Years: Applying a Multi-Domain Perspective', *Leadership Quarterly*, Summer 1995, pp. 219–47; R. C. Liden, R. T. Sparrowe and S. J. Wayne, 'Leader–Member Exchange Theory: The Past and Potential for the Future', in G. R. Ferris (ed.), *Research in Personnel and Human Resource Management*, vol. 15 (Greenwich, CT: JAI Press, 1997), pp. 47–119; and C. A. Schriesheim, S. L. Castro, X. Zhou and F. J. Yammarino, 'The Folly of Theorizing "A" but Testing "B": A Selective Level-of-Analysis Review of the Field and a Detailed Leader–Member Exchange Illustration', *Leadership Quarterly*, Winter 2001, pp. 515–51.

36. R. Liden and G. Graen, 'Generalizability of the Vertical Dyad Linkage Model of Leadership', *Academy of Management Journal*, September 1980, pp. 451–65; and R. C. Liden, S. J. Wayne and D. Stilwell, 'A Longitudinal Study of the Early Development of Leader–Member Exchanges', *Journal of Applied Psychology*, August 1993, pp. 662–74.

37. D. Duchon, S. G. Green and T. D. Taber, 'Vertical Dyad Linkage: A Longitudinal Assessment of Antecedents, Measures, and Consequences', *Journal of Applied Psychology*, February 1986, pp. 56–60; Liden, Wayne and Stilwell, 'A Longitudinal Study on the Early Development of Leader–Member Exchanges'; R. J. Deluga and J. T. Perry, 'The Role of Subordinate Performance and Ingratiation in Leader–Member Exchanges', *Group & Organization Management*, March 1994, pp. 67–86; T. N. Bauer and S. G. Green, 'Development of Leader–Member Exchange: A Longitudinal Test', *Academy of Management Journal*, December 1996, pp. 1538–67; and S. J. Wayne, L. M. Shore and R. C. Liden, 'Perceived Organizational Support and Leader–Member Exchange: A Social Exchange Perspective', *Academy of Management Journal*, February 1997, pp. 82–111.

38. See, for example, C. R. Gerstner and D. V. Day, 'Meta-Analytic Review of Leader–Member Exchange Theory: Correlates and Construct Issues', *Journal of Applied Psychology*, December 1997, pp. 827–44; C. Gomez and B. Rosen, 'The Leader–Member Exchange as a Link Between Managerial Trust and Employee Empowerment', *Group & Organization Management*, March 2001, pp. 53–69; and J. M. Maslyn and M. Uhl-Bien, 'Leader–Member Exchange and Its Dimensions: Effects of Self-Effort and Other's Effort on Relationship Quality', *Journal of Applied Psychology*, August 2001, pp. 697–708.

39. D. Eden, 'Leadership and Expectations: Pygmalion Effects and Other Self-Fulfilling Prophecies in Organizations', *Leadership Quarterly*, Winter 1992, pp. 278–79.

40. R. J. House, 'A Path–Goal Theory of Leader Effectiveness', *Administrative Science Quarterly*, September 1971, pp. 321–38; R. J. House and T. R. Mitchell, 'Path–Goal Theory of Leadership', *Journal of Contemporary Business*, Autumn 1974, pp. 81–97; and R. J. House, 'Path–Goal Theory of Leadership: Lessons, Legacy, and a Reformulated Theory', *Leadership Quarterly*, Fall 1996, pp. 323–52.

41. J. C. Wofford and L. Z. Liska, 'Path–Goal Theories of Leadership: A Meta-Analysis', *Journal of Management*, Winter 1993, pp. 857–76.

42. V. H. Vroom and P. W. Yetton, *Leadership and Decision-Making* (Pittsburgh: University of Pittsburgh Press, 1973).

43. V. H. Vroom and A. G. Jago, *The New Leadership: Managing Participation in Organizations* (Englewood Cliffs, NJ: Prentice Hall, 1988). See also V. H. Vroom and A. G. Jago, 'Situation Effects and Levels of Analysis in the Study of Leader Participation', *Leadership Quarterly*, Summer 1995, pp. 169–81.

44. See, for example, R. H. G. Field, 'A Test of the Vroom-Yetton Normative Model of Leadership', *Journal of Applied Psychology*, October 1982, pp. 523–32; C. R. Leana, 'Power Relinquishment versus Power Sharing: Theoretical Clarification and Empirical Comparison of Delegation

and Participation', *Journal of Applied Psychology*, May 1987, pp. 228–33; J. T. Ettling and A. G. Jago, 'Participation Under Conditions of Conflict: More on the Validity of the Vroom-Yetton Model', *Journal of Management Studies*, January 1988, pp. 73–83; and R. H. G. Field and R. J. House, 'A Test of the Vroom-Yetton Model Using Manager and Subordinate Reports', *Journal of Applied Psychology*, June 1990, pp. 362–66.

45. House and Aditya, 'The Social Scientific Study of Leadership', p. 428.

PHOTO CREDITS

340 Richard Branson, Virgin Group Chairman and Life President. With thanks to Virgin Blue Airlines; **345** Courtesy of the Commonwealth of Australia Department of Defence.

CHAPTER 12

Contemporary Issues in Leadership

CHAPTER OUTLINE

Trust: The foundation of leadership

Leaders as shapers of meaning

Emotional intelligence and leadership effectiveness

Contemporary leadership roles

Moral leadership

On-line leadership: Some speculative thoughts

Challenges to the leadership construct

Finding and creating effective leaders

LEARNING OBJECTIVES

After studying this chapter, you should be able to:

1. Identify the five dimensions of trust
2. Explain how framing influences leadership effectiveness
3. Define the qualities of a charismatic leader
4. Contrast transformational with transactional leadership
5. Identify the skills that visionary leaders exhibit
6. Identify the four roles that team leaders perform
7. Explain the role of a mentor
8. Describe how on-line leadership differs from face-to-face leadership
9. Identify when leadership may not be necessary
10. Explain how to find and create effective leaders

Leaders are visionaries with a poorly developed sense of fear and no concept of the odds against them.

R. Jarvik

Former New York city mayor Rudy Guiliani is a 21st century leader.

People around the world will appreciate the impact that the events of 11 September 2001 ('September 11') had on New York City and how various leaders rose to prominence. Rudolph W. Guiliani (see photo) was elected mayor of New York City in 1993 on a law-and-order platform. And he did successfully bring law and order to the city. For example, by the end of his second term, in 2001, he had overseen a 57 per cent decline in felony crimes and a 68 per cent reduction in the city's murder rate. In a city that many said was ungovernable, Guiliani had turned around New York's fortunes. He boosted property values, redeveloped large parts of Manhattan, brought tourists back and restored the city's spirit. But he stepped on a lot of toes in the process. His arrogant, self-serving and combative style rubbed a lot of people the wrong way. He became known more for his uncontrollable temper and vindictiveness than for his success in improving life in New York City. However, any negative perceptions of Guiliani essentially disappeared on September 11.[1]

On September 11, the worst crime ever committed on American soil took place—terrorists flew hijacked commercial jets into the twin towers of the World Trade Center in New York City, and into the Pentagon in Washington, DC, killing almost 3,000 people. As shock, and then fear, gripped the nation, Rudy Guiliani stepped up and led the city and nation through the crisis. Within minutes after the first plane hit, Guiliani was on the scene directing operations. Without regard for his own safety, he established a makeshift command centre and a temporary morgue, found a million pairs of gloves, dust masks and respirators, threw up protections against another attack, and tamed the mobs that wanted vengeance. One of the public's strongest memories of that first day was of Guiliani, on the streets of New York, trying to reassure the public, with his hair and suit still covered in the silt from the fallen buildings. In the weeks that followed, Guiliani provided the leadership that the public craved. Day after day, his mastery of the details of rescue and recovery, plus his calm explanations of awful news, helped to reassure a traumatised city that the crisis was under control. He found just the right balance between being a hard-nosed administrator and a caring and emotional leader. He consoled widows, widowers and survivors; he attended close to 200 funerals, wakes and memorial services; he revisited the attack site to mingle with rescue workers; he urged residents to dine out; and he reached out to tourists to come back to the city. In addition to the decisiveness and honesty he had always displayed, he now showed traits that the public had rarely seen in him before—compassion, fearlessness, calmness and openness. He put in 20-hour days and showed an uncanny ability to be consistently visible. Maybe most importantly, Guiliani was able to find the words and tap into emotions to help people better cope with the tragedy. He conveyed optimism and created, as one writer put it, 'an illusion that we were bound to win'. For example, on that first day following the attack, he said: 'Tomorrow, New York is going to be here. And we're going to rebuild, and we're going to be stronger than we were before ... I want the people of New York to be an example to the rest of the country, and the rest of the world, that terrorism can't stop us.' Within days, Guiliani almost unilaterally managed to create the sense that New York City was getting back to normalcy.

Time magazine may have summarised Guiliani's leadership role best when, in naming him its 2001 Person of the Year, it said: '... for having more faith in us than we had in ourselves, for being brave when required and rude where appropriate and tender without being trite, for not sleeping and not quitting and not shrinking from the pain all around him.'

Former New York City mayor Rudy Guiliani is a 21st-century leader. He called upon his experience, charisma and ability to create meaning out of tragedy and to help a city and nation recover. In this chapter, we address contemporary leadership topics such as charisma and the ability to create meaning in new or difficult situations. We will also discuss emotional intelligence and leadership effectiveness, contemporary leadership roles, moral leadership, and challenges to the leadership construct. First, however, we turn our attention to the topic of trust. We begin here because recent evidence indicates that trust is the foundation of leadership. Unless followers trust their leaders, they will be unresponsive to a 'leader's' influence efforts.

Trust: The Foundation of Leadership

LEARNING OBJECTIVE

1

Identify the five
dimensions of trust

Trust, or lack of trust, is an increasingly important leadership issue in today's organisations. In this section, we define *trust* and provide you with some guidelines for helping to build credibility and trust.

WHAT IS TRUST?

trust
A positive expectation
that another won't act
opportunistically.

Trust is a positive expectation that another will not—through words, actions or decisions—act opportunistically.[2] The two most important elements of our definition are that it implies familiarity and risk.

The phrase *positive expectation* in our definition assumes knowledge and familiarity about the other party. Trust is a history-dependent process based on relevant but limited samples of experience.[3] It takes time to form, building incrementally and accumulatively. Most of us find it hard, if not impossible, to trust someone immediately if we don't know anything about them. At the extreme, in the case of total ignorance, we can gamble but we can't trust.[4] But as we get to know someone, and the relationship matures, we gain confidence in our ability to make a positive expectation.

The term *opportunistically* refers to the inherent risk and vulnerability in any trusting relationship. Trust involves making oneself vulnerable as when, for example, we disclose intimate information or rely on another's promises.[5] By its very nature, trust provides the opportunity for disappointment or to be taken advantage of.[6] But trust isn't taking risk per se; rather, it is a *willingness* to take risk.[7] So, when we trust someone, we expect that they won't take advantage of us. This willingness to take risks is common to all trust situations.[8]

What are the key dimensions that underlie the concept of trust? Recent evidence has identified five: integrity, competence, consistency, loyalty and openness[9] (see Figure 12.1).

Integrity refers to honesty and truthfulness. Of all five dimensions, this one seems to be most critical when someone assesses another's trustworthiness.[10] 'Without a perception of the other's "moral character" and "basic honesty," other dimensions of trust [are] meaningless.'[11]

FIGURE 12.1 **Trust dimensions**

Competence encompasses an individual's technical and interpersonal knowledge and skills. Do they know what they are talking about? You are unlikely to listen to or depend upon someone whose abilities you don't respect. You need to believe that the person has the skills and abilities to carry out what they say they will do.

Consistency relates to an individual's reliability, predictability and good judgment in handling situations. 'Inconsistencies between words and action decrease trust.'[12] This dimension is particularly relevant for managers. 'Nothing is noticed more quickly . . . than a discrepancy between what executives preach and what they expect their associates to practice.'[13]

Loyalty is the willingness to protect and save face for another person. Trust requires that you can depend on someone not to act opportunistically.

The final dimension of trust is *openness*. Can you rely on the person to give you the full truth?

TRUST AND LEADERSHIP

Morale had plummeted at the headquarters of the global car manufacturer, DaimlerChrysler, largely due to comments by DaimlerChrysler chairman Jurgen Schrempp.[14] When Daimler-Benz and Chrysler merged, Schrempp called it 'a merger of equals'. But in the autumn of 2000, he admitted that he had lied. Schrempp now says he never really intended for the combined companies to be equals. If he had been honest, he says, there would have been no deal and he couldn't have made Chrysler into just another Daimler operating unit. With these words, Schrempp has decimated any trust that he may have had with his Chrysler employees.

As the DaimlerChrysler example illustrates, trust is a primary attribute associated with leadership; and when this trust is broken, it can have serious adverse effects on a group's performance.[15] In our discussion of traits in the previous chapter, honesty and integrity were among the six traits found to be consistently associated with leadership. It appears increasingly evident that it is impossible to lead people who don't trust you.

As one author noted: 'Part of the leader's task has been, and continues to be, working with people to find and solve problems, but whether leaders gain access to the knowledge and creative thinking they need to solve problems depends on how much people trust them. Trust and trustworthiness modulate the leader's access to knowledge and cooperation.'[16]

When followers trust a leader, they are willing to be vulnerable to the leader's actions—confident that their rights and interests won't be abused.[17] People are unlikely to look up to or follow someone whom they perceive as dishonest or who is likely to take advantage of them. Honesty, for example, consistently ranks at the top of most people's list of characteristics they admire in their leaders. 'Honesty is absolutely essential to leadership. If people are going to follow someone willingly, whether it be into battle or into the boardroom, they first want to assure themselves that the person is worthy of their trust.'[18] Now, more than ever, managerial and leadership effectiveness depends on the ability to gain the trust of followers.[19] For example, reengineering, downsizing and the increased use of temporary employees have undermined a lot of employees' trust in management. A recent nationwide survey of Australian managers found that managers don't feel their staff trust them. Similarly, a survey of US employees found that only half trusted their senior managers.[20] In times of change and instability, people turn to personal relationships for guidance; and the quality of these relationships is largely determined by level of trust. Additionally, contemporary management practices such as empowerment and the use of work teams require trust to be effective. Finally, of course, has been the recent and unprecedented revelations of misdeeds by senior managers in many large corporations around the world. Leaders at Enron, WorldCom, Dynergy, OneTel, HIH Insurance, Arthur Andersen Consultants and Tyco International were accused of engaging in an assortment of activities—from secret loans to insider trading, manipulating profit figures and evading taxes—that shook the confidence of employees as well as investors, suppliers and customers in the trustworthiness of these firms' senior executives.

THREE TYPES OF TRUST

There are three types of trust in organisational relationships: *deterrence*-based, *knowledge*-based and *identification*-based.[21]

Deterrence-based trust

deterrence-based trust
Trust based on fear of reprisal if the trust is violated.

The most fragile relationships are contained in **deterrence-based trust**. One violation or inconsistency can destroy the relationship. This form of trust is based on fear of reprisal if the trust is violated. Individuals who are in this type of relationship do what they say because they fear the consequences from not following through on their obligations.

Deterrence-based trust will work only to the degree that punishment is possible, consequences are clear, and the punishment is actually imposed if the trust is violated. To be sustained, the potential loss of future interaction with the other party must outweigh the profit potential that comes from violating expectations. Moreover, the potentially harmed party must be willing to introduce harm (for example, I have no qualms about speaking badly of you if you betray my trust) to the person acting distrustfully.

Most new relationships begin on a base of deterrence. Take, as an illustration, a situation where you are selling your car to a friend of a friend. You don't know the buyer, so you might be motivated to refrain from telling this buyer all the problems with the car that you know about. Such behaviour would increase your chances of selling the car and securing the highest price. But you don't withhold information. You openly share the car's flaws. Why? Probably because of fear of reprisal. If the buyer later thinks you deceived him, he is likely to share this with your mutual friend. If you knew that the buyer would never say anything to the mutual friend, you might be tempted to take advantage of the opportunity. If it is clear that the buyer would tell and that your mutual friend would think considerably less of you for taking advantage of this buyer–friend, your honesty could be explained in deterrence terms.

Another example of deterrence-based trust is a new manager–employee relationship. As an employee, you typically trust a new boss even though there is little experience on which to base that trust. The bond that creates this trust lies in the authority held by the boss and the punishment he or she can impose if you fail to fulfil your job-related obligations.

Knowledge-based trust

knowledge-based trust
Trust based on behavioural predictability that comes from a history of interaction.

Most organisational relationships are rooted in **knowledge-based trust**. That is, trust is based on the behavioural predictability that comes from a history of interaction. It exists when you have adequate information about someone to understand them well enough to be able to accurately predict their behaviour.

Knowledge-based trust relies on information rather than deterrence. Knowledge of the other party and predictability of their behaviour replaces the contracts, penalties and legal arrangements that are more typical of deterrence-based trust. This knowledge develops over time, largely as a function of experience that builds confidence of trustworthiness and predictability. The better you know someone, the more accurately you can predict what they will do. Predictability enhances trust—even if the other is predictably untrustworthy—because the ways in which the other will violate the trust can be predicted! The more communication and regular interaction you have with someone else, the more this form of trust can be developed and depended upon.

Interestingly, at the knowledge-based level, trust isn't necessarily broken by inconsistent behaviour. If you believe you can adequately explain or understand another's apparent violation, you can accept it, forgive the person and move on in the relationship. However, the same inconsistency at the deterrence level is likely to irrevocably break the trust.

In an organisational context, most manager–employee relationships are knowledge-based. Both parties have enough experience working with each other that they know what to expect. A long history of consistently open and honest interactions, for example, isn't likely to be permanently destroyed by a single violation.

Identification-based trust

The highest level of trust is achieved when there is an emotional connection between the parties. It allows one party to act as an agent for the other and to substitute for that person in interpersonal transactions. This is called **identification-based trust**. Trust exists because the parties understand each other's intentions and appreciate the other's wants and desires. This mutual understanding is developed to the point that each can effectively act for the other.

Controls are minimal at this level. You don't need to monitor the other party, because there exists unquestioned loyalty.

The best example of identification-based trust is a long-term, happily married couple. A husband comes to learn what is important to his wife and anticipates those actions. She, in turn, trusts that he will anticipate what is important to her without having to ask. Increased identification enables each to think like the other, feel like the other and respond like the other.

You see identification-based trust occasionally in organisations among people who have worked together for long periods of time and have a depth of experience that allows them to know each other well. This is also the type of trust that managers ideally seek in teams. Team members are so comfortable and trusting of each other that they can anticipate each other and freely act in each other's absence. Realistically, in the current work world, most large corporations have broken the bonds of identification trust they may have built with long-term employees. Broken promises have led to a breakdown in what was, at one time, a bond of unquestioned loyalty. It's likely to have been replaced with knowledge-based trust.

identification-based trust
Trust based on a mutual understanding of each other's intentions and appreciation of the other's wants and desires.

Leaders as Shapers of Meaning

In the previous chapter, we depicted leadership as an influence process. More recently, leadership has increasingly become viewed as the management of meaning. That is, leaders are seen as individuals who define organisational reality through the articulation of a vision.[22] This approach of 'leaders as shapers of meaning' tends to have a bias. It is directed predominantly towards leaders at the top of organisations. As such, it probably has more direct relevance to explaining the success and failures of chief executives than of first-line supervisors. However, lower-level managers can create visions to lead their units. It is just harder to define such visions and to align them with the larger goals of the organisation as a whole.

The Real Deal

Various impacts of trust in the workplace

Staff from *Human Capital Australia* magazine brought together two of Australia's leading HR practitioners, Sean Bowman, HR director at Lion Nathan (beer and wines), and Michael O'Shaughnessy, director of employee relations at McDonald's (fast food) to share their thoughts on trust in the workplace. Three interesting points relevant to the practice of effective leadership emerged from their discussions regarding retention, competitive behaviour and communicating facts about the business.

While we might expect people to leave an organisation where there is little trust in the leadership, the reverse may not be so when there is high trust. Michael O'Shaughnessy indicated a disconnect between trust and retention at McDonald's. From their staff survey results, he says that staff are proud to work for the company and there is a high degree of trust, but retention is decreasing at all levels. Retention seems to be influenced by factors such as market forces, rather than trust. McDonald's is a great training ground, and when other fast-food chains start up, such as Subway and Starbucks, store managers, in particular, are attracted to such new opportunities. While trust and loyalty are desirable in any workplace, leaders need to be aware that other factors need to be addressed if they are to retain good staff.

In the light of corporate collapses and company downsizing, the spotlight has been put on competitive behaviour in firms and what this may mean for trust in the workplace. Sean Bowman was one of 20 in a group that went on a tour of best practice companies. The group visited Enron in the United States before its infamous collapse. At the time of the visit, Enron was listed as the Most Innovative Company in the World in *Fortune* magazine. Sean's group saw signs of an impending implosion in Enron. The company proudly and purposely developed a very competitive culture where staff aggressively competed against each other for advantage, and where the top leadership were given excessive rewards compared to the majority of staff. While the leadership at Lion Nathan believes it is possible to achieve short-term and sustainable results, Sean Bowman highlights potential problems where reward systems and internal competition can affect trust and sustainability.

Communicating the facts about the organisation is important to maintaining positive levels of trust through building a climate of openness, transparency and achievement. Lion Nathan has consciously taken steps to communicate more around the company's strategic vision and provide more tangible milestones regarding its progress towards it. Every six months, Lion Nathan's CEO goes out and talks to staff about the company's vision, strategy and results. The willingness by senior leaders to share information with staff at all levels is an important facet of building trust in working relationships.

Source: 'HR at the Table', *Human Capital Australia*, June 2003, <www.hcamag.com>.

In this section, we present three contemporary leadership theories whose common component is that they present leaders as using words, ideas and their physical presence to 'charge the troops'. To better help you understand the power of words in inspiring others, we first need to review the concept of *framing*.

LEARNING OBJECTIVE

2

Explain how framing influences leadership effectiveness

FRAMING ISSUES

British Prime Minister Winston Churchill's famous words from one of his wartime speeches, 'We shall fight on the beaches. We shall fight in the fields and in the streets. We shall fight in the hills. We shall never surrender', have been referred to over the years to signify the spirit of the people of Great Britain in defending their homeland during the Second World War. His words created an image of what a country can do in times of crisis. What Churchill did was *frame* the defence of Great Britain in a way that touched the hearts and minds of the population.

Framing is a way to use language to manage meaning.[23] It is a way for leaders to influence how events are seen and understood. It involves the selection and highlighting of one or more aspects of a subject while excluding others. Framing is analogous to what a photographer does. The visual world that exists is essentially ambiguous. When the photographer aims her camera and focuses on a specific shot, she frames her photo. Others then see what she wanted them to see. They see her point of view. That is precisely what leaders do when they frame an issue. They choose which aspects or portion of the subject they want others to focus on and which portions they want to be excluded.

framing
A way to use language to
manage meaning.

Barristers make their living by framing issues. Barristers acting for the accused, for example, shape their arguments so as to get the jury to see their client in the most favourable terms. They include 'facts' that might help the jury find their client 'not guilty'. They exclude facts that might reflect unfavourably on their client. And they try to provide alternative interpretations to the 'facts' that the prosecution argues makes their client guilty.

Lobbying groups also provide rich illustrations of the framing concept. The movie *Bowling For Columbine* was released in Australasia in 2003. It is an entertaining documentary on the politics of gun ownership in the United States. Despite the satirical portrait of the National Rifle Association (NRA), its leadership has historically been very successful in limiting gun controls in the United States, much more so that their counterparts in Australia and New Zealand. They have done this not by focusing on shootings, deaths or even self-defence. They have succeeded by framing gun control as a first amendment 'freedom' issue. To the degree that the NRA can shape public opinion to think of gun controls as taking away a citizen's right to bear arms, they have been able to minimise gun control regulations. In a similar vein, original opponents of abortion rallied their cause by describing themselves as 'anti-abortion' advocates. In response, and realising the negative imagery from using the label 'pro-abortion', supporters reframed the issue by referring to themselves as 'pro-choice'.

So, why is framing relevant to leadership today? Because in the complex and chaotic environment in which an increasing number of leaders work, there is typically considerable manoeuvrability with respect to 'the facts'. What is real is often what the leader says is real. What is important is what they choose to say is important. Leaders can use language to influence followers' perceptions of the world, the meaning of events, beliefs about causes and consequences, and visions of the future. It is through framing that leaders determine whether people notice problems, how they understand and remember problems, and how they act upon them.[24] Thus, framing is a powerful tool by which leaders influence how others see and interpret reality.

LEARNING OBJECTIVE

3

Define the qualities
of a charismatic
leader

CHARISMATIC LEADERSHIP

Bob Hawke (former Prime Minister of Australia), Lee Kuan Yew (former Prime Minister of Singapore), Aung San Suu Kyi (opposition politician in Burma/Myanmar), Steve Jobs (co-founder of Apple Computer), James Strong (former CEO of Qantas Airlines) and Nicholas Milton (winner of the Symphony Australia Conducting Competition and Westfield Young Conductor of the Year) are individuals frequently cited as being charismatic leaders. What do they have in common?

What is charismatic leadership?

According to **charismatic leadership** theory, followers make attributions of heroic or extraordinary leadership abilities when they observe certain behaviours.[25] While there have been a number of studies that have attempted to identify personal characteristics of the charismatic leader, the best documented has isolated five such characteristics—they have a vision, are willing to take risks to achieve that vision, are sensitive to both environmental constraints and follower needs, and exhibit behaviours that are out of the ordinary—that differentiate charismatic leaders from non-charismatic ones.[26] These characteristics are described in Table 12.1.

charismatic leadership
Followers make
attributions of heroic or
extraordinary leadership
abilities when they
observe certain
behaviours.

During his period as chief executive of Qantas, James Strong was seen by many of his staff as a charismatic leader. He saw the importance of developing a competitive executive team in order to confront the challenges of privatisation, the merge between Qantas and Australian Airlines, and the increasing difficulties of sustaining a competitive advantage in the global airline industry.

How do charismatic leaders actually influence followers? The evidence suggests a four-step process.[27] It begins by the leader articulating an appealing vision. This vision provides a sense of continuity for followers by linking the present with a better future for the organisation. The leader then communicates high performance expectations and expresses confidence that followers can attain them. This enhances follower self-esteem and self-confidence. Next, the leader conveys, through words and actions, a new set of values and, by their behaviour, sets an example for followers to imitate. Finally, the charismatic leader makes self-sacrifices and engages in unconventional behaviour to demonstrate courage and convictions about the vision.

What can we say about the charismatic leader's effect on their followers? There is an increasing body of research that shows impressive correlations between charismatic leadership and high performance and satisfaction among followers.[28] People working for charismatic leaders are motivated to exert extra work effort and, because they like and respect their leader, express greater satisfaction.

Are charismatic leaders born or made?

If charisma is desirable, can people learn to be charismatic leaders? Or are charismatic leaders born with their qualities? While a small minority still think charisma cannot be learned, most experts believe that individuals can be trained to exhibit charismatic behaviours and can thus

TABLE 12.1	**Key characteristics of charismatic leaders**

1. *Vision and articulation.* Has a vision—expressed as an idealised goal—that proposes a future better than the status quo; and is able to clarify the importance of the vision in terms that are understandable to others.

2. *Personal risk.* Willing to take on high personal risk, incur high costs, and engage in self-sacrifice to achieve the vision.

3. *Environmental sensitivity.* Able to make realistic assessments of the environmental constraints and resources needed to bring about change.

4. *Sensitivity to follower needs.* Perceptive of others' abilities and responsive to their needs and feelings.

5. *Unconventional behaviour.* Engages in behaviours that are perceived as novel and counter to norms.

Source: Based on J. A. Conger and R. N. Kanungo, *Charismatic Leadership in Organizations* (Thousand Oaks, CA: Sage, 1998), p. 94.

enjoy the benefits that accrue to being labelled 'a charismatic leader'.[29] For example, one set of authors proposes that a person can learn to become charismatic by following a three-step process.[30] First, an individual needs to develop the aura of charisma by maintaining an optimistic view; using passion as a catalyst for generating enthusiasm; and communicating with the whole body, not just with words. Second, an individual draws others in by creating a bond that inspires others to follow. And third, the individual brings out the potential in followers by tapping into their emotions. This approach seems to work as evidenced by researchers who have succeeded in actually scripting undergraduate business students to 'play' charismatic.[31] The students were taught to articulate an overarching goal, communicate high performance expectations, exhibit confidence in the ability of followers to meet these expectations, and empathise with the needs of their followers; they learned to project a powerful, confident and dynamic presence; and they practised using a captivating and engaging voice tone. To further capture the dynamics and energy of charisma, the leaders were trained to evoke charismatic non-verbal characteristics: they alternated between pacing and sitting on the edges of their desks, leaned towards the subjects, maintained direct eye contact, and had relaxed postures and animated facial expressions. These researchers found that these students could learn how to project charisma. Moreover, followers of these leaders had higher task performance, task adjustment, and adjustment to the leader and to the group than did followers who worked under groups led by non-charismatic leaders.

When charisma is needed

Charismatic leadership may not always be needed to achieve high levels of employee performance. Charisma appears to be most appropriate when the follower's task has an ideological component or when the environment involves a high degree of stress and uncertainty.[32] This may explain why, when charismatic leaders surface, it is more likely to be in politics, religion or wartime, or when a business firm is in its infancy or facing a life-threatening crisis. In the 1970s, Prime Minister Gough Whitlam offered a vision for Higher Education by offering access to all Australians. In the early 1970s, when Chrysler Corp., in the United States, was on the brink of bankruptcy, it needed a charismatic leader with unconventional ideas such as Lee Iacocca to reinvent the company. In contrast, General Motors' failure to directly address its problems in the late 1990s—such as GM's inability to launch new vehicles on time, deep-seated aversion to change, and lacklustre financial performance—were frequently attributed to CEO John Smith, Jr and his *lack* of charisma.[33]

TRANSFORMATIONAL LEADERSHIP

Another stream of research has been focused on differentiating transformational leaders from transactional leaders.[34] Because transformational leaders are also charismatic, there is some overlap between this topic and our previous discussion of charismatic leadership.

Most of the leadership theories presented in the previous chapter—for example, the Ohio State studies, Fiedler's model, path–goal theory and the leader-participation model—have concerned **transactional leaders**. These kinds of leaders guide or motivate their followers in the direction of established goals by clarifying role and task requirements. There is also another type of leader who inspires followers to transcend their own self-interests for the good of the organisation, and who is capable of having a profound and extraordinary effect on their followers. These are **transformational leaders** such as Jo Horgan at Mecca Cosmetica, Andrea Jung at Avon and Richard Branson of the Virgin Group. They pay attention to the concerns and developmental needs of individual followers; they change followers' awareness of issues by helping them to look at old problems in new ways; and they are able to excite, arouse and inspire followers to put out extra effort to achieve group goals. Table 12.2 briefly identifies and defines the four characteristics that differentiate these two types of leaders.

Transactional and transformational leadership shouldn't be viewed as opposing approaches to getting things done.[35] Transformational leadership is built *on top of* transactional leadership—it

---

LEARNING OBJECTIVE

4

Contrast transformational with transactional leadership

transactional leaders
Leaders who guide or motivate their followers in the direction of established goals by clarifying role and task requirements.

transformational leaders
Leaders who inspire followers to transcend their own self-interests and who are capable of having a profound and extraordinary effect on followers.

OB Controversies

The decline of the charismatic leader

Up until recently, the business literature has encouraged managers to become transformational leaders and the popular press had regularly featured profiles of charismatic executives such as Jack Welch, formerly of General Electric, and James Strong, formerly of Qantas. Even politicians are recognised as charismatic role models. For example, former Prime Minister Lee Kuan Yew of Singapore was seen as an influential and charismatic figure in the Southeast Asian region.

However, according to David James of *Business Review Weekly*, charismatic and visionary leaders are in decline and self-effacing leaders are in. He credits Harry Onsman, author of *The Uncertain Art of Management*, as recognising that the charismatic leader died of stress. The chief executive officer of Wesfarmers believes that the language of vision strongly associated with the charismatic types is hardly used any more. Wesfarmers is one of Australia's largest public companies with business interests in coal mining, gas processing and distribution, and retailing of home and garden improvement products and building materials.

Professor of strategic management, Graham Hubbard, recently studied business leadership in Australia and concluded that there isn't a strong link between charisma and organisational success if a 20-year perspective on performance is taken. There is a need to focus on management teams rather than solely on chief executives. Chief executives come and go, and even the likes of Jack Welch has subsequently run into personal dramas that don't match with the aura described in the books about his leadership style. The former chief executive of Asea Brown Boveri, Percy Barnevik, has also had his reputation tarnished since being hailed as a hero manager. Stakeholders are looking for self-effacing, humble and quietly confident management. While the current chief executives of Woolworths and Qantas don't have a high-profile status, they are recognised by Hubbard for their effectiveness in getting results. The same could be said for Singapore's current Prime Minister Goh who has little of the charisma associated with former Prime Minister Lee, but has proved to be highly competent and effective.

According to James, there are several reasons for questioning the attribute of charisma. First, the large investors who were burned in the bull markets in the late 1990s are less tolerant of charismatic leaders. The second reason is that 'the leaders themselves appear to have less self-belief that they can provide this style of management in difficult market conditions, and are unsure what visionary leadership is'.

Sources: David James, 'Charisma vs. Performance', *Business Review Weekly*, 17 April 2003, pp. 72–74; Niccolo Mele, 'Singapore's Utilitarian Leadership', <www.wm.edu/SO/Eleutheria/issue1/sing.htm>; and G. Hubbard, D. Samuel, S. Heap and G. Cocks, *The First XI: Winning Organisations in Australia* (Brisbane: John Wiley and Sons, 2002).

produces levels of follower effort and performance that go beyond what would occur with a transactional approach alone. Moreover, transformational leadership is more than charisma. 'The purely charismatic [leader] may want followers to adopt the charismatic's world view and go no further; the transformational leader will attempt to instill in followers the ability to question not only established views but eventually those established by the leader.'[36]

The evidence supporting the superiority of transformational leadership over the transactional variety is overwhelmingly impressive. For example, a number of studies with US, Canadian and German military officers found, at every level, that transformational leaders were evaluated as more effective than their transactional counterparts.[37] In 2001, over 1,900 members of the Australian Institute of Management were surveyed; the study concluded that business leaders are more aware of and willing to use transformational leadership behaviours to get results.[38] In summary, the overall evidence indicates that transformational leadership is more strongly correlated than transactional leadership with lower turnover rates, higher productivity and higher employee satisfaction.[39]

TABLE 12.2   **Characteristics of transactional and transformational leaders**

Transactional Leader

Contingent Reward: Contracts exchange of rewards for effort, promises rewards for good performance, recognises accomplishments.

Management by Exception (active): Watches and searches for deviations from rules and standards, takes corrective action.

Management by Exception (passive): Intervenes only if standards are not met.

Laissez-faire: Abdicates responsibilities, avoids making decisions.

Transformational Leader

Charisma: Provides vision and sense of mission, instills pride, gains respect and trust.

Inspiration: Communicates high expectations, uses symbols to focus efforts, expresses important purposes in simple ways.

Intellectual Stimulation: Promotes intelligence, rationality and careful problem solving.

Individualised Consideration: Gives personal attention, treats each employee individually, coaches, advises.

Source: Reprinted from B. M. Bass, 'From Transactional to Transformational Leadership: Learning to Share the Vision', *Organizational Dynamics*, Winter 1990, p. 22. With permission from Elsevier Science.

VISIONARY LEADERSHIP

The term *vision* appeared in our previous discussion of charismatic leadership. But visionary leadership goes beyond charisma. In this section, we review recent revelations about the importance of visionary leadership.

Defining visionary leadership

Visionary leadership is the ability to create and articulate a realistic, credible, attractive vision of the future for an organisation or organisational unit that grows out of and improves upon the present.[40] This vision, if properly selected and implemented, is so energising that it 'in effect jump-starts the future by calling forth the skills, talents, and resources to make it happen'.[41]

A review of various definitions finds that a vision differs from other forms of direction setting in several ways:

A vision has clear and compelling imagery that offers an innovative way to improve, which recognizes and draws on traditions, and connects to actions that people can take to realize change. Vision taps people's emotions and energy. Properly articulated, a vision creates the enthusiasm that people have for sporting events and other leisure-time activities, bringing this energy and commitment to the workplace.[42]

Qualities of a vision

The key properties of a vision seem to be inspirational possibilities that are value-centred, realisable, with superior imagery and articulation.[43] Visions should be able to create possibilities that are inspirational, unique and offer a new order that can produce organisational distinction. A vision is likely to fail if it doesn't offer a view of the future that is clearly and demonstrably better for the organisation and its members. Desirable visions fit the times and circumstances and reflect the uniqueness of the organisation. People in the organisation must also believe that the vision is

Michael Dell's vision was of a computer company whose business model included bypassing traditional retail distributors and selling customised PCs directly to consumers and firms. It was new, it was unique, and it was attainable. Dell, headquartered in Austin, Texas, was founded in 1984 and is now a $31 billion company that employs nearly 35,000 people around the globe.

attainable. It should be perceived as challenging, yet doable. Visions that have clear articulation and powerful imagery are more easily grasped and accepted.

What are some examples of visions? From his beginnings in the Australian media business, Rupert Murdoch had a vision of the future of the communication industry by combining entertainment and media. Through his News Corporation, Murdoch has successfully integrated a broadcast network, TV stations, movie studio, publishing, and global satellite distribution. Singapore entrepreneur Ron Sim, founder and chairman of Osim, a Singapore-based health products firm, has a vision for the iMedic—a high-tech massage chair that has proved to be a phenomenal success for his company with Hong Kong and Singapore consumers. He wants it to be the preferred massage chair for all of China and has engaged China's most celebrated film actress, Gong Li, to promote his vision. Michael Dell has created a vision of a business that allows Dell Computer to sell and deliver a finished PC directly to a customer in fewer than eight days in countries across the South Pacific and Asia.

Qualities of a visionary leader

What skills do visionary leaders exhibit? Once the vision is identified, these leaders appear to have three qualities that are related to effectiveness in their visionary roles.[44] First is the ability to explain the vision to others. The leader needs to make the vision clear in terms of required actions and aims through clear oral and written communication. Second is to be able to express the vision not just verbally but through the leader's behaviour. This requires behaving in ways that continually convey and reinforce the vision. The third skill is being able to extend the vision to different leadership contexts. This is the ability to sequence activities so that the vision can be applied in a variety of situations. For example, the vision has to be as meaningful to the people in accounting as to those in marketing, and to employees in Sydney as well as in Kuala Lumpur.

Emotional Intelligence and Leadership Effectiveness

We introduced emotional intelligence (EI) in our discussion of emotions in a previous chapter. We revisit the topic here because of recent studies indicating that EI—more than IQ, expertise or any other single factor—is the best predictor of who will emerge as a leader.[45]

As our trait research demonstrated in the previous chapter, leaders need basic intelligence and job-relevant knowledge. But IQ and technical skills are 'threshold capabilities'. They are necessary but not sufficient requirements for leadership. It is the possession of the five components of EI—self-awareness, self-management, self-motivation, empathy and social skills—that allows an individual to become a star performer. Without EI, a person can have outstanding training, a highly analytical mind, a long-term vision and an endless supply of terrific ideas, but still not make a great leader. This is especially true as individuals move up in an organisation. The evidence indicates that the higher the rank of a person considered to be a star performer, the more that EI capabilities surface as the reason for their effectiveness. Specifically, when star performers were compared with average ones in senior management positions, nearly 90 per cent of the difference in their effectiveness was attributable to EI factors, rather than basic intelligence.

Interestingly, it has been pointed out that the maturing of Rudolph Guiliani's leadership effectiveness closely followed the development of his emotional intelligence. For the better part of the eight years he was mayor of New York City, Guiliani ruled with an iron fist.

He talked tough, picked fights, and demanded results. The result was a city that was cleaner, safer, and better governed—but also more polarized. Critics called Guiliani a tin-eared tyrant. In the eyes of many, something important was missing from his leadership. That something, his critics acknowledged, emerged as the World Trade Center collapsed. It was a newfound compassion to complement his command: a mix of resolve, empathy, and inspiration that brought comfort to millions.[46]

It is likely that Guiliani's emotional capacities and compassion for others were stimulated by a series of personal hardships—including prostate cancer and the highly visible breakup of his marriage—that had taken place less than a year before the terrorist attack on the World Trade Center.[47]

EI has shown to be positively related to job performance at all levels. But it appears to be especially relevant in jobs that demand a high degree of social interaction. And, of course, that's what leadership is all about. Great leaders demonstrate their EI by exhibiting all five of its key components:

Myth *or* Science?

'Men make better leaders than women'

This statement is false. There is no evidence to support the myth that men make better leaders than women.

The evidence indicates that the similarities in leadership style between men and women tend to outweigh the differences. But where there are differences, those differences tend to favour women, not men![48] Studies show that female leaders, when rated by their peers, underlings and bosses, score higher than their male counterparts on almost every important dimension of leadership—including goal setting, motivating others, fostering communication, producing high-quality work, listening to others and mentoring.

Women tend to use a more democratic leadership style. They encourage participation, share power and information, and attempt to enhance followers' self-worth. They prefer to lead through inclusion and rely on their charisma, expertise, contacts and interpersonal skills to influence others. Men, on the other hand, are more likely to use a directive command-and-control style. They rely on the formal authority of their managerial position for their influence base.

In today's organisations, flexibility, teamwork, trust and information sharing are replacing rigid structures, competitive individualism, control and secrecy. The best leaders listen, motivate, and provide support to their people. That is, they display EI. And, in contrast to men, women score somewhat higher on EI. As a specific example, the expanded use of cross-functional teams in organisations means that effective leaders must become skilful negotiators. The leadership styles women typically use can make them better at negotiating, as they tend to treat negotiations in the context of a continuing relationship—trying hard to make the other party a winner in its own and others' eyes.

- *Self-awareness:* Exhibited by self-confidence, realistic self-assessment and a self-deprecating sense of humour.
- *Self-management:* Exhibited by trustworthiness and integrity, comfort with ambiguity and openness to change.
- *Self-motivation:* Exhibited by a strong drive to achieve, optimism and high organisational commitment.
- *Empathy:* Exhibited by expertise in building and retaining talent, cross-cultural sensitivity, and service to clients and customers.
- *Social skills:* Exhibited by the ability to lead change, persuasiveness, and expertise in building and leading teams.

The recent evidence makes a strong case for concluding that EI is an essential element in leadership effectiveness. As such, it should probably be added to the list of traits associated with leadership that we described in the previous chapter.

Contemporary Leadership Roles

What unique demands do teams place on leaders? Why are many effective leaders also active mentors? And how can leaders develop self-leadership skills in their employees? In this section, we briefly address these three leadership-role issues.

LEARNING OBJECTIVE

6

Identify the four roles that team leaders perform

PROVIDING TEAM LEADERSHIP

Leadership is increasingly taking place within a team context. As teams grow in popularity, the role of the leader in guiding team members takes on heightened importance.[49] And the role of team leader is different from the traditional leadership role performed by first-line supervisors, as J. D. Bryant, a supervisor at one of Texas Instruments' factories, found out.[50] Texas Instruments Inc. is a world leader in digital signal processing and analog technologies and has production facilities and sales offices worldwide. One day, J. D was happily overseeing a staff of 15 circuit-board assemblers. The next day he was informed the company was moving to teams and that he was to become a 'facilitator'. 'I'm supposed to teach the teams everything I know and then let them make their own decisions,' he said. Confused about his new role, he admitted: 'There was no clear plan on what I was supposed to do.' In this section, we consider the challenge of being a team leader and review the new roles that team leaders take on.

Many leaders aren't equipped to handle the change to teams. As one prominent consultant noted, '[E]ven the most capable managers have trouble making the transition because all the command-and-control type things they were encouraged to do before are no longer appropriate. There's no reason to have any skill or sense of this.'[51] This same consultant estimated that 'probably 15 percent of managers are natural team leaders; another 15 percent could never lead a team because it runs counter to their personality. [They are unable to sublimate their dominating style for the good of the team.] Then there's that huge group in the middle: Team leadership doesn't come naturally to them, but they can learn it.'[52]

The challenge for most managers, then, is to learn how to become an effective team leader. They have to learn skills such as the patience to share information, to trust others, to give up authority, and understanding when to intervene. Effective leaders have mastered the difficult balancing act of knowing when to leave their teams alone and when to intercede. New team leaders may try to retain too much control at a time when team members need more autonomy, or they may abandon their teams at times when the teams need support and help.[53]

A study of 20 organisations that had reorganised themselves around teams found certain common responsibilities that all leaders had to assume. These included coaching, facilitating, handling disciplinary problems, reviewing team/individual performance, training and communication.[54] Many of these responsibilities apply to managers in general. A more meaningful way to describe the team leader's job is to focus on two priorities: managing the team's external boundary and facilitating the team process.[55] We have broken these priorities down into four specific roles.

First, team leaders are *liaisons with external constituencies*. These include upper management, other internal teams, customers and suppliers. The leader represents the team to other constituencies, secures needed resources, clarifies others' expectations of the team, gathers information from the outside, and shares this information with team members.

Second, team leaders are *troubleshooters*. When the team has problems and asks for assistance, team leaders sit in on meetings and help try to resolve the problems. This rarely relates to technical or operation issues because the team members typically know more about the tasks being done than does the team leader. Where the leader is most likely to contribute is by asking penetrating questions, helping the team to talk through problems, and by getting needed resources from external constituencies. For example, when a team in an aerospace firm found itself short-handed, its team leader took responsibility for getting more staff. He presented the team's case to upper management and got the approval through the company's human resources department.

Third, team leaders are *conflict managers*. When disagreements surface, they help to process the conflict. What is the source of the conflict? Who is involved? What are the issues? What resolution options are available? What are the advantages and disadvantages of each? By getting team members to address questions such as these, the leader minimises the disruptive aspects of intra-team conflicts.

Finally, team leaders are *coaches*. They clarify expectations and roles, teach, offer support, cheerlead, and do whatever else is necessary to help team members improve their work performance.

MENTORING

Many leaders create mentoring relationships. A **mentor** is a senior employee who sponsors and supports a less-experienced employee (a protégé). The mentoring role includes coaching, counselling and sponsorship.[56] As a coach, mentors help to develop their protégés' skills. As counsellors, mentors provide support and help to bolster protégés' self-confidence. And as sponsors, mentors actively intervene on behalf of their protégés, lobby to get their protégés visible assignments, and politic to get them rewards such as promotions and salary increases.

Successful mentors are good teachers. They can present ideas clearly, listen well, and empathise with the problems of their protégés. They also share experiences with the protégé, act as role models, share contacts, and provide guidance through the political maze of the organisation. They provide advice and guidance on how to survive and get ahead in the organisation and act as a sounding board for ideas that a protégé may be hesitant to share with their direct supervisor. A mentor vouches for a protégé, answers for them in the highest circles within the organisation, and makes appropriate introductions.

Some organisations have formal mentoring programs where mentors are officially assigned to new or high-potential employees. For example, at Edward Jones, a financial services firm with 24,000 employees, mentors are assigned to new employees after recruits have completed the company's initial two-month home study program and five-day customer-service seminar.[57] The new employees shadow their mentor for three weeks to specifically learn the company's way of doing business. However, in contrast to Edward Jones's formal system, most organisations rely on informal mentoring—with senior managers personally selecting an employee and taking that employee on as a protégé.

The most effective mentoring relationships exist outside the immediate boss–subordinate interface.[58] The boss–subordinate context has an inherent conflict of interest and tension, mostly attributable to managers' directly evaluating the performance of subordinates, that limits openness and meaningful communication.

LEARNING OBJECTIVE

7

Explain the role of a mentor

mentor
A senior employee who sponsors and supports a less-experienced employee.

Relationships in the workplace can have powerful consequences. When staff are willing to seek out and work with a competent mentor, their prospects for career development can be significantly enhanced.

Why would a leader want to be a mentor? There are personal benefits to the leader, as well as benefits for the organisation. The mentor–protégé relationship gives the mentor unfiltered access to the attitudes and feelings of lower-ranking employees. Protégés can provide early warning signals of potential problems. They provide timely information to upper managers that short-circuits the formal channels. So, the mentor–protégé relationship is a valuable communication channel that allows mentors to have news of problems before they become common knowledge to others in upper management. In addition, in terms of leader self-interest, mentoring can provide personal satisfaction to senior executives. In the latter stages of their career, managers are often allowed the luxury of playing the part of elder statesperson. They are respected for their judgment, built up over many years and through varied experiences. The opportunity to share this knowledge with others can be personally rewarding for the mentor. From the organisation's standpoint, mentoring provides a support system for high-potential employees. Where mentors exist, protégés are often more motivated, better politically grounded and less likely to quit. For example, one study found that where a significant mentoring relationship existed, the protégés had more favourable and frequent promotions, were paid significantly more than those who weren't mentored, and had a greater level of commitment to the organisation and greater career success.[59]

Are all employees in an organisation equally likely to participate in a mentoring relationship? Unfortunately, the answer is 'no'.[60] Evidence indicates that minorities and women are less likely to be chosen as protégés than are white males and thus are less likely to accrue the benefits of mentorship. Mentors tend to select protégés who are similar to themselves on criteria such as background, education, gender, race, ethnicity and religion. 'People naturally move to mentoring and can more easily communicate with those with whom they most closely identify.'[61] In the United States, for example, upper-management positions in most organisations have been traditionally staffed by white males, so it is hard for minorities and women to be selected as protégés. In addition, in terms of cross-gender mentoring, senior male managers may select male protégés to minimise problems such as sexual attraction or gossip. Organisations have responded to this dilemma by increasing formal mentoring programs and providing training and coaching for potential mentors of special groups such as minorities and women.

SELF-LEADERSHIP

self-leadership
A set of processes through which individuals control their own behaviour.

Is it possible for people to lead themselves? An increasing body of research suggests that many can.[62] Proponents of **self-leadership** propose that there are a set of processes through which individuals control their own behaviour. And effective leaders (or what advocates like to call *superleaders*) help their followers to lead themselves. They do this by developing leadership capacity in others and nurturing followers so that they no longer need to depend on formal leaders for direction and motivation.

How do leaders create self-leaders? The following have been suggested:[63]

1. *Model self-leadership.* Practise self-observation, setting challenging personal goals, self-direction and self-reinforcement. Then display these behaviours and encourage others to rehearse and then produce them.
2. *Encourage employees to create self-set goals.* Having quantitative, specific goals is the most important part of self-leadership.
3. *Encourage the use of self-rewards to strengthen and increase desirable behaviours.* In contrast, self-punishment should be limited only to occasions when the employee has been dishonest or destructive.
4. *Create positive thought patterns.* Encourage employees to use mental imagery and self-talk to further stimulate self-motivation.
5. *Create a climate of self-leadership.* Redesign the work to increase the natural rewards of a job and focus on these naturally rewarding features of work to increase motivation.
6. *Encourage self-criticism.* Encourage individuals to be critical of their own performance.

The underlying assumptions behind self-leadership are that people are responsible, capable and able to exercise initiative without the external constraints of bosses, rules or regulations. Given the proper support, individuals can monitor and control their own behaviour.

The importance of self-leadership has increased with the expanded popularity of teams. Empowered, self-managed teams need individuals who are themselves self-directed. Management can't expect individuals who have spent their organisational lives under boss-centred leadership to suddenly adjust to self-managed teams. Therefore, training in self-leadership is an excellent means to help employees make the transition from dependence to autonomy.

Moral Leadership

The topic of leadership and ethics has surprisingly received little attention. Only recently have ethicists and leadership researchers begun to consider the ethical implications in leadership.[64] Why now? One reason may be the growing general interest in ethics throughout the field of management. Another reason may be the discovery by probing biographers that many of our past leaders suffered from ethical shortcomings. In the political arena, the impeachment hearings in the United States of President Bill Clinton on grounds of perjury and other charges have done nothing to lessen concern about ethical leadership. In the business arena, events leading to the eventual bankruptcy of Enron Corp.—where executives at Enron, its accounting firm of Arthur Andersen and its law firm of Vinson & Elkins appear to have engaged in a multitude of unethical practices—has increased the public's and politicians' concerns about ethical standards in business worldwide. And in the public sector, various Australian states have had royal commissions into police corruption.

Ethics touches on leadership at a number of junctures. Transformational leaders, for example, have been described by one authority as fostering moral virtue when they try to change the attitudes and behaviours of followers.[65] Charisma, too, has an ethical component. Unethical leaders are more likely to use their charisma to enhance *power over* followers, directed towards self-serving ends. Ethical leaders are considered to use their charisma in a socially constructive way to serve others.[66] There is also the issue of abuse of power by leaders—for example, when they give themselves large salaries and bonuses while, at the same time, they seek to cut costs by laying off long-time employees. And, of course, the topic of trust explicitly deals with honesty and integrity in leadership.

Leadership effectiveness needs to address the *means* that a leader uses in trying to achieve goals, as well as the content of those goals. For example, Bill Gates's success in leading Microsoft to domination of the world's software business has been achieved by means of an extremely demanding work culture. Microsoft's culture demands long work hours by employees and is intolerant of individuals who want to balance work and their personal life. Microsoft's competitors and US government regulators have also pinpointed this pressurised and competitive culture as the source of numerous unethical practices—from using its control of its Windows' operating system to favour Microsoft's partners and subsidiaries, to encouraging its sales force to 'crush' its rivals. Importantly, Microsoft's culture mirrors the personality of its chairman and co-founder, Gates. In addition, ethical leadership must address the content of a leader's goals. Are the changes that the leader seeks for the organisation morally acceptable? Is a business leader effective if they build an organisation's success by selling products that damage the health of users? This question, for example, might be asked of tobacco executives. Or is a military leader successful by winning a war that shouldn't have been fought in the first place?

Leadership isn't value-free. Before we judge any leader to be effective, we should consider both the means used by the leader to achieve their goals and the moral content of those goals.

LEARNING OBJECTIVE

8

Describe how on-line leadership differs from face-to-face leadership

On-line Leadership: Some Speculative Thoughts

How do you lead people who are physically separated from you and where interactions are basically reduced to written digital communications? This is a question that, so far, has received little attention from OB researchers.[67] Leadership research has been directed almost exclusively to face-to-face and verbal situations. But we can't ignore the reality that today's managers and their employees are increasingly being linked by networks rather than geographical proximity. Obvious examples include managers who regularly use e-mail to communicate with their staff, managers overseeing virtual projects or teams, and managers whose telecommuting employees are linked to the office by a computer and modem.

If leadership is important to inspiring and motivating dispersed employees, we need to offer some guidance as to how leadership in this context might function. Keep in mind, however, that the dearth of research on this topic forces us to engage in considerable speculation. The intention here isn't to provide you with definitive guidelines for leading on-line. Rather, it is to introduce you to an increasingly important issue and get you to think about how leadership changes when relationships are defined by network interactions.

In face-to-face communications, harsh *words* can be softened by non-verbal action. A smile and comforting gestures, for example, can lessen the blow behind strong words such as *disappointed*, *unsatisfactory*, *inadequate* or *below expectations*. That non-verbal component doesn't exist with on-line interactions. The *structure* of words in a digital communication also has the power to motivate or demotivate the receiver. Is the message made up of full sentences or phrases? The latter, for example, is likely to be seen as curt and more threatening. Similarly, a message in all caps is the equivalent of shouting. The manager who inadvertently sends her message in short phrases, all in caps, may get a very different response than if she had sent that same message in full sentences, using upper and lowercase letters.

Leaders need to be sure that the *tone* of their message correctly reflects the emotions they want to send. Is the message formal or informal? Does it match the verbal style of the sender? Does it convey the appropriate level of importance or urgency? The fact that many people's writing style is very different from their interpersonal style is certainly a potential problem. One of your authors, for example, has observed a number of very warm and charismatic leaders who aren't comfortable with the written word and tend to make their written communications much more formal than their verbal style. This not only creates confusion for employees, but undoubtedly also hinders the leaders' overall effectiveness.

Finally, on-line leaders must choose a *style*. Do they use emoticons, abbreviations, jargon, and the like? Do they adapt their style to their audience? Observation suggests that some managers are having difficulty adjusting to computer-related communications. For example, they are using the same style with their bosses that they are using with their staff, with unfortunate consequences. Or they are selectively using digital communications to 'hide' when delivering bad news.

We know that messages convey more than surface information. From a leadership standpoint, messages can convey trust or lack of trust, status, task directives or emotional warmth. Concepts such as task structure, supportive behaviour and vision can be conveyed in written form as well as verbally. It may even be possible for leaders to convey charisma through the written word. But to effectively convey on-line leadership, managers must recognise that they have choices in the words, structure, tone and style of their digital communications. They also need to develop the skills of 'reading between the lines' in the messages they receive. In the same way that EI taps an individual's ability to monitor and assess others' emotions, effective on-line leaders need to develop the skill of deciphering the emotional components of messages.

Any discussion of on-line leadership needs also to consider the possibility that the digital age can turn non-leaders into leaders. Some managers, whose face-to-face leadership skills are less than satisfactory, may shine on-line. Their talents may lie in their writing skills and ability to read the messages behind written communiqués. Nothing in the mainstream leadership literature addresses this unique situation.

We propose that on-line leaders have to think through carefully what actions they want their digital messages to initiate. Although the networked communication is a relatively new form, it is a powerful channel. When used properly, it can build and enhance an individual's leadership effectiveness. But when misused, it has the potential to undermine a great deal of what a leader has been able to achieve through their verbal actions.

This discussion leads us to the tentative conclusion that, for an increasing number of managers, good interpersonal skills may include the abilities to communicate warmth, emotion, trust and leadership through written words on a computer screen and to read emotions in others' messages. In this 'new world' of communications, writing skills are likely to become an extension of interpersonal skills.

Challenges to the Leadership Construct

A noted management expert takes issue with the omnipotent role that academicians, practising managers and the general public have given to the concept of leadership. He says, 'In the 1500s, people ascribed all events they didn't understand to God. Why did the crops fail? God. Why did someone die? God. Now our all-purpose explanation is leadership.'[68] He notes that when a company succeeds, people need someone to give the credit to. And that's typically the firm's CEO. Similarly, when a company does poorly, they need someone to blame. CEOs also play this role. But much of an organisation's success or failure is due to factors outside the influence of leadership. In many cases, success or failure is just a matter of being in the right or wrong place at a given time. For example, when the demand for microchips was growing at 60 per cent or more a year, leaders at microchip makers such as Intel and Motorola were considered geniuses. Similarly, the CEOs at PC makers such as Compaq and Gateway were lauded in the 1990s, when demand for PCs was exploding. But by 2001, these same leaders were being widely criticised for the decline in their company's business. And many CEOs were replaced as profits sank. The key leadership question would be: in a recession, when consumers and business are widely cutting back on technology purchases, how is firing a CEO going to increase the demand for chips and PCs? The answer is, it can't.

In this section, we present two perspectives that challenge the widely accepted belief in the importance of leadership. The first argument proposes that leadership is more about appearances than reality. You don't have to *be* an effective leader, as long as you *look* like one! The second argument directly attacks the notion that some leadership *will always* be effective *regardless* of the situation. This argument contends that in many situations, whatever actions leaders exhibit are irrelevant.

LEADERSHIP AS AN ATTRIBUTION

attribution theory of leadership
The idea that leadership is merely an attribution that people make about other individuals.

We introduced attribution theory in a previous chapter. As you may remember, it deals with the ways in which people try to make sense out of cause-and-effect relationships. We said that when something happens, we want to attribute it to something else. The **attribution theory of leadership** says that leadership is merely an attribution that people make about other individuals.[69] The attribution framework has shown that people characterise leaders as having such traits as intelligence, outgoing personality, strong verbal skills, aggressiveness, understanding and industriousness.[70] Similarly, the high–high leader (high on both task and people dimensions) presented in the previous chapter has been found to be consistent with attributions of what makes a good leader.[71] That is, regardless of the situation, a high–high leadership style tends to be perceived as best. At the organisational level, the attribution framework accounts for the conditions under which people use leadership to explain organisational outcomes. Those conditions are extremes in organisational performance. When an organisation has either extremely negative or extremely positive performance, people are prone to make leadership attributions to explain the performance.[72] As noted earlier, this tendency helps to account for the vulnerability of CEOs when their organisations suffer a major financial setback, regardless of whether they had much to do with it; and also accounts for why these CEOs tend to be given credit for extremely positive financial results—again, regardless of how much or how little they contributed.

One of the more interesting findings in the attribution model of leadership literature is the perception that effective leaders are generally considered consistent or unwavering in their decisions.[73] One of the explanations for why John Howard (during his first term as Australian Prime Minister) was perceived as a leader was that he was fully committed, steadfast, and consistent in the decisions he made and the goals he set.

Following the attribution theory of leadership, we would say that what is important in being characterised as an 'effective leader' is projecting the *appearance* of being a leader, rather than focusing on *actual accomplishments*. Those who aspire to be a leader can attempt to shape the perception that they are smart, personable, verbally adept, aggressive, hard-working and consistent in their style. And by doing so, they increase the probability that their bosses, colleagues and employees will *view them* as an effective leader.

LEARNING OBJECTIVE
9
Identify when leadership may not be necessary

SUBSTITUTES AND NEUTRALISERS TO LEADERSHIP

Contrary to the arguments made throughout this and the previous chapter, leadership may not always be important. Data from numerous studies collectively demonstrate that, in many situations, whatever actions leaders exhibit are irrelevant. Certain individual, job and organisational variables can act as *substitutes* for leadership or *neutralise* the leader's effect to influence their followers.[74]

Neutralisers make it impossible for leader behaviour to make any difference to follower outcomes. They negate the leader's influence. Substitutes, on the other hand, make a leader's influence not only impossible but also unnecessary. They act as a replacement for the leader's influence. For example, characteristics of employees, such as their experience, training, 'professional' orientation, or indifference towards organisational rewards, can substitute for, or neutralise the effect of, leadership. Experience and training can replace the need for a leader's support or ability to create structure and reduce task ambiguity. Jobs that are inherently unambiguous and routine, or that are intrinsically satisfying, may place fewer demands on the leadership variable. Organisational characteristics such as explicit formalised goals, rigid rules and procedures, and cohesive work groups can also replace formal leadership (see Table 12.3).

This recent recognition that leaders don't always have an impact on follower outcomes shouldn't be that surprising. After all, we have introduced a number of variables in this text—attitudes, personality, ability and group norms, to name but a few—that have been documented as having an effect on employee performance and satisfaction. Yet, supporters of the leadership

TABLE 12.3	Substitutes and neutralisers for leadership	
Defining Characteristics	Relationship-oriented Leadership	Task-oriented Leadership
Individual		
Experience/training	No effect on	Substitutes for
Professionalism	Substitutes for	Substitutes for
Indifference to rewards	Neutralises	Neutralises
Job		
Highly structured task	No effect on	Substitutes for
Provides its own feedback	No effect on	Substitutes for
Intrinsically satisfying	Substitutes for	No effect on
Organisation		
Explicit formalised goals	No effect on	Substitutes for
Rigid rules and procedures	No effect on	Substitutes for
Cohesive work groups	Substitutes for	Substitues for

Source: Based on S. Kerr and J. M. Jermier, 'Substitutes for Leadership: Their Meaning and Measurement', *Organizational Behavior and Human Performance*, December 1978, p. 378.

concept place an undue burden on this variable for explaining and predicting behaviour. It is too simplistic to consider employees as guided to goal accomplishments solely by the actions of their leader. It is important, therefore, to recognise explicitly that leadership is merely another independent variable in our overall OB model. In some situations, it may contribute a lot to explaining employee productivity, absence, turnover, satisfaction and citizenship behaviour, but in other situations, it may contribute little towards that end.

Finding and Creating Effective Leaders

LEARNING OBJECTIVE
10
Explain how to find and create effective leaders

We have covered a lot of ground in these two chapters on leadership. But the ultimate goal of our review is to answer this question: How can organisations find or create effective leaders? Let's try to answer that question.[75]

SELECTION

The entire process that organisations go through to fill management positions is essentially an exercise in trying to identify individuals who will be effective leaders. Your search might begin by reviewing the specific requirements for the position to be filled. What knowledge, skills and abilities are needed to do the job effectively? You should try to analyse the situation in order to find candidates who will make a proper match.

Testing is useful for identifying and selecting leaders. Personality tests can be used to look for traits associated with leadership—ambition and energy, desire to lead, honesty and integrity, self-confidence, intelligence and job-relevant knowledge. Testing to find a leadership-candidate's score on self-monitoring also makes sense. High self-monitors are likely to outperform their low-scoring counterparts because the former is better at reading situations and adjusting their behaviour accordingly. You can additionally assess candidates for emotional intelligence. Given the importance of social skills to managerial effectiveness, candidates with a high EI should have an advantage, especially in situations requiring transformational leadership.[76]

Interviews additionally provide an opportunity to evaluate leadership candidates. For example, we know that experience is a poor predictor of leader effectiveness, but situation-specific experience is relevant. You can use the interview to determine if a candidate's prior experience fits with the situation you are trying to fill. Similarly, the interview is a reasonably good vehicle for identifying the degree to which a candidate has leadership traits such as ambition, self-confidence, a vision, the verbal skills to frame issues or a charismatic physical presence.

We know the importance of situational factors in leadership success. And we should use this knowledge to match leaders to situations. Does the situation require a change-focused leader? If so, look for transformational qualities. If not, look for transactional qualities. You might also ask: is leadership actually important in this specific position? There may be situational factors that substitute for or neutralise leadership. If there are, then the leader essentially performs a figure-head or symbolic role, and the importance of selecting the 'right' person isn't particularly crucial.

TRAINING

Organisations, in aggregate, spend billions of dollars, yen and euros on leadership training and development.[77] These efforts take many forms—from $50,000 executive leadership programs offered by universities such as Melbourne University and the University of New South Wales, to sailing experiences at the Outward Bound School. Although much of the money spent on training may provide dubious benefits, our review suggests that there are some things management can do to get the maximum effect from their leadership-training budgets.[78]

First, let's recognise the obvious. People aren't equally trainable. Leadership training of any kind is likely to be more successful with individuals who are high self-monitors than with low self-monitors. Such individuals have the flexibility to change their behaviour.

What kinds of things can individuals learn that might be related to higher leader effectiveness? It may be a bit optimistic to believe that we can teach 'vision creation', but we can teach implementation skills. We can train people to develop 'an understanding about content themes critical to effective visions'.[79] We also can teach skills such as trust building and mentoring. And leaders can be taught situational-analysis skills. They can learn how to evaluate situations, how to modify situations to make them fit better with their style, and how to assess which leader behaviours might be most effective in given situations.

On an optimistic note, there is evidence suggesting that behavioural training through modelling exercises can increase an individual's ability to exhibit charismatic leadership qualities. The success of the researchers mentioned earlier (see 'Are charismatic leaders born or made?') in actually scripting undergraduate business students to 'play' charismatic is a case in point.[80]

Summary and Implications for Managers

Effective managers today must develop trusting relationships with those whom they seek to lead. Why? Because as organisations have become less stable and predictable, strong bonds of trust are likely to be replacing bureaucratic rules in defining expectations and relationships. Managers who aren't trusted aren't likely to be effective leaders.

Organisations are increasingly searching for managers who can exhibit transformational leadership qualities. They want leaders with visions, and the charisma to carry out those visions. And while true leadership effectiveness may be a result of exhibiting the right behaviours at the right time, the evidence is quite strong that people have a relatively uniform perception of what a leader should look like. They attribute 'leadership' to people who are smart, personable, verbally adept, and the like. To the degree that managers project these qualities, others are likely to deem them leaders.

For managers concerned with how to fill key positions in their organisation with effective leaders, we have shown that tests and interviews help to identify people with leadership qualities. In addition to focusing on leadership selection, managers should also consider investing in leadership training. Many individuals with leadership potential can enhance their skills through formal courses, workshops, rotating job responsibilities, coaching and mentoring.

Point

GOOD LEADERSHIP IS CULTURALLY-BOUND

Leaders must adapt their style to different national cultures. What works in China, for example, isn't likely to work in Canada, Australia or Malaysia. Can you imagine, for example, executives at a large Australian department store chain, such as Myer, being effective by humiliating their employees? But that works at the Asia Department Store in central China.[a] Executives there blatantly brag about practising 'heartless' management, requiring new employees to undergo two to four weeks of military-type training in order to increase their obedience, and conduct the store's in-house training sessions in a public place where employees can openly suffer embarrassment from their mistakes.

National culture affects leadership style by way of the follower. Leaders cannot choose their styles at will. They are constrained by the cultural conditions that their followers have come to expect. For example, Korean leaders are expected to be paternalistic towards employees; Arab leaders who show kindness or generosity without being asked to do so are seen by other Arabs as weak; and Japanese leaders are expected to be humble and to speak infrequently.[b]

Consistent with the contingency approach, leaders need to adjust their style to the unique cultural aspects of a country. For example, a manipulative or autocratic style is compatible with high power distance, and we find high power distance scores in Russia, Spain, and Arab, Far Eastern and most Latin countries. Power distance rankings should also be good indicators of employee willingness to accept participative leadership. Participation is likely to be most effective in low power distance cultures such as exist in Norway, Finland, Denmark and Sweden.

Sources: [a] 'Military-Style Management in China', *Asia Inc.*, March 1995, p. 70.

[b] R. J. House, 'Leadership in the Twenty-First Century', in A. Howard (ed.), *The Changing Nature of Work* (San Francisco: Jossey-Bass, 1995), pp. 442–44; and M. F. Peterson and J. G. Hunt, 'International Perspectives on International Leadership', *Leadership Quarterly*, Fall 1997, pp. 203–31.

Counterpoint

The GLOBE research program has gathered data on approximately 18,000 middle managers in 825 organisations, covering 62 countries. It is the most comprehensive cross-cultural study of leadership ever undertaken, so its findings shouldn't be quickly dismissed. It's illuminating that one of the results coming from the GLOBE program is that there are some universal aspects to leadership. Specifically, a number of the elements making up transformational leadership appear to be associated with effective leadership regardless of what country the leader is in.[c] This conclusion is very important because it flies in the face of the contingency view that leadership style needs to adapt to cultural differences.

What elements of transformational leadership appear universal? Vision, foresight, providing encouragement, trustworthiness, dynamism, positiveness and proactiveness. The results led two members of the GLOBE team to conclude that 'effective business leaders in any country are expected by their subordinates to provide a powerful and proactive vision to guide the company into the future, strong motivational skills to stimulate all employees to fulfill the vision, and excellent planning skills to assist in implementing the vision'.[d]

What might explain the universal appeal of these transformational leader attributes? It has been suggested that pressures towards common technologies and management practices, as a result of global competition and multinational influences, may make some aspects of leadership universally accepted. If true, we may be able to select and train leaders in a universal style and thus significantly raise the quality of leadership worldwide.

Sources: [c] R. J. House, P. J. Hanges, S. A. Ruiz-Quintanilla, P. W. Dorfman and Associates, 'Culture Specific and Cross-Culturally Generalizable Implicit Leadership Theories: Are the Attributes of Charismatic/Transformational Leadership Universally Endorsed?', *Leadership Quarterly*, Summer 1999, pp. 219–56; and D. E. Carl and M. Javidan, 'Universality of Charismatic Leadership: A Multi-Nation Study', paper presented at the National Academy of Management Conference, Washington, DC, August 2001.

[d] Carl and Javidan, 'Universality of Charismatic Leadership', p. 29.

For Discussion

1. Contrast the three types of trust. Relate them to your experience in personal relationships.
2. What role do you think training plays in an individual's ability to trust others? For example, does the training of lawyers, accountants, law enforcement personnel and social workers take different approaches towards trusting others? Explain.
3. How might an understanding of knowledge-based trust explain the reluctance of a person to change jobs?
4. 'It's not possible to be both a trusting boss and a politically astute leader. One requires openness and the other requires concealment.' Do you agree or disagree with this statement? Explain.
5. What could you do if you wanted others to perceive you as a charismatic leader?
6. When is charisma needed?
7. What are the qualities of a vision?
8. How does a leader increase self-leadership among their followers?
9. How does EI relate to leadership effectiveness?
10. How does one become an effective leader?
11. Why would a leader want to be a mentor?
12. As a new employee in an organisation, why might you want to acquire a mentor? Why might women and minorities have more difficulty in finding a mentor than white males?
13. How is leadership an attribution?
14. Contrast substitutes and neutralisers for leadership.
15. Is there an ethical problem if leaders focus more on looking like a leader than actually being one? Discuss.

Exercises

Exercise 12a
PRACTISING TO BE CHARISMATIC

People who are charismatic engage in the following behaviours:
• They project a powerful, confident and dynamic presence. This has both verbal and non-verbal components. Those with charisma use a captivating and engaging voice tone. They convey confidence. They also talk directly to people, maintaining direct eye contact and holding their body posture in a way that says they are sure of themselves. They speak clearly, avoid stammering, and avoid sprinkling their sentences with non-content phrases such as 'ahhh' and 'you know'.

- They articulate an overarching goal. They have a vision for the future, unconventional ways of achieving the vision, and the ability to communicate the vision to others.

     The vision is a clear statement of where they want to go and how they are going to get there. They are able to persuade others how the achievement of this vision is in the others' self-interest.

     They look for fresh and radically different approaches to problems. The road to achieving their vision is novel but also appropriate to the context.

     They not only have a vision but they are able to get others to buy into it.

- They convey high performance expectations and confidence in others' ability to meet these expectations. They demonstrate their confidence in people by stating ambitious goals for them individually and as a group. They convey absolute belief that they will achieve their expectations.

- They are sensitive to the needs of followers. Charismatic leaders get to know their followers individually. They understand their individual needs and are able to develop intensely personal relationships with each. They do this through encouraging followers to express their points of view, by being approachable, by genuinely listening to and caring about their followers' concerns, and by asking questions so that they can learn what is really important to them.

Now that you know what charismatic leaders do, you get the opportunity to practise projecting charisma.

1. The class members should divide into pairs.
2. Student A's task is to 'lead' Student B through a new-student orientation to your university. The orientation should last about ten to 15 minutes. Assume that Student B is new to your university and is unfamiliar with the campus. Remember, Student A should attempt to project themself as charismatic.
3. Roles now reverse and Student B's task is to 'lead' Student A in a ten- to 15-minute program on how to study more effectively for exams. Take a few minutes to think about what has worked well for you and assume that Student A is a new student interested in improving their study habits. Again, remember that Student B should attempt to project themself as charismatic.
4. When both role plays are complete, each pair should assess how well they did in projecting charisma and how they might improve.

Source: This exercise is based on J. M. Howell and P. J. Frost, 'A Laboratory Study of Charismatic Leadership', *Organizational Behavior and Human Decision Processes*, April 1989, pp. 243–69.

Exercise 12b
AFFIRMATION OF TRUST

Divide into groups of 8 to 12 members each.

A. Each group has 20 minutes to discuss the following four topics:
   1. What kind of situations cause you to be afraid?
   2. What kind of situations cause you to feel insecure?
   3. What makes you happy?
   4. What makes you cry?
B. Each group member should remove a shoe and place it alongside the shoes of other members in a designated place, outside the group's meeting area. Each member should identify their shoe by writing their name on a slip of paper and putting it in front of their shoe.
C. Review the five-item 'Affirmation of Trust' listing that follows this exercise. Each member should:
   1. Write down the name of a person in your group on a slip of paper. Under their name, write the letters A to E in a vertical column. Next to each letter, rate your perception of that person (based on your experience in class as well as their responses to this activity) on a scale of 1 to 5 (1 being low) using the 'Affirmation of Trust' listing. Sign your name to the bottom of the slip. Deposit this slip of paper in the other member's shoe.
   2. Repeat the above for all the other members of the group.
D. After all members have distributed their slips, each one retrieves their own shoe with the slips left in. Read each of the slips directed to you by the other members of your group and record the summary results.
E. Group members now discuss their reactions to their slips with the group. To what degree do they align with your self-perceptions? To what degree do the various statements converge and agree? What have you learned from this feedback that could help you build trust with others?

AFFIRMATION OF TRUST LIST

A. Open
B. Speaks his or her feelings
C. Tells the truth
D. Consistent
E. Demonstrates competence

Source: Based on J. W. Pfeiffer and J. E. Jones (eds), *A Handbook of Structured Experiences for Human Relations Training*, vol. VI (La Jolla, CA: University Associates, 1977), pp. 110–13.

Case Study 12

When the East Comes to Lead the West

James Ong was busy planning the strategic management three-day retreat that was to run in two weeks time. He asked Gail Lambert, his director of human resources, to join him, since he wanted to get her ideas on the workshop. He had to be certain it would go well.

James was selected to be the managing director of Solarpower, a growing Australian company, two years ago after it was purchased by a Malaysian company. He was selected because he had lived in Australia for four years while doing his undergraduate business degree. He had recently completed an MBA program in Singapore, so he had the right qualifications. He and his wife and young son moved back to Australia and he enjoyed the quality of life in Australia. James was also a devout Buddhist and tried to reflect its precepts in his working life.

In his first year, James didn't make many changes. He wanted to know how Solarpower did things and to show the mostly Australian workforce that he wasn't a threat. After some time, however, it was obvious to James that some changes were necessary. The company was doing OK, but wasn't actively marketing its products on the world market. There was no strategic plan, and the workforce seemed content to do what they had done for the last ten years. Competition was rapidly moving into the Australian solar business and was eating into their market.

The previous chief executive manager had had an 'in-group', all the members of which were Australian. None had any university training in management, and while they were competent and friendly to each other they weren't very innovative. The marketing manager had a great deal of expertise in the Australian market. He had tried the international market without a great deal of success and now felt that Solarpower should concentrate on the growing Australian market in order to minimise the effect of local and international competition in Australia. James had a very supportive style but was beginning to think he needed to be more directive if the company was to move ahead in the way he knew it could.

He hired a financial controller from Singapore who had an MBA degree and had recently immigrated to Australia. He also hired Gail Lambert as the new manager of human resources, and Gail immediately began to encourage the hiring of more ethnic groups and women at Solarpower. She was now introducing a new performance management system based on a problem-solving approach, rather than an appraisal system that had been tried and then let wane.

James had a strong belief that solar products were not only good business but also an important contributor to easing the ecological problems that many industrial nations were facing. He wanted to expand from hot water heaters to a wide range of solar products (calculators, computers, cars, electricity generation, and so on). He was very impressed with leaders like Ricardo Semler, the CEO of Semco. He felt that Solarpower was in a business that could operate with a similar view. He wanted new workplace agreements that would reward staff members who met their section and corporate goals.

James wanted to outline a new vision for Solarpower at this strategic planning workshop. He wanted Gail's advice on which external consultants they might contact to help plan and facilitate the workshop. Gail also told James about some rumours she had heard. Several of the middle-level managers had expressed scepticism about the management retreat leading to anything. In previous years they had gone away and talked about the future of the business; each director gave a short review of the status of the business, and that was about it. In addition, there was some antagonism about James and the 'Gang of Four', which was considered to include Richard (the financial manager), Walter (the quality manager), Gail and James. There were some light-hearted jokes about the 'SNAILs', the Sensitive New Age Innovative Leaders, who were all concerned about multiculturalism, ISO9000, ecology and women's equality but didn't know very much about how to make profitable solar heaters.

After his discussion with Gail, James decided to ask you and your consulting team to plan and facilitate the strategic planning workshop.

Questions

1. Are any of the leadership issues mentioned in the chapter relevant to this case? Do they help to explain any of the problems that James found?
2. What do you recommend James do during the three days of the workshop? Are there also some longer-term things that he should put in place to help develop Solarpower and his managers?
3. What other problems and issues should James consider regarding the development of his managers in the future?

Web Workout

1. Who's hot and who's not? Find five companies whose CEOs have left (for reasons other than normal retirement) in the past 12 months. Assess their company's profit performance against the average for their industry group. A web search using terms such as *CEO + turnover* or *resignation* will yield a number of results. To find the share price performance, you can then use any of a number of on-line services such as <www.cnnfn.com>. What did this exercise tell you? Be prepared to discuss in class.
2. Do you trust your employer? How would your organisation know if you trusted it or not? Go to <http://management.about.com/library/weekly/aa022900.htm> to learn more about how an organisation can determine if its employees trust it. Be sure to link on and read the *Seattle Times* companion article. Write a few paragraphs addressing why you do or don't trust your organisation using the guidelines in the articles as a springboard for ideas. Bring your work to class for further discussion.
3. Trust no one? For some employees it is their new motto. Find out why at <http://careers.usatoday.com/service/usa/national/content/news/onthejob/2002-02-05-employee-trust>. Write a short reaction paper as to why you agree or don't agree with the article (or parts of the article). Can you relate any of what is discussed to your own working career? If so, include that in your paper as well. What will be your strategy when selecting your next employer? Bring your paper to class for further discussion.
4. Write a short paper on the connection between charismatic leadership and impression management. Performing a search using the key words *charismatic + leadership + impression + management* will get you off to a good start. Try using the terms in different combinations to get additional links. Be prepared to discuss your findings in class.
5. Select one of the links at <www.css.edu/users/dswenson/web/Leadlink.htm>, which is a huge resource of on-line leadership resources. Once you have selected a topic, prepare a five-minute presentation to give to the class on that topic. Develop a handout, or print off selections from the website to distribute so that every member of the class will have their own 'leadership resource library' once the presentations are completed. Try to keep your handout to two pages or less.
6. A very royal vision! Visit <www.findarticles.com/cf_trvgnt/m0VOU/1997_March_17/47217411/p1/article.jhtml>. Read what CEO and chairman Richard Fain of Royal Caribbean Cruise Lines has to say about his company's vision. Analyse the case presented using the criteria for visionary leadership as discussed in the text. Bring your work to class for further discussion.

KSS Program

KNOW THE CONCEPTS   SELF-AWARENESS   SKILLS APPLICATIONS

Developing trust

After you have read this chapter, take Self-Assessment #29 ('Do Others See Me as Trusting?') on your enclosed CD-Rom and complete the skill-building module entitled 'Developing Trust' on page 641.

NOTES

1. This opening vignette is based on J. Steinhauer, 'In Crisis, Guiliani's Popularity Overflows City', *New York Times*, 20 September 2001, p. A1; C. Jones, 'Guiliani Exits as National Icon', *USA Today*, 28 December 2001, p. 3A; D. Barry, 'A Man Who Became More Than a Mayor', *New York Times*, 31 December 2001, p. A1; and E. Pooley, 'Mayor of the World', *Time*, 31 December 2001.

2. Based on S. D. Boon and J. G. Holmes, 'The Dynamics of Interpersonal Trust: Resolving Uncertainty in the Face of Risk', in R. A. Hinde and J. Groebel (eds), *Cooperation and Prosocial Behaviour* (Cambridge, UK: Cambridge University Press, 1991), p. 194; D. J. McAllister, 'Affect- and Cognition-Based Trust as Foundations for Interpersonal Cooperation in Organizations', *Academy of Management Journal*, February 1995, p. 25; and D. M. Rousseau, S. B. Sitkin, R. S. Burt and C. Camerer, 'Not So Different After All: A Cross-Discipline View of Trust', *Academy of Management Review*, July 1998, pp. 393–404.

3. J. B. Rotter, 'Interpersonal Trust, Trustworthiness, and Gullibility', *American Psychologist*, January 1980, pp. 1–7.

4. J. D. Lewis and A. Weigert, 'Trust as a Social Reality', *Social Forces*, June 1985, p. 970.

5. J. K. Rempel, J. G. Holmes and M. P. Zanna, 'Trust in Close Relationships', *Journal of Personality and Social Psychology*, July 1985, p. 96.

6. M. Granovetter, 'Economic Action and Social Structure: The Problem of Embeddedness', *American Journal of Sociology*, November 1985, p. 491.

7. R. C. Mayer, J. H. Davis and F. D. Schoorman, 'An Integrative Model of Organizational Trust', *Academy of Management Review*, July 1995, p. 712.

8. C. Johnson-George and W. Swap, 'Measurement of Specific Interpersonal Trust: Construction and Validation of a Scale to Assess Trust in a Specific Other', *Journal of Personality and Social Psychology*, September 1982, p. 1306.

9. P. L. Schindler and C. C. Thomas, 'The Structure of Interpersonal Trust in the Workplace', *Psychological Reports*, October 1993, pp. 563–73.

10. H. H. Tan and C. S. F. Tan, 'Toward the Differentiation of Trust in Supervisor and Trust in Organization', *Genetic, Social, and General Psychology Monographs*, May 2000, pp. 241–60.

11. J. K. Butler, Jr and R. S. Cantrell, 'A Behavioral Decision Theory Approach to Modeling Dyadic Trust in Superiors and Subordinates', *Psychological Reports*, August 1984, pp. 19–28.

12. D. McGregor, *The Professional Manager* (New York: McGraw-Hill, 1967), p. 164.

13. B. Nanus, *The Leader's Edge: The Seven Keys to Leadership in a Turbulent World* (Chicago: Contemporary Books, 1989), p. 102.

14. 'Chrysler: Not Quite So Equal', *Business Week*, 13 November 2000, p. 14.

15. See, for example, K. T. Dirks and D. L. Ferrin, 'The Effects of Trust in Leadership on Employee Performance, Behavior, and Attitudes: A Meta-Analysis', paper presented at the Academy of Management Conference, Toronto, Canada, August 2000; and J. B. Cunningham and J. MacGregor, 'Trust and the Design of Work: Complementary Constructs in Satisfaction and Performance', *Human Relations*, December 2000, pp. 1575–91.

16. D. E. Zand, *The Leadership Triad: Knowledge, Trust, and Power* (New York: Oxford University Press, 1997), p. 89.

17. Based on L. T. Hosmer, 'Trust: The Connecting Link between Organizational Theory and Philosophical Ethics', *Academy of Management Review*, April 1995, p. 393; and R. C. Mayer, J. H. Davis and F. D. Schoorman, 'An Integrative Model of Organizational Trust', *Academy of Management Review*, July 1995, p. 712.

18. J. M. Kouzes and B. Z. Posner, *Credibility: How Leaders Gain and Lose It, and Why People Demand It* (San Francisco: Jossey-Bass, 1993), p. 14.

19. J. Brockner, P. A. Siegel, J. P. Daly, T. Tyler and C. Martin, 'When Trust Matters: The Moderating Effect of Outcome Favorability', *Administrative Science Quarterly*, September 1997, p. 558; S. Armour, 'Employees' New Motto: Trust No One', *USA Today*, 5 February 2002, p. 1B; J. Scott, 'Once Bitten, Twice Shy: A World of Eroding Trust', *New York Times*, 21 April 2002, p. WK5; and J. A. Byrne, 'Restoring Trust in Corporate America', *Business Week*, 24 June 2002, pp. 30–35.

20. <www.aimqld.com.au/home/news_abls.htm>; and 'WorkUSA 2000 Survey Finds Only Half of U.S. Workers are Committed to Employers', <www.watsonwyatt.com>, 11 January 2000.

21. This section is based on D. Shapiro, B. H. Sheppard and L. Cheraskin, 'Business on a Handshake', *Negotiation Journal*, October 1992, pp. 365–77; R. J. Lewicki and B. B. Bunker, 'Developing and Maintaining Trust in Work Relationships', in R. M. Kramer and T. R. Tyler (eds),

Trust in Organizations (Thousand Oaks, CA: Sage, 1996), pp. 119–24; and J. Child, 'Trust—The Fundamental Bond in Global Collaboration', *Organizational Dynamics*, vol. 29, no. 4, 2001, pp. 274–88.

22. A. Bryman, 'Leadership in Organizations', in S. R. Clegg, C. Hardy and W. R. Nord (eds), *Managing Organizations: Current Issues* (Thousand Oaks, CA: Sage, 1999), p. 30.

23. See R. M. Entman, 'Framing: Toward Clarification of a Fractured Paradigm', *Journal of Communication*, Autumn 1993, pp. 51–58; and G. T. Fairhurst and R. A. Starr, *The Art of Framing: Managing the Language of Leadership* (San Francisco: Jossey-Bass, 1996), p. 21.

24. Fairhurst and Starr, *The Art of Framing*, p. 4.

25. J. A. Conger and R. N. Kanungo, 'Behavioral Dimensions of Charismatic Leadership', in J. A. Conger, R. N. Kanungo and Associates, *Charismatic Leadership* (San Francisco: Jossey-Bass, 1988), p. 79.

26. J. A. Conger and R. N. Kanungo, *Charismatic Leadership in Organizations* (Thousand Oaks, CA: Sage, 1998); and R. Awamleh and W. L. Gardner, 'Perceptions of Leader Charisma and Effectiveness: The Effects of Vision Content, Delivery, and Organizational Performance', *Leadership Quarterly*, Fall 1999, pp. 345–73.

27. B. Shamir, R. J. House and M. B. Arthur, 'The Motivational Effects of Charismatic Leadership: A Self-Concept Theory', *Organization Science*, November 1993, pp. 577–94.

28. R. J. House, J. Woycke and E. M. Fodor, 'Charismatic and Noncharismatic Leaders: Differences in Behavior and Effectiveness', in Conger and Kanungo, *Charismatic Leadership*, pp. 103–04; D. A. Waldman, B. M. Bass and F. J. Yammarino, 'Adding to Contingent-Reward Behavior: The Augmenting Effect of Charismatic Leadership', *Group & Organization Studies*, December 1990, pp. 381–94; S. A. Kirkpatrick and E. A. Locke, 'Direct and Indirect Effects of Three Core Charismatic Leadership Components on Performance and Attitudes', *Journal of Applied Psychology*, February 1996, pp. 36–51; and R. J. Deluga, 'American Presidential Machiavellianism: Implications for Charismatic Leadership and Rated Performance', *Leadership Quarterly*, Fall 2001, pp. 339–63.

29. J. A. Conger and R. N. Kanungo, 'Training Charismatic Leadership: A Risky and Critical Task', in Conger and Kanungo (eds), *Charismatic Leadership*, pp. 309–23; and S. Caudron, 'Growing Charisma', *Industry Week*, 4 May 1998, pp. 54–55.

30. R. J. Richardson and S. K. Thayer, *The Charisma Factor: How to Develop Your Natural Leadership Ability* (Upper Saddle River, NJ: Prentice Hall, 1993).

31. J. M. Howell and P. J. Frost, 'A Laboratory Study of Charismatic Leadership', *Organizational Behavior and Human Decision Processes*, April 1989, pp. 243–69.

32. R. J. House, 'A 1976 Theory of Charismatic Leadership', in J. G. Hunt and L. L. Larson (eds), *Leadership: The Cutting Edge* (Carbondale: Southern Illinois University Press, 1977), pp. 189–207; and House and Aditya, 'The Social Scientific Study of Leadership', p. 441.

33. See A. Taylor III, 'Is Jack Smith the Man to Fix GM?', *Fortune*, 3 August 1998, pp. 86–92.

34. See, for example, B. M. Bass, *Leadership and Performance Beyond Expectations* (New York: Free Press, 1985); B. M. Bass, 'From Transactional to Transformational Leadership: Learning to Share the Vision', *Organizational Dynamics*, Winter 1990, pp. 19–31; F. J. Yammarino, W. D. Spangler and B. M. Bass, 'Transformational Leadership and Performance: A Longitudinal Investigation', *Leadership Quarterly*, Spring 1993, pp. 81–102; J. C. Wofford, V. L. Goodwin and J. L. Whittington, 'A Field Study of a Cognitive Approach to Understanding Transformational and Transactional Leadership', *Leadership Quarterly*, vol. 9, no. 1, 1998, pp. 55–84; and N. M. Ashkanasy and B. Tse, 'Transformational Leadership as Management of Emotion: A Conceptual Review', in N. M. Ashkanasy, C. E. J. Hartel and W. J. Zerbe (eds), *Emotions in the Workplace: Research, Theory, and Practice* (Westport, CT: Quorum Books, 2000), pp. 221–35.

35. B.M. Bass, 'Leadership: Good, Better, Best', *Organizational Dynamics*, Winter 1985, pp. 26–40; and J. Seltzer and B. M. Bass, 'Transformational Leadership: Beyond Initiation and Consideration', *Journal of Management*, December 1990, pp. 693–703.

36. B. J. Avolio and B. M. Bass, 'Transformational Leadership, Charisma and Beyond', working paper, School of Management, State University of New York, Binghamton, 1985, p. 14.

37. Cited in B. M. Bass and B. J. Avolio, 'Developing Transformational Leadership: 1992 and Beyond', *Journal of European Industrial Training*, January 1990, p. 23.

38. <www.aimvic.com.au/apps/uploadedFiles/News/248/ABLS_Executive_Summary_web_version.pdf>.

39. Bass and Avolio, 'Developing Transformational Leadership'; K. B. Lowe, K. G. Kroeck and N. Sivasubramaniam, 'Effectiveness Correlates of Transformational and Transactional Leadership: A Meta-Analytic Review of the MLQ Literature', *Leadership Quarterly*, Fall 1996, pp. 385–425; and T. A. Judge and J. E. Bono, 'Five-Factor Model of Personality and Transformational Leadership', *Journal of Applied Psychology*, October 2000, pp. 751–65.

40. This definition is based on M. Sashkin, 'The Visionary Leader', in Conger and Kanungo (eds), *Charismatic Leadership*, pp. 124–25; B. Nanus, *Visionary Leadership* (New York: Free Press, 1992), p. 8; N. H. Snyder and M. Graves, 'Leadership and Vision', *Business Horizons*, January–February 1994, p. 1; and J. R. Lucas, 'Anatomy of a Vision Statement', *Management Review*, February 1998, pp. 22–26.

41. Nanus, *Visionary Leadership*, p. 8.

42. P. C. Nutt and R. W. Backoff, 'Crafting Vision', *Journal of Management Inquiry*, December 1997, p. 309.

43. Ibid, pp. 312–14.
44. Based on Sashkin, 'The Visionary Leader', pp. 128–30; and J. R. Baum, E. A. Locke and S. A. Kirkpatrick, 'A Longitudinal Study of the Relation of Vision and Vision Communication to Venture Growth in Entrepreneurial Firms', *Journal of Applied Psychology*, February 1998, pp. 43–54.
45. This section is based on D. Goleman, *Working with Emotional Intelligence* (New York: Bantam, 1998); D. Goleman, 'What Makes a Leader?', *Harvard Business Review*, November–December 1998, pp. 93–102; J. M. George, 'Emotions and Leadership: The Role of Emotional Intelligence', *Human Relations*, August 2000, pp. 1027–55; D. R. Caruso, J. D. Mayer and P. Salovey, 'Emotional Intelligence and Emotional Leadership', in R. E. Riggio, S. E. Murphy and F. J. Pirozzolo (eds), *Multiple Intelligences and Leadership* (Mahwah, NJ: Lawrence Erlbaum, 2002), pp. 55–74; and D. Goleman, R. E. Boyatzis and A. McKee, *Primal Leadership: Realizing the Power of Emotional Intelligence* (Boston: Harvard Business School Press, 2002).
46. 'The Secret Skill of Leaders', *U.S. News & World Report*, 14 January 2002, p. 8.
47. Ibid.
48. A. H. Eagly and B. T. Johnson, 'Gender and Leadership Style: A Meta-Analysis', *Psychological Bulletin*, September 1990, pp. 233–56; J. D. Mayer, D. R. Caruso and P. Salovey, 'Emotional Intelligence Meets Traditional Standards for an Intelligence', *Intelligence*, vol. 27, 1999, pp. 267–98; H. Fisher, *The First Sex: The Natural Talents of Women and How They Are Changing the World* (New York: Ballantine, 2000); and R. Sharpe, 'As Leaders, Women Rule', *Business Week*, 20 November 2000, pp. 75–84.
49. See, for example, J. H. Zenger, E. Musselwhite, K. Hurson and C. Perrin, *Leading Teams: Mastering the New Role* (Homewood, IL: Business One Irwin, 1994); M. Frohman, 'Nothing Kills Teams Like Ill-Prepared Leaders', *Industry Week*, 2 October 1995, pp. 72–76; and S. Taggar, R. Hackett and S. Saha, 'Leadership Emergence in Autonomous Work Teams: Antecedents and Outcomes', *Personnel Psychology*, Winter 1999, pp. 899–926.
50. S. Caminiti, 'What Team Leaders Need to Know', *Fortune*, 20 February 1995, pp. 93–100.
51. Ibid, p. 93.
52. Ibid, p. 100.
53. N. Steckler and N. Fondas, 'Building Team Leader Effectiveness: A Diagnostic Tool', *Organizational Dynamics*, Winter 1995, p. 20.
54. R. S. Wellins, W. C. Byham and G. R. Dixon, *Inside Teams* (San Francisco: Jossey-Bass, 1994), p. 318.
55. Steckler and Fondas, 'Building Team Leader Effectiveness', p. 21.
56. See, for example, L. J. Zachary, *The Mentor's Guide: Facilitating Effective Learning Relationships* (San Francisco: Jossey-Bass, 2000); and M. Murray, *Beyond the Myths and Magic of Mentoring: How to Facilitate an Effective Mentoring Process*, rev. ed. (New York: Wiley, 2001).
57. K. McLaughlin, 'Training Top 50: Edward Jones', *Training*, March 2001, pp. 78–79.
58. J. A. Wilson and N. S. Elman, 'Organizational Benefits of Mentoring', *Academy of Management Executive*, November 1990, p. 90; and J. Reingold, 'Want to Grow as a Leader? Get a Mentor?', *Fast Company*, January 2001, pp. 58–60.
59. G. F. Dreher and R. A. Ash, 'A Comparative Study of Mentoring Among Men and Women in Managerial, Professional, and Technical Positions', *Journal of Applied Psychology*, October 1990, pp. 539–46.
60. See, for example, D. A. Thomas, 'The Impact of Race on Managers' Experiences of Developmental Relationships: An Intra-Organizational Study', *Journal of Organizational Behavior*, November 1990, pp. 479–92; K. E. Kram and D. T. Hall, 'Mentoring in a Context of Diversity and Turbulence', in E. E. Kossek and S. A. Lobel, *Managing Diversity* (Cambridge, MA: Blackwell, 1996), pp. 108–36; M. N. Ruderman and M. W. Hughes-James, 'Leadership Development Across Race and Gender', in C. D. McCauley, R. S. Moxley and E. Van Velsor (eds), *The Center for Creative Leadership Handbook of Leadership Development* (San Francisco: Jossey-Bass, 1998), pp. 291–335; and B. R. Ragins and J. L. Cotton, 'Mentor Functions and Outcomes: A Comparison of Men and Women in Formal and Informal Mentoring Relationships', *Journal of Applied Psychology*, August 1999, pp. 529–50.
61. Wilson and Elman, 'Organizational Benefits of Mentoring', p. 90.
62. See C. C. Manz, 'Self-Leadership: Toward an Expanded Theory of Self-Influence Processes in Organizations', *Academy of Management Review*, July 1986, pp. 585–600; C. C. Manz and H. P. Sims, Jr, 'Superleadership: Beyond the Myth of Heroic Leadership', *Organizational Dynamics*, Spring 1991, pp. 18–35; H. P. Sims, Jr and C. C. Manz, *Company of Heroes: Unleashing the Power of Self-Leadership* (New York: Wiley, 1996); M. Uhl-Bien and G. B. Graen, 'Individual Self-Management: Analysis of Professionals' Self-Managing Activities in Functional and Cross-Functional Work Teams', *Academy of Management Journal*, June 1998, pp. 340–50; G. Dessler, 'How to Earn Your Employees' Commitment', *Academy of Management Executive*, May 1999, pp. 58–67; and C. C. Manz and H. P. Sims, Jr, *The New Superleadership: Leading Others to Lead Themselves* (San Francisco: Berrett-Koehler, 2001).
63. Based on Manz and Sims, Jr, 'Superleadership'.
64. This section is based on R. B. Morgan, 'Self- and Co-Worker Perceptions of Ethics and Their Relationships to Leadership and Salary', *Academy of Management Journal*, February 1993, pp. 200–14; E. P. Hollander, 'Ethical Challenges in the Leader–Follower Relationship', *Business Ethics Quarterly*, January 1995, pp. 55–65; J. C. Rost, 'Leadership: A Discussion About Ethics', *Business Ethics Quarterly*, January

1995, pp. 129–42; R. N. Kanungo and M. Mendonca, *Ethical Dimensions of Leadership* (Thousand Oaks, CA: Sage Publications, 1996); J. B. Ciulla (ed.), *Ethics: The Heart of Leadership* (New York: Praeger Publications, 1998); and J. D. Costa, *The Ethical Imperative: Why Moral Leadership Is Good Business* (Cambridge, MA: Perseus Press, 1999).

65. J. M. Burns, *Leadership* (New York: Harper & Row, 1978).

66. J. M. Howell and B. J. Avolio, 'The Ethics of Charismatic Leadership: Submission or Liberation?', *Academy of Management Executive*, May 1992, pp. 43–55.

67. An exception is B. J. Avolio, S. Kahai and G. E. Dodge, 'E-Leadership: Implications for Theory, Research, and Practice', *Leadership Quarterly*, Winter 2000, pp. 615–68.

68. Comment by Jim Collins and cited in J. Useem, 'Conquering Vertical Limits', *Fortune*, 19 February 2001, p. 94.

69. See, for example, J. C. McElroy, 'A Typology of Attribution Leadership Research', *Academy of Management Review*, July 1982, pp. 413–17; J. R. Meindl and S. B. Ehrlich, 'The Romance of Leadership and the Evaluation of Organizational Performance', *Academy of Management Journal*, March 1987, pp. 91–109; R. G. Lord and K. J. Maher, *Leadership and Information Processing: Linking Perception and Performance* (Boston: Unwin Hyman, 1991); B. Shamir, 'Attribution of Influence and Charisma to the Leader: The Romance of Leadership Revisited', *Journal of Applied Social Psychology*, March 1992, pp. 386–407; and J. R. Meindl, 'The Romance of Leadership as a Follower-Centric Theory: A Social Constructionist Approach', *Leadership Quarterly*, Fall 1995, pp. 329–41.

70. R. G. Lord, C. L. DeVader and G. M. Alliger, 'A Meta-Analysis of the Relation Between Personality Traits and Leadership Perceptions: An Application of Validity Generalization Procedures', *Journal of Applied Psychology*, August 1986, pp. 402–10.

71. G. N. Powell and D. A. Butterfield, 'The "High-High" Leader Rides Again!', *Group & Organization Studies*, December 1984, pp. 437–50.

72. J. R. Meindl, S. B. Ehrlich and J. M. Dukerich, 'The Romance of Leadership', *Administrative Science Quarterly*, March 1985, pp. 78–102.

73. B. M. Staw and J. Ross, 'Commitment in an Experimenting Society: A Study of the Attribution of Leadership from Administrative Scenarios', *Journal of Applied Psychology*, June 1980, pp. 249–60; and J. Pfeffer, *Managing with Power* (Boston: Harvard Business School Press, 1992), p. 194.

74. S. Kerr and J. M. Jermier, 'Substitutes for Leadership: Their Meaning and Measurement', *Organizational Behavior and Human Performance*, December 1978, pp. 375–403; P. M. Podsakoff, S. B. MacKenzie and W. H. Bommer, 'Meta-Analysis of the Relationships Between Kerr and Jermier's Substitutes for Leadership and Employee Attitudes, Role Perceptions, and Performance', *Journal of Applied Psychology*, August 1996, pp. 380–99; and J. M. Jermier and S. Kerr, 'Substitutes for Leadership: Their Meaning and Measurement—Contextual Recollections and Current Observations', *Leadership Quarterly*, vol. 8, no. 2, 1997, pp. 95–101.

75. For one prominent scholar's view on this topic, see F. E. Fiedler, 'Research on Leadership Selection and Training: One View of the Future', *Administrative Science Quarterly*, June 1996, pp. 241–50.

76. B. M. Bass, 'Cognitive, Social, and Emotional Intelligence of Transformational Leaders', in R. E. Riggio, S. E. Murphy and F. J. Pirozzolo (eds), *Multiple Intelligences and Leadership* (Mahwah, NJ: Lawrence Erlbaum, 2002), pp. 113–14.

77. See, for example, R. Lofthouse, 'Herding the Cats', *EuroBusiness*, February 2001, pp. 64–65; and M. Delahoussaye, 'Leadership in the 21st Century', *Training*, September 2001, pp. 60–72.

78. See, for example, A. A. Vicere, 'Executive Education: The Leading Edge', *Organizational Dynamics*, Autumn 1996, pp. 67–81; J. Barling, T. Weber and E. K. Kelloway, 'Effects of Transformational Leadership Training on Attitudinal and Financial Outcomes: A Field Experiment', *Journal of Applied Psychology*, December 1996, pp. 827–32; and D. V. Day, 'Leadership Development: A Review in Context', *Leadership Quarterly*, Winter 2000, pp. 581–613.

79. M. Sashkin, 'The Visionary Leader', in J. A. Conger, R. N. Kanungo and Associates (eds), *Charismatic Leadership* (San Francisco: Jossey-Bass, 1988), p. 150.

80. Howell and Frost, 'A Laboratory Study of Charismatic Leadership'.

PHOTO CREDITS

CHAPTER 13

Power and Politics

CHAPTER OUTLINE

A definition of power
Contrasting leadership and power
Bases of power
Dependency: The key to power
Power tactics
Power in groups: Coalitions
Sexual harassment: Unequal power in the workplace
Politics: Power in action

LEARNING OBJECTIVES

After studying this chapter, you should be able to:

1. Contrast leadership and power
2. Define the seven bases of power
3. Clarify what creates dependency in power relationships
4. List seven power tactics and their contingencies
5. Explain how sexual harassment is about the abuse of power
6. Describe the importance of a political perspective
7. List the individual and organisational factors that stimulate political behaviour
8. Explain how defensive behaviours can protect an individual's self-interest
9. Identify seven techniques for managing the impression one makes on others
10. List the three questions that can help determine if a political action is ethical

Sincerity is the key to success. If you can fake that, you've got it made.

G. Marx

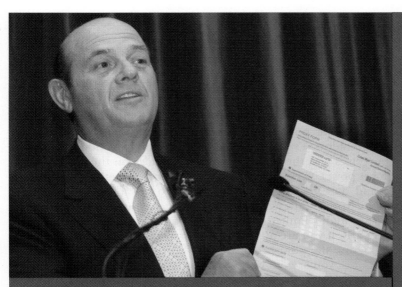

Solomon Lew tried desperately to get Coles Myer shareholders to reinstate him on the board of directors.

In November 2002, Solomon Lew was voted off the board of directors of one of Australia's largest retail chains, Coles Myer. Lew is a prominent businessman in his own right and his net worth was valued at $813 million in the *Business Review Weekly's* Rich 200 list in 2002. His battle with former chairman Stan Wallis illustrated the intensity of the politics that occurred in and around the boardroom, with Wallis reportedly going to each director and asking them not to support Lew's re-election to the board. Current chairman Rick Allert also supported Lew's removal. Lew has vast experience in the retail industry and felt that the company was making many mistakes. He invested over $10 million of his own money in a very public campaign to get re-elected. While he had a lot of support from the small shareholders, his agenda didn't align with the institutional investors who knew that their support for Lew would almost certainly mean the removal of the key players currently on the board. It is uncertain what effect such an upheaval would have had on the value of Coles Myer's shares in the immediate term.

Such battles in boardrooms around the Asia-Pacific region are not uncommon. The stakes are high for investors, and board members are coming under increasing scrutiny as to their contribution to the success of the company. What *is* rare is the very public display of the politics involved, with Lew appealing for support through the media. Who is right and who is wrong? The answer depends on whose perspective prevails by gathering enough support to control the company.[1]

Power has been described as the last dirty word. It is easier for most of us to talk about money than it is to talk about power. People who have it deny it, people who want it try not to appear to be seeking it, and those who are good at getting it are secretive about how they got it.[2]

A major theme of this chapter is that power is a natural factor in any group or organisation. As such, you need to know how it is acquired and exercised if you are going to fully understand organisational behaviour. Although you may have heard the phrase 'power corrupts, and absolute power corrupts absolutely', power isn't always bad. As one author has noted, most medicines can kill if taken in the wrong amount, and thousands die each year in automobile accidents, but we don't abandon chemicals or cars because of the dangers associated with them. Rather, we consider danger an incentive to get training and information that will help us to use these forces productively.[3] The same applies to power. It's a reality of organisational life and it's not going to go away. Moreover, by learning how power works in organisations, you'll be better able to use your knowledge to help you be a more effective manager.

A Definition of Power

Power refers to a capacity that A has to influence the behaviour of B, so that B acts in accordance with A's wishes.[4] This definition implies a *potential* that needn't be actualised to be effective and a *dependency* relationship.

Power may exist, but not be used. It is, therefore, a capacity or potential. One can have power but not impose it.

Probably the most important aspect of power is that it is a function of **dependency**. The greater B's dependence on A, the greater is A's power in the relationship. Dependence, in turn, is based on alternatives that B perceives and the importance that B places on the alternative(s) that A controls. A person can have power over you only if they control something you desire. If you want a university degree and have to pass a certain course to get it, and your current lecturer is the only faculty member in the university who teaches that course, the lecturer has power over you. Your alternatives are highly limited and you place a high degree of importance on obtaining a passing grade. Similarly, if you are attending university on funds totally provided by your parents, you probably recognise the power that they hold over you. You are dependent on them for financial support. But once you are out of school, have a job and are making a good income, your parents' power is reduced significantly. Who among us, though, hasn't known or heard of the rich relative who is able to control a large number of family members merely through the implicit or explicit threat of 'writing them out of the will'?

Contrasting Leadership and Power

A careful comparison of our description of power with our description of leadership in the previous two chapters reveals that the concepts are closely intertwined. Leaders use power as a means of attaining group goals. Leaders achieve goals, and power is a means of facilitating their achievement.

What differences are there between the two terms? One difference relates to goal compatibility. Power doesn't require goal compatibility, merely dependence. Leadership, on the other hand, requires some congruence between the goals of the leader and those being led. A second difference relates to the direction of influence. Leadership focuses on the downward influence on one's followers. It minimises the importance of lateral and upward influence patterns. Power does not. Still another difference deals with research emphasis. Leadership research, for the most part, emphasises style. It seeks answers to questions such as: How supportive should a leader be? How much decision making should be shared with followers? In contrast, the research on power has tended to encompass a broader area and to focus on tactics for gaining compliance. It has gone beyond the individual as exerciser, because power can be used by groups as well as by individuals to control other individuals or groups.

Bases of Power

Where does power come from? What is it that gives an individual or a group influence over others? We answer these questions by dividing the bases or sources of power into two general groupings—formal and personal—and then breaking each of these down into more specific categories.[5]

FORMAL POWER

Formal power is based on an individual's position in an organisation. Formal power can come from the ability to coerce or reward, from formal authority or from control of information.

Coercive power

The **coercive power** base is dependent on fear. One reacts to this power out of fear of the negative results that might occur if one failed to comply. It rests on the application, or the threat of application, of physical sanctions such as the infliction of pain, the generation of frustration through restriction of movement, or the controlling by force of basic physiological or safety needs.

At the organisational level, A has coercive power over B if A can dismiss, suspend or demote B, assuming that B values his or her job. Similarly, if A can assign B work activities that B finds unpleasant or treat B in a manner that B finds embarrassing, A possesses coercive power over B.

coercive power
A power base dependent on fear.

Reward power

The opposite of coercive power is **reward power**. People comply with the wishes or directives of another because doing so produces positive benefits; therefore, one who can distribute rewards that others view as valuable will have power over those others. These rewards can be either financial—such as controlling pay rates, raises and bonuses; or non-financial—including merit recognition, promotions, interesting work assignments, friendly colleagues, and preferred work shifts or sales territories.[6]

Coercive power and reward power are actually counterparts of each other. If you can remove something of positive value from another or inflict something of negative value on them, you have coercive power over that person. If you can give someone something of positive value or remove something of negative value, you have reward power over that person.

reward power
Compliance achieved based on the ability to distribute rewards that others view as valuable.

Legitimate power

In formal groups and organisations, probably the most frequent access to one or more of the power bases is one's structural position. This is called **legitimate power**. It represents the formal authority to control and use organisational resources.

Positions of authority include coercive and reward powers. Legitimate power, however, is broader than the power to coerce and reward. Specifically, it includes acceptance by members in an organisation of the authority of a position. When school principals, bank managers or army captains speak (assuming that their directives are viewed to be within the authority of their positions), teachers, bank tellers and first lieutenants listen and usually comply.

legitimate power
The power a person receives as a result of their position in the formal hierarchy of an organisation.

Information power

The fourth source of formal power—**information power**—comes from access to and control over information. People in an organisation who have data or knowledge that others need can make those others dependent on them. Managers, for example, because of their access to privileged sales, cost, salary, profit and similar data, can use this information to control and shape subordinates' behaviour. Similarly, departments that possess information that is critical to a company's performance in times of high uncertainty—for example, the legal department when a firm faces a major lawsuit or the human resources department during critical labour negotiations—will gain increased power in their organisation until those uncertainties are resolved.

information power
Power that comes from access to and control over information.

PERSONAL POWER

You don't have to have a formal position in an organisation to have power. Many of the most competent and productive chip designers at Intel, for example, have power, but they aren't managers and have no formal power. What they have is personal power—power that comes from an individual's unique characteristics. In this section, we look at three bases of personal power—expertise, the respect and admiration of others, and charisma.

Expert power

Expert power is influence wielded as a result of expertise, special skill or knowledge. Expertise has become one of the most powerful sources of influence as the world has become more

expert power
Influence based on special skills or knowledge.

technologically oriented. As jobs become more specialised, we become increasingly dependent on experts to achieve goals. So, although it is generally acknowledged that physicians have expertise and hence expert power—most of us follow the advice that our doctor gives us—you should also recognise that computer specialists, tax accountants, economists, industrial psychologists and other specialists are able to wield power as a result of their expertise.

Referent power

referent power
Influence based on possession by an individual of desirable resources or personal traits.

Referent power is based on identification with a person who has desirable resources or personal traits. If I like, respect and admire you, you can exercise power over me because I want to please you.

Referent power develops out of admiration of another and a desire to be like that person. It helps to explain, for example, why celebrities are paid millions of dollars to endorse products in commercials. Marketing research shows that people such as golfing young guns Karrie Webb and Aaron Baddeley and international soccer star David Beckham have the power to influence your choice of sunglasses, mobile phone and athletic shoes . . . With a little practice, we could probably deliver as smooth a sales pitch as these celebrities, but the buying public doesn't identify with us.

Charismatic power

charismatic power
An extension of referent power stemming from an individual's personality and interpersonal style.

The final base of power is charisma. **Charismatic power** is really an extension of referent power stemming from an individual's personality and interpersonal style. As we noted in the previous chapter, charismatic leaders get others to follow them because they can articulate attractive visions, take personal risks, demonstrate environmental and follower sensitivity, and are willing to engage in behaviour that most others consider unconventional. But many organisations will have people with charismatic qualities who, while not in formal leadership positions, nevertheless are able to exert influence over others because of the strength of their heroic qualities.

LEARNING OBJECTIVE

3

Clarify what creates dependency in power relationships

Dependency: The Key to Power

Earlier in this chapter it was said that probably the most important aspect of power is that it is a function of dependence. In this section, we show how an understanding of dependency is central to furthering your understanding of power itself.

THE GENERAL DEPENDENCY POSTULATE

Let's begin with a general postulate: *The greater* B*'s dependency on* A, *the greater the power* A *has over* B. When you possess anything that others require but that you alone control, you make them dependent on you and, therefore, you gain power over them.[7] Dependency, then, is inversely proportional to the alternative sources of supply. If something is plentiful, possession of it won't increase your power. If everyone is intelligent, intelligence gives no special advantage. Similarly, among the super-rich, money is no longer power. But, as the old saying goes, 'In the land of the blind, the one-eyed man is king!' If you can create a monopoly by controlling information, prestige, or anything that others crave, they become dependent on you. Conversely, the more that you can expand your options, the less power you place in the hands of others. This explains, for example, why most organisations develop multiple suppliers rather than give their business to only one. It also explains why so many of us aspire to financial independence. Financial independence reduces the power that others can have over us.

WHAT CREATES DEPENDENCY?

Dependency is increased when the resource you control is important, scarce and non-substitutable.[8]

Importance

If nobody wants what you've got, it's not going to create dependency. To create dependency, therefore, the thing(s) you control must be perceived as being important. Organisations, for example, actively seek to avoid uncertainty.[9] We should, therefore, expect that the individuals or groups who can absorb an organisation's uncertainty will be perceived as controlling an important resource. For example, a study of industrial organisations found that the marketing departments in these firms were consistently rated as the most powerful.[10] It was concluded by the researcher that the most critical uncertainty facing these firms was selling their products. This might suggest that engineers, as a group, would be more powerful at a manufacturing establishment such as Honda or General Motors (Holden) than at a retail chain such as Woolworths or Dairy Farm International's Cold Storage supermarket chain in Singapore. These inferences appear to be generally valid. The production facilities of organisations such as Honda and General Motors (Holden), which are heavily technologically oriented, are highly dependent on their engineers to maintain products' technical advantages and quality. Therefore, at both organisations, engineers are clearly a powerful group. At Woolworths and Cold Storage, marketing is the name of the game; hence, marketers are the most powerful occupational group.

Scarcity

As noted previously, if something is plentiful, possession of it won't increase your power. A resource needs to be perceived as scarce to create dependency. This can help to explain how low-ranking members in an organisation who have important knowledge not available to high-ranking members gain power over the high-ranking members. Possession of a scarce resource—in this case, important knowledge—makes the high-ranking member dependent on the low-ranking member. This also helps to make sense out of behaviours of low-ranking members that otherwise might seem illogical, such as destroying the procedure manuals that describe how a job is done, refusing to train people in their jobs or even to show others exactly what they do, creating specialised language and terminology that inhibit others from understanding their jobs, or operating in secrecy so that an activity will appear more complex and difficult than it really is.

The scarcity–dependency relationship can further be seen in the power of occupational categories. Individuals in occupations in which the supply of personnel is low relative to demand can negotiate compensation and benefit packages that are far more attractive than can those in occupations for which there is an abundance of candidates. University administrators have no problem today finding lecturers for English or marketing courses. The market for computer-engineering lecturers, in contrast, is extremely tight, with the demand high and the supply limited. The result is that the bargaining power of computer-engineering faculty allows them to negotiate higher salaries, lighter teaching loads and other benefits.

Non-substitutability

The more that a resource has no viable substitutes, the more power is provided by having control over that resource. Higher education again provides an excellent example. At universities in which there are strong pressures for the faculty to publish, we can say that a department head's power over a faculty member is inversely related to that member's publication record. The more recognition the faculty member receives through publication, the more mobile they are. That is, since other universities want faculty who are highly published and visible, there is an increased demand for their services. Although the concept of tenure can act to alter this relationship by restricting the department head's alternatives, faculty members who have few or no publications have the least mobility and are subject to the greatest influence from their superiors.

LEARNING OBJECTIVE

4

List seven power
tactics and their
contingencies

power tactics
Ways in which individuals
translate power bases
into specific actions.

Power Tactics

In this section we move to the topic of **power tactics** to learn how employees translate their power bases into specific actions. Recent research indicates that there are standardised ways by which power holders attempt to get what they want.[11]

When 165 managers were asked to write essays describing an incident in which they influenced their bosses, co-workers or employees, a total of 370 power tactics grouped into 14 categories were identified. These answers were condensed, rewritten into a 58-item questionnaire, and given to over 750 employees. These respondents were not only asked how they went about influencing others at work, but also for the possible reasons for influencing the target person. The results, which are summarised here, give us considerable insight into power tactics—how managerial employees influence others, and the conditions under which one tactic is chosen over another.[12]

The findings identified seven tactical dimensions or strategies:
- *Reason:* Use of facts and data to make a logical or rational presentation of ideas.
- *Friendliness:* Use of flattery, creation of goodwill, acting humble and being friendly prior to making a request.
- *Coalition:* Getting the support of other people in the organisation to back up the request.
- *Bargaining:* Use of negotiation through the exchange of benefits or favours.
- *Assertiveness:* Use of a direct and forceful approach, such as demanding compliance with requests, repeating reminders, ordering individuals to do what is asked, and pointing out that rules require compliance.
- *Higher authority:* Gaining the support of higher levels in the organisation to back up requests.
- *Sanctions:* Use of organisationally derived rewards and punishments such as preventing or promising a salary increase, threatening to give an unsatisfactory performance evaluation or withholding a promotion.

The researchers found that employees don't rely on the seven tactics equally. However, as shown in Table 13.1, the most popular strategy was the use of reason, regardless of whether the influence was directed upwards or downwards. In addition, researchers have uncovered five contingency variables that affect the selection of a power tactic: (1) the manager's relative power;

TABLE 13.1   Usage of power tactics: From most to least popular

	When Managers Influenced Superiors*	When Managers Influenced Subordinates
Most popular	Reason	Reason
	Coalition	Assertiveness
	Friendliness	Friendliness
	Bargaining	Coalition
	Assertiveness	Bargaining
	Higher authority	High authority
Least popular		Sanctions

* 'Sanctions' is omitted in the scale that measures upward influence.

Source: Reprinted from 'Patterns of Managerial Influence: Shotgun Managers, Tacticians, and Bystanders', by D. Kipnis et al, *Organizational Dynamics*, Winter 1984, p. 62. © 1984 with permission from Elsevier Science.

(2) the manager's objectives for wanting to influence; (3) the manager's expectation of the target person's willingness to comply; (4) the organisation's culture; and (5) cross-cultural differences.

A manager's relative power has an impact on the selection of tactics in two ways. First, managers who control resources that are valued by others, or who are perceived to be in positions of dominance, use a greater variety of tactics than do those with less power. Second, managers with power use assertiveness with greater frequency than do those with less power. Initially, we can expect that most managers will attempt to use simple requests and reason. Assertiveness is a backup strategy, used when the target of influence refuses or appears reluctant to comply with the request. Resistance leads to managers using more directive strategies. Typically, they shift from using simple requests to insisting that their demands be met. But the manager with relatively little power is more likely to stop trying to influence others when he or she encounters resistance because they perceive the costs associated with assertiveness as being unacceptable.

Managers vary their power tactics in relation to their objectives. When managers seek benefits from a superior, they tend to rely on kind words and the promotion of pleasant relationships—that is, they use friendliness. In comparison, managers attempting to persuade their superiors to accept new ideas usually rely on reason. This matching of tactics to objectives also holds true for downward influence. For example, managers use reason to sell ideas to employees and friendliness to obtain favours.

Managers' expectations of success guide their choice of tactics. When past experience indicates a high probability of success, managers use simple requests to gain compliance. When success is less predictable, managers are more tempted to use assertiveness and sanctions to achieve their objectives.

We know that cultures within organisations differ markedly—for example, some are warm, relaxed and supportive; others are formal and conservative. The organisational culture in which a manager works, therefore, will have a significant bearing on defining which tactics are considered appropriate. Some cultures encourage the use of friendliness, some encourage reason, and still others rely on sanctions and assertiveness. So, the organisation itself will influence which subset of power tactics is viewed as acceptable for use by managers.

Finally, evidence indicates that people in different countries tend to prefer different power tactics. For example, a study comparing managers in the United States and China found that the Americans perceived reason to be most effective, whereas Chinese managers preferred coalition tactics and higher authority.[13] These differences tend to be consistent with the values in these two countries. Reason is consistent with the preference of Americans for direct confrontation and the use of rational persuasion to influence others and resolve differences. Similarly, coalition tactics and higher authority are consistent with the Chinese preference for using indirect approaches for difficult or controversial requests.

Power in Groups: Coalitions

Those 'out of power' and seeking to be 'in' will first try to increase their power individually. Why share the spoils if one doesn't have to? But if this proves ineffective, the alternative is to form a **coalition**—an informal group bound together by the active pursuit of a single issue.[14] The logic of a coalition? There is strength in numbers.

coalition
An informal group bound together by the active pursuit of a single issue.

The natural way to gain influence is to become a power holder. Therefore, those who want power will attempt to build a personal power base. But, in many instances, this may be difficult, risky, costly or impossible. In such cases, efforts will be made to form a coalition of two or more 'outs' who, by joining together, can combine their resources to increase rewards for themselves.[15] Successful coalitions have been found to contain fluid membership and are able to form swiftly, achieve their target issue and quickly disappear.[16]

What predictions can we make about coalition formation?[17] First, coalitions in organisations often seek to maximise their size. In political science theory, coalitions move the other way—they

The Real Deal

Kylie's Influence at Ergon Energy

Kylie Hull graduated from the University of Southern Queensland with a Master of Management degree. She studied courses in human resource management and leadership to support her work at Ergon Energy in her various roles as project manager, change manager and organisational development manager. Ergon Energy is the largest and most diverse electricity network in Australia, supplying electricity to more than 560,000 customers. It has assets of approximately $2.8 billion. The organisation presents many challenges for Kylie in her work.

Kylie's role as a facilitator of change at Ergon Energy is one of influencing people and developing constructive relationships. She is very aware of the power dynamics in work relationships and of how they can affect work outcomes. As a young female, Kylie finds it difficult to gain respect from her associates, who are predominantly middle-aged men. Some of them are old enough to be Kylie's father. She feels that it isn't an issue of having to earn respect in this environment, but of having to earn *the right* to earn respect. She has been told that she is a young girl who won't be able to make it in a man's world.

Kylie admits that she has made mistakes in her work, which involves developing the capability of staff, implementing performance management systems and introducing leadership development programs. She has had good role models, who have reflected the positive side of power and influence in that these people encourage staff to stretch themselves and provide them with learning opportunities without the threat of punishment. Kylie's experiences have demonstrated the significance of power and influence in organisations, and that working with people is a power game. Respect comes with the contribution a person makes to a group through their ability to influence desired outcomes. In 2002, Kylie won the HR Partners Award for HR 'Young Gun' of the Year.

Source: Craig Donaldson, 'Charging Ahead: Challenges of a HR Young Gun', *Human Resources*, no. 37, August 2003, pp. 10–11. Reproduced with permission.

try to minimise their size. They tend to be just large enough to exert the power necessary to achieve their objectives. But legislatures are different from organisations. Specifically, decision making in organisations doesn't end just with selection from among a set of alternatives. The decision must also be implemented. In organisations, the implementation of and commitment to the decision is at least as important as the decision itself. It's necessary, therefore, for coalitions in organisations to seek a broad constituency to support the coalition's objectives. This means expanding the coalition to encompass as many interests as possible. This coalition expansion to facilitate consensus building, of course, is more likely to occur in organisational cultures in which cooperation, commitment and shared decision making are highly valued. In autocratic and hierarchically controlled organisations, this search for maximising the coalition's size is less likely to be sought.

Another prediction about coalitions relates to the degree of interdependence within the organisation. More coalitions will likely be

Kylie Hull won the HR Partners Award for HR "young guns" of the year. She was recognised for her ability to influence positive changes in her workplace.

created when there is a great deal of task and resource interdependence. In contrast, there will be less interdependence among sub-units and less coalition formation activity when sub-units are largely self-contained or resources are abundant.

Finally, coalition formation will be influenced by the actual tasks that workers do. The more routine the task of a group, the greater the likelihood that coalitions will form. The more that the work that people do is routine, the greater their substitutability for each other and, thus, the greater their dependence. To offset this dependence, they can be expected to resort to a coalition. This helps to explain the historical appeal of labour unions, especially among low-skilled workers. Such employees are better able to negotiate improved wages, benefits and working conditions as a united coalition than if they acted individually. A one-person 'strike' has little power over management. However, if a firm's entire workforce goes on strike, management has a serious problem.

LEARNING OBJECTIVE
5
Explain how sexual harassment is about the abuse of power

Sexual Harassment: Unequal Power in the Workplace

The issue of sexual harassment got increasing attention by corporations and the media in the 1980s because of the growing ranks of female employees, especially in non-traditional work environments. This became very apparent to the public with the increasing number of women recruited into the Australian Defence Forces. In 1992, charges of sexual harassment were made by three women serving on HMAS *Swan*. Both male and female co-workers blamed the women's morality, rather than sexual violence in the workplace. While no convictions were made from the subsequent court-martial, the event triggered substantial reforms regarding sexual harassment in the armed services, particularly in relation to young recruits at the Royal Military College at Duntroon, Canberra.[18]

Sexual harassment is defined as any unwanted activity of a sexual nature that affects an individual's employment. In the light of the case in the United States where Professor Anita Hill accused Supreme Court judge Clarence Thomas of sexual harassment, the US Supreme Court helped to clarify this definition by adding that the key test for determining if sexual harassment has occurred is whether comments or behaviour in a work environment 'would reasonably be perceived, and is perceived, as hostile or abusive'.[19] But

sexual harassment
Unwelcome advances, requests for sexual favours, and other verbal or physical conduct of a sexual nature.

there continues to be disagreement as to what *specifically* constitutes sexual harassment. Organisations have generally made considerable progress in the past decade towards limiting overt forms of sexual harassment. This includes unwanted physical touching, recurring requests for dates when it is made clear the person isn't interested, and coercive threats that a person will lose their job if they refuse a sexual proposition. The problems today are likely to surface around more subtle forms of sexual harassment—unwanted looks or comments, off-colour jokes, sexual artifacts such as posting pin-ups in the workplace, or misinterpretations of where the line between 'being friendly' ends and 'harassment' begins.

Effective relationships are important for a healthy work environment. Sometimes, however, relationships can be strained by unwanted behaviour of a sexual nature. Managers must guard against any potential for sexual harassment.

Most studies confirm that the concept of power is central to understanding sexual harassment.[20] This seems to be true whether the harassment comes from a supervisor, a co-worker or even an employee.

The supervisor–employee dyad best characterises an unequal power relationship, where formal power gives the supervisor the capacity to reward and coerce. Supervisors give employees their assignments, evaluate their performance, make recommendations for salary adjustments and promotions, and even decide whether or not an employee retains their job. These decisions give a supervisor power. Since employees want favourable performance reviews, salary increases, and the like, it is clear that supervisors control resources that most employees consider important and scarce. It is also worth noting that individuals who occupy high-status roles (such as management positions and sports coaches) sometimes believe that sexually harassing employees is merely an extension of their right to make demands on lower-status individuals. Because of power inequities, sexual harassment by one's boss typically creates the greatest difficulty for those who are being harassed. If there are no witnesses, it is the victim's word against the harasser's. Are there others this boss has harassed and, if so, will they come forward? Because of the supervisor's control over resources, many of those who are harassed are afraid of speaking out for fear of retaliation by the supervisor. The Australian media has recently highlighted the accusations of sexual harassment made against two prominent swimming coaches.

Although co-workers don't have legitimate power, they can have influence and use it to sexually harass peers. In fact, although co-workers appear to engage in somewhat less severe forms of harassment than do supervisors, co-workers are the most frequent perpetrators of sexual harassment in organisations. How do co-workers exercise power? Most often it's by providing or withholding information, cooperation and support. For example, the effective performance of most jobs requires interaction and support from co-workers. This is especially true nowadays because work is often assigned to teams. By threatening to withhold or delay providing information that is necessary for the successful achievement of your work goals, co-workers can exert power over you.

Although it doesn't get nearly the attention that harassment by a supervisor does, women in positions of power can be subjected to sexual harassment from males who occupy less powerful positions within the organisation. This is usually achieved by the employee devaluing the woman through highlighting traditional gender stereotypes (such as helplessness, passivity, lack of career commitment). An employee may engage in such practices to attempt to gain some power over the higher-ranking female or to minimise power differentials.

The topic of sexual harassment is about power. It is about an individual controlling or threatening another individual. It is wrong. And whether perpetrated against women or men, it is illegal. But you can understand how sexual harassment surfaces in organisations if you analyse it in terms of power.

Politics: Power in Action

When people get together in groups, power will be exerted. People want to carve out a niche from which to exert influence, to earn rewards and to advance their careers.[21] When employees in organisations convert their power into action, we describe them as being engaged in politics. Those with good political skills have the ability to use their bases of power effectively.[22]

DEFINITION

political behaviour
Activities that are not required as part of one's formal role in the organisation, but that influence, or attempt to influence, the distribution of advantages and disadvantages within the organisation.

There has been no shortage of definitions for organisational politics. Essentially, however, they have focused on the use of power to affect decision making in the organisation or on behaviours by members that are self-serving and organisationally non-sanctioned.[23] For our purposes, we shall define **political behaviour** in organisations as activities that are not required as part of one's formal role in the organisation, but that influence, or attempt to influence, the distribution of advantages and disadvantages within the organisation.[24]

This definition encompasses key elements from what most people mean when they talk about organisational politics. Political behaviour is outside one's specified job requirements. The behaviour requires some attempt to use one's power bases. In addition, our definition encompasses efforts to influence the goals, criteria or processes used for *decision making* when we state that politics is concerned with 'the distribution of advantages and disadvantages within the organisation'. Our definition is broad enough to include varied political behaviours such as withholding key information from decision makers, joining a coalition, whistle blowing, spreading rumours, leaking confidential information about organisational activities to the media, exchanging favours with others in the organisation for mutual benefit, and lobbying on behalf of or against a particular individual or decision alternative.

A final comment relates to what has been referred to as the 'legitimate–illegitimate' dimension in political behaviour.[25] **Legitimate political behaviour** refers to normal, everyday politics—complaining to your supervisor, bypassing the chain of command, forming coalitions, obstructing organisational policies or decisions through inaction or excessive adherence to rules, and developing contacts outside the organisation through one's professional activities. On the other hand, there are also **illegitimate political behaviours** that violate the implied rules of the game. Those who pursue such extreme activities are often described as individuals who 'play tough'. Illegitimate activities include sabotage, whistle blowing, and symbolic protests such as wearing unorthodox dress or protest buttons, and groups of employees simultaneously calling in sick.

The vast majority of all organisational political actions are of the legitimate variety. The reasons are pragmatic: the extreme illegitimate forms of political behaviour pose a very real risk of loss of organisational membership or extreme sanctions against those who use them and then fall short in having enough power to ensure that they work.

> **legitimate political behaviour**
> Normal, everyday politics.
>
> **illegitimate political behaviour**
> Extreme political behaviour that violates the implied rules of the game.

> **LEARNING OBJECTIVE**
>
> **6**
> Describe the importance of a political perspective

THE REALITY OF POLITICS

Politics is a fact of life in organisations. People who ignore this fact of life do so at their own peril. But why, you may wonder, must politics exist? Isn't it possible for an organisation to be politics-free? It's *possible*, but most unlikely.

Organisations are made up of individuals and groups with different values, goals and interests.[26] This sets up the potential for conflict over resources. Departmental budgets, space allocations, project responsibilities and salary adjustments are just a few examples of the resources about whose allocation organisational members will disagree.

Resources in organisations are also often limited, which turns potential conflict into real conflict.[27] If resources were abundant, then all the various constituencies within the organisation could satisfy their goals. But because they are limited, not everyone's interests can be provided for. Furthermore, whether true or not, gains by one individual or group are often *perceived* as being at the expense of others within the organisation. These forces create a competition among members for the organisation's limited resources.

Maybe the most important factor leading to politics within organisations is the realisation that most of the 'facts' that are used to allocate the limited resources are open to interpretation. What, for example, is *good* performance? What is an *adequate* improvement? What constitutes an *unsatisfactory* job? One person's view that an act is a 'selfless effort to benefit the organisation' is seen by another as a 'blatant attempt to further one's interest'.[28] The coach of any major Rugby League team knows that a goal-kicker with an 82 per cent kicking success rate is a high performer and a kicker with a 50 per cent kicking rate is a poor performer. You don't need to be a rocket scientist to know you should keep the goal-kicker with an 82 per cent success rate and relegate the 50 per cent kicker down to reserve grade. However, what if you have to choose between players with 79 per cent and 82 per cent kicking success? Then other factors—less objective ones—come into play: tackling rates, game expertise, attitude, potential, ability to perform in the

OB Controversies

Even Jacques Nasser had a boss

Everything is controversial when it comes to power and politics. In particular, don't upset the people who control 40 per cent of your company's shares! That's the lesson Australian Jacques Nasser has learned after being ousted from his position as CEO at Ford Motor Co.

Nasser had spent 33 years at Ford, working his way up through the company's international division after beginning his career in Melbourne as a financial analyst. He held a variety of roles, including senior leadership positions in Europe, Australia, the Philippines, Thailand, Japan, South Africa, Venezuela, Mexico and Brazil, before gaining the top position at Ford. He built his reputation as an aggressive cost cutter. That reputation, plus his vision and commitment to reinventing Ford, were the primary reasons he was appointed CEO in January 1999. But on his watch, the company's performance suffered serious setbacks. He took his eye off 'the ball'—Ford's basic product line—and spent US$13 billion of the company's US$15 billion cash reserves to acquire Jaguar, Aston Martin, Volvo and Land Rover. In the interim, Ford's product quality slipped badly and production efficiency seriously eroded. In three years, Nasser had burned through Ford's cash reserves, leaving the company little money to invest in the new models that are the lifeblood of the automobile business.

As CEO, Nasser's style managed to anger almost every core relationship Ford Motor had. Relations with the company's unions, dealers, white-collar employees and suppliers all suffered as he focused on them to reduce costs. By the autumn of 2001, it became increasingly clear to William Clay Ford, Jr, the 44-year-old company chairman and great-grandson of the company's founder, Henry Ford, that Nasser lacked the political skills to lead the company out of its problems. Nasser undermined relationships that the company highly valued and financial losses were mounting. He alienated many people with the decisions he made. Most importantly, he alienated Mr Ford, whose family controlled 40 per cent of the company's voting shares. On 30 October 2001, Mr Ford called Nasser into his office and ended Nasser's 33-year career with the company. As one financial analyst concluded in assessing Nasser's demise at Ford, 'This is an old school industrial company. You have to be diplomatic. This is a big organisation, and there are politics you have to deal with.' Jacques Nasser didn't have those political skills. And he failed to maintain the support of the one person with the power to give him the boot. The controversial issue is, who really runs a company from a political perspective?

Sources: Based on J. B. White and N. Shirouzu, 'A Stalled Revolution by Nasser Puts a Ford in the Driver's Seat', *Wall Street Journal,* 31 October 2001, p. A1; B. Yates, 'It's Curtains for "Jac the Knife"', *Wall Street Journal,* 31 October 2001, p. A24; D. Hakim, 'Left in Nasser's Exhaust at Ford', *New York Times,* 1 November 2001, p. C4; and <www.ceiconference.com/speakers/nasser.htm>, accessed 30 July 2003.

scrum, loyalty to the team, and so on. Managerial decisions more closely resemble choosing between the 79 per cent and the 82 per cent goal-kicker than deciding between a 50 per cent and an 82 per cent goal-kicker. It is in this large and ambiguous middle ground of organisational life—where the facts *don't* speak for themselves—that politics flourish (see Table 13.2).

Finally, because most decisions have to be made in a climate of ambiguity—where facts are rarely fully objective, and thus are open to interpretation—people within organisations will use whatever influence they can to taint the facts to support their goals and interests. That, of course, creates the activities we call *politicking*.

Therefore, to answer the earlier question of whether it is possible for an organisation to be politics-free, we can say 'yes', if all members of that organisation hold the same goals and interests, if organisational resources aren't scarce, and if performance outcomes are completely clear and objective. But that doesn't describe the organisational world that most of us live in.

TABLE 13.2   Politics is in the eye of the beholder

A behaviour that one person labels as 'organisational politics' is very likely to be characterised as an instance of 'effective management' by another. The fact is not that effective management is necessarily political, although in some cases it might be. Rather, a person's reference point determines what they classify as organisational politics. Take a look at the following labels used to describe the same phenomenon. These suggest that politics, like beauty, is in the eye of the beholder.

'Political' Label	'Effective Management' Label
1. Blaming others	1. Fixing responsibility
2. 'Sucking up'	2. Developing working relationships
3. Apple polishing	3. Demonstrating loyalty
4. Passing the buck	4. Delegating authority
5. Covering your rear	5. Documenting decisions
6. Creating conflict	6. Encouraging change and innovation
7. Forming coalitions	7. Facilitating teamwork
8. Whistle blowing	8. Improving efficiency
9. Scheming	9. Planning ahead
10. Overachieving	10. Competent and capable
11. Ambitious	11. Career-minded
12. Opportunistic	12. Astute
13. Cunning	13. Practical-minded
14. Arrogant	14. Confident
15. Perfectionist	15. Attentive to detail

Source: This table is based on T. C. Krell, M. E. Mendenhall and J. Sendry, 'Doing Research in the Conceptual Morass of Organizational Politics', paper presented at the Western Academy of Management Conference, Hollywood, California, April 1987.

FACTORS CONTRIBUTING TO POLITICAL BEHAVIOUR

Not all groups or organisations are equally political. In some organisations, for example, politicking is overt and rampant, while in others, politics plays a small role in influencing outcomes. Why is there this variation? Recent research and observation have identified a number of factors that appear to encourage political behaviour. Some are individual characteristics, derived from the unique qualities of the people the organisation employs; others are a result of the organisation's culture or internal environment. Figure 13.1 illustrates how both individual and organisational factors can increase political behaviour and provide favourable outcomes (increased rewards and averted punishments) for both individuals and groups in the organisation.

Individual factors

At the individual level, researchers have identified certain personality traits, needs and other factors that are likely to be related to political behaviour. In terms of traits, we find that employees who are high self-monitors, possess an internal locus of control, and have a high need for power are more likely to engage in political behaviour.[29]

The high self-monitor is more sensitive to social cues, exhibits higher levels of social conformity, and is more likely to be skilled in political behaviour than the low self-monitor. Individuals with an internal locus of control, because they believe they can control their environment, are more prone to take a proactive stance and attempt to manipulate situations in their favour. Not surprisingly, the Machiavellian personality—which is characterised by the will to manipulate and the desire for power—is comfortable using politics as a means to further their self-interest.

Myth *or* Science?

'It's not *what* you know, it's *who* you know'

This statement is somewhat true. While knowledge of *facts* is an increasingly important source of power in an information-based society, knowing the *right people* increases your chances of getting ahead.

Networking is the term usually used to refer to establishing effective relationships with key people inside and/or outside the organisation. And networking has been found to be the most important activity performed by managers who were promoted the fastest.[30]

A study of general managers found that they fully understood the importance of networking.[31] They established a wide political network of key people from both inside and outside their organisations. This network provided these managers with information and established cooperative relationships that could enhance their careers. The managers did favours for these contacts, stressed the obligations of these contacts to them, and 'called in' these obligations when support was needed.

Research also indicates that a person's location within an organisation is an important determinant of their influence.[32] Being in the right place increases your ability to know 'the right people'. This would further support the importance of contacts over knowledge of facts in gaining influence.

The above evidence should not be interpreted as a rejection of job-relevant expertise. Rather, it indicates that 'who you know' is an important *additional* factor in organisational life. People who want to get ahead or build their political power within an organisation should spend time and effort in developing a network of contacts.

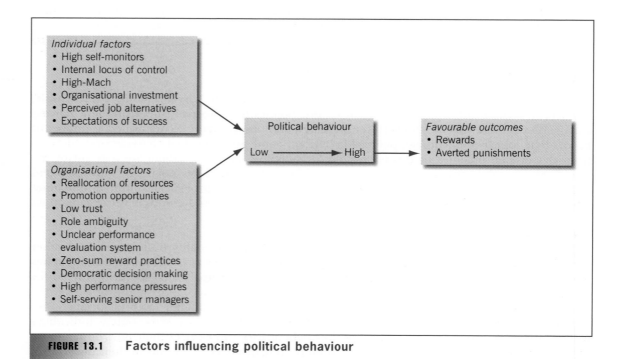

FIGURE 13.1 **Factors influencing political behaviour**

In addition, an individual's investment in the organisation, perceived alternatives and expectations of success will influence the degree to which they will pursue illegitimate means of political action.[33] The more a person has invested in the organisation in terms of expectations of increased future benefits, the more they have to lose if forced out and the less likely they are to use illegitimate means. The more alternative job opportunities an individual has—due to a favourable job market or the possession of scarce skills or knowledge, a prominent reputation or influential contacts outside the organisation—the more likely they are to risk illegitimate political actions. Finally, if an individual has a low expectation of success in using illegitimate means, it is unlikely that they will attempt to do so. High expectations of success in the use of illegitimate means are most likely to be the province of both experienced and powerful individuals with polished political skills and inexperienced and naive employees who misjudge their chances.

Organisational factors

Political activity is probably more a function of the organisation's characteristics than of individual difference variables. Why? Because many organisations have a large number of employees with the individual characteristics we listed, yet the extent of political behaviour varies widely.

Although we acknowledge the role that individual differences can play in fostering politicking, the evidence more strongly supports that certain situations and cultures promote politics. More specifically, when an organisation's resources are declining, when the existing pattern of resources is changing, and when there is opportunity for promotions, politics is more likely to surface.[34] In addition, cultures characterised by low trust, role ambiguity, unclear performance evaluation systems, zero-sum reward allocation practices, democratic decision making, high pressures for performance, and self-serving senior managers will create breeding grounds for politicking.[35]

When organisations downsize to improve efficiency, reductions in resources have to be made. Threatened with the loss of resources, people may engage in political actions to safeguard what they have. But any changes, especially those that imply significant reallocation of resources within the organisation, are likely to stimulate conflict and increase politicking.

Promotion decisions have consistently been found to be one of the most political actions in organisations. The opportunity for promotions or advancement encourages people to compete for a limited resource and to try to positively influence the decision outcome.

The less trust there is within the organisation, the higher the level of political behaviour and the more likely that the political behaviour will be of the illegitimate kind. So, high trust should suppress the level of political behaviour in general and inhibit illegitimate actions in particular.

Role ambiguity means that the prescribed behaviours of the employee are not clear. There are fewer limits, therefore, to the scope and functions of the employee's political actions. Because political activities are defined as those not required as part of one's formal role, the greater the role ambiguity, the more one can engage in political activity with little chance of it being visible.

The practice of performance evaluation is far from a perfect science. The more that organisations use subjective criteria in the appraisal, emphasise a single outcome measure, or allow significant time to pass between the time of an action and its appraisal, the greater the likelihood that an employee can get away with politicking. Subjective performance criteria create ambiguity. The use of a single outcome measure encourages individuals to do whatever is necessary to 'look good' on that measure, but often at the expense of performing well on other important parts of the job that are not being appraised. The amount of time that elapses between an action and its appraisal is also a relevant factor. The longer the time, the more unlikely that the employee will be held accountable for their political behaviours.

The more that an organisation's culture emphasises the zero-sum or win–lose approach to reward allocations, the more employees will be motivated to engage in politicking. The zero-sum approach treats the reward 'pie' as fixed, so that any gain one person or group achieves has to come at the expense of another person or group. If I win, you must lose! If $15,000 in annual raises is to be distributed among five employees, then any employee who gets more than $3,000

Ansett Airlines went out of business with the loss of over 15,000 jobs. The circumstances surrounding its failure and the uncertain climate that was created, provides the opportunity for intensive political activity as people act to protect their own interests.

takes money away from one or more of the others. Such a practice encourages making others look bad and increasing the visibility of what you do.

Since the mid-1970s, there has been a general move in Australia and among most developed nations towards making organisations less autocratic. Managers in these organisations are being asked to behave more democratically. They are told that they should allow employees to advise them on decisions and that they should rely to a greater extent on group input into the decision process. Such moves towards democracy, however, aren't necessarily embraced by all individual managers. Many managers sought their positions in order to have legitimate power so as to be able to make unilateral decisions. They fought hard and often paid high personal costs to achieve their influential positions. Sharing their power with others runs directly against their desires. The result is that managers, especially those who began their careers in the 1950s and 1960s, may use the required committees, conferences and group meetings in a superficial way, as arenas for manoeuvring and manipulating.

The more pressure that employees feel to perform well, the more likely they are to engage in politicking. When people are held strictly accountable for outcomes, this puts great pressure on them to 'look good'. If a person perceives that their entire career is riding on next quarter's sales figures or next month's plant productivity report, there is motivation to do whatever is necessary to make sure the numbers come out favourably.

Finally, when employees see the people on top engaging in political behaviour, especially when they do so successfully and are rewarded for it, a climate is created that supports politicking. Politicking by top management, in a sense, gives permission to those lower in the organisation to play politics by implying that such behaviour is acceptable.

HOW DO PEOPLE RESPOND TO ORGANISATIONAL POLITICS?

Trish O'Donnell loves her job as a writer on a weekly television comedy series but hates the internal politics. 'A couple of the writers here spend more time kissing up to the executive producer than doing any work. And our head writer clearly has his favourites. While they pay me a lot and I get to really use my creativity, I'm sick of having to be on alert for backstabbers and constantly having to self-promote my contributions. I'm tired of doing most of the work and getting little of the credit.'

Are Trish O'Donnell's comments typical of people who work in highly politicised workplaces? We all know of friends or relatives who regularly complain about the politics at their job. But how do people in general react to organisational politics? Let's look at the evidence.

In our discussion earlier in this chapter of factors that contribute to political behaviour, we focused on the favourable outcomes for individuals who successfully engage in politicking. But for most people—who have modest political skills or are unwilling to play the politics game—

outcomes tend to be predominantly negative. Figure 13.2 summarises the extensive research on the relationship between the perception of organisational politics and individual outcomes.[36] There is, for example, very strong evidence indicating that perceptions of organisational politics are negatively related to job satisfaction.[37] The perception of politics also tends to increase job anxiety or stress. This seems to be due to the perception that, by not engaging in politics, a person may be losing ground to others who are active politickers; or, conversely, because of the additional pressures individuals feel because of having entered into and competing in the political arena.[38] Not surprisingly, when politicking becomes too much to handle, it can lead to employees quitting. Finally, there is preliminary evidence suggesting that politics leads to self-reported declines in employee performance.[39] Perceived organisational politics appears to have a demotivating effect on individuals, thus leading to decreased performance levels.

In addition to the above conclusions, several interesting qualifiers have been noted. First, the politics–performance relationship appears to be moderated by an individual's understanding of the 'hows' and 'whys' of organisational politics. 'An individual who has a clear understanding of who is responsible for making decisions and why they were selected to be the decision makers would have a better understanding of how and why things happen the way they do than someone who does not understand the decision-making process in the organization.'[40] When both politics and understanding are high, performance is likely to increase because the individual will see political actions as an opportunity. This is consistent with what you might expect among individuals with well-honed political skills. But when understanding is low, individuals are more likely to see politics as a threat, which would have a negative effect on job performance.[41] Second, when politics is seen as a threat and consistently responded to with defensiveness, negative outcomes are almost sure to surface eventually. When people perceive politics as a threat rather than as an opportunity, they often respond with **defensive behaviours**—reactive and protective behaviours to avoid action, blame or change.[42] (Table 13.3 provides some examples of these defensive behaviours.) And defensive behaviours are often associated with negative feelings towards the job and work environment.[43] In the short run, employees may find that defensiveness protects their self-interest. But in the long run, it wears them down. People who consistently rely on defensiveness find that, eventually, it is the only way they know how to behave. At that point, they lose the trust and support of their peers, bosses, employees and clients.

Are our conclusions about responses to politics globally valid? Should we expect employees in Israel, for example, to respond the same way to workplace politics that employees in Singapore or New Zealand do? Almost all our conclusions on employee reactions to organisational politics are based on studies conducted in North America. The few studies that have included other countries suggest some minor modifications.[44] Israelis and Britons, for example, seem to generally respond, as do North Americans. That is, the perception of organisational politics among employees in these countries is related to decreased job satisfaction and increased turnover.[45] But in countries that are more politically unstable, employees seem to demonstrate greater tolerance of intense political processes in the workplace. This is likely to be because people in these countries are used to power struggles and have more experience in coping with them.[46] This suggests that people from politically turbulent countries in the Middle East or Latin America might be more accepting of organisational politics, and even more willing to use aggressive political tactics in the workplace, than people from countries such as Great Britain or Switzerland.

FIGURE 13.2 **Employee responses to organisational politics**

defensive behaviours
Reactive and protective behaviours to avoid action, blame or change.

TABLE 13.3	**Defensive behaviours**

Avoiding Action

Overconforming. Strictly interpreting your responsibility by saying things like, 'The rules clearly state . . .' or 'This is the way we've always done it.'

Buck passing. Transferring responsibility for the execution of a task or decision to someone else.

Playing dumb. Avoiding an unwanted task by falsely pleading ignorance or inability.

Stretching. Prolonging a task so that one appears to be occupied—for example, turning a two-week task into a four-month job.

Stalling. Appearing to be more or less supportive publicly while doing little or nothing privately.

Avoiding Blame

Buffing. This is a nice way to refer to 'covering your rear'. It describes the practice of rigorously documenting activity to project an image of competence and thoroughness.

Playing safe. Evading situations that may reflect unfavourably. It includes taking on only projects with a high probability of success, having risky decisions approved by superiors, qualifying expressions of judgment, and taking neutral positions in conflicts.

Justifying. Developing explanations that lessen one's responsibility for a negative outcome and/or apologising to demonstrate remorse.

Scapegoating. Placing the blame for a negative outcome on external factors that are not entirely blameworthy.

Misrepresenting. Manipulation of information by distortion, embellishment, deception, selective presentation or obfuscation.

Avoiding Change

Prevention. Trying to prevent a threatening change from occurring.

Self-protection. Acting in ways to protect one's self-interest during change by guarding information or other resources.

LEARNING OBJECTIVE

Identify seven techniques for managing the impression one makes on others

IMPRESSION MANAGEMENT

We know that people have an ongoing interest in how others perceive and evaluate them. For example, North Americans spend billions of dollars on diets, health club memberships, cosmetics and plastic surgery—all intended to make them more attractive to others.[47] Being perceived positively by others should also have benefits for people in organisations. It might, for example, help them initially to get the jobs they want in an organisation and, once hired, to get favourable evaluations, superior salary increases and more rapid promotions. In a political context, it might help to sway the distribution of advantages in their favour.

impression management
The process by which individuals attempt to control the impression others form of them.

The process by which individuals attempt to control the impression others form of them is called **impression management**.[48] It is a subject that has gained the attention of OB researchers only recently.[49]

Is everyone concerned with impression management (IM)? No! Who, then, might we predict to engage in IM? No surprise here! It's our old friend, the high self-monitor.[50] Low self-monitors tend to present images of themselves that are consistent with their personalities, regardless of the beneficial or detrimental effects for them. In contrast, high self-monitors are good at reading situations and moulding their appearances and behaviour to fit each situation.

Given that you want to control the impression others form of you, what techniques could you use? Table 13.4 summarises some popular IM techniques and provides an example of each.

TABLE 13.4   Impression management (IM) techniques

Conformity

Agreeing with someone else's opinion in order to gain their approval.

Example: A manager tells his boss, 'You're absolutely right on your reorganisation plan for the Victorian regional office. I couldn't agree with you more.'

Excuses

Explanations of a predicament-creating event aimed at minimising the apparent severity of the predicament.

Example: Sales manager to boss, 'We failed to get the ad in the paper on time, but no one responds to those ads anyway.'

Apologies

Admitting responsibility for an undesirable event and simultaneously seeking to get a pardon for the action.

Example: Employee to boss, 'I'm sorry I made a mistake on the report. Please forgive me.'

Self-promotion

Highlighting one's best qualities, downplaying one's deficits, and calling attention to one's achievements.

Example: A salesperson tells his boss: 'Matt worked unsuccessfully for three years to try to get that account. I sewed it up in six weeks. I'm the best closer this company has.'

Flattery

Complimenting others about their virtues in an effort to make oneself appear perceptive and likeable.

Example: New sales trainee to peer, 'You handled that client's complaint so tactfully! I could never have handled that as well as you did.'

Favours

Doing something nice for someone to gain that person's approval.

Example: Salesperson to prospective client, 'I've got two tickets to the theatre tonight that I can't use. Take them. Consider it a thank-you for taking the time to talk with me.'

Association

Enhancing or protecting one's image by managing information about people and things with which one is associated.

Example: A job applicant says to an interviewer, 'What a coincidence. Your boss and I were flatmates at university.'

Sources: Based on B. R. Schlenker, *Impression Management* (Monterey, CA: Brooks/Cole, 1980); W. L. Gardner and M. J. Martinko, 'Impression Management in Organizations', *Journal of Management*, June 1988, p. 332; and R. B. Cialdini, 'Indirect Tactics of Image Management: Beyond Basking', in R. A. Giacalone and P. Rosenfeld (eds), *Impression Management in the Organization* (Hillsdale, NJ: Lawrence Erlbaum Associates, 1989), pp. 45–71.

Keep in mind that IM doesn't imply that the impressions people convey are necessarily false (although, of course, they sometimes are).[51] Excuses, for example, may be offered with sincerity. Referring to the example used in Table 13.4, you can *actually* believe that advertisements contribute little to sales in your region. But misrepresentation can have a high cost. If the image claimed is false, you may be discredited.[52] If you 'cry wolf' once too often, no one is likely to believe you when the wolf really comes. So, the impression manager must be cautious not to be perceived as insincere or manipulative.[53]

Are there *situations* in which individuals are more likely to misrepresent themselves or more likely to get away with it? Yes—situations that are characterised by high uncertainty or ambiguity provide relatively little information for challenging a fraudulent claim and reduce the risks associated with misrepresentation.[54]

Most of the studies undertaken to test the effectiveness of IM techniques have been limited to determining whether IM behaviour is related to job interview success. Employment interviews make a particularly relevant area of study, since applicants are clearly attempting to present positive images of themselves and there are relatively objective outcome measures (written assessments and typically a hire–don't hire recommendation).

The evidence indicates that IM behaviour works.[55] In one study, for example, interviewers felt that applicants for a position as a customer service representative who used IM techniques performed better in the interview, and they seemed somewhat more inclined to hire these people.[56] Moreover, when the researchers considered applicants' credentials, they concluded that it was the IM techniques alone that influenced the interviewers. That is, it didn't seem to matter if applicants were well or poorly qualified. If they used IM techniques, they did better in the interview.

Another employment interview study looked at whether certain IM techniques work better than others.[57] The researchers compared applicants who used IM techniques that focused the conversation on themselves (called a *controlling style*) to applicants who used techniques that focused on the interviewer (referred to as a *submissive style*). The researchers hypothesised that applicants who used the controlling style would be more effective because of the implicit expectations inherent in employment interviews. We tend to expect job applicants to use self-enhancement, self-promotion and other active controlling techniques in an interview because they reflect self-confidence and initiative. The researchers predicted that these active controlling techniques would work better for applicants than submissive tactics such as conforming their opinions to those of the interviewer and offering favours to the interviewer. The results confirmed the researchers' predictions. Applicants who used the controlling style were rated higher by interviewers on factors such as motivation, enthusiasm and even technical skills—and they received more job offers. Another study confirmed the value of a controlling style over a submissive one.[58] Specifically, recent university graduates who used more self-promotion tactics got higher evaluations by interviewers and more follow-up job-site visits, even after adjusting for grade point average, gender and job type.

LEARNING OBJECTIVE

10

List the three questions that can help determine if a political action is ethical

THE ETHICS OF BEHAVING POLITICALLY

We conclude our discussion of politics by providing some ethical guidelines for political behaviour. Although there are no clear-cut ways to differentiate ethical from unethical politicking, there are some questions you should consider.

Figure 13.3 illustrates a decision tree to guide ethical actions.[59] This tree is built on the three ethical decision criteria—utilitarianism, rights and justice—presented in a previous chapter. The first question you need to answer addresses self-interest versus organisational goals. Ethical actions are consistent with the organisation's goals. Spreading untrue rumours about the safety of a new product introduced by your company, in order to make that product's design team look bad, is unethical. However, there may be nothing unethical if a department head exchanges work favours with her division's purchasing manager in order to get a critical contract processed quickly.

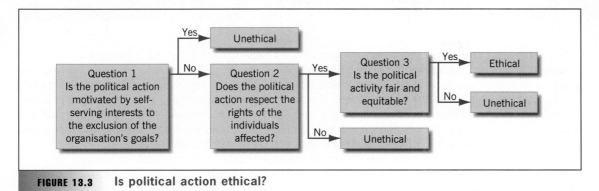

FIGURE 13.3   **Is political action ethical?**

Source: Adapted from G. F. Cavanagh, D. Moberg and M. Valasquez, 'The Ethics of Organizational Politics', *Academy of Management Review*, July 1981, p. 368. Copyright © 1981 by Academy of Management. Reproduced with permission of Academy of Management in the format Textbook via Copy Clearance Center.

The second question concerns the rights of other parties. If the department head described in the previous paragraph went down to the mail room during her lunch hour and read through the mail directed to the purchasing manager—with the intent of 'getting something on him' so that he would expedite the contract—she would be acting unethically. She would have violated the purchasing manager's right to privacy.

The final question that needs to be addressed relates to whether the political activity conforms to standards of equity and justice. The department head who inflates the performance evaluation of a favoured employee and deflates the evaluation of a disfavoured employee—and then uses these evaluations to justify giving the former a big raise and nothing to the latter—has treated the disfavoured employee unfairly.

Unfortunately, the answers to the questions in Figure 13.3 are often argued in ways to make unethical practices seem ethical. Powerful people, for example, can become very good at explaining self-serving behaviours in terms of the organisation's best interests. Similarly, they can persuasively argue that unfair actions are really fair and just. Our point is that immoral people can justify almost any behaviour. Those who are powerful, articulate and persuasive are most vulnerable because they are likely to be able to get away with unethical practices successfully. When faced with an ethical dilemma regarding organisational politics, try to answer the questions in Figure 13.3 truthfully. If you have a strong power base, recognise the ability of power to corrupt. Remember, it's a lot easier for the powerless to act ethically, if for no other reason than they typically have very little political discretion to exploit.

Summary and Implications for Managers

If you want to get things done in a group or organisation, it helps to have power. As a manager who wants to maximise your power, you will want to increase others' dependence on you. You can, for example, increase your power in relation to your boss by developing knowledge or a skill that she needs and for which she perceives no ready substitute. But power is a two-way street. You won't be alone in attempting to build your power bases. Others, particularly employees and peers, will be seeking to make you dependent on them. The result is a continual battle. While you seek to maximise others' dependence on you, you will be seeking to minimise your dependence on others. And, of course, others you work with will be trying to do the same.

Few employees relish being powerless in their job and organisation. It's been argued, for example, that when people in organisations are difficult, argumentative and temperamental, it may be because they are in positions of powerlessness; positions in which the performance expectations placed on them exceed their resources and capabilities.[60]

There is evidence that people respond differently to the various power bases.[61] Expert, referent and charismatic forms of power are derived from an individual's personal qualities. In contrast, coercion, reward, legitimate and information power are essentially organisationally derived. Since people are more likely to enthusiastically accept and commit to an individual whom they admire or whose knowledge they respect (rather than someone who relies on their position for influence), the effective use of expert, referent and charismatic power should lead to higher employee performance, commitment and satisfaction.[62] Competence especially appears to offer wide appeal, and its use as a power base results in high performance by group members. The message for managers seems to be: develop and use your expert power base!

The power of your boss may also play a role in determining your job satisfaction. 'One of the reasons many of us like to work for and with people who are powerful is that they are generally more pleasant—not because it is their native disposition, but because the reputation and reality of being powerful permits them more discretion and more ability to delegate to others.'[63]

The effective manager accepts the political nature of organisations. By assessing behaviour in a political framework, you can better predict the actions of others and use this information to formulate political strategies that will gain advantages for you and your work unit.

Some people are significantly more 'politically astute' than others. Those who are good at playing politics can be expected to get higher performance evaluations and, hence, larger salary increases and more promotions than the politically naive or inept.[64] The politically astute are also likely to exhibit higher job satisfaction. For employees with modest political skills or who are unwilling to play the politics game, the perception of organisational politics is generally related to lower job satisfaction and self-reported performance, increased anxiety and higher turnover.

Point

CREATING 'SPECIAL DEALS' FOR RESULTS

In countries such as France, Belgium and the Netherlands, terms of employment are largely mandated by law and hence highly standardised. In contrast, in countries such as Australia, Great Britain and New Zealand, managers have considerable leeway to negotiate idiosyncratic deals with employees. And in these latter countries, managers are increasingly using this latitude to customise their treatment of 'special' individuals.

Two trends help to explain the growth in special deals for certain employees. First, the demand for knowledge workers with distinctive competencies in a highly competitive market means workers have greater power to negotiate employment conditions suited to their tastes and preferences. Second, the decline in unionisation and the weakening of the job security-based model of organisational careers have led to less standardised conditions of employment.

In order to hire, motivate and keep highly skilled workers, managers are negotiating special treatment for certain employees. Examples of this special treatment include higher pay than others for doing similar work, allowing an employee to work from home several days a week, permitting an employee to leave early to fulfil family obligations, upgraded travel arrangements, and allowing certain employees to spend time on personal projects during work time.

What do these employees have that allow them to make idiosyncratic arrangements? It can be unique credentials, special skills, high status, important contacts or high marketability. But it must also include the willingness of an employee or prospective employee to speak up. These deals are typically proposed as bargaining chips when negotiating initial employment terms or after the employee has been on the job a while, built a trusting relationship with their manager and become a valued performer.

These special deals have advantages for both employees and managers. They provide greater rewards for employees and allow them to tailor their job to better meet their personal needs. They also give individual managers greater latitude in motivating their employees and flexibility to adapt to changing circumstances.

Source: This is largely based on D. M. Rousseau, 'The Idiosyncratic Deal: Flexibility versus Fairness?', *Organizational Dynamics*, Spring 2001, pp. 260–73.

Counterpoint

Talk about opening up a can of worms! Making special deals with certain employees is bound to undermine whatever trust there is in an organisation. Although management may desire flexibility in its relationships with employees, maintaining standardised practices is more likely to provide the appearance of fairness that is needed to create a climate of trust. And customisation of employment relationships, under the guise of flexibility, only increases politics in the workplace.

There is no shortage of arguments against special deals for special employees. Here are just a few.

- Special deals give too much power to managers. They allow managers to negotiate favourable treatment with employees they like. Although these employees may also be high performers, if they are not, it contributes to politicising the work environment.
- Special deals are unlikely to be perceived as fair by those who don't receive them. One person's merit is another's favouritism.
- Special deals reward the wrong behaviours. They encourage employees to 'kiss up' to their boss and to treat every attempt to get a raise or time off as a bargaining opportunity.
- Special deals tend to go to aggressive employees, whether or not they are contributing the most. Shy, quiet and less demanding employees who are good performers are likely to be excluded.
- Special deals aren't cost-free. Resources in organisations are limited. One employee's gain is often at another's expense. So, allowing one employee in a department to take off two hours early every Thursday afternoon to coach his son's soccer team often means that others in that department will have to take up some of his work. This has the potential to create conflicts. For example, evidence indicates that many single and childless employees resent the 'family-friendly' benefits—such as helping to find an employee's spouse employment or paid child-care—that many companies offer to married workers and those with children.

Our position is that special deals undermine trust and cooperation at work. They create the appearance, if not the actuality, that those with power get favoured treatment. We have spent three-quarters of a century building formalised human resource systems that ensure consistent treatment of the workforce. These systems are critical to promoting fairness, cooperation and efficiency. Using idiosyncratic deals to supposedly enhance flexibility is a major step towards trashing these systems.

For Discussion

1. What is power? How do you get it?
2. Contrast power tactics with power bases. What are some of the key contingency variables that determine which tactic a power holder is likely to use?
3. Which power bases lie with the individual? Which are derived from the organisation?
4. State the general dependency postulate. What does it mean?

5. What creates dependency? Give an applied example.
6. What is a coalition? When is it likely to develop?
7. How are power and politics related?
8. Define political behaviour. Why is politics a fact of life in organisations?
9. What factors contribute to political activity?
10. What is impression management? What type of people are most likely to engage in IM?
11. Based on the information presented in this chapter, what would you do as a recent university graduate entering a new job to maximise your power and accelerate your career progress?
12. 'Politics is not inherently bad. It is merely a way to get things accomplished within organisations.' Do you agree or disagree? Defend your position.
13. You are a sales representative for an international software company. After four excellent years, sales in your territory are off 30 per cent this year. Describe three defensive responses you might use to reduce the potential negative consequences of this decline in sales.
14. 'Sexual harassment should not be tolerated at the workplace.' 'Workplace romances are a natural occurrence in organisations.' Are both of these statements true? Can they be reconciled?

Exercises

Exercise 13a
UNDERSTANDING POWER DYNAMICS

1. Creation of groups
Each student is to give a dollar coin (or similar value of currency) to the lecturer. Students are then divided into three groups based on criteria given by the lecturer, assigned to their work areas, and instructed to read the following rules and tasks. The money is divided into thirds, giving two-thirds of it to the top group, one-third to the middle group, and none to the bottom group.

2. Conduct exercise   Groups go to their assigned workplaces and have 30 minutes to complete their tasks.

Rules
a. Members of the top group are free to enter the space of either of the other groups and to communicate whatever they wish, whenever they wish. Members of the middle group may enter the space of the lower group when they wish, but must request permission to enter the top group's space (which the top group can refuse). Members of the lower group may not disturb the top group in any way unless specifically invited by the top group. The lower group does have the right to knock on the door of the middle group and request permission to communicate with them (which can also be refused).
b. The members of the top group have the authority to make any change in the rules that they wish, at any time, with or without notice.

Tasks
a. *Top group.* To be responsible for the overall effectiveness and learning from the exercise, and to decide how to use its money.
b. *Middle group.* To assist the top group in providing for the overall welfare of the organisation, and to decide how to use its money.
c. *Bottom group.* To identify its resources and to decide how best to provide for learning and the overall effectiveness of the organisation.

3. Debriefing
Each of the three groups chooses two representatives to go to the front of the class and discuss the following questions:
a. Summarise what occurred within and among the three groups.
b. What are some of the differences between being in the top group versus being in the bottom group?
c. What can we learn about power from this experience?

d. How accurate do you think this exercise is to the reality of resource allocation decisions in large organisations?

Source: This exercise is adapted from L. Bolman and T. E. Deal, *Exchange*, vol. 3, no. 4, 1979, pp. 38–42. Reprinted by permission of Sage Publications, Inc.

Exercise 13b
POWER ORIENTATION TEST

For each statement, students are asked to circle the number that most closely resembles their attitude towards the issue contained in each statement.

		Disagree		Agree	
Statement	**A Lot**	**A Little**	**Neutral**	**A Little**	**A Lot**
1. The best way to handle people is to tell them what they want to hear.	1	2	3	4	5
2. When you ask someone to do something for you, it's best to give the real reason for wanting it rather than giving reasons that might carry more weight.	1	2	3	4	5
3. Anyone who completely trusts anyone else is asking for trouble.	1	2	3	4	5
4. It's hard to get ahead without cutting corners here and there.	1	2	3	4	5
5. It's safest to assume that all people have a vicious streak, and it will come out when they are given a chance.	1	2	3	4	5
6. One should take action only when it is morally right.	1	2	3	4	5
7. Most people are basically good and kind.	1	2	3	4	5
8. There is no excuse for lying to someone else.	1	2	3	4	5
9. Most people more easily forget the death of their father than the loss of their property.	1	2	3	4	5
10. Generally speaking, people won't work hard unless they are forced to do so.	1	2	3	4	5

Refer to Appendix C for scoring directions and key.

Source: R. Christie and F. L. Geis, *Studies in Machiavellianism.* © Academic Press, 1970. Reprinted by permission of Elsevier.

Case Study 13

Damned If You Do; Damned If You Don't

Fran Gilson has spent 15 years with a national retail grocery chain.* Starting out as a part-time cashier while attending university, she has risen up through the ranks of this 50-store chain. Today, at the age of 34, she is a regional manager, overseeing seven stores and earning approximately $75,000 a year. Fran also thinks she's ready to take on more responsibility. About five weeks ago, she was contacted by an executive-search recruiter enquiring about her interest in the position of regional manager for a national chemist/pharmaceutical retail chain of stores. She would be responsible for more than 100 stores in five regions. She agreed to meet with the recruiter. This led to two meetings with top executives at the national chain. The recruiter called Fran two days ago to tell her she was one of the two finalists for the job.

The only person at her present company who knows that Fran is looking at this other job is her good friend and colleague, Ken Hamilton. Ken is director of finance for the grocery chain. 'It's a dream job,' Fran told Ken. 'It's a lot more responsibility and it's a good company to work for. The regional office is just 35 kilometres from here, so I wouldn't have to move, and the pay is first-rate. With the performance bonus, I could make nearly $200,000 a year. But best of all, the job provides terrific visibility. I'd be their only female regional manager. The job would allow me to be a more visible role model for young women and give me a bigger voice in opening up doors for women and ethnic minorities in retailing management.'

Since Fran considered Ken a close friend and wanted to keep the fact that she was looking at another job secret, she asked Ken last week if she could use his name as a reference. Ken said, 'Of course. I'll give you a great recommendation. We'd hate to lose you here, but you've got a lot of talent. They'd be lucky to get someone with your experience and energy.' Fran passed Ken's name on to the executive recruiter as her only reference at her present job. She made it very clear to the recruiter that Ken was the only person who knew she was considering another job. The top management of Fran's present company is conservative and places a high value on loyalty. If anyone heard she was talking to another company, it might seriously jeopardise her chances for promotion. But she trusted Ken completely. It's against this backdrop that this morning's incident became more than just a question of sexual harassment. It became a full-blown ethical and political dilemma for Fran.

Jennifer Chung has been a financial analyst in Ken's department for five months. Fran met Jennifer through Ken. The three have chatted together on a number of occasions in the coffee room. Fran's impression of Jennifer is quite positive. In many ways, Jennifer strikes Fran as a lot like she was ten years ago. This morning, Fran came to work around 6.30 am, as she usually does. It allows her to get a lot accomplished before 'the troops' roll in at 8 am. At about 6.45, Jennifer came into Fran's office. It was immediately evident that something was wrong. Jennifer was very nervous and uncomfortable, which was most unlike her. She asked Fran if they could talk. Fran sat her down and listened to her story.

What Fran heard was hard to believe, but she had no reason to think Jennifer was lying. Jennifer said that Ken began making off-colour comments to her when they were alone within a month after Jennifer joined the company. From there it got progressively worse. Ken would leer at her. He put his arm over her shoulder when they were reviewing reports. He patted her backside. Every time one of these occurrences happened, Jennifer would ask him to stop and not do it again, but it fell on deaf ears. Yesterday, Ken reminded Jennifer that her six-month probationary review was coming up. 'He told me that if I didn't sleep with him that I couldn't expect a very favourable evaluation.' She told Fran that all she could do was go to the ladies' room and cry.

Jennifer said that she had come to Fran because she didn't know what to do or to whom to turn. 'You're a friend of Ken's and the highest-ranking woman here. Will you help me?' Fran had never heard anything like this about Ken before. About all she knew regarding his personal life was that he was in his late thirties, single, and involved in a long-term relationship.

Questions

1. Analyse Fran's situation in a purely legalistic sense. You might want to talk to friends or relatives who are in management or the legal profession for advice in this analysis.
2. Analyse Fran's dilemma in political terms.
3. Analyse Fran's situation in an ethical sense. What is the ethically right thing for her to do? Is that also the politically right thing to do?
4. If you were Fran, what would you do?

* The identity of this organisation and the people described are disguised for obvious reasons.

Web Workout

1. Information and policies concerning sexual harassment are often joked about, scorned and, more importantly, misunderstood. Learn about current trends in sexual harassment issues from *HRMagazine*, the Society for Human Resources' (SHRM) monthly publication to its members. Go to <www.shrm.org/>.
2. Knowing about 'personal power' is one thing; applying it to everyday work life is another. Learn how Craig Ohlson of Activation does it to be the top salesperson in a featured article in *Inc.* magazine. Point to <www.inc.com/magazine/19950201/2142.html> to read the article. Write a short reaction paper describing the power tactics Craig uses to influence his customers. Could any of his methods be applied to an activity you are involved in? Why or why not?
3. Power and gender equity are hot topics among HR professionals. These aren't necessarily sexual harassment issues, but systemic organisational issues of concern. To learn more, go to <www.workforce.com/archive/article/22/02/97.php>. Are there issues discussed that you haven't considered previously? Write a short journal entry of two or three paragraphs about what you learned from the article.
4. Ethics in the boardroom? You bet, despite the bad news we hear from the media on a daily basis. CEOs are talking about, and doing something about, ethics every day. Point to <www.refresher.com/!cirihal5.html> to learn how to apply an ethical framework to your activities. Click on the link for spiritualityhealth.com and take the self-test to become more aware of your own personal values. Write three things in a short journal entry you learned about yourself after reading this website.
5. Are smart people overrated? That was the question put forth by *New Yorker* magazine in the article, 'The Talent Myth'. Read this article at <www.newyorker.com/fact/content/?020722fa_fact>. Make a list of every impression management behaviour you spot in the article. Then make a list of IM techniques you plan to develop in the next few years. Bring both lists to class for discussion.
6. Go to <www.itstime.com/oct97map.htm> and develop your own personal power map for an organisation you are involved (or have been involved) with. Bring it to class for discussion.

KSS Program

KNOW THE CONCEPTS   SELF-AWARENESS   SKILLS APPLICATIONS

Building your power base
After you have read this chapter, take Self-Assessment #31 (How Power-oriented Am I?) on your enclosed CD-Rom and complete the skill-building module entitled 'Becoming Politically Adept' on page 643.

NOTES

1. Adele Ferguson, 'Away From the Boardroom, *Business Review Weekly*, vol. 25, no. 7, February 27, 2003, pp. 28–33.

2. R. M. Kanter, 'Power Failure in Management Circuits', *Harvard Business Review*, July–August 1979, p. 65.

3. J. Pfeffer, 'Understanding Power in Organizations', *California Management Review*, Winter 1992, p. 35.

4. Based on B. M. Bass, *Bass & Stogdill's Handbook of Leadership*, 3rd ed. (New York: Free Press, 1990).

5. J. R. P. French, Jr and B. Raven, 'The Bases of Social Power', in D. Cartwright (ed.), *Studies in Social Power* (Ann Arbor, MI: University of Michigan, Institute for Social Research, 1959), pp. 150–67; and B. J. Raven, 'The Bases of Power: Origins and Recent Developments', *Journal of Social Issues*, vol. 49, 1993, pp. 227–51.

6. E. A. Ward, 'Social Power Bases of Managers: Emergence of a New Factor', *Journal of Social Psychology*, February 2001, pp. 144–47.

7. R. E. Emerson, 'Power–Dependence Relations', *American Sociological Review*, vol. 27, 1962, pp. 31–41.

8. H. Mintzberg, *Power In and Around Organizations* (Upper Saddle River, NJ: Prentice Hall, 1983), p. 24.

9. R. M. Cyert and J. G. March, *A Behavioral Theory of the Firm* (Upper Saddle River, NJ: Prentice Hall, 1963).

10. C. Perrow, 'Departmental Power and Perspective in Industrial Firms', in M. N. Zald (ed.), *Power in Organizations* (Nashville, TN: Vanderbilt University Press, 1970).

11. See, for example, D. Kipnis, S. M. Schmidt, C. Swaffin-Smith and I. Wilkinson, 'Patterns of Managerial Influence: Shotgun Managers, Tacticians, and Bystanders', *Organizational Dynamics*, Winter 1984, pp. 58–67; D. Kipnis and S. M. Schmidt, 'Upward-Influence Styles: Relationship with Performance Evaluations, Salary, and Stress', *Administrative Science Quarterly*, December 1988, pp. 528–42; G. Yukl and C. M. Falbe, 'Influence Tactics and Objectives in Upward, Downward, and Lateral Influence Attempts', *Journal of Applied Psychology*, April 1990, pp. 132–40; S. J. Wayne, R. C. Liden, I. K. Graf and G. R. Ferris, 'The Role of Upward Influence Tactics in Human Resource Decisions', *Personnel Psychology*, Winter 1997, pp. 979–1006; and G. Blickle, 'Influence Tactics Used by Subordinates: An Empirical Analysis of the Kipnis and Schmidt Subscales', *Psychological Reports*, February 2000, pp. 143–54.

12. This section is adapted from Kipnis, Schmidt, Swaffin-Smith and Wilkinson, 'Patterns of Managerial Influence'.

13. P. P. Fu and G. Yukl, 'Perceived Effectiveness of Influence Tactics in the United States and China', *Leadership Quarterly*, Summer 2000, pp. 251–66.

14. Based on W. B. Stevenson, J. L. Pearce and L. W. Porter, 'The Concept of "Coalition" in Organization Theory and Research', *Academy of Management Review*, April 1985, pp. 261–63.

15. S. B. Bacharach and E. J. Lawler, 'Political Alignments in Organizations', in R. M. Kramer and M. A. Neale (eds), *Power and Influence in Organizations* (Thousand Oaks, CA: Sage, 1998), pp. 75–77.

16. J. K. Murnighan and D. J. Brass, 'Intraorganizational Coalitions', in M. H. Bazerman, R. J. Lewicki and B. H. Sheppard (eds), *Research on Negotiation in Organizations* (Greenwich, CT: JAI Press, 1991).

17. See J. Pfeffer, *Power in Organizations* (Marshfield, MA: Pitman, 1981), pp. 155–57.

18. Shelly Simonds, 'Doubts about Navy's Equality Move', *ANU Reporter*, vol. 28, no. 9, <http://info.anu.edu.au/mac/Newsletters_and_Journals/ANU_Reporter/_pdf/vol_28_no_09/navy.html>.

19. For recent reviews of the literature, see L. F. Fitzgerald and S. L. Shullman, 'Sexual Harassment: A Research Analysis and Agenda for the 1990s', *Journal of Vocational Behavior*, February 1993, pp. 5–27; S. Silverstein and S. Christian, 'Harassment Ruling Raises Free-Speech Issues', *Los Angeles Times*, 11 November 1993, p. D2; and M. L. Lengnick-Hall, 'Sexual Harassment Research: A Methodological Critique', *Personnel Psychology*, Winter 1995, pp. 841–64.

20. The following section is based on J. N. Cleveland and M. E. Kerst, 'Sexual Harassment and Perceptions of Power: An Under-Articulated Relationship', *Journal of Vocational Behavior*, February 1993, pp. 49–67.

21. S. A. Culbert and J. J. McDonough, *The Invisible War: Pursuing Self-Interest at Work* (New York: John Wiley, 1980), p. 6.

22. Mintzberg, *Power In and Around Organizations*, p. 26. See also K. M. Kacmar and R. A. Baron, 'Organizational Politics: The State of the Field, Links to Related Processes, and an Agenda for Future Research', in G. R. Ferris (ed.), *Research in Personnel and Human Resources Management*, vol. 17 (Greenwich, CT: JAI Press, 1999), pp. 1–39.

23. S. B. Bacharach and E. J. Lawler, 'Political Alignments in Organizations', in R. M. Kramer and M. A. Neale (eds), *Power and Influence in Organizations* (Thousand Oaks, CA: Sage, 1998), pp. 68–69.

24. D. Farrell and J. C. Petersen, 'Patterns of Political Behavior in Organizations', *Academy of Management Review*, July 1982, p. 405. For analyses of the controversies underlying the definition of organisational politics, see A. Drory and T. Romm, 'The Definition of Organizational Politics: A Review', *Human Relations*, November 1990, pp. 1133–54; and R. S. Cropanzano, K. M. Kacmar and D. P. Bozeman, 'Organizational Politics, Justice, and Support: Their Differences and Similarities', in R. S. Cropanzano and K. M. Kacmar (eds), *Organizational Politics, Justice and Support: Managing Social Climate at Work* (Westport, CT: Quorum Books, 1995), pp. 1–18.

25. Farrell and Peterson, 'Patterns of Political Behavior', pp. 406–07; and A. Drory, 'Politics in Organization and Its Perception Within the Organization', *Organization Studies*, vol. 9, no. 2, 1988, pp. 165–79.

26. Pfeffer, *Power in Organizations*.

27. Drory and Romm, 'The Definition of Organizational Politics'.

28. K. K. Eastman, 'In the Eyes of the Beholder: An Attributional Approach to Ingratiation and Organizational Citizenship Behavior', *Academy of Management Journal*, October 1994, pp. 1379–91; and M. C. Bolino, 'Citizenship and Impression Management: Good Soldiers or Good Actors?', *Academy of Management Review*, January 1999, pp. 82–98.

29. See, for example, G. Biberman, 'Personality and Characteristic Work Attitudes of Persons with High, Moderate, and Low Political Tendencies', *Psychological Reports*, October 1985, pp. 1303–10; R. J. House, 'Power and Personality in Complex Organizations', in B. M. Staw and L. L. Cummings (eds), *Research in Organizational Behavior*, vol. 10 (Greenwich, CT: JAI Press, 1988), pp. 305–57; and G. R. Ferris, G. S. Russ and P. M. Fandt, 'Politics in Organizations', in R.A. Giacalone and P. Rosenfeld (eds), *Impression Management in the Organization* (Hillsdale, NJ: Lawrence Erlbaum Associates, 1989), pp. 155–56.

30. F. Luthans, R. M. Hodgetts and S.A. Rosenkrantz, *Real Managers* (Cambridge, MA: Allinger, 1988).

31. J. P. Kotter, *The General Managers* (New York: The Free Press, 1982).

32. D. J. Brass, 'Being in the Right Place: A Structural Analysis of Individual Influence in an Organization', *Administrative Science Quarterly*, December 1984, pp. 518–39; and N. E. Friedkin, 'Structural Bases of Interpersonal Influence in Groups: A Longitudinal Case Study', *American Sociological Review*, vol. 58, 1993, pp. 861–72.

33. Farrell and Petersen, 'Patterns of Political Behavior', p. 408.

34. S. C. Goh and A. R. Doucet, 'Antecedent Situational Conditions of Organizational Politics: An Empirical Investigation', paper presented at the Annual Administrative Sciences Association of Canada Conference, Whistler, B.C., May 1986; C. Hardy, 'The Contribution of Political Science to Organizational Behavior', in J. W. Lorsch (ed.), *Handbook of Organizational Behavior* (Englewood Cliffs, NJ: Prentice Hall, 1987), p. 103; and G. R. Ferris and K. M. Kacmar, 'Perceptions of Organizational Politics', *Journal of Management*, March 1992, pp. 93–116.

35. See, for example, Farrell and Petersen, 'Patterns of Political Behavior', p. 409; P. M. Fandt and G. R. Ferris, 'The Management of Information and Impressions: When Employees Behave Opportunistically', *Organizational Behavior and Human Decision Processes*, February 1990, pp. 140–58; and Ferris, Russ and Fandt, 'Politics in Organizations', p. 147.

36. G. R. Ferris, G. S. Russ and P. M. Fandt, 'Politics in Organizations', in R. A. Giacalone and P. Rosenfeld (eds), *Impression Management in Organizations* (Newbury Park, CA: Sage, 1989), pp. 143–70; and K. M. Kacmar, D. P. Bozeman, D. S. Carlson and W. P. Anthony, 'An Examination of the Perceptions of Organizational Politics Model: Replication and Extension', *Human Relations*, March 1999, pp. 383–416.

37. Kacmar and Baron, 'Organizational Politics'; and M. Valle and L. A. Witt, 'The Moderating Effect of Teamwork Perceptions on the Organizational Politics–Job Satisfaction Relationship', *Journal of Social Psychology*, June 2001, pp. 379–88.

38. G. R. Ferris, D. D. Frink, M. C. Galang, J. Zhou, K. M. Kacmar and J. L. Howard, 'Perceptions of Organizational Politics: Prediction, Stress-Related Implications, and Outcomes', *Human Relations*, February 1996, pp. 233–66; and Kacmar, Bozeman, Carlson and Anthony, 'An Examination of the Perceptions of Organizational Politics Model', p. 388.

39. Kacmar, Bozeman, Carlson and Anthony, 'An Examination of the Perceptions of Organizational Politics Model'.

40. Ibid, p. 389.

41. Ibid, p. 409.

42. B. E. Ashforth and R. T. Lee, 'Defensive Behavior in Organizations: A Preliminary Model', *Human Relations*, July 1990, pp. 621–48.

43. M. Valle and P. L. Perrewe, 'Do Politics Perceptions Relate to Political Behaviors? Tests of an Implicit Assumption and Expanded Model', *Human Relations*, March 2000, pp. 359–86.

44. See T. Romm and A. Drory, 'Political Behavior in Organizations: A Cross-Cultural Comparison', *International Journal of Value Based Management*, vol. 1, 1988, pp. 97–113; and E. Vigoda, 'Reactions to Organizational Politics: A Cross-Cultural Examination in Israel and Britain', *Human Relations*, November 2001, pp. 1483–518.

45. Vigoda, 'Reactions to Organizational Politics', p. 1512.

46. Ibid, p. 1510.

47. M. R. Leary and R. M. Kowalski, 'Impression Management: A Literature Review and Two-Component Model', *Psychological Bulletin*, January 1990, pp. 34–47.

48. Ibid, p. 34.

49. See, for example, B. R. Schlenker, *Impression Management: The Self-Concept, Social Identity, and Interpersonal Relations* (Monterey, CA: Brooks/Cole, 1980); W. L. Gardner and M. J. Martinko, 'Impression Management in Organizations', *Journal of Management*, June 1988, pp. 321–38; Leary and Kowalski, 'Impression Management: A Literature Review and Two-Component Model', pp. 34–47; P. R. Rosenfeld, R. A. Giacalone and C. A. Riordan, *Impression Management in Organizations: Theory, Measurement, and Practice* (New York: Routledge, 1995); C. K. Stevens and A. L. Kristof, 'Making the Right Impression: A Field Study of Applicant Impression Management During Job Interviews', *Journal of Applied Psychology*, October 1995, pp. 587–606; and D. P. Bozeman and K. M. Kacmar,

'A Cybernetic Model of Impression Management Processes in Organizations', *Organizational Behavior and Human Decision Processes*, January 1997, pp. 9–30.

50. M. Snyder and J. Copeland, 'Self-Monitoring Processes in Organizational Settings', in Giacalone and Rosenfeld, *Impression Management in the Organization*, p. 11; E. D. Long and G. H. Dobbins, 'Self-Monitoring, Impression Management, and Interview Ratings: A Field and Laboratory Study', in J. L. Wall and L. R. Jauch (eds), *Proceedings of the 52nd Annual Academy of Management Conference*, Las Vegas, August 1992, pp. 274–78; A. Montagliani and R. A. Giacalone, 'Impression Management and Cross-Cultural Adaptation', *Journal of Social Psychology*, October 1998, pp. 598–608; and W. H. Turnley and M. C. Bolino, 'Achieved Desired Images While Avoiding Undesired Images: Exploring the Role of Self-Monitoring in Impression Management', *Journal of Applied Psychology*, April 2001, pp. 351–60.

51. Leary and Kowalski, 'Impression Management', p. 40.

52. Gardner and Martinko, 'Impression Management in Organizations', p. 333.

53. R. A. Baron, 'Impression Management by Applicants During Employment Interviews: The "Too Much of a Good Thing" Effect', in R. W. Eder and G. R. Ferris (eds), *The Employment Interview: Theory, Research, and Practice* (Newbury Park, CA: Sage Publishers, 1989), pp. 204–15.

54. Ferris, Russ and Fandt, 'Politics in Organizations'.

55. Baron, 'Impression Management by Applicants During Employment Interviews'; D. C. Gilmore and G. R. Ferris, 'The Effects of Applicant Impression Management Tactics on Interviewer Judgments', *Journal of Management*, December 1989, pp. 557–64; and Stevens and Kristof, 'Making the Right Impression: A Field Study of Applicant Impression Management During Job Interviews'.

56. Gilmore and Ferris, 'The Effects of Applicant Impression Management Tactics on Interviewer Judgments'.

57. K. M. Kacmar, J. E. Kelery and G. R. Ferris, 'Differential Effectiveness of Applicant IM Tactics on Employment Interview Decisions', *Journal of Applied Social Psychology*, 16–31 August 1992, pp. 1250–72.

58. Stevens and Kristof, 'Making the Right Impression: A Field Study of Applicant Impression Management During Job Interviews'.

59. This figure is based on G. F. Cavanagh, D. J. Moberg and M. Valasquez, 'The Ethics of Organizational Politics', *Academy of Management Journal*, June 1981, pp. 363–74.

60. R. M. Kanter, *Men and Women of the Corporation* (New York: Basic Books, 1977).

61. See, for example, C. M. Falbe and G. Yukl, 'Consequences for Managers of Using Single Influence Tactics and Combinations of Tactics', *Academy of Management Journal*, August 1992, pp. 638–52.

62. See J. G. Bachman, D. G. Bowers and P. M. Marcus, 'Bases of Supervisory Power: A Comparative Study in Five Organizational Settings', in A. S. Tannenbaum (ed.), *Control in Organizations* (New York: McGraw-Hill, 1968), p. 236; M. A. Rahim, 'Relationships of Leader Power to Compliance and Satisfaction with Supervision: Evidence from a National Sample of Managers', *Journal of Management*, December 1989, pp. 545–56; and P. A. Wilson, 'The Effects of Politics and Power on the Organizational Commitment of Federal Executives', *Journal of Management*, Spring 1995, pp. 101–18.

63. Pfeffer, *Managing with Power*, p. 137.

64. See, for example, N. Gupta and G. D. Jenkins, Jr, 'The Politics of Pay', *Compensation & Benefits Review*, March/April 1996, pp. 23–30.

PHOTO CREDITS
383 AAP Images/Julian Smith.

Conflict and Negotiation

CHAPTER OUTLINE

A definition of conflict
Transitions in conflict thought
Functional versus dysfunctional conflict
The conflict process
Negotiation

LEARNING OBJECTIVES

After studying this chapter, you should be able to:
1. Define conflict
2. Differentiate between the traditional, human relations and interactionist views of conflict
3. Contrast task, relationship and process conflict
4. Outline the conflict process
5. Describe the five conflict-handling intentions
6. Contrast distributive and integrative bargaining
7. Identify the five steps in the negotiation process
8. Describe cultural differences in negotiations

I don't want any yes-men around me. I want everybody to tell me the truth even if it costs them their jobs.
S. Goldwyn

Australian Competition & Consumer Commission

As the former chairman of the ACCC, Allan Fels is no stranger to the topic of conflict and negotiation.

In the 20th century, as capitalism burgeoned and globalisation took hold, large corporations had a major impact on national economies around the globe. In the face of hypercompetition, international cartels and the CEOs of multinational companies have pushed the limits of what is legal and morally justifiable in their quest for profits and personal rewards. Allan Fels, the former chairman of the Australian Competition & Consumer Commission (ACCC), says that 'preserving competition and consumer welfare in the face of these phenomena has prompted many developed nations to turn to criminal prosecution to temper the activities of those whose only interest is squeezing their competitors and consumers'.[1]

Justice Daryl Dawson's review of Australia's competition laws has been generally accepted by big business, small business and the ACCC. The Dawson review of competition law intends to bring Australia into line with its trading partners by allowing prison sentences to be imposed on those convicted of hard-core cartel behaviour.

While it is important to have checks and balances in the system, it can mean a heavy price for those people charged with keeping an eye on competition. Ask Allan Fels about the constant conflict that occurs between the ACCC and big business leaders. As James Thomson explained in *Business Review Weekly*:

> For many in the business community, April 23, 2002, was the day that Allan Fels, the chairman of the Australian Competition & Consumer Commission (ACCC), went too far. In the largest operation of its kind ever undertaken by the ACCC, 90 officials stormed into 11 sites in Sydney, Melbourne and Newcastle belonging to the oil companies Caltex Australia, Mobil Oil Australia and Shell Australia. Acting on information from a whistleblower, the officials copied and inspected documents they believed pertained to collusion, market sharing and price fixing.[2]

The story got wide media coverage. Sydney's *Daily Telegraph* newspaper carried a photograph on its front page with the caption, 'ACCC officers carry boxes of documents from Caltex's headquarters.' But the caption was misleading. As Fels later acknowledged, the officials were carrying boxes containing

ACCC property. No evidence was removed from Caltex's offices on that day. The chairman of Caltex, Dick Warburton, cried foul and accused Fels of using a 'trumped-up photograph to destroy Caltex's reputation'.

Conflict can be a serious problem between organisations and within an organisation. It can create chaotic conditions that make it nearly impossible for employees and organisations to work together. On the other hand, conflict also has a less-well-known positive side. We will explain the difference between negative and positive conflicts in this chapter and provide a guide to help you understand how conflicts develop. We will also present a topic closely akin to conflict—negotiation. But first, let's clarify what we mean by conflict.

LEARNING OBJECTIVE

1

Define conflict

A Definition of Conflict

There has been no shortage of definitions of conflict.[3] Despite the divergent meanings the term has acquired, several common themes underlie most definitions. Conflict must be perceived by the parties to it; whether or not conflict exists is a perception issue. If no one is aware of a conflict, then it is generally agreed that no conflict exists. Additional commonalities in the definitions are opposition or incompatibility and some form of interaction.[4] These factors set the conditions that determine the beginning point of the conflict process.

conflict
A process that begins when one party perceives that another party has negatively affected, or is about to negatively affect, something that the first party cares about.

We can define **conflict**, then, as a process that begins when one party perceives that another party has negatively affected, or is about to negatively affect, something that the first party cares about.[5]

This definition is purposely broad. It describes that point in any ongoing activity when an interaction 'crosses over' to become an inter-party conflict. It encompasses the wide range of conflicts that people experience in organisations—incompatibility of goals, differences over interpretations of facts, disagreements based on behavioural expectations, and the like. Finally, our definition is flexible enough to cover the full range of conflict levels—from overt and violent acts to subtle forms of disagreement.

LEARNING OBJECTIVE

2

Differentiate between the traditional, human relations and interactionist views of conflict

Transitions in Conflict Thought

It is entirely appropriate to say that there has been 'conflict' over the role of conflict in groups and organisations. One school of thought has argued that conflict must be avoided—that it indicates a malfunctioning within the group. We call this the *traditional* view. Another school of thought, the *human relations* view, argues that conflict is a natural and inevitable outcome in any group and that it need not be negative, but rather has the potential to be a positive force in determining group performance. The third, and most recent, perspective proposes not only that conflict can be a positive force in a group but explicitly argues that some conflict is *absolutely necessary* for a group to perform effectively. We label this third school the *interactionist* approach. Let's take a closer look at each of these views.

THE TRADITIONAL VIEW

The early approach to conflict assumed that all conflict was bad. Conflict was viewed negatively, and it was used synonymously with such terms as *violence, destruction* and *irrationality* to reinforce its negative connotation. Conflict, by definition, was harmful and was to be avoided.

The **traditional** view was consistent with the attitudes that prevailed about group behaviour in the 1930s and 1940s. Conflict was seen as a dysfunctional outcome resulting from poor communication, a lack of openness and trust between people, and the failure of managers to be responsive to the needs and aspirations of their employees.

The view that all conflict is bad certainly offers a simple approach to looking at the behaviour of people who create conflict. Since all conflict is to be avoided, we need merely direct our attention to the causes of conflict and correct these malfunctionings in order to improve group and organisational performance. Although research studies now provide strong evidence to dispute that this approach to conflict reduction results in high group performance, many of us still evaluate conflict situations using this outmoded standard.

THE HUMAN RELATIONS VIEW

The **human relations** position argued that conflict was a natural occurrence in all groups and organisations. Since conflict was inevitable, the human relations school advocated acceptance of conflict. Proponents rationalised its existence: it cannot be eliminated, and there are even times when conflict may benefit a group's performance. The human relations view dominated conflict theory from the late 1940s to the mid-1970s.

THE INTERACTIONIST VIEW

While the human relations approach accepted conflict, the **interactionist** approach encourages conflict on the grounds that a harmonious, peaceful, tranquil and cooperative group is prone to becoming static, apathetic and non-responsive to needs for change and innovation.[6] The main contribution of the interactionist approach, therefore, is encouraging group leaders to maintain an ongoing minimum level of conflict—enough to keep the group viable, self-critical and creative.

Given the interactionist view—and it is the one that we shall take in this chapter—it becomes evident that to say conflict is all good or bad is inappropriate and naive. Whether a conflict is good or bad depends on the type of conflict.

Functional versus Dysfunctional Conflict

The interactionist view doesn't propose that all conflicts are good. Rather, some conflicts support the goals of the group and improve its performance; these are **functional**, constructive forms of conflict. In addition, there are conflicts that hinder group performance; these are **dysfunctional** or destructive forms of conflict.

What differentiates functional from dysfunctional conflict? The evidence indicates that you need to look at the *type* of conflict.[7] Specifically, there are three types: task, relationship and process.

Task conflict relates to the content and goals of the work. **Relationship conflict** focuses on interpersonal relationships. **Process conflict** relates to how the work gets done. Studies demonstrate that relationship conflicts are almost always dysfunctional. Why? It appears that the friction and interpersonal hostilities inherent in relationship conflicts increase personality clashes and decrease mutual understanding, which hinders the completion of organisational tasks. On the other hand, low levels of process conflict and low to moderate levels of task conflict are

---

traditional view of conflict
The belief that all conflict is harmful and must be avoided.

human relations view of conflict
The belief that conflict is a natural and inevitable outcome in any group.

interactionist view of conflict
The belief that conflict is not only a positive force in a group but that it is absolutely necessary for a group to perform effectively.

functional conflict
Conflict that supports the goals of the group and improves its performance.

dysfunctional conflict
Conflict that hinders group performance.

LEARNING OBJECTIVE 3

Contrast task, relationship and process conflict

task conflict
Conflicts over content and goals of the work.

relationship conflict
Conflict based on interpersonal relationships.

process conflict
Conflict over how work gets done.

OB Controversies

Avoiding the Christmas party blues

The potential for conflict resides within organisations. As long as you have people working together, there is always the potential for disagreement, and even open hostility, for a variety of reasons. This is very apparent at the end-of-year office Christmas party.

A chief executive officer of the fashion chain store New Look, based in the United Kingdom, had a party he will never forget. He was sacked for touching a female manager and for committing other unacceptable behaviours. Being drunk and foolhardy was no excuse for his actions. According to a representative of the law firm Corrs Chambers Westgarth, alcohol and longstanding workplace tensions can provide a powerful cocktail for an embarrassing celebration resulting in charges of sexual harassment and the threat of legal action. Managers need to be wary of office parties, because of their potential to bring to the surface conflicts that have been simmering under normal work circumstances. They have a legal responsibility for what goes on. One survey suggested that 93 per cent of respondents indicated they had experienced embarrassing behaviour from professional colleagues at office parties.

Managers can avoid such destructive conflicts by setting definite start and finish times and ensuring that all staff are aware of the acceptable standards of behaviour. Alcohol consumption needs to be managed. This can be done by providing food and entertainment and providing advice to anyone drinking heavily. The point is to have fun, but be clear about the fine line between fun and conflict.

Source: Adapted from Anonymous, ''Tis the Season to be Merry', *Human Resources*, January 2002, p. 7. Reproduced with permission.

functional. For process conflict to be productive, it must be kept low. Intense arguments about who should do what become dysfunctional when they create uncertainty about task roles, increase the time required to complete tasks, and lead to members working at cross purposes. Low to moderate levels of task conflict consistently demonstrate a positive effect on group performance because they stimulate discussion of ideas that help groups to perform better.

LEARNING OBJECTIVE

4

Outline the conflict process

The Conflict Process

conflict process
Process with five stages: potential opposition or incompatibility, cognition and personalisation, intentions, behaviour and outcomes.

The **conflict process** can be seen as comprising five stages: potential opposition or incompatibility, cognition and personalisation, intentions, behaviour and outcomes. The process is illustrated in Figure 14.1.

STAGE I: POTENTIAL OPPOSITION OR INCOMPATIBILITY

The first step in the conflict process is the presence of conditions that create opportunities for conflict to arise. They *need not* lead directly to conflict, but one of these conditions is necessary if conflict is to surface. For simplicity's sake, these conditions (which also may be looked at as causes or sources of conflict) have been condensed into three general categories: communication, structure and personal variables.[8]

Communication

Susan had worked in financial management at Herron Pharmaceuticals Pty Ltd for three years. She enjoyed her work in large part because her boss, Andrew Kronios, was a great person to work for. Then, six months ago, Andrew got promoted and Rodney Wong took his place. Susan says her job is a lot more frustrating now. 'Andrew and I were on the same wavelength. It's not that

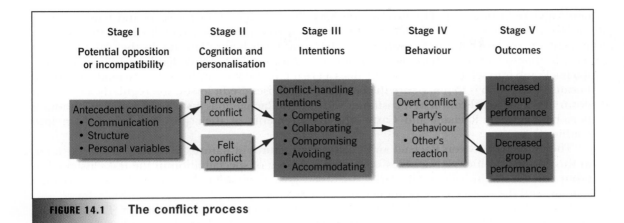

Stage I	Stage II	Stage III	Stage IV	Stage V
Potential opposition or incompatibility	Cognition and personalisation	Intentions	Behaviour	Outcomes

FIGURE 14.1   **The conflict process**

way with Rodney. He tells me something and I do it. Then he tells me I did it wrong. I think he means one thing but says something else. It's been like this since the day he arrived. I don't think a day goes by when he isn't yelling at me for something. You know, there are some people you just find it easy to communicate with. Well, Rodney isn't one of those!'

Susan's comments illustrate that communication can be a source of conflict. It represents the opposing forces that arise from semantic difficulties, misunderstandings and 'noise' in the communication channels. Much of this discussion can be related back to our comments on communication in a previous chapter.

A review of the research suggests that differing word connotations, jargon, insufficient exchange of information, and noise in the communication channel are all barriers to communication and potential antecedent conditions to conflict. Evidence demonstrates that semantic difficulties arise as a result of differences in training, selective perception and inadequate information about others. Research has further demonstrated a surprising finding: the potential for conflict increases when either too little or too much communication takes place. Apparently, an increase in communication is functional up to a point, whereupon it is possible to overcommunicate, with a resultant increase in the potential for conflict. Too much information, as well as too little, can lay the foundation for conflict. Furthermore, the channel chosen for communicating can have an influence on stimulating opposition. The filtering process that occurs as information is passed between members, and the divergence of communications from formal or previously established channels, offer potential opportunities for conflict to arise.

Structure

Rachael and Carly both work at AMART Furniture—a large discount furniture retailer. Rachael is a salesperson on the floor; Carly is the

A lot of conflicts like this one between two department heads, are due to structural relationships created by diverse goals. The HR director waits for money for staff training while the marketing director wants an increased budget for advertising.

company credit manager. The two women have known each other for years and have much in common—they live within two blocks of each other, and their oldest daughters attend the same school and are best friends. In reality, if Rachael and Carly had different jobs they might be best friends themselves, but these two women are consistently fighting battles with each other. Rachael's job is to sell furniture and she does a great job. But most of her sales are made on credit. Because Carly's job is to make sure the company minimises credit losses, she regularly has to turn down the credit application of a customer with whom Rachael has just closed a sale. It's nothing personal between Rachael and Carly—the requirements of their jobs just bring them into conflict.

The conflicts between Rachael and Carly are structural in nature. The term *structure* is used, in this context, to include variables such as size, degree of specialisation in the tasks assigned to group members, jurisdictional clarity, member/goal compatibility, leadership styles, reward systems, and the degree of dependence between groups.

Research indicates that size and specialisation act as forces to stimulate conflict. The larger the group and the more specialised its activities, the greater the likelihood of conflict. Tenure and conflict have been found to be inversely related. The potential for conflict tends to be greatest when group members are younger and when turnover is high.

The greater the ambiguity in precisely defining where responsibility for actions lies, the greater the potential for conflict to emerge. Such jurisdictional ambiguities increase inter-group fighting for control of resources and territory.

Groups within organisations have diverse goals. For example, supply management is concerned with the timely acquisition of inputs at low prices, marketing's goals concentrate on disposing of outputs and increasing revenues, quality control's attention is focused on improving quality and ensuring that the organisation's products meet standards, and production units seek efficiency of operations by maintaining a steady production flow. This diversity of goals among groups is a major source of conflict. When groups within an organisation seek diverse ends, some of which—like sales and credit at AMART Furniture—are inherently at odds, there are increased opportunities for conflict.

There is some indication that a close style of leadership—tight and continuous observation with general control of others' behaviours—increases conflict potential, but the evidence isn't particularly strong. Too much reliance on participation may also stimulate conflict. Research tends to confirm that participation and conflict are highly correlated, apparently because participation encourages the promotion of differences. Reward systems, too, are found to create conflict when one member's gain is at another's expense. Finally, if a group is dependent on another group (in contrast to the two being mutually independent), or if interdependence allows one group to gain at another's expense, opposing forces are stimulated.

Personal variables

Did you ever meet someone to whom you took an immediate dislike? Most of the opinions they expressed, you disagreed with. Even insignificant characteristics—the sound of their voice, the smirk when they smiled, their personality—annoyed you. We've all met people like that. When you have to work with such individuals, there is often the potential for conflict.

Our last category of potential sources of conflict is personal variables. They include the individual value systems that each person has and the personality characteristics that account for individual idiosyncrasies and differences.

The evidence indicates that certain personality types—for example, individuals who are highly authoritarian and dogmatic—lead to potential conflict. Most important, and probably the most overlooked variable in the study of social conflict, is differing value systems. Value differences, for example, are the best explanation of diverse issues such as prejudice, disagreements over one's contribution to the group and the rewards one deserves, and assessments of whether this particular book is any good. That an employee thinks he is worth $55,000 a year but his boss believes him to be worth $50,000, and that Ann thinks this book is interesting to read while Jennifer views

Myth *or* Science?

'The source of most conflicts is lack of communication'

This statement is probably false. A popular myth in organisations is that poor communication is the primary source of conflicts. And certainly, problems in the communication process do act to retard collaboration, stimulate misunderstandings and create conflicts. But a review of the literature suggests that within organisations, structural factors and individual value differences are probably greater sources of conflict.[9]

Conflicts in organisations are frequently structurally derived. For example, conflicts between people in marketing and finance are typically due to their different departmental goals. Marketing staff seek to promote and advertise the company's products and services and always argue for big budget allocations on the basis of 'no customers, no business'. And the finance department's goal of controlling costs and directing budget priorities impinges on the marketing department's objective.

When people have to work together but are pursuing diverse goals, conflicts ensue. Similarly, increased organisational size, routinisation, work specialisation and zero-sum reward systems are all examples of structural factors that can lead to conflicts.

Many conflicts that are attributed to poor communication are, on closer examination, due to value differences. For example, prejudice is a value-based source of conflict. When managers incorrectly treat a value-based conflict as a communication problem, the conflict is rarely eliminated. On the contrary, increased communication efforts are only likely to crystallise and reinforce differences. 'Before this conversation, I thought you might be closed-minded. Now I *know* you are!'

Lack of communication can be a source of conflict. But managers should first look to structural or value-based explanations, since they are more prevalent in organisations.

it as rubbish, are all value judgments. And differences in value systems are important sources for creating the potential for conflict.

STAGE II: COGNITION AND PERSONALISATION

If the conditions cited in Stage I negatively affect something that one party cares about, then the potential for opposition or incompatibility becomes actualised in the second stage. The antecedent conditions can lead to conflict only when one party or more is affected by, and aware of, the conflict.

As we noted in our definition of conflict, perception is required. Therefore, one or more of the parties must be aware of the existence of the antecedent conditions. However, because a conflict is **perceived** doesn't mean that it is personalised. In other words, '*A* may be aware that *B* and *A* are in serious disagreement . . . but it may not make *A* tense or anxious, and it may have no effect whatsoever on *A*'s affection toward *B*.'[10] It is at the **felt** level, when individuals become emotionally involved, that parties experience anxiety, tension, frustration or hostility.

Keep in mind two points. First, Stage II is important because it's where conflict issues tend to be defined. This is the place in the process where the parties decide what the conflict is about.[11] And, in turn, this 'sense making' is critical, because the way a conflict is defined goes a long way towards establishing the sort of outcomes that might settle it. For example, if I define our salary disagreement as a zero-sum situation—that is, if you get the increase in pay you want, there will be just that amount less for me—I am going to be far less willing to compromise than if I frame the conflict as a potential win–win situation (that is, the dollars in the salary pool might be increased so that both of us could get the added pay we want). So, the definition of a conflict is

perceived conflict
Awareness by one or more parties of the existence of conditions that create opportunities for conflict to arise.

felt conflict
Emotional involvement in a conflict creating anxiety, tension, frustration or hostility.

important, because it typically delineates the set of possible settlements. Our second point is that emotions play a major role in shaping perceptions.[12] For example, negative emotions have been found to produce oversimplification of issues, reductions in trust, and negative interpretations of the other party's behaviour.[13] In contrast, positive feelings have been found to increase the tendency to see potential relationships among the elements of a problem, to take a broader view of the situation and to develop more innovative solutions.[14]

STAGE III: INTENTIONS

LEARNING OBJECTIVE

5

Describe the five conflict-handling intentions

intentions
Decisions to act in a given way.

Intentions intervene between people's perceptions and emotions and their overt behaviour. These intentions are decisions to act in a given way.[15] Why are intentions separated out as a distinct stage? You have to infer the other's intent in order to know how to respond to that other's behaviour. A lot of conflicts are escalated merely by one party attributing the wrong intentions to the other party. In addition, there is typically a great deal of slippage between intentions and behaviour, so behaviour doesn't always accurately reflect a person's intentions.

Figure 14.2 represents one author's effort to identify the primary conflict-handling intentions. Using two dimensions—*cooperativeness* (the degree to which one party attempts to satisfy the other party's concerns) and *assertiveness* (the degree to which one party attempts to satisfy their own concerns)—five conflict-handling intentions can be identified: *competing* (assertive and uncooperative), *collaborating* (assertive and cooperative), *avoiding* (unassertive and uncooperative), *accommodating* (unassertive and cooperative) and *compromising* (mid-range on both assertiveness and cooperativeness).[16]

Competing

competing
A desire to satisfy one's interests, regardless of the impact on the other party to the conflict.

When one person seeks to satisfy their own interests, regardless of the impact on the other parties to the conflict, they are **competing**. Examples include intending to achieve your goal at the sacrifice of the other's goal, attempting to convince another that your conclusion is correct and that theirs is mistaken, and trying to make someone else accept blame for a problem.

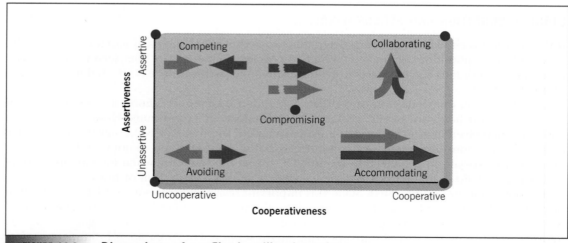

FIGURE 14.2 **Dimensions of conflict-handling intentions**

Source: K. Thomas, 'Conflict and Negotiation Processes in Organizations', in M. D. Dunnette and L. M. Hough (eds), *Handbook of Industrial and Organizational Psychology*, 2nd ed., vol. 3 (Palo Alto, CA: Consulting Psychologists Press, 1992), p. 668. Reproduced with permission.

Collaborating

When the parties to a conflict each desire to fully satisfy the concerns of all parties, we have cooperation and the search for a mutually beneficial outcome. In **collaborating**, the intention of the parties is to solve the problem by clarifying differences rather than by accommodating various points of view. Examples include attempting to find a win–win solution that allows both parties' goals to be completely achieved, and seeking a conclusion that incorporates the valid insights of both parties.

collaborating
A situation in which the parties to a conflict each desire to satisfy fully the concerns of all parties.

Avoiding

A person may recognise that a conflict exists and want to withdraw from it or suppress it. Examples of **avoiding** include trying to ignore a conflict, and avoiding others with whom you disagree.

avoiding
The desire to withdraw from or suppress a conflict.

Accommodating

When one party seeks to appease an opponent, that party may be willing to place the opponent's interests above their own. In other words, in order for the relationship to be maintained, one party is willing to be self-sacrificing. We refer to this intention as **accommodating**. Examples are a willingness to sacrifice your goal so that the other party's goal can be attained, supporting someone else's opinion despite your reservations about it, and forgiving someone for an infraction and allowing subsequent ones.

accommodating
The willingness of one party in a conflict to place the opponent's interests above their own.

Compromising

When each party to the conflict seeks to give up something, sharing occurs, resulting in a compromised outcome. In **compromising**, there is no clear winner or loser. Rather, there is a willingness to ration the object of the conflict and accept a solution that provides incomplete satisfaction of both parties' concerns. The distinguishing characteristic of compromising, therefore, is that each party intends to give up something. Examples might be willingness to accept a raise of $3 an hour rather than $5, to acknowledge partial agreement with a specific viewpoint, and to take partial blame for an infraction.

compromising
A situation in which each party to a conflict is willing to give up something.

Intentions provide general guidelines for parties in a conflict situation. They define each party's purpose. Yet, people's intentions aren't fixed. During the course of a conflict, they might change because of reconceptualisation or because of an emotional reaction to the behaviour of the other party. However, research indicates that people have an underlying disposition to handle conflicts in certain ways.[17] Specifically, individuals have preferences among the five conflict-handling intentions just described; these preferences tend to be relied on quite consistently, and a person's intentions can be predicted rather well from a combination of intellectual and personality characteristics. So, it may be more appropriate to view the five conflict-handling intentions as relatively fixed, rather than as a set of options from which individuals choose to fit an appropriate situation. That is, when confronting a conflict situation, some people want to win it all at any cost, some want to find an optimal solution, some want to run away, others want to be obliging, and still others want to 'split the difference'.

STAGE IV: BEHAVIOUR

When most people think of conflict situations, they tend to focus on Stage IV. Why? Because this is where conflicts become visible. The behaviour stage includes the statements, actions and reactions made by the conflicting parties.

These conflict behaviours are usually overt attempts to implement each party's intentions. But these behaviours have a stimulus quality that is separate from intentions. As a result of miscalculations or unskilled enactments, overt behaviours sometimes deviate from original intentions.[18]

It helps to think of Stage IV as a dynamic process of interaction. For example, you make a demand on me; I respond by arguing; you threaten me; I threaten you back; and so on. Figure 14.3

Annihilatory conflict	Overt efforts to destroy the other party
	Aggressive physical attacks
	Threats and ultimatums
	Assertive verbal attacks
	Overt questioning or challenging of others
	Minor disagreements or misunderstandings
No conflict	

FIGURE 14.3   Conflict intensity continuum

Sources: Based on S. P. Robbins, *Managing Organizational Conflict: A Nontraditional Approach* (Upper Saddle River, NJ: Prentice Hall, 1974), pp. 93–97; and F. Glasl, 'The Process of Conflict Escalation and the Roles of Third Parties', in G. B. J. Bomers and R. Peterson (eds), *Conflict Management and Industrial Relations* (Boston: Kluwer-Nojhoff, 1982), pp. 119–40.

provides a way of visualising conflict behaviour. All conflicts exist somewhere along this continuum. At the lower part of the continuum, we have conflicts characterised by subtle, indirect and highly controlled forms of tension. An illustration might be a student questioning in class a point the lecturer has just made. Conflict intensities escalate as they move upward along the continuum until they become highly destructive. Strikes, riots and wars clearly fall in this upper range. For the most part, you should assume that conflicts that reach the upper ranges of the continuum are almost always dysfunctional. Functional conflicts are typically confined to the lower range of the continuum.

conflict management
The use of resolution and stimulation techniques to achieve the desired level of conflict.

If a conflict is dysfunctional, what can the parties do to de-escalate it? Or, conversely, what options exist if conflict is too low and needs to be increased? This brings us to **conflict management** techniques. Table 14.1 lists the main resolution and stimulation techniques that allow managers to control conflict levels. Note that several of the resolution techniques were described earlier as conflict-handling intentions. This, of course, shouldn't be surprising. Under ideal conditions, a person's intentions should translate into comparable behaviours.

STAGE V: OUTCOMES

The action–reaction interplay between the conflicting parties results in consequences. As our model (see Figure 14.1) demonstrates, these outcomes may be functional in that the conflict results in an improvement in the group's performance, or dysfunctional in that it hinders group performance.

Functional outcomes

How might conflict act as a force to increase group performance? It is hard to visualise a situation in which open or violent aggression could be functional. But there are a number of instances in which it is possible to envision how low or moderate levels of conflict could improve the effectiveness of a group. Because people often find it difficult to think of instances in which conflict can be constructive, let's consider some examples and then review the research evidence. Note how all of these examples focus on task and process conflicts, and exclude the relationship variety.

Conflict is constructive when it improves the quality of decisions, stimulates creativity and innovation, encourages interest and curiosity among group members, provides the medium through which problems can be aired and tensions released, and fosters an environment of self-

TABLE 14.1	Conflict management techniques
Conflict Resolution Techniques	
Problem solving	Face-to-face meeting of the conflicting parties for the purpose of identifying the problem and resolving it through open discussion.
Superordinate goals	Creating a shared goal that cannot be attained without the cooperation of each of the conflicting parties.
Expansion of resources	When a conflict is caused by the scarcity of a resource—say, money, promotion opportunities, office space—expansion of the resource can create a win–win solution.
Avoidance	Withdrawal from, or suppression of, the conflict.
Smoothing	Playing down differences while emphasising common interests between the conflicting parties.
Compromise	Each party to the conflict gives up something of value.
Authoritative command	Management uses its formal authority to resolve the conflict and then communicates its desires to the parties involved.
Altering the human variable	Using behavioural change techniques such as human relations training to alter attitudes and behaviours that cause conflict.
Altering the structural variables	Changing the formal organisation structure and the interaction patterns of conflicting parties through job redesign, transfers, creation of coordinating positions and the like.
Conflict Stimulation Techniques	
Communication	Using ambiguous or threatening messages to increase conflict levels.
Bringing in outsiders	Adding employees to a group whose backgrounds, values, attitudes or managerial styles differ from those of present members.
Restructuring the organisation	Realigning work groups, altering rules and regulations, increasing interdependence, and making similar structural changes to disrupt the status quo.
Appointing a devil's advocate	Designating a critic to purposely argue against the majority positions held by the group.

Source: Based on S. P. Robbins, *Managing Organizational Conflict: A Nontraditional Approach* (Upper Saddle River, NJ: Prentice Hall, 1974), pp. 59–89.

evaluation and change. The evidence suggests that conflict can improve the quality of decision making by allowing all points, particularly the ones that are unusual or held by a minority, to be weighed in important decisions.[19] Conflict is an antidote for groupthink. It doesn't allow the group to passively 'rubber-stamp' decisions that may be based on weak assumptions, inadequate consideration of relevant alternatives or other debilities. Conflict challenges the status quo and therefore furthers the creation of new ideas, promotes reassessment of group goals and activities, and increases the probability that the group will respond to change.

For an example of a company that suffered because it had too little functional conflict, you don't have to look further than automobile behemoth General Motors.[20] Many of GM's problems, from the late 1960s to the late 1990s, can be traced to a lack of functional conflict. It hired and promoted individuals who were 'yes-men', loyal to GM to the point of never questioning company actions. Managers were, for the most part, homogeneous: conservative white males who resisted change—they preferred looking back to past successes rather than forward to new challenges. They were almost sanctimonious in their belief that what had worked in the past would continue to work in the future. Moreover, by sheltering executives in the company's corporate offices and encouraging them to socialise with others inside the GM ranks, the company further insulated managers from conflicting perspectives.

Research studies in diverse settings confirm the functionality of conflict. Consider the following findings.

The comparison of six major decisions made during the administration of four different US presidents found that conflict reduced the chance that groupthink would negatively affect sound policy decisions. The comparisons demonstrated that conformity among presidential advisers was related to poor decisions, whereas an atmosphere of constructive conflict and critical thinking surrounded the well-developed decisions.[21]

There is evidence indicating that conflict can also be positively related to productivity. For example, it was demonstrated that, among established groups, performance tended to improve more when there was conflict among members than when there was fairly close agreement. The investigators observed that when groups analysed decisions that had been made by the individual members of that group, the average improvement among the high-conflict groups was 73 per cent greater than was that of those groups characterised by low-conflict conditions.[22] Others have found similar results: groups composed of members with different interests tend to produce higher-quality solutions to a variety of problems than do homogeneous groups.[23]

The preceding leads us to predict that the increasing cultural diversity of the workforce should provide benefits to organisations. And that's what the evidence indicates. Research demonstrates that heterogeneity among group and organisation members can increase creativity, improve the quality of decisions, and facilitate change by enhancing member flexibility.[24] For example, researchers compared decision-making groups composed of all-Anglo individuals with groups that also contained members from Asian, Hispanic and black ethnic groups. The ethnically diverse groups produced more effective and more feasible ideas, and the unique ideas they generated tended to be of higher quality than the unique ideas produced by the all-Anglo group.

Similarly, studies of professionals—systems analysts, and research and development scientists—support the constructive value of conflict. An investigation of 22 teams of systems analysts found that the more incompatible groups were likely to be more productive.[25] Research and development scientists have been found to be most productive when there is a certain amount of intellectual conflict.[26]

Dysfunctional outcomes

The destructive consequences of conflict on a group's or organisation's performance are generally well known. A reasonable summary might state: uncontrolled opposition breeds discontent, which acts to dissolve common ties, and eventually leads to the destruction of the group. And, of course, there is a substantial body of literature to document how conflict—the dysfunctional varieties—can reduce group effectiveness.[27] Among the more undesirable consequences are a retarding of communication, reductions in group cohesiveness, and subordination of group goals to the primacy of infighting between members. At the extreme, conflict can bring group functioning to a halt and potentially threaten the group's survival.

The demise of an organisation as a result of too much conflict isn't as unusual as it might first appear. For example, the US law firm Shea & Gould closed down solely because the 80 partners just couldn't get along.[28] As one legal consultant, familiar with the organisation, said: 'This was a firm that had basic and principled differences among the partners that were basically irreconcilable.' That same consultant also addressed the partners at their last meeting: 'You don't have an economic problem,' he said. 'You have a personality problem. You hate each other!'

The Real Deal

Can you suffer from an absence of conflict?

This company might well have been the 'poster boy' for the New Economy firm. Begun in 1994, Yahoo! is a clever service for searching the then-fledgling World Wide Web. By 1999, it had become one of the best-known brand names on the Internet and was used by 185 million people worldwide. The company's market value had rocketed to an eye-popping US$134 billion.

The implosion of dot.com shares and the subsequent economic recession hit Yahoo! hard. By the spring of 2001, the share price was down 92 per cent from its peak and advertising sales were plunging. The company still had a valuable brand name, easy-to-use and high-quality services, and a record of profitability. Yet, its most critical problem was now exposed for everyone to see: Yahoo! was too insulated and void of functional conflict.

Yahoo! suffered from having managers and staff who were too comfortable with each other. It is a tone that had been directly set at the top by the company's CEO, Tim Koogle. Yahoo!'s corporate mentality was one of non-confrontation. This kept new ideas from percolating upward and held dissent to a minimum. It began with the company's inbred board—made up of a small group of insiders and friends of insiders. There was no one on the board with the courage or perspective to challenge company practices. This intense closeness by insiders also made it hard for the company to attract or retain experienced managers. Many left when they were unable to penetrate the company's inner sanctum. Yahoo!'s top European and Asian executives and many middle managers also left, amid complaints that the top team wouldn't delegate authority.

The company is 'very insular', says a former executive. 'They see the world through the Yahoo! lens.' This insularity also carries over into an arrogant attitude of 'we know better than anyone else'. Over the years, its Yahoo!-way-or-the-highway approach stifled new ideas and frustrated talented people who were outside the power core.

Yahoo! took the first step towards changing its conflict-free climate in March 2001 when it announced that it would launch a search for a new chief executive to replace Koogle.

Sources: Based on K. Swisher, 'Yahoo! May Be Down, But Don't Count It Out', *Wall Street Journal*, 9 March 2001, p. B1; and M. Mangalindan and S. L. Hwang, 'Coterie of Early Hires Made Yahoo! A Hit but an Insular Place', *Wall Street Journal*, 9 March 2001, p. A1.

Yahoo! suffered from having managers and staff who were too comfortable with each other. It began a search for a CEO who could stimulate constructive conflict.

www.yahoo.com.au

Creating functional conflict

We briefly mentioned conflict stimulation as part of Stage IV of the conflict process. In this section we ask: If managers accept the interactionist view towards conflict, what can they do to encourage functional conflict in their organisations?[29]

There seems to be general agreement that creating functional conflict is a tough job, particularly in large corporations. As one consultant put it, 'A high proportion of people who get to the top are conflict avoiders. They don't like hearing negatives, they don't like saying or thinking negative things. They frequently make it up the ladder in part because they don't irritate people on the way up.' Another suggests that at least seven out of ten people in business hush up when their opinions are at odds with those of their superiors, allowing bosses to make mistakes even when they know better. This is a concern for businesses around the world.

Such anti-conflict cultures may have been tolerable in the past but not in today's fiercely competitive global economy. Organisations that don't encourage and support dissent may find their survival threatened. Let's look at some approaches organisations are using to encourage their people to challenge the system and develop fresh ideas.

The Walt Disney Company purposely encourages big, unruly and disruptive meetings to create friction and stimulate creative ideas. The computer company Hewlett-Packard rewards dissenters by recognising go-against-the-grain types, or people who stay with the ideas they believe in even when those ideas are rejected by management. Staff at the Beechworth Bakery in Victoria are also encouraged by the proprietor, Tom O'Toole, to criticise their bosses if service or products aren't up to standard. IBM also has a formal system that encourages dissension. Employees can question their boss with impunity. If the disagreement can't be resolved, the system provides a third party for counsel.

Royal Dutch Shell Group, General Electric and Anheuser-Busch build devil's advocates into the decision process. For example, when the policy committee at Anheuser-Busch considers a major move, such as getting into or out of a business or making a major capital expenditure, it often assigns teams to make the case for each side of the question. This process frequently results in decisions and alternatives that hadn't been considered previously.

One common ingredient in organisations that successfully create functional conflict is that they reward dissent and punish conflict avoiders. The real challenge for managers, however, is when they hear news that they don't want to hear. The news may make their blood boil or their hopes collapse, but they can't show it. They have to learn to take the bad news without flinching. No tirades, no tight-lipped sarcasm, no eyes rolling upward, no gritting of teeth. Rather, managers should ask calm, even-tempered questions: 'Can you tell me more about what happened?' 'What do you think we ought to do?' A sincere 'Thank you for bringing this to my attention' will probably reduce the likelihood that managers will be cut off from similar communications in the future.

| Negotiation

Negotiation permeates the interactions of almost everyone in groups and organisations. There's the obvious: labour bargains with management. There's the not so obvious: managers negotiate with employees, peers and bosses; salespeople negotiate with customers; purchasing agents negotiate with suppliers. And there's the subtle: a worker agrees to answer a colleague's phone for a few minutes in exchange for some past or future benefit. In today's team-based organisations, in which members are increasingly finding themselves having to work with colleagues over whom they have no direct authority and with whom they may not even share a common boss, negotiation skills become critical.

We will define **negotiation** as a process in which two or more parties exchange goods or services and attempt to agree on the exchange rate for them.[30] Note that we use the terms *negotiation* and *bargaining* interchangeably.

negotiation
A process in which two or more parties exchange goods or services and attempt to agree on the exchange rate for them.

In this section, we will contrast two bargaining strategies, provide a model of the negotiation process, ascertain the role of personality traits on bargaining, review gender and cultural differences in negotiation, and take a brief look at third-party negotiations.

BARGAINING STRATEGIES

There are two general approaches to negotiation—*distributive bargaining* and *integrative bargaining*.[31] These are compared in Table 14.2.

Distributive bargaining

You see a used car advertised for sale in the newspaper. It appears to be just what you have been looking for. You go out to see the car. It's great and you want it. The owner tells you the asking price. You don't want to pay that much. The two of you then negotiate over the price. The negotiating strategy you are engaging in is called **distributive bargaining**. Its most identifying feature is that it operates under zero-sum conditions. That is, any gain I make is at your expense, and vice versa. Referring back to the used car example, every dollar you can get the seller to cut from the car's price is a dollar you save. Conversely, every dollar more the seller can get from you comes at your expense. So, the essence of distributive bargaining is negotiating over who gets what share of a fixed pie.

Probably the most widely cited example of distributive bargaining is in labour–management negotiations over wages. Typically, labour's representatives come to the bargaining table determined to get as much money as possible out of management. Since every cent more that labour negotiates increases management's costs, each party bargains aggressively and treats the other as an opponent who must be defeated.

The essence of distributive bargaining is depicted in Figure 14.4. Parties *A* and *B* represent two negotiators. Each has a *target point* that defines what they would like to achieve. Each also has a *resistance point*, which marks the lowest outcome that is acceptable—the point below which they would break off negotiations rather than accept a less-favourable settlement. The area between these two points makes up each one's aspiration range. As long as there is some overlap between *A* and *B*'s aspiration ranges, there exists a settlement range in which each one's aspirations can be met.

When engaged in distributive bargaining, one's tactics focus on trying to get one's opponent to agree to one's specific target point or to get as close to it as possible. Examples of such tactics are persuading your opponent of the impossibility of getting to their target point and the advisability of accepting a settlement near yours; arguing that your target is fair, while your opponent's isn't; and attempting to get your opponent to feel emotionally generous towards you and thus accept an outcome close to your target point.

LEARNING OBJECTIVE

6

Contrast distributive and integrative bargaining

distributive bargaining Negotiation that seeks to divide up a fixed amount of resources; a win–lose situation.

TABLE 14.2	**Distributive versus integrative bargaining**	
Bargaining Characteristic	**Distributive Characteristic**	**Integrative Characteristic**
Available resources	Fixed amount of resources to be divided	Variable amount of resources to be divided
Primary motivations	I win, you lose	I win, you win
Primary interests	Opposed to each other	Convergent or congruent with each other
Focus of relationships	Short term	Long term

Source: Based on R. J. Lewicki and J. A. Litterer, *Negotiation* (Homewood, IL: Irwin, 1985), p. 280.

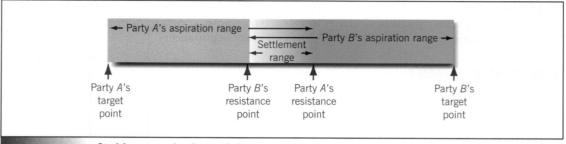

FIGURE 14.4   **Staking out the bargaining zone**

Integrative bargaining

A sales representative for a women's sportswear manufacturer has just finalised a $15,000 order from a small clothing retailer. The sales rep phones in the order to her firm's credit department. She is told that the firm can't approve credit to this customer because of a past slow-payment record. The next day, the sales rep and the firm's credit manager meet to discuss the problem. The sales rep doesn't want to lose the business. Neither does the credit manager, but he also doesn't want to get stuck with an uncollectable debt. The two openly review their options. After considerable discussion, they agree on a solution that meets both their needs: the credit manager will approve the sale, but the clothing store's owner will provide a bank guarantee that will ensure payment if the account isn't paid within 60 days.

integrative bargaining
Negotiation that seeks one or more settlements that can create a win–win solution.

This sales–credit negotiation is an example of **integrative bargaining**. In contrast to distributive bargaining, integrative problem solving operates under the assumption that there exists one or more settlements that can create a win–win solution.

In terms of intraorganisational behaviour, all things being equal, integrative bargaining is preferable to distributive bargaining. Why? Because the former builds long-term relationships and facilitates working together in the future. It bonds negotiators and allows each to leave the bargaining table feeling that they have achieved a victory. Distributive bargaining, on the other hand, leaves one party a loser. It tends to build animosities and deepen divisions when people have to work together on an ongoing basis.

Why, then, don't we see more integrative bargaining in organisations? The answer lies in the conditions necessary for this type of negotiation to succeed. These include parties who are open with information and candid about their concerns, a sensitivity by both parties to the other's needs, the ability to trust one another, and a willingness by both parties to maintain flexibility.[32] Since these conditions often don't exist in organisations, it isn't surprising that negotiations often take on a win-at-any-cost dynamic.

Australian and French trade negotiators have moved from distributative to more integrative. Slowly, as relations between the two countries improve, the various leaders and their negotiation teams have become more open, candid and sensitive to each other's needs.

THE NEGOTIATION PROCESS

LEARNING OBJECTIVE

7

Identify the five steps in the negotiation process

Figure 14.5 provides a simplified model of the negotiation process. It views negotiation as made up of five steps: (1) preparation and planning; (2) definition of ground rules; (3) clarification and justification; (4) bargaining and problem solving; and (5) closure and implementation.[33]

Preparation and planning

Before you start negotiating, you need to do your homework. What is the nature of the conflict? What is the history leading up to this negotiation? Who is involved and what are their perceptions of the conflict?

What do you want from the negotiation? What are *your* goals? If you are a supply manager at Dell Computer, for example, and your goal is to get a significant cost reduction from your supplier of keyboards, make sure that this goal stays paramount in your discussions and doesn't get overshadowed by other issues. It often helps to put your goals in writing and develop a range of outcomes—from 'most hopeful' to 'minimally acceptable'—to keep your attention focused.

You also want to prepare an assessment of what you think are the goals of the other party to your negotiation. What are they likely to ask for? How entrenched are they likely to be in their position? What intangible or hidden interests may be important to them? What might they be willing to settle on? When you can anticipate your opponent's position, you are better equipped to counter their arguments with the facts and figures that support your position.

The importance of sizing up the other party is illustrated by the experience of Keith Rosenbaum, a partner in a major American law firm. 'Once when we were negotiating to buy a business, we found that the owner was going through a nasty divorce. We were on good terms with the wife's attorney and we learned the seller's net worth. California is a community-property-law state, so we knew he had to pay her half of everything. We knew his time frame. We knew what he was willing to part with and what he was not. We knew a lot more about him than he would have wanted us to know. We were able to twist him a little bit, and get a better price.'[34]

Once you have gathered your information, use it to develop a strategy. For example, expert chess players have a strategy. They know ahead of time how they will respond to any given situation. As part of your strategy, you should determine yours and the other side's *Best Alternative To a Negotiated Agreement* (**BATNA**).[35] Your BATNA determines the lowest value acceptable to you for a negotiated agreement. Any offer you receive that is higher than your BATNA is better than an impasse. Conversely, you shouldn't expect success in your negotiation effort unless you are able to make the other side an offer they find more attractive than their BATNA. If you go into your negotiation having a good idea of what the other party's BATNA is, even if you are not able to meet theirs, you might be able to get them to change it.

BATNA
The best alternative to a negotiated agreement; the lowest acceptable value to an individual for a negotiated agreement.

Definition of ground rules

Once you have done your planning and developed a strategy, you are ready to begin defining the ground rules and procedures with the other party over the negotiation itself. Who will do the negotiating? Where will it take place? What time constraints, if any, will apply? To what issues will negotiation be limited? Will there be a specific procedure to follow if an impasse is reached? During this phase, the parties will also exchange their initial proposals or demands.

Clarification and justification

When initial positions have been exchanged, both you and the other party will explain, amplify, clarify, bolster and justify your original demands. This needn't be confrontational. Rather, it is an opportunity

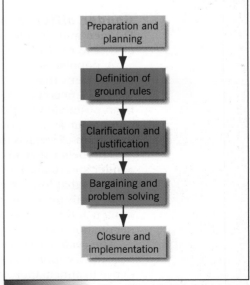

FIGURE 14.5   **The negotiation process**

for educating and informing each other on the issues, why they are important, and how each arrived at their initial demands. This is the point at which you might want to provide the other party with any documentation that helps to support your position.

Bargaining and problem solving

The essence of the negotiation process is the actual give-and-take in trying to hash out an agreement. It is here where concessions will undoubtedly need to be made by both parties.

Closure and implementation

The final step in the negotiation process is formalising the agreement that has been worked out and developing any procedures that are necessary for implementation and monitoring. For major negotiations—which would include everything from labour–management negotiations, to bargaining over lease terms, to buying a piece of real estate, to negotiating a job offer for a senior-management position—this will require hammering out the specifics in a formal contract. For most cases, however, closure of the negotiation process is nothing more formal than a handshake.

ISSUES IN NEGOTIATION

We conclude our discussion of negotiation by reviewing four contemporary issues in negotiation: the role of personality traits, gender differences in negotiating, the effect of cultural differences on negotiating styles, and the use of third parties to help resolve differences.

The role of personality traits in negotiation

Can you predict an opponent's negotiating tactics if you know something about their personality? It's tempting to answer 'yes' to this question. For example, you might assume that high risk takers would be more aggressive bargainers who make fewer concessions. Surprisingly, the evidence doesn't support this intuition.[36]

Overall assessments of the personality–negotiation relationship find that personality traits have no significant direct effect on either the bargaining process or the negotiation outcomes. This conclusion is important. It suggests that you should concentrate on the issues and the situational factors in each bargaining episode and not on your opponent's personality.

Gender differences in negotiations

Do men and women negotiate differently? And does gender affect negotiation outcomes? The answer to the first question appears to be 'no'.[37] The answer to the second is a qualified 'yes'.[38]

A popular stereotype held by many is that women are more cooperative and pleasant in negotiations than are men. The evidence doesn't support this belief. However, men have been found to negotiate better outcomes than women, although the difference is quite small. It's been postulated that this difference might be due to men and women placing divergent values on outcomes. 'It is possible that a few hundred dollars more in salary or the corner office is less important to women than forming and maintaining an interpersonal relationship.'[39]

The belief that women are 'nicer' than men in negotiations is probably due to confusing gender and the lack of power typically held by women in most large organisations. The research indicates that low-power managers, regardless of gender, attempt to placate their opponents and to use softly persuasive tactics rather than direct confrontation and threats. In situations in which women and men have similar power bases, there shouldn't be any significant differences in their negotiation styles.

The evidence suggests that women's attitudes towards negotiation and towards themselves as negotiators appear to be quite different from men's. Managerial women demonstrate less confidence in anticipation of negotiating and are less satisfied with their performance after the process is complete, even when their performance and the outcomes they achieve are similar to those for men.

Cultural differences in negotiations

Although there appears to be no significant direct relationship between an individual's personality and negotiation style, cultural background does seem to be relevant. Negotiating styles clearly vary across national cultures.[40]

LEARNING OBJECTIVE

8

Describe cultural differences in negotiations

The French like conflict. They frequently gain recognition and develop their reputations by thinking and acting against others. As a result, the French tend to take a long time in negotiating agreements and they aren't overly concerned about whether their opponents like or dislike them.[41] The Chinese also draw out negotiations, but that's because they believe negotiations never end. Just when you think you have pinned down every detail and reached a final solution with a Chinese executive, that executive might smile and start the process all over again. Like the Japanese, the Chinese negotiate to develop a relationship and a commitment to work together rather than to tie up every loose end.[42] Americans are known around the world for their impatience and their desire to be liked.[43] Astute negotiators from other countries often turn these characteristics to their advantage by dragging out negotiations and making friendship conditional on the final settlement. Figure 14.6 offers some insights into how managers can have trouble in cross-cultural negotiations.

The cultural context of the negotiation significantly influences the amount and type of preparation for bargaining, the relative emphasis on task versus interpersonal relationships, the tactics used, and even where the negotiation should be conducted. To further illustrate some of these differences, let's look at two studies that compare the influence of culture on business negotiations.

The first study compared North Americans, Arabs and Russians.[44] Among the factors that were looked at were their negotiating style, how they responded to an opponent's arguments, their approach to making concessions, and how they handled negotiating deadlines. North Americans tried to persuade by relying on facts and appealing to logic. They countered opponents' arguments with objective facts. They made small concessions early in the negotiation to establish a relationship, and usually reciprocated opponents' concessions. North Americans treated deadlines as very important. The Arabs tried to persuade by appealing to emotion. They countered opponent's arguments with subjective feelings. They made concessions throughout the bargaining process and almost always reciprocated opponents' concessions. Arabs approached deadlines very casually. The Russians based their arguments on asserted ideals. They made few, if any, concessions. Any concession offered by an opponent was viewed as a weakness and was almost never reciprocated. Finally, the Russians tended to ignore deadlines.

- Some managers use small talk in meetings and lots of it. This tests the patience of Israelis who are used to the fast pace of meetings. While Americans encourage informal and spontaneous chatter, the British see this as unnecessary.

- Some managers like to be loud and vocal. Indian managers can sound argumentative and like to interrupt one another. They may feel others aren't paying attention if they don't join in the conversation. However, with Malaysian and Japanese executives, short intervals of silence should be observed during negotiations.

- Some managers like to offer praise before they start to criticise someone. To some Europeans such as French, Germans and Italians, this can cause some concern as it can be seen as a manipulative tactic.

- Some managers like to organise their meetings with visitors and have all attendees wear name tags. To some Europeans, this can be taken as childish behaviour.

FIGURE 14.6   **How managers can have trouble in cross-cultural negotiations**

Source: Based on L. Khosla, 'You Say Tomato', *Forbes*, 21 May 2001, p. 36.

The second study looked at verbal and non-verbal negotiation tactics exhibited by North Americans, Japanese and Brazilians during half-hour bargaining sessions.[45] Some of the differences were particularly interesting. For example, the Brazilians, on average, said 'no' 83 times, compared to five times for the Japanese and nine times for the North Americans. The Japanese displayed more than five periods of silence lasting longer than ten seconds during the 30-minute sessions. North Americans averaged 3.5 such periods; the Brazilians had none. The Japanese and North Americans interrupted their opponent about the same number of times, but the Brazilians interrupted 2.5 to 3 times more often than the North Americans and the Japanese. Finally, while the Japanese and the North Americans had no physical contact with their opponents during negotiations except for handshaking, the Brazilians touched each other almost five times every half-hour.

Third-party negotiations

To this point, we have discussed bargaining in terms of direct negotiations. Occasionally, however, individuals or group representatives reach a stalemate and are unable to resolve their differences through direct negotiations. In such cases, they may turn to a third party to help them find a solution. There are four basic third-party roles: mediator, arbitrator, conciliator and consultant.[46]

mediator
A neutral third party who facilitates a negotiated solution by using reasoning, persuasion and suggestions for alternatives.

A **mediator** is a neutral third party who facilitates a negotiated solution by using reasoning and persuasion, suggesting alternatives, and the like. Mediators are widely used in labour–management negotiations and in civil court disputes.

The overall effectiveness of mediated negotiations is fairly impressive. The settlement rate is approximately 60 per cent, with negotiator satisfaction at about 75 per cent. But the situation is the key to whether or not mediation will succeed; the conflicting parties must be motivated to bargain and resolve their conflict. In addition, conflict intensity can't be too high; mediation is most effective under moderate levels of conflict. Finally, perceptions of the mediator are important; to be effective, the mediator must be perceived as neutral and non-coercive.

arbitrator
A third party to a negotiation who has the authority to dictate an agreement.

An **arbitrator** is a third party with the authority to dictate an agreement. Arbitration can be voluntary (requested) or compulsory (forced on the parties by law or contract).

The authority of the arbitrator varies according to the rules set by the negotiators. For example, the arbitrator might be limited to choosing one of the negotiator's last offers or to suggesting an agreement point that is non-binding, or free to choose and make any judgment they wish.

The big plus of arbitration over mediation is that it always results in a settlement. Whether or not there is a negative side depends on how 'heavy-handed' the arbitrator appears. If one party is left feeling overwhelmingly defeated, that party is certain to be dissatisfied and unlikely to graciously accept the arbitrator's decision. Therefore, the conflict may resurface at a later time.

conciliator
A trusted third party who provides an informal communication link between the negotiator and the opponent.

A **conciliator** is a trusted third party who provides an informal communication link between the negotiator and the opponent. This role was made famous by Robert Duval in the first *Godfather* film. As Don Corleone's adopted son and a lawyer by training, Duval acted as an intermediary between the Corleone family and the other Mafioso families. In Australia in the 1970s, when an industrial dispute between a union and an employer or industry seemed to be totally unresolvable, when arbitration had failed, and the impact of the dispute was causing huge financial losses and/or suffering by innocent parties (for example, during public transport strikes), Bob Hawke, the then president of the ACTU (Australian Council of Trade Unions), was often called upon by either or both of the disputing parties to act as an intermediary. Although he had no authority to conciliate the dispute, he was widely respected by most employers, industry groups and union leaders, and the general public. The respect he gained in this capacity was a significant factor in his election to Parliament and, later, in his becoming prime minister of Australia in 1983. Even since he retired from public office in 1995, he has often been called upon to act as a conciliator in very bitter negotiations.

Conciliation is used extensively in international, labour, family and community disputes. Comparing its effectiveness to mediation has proven difficult because the two overlap a great deal. In practice, conciliators typically act as more than mere communication conduits. They also engage in fact finding, interpreting messages, and persuading disputants to develop agreements.

A **consultant** is a skilled and impartial third party who attempts to facilitate problem solving through communication and analysis, aided by their knowledge of conflict management. In contrast to the previous roles, the consultant's role isn't to settle the issues but, rather, to improve relations between the conflicting parties so that they can reach a settlement themselves. Instead of putting forward specific solutions, the consultant tries to help the parties learn to understand and work with each other. Therefore, this approach has a longer-term focus: to build new and positive perceptions and attitudes between the conflicting parties.

consultant
An impartial third party, skilled in conflict management, who attempts to facilitate creative problem solving through communication and analysis.

Summary and Implications for Managers

Many people automatically assume that conflict is related to lower group and organisational performance. This chapter has demonstrated that this assumption is frequently incorrect. Conflict can be either constructive or destructive to the functioning of a group or unit. As shown in Figure 14.7, levels of conflict can be either too high or too low. Either extreme hinders performance. An optimal level is one at which there is enough conflict to prevent stagnation, stimulate creativity, allow tensions to be released, and initiate the seeds for change, yet not so much as to be disruptive or to deter coordination of activities.

Inadequate or excessive levels of conflict can hinder the effectiveness of a group or an organisation, resulting in reduced satisfaction of group members, increased absence and turnover rates, and, eventually, lower productivity. On the other hand, when conflict is at an optimal level, complacency and apathy should be minimised, motivation should be enhanced through the creation of a challenging and questioning environment with a vitality that makes work interesting, and there should be the amount of turnover needed to rid the organisation of misfits and poor performers.

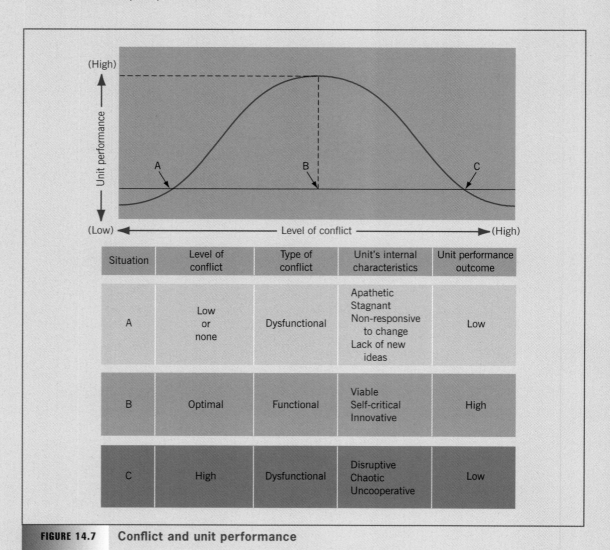

Situation	Level of conflict	Type of conflict	Unit's internal characteristics	Unit performance outcome
A	Low or none	Dysfunctional	Apathetic Stagnant Non-responsive to change Lack of new ideas	Low
B	Optimal	Functional	Viable Self-critical Innovative	High
C	High	Dysfunctional	Disruptive Chaotic Uncooperative	Low

FIGURE 14.7 **Conflict and unit performance**

What advice can we give managers faced with excessive conflict and the need to reduce it? Don't assume there is one conflict-handling intention that will always be best! You should select an intention appropriate for the situation. The following provides some guidelines:[47]

- Use *competition* when quick, decisive action is vital (in emergencies); on important issues, where unpopular actions need implementing (in cost cutting, enforcing unpopular rules, discipline); on issues vital to the organisation's welfare when you know you are right; and against people who take advantage of non-competitive behaviour.
- Use *collaboration* to find an integrative solution when both sets of concerns are too important to be compromised; when your objective is to learn; to merge insights from people with different perspectives; to gain commitment by incorporating concerns into a consensus; and to work through feelings that have interfered with a relationship.
- Use *avoidance* when an issue is trivial, or more important issues are pressing; when you perceive no chance of satisfying your concerns; when potential disruption outweighs the benefits of resolution; to let people cool down and regain perspective; when gathering information supersedes immediate decision; when others can resolve the conflict more effectively; and when issues seem tangential or symptomatic of other issues.
- Use *accommodation* when you find you are wrong and to allow a better position to be heard, to learn and to show your reasonableness; when issues are more important to others than to yourself and to satisfy others and maintain cooperation; to build social credits for later issues; to minimise loss when you are outmatched and losing; when harmony and stability are especially important; and to allow employees to develop by learning from mistakes.
- Use *compromise* when goals are important but not worth the effort of potential disruption of more assertive approaches; when opponents with equal power are committed to mutually exclusive goals; to achieve temporary settlements to complex issues; to arrive at expedient solutions under time pressure; and as a backup when collaboration or competition is unsuccessful.

Negotiation was shown to be an ongoing activity in groups and organisations. Distributive bargaining can resolve disputes, but it often negatively affects one or more negotiators' satisfaction because it is focused on the short term and is confrontational. Integrative bargaining, in contrast, tends to provide outcomes that satisfy all parties and build lasting relationships.

Point

CONFLICT BENEFITS ORGANISATIONS

Let's briefly review how stimulating conflict can provide benefits to the organisation.

- Conflict is a means by which to bring about radical change. It is an effective device by which management can drastically change the existing power structure, current interaction patterns and entrenched attitudes.
- Conflict facilitates group cohesiveness. While conflict increases hostility between groups, external threats tend to cause a group to pull together as a unit. Intergroup conflicts raise the extent to which members identify with their own group and increase feelings of solidarity.
- Conflict improves group and organisational effectiveness. The stimulation of conflict initiates the search for new means and goals, and clears the way for innovation. The successful solution of a conflict leads to greater effectiveness, to more trust and openness, to greater attraction of members for each other, and to depersonalisation of future conflicts.
- Conflict brings about a slightly higher, more constructive level of tension. When the level of tension is very low, the parties aren't sufficiently motivated to do something about a conflict.

Groups or organisations devoid of conflict are likely to suffer from apathy, stagnation, groupthink and other debilitating diseases. In fact, more organisations probably fail because they have too little conflict, not because they have too much. Take a look at a list of large organisations that have failed or suffered serious financial setbacks over the past decade or two. You see names such as General Motors, Kmart, Ansett Airlines, Greyhound and Digital Computer. The common thread running through these companies is that they stagnated. Their managements became complacent and unable or unwilling to facilitate change. These organisations could have benefited from functional conflict.

Counterpoint

It may be true that conflict is an inherent part of any group or organisation. It may not be possible to eliminate it completely. However, just because conflicts exist is no reason to deify them. All conflicts are dysfunctional, and it's one of management's main responsibilities to keep conflict intensity as low as humanly possible. A few points will support this case.

- The negative consequences of conflict can be devastating. The list of negatives associated with conflict is awesome. The most obvious are increased turnover, decreased employee satisfaction, inefficiencies between work units, sabotage, labour grievances and strikes, and physical aggression.
- Effective managers build teamwork. A good manager builds a coordinated team. Conflict works against such an objective. A successful work group is like a successful sports team; each member knows their role and supports their team-mates. When a team works well, the whole becomes greater than the sum of the parts. Management creates teamwork by minimising internal conflicts and facilitating internal coordination.
- Managers who accept and stimulate conflict don't survive in organisations. The whole argument on the value of conflict may be moot as long as the majority of senior executives in organisations have a traditional view of conflict. In the traditional view, any conflict will be seen as bad. Since the evaluation of a manager's performance is made by higher-level executives, those managers who don't succeed in eliminating conflicts are likely to be appraised negatively. This, in turn, will reduce opportunities for advancement. Any manager who aspires to move up in such an environment will be wise to follow the traditional view and eliminate any outward signs of conflict. Failure to follow this advice might result in the premature departure of the manager.

For Discussion

1. What are the disadvantages of conflict? What are its advantages?
2. What is the difference between functional and dysfunctional conflict? What determines functionality?
3. Under what conditions might conflict be beneficial to a group?
4. What are the components in the conflict process model? From your own experiences, give an example of how a conflict proceeded through the five stages.
5. How could a manager stimulate conflict in their department?
6. What defines the settlement range in distributive bargaining?
7. Why isn't integrative bargaining more widely practised in organisations?
8. How do men and women differ, if at all, in their approaches to negotiation?
9. What problems might Australians or New Zealanders have in negotiating with people from collectivist cultures such as China and Japan?
10. What can you do to improve your negotiating effectiveness?
11. Do you think competition and conflict are different? Explain.
12. 'Participation is an excellent method for identifying differences and resolving conflicts.' Do you agree or disagree? Discuss.

Exercise

A NEGOTIATION ROLE PLAY

This role play is designed to help you develop your negotiating skills. The class is to break into pairs. One person will play the role of Alex, the department supervisor. The other person will play CJ, Alex's boss.

The situation:
Alex and CJ work for the Nike Corporation. Alex supervises a research laboratory. CJ is the manager of research and development. Alex and CJ are former university runners who have worked for Nike for more than six years. CJ has been Alex's boss for two years.

One of Alex's employees, Lisa Roland, has greatly impressed Alex. Lisa was hired 11 months ago, is 24 years old and holds a master's degree in mechanical engineering. Her entry-level salary was $37,500 a year. She was told by Alex that, in accordance with company policy, she would receive an initial performance evaluation at six months and a comprehensive review after one year. She was also told that she could expect a salary adjustment at the time of the one-year evaluation, based on her performance record.

Alex's evaluation of Lisa after six months was very positive. Alex commented on the long hours Lisa was putting in, her cooperative spirit, the fact that others in the lab enjoyed working with her, and that she was making an immediate positive impact on the project to which she had been assigned. Now that Lisa's first anniversary is coming up, Alex has again reviewed Lisa's performance. Alex thinks Lisa may be the best new person the R&D group has ever hired. After only a year, Alex has ranked Lisa as the number-three performer in a department of 11.

Salaries in the department vary greatly. Alex, for instance, has a basic salary of $67,000, plus eligibility for a bonus that might add another $5,000 to $8,000 a year. The salary range of the 11 department members is $30,400 to $56,350. The lowest salary is a recent hire with a bachelor's degree in physics. The two people that Alex has rated above Lisa earn base salaries of $52,700 and $56,350. They are both 27 years old and have been at the Nike Corporation for three and four years, respectively. The median salary in Alex's department is $46,660.

Alex's role:

You want to give Lisa a big raise. Although she's young, she has proven to be an excellent addition to the department. You don't want to lose her. More importantly, she knows in general what other people in the department are earning and she thinks she's underpaid. The company typically gives one-year raises of 5 per cent, although 10 per cent isn't unusual and 20–30 per cent increases have been approved on occasion. You would like to get Lisa as large an increase as CJ will approve.

CJ's role:

All your supervisors typically try to squeeze you for as much money as they can for their people. You understand this because you did the same thing when you were a supervisor, but your boss wants to keep a lid on costs. He wants you to keep raises for recent hires generally in the 5–8 per cent range. In fact, he's sent a memo to all managers and supervisors saying this. However, your boss is also very concerned with equity and paying people what they are worth. You feel assured that he will support any salary recommendation you make, as long as it can be justified. Your goal, consistent with cost reduction, is to keep salary increases as low as possible.

The negotiation:

Alex has a meeting scheduled with CJ to discuss Lisa's performance review and salary adjustment. Take a couple of minutes to think through the facts in this exercise and to prepare a strategy. Then you have up to 15 minutes to conduct your negotiation. When your negotiation is complete, the class will compare the various strategies used and compare outcomes.

Case Study 14

Working at ThinkLink

Mallory Murray hadn't had much experience working as part of a team. A recent graduate of the University of Southern Queensland, her business program had focused primarily on individual projects and accomplishments. What little exposure she had had to teams was in her organisational behaviour, marketing research and strategy formulation courses. When she was interviewed by ThinkLink, an educational software firm, she didn't give much concern to the fact that ThinkLink made extensive use of cross-functional teams. During on-site interviews, she told interviewers and managers alike that she had limited experience on teams. But she did tell them she worked well with people and thought that she could be an effective team player. Unfortunately, Mallory Murray was mistaken.

Mallory joined ThinkLink as an assistant marketing manager for the company's high school core programs. These are essentially software programs designed to help students learn algebra and geometry. Mallory's boss is Lin Chen (marketing manager). Other members of the team she is currently working with include Todd Schlotsky (senior programmer), Laura Willow (advertising), Sean Traynor (director of strategic marketing), Joyce Rothman (co-founder of ThinkLink, who now works only part-time in the company, formerly a high school maths teacher, and the formal leader of this project) and Harlow Gray (educational consultant).

After her first week on the job, Mallory was seriously thinking about quitting. 'I never imagined how difficult it would be working with people who are so opinionated and competitive. Every decision seems to be a power contest. Sean, Joyce and Harlow are particularly troublesome. Sean thinks his rank entitles him to the last word. Joyce thinks her opinions should carry more weight because she was instrumental in creating the company. And Harlow views everyone as less knowledgeable than he is. Because he consults with a number of software firms and education departments, Harlow's a "know-it-all". To make things worse, Lin is passive and quiet. He rarely speaks up in meetings and appears to want to avoid any conflicts.'

'What makes my job particularly difficult,' Mallory went on, 'is that I don't have any specific job responsibilities. It seems that someone else is always interfering with what I'm doing or telling me how to do it. Our team has seven members—six chiefs and me!'

The project that Mallory's team is working on has a deadline of only six weeks away. Currently the team is at least two weeks behind schedule. Everyone is aware that there is a problem, but no one seems to be able to solve it. What is especially frustrating to Mallory is that neither Lin Chen nor Joyce Rothman is showing any leadership. Lin is preoccupied with a number of other projects, and Joyce can't seem to control Sean and Harlow's strong personalities.

Questions

1. Discuss cross-functional teams in terms of their propensity to create conflict.
2. What techniques or procedures might help to reduce conflict on cross-functional teams?
3. If you were Mallory, is there anything you could do to lessen the conflict on the core project? Elaborate.

Web Workout

1. Let's start out with a laugh. Go to despair.com and see what their commentary is for dysfunction. Point to <www.despair.com/demotivators/dysfunction.html>. While you are there, feel free to look at some of the other posters that 'spoof' traditional motivational posters found on the walls of businesses and schools.
2. How do you handle conflict when it arises? Seven guidelines for handling conflicts constructively can be found at <www.mediate.com/articles/jordan2.cfm>. Think of a conflict you are involved in or have been involved in recently. How could you have applied these guidelines to that situation? Is there room for improvement in your conflict management skills? Write a short reflection paper (or a paragraph or two) on one of the guidelines and how you plan to use it in future conflicts.

3. If you have never been involved in labour negotiations, it can be a challenging task—especially if you lack experience in the process. Preparation is key. Every manager should have an understanding of the process. Learn more at <www.mediate.com/articles/lynnK.cfm>. Are there lessons in this article that could be applied to any negotiation process—for example, buying a car, negotiating a contract with a vendor, etc? Think of a circumstance where you might find yourself explaining a negotiation process to a friend and the skills necessary to be successful. (Use the article for ideas.) Write out the scenario and skills and bring it to class.

4. Negotiating with other cultures requires an understanding of the culture and the individuals with whom you are negotiating. Point to <www.mediate.com/articles/lauchli.cfm> to learn more about negotiation and dispute resolution with the Chinese. As the book has discussed, the Chinese are a collectivist culture different from societies that have individualistic orientations. Make a note of two or three things of interest you learned from reading this page and bring it to class.

5. Read the article by Stella Ting-Toomey titled 'Intercultural Conflict Management: A Mindful Approach' at <www.personal.anderson.ucla.edu/richard.goodman/c4web/Mindful.htm>. Write a short synopsis of the three main points of the article. What is the most interesting or intriguing idea put forth in the paper? Do you agree or disagree with her assessments? Bring your written work to class for further discussion.

6. The University of Colorado offers a great deal of information regarding conflict management on their website. One page provides abstracts of selected readings on transformative conflict resolution. Some readings are more global in nature—others are geared to the organisation. Point to <www.colorado.edu/conflict/transform/abslist.htm> and select three abstracts of interest to you. Print them off and bring them to class. Prepare a short presentation on what you learned from the articles. Be prepared to talk about them before the class or in small groups.

KSS Program

KNOW THE CONCEPTS   SELF-AWARENESS   SKILLS APPLICATIONS

Negotiating

After you have read this chapter, take Self-Assessment #34 (What's My Preferred Conflict-handling Style?) on your enclosed CD-Rom and complete the skill-building module entitled 'Negotiating' on page 645.

NOTES

1. Allan Fels, 'Opinion: Crooks Should Do Time for Competition Crime', *Business Review Weekly*, vol. 25, no. 21, 12 June 2003.

2. James Thomson, 'Fuel for the Critics', *Business Review Weekly*, vol. 24, no. 25, June 12 2003.

3. See, for example, C. F. Fink, 'Some Conceptual Difficulties in the Theory of Social Conflict', *Journal of Conflict Resolution*, December 1968, pp. 412–60. For an updated review of the conflict literature, see J. A. Wall, Jr and R. R. Callister, 'Conflict and Its Management', *Journal of Management*, vol. 21, no. 3, 1995, pp. 515–58.

4. L. L. Putnam and M. S. Poole, 'Conflict and Negotiation', in F. M. Jablin, L. L. Putnam, K. H. Roberts and L. W. Porter (eds), *Handbook of Organizational Communication: An Interdisciplinary Perspective* (Newbury Park, CA: Sage, 1987), pp. 549–99.

5. K. W. Thomas, 'Conflict and Negotiation Processes in Organizations', in M. D. Dunnette and L. M. Hough (eds), *Handbook of Industrial and Organizational Psychology*, 2nd ed., vol. 3 (Palo Alto, CA: Consulting Psychologists Press, 1992), pp. 651–717.

6. For a comprehensive review of the interactionist approach, see C. De Dreu and E. Van de Vliert (eds), *Using Conflict in Organizations* (London: Sage Publications, 1997).

7. See K. A. Jehn, 'A Multimethod Examination of the Benefits and Detriments of Intragroup Conflict', *Administrative Science Quarterly*, June 1995, pp. 256–82; K. A. Jehn, 'A Qualitative Analysis of Conflict Types and Dimensions in Organizational Groups', *Administrative Science Quarterly*, September 1997, pp. 530–57; K. A. Jehn and E. A. Mannix, 'The Dynamic Nature of Conflict: A Longitudinal Study of Intragroup Conflict and Group Performance', *Academy of Management Journal*, April 2001, pp. 238–51; and C. K. W. De Dreu and A. E. M. Van Vianen, 'Managing Relationship Conflict and the Effectiveness of Organizational Teams', *Journal of Organizational Behavior*, May 2001, pp. 309–28.

8. See S. P. Robbins, *Managing Organizational Conflict: A Nontraditional Approach* (Englewood Cliffs, NJ: Prentice Hall, 1974), pp. 31–55; and Wall and Callister, 'Conflict and Its Management', pp. 517–23.

9. Robbins, *Managing Organizational Conflict*, pp. 31–55.

10. L. R. Pondy, 'Organizational Conflict: Concepts and Models', *Administrative Science Quarterly*, September 1967, p. 302.

11. See, for example, R. L. Pinkley, 'Dimensions of Conflict Frame: Disputant Interpretations of Conflict', *Journal of Applied Psychology*, April 1990, pp. 117–26; and R. L. Pinkley and G. B. Northcraft, 'Conflict Frames of Reference: Implications for Dispute Processes and Outcomes', *Academy of Management Journal*, February 1994, pp. 193–205.

12. R. Kumar, 'Affect, Cognition and Decision Making in Negotiations: A Conceptual Integration', in M. A. Rahim (ed.), *Managing Conflict: An Integrative Approach* (New York: Praeger, 1989), pp. 185–94.

13. Ibid.

14. P. J. D. Carnevale and A. M. Isen, 'The Influence of Positive Affect and Visual Access on the Discovery of Integrative Solutions in Bilateral Negotiations', *Organizational Behavior and Human Decision Processes*, February 1986, pp. 1–13.

15. Thomas, 'Conflict and Negotiation Processes in Organizations'.

16. Ibid.

17. See R. J. Sternberg and L. J. Soriano, 'Styles of Conflict Resolution', *Journal of Personality and Social Psychology*, July 1984, pp. 115–26; R. A. Baron, 'Personality and Organizational Conflict: Effects of the Type A Behavior Pattern and Self-Monitoring', *Organizational Behavior and Human Decision Processes*, October 1989, pp. 281–96; and R. J. Volkema and T. J. Bergmann, 'Conflict Styles as Indicators of Behavioral Patterns in Interpersonal Conflicts', *Journal of Social Psychology*, February 1995, pp. 5–15.

18. Thomas, 'Conflict and Negotiation Processes in Organizations'.

19. See, for example, R. A. Cosier and C. R. Schwenk, 'Agreement and Thinking Alike: Ingredients for Poor Decisions', *Academy of Management Executive*, February 1990, pp. 69–74; K. A. Jehn, 'Enhancing Effectiveness: An Investigation of Advantages and Disadvantages of Value-Based Intragroup Conflict', *International Journal of Conflict Management*, July 1994, pp. 223–38; R. L. Priem, D. A. Harrison and N. K. Muir, 'Structured Conflict and Consensus Outcomes in Group Decision Making', *Journal of Management*, vol. 21, no. 4, 1995, pp. 691–710; and K. A. Jehn and E. A. Mannix, 'The Dynamic Nature of Conflict: A Longitudinal Study of Intragroup Conflict and Group Performance', *Academy of Management Journal*, April 2001, pp. 238–51.

20. See, for example, C. J. Loomis, 'Dinosaurs?', *Fortune*, 3 May 1993, pp. 36–42.

21. I. L. Janis, *Victims of Groupthink* (Boston: Houghton Mifflin, 1972).

22. J. Hall and M. S. Williams, 'A Comparison of Decision-Making Performances in Established and Ad-Hoc Groups', *Journal of Personality and Social Psychology*, February 1966, p. 217.

23. R. L. Hoffman, 'Homogeneity of Member Personality and Its Effect on Group Problem-Solving', *Journal of Abnormal and Social Psychology*, January 1959, pp. 27–32; and R. L. Hoffman and N. R. F. Maier, 'Quality and Acceptance of Problem Solutions by Members of Homogeneous and Heterogeneous Groups', *Journal of Abnormal and Social Psychology*, March 1961, pp. 401–07.

24. See T. H. Cox and S. Blake, 'Managing Cultural Diversity: Implications for Organizational Competitiveness', *Academy of Management Executive*, August 1991, pp. 45–56; T. H. Cox, S. A. Lobel and P. L. McLeod, 'Effects of Ethnic Group Cultural Differences on Cooperative Behavior on a Group Task', *Academy of Management Journal*, December 1991, pp. 827–47; P. L. McLeod and S. A. Lobel, 'The Effects of Ethnic Diversity on Idea Generation in Small Groups', paper presented at the Annual Academy of Management Conference, Las Vegas, August 1992; C. Kirchmeyer and A. Cohen, 'Multicultural Groups: Their Performance and Reactions with Constructive Conflict', *Group & Organization Management*, June 1992, pp. 153–70; D. E. Thompson and L. E. Gooler, 'Capitalizing on the Benefits of Diversity through Workteams', in E. E. Kossek and S. A. Lobel (eds), *Managing Diversity: Human Resource Strategies for Transforming the Workplace* (Cambridge, MA: Blackwell, 1996), pp. 392–437; and L. H. Pelled, K. M. Eisenhardt and K. R. Xin, 'Exploring the Black Box: An Analysis of Work Group Diversity, Conflict, and Performance', *Administrative Science Quarterly*, March 1999, pp. 1–28.

25. R. E. Hill, 'Interpersonal Compatibility and Work Group Performance among Systems Analysts: An Empirical Study', *Proceedings of the Seventeenth Annual Midwest Academy of Management Conference*, Kent, OH, April 1974, pp. 97–110.

26. D. C. Pelz and F. Andrews, *Scientists in Organizations* (New York: Wiley, 1966).

27. See Wall and Callister, 'Conflict and Its Management', pp. 523–26 for evidence supporting the argument that conflict is almost uniformly dysfunctional.

28. M. Geyelin and E. Felsenthal, 'Irreconcilable Differences Force Shea & Gould Closure', *Wall Street Journal*, 31 January 1994, p. B1.

29. This section is based on F. Sommerfield, 'Paying the Troops to Buck the System', *Business Month*, May 1990, pp. 77–79; W. Kiechel III, 'How to Escape the Echo Chamber', *Fortune*, 18 June 1990, pp. 129–30; E. Van de Vliert and C. De Dreu, 'Optimizing Performance by Stimulating Conflict', *International Journal of Conflict Management*, July 1994, pp. 211–22; E. Van de Vliert, 'Enhancing Performance by Conflict-Stimulating Intervention', in De Dreu and Van de Vliert (eds), *Using Conflict in Organizations*, pp. 208–22; K. M. Eisenhardt, J. L. Kahwajy and L. J. Bourgeois III, 'How Management Teams Can Have a Good Fight', *Harvard Business Review*, July–August 1997, pp. 77–85; and S. Wetlaufer, 'Common Sense and Conflict', *Harvard Business Review*, January–February 2000, pp. 114–24.

30. J. A. Wall, Jr, *Negotiation: Theory and Practice* (Glenview, IL: Scott, Foresman, 1985).

31. R. E. Walton and R. B. McKersie, *A Behavioral Theory of Labor Negotiations: An Analysis of a Social Interaction System* (New York: McGraw-Hill, 1965).

32. Thomas, 'Conflict and Negotiation Processes in Organizations'.

33. This model is based on R. J. Lewicki, 'Bargaining and Negotiation', *Exchange: The Organizational Behavior Teaching Journal*, vol. 6, no. 2, 1981, pp. 39–40.

34. J. Lee, 'The Negotiators', *Forbes*, 11 January 1999, pp. 22–24.

35. M. H. Bazerman and M. A. Neale, *Negotiating Rationally* (New York: Free Press, 1992), pp. 67–68.

36. J. A. Wall, Jr and M. W. Blum, 'Negotiations', *Journal of Management*, June 1991, pp. 278–82.

37. C. Watson and L. R. Hoffman, 'Managers as Negotiators: A Test of Power versus Gender as Predictors of Feelings, Behavior, and Outcomes', *Leadership Quarterly*, Spring 1996, pp. 63–85.

38. A. E. Walters, A. F. Stuhlmacher and L. L. Meyer, 'Gender and Negotiator Competitiveness: A Meta-Analysis', *Organizational Behavior and Human Decision Processes*, October 1998, pp. 1–29; and A. F. Stuhlmacher and A. E. Walters, 'Gender Differences in Negotiation Outcome: A Meta-Analysis', *Personnel Psychology*, Autumn 1999, pp. 653–77.

39. Stuhlmacher and Walters, 'Gender Differences in Negotiation Outcome', p. 655.

40. See N. J. Adler, *International Dimensions of Organizational Behavior*, 4th ed. (Cincinnati, OH: Southwestern, 2002), pp. 208–56; and W. L. Adair, T. Okurmura and J. M. Brett, 'Negotiation Behavior When Cultures Collide: The United States and Japan', *Journal of Applied Psychology*, June 2001, pp. 371–85.

41. K. D. Schmidt, *Doing Business in France* (Menlo Park, CA: SRI International, 1987).

42. S. Lubman, 'Round and Round', *The Wall Street Journal*, 10 December 1993, p. R3.

43. P. R. Harris and R. T. Moran, *Managing Cultural Differences*, 4th ed. (Houston: Gulf Publishing, 1996), pp. 43–44.

44. E. S. Glenn, D. Witmeyer and K. A. Stevenson, 'Cultural Styles of Persuasion', *Journal of Intercultural Relations*, Fall 1977, pp. 52–66.

45. J. Graham, 'The Influence of Culture on Business Negotiations', *Journal of International Business Studies*, Spring 1985, pp. 81–96.

46. Wall and Blum, 'Negotiations', pp. 283–87.

47. K. W. Thomas, 'Toward Multidimensional Values in Teaching: The Example of Conflict Behaviors', *Academy of Management Review*, July 1977, p. 487.

Integrative Case Study A The Merger of Synergis and Abacus

MAREE BOYLE, The University of Queensland, Australia

Bill Jones, team leader and support coach at Synergis, an outstanding medium-sized management-consulting firm, walked into the managing director's office filled with apprehension. Alan Smith had called a meeting with him at short notice, with a cryptic message from his executive assistant about the nature of that meeting. It was unlike Alan not to provide Bill with details about meetings. Alan was a passionate believer in transparent communication and decision making. He had gained lot of respect from his employees because of his 'up-front' management style. As one long-time staff member commented: 'We may not like some of his decisions, but we always know where we stand with Alan.' Alan believed that in order for a knowledge-intensive firm such as Synergis to remain competitive and dynamic, open and collaborative communication and leadership styles were crucial to the continuing success of the firm.

Bill tried to dismiss a nagging feeling he'd had all day that something wasn't quite right. But when Bill examined his feelings closely, he realised he had regularly felt uneasy during the past few months. He had felt this way since the announcement of the merger between Synergis and Abacus. Initially, Synergis staff found it difficult to understand why there needed to be a merger between the two firms. Not only did they have very divergent organisational cultures, they were also at different stages of their organisational life cycles. Abacus was a mature, conservative business-consulting firm that had experienced slow growth in recent years. The owner of Abacus, Elliott West, was keen to form a productive alliance with a younger, more productive firm, and began to search for one that might fit the criteria.

Elliott was a self-made and uneducated entrepreneur. Although he had grown a very successful business, Elliott had always been in awe of the professional MBA-educated managers he hired to run his company. Elliott's feeling of inadequacy about his lack of education often led him to accept advice from his managers without questioning whether or not it was appropriate. The idea of a merger was 'sold' to him by the very ambitious and charismatic marketing manager, Nick Brown, who had been with Abacus for about a year. Elliott left all the negotiations with Synergis about the merger to his management team, and trusted them implicitly. He had met the Synergis team twice and was impressed by what he saw. There were times he thought that the outcomes of such a union would be almost too good to be true, but he dismissed the idea as negative thinking. Elliott also had doubts about the effect such a merger would have upon the staff of both companies. His management team were adamant that although there would be pain for current employees of Synergis, the Abacus way of doing things would have to prevail. Synergis had a lot to offer, but Elliott's managers warned of letting the younger employees of Synergis 'loose'. They explained to Elliott that individual employees had too much power and that Synergis wasn't centralised enough. If Elliott were to gain control of the merged entity, the Synergists would need to be 'brought into line'. The Abacus management team, in particular Nick Brown, developed a secret 'containment' plan that would be rolled out once the merger was official. They convinced Elliott that sufficient consultation had occurred with Synergist staff and that the executive staff were supportive of the plan. Despite having reservations about aspects of the plan, Elliott agreed for the plan to be implemented.

So, as Bill walked into the office and sat down in front of Alan, he realised why he had been feeling nervous. Alan looked as though he was about to deliver bad news. Alan told Bill that he had been informed by a disgruntled Abacus employee that senior management had a 'containment' plan ready to roll out once the merger was official. This plan would involve downsizing Bill's area, which conducted most of the research and development work central to maintaining Synergis's competitiveness. He also told Bill that the plan included moves to replace senior Synergis staff with middle managers from Abacus in order to reduce the costs of the merger. Bill was shocked at the news. He had met recently with his counterpart in Abacus and had no inkling that this would be a likely outcome of the merger. If anything, Abacus management seemed more than willing to cooperate with Synergis, particularly in relation to the merger of IT and HRM systems and procedures.

Alan and Bill arranged a meeting with Elliott later that week. When confronted with what Alan and Bill told him, Elliott first denied that such a plan existed. He then realised that the quality of some of the information he was receiving from his senior managers may be problematic. Instead of confronting them, particularly Nick, Elliott decided to do some investigations of his own. What he found startled him. Not only was Nick Brown feeding him false information, he had successfully convinced many of the Abacus staff members that he was the driving force behind Abacus, and that when the merger occurred he was the natural heir to the newly merged entity. He also presented an image of Elliott as 'past his prime' who needed 'looking after'.

Although angry and upset, Elliott decided not to retaliate. Instead, he worked with Alan and Bill over the next few weeks to develop an alternative 'containment' plan, as well as a proactive merger plan that concentrated on aligning the two distinct cultures. Elliott developed a sound working relationship with the two Synergis executives, and came to appreciate the level of expertise and culture of excellence that the Synergists would contribute to the newly formed organisation.

At the same time, Elliott continued to work with Nick Brown on planning the rollout. Nick had no knowledge of Elliott's secret meetings with Synergis, and assumed that Elliott would be making the announcement about the new CEO soon. He thought it strange that Elliott hadn't formally discussed it with him, but was confident that Elliott wouldn't consider anyone else for the position.

A month before the merger, Nick met with Elliott in his office. Elliott was quiet but firm when he informed Nick that it would be Alan, not himself, who would be the CEO of the new organisation, which would be called Synabis. Elliott also told Nick that he wouldn't be renewing his contract, which was due to expire in three months. Nick Brown's payout was considerably larger than was stipulated in his contract, but Elliott West was relieved he was now free of Nick's influence.

Activities for discussion, analysis and further research

1. What are the main kinds of power bases Elliott used to solve the problem of Nick Brown undermining his position?
2. What were the main power tactics used in this scenario? Which ones were the most successful? Why?
3. How were both legitimate and illegitimate political behaviour used together in this instance?
4. Describe how a power coalition formed in this case. Provide reasons for why it worked.
5. How could Elliott West have avoided the expensive termination payment for Nick Brown?
6. Demonstrate how 'truth' became a 'casualty' because of political action in this case.

Integrative Case Study B Developing Autonomous Work Teams at the Town of Kwinana

BRENDA SCOTT-LADD, Murdoch University, Australia

The introduction of semi-autonomous teams at the Town of Kwinana has led to major changes. From an employer faced with industrial unrest, poor customer service, inefficient work practices and low employee morale in 1995, the council has just picked up another award—one of several over the past three years.

About the Town of Kwinana

The Town of Kwinana is a 25-minute drive, 40 kilometres south of Perth, in Western Australia. Near the picturesque coast of Cockburn Sound, the municipality covers 118 square kilometres and has a combined suburban and rural population of approximately 21,000 people. Many locals commute to Perth, while others work in the surrounding industrial 'strip' or local community services. Currently, the municipality's operating revenue is about $20.8 million, and rate income is about $8 million per annum. Based on data from the Department of Employment and Workplace Relations, the unemployment rate of 13 per cent is the highest in the Perth metropolitan area. The Town of Kwinana employees are responsible for overseeing the collection of rates and providing services and information to ratepayers to ensure compliance with local, state and federal government legislation. Employees also ensure the construction and maintenance of public infrastructure by maintaining pathways, roads, parks and gardens. Additionally, there is a recreation and aquatic centre, a library, a family day-care and an aged-care facility that encompasses a nursing-home, hostel and aged persons units for purchase or rental.

Problems that led to change

Erica Brenchley, the current HR manager, who has worked for the Town of Kwinana in a number of capacities since 1987, reminisced that a lot has changed since 1995! The threat of rolling industrial action, with employees refusing to answer telephone calls, was just one symptom of bigger troubles. 'There were many problems! Due to regulation, our systems were centralised and bureaucratic. All decisions went through the CEO—even standard letters were signed by him and this led to delays.' Time delays were common, and information could be lost as it moved up and down the chain of command or between departments across the organisation. There were technological limitations. 'Staff had to access information from terminals linked to a main-frame which wasn't always up to date—especially during busy periods— which led to time delays in responding to ratepayer queries.' Employees were protective of *their job* and this sometimes meant they didn't share information. 'Our customers became angry and upset at being given what they saw as the "runaround".' Of course, confrontations with angry or upset ratepayers led to a negative response from employees!

'Another problem was that we still used a personnel approach to managing employees.' Despite policies being limited, rules had to be followed. 'Employees lived by the rules, as there was no room for negotiation!' Ratepayers had to deal with the municipal employees for advice and service related to municipal business. As Erica explained, 'Our customers had nowhere else to go—so they were taken for granted.' Internal problems led to inefficiencies, which cost the municipality money. The Town of Kwinana is by no means a wealthy socioeconomic area, and increasing rates to meet inefficient operations management costs wasn't desirable or a viable financial option. Given these circumstances, change needed to happen. 'We had to improve our customer service.'

Changes to the *Local Government Act* in 1995 paved the way for changes to work practices and allowed greater delegation. Entering enterprise bargaining negotiations gave the then CEO an opportunity to move towards ambitious restructuring and change. He appointed a competent and experienced HR manager to facilitate employee involvement as the first stage of moving towards semi-autonomous work teams. As legislative requirements prevent full autonomy, the aim was for employees to be involved, as much as possible, in the decisions affecting them. While this includes day-to-day operations and projects, it also extends to such issues as leave rosters, training and safety.

The structure

The municipality now has a workforce of 112 FTE (full-time equivalent) and a large number of casual employees spread over six different locations operating in 17 diverse teams. Previously, the structure operated with three divisions, these being: Commercial Operations, which incorporated the recreation centre, library, family day-care, nursing home and the arts centre); Customer Services, which incorporated health, planning, building and rangers; and Corporate Services, which incorporated finance, IT and admin/records. This led to four to five layers in the chain of command—for example, the accounts payable clerk reported to the finance manager, who reported to the corporate services manager, who in turn, reported to the CEO. The current structure is set out in Figure 1.

Developing semi-autonomous teams

The aim was to improve quality and customer service by developing natural work teams. In fact, there were two parallel team structures; with one being the natural work team supported by coaches, and a business team who focused on outcomes, with representatives from each work team. The business team linked change to strategic outcomes and the enterprise bargaining time frames. Coaches supported work teams in developing personalised goals at five levels, at their own pace, for their own work area. External consultants were engaged in the early stages to support employees and overcome the existing adversarial culture. Coaches were selected for their ability to function in this role, and in most cases weren't managers. They were given one day's training by an external 'Team Development Specialist', then met fortnightly to review and share their experiences. The longer-term objective was to be self-sufficient and build internal relationships, which has been achieved with two teams supported by one coach. While team meetings can be as frequent as weekly if the team believes there is a need to meet this often, the organisation requires monthly meetings as a minimum. The term *hit the road coaches* reinforced the role of coaches as one of being 'out there' working with the teams. Communication was intensive, with the coaches and business team rep providing two-way information to teams and an HR newsletter keeping employees informed across the organisation.

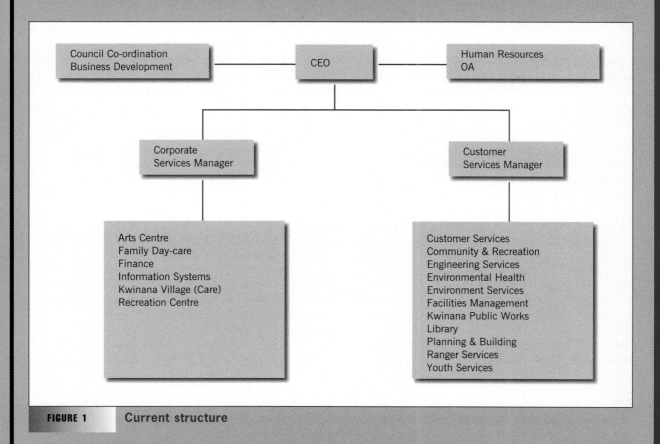

FIGURE 1   **Current structure**

Progressive development

The business team set key performance indicators (KPIs), or as they are called at Kwinana Council, 'team criteria levels', linked to the business plan. Each work team was set specific targets at five levels, and target requirements became more stringent as the levels progressed. Teams could only progress to the next level when an audit process demonstrated that they had achieved the set milestone. For example; a first-level target for the teams was to identify who their customers were; what their customers wanted or needed from them; and what they believed was their output or service. A third-level milestone could include meeting with a selection of customers every three months and measuring agreed business plan targets—for example, the teams' response times to meeting customer requests. At level five, teams needed to demonstrate that they met customer satisfaction requirements 95 per cent of the time, and to present evidence of cooperation with valued internal and external customers. An example at level five could be establishing a service agreement to target and deal with a cross-functional issue.

The change

The fruits of these changes are now being borne out. The Town of Kwinana has shared awards in a number of categories; namely, customer-service, process management and innovation, performance management and communication, in the 'Innovation' and 'Whole of Organisation' best practice in the Local Government Awards for the year 2002. This follows a number of other awards that demonstrate how much has changed since 1998. In that year, the Town achieved its first Local Government Award, when it received a gold certificate for its Worksafe plan following a 60 per cent reduction in workers' compensation claims. This was followed with a municipal WorkCare award in 1999, and ISO 9001 accreditation in 2000.

The organisation is justly proud of these awards, seeing them as recognition for substantial improvements in work practices and improved productivity. As Erica said, 'We have found that working in the semi-autonomous teams has given individual employees greater responsibility and accountability—the opportunity to discuss and have input into decisions has given them clearer direction.' Also, there is stronger identification with customers, and this emerges as a commitment to both the internal and external customer. 'They have a sense of being valued as individuals and have become more multi-skilled; they can perform a range of duties at various levels of skill and responsibility and these things have boosted morale and individuals' self-confidence. Because our employees are involved in decisions about their work, they understand just what level of contribution they do make to the organisation. An added bonus has been reduced concerns about job security—even if they left here, our employees know they are very marketable.'

Improvements in morale are further demonstrated through the marked reduction in internal conflicts and tensions, the increased level of flexibility and trust between employees and management, and the increased focus on 'the customer' with improved customer service. Cross-functional teams bring employees from across the organisation together in advance to plan, implement, monitor and review work processes, projects and specific issues. 'It's so different now! They know they can rely on others across the organisation as well as their team members.'

Lessons from the program's implementation

Despite the success of the program, it hasn't all been plain sailing. With hindsight, some valuable lessons have been learned. Early expectations of the pace of change were too high. 'In reality, a cultural change was required and this takes time.' Some initial targets needed to be redefined and broken down into more incremental steps. 'Not everyone wanted to change—at first we thought it was crucial for everyone to come on board—but we have learned to be more accepting,' Erica explained. 'It's OK for some people to take their own time.' It was a matter of gaining sufficient support to maintain the momentum. 'Teams have developed their own ways of operating; their own dispute resolution procedures; and, in most cases, it's the majority rules—but that's not always the case.' Some teams are more democratic than others! Further work is still required with some managers whose roles have changed through the development of the teams. While for some it was easy, others tended to cling to their previous roles, making the period of transition difficult for themselves and other employees. Some managers who didn't want to change left the organisation or stepped down. However, despite being uncomfortable and finding it difficult to adapt to the new role of coach and mentor instead of coordinator and controller, others have persevered. There is no doubt that the whole process of implementing the semi-autonomous teams has led to a significant cultural shift at the Town of Kwinana. However, change is continuous. The challenge now is to sustain the momentum and move on to the next phase. The

Town of Kwinana plans to do this by developing greater leadership skills in all team members. Hopefully, such an approach will help those few remaining employees who are struggling to adapt to the change, as well as better position the teams to continue to improve their levels of effectiveness in the future.

Activities for discussion, analysis and further research

1. Identify some of the advantages of building teams at the Town of Kwinana.
2. Identify the internal and external factors that influenced the development of semi-autonomous teams.
3. If you had been the external consultant who set up the work teams, what problems were you likely to encounter in starting the process, and how would you have approached the initial phases of team building?
4. If you had been a manager at the Town of Kwinana, what could you have done to assist your coach and team make the transition to semi-autonomous work teams, apart from the strategies implemented at the organisational level? In essence, this question is about how you, as a manager, could redefine your leadership role in a semi-autonomous team.
5. 'The structural changes have meant the Town of Kwinana has become more organic.' Develop a visual map of the Town of Kwinana's past structure and identify the strengths and weaknesses of such a structural change. As well as those identified in the case, explore other potential strengths and weaknesses.
6. Operating as autonomous work teams has both advantages and disadvantages for communication within the organisation. Compare and contrast strategies to maintain effective communication within and across the teams while minimising the risk of communication breakdowns.
7. If the Town of Kwinana invited you to tender a training program for the planned leadership development program, what outcomes and content would you consider vital?

Sources: This case study has been compiled with the support of the Town of Kwinana's CEO, Mr Rob Searle, and the assistance of the HR manager, Ms Erica Brenchley. Town of Kwinana unemployment statistics sourced from *Small Area Labour Markets, Australia*, Department of Employment and Workplace Relations, March Quarter 2002.

Integrative Case Study C Leadership and Inclusivity at the Papua New Guinea, Port Moresby Port Authority

ALLISON JAMES, Australian Maritime College, Australia

Papua New Guinea (PNG) occupies the eastern half of the island of New Guinea, just north of Australia, and many outlying islands. To the north and east are the islands of Manus, New Britain, New Ireland and Bougainville, all part of PNG. In December 1973, PNG became self-governing; it achieved complete independence from Britain in September 1975, becoming a full member of the Commonwealth.

General facts relating to trade

Capital and largest city: Port Moresby, 250,000; **Literacy rate:** 50 per cent; **Exports:** gold, copper, coffee, palm oil, copra, timber, lobster; **Imports:** food, machinery, transport equipment, fuels, chemicals, consumer goods; **Major trading partners:** Australia, UK, Japan, Singapore, New Zealand, US, South Korea, Germany.

PNG is spearheading a major shipping conference to boost trade and commerce in the Pacific Islands region. The Manufacturers Council of Papua New Guinea (MCPNG) said the conference would bring together government, shippers and the private sector to discuss shipping and air freight matters, as well as issues affecting the future development of trade and commerce in the region. The Council said:

> The Pacific Island countries are maritime nations and historically the island communities have survived because of the unhindered and extensive trading that existed between them. Now, one has to observe regulations such as customs, quarantine, other barriers to trade and of course the sabotage law . . . The opportunities created by the development of economic partnership agreements with the European Union and by the process of globalisation itself, will come to nothing if we do not take determined steps to guarantee the availability of appropriate and competitive marine transportation facilities.

The PNG Harbours Board

The PNG Harbours Board recognises itself as the gateway to the nation's prosperity, stating: '. . . it is reassuring to know that wherever in the world your hard earned export dollars are going, Papua New Guinea's Harbours Board is on hand with 20 ports nationwide to swiftly and safety handle your cargo . . .'

Port Moresby is the nation's capital, and its port is the largest of PNG's 20 ports. The Port Moresby Port Authority (PMPA) is facing a number of challenges. It is a statutory body, coming under the direct responsibility of the Minister of Transport. The primary goal of the port is to facilitate the safe and efficient handling of ships and the cargoes they carry. The port aims to provide a service that meets the needs of its users, in both range and quality, and to encourage the full use of the port.

Over the past five years, there has been a continual decline in vessel traffic. During the past two years, three shipping lines left for other competing facilities. However, the port continues to attract five international shipping lines.

The port's customers—ship owners, shippers and stevedores—see the port as an inaccessible, lethargic 'ivory tower'. One described the culture as a 'long-established command-control, listless culture'.

During the past five years, the port has recorded two profitable years, followed by three years with net losses. During these 'loss' years, the port faced growing competition from ports nationally and in neighbouring countries, particularly in the container trades. This competition will likely intensify, as two major competing ports have announced ambitious expansion plans for their container facilities. These ports have impressive marketing strategies with a strong emphasis on stakeholder management and the environment.

The port experienced its worst year for industrial disputes and person-days lost (two major disputes alone, lasting one and two weeks, respectively). A century-old tradition of 'worker versus boss' is a tough place to improve effectiveness, efficiency and customer focus.

PMPA established a formal staff and port worker-training program three years ago. To support the training program, the Board authorised an increase in the training budget of 2 per cent; however, this was terminated in 2002 due to the overall loss.

A new CEO has been appointed to facilitate a turnaround strategy.[1] Few of us will ever be confronted with a leadership challenge as problematic as that facing the CEO of PMPA; however, we may face opportunities for leadership that involve group dynamics that are just as complex.

The CEO is well aware that the environment in which organisations operate is dramatically changing. The increasing pressure of global competition, together with accelerating rates of change in areas such as technology, international affairs, business practices and the responsibilities of organisations to their employees and other stakeholders, demand that managers continually reconsider their leadership style, emphasising a need for innovative responses.

Why is it necessary to change? Leadership is really quite simple—right? Just as navigation was possible using the old Earth-centred view of the universe, so management and leadership are possible using the hierarchal pyramid approach for managing—right?

In the traditional approach, the 'chain of command' was instituted with clear lines of authority. Distinct functional divisions evolved. Communication and reporting lines were set in cement. 'Traditional' competencies—such as decisiveness, results-orientation, chain of command dependence, forcefulness, task-orientation, assertiveness, bottom-line focus—were considered desirable.

The CEO realises that a new approach to leadership is required to facilitate a turnaround. He needs to address what competencies are required for leaders in the 21st century and how these are different from the 'traditional' leadership styles described above. Leadership will remain a complex series of interactions between the leader, followers and the situation—the change in each of these will give leadership in the 21st century its special characteristics. He also realises that the relaxed, Islander approach may both assist and hinder the change.

He believes that an inclusive style of management—including the claims of all stakeholders—builds competitive advantage. The inclusive style seems to imply an overall holistic approach in both strategic and operational decision making for stakeholders both within and outside the organisation.

Note: [1] *Turnaround strategy* means to 'ride out the storm' and turn around the organisation from loss to success. *Turnaround* refers to survival measures recommended for financial troubles due to economic recessions, innovative breakthroughs by competitors, and internal problems (mismanagement, production inefficiencies, shortage of resources).

Activities for discussion, analysis and further research

1. Identify the leadership approach required to facilitate the change.
2. Explain how the CEO can use communication to improve effectiveness, efficiency and customer focus.
3. The CEO believes that part of the solution involves cross-functional teams. What are the benefits of these teams, and what might be the problems?
4. Outline the main types of power required by the CEO of PMPA. To guide your thinking, consider a situation in which you were a leader. What types of power were available to you? Which ones did you use most? What were the results in terms of follower commitment, compliance and resistance?
5. The level of staffing is more than adequate to meet the port's ongoing operational needs. The CEO knows that part of the turnaround will include a restructure and loss of at least one-third of the current workforce. What techniques or procedures can be used to manage the conflict?

The Organisation
Part

4

CHAPTER 15   FOUNDATIONS OF ORGANISATIONAL STRUCTURE

CHAPTER 16   ORGANISATIONAL CULTURE

CHAPTER 17   HUMAN RESOURCE POLICIES AND PRACTICES

CHAPTER 18   ORGANISATIONAL CHANGE AND STRESS MANAGEMENT

Foundations of Organisational Structure

CHAPTER OUTLINE

What is organisational structure?
Common organisational designs
New design options
Why do structures differ?
Organisational designs and employee behaviour

LEARNING OBJECTIVES

After studying this chapter, you should be able to:

1. Identify the six key elements that define an organisation's structure
2. Describe a simple structure
3. Explain the characteristics of a bureaucracy
4. Describe a matrix organisation
5. Explain the characteristics of a 'virtual' organisation
6. Summarise why managers want to create boundaryless organisations
7. List the factors that favour different organisation structures
8. Explain the behavioural implications of different organisational designs

One man's red tape is another man's system.
D. Waldo

As chief executive officer of Promina, Michael Wilkins appreciates the importance of having an effective organisational structure.

Royal & SunAlliance, a British company, is one of the world's largest international insurance groups. It focuses predominantly on property and casualty insurance and has some operations in life insurance. The group has significant market positions in the United Kingdom, the United States, Canada, Scandinavia and Australia/New Zealand. It employs over 40,000 staff, who deal with in excess of 20 million customers in 130 countries around the globe.

In 2003, Royal & SunAlliance announced a new organisational structure in Australia and New Zealand. Consequently, the Promina group was established as a separate insurance entity in the region. Michael Wilkins, the new managing director and chief executive for the combined Australian and New Zealand operations, said the restructure enhanced the ability of the New Zealand and Australian businesses to focus on market segments where they could continue to deliver quality products and services. 'This new organisational structure will allow each business within the Australasian group to have autonomy in relation to its operating functions, while being supported by an overarching corporate function that determines the group's overall strategic direction and priorities.' The marketing, general administration and other functions will be maintained locally in both Australia and New Zealand to service its diverse customer base in both regions.[1]

In Malaysia, Abdul Wahid Omar, a relatively young and up-and-coming chartered accountant, was appointed managing director and CEO of debt-laden United Engineers (M) Bhd (UEM), hence taking on the mammoth task of turning around the largest construction group in the country. The UEM-Renong Group's colossal debt of slightly over 30 billion Malaysian ringgit (RM) wasn't a good start for any new CEO. The group structure involved more than 34 operating companies, including 14 listed ones. After gaining a good understanding of the group (UEM, Renong, Time Engineering Bhd and Faber)—not only in terms of the businesses, the organisational structure and the financials, but also the nature of the inherent debt problems and business—he unveiled a group-wide restructuring scheme to address the issues.[2]

The CEOs in both of these situations have different challenges. They realise that their organisations have different structures and these structures have a bearing not only on employee attitudes and behaviour but also on the company's performance. Managers, in general, become aware of the need to change the structure to meet the requirements of their organisations. That is the theme of this chapter. In the following pages, we define the key components that make up an organisation's structure, present half a dozen or so structural design options from which managers can choose, identify the contingency factors that make certain structural designs preferable in varying situations, and conclude by considering the different effects that various organisational designs have on employee behaviour.

LEARNING OBJECTIVE

1

Identify the six key
elements that
define an
organisation's
structure

What is Organisational Structure?

**organisational
structure**
How job tasks are
formally divided, grouped
and coordinated.

An **organisational structure** defines how job tasks are formally divided, grouped and coordinated. There is an increasing number of organisations that have changed their structure from one where employees performed narrow, specialised tasks in separate departments, under the direct guidance of a department or section manager, to a team-based structure that relies more prominently on the self-managing capabilities of the team members. Managers need to address six key elements when they design their organisation's structure. These are: work specialisation, departmentalisation, chain of command, span of control, centralisation and decentralisation, and formalisation.[3] Table 15.1 presents each of these elements as answers to an important structural question. The following sections describe these six elements of structure.

WORK SPECIALISATION

Early last century, Henry Ford became rich and famous by building automobiles on an assembly line. Every Ford worker was assigned a specific, repetitive task. For example, one person would just put on the right-front wheel and someone else would install the right-front door. By breaking jobs up into small standardised tasks, which could be performed over and over again, Ford was able to produce cars at the rate of one every ten seconds while using employees who had relatively limited skills.

work specialisation
The degree to which
tasks in the organisation
are subdivided into
separate jobs.

Ford demonstrated that work can be performed more efficiently if employees are allowed to specialise. Today, we use the term **work specialisation**, or *division of labour*, to describe the degree to which tasks in the organisation are subdivided into separate jobs.

The essence of work specialisation is that, rather than an entire job being done by one individual, the job is broken down into a number of steps, each step being completed by a separate individual. In essence, individuals specialise in doing part of an activity rather than the entire activity.

By the late 1940s, most manufacturing jobs in industrialised countries were being done with high work specialisation. Management saw this as a way to make the most efficient use of its employees' skills. In most organisations, some tasks require highly developed skills; others can be performed by the untrained. If all workers were engaged in each step of, say, an organisation's manufacturing process, all would have to have the skills necessary to perform both the most demanding and the least demanding jobs. As a result, except when performing the most skilled or highly sophisticated tasks, employees would be working below their skill levels. And since skilled workers are paid more than unskilled workers and their wages tend to reflect their highest

TABLE 15.1	Six key questions that managers need to answer in designing an organisation structure	
Key Question		**The Answer is Provided by**
1. To what degree are tasks subdivided into separate jobs?		Work specialisation
2. On what basis will jobs be grouped together?		Departmentalisation
3. To whom do individuals and groups report?		Chain of command
4. How many individuals can a manager efficiently and effectively direct?		Span of control
5. Where does decision-making authority lie?		Centralisation and decentralisation
6. To what degree will there be rules and regulations to direct employees and managers?		Formalisation

level of skill, it represents an inefficient usage of organisational resources to pay highly skilled workers to do easy tasks.

Managers also looked for other efficiencies that could be achieved through work specialisation. Employee skills at performing a task successfully increase through repetition. Less time is spent in changing tasks, in putting away one's tools and equipment from a prior step in the work process, and in getting ready for another. Equally important, training for specialisation is more efficient from the organisation's perspective. It's easier and less costly to find and train workers to do specific and repetitive tasks. This is especially true of highly sophisticated and complex operations. For example, could Cessna produce one Citation jet a year if one person had to build the entire plane alone? Finally, work specialisation increases efficiency and productivity by encouraging the creation of special inventions and machinery.

For much of the first half of last century, managers viewed work specialisation as an unending source of increased productivity. And they were probably right. Because specialisation wasn't widely practised, its introduction almost always generated higher productivity. But by the 1960s, increasing evidence showed that a good thing can be carried too far. The point had been reached in some jobs where the human diseconomies from specialisation—which surface as boredom, fatigue, stress, low productivity, poor quality, increased absenteeism and high turnover—more than offset the economic advantages (see Figure 15.1). In such cases, productivity could be increased by enlarging, rather than narrowing, the scope of job activities. Additionally, a number of companies found that by giving employees a variety of activities to do, allowing them to do a whole and complete job, and by putting them into teams with interchangeable skills, they often achieved significantly higher output with increased employee satisfaction.

Most managers today see work specialisation as neither obsolete nor as an unending source of increased productivity. Rather, managers recognise the economies it provides in certain types of jobs and the problems it creates when it is carried too far. You will find, for example, high work specialisation being used by McDonald's to efficiently make and sell hamburgers and fries, and by medical specialists in most health-care organisations. However, information technology companies such as NEC (Australia) and service organisations such as Queensland Health have had success by broadening the scope of jobs and *reducing* specialisation. For example, employees in the electronics assembly career stream at NEC (Australia) are encouraged to undertake job rotation to broaden their skills and experience. At Queensland Health, nurses in intensive care units are at the cutting edge of technological innovation and require a much broader range of skills than was the case a decade ago.

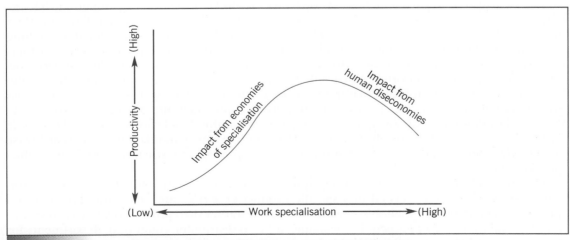

FIGURE 15.1   **Economies and diseconomies of work specialisation**

Most organisations try to group various jobs and functions together to gain efficiencies. Automobile production plants provide some of the best examples of grouping highly specialised tasks according to the segment of the production technology.

DEPARTMENTALISATION

Once you have divided jobs up through work specialisation, you need to group these jobs together so that common tasks can be coordinated. The basis by which jobs are grouped together is called **departmentalisation**.

One of the most popular ways to group activities is by the *function* performed. A manufacturing manager might organise a factory by separating engineering, accounting, manufacturing, personnel and purchasing specialists into common departments. Of course, departmentalisation by function can be used in all types of organisations. Only the functions change to reflect the organisation's objectives and activities. A hospital might have departments devoted to research, patient care, accounting, and so forth. A professional football organisation—for example, the Auckland Warriors, the Brisbane Lions, the Sydney Swans or the Jurong Soccer Club in Singapore—might have departments to handle specific activities such as staffing, including players, ticket sales, marketing, and travel and accommodation. The main advantage of this type of grouping is the efficiencies that can be obtained from putting similar activities together so

departmentalisation
The basis by which jobs are grouped together.

that administrators can focus their attention and skills. Functional departmentalisation seeks to achieve economies of scale by placing people with common skills and orientations into common units.

Tasks can also be departmentalised by the type of *product or service* the organisation produces. Large accounting firms, for example, can have a variety of departments which focus on their major product/service areas (for example, taxation, auditing and management consulting services), and these departments can be placed under the authority of one of the firm's partners who is a specialist in, and responsible for, everything having to do with the product/service line. When you think of Woolworths, you think of one of Australia's biggest grocery chains. But Woolworths is also a significant player in the liquor industry. Woolworths has created a new organisational structure for liquor retailing using four separate means of distribution: Woolworths Liquor and Safeway Liquor are departments within Woolworths supermarkets, while First Estate, BWS and Dan Murphy Cellars are free-standing stores. In relation to the total diverse Woolworths operation, these departments and stores represent sub-structures based on product differentiation.

The main advantage of this type of grouping is increased accountability for product performance, since all activities related to a specific product or service are under the direction of a single manager. If an organisation's activities are service- rather than product-related, each service would be autonomously grouped. For example, a Volvo distributor could have departments for new cars, second-hand cars, trucks and buses, and the like. Each would offer a common array of services under the direction of a particular service manager.

Another way to departmentalise is on the basis of *geography or territory*. The sales function, for example, may have western, southern, northern or eastern regions. It may be divided into North Island or South Island, as in New Zealand, or East or West, as in Malaysia. Each of these regions is, in effect, a department organised around geography. If an organisation's customers are scattered over a large geographic area, then this form of departmentalisation can be valuable.

If you have had the opportunity to visit an aluminium tubing plant, you will have noticed that production is generally organised into five departments: casting; press; tubing; finishing; and inspect, pack and ship. This is an example of *process* departmentalisation, because each department specialises in one specific phase in the production of aluminium tubing. The metal is cast in huge furnaces; sent to the press department, where it is extruded into aluminium pipe; transferred to the tube mill, where it is stretched into various sizes and shapes of tubing; moved to finishing, where it is cut and cleaned; and finally arrives in the inspect, pack and ship department. Since each process requires different skills, this method offers a basis for the homogeneous categorising of activities.

Process departmentalisation can be used for processing customers as well as products. If you have ever been to a state motor vehicle office to get a driver's licence, you probably went through several departments before you received your licence. Some years ago, applicants may have gone through three steps, each handled by a separate department—for example:

- validation by the motor vehicles division;
- processing by the licensing department; and
- payment collection by the finance department.

Today, applicants are more likely to be processed at a one-stop shop, a service counter where the one department completes all the processes necessary for the issue of a licence. This has been brought about by the availability of sophisticated information systems and photographic technology.

A final category of departmentalisation is to use the particular type of *customer* the organisation seeks to reach. Microsoft, for example, is organised around four customer markets: consumers, large corporations, software developers, and small businesses. A large law office can segment its staff on the basis of whether they service corporate or individual clients. The assumption underlying customer departmentalisation is that customers in each department have a common set of demands that can best be met by having specialists for each.

Large organisations may use all of the forms of departmentalisation we have described. A major Japanese electronics firm, for example, organises each of its divisions along functional lines and its manufacturing units around processes; it departmentalises sales around seven geographic regions; and divides each sales region into four customer groupings. Across organisations of all sizes, one strong trend has developed over the past decade. Rigid, functional departmentalisation is being increasingly complemented by teams that cross over traditional departmental lines. As tasks have become more complex, and more diverse skills are needed to accomplish those tasks, management has turned to cross-functional teams.

CHAIN OF COMMAND

Thirty years ago, the chain of command concept was a basic cornerstone in the design of organisations. As you will see, it has far less importance today. But contemporary managers should still consider its implications when they decide how best to structure their organisations.

The **chain of command** is an unbroken line of authority that extends from the top of the organisation to the lowest echelon and clarifies who reports to whom. It answers questions for employees such as 'Who do I go to if I have a problem?' and 'To whom am I responsible?'

You can't discuss the chain of command without discussing two complementary concepts: authority and unity of command. **Authority** refers to the rights inherent in a managerial position to give orders and to expect those orders to be obeyed. To facilitate coordination, each managerial position is given a place in the chain of command, and each manager is given a degree of authority in order to meet their responsibilities.

chain of command
The unbroken line of authority that extends from the top of the organisation to the lowest echelon and clarifies who reports to whom.

authority
The rights inherent in a managerial position to give orders and to expect the orders to be obeyed.

The **unity of command** principle helps to preserve the concept of an unbroken line of authority. It states that a person should have one and only one superior to whom they are directly responsible. If the unity of command is broken, a subordinate might have to cope with conflicting demands or priorities from several superiors. Times change and so do the basic tenets of organisational design. The concepts of chain of command, authority and unity of command have substantially less relevance today because of advancements in computer technology and the trend towards empowering employees.

The post-war, hierarchical organisation has been replaced by organisations with much flatter structures. While some functions, especially financial, are still centrally controlled, much of the responsibility is pushed down to frontline managers and those managers in the middle were simply removed.[4] This is also associated with the introduction of semi-autonomous work groups providing more empowerment, flexibility and autonomy to team members.[5]

A low-level employee today can access information in seconds that, 20 years ago, was available only to top managers. Similarly, computer technology increasingly allows employees anywhere in an organisation to communicate with anyone else without going through formal channels. Moreover, the concepts of authority and maintaining the chain of command are increasingly less relevant as operating employees are being empowered to make decisions that previously were reserved for management. Add to this the popularity of self-managed and cross-functional teams and the creation of new structural designs that include multiple bosses, and the unity of command concept takes on less relevance. Many organisations, of course, still find they can be most productive by enforcing the chain of command. There just seem to be fewer of them nowadays.

SPAN OF CONTROL

How many subordinates can a manager efficiently and effectively direct? This question of **span of control** is important because, to a large degree, it determines the number of levels and managers an organisation has. All things being equal, the wider or larger the span, the more efficient the organisation. An example can illustrate the validity of this statement.

Assume we have two organisations, both of which have approximately 4,100 operative-level employees. As Figure 15.2 illustrates, if one has a uniform span of four and the other a span of eight, the wider span would have two fewer levels and approximately 800 fewer managers. If the average manager was paid $50,000 a year, the wider span would save $40 million a year in management salaries! Obviously, wider spans are more efficient in terms of cost. However, at some point wider spans reduce effectiveness. That is, when the span becomes too large, employee performance suffers because supervisors no longer have the time to provide the necessary leadership and support.

Narrow or small spans have their advocates. By keeping the span of control to five or six employees, a manager can maintain close control.[6] But small spans have three main drawbacks. First, as already described, they are expensive because they add levels of management. Second, they make vertical communication in the organisation more complex. The added levels of hierarchy slow down decision making and tend to isolate upper management. Third, small spans of control encourage overly tight supervision and discourage employee autonomy.

Span of control is an important human resources concept that concerns managers everywhere, including athletic administrators where the proper supervision of employees is critical. Hugh Yoshida, director of athletics at the University of Hawaii, believes in a medium-level span of control using his associate and assistant director effectively. With 100 full-time employees, he depends a lot on his mid-level managers to implement policies and procedures for the athletics department. He believes that effective communication is essential to minimise 'direct reporting' through weekly administrative staff meetings, monthly coaches' meetings and quarterly departmental meetings. As in any organisation, 'mid-level' managers want access to the athletics director. Hugh believes that the meeting structure helps him to reduce the number of 'direct reports'.[7]

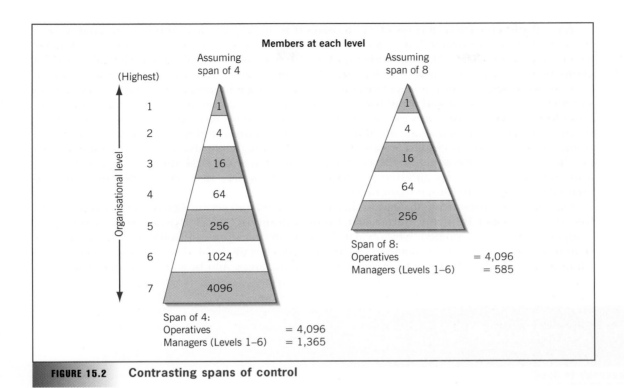

FIGURE 15.2 **Contrasting spans of control**

The trend in recent years has been towards larger spans of control.[8] For example, the Conciliation and Arbitration Commission ratified an award restructuring agreement with the Australian Taxation Office, replacing 93 classifications in the clerical administrative, clerical assistant and keyboard structure with an eight-level administrative service officer structure.[9] Among other things, these changes provided opportunities for job redesign in order to eliminate unnecessary supervision and mundane jobs.

Wide spans of control are consistent with recent efforts by companies to reduce costs, cut overheads, speed up decision making, increase flexibility, get closer to customers and empower employees. However, to ensure that performance doesn't suffer because of these wider spans, organisations have been investing heavily in employee training. Managers recognise that they can handle a wider span when employees know their jobs inside and out or can turn to their co-workers when they have questions.

CENTRALISATION AND DECENTRALISATION

In some organisations, top managers make all the decisions; lower-level managers merely carry out top management's directives. At the other extreme are organisations where decision making is pushed down to those managers who are closest to the action. The former organisations are highly centralised; the latter are decentralised.

The term **centralisation** refers to the degree to which decision making is concentrated at a single point in the organisation. The concept includes only formal authority—that is, the rights inherent in one's position. Typically, it is said that if top management makes the organisation's key decisions with little or no input from lower-level personnel, then the organisation is centralised. In contrast, the more that lower-level personnel provide input or are actually given the discretion to make decisions, the more **decentralisation** there is.

centralisation
The degree to which decision making is concentrated at a single point in the organisation.

decentralisation
Decision discretion is pushed down to lower-level employees.

An organisation characterised by centralisation is an inherently different structural animal from one that is decentralised. In a decentralised organisation, action can be taken more quickly to solve problems, more people provide input into decisions, and employees are less likely to feel alienated from those who make the decisions that affect their work lives.

Consistent with recent management efforts to make organisations more flexible and responsive, there has been a marked trend towards decentralising decision making. In large companies, lower-level managers are closer to the action and typically have more detailed knowledge about problems than do top managers. McDonald's is a well-known brand name and its stores occupy prime locations in many countries around the world. While major decisions are taken at corporate headquarters, the company believes in decentralisation and a local mindset. They realise that a mindset of 'one size fits all circumstances' isn't appropriate in a global operation and are focused on adapting to local environments.[10]

Organisations just starting up are also keen to get away from centralised hierarchies and install flat structures right from the start. Clear Communications (NZ) Ltd is a company set up to compete in the deregulated New Zealand telecommunications industry. In planning their requirements for the future, members of the executive staff decided to develop a network of teams as part of a flat structure where local decision making could be supported by e-mail.[11]

Myth *or* Science?

'Bureaucracy is dead'

This statement is false. Some bureaucratic characteristics are in decline. And bureaucracy is undoubtedly going through changes. But it's far from dead.

Bureaucracy is characterised by specialisation, formalisation, departmentalisation, centralisation, narrow spans of control, and adherence to a chain of command. Have these characteristics disappeared from today's modern organisations? No. In spite of the increased use of empowered teams and flattened structures, certain facts remain.[12]

1. *Large size prevails.* Organisations that succeed and survive tend to grow to a large size, and bureaucracy is efficient with large size. Small organisations and their non-bureaucratic structures are more likely to fail, so over time, small organisations may come and go but large bureaucracies stay. Moreover, while the average business today has considerably fewer employees than those of 30 years ago, these smaller firms are increasingly part of a large, multi-location organisation with the financial and technological resources to compete in a global marketplace.

2. *Environmental turbulence can be largely managed.* The impact of uncertainties in the environment on the organisation are substantially reduced by management strategies such as environmental scanning, strategic alliances, advertising and lobbying. This allows organisations facing dynamic environments to maintain bureaucratic structures and still be efficient.

3. *Bureaucracy's goal of standardisation can be increasingly achieved through hiring people who have undergone extensive educational training.* Rational discipline, rather than that imposed by rules and regulations, is internalised by hiring professionals with TAFE college and university training. They come preprogrammed. In addition, strong cultures help to achieve standardisation by substituting for high formalisation.

4. *Finally, technology maintains control.* Networked computers allow management to closely monitor the actions of employees without centralisation or narrow spans of control. Technology has merely replaced some previously bureaucratic characteristics, but without any loss of management control.

In spite of some changes, bureaucracy is alive and well in many venues. It continues to be a dominant structural form in manufacturing, service firms, hospitals, schools and universities, the armed forces and voluntary associations. Why? Because it is still the most efficient way to organise large-scale activities.[13]

FORMALISATION

Formalisation refers to the degree to which jobs within the organisation are standardised. If a job is highly formalised, then the job incumbent has a minimum amount of discretion over what is to be done, when it is to be done and how they should do it. Employees can be expected always to handle the same input in exactly the same way, resulting in a consistent and uniform output. There are explicit job descriptions, many organisational rules and clearly defined procedures covering work processes in organisations where there is high formalisation. Where formalisation is low, job behaviours are relatively nonprogrammed and employees have a great deal of freedom to exercise discretion in their work. Since an individual's discretion on the job is inversely related to the amount of behaviour in that job that is preprogrammed by the organisation, the greater the standardisation, the less input the employee has into how the work is to be done. Standardisation not only eliminates the possibility of employees engaging in alternative behaviours, but also removes the need for employees to consider alternatives.

The degree of formalisation can vary widely between and within organisations. Certain jobs, for example, are well known to have little formalisation. University textbook travellers—the representatives of publishers who call on faculty heads and academic staff to inform them of their company's new publications—have a great deal of freedom in their jobs. They have no standard sales spiel, and the extent of rules and procedures governing their behaviour may be little more than the requirement that they submit a weekly sales report and some suggestions on what to emphasise for the various new titles. At the other extreme are clerical and editorial positions in the same publishing houses, where employees are required to clock in at their workstations by 9 am or be docked a half-hour of pay and, once at that workstation, to follow a set of precise procedures dictated by management.

formalisation
The degree to which jobs within the organisation are standardised.

Common Organisational Designs

We now turn to describing three of the more common organisational designs found in use: the simple structure, the bureaucracy and the matrix structure.

LEARNING OBJECTIVE
2
Describe a simple structure

THE SIMPLE STRUCTURE

What do a small retail store, an electronics firm run by a hard-driving entrepreneur, a new law firm and an airline in the midst of a company-wide pilots' strike have in common? They probably all utilise the simple structure.

The **simple structure** is said to be characterised most by what it is *not*, rather than by what it *is*. The simple structure isn't elaborate.[14] It has a low degree of departmentalisation, wide spans of control, authority centralised in a single person and little formalisation. The simple structure is a 'flat' organisation; it usually has only two or three vertical levels, a loose body of employees, and one individual in whom the decision-making authority is centralised.

The simple structure is most widely practised in small businesses in which the manager and the owner are one and the same. This organisational design is illustrated in Figure 15.3, an organisation chart for a retail men's store. Although Jack Gold, who owns and manages this store, employs five full-time sales people, a cashier, and extra personnel for weekends and holidays, he runs the show.

IBM became a simple structure for more than a year back in the early 1990s.[15] When Louis Gerstner was hired as CEO in 1993, he immediately put the company into what he called 'survival mode'. 'We had to cut [US]$9 billion a year in expenses. We had to bring the company back, literally from the brink of death.' So Gerstner implemented a highly centralised, personalised leadership and organisational style. Said Gerstner: 'It was a benevolent dictatorship, with me as the dictator.'

simple structure
A structure characterised by a low degree of departmentalisation, wide spans of control, authority centralised in a single person and little formalisation.

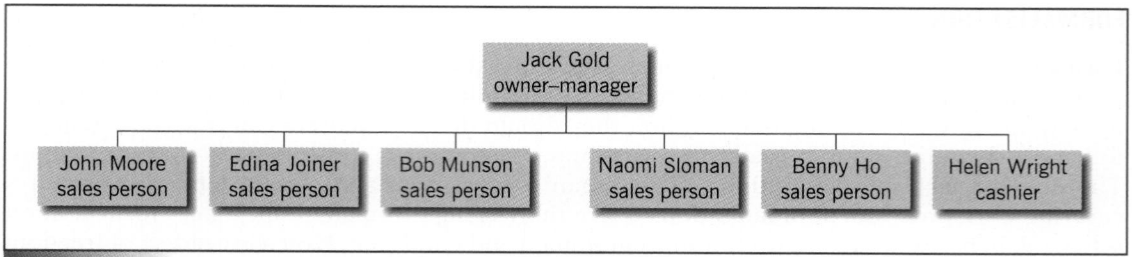

FIGURE 15.3   **A simple structure: Jack Gold's Men's Store**

The strength of the simple structure lies in its simplicity. It is fast, flexible and inexpensive to maintain, and accountability is clear. One main weakness is that it's difficult to maintain in anything other than small organisations. It becomes increasingly inadequate as an organisation grows, because its low formalisation and high centralisation tend to create information overload at the top. As size increases, decision making typically becomes slower and can eventually come to a standstill as the single executive tries to continue making all the decisions. This often proves to be the undoing of many small businesses. When an organisation begins to employ 50 or 100 people, it is very difficult for the owner–manager to make all the choices. If the structure isn't changed and made more elaborate, the firm often loses momentum and can eventually fail. The simple structure's other weakness is that it is risky: everything depends on one person. One heart attack can literally destroy the organisation's information and decision-making centre.

The simple structure isn't strictly limited to small organisations; it's just harder to make it work effectively in larger firms. One large company that seems to have succeeded with the simple structure is FutureKids, a franchise that offers computer literacy courses to young children. The headquarters contains a small number of staff providing support services to over 50 franchised learning centres around the country. Each learning centre is self-contained and runs as a small business. FutureKids Australia is a large business based on a simple structure design. By using franchised outlets, the company can expand operations considerably as a network of small businesses.

LEARNING OBJECTIVE

3

Explain the characteristics of a bureaucracy

bureaucracy
A structure with highly routine operating tasks achieved through specialisation, very formalised rules and regulations, tasks that are grouped into functional departments, centralised authority, narrow spans of control, and decision making that follows the chain of command.

THE BUREAUCRACY

Standardisation! That's the key concept underlying all bureaucracies. Take a look at the bank where you keep your accounts; the department store where you buy your clothes; or the government offices that collect your taxes, enforce health regulations or provide local fire protection. They all rely on standardised work processes for coordination and control.

The **bureaucracy** is characterised by highly routine operating tasks achieved through specialisation, very formalised rules and regulations, tasks that are grouped into functional departments, centralised authority, narrow spans of control, and decision making that follows the chain of command.

The primary strength of the bureaucracy lies in its ability to perform standardised activities in a highly efficient manner. Putting like specialities together in functional departments results in economies of scale, minimum duplication of personnel and equipment, and employees who have the opportunity to talk the same language among their peers. Further, bureaucracies can get by nicely with less talented—and, hence, less costly—middle- and lower-level managers. The pervasiveness of rules and regulations substitutes for managerial discretion. Standardised operations, coupled with high formalisation, allow decision making to be centralised. There is little need, therefore, for innovative and experienced decision makers below the level of senior executives.

One of the main weaknesses of bureaucracy is illustrated in the following dialogue between four executives in one company: 'You know, nothing happens in this place until we *produce* something,' said the production executive. 'Wrong,' commented the research and development manager. 'Nothing happens until we *design* something!' 'What are you talking about?' asked the marketing executive. 'Nothing happens here until we *sell* something!' Finally, the exasperated accounting manager responded, 'It doesn't matter what you produce, design or sell. No one knows what happens until we *tally up the results!*' This conversation highlights the fact that specialisation creates subunit conflicts. Functional unit goals can override the overall goals of the organisation.

The other main weakness of bureaucracy is something we have all experienced at one time or another when having to deal with people who work in these organisations: obsessive concern with following the rules. When cases arise that don't precisely fit the rules, there is no room for modification. The bureaucracy is efficient only as long as employees confront problems they have previously encountered and for which programmed decision rules have already been established.

THE MATRIX STRUCTURE

Another popular organisational design option is the **matrix structure**. You will find it being used in advertising agencies, aerospace firms, research and development laboratories, construction companies, hospitals, government agencies, universities, management consulting firms and entertainment companies.[16] Essentially, the matrix combines two forms of departmentalisation: functional and product.

The strength of functional departmentalisation lies in putting like specialists together, which minimises the number necessary while allowing the pooling and sharing of specialised resources across products. Its main disadvantage is the difficulty of coordinating the tasks of diverse functional specialists so that their activities are completed on time and within budget. Product departmentalisation, on the other hand, has exactly the opposite benefits and disadvantages. It facilitates coordination among specialities to achieve on-time completion and to meet budget targets. Further, it provides clear responsibility for all activities related to a product, but with duplication of activities and costs. The matrix attempts to gain the strengths of each while avoiding their weaknesses.

The most obvious structural characteristic of the matrix is that it breaks the unity of command concept. Employees in the matrix have two bosses: their functional department managers and their product managers. Therefore, the matrix has a dual chain of command.

Figure 15.4 shows the matrix form as used in a faculty of business in a university. The academic departments of accounting, marketing and so forth are functional units. Additionally, specific programs (that is, products) are overlaid on the functions. In this way, members in a matrix structure have a dual assignment—to their functional department and to their product groups. For example, a professor of accounting teaching an undergraduate course reports to the director of undergraduate programs as well as to the head of the accounting department.

The strength of the matrix lies in its ability to facilitate coordination when the organisation has a multiplicity of complex and interdependent activities. As an organisation gets larger, its information processing capacity can become overloaded. In a bureaucracy, complexity results in increased formalisation. The direct and frequent contact between different specialities in the matrix can make for better communication and more flexibility. Information permeates the organisation and more quickly reaches those people who need to take account of it. Further, the matrix reduces bureaupathologies. That is, the dual lines of authority reduce tendencies of departmental members to become so busy protecting their little worlds that the organisation's overall goals become secondary.

Another advantage of the matrix is that it facilitates the efficient allocation of specialists. When individuals with highly specialised skills are lodged in one functional department or product group, their talents are monopolised and underutilised. The matrix achieves the advantages of

LEARNING OBJECTIVE

4

Describe a matrix organisation

matrix structure
A structure that creates dual lines of authority and combines functional and product departmentalisation.

Programs Academic departments	Undergraduate	Master's	PhD	Research	Executive programs	Community-service programs
Accounting						
Administrative Studies						
Economics						
Finance						
Marketing						
Organisational Behaviour						
Quantitative Methods						

FIGURE 15.4   **Matrix structure for a faculty of business administration**

economies of scale by providing the organisation with both the best resources and an effective way of ensuring their efficient deployment.

The main disadvantages of the matrix lie in the confusion it creates, its propensity to foster power struggles, and the stress it places on individuals.[17] When you dispense with the unity of command concept, ambiguity is significantly increased and ambiguity often leads to conflict. For example, it's frequently unclear who reports to whom, and it's not unusual for product managers to fight over who gets the best specialists assigned to their products. Confusion and ambiguity also create the seeds of power struggles. Bureaucracy reduces the potential for power grabs by defining the rules of the game. When those rules are up for grabs, power struggles between functional and product managers result. For individuals who desire security and absence from ambiguity, this work climate can produce stress. Reporting to more than one boss introduces role conflict, and unclear expectations introduce role ambiguity. The comfort of bureaucracy's predictability is absent, replaced by insecurity and stress.

New Design Options

Since the early 1980s, senior managers in a number of organisations have been working to develop new structural options that can better help their firms to compete effectively. In this section, we describe three such structural designs: the team structure, the virtual organisation and the boundaryless organisation.

THE TEAM STRUCTURE

team structure
The use of teams as the central device to coordinate work activities.

Teams have become an extremely popular means around which to organise work activities. When management uses teams as its central coordination device, you have a **team structure**.[18] The primary characteristics of the team structure are that it breaks down departmental barriers and decentralises decision making to the level of the work team. Team structures also require employees to be generalists as well as specialists.[19] In smaller companies, the team structure can define

While the chief executive officer has prime responsibility for the performance of the company, most chief executives realise the value of developing an effective team of senior executives rather than relying on the skills and knowledge of specific individuals.

the entire organisation. For example, some of the larger management consulting and accounting firms organise on the basis of customer-focused teams. KPMG, one of the major international accounting firms, has formed a team of 25 specialists, including five senior police officers. The team has the expertise, flexibility and mobility to deal with wide-ranging cases of fraud.[20] Ernst & Young, another major international accounting firm, uses the team approach to management consulting. This allows it to mobilise various professional experts to go into an organisation at short notice to conduct internal assessments of the organisation's capabilities and current strengths and weaknesses.

More often, particularly among larger organisations, the team structure complements what is typically a bureaucracy. This allows the organisation to achieve the efficiency of bureaucracy's standardisation while gaining the flexibility that teams provide. To improve productivity at the operating level, for example, companies such as Kodak Australasia Pty Ltd, Motorola and Xerox have made extensive use of self-managed teams. Self-managed teams aren't unique to private industry. There are many examples where they have been implemented in the public sector. For example, certain sections of the Queensland Police Service have been experimenting with team-based structures. When companies such as Boeing or Hewlett-Packard need to design new products or coordinate major projects, they will structure activities around cross-functional teams. Qantas uses cross-functional teams to solve issues dealing with customer service.

THE VIRTUAL ORGANISATION

Why own when you can rent? That's the essence of the **virtual organisation** (also sometimes called the network or modular organisation), a small, core organisation that outsources major business functions.[21] In structural terms, the virtual organisation is highly centralised, with little or no departmentalisation.

The prototype of the virtual structure is today's movie-making organisation. In Hollywood's golden era, movies were made by huge, vertically integrated corporations. Studios such as MGM, Warner Brothers and 20th-Century Fox owned large movie lots and employed thousands of full-time specialists—set designers, camera people, film editors, directors and even actors. Nowadays, most movies are made by a collection of individuals and small companies who come together and make films project by project.[22] This structural form allows each project to be staffed with the talent most suited to its demands, rather than having to choose from just those people the studio employs. It minimises bureaucratic overhead since there is no lasting organisation to maintain. And it lessens long-term risks and their costs because there is no long term—a team is assembled for a finite period and then disbanded.

As a director of KJ Enterprising Solutions, Kathleen Jordan doesn't believe that working from home is a barrier to successful management consulting in Australia. She specialises in forming networks of specialist consultants, creating project teams and matching talents with the needs of

LEARNING OBJECTIVE

5

Explain the characteristics of a 'virtual' organisation

virtual organisation
A small, core organisation that outsources major business functions.

clients. Using her previous corporate experience, Jordan works from her home to organise teams of mainly home-based consultants. Her virtual organisation is a great combination of high expertise and low overheads. Christine Sather, a successful consultant with 14 years' experience in international marketing, has developed a network of professional advisers comprising a solicitor with international corporate expertise, an accountant offering business management and planning advice, a computer expert for technical support, and a diligent editor who helps Christine with her client presentations. Christine also believes in the merits of her virtual organisation.[23]

When large organisations use the virtual structure, they frequently use it to outsource manufacturing. Companies such as Nike, Reebok and Dell Computer are just a few of the thousands of companies that have found that they can do hundreds of millions of dollars in business without owning manufacturing facilities. Dell Computer, for example, owns no factories and merely assembles computers from outsourced parts. Mobil Oil Corporation has turned over maintenance of its refineries to another firm.

What's going on here? A quest for maximum flexibility. These virtual organisations have created networks of relationships that allow them to contract out manufacturing, distribution, marketing, or any other business function when management feels that others can do it better or more cheaply.

The virtual organisation stands in sharp contrast to the typical bureaucracy that has many vertical levels of management and where control is sought through ownership. In such organisations, research and development are done in-house, production occurs in company-owned plants, and sales and marketing are performed by the company's own employees. To support all this, management has to employ extra personnel, including accountants, human resource specialists and lawyers. The virtual organisation, however, outsources many of these functions and concentrates on what it does best. For most firms, that means focusing on design or marketing.

Figure 15.5 shows a virtual organisation in which management outsources all of the primary functions of the business. The core of the organisation is a small group of executives. Their job is to oversee directly any activities that are done in-house and to coordinate relationships with the organisations that manufacture, distribute and perform other crucial functions for the virtual organisation. The arrowed lines in Figure 15.5 represent those relationships, typically maintained under contracts. In essence, managers in virtual structures spend most of their time coordinating and controlling external relations, typically by way of computer network links.

The main advantage of the virtual organisation is its flexibility. For example, it allows someone with an innovative idea and little money—such as Michael Dell and his Dell Computer firm—to

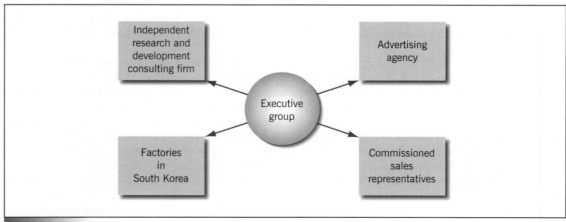

FIGURE 15.5 **A virtual organisation**

successfully compete against large companies such as IBM. The primary drawback of this structure is that it reduces management's control over key parts of its business.

THE BOUNDARYLESS ORGANISATION

General Electric (GE) chairman Jack Welch coined the term **boundaryless organisation** to describe his idea of what he wanted GE to become. Welch wanted to turn his company into a '[US]$60 billion family grocery store'.[24] That is, in spite of its monstrous size, he wanted to eliminate *vertical* and *horizontal* boundaries within GE and to break down *external* barriers between the company and its customers and suppliers. The boundaryless organisation seeks to eliminate the chain of command, have limitless spans of control and replace departments with empowered teams. And because it relies so heavily on information technology, some have begun calling this structure the T-form (or technology-based) organisation.[25]

While GE hasn't yet achieved this boundaryless state—and probably never will—it has made significant progress towards this end. So have other companies such as Hewlett-Packard, Telstra,

LEARNING OBJECTIVE

6

Summarise why managers want to create boundaryless organisations

boundaryless organisation
An organisation that seeks to eliminate the chain of command, have limitless spans of control, and replace departments with empowered teams.

OB Controversies

Does structure ensure accountability?

Australia's general insurance industry, the Australian public and HIH shareholders were devastated by the demise of HIH Insurance, which, after months of speculation, was placed in liquidation in March 2001. The failure of the company, with its $5.3 billion deficiency, constituted another attack on the reputation of the general insurance industry after well-documented reinsurance losses by GIO and Reinsurance Australia. These cases are part of a larger pool of recent corporate failures and scandals that includes Enron, WorldCom and OneTel.

As a consequence of the collapse, Justice Neville Owen of the Supreme Court of Western Australia was appointed Royal Commissioner to inquire into the failure of the HIH Insurance Group of companies. The Commission was asked to examine whether decisions or actions of directors, officers or associated advisers contributed to the failure, or were involved in any undesirable corporate governance practices.

There is an interesting and controversial structural issue raised by the Commission, as it was also asked to examine the adequacy and appropriateness of arrangements for the regulation and prudential supervision of the general insurance industry. The Australian Prudential Regulation Authority (APRA) has a responsibility for overseeing aspects of corporate governance in the industry as the prudential regulator of banks, insurance companies and superannuation funds, credit unions, building societies and friendly societies.

The Commission was told that in the three years before HIH collapsed, APRA ignored warnings from a company whistle blower, state regulators and its own junior staff, as well as media reports. The Commission also heard the claim that for all the influence that APRA had on the activities of HIH, APRA was ineffectual. While HIH was seen to fail because of incompetent and dishonest behaviour by many of its managers and board members, APRA was told of its responsibility for deficiencies in adequately resourcing its own organisational structure. In particular, an APRA branch manager attracted criticism for exacerbating existing problems in his under-staffed branch by his many distractions, including a university teaching post and international committee positions.

The structural issue relates to how the formation of departments and branches with clear goals and priorities, as in the case of APRA, can influence the behaviour of staff such as the branch manager. What role does structure play in balancing career aspirations with organisational priorities? How does an organisation's structure assist organisations such as APRA to learn from its experiences?

Source: Based on 'APRA Misled Minister, Failed in Duty to Prevent HIH Collapse', *AAP General News (Australia)*, 15 January 2003.

Like McDonalds, Coca Cola sees itself as a global corporation. As such, it needs to take on the attributes of a boundaryless organisation to meet the expectations of its customers around the world.

SingTel, Westpac and Motorola. Let's take a look at what a boundaryless organisation would look like and what some firms are doing to make it a reality.[26]

By removing *vertical* boundaries, management flattens the hierarchy. Status and rank are minimised. And the organisation looks more like a silo than a pyramid, where the grain at the top is no different from the grain at the bottom. Cross-hierarchical teams (which include top executives, middle managers, supervisors and operative employees), participative decision-making practices, and the use of 360-degree performance appraisals (where peers and others above and below the employee evaluate his or her performance) are examples of what GE is doing to break down vertical boundaries.

Functional departments create *horizontal* boundaries. The way to reduce these barriers is to replace functional departments with cross-functional teams and to organise activities around processes. For example, Xerox now develops new products through multidisciplinary teams that work in a single process focusing on the total project goals instead of fragmenting product development around narrow, functional tasks . Similarly, some units within the large telecommunications companies are now doing annual budgets based not on functions or departments, but on processes, such as the maintenance of a worldwide telecommunications network. Another way management can cut through horizontal barriers is to use lateral transfers and rotate people into and out of different functional areas. This turns specialists into generalists.

When fully operational, the boundaryless organisation also breaks down barriers to *external* constituencies and barriers created by geography. Globalisation, strategic alliances, customer–organisation linkages and telecommuting are all examples of practices that reduce external boundaries. Coca-Cola, for example, sees itself as a global corporation, not a US company. Firms such as Boeing and Microsoft each have strategic alliances or joint partnerships with dozens of companies. These alliances blur the distinction between one organisation and another as employees work on joint projects.

The one common technological thread that makes the boundaryless organisation possible is networked computers. They allow people to communicate across intraorganisational and interorganisational boundaries.[27] Electronic mail, for example, enables hundreds of employees to share information simultaneously and allows rank and file workers to communicate directly with senior executives. And interorganisational networks now make it possible for firms such as Procter & Gamble and Levi Strauss to monitor inventory levels of laundry soap and jeans, respectively, at retail stores owned by some of their clients because Procter & Gamble's and Levi's computer systems are networked to their clients' systems. The manager of Contract and Management Services (CAMS) in Western Australia has had a specific aim to make the company a boundaryless organisation. Through the use of the Internet and communications technology, staff are able to administer contracts and select tenders electronically without a client knowing where their service ends and the services of the suppliers begin.

Why Do Structures Differ?

LEARNING OBJECTIVE

7

List the factors that favour different organisation structures

In the previous sections, we described a variety of organisational designs. They ranged from the highly structured and standardised bureaucracy to the loose and amorphous boundaryless organisation. The other designs we discussed tend to exist somewhere between these two extremes.

Figure 15.6 reconceptualises our previous discussions by presenting two extreme models of organisational design. One extreme we call the **mechanistic model**. This model is generally synonymous with the bureaucracy in that it has extensive departmentalisation, high formalisation, a limited information network (mostly downward communication), and little participation by low-level members in decision making. At the other extreme is the **organic model**. This model looks a lot like the boundaryless organisation. It is flat, uses cross-hierarchical and cross-functional teams, has low formalisation, possesses a comprehensive information network (utilising lateral and upward communication as well as downward), and involves high participation in decision making.[28]

With these two models in mind, we are now prepared to address this question: Why are some organisations structured along more mechanistic lines while others have organic characteristics? What are the forces influencing the design that is chosen? In the following pages, we present the main forces that have been identified as causes or determinants of an organisation's structure.[29]

mechanistic model
A structure characterised by extensive departmentalisation, high formalisation, a limited information network and centralisation.

organic model
A structure that is flat, uses cross-hierarchical and cross-functional teams, has low formalisation, possesses a comprehensive information network, and relies on participative decision making.

STRATEGY

An organisation's structure is a means to help management achieve its objectives. Since objectives are derived from the organisation's overall strategy, it is only logical that strategy and structure should be closely linked. More specifically, structure should follow strategy. If management makes a significant change in its organisation's strategy, the structure will need to be modified to accommodate and support this change.[30] Most current strategy frameworks focus on three strategic options—innovation, cost minimisation and imitation—and the structural design that works best with each.[31]

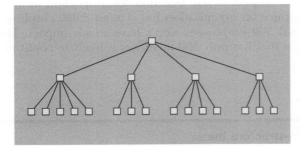
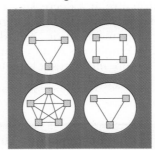

The mechanistic models

The organic models

- High specialisation
- Rigid departmentalisation
- Clear chain of command
- Narrow spans of control
- Centralisation
- High formalisation

- Cross-functional teams
- Cross-hierarchical teams
- Free flow of information
- Wide spans of control
- Decentralisation
- Low formalisation

FIGURE 15.6 **Mechanistic versus organic models**

innovation strategy
A strategy that emphasises the introduction of major new products and services.

cost-minimisation strategy
A strategy that emphasises tight cost controls, avoidance of unnecessary innovation or marketing expenses, and price cutting.

imitation strategy
A strategy that seeks to move into new products or new markets only after their viability has already been proven.

To what degree does an organisation introduce major new products or services? An **innovation strategy** doesn't mean a strategy merely for simple or cosmetic changes from previous offerings but, rather, one for meaningful and unique innovations. Obviously, not all firms pursue innovation. This strategy may appropriately characterise 3M Co., but it certainly isn't a strategy pursued by Reader's Digest or National Geographic.

An organisation pursuing a **cost-minimisation strategy** tightly controls costs, refrains from incurring unnecessary innovation or marketing expenses, and cuts prices in selling a basic product. This would describe the strategy pursued by the manufacturers of brake drums for trucks, such as the Toowoomba Foundry. Of course, competing in the brake drum market means that quality is a factor, as well as cost. Also, the sellers of generic grocery products would pursue a cost-minimisation strategy.

Organisations following an **imitation strategy** try to capitalise on the best of both of the previous strategies. They seek to minimise risk and maximise opportunity for profit. Their strategy is to move into new products or new markets only after viability has been proven by innovators. They take the successful ideas of innovators and copy them. Manufacturers of mass-marketed fashion goods that are rip-offs of designer styles follow the imitation strategy. This strategy also probably characterises such well-known firms as IBM and Caterpillar. They essentially follow their smaller and more innovative competitors with superior products, but only after their competitors have demonstrated that a market exists.

Table 15.2 describes the structural option that best matches each strategy. Innovators need the flexibility of the organic structure; cost minimisers seek the efficiency and stability of the mechanistic structure. Imitators combine the two structures. They use a mechanistic structure in order to maintain tight controls and low costs in their current activities, while at the same time they create organic subunits in which to pursue new undertakings.

ORGANISATION SIZE

Considerable evidence supports the idea that an organisation's size significantly affects its structure.[32] For example, large organisations—those typically employing 2,000 or more people—tend to have more specialisation, more departmentalisation, more vertical levels, and more rules and regulations than do small organisations. However, the relationship isn't linear. Rather, size affects structure at a decreasing rate. The impact of size becomes less important as an organisation expands. Why is this? Essentially, once an organisation has around 2,000 employees, it is already fairly mechanistic. An additional 500 employees won't have much impact. However, adding 500 employees to an organisation that has only 300 members is likely to result in a shift towards a more mechanistic structure.

TABLE 15.2	**Contemporary strategy–structure thesis**
Strategy	**Structural Option**
Innovation	*Organic:* A loose structure; low work specialisation, low formalisation, decentralised.
Cost minimisation	*Mechanistic:* Tight control; extensive work specialisation, high formalisation, high centralisation.
Imitation	*Mechanistic and organic:* Mix of loose with tight properties; tight controls over current activities and looser controls for new undertakings.

TECHNOLOGY

The term **technology** refers to how an organisation transfers its inputs into outputs. Every organisation has at least one technology for converting financial, human and physical resources into products or services. The Nissan Motor Co., for example, predominantly uses an assembly-line process to make its products. Universities, in contrast, may use a number of instructional technologies—the ever-popular formal lecture method, the case analysis method, the experiential exercise method, the programmed learning method, and so forth. In this section, we show how organisational structures adapt to their technology.

Numerous studies have been carried out on the technology–structure relationship.[33] The details of those studies are quite complex, so let's go straight to the bottom line and attempt to summarise what we know.

The common theme differentiating technologies is their *degree of routineness*. By this we mean that technologies tend towards either routine or non-routine activities. The former are characterised by automated and standardised operations. Non-routine activities are customised. They include such varied operations as furniture restoring, custom shoemaking and genetic research.

What relationships have been found between technology and structure? Although the relationship isn't overwhelmingly strong, we find that routine tasks are associated with taller and more departmentalised structures. The relationship between technology and formalisation, however, is stronger. Studies consistently show routineness to be associated with the presence of rule manuals, job descriptions and other formalised documentation. Finally, there has been found to be an interesting relationship between technology and centralisation. It seems logical that routine technologies would be associated with a centralised structure, whereas non-routine technologies, which rely more heavily on the knowledge of specialists, would be characterised by delegated decision authority.

This position has met with some support. However, a more generalisable conclusion is that the technology–centralisation relationship is moderated by the degree of formalisation. Formal regulations and centralised decision making are both control mechanisms, and management can substitute one for the other. Routine technologies should be associated with centralised control if there is a minimum of rules and regulations. However, if formalisation is high, routine technology can be accompanied by decentralisation. So, we would predict that routine technology would lead to centralisation, but only if formalisation is low.

technology
How an organisation transfers its inputs into outputs.

ENVIRONMENT

An organisation's **environment** is composed of those institutions or forces that are outside the organisation and potentially affect the organisation's performance. These typically include suppliers, customers, competitors, government regulatory agencies, public pressure groups, and the like.

Why should an organisation's structure be affected by its environment? Because of environmental uncertainty. Some organisations face relatively static technology environments—few forces in their environment are changing. There are, for example, no new competitors, no new technological breakthroughs by current competitors, or little activity by public pressure groups to influence the organisation. Other organisations face very dynamic environments—rapidly changing government regulations affecting their business, new competitors, difficulties in acquiring raw materials, continually changing product preferences by customers, and so on. Static environments create significantly less uncertainty for managers than do dynamic ones. And since uncertainty is a threat to an organisation's effectiveness, management will try to minimise it. One way to reduce environmental uncertainty is through adjustments in the organisation's structure.[34]

Recent research has helped to clarify what is meant by environmental uncertainty. Three key dimensions to any organisation's environment have been found: capacity, volatility and complexity.[35]

environment
Institutions or forces outside the organisation that potentially affect the organisation's performance.

The *capacity* of an environment refers to the degree to which it can support growth. Rich and growing environments generate excess resources, which can buffer the organisation in times of relative scarcity. Abundant capacity, for example, leaves room for an organisation to make mistakes; scarce capacity doesn't. In the year 2000, firms operating in the multimedia software business had relatively abundant environments, whereas those in the full-service brokerage business faced relative scarcity.

The degree of instability in an environment is captured in the *volatility* dimension. Where there is a high degree of unpredictable change, the environment is dynamic. This makes it difficult for management to predict accurately the probabilities associated with various decision alternatives. At the other extreme is a stable environment. The accelerated changes in Eastern Europe and the demise of the Cold War had dramatic effects on the defence industry in the early 1990s. This moved the environment of major defence contractors such as Lockheed Martin, General Dynamics and Northrop Grumman from relatively stable to dynamic.

Finally, the environment needs to be assessed in terms of *complexity*—that is, the degree of heterogeneity and concentration among environmental elements. *Simple* environments are homogeneous and concentrated. This might describe the tobacco industry, since there are relatively few players. It is easy for firms in this industry to keep a close eye on the competition. In contrast, environments characterised by heterogeneity and dispersion are called *complex*. This is essentially the current environment for firms competing in the Internet-connection business. Every day there seems to be another 'new kid on the block' with whom current Internet access providers have to deal.

Figure 15.7 summarises our definition of the environment along its three dimensions. The arrows in this figure indicate movement towards higher uncertainty. So, organisations that operate in environments characterised as scarce, dynamic and complex face the greatest degree of uncertainty. Why? Because they have little room for error, high unpredictability, and a diverse set of elements in the environment to constantly monitor.

Given this three-dimensional definition of environment, we can offer some general conclusions. There is evidence that relates the degrees of environmental uncertainty to different structural arrangements. Specifically, the more scarce, dynamic and complex the environment, the more organic a structure should be. The more abundant, stable and simple the environment, the more the mechanistic structure will be preferred.

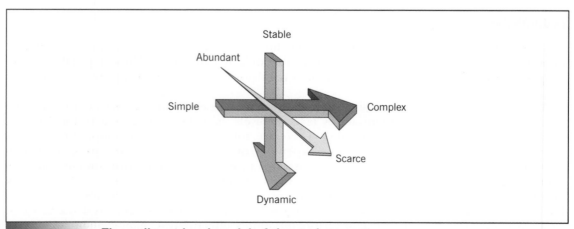

FIGURE 15.7   **Three-dimensional model of the environment**

The Real Deal

Developing a global structure

Rebecca Morrice Williams is in her thirties and has experience as a make-up artist. Who would think that a make-up artist would be heading up an unlisted public company, Becca Cosmetics Developments Ltd, from a warehouse in Perth? In 18 months, the company has developed a market capitalisation in the order of $6 million and has established an international cosmetics brand with a range of 160 make-up items selling in 45 stores around the world, including Singapore and New York. Currently, Perth is a cost-effective base and has access to a reliable logistics system.

Rebecca's experience as a make-up artist helped in developing some of the initial ideas and products for the business. She is keen to develop a business empire from the relative isolation of the west coast of Australia. One of the issues Rebecca has to confront is developing an effective organisational structure that can cope with growth and expansion in Europe and Asia and effectively connect the manufacturing and sales operations around the globe. While the company is small, employing 13 people in Perth and seven in its overseas bases, it won't stay small for long. The cosmetics are manufactured in Germany and assembled in Perth. The packaging for the various products is made in Italy.

Rebecca isn't the only person concerned with developing a suitable structure connecting a network of worldwide operations with Perth. David Demetrius heads a computing company that manufactures its products in Perth and has sales offices in London and New York. David lives in Brussels, where he provides the corporate leadership essential to grow the business for further success. He regards his mobile phone and e-mail as important integrating devices for his organisational structure.

Source: Belinda Hickman, 'Empire Built on Firm Foundation—Western Australia: A Special Report', *The Australian*, 24 March 2003, p. 26.

Organisational Designs and Employee Behaviour

LEARNING OBJECTIVE

8

Explain the behavioural implications of different organisational designs

We opened this chapter by implying that an organisation's structure can have profound effects on its members. In this section, we directly assess just what those effects might be.

A review of the evidence linking organisational structures to employee performance and satisfaction leads to a clear conclusion: you can't generalise! Not everyone prefers the freedom and flexibility of organic structures. Some people are most productive and satisfied when work tasks are standardised and ambiguity is minimised—that is, in mechanistic structures. So, any discussion of the effect of organisation design on employee behaviour has to address individual differences. To illustrate this point, let's consider employee preferences for work specialisation, span of control and centralisation.[36]

The evidence generally indicates that work specialisation contributes to higher employee productivity but at the price of reduced job satisfaction. However, this statement ignores individual differences and the type of job tasks people do.

As we noted previously, work specialisation isn't an unending source of higher productivity. Problems start to surface, and productivity begins to suffer, when the human diseconomies of doing repetitive and narrow tasks overtake the economies of specialisation. As the workforce has become more highly educated and desirous of jobs that are intrinsically rewarding, the point where productivity begins to decline seems to be reached more quickly than in decades past.

While more people today are undoubtedly turned off by overly specialised jobs than were their parents or grandparents, it would be naive to ignore the reality that there is still a segment of the workforce that prefers the routine and repetitiveness of highly specialised jobs. Some individuals want work that makes minimal intellectual demands and provides the security of routine. For these people, high work specialisation is a source of job satisfaction. The empirical question, of course, is whether this represents 2 per cent of the workforce or 52 per cent. Given that there is some self-selection operating in the choice of careers, we might conclude that negative behavioural outcomes from high specialisation are most likely to surface in professional jobs occupied by individuals with high needs for personal growth and diversity.

A review of the research indicates that it is probably safe to say that no evidence supports a relationship between span of control and employee performance. While it is intuitively attractive to argue that large spans might lead to higher employee performance because they provide more distant supervision and more opportunity for personal initiative, the research fails to support this notion. At this point, it is impossible to state that any particular span of control is best for producing high performance or high satisfaction among subordinates. The reason is, again, probably individual differences. That is, some people like to be left alone, whereas others prefer the security of a boss who is quickly available at all times. Consistent with several of the contingency theories of leadership discussed previously, we would expect factors such as employees' experiences and abilities and the degree of structure in their tasks to explain when wide or narrow spans of control are likely to contribute to their performance and job satisfaction. However, some evidence indicates that a manager's job satisfaction increases as the number of subordinates they supervise increases.

We find fairly strong evidence linking centralisation and job satisfaction. In general, organisations that are less centralised have a greater amount of participative decision making. And the evidence suggests that participative decision making is positively related to job satisfaction. But, again, individual differences surface. The decentralisation–satisfaction relationship is strongest with employees who have low self-esteem. Because low-self-esteem individuals have less confidence in their abilities, they place a higher value on shared decision making, which means they aren't held solely responsible for decision outcomes.

Our conclusion: to maximise employee performance and satisfaction, individual differences, such as experience, personality and the work task, should be taken into account. In addition, national culture influences preference for structure, so it, too, needs to be considered.[37] Organisations operating with people from high power distance cultures, such as found in Greece, France and most of Latin America, will find employees much more accepting of mechanistic structures than when employees come from low power distance countries. So, you need to consider cultural differences along with individual differences when making predictions on how structure will affect employee performance and satisfaction.

One obvious point needs to be made before we leave this topic. People don't select employers randomly. There is substantial evidence that individuals are attracted to, selected by and stay with organisations that suit their personal characteristics.[38] Job candidates who prefer predictability, for example, are likely to seek out and take employment in mechanistic structures, while those who want autonomy are more likely to end up in an organic structure. So, the effect of structure on employee behaviour is undoubtedly reduced when the selection process facilitates proper matching of individual characteristics with organisational characteristics.

Summary and Implications for Managers

The theme of this chapter has been that an organisation's internal structure contributes to explaining and predicting behaviour. That is, in addition to individual and group factors, the structural relationships in which people work have an important bearing on employee attitudes and behaviour.

What is the basis for the argument that structure has an impact on both attitudes and behaviour? To the degree that an organisation's structure reduces ambiguity for employees and clarifies such concerns as 'What am I supposed to do?', 'How am I supposed to do it?', 'To whom do I report?' and 'To whom do I go if I have a problem?', it shapes their attitudes and facilitates and motivates them to higher levels of performance.

Of course, structure also constrains employees to the extent that it limits and controls what they do. For example, organisations structured around high levels of formalisation and specialisation, strict adherence to the chain of command, limited delegation of authority and narrow spans of control give employees little autonomy. Controls in such organisations are tight, and behaviour will tend to vary within a narrow range. In contrast, organisations that are structured around limited specialisation, low formalisation, wide spans of control, and the like, provide employees with greater freedom and, thus, will be characterised by greater behavioural diversity.

Figure 15.8 visually summarises what we have discussed in this chapter. Strategy, size, technology and environment determine the type of structure an organisation will have. For simplicity's sake, we can classify structural designs around one of two models: mechanistic or organic. The specific effect of structural designs on performance and satisfaction is moderated by employees' individual preferences.

One last point: managers need to be reminded that structural variables such as work specialisation, span of control, formalisation and centralisation are objective characteristics that can be measured by organisational researchers. The findings and conclusions offered in this chapter, in fact, are directly a result of the work of these researchers. But employees don't objectively measure these structural characteristics! They observe things around them in an unscientific fashion and then form their own **implicit models** of what the organisation's structure is like. How many people did they have to have interviews with before they were offered their jobs? How many people work in their departments and buildings? Is there an organisation policy manual? If so, is it readily available and do people follow it closely? How is the organisation and its top management described in newspapers and periodicals? Answers to questions such as these, when combined with an employee's past experiences and comments made by peers, lead members to form an overall subjective image of what their organisation's structure is like. This image, though, may in no way resemble the organisation's actual objective structural characteristics.

The importance of these implicit models of organisation structure shouldn't be overlooked. People respond to their perceptions rather than to objective reality. The research, for example, on the relationship between many

implicit models of organisational structure Perceptions that people hold regarding structural variables formed by observing things around them in an unscientific fashion.

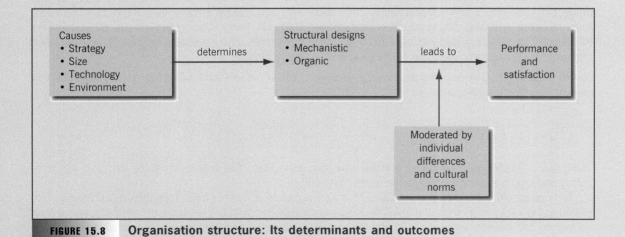

FIGURE 15.8 **Organisation structure: Its determinants and outcomes**

structural variables and subsequent levels of performance or job satisfaction is far from consistent. We explained some of this as being attributable to individual differences. However, an additional contributing cause to these inconsistent findings might be diverse perceptions of the objective characteristics. Researchers typically focus on actual levels of the various structural components, but these may be irrelevant if people interpret similar components differently. The bottom line, therefore, is to understand how employees interpret their organisation's structure. That should prove a more meaningful predictor of their behaviour than the objective characteristics themselves.

Point

TECHNOLOGY IS RESHAPING ORGANISATIONS

In today's chaotic, uncertain and high-tech world, there is essentially only one type of design that is going to survive. This is the electronically configured organic organisation.

We are undergoing a second Industrial Revolution and it will change every aspect of people's lives. The changes the large corporations used to take a decade to implement now occur in one to two years. Companies that are successful will be designed to thrive on change. And the structure of those organisations will have common characteristics.

Ten years from now there will be nothing but electronic organisations. Bricks-and-mortar organisations won't go away, but clicks-and-mortar will become the only means to survival. In addition, every organisation will need to keep its finger on the pulse of its customers. Customer priorities will change very rapidly. What customers will pay a premium for will become a commodity so rapidly that those who lose touch with their customers will be candidates for extinction. Consumers are gaining the ability to compare the prices of hundreds of competitors rather than just two or three. This is going to dramatically drive down prices. By the end of 2003, prices of consumer products in Britain, for example, will have come down 10–15 per cent since 2000. If firms don't improve their productivity to match these drops in prices, they will be out of business.

Technology allows firms to stay closer to the customer, to move jobs to where costs are lowest, and to make decisions much more rapidly. For example, executives at Cisco Systems can monitor expenses, gross margins, the supply chain and profitability in real time. There no longer need to be surprises. Every employee can make decisions that might have had to come from the top management ranks a few years ago. At the end of a quarter, individual product managers at Cisco can see exactly what the gross margins are on their products, whether they are below expectations, and determine the cause of any discrepancy. Quicker decision making at lower levels will translate into higher profit margins. So, instead of the CEO or chief financial officer making 50 to 100 different decisions in a quarter, managers throughout the organisation can make millions of decisions. Companies that don't adjust to create this capability will be non-competitive. Cisco Systems shipped its first product in 1986 and is now a multinational corporation, with over 35,000 employees in more than 115 countries, including Australia, Singapore, New Zealand and Malaysia. Today, Cisco solutions are the networking foundations for service providers, small to medium-size businesses, and enterprise customers, which include corporations, government agencies, utilities and educational institutions.

Source: Based on J. Chambers, 'Nothing Except E-Companies', *Business Week*, 28 August 2000, pp. 210–12. See also <www.cisco.com/global/AU/about/whois.shtml>.

Counterpoint

There is a saying that every generation thinks it has discovered sex. This seems also to be the case with technology and how it is going to change the world completely.

Technology will transform the structure of organisations at a much slower rate than many believe. For example, it is useful to go back and ask if the railroads changed the world. There were definitely changes in how commerce and industry were arranged. But life remained the same, and the way people related to each other remained the same.

There are changes occurring that will influence the way businesses organise. But the changes have been, and will continue to be, gradual. They may accelerate some, but we are not going to see a revolution in the design of organisations. Take the case of globalisation. It is significant, but it is also evolutionary. Has the formation of the European Union abolished national borders in the largest continental society in the Western world? No. France is still France, and Germany is still Germany. Things have changed, but things haven't changed.

The emphasis on speed has its limits. Brains don't speed up. The exchange of ideas doesn't really speed up, only the overhead that slowed down the exchange. When it comes down to the bulk of knowledge work, the 21st century works the same as the 20th century. You can reach people around the clock, but they won't think any better or faster just because you have reached them faster. The give and take remains a limiting factor.

The virtual organisation also has its limitations. When you farm out your data processing, manufacturing and other functions, you make your capabilities available to your competitors. So, virtualisation of work diminishes competitive advantages. It leads to rapidly spreading commoditisation of everything. Any function that an organisation uses to achieve a competitive advantage cannot be outsourced.

Look back over the past 40 years. People haven't changed. And our fundamental organisations haven't changed. On the fringes, there is more looseness in the organisation. But more hasn't changed than has. The changes we have seen have been slow and gradual. And that pace is likely to continue into the future.

Source: Based on A. Grove, 'I'm a Little Skeptical … Brains Don't Speed Up', *Business Week*, 28 August 2000, pp. 212–14.

For Discussion

1. How is the typical large corporation of today organised, in contrast to how that same organisation was probably organised in the 1960s?
2. Why isn't work specialisation an unending source of increased productivity?
3. Do you think most employees prefer high formalisation? Support your position.
4. All things being equal, which is more efficient: a wide or narrow span of control? Why?
5. In what ways can management departmentalise?
6. What is a matrix structure? When would management use it?
7. Contrast the virtual organisation with the boundaryless organisation.
8. What type of structure works best with an innovation strategy? A cost-minimisation strategy? An imitation strategy?
9. Summarise the size–structure relationship.
10. Define and give an example of what is meant by the term *technology*.
11. Summarise the environment–structure relationship.
12. 'Employees form implicit models of organisation structure.' What is the importance of this statement?

Exercise

WHAT SORT OF STRUCTURE DO YOU LIKE TO WORK IN?

Purpose:
To learn about one's experiences with, and feelings about, organisational structures.

Time required:
Approximately 75 minutes

Procedure:
• Your lecturer will separate class members into small groups of three to four students. Each group will then work in isolation.
• Each member of the group must complete the following questionnaire, 'Do you like working for a bureaucracy?'

- When group members have finished the questionnaire, they will discuss their experiences with and feelings about working in a bureaucracy.
- On the lecturer's instruction, each group will report back to the entire class listing a number of points and counterpoints in relation to working in a bureaucracy. The lecturer will record the points/counterpoints on the whiteboard.
- After each group has recorded their deliberations, the lecturer will ask the class to identify the attributes of an organisational structure that they would prefer to work in.

QUESTIONNAIRE: DO YOU LIKE WORKING FOR A BUREAUCRACY?

For each statement, check the response (either mostly agree or mostly disagree) that best represents your feelings:

	Mostly agree	Mostly disagree		Mostly agree	Mostly disagree
1. I value stability in my job.			**12.** Given a choice, I would prefer to make $60,000 per year as a senior executive in a small company to $90,000 as a staff specialist in a large company.		
2. I like a predictable organisation.					
3. The best job for me would be one in which the future is uncertain.					
4. The federal government would be a nice place to work.			**13.** I would regard wearing an employee badge with a number on it as a degrading experience.		
5. Rules, policies and procedures tend to frustrate me.			**14.** Parking spaces in a company carpark should be assigned on the basis of job level.		
6. I would enjoy working for a company that employed 85,000 people worldwide.			**15.** If an accountant works for a large organisation, they cannot be a true professional.		
7. Being self-employed would involve more risk than I'm willing to take.			**16.** Before accepting a job (given a choice), I would want to make sure the company had a very fine program of employee benefits.		
8. Before accepting a job, I would like to see an exact job description.					
9. I would prefer a job as a freelance house painter to one as a clerk for a government department involving motor vehicle registrations.			**17.** A company probably won't be successful unless it establishes a clear set of rules and procedures.		
10. Seniority should be as important as performance in determining pay increases and promotion.			**18.** Regular working hours and holidays are more important to me than finding thrills on the job.		
11. It would give me a feeling of pride to work for the largest and most successful company in its field.			**19.** You should respect people according to their rank.		
			20. Rules are meant to be broken.		

Refer to Appendix C for scoring directions and key.

Source: A. J. DuBrin, *Human Relations: A Job Oriented Approach* © 1978, pp. 687–88.

Reprinted by permission of Prentice Hall, Inc., Upper Saddle River, NJ.

Case Study 15

Working by the Rules

The trend today is away from rigid rules and procedures. Flexibility is the new gospel. While these statements may be true in general, not every manager is buying into it. One in particular is Stephen Reuning, head of the US recruiting firm, Diedre Moire Corporation.

New employees at Diedre Moire must copy Mr Reuning's 244-page Standard Operating Protocol—using longhand script, three times over. This manual covers everything that is expected of company employees—from procedures on how to greet customers, to how to sit during lunch, to hair and grooming tips, to what items should and shouldn't be on the employee's desk. It can take 100 hours or more for new employees to make their copies. After that, they still have to pass 12 oral exams on the content.

Reuning is obsessive about documenting everything. Since starting the firm 18 years ago, he has stored 45,000 pages of data on the firm's computer network. Every process, procedure, product, form, letter, brochure and agreement used by any Diedre Moire employee is documented, catalogued and stored so that it is readily available to any and all members of the firm.

Reuning's fascination with rules and control isn't for everyone. According to Reuning, half of the job candidates he interviews head for the door when told about the protocol requirements. Of those who stay, about one in five lasts beyond a year. One former employee, who lasted nine months, calls the company's environment more structured than the basic training he had in the army. 'They were robotic,' he says.

Those who stay make six-figure incomes and say that there is a comforting efficiency about the place. Customers also seem to appreciate the result. They like that employees are well-trained, systematic, and able to respond to almost any question.

Questions

1. What advantages, if any, does Reuning's system provide?
2. Why does his system work? What is its potential downside?
3. What type of employees do you think fit into Reuning's system?
4. What does flexibility in structure really mean?

Source: D. Morse, 'You Think You Have an Obsessive Boss? Meet Mr. Reuning', *Wall Street Journal*, 4 October 2000, p. A1. Wall Street Journal Eastern Edition (staff produced copy only) by D. Morse. Copyright © 2000 by Dow Jones & Co Inc. Reproduced with permission of Dow Jones & Co Inc in the format Testbook via Copyright Clearance Center.

Web Workout

1. E-mail has been an important tool for breaking down communication barriers between management and workers. However, e-mail is never private between parties—it can be viewed by others at any time. It is often 'archived' for years and can be accessed by organisations years later, should a problem ever arise. How do organisations do this and why? To read more about products that make this type of monitoring possible, point to <http://loper.org/~george/trends/1998/Oct/41.html>.

   Write a list of at least three pros and three cons for organisations pursuing this type of activity. Then write a short paragraph stating your views on this activity. Be prepared to debate this topic in class.

2. The chapter discusses span of control and the various advantages and disadvantages of wide versus narrow. Let us see how that looks in actual numbers. First, determine how many hierarchical levels there are in at least three organisations of varying sizes that you are currently involved with. One could be the TAFE college or university you attend, another where you work, and finally a club or other institution you belong to. Or, for one of the choices, select a non-profit organisation you have some interest in (for example, Red Cross,

LifeLine, Care Australia, etc). Obtain their hierarchical structure either by searching the World Wide Web (most annual reports have information on this), calling or visiting them, or drawing the structure yourself if you are involved in the organisation. Then point to the Simple Span of Control Calculator to plug in the numbers at <www.icce.rug.nl/qr/ssocc.html>. Don't worry about being exact—the idea is to see the span of control in real numbers. Bring this information to class for discussion.

3. We have learned that structure and span of control should relate to the organisation's goals and strategies for achieving those goals. So, how does an organisation know if they are in alignment according to those principles? Often, the organisation will conduct an audit. Read a report of one such audit at <www.metrokc.gov/auditor/1994/span.htm>. Print the report and answer the following questions: What type of structure is King County? What goals do you think they have as an organisation? On what did they base their conclusions? What do you think will happen next? Do you agree with the findings?

4. What are issues concerning virtual organisations? *VONET* is an on-line journal publishing the latest research on virtual organisations. One issue concerns the role of virtual and physical environments. Point to <www.virtual-organization.net/files/articles/gillen.pdf> to read the article in its entirety. Write a short reaction paper incorporating the issues raised in the article if the organisation in question were your university. How would the environment change for students, faculty/staff and administration? What would be the benefits or shortcomings? Be prepared to discuss your reactions in class.

5. What factors influence virtual teams? For a short analysis, point to <www.seanet.com/~daveg/articles.htm>. Write a short paragraph or two outlining why you would or wouldn't like working in a virtual environment. Do you see a time later in your career when you would prefer working in a virtual team? Why or why not?

KSS Program

KNOW THE CONCEPTS   SELF-AWARENESS   SKILLS APPLICATIONS

Delegating authority/empowerment

After you have read this chapter, take Self-Assessment #40 (How Willing am I to Delegate?] on your enclosed CD-Rom and complete the skill-building module entitled 'Delegating Authority' on page 646.

NOTES

 1. 'Wilko Takes Royal & Sun to Starting Gate', *The Daily Telegraph* (Sydney), 28 January 2003, p. 26.
 2. 'Up to the Task', *Malaysian Business*, 1 November 2002.
 3. See, for example, R. L. Daft, *Organization Theory and Design*, 6th ed. (Cincinnati, OH: South-Western College Publishing, 1998).
 4. D. James, 'Middle Managers or Those With Power Often Went First', *Business Review Weekly*, 22 March 2000, pp. 52–54.
 5. S. Thatcher, 'Team Up', *HRMonthly*, February 2003, p. 34.
 6. See, for example, L. Urwick, *The Elements of Administration* (New York: Harper & Row, 1944), pp. 52–53.
 7. E. Alden, 'Span of Control: A Critical Component of Athletic Management', <www.aldenandassoc.com/articles/span_control.htm>, accessed 3 April 2003.
 8. J. Child and R.G. McGrath, 'Organizations Unfettered: Organizational Form in an Information-Intensive Economy', *Academy of Management Journal*, December 2001, pp. 1135–48.
 9. J. Teicher, 'Award Restructuring and Organisational Change in the Australian Taxation Office (Melbourne Branch)', Management Paper no. 39, September 1991, Graduate School of Management, Monash University, Melbourne.
10. 'McDonald's Corporation Conference Call–Final', 17 January 2003.
11. A. Williams, 'Organisational Change as Market Response: CLEAR Communications (NZ)', in M. Patrickson, V. Bamber and G. Bamber (eds), *Organisational Change Strategies: Case Studies of Human Resource and Industrial Relations Issues* (Melbourne: Longman, 1995).
12. B. Harrison, *Lean and Mean: The Changing Landscape of Corporate Power in the Age of Flexibility* (New York: Basic Books, 1994); and S. P. Robbins and N. Barnwell, *Organisation Theory: Concepts and Cases*, 3rd ed. (Sydney: Prentice Hall, 1998), Chapter 11.
13. F. Hilmer and L. Donaldson, *Management Redeemed* (New York: Free Press, 1996).
14. H. Mintzberg, *Structure in Fives: Designing Effective Organizations* (Englewood Cliffs, NJ: Prentice Hall, 1983), p. 157.
15. S. Lohr, 'I.B.M. Chief Gerstner Recalls Difficult Days at Big Blue', *New York Times*, 31 July 2000, p. C5.

16. K. Knight, 'Matrix Organization: A Review', *Journal of Management Studies*, May 1976, pp. 111–30; L. R. Burns and D. R. Wholey, 'Adoption and Abandonment of Matrix Management Programs: Effects of Organizational Characteristics and Interorganizational Networks', *Academy of Management Journal*, February 1993, pp. 106–38; and R. E. Anderson, 'Matrix Redux', *Business Horizons*, November–December 1994, pp. 6–10.

17. See, for example, S. M. Davis and P. R. Lawrence, 'Problems of Matrix Organization', *Harvard Business Review*, May–June 1978, pp. 131–32.

18. S. A. Mohrman, S. G. Cohen and A. M. Mohrman, Jr, *Designing Team-Based Organizations* (San Francisco: Jossey-Bass, 1995); F. Ostroff, *The Horizontal Organization* (New York: Oxford University Press, 1999); and R. Forrester and A. B. Drexler, 'A Model for Team-Based Organization Performance', *Academy of Management Executive*, August 1999, pp. 36–49.

19. M. Kaeter, 'The Age of the Specialized Generalist', *Training*, December 1993, pp. 48–53.

20. C. Wood, 'KPMG Squad Brings the Villains to Account', *Business Review Weekly*, 23 September 1996, pp. 98–99.

21. See, for example, R. E. Miles and C. C. Snow, 'The New Network Firm: A Spherical Structure Built on Human Investment Philosophy', *Organizational Dynamics*, Spring 1995, pp. 5–18; G. G. Dess, A. M. A. Rasheed, K. J. McLaughlin and R. L. Priem, 'The New Corporate Architecture', *Academy of Management Executive*, August 1995, pp. 7–20; D. Pescovitz, 'The Company Where Everybody's a Temp', *New York Times Magazine*, 11 June 2000, pp. 94–96; W. F. Cascio, 'Managing a Virtual Workplace', *Academy of Management Executive*, August 2000, pp. 81–90; and D. Lyons, 'Smart and Smarter', *Forbes*, 18 March 2002, pp. 40–41.

22. J. Bates, 'Making Movies and Moving On', *Los Angeles Times*, 19 January 1998, p. A1.

23. Andrea Lane, 'The Consultancy Dream', *Business Review Weekly*, 4 May 1998, pp. 75–78.

24. 'GE: Just Your Average Everyday $60 Billion Family Grocery Store', *Industry Week*, 2 May 1994, pp. 13–18.

25. H. C. Lucas, Jr, *The T-form Organization: Using Technology to Design Organizations for the 21st Century* (San Francisco: Jossey-Bass, 1996).

26. This section is based on D. D. Davis, 'Form, Function and Strategy in Boundaryless Organizations', in A. Howard (ed.), *The Changing Nature of Work* (San Francisco: Jossey-Bass, 1995), pp. 112–38; P. Roberts, 'We Are One Company, No Matter Where We Are. Time and Space Are Irrelevant', *Fast Company*, April/May 1998, pp. 122–28; R. L. Cross, A. Yan and M. R. Louis, 'Boundary Activities in "Boundaryless" Organizations: A Case Study of a Transformation to a Team-Based Structure', *Human Relations*, June 2000, pp. 841–68; and R. Ashkenas, D. Ulrich, T. Jick and S. Kerr, *The Boundaryless Organization: Breaking the Chains of Organizational Structure*, revised and updated (San Francisco: Jossey-Bass, 2002).

27. See J. Lipnack and J. Stamps, *The TeamNet Factor* (Essex Junction, VT: Oliver Wight Publications, 1993); J. Fulk and G. DeSanctis, 'Electronic Communication and Changing Organizational Forms', *Organization Science*, July–August 1995, pp. 337–49; A. Cortese, 'Here Comes the Intranet', *Business Week*, 26 February 1996, pp. 76–84; and M. Hammer, *The Agenda* (New York: Crown Business, 2001).

28. T. Burns and G. M. Stalker, *The Management of Innovation* (London: Tavistock, 1961); and J. A. Courtright, G. T. Fairhurst and L. E. Rogers, 'Interaction Patterns in Organic and Mechanistic Systems', *Academy of Management Journal*, December 1989, pp. 773–802.

29. This analysis is referred to as a contingency approach to organisation design. See, for example, I. M. Pennings, 'Structural Contingency Theory: A Reappraisal', in B. M. Staw and L. L. Cummings (eds), *Research in Organizational Behavior*, vol. 14 (Greenwich, CT: JAI Press, 1992), pp. 267–309.

30. The strategy–structure thesis was originally proposed in A. D. Chandler, Jr, *Strategy & Structure: Chapters in the History of the Industrial Enterprise* (Cambridge, MA: MIT Press, 1962). For an updated analysis, see T. L. Amburgey and T. Dacin, 'As the Left Foot Follows the Right? The Dynamics of Strategic and Structural Change', *Academy of Management Journal*, December 1994, pp. 1427–52.

31. See R. E. Miles and C. C. Snow, *Organizational Strategy, Structure, and Process* (New York: McGraw-Hill, 1978); D. Miller, 'The Structural and Environmental Correlates of Business Strategy', *Strategic Management Journal*, January–February 1987, pp. 55–76; D. C. Galunic and K. M. Eisenhardt, 'Renewing the Strategy–Structure–Performance Paradigm', in B. M. Staw and L. L. Cummings (eds), *Research in Organizational Behavior*, vol. 16 (Greenwich, CT: JAI Press, 1994), pp. 215–55; and I. C. Harris and T. W. Ruefli, 'The Strategy/Structure Debate: An Examination of the Performance Implications', *Journal of Management Studies*, June 2000, pp. 587–603.

32. See, for example, P. M. Blau and R. A. Schoenherr, *The Structure of Organizations* (New York: Basic Books, 1971); D. S. Pugh, 'The Aston Program of Research: Retrospect and Prospect', in A. H. Van de Ven and W. F. Joyce (eds), *Perspectives on Organization Design and Behavior* (New York: Wiley, 1981), pp. 135–66; R. Z. Gooding and J. A. Wagner III, 'A Meta-analytic Review of the Relationship Between Size and Performance: The Productivity and Efficiency of Organizations and Their Subunits', *Administrative Science Quarterly*, December 1985, pp. 462–81; and A. C. Bluedorn, 'Pilgrim's Progress: Trends and Convergence in Research on Organizational Size and Environments', *Journal of Management*, Summer 1993, pp. 163–92.

33. See J. Woodward, *Industrial Organization: Theory and Practice* (London: Oxford University Press, 1965); C. Perrow, 'A Framework for the Comparative Analysis of Organizations', *American Sociological Review*, April 1967, pp. 194–208; J. D. Thompson, *Organizations in Action* (New York: McGraw-Hill, 1967); J. Hage and M. Aiken, 'Routine Technology, Social Structure, and Organizational Goals', *Administrative*

Science Quarterly, September 1969, pp. 366–77; C. C. Miller, W. H. Glick, Y. Wang and G. P. Huber, 'Understanding Technology–Structure Relationships: Theory Development and Meta-analytic Theory Testing', *Academy of Management Journal*, June 1991, pp. 370–99; and K. H. Roberts and M. Grabowski, 'Organizations, Technology, and Structuring', in S. R. Clegg, C. Hardy and W. R. Nord (eds), *Managing Organizations: Current Issues* (Thousand Oaks, CA: Sage, 1999), pp. 159–71.

34. See F. E. Emery and E. Trist, 'The Causal Texture of Organizational Environments', *Human Relations*, February 1965, pp. 21–32; P. Lawrence and J. W. Lorsch, *Organization and Environment: Managing Differentiation and Integration* (Boston: Harvard Business School, Division of Research, 1967); and Bluedorn, 'Pilgrim's Progress'.

35. G. G. Dess and D. W. Beard, 'Dimensions of Organizational Task Environments', *Administrative Science Quarterly*, March 1984, pp. 52–73; E. A. Gerloff, N. K. Muir and W. D. Bodensteiner, 'Three Components of Perceived Environment Uncertainty: An Exploratory Analysis of the Effects of Aggregation', *Journal of Management*, December 1991, pp. 749–68; and O. Shenkar, N. Aranya and T. Almor, 'Construct Dimensions in the Contingency Model: An Analysis Comparing Metric and Non-metric Multivariate Instruments', *Human Relations*, May 1995, pp. 559–80.

36. See, for example, L. W. Porter and E. E. Lawler, III, 'Properties of Organization Structure in Relation to Job Attitudes and Job Behavior', *Psychological Bulletin*, July 1965, pp. 23–51; L. R. James and A. P. Jones, 'Organization Structure: A Review of Structural Dimensions and Their Conceptual Relationships with Individual Attitudes and Behavior', *Organizational Behavior and Human Performance*, June 1976, pp. 74–113; D. R. Dalton, W. D. Todor, M. J. Spendolini, G. J. Fielding and L. W. Porter, 'Organization Structure and Performance: A Critical Review', *Academy of Management Review*, January 1980, pp. 49–64; W. Snizek and J. H. Bullard, 'Perception of Bureaucracy and Changing Job Satisfaction: A Longitudinal Analysis', *Organizational Behavior and Human Performance*, October 1983, pp. 275–87; and D. B. Turban and T. L. Keon, 'Organisational Attractiveness: An Interactionist Perspective', *Journal of Applied Psychology*, April 1994, pp. 184–93.

37. See, for example, P. R. Harris and R. T. Moran, *Managing Cultural Differences*, 4th ed. (Houston, TX: Gulf Publishing, 1996).

38. See, for example, B. Schneider, 'The People Make the Place', *Personnel Psychology*, Autumn 1987, pp. 437–53; B. Schneider, H. W. Goldstein and D. B. Smith, 'The ASA Framework: An Update', *Personnel Psychology*, Winter 1995, pp. 747–73; and J. Schaubroeck, D. C. Ganster and J. R. Jones, 'Organization and Occupation Influences in the Attraction–Selection–Attrition Process', *Journal of Applied Psychology*, December 1998, pp. 869–91.

PHOTO CREDITS

468 Beetle assembly line, Mexico; **480** Trademarks of The Coca-Cola Company are used with permission. The Coca-Cola Company is not the producer of this publication, nor does it endorse the contents.

Organisational Culture

CHAPTER **16**

CHAPTER OUTLINE

Institutionalisation: A forerunner of culture
What is organisational culture?
Impact of major religions on culture
What do cultures do?
Creating and sustaining culture
How employees learn culture
Creating an ethical organisational culture
Creating a customer-responsive culture
Spirituality and organisational culture

LEARNING OBJECTIVES

After studying this chapter, you should be able to:

1. Describe institutionalisation and its relationship to organisational culture
2. Define the common characteristics making up organisational culture
3. Contrast strong and weak cultures
4. Identify the impact of major world religions and their role in reinforcing international diversity
5. Identify the functional and dysfunctional effects of organisational culture on people and the organisation
6. Explain the factors that determine and maintain an organisation's culture
7. Outline the various socialisation alternatives available to management
8. Clarify how culture is transmitted to employees
9. Describe a customer-responsive culture
10. Identify characteristics of a spiritual culture

*In any organisation, there are the ropes
to skip and the ropes to know.*
R. Ritti and G. Funkhouser

Jorma Ollila, CEO of Nokia——visionary, master-manager and shaper of the future.

Nokia is a true global success story.[1] Founded in 1885 in southern Finland, the company began as a paper manufacturer. In the 1920s it added manufacturing of rubber boots, raincoats and hunting rifles. It went into consumer electronics in the 1950s by making television sets. But it didn't find its current niche until the late 1980s, when management decided to change strategies—to transform Nokia by focussing on the emerging market for mobile phones and networks. Jorma Ollila, who was then the company's chief financial officer, was put in charge of the mobile phone business. He became CEO in 1992 and the rest, as they say, is history.

Management's revised strategy has proven an overwhelming success. Nokia is now the world's leading manufacturer of mobile phones. With 35 per cent of the world's mobile phone market, its annual sales have reached US$28.1 billion, with pre-tax profits of over US$3.1 billion.

Part of Nokia's success was undoubtedly due to being in the right place at the right time. What, then, explains Nokia's remarkable performance? A major part of the answer is Nokia's strong organisational culture. Ollila has carefully shaped Nokia's culture around four core values: customer satisfaction, achievement, respect for the individual, and continuous learning. Ollila believes Nokia has outpaced its competitors because the firm is more customer-focused, resulting in more desirable products. The company focuses on making things that are better suited to customer needs and on rapidly responding as those needs change. For example, Nokia was first to the market with phones that didn't require two hands to use and with switchable covers and changeable ringing tones.

Talk with Nokia employees and they speak about similar aspects of what they like about working at the company: Respect for individual employees. Opportunities for personal growth and responsibility. Teamwork. A feeling of family. Freedom to be creative. Minimal rules and regulations. Little or no hierarchy. 'You join Nokia, and no one will give you a very accurate job description,' says a company market relations manager. 'You don't know who your boss is. So you live in this state of confusion—it never goes away. You have to adapt to it.' Nokia prides itself on attracting employees who can deal with ambiguity; then the company continually emphasises the importance of flexibility by minimising formalisation.

To facilitate the company's desire to create a family-like environment, Nokia provides a rich array of benefits and services to facilitate work/life balance. There are on-site saunas, 24-hour gyms, cafeterias with company-subsidised meals, and a staff physician in many locations. Telecommuting is also widely practised. For example, although Nokia's headquarters is in Finland, its design director works out of Los Angeles.

A strong organisational culture such as Nokia provides employees with an understanding of 'the way things are done around here'. It provides stability to an organisation. But, for some organisations, it can also be a major barrier to change. In this chapter, we show that every organisation has a culture and, depending on its strength, it can have a significant influence on the attitudes and behaviours of organisation members.

Institutionalisation: A Forerunner of Culture

The idea of viewing organisations as cultures—where there is a system of shared meaning among members—is a relatively recent phenomenon. Until the mid-1980s, organisations were, for the most part, simply thought of as rational means by which to coordinate and control a group of people. They had vertical levels, departments, authority relationships, and so forth. But organisations are more. They have personalities, too, just like individuals. They can be rigid or flexible, unfriendly or supportive, innovative or conservative. Virgin Blue Airline offices and people *are* different from the offices and people at Qantas. The University of Sydney and the University of Technology Sydney are in the same business—post-secondary education—and separated only by the width of Parramatta Road on the outskirts of the Sydney CBD, but each has a unique feeling and character beyond its structural characteristics. Organisational theorists now acknowledge this by recognising the important role that culture plays in the lives of organisation members. Interestingly, though, the origin of culture as an independent variable affecting an employee's attitudes and behaviour can be traced back more than 50 years to the notion of **institutionalisation**.[2]

institutionalisation
When an organisation takes on a life of its own, apart from any of its members, and acquires immortality.

When an organisation becomes institutionalised, it takes on a life of its own, apart from its founders or any of its members. Ross Perot created Electronic Data Systems (EDS) in the early 1960s, but he left in 1987 to found a new company, Perot Systems. EDS has continued to thrive despite the departure of its founder. Sony, Qantas, BHP Billiton, AMP, McDonald's and Disney are examples of organisations that have existed beyond the life of their founder or any one member.

In addition, when an organisation becomes institutionalised, it becomes valued for itself, not merely for the goods or services it produces. It acquires a quasi-form of immortality. If its original goals are no longer relevant, it doesn't go out of business. Rather, it redefines itself. A classic example is the Toowoomba Foundry in Queensland. It was originally created to manufacture windmills and water pumps. When demand for these products declined, the Toowoomba Foundry didn't close down. It merely redefined its objectives and redirected itself into other types of manufacturing, including contracts for steam engines and steel railway sleepers for Queensland Rail. With well over 100 years in manufacturing, the Toowoomba Foundry took on an existence that went well beyond its original mission to manufacture irrigation equipment for the agricultural industry.

Institutionalisation operates to produce common understandings among members about what is appropriate and, fundamentally, meaningful behaviour.[3] So, when an organisation takes on institutional permanence, acceptable modes of behaviour become largely self-evident to its members. As we will see, this is essentially the same thing that organisational culture does. So, an understanding of what makes up an organisation's culture, and how it is created, sustained and learned, will enhance our ability to explain and predict the behaviour of people at work.

What is Organisational Culture?

A number of years back, an executive was asked to explain what he thought the term *organisational culture* meant. He gave essentially the same answer that a Supreme Court Justice once gave in attempting to define pornography: 'I can't define it, but I know it when I see it.' This executive's approach to defining organisational culture isn't acceptable for our purposes. We need a basic definition to provide a point of departure for our quest to better understand the phenomenon. In this section, we propose a specific definition and review several peripheral issues that revolve around this definition.

A DEFINITION

There seems to be wide agreement that **organisational culture** refers to a system of shared meaning held by members that distinguishes the organisation from other organisations.[4] This system of shared meaning is, on closer examination, a set of key characteristics that the organisation values. The research suggests that there are seven primary characteristics that, in aggregate, capture the essence of an organisation's culture.[5]

1. *Innovation and risk taking:* the degree to which employees are encouraged to be innovative and take risks.
2. *Attention to detail:* the degree to which employees are expected to exhibit precision, analysis and attention to detail.
3. *Outcome orientation:* the degree to which management focuses on results or outcomes, rather than on the techniques and processes used to achieve those outcomes.
4. *People orientation:* the degree to which management decisions take into consideration the effect of outcomes on people within the organisation.
5. *Team orientation:* the degree to which work activities are organised around teams, rather than individuals.
6. *Aggressiveness:* the degree to which people are aggressive and competitive, rather than easygoing.
7. *Stability:* the degree to which organisational activities emphasise maintaining the status quo in contrast to growth.

Each of these characteristics exists on a continuum from low to high. Appraising the organisation on these seven characteristics, then, gives a composite picture of the organisation's culture. This picture becomes the basis for feelings of shared understanding that members have about the organisation, how things are done in it, and the way members are supposed to behave. Table 16.1 demonstrates how these characteristics can be mixed to create highly diverse organisations.

CULTURE IS A DESCRIPTIVE TERM

Organisational culture is concerned with how employees perceive the characteristics of an organisation's culture, not with whether or not they like them. That is, it's a descriptive term. This is important, because it differentiates this concept from that of job satisfaction.

Research on organisational culture has sought to measure how employees see their organisation: Does it encourage teamwork? Does it reward innovation? Does it stifle initiative?

In contrast, job satisfaction seeks to measure affective responses to the work environment. It is concerned with how employees feel about the organisation's expectations, reward practices, and the like. Although the two terms undoubtedly have overlapping characteristics, keep in mind that the term *organisational culture* is descriptive, while *job satisfaction* is evaluative.

DO ORGANISATIONS HAVE UNIFORM CULTURES?

Organisational culture represents a common perception held by the organisation's members. This was made explicit when we defined culture as a system of *shared* meaning. We should expect, therefore, that individuals with different backgrounds or at different levels in the organisation would tend to describe the organisation's culture in similar terms.[6]

Acknowledgment that organisational culture has common properties doesn't mean, however, that there cannot be subcultures within any given culture. Most large organisations have a dominant culture and numerous sets of subcultures.[7]

A **dominant culture** expresses the core values that are shared by a majority of the organisation's members. When we talk about an organisation's culture, we are referring to its dominant culture. It is this macro view of culture that gives an organisation its distinct personality.[8]

organisational culture
A system of shared meaning held by members that distinguishes the organisation from other organisations.

LEARNING OBJECTIVE
2
Define the common characteristics making up organisational culture

dominant culture
Expresses the core values that are shared by a majority of the organisation's members.

TABLE 16.1   **Contrasting organisational cultures**

Organisation A

This organisation is a manufacturing firm. Managers are expected to fully document all decisions; and 'good managers' are those who can provide detailed data to support their recommendations. Creative decisions that incur significant change or risk are not encouraged. Because managers of failed projects are openly criticised and penalised, managers try not to implement ideas that deviate much from the status quo. One lower-level manager quoted an often-used phrase in the company: 'If it ain't broke, don't fix it.'

There are extensive rules and regulations in this firm that employees are required to follow. Managers supervise employees closely to ensure there are no deviations. Management is concerned with high productivity, regardless of the impact on employee morale or turnover.

Work activities are designed around individuals. There are distinct departments and lines of authority, and employees are expected to minimise formal contact with other employees outside their functional area or line of command. Performance evaluations and rewards emphasise individual effort, although seniority tends to be the primary factor in the determination of pay raises and promotions.

Organisation B

This organisation is also a manufacturing firm. Here, however, management encourages and rewards risk taking and change. Decisions based on intuition are valued as much as those that are well rationalised. Management prides itself on its history of experimenting with new technologies and its success in regularly introducing innovative products. Managers or employees who have a good idea are encouraged to 'run with it'. And failures are treated as 'learning experiences'. The company prides itself on being market-driven and rapidly responsive to the changing needs of its customers.

There are few rules and regulations for employees to follow, and supervision is loose because management believes that its employees are hardworking and trustworthy. Management is concerned with high productivity but believes that this comes through treating its people right. The company is proud of its reputation as being a good place to work.

Job activities are designed around work teams, and team members are encouraged to interact with people across functions and authority levels. Employees talk positively about the competition between teams. Individuals and teams have goals, and bonuses are based on achievement of these outcomes. Employees are given considerable autonomy in choosing the means by which the goals are attained.

---

subcultures
Minicultures within an organisation, typically defined by department designations and geographical separation.

core values
The primary or dominant values that are accepted throughout the organisation.

Subcultures tend to develop in large organisations to reflect common problems, situations or experiences that members face. These subcultures are likely to be defined by department designations and geographical separation. The purchasing department, for example, can have a subculture that is uniquely shared by members of that department. It will include the **core values** of the dominant culture, plus additional values unique to members of the purchasing department. Similarly, an office or unit of the organisation that is physically separated from the organisation's main operations may take on a different personality. Again, the core values are essentially retained, but they are modified to reflect the separated unit's distinct situation.

If organisations had no dominant culture and were composed only of numerous subcultures, the value of organisational culture as an independent variable would be significantly lessened because there would be no uniform interpretation of what represented appropriate and inappropriate behaviour. It is the 'shared meaning' aspect of culture that makes it such a potent device for guiding and shaping behaviour. That's what allows us to say that Microsoft's culture values aggressiveness and risk taking[9] and then to use that information to better understand the behaviour of Microsoft executives and employees. But we cannot ignore the reality that many organisations also have subcultures that can influence the behaviour of members.

STRONG VERSUS WEAK CULTURES

It has become increasingly popular to differentiate between strong and weak cultures.[10] The argument here is that strong cultures have a greater impact on employee behaviour and are more directly related to reduced turnover.

In a **strong culture**, the organisation's core values are both intensely held and widely shared.[11] The more members who accept the core values and the greater their commitment to those values is, the stronger the culture is. Consistent with this definition, a strong culture will have a great influence on the behaviour of its members because the high degree of sharedness and intensity creates an internal climate of high behavioural control. For example, the Australian company Officeworks is fast developing one of the strongest service cultures in the office-supplies retailing industry. Officeworks employees know in no uncertain terms what is expected of them, and these expectations go a long way in shaping their behaviour.

One specific result of a strong culture should be lower employee turnover. A strong culture demonstrates high agreement among members about what the organisation stands for. Such unanimity of purpose builds cohesiveness, loyalty and organisational commitment. These qualities, in turn, lessen employees' propensity to leave the organisation.[12]

strong culture
Culture in which the core values are intensely held and widely shared.

LEARNING OBJECTIVE
3
Contrast strong and weak cultures

CULTURE VERSUS FORMALISATION

A strong organisational culture increases behavioural consistency. In this sense, we should recognise that a strong culture can act as a substitute for formalisation.

In a previous chapter, we discussed how formalisation's rules and regulations act to regulate employee behaviour. High formalisation in an organisation creates predictability, orderliness and consistency. Our point here is that a strong culture achieves the same end without the need for written documentation. Therefore, we should view formalisation and culture as two different roads to a common destination. The stronger an organisation's culture, the less management need be concerned with developing formal rules and regulations to guide employee behaviour. Those guides will be internalised in employees when they accept the organisation's culture.

ORGANISATIONAL CULTURE VERSUS NATIONAL CULTURE

Throughout this book we have argued that national differences—that is, national cultures—must be taken into account if accurate predictions are to be made about organisational behaviour in different countries. But does national culture override an organisation's culture? Is an IBM facility in Germany, for example, more likely to reflect German ethnic culture or IBM's corporate culture?

The research indicates that national culture has a greater impact on employees than does their organisation's culture.[13] German employees at an IBM facility in Munich, therefore, will be influenced more by German culture than by IBM's culture. This means that as influential as organisational culture is in shaping employee behaviour, national culture is even more influential. The positive to draw from this is that those diverse national cultures around the world influencing employees within the local operations help to make the company globally more flexible and adaptable to the world economy and events.

The preceding conclusion has to be qualified to reflect the self-selection that goes on at the hiring stage.[14] A British multinational corporation, for example, is likely to be less concerned with hiring the 'typical Italian' for its Italian operations than in hiring an Italian who fits with the corporation's way of doing things. We should expect, therefore, that the employee selection process would be used by multinationals to find and hire job applicants who are a good fit with

LEARNING OBJECTIVE

4

Identify the impact of major world religions and their role in reinforcing international diversity

their organisation's dominant culture, even if such applicants are somewhat atypical for members of their country.

Impact of Major Religions on Culture

Trying to determine whether religions shape cultures or are shaped by cultures would be a pointless exercise. This is because most of the world's major religions are so intertwined with culture as to make distinctions almost impossible. At the same time, an appreciation of the major religions of the world can provide managers with some insight into how people of different cultures view the world around them. It can also help to explain some of the differences between cultures when diverse religions are involved.

Animism

animism
Belief in souls of people, spirits of the dead and ancestors, and spirits in inanimate objects.

Animism involves a belief in the souls of people, spirits of the dead and ancestors, and the spirits in inanimate objects such as trees, the soil, rivers and rocks. Usually found in nomadic and/or ancient agricultural societies, it still exerts significant influence over the cultures of many indigenous peoples in Asia, Africa, the Pacific and the Americas. Ancestor worship and shamanism are other features of animism that can be seen in more recent religions.[15]

Buddhism

Buddhism
Philosophy of living involving prayer, meditation and moral living.

First taught by the Buddha in the sixth century BC in India, **Buddhism** recognises that suffering is the natural condition for all creatures.[16] Through good works, meditation and prayer, moral living and service to others, it is possible for the endless cycle of death and rebirth to be broken and Nirvana (oneness with the universe) to be achieved. More a philosophy about life than a religion as such, Buddhism is practised, often with other religions, throughout Asia. Because of its inward personal focus and peaceful tenets, focused on achieving personal enlightenment, it coexists with other religions quite easily.

Christianity

Christianity
Religion based on belief in the deity and eternal life.

Building on the writings of the Jewish faith, **Christianity** commenced with the death of Christ approximately 2,000 years ago. Although claiming devotees in most parts of the world, Christian beliefs have been fragmented by numerous schisms that have created different Christian churches with very distinct variations. Promising deliverance from the suffering of this world and atonement for wrongdoing, it is a very popular religion. It is also very individualistic, with its main emphasis being on the salvation of the individual, rather than on groups, families or society at large.

Confucianism

Confucianism
Philosophy of moral living, social obedience and filial piety.

Like Buddhism, **Confucianism** is more an ethical code or philosophy for harmonious human relations. Developed by Confucius (552–479 BC) over the course of his life of public service, it emphasised the relationship between people, ethical behaviours, filial piety, and the family as the foundation of all of society. The five natural laws for ethical behaviour in the family, according to Confucian principles, were: loyalty between sovereign and subject; intimacy between father and son; difference between husband and wife; precedence based on age; and trust between friends. The influence of Confucianism spans almost all of Asia, often coexisting with other religions such as Buddhism, Hinduism, animism, Taoism and Shintoism.

Hinduism

Hinduism
Religion predicated on reincarnation and progression of the soul through death and rebirth.

The origins of Hindu beliefs on the Indian subcontinent aren't exactly known but appear to be a blend of animism, polytheism, mysticism, and a plethora of divinities, goddesses and saints (*saddhu*). Central to **Hinduism** is the death and rebirth cycle of life with its reliance on a strict caste system for the ordering of social life.[17] For those who lead moral and righteous lives, practise ritual cleansing and purification, and perform rituals of worship and meditation, each rebirth will be at a higher level in the caste system, ideally leading to permanent union with the gods.

Islam
Springing originally from the same prophets as for the Jewish faith, **Islam** (or the religion of Muslims) was defined by the prophet Mohammed. Based on the writings of the Holy Koran, all Muslims pledge total submission to a single God, called Allah. Suffering and tragedy are the lessons from which all Muslims learn submission to the will of God. As such, Islam and the control of society by a select few are often linked, as can be seen in many Arab and Middle East societies.

Islam
Religion recognising a single deity and total subjugation of will to this deity

Shintoism
Shintoism is a distinctly Japanese religion, rarely found elsewhere. Commonly practised alongside Buddhism, Taoism and even Christianity, the Shinto religion is a mixture of ancestor worship, Eastern medicines, shamanism and the worship of nature.[18] The choice of religious observance (Shinto, Buddhism, Zen or Christianity) depends on the view of the individual as to the most appropriate religion for a particular aspect of spiritual or physical need at the time.

Shintoism
Mixture of ancestor worship, medical practices, shamanism and worship of nature.

Taoism
Taoism is similar to Buddhism and Confucianism in that it is primarily focused on the philosophical aspects of the person's ethical behaviours, particularly sincerity and honesty. Taoism teachings also centre on the role of nature in the spiritual lives of its followers.

Taoism
Philosophy of life based on ethical behaviour and the role of nature.

Zen
A form of Buddhism introduced into Japan in the 12th century, **Zen** advocates the development of enlightenment and understanding of the universe through self-contemplation and meditation. Zen has become increasingly widely known and practised in the Western world, particularly by those persons disenchanted with materialism and organised religions.

Zen
A derivative of Buddhism, involving self-contemplation and meditation to find enlightenment.

Space prevents a wider discussion of these major religions. Each has numerous variants (for example, Christianity is divided into Protestant and Roman Catholic, Roman Catholic and Eastern Orthodoxy, Russian Orthodoxy and Greek Orthodoxy—the list is almost infinite). Irrespective of which religion(s) are followed by individuals, they have profound impacts on the broader societal values, customs, structures and cultures. By being aware of the importance of different religions in different cultures, managers in global organisations can come to appreciate the diversity and subtleties of various ideas, values, customs and practices for employees from those countries.

What Do Cultures Do?

We have alluded to the impact of organisational culture on behaviour. We have also explicitly argued that a strong culture should be associated with reduced turnover. In this section, we will more carefully review the functions that culture performs and assess whether culture can be a liability for an organisation.

CULTURE'S FUNCTIONS

Culture performs a number of functions within an organisation. First, it has a boundary-defining role—that is, it creates distinctions between one organisation and others. Second, it conveys a sense of identity for organisation members. Third, culture facilitates the generation of commitment to something larger than one's individual self-interest. Fourth, it enhances the stability of the social system. Culture is the social glue that helps to hold the organisation together by providing appropriate standards for what employees should say and do. Finally, culture serves as a sense-making and control mechanism that guides and shapes the attitudes and behaviour of employees. It is this last function that is of particular interest to us.[19] As the following quote makes clear, culture defines the rules of the game:

> Culture by definition is elusive, intangible, implicit, and taken for granted. But every organisation develops a core set of assumptions, understandings, and implicit rules that govern day-to-day behaviour in the workplace. . . . Until newcomers learn the rules, they are not accepted as full-fledged members of the organisation. Transgressions of the rules on the part of high-level executives or front-line employees result in universal disapproval and powerful penalties. Conformity to the rules becomes the primary basis for reward and upward mobility.[20]

The role of culture in influencing employee behaviour appears to be increasingly important in today's workplace.[21] As organisations have widened spans of control, flattened structures, introduced teams, reduced formalisation and empowered employees, the *shared meaning* provided by a strong culture ensures that everyone is pointed in the same direction.

As we show later in this chapter, who receives a job offer to join the organisation, who is appraised as a high performer and who gets the promotion are all strongly influenced by the individual–organisation 'fit'—that is, whether the applicant or employee's attitudes and behaviour are compatible with the culture. It's not a coincidence that employees at Sea World and Movie-World theme parks appear to be almost universally attractive, clean, and wholesome looking, with bright smiles. That's the image the management of the theme park seeks. The company selects employees who will maintain that image. And once on the job, a strong culture, supported by formal rules and regulations, ensures that the theme park employees will act in a relatively uniform and predictable way.

LEARNING OBJECTIVE

5

Identify the functional and dysfunctional effects of organisational culture on people and the organisation

CULTURE AS A LIABILITY

We are treating culture in a non-judgmental manner. We haven't said that it's good or bad, only that it exists. Many of its functions, as outlined, are valuable for both the organisation and the employee. Culture enhances organisational commitment and increases the consistency of employee behaviour. These are clearly benefits to an organisation. From an employee's standpoint, culture is valuable because it reduces ambiguity. It tells employees how things are done and what is important. But we shouldn't ignore the potentially dysfunctional aspects of culture, especially a strong one, on an organisation's effectiveness.

Barrier to change

Culture is a liability when the shared values aren't in agreement with those that will further the organisation's effectiveness. This is most likely to occur when an organisation's environment is dynamic. When an environment is undergoing rapid change, an organisation's entrenched culture may no longer be appropriate. So, consistency of behaviour is an asset to an organisation when it faces a stable environment. It may, however, burden the organisation and make it difficult to respond to changes in the environment. This helps to explain the challenges that executives at organisations such as Westpac, Suncorp-Metway, Coles Myer, Arnott's and Qantas have had in recent years in adapting to upheavals in their environment.[22] These organisations have strong cultures that worked well for them in the past. But these strong cultures become barriers to change when 'business as usual' is no longer effective.

Barrier to diversity

Hiring new employees who, because of race, gender, disability or other differences, are not like the majority of the organisation's members creates a paradox.[23] Management wants new employees to accept the organisation's core cultural values. Otherwise, these employees are unlikely to fit in or be accepted. But at the same time, management wants to openly acknowledge and demonstrate support for the differences that these employees bring to the workplace.

Myth *or* Science?

'Success breeds success'

This statement isn't always true. Generally speaking, success creates positive momentum. People like being associated with a successful team or organisation, which allows winning teams and organisations to get the best new recruits. Microsoft's incredible success in the 1990s made it a highly desirable place to work. They had their pick among the 'best and the brightest' job applicants when filling job slots. Success led to further successes. Microsoft's experience is generalisable across decades to other companies. In the 1960s, when General Motors controlled nearly 50 per cent of the US automobile market, GM was the most sought-after employer by newly minted MBAs. In the early 1990s, Motorola was routinely described as one of the best-managed and successful companies, and it was able to attract the best and the brightest engineers and professionals.

But success often breeds failure, especially in organisations with strong cultures. Organisations that have tremendous successes begin to believe in their own invulnerability. They often become arrogant. They lose their competitive edge. Their strong cultures reinforce past practices and make change difficult. 'Why change? It worked in the past. If it ain't broke, don't fix it.'

The corporate highway is littered with companies that let arrogance undermine previous successes. JC Penney and Sears once ruled the US retail-department-store market. Their executives considered their markets immune to competition. Beginning in the mid-1970s in the United States, Wal-Mart did a pretty effective job of humbling Penney and Sears' management. General Motors executives, safe and cloistered in their Detroit headquarters, ignored the aggressive efforts by Japanese automobile firms to penetrate its markets. The result? GM's market share has been in a free fall for three decades. Motorola may have been the high-tech darling of the early 1990s, when it dominated world markets for semiconductors and analog cellular phones, but the company became arrogant. It stumbled badly in the digital market, failed to listen to the needs of its customers, and overextended itself in Asia. In the first quarter of 2001 the company lost US$206 million and was in the process of cutting 22,000 jobs worldwide.

Sources: D. Miller, 'What Happens after Success: The Perils of Excellence', *Journal of Management Studies*, May 1994, pp. 11–38; D. Roth, 'From Poster Boy to Whipping Boy: Burying Motorola', *Fortune*, 6 July 1998, p. 28; and J. Howell-Jones, 'Motorola Cuts Jobs as Profits Plummet', <www.vnunet.com>, 19 April 2001.

Strong cultures put considerable pressure on employees to conform. They limit the range of values and styles that are acceptable. In some instances, such as the widely publicised Texaco case (which was settled on behalf of 1,400 employees for US$176 million) in which senior managers made disparaging remarks about minorities, a strong culture that condones prejudice can even undermine formal corporate diversity policies.[24]

Organisations seek out and hire diverse individuals because of the alternative strengths these people bring to the workplace. Yet these diverse behaviours and strengths are likely to diminish in strong cultures as people attempt to fit in. Strong cultures, therefore, can be liabilities when they effectively eliminate the unique strengths that people of different backgrounds bring to the organisation. Moreover, strong cultures can also be liabilities when they support institutional bias or become insensitive to people who are different.

Barrier to acquisitions and mergers

Historically, the key factors that management looked at in making acquisition or merger decisions were related to financial advantages or product synergy. In recent years, cultural compatibility has become the primary concern.[25] While a favourable financial statement or product line may be the initial attraction of an acquisition candidate, whether the acquisition actually works seems to have more to do with how well the two organisations' cultures match up.

A number of acquisitions consummated in the 1990s have already failed. And the primary cause is conflicting organisational cultures.[26] For example, AT&T's 1991 acquisition of NCR was a disaster. AT&T's unionised employees objected to working in the same building as NCR's non-union staff. Meanwhile, NCR's conservative, centralised culture didn't take kindly to AT&T's insistence on calling supervisors 'coaches' and removing executives' office doors. By the time AT&T finally sold NCR, the failure of the deal had cost AT&T more than US$3 billion. In 1998, Daimler-Benz paid US$36 billion for Chrysler Corp. But precision engineering drove Daimler's culture, whereas Chrysler's strength was salesmanship. Instead of the hoped-for synergies and cost savings, the merger didn't work. It wiped out US$60 billion in market value as Chrysler went from being the most profitable car maker in the United States to its biggest money loser. Prognosticators are already forecasting hard times for the recent Hewlett-Packard and Compaq merger. Critics question whether Compaq's confrontational culture will clash with HP's congenial, egalitarian one.[27]

Creating and Sustaining Culture

An organisation's culture doesn't pop out of thin air. Once established, it rarely fades away. What forces influence the creation of a culture? What reinforces and sustains these forces once they are in place? We answer both of these questions in this section.

HOW A CULTURE BEGINS

An organisation's current customs, traditions and general way of doing things are largely due to what it has done before and the degree of success it has had with those endeavours. This leads us to the ultimate source of an organisation's culture: its founders.[28]

The founders of an organisation traditionally have a major impact on that organisation's early culture. They have a vision of what the organisation should be. They are unconstrained by previous customs or ideologies. The small size that typically characterises new organisations further facilitates the founders' imposition of their vision on all organisational members.

Culture creation occurs in three ways.[29] First, founders hire and keep only employees who think and feel the same way they do. Second, they indoctrinate and socialise these employees to their way of thinking and feeling. And finally, the founders' own behaviour acts as a role model that encourages employees to identify with them and thereby internalise their beliefs, values and assumptions. When the organisation succeeds, the founders' vision becomes seen as a primary determinant of that success. At this point, the founders' entire personality becomes embedded in the culture of the organisation.

The culture at Hyundai, the giant Korean conglomerate, is largely a reflection of its founder Chung Ju Yung. Hyundai's fierce, competitive style, and its disciplined, authoritarian nature are the same characteristics often used to describe Chung. Other contemporary examples of founders who have had an immeasurable impact on their organisation's culture would include Bill Gates at Microsoft, Ingvar Kamprad at IKEA, Gerry Harvey at Harvey Norman, Dick Smith at the Dick Smith retail chain, Mary Kay at Mary Kay Cosmetics, and Richard Branson at the Virgin Group.

KEEPING A CULTURE ALIVE

Once a culture is in place, there are practices within the organisation that act to maintain it by giving employees a set of similar experiences.[30] For example, many of the human resource practices discussed in the previous chapter reinforce the organisation's culture. The selection process, performance evaluation criteria, training and career development activities, and promotion procedures ensure that those hired fit in with the culture, reward those who support it, and penalise (and even expel) those who challenge it. Three forces play a particularly important part in sustaining a culture: selection practices, the actions of top management, and socialisation methods. Let's take a closer look at each.

Selection

The explicit goal of the selection process is to identify and hire individuals who have the knowledge, skills and abilities to perform the jobs within the organisation successfully. Typically, more than one candidate will be identified who meets any given job's requirements. When that point is reached, it would be naive to ignore that the final decision as to who is hired will be significantly influenced by the decision maker's judgment of how well the candidates will fit into the organisation. This attempt to ensure a proper match, whether purposely or inadvertently, results in the hiring of people who have values essentially consistent with those of the organisation, or at least a good portion of those values.[31] In addition, the selection process provides information to applicants about the organisation. Candidates learn about the organisation and, if they perceive a conflict between their values and those of the organisation, they can self-select themselves out of the applicant pool. Selection, therefore, becomes a two-way street, allowing employer or applicant to abrogate a marriage if there appears to be a mismatch. In this way, the selection process sustains an organisation's culture by selecting out those individuals who might attack or undermine its core values.

For example, applicants for entry-level positions in brand management at Procter & Gamble (P&G) experience an exhaustive application and screening process. Their interviewers are part of an elite cadre who have been selected and trained extensively via lectures, videotapes, practice interviews and role plays to identify applicants who will successfully fit in at P&G. Applicants are interviewed in depth for qualities such as their ability to 'turn out high volumes of excellent work', 'identify and understand problems' and 'reach thoroughly substantiated and well-reasoned conclusions that lead to action'. P&G values rationality and seeks applicants who think that way. University graduate applicants receive two interviews and a general knowledge test on campus before being flown to head office for three more one-on-one interviews and a group interview at lunch. Each encounter seeks corroborating evidence of the traits that the firm believes correlate highly with 'what counts' for success at P&G.[32]

Applicants for positions at Compaq Computer are carefully chosen for their ability to fit into the company's teamwork-oriented culture. As one executive put it, 'We can find lots of people who are competent.... The No. 1 issue is whether they fit into the way we do business.'[33] At Compaq, that means job candidates who are easy to get along with and who feel comfortable with the company's consensus management style. To increase the likelihood that loners and those with big egos get screened out, it's not unusual for an applicant to be interviewed by 15 people, who represent all departments of the company and a variety of seniority levels.[34]

Top management

The actions of top management also have a major impact on the organisation's culture.[35] Through what they say and how they behave, senior executives establish norms that filter down through the organisation as to whether risk taking is desirable; how much freedom managers should give their employees; what is appropriate dress; what actions will pay off in terms of pay raises, promotions and other rewards; and the like.

For example, Robert A. Keirlin has been called 'the cheapest CEO in America'.[36] Keirlin is chairman and CEO of Fastenal Co., the largest speciality retailer of nuts and bolts in the United States, with 6,500 employees. He takes a salary of only US$60,000 a year. He owns only three suits, each of which he bought used. He clips grocery coupons, drives a Toyota, and stays in low-priced motels when he travels on business. Does Keirlin need to pinch pennies? No. The market value of his shares in Fastenal is about US$300 million. But the man prefers a modest personal lifestyle. And he prefers the same for his company. Keirlin argues that his behaviour should send a message to all his employees: we don't waste things in this company. Keirlin sees himself as a role model for frugality, and employees at Fastenal have learned to follow his example.

Adventurer, explorer, entrepreneur—Dick Smith is all these. Unashamedly Australian, he not only puts his own stamp on the culture of his companies but for his latest venture he even put his name and face.

Socialisation

No matter how good a job the organisation does in recruiting and selection, new employees aren't fully indoctrinated in the organisation's culture. Maybe most important, because they are unfamiliar with the organisation's culture, new employees are potentially likely to disturb the beliefs and customs that are in place. The organisation will, therefore, want to help new employees adapt to its culture. This adaptation process is called **socialisation**.[37]

All army recruits (whether in Australia, Singapore, Taiwan, or any other country) must go through boot camp, where they 'prove' their commitment. Of course, at the same time, the army trainers are indoctrinating new recruits in the 'army way' of doing things. New Sanyo employees go through an intensive five-month training program (trainees eat and sleep together in company-subsidised dormitories and are required to take holidays together at company-owned resorts) where they learn the Sanyo way of doing everything—from how to speak to superiors to proper grooming and dress.[38] The company considers this program essential for transforming young employees, fresh out of school, into dedicated *kaisha senshi*, or corporate warriors. All new employees at Starbucks, the large coffee chain, go through 24 hours of training.[39] Classes are offered on everything necessary to turn new employees into brewing consultants. They learn the Starbucks philosophy, the company jargon (including phrases such as 'half-decaf double tall almond skim mocha'), and even how to help customers make decisions about beans, grind and espresso machines. The result is employees who understand Starbucks' culture and who project an enthusiastic and knowledgeable interface with customers. For new incoming employees in the upper ranks, companies often put considerably more time and effort into the socialisation process. At The Limited (an on-line gift and collectables retailer), newly hired vice presidents and regional directors go through an intensive one-month program, called 'onboarding', designed to immerse these executives in The Limited's culture.[40] During this month they have no direct responsibilities for tasks associated with their new positions. Instead, they spend all their work time meeting with other senior leaders and mentors, working the floors of retail stores, evaluating employee and customer habits, investigating the competition, and studying The Limited's past and current operations.

As we discuss socialisation, keep in mind that the most critical socialisation stage is at the time of entry into the organisation. This is when the organisation seeks to mould the outsider into an employee 'in good standing'. Employees who fail to learn the essential or pivotal role behaviours risk being labelled 'nonconformists' or 'rebels', which often leads to expulsion. But the organisation will be socialising every employee, though maybe not as explicitly, throughout his or her entire career in the organisation. This further contributes to sustaining the culture.

Socialisation can be conceptualised as a process made up of three stages: pre-arrival, encounter and metamorphosis.[41] The first stage encompasses all the learning that occurs before a new member joins the organisation. In the second stage, the new employee sees what the

socialisation
The process that adapts employees to the organisation's culture.

LEARNING OBJECTIVE

7

Outline the various socialisation alternatives available to management organisation is really like and confronts the possibility that expectations and reality may diverge. In the third stage, the relatively long-lasting changes take place. The new employee masters the skills required for their job, successfully performs their new roles, and makes the adjustments to their work group's values and norms.[42] This three-stage process has an impact on the new employee's work productivity, commitment to the organisation's objectives and eventual decision to stay with the organisation. Figure 16.1 depicts this process.

The **pre-arrival stage** explicitly recognises that each individual arrives with a set of values, attitudes and expectations. These cover both the work to be done and the organisation. For example, in many jobs, particularly professional work, new members will have undergone a considerable degree of prior socialisation in training and in school. One of the main purposes of a business school, for example, is to socialise business students to the attitudes and behaviours that business firms want. If business executives believe that successful employees value the profit ethic, are loyal, will work hard, and desire to achieve, they can hire individuals out of business schools who have been pre-moulded in this pattern. But pre-arrival socialisation goes beyond the specific job. The selection process is used in most organisations to inform prospective employees about the organisation as a whole. In addition, as noted previously, the selection process acts to ensure the inclusion of the 'right type'—those who will fit in. 'Indeed, the ability of the individual to present the appropriate face during the selection process determines his ability to move into the organisation in the first place. Thus, success depends on the degree to which the aspiring member has correctly anticipated the expectations and desires of those in the organisation in charge of selection.'[43]

On entry into the organisation, the new member enters the **encounter stage**. Here the individual confronts the possible dichotomy between their expectations—about their job, their fellow employees, their supervisor, and the organisation in general—and reality. If expectations prove to have been more or less accurate, the encounter stage merely provides a reaffirmation of the perceptions gained earlier. However, this is often not the case. Where expectations and reality differ, the new employee must undergo socialisation that will detach them from their previous assumptions and replace them with another set that the organisation deems desirable. At the extreme, a new member may become totally disillusioned with the actualities of their job and resign. Proper selection should significantly reduce the probability of the latter occurrence.

Finally, the new member must work out any problems discovered during the encounter stage. This may mean going through changes—hence, we call this the **metamorphosis stage**. The options presented in Table 16.2 are alternatives designed to bring about the desired metamorphosis. Note, for example, that the more management relies on socialisation programs that are formal, collective, fixed, serial and emphasise divestiture, the greater the likelihood that newcomers' differences and perspectives will be stripped away and replaced by standardised and predictable behaviours. Careful selection by management of newcomers' socialisation

pre-arrival stage
The period of learning in the socialisation process that occurs before a new employee joins the organisation.

encounter stage
The stage in the socialisation process in which a new employee sees what the organisation is really like and confronts the possibility that expectations and reality may diverge.

metamorphosis stage
The stage in the socialisation process in which a new employee changes and adjusts to the job, work group and organisation.

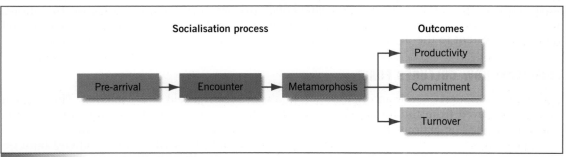

FIGURE 16.1   **A socialisation model**

TABLE 16.2	Entry socialisation options

Formal versus Informal. The more a new employee is segregated from the ongoing work setting and differentiated in some way to make explicit their newcomers' role, the more formal socialisation is. Specific orientation and training programs are examples. Informal socialisation puts the new employee directly into their job, with little or no special attention.

Individual versus Collective. New members can be socialised individually. This describes how it's done in many professional offices. They can also be grouped together and processed through an identical set of experiences, as in an army training camp.

Fixed versus Variable. This refers to the time schedule in which newcomers make the transition from outsider to insider. A fixed schedule establishes standardised stages of transition. This characterises rotational training programs. It also includes probationary periods, such as the eight- to ten-year 'associate' status used by accounting and law firms before deciding on whether or not a candidate is made a partner. Variable schedules give no advance notice of their transition timetable. Variable schedules describe the typical promotion system, where one isn't advanced to the next stage until one is 'ready'.

Serial versus Random. Serial socialisation is characterised by the use of role models who train and encourage the newcomer. Apprenticeship and mentoring programs are examples. In random socialisation, role models are deliberately withheld. The new employee is left on their own to figure things out.

Investiture versus Divestiture. Investiture socialisation assumes that the newcomer's qualities and qualifications are the necessary ingredients for job success, so these qualities and qualifications are confirmed and supported. Divestiture socialisation tries to strip away certain characteristics of the recruit. Initiation rites for 'newcomers' go through divestiture socialisation to shape them into the proper role.

Sources: Based on J. Van Maanen, 'People Processing: Strategies of Organizational Socialization', *Organizational Dynamics*, Summer 1978, pp. 19–36; and E. H. Schein, 'Organizational Culture', *American Psychologist*, February 1990, p. 116.

experiences can—at the extreme—create conformists who maintain traditions and customs, or inventive and creative individualists who consider no organisational practice sacred.

We can say that metamorphosis and the entry socialisation process is complete when the new member has become comfortable with the organisation and their job. They have internalised the norms of the organisation and their work group, and understand and accept these norms. The new member feels accepted by their peers as a trusted and valued individual, is confident that they have the competence to complete the job successfully, and understands the system—not only their own tasks, but the rules, procedures and informally accepted practices as well. Finally, they know how they will be evaluated—that is, what criteria will be used to measure and appraise their work. They know what is expected, and what constitutes a job 'well done'. As Figure 16.2 shows, successful metamorphosis should have a positive impact on the new employee's productivity and their commitment to the organisation, and reduce their propensity to leave the organisation.

SUMMARY: HOW CULTURES FORM

Figure 16.2 summarises how an organisation's culture is established and sustained. The original culture is derived from the founder's philosophy. This, in turn, strongly influences the criteria used in hiring. The actions of the current top management set the general climate of what is acceptable behaviour and what is not. How employees are to be socialised will depend both on the degree of success achieved in matching new employees' values to those of the organisation in the selection process and on top management's preference for socialisation methods.

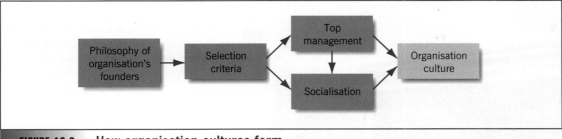

FIGURE 16.2   How organisation cultures form

OB Controversies

Are the cultures of global companies becoming the same?

An intriguing question is whether the increased number of global companies and globalisation is leading to a more common organisational culture worldwide and to convergence of cultures. The speed at which fashions spread globally is an indication of the commonality of shared values, at least in fashion statements. Could the same be true of organisational cultures—are they becoming more similar? The research suggests that the answer is 'no', at least for now. Hofstede's research (discussed in Chapter 3) identified that one of the key dimensions of national culture is the difference on the individualism–collectivism continuum. This has bearing on the risk preferences and decision-making styles of managers within those cultures. This isn't significantly altered by global commerce. Likewise, employees aren't likely to adopt different corporate values and shared meanings if they are in conflict with the national cultures in which they are embedded. The GLOBE research program reveals similar findings—that employees of global companies will tend to retain their national cultural values even when working in a global context. This suggests that employees with similar sets of cultural values will tend to 'cluster' within the international company, leading to 'pockets' of shared values that may or may not reflect the intended or desired global organisational set of cultural values. Managers and executives need to look closely at this issue to ensure the greatest 'fit' among the different cultural value 'sets' across the company.

Source: P. J. D. Drenth and D. N. Den Hartog, 'Culture and Organizational Differences', in W. J. Lonner and D. L. Dinnel (eds), *Merging Past, Present and Future in Cross-Cultural Psychology: Selected Papers from the 14th International Congress of the International Association for Cross-Cultural Psychology* (Lisse, Netherlands, 1999), pp. 489–502. Reproduced with permission by Swets and Zeitlinger Publishers.

How Employees Learn Culture

LEARNING OBJECTIVE

8

Clarify how culture is transmitted to employees

Culture is transmitted to employees in a number of forms, the most potent being stories, rituals, material symbols and language.

STORIES

During the days when Henry Ford II was chairman of the Ford Motor Co., one would have been hard pressed to find a manager who hadn't heard the story about Mr Ford reminding his executives, when they got too arrogant, that 'It's my name that's on the building.' The message was clear: Henry Ford II ran the company!

Started in Adelaide in 1985, Anthony and Sylvia Toop set out to create the best real estate company in Australia. They succeeded by being innovative, nimble, risk-taking and prepared to challenge the boundaries in order to provide clients with unmatched service delivery.

Nike has a number of senior executives who spend much of their time serving as corporate storytellers. And the stories they tell are meant to convey what Nike is about.[44] When they tell the story of how co-founder (and University of Oregon athletics coach) Bill Bowerman went to his workshop and poured rubber into his wife's waffle iron to create a better running shoe, they are talking about Nike's spirit of innovation. When new hires hear tales of running star Steve Prefontaine's battles to make running a professional sport and to attain better-performance equipment, they learn of Nike's commitment to helping athletes.

Nordstrom employees are fond of the following story, which strongly conveys the company's policy towards customer returns. When this speciality retail chain was in its infancy, a customer came in and wanted to return a set of automobile tyres. The sales clerk was a little uncertain how to handle the problem. As the customer and sales clerk were talking, Mr Nordstrom walked by and overheard the conversation. He immediately interceded, asking the customer how much he had paid for the tyres. He then instructed the clerk to take the tyres back and provide a full cash refund. After the customer had received his refund and left, the perplexed clerk looked at the boss. 'But, Mr Nordstrom, we don't sell tyres!' 'I know,' replied the boss, 'but we do whatever we need to do to make the customer happy. I mean it when I say we have a no-questions-asked return policy.' Nordstrom then picked up the telephone and called a friend in the auto parts business to see how much he could get for the tyres.

Stories such as these circulate through many organisations. They typically contain a narrative of events about the organisation's founders, rule breaking, rags-to-riches successes, reductions in the workforce, relocation of employees, reactions to past mistakes, and organisational coping.[45] These stories anchor the present in the past and provide explanations and legitimacy for current practices. For the most part, these stories develop spontaneously. But some organisations actually try to manage this element of culture learning. For example, Krispy Kreme, a large doughnut maker in the United States, has a full-time 'Minister of Culture' whose primary responsibility is to tape interviews with customers and employees.[46] The stories these people tell are then put in the company's video magazine, which describes Krispy Kreme's history and values. Toop & Toop, an Adelaide real estate firm, has a 'Complaints Chairman', a position that is rotated monthly, whose primary responsibility is to meet with customers and resolve their complaints.[47] The stories these people tell are then circulated to all staff, and new procedures and policies are devised which are based on these values.

RITUALS

rituals
Repetitive sequences of activities that express and reinforce the key values of the organisation, which goals are most important, and which people are important and which are expendable.

Rituals are repetitive sequences of activities that express and reinforce the key values of the organisation—what goals are most important, which people are important, and which people are expendable.[48]

University faculty members undergo a lengthy ritual in their quest for permanent employment, or tenure. Typically, the faculty member is on probation for up to five years. At the end of that period, the member's colleagues, supervisors and senior managers must make one of two choices: grant the tenured appointment or terminate the academic's contract. What does it take to obtain tenure? It usually requires satisfactory teaching performance, service to the department and university, and scholarly activity. But, of course, what satisfies the requirements for tenure in one department at one university may be appraised as inadequate in another. The key is that the tenure decision, in essence, asks those who are tenured to assess whether the candidate has demonstrated, based on many years of performance, whether he or she fits in. Colleagues who have been socialised properly will have proved themselves worthy of being granted tenure. Every year, hundreds of faculty members at universities are denied tenure. In some cases, this action is a result of poor performance across the board. More often, however, the decision can be traced to the faculty member's not doing well in the areas that the tenured faculty believe are important. The lecturer who spends dozens of hours each week preparing for class and achieves outstanding evaluations by students, but who neglects his or her own research and publication activities, may be passed over for tenure. What has happened, simply, is that the academic has failed to adapt to the norms set by the department. The astute faculty member will assess early on in the probationary period what attitudes and behaviours his or her colleagues and supervisors want and will then proceed to give them what they want. And, of course, by demanding certain attitudes and behaviours, the tenured faculty have made significant strides towards standardising tenure candidates.

One of the better-known corporate rituals is Wal-Mart's company chant. Begun by the company's founder, Sam Walton, as a way to motivate and unite his workforce, 'Gimme a W, gimme an A, gimme an L, gimme a squiggle, give me an M, A, R, T!' has become a company ritual that bonds Wal-Mart workers and reinforces Sam Walton's belief in the importance of his employees to the company's success. Similar corporate chants are used by IBM, Ericsson, Novell, Deutsche Bank and PricewaterhouseCoopers.[49]

MATERIAL SYMBOLS

The headquarters of Alcoa doesn't look like your typical head office operation. There are few individual offices, even for senior executives. It is essentially made up of cubicles, common areas and meeting rooms. This informal corporate headquarters conveys to employees that Alcoa values openness, equality, creativity and flexibility.

Some corporations provide their top executives with chauffeur-driven limousines and, when they travel by air, unlimited use of the corporate jet or first-class commercial airline travel. Others may not get to ride in limousines or private jets, but they might still get a car and airfares paid for by the company. Only the car is a Commodore (with no driver) and the airline seat is in the economy section of a commercial airliner.

The layout of corporate headquarters, the types of automobiles top executives are given, and the presence or absence of corporate aircraft are a few examples of material symbols. Others include the size of offices, the elegance of furnishings, executive perks, and attire.[50] These material symbols convey to employees who is important, the degree of egalitarianism desired by top management, and the kinds of behaviour (for example, risk taking, conservative, authoritarian, participative, individualistic, social) that are appropriate.

LANGUAGE

Many organisations and units within organisations use language as a way to identify members of a culture or subculture. By learning this language, members attest to their acceptance of the culture and, in so doing, help to preserve it. Librarians are a rich source of terminology foreign to people outside their profession. They sprinkle their conversations liberally with acronyms such as ARL (Association for Research Libraries), OCLC (a centre in the United States that does cooperative cataloguing) and OPAC (for On-line Patron Accessing Catalogue). If you are a new employee at Boeing, you will find yourself learning a whole unique vocabulary of acronyms, including: BOLD (Boeing On-Line Data); CATIA (computer-graphics-aided three-dimensional interactive application); MAIDS (manufacturing assembly and installation data system); POP (purchased outside production); and SLO (service level objectives).[51]

Organisations, over time, often develop unique terms to describe equipment, offices, key personnel, suppliers, customers, or products that relate to its business. New employees are frequently overwhelmed with acronyms and jargon that, after six months on the job, have become fully part of their language. Once assimilated, this terminology acts as a common denominator that unites members of a given culture or subculture.

Creating an Ethical Organisational Culture

The content and strength of a culture influences an organisation's ethical climate and the ethical behaviour of its members.[52]

An organisational culture most likely to shape high ethical standards is one that is high in risk tolerance, low to moderate in aggressiveness, and focuses on means as well as outcomes. Managers in such a culture are supported for taking risks and innovating, are discouraged from engaging in unbridled competition, and will pay attention to *how* goals are achieved as well as to *what* goals are achieved.

A strong organisational culture will exert more influence on employees than a weak one. If the culture is strong and supports high ethical standards, it should have a very powerful and positive influence on employee behaviour. Johnson & Johnson, for example, has a strong culture that has long stressed corporate obligations to customers, employees, the community and shareholders, in that order. When poisoned Tylenol (a Johnson & Johnson product similar to Paracetamol) was found on store shelves in the United States, employees at Johnson & Johnson independently pulled the product from these stores before management had even issued a statement concerning the product tampering. No one had to tell these individuals what was morally right; they knew what Johnson & Johnson would expect them to do. In contrast, it wasn't until the Australian government issued a national recall of Pan Pharmaceuticals' health-care products that their products were removed from store shelves, despite earlier rumours of unethical manufacturing practices.

What can management do to create a more ethical culture? We suggest a combination of the following practices:

Be a visible role model. Employees will look to top-management behaviour as a benchmark for defining appropriate behaviour. When senior management is seen as taking the ethical high-road, it provides a positive message for all employees.

Communicate ethical expectations. Ethical ambiguities can be minimised by creating and disseminating an organisational code of ethics. It should state the organisation's primary values and the ethical rules that employees are expected to follow.

Provide ethical training. Set up seminars, workshops, and similar ethical training programs. Use these training sessions to reinforce the organisation's standards of conduct; to clarify what practices are and are not permissible; and to address possible ethical dilemmas.

Visibly reward ethical acts and punish unethical ones. Performance appraisals of managers should include a point-by-point evaluation of how their decisions measure up against the organisation's code of ethics. Appraisals must include the means taken to achieve goals, as well as the ends themselves. People who act ethically should be visibly rewarded for their behaviour. Just as importantly, unethical acts should be conspicuously punished.

Provide protective mechanisms. The organisation needs to provide formal mechanisms so that employees can discuss ethical dilemmas and report unethical behaviour without fear of reprimand. This might include creation of ethical counsellors, ombudsmen or ethical officers.

The Real Deal

Enron and the creation of an unethical culture

Enron Corp., which in December 2001 became the largest-ever bankruptcy in the United States, didn't fail solely because of improper accounting practices, although that was certainly a major contributor. It also failed because it had a culture that pushed executives into unethical behaviour.

During Enron's heyday in the late 1990s, the press regularly praised the company for its entrepreneurial culture: smart, sassy, creative and risk-taking. But a post-mortem analysis reveals a different culture—an unrelenting emphasis on earnings growth and individual initiative. Instead of rewarding new ideas, the company encouraged unethical corner cutting. How? First, it pressured executives to make their numbers. Second, it instilled lax controls over how those numbers were created. Third, it bred a 'yes-man' culture among executives. People were afraid to speak out on questionable practices for fear that it would adversely affect their performance evaluations and the size of their bonuses. Fourth, bonuses and money became the Almighty God. The company sought out and rewarded people who placed a high value on money. Jeff Skilling, the CEO who created Enron's 'in-your-face' culture, is quoted as saying, 'All that matters is money. You can buy loyalty with money.' Fifth, although managers were supposed to be graded on teamwork, the culture was heavily built around star players, with little value attached to team-building. The organisation rewarded highly competitive people who were less likely to share power, authority or information. Finally, the company continually set itself wildly optimistic expectations for growth and then drove executives to find ways to meet them. 'You've got someone at the top saying the stock price is the most important thing, which is driven by earnings,' said one insider. 'Whoever could provide earnings quickly would be promoted.'

One former Enron employee summed up the Enron culture this way: 'If your boss was [fudging], and you have never worked anywhere else, you just assume that everybody fudges earnings. Once you get there and you realised how it was, do you stand up and lose your job? It was scary. It was easy to get into "Well, everybody else is doing it, so maybe it isn't so bad."'

Sources: Based on W. Zellner, 'Jeff Skilling: Enron's Missing Man', *Business Week*, 11 February 2002, pp. 38–40; and J. A. Byrne, 'The Environment Was Ripe for Abuse', *Business Week*, 25 February 2002, pp. 118–20.

LEARNING OBJECTIVE

9

Describe a customer-responsive culture

Creating a Customer-responsive Culture

French retailers have a well-established reputation for indifference to customers.[53] Sales people, for example, routinely make it clear to customers that their phone conversations shouldn't be interrupted. Just getting any help at all from a sales person can be a challenge. And no one in France finds it particularly surprising that the owner of a Paris store should complain that he was unable to work on his books all morning because he kept being bothered *by customers*!

Most organisations today are trying very hard to take the opposite approach to the French in dealing with their clients or customers. They are attempting to create a customer-responsive culture because they recognise that this is the path to customer loyalty and long-term profitability. Companies that have created such cultures— such as Woolworth's, Big W, Johnson & Johnson, Optus, Marriott Hotels, the Gold Coast theme parks and Dick Smith Foods—have built a strong and loyal customer base and have generally outperformed their competitors in revenue growth and financial performance. In this section, we will briefly identify the variables that shape customer-responsive cultures and offer some suggestions that management can follow for creating such cultures.

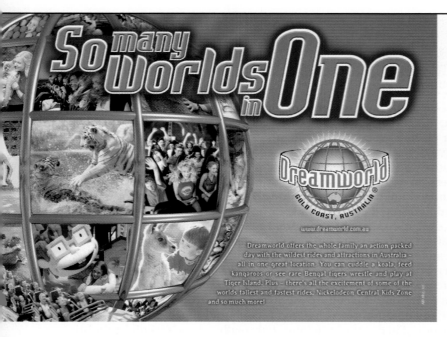

At Dreamworld the patron is not a customer or a visitor—they are a valued guest. Total focus on their guests' needs and desires earns for Dreamworld unique loyalty and repeat trips from all their guests.

KEY VARIABLES SHAPING CUSTOMER-RESPONSIVE CULTURES

A review of the evidence finds that half a dozen variables are routinely evident in customer-responsive cultures.[54]

First is the type of employees themselves. Successful, service-oriented organisations hire employees who are outgoing and friendly. Second is low formalisation. Service employees need to have the freedom to meet changing customer-service requirements. Rigid rules, procedures and regulations make this difficult. Third is an extension of low formalisation—it's the widespread use of empowerment. Empowered employees have the decision discretion to do what's necessary to please the customer. Fourth are good listening skills. Employees in customer-responsive cultures have the ability to listen to and understand messages sent by the customer. Fifth is role clarity. Service employees act as 'boundary spanners' between the organisation and its customers. They have to acquiesce to the demands of both their employer and the customer. This can create considerable role ambiguity and conflict, which reduces employees' job satisfaction and can hinder employee service performance. Successful customer-responsive cultures reduce employee uncertainty about the best way to perform their jobs and the importance of job activities. Finally, customer-responsive cultures have employees who exhibit organisational citizenship behaviour. They are conscientious in their desire to please the customer. And they are willing to take the initiative, even when it's outside their normal job requirements, to satisfy a customer's needs.

In summary, customer-responsive cultures hire service-oriented employees with good listening skills and the willingness to go beyond the constraints of their job description to do what's necessary to please the customer. It then clarifies their roles, frees them up to meet changing customer needs by minimising rules and regulations, and provides them with a wide range of decision discretion to do their job as they see fit.

MANAGERIAL ACTION

Based on the previously identified characteristics, we can suggest a number of actions that management can take if it wants to make its culture more customer-responsive. These actions are designed to create employees with the competence, ability and willingness to solve customer problems as they arise.

Selection

The place to start in building a customer-responsive culture is hiring service-contact people with the personality and attitudes consistent with a high service orientation. Singapore Airlines is a shining example of a company that has focused its hiring process on selecting out job candidates whose personalities aren't people-friendly. Job applicants go through an extensive interview process at Singapore Airlines in which company employees and executives carefully assess whether candidates have the charming and friendly personality that it wants in all its employees.

Studies show that friendliness, enthusiasm and attentiveness in service employees positively affect customers' perceptions of service quality.[55] So, managers should look for these qualities in applicants. In addition, job candidates should be screened so that new hires have the patience, concern about others and listening skills that are associated with customer-oriented employees.

Training and socialisation

Organisations that are trying to become more customer-responsive don't always have the option of hiring all new employees. More typically, management is faced with the challenge of making its current employees more customer-focused. In such cases, the emphasis will be on training, rather than hiring. This describes the dilemma that senior executives at companies such as General Motors-Holden, National Australia Bank and Suncorp-Metway have faced in the past decade as they have attempted to move away from their product focus. The content of these training programs will vary widely but should focus on improving product knowledge, active listening, showing patience and displaying emotions.

In addition, even new employees who have a customer-friendly attitude may need to understand management's expectations. So, all new service-contact people should be socialised into the organisation's goals and values. Lastly, even the most customer-focused employees can lose direction every once in a while. This should be addressed with regular training updates in which the organisation's customer-focused values are restated and reinforced.

Structural design

Organisation structures need to give employees more control. This can be achieved by reducing rules and regulations. Employees are better able to satisfy customers when they have some control over the service encounter. So, management needs to allow employees to adjust their behaviour to the changing needs and requests of customers. What customers *don't* want to hear are responses such as 'I can't handle this. You need to talk to someone else'; or 'I'm sorry, but that's against our company policy.'

Empowerment

Consistent with low formalisation is empowering employees with the discretion to make day-to-day decisions about job-related activities. This is a necessary component of a customer-responsive culture, because it allows service employees to make on-the-spot decisions to satisfy customers completely.[56]

Leadership

Leaders convey the organisation's culture through both what they say and what they do. Effective leaders in customer-responsive cultures deliver by conveying a customer-focused vision and demonstrating by their continual behaviour that they are committed to customers.

In almost every organisation that has successfully created and maintained a strong customer-responsive culture, its chief executive officer has played a major role in championing the message. For example, in the United States, DuPont's CEO, Richard Heckert, led the charge to change the mentality of his company's employees from emphasising research and product development to focusing on marketing and customer needs.[57]

Performance evaluation

There is an impressive amount of evidence demonstrating that behaviour-based performance evaluations are consistent with improved customer service.[58] Behaviour-based evaluations appraise employees on the basis of how they behave or act—on criteria such as effort, commitment, teamwork, friendliness, and the ability to solve customer problems—rather than on the measurable outcomes they achieve. Why are behaviours superior to outcomes for improving service? Because it gives employees the incentive to engage in behaviours that are conducive to improved service quality, and it gives employees more control over the conditions that affect their performance evaluations.[59]

In addition, a customer-responsive culture will be fostered by using 360-degree evaluations that include input from customers. Just the fact that employees know that part of their performance appraisal will include evaluations from customers is likely to make those employees more concerned with satisfying customer needs. Of course, this should only be used with employees who have direct contact with customers.

Reward systems

Finally, if management wants employees to give good service, it has to reward good service. It needs to provide ongoing recognition to employees who have demonstrated extraordinary effort to please customers and who have been singled out by customers for 'going the extra mile'. And it needs to make pay and promotions contingent on outstanding customer service.

Spirituality and Organisational Culture

What do Westpac, McKinsey & Company, Hewlett-Packard, Wetherill Associates and CPA Australia have in common? They are among a growing number of organisations that have embraced workplace spirituality.

WHAT IS WORKPLACE SPIRITUALITY?

workplace spirituality
The recognition that people have an inner life that nourishes and is nourished by meaningful work that takes place in the context of community.

Workplace spirituality is *not* about organised religious practices. It's not about God or theology. **Workplace spirituality** recognises that people have an inner life that nourishes and is nourished by meaningful work that takes place in the context of community.[60] Organisations that promote a spiritual culture recognise that people have both a mind and a spirit, seek to find meaning and purpose in their work, and desire to connect with other human beings and be part of a community.

WHY SPIRITUALITY NOW?

Historical models of management and organisational behaviour had no room for spirituality. As we noted in our discussion of emotions in Chapter 4, the myth of rationality assumed that the well-run organisation eliminated feelings. Similarly, concern about an employee's inner life had no role in the perfectly rational model. But just as we have now come to realise that the study of emotions improves our understanding of organisational behaviour, an awareness of spirituality can help you to better understand employee behaviour in the 21st century.

Of course, employees have always had an inner life. So, why has the search for meaning and purposefulness in work surfaced now? There are a number of reasons. We summarise them in Table 16.3.

LEARNING OBJECTIVE

10

Identify characteristics of a spiritual culture

CHARACTERISTICS OF A SPIRITUAL ORGANISATION

The concept of workplace spirituality draws on our previous discussions of topics such as values, ethics, motivation, leadership, work/life balance and job satisfaction. As you will see, for example, spiritual organisations are concerned with helping people to develop and reach their full potential. This is analogous to Maslow's description of self-actualisation that we discussed in relation to motivation. Similarly, organisations that are concerned with spirituality are more likely to directly address problems created by work/life conflicts.

TABLE 16.3	**Reasons for the growing interest in spirituality**

- As a counterbalance to the pressures and stress of a turbulent pace of life. Contemporary lifestyles—single-parent families, geographic mobility, the temporary nature of jobs, new technologies that create distance between people—underscore the lack of community many people feel and increases the need for involvement and connection.
- Ageing baby-boomers, reaching mid-life, are looking for something in their life.
- Formalised religion hasn't worked for many people and they continue to look for anchors to replace lack of faith and to fill a growing feeling of emptiness.
- Job demands have made the workplace dominant in many people's lives, yet they continue to question the meaning of work.
- The desire to integrate personal life values with one's professional life.
- In times of economic plenty, more people have the luxury to engage in a search to reach their full potential.

What differentiates spiritual organisations from their non-spiritual counterparts? Although research on this question is only preliminary, our review identified five cultural characteristics that tend to be evident in spiritual organisations.[61]

Strong sense of purpose

Spiritual organisations build their cultures around a meaningful purpose. While profits may be important, they are not the primary values of the organisation. Bunnings, for example, is strongly committed to providing the lowest prices, sustainable solutions and a pleasant experience for customers. The Body Shop has closely intermeshed socially responsible behaviour into its producing and selling of personal-care products, particularly in its support for the children's charity Children on the Edge. Dick Smith strives to sell consumer products that are made entirely in Australia to support Australian employment.

Focus on individual development

Spiritual organisations recognise the worth and value of people. They aren't just providing jobs. They seek to create cultures in which employees can continually learn and grow. Recognising the importance of people, they also try to provide employment security. Hewlett-Packard, for example, has gone to extremes to try to minimise the effect of economic downturns on its staff. The company has handled temporary downturns through voluntary attrition and shortened work weeks (shared by all); and longer-term declines through early retirements and buy-outs.

Trust and openness

Spiritual organisations are characterised by mutual trust, honesty and openness. Managers aren't afraid to admit mistakes. And they tend to be extremely up-front with their employees, customers and suppliers. The president of Wetherill Associates, a highly successful automotive parts distribution firm, says: 'We don't tell lies here, and everyone knows it. We are specific and honest about quality and suitability of the product for our customers' needs, even if we know they might not be able to detect any problem.'[62]

Employee empowerment

The high-trust climate in spiritual organisations, when combined with the desire to promote employee learning and growth, leads to management empowering employees to make most work-related decisions. Managers in spiritually based organisations are comfortable delegating authority to individual employees and teams. They trust their employees to make thoughtful and conscientious decisions. As a case in point, employees of Southwest Airlines in the United States—including flight attendants, customer service representatives and baggage handlers—are encouraged to take whatever action they deem necessary to meet customer needs or to help fellow workers, even if it means breaking company policies.

Toleration of employee expression
The final characteristic that differentiates spiritually based organisations is that they don't stifle employee emotions. They allow people to be themselves—to express their moods and feelings without guilt or fear of reprimand. Employees at the Flight Centre, for example, are encouraged to express their sense of humour on the job, to act spontaneously and to make their work fun.

CRITICISMS OF SPIRITUALITY

Critics of the spirituality movement in organisations have focused on two issues. First is the question of legitimacy. Specifically, do organisations have the right to impose spiritual values on their employees? Second is the question of economics. Are spirituality and profits compatible?

On the first question, there is clearly the potential for an emphasis on spirituality to make some employees uneasy. Critics might argue that secular institutions, especially business firms, have no business imposing spiritual values on employees. This criticism is undoubtedly valid when spirituality is defined as bringing religion and God into the workplace.[63] However, the criticism seems less stinging when the goal is limited to helping employees find meaning in their work lives. If the concerns listed in Table 16.3 truly characterise a growing segment of the workforce, then maybe the time is right for organisations to help employees find meaning and purpose in their work and to use the workplace as a source of community.

The issue of whether spirituality and profits are compatible objectives is certainly relevant for managers and investors in business. The evidence, although limited, indicates that the two objectives may be very compatible. A recent research study by a major consulting firm found that companies that introduced spiritually based techniques improved productivity and significantly reduced turnover.[64] Another study found that organisations that provide their employees with opportunities for spiritual development outperformed those that didn't.[65] Other studies also report that spirituality in organisations was positively related to creativity, employee satisfaction, team performance and organisational commitment.[66] And if you are looking for a single case to make the argument for spirituality, it's hard to beat Southwest Airlines. Southwest has one of the lowest employee turnover rates in the airline industry; it consistently has the lowest labour costs per distance flown of any major airline; it regularly outpaces its competitors for achieving on-time arrivals and fewest customer complaints; and it has proven itself to be the most consistently profitable airline in the United States.[67]

Summary and Implications for Managers

Figure 16.3 depicts organisational culture as an intervening variable. Employees form an overall subjective perception of the organisation based on factors such as degree of risk tolerance, team emphasis and support of people. This overall perception becomes, in effect, the organisation's culture or personality. These favourable or unfavourable perceptions then affect employee performance and satisfaction, with the impact being greater for stronger cultures.

Just as people's personalities tend to be stable over time, so too do strong cultures. This makes strong cultures difficult for managers to change. When a culture becomes mismatched to its environment, management will want to change it. But as the Point–Counterpoint debate following this section demonstrates, changing an organisation's culture is a long and difficult process. The result, at least in the short term, is that managers should treat their organisation's culture as relatively fixed.

One of the more important managerial implications of organisational culture relates to selection decisions. Recruiting individuals whose values don't align with those of the organisation is likely to lead to employees who lack motivation and commitment and who are dissatisfied with their jobs and the organisation.[68] Not surprisingly, employee 'misfits' have considerably higher turnover rates than individuals who perceive a good fit.[69]

We should also not overlook the influence that socialisation has on employee performance. An employee's performance depends to a considerable degree on knowing what he should or shouldn't do. Understanding the right way to do a job indicates proper socialisation. Furthermore, the appraisal of an individual's performance includes how well the person fits into the organisation. Can he or she get along with fellow employees? Does he or she have acceptable work habits and demonstrate the right attitude? These qualities differ between jobs and organisations. For example, on some jobs, employees will be evaluated more favourably if they are aggressive and outwardly indicate that they are ambitious. On another job, or on the same job in another organisation, such an approach may be evaluated negatively. As a result, proper socialisation becomes a significant factor in influencing both actual job performance and how others perceive it.

Point

ORGANISATIONAL CULTURES CAN'T BE CHANGED

An organisation's culture is made up of relatively stable characteristics. It develops over many years and is rooted in deeply held values to which employees are strongly committed. In addition, there are a number of forces continually operating to maintain a given culture. These include written statements about the organisation's mission and philosophy, the design of physical spaces and buildings, the dominant leadership style, hiring criteria, past promotion practices, entrenched rituals, popular stories about key people and events, the organisation's historic performance evaluation criteria and its formal structure.

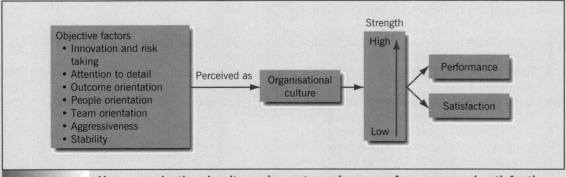

FIGURE 16.3 How organisational cultures impact employee performance and satisfaction

Selection and promotion policies are particularly important devices that work against cultural change. Employees chose the organisation because they perceived their values to be a 'good fit' with the organisation. They become comfortable with that fit and will strongly resist efforts to disturb the equilibrium. The terrific difficulties that organisations such as General Motors-Holden, Australia Post and Telstra have had in trying to reshape their cultures attest to this dilemma. These organisations historically tended to attract individuals who desired situations that were stable and highly structured. Those in control in organisations will also select senior managers who will continue the current culture. Even attempts to change a culture by going outside the organisation to hire a new chief executive are unlikely to be effective. The evidence indicates that the culture is more likely to change the executive, than the other way around.

Our argument shouldn't be viewed as saying that culture can *never* be changed. In the unusual case in which an organisation confronts a survival-threatening crisis—a crisis that is universally acknowledged as a true life-or-death situation—members of the organisation will be responsive to efforts at cultural change. However, anything less than a crisis is unlikely to be effective in bringing about cultural change.

Counterpoint

Changing an organisation's culture is extremely difficult, but cultures *can* be changed. The evidence suggests that cultural change is most likely to take place when most or all of the following conditions exist:

- *A dramatic crisis.* This is the shock that undermines the status quo and calls into question the relevance of the current culture. Examples of these crises might be a surprising financial setback, the loss of a major customer, or a dramatic technological breakthrough by a competitor.
- *Turnover in leadership.* New top leadership, which can provide an alternative set of key values, may be perceived as more capable of responding to the crisis.
- *Young and small organisations.* The younger the organisation is, the less entrenched its culture will be. Similarly, it's easier for management to communicate its new values when the organisation is small.
- *Weak culture.* The more widely held a culture is and the higher the agreement among members on its values, the more difficult it will be to change. Conversely, weak cultures are more amenable to change than strong ones.

If the above conditions exist, the following actions may lead to change: new stories and rituals need to be set in place by top management; employees should be selected and promoted who espouse the new values; the reward system needs to be changed to support the new values; and current subcultures need to be undermined through transfers, job rotation and terminations.

Under the best of conditions, these actions won't result in an immediate or dramatic shift in the culture. This is because, in the final analysis, cultural change is a lengthy process—measured in years, rather than in months. But cultures can be changed. The success that new leadership had in turning around the cultures at companies such as Harley-Davidson, IBM, Optus and Electronic Data Systems attests to this claim.

For Discussion

1. What is the difference between job satisfaction and organisational culture?
2. Can an employee survive in an organisation if they reject its core values? Explain.
3. If management sought a culture characterised as innovative and autonomous, what might its socialisation program look like?
4. Today's workforce is increasingly made up of part-time or contingent employees. Is organisational culture really important if the workforce is mostly temporary staff?
5. What defines an organisation's subcultures?
6. Contrast organisational culture with national culture.
7. How can culture be a liability to an organisation?
8. How does a strong culture affect an organisation's efforts to improve diversity?
9. What benefits can socialisation provide for the organisation? For the new employee?

10. Can you identify a set of characteristics that describes your university's culture? Compare them with several of your peers. How closely do they agree?
11. How is language related to organisational culture?
12. How can management create an ethical culture?
13. What criticisms have been targeted against bringing spirituality to the workplace?
14. 'We should be opposed to the manipulation of individuals for organisational purposes, but a degree of social uniformity enables organisations to work better.' Do you agree or disagree with this statement? What are its implications for organisational culture? Discuss.

Exercise

RATE YOUR CLASSROOM CULTURE

Listed here are 14 statements. Using the five-item scale (from Strongly Agree to Strongly Disagree), respond to each statement by circling the number that best represents your opinion.

	Strongly Agree	Agree	Neutral	Disagree	Strongly Disagree
1. I feel comfortable challenging statements made by my lecturer.	5	4	3	2	1
2. My lecturer heavily penalises assignments that aren't turned in on time.	1	2	3	4	5
3. My lecturer believes that 'it's final results that count'.	1	2	3	4	5
4. My lecturer is sensitive to my personal needs and problems.	5	4	3	2	1
5. A large portion of my final grade depends on how well I work with others in the class.	5	4	3	2	1
6. I often feel nervous and tense when I come to class.	1	2	3	4	5
7. My lecturer seems to prefer stability over change.	1	2	3	4	5
8. My lecturer encourages me to develop new and different ideas.	5	4	3	2	1
9. My lecturer has little tolerance for sloppy thinking.	1	2	3	4	5
10. My lecturer is more concerned with how I came to a conclusion than the conclusion itself.	5	4	3	2	1
11. My lecturer treats all students alike.	1	2	3	4	5
12. My lecturer frowns on class members helping each other with assignments.	1	2	3	4	5
13. Aggressive and competitive people have a distinct advantage in this class.	1	2	3	4	5
14. My lecturer encourages me to see the world differently.	5	4	3	2	1

Refer to Appendix C for scoring directions and key.

Case Study 16

Socially Responsible—and Profitable!

Working for The Body Shop, a niche retailer selling personal-care products with an annual turnover in excess of $80 million a year, is an experience most employees are very enthusiastic about. Employing over 600 casuals, part-timers and permanent employees, most enthusiastically report what a wonderful place The Body Shop is to work in—a virtual employees' paradise. What is it that causes The Body Shop's employees to be so committed and loyal to the company? Interviews with a number of employees suggest some common themes for the company's success with its people.

The Body Shop values its people. Staff know that they can come and go from the company when they need to, particularly when pursuing community work. Romanian-born Australian Carmelia Safrone has twice been involved in the company's Children on the Edge program, where volunteers from the company travel to Romania to help socialise and uplift groups of abandoned children in the former communist country. She joins volunteers from the company from 20 different countries, all with the company's support.

Closer to home, employees feel that the company values them, and they value the company's commitment to both their employees and to social and environmental causes. This employee loyalty and commitment shows. As Sturt Harker from the consulting firm PricewaterhouseCoopers observed, 'A big positive for The Body Shop is that the staff seem to fit the culture. It seems to me their people believe in the concept, they believe in the brands. Certainly when I shop there, they know the products.'

The company's mission statement embodies its social and environmental charter, stating clearly that it aims to campaign passionately for the protection of environmental issues as well as human and civil rights. The company embodies this in its corporate culture, not only in its community activities, but also in how it treats its employees. It stresses a balance between lifestyle and work. Employees are supported at every level, and more regular hours are stressed. When the shop closes at 6 pm, that's it for the day—your own life begins, free from requests for overtime and out-of-hours phone calls or call-backs. Employees are encouraged to pursue their own issues and interests with the same passion the company shows in pursuing its social and environmental issues, and employees know that when occasionally there is an overlap, the company will support their choices. It's no wonder that this non-unionised company has high staff tenure and low turnover rates that are the envy of the retail industry!

Questions

1. Describe the culture of The Body Shop.
2. What specific forces created this culture? What maintains it?
3. Describe the culture that the competitors of The Body Shop have.
4. Do you think The Body Shop will succeed or fail in the future with this culture? Why?

Source: Parts of this case are based on N. Way, 'Staffing: The Kings of Culture', *Business Review Weekly*, 7 April 2000.

Web Workout

1. The report at <www.aimnt.com.au/home/news_abls.htm> contends that trust is a foundation of organisational culture. Do you agree with this view? What implications does a finding of low levels of trust have for Australian organisations generally?
2. The culture of an organisation can pose very real dangers for people outside of the organisation. Visit the site <www.aviation.unsw.edu.au/uniken_boyd.html> and assess how important culture is to the community generally.
3. Developing a customer-responsive culture isn't restricted to organisations only. Have a read of how the local government of a holiday resort region in South Australia plans to use a community-wide customer-responsive culture to develop and grow the community's economic prosperity at <www.holdfast.sa.gov.au/about_us/pdf/strategic_plan.pdf>.
4. Visit the site <www.une.edu.au/clg/lgconf/papers/morrison.htm>. How do the building blocks of a culture affect the built environment of a region or country? Should we look at the built environment as an expression or a determinant of a culture?
5. Visit the site <http://northernway.org/workplace.html> and analyse the various themes that are emerging within the workplace spirituality theme. Are we dealing with one title for numerous issues?

KSS Program

KNOW THE CONCEPTS   SELF-AWARENESS   SKILLS APPLICATIONS

Reading an organisation's culture

After you have read this chapter, take Self-Assessment #42 (What's the Right Organisational Culture For Me?) on your enclosed CD-Rom and complete the skill-building module entitled 'Reading an Organisation's Culture' on page 647.

NOTES

1. Based on J. Fox, 'Nokia's Secret Code', *Fortune*, 1 May 2000, pp. 161–74; M. Moskowitz and R. Levering, 'Best Companies to Work For', *Fortune*, 4 February 2002; P. Taylor, 'Nokia Goes from Humble Origins to Global Success', *Financial Times*, 7 March 2002, p. 22; and <www.nokia.co.uk>.
2. P. Selznick, 'Foundations of the Theory of Organizations', *American Sociological Review*, February 1948, pp. 25–35.
3. See L. G. Zucker, 'Organizations as Institutions', in S. B. Bacharach (ed.), *Research in the Sociology of Organizations* (Greenwich, CT: JAI Press, 1983), pp. 1–47; A. J. Richardson, 'The Production of Institutional Behavior: A Constructive Comment on the Use of Institutionalization Theory in Organizational Analysis', *Canadian Journal of Administrative Sciences*, December 1986, pp. 304–16; L. G. Zucker, *Institutional Patterns and Organizations: Culture and Environment* (Cambridge, MA: Ballinger, 1988); and R. L. Jepperson, 'Institutions, Institutional Effects, and Institutionalism', in W. W. Powell and P. J. DiMaggio (eds), *The New Institutionalism in Organizational Analysis* (Chicago: University of Chicago Press, 1991), pp. 143–63.
4. See, for example, H. S. Becker, 'Culture: A Sociological View', *Yale Review*, Summer 1982, pp. 513–27; and E. H. Schein, *Organizational Culture and Leadership* (San Francisco: Jossey-Bass, 1985), p. 168.
5. This seven-item description is based on C. A. O'Reilly III, J. Chatman and D. F. Caldwell, 'People and Organizational Culture: A Profile Comparison Approach to Assessing Person–Organization Fit', *Academy of Management Journal*, September 1991, pp. 487–516; and J. A. Chatman and K. A. Jehn, 'Assessing the Relationship between Industry Characteristics and Organizational Culture: How Different Can You Be?', *Academy of Management Journal*, June 1994, pp. 522–53. For a review of cultural dimensions, see N. M. Ashkanasy, C. P. M. Wilderom and M. F. Peterson (eds), *Handbook of Organizational Culture and Climate* (Thousand Oaks, CA: Sage, 2000), pp. 131–45.
6. The view that there will be consistency among perceptions of organisational culture has been called the 'integration' perspective. For a review of this perspective and conflicting approaches, see D. Meyerson and J. Martin, 'Cultural Change: An Integration of Three Different Views', *Journal of Management Studies*, November 1987, pp. 623–47; and P. J. Frost, L. F. Moore, M. R. Louis, C. C. Lundberg and J. Martin (eds), *Reframing Organizational Culture* (Newbury Park, CA: Sage Publications, 1991).
7. See J. M. Jermier, J. W. Slocum, Jr, L. W. Fry and J. Gaines, 'Organizational Subcultures in a Soft Bureaucracy: Resistance Behind the Myth and Facade of an Official Culture', *Organization Science*, May 1991, pp. 170–94; S. A. Sackmann, 'Culture and Subcultures: An Analysis of Organizational Knowledge', *Administrative Science Quarterly*, March 1992, pp. 140–61; R. F. Zammuto, 'Mapping Organizational Cultures

and Subcultures: Looking Inside and Across Hospitals', paper presented at the 1995 National Academy of Management Conference, Vancouver, BC, August 1995; and G. Hofstede, 'Identifying Organizational Subcultures: An Empirical Approach', *Journal of Management Studies*, January 1998, pp. 1–12.

8. T. A. Timmerman, 'Do Organizations Have Personalities?', paper presented at the 1996 National Academy of Management Conference, Cincinnati, OH, August 1996.

9. S. Hamm, 'No Letup—and No Apologies', *Business Week*, 26 October 1998, pp. 58–64; and C. Carlson, 'Former Intel Exec Slams Microsoft Culture', *eWeek.com*, 26 March 2002.

10. See, for example, G. G. Gordon and N. DiTomaso, 'Predicting Corporate Performance from Organizational Culture', *Journal of Management Studies*, November 1992, pp. 793–98; and J. B. Sorensen, 'The Strength of Corporate Culture and the Reliability of Firm Performance', *Administrative Science Quarterly*, March 2002, pp. 70–91.

11. Y. Wiener, 'Forms of Value Systems: A Focus on Organizational Effectiveness and Cultural Change and Maintenance', *Academy of Management Review*, October 1988, p. 536.

12. R. T. Mowday, L. W. Porter and R. M. Steers, *Employee–Organization Linkages: The Psychology of Commitment, Absenteeism, and Turnover* (New York: Academic Press, 1982).

13. See N. J. Adler, *International Dimensions of Organizational Behavior*, 4th ed. (Cincinnati, OH: Southwestern, 2002), pp. 67–69.

14. S. C. Schneider, 'National vs. Corporate Culture: Implications for Human Resource Management', *Human Resource Management*, Summer 1988, p. 239.

15 Tapp, 'Karma and Cosmology: Anthropology and Religion', in G. Evans (ed.), *Asia's Cultural Mosaic: An Anthropological Introduction* (Singapore: Simon & Schuster (Asia), 1993), pp. 287–306.

16. T. Lowenstein, *The Vision of the Buddha: Philosophy and Meditation* (London: Macmillan, 1996).

17. Tapp, 'Karma and Cosmology', pp. 298–300.

18. J. Hendry, 'Japan: The Anthropology of Modernity', in G. Evans (ed.), *Asia's Cultural Mosaic: An Anthropological Introduction* (Singapore: Simon & Schuster (Asia), 1993), pp. 345–66.

19. See C. A. O'Reilly and J. A. Chatman, 'Culture as Social Control: Corporations, Cults, and Commitment', in B. M. Staw and L. L. Cummings (eds), *Research in Organizational Behavior*, vol. 18 (Greenwich, CT: JAI Press, 1996), pp. 157–200.

20. T. E. Deal and A. A. Kennedy, 'Culture: A New Look Through Old Lenses', *Journal of Applied Behavioral Science*, November 1983, p. 501.

21. J. Case, 'Corporate Culture', *INC.*, November 1996, pp. 42–53.

22. See, for example, P. L. Moore, 'She's Here to Fix the Xerox', *Business Week*, 6 August 2001, pp. 47–48; and C. Ragavan, 'FBI Inc.', *U.S. News & World Report*, 18 June 2001, pp. 15–21.

23. See C. Lindsay, 'Paradoxes of Organizational Diversity: Living within the Paradoxes', in L. R. Jauch and J. L. Wall (eds), *Proceedings of the 50th Academy of Management Conference* (San Francisco: 1990), pp. 374–78; T. Cox, Jr, *Cultural Diversity in Organizations: Theory, Research & Practice* (San Francisco: Berrett-Koehler, 1993), pp. 162–70; and L. Grensing-Pophal, 'Hiring to Fit Your Corporate Culture', *HRMagazine*, August 1999, pp. 50–54.

24. K. Labich, 'No More Crude at Texaco', *Fortune*, 6 September 1999, pp. 205–12; and 'Rooting Out Racism', *Business Week*, 10 January 2000, p. 66.

25. A. F. Buono and J. L. Bowditch, *The Human Side of Mergers and Acquisitions: Managing Collisions between People, Cultures, and Organizations* (San Francisco: Jossey-Bass, 1989); S. Cartwright and C. L. Cooper, 'The Role of Culture Compatibility in Successful Organizational Marriages', *Academy of Management Executive*, May 1993, pp. 57–70; R. J. Grossman, 'Irreconcilable Differences', *HRMagazine*, April 1999, pp. 42–48; J. Veiga, M. Lubatkin, R. Calori and P. Very, 'Measuring Organizational Culture Clashes: A Two-Nation Post-Hoc Analysis of a Cultural Compatibility Index', *Human Relations*, April 2000, pp. 539–57; and E. Krell, 'Merging Corporate Cultures', *Training*, May 2001, pp. 68–78.

26. D. Carey and D. Ogden, 'A Match Made in Heaven? Find Out Before You Merge', *Wall Street Journal*, 30 November 1998, p. A22; and M. Arndt, 'Let's Talk Turkeys', *Business Week*, 11 December 2000, pp. 44–46.

27. 'Carly's Last Stand?', *Business Week*, 24 December 2001, p. 65.

28. E. H. Schein, 'The Role of the Founder in Creating Organizational Culture', *Organizational Dynamics*, Summer 1983, pp. 13–28.

29. E. H. Schein, 'Leadership and Organizational Culture', in F. Hesselbein, M. Goldsmith and R. Beckhard (eds), *The Leader of the Future* (San Francisco: Jossey-Bass, 1996), pp. 61–62.

30. See, for example, J. R. Harrison and G. R. Carroll, 'Keeping the Faith: A Model of Cultural Transmission in Formal Organizations', *Administrative Science Quarterly*, December 1991, pp. 552–82.

31. B. Schneider, 'The People Make the Place', *Personnel Psychology*, Autumn 1987, pp. 437–53; D. E. Bowen, G. E. Ledford, Jr and B. R. Nathan, 'Hiring for the Organization, Not the Job', *Academy of Management Executive*, November 1991, pp. 35–51; B. Schneider, H. W. Goldstein and D. B. Smith, 'The ASA Framework: An Update', *Personnel Psychology*, Winter 1995, pp. 747–73; A. L. Kristof,

'Person–Organization Fit: An Integrative Review of Its Conceptualizations, Measurement, and Implications', *Personnel Psychology*, Spring 1996, pp. 1–49; D. M. Cable and T. A. Judge, 'Interviewers' Perceptions of Person–Organization Fit and Organizational Selection Decisions', *Journal of Applied Psychology*, August 1997, pp. 546–61; J. Schaubroeck, D. C. Ganster and J. R. Jones, 'Organization and Occupation Influences in the Attraction–Selection–Attrition Process', *Journal of Applied Psychology*, December 1998, pp. 869–91; and J. Harris and J. Brannick, *Finding and Keeping Great Employees* (New York: AMACOM, 1999).

32. R. Pascale, 'The Paradox of "Corporate Culture": Reconciling Ourselves to Socialization', *California Management Review*, Winter 1985, pp. 26–27.

33. 'Who's Afraid of IBM?', *Business Week*, 29 June 1987, p. 72.

34. Ibid.

35. D. C. Hambrick and P. A. Mason, 'Upper Echelons: The Organization as a Reflection of Its Top Managers', *Academy of Management Review*, April 1984, pp. 193–206; B. P. Niehoff, C. A. Enz and R. A. Grover, 'The Impact of Top-Management Actions on Employee Attitudes and Perceptions', *Group & Organization Studies*, September 1990, pp. 337–52; and H. M. Trice and J. M. Beyer, 'Cultural Leadership in Organizations', *Organization Science*, May 1991, pp. 149–69.

36. J. S. Lublin, 'Cheap Talk', *Wall Street Journal*, 11 April 2002, p. B14.

37. K. Walters, 'Complaints: Customer Anger Can Be a Healthy Sign', *Business Review Weekly*, 6 August 1999.

38. See, for example, J. P. Wanous, *Organizational Entry*, 2nd ed. (New York: Addison-Wesley, 1992); G. T. Chao, A. M. O'Leary-Kelly, S. Wolf, H. J. Klein and P. D. Gardner, 'Organizational Socialization: Its Content and Consequences', *Journal of Applied Psychology*, October 1994, pp. 730–43; B. E. Ashforth, A. M. Saks and R. T. Lee, 'Socialization and Newcomer Adjustment: The Role of Organizational Context', *Human Relations*, July 1998, pp. 897–926; D. A. Major, 'Effective Newcomer Socialization into High-Performance Organizational Cultures', in N. M. Ashkanasy, C. P. M. Wilderom and M. F. Peterson (eds), *Handbook of Organizational Culture & Climate* (Thousand Oaks, CA: Sage, 2000), pp. 355–68; and D. M. Cable and C. K. Parsons, 'Socialization Tactics and Person–Organization Fit', *Personnel Psychology*, Spring 2001, pp. 1–23.

39. B. Filipczak, 'Trained by Starbucks', *Training*, June 1995, pp. 73–79; and S. Gruner, 'Lasting Impressions', *INC.*, July 1998, p. 126.

40. K. Rhodes, 'Breaking in the Top Dogs', *Training*, February 2000, pp. 67–74.

41. J. Van Maanen and E. H. Schein, 'Career Development', in J. R. Hackman and J. L. Suttle (eds), *Improving Life at Work* (Santa Monica, CA: Goodyear, 1977), pp. 58–62.

42. D. C. Feldman, 'The Multiple Socialization of Organization Members', *Academy of Management Review*, April 1981, p. 310.

43. Van Maanen and Schein, 'Career Development', p. 59.

44. E. Ransdell, 'The Nike Story? Just Tell It!', *Fast Company*, January–February 2000, pp. 44–46.

45. D. M. Boje, 'The Storytelling Organization: A Study of Story Performance in an Office-Supply Firm', *Administrative Science Quarterly*, March 1991, pp. 106–26; and C. H. Deutsch, 'The Parables of Corporate Culture', *The New York Times*, 13 October 1991, p. F25.

46. 'Job Titles of the Future: Minister of Culture', *Fast Company*, September 1998, p. 64.

47. Ibid.

48. See K. Kamoche, 'Rhetoric, Ritualism, and Totemism in Human Resource Management', *Human Relations*, April 1995, pp. 367–85.

49. V. Matthews, 'Starting Every Day with a Shout and a Song', *Financial Times*, 2 May 2001, p. 11; and M. Gimein, 'Sam Walton Made Us a Promise', *Fortune*, 18 March 2002, pp. 121–30.

50. A. Rafaeli and M. G. Pratt, 'Tailored Meanings: On the Meaning and Impact of Organizational Dress', *Academy of Management Review*, January 1993, pp. 32–55.

51. 'DCACronyms', April 1997, Rev. D; published by The Boeing Co.

52. See B. Victor and J. B. Cullen, 'The Organizational Bases of Ethical Work Climates', *Administrative Science Quarterly*, March 1988, pp. 101–25; L. K. Trevino, 'A Cultural Perspective on Changing and Developing Organizational Ethics', in W. A. Pasmore and R. W. Woodman (eds), *Research in Organizational Change and Development*, vol. 4 (Greenwich, CT: JAI Press, 1990); and M. W. Dickson, D. B. Smith, M. W. Grojean and M. Ehrhart, 'An Organizational Climate Regarding Ethics: The Outcome of Leader Values and the Practices That Reflect Them', *Leadership Quarterly*, Summer 2001, pp. 197–217.

53. S. Daley, 'A Spy's Advice to French Retailers: Politeness Pays', *New York Times*, 26 December 2000, p. A4.

54. Based on M. J. Bitner, B. H. Booms and L. A. Mohr, 'Critical Service Encounters: The Employee's Viewpoint', *Journal of Marketing*, October 1994, pp. 95–106; M. D. Hartline and O. C. Ferrell, 'The Management of Customer-Contact Service Employees: An Empirical Investigation', *Journal of Marketing*, October 1996, pp. 52–70; M. L. Lengnick-Hall and Cynthia A. Lengnick-Hall, 'Expanding Customer Orientation in the HR Function', *Human Resource Management*, Fall 1999, pp. 201–14; B. Schneider, D. E. Bowen, M. G. Ehrhart and K. M. Holcombe, 'The Climate for Service: Evolution of a Construct', in N. M. Ashkanasy, C. P. M. Wilderom and M. F. Peterson (eds), *Handbook of Organizational Culture and Climate* (Thousand Oaks, CA: Sage, 2000), pp. 21–36; M. D. Hartline, J. G. Maxham III and D. O. McKee, 'Corridors of Influence in the Dissemination of Customer-Oriented Strategy to Customer Contact Service Employees', *Journal of Marketing*, April 2000, pp. 35–50;

and L. A. Bettencourt, K. P. Gwinner and M. L. Meuter, 'A Comparison of Attitude, Personality, and Knowledge Predictors of Service-Oriented Organizational Citizenship Behaviors', *Journal of Applied Psychology*, February 2001, pp. 29–41.

55. D. E. Bowen and B. Schneider, 'Boundary-Spanning-Role Employees and the Service Encounter: Some Guidelines for Future Management and Research', in J. Czepiel, M. R. Solomon and C. F. Surprenant (eds), *The Service Encounter* (New York: Lexington Books, 1985), pp. 127–47; W.-C. Tsai, 'Determinants and Consequences of Employee Displayed Positive Emotions', *Journal of Management*, vol. 27, no. 4, 2001, pp. 497–512; and S. D. Pugh, 'Service with a Smile: Emotional Contagion in the Service Encounter', *Academy of Management Journal*, October 2001, pp. 1018–27.

56. Hartline and Ferrell, 'The Management of Customer-Contact Service Employees', p. 56; and R. C. Ford and C. P. Heaton, 'Lessons from Hospitality That Can Serve Anyone', *Organizational Dynamics*, Summer 2001, pp. 41–42.

57. E. E. Messikomer, 'DuPont's "Marketing Community"', *Business Marketing*, October 1987, pp. 90–94.

58. See, for example, E. Anderson and R. L. Oliver, 'Perspectives on Behavior-Based Versus Outcome-Based Salesforce Control Systems', *Journal of Marketing*, October 1987, pp. 76–88; W. R. George, 'Internal Marketing and Organizational Behavior: A Partnership in Developing Customer-Conscious Employees at Every Level', *Journal of Business Research*, January 1990, pp. 63–70; and K. K. Reardon and B. Enis, 'Establishing a Company-Wide Customer Orientation Through Persuasive Internal Marketing', *Management Communication Quarterly*, February 1990, pp. 376–87.

59. Hartline and Ferrell, 'The Management of Customer-Contact Service Employees', p. 57.

60. D. P. Ashmos and D. Duchon, 'Spirituality at Work: A Conceptualization and Measure', *Journal of Management Inquiry*, June 2000, p. 139.

61. This section is based on I. A. Mitroff and E. A. Denton, *A Spiritual Audit of Corporate America: A Hard Look at Spirituality, Religion, and Values in the Workplace* (San Francisco: Jossey-Bass, 1999); J. Milliman, J. Ferguson, D. Trickett and B. Condemi, 'Spirit and Community at Southwest Airlines: An Investigation of a Spiritual Values-Based Model', *Journal of Organizational Change Management*, vol. 12, no. 3, 1999, pp. 221–33; E. H. Burack, 'Spirituality in the Workplace', *Journal of Organizational Change Management*, vol. 12, no. 3, 1999, pp. 280–91; and F. Wagner-Marsh and J. Conley, 'The Fourth Wave: The Spiritually-Based Firm', *Journal of Organizational Change Management*, vol. 12, no. 3, 1999, pp. 292–302.

62. Cited in Wagner-Marsh and Conley, 'The Fourth Wave', p. 295.

63. M. Conlin, 'Religion in the Workplace: The Growing Presence of Spirituality in Corporate America', *Business Week*, 1 November 1999, pp. 151–58; and P. Paul, 'A Holier Holiday Season', *American Demographics*, December 2001, pp. 41–45.

64. Cited in Conlin, 'Religion in the Workplace', p. 153.

65. C. P. Neck and J. F. Milliman, 'Thought Self-Leadership: Finding Spiritual Fulfillment in Organizational Life', *Journal of Managerial Psychology*, vol. 9, no. 8, 1994, p. 9.

66. D. W. McCormick, 'Spirituality and Management', *Journal of Managerial Psychology*, vol. 9, no. 6, 1994, p. 5; E. Brandt, 'Corporate Pioneers Explore Spiritual Peace', *HRMagazine*, vol. 41, no. 4, 1996, p. 82; P. Leigh, 'The New Spirit at Work', *Training and Development*, vol. 51, no. 3, 1997, p. 26; P. H. Mirvis, 'Soul Work in Organizations', *Organization Science*, vol. 8, no. 2, 1997, p. 193; and J. Millman, A. Czaplewski and J. Ferguson, 'An Exploratory Empirical Assessment of the Relationship Between Spirituality and Employee Work Attitudes', paper presented at the National Academy of Management Meeting, Washington, DC, August 2001.

67. Cited in Milliman, et al, 'Spirit and Community at Southwest Airlines'.

68. J. A. Chatman, 'Matching People and Organizations: Selection and Socialization in Public Accounting Firms', *Administrative Science Quarterly*, September 1991, pp. 459–84; and B. Z. Posner, 'Person–Organization Values Congruence: No Support for Individual Differences as a Moderating Influence', *Human Relations*, April 1992, pp. 351–61.

69. J. E. Sheridan, 'Organizational Culture and Employee Retention', *Academy of Management Journal*, December 1992, pp. 1036–56.

PHOTO CREDITS

17

Human Resource Policies and Practices

CHAPTER OUTLINE

Human resources management
Selection practices
Training and development programs
Career development
Performance evaluation
Employee relations interface
International human resource practices: Selected issues
Managing diversity in organisations

LEARNING OBJECTIVES

After studying this chapter, you should be able to:

1. Contrast job descriptions with job specifications
2. List the advantages of performance-simulation tests over written tests
3. Define four general skill categories
4. Describe how career planning has changed in the past 20 years
5. Explain the purposes of performance evaluation
6. Describe actions that can improve the performance-evaluation process
7. Clarify how the existence of a union affects employee behaviour
8. Identify the content in a typical diversity-training program

After listening to my employees, I have to conclude that I have only three types of people working for me: Stars, All-Stars, and Superstars! How is it possible for all my people to be above average?

An anonymous boss

Mention retrenchments and you upset employee's sense of security, not to mention decrease productivity. However, failure by management to reduce staffing levels can lead to a business failure as happened at Moulinex.

Employee layoffs are often a necessary evil if an organisation is to maintain its competitiveness. In Australia, for example, executives at a number of major companies—including Qantas, National Australia Bank, Westpac, Suncorp-Metway and Mitsubishi Australia—have laid off thousands of employees in the past several years. But executives in France don't have the same freedom to fire employees as do their Australian counterparts. While much has been said about global competitiveness and the breakdown of economic barriers between countries, laws continue to vary from nation to nation. And what is an acceptable human resource management practice in one country may be totally unacceptable in another.

Take the recent case of French appliance-maker Moulinex.[1] The company employed 8,800 people. But it was having difficulty making money. In 2000, for example, it lost A$200 million on sales of A$1.8 billion. To survive, the company needed to reduce capacity and close up several of its unprofitable factories. Yet, it couldn't. Why? The French government, under pressure from the country's strong trade unions, enacted laws that make laying off workers incredibly difficult. French labour laws require companies to pursue lengthy negotiations with unions over planned job reductions and the government has a final say so in factory closings. As Moulinex's financial status deteriorated throughout the 1990s, French authorities repeatedly blocked management's efforts to close factories. In August 2001, for example, the government rejected Moulinex's plan to shut down a refrigerator factory and lay off 670 workers. Instead, the company was ordered to resume talks with its trade unions.

Unable to get its costs in line, Moulinex declared bankruptcy in October 2001. A bankruptcy court approved the sale of most of Moulinex's assets and brands to French rival SEB. However, nearly two-thirds of Moulinex's employees lost their jobs permanently.

The message of this chapter is that human resource policies and practices—such as employee selection, training, performance evaluation and employee relations—influence an organisation's effectiveness.[2] And as illustrated in the case of Moulinex, we will also look at how human resource practices differ across cultures. We begin our discussion with a brief definition of human resource management and then look at the various key aspects of human resource management.

Human Resources Management

Many definitions abound as to what human resources management (HRM) actually is. For example, Stone defines HRM as 'managing people within the employer–employee relationship . . . specifically [to] involve the productive utilisation of people in achieving the organisation's objectives and the satisfaction of individual needs'.[3] As such, HRM will draw very heavily on the theories and models of OB to effectively manage the organisation's human resources in the most productive manner and to maximise individual satisfaction. Specifically, HRM will affect individuals and groups through the organisation's policies and practices in how it recruits, selects, develops and compensates employees. In Figure 17.1, we present a model of the HRM process showing its key components.

Our interest in OB is the impact of HRM on individuals and groups, and how OB can improve the various practices and policies used by managers and human resources professionals. As such, we look more closely at selection practices, training and development, career development, performance evaluation, the employee relations interface, diversity, and some selected issues in international HRM practices which are key aspects of HRM.

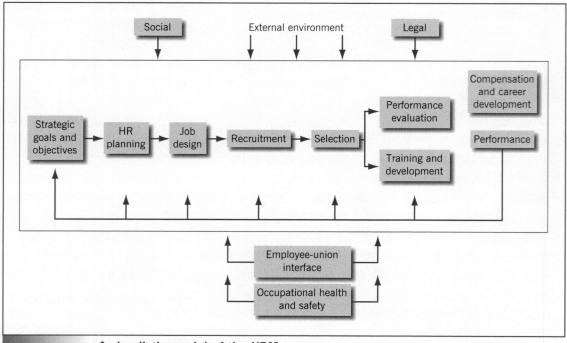

FIGURE 17.1 **A simplistic model of the HRM process**

LEARNING OBJECTIVE

1

Contrast job descriptions with job specifications

Selection Practices

The objective of effective selection is to match individual characteristics (ability, experience, and so on) with the requirements of the job.[4] When management fails to get a proper match, both employee performance and satisfaction suffer. In this search to achieve the right individual–job fit, where does management begin? The answer is to assess the demands and requirements of the job. The process of assessing the activities within a job is called *job analysis*.

JOB ANALYSIS

Job analysis involves developing a detailed description of the tasks involved in a job, determining the relationship of a given job to other jobs, and ascertaining the knowledge, skills and abilities necessary for an employee to successfully perform the job.[5]

How is this information attained? Table 17.1 describes the more popular job analysis methods.

Information gathered by using one or more of the job analysis methods results in the organisation being able to create a **job description** and **job specification**. The former is a written statement of what a job holder does, how it is done and why it is done. It should accurately portray job content, environment and conditions of employment. The job specification states the minimum acceptable qualifications that an employee must possess to perform a given job successfully. It identifies the knowledge, skills and abilities needed to do the job effectively. So, job descriptions identify characteristics of the job, whereas job specifications identify characteristics of the successful job incumbent.

The job description and specification have historically been important documents for guiding the selection process. The job description can be used to describe the job to potential candidates. The job specification keeps the attention of those doing the selection on the list of qualifications necessary for an incumbent to perform a job and assists in determining whether candidates are qualified. However, there are signs that these documents may be declining in importance. Because job analysis is a static view of the job as it currently exists, job descriptions and specifications are also static documents. To facilitate flexibility, organisations are increasingly hiring for organisational needs, rather than for specific individual jobs.[6] Organisations want their permanent employees to be able to do a variety of tasks and to be able to move smoothly from project to project and from one team to another. In such a climate, organisations will tend to seek new employees who, in addition to job-relevant skills, have personalities and attitudes that fit with the organisation's culture and who display organisational citizenship behaviours. Traditional job analysis can identify current job-relevant skills but is inadequate for identifying these other contextual factors that managers are increasingly looking for in new employees.

SELECTION DEVICES

What do application forms, interviews, employment tests, background checks and personal letters of recommendation have in common? Each is a device for obtaining information about a job applicant that can help the organisation to determine whether the applicant's skills, knowledge and abilities are appropriate for the job in question. In this section, we review the more important of these selection devices—interviews, written tests and performance-simulation tests.

Interviews
In Korea, Japan and many other Asian countries, employee interviews traditionally haven't been part of the selection process. Decisions were made almost entirely on the basis of exam scores,

job analysis
Developing a detailed description of the tasks involved in a job, determining the relationship of a given job to other jobs, and ascertaining the knowledge, skills and abilities necessary for an employee to perform the job successfully.

job description
A written statement of what a job holder does, how it is done and why it is done.

job specification
A statement of the minimum acceptable qualifications that an employee must possess to perform a given job successfully.

TABLE 17.1	**Popular job analysis methods**

Observation. An analyst watches employees directly or reviews films of workers on the job.
Interviews. Selected job incumbents are extensively interviewed, and the results of a number of interviews are combined into a single job analysis.
Diaries. Job incumbents record their daily activities, and the amount of time spent on each, in a diary or log.
Questionnaires. Incumbents check or rate the items they perform in their jobs from a long list of possible task items.

Myth *or* Science?

'It's first impressions that count'

This statement is true. When we meet someone for the first time, we notice a number of things about that person—physical characteristics, clothes, firmness of handshake, gestures, tone of voice, and the like. We then use these impressions to fit the person into ready-made categories. And this early categorisation, formed quickly and on the basis of minimal information, tends to hold greater weight than impressions and information received later.

The best evidence on first impressions comes from research on employment interviews. Findings clearly demonstrate that first impressions count. For example, the primacy effect is potent. That is, the first information presented affects later judgments more than information presented later.

Research on applicant appearance confirms the power of first impressions. Studies have looked at assessments made of applicants before the actual interview—that brief period in which the applicant walks into an interview room, exchanges greetings with the interviewer, sits down and engages in minor chit-chat. The evidence indicates that the way applicants walk, talk, dress and look can have a great impact on the interviewer's evaluation of applicant qualifications. Facial attractiveness seems to be particularly influential. Applicants who are highly attractive are evaluated as more qualified for a variety of jobs than persons who are unattractive.

A final body of confirmative research finds that interviewers' post-interview evaluations of applicants conform, to a substantial degree, to their pre-interview impressions. That is, those first impressions carry considerable weight in shaping the interviewers' final evaluations, regardless of what actually transpired in the interview itself. This latter conclusion assumes that the interview elicits no highly negative information.

Sources: R. E. Carlson, 'Effect of Interview Information in Altering Valid Impressions', *Journal of Applied Psychology*, February 1971, pp. 66–72; M. London and M. D. Hakel, 'Effects of Applicant Stereotypes, Order, and Information on Interview Impressions', *Journal of Applied Psychology*, April 1974, pp. 157–62; E. C. Webster, *The Employment Interview: A Social Judgment Process* (Ontario, Canada: S.I.P., 1982); N. R. Bardack and F. T. McAndrew, 'The Influence of Physical Attractiveness and Manner of Dress on Success in a Simulated Personnel Decision', *Journal of Social Psychology*, August 1985, pp. 777–78; R. Bull and N. Rumsey, *The Social Psychology of Facial Appearance* (London: Springer-Verlag, 1988); T. W. Dougherty, R. J. Ebert and J. C. Callender, 'Policy Capturing in the Employment Interview', *Journal of Applied Psychology*, February 1986; and T. M. Macan and R. L. Dipboye, 'The Relationship of the Interviewers' Preinterview Impressions to Selection and Recruitment Outcomes', *Personnel Psychology*, Autumn 1990, pp. 745–69.

scholastic accomplishments and letters of recommendation. This isn't the case, however, throughout most of the world. It's probably correct to say that most of us don't know anyone who has gotten a job without at least one interview. You may have an acquaintance who got a part-time or summer job through a close friend or relative without having to go through an interview, but such instances are rare. Of all the selection devices that organisations use to differentiate candidates, the interview continues to be the one most frequently used.[7] Even companies in Asian countries have begun to rely on employee interviews as a screening device.[8]

Not only is the interview widely used, it also seems to carry a great deal of weight. That is, the results tend to have a disproportionate amount of influence on the selection decision. The candidate who performs poorly in the employment interview is likely to be cut from the applicant pool, regardless of his or her experience, test scores or letters of recommendation. Conversely, 'all too often, the person most polished in job-seeking techniques, particularly those used in the interview process, is the one hired, even though he or she may not be the best candidate for the position'.[9]

These findings are important because of the unstructured manner in which the selection interview is frequently conducted.[10] The unstructured interview—short in duration, casual and made up of random questions—has been proven to be an ineffective selection device.[11] The data gathered from such interviews are typically biased and often unrelated to future job performance. Without structure, a number of biases can distort results. These biases include interviewers tending to favour applicants who share their attitudes, giving unduly high weight to negative information, and allowing the order in which applicants are interviewed to influence evaluations.[12] By having interviewers use a standardised set of questions, providing interviewers with a uniform method of recording information, and standardising the rating of the applicant's qualifications, the variability in results across applicants is reduced and the validity of the interview as a selection device is greatly enhanced.

The evidence indicates that interviews are most valuable for assessing an applicant's applied mental skills, level of conscientiousness and interpersonal skills.[13] When these qualities are related to job performance, the validity of the interview as a selection device is increased. For example, these qualities have demonstrated relevance for performance in upper managerial positions. This may explain why applicants for senior management positions typically undergo dozens of interviews with executive recruiters, board members and other company executives before a final decision is made. It can also explain why organisations that design work around teams may similarly put applicants through an unusually large number of interviews.

In practice, most organisations use interviews for more than a 'prediction-of-performance' device.[14] Companies as diverse as Virgin Blue, Disney, Microsoft and the Australian Taxation Office use the interview to assess applicant–organisation fit. So, in addition to specific, job-relevant skills, organisations are looking at candidates' personality characteristics, personal values, and the like to find individuals who fit with the organisation's culture and image.

In summary, then, the selection interview is a significant tool to initiate and develop the successful recruit's psychological contract to remain with the new employer. Given the high cost of recruitment, selection and induction costs, it may well be a valid trade-off between less-than-optimal reliability and validity of the selection interview with improved recruit retention rates post-induction.

Written tests

Typical written tests are tests of intelligence, aptitude, ability, interest and integrity. Long popular as selection devices, they suffered a decline in use from the late 1960s. The reason was that such tests were frequently characterised as discriminating, and many organisations hadn't validated such tests as being job-related.

Tests in intellectual ability, spatial and mechanical ability, perceptual accuracy and motor ability have shown to be moderately valid predictors for many semiskilled and unskilled operative jobs in industrial organisations.[15] Intelligence tests have proven to be particularly good predictors for jobs that require cognitive complexity.[16] Japanese automobile makers, when staffing factories in the United States, have relied heavily on written tests to predict candidates who will be high performers.[17] Getting a job with Toyota, for example, can take up to three days of testing and interviewing. Written tests typically focus on skills such as reading, mathematics, mechanical dexterity and ability to work with others.

The old saying "the proof is in the pudding" is typified by work sampling tests. Potential employees are given the opportunity to demonstrate their abilities and competencies in practical tests.

As ethical problems have increased in organisations, integrity tests have gained in popularity. These are paper-and-pencil tests that measure factors such as dependability, carefulness, responsibility and honesty. The evidence is impressive that these tests are powerful in predicting supervisory ratings of job performance and counterproductive employee behaviour on the job, such as theft, discipline problems and excessive absenteeism.[18]

LEARNING OBJECTIVE

2

List the advantages of performance-simulation tests over written tests

Performance-simulation tests

What better way is there to find out if an applicant can do a job successfully than by having them do it? That's precisely the logic of performance-simulation tests.

Although more complicated to develop and more difficult to administer than written tests, performance-simulation tests have increased in popularity during the past two decades. This appears to be due to the fact that they are based on job analysis data and, therefore, more easily meet the requirement of job-relatedness than do most written tests.

The two best-known performance-simulation tests are work sampling and assessment centres. The former is suited to routine jobs, while the latter is relevant for the selection of managerial personnel.

work sampling
Creating a miniature replica of a job to evaluate the performance abilities of job candidates.

Work sampling tests are hands-on simulations of part or all of the job that must be performed by applicants. By carefully devising work samples based on job analysis data, management determines the knowledge, skills and abilities needed for each job. Then each work sample element is matched with a corresponding job performance element. Work samples are widely used in the hiring of skilled workers, such as welders, machinists, carpenters and electricians. Job candidates for production jobs at a BMW factory in the United States are given work sample tests.[19] Candidates are given 90 minutes to perform a variety of typical work tasks on a specially built simulated assembly line. High school students in Queensland are given the opportunity to undertake a structured work placement where the student participates in specific tasks in an organisation. This can involve a work sampling placement, where students have the opportunity to test personal vocational preferences through performing tasks in their assigned workplace. Students select placements according to their future occupational aspirations, and this provides a great opportunity for the clarification of their employment goals and to gain first-hand information about what it means to work, as well as about the work processes of the organisation and the work environment.[20]

The results from work sample experiments are impressive. Studies almost consistently demonstrate that work samples yield validities superior to written aptitude and personality tests.[21]

assessment centres
A set of performance-simulation tests designed to evaluate a candidate's managerial potential.

A more elaborate set of performance simulation tests, specifically designed to evaluate a candidate's managerial potential, is administered in assessment centres. In **assessment centres**, line executives, supervisors and/or trained psychologists evaluate candidates as they go through one to several days of exercises that simulate real problems that they would confront on the job.[22] Based on a list of descriptive dimensions that the actual job incumbent has to meet, activities might include interviews, in-basket problem-solving exercises, leaderless group discussions and business decision games. For example, a candidate might be required to play the role of a manager who must decide how to respond to ten memos in his or her in-basket within a two-hour period.

How valid is the assessment centre as a selection device? The evidence on the effectiveness of assessment centres is impressive. They have consistently demonstrated results that predict later job performance in managerial positions.[23]

Training and Development Programs

Competent employees don't remain competent forever. Skills deteriorate and can become obsolete. That's why organisations spend billions of dollars each year on formal training. For example, it was reported that 68 per cent of workplaces in Australia provided training in 1995, up from

OB Controversies

Is it unethical to 'shape' your resume?

When does 'putting a positive spin' on your accomplishments step over the line to become misrepresentation or lying? Does a resume have to be 100 per cent truthful? Consider the following three situations.

Sean left a job for which his title was 'credit clerk'. When looking for a new job, he describes his previous title as 'credit analyst'. He thinks it sounds more impressive. Is this retitling of a former job wrong?

About eight years ago, Emily took nine months off between jobs to travel overseas. Afraid that people might consider her unstable or lacking in career motivation, she put down on her resume that she was engaged in 'independent consulting activities' during the period. Was she wrong?

Michael is 50 years old with an impressive career record. He spent five years at university 30 years ago, but he never got a degree. He is being considered for a $175,000-a-year managerial position at another firm. He knows that he has the ability and track record to do the job, but he won't get the interview if he admits to not having a university degree. He knows that the probability that anyone would check his university records, at this point in his career, is very low. Should he put on his resume that he completed his degree?

58 per cent only five years before.[24] Other studies reveal that larger organisations and those in the information technology sector spend far more on training for their employees than do smaller organisations.[25] In 1997, the last time training was measured in Australia, it was estimated that organisations spent over $7.4 billion on structured training for their employees annually.[26]

TYPES OF TRAINING

Training can include everything from teaching employees basic reading skills to advanced courses in executive leadership. The following summarises four general skill categories—basic literacy, technical, interpersonal and problem solving. In addition, we briefly discuss ethics training.

Basic literacy skills

A recent report by the Australian Bureau of Statistics found that nearly 50 per cent of the Australian population read very poorly or not at all.[27] Most workplace demands require a Year 10 or Year 11 reading level, but about 17 per cent of Australians between the ages of 21 and 25 can't read at even the Year 8 level.[28] This problem, of course, isn't unique to Australia. It's a worldwide problem—from the most developed countries to the least.[29] For many Third World countries, where few workers can read or have gone beyond the equivalent of the third grade, widespread illiteracy means there is almost no hope for these countries to compete in a global economy.

Organisations are increasingly having to provide basic reading and maths skills for their employees. For example, jobs at the world-famous firearms manufacturing company Smith and Wesson have become more complex.[30] Employees need improved maths skills for understanding numerical control equipment, better reading and writing skills to interpret process sheets, and better oral communication skills for working in teams. A literacy audit showed that employees needed to have at least an eighth-grade reading level to do typical workplace tasks. Yet, 30 per cent of the company's 676 workers with no degree scored below eighth-grade levels in either reading or mathematics. These employees were told that they wouldn't lose their jobs, but they

LEARNING OBJECTIVE

3

Define four general skill categories

had to take basic skill classes, paid for by the company and provided on company time. After the first round of classes, 70 per cent of attendees brought their skills up to the target level. And these improved skills allowed employees to do a better job. They displayed greater ease in writing and reading charts, graphs and bulletin boards, increased abilities to use fractions and decimals, better overall communication and a significant increase in confidence.

Technical skills

Most training is directed at upgrading and improving an employee's technical skills. Technical training has become increasingly important today, for two reasons—new technology and new structural designs.

Jobs change as a result of new technologies and improved methods. For example, many automotive repair personnel have had to undergo extensive training to fix and maintain recent models with computer-monitored engines, electronic stabilising systems and other innovations. Similarly, computer-controlled equipment has required millions of production employees to learn a whole new set of skills.

In addition, technical training has become increasingly important because of changes in organisation design. As organisations flatten their structures, expand their use of teams and break down traditional departmental barriers, employees need to learn a wider variety of tasks and need an increased knowledge of how their organisation operates. For example, the restructuring of jobs at Miller Brewing Company around empowered teams has led management to introduce a comprehensive business literacy program to help employees better understand competition, the state of the beer industry, where the company's revenues come from, how costs are calculated, and where employees fit into the company's value chain.[31]

The managing director of Air Liquide Australia, Dennis Cliche, has used a business literacy program called Zodiak that has helped his employees better understand how their personal performance fits with his strategic priorities for the company. The program uses a board game to simulate three years in the life of an imaginary business. Employees come together in half-day sessions where they run this imaginary business and learn to deal with crises and make critical decisions. Amcor, Visy Industries and Western Power are some of the other companies to use this approach to business literacy training.[32]

Interpersonal skills

Almost all employees belong to a work unit. To some degree, their work performance depends on their ability to effectively interact with their co-workers and their boss. Some employees have excellent interpersonal skills, but others require training to improve theirs. This includes learning how to be a better listener, how to communicate ideas more clearly, and how to be a more effective team player.

Problem-solving skills

Managers, as well as many employees who perform non-routine tasks, have to solve problems on their jobs. When people require these skills but are

Problem-solving skills can be learned and improved as shown in the Zodiak program. Various techniques set learners unstructured and unusual tasks to perform, stimulating skill development and an awareness of the opportunities such skills present participants.

deficient in them, they can participate in problem-solving training. This would include activities to sharpen their logic, reasoning and problem-defining skills, as well as their abilities to assess causation, develop alternatives, analyse these, and select solutions. Problem-solving training has become a basic part of almost every organisational effort to introduce self-managed teams or implement total quality management programs.

What about ethics training?

A survey carried out in the late 1990s found that about 75 per cent of employees working in the 1,000 largest US corporations receive ethics training.[33] No similar studies have been conducted in Australia, but it is likely, based on the existence of legislation requiring the development of codes of conduct for public sector organisations (for example, the *Public Sector Ethics Act 1994*), that many Australian public sector and private organisations have started at least some basic level of training in ethical behaviour. But despite this, the evidence isn't clear about whether ethics can be taught.

Critics argue that ethics are based on values, and value systems are fixed at an early age. By the time employers hire people, their ethical values have already been well established. The critics also claim that ethics cannot be formally 'taught', but must be learned by example.

Supporters of ethics training argue that values can be learned and changed after early childhood. And even if they couldn't, ethics training would be effective because it helps employees to recognise ethical dilemmas and become more aware of the ethical issues underlying their actions, and it reaffirms an organisation's expectations that members will act ethically.

TRAINING METHODS

Training methods are most readily classified as formal or informal, and on-the-job or off-the-job.

Historically, training meant *formal training*. It is planned in advance and has a structured format. However, recent evidence indicates that 70 per cent of workplace learning is made up of *informal training*—unstructured, unplanned, and easily adapted to situations and individuals—for teaching skills and keeping employees current.[34] In reality, most informal training is nothing other than employees helping each other out. They share information and solve work-related problems with one another. Maybe the most important outcome of this trend is that many managers are now supportive of what used to be considered 'idle chatter'. At a Siemens plant in the United States, for example, management now recognises that people needn't be on the production line to be working.[35] Discussions around the water cooler or in the cafeteria weren't, as managers thought, about non-work topics such as sports or politics. They largely focused on solving work-related problems. Siemens' management now encourages such casual meetings.

On-the-job training includes job rotation, apprenticeships, understudy assignments and formal mentoring programs. But the primary drawback of these on-the-job training methods is that they often disrupt the workplace. So, organisations invest in *off-the-job training*. The $7.4 billion figure we cited earlier for training costs was largely spent on the formal off-the-job variety. What types of training might this include? The most popular continues to be live classroom lectures. But it also encompasses videotapes, public seminars, self-study programs, Internet courses, satellite-beamed television classes, and group activities that use role plays and case studies. In recent years, the fastest-growing means for delivering training is probably computer-based or *e-learning*.[36] Cisco Systems, an Internet networking company based in San Francisco, for example, has created a website on its corporate intranet that provides a curriculum of training courses, with content organised for job titles, specific technologies and products.[37] This system would allow, for example, a Cisco sales person, who was making a call on a customer later in the day, to download a 20-minute chunk of information describing a new product feature and then watch it on a desktop computer.

INDIVIDUALISE FORMAL TRAINING TO FIT THE EMPLOYEE'S LEARNING STYLE

The way that *you* process, internalise, and remember new and difficult material isn't necessarily the same way that *I* do. This fact means that effective formal training should be individualised to reflect the learning style of the employee.[38]

Some examples of different learning styles include reading, watching, listening and participating. Some people absorb information better when they read about it. They are the kind of people who can learn to use computers by sitting in their study and reading manuals. Some people learn best by observation. They watch others and then emulate the behaviours they have seen. Such people can watch someone use a computer for a while, then copy what they have seen. Listeners rely heavily on their auditory senses to absorb information. They would prefer to learn how to use a computer, for example, by listening to an audiotape. People who prefer a participating style learn by doing. They want to sit down, turn on the computer, and gain hands-on experience by practising.

You can translate these styles into different learning methods. To maximise learning, readers should be given books or other reading material to review; watchers should get the opportunity to observe individuals modelling the new skills either in person or on video; listeners will benefit from hearing lectures or audiotapes; and participants will benefit most from experiential opportunities in which they can simulate and practise the new skills.

These different learning styles are obviously not mutually exclusive. In fact, good teachers recognise that their students learn differently and, therefore, provide multiple learning methods. They assign readings before class; give lectures; use visual aids to illustrate concepts; and have students participate in group projects, case analyses, role plays and experiential learning exercises. If you know the preferred style of an employee, you can design their formal training program to optimise this preference. If you don't have that information, it's probably best to design the program to use a variety of learning styles. Over-reliance on a single style places individuals who don't learn well from that style at a disadvantage.

LEARNING OBJECTIVE

4

Describe how career planning has changed in the past 20 years

| Career Development

Few human resource issues have changed as much in the past decade or two as the role of the organisation in its employees' careers.[39] It has gone from paternalism—in which the organisation took nearly complete responsibility for managing its employees' careers—to supporting individuals as they take personal responsibility for their future. And careers themselves have gone from a series of upward moves with increasing income, authority, status and security to one in which people adapt quickly, learn continuously and change their work identities over time.

For much of the 20th century, companies recruited young workers with the intent that they would spend their entire career inside that single organisation. For those with the right credentials and motivation, they created promotion paths dotted with ever-increasing responsibility. Employers would provide the training and opportunities, and employees would respond by demonstrating loyalty and hard work. This arrangement has undergone serious decay. High uncertainty now limits the ability of organisations to accurately forecast future needs. Management seeks flexibility over permanence. Meanwhile, flattened hierarchies have reduced promotion opportunities. The result is that, today, career planning is something increasingly being done by individual employees rather than by their employers. It has become the employee's responsibility to keep their skills, abilities and knowledge current, and to prepare for tomorrow's new tasks.

The organisation's responsibilities

What, if any, responsibility does the organisation have for career development under these new rules? Basically, the organisation's responsibility is to build employee self-reliance and to help employees maintain their marketability through continual learning.

The essence of a progressive career development program is built on providing support for employees to continually add to their skills, abilities and knowledge. This support includes:

1. *Clearly communicating the organisation's goals and future strategies.* When people know where the organisation is headed, they are better able to develop a personal plan to share in that future.
2. *Creating growth opportunities.* Employees should have the opportunity to get new, interesting and professionally challenging work experiences.
3. *Offering financial assistance.* The organisation should offer tuition reimbursement to help employees keep current.
4. *Providing the time for employees to learn.* Organisations should be generous in providing paid time off from work for off-the-job training. In addition, workloads shouldn't be so demanding that they preclude employees from having the time to develop new skills, abilities and knowledge.

The employee's responsibilities

Today's employees should manage their own careers like entrepreneurs managing a small business. They should think of themselves as self-employed, even if they are employed in a large organisation.[40] In a world of 'free agency', the successful career will be built on maintaining flexibility and keeping skills and knowledge up to date. The following suggestions are consistent with the view that you, and only you, hold primary responsibility for your career.[41]

1. *Know yourself.* Know your strengths and weaknesses. What talents can you bring to an employer? Personal career planning begins by being honest with yourself.
2. *Manage your reputation.* Without appearing as a braggart, let others both inside and outside your current organisation know about your achievements. Make you and your accomplishments visible.
3. *Build and maintain network contacts.* In a world of high mobility, you need to develop contacts. Join national and local professional associations, attend conferences, and network at social gatherings.
4. *Keep current.* Develop the specific skills and abilities that are in high demand. Avoid learning organisation-specific skills that can't be transferred quickly to other employers.
5. *Balance your specialist and generalist competencies.* You need to stay current within your technical speciality. But you also need to develop general competencies that give you the versatility to react to an ever-changing work environment. Overemphasis in a single functional area, or even in a narrow industry, can limit your mobility.
6. *Document your achievements.* Employers are increasingly looking to what you have accomplished, rather than the titles you have held. Seek jobs and assignments that will provide increasing challenges and that will also offer objective evidence of your competencies.
7. *Keep your options open.* Always have contingency plans prepared that you can call on when needed. You never know when your group will be eliminated, your department downsized, your project cancelled, or your company acquired in a takeover. 'Hope for the best, but be prepared for the worst' may be a cliché, but it's still not bad advice.

Performance Evaluation

Would you study differently or exert a different level of effort for a university course graded on a pass–fail basis than for one for which letter grades from A to F are used? When we ask that question of students, we usually get an affirmative answer. Students typically tell us that they study harder when letter grades are at stake. In addition, they tell us that when they take a course on a pass–fail basis, they tend to do just enough to ensure a passing grade.

This finding illustrates how performance evaluation systems influence behaviour. The main determinants of your in-class behaviour and out-of-class studying effort at university are the criteria and techniques your lecturer uses to evaluate your performance. Of course, what applies in the university context also applies to employees at work. In this section, we show how the choice

The Real Deal

Forced rankings gain in popularity

It's become one of the fastest-growing trends in performance evaluation. Companies such as Ford, GE, Microsoft, Sun Microsystems and Conoco are among the 20 per cent of US companies that now rank their employees from best to worst and then use those rankings to determine pay and make other human resource decisions.

Many top executives became frustrated by managers who rated all their employees 'above average'. In addition, executives wanted to create a system that would increase the organisation's competitiveness—one that would reward the very best performers and encourage poor performers to leave. So, they are turning to forced rankings, or what has been called 'rank and yank' by its critics.

For example, all 18,000 of Ford Motor's managers undergo this process. These managers are divided into groups of 30 to 50, then rated. For each group, 10 per cent have to get an A, 80 per cent a B, and 10 per cent a C. Anyone receiving a C is restricted from getting a pay raise, and two consecutive years of a C rating results in either a demotion or termination.

The most well-known 'rank and yank' program is GE's '20–70–10 plan'. The company forces the heads of each of its divisions to review all managers and professional employees, and to identify their top 20 per cent, middle 70 per cent and bottom 10 per cent. GE then does everything possible to keep and reward its top performers and fires all bottom-group performers. The company's former CEO stated, 'A company that bets its future on its people must remove the lower 10 per cent, and keep removing it every year—always raising the bar of performance and increasing the quality of its leadership.'

Proponents see these forced rankings and elimination of weak performers as a way to continually improve an organisation's workforce and to reward those who are most deserving. Critics, on the other hand, argue that these programs are harsh, arbitrary and create a 'zero-sum game' that discourages cooperation. Critics also say that these programs run counter to the belief, held by many, that almost any worker is salvageable.

Sources: Based on R. Abelson, 'Companies Turn to Grades, and Employees Go to Court', *New York Times*, 19 March 2001, p. A1; D. Jones, 'More Firms Cut Workers Ranked at Bottom to Make Way for Talent', *USA Today*, 30 May 2001, p. 1B; and J. Greenwald, 'Rank and Fire', *Time*, 18 June 2001, pp. 38–40.

LEARNING OBJECTIVE

5

Explain the purposes of performance evaluation

of a performance evaluation system and the way it is administered can be an important force influencing employee behaviour.

PURPOSES OF PERFORMANCE EVALUATION

Performance evaluation serves a number of purposes in organisations (see Table 17.2).[42] Management uses evaluations for general *human resource decisions.* Evaluations provide input into important decisions such as promotions, transfers and terminations. Evaluations *identify training and development needs.* They pinpoint employee skills and competencies that are currently inadequate but for which programs can be developed to remedy. Performance evaluations can be used as a *criterion against which selection and development programs are validated.* Newly hired employees who perform poorly can be identified through performance evaluation. Similarly, the effectiveness of training and development programs can be determined by assessing how well employees who have participated do on their performance evaluation. Evaluations also fulfil the purpose of *providing feedback to employees* on how the organisation views their performance. Furthermore, performance evaluations are used as the *basis for reward allocations.* Decisions as to who gets merit pay increases and other rewards are frequently determined by performance evaluations.

TABLE 17.2	Primary uses for performance evaluations
Use	**Per cent***
Compensation	85.6
Performance feedback	65.1
Training	64.3
Promotion	45.3
Human resource planning	43.1
Retention/discharge	30.3
Research	17.2

* Based on responses from 600 organisations.

Source: Based on 'Performance Appraisal: Current Practices and Techniques', *Personnel*, May–June 1984, p. 57.

Each of these functions of performance evaluation is important. Yet, their importance to us depends on the perspective we are taking. Several are clearly relevant to human resource management decisions. But our interest is in organisational behaviour. As a result, we shall be emphasising performance evaluation in its role as a mechanism for providing feedback and as a determinant of reward allocations.

PERFORMANCE EVALUATION AND MOTIVATION

In discussing motivation in an earlier chapter of this book, some attention was given to the expectancy model of motivation. We argued that this model currently offers one of the best explanations of what conditions the amount of effort an individual will exert on their job. A vital component of this model is performance, specifically the effort–performance and performance–reward links.

But what defines *performance?* In the expectancy model, it is the individual's performance evaluation. To maximise motivation, people need to perceive that the effort they exert leads to a

TABLE 17.3	Performance management at AMP

Performance management at AMP, Australia's largest insurance company, consists of four integrated components:
1. *The performance agreement:* The manager and the employee determine outcomes and performance indicators consistent with the business strategies, ranking each in terms of priority and identifying any training needs to accomplish the goals.
2. *Coaching and feedback:* Encouragement and reinforcement are given for successful outcomes and attainments.
3. *Performance evaluation:* The employee meets with the manager to review performance results, skill development, training outcomes, career goals and value of outcomes to the business. Generally this occurs twice a year, with the mid-year appraisal agreeing on the performance rating and the end-of-year appraisal establishing the final rating.
4. *Pay reviews:* Based on the final performance rating, decisions are made regarding both fixed pay and bonus pay levels for the employee.

Source: This table is based on M. McInerney, 'The AMP Story: Going Global with Performance Management', *HRMonthly*, May 2000, p. 20.

favourable performance evaluation and that the favourable evaluation will lead to the rewards that they value (see Table 17.3 for an example).

Following the expectancy model of motivation, if the objectives that employees are expected to achieve are unclear, if the criteria for measuring those objectives are vague, and if the employees lack confidence that their efforts will lead to a satisfactory appraisal of their performance or believe that there will be an unsatisfactory payoff by the organisation when their performance objectives are achieved, we can expect individuals to work considerably below their potential.

In the real world of organisations, one explanation for why many employees may not be motivated is that the performance evaluation process is often more political than objective. Many managers will subordinate objective accuracy for self-serving ends—deliberately manipulating evaluations to get the outcomes they want.[43]

WHAT DO WE EVALUATE?

The criteria or criterion that management chooses to evaluate, when appraising employee performance, will have a major influence on what employees do. Two examples illustrate this.

In a public employment agency, which served workers seeking employment and employers seeking workers, employment interviewers were appraised by the number of interviews they conducted. Consistent with the thesis that the evaluating criteria influence behaviour, interviewers emphasised the *number* of interviews conducted, rather than the *placements* of clients in jobs.[44]

A management consultant specialising in police research noticed that, in one community, officers would come on duty for their shift, proceed to get into their police cars, drive to the highway that cut through the town, and speed back and forth along this highway for their entire shift. Clearly, this fast cruising had little to do with good police work, but this behaviour made considerably more sense once the consultant learned that the community's city council used mileage on police vehicles as an evaluative measure of police effectiveness.[45]

These examples demonstrate the importance of criteria in performance evaluation. This, of course, leads to the question: what should management evaluate? The three most popular sets of criteria are individual task outcomes, behaviours and traits.

Individual task outcomes

If ends count, rather than means, then management should evaluate an employee's task outcomes. Using task outcomes, a plant manager could be judged on criteria such as quantity produced, scrap generated, and cost per unit of production. Similarly, a sales person could be assessed on overall sales volume in their territory, dollar increase in sales, and number of new accounts established.

Behaviours

In many cases, it is difficult to identify specific outcomes that can be directly attributable to an employee's actions. This is particularly true of personnel in advisory or support positions and individuals whose work assignments are intrinsically part of a group effort. In the latter case, the group's performance may be readily evaluated, but the contribution of each group member may be difficult or impossible to identify clearly. In such instances, it's not unusual for management to evaluate the employee's behaviour. Using the previous examples, behaviours of a factory manager that could be used for performance evaluation purposes might include promptness in submitting their monthly reports or the leadership style that the manager exhibits. Pertinent sales-person behaviours could be the average number of contact calls made per day or sick days used per year.

Note that these behaviours needn't be limited to those directly related to individual productivity.[46] As we pointed out in our previous discussion on organisational citizenship behaviour, helping others, making suggestions for improvements, and volunteering for extra duties make work groups and organisations more effective. So, including subjective or contextual factors in a performance evaluation—as long as they contribute to organisational effectiveness—may not only make sense; they may also improve coordination, teamwork, cooperation and overall organisational performance.

Traits

The weakest set of criteria, yet one that is still widely used by organisations, is individual traits.[47] We say they are weaker than either task outcomes or behaviours because they are furthest removed from the actual performance of the job itself. Traits such as having 'a good attitude', showing 'confidence', being 'dependable', 'looking busy' or possessing 'a wealth of experience' may or may not be highly correlated with positive task outcomes, but only the naive would ignore the reality that such traits are frequently used in organisations as criteria for assessing an employee's level of performance.

WHO SHOULD DO THE EVALUATING?

Who should evaluate an employee's performance? The obvious answer would seem to be their immediate boss. By tradition, a manager's authority typically has included appraising sub-ordinates' performance. The logic behind this tradition seems to be that since managers are held responsible for their employees' performance, it only makes sense that these managers do the evaluating of that performance. But that logic may be flawed. Others may actually be able to do the job better.

Immediate superior

The majority of performance evaluations at the lower and middle levels of organisations continue to be conducted by an employee's immediate boss.[48] Yet, a number of organisations are recognising the drawbacks to using this source of evaluation. For example, many bosses feel unqualified to evaluate the unique contributions of each of their employees. Others resent being asked to 'play God' with their employees' careers. In addition, with many of today's organisations using self-managed teams, telecommuting and other organising devices that distance bosses from their employees, an employee's immediate superior may not be the most reliable judge of that employee's performance.

Peers

Peer evaluations are one of the most reliable sources of appraisal data. Why? First, peers are close to the action. Daily interactions provide them with a comprehensive view of an employee's job performance. Second, using peers as raters results in a number of independent judgments. A boss can offer only a single evaluation, but peers can provide multiple appraisals. And the average of several ratings is often more reliable than a single evaluation. On the downside, peer evaluations can suffer from co-workers' unwillingness to evaluate one another and from biases based on friendship or animosity.

Self-evaluation

Having employees evaluate their own performance is consistent with values such as self-management and empowerment. Self-evaluations get high marks from employees themselves; they tend to lessen employees' defensiveness about the appraisal process; and they make excellent vehicles for stimulating job performance discussions between employees and their superiors. However, as you might guess, they suffer from over-inflated assessment and self-serving bias. Moreover, self-evaluations are often low in agreement with superiors' ratings.[49] Because of these serious drawbacks, self-evaluations are probably better suited to developmental uses than for evaluative purposes.

Immediate subordinates

A fourth judgment source is an employee's immediate subordinates. Its proponents argue that it is consistent with recent trends towards enhancing honesty, openness and empowerment in the workplace.

Immediate subordinates' evaluations can provide accurate and detailed information about a manager's behaviour because the evaluators typically have frequent contact with the person being evaluated. The obvious problem with this form of rating is fear of reprisal from bosses who are given unfavourable evaluations. Therefore, respondent anonymity is crucial if these evaluations are to be accurate.

360-degree evaluations

The latest approach to performance evaluation is the use of 360-degree evaluations.[50] This approach provides for performance feedback from the full circle of daily contacts that an employee might have, ranging from mailroom personnel to customers to bosses to peers (see Figure 17.2). The number of appraisals can be as few as three or four evaluations or as many as 25, with most organisations collecting five to ten per employee.

A recent survey shows that about 43 per cent of Australian organisations are using full 360-degree programs, but the trend is growing.[51] Companies currently using this approach in Australia report that their main concern is to improve and develop their employees, and 37 per cent of organisations see 360-degree feedback as a positive contributor to employee development.[52]

What is the appeal of 360-degree evaluations? They fit well into organisations that have introduced teams, employee involvement and quality-management programs. By relying on feedback from co-workers, customers and subordinates, these organisations are hoping to give everyone more of a sense of participation in the review process and to gain more accurate readings on employee performance. On this later point, 360-degree evaluations are consistent with evidence

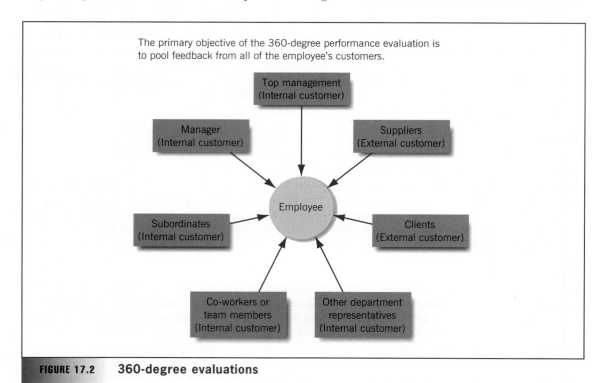

FIGURE 17.2   **360-degree evaluations**

Source: Adapted from *Personnel Journal*, November 1994, p. 100.

that employee performance varies across contexts and that people behave differently with different constituencies.[53] The use of multiple sources, therefore, is more likely to capture this variety of behaviour accurately.

METHODS OF PERFORMANCE EVALUATION

The previous sections explained *what* we evaluate and *who* should do the evaluating. Now we ask: *how* do we evaluate an employee's performance? That is, what are the specific techniques for evaluation? This section reviews the main performance evaluation methods.

Written essays

Probably the simplest method of evaluation is to write a narrative describing an employee's strengths, weaknesses, past performance, potential, and suggestions for improvement. The written essay requires no complex forms or extensive training to complete. But the results often reflect the ability of the writer. A good or bad appraisal may be determined as much by the evaluator's writing skill as by the employee's actual level of performance.

Critical incidents

Critical incidents focus the evaluator's attention on the behaviours that are key in making the difference between executing a job effectively and executing it ineffectively. That is, the appraiser writes down anecdotes that describe what the employee did that was especially effective or ineffective. The key here is that only specific behaviours, not vaguely defined personality traits, are cited. A list of critical incidents provides a rich set of examples from which the employee can be shown the behaviours that are desirable and those that call for improvement.

critical incidents
Evaluating the behaviours that are key in making the difference between executing a job effectively and executing it ineffectively.

Graphic rating scales

One of the oldest and most popular methods of evaluation is the use of **graphic rating scales**. In this method, a set of performance factors, such as quantity and quality of work, depth of knowledge, cooperation, loyalty, attendance, honesty and initiative, is listed. The evaluator then goes down the list and rates each on incremental scales. The scales typically specify five points, so a factor such as *job knowledge* might be rated 1 ('poorly informed about work duties') to 5 ('has complete mastery of all phases of the job').

Why are graphic ratings scales so popular? Although they don't provide the depth of information that essays or critical incidents do, they are less time-consuming to develop and administer. They also allow for quantitative analysis and comparison.

graphic rating scales
An evaluation method in which the evaluator rates performance factors on an incremental scale.

Behaviourally anchored rating scales

Behaviourally anchored rating scales (BARS) combine the main elements from the critical incident and graphic rating scale approaches: the appraiser rates the employees based on items along a continuum, but the points are examples of actual behaviour on the given job rather than general descriptions or traits.

BARS specify definite, observable and measurable job behaviour. Examples of job-related behaviour and performance dimensions are found by asking participants to give specific illustrations of effective and ineffective behaviour regarding each performance dimension. These behavioural examples are then translated into a set of performance dimensions, each dimension having varying levels of performance. The results of this process are behavioural descriptions, such as *anticipates, plans, executes, solves immediate problems, carries out orders* and *handles emergency situations*.

behaviourally anchored rating scales (BARS)
Scales that combine the main elements from the critical incident and graphic rating scale approaches: the appraiser rates the employees based on items along a continuum, but the points are examples of actual behaviour on the given job, rather than general descriptions or traits.

Forced comparisons

Forced comparisons evaluate one individual's performance against the performance of another or others. It is a relative, rather than an absolute, measuring device. The three most popular comparisons are group order ranking, individual ranking and paired comparisons.

group order ranking
An evaluation method that places employees into a particular classification, such as quartiles.

individual ranking
An evaluation method that rank-orders employees from best to worst.

paired comparison
An evaluation method that compares each employee with every other employee and assigns a summary ranking based on the number of superior scores that the employee achieves.

The **group order ranking** requires the evaluator to place employees into a particular classification, such as top one-fifth or second one-fifth. This method is often used in recommending students to undertake postgraduate studies. Evaluators are asked whether the student ranks in the top 5 per cent of the class, the next 5 per cent, the next 15 per cent, and so forth. But when used by managers to appraise employees, managers deal with all their subordinates. Therefore, if a rater has 20 employees, only four can be in the top fifth and, of course, four must also be relegated to the bottom fifth.

The **individual ranking** approach rank-orders employees from best to worst. If the manager is required to appraise 30 employees, this approach assumes that the difference between the first and second employee is the same as that between the 21st and 22nd. Even though some of the employees may be closely grouped, this approach allows for no ties. The result is a clear ordering of employees, from the highest performer down to the lowest.

The **paired comparison** approach compares each employee with every other employee and rates each as either the superior or the weaker member of the pair. After all paired comparisons are made, each employee is assigned a summary ranking based on the number of superior scores they achieved. This approach ensures that each employee is compared against every other, but it can obviously become unwieldy when many employees are being compared.

Multi-person comparisons can be combined with one of the other methods to blend the best from both absolute and relative standards. For example, recent studies of the top universities in the United States have found widespread evidence of grade inflation.[54] In one recent year, 46 per cent of all undergraduate grades at Harvard were A's. At Princeton, 43 per cent of all undergraduate grades were A's, with only 12 per cent below the B range. One way for these universities to deal with this problem would be to require academics to include not only an absolute letter grade but also relative data on class size and rank. So, a prospective employer or graduate school could look at two students who each got an 'A' in their physical geology courses and draw considerably different conclusions about each because next to one grade it says 'ranked 2nd out of 26', while the other says 'ranked 14th out of 30'. Obviously, the former student performed better, relatively, than did the latter.

LEARNING OBJECTIVE

6

Describe actions that can improve the performance-evaluation process

SUGGESTIONS FOR IMPROVING PERFORMANCE EVALUATIONS

The performance evaluation process is a potential minefield of problems. For example, evaluators can make leniency, halo, and similarity errors, or use the process for political purposes. They can unconsciously inflate evaluations (positive leniency), understate performance (negative leniency), or allow the assessment of one characteristic to unduly influence the assessment of other characteristics (the halo error). Some appraisers bias their evaluations by unconsciously favouring people who have qualities and traits similar to themselves (the similarity error). And, of course, some evaluators see the evaluation process as a political opportunity to overtly reward or punish employees they like or dislike. Although there are no protections that will *guarantee* accurate performance evaluations, the following suggestions can significantly help to make the process more objective and fair.

Emphasise behaviours rather than traits

Many traits often considered to be related to good performance may, in fact, have little or no performance relationship. For example, traits such as loyalty, initiative, courage, reliability and self-expression are intuitively appealing as characteristics in employees. But the relevant question is: are individuals who are evaluated as high on those traits higher performers than those who rate low? We can't answer this question easily. We know that there are employees who rate high on these characteristics and are poor performers. We can find others who are excellent performers but don't score well on traits such as these. Our conclusion is that traits such as loyalty and initiative may be prized by managers, but there is no evidence to support that certain traits will be adequate synonyms for performance in a large cross-section of jobs.

Another weakness of trait evaluation is the judgment itself. What is 'loyalty'? When is an employee 'reliable'? What you consider to be 'loyalty', I may not. So, traits suffer from weak inter-rater agreement.

Document performance behaviours in a diary

Diaries help evaluators to better organise information in their memory. The evidence indicates that by keeping a diary of specific critical incidents for each employee, evaluations tend to be more accurate and less prone to rating errors.[55] Diaries, for example, tend to reduce leniency and halo errors because they encourage the evaluator to focus on performance-related behaviours rather than on traits.

Use multiple evaluators

As the number of evaluators increases, the probability of attaining more accurate information increases. If rater error tends to follow a normal curve, an increase in the number of appraisers will tend to find the majority congregating about the middle. You see this approach being used in athletic competitions in such sports as diving and gymnastics. A set of evaluators judges a performance, the highest and lowest scores are dropped, and the final performance evaluation is made up from the cumulative scores of those remaining. The logic of multiple evaluators applies to organisations as well.

If an employee has had ten supervisors, nine having rated her excellent and one poor, we can discount the value of the one poor evaluation. Therefore, by moving employees about within the organisation so as to gain a number of evaluations, or by using multiple assessors (as provided in 360-degree appraisals), we increase the probability of achieving more valid and reliable evaluations.

Evaluate selectively

Appraisers should evaluate only in areas in which they have some expertise.[56] If raters make evaluations on only the dimensions on which they are in a good position to rate, we increase the inter-rater agreement and make the evaluation a more valid process. This approach also recognises that different organisational levels often have different orientations towards those being rated and observe them in different settings. In general, therefore, we would recommend that appraisers should be as close as possible, in terms of organisational level, to the individual being evaluated. Conversely, the more levels that separate the evaluator and the person being evaluated, the less opportunity the evaluator has to observe the individual's behaviour and, not surprisingly, the greater the possibility for inaccuracies.

Train evaluators

If you can't *find* good evaluators, the alternative is to *make* good evaluators. There is substantial evidence that training evaluators can make them more accurate raters.[57]

Common errors such as halo and leniency have been minimised or eliminated in workshops where managers practise observing and rating behaviours. These workshops typically run from one to three days, but allocating many hours to training may not always be necessary. One case has been cited in which both halo and leniency errors were decreased immediately after exposing evaluators to explanatory training sessions lasting only five minutes.[58] But the effects of training appear to diminish over time.[59] This suggests the need for regular refresher sessions.

Provide employees with due process

The concept of *due process* can be applied to appraisals to increase the perception that employees are treated fairly.[60] Three features characterise due process systems: (1) individuals are provided with adequate notice of what is expected of them; (2) all relevant evidence to a proposed violation is aired in a fair hearing so that the individuals affected can respond; and (3) the final decision is based on the evidence and is free from bias.

There is considerable evidence that evaluation systems often violate employees' due process by providing them with infrequent and relatively general performance feedback, allowing them little input into the appraisal process, and knowingly introducing bias into performance ratings. However, when due process has been part of the evaluation system, employees report positive reactions to the appraisal process, perceive the evaluation results as more accurate, and express increased intent to remain with the organisation.

PROVIDING PERFORMANCE FEEDBACK

For many managers, few activities are more unpleasant than providing performance feedback to employees.[61] In fact, unless pressured by organisational policies and controls, managers are likely to ignore this responsibility.[62]

Why the reluctance to give performance feedback? There seem to be at least three reasons. First, managers are often uncomfortable discussing performance weaknesses directly with employees. Given that almost every employee could stand to improve in some areas, managers fear a confrontation when presenting negative feedback. This apparently even applies when people give negative feedback to a computer! Bill Gates reports that Microsoft conducted a project that required users to rate their experience with a computer. 'When we had the computer the users had worked with ask for an evaluation of its performance, the responses tended to be positive. But when we had a second computer ask the same people to evaluate their encounters with the first machine, the people were significantly more critical. Their reluctance to criticise the first computer "to its face" suggested that they didn't want to hurt its feelings, even though they knew it was only a machine.'[63] Second, many employees tend to become defensive when their weaknesses are pointed out. Instead of accepting the feedback as constructive and a basis for improving performance, some employees challenge the evaluation by criticising the manager or redirecting blame to someone else. A survey of 151 area managers in Philadelphia, for example, found that 98 per cent of these managers encountered some type of aggression after giving employees negative appraisals.[64] Finally, employees tend to have an inflated assessment of their own performance. Statistically speaking, half of all employees must be below-average performers. But the evidence indicates that the average employee's estimate of his or her own performance level generally falls around the 75th percentile.[65] So, even when managers are providing good news, employees are likely to perceive it as not good enough.

The solution to the performance feedback problem isn't to ignore it, but to train managers in how to conduct constructive feedback sessions. An effective review—one in which the employee perceives the appraisal as fair, the manager as sincere and the climate as constructive—can result in the employee leaving the interview in an upbeat mood, informed about the performance areas in which they need to improve, and determined to correct the deficiencies.[66] In addition, the performance review should be designed more as a

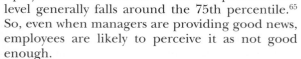

Carefully planned and implemented effective employee appraisals raise both individual and organisation performance, increase commitment and boost motivation through feedback.

counselling activity than a judgment process. This can best be accomplished by allowing the review to evolve out of the employee's own self-evaluation.

WHAT ABOUT TEAM PERFORMANCE EVALUATIONS?

Performance evaluation concepts have been almost exclusively developed with only individual employees in mind. This reflects the historic belief that individuals are the core building block around which organisations are built. But as we have described throughout this book, more and more organisations are restructuring themselves around teams. In organisations that use teams, how should they evaluate performance? Four suggestions have been offered for designing a system that supports and improves the performance of teams.[67]

1. *Tie the team's results to the organisation's goals.* It is important to find measurements that apply to important goals that the team is supposed to accomplish.
2. *Begin with the team's customers and the work process the team follows to satisfy customers' needs.* The final product the customer receives can be evaluated in terms of the customer's requirements. The transactions between teams can be evaluated based on delivery and quality. And the process steps can be evaluated based on waste and cycle time.
3. *Measure both team and individual performance.* Define the roles of each team member in terms of accomplishments that support the team's work process. Then assess each member's contribution and the team's overall performance. Remember that individual skills are necessary for team success but are not sufficient for good team performance.[68]
4. *Train the team to create its own measures.* Having the team define its objectives and those of each member ensures that everyone understands their role on the team and helps the team to develop into a more cohesive unit.

Employee Relations Interface

Trade unions are a vehicle by which employees act collectively to protect and promote their interests. Currently, in the United States, about 13 per cent of the private sector workforce belongs to and is represented by a union. This number is considerably higher in other countries. For example, the comparable figures for Canada and Australia are 37 per cent and 26 per cent, respectively.[69]

For employees who are members of a trade union, wage levels and conditions of employment are explicitly articulated in a contract that is negotiated, through collective bargaining, between representatives of the trade union and the organisation's management. Where a trade union exists, it influences a number of organisational activities.[70] Recruitment sources, hiring criteria, work schedules, job design, redress procedures, safety rules, and eligibility for training programs are examples of activities that are influenced by unions. Trade unions, having to contend with declining job markets in industries where they were historically strong—such as steel, manufacturing, transport, construction, textiles and footwear—have focused their attention in recent years on improving stagnant wages, discouraging corporate downsizings, minimising the outsourcing of jobs, protecting employee entitlements from corporate bankruptcies and coping with job obsolescence.[71]

The most obvious and pervasive area of employees' influence, especially in enterprise bargaining, is wage rates and working conditions. Where trade unions exist, performance evaluation systems tend to be less complex because they play a relatively small part in reward decisions. Wage rates, when determined through collective bargaining, emphasise seniority and downplay performance differences. Also, similar patterns across individual enterprise agreements tend to appear where the industry is heavily unionised, suggesting there is still strong trade union support in some industries.

Figure 17.3 shows what impact a union has on an employee's performance and job satisfaction. The union contract affects motivation through determination of wage rates, seniority rules,

trade union
An organisation, made up of employees, that acts collectively to protect and promote employee interests.

LEARNING OBJECTIVE
7
Clarify how the existence of a union affects employee behaviour

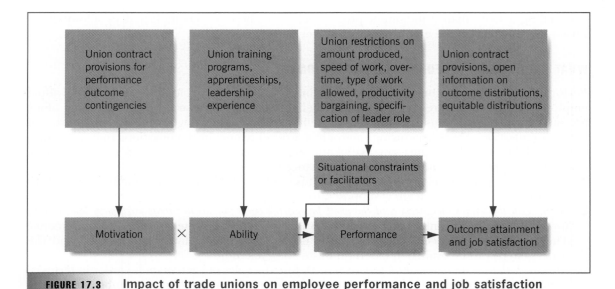

FIGURE 17.3   **Impact of trade unions on employee performance and job satisfaction**

Source: T. H. Hammer, 'Relationships between Local Union Characteristics and Worker Behavior and Attitudes', *Academy of Management Journal,* December 1978, p. 573. Copyright © 1978 by Academy of Management. Reproduced by permission of Academy of Management in the format Textbook via the Copyright Clearance Center.

layoff procedures, promotion criteria and security provisions. Unions can influence the competence with which employees perform their jobs by offering special training programs to their members, by requiring apprenticeships, and by allowing members to gain leadership experience through union organisational activities. The actual level of employee performance will be further influenced by collective bargaining restrictions placed on the amount of work produced, the speed with which work can be done, overtime allowances per worker, and the kind of tasks a given employee is allowed to perform.

The research evaluating the specific effect of unions on productivity is mixed.[72] Some studies found that unions had a positive effect on productivity as a result of improvements in employee relations, as well as improvements in the quality of the workforce. In contrast, other studies have shown that trade unions have a negative impact on productivity by reducing the effectiveness of some productivity-enhancing managerial practices and by contributing to a poorer employee relations climate. The evidence, then, is too inconsistent to draw any meaningful conclusions.

Are union members more satisfied with their jobs than their non-union counterparts? The answer to this question is more complicated than a simple 'yes' or 'no'. The evidence consistently demonstrates that unions have only indirect effects on job satisfaction.[73] They increase pay satisfaction but negatively affect satisfaction with the work itself (by decreasing job scope perceptions), satisfaction with co-workers and supervision (through less favourable perceptions of supervisory behaviour), and satisfaction with promotions (through the lower importance placed on promotions).

International Human Resource Practices: Selected Issues

Many of the human resource policies and practices discussed in this chapter have to be modified to reflect societal differences.[74] To illustrate this point, let's briefly look at the universality of selection practices and the importance of performance evaluation in different cultures.

SELECTION

A recent study of 300 large organisations in 22 countries demonstrated that selection practices differ by nation.[75] A few common procedures were found. For example, the use of educational qualifications in screening candidates seems to be a universal practice. For the most part, however, different countries tend to emphasise different selection techniques. Structured interviews, as a case in point, were popular in some countries and non-existent in others. The authors of the study suggested that 'certain cultures may find structured interviews antithetical to beliefs about how one should conduct an interpersonal interaction or the extent to which one should trust the judgment of the interviewer'.[76]

The above study, when combined with earlier research, tells us that there are no widely accepted universal selection practices. Moreover, global firms that attempt to implement standardised worldwide selection practices can expect to face considerable resistance from local managers. Policies and practices need to be modified to reflect culture-based norms and social values, as well as legal and economic differences.

PERFORMANCE EVALUATION

We previously examined the role that performance evaluation plays in motivation and in affecting behaviour. Caution must be used, however, in generalising across cultures. Why? Because many cultures aren't particularly concerned with performance appraisal or, if they are, they don't look at it the same way as do managers in Australia.

Let's look at four cultural dimensions: individualism/collectivism, a person's relationship to the environment, time orientation, and focus of responsibility.

Individual-oriented cultures such as Australia or New Zealand emphasise formal performance evaluation systems to a greater degree than informal systems. They advocate, for example, written evaluations performed at regular intervals, the results of which are shared with employees and used in the determination of rewards. On the other hand, the collectivist cultures that dominate many parts of Asia and much of Latin America are characterised by more informal systems—downplaying formal feedback and disconnecting reward allocations from performance ratings. Japanese technology giant Fujitsu, for example, introduced a formal, performance-based evaluation system in Japan in the mid-1990s. But the company recently began to dismantle it, recognising that it 'had proved flawed and a poor fit with Japanese [collectivist] business culture'.[77]

Australian and Canadian organisations hold people responsible for their actions, because people in these countries believe that they can dominate their environment. In Middle Eastern countries, on the other hand, performance evaluations aren't likely to be widely used because managers in these countries tend to see people as subjugated to their environment.

Some countries, such as Australia and New Zealand, have a short-term time orientation. Performance evaluations are likely to be frequent in such a culture—at least once a year. In Japan, however, where people hold a long-term time frame, performance appraisals may occur only every five or ten years.

Israel's culture values group activities much more than does the culture of Australia, New Zealand or Canada. So, while Australian managers emphasise the individual in performance evaluations, their counterparts in Israel are much more likely to emphasise group contributions and performance.

Managing Diversity in Organisations

David Morris and his father, Saul, started Habitat International, a company manufacturing a grass-like indoor–outdoor carpet, in 1981. From the beginning, the Morrises hired refugees from Cambodia, Bosnia and Laos, many of whom didn't speak English. But when a social-service worker suggested in 1984 that the company hire mentally challenged people, Saul balked. Hiring someone with a condition such as Down's syndrome seemed too chancy. But David thought otherwise. He talked his dad into giving it a try.[78]

The first group of eight mentally disabled workers came in with their job coach from the social-services agency and went straight to work boxing mats. Two weeks later, says Saul, employees were coming to him and wondering why the company couldn't 'hire more people like this, who care, do their work with pride, and smile?'.

Today, 75 per cent of Habitat's employees have some kind of disability. People with schizophrenia, for example, are driving forklifts next to employees with autism or cerebral palsy. Meanwhile, the Morris father–son team are doing good things both for these people and for themselves. The disabled employees have enhanced self-esteem and are now self-sufficient enough to be off government aid, and the Morrises enjoy the benefits of a dedicated, hardworking workforce. 'We have practically zero absenteeism and very little turnover,' says David.

Habitat International illustrates the role of employee-selection in increasing diversity. But effective diversity programs go well beyond merely hiring a diverse workforce. They also include managing work/life conflicts and providing diversity training. These seem to be common characteristics among major organisations that have developed reputations as diversity leaders—including American Express, Transfield, Johnson & Johnson, IBM, Australian Catholic University and Marriott International.[79]

FAMILY-FRIENDLY WORKPLACES

We introduced work/life balance earlier in this book and discussed the forces that are blurring the lines between work life and personal life. In this section we want to elaborate on this issue—specifically focusing on what organisations can do to create family-friendly workplaces, thereby helping employees to reduce work/life conflicts.

Work/life conflicts grabbed management's attention in the 1980s, largely as a result of the growing number of women with dependent children entering the workforce. In response, most major organisations took actions to make their workplaces more family-friendly.[80] They introduced programs such as on-site child-care, summer day camps, flexitime, job sharing, leaves for school functions, telecommuting and part-time employment. But organisations quickly realised that work/life conflicts weren't only experienced by female employees with children. Male workers and women without children were also facing this problem. Heavy workloads and increased travel demands, for example, were making it increasingly hard for a wide range of employees to meet both work and personal responsibilities. A Harvard study, for example, found that 82 per cent of men between the ages of 20 and 39 said that a 'family-friendly' schedule was their most important job criterion.[81] Even among employees who seemed to be able to 'do it all', many were experiencing guilt or stress.[82]

Today's progressive workplace is being modified to accommodate the varied needs of a diverse workforce. This includes providing a wide range of scheduling options and benefits that allow employees more flexibility at work and which allow them to better balance or integrate their work and personal lives. Table 17.4 lists some examples of initiatives that organisations are providing to help their employees reduce work/life conflicts.

The Australian Catholic University (ACU), to cite one example, achieved its role as a diversity leader with its groundbreaking family-friendly policies that were incorporated into the university's enterprise bargaining agreements. Specifically, the ACU offered all female employees up to one year's paid maternity leave—at a time when nearly half of all women in the Australian workforce were lucky to get six weeks' paid maternity leave. While the ACU was rather private about its reasons, the fact that it faced future shortages of good academics and with a value set from the Catholic Church that promotes family values, the strategy makes good business sense. It even helped to drive the diversity agenda, with the main political parties being forced to re-examine their political policies with regards to family-friendly work practices.

Recent research on work/life conflicts has provided new insights for managers into what works and when. For example, evidence indicates that time pressures aren't the primary problem underlying work/life conflicts.[83] The main problem is the psychological interference of work into the family domain, and vice versa. People are worrying about personal problems at work and thinking about work problems at home. So, Dad may physically make it home in time for dinner, but his mind is elsewhere while he's at the dinner table. This suggests that organisations should spend less effort helping employees with time-management issues and more effort in helping them to clearly segment their lives. Keeping workloads reasonable, reducing work-related travel, and offering on-site quality child-care are examples of practices that can help in this endeavour. Also, not surprisingly, people have been found to differ in their preference for scheduling options and benefits.[84] Some people prefer organisational initiatives that better segment work from their personal lives. Others prefer initiatives that facilitate integration. For example, flexitime segments because it allows employees to schedule work hours that are less likely to conflict with personal responsibilities. On the other hand, on-site child-care integrates by blurring the boundaries between work and family responsibilities. People who prefer segmentation are more likely to be satisfied and committed to their work when offered options such as flexitime, job sharing and part-time hours. People who prefer integration are more likely to respond positively to options such as on-site child-care, gym facilities and company-sponsored family picnics.

Given the opportunity to make a productive contribution, Gwen, a sufferer of manic-depression leads a happier life while at the same time being a highly productive and valued employee.

TABLE 17.4	Work/life initiatives	
Strategy	**Program or Policy**	**Example**
Time-based strategies	Flexitime Job sharing Part-time work Leave for new parents Telecommuting Closing factories/offices for special occasions	IBM Australia gives employees flexibility over start/finish times, the ability to switch from full-time to part-time work (and back again) and telecommuting options. Almost all PeopleSoft employees in Australia use flexitime. BP Australia schedules regular nine-day fortnights and 'No-Meeting-Fridays' to help employees reduce stress, schedule business trips and improve work/life balance. Women at the Australian Catholic University can be paid full pay for 12 weeks and then 60 per cent of their salary for the remainder of up to 12 months for the birth of their child. Fathers who are sole parents are also able to benefit from these entitlements. Fujitsu Australia holds an off-site celebration for all its employees on the 20th of June each year to commemorate its Foundation Day and to present employee service and recognition awards.
Information-based strategies	Intranet work/life website Relocation assistance Elder-care resources	Ernst & Young provides intranet work/life websites that include information on how to write flexible work arrangements proposals, find a job share partner, etc.
Money-based strategies	Vouchers for child-care Flexible benefits Adoption assistance Discounts for child-care tuition Leave with pay	At Adventis Australia, employees are paid for up to six months' child-care, by far the most generous private employer to date.
Direct services	On-site child-care Emergency back-up care On-site health/beauty services Concierge services Take-away dinners	Australia Post conducts regular health risk assessments for staff and provides continual health and well-being promotions through seminars held at lunchtime and reminders in employees' pay slips. Adventis Australia provides its employees with child-care, a dry-cleaning service, masseuse, an accountant for tax returns and a car washing service. Fujitsu provides employees with 'Dinner-forTwo' awards to recognise outstanding performance. Genentech has an on-site hair salon.
Culture-change strategies	Training for managers to help employees deal with work–life conflicts Tie manager pay to employee satisfaction Focus on employees' actual performance, not 'face time'	Lucent, Marriott, Merck, Pfizer, Prudential and Xerox, among others, tie manager pay to employee satisfaction. Deloitte Touche Tohmatsu has identified its seven core values (called Deloitte Signals) and trains all employees in the strategies to achieve these values—including how to have fun and celebrate. Staff are rewarded for results, not for time spent at the office. Fujitsu Australia awards employees with 'Weekend Away' awards when an individual's ability to maintain work/life balance has been adversely affected.

Sources: Based on C. A. Thompson, 'Managing the Work–Life Balancing Act: An Introductory Exercise', *Journal of Management Education*, April 2002, p. 210; R. Levering and M. Moskowitz, 'The Best in the Worst of Times', *Fortune*, 4 February 2002, pp. 60–90; and various websites.

DIVERSITY TRAINING

LEARNING OBJECTIVE

8

Identify the content
in a typical
diversity-training
program

The centrepiece of most diversity programs is training. For example, a relatively recent survey found that, among companies with diversity initiatives, 93 per cent used training as part of their programs.[85] Diversity training programs are generally intended to provide a vehicle for increasing awareness and examining stereotypes. Participants learn to value individual differences, increase their cross-cultural understanding and confront stereotypes.[86] In today's global economy, diversity training can be particularly helpful in accelerating cooperation in multinational work teams, facilitating group learning and reducing cultural misunderstandings.[87]

The typical program lasts from half a day to three days and includes role-playing exercises, lectures, discussions, and sharing of experiences. For example, a training exercise at Hartford Insurance that sought to increase sensitivity to ageing asked participants to respond to the following four questions: (1) If you didn't know how old you are, how old would you guess you are? In other words, how old do you feel inside? (2) When I was 18, I thought middle age began at age _____. (3) Today, I think middle age begins at age _____. (4) What would be your first reaction if someone called you 'an older worker'?[88] Answers to these questions were then used to analyse age-related stereotypes. In another program designed to raise awareness of the power of stereotypes, each participant was asked to write an anonymous paper detailing all groups— women, born-again Christians, indigenous persons, gays, disabled persons, men—to which they had attached stereotypes.[89] They were also asked to explain why they had had trouble working with certain groups in the past. Based on responses, guest speakers were brought into the class to shatter the stereotypes directed at each group. This was followed by extensive discussion.

Summary and Implications for Managers

An organisation's human resource policies and practices represent important forces for shaping employee behaviour and attitudes. In this chapter, we specifically discussed the influence of selection practices, training and development programs, performance evaluation systems and the existence of a union.

Selection practices

An organisation's selection practices will determine who gets hired. If properly designed, they will identify competent candidates and accurately match them to the job and the organisation. The use of the proper selection devices will increase the probability that the right person will be chosen to fill a slot.

Although employee selection is far from a science, some organisations fail to design their selection systems so as to maximise the likelihood that the right person–job fit will be achieved. When errors are made, the chosen candidate's performance may be less than satisfactory. Training may be necessary to improve the candidate's skills. At worst, the candidate will prove unacceptable and a replacement will need to be found. Similarly, when the selection process results in the hiring of less-qualified candidates or individuals who don't fit into the organisation, those chosen are likely to feel anxious, tense and uncomfortable. This, in turn, is likely to increase dissatisfaction with the job.

Training and development programs

Training programs can affect work behaviour in two ways. The most obvious is by directly improving the skills necessary for the employee to successfully complete their job. An increase in ability improves the employee's potential to perform at a higher level. Of course, whether that potential becomes realised is largely an issue of motivation.

A second benefit from training is that it increases an employee's self-efficacy. As you will remember from the chapter on motivation, self-efficacy is a person's expectation that they can successfully execute the behaviours required to produce an outcome.[90] For employees, those behaviours are work tasks and the outcome is effective job performance. Employees with high self-efficacy have strong expectations about their abilities to perform successfully in new situations. They are confident and expect to be successful. Training, then, is a means to positively affect self-efficacy, because employees may be more willing to undertake job tasks and exert a high level of effort. Or, in expectancy terms (see the chapter on motivation), individuals are more likely to perceive their effort as leading to performance.

We also discussed career development in this chapter. We noted the significant decline in formal programs intended to guide an employee's career within a single organisation. But employees still value career planning and development. So, organisations can increase employee commitment, loyalty and satisfaction by encouraging and guiding employees in developing a self-managed career plan, and by clearly communicating the organisation's goals and future strategies, giving employees growth experiences, offering financial assistance to help employees keep their knowledge and skills current, and providing paid time off from work for off-the-job training.

Performance evaluation

A major goal of performance evaluation is to assess accurately an individual's performance contribution as a basis for making reward allocation decisions. If the performance evaluation process emphasises the wrong criteria or inaccurately appraises actual job performance, employees will be over-rewarded or under-rewarded. As demonstrated in the chapter on motivation, in our discussion of equity theory, this can lead to negative consequences, such as reduced effort, increases in absenteeism or a search for alternative job opportunities. In addition, the content of the performance evaluation has been found to influence employee performance and satisfaction.[91] Specifically, performance and satisfaction are increased when the evaluation is based on behavioural, results-oriented criteria, when career issues as well as performance issues are discussed, and when the employee has an opportunity to participate in the evaluation.

Employee relations interface

The existence of a trade union in an organisation adds another variable in our search to explain and predict employee behaviour. The trade union has been found to be an important contributor to employees' perceptions, attitudes and behaviour.

The power of the trade union surfaces in the collective bargaining agreement or enterprise bargaining agreement that it negotiates with management. Much of what an employee can and cannot do on the job is formally stipulated in this agreement. In addition, the informal norms that union cohesiveness fosters can encourage or discourage high productivity, organisational commitment and morale.

Point

IT'S TIME TO ABOLISH PERFORMANCE EVALUATIONS!

Performance evaluations have failed us. They take up a lot of management's valuable time and effort. And instead of providing valid and reliable information for human resource decisions, more often they do nothing other than demotivate employees. As practised today, performance evaluations provide management with essentially worthless data and make employees angry, jealous and cynical.

There is no shortage of good reasons why performance evaluations should be eliminated.[a] The whole process, for example, is political. Management uses it for ulterior purposes—to cover themselves against law suits, to justify different levels of pay, to reward allies and to punish enemies. Employees see the process as a sham that can be manipulated for political purposes. So, most employees put little value in the process or in the final results.

Performance evaluations are subjective. In spite of efforts to formalise and systematise the process, rater errors continue to make any results highly suspicious. Evaluation results also tend to be inflated and non-differentiating. It is typical for 80 per cent or more of employees to be rated above average. This tends to over-value most people's contribution and overlook those who are under-performing.

Employees aren't immune to the influences of regular performance evaluations. Regardless of their validity, most employees still want to receive favourable evaluations. This often encourages employees to misdirect their efforts in order to look good on the criteria management has chosen to appraise. This, of course, helps to explain many behaviours that actually undermine an organisation's overall performance—such as following rules that don't make any sense, or engaging in practices that forgo a large payoff in the long term in order to gain a small payoff immediately.

Performance evaluations were a good fit in the management world of the 1950s and 1960s—a world of bureaucratic organisations run by command-and-control post-Taylorist managers. In today's climate of teamwork, commitment, trust and empowerment, performance evaluations are obsolete and should be abolished.

Source: [a] Much of this argument is based on T. Coens and M. Jenkins, *Abolishing Performance Appraisals* (San Francisco: Berrett-Koehler, 2000).

Counterpoint

If you eliminate performance evaluations, with what do you replace it? We still need some measure of an employee's contribution. We need to hold people accountable for previous commitments they have made to their work group and organisation; and employees would still need some form of feedback on how they can improve if they come up short on meeting those commitments.

Many of the negatives associated with performance evaluations can be corrected by following what we have learned that can make appraisals more valid and reliable, and by focusing on development rather than evaluation.

Much of the criticism unleashed against performance evaluations is due to the way the process is handled. For example, having employees participate in setting their work goals and having them engage in self-evaluation makes the process more democratic and less threatening. By using comparative rankings, management can minimise the effect of inflationary ratings. And the use of multiple evaluators lessens the likelihood of political influence and increases the validity of the results.

In addition, performance appraisals should be used for more than merely evaluation. That is, they should do more than just try to identify what's wrong. They should also be used for development purposes—helping employees to learn how they can improve. When the appraisal process focuses more on development than evaluation, much of the criticism aimed at the process will subside. In a developmental role, managers no longer have to play God. Rather, they become a supportive coach helping employees to improve their performance.

The arguments against performance evaluation are misdirected. The concept is solid. What needs to be abolished is the mismanagement of the process. By emphasising development rather than evaluation, and by making sure that best practices are followed, the performance evaluation can be a valuable tool for improving both employee and organisational performance.

For Discussion

1. How could the phrase 'the best predictor of future behaviour is past behaviour' guide you in managing human resources?
2. What are assessment centres? Why do you think they might be more effective for selecting managers than traditional written tests?
3. Contrast formal and informal training.
4. What can organisations do to help employees develop their careers?
5. What can individuals do to foster their own career development?
6. Why do organisations evaluate employees?
7. What are the advantages and disadvantages of the following performance evaluation methods: (a) written essays, (b) graphic rating scales, and (c) behaviourally anchored rating scales?
8. How can management effectively evaluate individuals when they work as part of a team?
9. What problems, if any, can you see developing as a result of using 360-degree evaluations?
10. What impact do trade unions have on an organisation's reward system and on enterprise bargaining agreements?

Exercise

EVALUATING PERFORMANCE AND PROVIDING FEEDBACK

Objective:
To experience the assessment of performance and observe the providing of performance feedback.

Time:
Approximately 30 minutes.

Procedure:
A class leader is to be selected. They may be either a volunteer or someone chosen by your lecturer. The class leader will preside over the class discussion and perform the role of manager in the evaluation review.

Your lecturer will leave the room. The class leader is then to spend up to 15 minutes helping the class to evaluate your lecturer. Your lecturer understands that this is only a class exercise and is prepared to accept criticism (and, of course, any praise you may want to convey). Your lecturer also recognises that the leader's evaluation is actually a composite of many students' input. So, be open and honest in your evaluation and have confidence that your lecturer won't be vindictive.

Research has identified seven performance dimensions to the university lecturer's job: (1) lecturer knowledge, (2) testing procedures, (3) student–lecturer relations, (4) organisational skills, (5) communication skills, (6) subject relevance, and (7) utility of assignments. The discussion of your lecturer's performance should focus on these seven dimensions. The leader may want to take notes for personal use but won't be required to give the lecturer any written documentation.

When the 15-minute class discussion is complete, the leader will invite the lecturer back into the room. The performance review will begin as soon as the lecturer walks through the door, with the class leader becoming the manager and the lecturer playing himself or herself.

When completed, class discussion will focus on performance evaluation criteria and how well your class leader did in providing performance feedback.

Case Study 17

Is This Any Way to Run a Business?

SAS Institute Inc. is probably the least-well-known major software company in the world. The company makes statistical analysis software (hence the acronym SAS). And it is growing very rapidly. From 1,900 employees five years ago, it now has 5,400. But SAS isn't your typical software company. It's not your typical *anything* company!

At its headquarters, just outside Raleigh, North Carolina, there is a 36,000-square-foot gym for employees. There is a large, hardwood aerobic floor; two full-length basketball courts; pool tables; a private, sky-lighted yoga room; and workout areas. Outside, there are soccer and softball fields. Massages are available several times a week, and classes are offered in golf, African dance, tennis and tai chi. The company also operates the largest on-site day-care facility in the state. To encourage families to eat lunch together, the SAS cafeteria supplies baby seats and high chairs. To encourage families to eat dinner together, the company has a seven-hour workday, five days a week. Unlike many work-obsessive software firms, most SAS employees leave the office by 5 pm. Management likes to call its workplace culture 'relaxed'.

The list of employee amenities at SAS goes on and on. Unlimited soft drinks, coffee, tea and juice. An extra one-week paid holiday between Christmas and New Year's Day. An on-site health clinic staffed with six nurse practitioners and two doctors providing free medical service. Zero cost to employees for health insurance. Dirty workout clothes laundered overnight at no charge. Casual dress every day. Elder-care advice and referrals. Unlimited sick days, and use of sick days to care for sick family members.

Is this any way to run a business? Management thinks so. SAS's strategy is to make it impossible for people not to do their work. Even though the company provides no share options and salaries no better than competitive, the company has built an unbelievably loyal workforce. Whereas competitors typically have turnover rates above 30 per cent, SAS's rate has never been higher than 5 per cent. Management claims that it saves US$67 million a year just in employee replacement-related costs such as recruitment, interviews, moving costs for new hires, and lost work time. That gives it an extra US$12,500 per year per employee to spend on benefits.

Just in case anyone wonders if the company makes any money, we will add the following. SAS is owned by just two people—Jim Goodnight and John Sall. *Forbes* magazine recently listed Goodnight, with US$3 billion, as number 43 on its list of the 400 richest people in America. Sall, with US$1.5 billion, was number 110.

Questions

1. One critic calls SAS 'a big brother approach to managing people'. Is the company too paternalistic? Can a company *be* too paternalistic?
2. When, if ever, do work/life initiatives become paternalistic?
3. What negatives, if any, would you find working for SAS?
4. Are progressive HR practices such as those at SAS a *cause* or a *result* of high profits? Discuss.
5. Microsoft is an unbelievably successful software company. But no one would ever call their culture relaxed. It is 'frantic'. Employees regularly put in 12–14-hour days, six and seven days a week. How does Microsoft keep people? Do you think SAS and Microsoft attract different types of employees? Explain.

Source: Based on C. Fishman, 'Sanity Inc.', *Fast Company*, January 1999, pp. 85–96.

Web Workout

1. How does the project outline document provided by Sun at <www.sun.com/service/servicelist/ses/jobanalysis-au-eng-20020924.pdf> mirror the theory discussed in the textbook? Are there any differences?
2. Go to page 9 of the document at <www.hrobjective.com/en/HRO_TrainingBrochure.pdf>. Identify the key aspects of interpersonal skills training. How might you benefit from such a training program?
3. At the site <http://flexibility.com.au/newsletter-issue3.html>, there is an interview with the former CEO of Westpac, Bob Joss. What were the business objectives identified by him for implementing flexible work practices at Westpac? How successful were they?
4. Discuss the various approaches to ethics training identified at <www.iipe.org/conference2002/papers/Boyd2.pdf>. How effective would you expect these to be in reality? Why?
5. Identify the performance benefits that organisations can achieve by managing diversity outlined in the report at <www.diversityaustralia.gov.au/_inc/doc_pdf/corporate_v/add_value_hrm_tool.pdf>. Read the case studies included in the report and assess for yourself the value of diversity management.

KSS Program

KNOW THE CONCEPTS   SELF-AWARENESS   SKILLS APPLICATIONS

Interviewing skills
After you have read this chapter, take Self-Assessment #17 (What's My Decision-making Style?) on your enclosed CD-Rom and complete the skill-building module entitled 'Selection Interviewing' on page 649.

NOTES

1. C. Matlack, 'The High Cost of France's Aversion to Layoffs', *Business Week*, 5 November 2001, p. 56.
2. See B. Becker and B. Gerhart, 'The Impact of Human Resource Management on Organizational Performance: Progress and Prospects', *Academy of Management Journal*, August 1996, pp. 779–801; J. T. Delaney and M. A. Huselid, 'The Impact of Human Resource Management Practices on the Perceptions of Organizational Performance', *Academy of Management Journal*, August 1996, pp. 949–69; and M. A. Huselid, S. E. Jackson and R. S. Schuler, 'Technical and Strategic Human Resource Management Effectiveness as Determinants of Firm Performance', *Academy of Management Journal*, February 1997, pp. 171–88.
3. R. J. Stone, *Human Resources Management* (Brisbane: John Wiley & Sons, 1995), p. 4.
4. See, for example, C. T. Dortch, 'Job-Person Match', *Personnel Journal*, June 1989, pp. 49–57; and S. Rynes and B. Gerhart, 'Interviewer Assessments of Applicant "Fit": An Exploratory Investigation', *Personnel Psychology*, Spring 1990, pp. 13–34.
5. See, for example, J. V. Ghorpade, *Job Analysis: A Handbook for the Human Resource Director* (Englewood Cliffs, NJ: Prentice Hall, 1988).
6. D. E. Bowen, G. E. Ledford, Jr and B. R. Nathan, 'Hiring for the Organization, Not the Job', *Academy of Management Executive*, November 1991, pp. 35–51; E. E. Lawler III, 'From Job-Based to Competency-Based Organizations', *Journal of Organizational Behavior*, January 1994, pp. 3–15; D. M. Cable and T. A. Judge, 'Interviewers' Perceptions of Person–Organization Fit and Organizational Selection Decisions', *Journal of Applied Psychology*, August 1997, pp. 546–61; and A. L. Kristof-Brown, 'Perceived Applicant Fit: Distinguishing Between Recruiters' Perceptions of Person–Job and Person–Organization Fit', *Personnel Psychology*, Autumn 2000, pp. 643–71.
7. R. A. Posthuma, F. P. Moregeson and M. A. Campion, 'Beyond Employment Interview Validity: A Comprehensive Narrative Review of Recent Research and Trend Over Time', *Personnel Psychology*, Spring 2002, p. 1.
8. L. Yoo-Lim, 'More Companies Rely on Employee Interviews', *Business Korea*, November 1994, pp. 22–23.
9. T. J. Hanson and J. C. Balestreri-Spero, 'An Alternative to Interviews', *Personnel Journal*, June 1985, p. 114. See also T. W. Dougherty, D. B. Turban and J. C. Callender, 'Confirming First Impressions in the Employment Interview: A Field Study of Interviewer Behavior', *Journal of Applied Psychology*, October 1994, pp. 659–65.
10. K. I. van der Zee, A. B. Bakker and P. Bakker, 'Why are Structured Interviews So Rarely Used in Personnel Selection?', *Journal of Applied Psychology*, February 2002, pp. 176–84.
11. See M. A. McDaniel, D. L. Whetzel, F. L. Schmidt and S. D. Maurer, 'The Validity of Employment Interviews: A Comprehensive Review and Meta-Analysis', *Journal of Applied Psychology*, August 1994, pp. 599–616; J. M. Conway, R. A. Jako and D. F. Goodman, 'A Meta-Analysis of Interrater and Internal Consistency Reliability of Selection Interviews', *Journal of Applied Psychology*, October 1995, pp. 565–79; M. A. Campion, D. K. Palmer and J. E. Campion, 'A Review of Structure in the Selection Interview', *Personnel Psychology*, Autumn 1997, pp. 655–702; F. L. Schmidt and J. E. Hunter, 'The Validity and Utility of Selection Methods in Personnel Psychology: Practical and Theoretical

Implications of 85 Years of Research Findings', *Psychological Bulletin*, September 1998, pp. 262–74; and A. I. Huffcutt and D. J. Woehr, 'Further Analysis of Employment Interview Validity: A Quantitative Evaluation of Interviewer-Related Structuring Methods', *Journal of Organizational Behavior*, July 1999, pp. 549–60.

12. R. L. Dipboye, *Selection Interviews: Process Perspectives* (Cincinnati: South-Western Publishing, 1992), pp. 42–44; and Posthuma, Moregeson and Campion, 'Beyond Employment Interview Validity', pp. 1–81.

13. A. I. Huffcutt, J. M. Conway, P. L. Roth and N. J. Stone, 'Identification and Meta-Analytic Assessment of Psychological Constructs Measured in Employment Interviews', *Journal of Applied Psychology*, October 2001, p. 910.

14. See G. A. Adams, T. C. Elacqua and S. M. Colarelli, 'The Employment Interview as a Sociometric Selection Technique', *Journal of Group Psychotherapy*, Fall 1994, pp. 99–113; R. L. Dipboye, 'Structured and Unstructured Selection Interviews: Beyond the Job–Fit Model', *Research in Personnel Human Resource Management*, vol. 12, 1994, pp. 79–123; and B. Schneider, D. B. Smith, S. Taylor and J. Fleenor, 'Personality and Organizations: A Test of the Homogeneity of Personality Hypothesis', *Journal of Applied Psychology*, June 1998, pp. 462–70.

15. E. E. Ghiselli, 'The Validity of Aptitude Tests in Personnel Selection', *Personnel Psychology*, Winter 1973, p. 475.

16. R. J. Herrnstein and C. Murray, *The Bell Curve: Intelligence and Class Structure in American Life* (New York: Free Press, 1994); and M. J. Ree, J. A. Earles and M. S. Teachout, 'Predicting Job Performance: Not Much More Than g', *Journal of Applied Psychology*, August 1994, pp. 518–24.

17. J. Flint, 'Can You Tell Applesauce From Pickles?', *Forbes*, 9 October 1995, pp. 106–08.

18. D. S. Ones, C. Viswesvaran and F. L. Schmidt, 'Comprehensive Meta-Analysis of Integrity Test Validities: Findings and Implications for Personnel Selection and Theories of Job Performance', *Journal of Applied Psychology*, August 1993, pp. 679–703; P. R. Sackett and J. E. Wanek, 'New Developments in the Use of Measures of Honesty, Integrity, Conscientiousness, Dependability, Trustworthiness, and Reliability for Personnel Selection', *Personnel Psychology*, Winter 1996, pp. 787–829; and Schmidt and Hunter, 'The Validity and Utility of Selection Methods in Personnel Psychology'.

19. P. Carbonara, 'Hire for Attitude, Train for Skill', *Fast Company, Greatest Hits*, vol. 1, 1997, p. 68.

20. <http://education.qld.gov.au/students/placement/work/workex.html>, accessed 15 September 2003.

21. J. J. Asher and J. A. Sciarrino, 'Realistic Work Sample Tests: A Review', *Personnel Psychology*, Winter 1974, pp. 519–33; and I. T. Robertson and R. S. Kandola, 'Work Sample Tests: Validity, Adverse Impact and Applicant Reaction', *Journal of Occupational Psychology*, Spring 1982, pp. 171–82.

22. See, for example, A. C. Spychalski, M. A. Quinones, B. B. Gaugler and K. Pohley, 'A Survey of Assessment Center Practices in Organizations in the United States', *Personnel Psychology*, Spring 1997, pp. 71–90; and C. Woodruffe, *Development and Assessment Centres: Identifying and Assessing Competence* (London: Institute of Personnel and Development, 2000).

23. B. B. Gaugler, D. B. Rosenthal, G. C. Thornton and C. Benson, 'Meta-Analysis of Assessment Center Validity', *Journal of Applied Psychology*, August 1987, pp. 493–511; G. C. Thornton, *Assessment Centers in Human Resource Management* (Reading, MA: Addison-Wesley, 1992); W. Arthur, Jr, D. J. Woehr and R. Maldegen, 'Convergent and Discriminant Validity of Assessment Center Dimensions: A Conceptual and Empirical Reexamination of the Assessment Center Construct-Related Validity Paradox', *Journal of Management*, vol. 26, no. 4, 2000, pp. 813–35; and P. G. W. Jansen and B. A. M. Stoop, 'The Dynamics of Assessment Center Validity: Results of a 7-Year Study', *Journal of Applied Psychology*, August 2001, pp. 741–53.

24. A. Morehead, M. Steele, M. Alexander, K. Stephen and L. Duffin, *Changes at Work* (Melbourne: Longman, 1997).

25. R. R. Collins and B. K. Hackman, 'National Survey of Training and Development Practices: July 1991', *Training and Development in Australia*, December 1991, pp. 15–22.

26. Australian Bureau of Statistics, 1998, *Education and Training Experience Australia 1997*, Canberra, AGPS.

27. Ibid.

28. Ibid.

29. A. Bernstein, 'The Time Bomb in the Workforce: Illiteracy', *Business Week*, 25 February 2002, p. 122; M. Norton, 'So—How Many People Can't Read?', in Australian Bureau of Statistics, 1996, *Aspects of Literacy: Assessed Skill Levels Australia*, Cat. No. 4228.0, Canberra, AGPS.

30. Baynton, 'America's $60 Billion Problem', p. 52.

31. J. Barbarian, 'Mark Spear: Director of Management and Organizational Development, Miller Brewing Co.', *Training*, October 2001, pp. 34–38.

32. J. Thomson, 'Bright Idea', *Business Review Weekly*, 19 September 2002, p. 19.

33. G. R. Weaver, L. K. Trevino and P. L. Cochran, 'Corporate Ethics Practices in the Mid-1990's: An Empirical Study of the Fortune 1000', *Journal of Business Ethics*, February 1999, pp. 283–94.

34. K. Dobbs, 'The U.S. Department of Labor Estimates that 70 Percent of Workplace Learning Occurs Informally', *Sales & Marketing Management*, November 2000, pp. 94–98.

35. S. J. Wells, 'Forget the Formal Training. Try Chatting at the Water Cooler', *New York Times*, 10 May 1998, p. BU-11.

36. See, for example, K. G. Brown, 'Using Computers to Deliver Training: Which Employees Learn and Why?', *Personnel Psychology*, Summer 2001, pp. 271–96; and 'The Delivery: How U.S. Organizations Use Classrooms and Computers in Training', *Training*, October 2001, pp. 66–72.

37. A. Muoio, 'Cisco's Quick Study', *Fast Company*, October 2000, pp. 287–95.

38. D. A. Kolb, 'Management and the Learning Process', *California Management Review*, Spring 1976, pp. 21–31; and B. Filipczak, 'Different Strokes: Learning Styles in the Classroom', *Training*, March 1995, pp. 43–48.

39. D. T. Hall and Associates (ed.), *The Career Is Dead—Long Live the Career* (San Francisco: Jossey-Bass, 1996); and S. E. Sullivan, 'The Changing Nature of Careers: A Review and Research Agenda', *Journal of Management*, vol. 25, no. 3, 1999, pp. 457–84.

40. T. Peters, *The Brand You* (New York: Knopf, 1999).

41. Based on P. Hirsch, *Pack Your Own Parachute: How to Survive Mergers, Takeovers, and Other Corporate Disasters* (Reading, MA: Addison-Wesley, 1987); R. Henkoff, 'Winning the New Career Game', *Fortune*, 12 July 1993, pp. 46–49; and H. Lancaster, 'As Company Programs Fade, Workers Turn to Guild-like Groups', *Wall Street Journal*, 16 January 1996, p. B1.

42. W. F. Cascio, *Applied Psychology in Human Resource Management*, 5th ed. (Upper Saddle River, NJ: Prentice Hall, 1998), p. 59.

43. See, for example, C. O. Longnecker, H. P. Sims and D. A. Gioia, 'Behind the Mask: The Politics of Employee Appraisal', *Academy of Management Executive*, August 1987, pp. 183–93; P. Villanova and H. Bernardin, 'Impression Management in the Context of Performance Appraisal', in R. A. Giacalone and P. Rosenfeld (eds), *Impression Management in the Organization* (Hillsdale, NJ: Lawrence Erlbaum, 1989), pp. 299–314; and P. Villanova and H. Bernardin, 'Performance Appraisal: The Means, Motive, and Opportunity to Manage Impressions', in R. A. Giacalone and P. Rosenfeld (eds), *Applied Impression Management: How Image-Making Affects Managerial Decisions* (Newbury Park, CA: Sage, 1991), pp. 81–96.

44. P. M. Blau, *The Dynamics of Bureaucracy*, rev. ed. (Chicago: University of Chicago Press, 1963).

45. 'The Cop-Out Cops', *National Observer*, 3 August 1974.

46. See W. C. Borman and S. J. Motowidlo, 'Expanding the Criterion Domain to Include Elements of Contextual Performance', in N. Schmitt and W. C. Borman (eds), *Personnel Selection in Organizations* (San Francisco: Jossey-Bass, 1993), pp. 71–98; W. H. Bommer, J. L. Johnson, G. A. Rich, P. M. Podsakoff and S. B. MacKenzie, 'On the Interchangeability of Objective and Subjective Measures of Employee Performance: A Meta-Analysis', *Personnel Psychology*, Autumn 1995, pp. 587–605.

47. A. H. Locher and K. S. Teel, 'Appraisal Trends', *Personnel Journal*, September 1988, pp. 139–45.

48. G. P. Latham and K. N. Wexley, *Increasing Productivity through Performance Appraisal* (Reading, MA: Addison-Wesley, 1981), p. 80.

49. See review in R. D. Bretz, Jr, G. T. Milkovich and W. Read, 'The Current State of Performance Appraisal Research and Practice: Concerns, Directions, and Implications', *Journal of Management*, June 1992, p. 326.

50. See, for example, W. W. Tornow and M. London (eds), *Maximizing the Value of 360-Degree Feedback* (San Francisco: Jossey-Bass, 1998); J. Ghorpade, 'Managing Five Paradoxes of 360-Degree Feedback', *Academy of Management Executive*, February 2000, pp. 140–50; J. D. Facteau and S. B. Craig, 'Are Performance Appraisal Ratings from Different Rating Sources Compatible?', *Journal of Applied Psychology*, April 2001, pp. 215–27; J. F. Brett and L. E. Atwater, '360-Degree Feedback: Accuracy, Reactions, and Perceptions of Usefulness', *Journal of Applied Psychology*, October 2001, pp. 930–42; and C. Wingrove, 'Untangling the Myths of 360: Straight Talk for Successful Outcomes', *Compensation & Benefits Review*, November–December 2001, pp. 34–37.

51. C. Trafford, '360-degree Feedback Provides Tools to Focus Development Efforts', *HRMonthly*, October 1997, pp. 32–33.

52. Ibid.

53. D. V. Day, 'Leadership Development: A Review in Context', *Leadership Quarterly*, Winter 2000, pp. 587–89.

54. 'Ivy League Grade Inflation', *USA Today*, 8 February 2002, p. 11A.

55. A. S. DeNisi and L. H. Peters, 'Organization of Information in Memory and the Performance Appraisal Process: Evidence from the Field', *Journal of Applied Psychology*, December 1996, pp. 717–37.

56. See, for example, J. W. Hedge and W. C. Borman, 'Changing Conceptions and Practices in Performance Appraisal', in A. Howard (ed.), *The Changing Nature of Work* (San Francisco: Jossey-Bass, 1995), pp. 453–59.

57. See, for example, D. E. Smith, 'Training Programs for Performance Appraisal: A Review', *Academy of Management Review*, January 1986, pp. 22–40; T. R. Athey and R. M. McIntyre, 'Effect of Rater Training on Rater Accuracy: Levels-of-Processing Theory and Social Facilitation Theory Perspectives', *Journal of Applied Psychology*, November 1987, pp. 567–72; and D. J. Woehr, 'Understanding Frame-of-Reference Training: The Impact of Training on the Recall of Performance Information', *Journal of Applied Psychology*, August 1994, pp. 525–34.

58. H. J. Bernardin, 'The Effects of Rater Training on Leniency and Halo Errors in Student Rating of Instructors', *Journal of Applied Psychology*, June 1978, pp. 301–08.

59. Ibid; and J. M. Ivancevich, 'Longitudinal Study of the Effects of Rater Training on Psychometric Error in Ratings', *Journal of Applied Psychology*, October 1979, pp. 502–08.

60. M. S. Taylor, K. B. Tracy, M. K. Renard, J. K. Harrison and S. J. Carroll, 'Due Process in Performance Appraisal: A Quasi-Experiment in Procedural Justice', *Administrative Science Quarterly*, September 1995, pp. 495–523.

61. J. S. Lublin, 'It's Shape-up Time for Performance Reviews', *Wall Street Journal*, 3 October 1994, p. B1.

62. Much of this section is based on H. H. Meyer, 'A Solution to the Performance Appraisal Feedback Enigma', *Academy of Management Executive*, February 1991, pp. 68–76.

63. B. Gates, *The Road Ahead* (New York: Viking, 1995), p. 86.

64. T. D. Schelhardt, 'It's Time to Evaluate Your Work, and All Involved Are Groaning', *Wall Street Journal*, 19 November 1996, p. A1.

65. R. J. Burke, 'Why Performance Appraisal Systems Fail', *Personnel Administration*, June 1972, pp. 32–40.

66. B. R. Nathan, A. M. Mohrman, Jr and J. Milliman, 'Interpersonal Relations as a Context for the Effects of Appraisal Interviews on Performance and Satisfaction: A Longitudinal Study', *Academy of Management Journal*, June 1991, pp. 352–69. See also B. D. Cawley, L. M. Keeping and P. E. Levy, 'Participation in the Performance Appraisal Process and Employee Reactions: A Meta-Analytic Review of Field Investigations', *Journal of Applied Psychology*, August 1998, pp. 615–33.

67. J. Zigon, 'Making Performance Appraisal Work for Teams', *Training*, June 1994, pp. 58–63.

68. E. Salas, T. L. Dickinson, S. A. Converse and S. I. Tannenbaum, 'Toward an Understanding of Team Performance and Training', in R. W. Swezey and E. Salas (eds), *Teams: Their Training and Performance* (Norwood, NJ: Ablex, 1992), pp. 3–29.

69. D. A. DeCenzo and S. P. Robbins, *Human Resource Management*, 7th ed. (New York: Wiley, 2002), p. 436.

70. Much of the material in this section was adapted from T. H. Hammer, 'Relationship between Local Union Characteristics and Worker Behavior and Attitudes', *Academy of Management Journal*, December 1978, pp. 560–77.

71. See B. B. Auster and W. Cohen, 'Rallying the Rank and File', *U.S. News & World Report*, 1 April 1996, pp. 26–28; and M. A. Verespej, 'Wounded and Weaponless', *Industry Week*, 16 September 1996, pp. 46–58.

72. See J. B. Arthur and J. B. Dworkin, 'Current Topics in Industrial and Labor Relations Research and Practice', *Journal of Management*, September 1991, pp. 530–32.

73. See, for example, C. J. Berger, C. A. Olson and J. W. Boudreau, 'Effects of Unions on Job Satisfaction: The Role of Work-Related Values and Perceived Rewards', *Organizational Behavior and Human Performance*, December 1983, pp. 289–324; and M. G. Evans and D. A. Ondrack, 'The Role of Job Outcomes and Values in Understanding the Union's Impact on Job Satisfaction: A Replication', *Human Relations*, May 1990, pp. 401–18.

74. See, for example, M. Mendonca and R. N. Kanungo, 'Managing Human Resources: The Issue of Cultural Fit', *Journal of Management Inquiry*, June 1994, pp. 189–205; and N. Ramamoorthy and S. J. Carroll, 'Individualism/Collectivism Orientations and Reactions toward Alternative Human Resource Management Practices', *Human Relations*, May 1998, pp. 571–88.

75. A. M. Ryan, L. McFarland, H. Baron and R. Page, 'An International Look at Selection Practices: Nation and Culture as Explanations for Variability in Practice', *Personnel Psychology*, Summer 1999, pp. 359–92.

76. Ibid, p. 386.

77. M. Tanikawa, 'Fujitsu Decides to Backtrack on Performance-Based Pay', *New York Times*, 22 March 2001, p. W1.

78. N. B. Henderson, 'An Enabling Work Force', *Nation's Business*, June 1998, p. 93.

79. See L. Urresta and J. Hickman, 'The Diversity Elite', *Fortune*, 3 August 1998, pp. 114–22.

80. C. Oglesby, 'More Options for Moms Seeking Work–Family Balance', <www.cnn.com>, 10 May 2001.

81. 'On the Daddy Track', *Wall Street Journal*, 11 May 2000, p. A1.

82. M. B. Grover, 'Daddy Stress', *Forbes*, 6 September 1999, pp. 202–08.

83. S. D. Friedman and J. H. Greenhaus, *Work and Family—Allies or Enemies?* (New York: Oxford University Press, 2000).

84. N. P. Rothbard, T. L. Dumas and K. W. Phillips, 'The Long Arm of the Organization: Work–Family Policies and Employee Preferences for Segmentation', paper presented at the 61st Annual Academy of Management Meeting, Washington, DC, August 2001.

85. Cited in 'Survey Shows 75% of Large Corporations Support Diversity Programs', *Fortune*, 6 July 1998, p. S14.

86. See, for example, S. Nelton, 'Nurturing Diversity', *Nation's Business*, June 1995, pp. 25–27; J. K. Ford and S. Fisher, 'The Role of Training in a Changing Workplace and Workforce: New Perspectives and Approaches', in E. E. Kossek and S. A. Lobel (eds), *Managing Diversity* (Cambridge, MA: Blackwell Publishers, 1996), pp. 164–93.

87. R. Koonce, 'Redefining Diversity', *T+D*, December 2001, p. 25.

88. B. Hynes-Grace, 'To Thrive, Not Merely Survive', in *Textbook Authors Conference Presentations* (Washington, DC: 21 October 1992), sponsored by the American Association of Retired Persons, p. 12.

89. 'Teaching Diversity: Business Schools Search for Model Approaches', *Newsline*, Fall 1992, p. 21.

90. A. Bandura, 'Self-Efficacy: Towards a Unifying Theory of Behavioral Change', *Psychological Review*, March 1977, pp. 191–215; and P. C. Earley, 'Self or Group? Cultural Effects of Training on Self-Efficacy and Performance', *Administrative Science Quarterly*, March 1994, pp. 89–117.

91. Nathan, Mohrman and Milliman, 'Interpersonal Relations as a Context for the Effects of Appraisal Interviews on Performance and Satisfaction: A Longitudinal Study'; and Cawley, Keeping and Levy, 'Participation in the Performance Appraisal Process and Employee Reactions'.

PHOTO CREDITS

531 AAP Image.

18

Organisational Change and Stress Management

CHAPTER OUTLINE

Forces for change
Managing planned change
Resistance to change
Approaches to managing organisational change
Contemporary change issues for today's managers
Work stress and its management

LEARNING OBJECTIVES

After studying this chapter, you should be able to:
1. Describe forces that act as stimulants to change
2. Summarise sources of individual and organisational resistance to change
3. Summarise Lewin's three-step change model
4. Explain the values underlying most OD efforts
5. Identify properties of innovative organisations
6. List characteristics of a learning organisation
7. Define knowledge management and explain its importance
8. Describe potential sources of stress
9. Explain individual difference variables that moderate the stress–outcome relationship

Most people hate any change that doesn't jingle in their pockets.

Anonymous

Geoff Bell recognised the challenge of cultural change at the Sydney Markets.

Geoff Bell was a colonel in the Australian Army who is used to working with and giving directions to people; in fact, up to 300 of them. In 1999, he left the army for a job in Sydney, which enabled his family to settle down in the one place. This was particularly important for his children in their high school years. Geoff became chief executive officer of the Sydney Markets, where growers from all over Australia and from overseas send one million tonnes of fresh produce worth $1.8 billion each year to these markets for sale to thousands of buyers. Growers have a choice of sending their produce to any one of 137 wholesalers and, currently, some 400 growers directly sell their produce to retailers and consumers.

One of the first challenges that Geoff saw on his arrival at the markets was to change the culture of how the markets were run. As CEO responsible for operating the markets, he was concerned that the people at the markets had a process orientation rather than an outcome orientation. There needed to be more focus on the wholesalers and growers. This was a change management exercise and his background in the army gave him the experience to develop such a culture.

He believes that systems are systems and people are people, and it is a question of adapting systems and leadership styles to suit the different contexts. In the army, he had experience with strategic planning at a national level, particularly with developing infrastructure and implementing change management projects. Today, the Sydney Markets are seen as a thriving enterprise that recognises the needs of the growers, wholesalers, retailers and consumers alike, with a clear set of values about operational excellence, innovation and business development, cooperation and teamwork, and strong leadership and management based on honesty and integrity at all levels within the company.[1]

This chapter is about organisational change and stress. We describe environmental forces that are requiring managers to implement comprehensive change programs. We also consider why people and organisations often resist change and how this resistance can be overcome. We review various processes for managing organisational change. We also discuss contemporary change issues for today's managers. Then we move to the topic of stress .We elaborate on the sources and consequences of stress. Finally, we conclude this chapter with a discussion of what individuals and organisations can do to better manage stress levels.

Forces for Change

Management students around the world should be familiar with Amazon.com because they can get the latest in management texts through the convenience of Internet ordering and supply. In January 2000, *Time* magazine described Amazon.com as a breakthrough concept and named its founder and CEO, Jeff Bezos, as the *Time* Person of the Year. Twelve months later, Amazon's shares had dropped 80 per cent in value, its survival was uncertain, and Bezos himself was saying that the media had now made him the Piñata of the Year. Bezos's experience offers a chilling illustration of the rapid forces of change in the 21st century.

More and more organisations today face a dynamic and changing environment. This, in turn, is requiring these organisations to adapt. 'Change or die!' is the rallying cry among today's managers worldwide. Table 18.1 summarises six specific forces that are acting as stimulants for change.

In a number of places in this book, we have discussed the *changing nature of the workforce*. For example, almost every organisation is having to adjust to a multicultural environment. Human resource policies and practices have to change in order to attract and keep this more diverse workforce. And many companies are having to spend large amounts of money on training to upgrade reading, maths, computer and other skills of employees.

Technology is changing jobs and organisations. For example, computers are now commonplace in almost every organisation; and cell or mobile phones and hand-held PDAs (Personal Digital Assistants) are being increasingly perceived as necessities by a large segment of the population. For the longer term, recent breakthroughs in deciphering the human genetic code offer the potential for pharmaceutical companies to produce drugs designed for specific individuals and create serious ethical dilemmas for insurance companies as to who is insurable and who isn't.

TABLE 18.1 **Forces for change**	
Force	**Examples**
Nature of the workforce	• More cultural diversity • Increase in professionals • Many new entrants with inadequate skills
Technology	• Faster and cheaper computers • New mobile communication devices • Deciphering of the human genetic code
Economic shocks	• Rise and fall of dot.com shares • Decline in the value of the euro • Collapse of Enron Corporation
Competition	• Global competitors • Mergers and consolidations • Growth of e-commerce
Social trends	• Internet chat rooms • Retirement of baby-boomers • Increased interest in urban living
World politics	• Escalation of hostilities in the Middle East • Opening of markets in China • The war on terrorism following September 11

We live in an 'age of discontinuity'. In the 1950s and 1960s, the past was a pretty good prologue to the future. Tomorrow was essentially an extended trend line from yesterday. That's no longer true. Beginning in the early 1970s, with the overnight quadrupling of world oil prices, *economic shocks* have continued to impose changes on organisations. In recent years, for example, new dot.com businesses have been created, turned tens-of-thousands of investors into overnight millionaires, and then crashed. Western European countries created the euro to counter the dominance of the US dollar on world financial markets. The collapse of Enron Corp. in the United States and HIH Insurance and OneTel in Australia has made executive ethics, managerial controls, responsibility of board members, manipulation of earnings, and conflicts of interest between firms and their auditors topics of concern for all corporate executives.

Competition is changing. The global economy means that competitors are as likely to come from across the ocean as from across town. Heightened competition also makes it necessary for established organisations to defend themselves against both traditional competitors who develop new products and services and small, entrepreneurial firms with innovative offerings. Successful organisations will be the ones that can change in response to the competition. They will be fast on their feet, capable of developing new products rapidly and getting them to market quickly. They will rely on short production runs, short product cycles and an ongoing stream of new products. In other words, they will be flexible. They will require an equally flexible and responsive workforce that can adapt to rapidly, and even radically, changing conditions.

Social trends don't remain static. For example, in contrast to just ten years ago, people are meeting and sharing information in Internet chat rooms; baby-boomers have begun to retire; and many baby-boomer and Generation Xers are leaving the suburbs and moving to the cities Throughout this book, we have argued strongly for the importance of seeing OB in a global context. Business schools have been preaching a global perspective since the early 1980s, but no one—not even the strongest proponents of globalisation—could have imagined how *world politics* would change in recent years. We have seen the breakup of the Soviet Union; the opening up of South Africa and China; almost daily suicide bombings in the Middle East; and, of course, the rise of Muslim fundamentalism. The attacks on New York and Washington on 11 September 2001, the subsequent war on terrorism and Iraq, and the Bali bombings of 12 October 2002, have led to changes in business practices related to the creation of backup systems, employee security, employee stereotyping and profiling, and post-terrorist-attack anxiety.

Managing Planned Change

A group of housekeeping employees who work for a small hotel confronted the owner: 'It's very hard for most of us to maintain rigid 7-to-4 work hours,' said their spokeswoman. 'Each of us has significant family and personal responsibilities. And rigid hours don't work for us. We're going to begin looking for someplace else to work if you don't set up flexible work hours.' The owner listened thoughtfully to the group's ultimatum and agreed to its request. The next day, the owner introduced a flexitime plan for these employees.

A major automobile manufacturer spent several billion dollars to install state-of-the-art robotics. One area that would receive the new equipment was quality control. Sophisticated computer-controlled equipment would be put in place to significantly improve the company's ability to find and correct defects. Because the new equipment would dramatically change the jobs of the people working in the quality-control area, and because management anticipated considerable employee resistance to the new equipment, executives were developing a program to help people become familiar with the equipment and to deal with any anxieties they might be feeling.

change
Making things different.

Both of the previous scenarios are examples of **change**. That is, both are concerned with making things different. However, only the second scenario describes a **planned change**. Many changes in organisations are like the one that occurred at the hotel—they just happen. Some organisations treat all change as an accidental occurrence. We are concerned with change

planned change
Change activities that are intentional and goal-oriented.

YOU'RE NOT CHAINED TO YOUR DESK. YOU'RE WIRED TO IT.

The new ThinkPad® X31 with easier wireless connectivity.

The ThinkPad X31 is powered by Intel® Centrino™ Mobile Technology.

IBM is a well known brand name in the computer industry yet this great computer company has gone through profound changes in the past 40 years due to the technological developments associated with computers.

activities that are proactive and purposeful. In this chapter, we address change as an intentional, goal-oriented activity.

What are the goals of planned change? Essentially, there are two. First, it seeks to improve the ability of the organisation to adapt to changes in its environment. Second, it seeks to change employee behaviour.

If an organisation is to survive, it must respond to changes in its environment. When competitors introduce new products or services, government agencies enact new laws, important sources of supply go out of business, or similar environmental changes take place, the organisation needs to adapt. Efforts to stimulate innovation, empower employees and introduce work teams are examples of planned-change activities directed at responding to changes in the environment.

Because an organisation's success or failure is essentially due to the things that its employees do or fail to do, planned change also is concerned with changing the behaviour of individuals and groups within the organisation. Later in this chapter, we review a number of techniques that organisations can use to get people to behave differently in the tasks they perform and in their interactions with others.

change agents
Persons who act as catalysts and assume the responsibility for managing change activities.

Who in organisations are responsible for managing change activities? The answer is: **change agents**.[2] Change agents can be managers or non-managers, employees of the organisation or outside consultants. For major change efforts, internal management often will hire the services of outside consultants to provide advice and assistance. Because they are from the outside, these individuals can offer an objective perspective often unavailable to insiders. Outside consultants, however, are disadvantaged because they usually have an inadequate understanding of the organisation's history, culture, operating procedures and personnel. Outside consultants also may be prone to initiating more drastic changes—which can be a benefit or a disadvantage—because they don't have to live with the repercussions after the change is implemented. In contrast, internal staff specialists or managers, when acting as change agents, may be more thoughtful (and possibly more cautious) because they have to live with the consequences of their actions.

LEARNING OBJECTIVE

2

Summarise sources of individual and organisational resistance to change

Resistance to Change

One of the most well-documented findings from studies of individual and organisational behaviour is that organisations and their members resist change. In a sense, this is positive. It provides a degree of stability and predictability to behaviour. If there weren't some resistance, organisational behaviour would take on the characteristics of chaotic randomness. Resistance to change can also be a source of functional conflict. For example, resistance to a reorganisation plan or a change in a product line can stimulate a healthy debate over the merits of the idea and result in a better decision. But there is a definite downside to resistance to change. It hinders adaptation and progress, and can generate unhealthy levels of stress throughout the organisation.

Resistance to change doesn't necessarily surface in standardised ways. Resistance can be overt, implicit, immediate or deferred. It is easiest for management to deal with resistance when it is overt and immediate. For example, a change is proposed and employees quickly respond by voicing complaints, engaging in a work slowdown, threatening to go on strike, or the like. The greater challenge is managing resistance that is implicit or deferred. Implicit resistance efforts are more subtle—loss of loyalty to the organisation, loss of motivation to work, increased errors or mistakes, increased absenteeism due to 'sickness'—and hence are more difficult to recognise. Similarly, deferred actions cloud the link between the source of the resistance and the reaction to it. A change may produce what appears to be only a minimal reaction at the time it is initiated, but then resistance surfaces weeks, months or even years later. Or a single change that in and of itself might have little impact becomes the straw that breaks the camel's back. Reactions to change can build up and then explode in some response that seems totally out of proportion to the change action it follows. The resistance, of course, has merely been deferred and stockpiled. What surfaces is a response to an accumulation of previous changes.

Let's look at the sources of resistance. For analytical purposes, we have categorised them by individual and organisational sources. In the real world, the sources often overlap.

INDIVIDUAL RESISTANCE

Individual sources of resistance to change reside in basic human characteristics such as perceptions, personalities and needs. The following summarises five reasons why individuals may resist change (see Figure 18.1).

Habit

Every day, when you go to work or school, do you continually use the same route and streets? Probably. If you are like most people, you find a single route and you use it regularly.

As human beings, we are creatures of habit. Life is complex enough; we don't need to consider the full range of options for the hundreds of decisions we have to make every day. To cope with this complexity, we all rely on habits or programmed responses. But when confronted with change, this tendency to respond in our accustomed ways becomes a source of resistance. So, when your department is moved to a new office building on the other side of town, it means you are likely to have to change many habits: waking up ten minutes earlier, taking a new route to work, finding a new parking place, adjusting to the new office layout, developing a new lunchtime routine, and so on.

Security

People with a high need for security are likely to resist change because it threatens their feelings of safety. When Ericcson, one of the world's leading suppliers of telecommunications, announces it is laying off 17,000 people, or General Motors-Holden introduces new robotic equipment, many employees at these firms may fear that their jobs are in jeopardy.

Economic factors

Another source of individual resistance is concern that changes will lower one's income. Changes in job tasks or established work routines also can arouse economic fears if people are concerned that they won't be able to perform the new tasks or routines to their previous standards, especially when pay is closely tied to productivity.

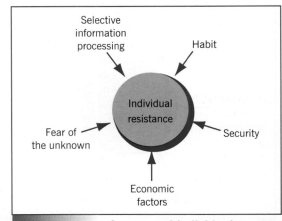

FIGURE 18.1   Sources of individual resistance to change

Fear of the unknown

Changes substitute ambiguity and uncertainty for the known. The transition from high school to university is typically such an experience. By the time we are in Year 12 in high school, we understand how things work. You might not have liked high school, but at least you understood the system. Then you move on to university and face a whole new and uncertain system. You have traded the known for the unknown and the fear or insecurity that goes with it.

Employees in organisations hold the same dislike for uncertainty. If, for example, the introduction of quality management means production workers will have to learn statistical process control techniques, some may fear they will be unable to do so. They may, therefore, develop a negative attitude towards a quality-management program or behave dysfunctionally if required to use statistical techniques.

Selective information processing

As we learned earlier in the book, individuals shape their world through their perceptions. Once they have created this world, it resists change. So, individuals are guilty of selectively processing information in order to keep their perceptions intact. They hear what they want to hear. They ignore information that challenges the world they have created. To return to the production workers who are faced with the introduction of quality management, they may ignore the arguments their managers make in explaining why a knowledge of statistics is necessary or the potential benefits the change will provide them.

ORGANISATIONAL RESISTANCE

Organisations, by their very nature, are conservative.[3] They actively resist change. You don't have to look far to see evidence of this phenomenon. Government agencies want to continue doing what they have been doing for years, whether the need for their service changes or remains the same. Organised religions are deeply entrenched in their history. Attempts to change church doctrine require great persistence and patience. Educational institutions, which exist to open minds and challenge established doctrine, are themselves extremely resistant to change. And the majority of business firms appear highly resistant to change.

Six main sources of organisational resistance have been identified.[4] They are shown in Figure 18.2.

FIGURE 18.2 Sources of organisational resistance to change

Structural inertia

Organisations have built-in mechanisms to produce stability. For example, the selection process systematically selects certain people in and certain people out. Training and other socialisation techniques reinforce specific role requirements and skills. Formalisation provides job descriptions, rules and procedures for employees to follow.

The people who are hired into an organisation are chosen for fit; they are then shaped and directed to behave in certain ways. When an organisation is confronted with change, this structural inertia acts as a counterbalance to sustain stability.

Limited focus of change

Organisations are made up of a number of interdependent subsystems. You can't change one without affecting the others. For example, if management changes the technological processes without simultaneously modifying the organisation's structure to match, the change in technology isn't likely to be accepted. So, limited changes in subsystems tend to get nullified by the larger system.

Group inertia

Even if individuals want to change their behaviour, group norms may act as a constraint. An individual union member, for example, may be willing to accept changes in his job suggested by management. But if union norms dictate resisting any unilateral change made by management, he is likely to resist.

Threat to expertise

Changes in organisational patterns may threaten the expertise of specialised groups. The introduction of decentralised personal computers, which allow managers to gain access to information directly from a company's mainframe, is an example of a change that was strongly resisted by many information systems departments in the early 1980s. Why? Because decentralised end-user computing was a threat to the specialised skills held by those in the centralised information systems departments.

Threat to established power relationships

Any redistribution of decision-making authority can threaten long-established power relationships within the organisation. The introduction of participative decision making or self-managed work teams is the kind of change that is often seen as threatening by supervisors and middle managers.

Threat to established resource allocations

Groups in the organisation that control sizeable resources often see change as a threat. They tend to be content with the way things are. Will the change, for example, mean a reduction in their budgets or a cut in their staff size? Those that most benefit from the current allocation of resources often feel threatened by changes that may affect future allocations.

OVERCOMING RESISTANCE TO CHANGE

Six tactics have been suggested for use by change agents in dealing with resistance to change.[5] Let's review them briefly.

Education and communication

Resistance can be reduced through communicating with employees to help them see the logic of a change. This tactic basically assumes that the source of resistance lies in misinformation or poor communication: if employees receive the full facts and get any misunderstandings cleared up, resistance will subside. Communication can be achieved through one-on-one discussions, memos, group presentations or reports. Does it work? It does, provided that the source of resistance is inadequate communication and that management–employee relations are characterised by mutual trust and credibility. If these conditions don't exist, the change is unlikely to succeed.

Participation

It is difficult for individuals to resist a change decision in which they participated. Prior to making a change, those opposed can be brought into the decision process. Assuming that the participants have the expertise to make a meaningful contribution, their involvement can reduce resistance, obtain commitment and increase the quality of the change decision. However, against these advantages are the negatives: potential for a poor solution and great time consumption.

Facilitation and support

Change agents can offer a range of supportive efforts to reduce resistance. When employees' fear and anxiety are high, employee counselling and therapy, new-skills training, or a short paid leave of absence may facilitate adjustment. The drawback of this tactic is that, as with the others, it is time-consuming. In addition, it is expensive, and its implementation offers no assurance of success.

Negotiation

Another way for the change agent to deal with potential resistance to change is to exchange something of value for a lessening of the resistance. For example, if the resistance is centred in a few powerful individuals, a specific reward package can be negotiated that will meet their individual needs. Negotiation as a tactic may be necessary when resistance comes from a powerful source. Yet, one cannot ignore its potentially high costs. In addition, there is the risk that, once a change agent negotiates with one party to avoid resistance, they are open to the possibility of being blackmailed by other individuals in positions of power.

Manipulation and cooptation

Manipulation refers to covert influence attempts. Twisting and distorting facts to make them appear more attractive, withholding undesirable information, and creating false rumours to get employees to accept a change are all examples of manipulation. If corporate management threatens to close down a particular factory if that factory's employees fail to accept an across-the-board pay cut, and if the threat is actually untrue, management is using manipulation. *Cooptation*, on the other hand, is a form of both manipulation and participation. It seeks to 'buy off' the leaders of a resistance group by giving them a key role in the change decision. The leaders' advice is sought, not to seek a better decision, but to get their endorsement. Both manipulation and cooptation are relatively inexpensive and easy ways to gain the support of adversaries, but the tactics can backfire if the targets become aware that they are being tricked or used. Once discovered, the change agent's credibility may drop to zero.

Coercion

Last on the list of tactics is coercion—that is, the application of direct threats or force on the resisters. If the corporate management mentioned in the previous discussion really is determined to close a factory if employees don't acquiesce to a pay cut, then coercion would be the label attached to its change tactic. Other examples of coercion are threats of transfer, loss of promotions, negative performance evaluations and a poor letter of recommendation. The advantages and drawbacks of coercion are approximately the same as those mentioned for manipulation and cooptation.

THE POLITICS OF CHANGE

No discussion of resistance to change would be complete without a brief mention of the politics of change. Because change invariably threatens the status quo, it inherently implies political activity.[6]

Internal change agents typically are individuals high in the organisation who have a lot to lose from change. They have, in fact, risen to their positions of authority by developing skills and behavioural patterns that are favoured by the organisation. Change is a threat to those skills and patterns. What if they are no longer the ones the organisation values? Change creates the potential for others in the organisation to gain power at their expense.

Politics suggests that the impetus for change is more likely to come from outside change agents, from employees who are new to the organisation (and have less invested in the status quo), or from managers slightly removed from the main power structure. Managers who have spent their entire careers with a single organisation and eventually achieve a senior position in the hierarchy are often major impediments to change. Change, itself, is a very real threat to their status and position. Yet, they may be expected to implement changes to demonstrate that they are not merely caretakers. By acting as change agents, they can symbolically convey to various constituencies—shareholders, suppliers, employees, customers—that they are on top of problems and adapting to a dynamic environment. Of course, as you might guess, when forced to introduce change, these long-time power holders tend to implement incremental changes. Radical change is too threatening.

Power struggles within the organisation will determine, to a large degree, the speed and quantity of change. You should expect that long-time career executives will be sources of resistance. This, incidentally, explains why boards of directors that recognise the imperative for the rapid introduction of radical change in their organisations frequently turn to outside candidates for new leadership.[7]

Approaches to Managing Organisational Change

Now we turn to several popular approaches to managing change: Lewin's classic three-step model of the change process, action research and organisational development.

LEWIN'S THREE-STEP MODEL

Kurt Lewin argued that successful change in organisations should follow three steps: **unfreezing** the status quo, *movement* to a new state, and **refreezing** the new change to make it permanent[8] (see Figure 18.3). The value of this model can be seen in the following example when the management of a large oil company decided to reorganise its marketing function in Australia.

The oil company had three regional offices located on the east coast of Australia—in Sydney, Brisbane and Melbourne—and an office in Perth and another in Adelaide, serving Australia's western and central regions, respectively. The decision was made to consolidate the divisions into a single office to be located in Sydney. The reorganisation meant transferring over 150 employees, eliminating some duplicate managerial positions and instituting a new hierarchy of command. As you might guess, a move of this magnitude was difficult to keep secret. The rumour of its occurrence preceded the announcement by several months. The decision itself was made unilaterally. It came from the executive offices in Singapore. Those people affected had no say whatsoever in the choice. For those in Brisbane or Melbourne, who may have disliked the decision and its consequences—the problems inherent in transferring to another city, pulling youngsters out of school, making new friends, having new co-workers, undergoing the reassignment of responsibilities—their only recourse was to quit. Less than 10 per cent did.

The status quo can be considered to be an equilibrium state. To move from this equilibrium—to overcome the pressures of both individual resistance and group conformity—unfreezing is necessary. It can be achieved in one of three ways (see Figure 18.4). The **driving forces**, which direct behaviour away from the status quo, can be increased. The **restraining forces**, which hinder movement from the existing equilibrium, can be decreased. A third alternative is to combine the first two approaches.

The oil company's management could expect employee resistance to the consolidation. To deal with that resistance, management could use positive incentives to encourage employees to accept the change. For example, increases in pay can be offered to those who accept the transfer. Very liberal moving expenses can be paid by the company. Management might offer low-cost mortgage funds to allow employees to buy new homes in Sydney. Of course, management might also consider unfreezing acceptance of the status quo by removing restraining forces. Employees

unfreezing
Change efforts to overcome the pressures of both individual resistance and group conformity.

refreezing
Stabilising a change intervention by balancing driving and restraining forces.

driving forces
Forces that direct behaviour away from the status quo.

restraining forces
Forces that hinder movement from the existing equilibrium.

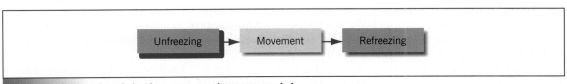

FIGURE 18.3   Lewin's three-step change model

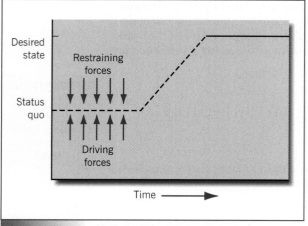

Desired state

Restraining forces

Status quo

Driving forces

Time ⟶

FIGURE 18.4   **Unfreezing the status quo**

could be counselled individually. Each employee's concerns and apprehensions could be heard and specifically clarified. Assuming that most of the fears are unjustified, the counsellor could assure the employees that there was nothing to fear and then demonstrate, through tangible evidence, that restraining forces are unwarranted. If resistance is extremely high, management may have to resort to both reducing resistance and increasing the attractiveness of the alternative if the unfreezing is to be successful.

Once the consolidation change has been implemented, if it is to be successful the new situation needs to be refrozen so that it can be sustained over time. Unless this last step is taken, there is a very high chance that the change will be short-lived and that employees will attempt to revert to the previous equilibrium state. The objective of refreezing, then, is to stabilise the new situation by balancing the driving and restraining forces.

How could the oil company's management refreeze its consolidation change? By systematically replacing temporary forces with permanent ones. For example, management might impose a permanent upward adjustment of salaries. The formal rules and regulations governing behaviour of those affected by the change should also be revised to reinforce the new situation. Over time, of course, the work group's own norms will evolve to sustain the new equilibrium. But until that point is reached, management will have to rely on more formal mechanisms.

ACTION RESEARCH

action research
A change process based on systematic collection of data and then selection of a change action based on what the analysed data indicate.

Action research refers to a change process based on the systematic collection of data and then selection of a change action based on what the analysed data indicate.[9] Their importance lies in providing a scientific methodology for managing planned change.

The process of action research consists of five steps: diagnosis, analysis, feedback, action and evaluation. (You will note that these steps closely parallel the scientific method.)

The change agent, often an outside consultant in action research, begins by gathering information about problems, concerns and needed changes from members of the organisation. This *diagnosis* is analogous to the doctor's search to find specifically what ails a patient. In action research, the change agent asks questions, interviews employees, reviews records, and listens to the concerns of employees.

Diagnosis is followed by *analysis*. What problems do people key in on? What patterns do these problems seem to take? The change agent synthesises this information into primary concerns, problem areas and possible actions.

Action research includes extensive involvement of the change targets. That is, the people who will be involved in any change program must be actively involved in determining what the problem is and participating in creating the solution. So, the third step—*feedback*—requires sharing with employees what has been found from steps one and two. The employees, with the help of the change agent, develop action plans for bringing about any needed change.

Now the *action* part of action research is set in motion. The employees and the change agent carry out the specific actions to correct the problems that have been identified.

The final step, consistent with the scientific underpinnings of action research, is *evaluation* of the action plan's effectiveness. Using the initial data gathered as a benchmark, any subsequent changes can be compared and evaluated.

Action research provides at least two specific benefits for an organisation. First, it is problem-focused. The change agent objectively looks for problems and the type of problem determines the type of change action. While this may seem intuitively obvious, a lot of change activities aren't

OB Controversies

Treating people with respect at Qantas

The world's major airlines are well aware of the need to manage change effectively. The airline industry is prone to all sorts of events that can have an effect on tourist and business travel arrangements. For example, in 2003, Qantas Airways Ltd announced it would slash international operations by about 20 per cent because of the global downturn caused by fears of terrorism, the war in Iraq and the worsening Severe Acute Respiratory Syndrome (SARS) outbreak. The SARS virus, which has claimed many lives and infected thousands of people worldwide, was seen to be a greater potential threat to the airline industry in the Asia-Pacific region than war. Consequently, Qantas announced that it would cut jobs. Other airlines to announce job cuts included Cathy Pacific and Singapore Airlines.

The 21st century has been a turbulent time for the airline industry in Australia. In February 2001, Qantas announced 1,200 job reductions to be managed through natural attrition. In September 2001, Australia witnessed the collapse of Ansett Airlines with the loss of over 13,500 jobs. In November 2001, Qantas announced the loss of 2,000 jobs. In February 2003, Qantas announced that the workforce would be temporarily reduced through the equivalent of 1,500 staff taking leave. This was followed by an announcement in April 2003, that Qantas would make 1,000 staff redundant, eliminate 400 positions through attrition and convert 300 jobs from full-time to part-time. This should be seen in the context of the global aviation industry shedding more than 400,000 jobs between the terrorist attacks in the United States on 11 September 2001 and the beginning of the war against Iraq in 2003.

The OB controversy concerns the quandary that airline managers find themselves in. Redundancies, they are told, are a necessary response to environmental changes, yet the same managers must deal with the mistrust and anxiety that redundancies cause. Qantas chief executive Geoff Dixon stated that redundancies were part of a continuing restructuring program in response to changes in the aviation marketplace and that the aim is to protect the jobs of the vast majority of the 35,000 Qantas employees as well as meeting the needs of the many Qantas shareholders. Unions representing air crews, baggage handlers, ground staff and maintenance workers consider industrial action and claim that they are being left in the dark.

Dixon said that in order to remain one of the more successful airlines in the world, Qantas management must ensure that the labour and capital expenditure base matches the current reality of market activity. How do airline managers treat staff as appreciated contributors to the success of their airline, rather than as a labour expenditure, in a time when every airline needs their staff to be fully committed?

Source: Based on 'Qantas Axes 1,400 Jobs as Impact of SARS Virus and Iraq War Bite', *Agence France Presse English*, 9 April 2003; and Geoff Easdown and Susie O'Brien, 'Job Axe Falls at Qantas SARS, War Blow to Travel', *Herald Sun* (Melbourne), 10 April 2003, pp. 003.

Like many of the world's international airlines, Qantas is continuously challenged with the task of reducing costs and improving the quality of service. The paradox of managing change at Qantas is treating staff as a cost and an asset.

done this way. Rather, they are solution-centred. The change agent has a favourite solution—for example, implementing flexitime, teams or a process reengineering program—and then seeks out problems that their solution fits. Second, because action research so heavily involves employees in the process, resistance to change is reduced. In fact, once employees have actively participated in the feedback stage, the change process typically takes on a momentum of its own. The employees and groups that have been involved become an internal source of sustained pressure to bring about the change.

LEARNING OBJECTIVE

4

Explain the values underlying most OD efforts

ORGANISATIONAL DEVELOPMENT

No discussion of managing change would be complete without including organisational development. **Organisational development (OD)** isn't an easily defined single concept. Rather, it is a term used to encompass a collection of planned-change interventions built on humanistic–democratic values that seek to improve organisational effectiveness and employee well-being.[10]

organisational development (OD)
A collection of planned-change interventions, built on humanistic–democratic values, that seeks to improve organisational effectiveness and employee well-being.

The OD paradigm values human and organisational growth, collaborative and participative processes, and a spirit of enquiry.[11] The change agent may be directive in OD; however, there is a strong emphasis on collaboration. Table 18.2 briefly identifies the underlying values in most OD efforts.

What are some of the OD techniques or interventions for bringing about change? In the following pages, we present six interventions that change agents might consider using.

Sensitivity training

sensitivity training
Training groups that seek to change behaviour through unstructured group interaction.

It can go by a variety of names—**sensitivity training**, laboratory training, encounter groups or T-groups (training groups)—but all refer to a method of changing behaviour through unstructured group interaction.[12] Members are brought together in a free and open environment in which participants discuss themselves and their interactive processes, loosely directed by a professional behavioural scientist. The group is process-oriented, which means that individuals learn through observing and participating, rather than by being told. The professional creates the opportunity for participants to express their ideas, beliefs and attitudes. He or she does not accept—in fact, overtly rejects—any leadership role.

The objectives of the T-groups are to provide the subjects with increased awareness of their own behaviour and how others perceive them, greater sensitivity to the behaviour of others, and increased understanding of group processes. Specific results sought include increased ability to empathise with others, improved listening skills, greater openness, increased tolerance of individual differences, and improved conflict-resolution skills.

If individuals lack awareness of how others perceive them, then the successful T-group can effect more realistic self-perceptions, greater group cohesiveness and a reduction in dysfunctional interpersonal conflicts. Furthermore, it will ideally result in a better integration between the individual and the organisation.

TABLE 18.2   Underlying values of OD

1. *Respect for people.* Individuals are perceived as being responsible, conscientious and caring. They should be treated with dignity and respect.
2. *Trust and support.* The effective and healthy organisation is characterised by trust, authenticity, openness and a supportive climate.
3. *Power equalisation.* Effective organisations de-emphasise hierarchical authority and control.
4. *Confrontation.* Problems shouldn't be swept under the rug. They should be openly confronted.
5. *Participation.* The more that people who will be affected by a change are involved in the decisions surrounding that change, the more they will be committed to implementing those decisions.

Survey feedback

One tool for assessing attitudes held by organisational members, identifying discrepancies among member perceptions and solving these differences is the **survey feedback** approach.[13]

Everyone in an organisation can participate in survey feedback, but of key importance is the organisational family—the manager of any given unit and the employees who report directly to them. A questionnaire is usually completed by all members in the organisation or unit. Organisation members may be asked to suggest questions or may be interviewed to determine what issues are relevant. The questionnaire typically asks members for their perceptions and attitudes on a broad range of topics, including decision-making practices; communication effectiveness; coordination between units; and satisfaction with the organisation, job, peers and their immediate supervisor.

The data from this questionnaire are tabulated with data pertaining to an individual's specific 'family' and to the entire organisation and distributed to employees. These data then become the springboard for identifying problems and clarifying issues that may be creating difficulties for people. Particular attention is given to the importance of encouraging discussion and ensuring that discussions focus on issues and ideas, and not on attacking individuals.

Finally, group discussion in the survey feedback approach should result in members identifying possible implications of the questionnaire's findings. Are people listening? Are new ideas being generated? Can decision making, interpersonal relations or job assignments be improved? Answers to questions like these, it is hoped, will result in the group agreeing on commitments to various actions that will remedy the problems that are identified.

survey feedback
The use of questionnaires to identify discrepancies among member perceptions; discussion follows and remedies are suggested.

Process consultation

No organisation operates perfectly. Managers often sense that their unit's performance can be improved, but they are unable to identify what can be improved and how it can be improved. The purpose of **process consultation** is for an outside consultant to assist a client, usually a manager, 'to perceive, understand, and act upon process events' with which they must deal.[14] These might include work flow, informal relationships among unit members and formal communication channels.

Process consultation (PC) is similar to sensitivity training in its assumption that organisational effectiveness can be improved by dealing with interpersonal problems and in its emphasis on involvement. But PC is more task-directed than is sensitivity training.

Consultants in PC are there to 'give the client "insight" into what is going on around him, within him, and between him and other people'.[15] They don't solve the organisation's problems. Rather, the consultant is a guide or coach who advises on the process to help the client solve their own problems.

The consultant works with the client in *jointly* diagnosing what processes need improvement. The emphasis is on 'jointly', because the client develops a skill at analysing processes within their unit that can be continually called on long after the consultant is gone. In addition, by having the client actively participate in both the diagnosis and the development of alternatives, there will be greater understanding of the process and the remedy and less resistance to the action plan chosen.

Importantly, the process consultant need not be an expert in solving the particular problem that is identified. The consultant's expertise lies in diagnosis and in developing a helping relationship. If the specific problem uncovered requires technical knowledge outside the client's and consultant's expertise, the consultant helps the client to locate such an expert and then instructs the client in how to get the most out of this expert resource.

process consultation
A consultant assists a client to understand process events with which they must deal and identify processes that need improvement.

Team building

As we have noted in numerous places throughout this book, organisations are increasingly relying on teams to accomplish work tasks. **Team building** uses high-interaction group activities to increase trust and openness among team members.[16]

team building
High interaction among team members to increase trust and openness.

Team building can be applied within groups or at the intergroup level, at which activities are interdependent. For our discussion, we emphasise the intragroup level and leave intergroup development to the next section. As a result, our interest concerns applications to organisational families (command groups), as well as to committees, project teams, self-managed teams and task groups.

Not all group activity has interdependence of functions. To illustrate, consider a football team and an athletics team. Although members on both teams are concerned with the team's total output, they function differently. The football team's output depends synergistically on how well each player does his particular job in concert with his teammates. On the other hand, an athletics team's performance is determined largely by the mere addition of the performances of the individual members.[17]

Team building is applicable to the case of interdependence, such as in football. The objective is to improve coordination efforts of members, which will result in increasing the team's performance.

The activities considered in team building typically include goal setting, development of interpersonal relations among team members, role analysis to clarify each member's role and responsibilities, and team process analysis. Of course, team building may emphasise or exclude certain activities, depending on the purpose of the development effort and the specific problems with which the team is confronted. Basically, however, team building attempts to use high interaction among members to increase trust and openness.

It may be beneficial to begin by having members attempt to define the goals and priorities of the team. This will bring to the surface different perceptions of what the team's purpose may be. Following this, members can evaluate the team's performance—how effective is the team in structuring priorities and achieving its goals? This should identify potential problem areas. This self-critique discussion of means and ends can be done with members of the total team present or, when large size impinges on a free interchange of views, may initially take place in smaller groups followed by the sharing of their findings with the total team.

Team building can also address itself to clarifying each member's role on the team. Each role can be identified and clarified. Previous ambiguities can be brought to the surface. For some individuals, it may offer one of the few opportunities they have had to think through thoroughly what their job is all about and what specific tasks they are expected to carry out if the team is to optimise its effectiveness.

Still another team-building activity can be similar to that performed by the process consultant—that is, to analyse key processes that go on within the team in order to identify the way work is performed and how these processes might be improved to make the team more effective.

Intergroup development

A major area of concern in OD is the dysfunctional conflict that exists between groups. As a result, this has been a subject to which change efforts have been directed.

intergroup development
OD efforts to change the attitudes, stereotypes and perceptions that groups have of each other.

Intergroup development seeks to change the attitudes, stereotypes and perceptions that groups have of each other. For example, in one company, the engineers saw the accounting department as composed of shy and conservative types, and the human resources department as having a bunch of 'softies who are more concerned that some protected group of employees might get their feelings hurt than with the company making a profit'. Such stereotypes can have an obvious negative impact on the coordination efforts between the departments.

Although there are several approaches for improving intergroup relations,[18] a popular method emphasises problem solving.[19] In this method, each group meets independently to develop lists of its perception of itself, the other group, and how it believes the other group perceives it. The groups then share their lists, after which similarities and differences are discussed. Differences are clearly articulated, and the groups look for the causes of the disparities.

Are the groups' goals at odds? Were perceptions distorted? On what basis were stereotypes formulated? Have some differences been caused by misunderstandings of intentions? Have words and concepts been defined differently by each group? Answers to questions like these clarify the exact nature of the conflict. Once the causes of the difficulty have been identified, the groups can move to the integration phase—working to develop solutions that will improve relations between the groups.

Subgroups, with members from each of the conflicting groups, can now be created for further diagnosis and to begin to formulate possible alternative actions that will improve relations.

Appreciative inquiry

Most OD approaches are problem-centred. They identify a problem or set of problems, then look for a solution. **Appreciative inquiry** accentuates the positive.[20] Rather than looking for problems to fix, this approach seeks to identify the unique qualities and special strengths of an organisation, which can then be built on to improve performance. That is, it focuses on an organisation's successes rather than on its problems.

Advocates of appreciative inquiry (AI) argue that problem-solving approaches always ask people to look backward at yesterday's failures, to focus on shortcomings, and rarely result in new visions. Instead of creating a climate for positive change, action research and OD techniques such as survey feedback and process consultation end up placing blame and generating defensiveness. AI proponents claim it makes more sense to refine and enhance what the organisation is already doing well. This allows the organisation to change by playing to its strengths and competitive advantages.

The AI process essentially consists of four steps, often played out in a large-group meeting over a two- or three-day time period, and overseen by a trained change agent. The first step is one of *discovery*. The idea is to find out what people think are the strengths of the organisation. For example, employees are asked to recount times they felt the organisation worked best or when they specifically felt most satisfied with their jobs. The second step is *dreaming*. The information from the discovery phase is used to speculate on possible futures for the organisation. For example, people are asked to envision the organisation in five years and to describe what is different. The third step is *design*. Based on the dream articulation, participants focus on finding a common vision of how the organisation will look and agree on its unique qualities. The fourth stage seeks to define the organisation's *destiny*. In this final step, participants discuss how the organisation is going to fulfil its dream. This typically includes the writing of action plans and development of implementation strategies.

AI has proven to be an effective change strategy in organisations such as the telecommunications company GTE, the international cosmetics company Avon operating in Mexico, and the Brazilian food wholesaler Nutrimental Foods. For example, executives at Nutrimental Foods closed their factories and offices for a day and invited all employees, plus a large group of customers and other constituents, to meet in a vacated warehouse. After an hour of instruction by an AI consultant, the 700 participants broke into teams and interviewed each other for half a day. This generated several hundred conclusions about what the company did well. At the end of the day their work was handed off to a group of 150, who were given four days to shape the information into a new and bolder corporate vision. The process ended up generating three new strategic business initiatives. And management reports that six months after this AI exercise, company sales had increased by several million dollars and profits were up by 300 per cent.[21]

AI has also been used as a fundamental part of the planning process for creating a new faculty in an Australian university.[22] The planning dean of the university had been exposed to AI on a recent 'Women in Leadership' program. She was charged with overseeing the amalgamation of several existing faculties into one. She saw the potential of the AI process for providing an inclusive and generative approach to developing the new organisational unit. She wanted a consultative process so as to provide voice and space for all participants, and she wanted a deliverable in the form of a new faculty blueprint based on the 'best of' what existed and to which everyone was committed.

appreciative inquiry
Seeks to identify the unique qualities and special strengths of an organisation, which can then be built on to improve performance.

Contemporary Change Issues for Today's Managers

Talk to managers. Read the popular business periodicals. What you will find is that three issues have risen above the rest as current change topics. They are: stimulating organisational *innovation*, building a *learning organisation* and creating *knowledge-management* systems. In the following pages, we take a look at these topics. Then we address the question: is managing change culture-bound?

LEARNING OBJECTIVE

5

Identify properties
of innovative
organisations

STIMULATING INNOVATION

The relevant question is: how can an organisation become more innovative? What is the secret of companies such as the global pharmaceutical company Pfizer, Corning, General Electric, DuPont and 3M that consistently generate new products with very low failure rates? Although there is no guaranteed formula, certain characteristics surface again and again when researchers study innovative organisations. We have grouped them into structural, cultural and human resource categories. Our message to change agents is that they should consider introducing these characteristics into their organisation if they want to create an innovative climate. Before we look at these characteristics, however, let's clarify what we mean by innovation.

Definition

innovation
A new idea applied to
initiating or improving a
product, process or
service.

We said that *change* refers to making things different. **Innovation** is a more specialised kind of change. Innovation is a new idea applied to initiating or improving a product, process or service.[23] So, all innovations involve change, but not all changes necessarily involve new ideas or lead to significant improvements. Innovations in organisations can range from small, incremental improvements, such as Arnott's extension of the line of Tim Tam biscuits to include dark chocolate, double-choc and caramel versions, up to radical breakthroughs, such as Jeff Bezos's idea in 1994 to create Amazon.com, an on-line bookstore. Keep in mind that while our examples are mostly of product innovations, the concept of innovation also encompasses new production process technologies, new structures or administrative systems, and new plans or programs pertaining to organisational members.

Sources of innovation

Structural variables have been the most studied potential source of innovation.[24] A comprehensive review of the structure–innovation relationship leads to the following conclusions.[25] First, organic structures positively influence innovation. Because they are lower in vertical differentiation, formalisation and centralisation, organic organisations facilitate the flexibility, adaptation and cross-fertilisation that make the adoption of innovations easier. Second, long tenure in management is associated with innovation. Managerial tenure apparently provides legitimacy and knowledge of how to accomplish tasks and obtain desired outcomes. Third, innovation is nurtured when there are slack resources. Having an abundance of resources allows an organisation to afford to purchase innovations, bear the cost of instituting innovations and absorb failures. Finally, inter-unit communication is high in innovative organisations.[26] These organisations are high users of committees, task forces, cross-functional teams, and other mechanisms that facilitate interaction across departmental lines.

Innovative organisations tend to have similar *cultures*. They encourage experimentation and embrace new technology. They reward both successes and failures. They celebrate mistakes. At Hewlett-Packard, the computer company, for example, top management has successfully built a corporate culture that supports people who try something that doesn't work out.[27] Unfortunately, in too many organisations, people are rewarded for the absence of failures, rather than for the presence of successes. Such cultures extinguish risk taking and innovation. People will suggest and try new ideas only when they feel such behaviours exact no penalties. Managers in innovative organisations recognise that failures are a natural by-product of venturing into the unknown.

Within the *human resources* category, we find that innovative organisations actively promote the training and development of their members so that they keep current, offer high job security so that employees don't fear getting fired for making mistakes, and encourage individuals to become champions of change. Once a new idea is developed, **idea champions** actively and enthusiastically promote the idea, build support, overcome resistance and ensure that the innovation is implemented.[28] The evidence indicates that champions have common personality characteristics: extremely high self-confidence, persistence, energy, and a tendency to take risks. Idea champions also display characteristics associated with transformational leadership. They inspire and energise others with their vision of the potential of an innovation and through their strong personal conviction in their mission. They are also good at gaining the commitment of others to support their mission. In addition, idea champions have jobs that provide considerable decision-making discretion. This autonomy helps them to introduce and implement innovations in organisations.[29]

idea champions
Individuals who take an innovation and actively and enthusiastically promote the idea, build support, overcome resistance and ensure that the idea is implemented.

CREATING A LEARNING ORGANISATION

The learning organisation has recently developed a groundswell of interest from managers and organisation theorists looking for new ways to successfully respond to a world of interdependence and change.[30] In this section, we describe what a learning organisation looks like and methods for managing learning.

LEARNING OBJECTIVE

6

List characteristics of a learning organisation

What is a learning organisation?

A **learning organisation** is an organisation that has developed the continuous capacity to adapt and change. Just as individuals learn, so too do organisations. 'All organizations learn, whether they consciously choose to or not—it is a fundamental requirement for their sustained existence.'[31] However, some organisations, such as Corning, Electronic Arts, General Electric, Singapore Police, BP Australia and the US Army, just do it better than others. For example, BP Australia sees itself as a leader in developing their graduate recruits for competitive advantage. The company sees their learning and development as two key elements of BP Australia's long-term strategy. As the company explains to potential recruits, 'It's not just about moving you upwards from one level to the next, it's about moving in directions that best suit you as well as the business. We create and support a long-term career relationship with you, where you can apply what you've learned, use your initiative and continue to develop.'[32]

learning organisation
An organisation that has developed the continuous capacity to adapt and change.

Most organisations engage in what has been called **single-loop learning**.[33] When errors are detected, the correction process relies on past routines and present policies. In contrast, learning organisations use **double-loop learning**. When an error is detected, it is corrected in ways that involve the modification of the organisation's objectives, policies and standard routines. Double-loop learning challenges deeply rooted assumptions and norms within an organisation. In this way, it provides opportunities for radically different solutions to problems and dramatic jumps in improvement.

single-loop learning
Errors are corrected using past routines and present policies.

double-loop learning
Errors are corrected by modifying the organisation's objectives, policies and standard routines.

Table 18.3 summarises the five basic characteristics of a learning organisation. It is an organisation in which people put aside their old ways of thinking, learn to be open with each other, understand how their organisation really works, form a plan or vision that everyone can agree on, and then work together to achieve that vision.[34]

Proponents of the learning organisation envision it as a remedy for three fundamental problems inherent in traditional organisations: fragmentation, competition and reactiveness.[35] First, *fragmentation* based on specialisation creates 'walls' and 'chimneys' that separate different functions into independent and often warring fiefdoms. Second, an overemphasis on *competition* often undermines collaboration. Members of the management team compete with one another

Amazon.com developed a reputation as an innovative company. It was one of the first retailers to fully exploit the opportunity of selling books online, hence reaching customers from all over the world.

to show who is right, who knows more or who is more persuasive. Divisions compete with one another when they ought to cooperate and share knowledge. Team project leaders compete to show who is the best manager. And third, *reactiveness* misdirects management's attention to problem solving, rather than creation. The problem solver tries to make something go away, while a creator tries to bring something new into being. An emphasis on reactiveness pushes out innovation and continuous improvement and, in its place, encourages people to run around 'putting out fires'.

It may help to better understand what a learning organisation is if you think of it as an *ideal* model that builds on a number of previous OB concepts. No company has successfully achieved all the characteristics described in Table 18.3. As such, you should think of a learning organisation as an ideal to strive towards, rather than a realistic description of structured activity. Note, too, how learning organisations draw on previous OB concepts such as quality management, organisational culture, the boundaryless organisation, functional conflict and transformational leadership. For example, the learning organisation adopts quality management's commitment to continuous improvement. Learning organisations are also characterised by a specific culture that values risk taking, openness and growth. It seeks 'boundarylessness' through breaking down barriers created by hierarchical levels and fragmented departmentation. A learning organisation supports the importance of disagreements, constructive criticism and other forms of functional conflict. And transformational leadership is needed in a learning organisation to implement the shared vision.

TABLE 18.3	**Characteristics of a learning organisation**
1.	There exists a shared vision which everyone agrees on.
2.	People discard their old ways of thinking and the standard routines they use for solving problems or doing their jobs.
3.	Members think of all organisational processes, activities, functions and interactions with the environment as part of a system of interrelationships.
4.	People openly communicate with each other (across vertical and horizontal boundaries) without fear of criticism or punishment.
5.	People sublimate their personal self-interest and fragmented departmental interests to work together to achieve the organisation's shared vision.

Source: Based on P. M. Senge, *The Fifth Discipline* (New York: Doubleday, 1990).

The Real Deal

Singapore Police strive to be a learning organisation

Recently Prime Minister Goh Chok Tong of Singapore stated that there was an imperative for being in time for tomorrow. He was referring to the need for governments and business to learn to deal with the ideas and technology of the information age. Singapore has been a case study in development, growth and prosperity in the Asia-Pacific region for the past 30 years. Its government has also been keen to embrace the concept of organisational learning and has encouraged public sector agencies to become learning organisations in order to meet the demands placed upon them in the 21st century.

However, it still may be surprising to some that the Singapore Police Force has been one of the first to embrace the concept with enthusiasm. Under the current commissioner of police, the Force has set about overcoming barriers to learning and developing the sort of capability promoted by the five disciplines framework established by Peter Senge. The disciplines of Personal Mastery, Mental Models, Shared Visions, Team Learning and Stems Thinking were intuitive to members of the Force.

Some of the obstacles to learning were embedded in the culture of the organisation. Most police services are based on an authoritarian and hierarchical command structure. They are structured in specialised areas that promote a parochial outlook within the different units. As the commissioner points out, respect comes from fear rather than admiration, and deference to authority can be a barrier to effective learning. Also, in the Asian culture, saving face can act against effective decision making.

An interesting aspect of the implementation of the learning organisation concepts was that the 'processes and interactions between the commissioner and his division commanders and staff directors were reinvented along the principles of the learning organization. However, for processes between these commanders or directors and their staff, the former would have the independence to decide if they wanted to adopt the new principles or how far they wanted to go. They were not measured, judged, or penalized for the approach and extent to which they were prepared to go.' The case of the Singapore Police Force highlights the importance of the will and support of senior management to embrace change and put faith in subordinates to achieve their true potential.

Sources: Based on Khoo Boon Hui and Tan Tay Keong, 'Learning and Innovation in Public Institutions: Lessons from Singapore', in M. Asher (ed.), *Public Policy in Asia: Implications for Business and Government* (Singapore: Quorum Books, 2002), pp. 175–92; and Peter Senge, *The Fifth Disciple: The Art and Practice of the Learning Organisation* (Sydney: Random House, 1994).

The Singapore Police Force has been one of the first police services in the world to embrace the concept of the learning organisation. The Police Commissioner is the driving force behind innovation and change among all ranks in the force.

Managing learning

How do you change an organisation to make it into a continual learner? What can managers do to make their firms learning organisations?

- *Establish a strategy.* Management needs to make explicit its commitment to change, innovation and continuous improvement.
- *Redesign the organisation's structure.* The formal structure can be a serious impediment to learning. By flattening the structure, eliminating or combining departments, and increasing the use of cross-functional teams, interdependence is reinforced and boundaries between people are reduced.
- *Reshape the organisation's culture.* As noted earlier, learning organisations are characterised by risk taking, openness and growth. Management sets the tone for the organisation's culture both by what it says (strategy) and what it does (behaviour). Managers need to demonstrate by their actions that taking risks and admitting failures are desirable traits. That means rewarding people who take chances and make mistakes. And management needs to encourage functional conflict. 'The key to unlocking real openness at work,' says one expert on learning organisations, 'is to teach people to give up having to be in agreement. We think agreement is so important. Who cares? You have to bring paradoxes, conflicts, and dilemmas out in the open, so collectively we can be more intelligent than we can be individually.'[36]

Some may be surprised at this selection, but an excellent illustration of a learning organisation is the US Army.[37] This organisation's environment has changed dramatically in the past several decades. Most significantly, the Soviet threat, which was a major justification for the army's military buildup, is largely gone. Now army soldiers are more likely to be peacekeeping in Africa or the Middle East, or helping to fight fires in the Pacific Northwest. In response to this new mission, the army's high command has redesigned its structure. Its formerly rigid, hierarchical, war-based command-and-control structure has been replaced with an adaptive and flexible structure to match its more varied objectives. In addition, everyone from PFCs to brigadier generals has gone through team training to make the army's culture more egalitarian. For example, soldiers are now encouraged to question authority and have been given new skills that allow them to make decisions in the field. The 'new army' is developing soldiers and officers who can adapt rapidly to different tasks and missions—fighting, peacekeeping, humanitarian rescue—and who can quickly improvise in complex and ambiguous situations. The current war on terrorism involving the United States, the United Kingdom, Australia and their allies has placed significant demands on these countries' defence forces, in that they require innovative means for dealing with conflicts that don't represent the scenarios of traditional warfare.

LEARNING OBJECTIVE

7

Define knowledge management and explain its importance

KNOWLEDGE MANAGEMENT

Siemens, the global telecommunications giant, recently won a US$460,000 contract in Switzerland to build a telecommunications network for two hospitals in spite of the fact that its bid was 30 per cent higher than the competition. The secret to Siemens' success was its knowledge-management system.[38] This system allowed Siemens' people in the Netherlands to draw on their experience and provide the Swiss sales reps with technical data that proved that the Siemens' network would be substantially more reliable than the competition's.

Siemens is one of a growing number of companies—including Unilever Malaysia, Boeing Australia, British Telecom, Sony Technologies Malaysia, IBM, Whirlpool, Intel, Volkswagen and KPMG Singapore—that have realised the value of knowledge management (KM).

knowledge management
A process of organising and distributing an organisation's collective wisdom so that the right information gets to the right people at the right time.

What is **knowledge management**? It is a process of organising and distributing an organisation's collective wisdom so that the right information gets to the right people at the right time.[39] When done properly, KM provides an organisation with both a competitive edge and improved organisational performance, because it makes its employees smarter.

Knowledge management is increasingly important today, for at least three reasons.[40] First, in many organisations, intellectual assets are now as important as physical or financial assets.

Organisations that can quickly and efficiently tap into their employees' collective experience and wisdom are more likely to 'outsmart' their competition. Second, as baby-boomers begin to leave the workforce, there is an increasing awareness that they represent a wealth of knowledge that will be lost if there are no attempts to capture it. And third, a well-designed KM system will reduce redundancy and make the organisation more efficient. For example, when employees in a large organisation undertake a new project, they needn't start from scratch. A knowledge-management system can allow them to access what previous employees have learned and reduce wasteful time spent retracing a path that has already been travelled.

How does an organisation record the knowledge and expertise of its employees and make that information easily accessible? It needs to develop computer databases of pertinent information that employees can readily access; it needs to create a culture that supports and rewards sharing; and it has to develop mechanisms that allow employees who have developed valuable expertise and insights to share them with others.

KM begins by identifying what knowledge matters to the organisation.[41] As with process reengineering, management needs to review processes to identify those that provide the most value. Then it can develop computer networks and databases that can make that information readily available to the people who most need it. But KM won't work unless the culture supports sharing of information.[42] Remember, information that is important and scarce can be a potent source of power. And people who hold that power are often reluctant to share it with others. So, KM requires an organisational culture that promotes, values and rewards sharing knowledge. Finally, KM must provide the mechanisms and the motivation for employees to share knowledge that employees find useful on the job and enables them to achieve better performance.[43] *More* knowledge isn't necessarily *better* knowledge. Information overload needs to be avoided by designing the system to capture only pertinent information and then organising it so that it can be quickly accessed by the people whom it can help.

When Lynn Odland, the former chief executive officer and now chairman of Deloitte Touche Tohmatsu in Australia, went about changing the culture of the firm, one of the primary aims for Peter May, the new human resources director, was to restore the company's confidence in the HR management functions. The HR director saw that one of his main roles was to determine what sort of people the company would need for the future, and then to set about sourcing agile consultants and business advisers. This was in keeping with changing the culture from that of a traditional auditing firm to that of a consulting firm. The HR director also saw an opportunity and a need to repair knowledge-management networks within the company. This involved a change of emphasis from a focus on technology to a focus on connecting people. Peter May recognises the importance of knowledge management in the consulting and professional services arena, and his real challenge is building the right human capabilities for the future and developing human capital for the business.[44]

MANAGING CHANGE: IT IS CULTURE-BOUND

A number of change issues we have discussed in this chapter are culture-bound. To illustrate, let's briefly look at five questions: (1) Do people believe that change is possible? (2) If change is possible, how long will it take to bring it about? (3) Is resistance to change greater in some cultures than in others? (4) Does culture influence how change efforts will be implemented? (5) Do successful idea champions do things differently in different cultures?

Do people believe that change is possible? Remember that cultures vary in terms of beliefs about their ability to control their environment. In cultures in which people believe that they can dominate their environment, individuals will take a proactive view of change. This, for example, would describe Australia and New Zealand. In many other countries, such as Iran, Pakistan and Thailand, people see themselves as subjugated to their environment and thus will tend to take a passive approach towards change.

If change is possible, how long will it take to bring it about? A culture's time orientation can help us to answer this question. Societies that focus on the long term, such as Japan, will demonstrate considerable patience while waiting for positive outcomes from change efforts. In societies with a short-term focus, such as Australia and New Zealand, people expect quick improvements and will seek change programs that promise fast results.

Is resistance to change greater in some cultures than in others? Resistance to change will be influenced by a society's reliance on tradition. Italians, for example, focus on the past, whereas Australians emphasise the present. Such a reliance on tradition could mean, therefore, that Italians should generally be more resistant to change efforts than their Australian counterparts.

Does culture influence how change efforts will be implemented? Power distance can help with this issue. In high-power-distance cultures, such as Hong Kong or Singapore, change efforts will tend to be autocratically implemented by top management. In contrast, low-power-distance cultures value democratic methods. We would predict, therefore, a greater use of participation in countries such as Australia and New Zealand.

Finally, do successful idea champions do things differently in different cultures? The evidence indicates that the answer is 'yes'.[45] People in collectivist cultures, in contrast to individualistic cultures, prefer appeals for cross-functional support for innovation efforts; people in high-power-distance cultures prefer champions to work closely with those in authority to approve innovative activities before work is conducted on them; and the higher the uncertainty avoidance of a society, the more champions should work within the organisation's rules and procedures to develop the innovation. These findings suggest that effective managers will alter their organisation's championing strategies to reflect cultural values. So, for example, while idea champions in Russia might succeed by ignoring budgetary limitations and working around confining procedures, champions in Austria, Denmark, Germany or other cultures high in uncertainty avoidance will be more effective by closely following budgets and procedures.

Work Stress and its Management

Most of us are aware that employee stress is an increasing problem in organisations. It is an important aspect of managing change. Friends may tell us that they are stressed out from greater workloads and from having to work longer hours because of downsizing at their company. Table 18.4 illustrates the results of a survey of employees in the United States and their responses to pressures at work.

Our parents talk about the lack of job stability in today's world and reminisce about a time when a job with a large company implied lifetime security. We read surveys in which employees complain about the stress created in trying to balance work and family responsibilities.[46] We also see the tension between employer groups and employee unions on the impact of stress in the workplace. The Australian Chamber of Commerce and Industry, Australia's main employer

TABLE 18.4	Too much work, too little time
With companies downsizing workers, those who remain find their jobs are demanding increasing amounts of time and energy. A national sample of US employees finds that they:	
Feel overworked	54%
Are overwhelmed by workload	55%
Lack time for reflection	59%
Don't have time to complete tasks	56%
Must multitask too much	45%

Source: Reprinted from *Business Week*, 16 July 2001, p. 12 by special permission. Copyright © 2001 by The McGraw Hill Companies, Inc.

Stress is a dynamic condition associated with constraints and demands. Over recent years more and more people have been complaining about the increased demands and complexity related to their work.

group, is calling for tighter controls on workplace stress claims, because they increase business costs. Stress-related levels of compensation have been rising. In the United Kingdom and the European Union, more than 41 million workers were reported to suffer from workplace stress. However, the Australian Council of Trade Unions (ACTU) is concerned about the causal links between stress and illness, indicating that Australians are working longer and harder than ever, and more than workers in most other countries, and hence are reporting more stress-related conditions.[47]

In this section, we will look at the causes and consequences of stress, and then consider what individuals and organisations can do to reduce it.

WHAT IS STRESS?

Stress is a dynamic condition in which an individual is confronted with an opportunity, constraint or demand related to what they desire and for which the outcome is perceived to be both uncertain and important.[48] This is a complicated definition. Let's look at its components more closely.

Stress isn't necessarily bad in and of itself. Although stress is typically discussed in a negative context, it also has a positive value.[49] It is an opportunity when it offers potential gain. Consider, for example, the superior performance that an athlete or stage performer gives in 'clutch' situations. Such individuals often use stress positively to rise to the occasion and perform at or near their maximum. Similarly, many professionals see the pressures of heavy workloads and deadlines as positive challenges that enhance the quality of their work and the satisfaction they get from their job.

More typically, stress is associated with **constraints** and **demands**. The former prevent you from doing what you desire. The latter refers to the loss of something desired. So, when you take a test at university or undergo your annual performance review at work, you feel stress because you confront opportunities, constraints and demands. A good performance review may lead to a promotion, greater responsibilities and a higher salary. But a poor review may prevent you from getting the promotion. An extremely poor review might even result in your being fired.

Two conditions are necessary for potential stress to become actual stress.[50] There must be uncertainty over the outcome, and the outcome must be important. Regardless of the conditions, it is only when there is doubt or uncertainty regarding whether the opportunity will be seized, the constraint removed, or the loss avoided that there is stress. That is, stress is highest for individuals who perceive that they are uncertain as to whether they will win or lose, and lowest for individuals who think that winning or losing is a certainty. But importance is also critical. If winning or losing is an unimportant outcome, there is no stress. If keeping your job or earning a promotion doesn't hold any importance to you, you have no reason to feel stress over having to undergo a performance review.

stress
A dynamic condition in which an individual is confronted with an opportunity, constraint or demand related to what they desire and for which the outcome is perceived to be both uncertain and important.

constraints
Forces that prevent individuals from doing what they desire.

demands
The loss of something desired.

UNDERSTANDING STRESS AND ITS CONSEQUENCES

What causes stress? What are its consequences for individual employees? Why is it that the same set of conditions that creates stress for one person seems to have little or no effect on another person? Figure 18.5 provides a model that can help to answer questions such as these.[51]

The model identifies three sets of factors—environmental, organisational and individual—that act as *potential* sources of stress. Whether they become *actual* stress depends on individual differences, such as job experience and personality. When stress is experienced by an individual, its symptoms can surface as physiological, psychological and behavioural outcomes.

POTENTIAL SOURCES OF STRESS

LEARNING OBJECTIVE

8

Describe potential
sources of stress

As the model in Figure 18.5 shows, there are three categories of potential stressors: environmental, organisational and individual. Let's take a look at each.[52]

Environmental factors

Just as environmental uncertainty influences the design of an organisation's structure, it also influences stress levels among employees in that organisation. Changes in the business cycle create *economic uncertainties*. When the economy is contracting, for example, people become increasingly anxious about their job security. *Political uncertainties* don't tend to create stress among Australians or New Zealanders as they do for employees in countries such as Colombia and Fiji. The obvious reason is that Australia and New Zealand have stable political systems, in which change is typically implemented in an orderly manner. Yet, political threats and changes, even in countries seen to be politically stable, can induce stress. For example, the recent dramatic rise and fall of the political party One Nation in Australia increased stress among many Australian communities because of the policies that the party's politicians espoused. Some of the policies were perceived by local and overseas communities as racist and generated divisive debates over immigration and the treatment of refugees.

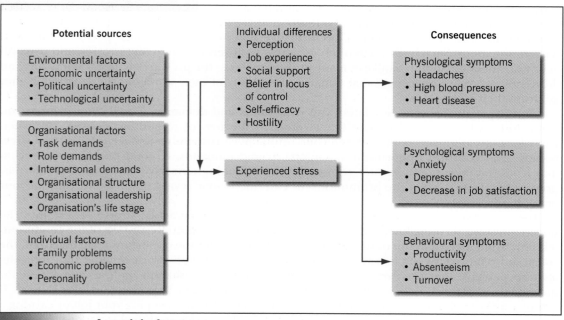

FIGURE 18.5   A model of stress

Technological uncertainty is a third type of environmental factor that can cause stress. Because new innovations can make an employee's skills and experience obsolete in a very short time, computers, robotics, automation and similar forms of technological innovation are a threat to many people and cause them stress. *Terrorism* is an increasing source of environmental-induced stress in the 21st century. Employees in the Middle East, for example, have long faced this threat and have learned to cope with it. For Americans, on the other hand, 11 September 2001 opened the door to new terrorism-related stresses—such as working in skyscrapers, flying, attending large public events, and concern about security.

Organisational factors

There is no shortage of factors within the organisation that can cause stress. Pressures to avoid errors or to complete tasks in a limited time, work overload, a demanding and insensitive boss, and unpleasant co-workers are a few examples. We have categorised these factors around task, role and interpersonal demands; organisational structure; organisational leadership; and the organisation's life stage.[53]

Task demands are factors related to a person's job. They include the design of the individual's job (autonomy, task variety, degree of automation), working conditions and the physical work layout. Assembly lines, for example, can put pressure on people when the line's speed is perceived as excessive. Similarly, working in an overcrowded room or in a visible location where interruptions are constant can increase anxiety and stress. Some jobs are also subject to workplace violence. For example, employees in health-care organisations may be confronted with aggressive patients, and hospitality staff in hotels and restaurants may be confronted with drunken, potentially violent customers as part of the job tasks they perform.

Role demands relate to pressures placed on a person as a function of the particular role they play in the organisation. Role conflicts create expectations that may be hard to reconcile or satisfy—for example, when the responsibilities of a particular job outweigh the knowledge and skills of the incumbent. Role overload is experienced when the employee is expected to do more than time permits. Role ambiguity is created when role expectations aren't clearly understood and the employee isn't sure what he or she is to do.

Interpersonal demands are pressures created by other employees. Lack of social support from colleagues and poor interpersonal relationships can cause considerable stress, especially among employees with a high social need. Workplace bullying has been getting a lot of attention recently because of the unacceptable pressures some people are putting on their colleagues through intimidating tactics.

Organisational structure defines the level of differentiation in the organisation, the degree of rules and regulations, and where decisions are made. Excessive rules and lack of participation in decisions that affect an employee are examples of structural variables that might be potential sources of stress.

Organisational leadership represents the managerial style of the organisation's senior executives. Some chief executive officers create a culture characterised by tension, fear and anxiety. They establish unrealistic pressures to perform in the short run, impose excessively tight controls and routinely fire employees who don't 'measure up'.

Organisations go through a cycle. They are established, grow, become mature and eventually decline. An *organisation's life stage*—that is, where it is in this four-stage cycle—creates different problems and pressures for employees. The establishment and decline stages are particularly stressful. The former is characterised by a great deal of excitement and uncertainty, while the latter typically requires cutbacks, layoffs and a different set of uncertainties. Stress tends to be least in the maturity stage, during which uncertainties are at their lowest ebb.

Individual factors

The typical individual works about 40 to 50 hours a week. But the experiences and problems that people encounter in those other 120-plus non-work hours each week can spill over to the job. Our

LEARNING OBJECTIVE

9

Explain individual difference variables that moderate the stress–outcome relationship final category, then, encompasses factors in the employee's personal life. Primarily, these factors are family issues, personal economic problems and inherent personality characteristics.

National surveys consistently show that people hold *family* and personal relationships dear. Marital difficulties, the breaking off of a relationship, and discipline troubles with children are examples of relationship problems that create stress for employees that aren't left at the front door when they arrive at work.

Economic problems created by individuals overextending their financial resources is another set of personal troubles that can create stress for employees and distract their attention from their work. Regardless of income level—people who make $100,000 a year seem to have as much trouble handling their finances as those who earn $30,000—some people are poor money managers or have wants that always seem to exceed their earning capacity.

Studies in three diverse organisations found that stress symptoms reported prior to beginning a job accounted for most of the variance in stress symptoms reported nine months later.[54] This led the researchers to conclude that some people may have an inherent tendency to accentuate negative aspects of the world in general. If this is true, then a significant individual factor that influences stress is a person's basic disposition. That is, stress symptoms expressed on the job may actually originate in the person's personality.

Stressors are additive

A fact that tends to be overlooked when stressors are reviewed individually is that stress is an additive phenomenon.[55] Stress builds up. Each new and persistent stressor adds to an individual's stress level. So, a single stressor may be relatively unimportant in and of itself, but if it is added to an already high level of stress, it can be 'the straw that breaks the camel's back'. If we want to appraise the total amount of stress an individual is under, we have to sum up their opportunity stresses, constraint stresses and demand stresses.

INDIVIDUAL DIFFERENCES

Some people thrive on stressful situations, while others are overwhelmed by them. What is it that differentiates people in terms of their ability to handle stress? What individual difference variables moderate the relationship between *potential* stressors and *experienced* stress? At least six variables—perception, job experience, social support, belief in locus of control, self-efficacy and hostility—have been found to be relevant moderators.

Previously, we demonstrated that employees react in response to their perception of reality, rather than to reality itself. *Perception*, therefore, will moderate the relationship between a potential stress condition and an employee's reaction to it. For example, one person's fear that he will lose his job because his company is laying off personnel may be perceived by another as an opportunity to get a large severance allowance and start his own business. So, stress potential doesn't lie in objective conditions; it lies in an employee's interpretation of those conditions.

The evidence indicates that *experience* on the job tends to be negatively related to work stress. Why? Two explanations have been offered.[56] First is the idea of selective withdrawal. Voluntary turnover is more probable among people who experience more stress. Therefore, people who remain with the organisation longer are those with more stress-resistant traits or those who are more resistant to the stress characteristics of their organisation. Second, people eventually develop coping mechanisms to deal with stress. Because this takes time, senior members of the organisation are more likely to be fully adapted and should experience less stress.

There is increasing evidence that *social support*—that is, collegial relationships with co-workers or supervisors—can buffer the impact of stress.[57] The logic underlying this moderating variable is that social support acts as a palliative, mitigating the negative effects of even high-strain jobs.

Locus of control was introduced in a previous chapter as a personality attribute. Those with an internal locus of control believe that they control their own destiny. Those with an external locus believe that their lives are controlled by outside forces. Evidence indicates that internals perceive their jobs to be less stressful than do externals.[58] When internals and externals confront a similar stressful situation, the internals are likely to believe that they can have a significant effect on the results. They, therefore, act to take control of events. In contrast, externals are more likely to be passive and to feel helpless.

Self-efficacy has also been found to influence stress outcomes. You will remember from an earlier chapter that this term refers to an individual's belief that they are capable of performing a task. Recent evidence indicates that individuals with strong self-efficacy reacted less negatively to the strain created by long work hours and work overload than did those with low levels of self-efficacy.[59] That is, confidence in one's own abilities appears to decrease stress. As with an internal locus of control, strong efficacy confirms the power of self-beliefs in moderating the effect of a high-strain situation.

Some people's personality includes a high degree of hostility and anger. These people are chronically suspicious and mistrustful of others. Evidence indicates that this *hostility* significantly increases a person's stress and risk for heart disease.[60] More specifically, people who are quick to anger, maintain a persistently hostile outlook, and project a cynical mistrust of others are more likely to experience stress in situations.

CONSEQUENCES OF STRESS

Stress shows itself in a number of ways. For example, an individual who is experiencing a high level of stress may develop high blood pressure, ulcers, irritability, difficulty in making routine decisions, loss of appetite, accident-proneness, and the like. These symptoms can be subsumed under three general categories: physiological, psychological and behavioural symptoms.[61]

Physiological symptoms

Most of the early concern with stress was directed at physiological symptoms. This was predominantly due to the fact that the topic was researched by specialists in the health and medical sciences. This research led to the conclusion that stress could create changes in metabolism, increase heart and breathing rates, increase blood pressure, bring on headaches and induce heart attacks.

The link between stress and particular physiological symptoms isn't clear. There are few, if any, consistent relationships.[62] This is attributed to the complexity of the symptoms and the difficulty of objectively measuring them. But of greater relevance is the fact that physiological symptoms have the least direct relevance to students of OB. Our concern is with attitudes and behaviours. Therefore, the two other categories of symptoms are more important to us.

Psychological symptoms

Stress can cause dissatisfaction. Job-related stress can cause job-related dissatisfaction. Job dissatisfaction, in fact, is 'the simplest and most obvious psychological effect' of stress.[63] But stress shows itself in other psychological states—for example, tension, anxiety, irritability, boredom and procrastination.

The evidence indicates that when people are placed in jobs that make multiple and conflicting demands, or in which there is a lack of clarity about the incumbent's duties, authority and responsibilities, both stress and dissatisfaction are increased.[64] Similarly, the less control people have over the pace of their work, the greater the stress and dissatisfaction. While more research is needed to clarify the relationship, the evidence suggests that jobs that provide a low level of variety, significance, autonomy, feedback and identity to incumbents create stress and reduce satisfaction and involvement in the job.[65]

Behavioural symptoms

Behaviour-related stress symptoms include changes in productivity, absence and turnover, as well as changes in eating habits, increased smoking or consumption of alcohol, rapid speech, fidgeting and sleep disorders. In dollar terms, we cannot underestimate the cost of job stress. For example, recent estimates indicate that workplace stress costs US employers US$200 billion annually in absenteeism, reduced productivity, employee turnover, accidents, workers' compensation, and direct medical, legal and insurance fees.[66] While not as high as the American estimates, work-related illnesses in Australia cost $15 billion a year in compensation claims, reduced productivity, absenteeism, added health insurance premiums and direct medical expenses.[67] Stress has also been identified as the fastest-growing reason for unscheduled work absences.[68]

There has been a significant amount of research investigating the stress–performance relationship. The most widely studied pattern in the stress–performance literature is the inverted-U relationship.[69] This is shown in Figure 18.6.

The logic underlying the inverted U is that low to moderate levels of stress stimulate the body and increase its ability to react. Individuals then often perform their tasks better, more intensely or more rapidly. But too much stress places unattainable demands or constraints on a person, which result in lower performance. This inverted-U pattern may also describe the reaction to stress over time, as well as to changes in stress intensity. That is, even moderate levels of stress can have a negative influence on performance over the long term, as the continued intensity of the stress wears down the individual and saps their energy resources. An athlete may be able to use the positive effects of stress to obtain a higher performance during every Saturday's game in the autumn season, or a sales executive may be able to psych herself up for her presentation at the annual national meeting. But moderate levels of stress experienced continually over long periods, as typified by the emergency room staff in a large urban hospital, can result in lower performance. This may explain why emergency room staffs at such hospitals are frequently rotated and why it is unusual to find individuals who have spent the bulk of their career in such an environment. In effect, to do so would expose the individual to the risk of 'career burnout'.

In spite of the popularity and intuitive appeal of the inverted-U model, it doesn't get a lot of empirical support.[70] At this time, managers should be careful in assuming that this model accurately depicts the stress–performance relationship.

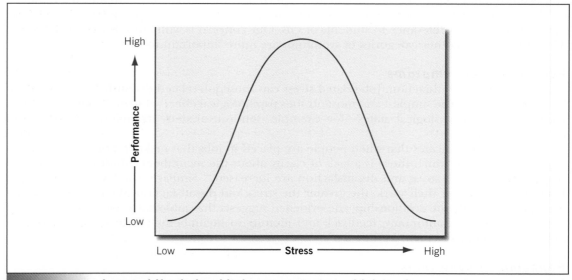

FIGURE 18.6   **Inverted-U relationship between stress and job performance**

MANAGING STRESS

From the organisation's standpoint, management may not be concerned when employees experience low to moderate levels of stress. The reason, as we showed earlier, is that such levels of stress may be functional and lead to higher employee performance. But high levels of stress, or even low levels sustained over long periods, can lead to reduced employee performance and, thus, require action by management.

While a limited amount of stress may benefit an employee's performance, don't expect employees to see it that way. From the individual's standpoint, even low levels of stress are likely to be perceived as undesirable. It is not unlikely, therefore, for employees and management to have different notions of what constitutes an acceptable level of stress on the job. What management may consider to be 'a positive stimulus that keeps the adrenalin running' is very likely to be seen as 'excessive pressure' by the employee. Keep this in mind as we discuss individual and organisational approaches towards managing stress.[71]

Individual approaches

An employee can take personal responsibility for reducing their stress level. Individual strategies that have proven effective include implementing time-management techniques, increasing physical exercise, relaxation training, and expanding the social support network.

Many people manage their time poorly. The things they have to accomplish in any given day or week aren't necessarily beyond completion if they manage their time properly. The well-organised employee, like the well-organised student, can often accomplish twice as much as the person who is poorly organised. So, an understanding and utilisation of basic *time-management* principles can help individuals to better cope with tensions created by job demands.[72] A few of the more well-known time-management principles are: (1) making daily lists of activities to be accomplished; (2) prioritising activities by importance and urgency; (3) scheduling activities according to the priorities set; and (4) knowing your daily cycle, and handling the most demanding parts of your job during the high part of your cycle when you are most alert and productive.[73]

Non-competitive physical exercise such as aerobics, walking, jogging, swimming and riding a bicycle have long been recommended by doctors as a way to deal with excessive stress levels. These forms of *physical exercise* increase heart capacity, lower the at-rest heart rate, provide a mental diversion from work pressures, and offer a means to 'let off steam'.[74]

Individuals can teach themselves to reduce tension through *relaxation techniques* such as meditation, hypnosis and biofeedback. The objective is to reach a state of deep relaxation, in which one feels physically relaxed, somewhat detached from the immediate environment and detached from body sensations.[75] Deep relaxation for 15 or 20 minutes a day releases tension and provides a person with a pronounced sense of peacefulness. Importantly, significant changes in heart rate, blood pressure and other physiological factors result from achieving the condition of deep relaxation.

As we noted earlier in this chapter, having friends, family or work colleagues to talk to provides an outlet when stress levels become excessive. Expanding your *social support network*, therefore, can be a means for tension reduction. It provides you with someone to listen to your problems and to offer a more objective perspective on the situation.

Organisational approaches

Several of the factors that cause stress—particularly task and role demands, and organisational structure—are controlled by management. As such, they can be modified or changed. Strategies that management might want to consider include improved personnel selection and job placement, training, use of realistic goal setting, redesigning of jobs, increased employee involvement, improved organisational communication, offering employee sabbaticals, and establishment of corporate wellness programs.

Certain jobs are more stressful than others, but, as we learned earlier in this chapter, individuals differ in their response to stress situations. We know, for example, that individuals with little experience or an external locus of control tend to be more prone to stress. *Selection and placement* decisions should take these facts into consideration. Obviously, management shouldn't restrict hiring to only experienced individuals with an internal locus, but such individuals may adapt better to high-stress jobs and perform those jobs more effectively. Similarly, *training* can increase an individual's self-efficacy and thus lessen job strain.

We discussed *goal setting* in a previous chapter. Based on an extensive amount of research, we concluded that individuals perform better when they have specific and challenging goals and receive feedback on how well they are progressing towards these goals. The use of goals can reduce stress as well as provide motivation. Specific goals that are perceived as attainable clarify performance expectations. In addition, goal feedback reduces uncertainties about actual job performance. The result is less employee frustration, role ambiguity and stress.

Redesigning jobs to give employees more responsibility, more meaningful work, more autonomy and increased feedback can reduce stress, because these factors give the employee greater control over work activities and lessen dependence on others. But as we noted in our discussion of work design, not all employees want enriched jobs. The right redesign, then, for employees with a low need for growth might be less responsibility and increased specialisation. If individuals prefer structure and routine, reducing skill variety should also reduce uncertainties and stress levels. An extension of job redesign, which has received considerable recent attention, is allowing workers to take short naps during the work day.[76] Nap time, apparently, isn't just for pre-school kids, anymore! An increasing number of companies are finding that allowing employees to catch 10 to 30 minutes of sleep in the afternoon increases productivity and makes them less prone to making errors.

Role stress is detrimental to a large extent, because employees feel uncertain about goals, expectations, how they will be evaluated, and the like. By giving these employees a voice in the decisions that directly affect their job performances, management can increase employee control and reduce this role stress. So, managers should consider *increasing employee involvement* in decision making.[77]

Increasing formal *organisational communication* with employees reduces uncertainty by lessening role ambiguity and role conflict. Given the importance that perceptions play in moderating the stress–response relationship, management can also use effective communications as a means to shape employee perceptions. Remember that what employees categorise as demands, threats or opportunities are merely an interpretation, and that interpretation can be affected by the symbols and actions communicated by management.

What some employees need is an occasional escape from the frenetic pace of their work. In recent years, companies such as financial consultants Charles Schwab, the global chemical, materials and energy company Du Pont, and the footwear company Nike have begun to provide extended voluntary leaves.[78] These *sabbaticals*—ranging in length from a few weeks to several months—allow employees to travel, relax, or pursue personal projects that consume time beyond normal holiday allowances. Proponents argue that these sabbaticals can revive and rejuvenate workers who might be headed for burnout.

wellness programs
Organisationally supported programs that focus on the employee's total physical and mental condition.

Our final suggestion is to offer organisationally supported **wellness programs**. These programs focus on the employee's total physical and mental condition.[79] For example, they typically provide workshops to help people quit smoking, control alcohol use, lose weight, eat better and develop a regular exercise program. The assumption underlying most wellness programs is that employees need to take personal responsibility for their physical and mental health. The organisation is merely a vehicle to facilitate this end.

Organisations, of course, aren't altruistic. They expect a payoff from their investment in wellness programs. And most of those firms that have introduced wellness programs have found significant benefits. For example, in the United States, Johnson & Johnson calculated the following annual savings in insurance premiums when an employee exchanges bad habits for healthy ones: quitting smoking (US$1,110); starting to exercise (US$260); lowering cholesterol from 240 to 190 milligrams (US$1,200); and slimming down from obese to normal weight (US$177).[80] Xerox reports that savings in medical expenses are five times the cost of its wellness programs.[81]

Summary and Implications for Managers

The need for change has been implied throughout this text. 'A casual reflection on change should indicate that it encompasses almost all of our concepts in the organizational behavior literature. Think about leadership, motivation, organizational environments, and roles. It is impossible to think about these and other concepts without inquiring about change.'[82]

If environments were perfectly static, if employees' skills and abilities were always up to date and incapable of deteriorating, and if tomorrow were always exactly the same as today, organisational change would have little or no relevance to managers. But the real world is turbulent, requiring organisations and their members to undergo dynamic change if they are to perform at competitive levels.

Managers are the primary change agents in most organisations. By the decisions they make and their role-modelling behaviours, they shape the organisation's change culture. For example, management decisions related to structural design, cultural factors and human resource policies largely determine the level of innovation within the organisation. Similarly, management decisions, policies and practices will determine the degree to which the organisation learns and adapts to changing environmental factors.

We found that the existence of work stress, in and of itself, need not imply lower performance. The evidence indicates that stress can be either a positive or a negative influence on employee performance. For many people, low to moderate amounts of stress enable them to perform their jobs better, by increasing their work intensity, alertness and ability to react. However, a high level of stress, or even a moderate amount sustained over a long period, eventually takes its toll, and performance declines. The impact of stress on satisfaction is far more straightforward. Job-related tension tends to decrease general job satisfaction.[83] Even though low to moderate levels of stress may improve job performance, employees find stress dissatisfying.

Point

MANAGING CHANGE IS AN EPISODIC ACTIVITY

Organisational change is an episodic activity. That is, it starts at some point, proceeds through a series of steps, and culminates in some outcome that those involved hope is an improvement over the starting point. It has a beginning, a middle and an end.

Lewin's three-step model represents a classic illustration of this perspective. Change is seen as a break in the organisation's equilibrium. The status quo has been disturbed, and change is necessary to establish a new equilibrium state. The objective of refreezing is to stabilise the new situation by balancing the driving and restraining forces.

Some experts have argued that organisational change should be thought of as balancing a system made up of five interacting variables within the organisation—people, tasks, technology, structure and strategy. A change in any one variable has repercussions on one or more of the others. This perspective is episodic in that it treats organisational change as essentially an effort to sustain an equilibrium. A change in one variable begins a chain of events that, if properly managed, requires adjustments in the other variables to achieve a new state of equilibrium.

Another way to conceptualise the episodic view of looking at change is to think of managing change as analogous to captaining a ship. The organisation is like a large ship travelling up the Strait of Malacca to a specific port. The ship's captain has made this exact trip hundreds of times before with the same crew. Every once in a while, however, a storm will appear, and the crew has to respond. The captain will make the appropriate adjustments—that is, implement changes—and, having manoeuvred through the storm, will return to calm waters. Like this ship's voyage, managing an organisation should be seen as a journey with a beginning and an end, and implementing change as a response to a break in the status quo and needed only occasionally.

Counterpoint

The episodic approach may be the dominant paradigm for handling organisational change, but it has become obsolete. It applies to a world of certainty and predictability. The episodic approach was developed in the 1950s and 1960s, and it reflects the environment of those times. It treats change as the occasional disturbance in an otherwise peaceful world. However, this paradigm has little resemblance to today's environment of constant and chaotic change.[a]

If you want to understand what it is like to manage change in today's organisations, think of it as equivalent to permanent white-water rafting.[b] The organisation isn't a large ship, but more akin to a 15-metre raft. Rather than sailing a calm sea, this raft must traverse a raging river made up of an uninterrupted flow of permanent white-water rapids. To make things worse, the raft is manned by ten people who have never worked together or travelled the river before, much of the trip is in the dark, the river is dotted by unexpected turns and obstacles, the exact destination of the raft isn't clear, and at irregular intervals the raft needs to pull to shore, where some new crew members are added and others leave. Change is a natural state, and managing change is a continual process. That is, managers never get the luxury of escaping the white-water rapids.

The stability and predictability characterised by the episodic perspective no longer captures the world we live in. Disruptions in the status quo aren't occasional, temporary, and followed by a return to an equilibrium state. There is, in fact, no equilibrium state. Managers today face constant change, bordering on chaos. They are being forced to play a game they have never played before, governed by rules that are created as the game progresses.

Sources: [a] For contrasting views on episodic and continuous change, see K. E. Weick and R. E. Quinn, 'Organizational Change and Development', in J. T. Spence, J. M. Darley and D. J. Foss (eds), *Annual Review of Psychology*, vol. 50 (Palo Alto, CA: Annual Reviews, 1999), pp. 361–86.

[b] This perspective is based on P. B. Vaill, *Managing as a Performing Art: New Ideas for a World of Chaotic* Change (San Francisco: Jossey-Bass, 1989).

For Discussion

1. What is meant by the phrase 'we live in an age of discontinuity'?
2. 'Resistance to change is an irrational response.' Do you agree or disagree? Explain.
3. Why is participation considered such an effective technique for lessening resistance to change?
4. Why does change so frequently become a political issue in organisations?
5. How does Lewin's three-step model of change deal with resistance to change?
6. In an organisation that has a history of 'following the leader', what changes can be made to foster innovation?
7. 'Learning organisations attack fragmentation, competitiveness and reactiveness.' Explain this statement.
8. What characteristics distinguish organisational development?
9. How does an organisation build a knowledge-management system?
10. How are opportunities, constraints and demands related to stress? Give an example of each.
11. What can organisations do to reduce employee stress?

Exercise

POWER AND THE CHANGING ENVIRONMENT

Objectives:
1. To describe the forces for change influencing power differentials in organisational and interpersonal relationships.
2. To understand the effect of technological, legal/political, economic and social changes on the power of individuals within an organisation.

The situation:
Your organisation manufactures golf carts and sells them to country clubs, golf courses and consumers. Your team is faced with the task of assessing how environmental changes will affect individuals' organisational power. Read each of the five scenarios and then, for each, identify the five members in the organisation whose power will increase most in light of the environmental condition(s).

(m) = male   (f) = female

Advertising expert (m)	Accountant-CPA (m)	Product designer (m)
Chief financial officer (f)	General manager (m)	In-house lawyer (m)
Securities analyst (m)	Marketing manager (f)	Public relations expert (m)
Operations manager (f)	Computer programmer (f)	Human resource manager (f)
Corporate trainer (m)	Industrial engineer (m)	Chemist (m)

1. New computer-aided manufacturing technologies are being introduced in the workplace during the upcoming two to 18 months.
2. New emission standards are being legislated by the government.
3. Sales are way down; the industry appears to be shrinking.
4. The company is planning to go international in the next 12 to 18 months.
5. The Equal Employment Opportunity Commission is applying pressure to balance the male–female population in the organisation's upper hierarchy by threatening to publicise the predominance of men in upper management.

The procedure:
1. Divide the class into teams of three to four students each.
2. Teams should read each scenario and identify the five members whose power will increase most in light of the external environmental condition described.
3. Teams should then address the question: Assuming that the five environmental changes are taking place at once, which five members of the organisation will now have the most power?
4. After 20 to 30 minutes, representatives of each team will be selected to present and justify their conclusions to the entire class. Discussion will begin with scenario 1 and proceed through to scenario 5 and the 'all at once' scenario.

Source: Adapted from J. E. Barbuto, Jr, 'Power and the Changing Environment', *Journal of Management Education*, April 2000, pp. 288–96.

Case Study 18

The Kingaroy Art & Card Company

At first Tammy Reinhold didn't believe the rumours. Now that the rumours were confirmed, she was in denial. 'I can't believe it,' she said. 'I've worked as a greeting-card artist here for 17 years. I love what I do. Now they tell me that I'm going to have to do all my work on a computer.'

Tammy wasn't alone in her fear. The company's other two artists, Mike Tomaski and Maggie Lyall, were just as concerned. Each had graduated from art school near the top of their class. They came to work for Kingaroy Art & Card Company right out of school—Mike in 1976, Tammy in 1983 and Maggie in 1988. They chose the company, which had been around for more than 50 years, because of its reputation as a good place to work. The company also had never had a layoff.

Kingaroy Art & Card Company is a small maker of greeting cards and speciality wrapping paper. It has modest resources and modest ambitions. Management has always pursued progress slowly. Maybe that's why it was so late in introducing computerised technology to its production operations. And why it now decided that it no longer wanted its artists to do hand-rendered work. Management had bought three high-powered Macintosh computers and equipped them with the latest graphics and photo-manipulation software, including Photoshop, Quark and Illustrator.

Courtland Gray, the company's owner, called Tammy, Mike and Maggie into his office that morning. He told them about the changes that were going to be made. Gray acknowledged that the three of them were going to have a lot to learn to be able to do all their work on computers. But he stressed that the changes would dramatically speed up the art-production and photo-layout processes and eventually result in significant cost savings. He offered to send them to a one-week course in Brisbane specifically designed to train artists in the new technology. He also said he expected all of the company's art and photo operations to be completely digitalised within three months.

Tammy wasn't stupid. She had been following the trends in graphic art. More and more work was being done on computers. She just thought, as did Mike and Maggie, that she might escape having to learn these programs. After all, Kingaroy Art & Card isn't Hallmark. But Tammy was wrong. Technology was coming to Kingaroy Art & Card Company and there wasn't much she could do about it—other than complain or look for another job!

Questions

1. Explain Tammy's resistance.
2. Evaluate the way Courtland Gray handled the change.
3. What, if anything, would you have done differently if you were in Courtland Gray's position?

Web Workout

1. What would be your strategy if you were called upon to be a 'change agent' for your organisation? How would you begin, gather information and create buy-in for your ideas? Go to FastCompany's website, which features an article on this topic at <www.fastcompany.com/online/05/changetips.html>. Even more interesting, read several of the reader responses linked at the bottom of the page. Write a short reaction paper on why you think there is such a difference from the article's perspective versus the readers' comments. What OB strategies would you use as change agent to address some of those readers' concerns?
2. Resistance to change is a concern when making organisational changes—but, as we read in the text, it is to be expected. Read about the Theory of Constraints (TOC) model used by some organisations to better know where resistance is and how to develop a strategy for addressing it. Visit <www.focusedperformance.com/articles/resistance.html> to find an article on TOC and how to take advantage of resistance. Print and bring to class for further discussion.

3. What is the difference between learning organisations and organisational learning? For a brief overview of the two, go to <www.brint.com/papers/orglrng.htm>. Develop a table outlining the differences between the two and bring to class for further discussion.

4. Write a two-page paper on knowledge management. It can be a general paper, or you can choose to focus on different aspects of KM, such as the challenges of such a system or how KM enhances organisational effectiveness or innovation. For an overview on knowledge management, go to <www.outsights.com/systems/kmgmt/kmgmt.htm> as a place to start. Don't hesitate to do your own search—there are many, many interesting sites on this topic.

5. Knowledge management requires a commitment to the continuing development of an organisation's intellectual resources—people! This often means more training, and it needs to be better and faster. Visit <www.reengineering.com/articles/jul96/spotlight.htm> to learn about the concept of JITT, or Just In Time Training. Write a few paragraphs on what you learned from the page. Also, did anything you learned surprise you? Print and bring to class.

6. Dealing with individual stress requires a knowledge of various coping skills and the willingness to put them into practice. Visit <www.shpm.com/articles/stress/stress2.html> for tips on how to deal with everyday stressors. For tips on how to deal with 'college blues', visit the International Stress Management Association's journal archives at <www.isma-usa.org/article0701.htm>.

KSS Program

KNOW THE CONCEPTS   SELF-AWARENESS   SKILLS APPLICATIONS

Managing resistance to change

After you have read this chapter, take Self-Assessment #47 (How Well Do I Respond to Turbulent Change?) on your enclosed CD-Rom and complete the skill-building module entitled 'Managing Resistance to Change' on page 650.

NOTES

1. Anonymous, 'Geoff Bell', *Management Today*, March 2003, p. 33; and <www.sydneymarkets.com.au/html/about_us.html>, accessed 24 April 2003.

2. See, for example, K. H. Hammonds, 'Practical Radicals', *Fast Company*, September 2000, pp. 162–74; and P. C. Judge, 'Change Agents', *Fast Company*, November 2000, pp. 216–26.

3. R. H. Hall, *Organizations: Structures, Processes, and Outcomes*, 4th ed. (Upper Saddle River, NJ: Prentice Hall, 1987), p. 29.

4. D. Katz and R. L. Kahn, *The Social Psychology of Organizations*, 2nd ed. (New York: Wiley, 1978), pp. 714–15.

5. J. P. Kotter and L. A. Schlesinger, 'Choosing Strategies for Change', *Harvard Business Review*, March–April 1979, pp. 106–14.

6. See J. Pfeffer, *Managing with Power: Politics and Influence in Organizations* (Boston: Harvard Business School Press, 1992), pp. 7 and 318–20; and D. Knights and D. McCabe, 'When "Life Is but a Dream": Obliterating Politics Through Business Process Reengineering?', *Human Relations*, June 1998, pp. 761–98.

7. See, for example, W. Ocasio, 'Political Dynamics and the Circulation of Power: CEO Succession in U.S. Industrial Corporations, 1960–1990', *Administrative Science Quarterly*, June 1994, pp. 285–312.

8. K. Lewin, *Field Theory in Social Science* (New York: Harper & Row, 1951).

9. See, for example, A. B. Shani and W. A. Pasmore, 'Organization Inquiry: Towards a New Model of the Action Research Process', in D. D. Warrick (ed.), *Contemporary Organization Development: Current Thinking and Applications* (Glenview, IL: Scott, Foresman, 1985), pp. 438–48.

10. For a sampling of various OD definitions, see J. I. Porras and P. J. Robertson, 'Organizational Development: Theory, Practice, and Research', in M. D. Dunnette and L. M. Hough (eds), *Handbook of Industrial & Organizational Psychology*, 2nd ed., vol. 3 (Palo Alto: Consulting Psychologists Press, 1992), pp. 721–23; N. Nicholson (ed.), *Encyclopedic Dictionary of Organizational Behavior* (Malden, MA: Blackwell, 1998), pp. 359–61; and G. Farias and H. Johnson, 'Organizational Development and Change Management', *Journal of Applied Behavioral Science*, September 2000, pp. 376–79.

11. See, for example, W. A. Pasmore and M. R. Fagans, 'Participation, Individual Development, and Organizational Change: A Review and Synthesis', *Journal of Management*, June 1992, pp. 375–97; T. G. Cummings and C .G. Worley, *Organization Development and Change*, 5th ed. (Minneapolis: West, 1993); and W. W. Burke, *Organization Development: A Process of Learning and Changing*, 2nd ed. (Reading, MA: Addison-Wesley, 1994).

12. R. T. Golembiewski and A. Blumberg (eds), *Sensitivity Training and the Laboratory Approach*, 2nd ed. (Itasca, IL: Peacock, 1973).

13. J. E. Edwards and M. D. Thomas, 'The Organizational Survey Process: General Steps and Practical Considerations', in P. Rosenfeld, J. E. Edwards and M. D. Thomas (eds), *Improving Organizational Surveys: New Directions, Methods, and Applications* (Newbury Park, CA: Sage, 1993), pp. 3–28.

14. E. H. Schein, *Process Consultation: Its Role in Organizational Development*, 2nd ed. (Reading, MA: Addison-Wesley, 1988), p. 9. See also E. H. Schein, *Process Consultation Revisited: Building Helpful Relationships* (Reading, MA: Addison-Wesley, 1999).

15. Ibid.

16. W. Dyer, *Team Building: Issues and Alternatives* (Reading, MA: Addison-Wesley, 1994).

17. N. Margulies and J. Wallace, *Organizational Change: Techniques and Applications* (Glenview, IL: Scott, Foresman, 1973), pp. 99–100.

18. See, for example, E. H. Neilsen, 'Understanding and Managing Intergroup Conflict', in J. W. Lorsch and P. R. Lawrence (eds), *Managing Group and Intergroup Relations* (Homewood, IL: Irwin-Dorsey, 1972), pp. 329–43.

19. R. R. Blake, J. S. Mouton and R. L. Sloma, 'The Union–Management Intergroup Laboratory: Strategy for Resolving Intergroup Conflict', *Journal of Applied Behavioral Science*, no. 1, 1965, pp. 25–57.

20. See, for example, D. Whitney and C. Schau, 'Appreciative Inquiry: An Innovative Process for Organization Change', *Employment Relations Today*, Spring 1998, pp. 11–21; R. Zemke, 'Don't Fix That Company!', *Training*, June 1999, pp. 26–33; and D. L. Cooperrider and D. Whitney, *Collaborating for Change: Appreciative Inquiry* (San Francisco: Berrett-Koehler, 2000).

21. Zemke, 'Don't Fix That Company!', p. 31.

22. Mellish, <www.mellish.com.au/Resources/appinqaustuni.htm>, accessed 1 May 2003.

23. See, for example, A. Van de Ven, 'Central Problems in the Management of Innovation', *Management Science*, vol. 32, 1986, pp. 590–607; and R. M. Kanter, 'When a Thousand Flowers Bloom: Structural, Collective and Social Conditions for Innovation in Organizations', in B. M. Staw and L. L. Cummings (eds), *Research in Organizational Behavior*, vol. 10 (Greenwich, CT: JAI Press, 1988), pp. 169–211.

24. F. Damanpour, 'Organizational Innovation: A Meta-Analysis of Effects of Determinants and Moderators', *Academy of Management Journal*, September 1991, p. 557.

25. Ibid, pp. 555–90.

26. See also P. R. Monge, M. D. Cozzens and N. S. Contractor, 'Communication and Motivational Predictors of the Dynamics of Organizational Innovation', *Organization Science*, May 1992, pp. 250–74.

27. J. H. Sheridan, 'Lew Platt: Creating a Culture for Innovation', *Industry Week*, 19 December 1994, pp. 26–30.

28. J. M. Howell and C. A. Higgins, 'Champions of Change', *Business Quarterly*, Spring 1990, pp. 31–32; and D. L. Day, 'Raising Radicals: Different Processes for Championing Innovative Corporate Ventures', *Organization Science*, May 1994, pp. 148–72.

29. Howell and Higgins, 'Champions of Change'.

30. See, for example, the special edition on organisational learning in *Organizational Dynamics*, Autumn 1998; P. Senge, *The Dance of Change: The Challenges to Sustaining Momentum in Learning Organizations* (New York: Doubleday/Currency, 1999); A. M. Webber, 'Will Companies Ever Learn?', *Fast Company*, October 2000, pp. 275–82; and R. Snell, 'Moral Foundations of the Learning Organization', *Human Relations*, March 2001, pp. 319–42.

31. D. H. Kim, 'The Link Between Individual and Organizational Learning', *Sloan Management Review*, Fall 1993, p. 37.

32. See <www.bp.com.au/careers/program.asp>.

33. C. Argyris and D. A. Schon, *Organizational Learning* (Reading, MA: Addison-Wesley, 1978).

34. B. Dumaine, 'Mr. Learning Organization', *Fortune*, 17 October 1994, p. 148.

35. F. Kofman and P. M. Senge, 'Communities of Commitment: The Heart of Learning Organizations', *Organizational Dynamics*, Autumn 1993, pp. 5–23.

36. Dumaine, 'Mr. Learning Organization', p. 154.

37. L. Smith, 'New Ideas from the Army (Really)', *Fortune*, 19 September 1994, pp. 203–12; and L. Baird, P. Holland and S. Deacon, 'Imbedding More Learning into the Performance Fast Enough to Make a Difference', *Organizational Dynamics*, Spring 1999, pp. 19–32.

38. See J. Ewing, 'Sharing the Wealth', *BusinessWeek e.biz*, 19 March 2001, pp. EB36–40; and D. Tapscott, D. Ticoll and A. Lowy, *Digital Capital: Harnessing the Power of Business Webs* (Boston: Harvard Business School Press, 2000).

39. See B. Roberts, 'Pick Employees' Brains', *HRMagazine*, February 2000, p. 115; and L. Empson, 'Introduction: Knowledge Management in Professional Service Firms', *Human Relations*, July 2001, pp. 811–16.

40. Roberts, 'Pick Employees' Brains', pp. 115–16; B. Fryer, 'Get Smart', *INC. Technology 1999*, no. 3, p. 65; and D. Zielinski, 'Have You Shared a Bright Idea Today?', *Training*, July 2000, p. 65.

41. Fryer, 'Get Smart', p. 63.

42. Roberts, 'Pick Employees' Brains', p. 117; and D. W. DeLong and L. Fahey, 'Diagnosing Cultural Barriers to Knowledge Management', *Academy of Management Executive*, November 2000, pp. 113–27.

43. J. Gordon, 'Intellectual Capital and You', *Training*, September 1999, p. 33.

44. Emily Ross, 'The New Heavyweight Titles', *Business Review Weekly*, vol. 24, no. 28, July 2002, pp. 60–63.

45. See S. Shane, S. Venkataraman and I. MacMillan, 'Cultural Differences in Innovation Championing Strategies', *Journal of Management*, vol. 21, no. 5, 1995, pp. 931–52.

46. See, for example, K. Slobogin, 'Many U.S. Employees Feel Overworked, Stressed, Study Says', <www.cnn.com>, accessed 16 May 2001.

47. Meaghan Shaw, 'Bosses Seek Tough Stance on Work Stress', *The Age*, 14 January 2002.

48. Adapted from R. S. Schuler, 'Definition and Conceptualization of Stress in Organizations', *Organizational Behavior and Human Performance*, April 1980, p. 189. For an updated review of definitions, see R. L. Kahn and P. Byosiere, 'Stress in Organizations', in M. D. Dunnette and L. M. Hough (eds), *Handbook of Industrial and Organizational Psychology*, 2nd ed., vol. 3 (Palo Alto, CA: Consulting Psychologists Press, 1992), pp. 573–80.

49. See, for example, M. A. Cavanaugh, W. R. Boswell, M. V. Roehling and J. W. Boudreau, 'An Empirical Examination of Self-Reported Work Stress Among U.S. Managers', *Journal of Applied Psychology*, February 2000, pp. 65–74.

50. Schuler, 'Definition and Conceptualization of Stress in Organizations', p. 191.

51. This model is based on D. F. Parker and T. A. DeCotiis, 'Organizational Determinants of Job Stress', *Organizational Behavior and Human Performance*, October 1983, p. 166, S. Parasuraman and J. A. Alutto, 'Sources and Outcomes of Stress in Organizational Settings: Toward the Development of a Structural Model', *Academy of Management Journal*, June 1984, p. 333; and Kahn and Byosiere, 'Stress in Organizations', p. 592.

52. This section is adapted from C. L. Cooper and R. Payne, *Stress at Work* (London: Wiley, 1978); Parasuraman and Alutto, 'Sources and Outcomes of Stress in Organizational Settings', pp. 330–50; and S. Cartwright and C. L. Cooper, *Managing Workplace Stress* (Thousand Oaks, CA: Sage, 1997).

53. See, for example, D. R. Frew and N. S. Bruning, 'Perceived Organizational Characteristics and Personality Measures as Predictors of Stress/Strain in the Work Place', *Journal of Management*, Winter 1987, pp. 633–46; and M. L. Fox, D. J. Dwyer and D. C. Ganster, 'Effects of Stressful Job Demands and Control of Physiological and Attitudinal Outcomes in a Hospital Setting', *Academy of Management Journal*, April 1993, pp. 289–318.

54. D. L. Nelson and C. Sutton, 'Chronic Work Stress and Coping: A Longitudinal Study and Suggested New Directions', *Academy of Management Journal*, December 1990, pp. 859–69.

55. H. Selye, *The Stress of Life*, rev. ed. (New York: McGraw-Hill, 1956).

56. S. J. Motowidlo, J. S. Packard and M. R. Manning, 'Occupational Stress: Its Causes and Consequences for Job Performance', *Journal of Applied Psychology*, November 1987, pp. 619–20.

57. See, for example, R. C. Cummings, 'Job Stress and the Buffering Effect of Supervisory Support', *Group & Organization Studies*, March 1990, pp. 92–104; M. R. Manning, C. N. Jackson and M. R. Fusilier, 'Occupational Stress, Social Support, and the Cost of Health Care', *Academy of Management Journal*, June 1996, pp. 738–50; and P. D. Bliese and T. W. Britt, 'Social Support, Group Consensus and Stressor-Strain Relationships: Social Context Matters', *Journal of Organizational Behavior*, June 2001, pp. 425–36.

58. See L. R. Murphy, 'A Review of Organizational Stress Management Research', *Journal of Organizational Behavior Management*, Fall–Winter 1986, pp. 215–27.

59. S. M. Jex and P. D. Bliese, 'Efficacy Beliefs as a Moderator of the Impact of Work-Related Stressors: A Multilevel Study', *Journal of Applied Psychology*, June 1999, pp. 349–61.

60. R. Williams, *The Trusting Heart: Great News About Type A Behavior* (New York: Times Books, 1989).

61. Schuler, 'Definition and Conceptualization of Stress', pp. 200–05; and Kahn and Byosiere, 'Stress in Organizations', pp. 604–10.

62. See T. A. Beehr and J. E. Newman, 'Job Stress, Employee Health, and Organizational Effectiveness: A Facet Analysis, Model, and Literature Review', *Personnel Psychology*, Winter 1978, pp. 665–99; and B. D. Steffy and J. W. Jones, 'Workplace Stress and Indicators of Coronary-Disease Risk', *Academy of Management Journal*, September 1988, pp. 686–98.

63. Steffy and Jones, 'Workplace Stress and Indicators of Coronary-Disease Risk', p. 687.

64. C. L. Cooper and J. Marshall, 'Occupational Sources of Stress: A Review of the Literature Relating to Coronary Heart Disease and Mental Ill Health', *Journal of Occupational Psychology*, vol. 49, no. 1, 1976, pp. 11–28.

65. J. R. Hackman and G. R. Oldham, 'Development of the Job Diagnostic Survey', *Journal of Applied Psychology*, April 1975, pp. 159–70.

66. Cited in *Fast Company*, March 2000, p. 219.

67. <www2.agsm.edu.au/agsm/web.nsf/Content/News-LatestNews-WorkplaceStress%3F>.

68. 'Reasons for Unscheduled Absences', *Business Week Frontier*, 8 November 1999, p. F6.

69. See, for example, J. M. Ivancevich and M. T. Matteson, *Stress and Work* (Glenview, IL: Scott, Foresman, 1981); R. D. Allen, M. A. Hitt and C. R. Greer, 'Occupational Stress and Perceived Organizational Effectiveness in Formal Groups: An Examination of Stress Level and Stress Type', *Personnel Psychology*, Summer 1982, pp. 359–70; and L. A. Muse and S. G. Harris, 'The Relationship between Stress

and Job Performance: Has the Inverted U Theory Had a Fair Test?', paper presented at the Southern Management Association meeting, 1998.

70. S. E. Sullivan and R. S. Bhagat, 'Organizational Stress, Job Satisfaction and Job Performance: Where Do We Go From Here?', *Journal of Management*, June 1992, pp. 361–64; and M. Westman and D. Eden, 'The Inverted-U Relationship between Stress and Performance: A Field Study', *Work & Stress*, Spring 1996, pp. 165–73.

71. The following discussion has been influenced by J. E. Newman and T. A. Beehr, 'Personal and Organizational Strategies for Handling Job Stress', *Personnel Psychology*, Spring 1979, pp. 1–38; J. M. Ivancevich and M. T. Matteson, 'Organizational Level Stress Management Interventions: A Review and Recommendations', *Journal of Organizational Behavior Management*, Fall–Winter 1986, pp. 229–48; M. T. Matteson and J. M. Ivancevich, 'Individual Stress Management Interventions: Evaluation of Techniques', *Journal of Management Psychology*, January 1987, pp. 24–30; and J. M. Ivancevich, M. T. Matteson, S. M. Freedman and J. S. Phillips, 'Worksite Stress Management Interventions', *American Psychologist*, February 1990, pp. 252–61.

72. T. H. Macan, 'Time Management: Test of a Process Model', *Journal of Applied Psychology*, June 1994, pp. 381–91.

73. See, for example, G. Lawrence-Ell, *The Invisible Clock: A Practical Revolution in Finding Time for Everyone and Everything* (Seaside Park, NJ: Kingsland Hall, 2002).

74. J. Kiely and G. Hodgson, 'Stress in the Prison Service: The Benefits of Exercise Programs', *Human Relations*, June 1990, pp. 551–72.

75. E. J. Forbes and R. J. Pekala, 'Psychophysiological Effects of Several Stress Management Techniques', *Psychological Reports*, February 1993, pp. 19–27; and G. Smith, 'Meditation, the New Balm for Corporate Stress', *Business Week*, 10 May 1993, pp. 86–87.

76. See W. A. Anthony and C. W. Anthony, *The Art of Napping at Work* (Burdett, NY: Larson Publications, 2000); J. E. Brody, 'New Respect for the Nap, a Pause That Refreshes', *New York Times*, 4 January 2000, p. D7; and 'Nappers of the World, Lie Down and Be Counted!', *Training*, May 2000, p. 24.

77. S. E. Jackson, 'Participation in Decision Making as a Strategy for Reducing Job-Related Strain', *Journal of Applied Psychology*, February 1983, pp. 3–19.

78. S. Greengard, 'It's About Time', *Industry Week*, 7 February 2000, pp. 47–50.

79. See, for example, M. N. Martinez, 'Using Data to Create Wellness Programs That Work', *HRMagazine*, November 1999, pp. 106–09; and B. Leonard, 'Health Care Costs Increase Interest in Wellness Programs', *HRMagazine*, September 2001, pp. 35–36.

80. S. Tully, 'America's Healthiest Companies', *Fortune*, 12 June 1995, p. 104.

81. M. Freudenheim, 'Employers Focus on Weight as Workplace Health Issue', *New York Times*, 6 September 1999, p. A11.

82. P. S. Goodman and L. B. Kurke, 'Studies of Change in Organizations: A Status Report', in P. S. Goodman (ed.), *Change in Organizations* (San Francisco: Jossey-Bass, 1982), pp. 1–2.

83. Kahn and Byosiere, 'Stress in Organizations', pp. 605–08.

PHOTO CREDITS

Integrative Case Study A Accenture Practises What it Preaches

DR GLENICE J. WOOD, University of Ballarat, Australia

Challenges face Ms Hemstritch, the first female managing director in Australia for Accenture, one of the world's leading management consulting and technology services organisations. She has been newly appointed to the position to enhance the company's profile of organisational and human performance within Australia, and throughout the Asia-Pacific, at a time when the IT industry is emerging from a period of depression.

Accenture (formerly known as Andersen Consulting) employs 75,000 people in 47 countries, generating net revenues of over US$11 billion for the financial year ended 31 August 2001. The company operates through various business approaches, which include outsourcing expertise through alliances, ventures and other consulting capabilities. Such multifaceted approaches deliver innovative solutions to clients drawn from all industry sectors. In addition, Accenture focuses on working with clients, helping them to recognise, and capitalise on, important business and technology opportunities. Where complex and critical challenges are required, solutions are provided by Accenture's breadth of experience, industry knowledge, and familiarity with current and emerging technologies.

Ms Hemstritch takes on the role at a time of difficulty within the IT industry generally, and Accenture in particular. In Australia, the organisation has reduced its staff by 400, a step described by Ms Hemstritch as 'a painful but necessary moment in our lives to really get the size and the mix of skills right for the business that we have today' (Thorp, 2003, p. 29). Her view is that the organisation has been traditionally a project-focused consulting and systems integration business, and while it will continue to do this, she believes her new role is to ensure that the mix is altered so that outsourcing forms a more integral part of the business. She has been with the company since 1982, and has held several significant roles in the organisation, including heading up Communications and the high-tech group in the Asia-Pacific region, as well as being responsible for Telstra, a top client, managing 500 staff in the process.

The appointment of Ms Hemstritch as the first female managing director in Australia is evidence of Accenture's commitment to their stated objective to 'attract, retain and advance women by recognizing, fostering and maximizing their performance' (<www.careers3.accenture.com.au>). The organisation has taken seriously the challenge of creating a global work environment which is inclusive, and one visible manifestation of this perspective is the development of a program entitled Accenture's Great Place to Work for Women, which has been running for three years. Such a development came about through Accenture identifying and retaining its best talent as a strategic priority within the organisation, and the program is designed to support that goal.

The program operates worldwide and is specifically designed to ensure that the initiative is applicable in each geographical location. Thus, the program is customised in each location so as to offer the relevant information networking opportunities, policies and programs. In Australia, the program is included in the organisation's recruitment activities (Fenton-Jones, 2001).

This initiative is given serious credibility by enjoying the co-sponsorship of the company's chairman and CEO, and by being globally managed by Accenture's chief leadership officer. Such executive ownership ensures that the program continues to be aligned with the specified business objectives of the organisation. Currently, there are more than 29,000 female employees at Accenture worldwide, with the percentage of female partners increasing from 5.8 per cent in 1994 to 10 per cent in 2002. In terms of global promotions to the level of partner, women comprised 14.1 per cent, and they make up 17 per cent of Accenture's Management Committee, which is the senior leadership group. (<www.careers3.accenture.com.au>).

The innovativeness of the Great Place to Work for Women program has received recognition internationally. Catalyst, the international non-profit organisation whose charter is to advance women in business, has named Accenture as a Catalyst Award Winner for 2003, on the basis of its 'innovative approaches to recruiting, developing and advancing women in business' (<www.careers3.accenture.com.au>). Prior to designing the program, focus groups for and surveys of women employees were conducted, and external data analysis was incorporated. Amalgamation of the various sources of data was used to create a comprehensive action plan.

The program has been particularly welcomed in Australia, where a recent research study found that 83 per cent of respondents believed that Australian organisations were less effective at promoting women into senior management roles than were other global organisations (<www.womenfuture.com/about/aust_art.hrm>). Ongoing projects in the Great Place to Work for Women program include promoting flexible work arrangements, recruiting, pipeline management, networking, and participation in or sponsorship of external women's events. In addition, Accenture Australia are committed to developing and promoting an acceptance of the advancement of women in business (<www.accenture.com.au>).

Ms Hemstritch is keen to ensure the success of the Great Place to Work for Women program, so that Accenture draws from the entire talent base that is available within Australia. It would appear that the program is well on track for achieving its stated goal, and Ms Hemstritch is living proof of its success.

Sources: Adapted from Diana Thorp, 'Accenture Hires for Push in Outsourcing', *The Australian*, 25 February 2003, p. 29; M. Fenton-Jones, 'Clue to Closing Gender Gap', *Australian Financial Review*, 19 October 2001; and various websites.

Activities for discussion, analysis and further research

1. Describe the forces for change that are impacting on Accenture as it makes plans to accommodate future trends.
2. How would you characterise the culture at Accenture in terms of dominant and subcultures, and core values? Discuss three factors that would maintain the culture in this organisation.
3. In terms of career development, how has Accenture met its organisational responsibilities to the female employees who participate in the Great Place to Work for Women program? Describe three support mechanisms that Accenture has put in place to fulfil its responsibilities in this regard.
4. Would you describe Accenture as a learning organisation? Why, or why not?
5. Define organisational development (OD) and describe the main values it embodies. Explain how the OD intervention of intergroup development has been used successfully in this organisation.
6. Would you describe Accenture as a virtual organisation? A boundaryless organisation? Support your views.

Integrative Case Study B **Instrumentation Pty Ltd**

JOHN DUGAS, The University of Newcastle, Australia

Ken Wong, CEO of Instrumentation Pty Ltd, looked out of his mezzanine-level office window over the largest factory now controlled by his organisation. His thoughts raced back to five years before, when he had first joined the company. What a remarkable change had occurred in that time!

With manufacturing and service facilities in four Australian states and negotiations well advanced for their first offshore base in the People's Republic of China, Ken knew that the organisation would have yet more challenges ahead.

Way, way back, over 35 years ago, two Australian electrical engineers, Andrew Wallace and K. D. Marshall, had set up in a garage in one of their homes and produced gauges that monitored temperatures in steel-making furnaces. It was a matter of pride to the company founders, now both in their seventies and the two major shareholders in the organisation, that their device was selected by a specialist stainless steel maker over other instrument imports available from both the United States and Germany. The robust devices sold at 60 per cent of the cost of expensive imports and, backed up by local service, found a market niche with plain-talking steel makers in Newcastle and Wollongong, the two steel cities to the north and south of Sydney.

Many of those steel makers were now gone, the result of progressively tougher competition from offshore steel producers whose labour costs were well under those that the Australians had to pay.

Wallace and Marshall weren't really responding to changing international circumstances with their early business strategy choices, but they did have a desire to grow their business by extending the product range. Measuring instruments were required in cool rooms, in hospitals, and in military vessels of all shapes and sizes both on the land, in the air and on the water. Add to this other consumer leisure vehicles of all types — air, land, sea and river — and it was obvious that the market was large. Manufacturing and food processing, as well as utilities such as water, power and gas, and extractive industries such as mines, depended on appropriate measurement.

Instruments were ubiquitous. It was a matter of targeting the overpriced ones, the poorly supported ones, and the ones that didn't do the job, and then tapping into the organisation's key instrumentation engineering competences. And these were substantial. Marshall was the creative one, the engineering ideas man. But Wallace knew how to turn ideas into innovations. He was able to carry the concept through to reality, and to lock up the intellectual property and patents attendant on the innovation. The R&D department, a highly committed, hand-picked group, was the company's 'growth engine'. This expert and elite group in many respects drove the fortunes of the company. This wasn't to deny the importance of other organisational functions; but it was clear that without new ideas, or adaptations of existing ideas to different contexts, competitors would catch up. It was only a matter of time.

Over the years the business grew steadily, but not remarkably. The remarkable growth had only been relatively recently. The widespread application of information technology, combined with the ability to instantly transmit information, was the breakthrough that funded the company's recent rapid growth.

In business and in science, unmeasured is unknown, and with increasing emphasis on quality, manufacturers led the way in the demand for more precise measures of what they were doing. Measuring inputs and measuring processes enhanced the likelihood of predictable, quality outputs. Less waste, less recall, less consumer and public relations problems, mused Ken Wong.

He understood all of this — how the organisation had got where it had got. But so much remained to be done. In truth, the organisation still had some characteristics more aligned to a small business. With 360 people, and four, soon five, sites (one offshore) and an annual turnover exceeding $100 million, they weren't small. True, the growth had come mainly in the last four to six years, and particularly since the board of directors had embarked on a growth by acquisition strategy fuelled by ever-increasing revenues from their core business and a number of successful, patented products. One after the other, specialist instrument makers for specific fields had been brought in under the umbrella of Instrumentation Pty Ltd.

That meant a merging of organisational cultures. The process of combining smaller businesses, with their ways of doing things, with the larger business's ways of doing things had been repeated six times in the last six years. It was challenging. It wasn't just the cultures that had to be merged, but also the processes, and the 'legacy systems' of accounting, information technology, industrial relations, occupational health and safety, and even suppliers, among others. All were matters that had to be dealt with and were still being dealt with. On a forever basis, it would seem, thought Ken.

The people part of the business was the hardest. The R&D department was crucial to the company's level of innovation. Innovate or die. How true. But not just for products and service provision, but for organisational structures and processes, too, thought Ken. And it seemed to be speeding up, like a treadmill that goes faster as you run faster. More and more seemed to be coming at him. Ken reflected gloomily on the responses that he would give now to some of those work–life balance questions asked rhetorically at a recent seminar.

Ken's thoughts shifted to other aspects of the business. His departmental heads had their hands full, too. Line managers still hired for their own functional departments. He wondered at the duplication, at the effectiveness of this. There were gains that could plausibly be made by establishing a central human resources function. And, was it just HR that needed consideration? Given the increase in staff numbers, the increase in product range, and the move internationally, would the current structure with its manufacturing, sales, service, accounts and R&D departments still suffice? So much was happening, that plant maintenance, IT and purchasing, as well as HR, were jostling for more attention, more resources. Sure, training was ongoing, but was it as tightly integrated with the overall strategy direction of the organisation as it might be? And then there was performance management. Reward was tied to performance, but the implementation of the performance appraisal process wasn't all that it could be. Ken had heard rumblings. 'I must keep walking around the factory,' he thought, making a mental note.

It was great to be growing revenue, and potentially profits, but if Instrumentation Pty Ltd lost capability because of a less-than-appropriate structure, revenue, and ultimately business viability, would be impacted. That wasn't a happy prospect.

Then, there was the China move. The risk was high relative to earlier initiatives. Even very big players got burned there. Government regulations, the distance, the language, the inevitable cultural collision — how do you prepare for that? His own cultural background helped, of course, but this alone wouldn't be enough. Neither would his first-class honours degree in electrical engineering and his PhD in business administration. His command of both English and Chinese was excellent. His father's insistence that he learn his parents' tongue, as well as studying it as an elective as part of his university degree, had been an astute move.

Ken remembered how actively Marshall and Wallace had recruited him and thought that it wasn't only his father who had been shrewd. Deregulation, globalisation and engagement with Asia, among other 'big picture' phenomena, must have guided the founders and major shareholders to some extent in choosing him as the CEO nearly half a decade ago. All of this was still a huge 'ask'. How would he fare, he wondered?

Ken's mind snapped back to the present when his executive assistant announced on the intercom the arrival of the three government Austrade representatives from Canberra.

He quickly jotted down some bullet points about the issues he would raise at the next board meeting and then rose. He advanced briskly across the room and smiled politely to greet the visitors from the national capital as they walked into his office.

Activities for discussion, analysis and further research

1. What were Ken Wong's 'bullet point' issues?
2. What would appear to be the organisational structure of Instrumentation Pty Ltd?
3. Why does it have this structure?
4. Is this a suitable structure? Explain why or why not.
5. What are the challenges facing Instrumentation Pty Ltd, and Ken Wong in particular?
6. How might Ken Wong respond to these challenges?
7. Based on your knowledge of organisational behaviour and relevant theories about change, motivation and organisational structure, what recommendations would you make to Ken Wong to move Instrumentation forward?
8. Many aspects of Instrumentation Pty Ltd's situation are not unique. Do you agree with this statement. Explain why or why not.
9. What can you learn from Instrumentation Pty Ltd's circumstances?

Appendix A Historical Evolution of Organisational Behaviour

Why study history? As managers, our actions are guided by what we see in the future. However, we always view the places we are going by the images of the places we have already been or talked about. By *looking back* at the history of organisational behaviour, you can gain a great deal of insight into how the field got to where it is today. It will help you to understand, for example, how management came to impose rules and regulations on employees, why many workers in organisations do standardised and repetitive tasks on assembly lines, and why a number of organisations in recent years have replaced their assembly lines with team-based work units. In this appendix, you will find a brief description of how the theory and practice of OB has evolved.

So, where do we start? People and organised activities have been around for thousands of years, but we don't need to go back beyond the 18th or 19th century to find the roots of OB.

EARLY PRACTICES

There is no question that hundreds of people helped to plant the 'seeds' from which the OB 'garden' has grown.[1] Three individuals in the United Kingdom, however, were particularly important in promoting ideas that would eventually have a major influence in shaping the direction and boundaries of OB. These people were Adam Smith, Charles Babbage and Robert Owen.

Adam Smith

Adam Smith is more typically cited by economists for his contributions to classical economic doctrine, but his discussion in *The Wealth of Nations*,[2] published in 1776, includes a brilliant argument on the economic advantages that organisations and society would reap from the division of labour. Smith used the pin-manufacturing industry for his examples. He noted that ten individuals, each doing a specialised task, could produce about 48,000 pins a day among them. He proposed, however, that if each were working separately and independently, the ten individuals together would be lucky to make ten pins in one day. If each one had to draw the wire, straighten it, cut it, pound heads for each pin, sharpen the point, and solder the head and pin shaft, it would be quite a feat to produce ten pins a day!

Smith concluded that division of labour raised productivity by increasing each worker's skill and dexterity, by saving time that is commonly lost in changing tasks, and by encouraging the creation of labour-saving inventions and machinery. The extensive development of assembly-line production processes during the 20th century was undoubtedly stimulated by the economic advantages of job specialisation cited over 200 years ago by Adam Smith.

Charles Babbage

Charles Babbage was a British mathematics professor who expanded on the virtues of division of labour first articulated by Adam Smith. In his book *On the Economy of Machinery and Manufactures*,[3] published in 1832, Babbage added the following to Smith's list of the advantages that accrue from division of labour:

1. It reduces the time needed for learning a job.
2. It reduces the waste of material during the learning stage.
3. It allows for the attainment of high skill levels.
4. It allows a more careful matching of people's skills and physical abilities with specific tasks.

Moreover, Babbage proposed that the economies from specialisation should be as relevant to doing mental work as physical labour. Now, for example, we take specialisation among professionals for granted. When we have a skin rash, we go to a dermatologist. When we buy a home, we consult a solicitor who specialises in conveyancing. The lecturers you encounter in your business courses specialise in areas such as tax accounting, entrepreneurship, consumer behaviour and organisational behaviour. These applications of division of labour were unheard of in 18th-century England. But contemporary organisations around the world—in both manufacturing and service industries—make wide use of division of labour.

Robert Owen

Robert Owen was a Welsh entrepreneur who bought his first factory in 1789, when he was 18. He is important in the history of OB because he was one of the first industrialists to recognise how the growing factory system was demeaning to employees.

Repulsed by the harsh practices he saw in factories—such as the employment of young children (many under the age of ten), 13-hour work days and miserable working conditions—Owen became a reformer. He chided factory owners for treating their equipment better than their employees. He said that they would buy the best machines, but then buy the cheapest labour to run them. Owen argued that money spent on improving labour was one of the best investments that business executives could make. He claimed that showing concern for employees was profitable for management and would relieve human misery.

For his time, Owen was an idealist. What he proposed was a utopian workplace that would reduce the suffering of the working class. He was more than 100 years ahead of his time when he argued, in 1825, for regulated hours of work for all, child labour laws, public education, meals provided at work by the employer, and business involvement in community projects.[4]

THE CLASSICAL ERA

The classical era covered the period from about 1900 to the mid-1930s. It was during this period that the first general theories of management began to evolve. The classical contributors—who include Frederick Taylor, Henri Fayol, Max Weber, Mary Parker Follett and Chester Barnard—laid the foundation for contemporary management practices.

Scientific management

More than 90 years ago, Frederick W. Taylor wrote *Principles of Scientific Management*,[5] in which he described how the scientific method could be used to define the 'one best way' for a job to be done. In this section, we review Taylor's work.

As a mechanical engineer in a US steel company, Taylor was consistently appalled at the inefficiency of employees who used vastly different techniques to do the same job. They were prone to 'taking it easy' on the job. Taylor believed that individual output was only about one-third of what was possible. He set out to correct the situation by applying the scientific method to jobs on the shopfloor. He spent more than 20 years pursuing, with a passion, the 'one best way' for each job to be done.

What Taylor saw aroused his determination to improve the way things were done in the factory. At the time, there were no clear concepts of employee and management responsibilities. Virtually no effective work standards existed. Employees purposely worked at a slow pace. Management decisions were of the 'seat-of-the-pants' nature, based on hunch and intuition. Employees were placed on jobs with little or no concern for matching their abilities and aptitudes with the tasks they were required to do. Most importantly, management and workers considered themselves to be in continual conflict. Rather than cooperating to their mutual benefit, they perceived their relationship as a zero-sum game—any gain by one would be at the expense of the other.

Taylor sought to create a mental revolution among both the employees and management by defining clear guidelines for improving production efficiency. He defined four principles of management, listed in Table A.1; he argued that following these principles would result in the prosperity of both management and employees. Employees would earn more pay, and management would make more profits.

Probably the most widely cited example of scientific management has been Taylor's pig-iron experiment. The average daily output of 92 pounds (41.7 kg) of pig-iron loaded on to railway

TABLE A.1	Taylor's four principles of management

1. Develop a science for each element of an individual's work. (Previously, employees used the 'rule-of-thumb' method.)
2. Scientifically select and then train, teach and develop the employee. (Previously, employees chose their own work and trained themselves as best they could.)
3. Heartily cooperate with the employees so as to ensure that all work is done in accordance with the principles of the science that has been developed. (Previously, management and employees were in continual conflict.)
4. Divide work and responsibility almost equally between management and employees. Management takes over all work for which it is better fitted than the employees. (Previously, almost all the work and the greater part of the responsibility were thrown upon the employees.)

wagons was 12.5 tonnes per employee. Taylor believed that by scientifically analysing the job to determine the one best way to load pig-iron, the output could be increased to between 47 and 48 tonnes per day.

Taylor began his experiment by looking for a physically strong person who placed a high value on the dollar. The individual Taylor chose was a big, strong Dutch immigrant, whom he called Schmidt. Schmidt, like the other loaders, earned US$1.15 a day, which, even at the turn of the 20th century, was barely enough for a person to survive on. As the following quotation from Taylor's book demonstrates, Taylor used money—the opportunity to make US$1.85 a day—as the primary means to get employees like Schmidt to do exactly as they were told:

'Schmidt, are you a high-priced man?' 'Well, I don't know vat you mean.' 'Oh, yes you do. What I want to know is whether you are a high-priced man or not.' 'Well, I don't know vat you mean.' 'Oh, come now, you answer my questions. What I want to find out is whether you are a high-priced man or one of these cheap fellows here. What I want to know is whether you want to earn [US]$1.85 a day or whether you are satisfied with [US]$1.15, just the same as all those cheap fellows are getting.' 'Did I vant $1.85 a day? Vas dot a high-priced man? Well, yes. I vas a high-priced man.'[6]

Using money to motivate Schmidt, Taylor had him load the pig-iron, alternating various job factors to see what effect the changes had on Schmidt's daily output. On some days, Schmidt would lift the pig-iron by bending his knees, on other days he kept his legs straight and used his back. He experimented with rest periods, walking speed, carrying positions and other variables. After a long period of scientifically trying various combinations of procedures, techniques and tools, Taylor succeeded in obtaining the level of productivity he thought possible. By putting the right person on the job with the correct tools and equipment, by having the employee follow his instructions exactly, and by motivating the employee through the economic incentive of a significantly higher daily wage, Taylor was able to achieve his 48 tonnes objective.

Another Taylor experiment dealt with shovel sizes. Taylor noticed that every employee in the factory used the same size of shovel, regardless of the material he was moving. This made no sense to Taylor. If there was an optimum weight that would maximise an employee's shovelling output over an entire day, then Taylor thought the size of the shovel should vary, depending on the weight of the material being moved. After extensive experimentation, Taylor found that 21 pounds (9.5 kg) was the optimum shovel capacity. To achieve this optimum weight, heavy material such as iron ore would be moved with a small-faced shovel and light material such as coke with a large-faced shovel. Based on Taylor's findings, supervisors would no longer merely tell an employee to 'shovel that pile over there'. Depending on the material to be moved, the supervisor would now have to determine the appropriate shovel size and assign that size to the employee. The result, of course, was again significant increases in employee output.

Using similar approaches in other jobs, Taylor was able to define the one best way for doing each job. He could then, after selecting the right people for the job, train them to do it precisely in this one best way. To motivate employees, he favoured incentive wage plans. Overall, Taylor achieved consistent improvements in productivity in the range of 200 per cent or more. He reaffirmed the role of managers to plan and control and that of employees to perform as they were instructed. *Principles of Scientific Management*, as well as papers that Taylor wrote and presented, spread his ideas not only in the United States but also in France, Germany, Russia and Japan. One of the biggest boosts in interest in scientific management in the United States came during a 1910 hearing on railroad rates before the Interstate Commerce Commission. Appearing before the commission, an efficiency expert claimed that railroads could save US$1 million a day (equivalent to around $16 million a day in 1998 dollars) through the application of scientific management! The early acceptance of scientific management techniques by US manufacturing organisations, in fact, gave them a comparative advantage over foreign businesses that made US manufacturing efficiency the envy of the world—at least for 50 years or so!

Administrative theory

Administrative theory describes efforts to define the universal functions that managers perform and principles that constitute good management practice. The main contributor to administrative theory was a French industrialist named Henri Fayol.

Writing at about the same time as Taylor, Fayol proposed that all managers perform five management functions: they plan, organise, command, coordinate and control.[7] The importance of this simple insight is underlined by the fact that almost every introductory management textbook today uses these same five functions, or a very close variant of them, as a basic framework for describing what managers do.

In addition, Fayol described the practice of management as something distinct from accounting, finance, production, distribution, and other typical business functions. He argued that management was an activity common to all human undertakings in business, in government and even in the home. He then proceeded to state 14 principles of management which could be taught in schools and universities. These principles are shown in Table A.2.

Structural theory

While Taylor was concerned with management at the shop level (or what we today would describe as the job of a supervisor) and Fayol focused on general management functions, the German sociologist Max Weber (pronounced *Vayber*) was developing a theory of authority structures and describing organisational activity as based on authority relations.[8] He was one of the first to look at management and OB from a structural perspective.

Weber described an ideal type of organisation that he called a *bureaucracy*. Bureaucracy is a system characterised by division of labour, a clearly defined hierarchy, detailed rules and regulations, and impersonal relationships. Weber recognised that this 'ideal bureaucracy' didn't exist in reality but, rather, represented a selective reconstruction of the real world. He meant it to be taken as a basis for theorising about work and how work could be done in large groups. His theory became the design prototype for almost all of today's large organisations. The detailed features of Weber's ideal bureaucratic structure are outlined in Table A.3.

'Social man' theory

People such as Taylor, Fayol and Weber could be faulted for forgetting that human beings are the central core of every organisation and that human beings are social animals. Mary Parker Follett and Chester Barnard were two theorists who saw the importance of the social aspects of organisations. Their ideas were born late in the scientific management period but didn't achieve any large degree of recognition until the 1930s.[9]

TABLE A.2	Fayol's 14 principles of management

1. *Division of work:* This principle is the same as Adam Smith's 'division of labour'. Specialisation increases output by making employees more efficient.
2. *Authority:* Managers must be able to give orders. Authority gives them this right. With authority, however, goes responsibility. Wherever authority is exercised, responsibility arises.
3. *Discipline:* Employees must obey and respect the rules that govern the organisation. Good discipline is the result of effective leadership, a clear understanding between management and employees about the organisation's rules, and the judicious use of penalties for infractions of the rules.
4. *Unity of command:* Every employee should receive orders from only one superior.
5. *Unity of direction:* Each group of organisational activities that have the same objective should be directed by one manager using one plan.
6. *Subordination of individual interests to the general interests:* The interests of any one employee or group of employees should not take precedence over the interests of the organisation as a whole.
7. *Remuneration:* Workers must be paid a fair wage for their services.
8. *Centralisation:* Centralisation refers to the degree to which subordinates are involved in decision making. Whether decision making is centralised (to management) or decentralised (to employees) is a question of proper proportion. The problem is to find the optimum degree of centralisation for each situation.
9. *Scalar chain:* The line of authority from top management to the lowest ranks represents the scalar chain. Communications should follow this chain. However, if following the chain creates delays, cross-communications can be allowed if agreed to by all parties and managers are kept informed.
10. *Order:* People and materials should be in the right place at the right time.
11. *Equity:* Managers should be kind and fair to their employees.
12. *Stability of tenure of personnel:* High employee turnover is inefficient. Management should provide orderly personnel planning and ensure that replacements are available to fill vacancies.
13. *Initiative:* Employees who are allowed to originate and carry out plans will exert high levels of effort.
14. *Esprit de corps:* Promoting team spirit will build harmony and unity within the organisation.

TABLE A.3	Weber's ideal bureaucracy

1. *Division of labour:* Jobs are broken down into simple, routine and well-defined tasks.
2. *Authority hierarchy:* Offices or positions are organised in a hierarchy, each lower one being controlled and supervised by a higher one.
3. *Formal selection:* All organisational members are to be selected on the basis of technical qualifications demonstrated by training, education or formal examination.
4. *Formal rules and regulations:* To ensure uniformity and to regulate the actions of employees, managers must depend heavily on formal organisational rules.
5. *Impersonality:* Rules and controls are applied uniformly, avoiding involvement with personalities and personal preferences of employees.
6. *Career orientation:* Managers are professional officials rather than owners of the units they manage. They work for fixed salaries and pursue their careers within the organisation.

Mary Parker Follett

Mary Parker Follett was one of the earliest writers to recognise that organisations could be viewed from the perspective of individual and group behaviour.[10] A transitionalist writing during the time when scientific management dominated, Follett was a social philosopher who proposed more people-oriented ideas. Her ideas had clear implications for OB. Follett thought that organisations should be based on a group ethic rather than individualism. Individual potential, she argued, remained only potential until released through group association. The manager's job was to harmonise and coordinate group efforts. Managers and employees should view themselves as partners—as part of a common group. Therefore, managers should rely more on their expertise and knowledge than on the formal authority of their position to lead subordinates.

Follett's humanistic ideas have influenced the way we look at motivation, leadership, power and authority today. In fact, Japanese organisation and management styles, which were in vogue from the 1950s to the 1980s, were indebted to Follett. They placed a heavy emphasis on group togetherness and team effort.

Chester Barnard

Like Henri Fayol, Chester Barnard was a practitioner. He joined the American Telephone and Telegraph system in 1909 and became president of New Jersey Bell in 1927. Barnard had read Weber and was influenced by his writings. But unlike Weber, who had a mechanistic and impersonal view of organisations, Barnard saw organisations as social systems that require human cooperation. He expressed his views in *The Functions of the Executive*,[11] published in 1938.

Barnard viewed organisations as made up of people who have interacting social relationships. Managers' main roles were to communicate and to stimulate subordinates to high levels of effort. A major part of an organisation's success, as Barnard saw it, depended on obtaining cooperation from its personnel. Barnard also argued that success depended on maintaining good relations with people and institutions outside the organisation with whom the organisation regularly interacted. By recognising the organisation's dependence on investors, suppliers, customers and other external constituencies, Barnard introduced the idea that managers had to examine the environment and then adjust the organisation to maintain a state of equilibrium. So, for example, regardless of how efficient an organisation's production might be, if management failed to ensure a continuous input of materials and supplies or to find markets for its outputs, then the organisation's survival would be threatened. Much of the current interest in how the environment affects organisations and their employees can be traced to ideas initially suggested by Barnard.

THE BEHAVIOURAL ERA

The 'people side' of organisations came into its own during the period we will call the 'behavioural era'. As we show, this era was marked by the human relations movement and the widespread application in organisations of behavioural science research. While this behavioural era really didn't begin to take off until the 1930s, two earlier events deserve brief mention because they played an important part in the application and development of OB. These are the birth of the 'personnel office' around the turn of the 20th century and the creation of the field of industrial psychology with the publication of Hugo Münsterberg's textbook in 1913.

The birth of the 'personnel office'

In response to the growth of trade unionism at the turn of the 20th century, a few organisations—for example, H. J. Heinz and International Harvester—created the position of 'welfare secretary'. Welfare secretaries were supposed to assist employees by suggesting improvements in working conditions, housing, medical care, educational facilities and recreation. These people, who were the forerunners of today's personnel or human resource management directors, acted as a buffer between the organisation and its employees. The B. F. Goodrich Co. developed the first employment department in 1900, but its responsibilities consisted only of hiring. In 1902, the National

Cash Register Company established the first comprehensive labour department responsible for pay administration, grievances, employment and working conditions, health conditions, record keeping and employees' improvement.

The birth of industrial psychology

Hugo Münsterberg created the field of industrial psychology with the publication of his text *Psychology and Industrial Efficiency*[12] in 1913. In it, he argued for the scientific study of human behaviour to identify general patterns and to explain individual differences. Interestingly, Münsterberg saw a link between scientific management and industrial psychology. Both sought increased efficiency through scientific work analyses and through better alignment of individual skills and abilities with the demands of various jobs.

Münsterberg suggested the use of psychological tests to improve employee selection, the value of learning theory in the development of training methods, and the study of human behaviour in order to understand what techniques are most effective for motivating employees. Much of our current knowledge of selection techniques, employee training, job design and motivation is built on Münsterberg's work.

Human relations

The essence of the human relations movement was the belief that the key to higher productivity in organisations was increasing employee satisfaction. In addition to the Hawthorne studies, three people played important roles in conveying the message of human relations. These were Dale Carnegie, Abraham Maslow and Douglas McGregor. In this section, we briefly review the contribution of each. But first, we will briefly describe the very influential Hawthorne studies.

The Hawthorne studies

Without question, the most important contribution to the human relations movement within OB came out of the Hawthorne studies undertaken at the Western Electric Company's Hawthorne Works in Illinios. These studies, originally begun in 1924 but eventually expanded and carried on through the early 1930s, were initially devised by Western Electric industrial engineers to examine the effect of various illumination levels on employee productivity. Control and experimental groups were established. The experimental group was presented with varying illumination intensities, while the control group worked under a constant intensity. The engineers had expected individual output to be directly related to the intensity of light. However, they found that as the light level was increased in the experimental group, output for both groups rose. To the surprise of the engineers, as the light level was dropped in the experimental group, productivity continued to increase in both groups. In fact, a productivity decrease was observed in the experimental group only when the light intensity had been reduced to that of moonlight. The engineers concluded that illumination intensity was not directly related to group productivity, but they could not explain the behaviour they had witnessed.

In 1927 the Western Electric engineers asked Elton Mayo, an Australian-born Harvard professor, and his associates to join the study as consultants. Thus began a relationship that lasted until 1932 and encompassed numerous experiments covering the redesign of jobs, changes in the length of the work day and work week, introduction of rest periods, and individual versus group wage plans.[13] For example, one experiment was designed to evaluate the effect of a group piece-work incentive pay system on group productivity. The results indicated that the incentive plan had less effect on an employee's output than did group pressure and acceptance and the concomitant security. Social norms or standards of the group, therefore, were concluded to be the key determinants of individual work behaviour.

Scholars generally agree that the Hawthorne studies had a large and dramatic effect on the direction of OB and management practice. Mayo's conclusions were that behaviour and sentiments were closely related, that group influences significantly affected individual behaviour, that group standards established individual employee output, and that money was less a factor in determining output than were group standards, group sentiments and security. These conclusions led to a new emphasis on the human factor in the functioning of organisations and the attainment of their objectives. They also led to increased paternalism by management.

The Hawthorne studies had their critics. Attacks have been made on their procedures, analyses of findings and the conclusions they drew.[14] However, from a historical standpoint, it is of little importance whether the studies were academically sound or their conclusions justified. What is important is that they stimulated an interest in human factors.

Dale Carnegie

Dale Carnegie's book *How to Win Friends and Influence People*[15] was read by millions during the 1930s, 1940s and 1950s. During this same period, tens of thousands of managers and aspiring managers attended his management speeches and seminars. So, Carnegie's ideas deserve attention because of the wide audience they commanded.

Carnegie's essential theme was that the way to success was through winning the cooperation of others. He advised his audience to:
- make others feel important through a sincere appreciation of their efforts;
- strive to make a good first impression;
- win people to your way of thinking by letting others do the talking, being sympathetic, and 'never telling a man he is wrong'; and
- change people by praising their good traits and giving the offender the opportunity to save face.[16]

Abraham Maslow

Few university students haven't been exposed to the ideas of Abraham Maslow. A humanistic psychologist, Maslow proposed a theoretical hierarchy of five needs: physiological, safety, social, esteem and self-actualisation.[17] From a motivation standpoint, Maslow argued that each step in the hierarchy must be satisfied before the next can be activated, and that once a need was substantially satisfied, it no longer motivated behaviour. Moreover, he believed that self-actualisation—that is, achieving one's full potential—was the summit of a human being's existence. Managers who accepted Maslow's hierarchy attempted to alter their organisations and management practices to reduce barriers to employees' self-actualisation.

Douglas McGregor

Douglas McGregor is best known for his formulation of two sets of assumptions—theory X and theory Y—about human nature.[18] Briefly, theory X rests on an essentially negative view of people. It assumes that they have little ambition, dislike work, want to avoid responsibility, and need to be closely directed to work effectively. Theory Y, on the other hand, rests on a positive view of people. It assumes they can exercise self-direction, accept responsibility, and consider work to be as natural as rest or play. McGregor personally believed that theory Y assumptions best captured the true nature of employees and should guide management practice. As a result, he argued that managers should free up their employees to unleash their full creative and productive potential.

Behavioural science theorists

The final category within the behavioural era encompasses a group of researchers who, as Taylor did in scientific management, relied on the scientific method for the study of OB. Unlike members of the human relations movement, the behavioural science theorists engaged in *objective* research of human behaviour in organisations. They carefully attempted to keep their personal beliefs out of their work. They sought to develop rigorous research designs that could be replicated by other behavioural scientists in the hope that a science of OB could be built.

A full review of the contributions made by behavioural science theorists would cover hundreds of pages, since their work makes up a large part of today's foundations of OB. But to give you the flavour of their work, we briefly summarise the contributions of a few of the major theorists.

B. F. Skinner

People are more familiar with the name of B. F. Skinner than with that of any other behavioural scientist. Skinner's research on operant conditioning and behaviour modification had a significant effect on the design of organisational training programs and reward systems.[19]

Essentially, Skinner demonstrated that behaviour is a function of its consequences. He found that people will most likely engage in desired behaviour if they are rewarded for doing so; these rewards are most effective if they immediately follow the desired response; and behaviour that isn't rewarded, or is punished, is less likely to be repeated.

David McClelland

Harvard psychologist David McClelland tested the strength of individual achievement motivation by asking subjects to look at a set of somewhat ambiguous pictures and to write their own story about each picture. Based on these projective tests, McClelland found he was able to differentiate people with a high need to achieve—individuals who had a strong desire to succeed or achieve in relation to a set of standards—from people with a low need to achieve.[20] His research has been instrumental in helping organisations better match people with jobs and in redesigning jobs for high achievers so as to maximise their motivation potential. In addition, McClelland and his associates have successfully trained individuals to increase their achievement drive. For example, in India, people who underwent achievement training worked longer hours, initiated more new business ventures, made greater investments in productive assets, employed a larger number of employees, and saw a greater increase in their gross incomes than did a similar group who didn't undergo achievement training.

Fred Fiedler

Leadership is one of the most important and extensively researched topics in OB. The work of Fred Fiedler on the subject is significant for its emphasis on the situational aspects of leadership, as well as for its attempt to develop a comprehensive theory of leadership behaviour.[21]

From the mid-1960s to the late 1970s, Fiedler's contingency model dominated leadership research. He developed a questionnaire to measure an individual's inherent leadership orientation and identified three contingency variables that, he argued, determined what type of leader behaviour is most effective. In testing his model, Fiedler and his associates studied hundreds of groups. Dozens of researchers have attempted to replicate his results. Although some of the predictions from the model haven't stood up well under closer analysis, Fielder's model has been a major influence on current thinking and research on leadership.

Frederick Herzberg

With the possible exception of the Hawthorne studies, no single stream of research has had a greater impact on undermining the recommendations of scientific management than the work of Frederick Herzberg.[22]

Herzberg sought an answer to the question: 'What do individuals want from their jobs?' He asked hundreds of people that question in the late 1950s, and then carefully analysed their responses. He concluded that people preferred jobs that offered opportunities for recognition, achievement, responsibility and growth. Managers who concerned themselves with things like the organisation's policies, employee pay, creating narrow and repetitive jobs, and developing favourable working conditions might placate their employees but they wouldn't motivate them. According to Herzberg, if managers want to motivate their people, they should redesign jobs to allow employees to perform more and varied tasks. Much of the current interest in enriching jobs and improving the quality of work life can be traced to Herzberg's research.

J. Richard Hackman and Greg Oldham

While Herzberg's conclusions were greeted with enthusiasm, the methodology he used for arriving at those conclusions was far less enthusiastically embraced. It would be the work of J. Richard

Hackman and Greg Oldham in the 1970s that would provide an explanation of how job factors influence employee motivation and satisfaction, and would offer a valid framework for analysing jobs.[23] Hackman and Oldham's research also uncovered the core job dimensions—skill variety, task identity, task significance, autonomy and feedback—that have stood up well as guides in the design of jobs. More specifically, Hackman and Oldham found that among individuals with strong growth needs, jobs that score high on these five core dimensions lead to high employee performance and satisfaction.

OB TODAY: A CONTINGENCY PERSPECTIVE

We have demonstrated in this appendix that the present state of OB encompasses ideas introduced many, and sometimes hundreds of, years ago. So, don't think of one era's concepts as *replacing* an earlier era's; rather, view them as *extensions* and *modifications* of earlier ideas. Many of Taylor's scientific management principles, for example, can be applied today with impressive results.

This doesn't mean that those principles work as well in other organisations. If there is anything we have learned since the 1970s, it is that few ideas—no matter how attractive—are applicable to *all* organisations or to *all* jobs or to *all* types of employees. Today, OB must be studied and applied in a contingency framework.

Cricket fans know that a batter doesn't *always* try for a six. It depends on the score, the time in the match, and similar contingency variables. Similarly, you can't say that students always learn more in small classes than in large ones. An extensive body of research tells us that *contingency* factors such as course content and the teaching style of the lecturer influence the relationship between class size and learning effectiveness. Applied to OB, contingency theory recognises that there is no 'one best way' to manage people in organisations and no single set of simple principles that can be applied universally.[24]

A contingency approach to the study of OB is intuitively logical. Why? Because organisations obviously differ in size, objectives and environmental uncertainty. Similarly, employees differ in values, attitudes, needs and experiences. So, it would be surprising to find that there are universally applicable principles that work in *all* situations. But, of course, it's one thing to say 'it all depends' and another to say *what* it all depends upon.

The most popular OB topics for research investigation in recent years have been theories of motivation, leadership, job design and job satisfaction. The 1960s and 1970s saw the development of new theories, and in the present the emphasis has been on refining existing theories, clarifying previous assumptions and identifying relevant contingency variables. That is, researchers have been trying to identify the 'what' variables and which of those variables are relevant for understanding various behavioural phenomena. This essentially reflects the maturing of OB as a scientific discipline. The near-term future of OB research is likely to continue to focus on fine-tuning current theories so as to better help us understand those situations where they are most likely to be useful.

SUMMARY

While the seeds of organisational behaviour were planted more than 200 years ago, current OB theory and practice are essentially products of the 20th century.

Frederick Taylor's principles of scientific management were instrumental in engineering precision and standardisation into people's jobs. Henri Fayol defined the universal functions that all managers perform and the principles that constitute good management practice. Max Weber developed a theory of authority structures and described organisational activity based on authority relations.

The 'people side' of organisations came into its own in the 1930s, predominantly as a result of the Hawthorne studies. These studies led to a new emphasis on the human factor in organisations and increased paternalism by management. In the late 1950s, managers' attention was caught by the ideas of people such as Abraham Maslow and Douglas McGregor, who proposed that organisation structures and management practices had to be altered so as to bring out the full productive potential of employees. Motivation and leadership theories offered by David McClelland, Fred Fiedler, Frederick Herzberg and other behavioural scientists during the 1960s and 1970s provided managers with still greater insights into employee behaviour.

Most contemporary management and OB concepts are contingency-based. That is, they provide various recommendations dependent upon situational factors. As a maturing discipline, current OB research is emphasising the refinement of existing theories.

NOTES

1. See, for example, D. A. Wren, *The Evolution of Management Thought*, 4th ed. (New York: John Wiley & Sons, 1994), especially Chapters 13–18.

2. A. Smith, *An Inquiry into the Nature and Causes of the Wealth of Nations* (New York: Modern Library, 1937; orig. pub. 1776).

3. C. Babbage, *On the Economy of Machinery and Manufactures* (London: Charles Knight, 1832).

4. R. A. Owen, *A New View of Society* (New York: E. Bliss & White, 1825).

5. F. W. Taylor, *Principles of Scientific Management* (New York: Harper & Brothers, 1911).

6. Ibid, p. 44.

7. H. Fayol, *Industrial and General Administration* (Paris: Dunod, 1916).

8. M. Weber, *The Theory of Social and Economic Organizations*, ed. T. Parson, trans. A. M. Henderson and T. Parsons (New York: Free Press, 1947).

9. Wren, *The Evolution of Management Thought*, Chapter 14.

10. See, for example, M. P. Follett, *The New State: Group Organization the Solution of Popular Government* (London: Longmans, Green & Co., 1918). See also the review forum on Mary Parker Follett in *Organization*, February 1996, pp. 147–80.

11. C. I. Barnard, *The Functions of the Executive* (Cambridge, MA: Harvard University Press, 1938).

12. H. Münsterberg, *Psychology and Industrial Efficiency* (Boston: Houghton Mifflin, 1913).

13. E. Mayo, *The Human Problems of an Industrial Civilization* (New York: Macmillan, 1933); and F. J. Roethlisberger and W. J. Dickson, *Management and the Worker* (Cambridge, MA: Harvard University Press, 1939).

14. See, for example, A. Carey, 'The Hawthorne Studies: A Radical Criticism', *American Sociological Review*, June 1967, pp. 403–16; R. H. Franke and J. Kaul, 'The Hawthorne Experiments: First Statistical Interpretations', *American Sociological Review*, October 1978, pp. 623–43; B. Rice, 'The Hawthorne Defect: Persistence of a Flawed Theory', *Psychology Today*, February 1982, pp. 70–74; J. A. Sonnenfeld, 'Shedding Light on the Hawthorne Studies', *Journal of Occupational Behavior*, April 1985, pp. 111–30; and S. R. G. Jones, 'Was There a Hawthorne Effect?', *American Journal of Sociology*, November 1992, pp. 451–68.

15. D. Carnegie, *How to Win Friends and Influence People* (New York: Simon & Schuster, 1936).

16. Wren, *The Evolution of Management Thought*, p. 336.

17. A. Maslow, *Motivation and Personality* (New York: Harper & Row, 1954).

18. D. McGregor, *The Human Side of Enterprise* (New York: McGraw-Hill, 1960).

19. See, for example, B. F. Skinner, *Science and Human Behavior* (New York: Free Press, 1953); and B. F. Skinner, *Beyond Freedom and Dignity* (New York: Knopf, 1972).

20. D. C. McClelland, *The Achieving Society* (New York: Van Nostrand Reinhold, 1961); and D. C. McClelland and D. G. Winter, *Motivating Economic Achievement* (New York: Free Press, 1969).

21. F. E. Fiedler, *A Theory of Leadership Effectiveness* (New York: McGraw-Hill, 1967).

22. F. Herzberg, B. Mausner and B. Snyderman, *The Motivation to Work* (New York: John Wiley, 1959); and F. Herzberg, *The Managerial Choice: To Be Efficient or To Be Human*, rev. ed. (Salt Lake City, UT: Olympus, 1982).

23. J. R. Hackman and G. R. Oldham, 'Development of the Job Diagnostic Survey', *Journal of Applied Psychology*, April 1975, pp. 159–70.

24. See, for example, J. M. Shepard and J. G. Hougland, Jr, 'Contingency Theory: "Complex Man" or "Complex Organization"?', *Academy of Management Review*, July 1978, pp. 413–27; and H. L. Tosi, Jr and J. W. Slocum, Jr, 'Contingency Theory: Some Suggested Directions', *Journal of Management*, Spring 1984, pp. 9–26.

Appendix B Research in Organisational Behaviour

Some years back, a friend of one of the authors was excited because he had read about the findings from a research study that finally, once and for all, resolved the question of what it takes to make it to the top in a large corporation. Doubting that there was any simple answer to this question, but not wanting to dampen his enthusiasm, the friend was asked to tell what he had read. The answer, according to the friend, was participation in university athletics. You can imagine the scepticism that this response provoked, so the friend was asked to tell more about the study.

The study encompassed 1,700 successful senior executives at the 500 largest corporations in the United States. The researchers found that half of these executives had played university-level sports.[1] The friend, who happens to be good with statistics, maintained that since fewer than 2 per cent of all university students participate in inter-varsity athletics, the probability of this finding occurring by mere chance is less than one in 10 million! He concluded his analysis by suggesting that, based on this research, management students should be encouraged to get into shape and to become a member of one of the university sporting teams.

The friend was somewhat perturbed when it was suggested that his conclusions were likely to be flawed. These executives were all males who attended university in the 1940s and 1950s. Would his advice be meaningful to females in the 21st century? These executives also weren't your typical university students. For the most part, they had attended small, private elite universities, where a large proportion of the student body participated in inter-varsity sports. Moreover, maybe the researchers had confused the direction of causality. That is, maybe individuals with the motivation and ability to make it to the top of a large corporation are drawn to competitive activities such as university athletics.

The friend was guilty of misusing research data. Of course, he isn't alone. We are all continually bombarded with reports of experiments that link certain substances to cancer in mice, and with surveys that show changing attitudes towards sex among university students, for example. Many of these studies are carefully designed, with great caution taken to note the implications and limitations of the findings. But some studies are poorly designed, making their conclusions at best suspect, and at worst meaningless.

Rather than attempting to make you a researcher, the purpose of this appendix is to increase your awareness as a consumer of behavioural research. A knowledge of research methods will allow you to appreciate more fully the care in data collection that underlies the information and conclusions presented in this text. Moreover, an understanding of research methods will make you a more skilled evaluator of those OB studies you will encounter in business and professional journals. So, an appreciation of behavioural research is important because (1) it is the foundation upon which the theories in this text are built, and (2) it will benefit you in future years when you read reports of research and attempt to assess their value.

PURPOSE OF RESEARCH

Research is concerned with the systematic gathering of information. Its purpose is to help us in our search for the truth. While we will never find ultimate truth—in our case, that would be to know precisely how any person would behave in any organisational context—ongoing research adds to our body of OB knowledge by supporting some theories, contradicting others, and suggesting new theories to replace those that fail to gain support.

RESEARCH TERMINOLOGY

Researchers have their own vocabulary for communicating among themselves and with outsiders. The following briefly defines some of the more popular terms you are likely to encounter in behavioural science studies.[2]

Variable

A variable is any general characteristic that can be measured and that changes in either amplitude, intensity, or both. Some examples of OB variables found in this text are job satisfaction, employee productivity, work stress, ability, personality, and group norms.

Hypothesis

A tentative explanation of the relationship between two or more variables is called a hypothesis. The friend's statement that participation in university athletics leads to a top executive position in a large corporation is an example of a hypothesis. Until confirmed by empirical research, a hypothesis remains only a tentative explanation.

Dependent variable

A dependent variable is a response that is affected by an independent variable. In terms of the hypothesis, it is the variable that the researcher is interested in explaining. Referring back to our opening example, the dependent variable in the friend's hypothesis was executive succession. In organisational behaviour research, the most popular dependent variables are productivity, absenteeism, turnover, job satisfaction and organisational commitment.[3]

Independent variable

An independent variable is the presumed cause of some change in the dependent variable. Participating in university athletics was the independent variable in the friend's hypothesis. Popular independent variables studied by OB researchers include intelligence, personality, job satisfaction, experience, motivation, reinforcement patterns, leadership style, reward allocations, selection methods and organisation design.

You may have noticed we said that job satisfaction is frequently used by OB researchers as both a dependent and an independent variable. This isn't an error. It merely reflects that the label given to a variable depends on its place in the hypothesis. In the statement 'Increases in job satisfaction lead to reduced turnover', job satisfaction is an independent variable. However, in the statement 'Increases in money lead to higher job satisfaction', job satisfaction becomes a dependent variable.

Moderating variable

A moderating variable abates the effect of the independent variable on the dependent variable. It might also be thought of as the contingency variable: if X (independent variable), then Y (dependent variable) will occur, but only under conditions Z (moderating variable). To translate this into a real-life example, we might say that if we increase the amount of direct supervision in the work area (X), then there will be a change in worker productivity (Y), but this effect will be moderated by the complexity of the tasks being performed (Z).

Causality

A hypothesis, by definition, implies a relationship. That is, it implies a presumed cause and effect. This direction of cause and effect is called causality. Changes in the independent variable are assumed to cause changes in the dependent variable. However, in behavioural research, it's possible to make an incorrect assumption of causality when relationships are found. For example, early behavioural scientists found a relationship between employee satisfaction and productivity. They concluded that a happy employee was a productive employee. Follow-up research has supported the relationship but disconfirmed the direction of the arrow. The evidence more correctly suggests that high productivity leads to satisfaction, rather than the other way around.

Correlation coefficient

It's one thing to know that there is a relationship between two or more variables. It's another to know the strength of that relationship. The term *correlation coefficient* is used to indicate that strength, and is expressed as a number between –1.00 (a perfect negative relationship) and +1.00 (a perfect positive correlation).

When two variables vary directly with one another, the correlation will be expressed as a positive number. When they vary inversely—that is, one increases as the other decreases—the correlation will be expressed as a negative number. If the two variables vary independently of each other, we say that the correlation between them is zero.

For example, a researcher might survey a group of employees to determine the satisfaction of each with his or her job. Then, using company absenteeism reports, the researcher could correlate the job satisfaction scores against individual attendance records to determine whether employees who are more satisfied with their jobs have better attendance records than their counterparts who indicated lower job satisfaction. Let's suppose the researcher found a correlation coefficient between satisfaction and attendance of +0.50. Would that be a strong association? There is, unfortunately, no precise numerical cut-off separating strong and weak relationships. A standard statistical test would need to be applied to determine whether or not the relationship was a significant one.

A final point needs to be made before we move on: a correlation coefficient measures only the strength of association between two variables. A high value doesn't imply causality. The length of women's skirts and stock market prices, for example, have long been noted to be highly correlated, but one should be careful not to infer that a causal relationship between the two exists. In this instance, the high correlation is more happenstance than predictive.

Theory

The final term we introduce in this section is *theory*. Theory describes a set of systematically interrelated concepts or hypotheses that purports to explain and predict phenomena. In OB, theories are also frequently referred to as models. We use the two terms interchangeably.

There are no shortages of theories in OB. For example, we have theories to describe what motivates people, the most effective leadership styles, the best way to resolve conflicts, and how people acquire power. In some cases, we have half a dozen or more separate theories that purport to explain and predict a given phenomenon. In such cases, is one right and the others wrong? No! They tend to reflect science at work—researchers testing previous theories, modifying them, and, when appropriate, proposing new models that may prove to have higher explanatory and predictive powers. Multiple theories attempting to explain common phenomena merely attest that OB is an active discipline, still growing and evolving.

EVALUATING RESEARCH

As a potential consumer of behavioural research, you should follow the dictum of caveat emptor—let the buyer beware! In evaluating any research study, you need to ask three questions.[4]

Is it valid? Is the study actually measuring what it claims to be measuring? Employers have discarded many psychological tests in recent years because they have not been found to be valid measures of the applicants' ability to successfully do a given job. The validity issue is relevant to all research studies. So, if you find a study that links cohesive work teams with higher productivity, you want to know how each of these variables was measured and whether it is actually measuring what it is supposed to be measuring.

Is it reliable? Reliability refers to consistency of measurement. If you were to have your height measured every day with a wooden yardstick, you would get highly reliable results. On the other hand, if you were measured each day by an elastic tape measure, there would probably be considerable disparity between your height measurements from one day to the next. Your height, of course, doesn't change from day to day. The variability is due to the unreliability of the measuring device. So, if a company asked a group of its employees to complete a reliable job satisfaction questionnaire, and then to repeat the questionnaire six months later, we would expect the results to be very similar— provided nothing changed in the interim that might significantly affect employee satisfaction.

Is it generalisable? Are the results of the research study generalisable to groups of individuals other than those who participated in the original study? Be aware, for example, of the limitations that might exist in research that uses university students as subjects. Are the findings in such studies generalisable to full-time employees in real jobs? Similarly, how generalisable to the overall work population are the results from a study that assesses job stress among ten nuclear power plant engineers in the hamlet of Mahone Bay, Nova Scotia?

RESEARCH DESIGN

Doing research is an exercise in trade-offs. Richness of information typically comes with reduced generalisability. The more a researcher seeks to control for confounding variables, the less realistic his or her results are likely to be. High precision, generalisability and control almost always translate into higher costs. When researchers make choices about who they will study, where their research will be done, the methods they will use to collect data, and so on, they must make some concessions. Good research designs aren't perfect, but they do carefully reflect the questions being addressed. Keep these facts in mind as we review the strengths and weaknesses of five popular research designs: case studies, field surveys, laboratory experiments, field experiments and aggregate quantitative reviews.

Case study

You pick up a copy of Soichiro Honda's autobiography. In it he describes his impoverished childhood; his decisions to open a small garage, assemble motorcycles and eventually to build automobiles; and how this led to the creation of one of the largest and most successful corporations in the world. Or you are in a business class and the lecturer distributes a 50-page handout covering two companies: Dell Computer and Apple Computer. The handout details the two firms' histories, describes their product lines, production facilities, management philosophies and marketing strategies, and includes copies of their recent balance sheets and income statements (the US equivalents of our statement of financial position and statement of financial performance). The lecturer asks the class members to read the handout, analyse the data and determine why Dell has been more successful in recent years than Apple.

Soichiro Honda's autobiography and the Dell and Apple handouts are case studies. Drawn from real-life situations, case studies present an in-depth analysis of one setting. They are thorough descriptions, rich in details about an individual, a group or an organisation. The primary source of information in case studies is obtained through observation, occasionally backed up by interviews and a review of records and documents.

Case studies have their drawbacks. They are open to the perceptual bias and subjective interpretations of the observer. The reader of a case is captive to what the observer/case writer chooses to include and exclude. Cases also trade off generalisability for depth of information and richness of detail. Since it's always dangerous to generalise from a sample of one, case studies make it difficult to prove or reject a hypothesis. On the other hand, you can't ignore the in-depth analysis that cases often provide. They are an excellent device for initial exploratory research and for evaluating real-life problems in organisations.

Field survey

A lengthy questionnaire was created to assess the use of ethics policies, formal ethics structures, formalised activities such as ethics training, and executive involvement in ethics programs among billion-dollar corporations. The public affairs or corporate communications office of all Fortune 500 industrial firms and 500 service corporations in the United States were contacted to get the name and address of the 'officer most responsible for dealing with ethics and conduct issues' in each firm. The questionnaire, with a cover letter explaining the nature of the study, was mailed to these 1,000 officers. Of the total, 254 returned a completed questionnaire, for a response rate of just above 25 per cent. The results of the survey found, among other things, that 77 per cent had formal codes of ethics and 54 per cent had a single officer specifically assigned to deal with ethics and conduct issues.[5]

The preceding study illustrates a typical field survey. A sample of respondents (in this case, 1,000 corporate officers in the largest US publicly held corporations) was selected to represent a larger group that was under examination (billion-dollar US business firms). The respondents were then surveyed using a questionnaire or interviewed to collect data on particular characteristics (the content and structure of ethics programs and practices) of interest to the researchers. The standardisation of response items allows for data to be easily quantified, analysed and summarised, and for the researchers to make inferences from the representative sample about the larger population.

The field survey provides economies for doing research. It is less costly to sample a population than to obtain data from every member of that population. (There are, for example, more than 5,000 US business firms with sales in excess of a billion dollars; and some of these are privately held, don't release financial data to the public, and are therefore excluded from the *Fortune* list). Moreover, as the ethics study illustrates, field surveys provide an efficient way to find out how people feel about issues or how they say they behave. These data can then be easily quantified. But the field survey has a number of potential weaknesses. First, mailed questionnaires rarely obtain 100 per cent returns. Low response rates call into question whether conclusions based on respondents' answers are generalisable to non-respondents. Second, the format is better at tapping respondents' attitudes and perceptions than behaviours. Third, responses can suffer from social desirability—that is, people saying what they think the researcher wants to hear. Fourth, since field surveys are designed to focus on specific issues, they are a relatively poor means of acquiring depth of information. Finally, the quality of the generalisations is largely a factor of the population chosen. Responses from executives at Fortune 500 firms, for example, tell us nothing about small- or medium-sized firms or not-for-profit organisations. In summary, even a well-designed field survey trades off depth of information for breadth, generalisability and economic efficiencies.

Laboratory experiment

The following study is a classic example of the laboratory experiment. A researcher, Stanley Milgram, wondered how far individuals would go in following commands. If subjects were placed in the role of a teacher in a learning experiment and told by an experimenter to administer a shock to a learner each time that learner made a mistake, would the subjects follow the commands of the experimenter? Would their willingness to comply decrease as the intensity of the shock was increased?

To test these hypotheses, Milgram hired a set of subjects. Each was led to believe that the experiment was to investigate the effect of punishment on memory. Their job was to act as teachers and administer punishment whenever the learner made a mistake on the learning test.

Punishment was administered by an electric shock. The subject sat in front of a shock generator with 30 levels of shock—beginning at zero and progressing in 15-volt increments to a high of 450 volts. The demarcations of these positions ranged from 'Slight Shock' at 15 volts to 'Danger: Severe Shock' at 450 volts. To increase the realism of the experiment, the subjects received a sample shock of 45 volts and saw the learner—a pleasant, mild-mannered man about 50 years old—strapped into an 'electric chair' in an adjacent room. Of course, the learner was an actor, and the electric shocks were phoney, but the subjects didn't know this.

Taking their seat in front of the shock generator, the subject was directed to begin at the lowest shock level and to increase the shock intensity to the next level each time the learner made a mistake or failed to respond.

When the test began, the shock intensity rose rapidly because the learner made many errors. The subject got verbal feedback from the learner: At 75 volts, the learner began to grunt and moan; at 150 volts, he demanded to be released from the experiment; at 180 volts, he cried out that he could no longer stand the pain; and at 300 volts, he insisted that he be let out, yelled about his heart condition, screamed, and then failed to respond to further questions.

Most subjects protested and, fearful that they might kill the learner if the increased shocks were to bring on a heart attack, insisted they couldn't go on with their job. Hesitations or protests by the subject were met by the experimenter's statement, 'You have no choice, you must go on! Your job is to punish the learner's mistakes.' Of course, the subjects did have a choice. All they had to do was stand up and walk out.

The majority of the subjects dissented. But dissension isn't synonymous with disobedience. Sixty-two per cent of the subjects increased the shock level to the maximum of 450 volts. The average level of shock administered by the remaining 38 per cent was nearly 370 volts.[6]

In a laboratory experiment such as that conducted by Milgram, an artificial environment is created by the researcher. Then the researcher manipulates an independent variable under controlled conditions. Finally, since all other things are held equal, the researcher is able to conclude that any change in the dependent variable is due to the manipulation or change imposed on the independent variable. Note that, because of the controlled conditions, the researcher is able to imply causation between the independent and dependent variables.

The laboratory experiment trades off realism and generalisability for precision and control. It provides a high degree of control over variables and precise measurement of those variables. But findings from laboratory studies are often difficult to generalise to the real world of work. This is because the artificial laboratory rarely duplicates the intricacies and nuances of real organisations. Additionally, many laboratory experiments deal with phenomena that cannot be reproduced or applied to real-life situations.

Field experiment

The following is an example of a field experiment. The management of a large company is interested in determining the impact that a four-day work week would have on employee absenteeism. To be more specific, management wants to know if employees working four ten-hour days have lower absence rates than similar employees working the traditional five-day week of eight hours each day. Because the company is large, it has a number of manufacturing facilities that employ essentially similar workforces. Two of these are chosen for the experiment, both located in the greater Sydney area. Obviously, it wouldn't be appropriate to compare two similar-sized factories if one is in rural Tasmania and the other is in urban Singapore, because factors such as national culture, transportation and weather might be more likely to explain any differences found than changes in the number of days worked per week.

In one factory, the experiment was put into place—employees began the four-day week. At the other factory, which became the control group, no changes were made in the employees' five-day week. Absence data were gathered from the company's records at both locations for a period of 18 months. This extended time period lessened the possibility that any results would be distorted by the mere novelty of changes being implemented in the experimental plant. After 18 months, management found that absenteeism had dropped by 40 per cent at the experimental factory, and by only 6 per cent in the control factory. Because of the design of this study, management believed that the larger drop in absences at the experimental factory was due to the introduction of the compressed work week.

The field experiment is similar to the laboratory experiment, except it is conducted in a real organisation. The natural setting is more realistic than the laboratory setting, and this enhances validity but hinders control. Additionally, unless control groups are maintained, there can be a loss of control if extraneous forces intervene—for example, an employee strike, a major layoff or a corporate restructuring. Maybe the greatest concern with field studies has to do with organisational selection bias. Not all organisations are going to allow outside researchers to come in and study their employees and operations. This is especially true of organisations that have serious problems. Therefore, since most published studies in OB are done by outside researchers, the selection bias might work towards publication of studies conducted almost exclusively at successful and well-managed organisations.

Our general conclusion is that, of the four research designs we have discussed, the field experiment typically provides the most valid and generalisable findings and, except for its high cost, trades off the least to get the most.[7]

Aggregate quantitative reviews

What is the overall effect of organisational behaviour modification (OB Mod) on task performance? There have been a number of field experiments that have sought to throw light on this question. Unfortunately, the large range of effect from these various studies makes it hard to generalise.

To try to reconcile these diverse findings, two researchers reviewed all the empirical studies they could find on the impact of OB Mod on task performance over a 20-year period.[8] After discarding reports that had inadequate information, non-quantitative data, or didn't meet all the conditions associated with the principles of behavioural modification, the researchers narrowed their set to 19 studies that included data on 2,818 individuals. Using an aggregating technique called meta-analysis, the researchers were able to synthesise the studies quantitatively and conclude that the average person's task performance will rise from the 50th percentile to the 67th percentile after an OB Mod intervention.

The OB Mod–task performance review done by these researchers illustrates the use of meta-analysis, a quantitative form of literature review that enables researchers to look at validity findings from a comprehensive set of individual studies, and then apply a formula to them to determine if they consistently produced similar results.[9] If results prove to be consistent, researchers may conclude more confidently that validity is generalisable. Meta-analysis is a means for overcoming the potentially imprecise interpretations of qualitative reviews and to synthesise variations in quantitative studies. Additionally, the technique enables researchers to identify potential moderating variables between an independent and a dependent variable.

In the past 20 years, there has been a surge in the popularity of this research method. Why? It appears to offer a more objective means for doing traditional literature reviews. While the use of meta-analysis requires researchers to make a number of judgment calls, which can introduce a considerable amount of subjectivity into the process, there is no arguing that meta-analysis reviews have now become widespread in the OB literature.

ETHICS IN RESEARCH

Researchers aren't always tactful or candid with subjects when they do their studies. For example, questions in field surveys may be perceived as embarrassing by respondents or as an invasion of privacy. Also, researchers in laboratory studies have been known to deceive participants as to the true purpose of their experiment 'because they felt deception was necessary to get honest responses'.[10]

The 'learning experiments' conducted by Stanley Milgram were widely criticised by psychologists on ethical grounds. He lied to subjects, telling them his study was investigating learning, when, in fact, he was concerned with obedience. The shock machine he used was a fake. Even the 'learner' was an accomplice of Milgram's who had been trained to act as if he were hurt and in pain.

Professional associations such as the American Psychological Association, the American Sociological Association, the Academy of Management and the National Health & Medical Research Council of Australia have published formal guidelines for the conduct of research. Yet, the ethical debate continues. On one side are those who argue that strict ethical controls can damage the scientific validity of an experiment and cripple future research. Deception, for example, is often necessary to avoid contaminating results. Moreover, proponents of minimising ethical controls note that few subjects have been appreciably harmed by deceptive experiments. Even in Milgram's highly manipulative experiment, only 1.3 per cent of the subjects reported negative feelings about their experience. The other side of this debate focuses on the rights of participants. Those favouring strict ethical controls argue that no procedure should ever be emotionally or physically distressing to subjects, and that, as professionals, researchers are obliged to be completely honest with their subjects and to protect the subjects' privacy at all costs.

Now, let's take a look at a sampling of ethical questions relating to research. Do you think Milgram's experiment was unethical? Would you judge it unethical for a company to anonymously survey its employees with mail questionnaires on their intentions to quit their present job? Would your answer be any different if the company coded the survey responses to identify those who didn't reply so that they could send them follow-up questionnaires? Would it be unethical for management to hide a video camera on the production floor to study group interaction patterns (with the goal of using the data to design more effective work teams) without first telling employees that they were subjects of research?

SUMMARY

The subject of organisational behaviour is composed of a large number of theories that are research-based. Research studies, when cumulatively integrated, become theories, and theories are proposed and followed by research studies designed to validate them. The concepts that make up OB, therefore, are only as valid as the research that supports them.

The topics and issues in this text are, for the most part, largely derived from research. They represent the result of systematic information gathering, rather than merely hunch, intuition or opinion. This doesn't mean, of course, that we have all the answers to OB issues. Many require far more corroborating evidence. The generalisability of others is limited by the research methods used. But new information is being created and published at an accelerated rate. To keep up with the latest findings, we strongly encourage you to regularly review the latest research in organisational behaviour. The more academic work can be found in journals such as the *Academy of Management Journal, Academy of Management Review, Administrative Science Quarterly, Human Relations, Journal of Applied Psychology, Journal of Management, The Asia-Pacific Journal of Human Resources*, the *International Journal of Organisational Behaviour* and *Leadership Quarterly*. For more practical interpretations of OB research findings, you may want to read the *Academy of Management Executive, California Management Review, Harvard Business Review, Organizational Dynamics* and *Sloan Management Review*.

NOTES

1. J. A. Byrne, 'Executive Sweat', *Forbes*, 20 May 1985, pp. 198–200.
2. This discussion is based on material presented in E. Stone, *Research Methods in Organizational Behavior* (Santa Monica, CA: Goodyear, 1978).
3. B. M. Staw and G. R. Oldham, 'Reconsidering Our Dependent Variables: A Critique and Empirical Study', *Academy of Management Journal*, December 1978, pp. 539–59; and B. M. Staw, 'Organizational Behavior: A Review and Reformulation of the Field's Outcome Variables', in M. R. Rosenzweig and L. W. Porter (eds), *Annual Review of Psychology*, vol. 35 (Palo Alto, CA: Annual Reviews, Inc., 1984), pp. 627–66.
4. R. S. Blackburn, 'Experimental Design in Organizational Settings', in J. W. Lorsch (ed.), *Handbook of Organizational Behavior* (Englewood Cliffs, NJ: Prentice Hall, 1987), pp. 127–28.
5. G. R. Weaver, L. K. Trevino and P. L. Cochran, 'Corporate Ethics Practices in the Mid-1990's: An Empirical Study of the Fortune 1000', *Journal of Business Ethics*, February 1999, pp. 283–94.
6. S. Milgram, *Obedience to Authority* (New York: Harper & Row, 1974). For a critique of this research, see T. Blass, 'Understanding Behavior in the Milgram Obedience Experiment: The Role of Personality, Situations, and Their Interactions', *Journal of Personality and Social Psychology*, March 1991, pp. 398–413.
7. See, for example, W. N. Kaghan, A. L. Strauss, S. R. Barley, M. Y. Brannen and R. J. Thomas, 'The Practice and Uses of Field Research in the 21st Century Organization', *Journal of Management Inquiry*, March 1999, pp. 67–81.
8. A. D. Stajkovic and F. Luthans, 'A Meta-Analysis of the Effects of Organizational Behavior Modification on Task Performance, 1975–1995', *Academy of Management Journal*, October 1997, pp. 1122–49.
9. See, for example, R. A. Guzzo, S. E. Jackson and R. A. Katzell, 'Meta-Analysis Analysis', in L. L. Cummings and B. M. Staw (eds.), *Research in Organizational Behavior*, vol. 9 (Greenwich, CT: JAI Press, 1987), pp. 407–42; A. L. Beaman, 'An Empirical Comparison of Meta-Analytic and Traditional Reviews', *Personality and Social Psychology Bulletin*, June 1991, pp. 252–57; K. Zakzanis, 'The Reliability of Meta Analytic

Review', *Psychological Reports*, August 1998, pp. 215–22; and F. L. Schmidt and J. E. Hunter, 'Comparison of Three Meta-Analysis Methods Revisited: An Analysis of Johnson, Mullen, and Salas (1995)', *Journal of Applied Psychology*, February 1999, pp. 144–48.

10. For more on ethical issues in research, see T. L. Beauchamp, R. R. Faden, R. J. Wallace, Jr and L. Walters (eds), *Ethical Issues in Social Science Research* (Baltimore, MD: Johns Hopkins University Press, 1982); and D. Baumrind, 'Research Using Intentional Deception', *American Psychologist*, February 1985, pp. 165–74.

Appendix C Scoring Keys for Exercises

Exercise 1b
WHAT DO YOU KNOW ABOUT HUMAN BEHAVIOUR?

The correct answers to this exercise are as follows:

1.	T	6.	F	11.	F	16.	T
2.	F	7.	T	12.	T	17.	T
3.	F	8.	F	13.	F	18.	F
4.	F	9.	F	14.	F	19.	F
5.	F	10.	T	15.	F	20.	F

How well did you do? Most people get between 12 and 16 right. Did you beat the average?

The value of this exercise is to dramatise that some of what you 'know' about human behaviour is erroneous. The systematic study of OB will help you to sort out fact from fiction regarding the behaviour of people at work.

Exercise 13b
POWER ORIENTATION TEST

This test is designed to calculate your Machiavellianism (Mach) score. To obtain your score, add the number you have checked on questions 1, 3, 4, 5, 9 and 10. For the other four questions, reverse the numbers you have checked: 5 becomes 1, 4 is 2, 2 is 4, 1 is 5. Total your 10 numbers to find your score. The National Opinion Research Center, in the United States, which used this short form of the scale in a random sample of American adults, found that the national average was 25.

The results of research using the Mach test have found that: (1) men are generally more Machiavellian than women; (2) older adults tend to have lower Mach scores than younger adults; (3) there is no significant difference between high-Machs and low-Machs on measures of intelligence or ability; (4) Machiavellianism is not significantly related to demographic characteristics such as educational level or marital status; and (5) high-Machs tend to be in professions that emphasise the control and manipulation of individuals—for example, managers, lawyers, psychiatrists and behavioural scientists.

The lecturer can ask students to share their results and discuss them in terms of the use of the Mach test in the workplace.

Exercise 15
QUESTIONNAIRE: DO YOU LIKE WORKING FOR A BUREAUCRACY?

Give yourself one point for each statement for which you responded in the bureaucratic directions:

1.	Mostly agree	11.	Mostly agree
2.	Mostly agree	12.	Mostly disagree
3.	Mostly disagree	13.	Mostly disagree
4.	Mostly agree	14.	Mostly agree
5.	Mostly disagree	15.	Mostly disagree
6.	Mostly disagree	16.	Mostly agree
7.	Mostly agree	17.	Mostly disagree
8.	Mostly agree	18.	Mostly agree
9.	Mostly disagree	19.	Mostly agree
10.	Mostly agree	20.	Mostly disagree

A very high score (15 or over) suggests that you would enjoy working in a bureaucracy. A very low score (5 or lower) suggests that you would be frustrated by working in a bureaucracy, especially a large one.

Exercise 16
RATE YOUR CLASSROOM CULTURE

Calculate your total score by adding up the numbers you circled. Your score will fall between 14 and 70.

A high score (49 or above) describes an open, risk-taking, supportive, humanistic, team-oriented, easy-going, growth-oriented culture. A low score (35 or below) describes a closed, structured, task-oriented, individualistic, tense and stability-oriented culture. Note that differences count. So, a score of 60 is a more open culture than one that scores 50. Also, realise that one culture isn't preferable over the other. The 'right' culture depends on you and your preferences for a learning environment.

Form teams of five to seven members each. Compare your scores. How closely do they align? Discuss and resolve discrepancies. Based on your team's analysis, what type of student do you think would perform best in this class?

Skill-building Modules

I hear and I forget. I see and I remember. I do and I understand.

Confucius

This section on skill building has been added to help readers apply and use OB concepts. The 15 skills selected were chosen because of their relevance to developing competence in interpersonal skills and their linkage to one or more of the topic areas in this book.

To maximise the learning of skills, we suggest combining text content and self-assessment feedback with the skill-building modules in this section. The self-assessments are available on the website. Table SB-1 provides a matrix indicating the relevant self-assessment and skill module for Chapters 2 to 18 in your textbook.

For each of the 15 skills, we provide the following: (1) a brief interpretation of what your self-assessment results mean; (2) a review of basic skill concepts and specific behaviours associated with developing competence in the skill; (3) a short scenario designed to provide you with an opportunity to practise the behaviours associated with the skill; and (4) several reinforcement activities to give you additional opportunities to practise and learn the behaviours associated with the skill.

2 EFFECTIVE DISCIPLINING

Self-assessment interpretation

Complete the self-assessment (#26) on feedback skills. This instrument assesses how good you are at providing feedback to others.

TABLE SB-1	From knowledge to skills	
Skill-building Chapter/Topic	**Self-assessment**	**Module**
2. Individual Behaviour	Feedback Skills (#26)	Effective Disciplining
3. Values and Attitudes	Job Satisfaction (#11)	Changing Attitudes
4. Personality and Emotions	EI Score (#20)	Reading Emotions
5. Perception and Decisions	How Creative Am I? (#8)	Creative Problem-solving
6/7. Motivation	Personal Planning (#22)	Setting Goals
8/9. Groups and Teams	Leading a Team (#30)	Creating Effective Teams
10. Communication	Listening Skills (#25)	Active Listening
11. Basic Leadership	Leadership Style (#27)	Choosing a Leadership Style
12. Contemporary Leadership	Trusting? (#29)	Developing Trust
13. Power and Politics	Power Orientation (#31)	Becoming Politically Adept
14. Conflict and Negotiation	Conflict Style (#34)	Negotiating
15. Organisation Structure	Willingness to Delegate (#40)	Delegating Authority
16. Organisational Culture	Right Culture? (#42)	Reading an Organisation's Culture
17. HR Policies and Practices	Decision-making Style (#17)	Selection Interviewing
18. Organisational Change	Response to Change (#47)	Managing Resistance to Change

Strong feedback skills are an important part of disciplinary actions. If your strength/weakness ratio was 6/2 or higher, you already know a considerable amount about behaviours associated with effective disciplining.

Skills concepts and behaviours

If an employee's performance regularly isn't up to par or if an employee consistently ignores the organisation's standards and regulations, a manager may have to use discipline as a way to control behaviour. What exactly is *discipline?* It is actions taken by a manager to enforce the organisation's expectations, standards and rules. The most common types of discipline problems managers have to deal with include attendance (absenteeism, tardiness, abuse of sick leave), on-the-job behaviours (failure to meet performance goals, disobedience, failure to use safety devices, alcohol or drug abuse), and dishonesty (theft, lying to managers).

The essence of effective disciplining can be summarised by the following eight behaviours.[1]

1. *Respond immediately.* The more quickly a disciplinary action follows an offence, the more likely it is that the employee will associate the discipline with the offence rather than with you as the dispenser of the discipline. It is best to begin the disciplinary process as soon as possible after you notice a violation.
2. *Provide a warning.* You have an obligation to warn an employee before initiating disciplinary action. This means that the employee must be aware of the organisation's rules and accept its standards of behaviour. Disciplinary action is more likely to be interpreted by employees as fair when they have received a clear warning that a given violation will lead to discipline and when they know what that discipline will be.
3. *State the problem specifically.* Give the date, time, place, individuals involved, and any mitigating circumstances surrounding the violation. Be sure to define the violation in exact terms instead of just reciting company regulations or terms from a union contract. It is not the violation of the rules per se about which you want to convey concern. It is the effect that the rule violation has on the work unit's performance. Explain why the behaviour can't be continued by showing how it specifically affects the employee's job performance, the unit's effectiveness and the employee's colleagues.
4. *Allow the employee to explain their position.* Regardless of what facts you have uncovered, due process demands that you give the employee the opportunity to explain their position. From the employee's perspective, what happened? Why did it happen? What was their perception of the rules, regulations and circumstances?
5. *Keep the discussion impersonal.* Penalties should be connected with a given violation, not with the personality of the individual violator. That is, discipline should be directed at what the employee has done, not at the employee.
6. *Be consistent.* Fair treatment of employees demands that disciplinary action be consistent. If you enforce rule violations in an inconsistent manner, the rules will lose their impact, morale will decline, and employees will likely question your competence. Consistency, however, need not result in treating everyone exactly alike; doing that would ignore mitigating circumstances. It is reasonable to modify the severity of penalties to reflect the employee's past history, job performance record and the like. But the responsibility is yours to clearly justify disciplinary actions that might appear inconsistent to employees.
7. *Take progressive action.* Choose a punishment that is appropriate to the crime. Penalties should get progressively stronger if, or when, an offence is repeated. Typically, progressive disciplinary action begins with a verbal warning and then proceeds through a written reprimand, suspension, a demotion or pay cut, and finally, in the most serious cases, dismissal.
8. *Obtain agreement on change.* Disciplining should include guidance and direction for correcting the problem. Let the employee state what they plan to do in the future to ensure that the violation won't be repeated.

Practising the skill

Read through the following scenario, then practise your skill in a role-play conducted either in front of the class or in groups of two.

You are a team leader in the customer services department at Mountain View Brewery. Sandy is the newest member of your ten-person team, having been there only six weeks. Sandy came to Mountain View with good recommendations from his previous job as a customer support representative at a car dealership. However, not long after joining your team, Sandy was late in issuing an important purchasing order. When you talked to Sandy about it, you were told it was 'lost'. But you discovered it in Sandy's in-box, where it had been properly placed. Then, just last week, Sandy failed to make an immediate return call to an unhappy customer who could easily have been satisfied at that point. Instead, the customer worked himself into a rage and vented his unhappiness in a letter to the company's CEO. The latest incident with Sandy came up just yesterday. As part of your company's quality-improvement program, your team members prepare periodic reports on the service they provide to each customer and turn these reports over to an upper-management team who evaluates them. Sandy didn't meet the deadline for getting his report into this evaluation group and you received a call from one of the team members wanting to know where the report was. Because Sandy is still on probation for another six weeks, it appears that the time has come for the two of you to talk about his failure to meet expected work-performance goals.

Reinforcement activities

1. Talk with a manager at three different organisations. Ask each what guidance they have received from their organisations in disciplining employees. Have them describe specific employee discipline problems they have faced and how they have handled them.
2. Interview three of your current or past lecturers. Ask them about their approaches to discipline. How do they handle late papers, cheating, excessive absenteeism or other disciplinary problems?

3 CHANGING ATTITUDES

Self-assessment interpretation

Complete the self-assessment (#11) on job satisfaction. This instrument is designed to determine your general attitude about your job. Use the results to reflect on your attitudes towards your job and what, if anything, could be done to change your attitudes. This self-assessment will prepare you for thinking about how you might go about changing unfavourable attitudes that your employees might have.

Skill concepts and behaviours

Can you change unfavourable employee attitudes? Sometimes! It depends on who you are, the strength of the employee's attitude, the magnitude of the change, and the technique you choose to try to change the attitude.[2]

Employees are most likely to respond to change efforts made by someone who is liked, credible and convincing. If people like you, they are more apt to identify and adopt your message. Credibility implies trust, expertise and objectivity. So you are more likely to change an employee's attitude if that employee sees you as believable, knowledgeable about what you are talking about, and unbiased in your presentation. Finally, successful attitude change is enhanced when you present your arguments clearly and persuasively.

It is easier to change an employee's attitude if they aren't strongly committed to it. Conversely, the stronger the belief about the attitude, the harder it is to change it. In addition, attitudes that have been expressed publicly are more difficult to change because it requires one to admit that one has made a mistake.

It is easier to change attitudes when that change isn't very significant. To get an employee to accept a new attitude that varies greatly from their current position requires more effort. It may also threaten other deeply held attitudes and create increased dissonance.

One of the most widely used techniques for bringing about attitude change is oral persuasion. The following summarises actions you can take to be more persuasive:

1. *Use a positive, tactful tone.* Assume the person you are trying to persuade is intelligent and mature. Don't talk down to that person. Be respectful, direct, sincere and tactful.
2. *Present strong evidence to support your position.* You need to explain why what you want is important. Merely saying that a request is important or urgent isn't enough.
3. *Tailor your argument to the listener.* Effective persuasion demands flexibility. You have to select your argument for your specific listener. To whom are you talking? What are their goals, needs, interests, fears and aspirations? What are their preconceived views on this subject?
4. *Use logic.* While a logical, reasoned argument isn't guaranteed to persuade the subject, if you lack facts and reasons to support your argument, your persuasiveness will almost certainly be undermined.
5. *Use emotional appeals.* Presenting clear, rational and objective evidence in support of your view is often not enough. You should also appeal to a person's emotions. Try to reach inside the subject and understand their loves, hates, fears and frustrations. Then use that information to mould what you say and how you say it.

Practising the skill

Form into groups of two. Person A is to choose any topic that they feel strongly about and state their position on the topic in 30 words or less. Person B's task will be to attempt to change Person A's attitude on this topic. Person B will have ten minutes to make their case. When the time is up, the roles are reversed. Person B picks the topic and Person A has ten minutes to try to change Person B's attitude.

Potential topics (you can choose *either* side of a topic) include: politics, the economy, world events, social practices, or specific management issues such as organisations should require all employees to undergo regular drug testing, there is no such thing as organisational loyalty anymore, the customer is always right, and layoffs are an indication of management failures.

Reinforcement activities

1. Try to convince a friend or relative to go with you to see a movie or play that you know the subject doesn't want to see.
2. Try to convince a friend or relative to try a different brand of toothpaste.

4 READING EMOTIONS

Self-assessment interpretation

Complete the self-assessment (#20) on emotional intelligence. This instrument will provide you with insights into your EI score. The higher your EI score, the better you are at accurately reading others' emotions and feelings.

Skill concepts and behaviours

Understanding another person's felt emotions is a very difficult task. But we can learn to read others' display emotions. We do this by focusing on verbal, non-verbal and paralinguistic cues.[3]

1. *Ask about emotions.* The easiest way to find out what someone is feeling is to ask them. Saying something as simple as 'Are you OK? What's the problem?' can frequently provide you with the information to assess an individual's emotional state. But relying on a verbal response has two drawbacks. First, almost all of us conceal our emotions to some extent for privacy and to reflect social expectations. So we might be unwilling to share our true feelings. Second, even if we want to convey our feelings verbally, we may be unable to do so. Some people have

difficulty understanding their own emotions and, hence, are unable to express them verbally. So, at best, verbal responses provide only partial information.

2. *Look for non-verbal cues.* You are talking with a co-worker. Does the fact that his back is rigid, his teeth are clenched and his facial muscles are tight tell you something about his emotional state? It probably should. Facial expressions, gestures, body movements and physical distance are non-verbal cues that can provide additional insights into what a person is feeling. Facial expressions, for example, are a window into a person's feelings. Notice differences in facial features: the height of the cheeks, the raising or lowering of the brow, the turn of the mouth, the positioning of the lips and the configuration of muscles around the eyes. Even something as subtle as the distance at which someone chooses to position themself from you can convey their feelings, or lack, of intimacy, aggressiveness, repugnance or withdrawal.

3. *Look for how things are said.* A third source of information on a person's emotions is *paralanguage*. This is communication that goes beyond the specific spoken words. It includes pitch, amplitude, rate, and voice quality of speech. Paralanguage reminds us that people convey their feelings not only in *what* they say, but also in *how* they say it.

Practising the skill

Part A. Form groups of two. Each person is to spend a couple of minutes thinking of a time in the past when they were emotional about something. Examples might include being upset with a parent, sibling or friend; being excited or disappointed about an academic or athletic achievement; being angry with someone over an insult or slight; being disgusted by something someone has said or done; or being happy because of something good that happened.

Part B. Now you will conduct two role-plays. Each will be an interview. In the first, one person will play the interviewer and the other will play the job applicant. The job is for a summer management job with a large retail chain. Each role-play will last no longer than ten minutes. The interviewer is to conduct a normal job interview, except you are to continually rethink the emotional episode you envisioned in Part A. Try hard to convey this emotion while, at the same time, being professional in interviewing the job applicant.

Part C. Now reverse positions for the second role-play. The interviewer becomes the job applicant, and vice versa. The new interviewer will conduct a normal job interview, except that they will continually rethink the emotional episode chosen in Part A.

Part D. Spend ten minutes deconstructing the interview, with specific attention focused on what emotion(s) you think the other was conveying. What cues did you pick up? How accurate were you in reading those cues?

Reinforcement activities

1. Rent a DVD or video of an emotionally-laden film such as *Death of a Salesman* or *Twelve Angry Men*. Carefully watch the actors for clues to the emotions they are exhibiting. Try to determine the various emotions projected and explain how you arrived at your conclusion.
2. If you are currently working, spend a day specifically looking for emotional cues in interactions with colleagues. Did this improve communication?

5 CREATIVE PROBLEM-SOLVING

Self-assessment interpretation

Complete the self-assessment (#8) that evaluates your creativity. This instrument will determine the degree to which you display characteristics associated with a creative personality. The following will help you to tap into more of your creative talents.

Skill concepts and behaviours

The uniqueness and variety of problems that managers face demand that they be able to solve problems creatively. Creativity is partly a frame of mind. You need to expand your mind's capabilities—that is, open yourself up to new ideas. Every individual has the ability to improve their creativity, but many people simply don't try to develop that ability.

You can be more effective at solving problems creatively if you use the following ten suggestions.[4]

1. *Think of yourself as creative.* Research shows that if you think you can't be creative, you won't be. Believing in your ability to be creative is the first step in becoming more creative.

2. *Pay attention to your intuition.* Every individual has a subconscious mind that works well. Sometimes answers will come to you when you least expect them. Listen to that 'inner voice'. In fact, most creative people will keep a notepad near their bed and write down ideas when the thoughts come to them.

3. *Move away from your comfort zone.* Every individual has a comfort zone in which certainty exists. But creativity and the known often don't mix. To be creative, you need to move away from the status quo and focus your mind on something new.

4. *Determine what you want to do.* This includes such things as taking time to understand a problem before beginning to try to resolve it, getting all the facts in mind, and trying to identify the most important facts.

5. *Think outside the box.* Use analogies whenever possible. (For example, could you approach your problem like a fish out of water and look at what the fish does to cope? Or can you use the things you have to do to find your way when it's foggy to help you solve your problem?) Use different problem-solving strategies such as verbal, visual, mathematical or theatrical. Look at your problem from a different perspective or ask yourself what someone else, such as your grandmother, might do if faced with the same situation.

6. *Look for ways to do things better.* This may involve trying consciously to be original, not worrying about looking foolish, keeping an open mind, being alert to odd or puzzling facts, thinking of unconventional ways to use objects and the environment, discarding usual or habitual ways of doing things, and striving for objectivity by being as critical of your own ideas as you would those of someone else.

7. *Find several right answers.* Being creative means continuing to look for other solutions even when you think you have solved the problem. A better, more creative solution just might be found.

8. *Believe in finding a workable solution.* Like believing in yourself, you also need to believe in your ideas. If you don't think you can find a solution, you probably won't.

9. *Brainstorm with others.* Creativity isn't an isolated activity. Bouncing ideas off of others creates a synergistic effect.

10. *Turn creative ideas into action.* Coming up with creative ideas is only part of the process. Once the ideas are generated, they must be implemented. Keeping great ideas in your mind, or in notepads that no one will read, does little to expand your creative abilities.

Practising the skill

Every time the phone rings, your stomach clenches and your palms start to sweat. And it's no wonder! As sales manager for Brinkers, a machine tool parts manufacturer, you are besieged by calls from customers who are upset about late deliveries. Your boss, Carter Hererra, acts as both production manager and scheduler. Every time your sales representatives negotiate a sale, it's up to Carter to determine whether production can actually meet the delivery date the customer specifies. And Carter invariably says, 'No problem.' The good thing about this is that you make a lot of initial sales. The bad news is that production hardly ever meets the shipment dates that Carter authorises. And he doesn't seem to be all that concerned about the aftermath of late deliveries. He says, 'Our customers know they are getting outstanding quality at a great price. Just let them try to match that anywhere. It can't be done. So even if they have to wait a couple of extra days or weeks, they are still getting the best deal they can.' Somehow the customers don't see it that way. And they let you know about their unhappiness. Then it's up to you to try to soothe the relationship. You know this problem has to be taken care of, but what possible solutions are there? After all, how are you going to keep from making your manager mad or making the customers mad?

Reinforcement activities

1. Take 20 minutes to list as many medical or health-care-related jobs as you can that begin with the letter *r* (for instance, radiologist, registered nurse). If you run out of listings before the time is up, it's OK to quit early. But try to be as creative as you can.
2. List on a piece of paper some common terms that apply to both *water* and *finance*. How many were you able to come up with?

6–7 SETTING GOALS

Self-assessment interpretation

Complete the self-assessment (#22) on personal planning. This instrument is designed to get you to think about goal setting as it relates to your school and personal life. The better you are at your personal planning and goal setting, the better qualified you will be to help others.

Skill concepts and behaviours

Employees should have a clear understanding of what they are attempting to accomplish. Managers have the responsibility to see that this is done by helping employees set work goals.

You can be more effective at setting goals if you use the following eight suggestions.[5]

1. *Identify an employee's key job tasks.* Goal setting begins by defining what it is that you want your employees to accomplish. The best source for this information is each employee's job description.
2. *Establish specific and challenging goals for each key task.* Identify the level of performance expected of each employee. Specify the target towards which the employee is working.
3. *Specify the deadlines for each goal.* Putting deadlines on each goal reduces ambiguity. Deadlines, however, should not be set arbitrarily. Rather, they need to be realistic given the tasks to be completed.
4. *Allow the employee to participate actively.* When employees participate in goal setting, they are more likely to accept the goals. However, it must be sincere participation. That is, employees must perceive that you are truly seeking their input, not just going through the motions.
5. *Prioritise goals.* When you give someone more than one goal, it is important to rank the goals in order of importance. The purpose of prioritising is to encourage the employee to take action and expend effort on each goal in proportion to its importance.
6. *Rate goals for difficulty and importance.* Goal setting shouldn't encourage people to choose easy goals. Instead, goals should be rated for their difficulty and importance. When goals are rated, individuals can be given credit for trying difficult goals, even if they don't fully achieve them.
7. *Build in feedback mechanisms to assess goal progress.* Feedback lets employees know whether their level of effort is sufficient to attain the goal. Feedback should be both self-generated and supervisor-generated. Feedback should also be frequent and recurring.
8. *Link rewards to goal attainment.* It is natural for employees to ask, 'What's in it for me?' Linking rewards to the achievement of goals will help to answer that question.

Practising the skill

You worked your way through university while holding down a part-time job stacking shelves at Food Town supermarket chain. You liked working in the food industry, and when you graduated, you accepted a position with Food Town as a management trainee. Three years have passed and you have gained experience in the grocery store industry and in operating a large supermarket.

Several months ago, you received a promotion to store manager at one of the chain's locations. One of the things you have liked about Food Town is that it gives store managers a great deal of autonomy in running their stores. The company provides very general guidelines to its managers. Top management is concerned with the bottom line; for the most part, how you get there is up to you. Now that you are finally a store manager, you want to establish an MBO-type program in your store. You like the idea that everyone should have clear goals to work towards and then be evaluated against those goals.

Your store employs 70 people, although except for the managers, most work only 20 to 30 hours per week. You have six people reporting to you: an assistant manager; a weekend manager; and grocery, produce, meat and bakery managers. The only highly skilled jobs belong to the butchers, who have strict training and regulatory guidelines. Other less-skilled jobs include checkout operator, shelf stocker and maintenance.

Specifically describe how you would go about setting goals in your new position. Include examples of goals for the jobs of butcher, checkout operator and bakery manager.

Reinforcement activities

1. Set personal and academic goals you want to achieve by the end of this university term. Prioritise and rate them for difficulty.
2. Where do you want to be in five years? Do you have specific five-year goals? Establish three goals you want to achieve in five years. Make sure these goals are specific, challenging and measurable.

8–9 CREATING EFFECTIVE TEAMS

Self-assessment interpretation

Complete the self-assessment (#30) on leading a team. This instrument evaluates how well you diagnose team development and manage the various stages of that development. The higher your score, the better you are at creating effective teams.

Skill concepts and behaviours

Managers and team leaders need to be able to create effective teams. You can increase the effectiveness of your teams if you use the following nine behaviours.[6]

1. *Establish a common purpose.* An effective team needs a common purpose to which all members aspire. This purpose is a vision. It is broader than any specific goals. A common purpose provides direction, momentum and commitment for team members.
2. *Assess team strengths and weaknesses.* Team members will have different strengths and weaknesses. Knowing these strengths and weaknesses can help the team leader build on the strengths and compensate for the weaknesses.
3. *Develop specific individual goals.* Specific individual goals help lead team members to achieve higher performance. In addition, specific goals facilitate clear communication and help to maintain the focus on getting results.
4. *Get agreement on a common approach for achieving goals.* Goals are the ends a team strives to attain. Defining and agreeing on a common approach ensures that the team is unified on the *means* for achieving those ends.
5. *Encourage acceptance of responsibility for both individual and team performance.* Successful teams make members individually and jointly accountable for the team's purpose, goals and approach. Members understand what they are individually responsible for and what they are jointly responsible for.
6. *Build mutual trust among members.* When there is *trust*, team members believe in the integrity, character and ability of each other. When trust is lacking, members are unable to depend on each other. Teams that lack trust tend to be short-lived.
7. *Maintain an appropriate mix of team member skills and personalities.* Team members come to the team with different skills and personalities. To perform effectively, teams need three types of

skills. They need people with technical expertise, people with problem-solving and decision-making skills, and people with good interpersonal skills.

8. *Provide needed training and resources.* Team leaders need to make sure that their teams have both the training and the resources they need to accomplish their goals.

9. *Create opportunities for small achievements.* Building an effective team takes time. Team members have to learn to think and work as a team. New teams can't be expected to hit home runs every time they come to bat, especially at the beginning. Instead, team members should be encouraged to try for small achievements initially.

Practising the skill

You are the leader of a five-member project team that has been assigned the task of moving your engineering firm into the booming area of high-speed, inter-city rail construction. You and your team members have been researching the field, identifying specific business opportunities, negotiating alliances with equipment vendors, and evaluating high-speed rail experts and consultants from around the world. Throughout the process, Tonya, a highly qualified and respected engineer, has challenged a number of things you have said during team meetings and in the workplace. For example, at a meeting two weeks ago, you presented the team with a list of ten possible high-speed rail projects and started evaluating your organisation's ability to compete for them. Tonya contradicted virtually all your comments, questioned your statistics, and was quite pessimistic about the possibility of getting contracts on these projects. After this latest display of displeasure, two other group members, Bryan and Maggie, came to you and complained that Tonya's actions were damaging the team's effectiveness. You originally put Tonya on the team for her unique expertise and insight. You would like to find a way to reach her and get the team on the right track to its fullest potential.

Reinforcement activities

1. Interview three managers at different organisations. Ask them about their experiences in managing teams. Have each describe teams that they thought were effective and explain why they succeeded. Have each also describe teams that they thought were ineffective and give possible reasons for this.

2. Contrast a team, of which you have been a part, whose members trusted each other with another team whose members lacked trust in each other. How did these conditions develop? What were the consequences in terms of interaction patterns and performance?

10 ACTIVE LISTENING

Self-assessment interpretation

Complete the self-assessment (#25) on listening skills. The higher your score, the better listener you are.

Skill concepts and behaviours

Too many people take listening skills for granted. They confuse hearing with listening. Hearing is merely picking up sound vibrations. Listening is making sense out of what we hear; and it requires paying attention, interpreting and remembering. Active listening is hard work and requires you to 'get inside' the speaker's head in order to understand the communication from their point of view.

Eight specific behaviours are associated with active listening. You can be more effective at active listening if you use these behaviours.[7]

1. *Make eye contact.* We may listen with our ears, but others tend to judge whether we are really listening by looking at our eyes.

2. *Exhibit affirmative nods and appropriate facial expressions.* The effective active listener shows interest in what is being said through non-verbal signals.

3. *Avoid distracting actions or gestures.* When listening, don't look at your watch, shuffle papers, play with your pencil or engage in similar distractions. These actions make the speaker feel that you are bored or uninterested.

4. *Ask questions.* The critical listener analyses what they hear and asks questions. This behaviour provides clarification, ensures understanding, and assures the speaker that you are really listening.

5. *Paraphrase.* Restate *in your own words* what the speaker has said. The effective active listener uses phrases such as 'What I hear you saying is …' or 'Do you mean … ?' Paraphrasing is an excellent control device to check whether or not you are listening carefully and is also a control for accuracy of understanding.

6. *Avoid interrupting the speaker.* Let the speaker complete their thoughts before you try to respond. Don't try to second-guess where the speaker's thoughts are going.

7. *Don't over-talk.* Most of us would rather speak our own ideas than listen to what others say. Although talking might be more fun and silence might be uncomfortable, you can't talk and listen at the same time. The good active listener recognises this fact and doesn't over-talk.

8. *Make smooth transitions between the roles of speaker and listener.* In most work situations, you are continually shifting back and forth between the roles of speaker and listener. The effective active listener makes transitions smoothly from speaker to listener and back to speaker.

Practising the skill

Break into groups of two. This exercise is a debate. Person A can choose any contemporary issue. Some examples: business ethics, value of unions, stiffer university grading policies, money as a motivator. Person B then selects a position on this issue. Person A must automatically take the counter position. The debate is to proceed for eight to ten minutes, with only one catch. Before each person speaks, they must first summarise, in their own words and without notes, what the other has said. If the summary doesn't satisfy the speaker, it must be corrected until it does.

Reinforcement activities

1. In another class—preferably one with a lecture format—practise active listening. Ask questions, paraphrase, exhibit affirming non-verbal behaviours. Then ask yourself: Was this harder for me than a normal lecture? Did it affect my note taking? Did I ask more questions? Did it improve my understanding of the lecture's content? What was the lecturer's response?

2. Spend an entire day fighting your urge to talk. Listen as carefully as you can to everyone you talk to and respond as appropriately as possible in order to understand, not to make your own point. What, if anything, did you learn from this exercise?

11 CHOOSING AN EFFECTIVE LEADERSHIP STYLE

Self-assessment interpretation

Complete the self-assessment (#27) on leadership style. This instrument is designed to tap the degree to which you are task- or people-oriented. These results suggest your preferential style. But effective leadership depends on properly matching up leadership style with a situation that is congruent. By knowing your leadership tendency, you can put yourself into situations that will increase your likelihood for success.

Skill concepts and behaviours

Simply put, leadership style can be categorised as task- or people-oriented. Neither one is right for all situations. Although there are a number of situational variables that influence the choice of an effective leadership style, four variables seem most relevant:

1. *Task structure.* Structured tasks have procedures and rules that minimise ambiguity. The more structured a job is, the less need there is for a leader to provide task structure.

2. *Level of stress.* Situations differ in terms of time and performance stress. High-stress situations favour leaders with experience. Low stress favours a leader's intelligence.
3. *Level of group support.* Members of close-knit and supportive groups help each other out. They can provide both task support and relationship support. So, supportive groups make fewer demands on a leader.
4. *Follower characteristics.* Personal characteristics of followers—such as experience, ability and motivation—influence which leadership style will be most effective. Employees with extensive experience, strong abilities and high motivation don't require much task behaviour. They will be more effective with a people-oriented style. Conversely, employees with little experience, marginal abilities and low motivation will perform better when leaders exhibit task-oriented behaviour.

Practising the skill

You are a manufacturing manager in a large electronics plant.[8] The company's management is always searching for ways to increase efficiency. They recently installed new machines and set up a new, simplified work system, but to the surprise of everyone—including you—the expected increase in production wasn't realised. In fact, production has begun to drop, quality has fallen off, and the number of employee resignations has risen.

You don't think there is anything wrong with the machines. You have had reports from other companies that are using them, and they confirm your opinion. You have also had representatives from the firm that built the machines go over them, and they report that the machines are operating at peak efficiency.

You know that some aspect of the new work system must be responsible for the change, but you are getting no help from your immediate team members—four first-line supervisors who report to you and who are each in charge of a section—or your supply manager. The drop in production has been variously attributed to poor training of the operators, lack of an adequate system of financial incentives and poor morale. All of the individuals involved have deep feelings about this issue. Your team doesn't agree with you or with one another.

This morning you received a phone call from your division manager. He had just received your production figures for the past six months and was calling to express his concern. He indicated that the problem was yours to solve in any way that you think best, but that he would like to know within a week what steps you plan to take.

You share your division manager's concern with the falling productivity and know that your employees are also concerned. Using your knowledge of leadership concepts, which leadership style would you choose? Explain your reasons.

Reinforcement activities

1. Think of a group or team to which you currently belong or of which you have been a part. What type of leadership style did the leader of this group appear to exhibit? Give some specific examples of the types of leadership behaviours they used. Evaluate the leadership style. Was it appropriate for the group? Why or why not? What would you have done differently? Why?
2. Observe two sports team (either university or professional—one that you consider successful and the other unsuccessful). What leadership styles appear to be used in these team situations? Give some specific examples of the types of leadership behaviours you observe. How would you evaluate the leadership style? Was it appropriate for the team? Why or why not? To what degree do you think leadership style influenced the team's outcomes?

12 DEVELOPING TRUST

Self-assessment interpretation

Complete the self-assessment (#29) on whether others see you as trusting. The higher your score, the more you are perceived as a person who can be trusted.

Skill concepts and behaviours

Trust plays an important role in any manager's relationships with their employees. Given the importance of trust, today's managers should actively seek to develop it within their work group.

You can be more effective at developing trust among your employees if you follow these eight suggestions.[9]

1. *Practise openness.* Mistrust comes as much from what people don't know as from what they do know. Openness leads to confidence and trust. So, keep people informed, make the criteria on how decisions are made overtly clear, explain the rationale for your decisions, be candid about problems, and fully disclose relevant information.

2. *Be fair.* Before making decisions or taking actions, consider how others will perceive them in terms of objectivity and fairness. Give credit where credit is due, be objective and impartial in performance appraisals, and pay attention to equity perceptions in reward distributions.

3. *Speak your feelings.* Managers who convey only hard facts come across as cold and distant. If you share your feelings, others will see you as real and human. They will know who you are and their respect for you will increase.

4. *Tell the truth.* Being trustworthy means being credible. If honesty is critical to credibility, then you must be perceived as someone who tells the truth. Employees are more tolerant of hearing something 'they don't want to hear' than finding out that their manager lied to them.

5. *Show consistency.* People want predictability. Mistrust comes from not knowing what to expect. Take the time to think about your values and beliefs. Then let them consistently guide your decisions. When you know your central purpose, your actions will follow accordingly, and you will project a consistency that earns trust.

6. *Fulfil your promises.* Trust requires that people believe you are dependable. So, you need to ensure that you keep your word and commitments. Promises made must be promises kept.

7. *Maintain confidences.* You trust people who are discreet and on whom you can rely. So, if people make themselves vulnerable by telling you something in confidence, they need to feel assured that you won't discuss it with others or betray that confidence. If people perceive you as someone who leaks personal confidences or as someone who can't be depended on, you won't be perceived as trustworthy.

8. *Demonstrate competence.* Develop the admiration and respect of others by demonstrating technical and professional ability. Pay particular attention to developing and displaying your communication, negotiation and other interpersonal skills.

Practising the skill

You recently graduated from university with your degree in business administration. You have spent the past two summers working at Canberra Mutual Insurance (CMI), helping out on a number of different jobs while employees took their holidays. You have received and accepted an offer to join CMI full-time as supervisor of the policy renewal department.

CMI is a large insurance company. In the headquarters office alone, where you will be working, there are more than 500 employees. The company believes strongly in the personal development of its employees. This translates into a philosophy, emanating from the top executive offices, of trust and respect for all CMI employees. The company is also regularly atop most lists of 'best companies to work for', largely due to its progressive work/life programs and strong commitment to minimising layoffs.

In your new job, you will direct the activities of 18 policy-renewal clerks. Their jobs require little training and are highly routine. A clerk's responsibility is to ensure that renewal notices are sent on current policies, to tabulate any changes in premiums, to advise the sales division if a policy is to be cancelled as a result of non-response to renewal notices, and to answer questions and solve problems related to renewals.

The people in your work group range in age from 19 to 62, with a median age of 25. For the most part they are high school graduates with little prior working experience. They earn between $1,850 and $2,400 a month. You will be replacing a long-time CMI employee, Jan Allison. Jan is retiring after 37 years with CMI, the past 14 spent as a policy-renewal supervisor. Because you spent a few weeks in Jan's group last summer, you are familiar with her style and are acquainted with most of the department members. But people don't know you very well and are suspicious of the fact that you are fresh out of university and have little experience in the department. And the reality is that you got this job because management wanted someone with a degree to oversee the department. Your most vocal critic is Lillian Lantz. Lillian is well into her fifties, has been a policy renewal clerk for over a dozen years, and—as the 'grand old lady' of the department—carries a lot of weight with group members. You know that it will be very hard to lead this department without Lillian's support and confidence.

Identify specific actions you will take to win the trust and support of Lillian and the rest of the department.

Reinforcement activities

1. Keep a one-week log describing ways that your daily decisions and actions encouraged people to trust you or not to trust you. What things did you do that led to trust? What things did you do that may have led to distrust? How might you have changed your behaviour so that the situations of distrust could have been situations of trust?
2. Review recent issues of a business periodical (such as *Business Review Weekly*, *Fortune*, *Forbes* or *The Australian Financial Review*) for articles in which trust (or lack of trust) may have played a role. Find two articles and describe the situation. Explain how the person(s) involved might have used skills in developing trust to handle the situation.

13 BECOMING POLITICALLY ADEPT

Self-assessment interpretation

Complete the self-assessment (#31) on power orientation. This instrument is designed to calculate your Machiavellian score. The higher your score, the more likely you are to be manipulative and persuasive. A high Machiavellian score also indicates a strong willingness to engage in political behaviours.

Skill concepts and behaviours

Forget, for a moment, the ethics of politicking and any negative impressions you might have of people who engage in organisational politics. If you want to be more politically adept in your organisation, follow these eight suggestions:[10]

1. *Frame arguments in terms of organisational goals.* Effective politicking requires camouflaging your self-interest. No matter that your objective is self-serving; all the arguments you marshal in support of it must be framed in terms of the benefits that will accrue to the organisation. People whose actions appear to blatantly further their own interests at the expense of the organisation are almost universally denounced, are likely to lose influence, and often suffer the ultimate penalty of being expelled from the organisation.
2. *Develop the right image.* If you know your organisation's culture, you understand what the organisation wants and values from its employee—in terms of dress, associates to cultivate and those to avoid, whether to appear to be a risk taker or risk-aversive, the preferred leadership style, the importance placed on getting along well with others, and so forth. Then you are equipped to project the appropriate image. Because the assessment of your performance isn't always a fully objective process, you need to pay attention to style as well as substance.
3. *Gain control of organisational resources.* The control of organisational resources that are scarce and important is a source of power. Knowledge and expertise are particularly effective resources to control. They make you more valuable to the organisation and, therefore, more likely to gain security, advancement and a receptive audience for your ideas.
4. *Make yourself appear indispensable.* Because we are dealing with appearances rather than objective facts, you can enhance your power by appearing to be indispensable. You don't really have

to be indispensable, as long as key people in the organisation believe that you are. If the organisation's prime decision makers believe there is no ready substitute for what you are giving the organisation, they are likely to go to great lengths to ensure that your desires are satisfied.

5. *Be visible.* If you have a job that brings your accomplishments to the attention of others, that's great. However, if you don't have such a job, you will want to find ways to let others in the organisation know what you are doing by highlighting successes in routine reports, having satisfied customers relay their appreciation to senior executives, being seen at social functions, being active in your professional associations, and developing powerful allies who speak positively about your accomplishments. Of course, the skilled politician actively and successfully lobbies to get the projects that will increase their visibility.

6. *Develop powerful allies.* It helps to have powerful people on your side. Cultivate contacts with potentially influential people above you, at your own level and in the lower ranks. These allies often can provide you with information that is otherwise not readily available. In addition, there will be times when decisions will be made in favour of those with the greatest support. Having powerful allies can provide you with a coalition of support if and when you need it.

7. *Avoid 'tainted' members.* In almost every organisation, there are fringe members whose status is questionable. Their performance and/or loyalty is suspect. Keep your distance from such individuals. Given the reality that effectiveness has a large subjective component, your own effectiveness might be called into question if you are perceived as being too closely associated with tainted members.

8. *Support your boss.* Your immediate future is in the hands of your current boss. Because they evaluate your performance, you will typically want to do whatever is necessary to have your boss on your side. You should make every effort to help your boss succeed, to make them look good, support them if they are under siege, and spend the time to find out the criteria they will use to assess your effectiveness. Don't undermine your boss. And don't speak negatively of them to others.

Practising the skill

You used to be the star marketing manager for Hilton Electronics Limited. But for the past year, you have been outpaced again and again by Sean, a new manager in the design department, who has been accomplishing everything expected of him and more. Meanwhile, your best efforts to do your job well have been sabotaged and undercut by Maria—your and Sean's manager. For example, prior to last year's international consumer electronics show, Maria moved $30,000 from your budget to Sean's. Despite your best efforts, your marketing team couldn't complete all the marketing materials normally developed to showcase all of your organisation's new products at this important industry show. And Maria has chipped away at your staff and budget ever since. Although you have been able to meet most of your goals with less staff and budget, Maria has continued to slice away resources from your group. Just last week, she eliminated two positions in your team of eight marketing specialists to make room for a new designer and some extra equipment for Sean. Maria is clearly taking away your resources while giving Sean whatever he wants. You think it's time to do something, or soon you won't have any team or resources left.

Reinforcement activities

1. Keep a one-week journal of your behaviour, describing incidences when you tried to influence others around you. Assess each incident. Were you successful at these attempts to influence them? Why or why not? What could you have done differently?

2. Outline a specific action plan, based on concepts in this module, that would improve your career progression in the organisation in which you currently work or an organisation in which you think you would like to be employed.

14 NEGOTIATING

Self-assessment interpretation

Complete the self-assessment (#34) on your conflict style. The results suggest your preferred style for handling conflict. You will want to use this information to work against your natural tendencies when the situation requires a different style. Because negotiation is a method for resolving conflicts, knowing your preferred conflict style will give you insights into how you might handle negotiations.

Skill concepts and behaviours

You can be more effective at negotiating if you use the following five recommended behaviours.[11]

1. *Begin with a positive overture.* Studies on negotiation show that concessions tend to be reciprocated and lead to agreements. As a result, begin bargaining with a positive overture—perhaps a small concession—and then reciprocate the other party's concessions.

2. *Address problems, not personalities.* Concentrate on the negotiation issues, not on the personal characteristics of the individual with whom you are negotiating. When negotiations get tough, avoid the tendency to attack this person. Remember, it's that person's ideas or position that you disagree with, not them personally. Separate the people from the problem, and don't personalise differences.

3. *Pay little attention to initial offers.* Treat an initial offer as merely a point of departure. Everyone must have an initial position. These initial offers tend to be extreme and idealistic. Treat them as such.

4. *Emphasise win–win solutions.* Inexperienced negotiators often assume that their gain must come at the expense of the other party. That needn't be the case. There are often win–win solutions. But assuming a zero-sum game means missed opportunities for trade-offs that could benefit both sides. So, if conditions are supportive, look for an integrative solution. Frame options in terms of the other party's interests and look for solutions that can allow this person, as well as yourself, to declare a victory.

5. *Create an open and trusting climate.* Skilled negotiators are better listeners, ask more questions, focus their arguments more directly, are less defensive, and have learned to avoid words or phrases that can irritate the person with whom they are negotiating (such as 'generous offer', 'fair price' or 'reasonable arrangement'). In other words, they are better at creating the open and trusting climate that is necessary for reaching a win–win settlement.

Practising the skill

As marketing director for Done Right, a regional home-repair chain, you have come up with a plan you believe has significant potential for future sales. Your plan involves a customer information service designed to help people make their homes more environmentally sensitive. Then, based on homeowners' assessments of their homes' environmental impact, your firm will be prepared to help them deal with problems or concerns they may uncover. You are really excited about the competitive potential of this new service. You envision pamphlets, in-store appearances by environmental experts, as well as contests for consumers and school kids. After several weeks of preparations, you make your pitch to your boss, Nick Castro. You point out how the market for environmentally sensitive products is growing, and how this growing demand represents the perfect opportunity for Done Right. Nick seems impressed by your presentation, but he has expressed one major concern. He thinks your workload is already too heavy. He doesn't see how you are going to have enough time to start this new service and still be able to look after all of your other assigned marketing duties.

Reinforcement activities

1. Negotiate with a course instructor to raise the grade on an exam or paper on which you think you should have received a higher grade.

2. The next time you purchase a relatively expensive item (for example, a car, plasma TV or jewellery), negotiate a better price and gain some concessions such as an extended warranty, smaller down-payment, maintenance services, or the like.

15 DELEGATING AUTHORITY

Self-assessment interpretation

Complete the self-assessment (#40) on willingness to delegate. This instrument taps excuses for failing to delegate and errors managers use when delegation is done improperly. The higher your score, the better your delegation skills.

Skill concepts and behaviours

Managers get things done through other people. Because there are limits to any manager's time and knowledge, effective managers need to understand how to delegate. *Delegation* is the assignment of authority to another person to carry out specific duties. It allows an employee to make decisions. Delegation shouldn't be confused with participation. In participative decision making, there is a sharing of authority. In delegation, employees make decisions on their own.

A number of actions differentiate the effective delegator from the ineffective delegator. There are five behaviours that effective delegators will use.[12]

1. *Clarify the assignment.* The place to begin is to determine *what* is to be delegated and *to whom*. You need to identify the person who is most capable of doing the task and then determine whether they have the time and motivation to do the task. Assuming you have a willing and able individual, it is your responsibility to provide clear information on what is being delegated, the results you expect, and any time or performance expectations you may have. Unless there is an overriding need to adhere to specific methods, you should delegate only the results expected. Get agreement on what is to be done and the results expected, but let the employee decide the best way to complete the task.

2. *Specify the employee's range of discretion.* Every act of delegation comes with constraints. Although you are delegating to an employee the authority to perform some task or tasks, you are not delegating unlimited authority. You are delegating authority to act on certain issues within certain parameters. You need to specify what those parameters are so that the employee knows, in no uncertain terms, the range of their discretion.

3. *Allow the employee to participate.* One of the best sources for determining how much authority will be necessary to accomplish a task is the person who will be held accountable for that task. If you allow employees to participate in determining what is delegated, how much authority is needed to get the job done, and the standards by which they will be judged, you increase employee motivation, satisfaction and accountability for performance.

4. *Inform others that delegation has occurred.* Delegation shouldn't take place in a vacuum. Not only do you and the delegatee need to know specifically what has been delegated and how much authority has been given, but anyone else who may be affected by the delegation act also needs to be informed.

5. *Establish feedback channels.* The establishment of controls to monitor the employee's progress increases the likelihood that important problems will be identified early and that the task will be completed on time and to the desired specifications. Ideally, these controls should be determined at the time of the initial assignment. Agree on a specific time for the completion of the task and then set progress dates when the employee will report back on how well they are doing and any major problems that may have arisen. These controls can be supplemented with periodic checks to ensure that authority guidelines aren't being abused, organisational policies are being followed, proper procedures are being met, and the like.

Practising the skill

You are the director of research and development for a large pharmaceutical manufacturer. You have six people who report directly to you: Sue (your assistant), Dale (laboratory manager), Todd (quality standards manager), Linda (patent coordination manager), Ruben (market coordination manager) and Marah (senior projects manager). Dale is the most senior of the five managers and is generally acknowledged as the chief candidate to replace you if you are promoted or leave.

You have received your annual instructions from the CEO to develop next year's budget for your area. The task is relatively routine but takes quite a bit of time. In the past, you have always done the annual budget yourself. But this year, because your workload is exceptionally heavy, you have decided to try something different. You are going to assign budget preparation to one of your subordinate managers. The obvious choice is Dale. Dale has been with the company longest, is highly dependable, and, as your probable successor, is most likely to gain from the experience. The budget is due on your boss's desk in eight weeks. Last year it took you about 30 to 35 hours to complete. However, you have done a budget many times before. For a novice, it might take double that amount of time.

The budget process is generally straightforward. You start with last year's budget and modify it to reflect inflation and changes in departmental objectives. All the data that Dale will need are in your files, on-line, or can be obtained from your other managers.

You have just walked over to Dale's office and informed him of your decision. He seemed enthusiastic about doing the budget, but he also has a heavy workload. He told you, 'I'm regularly coming in around 7 am and it's unusual for me to leave before 7 pm. For the past five weekends, I've even come in on Saturday mornings to get my work done. I can do my best to try to find time to do the budget.'

Specify exactly what you would say to Dale and the actions you would take if Dale agrees to do the budget.

Reinforcement activities

1. When watching a DVD or video of a classic movie that has examples of 'managers' delegating assignments, pay explicit attention to the incidence of delegation. Was delegating done effectively? What was good about the practice? How might it have been improved? Examples of movies with delegation examples include *The Godfather*, *The Firm*, *Star Trek*, *Nine-to-Five* and *Working Girl*.
2. The next time you have to do a group project for a class, pay explicit attention to how tasks are delegated. Does someone assume a leadership role? If so, note how closely the delegation process is followed. Is delegation different in project or study groups than in typical work groups?

16 READING AN ORGANISATION'S CULTURE

Self-assessment interpretation

Complete the self-assessment (#42) on identifying the right organisational culture for you. The result will suggest whether you fit better in a more formal and structured culture or a more informal and flexible one. Your success and satisfaction in an organisation will be influenced by how well its culture fits your personal preference.

Skill concepts and behaviours

The ability to read an organisation's culture can be a valuable skill. For example, if you are looking for a job, you will want to choose an employer whose culture is compatible with your values and in which you will feel comfortable. If you can accurately assess a potential employer's culture before you make your job decision, you may be able to save yourself a lot of grief and reduce the likelihood of making a poor choice. Similarly, you will undoubtedly have business transactions with numerous organisations during your professional career, such as selling a product or service, negotiating a contract, arranging a joint work project, or merely seeking out who controls certain decisions in an organisation. The ability to assess another organisation's culture can be a definite plus in successfully performing those pursuits.

You can be more effective at reading an organisation's culture if you use the following behaviours. For the sake of simplicity, we are going to look at this skill from the perspective of a job applicant. We will assume that you are interviewing for a job, although these skills are generalisable to many situations. Here is a list of things you can do to help learn about an organisation's culture.[13]

1. *Do background work.* Get the names of former employees from friends or acquaintances, and talk with them. Also talk with members of professional trade associations to which the organisation's employees belong and executive recruiters who deal with the organisation. Look for clues in stories told in annual reports and other organisational literature; and check out the organisation's website for evidence of high turnover or recent management shake-ups.

2. *Observe the physical surroundings.* Pay attention to signs, posters, pictures, photos, style of dress, length of hair, degree of openness between offices, and office furnishings and arrangements.

3. *Make notes about the people you met.* Who did you meet? How did they expect to be addressed?

4. *How would you characterise the style of the people you met?* Are they formal? Casual? Serious? Jovial? Open? Reticent about providing information?

5. *Look at the organisation's human resources manual.* Are there formal rules and regulations printed there? If so, how detailed are they? What do they cover?

6. *Ask questions of the people you meet.* The most valid and reliable information tends to come from asking the same questions of many people (to see how closely their responses align). Questions that will give you insights into organisational processes and practices might include: What is the background of the founders? What is the background of current senior managers? What are these managers' functional specialities, and were they promoted from within or hired from outside? How does the organisation integrate new employees? Is there a formal orientation program? Are there formal employee training programs and, if so, how are they structured? How does your boss define their job success? How would you define fairness in terms of reward allocations? Can you identify some people here who are on the 'fast track'? What do you think has put them on the fast track? Can you identify someone in the organisation who seems to be considered a deviant, and how has the organisation responded to this person? Can you describe a decision that someone made that was well received? Can you describe a decision that didn't work out well, and what were the consequences for that decision maker? Could you describe a crisis or critical event that has occurred recently in the organisation, and how did top management respond?

Practising the skill

After spending your first three years after graduating from university as a freelance graphic designer, you are looking at pursuing a job as an account executive at a graphic design firm. You feel that the scope of assignments and potential for technical training far exceed what you would be able to do on your own, and you are looking to expand your skills and meet a brand-new set of challenges. However, you want to make sure you 'fit' into the organisation where you are going to be spending more than eight hours every work day. What is the best way for you to find a place where you will be happy and where your style and personality will be appreciated?

Reinforcement activities

1. If you are taking more than one course, assess the culture of the various classes in which you are enrolled. How do the classroom cultures differ?

2. Do some comparisons of the atmosphere or feeling you get from various organisations. Because of the number and wide variety that you will find, it will probably be easiest for you to do this exercise using restaurants, retail stores or banks. Based on the atmosphere that you observe, what type of organisational culture do you think these organisations might have? If you can, have three employees at each organisation describe their organisation's culture.

17 SELECTION INTERVIEWING

Self-assessment interpretation

Complete the self-assessment (#17) on decision-making style. This instrument taps your preferred style—from among directive, analytic, conceptual and behavioural decision making. The selection interview is an important activity in which most managers will engage. The purpose of the interview is to gain information to help you make an effective decision. High emphasis in one decision-style category shows your dominant style. If your answers spread out over the four response categories, you show flexibility. Consider how your style influences the way you approach and conduct selection interviews.

Skill concepts and behaviours

The interview is used almost universally as part of the employee-selection process. Not many of us have ever gotten a job without having gone through one or more interviews. Interviews can be valid and reliable selection tools, but they need to be structured and well organised.

You can be an effective interviewer if you use the following seven suggestions for interviewing job candidates.[14]

1. *Review the job description and job specifications.* Prior to the interview, be sure you have reviewed pertinent information about the job. This will provide you with valuable information on which to assess the job candidate. Furthermore, knowing the relevant job requirements can help to eliminate interview bias.

2. *Prepare a structured set of questions you want to ask all job applicants.* By having a set of prepared questions, you ensure that you will get the information you want. Furthermore, by asking similar questions, you are able to better compare all candidates' answers against a common base. Choose questions that can't be answered with merely a 'yes' or a 'no'. Avoid leading questions that telegraph the desired response (such as 'Would you say you have good interpersonal skills?') and bipolar questions that require the applicant to select an answer from only two choices (such as 'Do you prefer working with people or working alone?'). Because the best predictor of future behaviour is past behaviour, the best questions tend to be those that focus on previous experiences that are relevant to the current job. Examples might include: 'What have you done in previous jobs that demonstrates your creativity?' 'On your last job, what was it that you most wanted to accomplish but didn't? Why didn't you?'

3. *Before meeting a candidate, review their application form and resume.* This will help you to create a complete picture of the candidate in terms of what is represented on the resume or application and what the job requires. You can also begin to identify areas to explore during the interview. Areas that are not clearly defined on the resume or application but that are essential to the job need to be addressed in your discussion with the candidate.

4. *Open the interview by putting the applicant at ease and by providing a brief preview of the topics to be discussed.* Interviews are stressful for job candidates. Be friendly, and open the discussion with a few simple questions or statements that can break the ice. Once the applicant is fairly relaxed, provide a brief orientation. Preview what topics will be discussed, how long the interview will take, and explain if you will be taking notes. Encourage the applicant to ask questions.

5. *Ask your questions and listen carefully to the candidate's answers.* Select follow-up questions that flow naturally from the answers given. Focus on the candidate's responses as they relate to information you need to ensure that the person meets your job requirements. For example, if you feel that the applicant's response is superficial or inadequate, seek elaboration. Encourage greater response by saying, 'Tell me more about that issue.' To clarify information, you could say, 'You said working overtime was OK *sometimes*. Can you tell me specifically when you would be willing to work overtime?' If the applicant doesn't directly answer your question, follow up by repeating or paraphrasing the question. Also, never underestimate the power of silence in an interview. Inexperienced interviewers often talk too much. So, pause for at least a few

seconds after the applicant appears to have finished an answer. Your silence encourages the applicant to continue talking.

6. *Close the interview by telling the applicant what is going to happen next.* Applicants are anxious about the status of your hiring decision. Be up front with candidates regarding others who will be interviewed and the remaining steps in the hiring process. Let the person know your time frame for making a decision. In addition, tell the applicant how you will notify them about your decision.

7. *Write your evaluation of the applicant while the interview is still fresh in your mind.* Don't wait until the end of the day, after interviewing several people, to write your analysis of each person. The sooner you write your impressions after an interview, the better chance you have of accurately noting what occurred in the interview and your perceptions of the candidate.

Practising the skill

1. Form groups of three.
2. Take up to ten minutes to compose five challenging job interview questions that you think would be relevant in the hiring of new university graduates for a sales-management training program at Procter & Gamble. Each new hire will spend 18 to 24 months as a sales representative, calling on retail grocery accounts. After this training period, successful performers can be expected to be promoted to the position of district sales supervisor.
3. Exchange your five questions with another group.
4. Each group should allocate one of the following roles to their three members: interviewer, applicant and observer. The person playing the applicant should rough out a brief resume of their background and experience and give it to the interviewer.
5. Role-play a job interview. The interviewer should include, but not be limited to, the five questions provided by the other group.
6. After the interview, the observer should evaluate the interviewer's behaviours in terms of the previously described skill concepts.

Reinforcement activities

1. Talk to friends who have recently experienced a job interview. Find out what kinds of questions they were asked, how they responded, and what, if anything, they learned from the experience.
2. Interview a manager about the interview process they use in hiring new employees. What types of information does the manager try to get during an interview? (Be sure that, as you interview this manager, you are using the suggestions for good interviewing! Although you are not 'hiring' this person, you are looking for information, which is exactly what managers are looking for during a job interview.)

18 MANAGING RESISTANCE TO CHANGE

Self-assessment interpretation

Complete the self-assessment (#47) on how well you respond to turbulent change. The higher your score, the more comfortable you are with change. Not all people, of course, handle change well. Use your score to understand the type of changes that may intimidate people.

Skill concepts and behaviours

Managers play an important role in organisational change, often serving as change agents. However, managers may find that change is resisted by employees. After all, change represents ambiguity and uncertainty, or it threatens the status quo. How can this resistance to change be effectively managed?

You can be more effective at managing resistance to change if you use the following suggestions.[15]

1. *Assess the climate for change.* A major factor why some changes succeed and others fail is the readiness for change. Assessing the climate for change involves asking a number of questions. The more affirmative answers you get to the following questions, the more likely it is that change efforts will succeed.

    Is the sponsor of the change high up enough to have power to deal effectively with resistance? Is senior management supportive of the change and committed to it? Is there a strong sense of urgency from senior management about the need for change, and is this feeling shared by the rest of the organisation? Do managers have a clear vision of how the future will look different from the present? Are there objective measures in place to evaluate the change effort, and have reward systems been explicitly designed to reinforce them? Is the specific change effort consistent with other changes going on within the organisation? Are functional managers willing to sacrifice their self-interests for the good of the organisation as a whole? Does management pride itself on closely monitoring changes and actions taken by competitors? Are managers and employees rewarded for taking risks, being innovative, and looking for new and better solutions? Is the organisational structure flexible? Does communication flow both down *and* up in the organisation? Has the organisation successfully implemented major changes in the recent past? Is employee satisfaction and trust in management high? Is there a high degree of interaction and cooperation between organisational work units? Are decisions made quickly, and do decisions take into account a wide variety of suggestions?

2. *Choose an appropriate approach for managing the resistance to change.* There are six tactics that have been suggested for dealing with resistance to change. Each is designed to be appropriate for different conditions of resistance. These include *education and communication* (used when resistance comes from lack of information or inaccurate information), *participation* (used when resistance stems from people not having all the information they need or when they have the power to resist), *facilitation and support* (used when those with power will lose out in a change), *manipulation and co-optation* (used when any other tactic won't work or is too expensive) and *coercion* (used when speed is essential and change agents possess considerable power). Which one or more of these approaches will be effective depends on the source of the resistance to the change.

3. *During the time the change is being implemented and after the change is completed, communicate with employees regarding what support you may be able to provide.* Your employees need to know that you are there to support them during change efforts. Be prepared to offer the assistance that may be necessary to help your employees enact the change.

Practising the skill

You are the nursing supervisor at a community hospital employing both emergency room and floor nurses. Each of these teams of nurses tends to work almost exclusively with others doing the same job. In your professional reading, you have come across the concept of cross-training nursing teams and giving them more varied responsibilities, which in turn has been shown to improve patient care while at the same time lowering costs. You call the two team leaders, Sue and Scott, into your office to explain that you want the nursing teams to move to this approach. To your surprise, they are both opposed to the idea. Sue says she and the other emergency room nurses feel they are needed in the ER, where they fill the most vital role in the hospital. They work special hours when needed, do whatever tasks are required, and often work in difficult and stressful circumstances. They think the floor nurses have relatively easy jobs for the pay they receive. Scott, leader of the floor nurse team, tells you that his group believes the ER nurses lack the special training and extra experience that the floor nurses bring to the hospital. The floor nurses claim they have the heaviest responsibilities and do the most exacting work. Because they have ongoing contact with patients and families, they believe they shouldn't be called away from vital floor duties to help the ER nurses complete their tasks.

Reinforcement activities

1. Think about changes (major and minor) that you have dealt with over the past year. Perhaps these changes involved other people, and perhaps they were personal. Did you resist the change? Did others resist the change? How did you overcome your resistance, or the resistance of others, to the change?
2. Interview managers at three different organisations about changes they have implemented. What was their experience in implementing the changes? How did they manage resistance to the changes?

NOTES

1. Based on A. Belohlav, *The Art of Disciplining Your Employees* (Upper Saddle River, NJ: Prentice Hall, 1985); R. H. Lussier, 'A Discipline Model for Increasing Performance', *Supervisory Management*, August 1990, pp. 6–7; and J. J. Martocchio and T. A. Judge, 'When We Don't See Eye to Eye: Discrepancies between Supervisors and Subordinates in Absence Disciplinary Decisions', *Journal of Management*, vol. 21, no. 5, 1995, pp. 251–78.

2. Based on A. Bednar and W. H. Levie, 'Attitude-Change Principles', in C. Fleming and W. H. Levie, *Instructional Message Design: Principles from the Behavioral and Cognitive Sciences*, 2nd ed. (Upper Saddle River, NJ: Educational Technology Publications, 1993); and S. P. Robbins and P. L. Hunsaker, *Training in InterPersonal Skills*, 2nd ed. (Upper Saddle River, NJ: Prentice Hall, 1996), pp. 110–16.

3. Based on V. P. Richmond, J. C. McCroskey and S. K. Payne, *Nonverbal Behavior in Interpersonal Relations*, 2nd ed. (Englewood Cliffs, NJ: Prentice Hall, 1991), pp. 117–38; and L. A. King, 'Ambivalence over Emotional Expression and Reading Emotions in Situations and Faces', *Journal of Personality and Social Psychology*, March 1998, pp. 753–62.

4. Based on J. Calano and J. Salzman, 'Ten Ways to Fire Up Your Creativity', *Working Woman*, July 1989, p. 94; J. V. Anderson, 'Mind Mapping: A Tool for Creative Thinking', *Business Horizons*, January–February 1993, pp. 42–46; M. Loeb, 'Ten Commandments for Managing Creative People', *Fortune*, 16 January 1995, pp. 135–36; and M. Henricks, 'Good Thinking', *Entrepreneur*, May 1996, pp. 70–73.

5. Based on Robbins and Hunsaker, *Training in InterPersonal Skills*, pp. 54–57.

6. Ibid, pp. 200–07.

7. Ibid, pp. 36–39.

8. Based on V. H. Vroom, 'A New Look at Managerial Decision Making', *Organizational Dynamics*, Spring 1973, pp. 66–80. With permission.

9. Based on F. Bartolome, 'Nobody Trusts the Boss Completely—Now What?', *Harvard Business Review*, March–April 1989, pp. 135–42; and J. K. Butler, Jr, 'Toward Understanding and Measuring Conditions of Trust: Evolution of a Condition of Trust Inventory', *Journal of Management*, September 1991, pp. 643–63.

10. Based on H. Mintzberg, *Power In and Around Organizations* (Upper Saddle River, NJ: Prentice Hall, 1983), p. 24; and Robbins and Hunsaker, *Training in InterPersonal Skills*, pp. 131–34.

11. Based on J. A. Wall, Jr and M. W. Blum, 'Negotiations', *Journal of Management*, June 1991, pp. 278–82; and J. S. Pouliot, 'Eight Steps to Success in Negotiating', *Nation's Business*, April 1999, pp. 40–42.

12. Based on Robbins and Hunsaker, *Training in InterPersonal Skills*, pp. 93–95.

13. Based on A. L. Wilkins, 'The Culture Audit: A Tool for Understanding Organizations', *Organizational Dynamics*, Autumn 1983, pp. 24–38; H. M. Trice and J. M. Beyer, *The Culture of Work Organizations* (Upper Saddle River, NJ: Prentice Hall, 1993), pp. 358–62; H. Lancaster, 'To Avoid a Job Failure, Learn the Culture of a Company First', *Wall Street Journal*, 14 July 1998, p. B1; and D. M. Cable, L. Aiman-Smith, P. W. Mulvey and J. R. Edwards, 'The Sources and Accuracy of Job Applicants' Beliefs about Organizational Culture', *Academy of Management Journal*, December 2000, pp. 1076–85.

14. Based on W. C. Donaghy, *The Interview: Skills and Applications* (Glenview, IL: Scott, Foresman, 1984), pp. 245–80; J. M. Jenks and B. L. P. Zevnik, 'ABCs of Job Interviewing', *Harvard Business Review*, July–August 1989, pp. 38–42; and E. D. Pulakos and N. Schmitt, 'Experience-Based and Situational Interview Questions: Studies of Validity', *Personnel Psychology*, Summer 1995, pp. 289–308.

15. Based on J. P. Kotter and L. A. Schlesinger, 'Choosing Strategies for Change', *Harvard Business Review*, March–April 1979, pp. 106–14; and T. A. Stewart, 'Rate Your Readiness to Change', *Fortune*, 7 February 1994, pp. 106–10.

Glossary

Note: Number in brackets denotes the chapter in which the term appears.

ability (2) An individual's capacity to perform the various tasks in a job.

absenteeism (1) The failure to report to work.

accommodating (14) The willingness of one party in a conflict to place the opponent's interests above their own.

action research (18) A change process based on systematic collection of data and then selection of a change action based on what the analysed data indicate.

adjourning stage (8) The final stage in group development for temporary groups, characterised by concern with wrapping up activities rather than task performance.

affect (4) A broad range of feelings that people experience.

affective component of an attitude (3) The emotional or feeling segment of an attitude.

agreeableness (4) A personality dimension that describes someone who is good-natured, cooperative and trusting.

animism (16) Belief in souls of people, spirits of the dead and ancestors, and spirits in inanimate objects.

anthropology (1) The study of societies to learn about human beings and their activities.

appreciative inquiry (18) Seeks to identify the unique qualities and special strengths of an organisation, which can then be built on to improve performance.

arbitrator (14) A third party to a negotiation who has the authority to dictate an agreement.

assessment centres (17) A set of performance-simulation tests designed to evaluate a candidate's managerial potential.

attitude surveys (3) Eliciting responses from employees through questionnaires about how they feel about their jobs, work groups, supervisors and the organisation.

attitudes (3) Evaluative statements or judgments concerning objects, people or events (*see also* **attitude surveys**).

attribution theory (5) When individuals observe behaviour, they attempt to determine whether it is internally or externally caused.

attribution theory of leadership (12) The idea that leadership is merely an attribution that people make about other individuals.

authority (15) The rights inherent in a managerial position to give orders and to expect the orders to be obeyed.

availability heuristic (5) The tendency for people to base their judgments on information that is readily available to them.

avoiding (14) The desire to withdraw from or suppress a conflict.

BATNA (14) The best alternative to a negotiated agreement; the lowest acceptable value to an individual for a negotiated agreement.

behavioural component of an attitude (3) An intention to behave in a certain way towards someone or something.

behavioural theories of leadership (11) Theories proposing that specific behaviours differentiate leaders from non-leaders.

behaviourally anchored rating scales (BARS) (17) Scales that combine the main elements from the critical incident and graphic rating scale approaches: the appraiser rates the employees based on items along a continuum, but the points are examples of actual behaviour on the given job, rather than general descriptions or traits.

biographical characteristics (2) Personal characteristics—such as age, gender and marital status—that are objective and easily obtained from personnel records.

board representative (7) A form of representative participation; employees sit on a company's board of directors and represent the interests of the firm's employees.

boundaryless organisation (15) An organisation that seeks to eliminate the chain of command, have limitless spans of control, and replace departments with empowered teams.

bounded rationality (5) Individuals make decisions by constructing simplified models that extract the essential features from problems without capturing all their complexity.

brainstorming (8) An idea-generation process that specifically encourages any and all alternatives, while withholding any criticism of those alternatives.

Buddhism (16) Philosophy of living involving prayer, meditation and moral living.

bureaucracy (15) A structure with highly routine operating tasks achieved through specialisation, very formalised rules and regulations, tasks that are grouped into functional departments, centralised authority, narrow spans of control, and decision making that follows the chain of command.

centralisation (15) The degree to which decision making is concentrated at a single point in the organisation.

chain of command (15) The unbroken line of authority that extends from the top of the organisation to the lowest echelon and clarifies who reports to whom.

change (18) Making things different.

change agents (18) Persons who act as catalysts and assume the responsibility for managing change activities.

channel richness (10) The amount of information that can be transmitted during a communication episode.

charismatic leadership (12) Followers make attributions of heroic or extraordinary leadership abilities when they observe certain behaviours.

charismatic power (13) An extension of referent power stemming from an individual's personality and interpersonal style.

Christianity (16) Religion based on belief in the deity and eternal life.

classical conditioning (2) A type of conditioning in which an individual responds to some stimulus that wouldn't ordinarily produce such a response.

coalition (13) An informal group bound together by the active pursuit of a single issue.

coercive power (13) A power base dependent on fear.

cognitive component of an attitude (3) The opinion or belief segment of an attitude.

cognitive dissonance (3) Any incompatibility between two or more attitudes or between behaviour and attitudes.

cognitive evaluation theory (6) Allocating extrinsic rewards for behaviour that had been previously intrinsically rewarding tends to decrease the overall level of motivation.

cognitive resource theory (11) A theory of leadership that states that stress unfavourably affects a situation and that intelligence and experience can lessen the influence of stress on the leader.

cohesiveness (8) Degree to which group members are attracted to each other and are motivated to stay in the group.

cohorts (8) Individuals who, as part of a group, hold a common attribute.

collaborating (14) A situation in which the parties to a conflict each desire to satisfy fully the concerns of all parties.

collectivism (3) A national culture attribute that describes a tight social framework in which people expect others in groups of which they are a part to look after them and protect them (*see also* **culture**).

command group (8) A group composed of the individuals who report directly to a given manager.

communication (10) The transference and understanding of meaning.

communication apprehension (10) Undue tension and anxiety about oral communication, written communication, or both.

communication process (10) The steps between a source and a receiver that result in the transference and understanding of meaning.

comparable worth (7) A doctrine that holds that jobs equal in value to an organisation should be equally compensated, whether or not the work content of those jobs is similar.

competing (14) A desire to satisfy one's interests, regardless of the impact on the other party to the conflict.

compromising (14) A situation in which each party to a conflict is willing to give up something.

conceptual skills (1) The mental ability to analyse and diagnose complex situations.

conciliator (14) A trusted third party who provides an informal communication link between the negotiator and the opponent.

conflict (14) A process that begins when one party perceives that another party has negatively affected, or is about to negatively affect, something that the first party cares about.

conflict management (14) The use of resolution and stimulation techniques to achieve the desired level of conflict.

conflict process (14) Process with five stages: potential opposition or incompatibility, cognition and personalisation, intentions, behaviour and outcomes.

conforming (8) Adjusting one's behavior to align with the norms of the group.

Confucianism (16) Philosophy of moral living, social obedience and filial piety.

conscientiousness (4) A personality dimension that describes someone who is responsible, dependable, persistent and organised.

consideration (11) The extent to which a leader is likely to have job relationships characterised by mutual trust, respect for subordinates' ideas and regard for their feelings.

constraints (18) Forces that prevent individuals from doing what they desire.

consultant (14) An impartial third party, skilled in conflict management, who attempts to facilitate creative problem solving through communication and analysis.

contingency variables (1) Situational factors: variables that moderate the relationship between two or more other variables and improve the correlation.

continuous reinforcement (2) A desired behaviour is reinforced each time it is demonstrated.

contrast effects (5) Evaluation of a person's characteristics that are affected by comparisons with other people recently encountered who rank higher or lower on the same characteristics.

controlling (1) Monitoring activities to ensure they are being accomplished as planned and correcting any significant deviations.

core values (16) The primary or dominant values that are accepted throughout the organisation.

cost-minimisation strategy (15) A strategy that emphasises tight cost controls, avoidance of unnecessary innovation or marketing expenses, and price cutting.

creativity (5) The ability to produce novel and useful ideas.

critical incidents (17) Evaluating the behaviours that are key in making the difference between executing a job effectively and executing it ineffectively.

cross-functional teams (9) Employees from about the same hierarchical level, but from different work areas, who come together to accomplish a task.

decentralisation (15) Decision discretion is pushed down to lower-level employees.

decisions (5) The choices made from among two or more alternatives.

defensive behaviours (13) Reactive and protective behaviours to avoid action, blame or change.

demands (18) The loss of something desired.

departmentalisation (15) The basis by which jobs are grouped together.

dependency (13) B's relationship to A when A possesses something that B requires.

dependent variable (1) A response that is affected by an independent variable.

deterrence-based trust (12) Trust based on fear of reprisal if the trust is violated.

development-oriented leader (11) One who values experimentation, seeks new ideas, and generates and implements change.

deviant workplace behaviour (8) Antisocial actions by organisational members that intentionally violate established norms and that result in negative consequences for the organisation, its members, or both.

displayed emotions (4) Emotions that are organisationally required and considered appropriate in a given job.

distributive bargaining (14) Negotiation that seeks to divide up a fixed amount of resources; a win–lose situation.

distributive justice (6) Perceived fairness of the amount and allocation of rewards among individuals.

dominant culture (16) Expresses the core values that are shared by a majority of the organisation's members.

double-loop learning (18) Errors are corrected by modifying the organisation's objectives, policies and standard routines.

driving forces (18) Forces that direct behaviour away from the status quo.

dysfunctional conflict (14) Conflict that hinders group performance.

effectiveness (1) Achievement of goals.

efficiency (1) The ratio of effective output to the input required to achieve it.

electronic meeting (8) A meeting in which members interact on computers, allowing for anonymity of comments and aggregation of votes.

emotional intelligence (EI) (4) An assortment of non-cognitive skills, capabilities and competencies that influence a person's ability to succeed in coping with environmental demands and pressures.

emotional labour (4) A situation in which an employee expresses organisationally desired emotions during interpersonal transactions.

emotional stability (4) A personality dimension that characterises someone as calm, self-confident and secure (positive) versus nervous, depressed and insecure (negative).

emotions (4) Intense feelings that are directed at someone or something.

employee deviance (4) Voluntary actions that violate established norms and that threaten the organisation, its members, or both.

employee involvement program (7) A participative process that uses the entire capacity of employees and is designed to encourage increased commitment to the organisation's success.

employee-oriented leader (11) Emphasising interpersonal relations; taking a personal interest in the needs of employees and accepting individual differences among members.

empowering employees (1) Putting employees in charge of what they do.

encounter stage (16) The stage in the socialisation process in which a new employee sees what the organisation is really like and confronts the possibility that expectations and reality may diverge.

environment (15) Institutions or forces outside the organisation that potentially affect the organisation's performance.

equity theory (6) Individuals compare their job inputs and outcomes with those of others and then respond to eliminate any inequities.

ERG theory (6) There are three groups of core needs: existence, relatedness and growth.

escalation of commitment (5) An increased commitment to a previous decision in spite of negative information.

ethical dilemmas (1) Situations in which individuals are required to define right and wrong conduct.

exit (3) Dissatisfaction expressed through behaviour directed towards leaving the organisation.

expectancy theory (6) The strength of a tendency to act in a certain way depends on the strength of an expectation that the act will be followed by a given outcome and on the attractiveness of that outcome to the individual.

expert power (13) Influence based on special skills or knowledge.

externals (4) Individuals who believe that what happens to them is controlled by outside forces such as luck or chance.

extroversion (4) A personality dimension describing someone who is sociable, gregarious and assertive.

felt conflict (14) Emotional involvement in a conflict creating anxiety, tension, frustration or hostility.

felt emotions (4) An individual's actual emotions.

Fiedler contingency model (11) The theory that effective groups depend on a proper match between a leader's style of interacting with subordinates and the degree to which the situation gives control and influence to the leader.

filtering (10) A sender's manipulation of information so that it will be seen more favourably by the receiver.

five-stage group development model (8) Groups go through five distinct stages: forming, storming, norming, performing and adjourning.

fixed-interval schedule (2) Rewards are spaced at uniform time intervals.

fixed-ratio schedule (2) Rewards are initiated after a fixed or constant number of responses.

flexible benefits (7) Employees tailor their benefit program to meet their personal needs by picking and choosing from a menu of benefit options.

formal group (8) A designated work group defined by the organisation's structure.

formalisation (15) The degree to which jobs within the organisation are standardised.

forming stage (8) The first stage in group development, characterised by much uncertainty.

framing (12) A way to use language to manage meaning.

friendship group (8) Those brought together because they share one or more common characteristics.

functional conflict (14) Conflict that supports the goals of the group and improves its performance.

fundamental attribution error (5) The tendency to underestimate the influence of external factors and overestimate the influence of internal factors when making judgments about the behaviour of others.

gain sharing (7) An incentive plan in which improvements in group productivity determine the total amount of money that is allocated.

goal-setting theory (6) The theory that specific and difficult goals, with feedback, lead to higher performance.

grapevine (10) The organisation's informal communication network.

graphic rating scales (17) An evaluation method in which the evaluator rates performance factors on an incremental scale.

group demography (8) The degree to which members of a group share a common demographic attribute, such as age, sex, race, educational level, or length of service in the organisation, and the impact of this attribute on turnover.

group order ranking (17) An evaluation method that places employees into a particular classification, such as quartiles.

group(s) (8) Two or more individuals, interacting and interdependent, who have come together to achieve particular objectives (*see also* **work group**).

groupshift (8) A change in decision risk between the group's decision and the individual decision that members within the group would make; can be either towards conservatism or greater risk.

groupthink (8) Phenomenon in which the norm for consensus overrides the realistic appraisal of alternative courses of action.

halo effect (5) Drawing a general impression about an individual on the basis of a single characteristic.

heuristics (5) Judgmental shortcuts in decision making.

hierarchy of needs theory (6) There is a hierarchy of five needs—physiological, safety, social, esteem and self-actualisation; as each need is substantially satisfied, the next need becomes dominant.

high-context cultures (10) Cultures that rely heavily on non-verbal and subtle situational cues in communication.

higher-order needs (6) Needs that are satisfied internally; social, esteem and self-actualisation needs.

Hinduism (16) Religion predicated on reincarnation and progression of the soul through death and rebirth.

human relations view of conflict (14) The belief that conflict is a natural and inevitable outcome in any group.

human skills (1) The ability to work with, understand and motivate other people, both individually and in groups.

hygiene factors (6) Factors—such as company policy and administration, supervision and salary—that, when adequate in a job, placate workers. When these factors are adequate, people won't be dissatisfied.

idea champions (18) Individuals who take an innovation and actively and enthusiastically promote the idea, build support, overcome resistance and ensure that the idea is implemented.

identification-based trust (12) Trust based on a mutual understanding of each other's intentions and appreciation of the other's wants and desires.

illegitimate political behaviour (13) Extreme political behaviour that violates the implied rules of the game.

imitation strategy (15) A strategy that seeks to move into new products or new markets only after their viability has already been proven.

implicit models of organisational structure (15) Perceptions that people hold regarding structural variables formed by observing things around them in an unscientific fashion.

impression management (13) The process by which individuals attempt to control the impression others form of them.

independent variable (1) The presumed cause of some change in the dependent variable.

individual ranking (17) An evaluation method that rank-orders employees from best to worst.

individualism (3) A national culture attribute describing the degree to which people prefer to act as individuals rather than a member of groups.

informal group (8) A group that is neither formally structured nor organisationally determined; appears in response to the need for social contact.

information overload (10) A condition in which information inflow exceeds an individual's processing capacity.

information power (13) Power that comes from access to and control over information.

initiating structure (11) The extent to which a leader is likely to define and structure his or her role and those of subordinates in the search for goal attainment.

innovation (18) A new idea applied to initiating or improving a product, process or service.

innovation strategy (15) A strategy that emphasises the introduction of major new products and services.

institutionalisation (16) When an organisation takes on a life of its own, apart from any of its members, and acquires immortality.

instrumental values (3) Preferable modes of behaviour or means of achieving one's terminal values.

integrative bargaining (14) Negotiation that seeks one or more settlements that can create a win–win solution.

intellectual ability (2) The capacity to do mental activities.

intentions (14) Decisions to act in a given way.

interacting groups (8) Typical groups, in which members interact with each other face-to-face.

interactionist view of conflict (14) The belief that conflict is not only a positive force in a group but that it is absolutely necessary for a group to perform effectively.

interest group (8) Those working together to attain a specific objective with which each is concerned.

intergroup development (18) OD efforts to change the attitudes, stereotypes and perceptions that groups have of each other.

intermittent reinforcement (2) A desired behaviour is reinforced often enough to make the behaviour worth repeating, but not every time it is demonstrated.

internals (4) Individuals who believe that they control what happens to them.

intuition (1) A feeling not necessarily supported by research.

intuitive decision making (5) An unconscious process created out of distilled experience.

Islam (16) Religion recognising a single deity and total subjugation of will to this deity

job analysis (17) Developing a detailed description of the tasks involved in a job, determining the relationship of a given job to other jobs, and ascertaining the knowledge, skills and abilities necessary for an employee to perform the job successfully.

job characteristics model (6) Identifies five job characteristics and their relationship to personal and work outcomes.

job description (17) A written statement of what a job holder does, how it is done and why it is done.

job design (7) The way that tasks are combined to form complete jobs.

job enrichment (7) The increase of responsibility and higher-order skills required of jobs.

job involvement (3) The degree to which a person identifies with his or her job, actively participates in it, and considers his or her performance important to self-worth.

job rotation (7) The periodic shifting of an employee from one task to another.

job satisfaction (1) An individual's general attitude towards his or her job.

job specification (17) A statement of the minimum acceptable qualifications that an employee must possess to perform a given job successfully.

knowledge management (18) A process of organising and distributing an organisation's collective wisdom so that the right information gets to the right people at the right time.

knowledge-based trust (12) Trust based on behavioural predictability that comes from a history of interaction.

leader–member exchange (LMX) theory (11) Leaders create in-groups and out-groups, and subordinates with in-group status will have higher performance ratings, less turnover and greater job satisfaction.

leader–member relations (11) The degree of confidence, trust and respect subordinates have in their leader.

leader-participation model (11) A leadership theory that provides a set of rules to determine the form and amount of participative decision making in different situations.

leadership (11) The ability to influence a group towards the achievement of goals.

leading (1) A function that includes motivating employees, directing others, selecting the most effective communication channels and resolving conflicts.

learning (2) Any relatively permanent change in behaviour that occurs as a result of experience.

learning organisation (18) An organisation that has developed the continuous capacity to adapt and change.

least preferred co-worker (LPC) questionnaire (11) An instrument that purports to measure whether a person is task- or relationship-oriented.

legitimate political behaviour (13) Normal, everyday politics.

legitimate power (13) The power a person receives as a result of their position in the formal hierarchy of an organisation.

locus of control (4) The degree to which people believe they are masters of their own fate.

long-term orientation (3) A national culture attribute that emphasises the future, thrift and persistence.

low-context cultures (10) Cultures that rely heavily on words to convey meaning in communication.

lower-order needs (6) Needs that are satisfied externally; physiological and safety needs.

loyalty (3) Dissatisfaction expressed by passively waiting for conditions to improve.

Machiavellianism (4) Degree to which an individual is pragmatic, maintains emotional distance and believes that ends can justify means.

management by objectives (MBO) (7) A program that encompasses specific goals, participatively set, for an explicit time period, with feedback on goal progress.

managerial grid (11) A nine-by-nine matrix outlining 81 different leadership styles.

managers (1) Individuals who achieve goals through other people.

matrix structure (15) A structure that creates dual lines of authority and combines functional and product departmentalisation.

McClelland's theory of needs (6) Achievement, power and affiliation are three important needs that help to explain motivation.

mechanistic model (15) A structure characterised by extensive departmentalisation, high formalisation, a limited information network and centralisation.

mediator (14) A neutral third party who facilitates a negotiated solution by using reasoning, persuasion and suggestions for alternatives.

mentor (12) A senior employee who sponsors and supports a less-experienced employee.

metamorphosis stage (16) The stage in the socialisation process in which a new employee changes and adjusts to the job, work group and organisation.

model (1) An abstraction of reality. A simplified representation of some real-world phenomenon.

moods (4) Feelings that tend to be less intense than emotions and that lack a contextual stimulus.

motivating potential score (MPS) (6) A predictive index suggesting the motivation potential in a job.

motivation (6) The processes that account for an individual's intensity, direction and persistence of effort towards attaining a goal.

multiple intelligences (2) Intelligence contains four subparts: cognitive, social, emotional and cultural.

Myers-Briggs Type Indicator (MBTI) (4) A personality test that taps four characteristics and classifies people into one of 16 personality types.

need for achievement (6) The drive to excel, to achieve in relation to a set of standards, to strive to succeed.

need for affiliation (6) The desire for friendly and close interpersonal relationships.

need for power (6) The need to make others behave in a way that they would not have behaved otherwise.

neglect (3) Dissatisfaction expressed through allowing conditions to worsen.

negotiation (14) A process in which two or more parties exchange goods or services and attempt to agree on the exchange rate for them.

nominal group technique (8) A group decision-making method in which individual members meet face-to-face to pool their judgments in a systematic but independent fashion.

norming stage (8) The third stage in group development, characterised by close relationships and cohesiveness.

norms (8) Acceptable standards of behaviour within a group that are shared by the group's members.

OB Mod (2) The application of reinforcement concepts to individuals in the work setting.

openness to experience (4) A personality dimension that characterises someone in terms of imaginativeness, artistic ability, sensitivity and intellectualism.

operant conditioning (2) A type of conditioning in which desired voluntary behaviour leads to a reward or prevents a punishment.

opportunity to perform (6) High levels of performance are partially a function of an absence of obstacles that constrain the employee.

organic model (15) A structure that is flat, uses cross-hierarchical and cross-functional teams, has low formalisation, possesses a comprehensive information network, and relies on participative decision making.

organisation (1) A consciously coordinated social unit, composed of two or more people, that functions on a relatively continuous basis to achieve a common goal or set of goals.

organisational behaviour (OB) (1) A field of study that investigates the impact that individuals, groups and structure have on behaviour within organisations, for the purpose of applying such knowledge towards improving an organisation's effectiveness.

organisational citizenship behaviour (OCB) (1) Discretionary behaviour that isn't part of an employee's formal job requirements, but that nevertheless promotes the effective functioning of the organisation.

organisational commitment (3) The degree to which an employee identifies with a particular organisation and its goals, and wishes to maintain membership in the organisation.

organisational culture (16) A system of shared meaning held by members that distinguishes the organisation from other organisations.

organisational development (OD) (18) A collection of planned-change interventions, built on humanistic–democratic values, that seeks to improve organisational effectiveness and employee well-being.

organisational structure (15) How job tasks are formally divided, grouped and coordinated.

organising (1) Determining what tasks are to be done, who is to do them, how the tasks are to be grouped, who reports to whom, and where decisions are to be made.

paired comparison (17) An evaluation method that compares each employee with every other employee and assigns a summary ranking based on the number of superior scores that the employee achieves.

participative management (7) A process in which subordinates share a significant degree of decision-making power with their immediate superiors.

path–goal theory (11) The theory that it is the leader's job to assist followers in attaining their goals and to provide the necessary direction and/or support to ensure that their goals are compatible with the overall objectives of the group or organisation.

perceived conflict (14) Awareness by one or more parties of the existence of conditions that create opportunities for conflict to arise.

perception (5) A process by which individuals organise and interpret their sensory impressions in order to give meaning to their environment.

performing stage (8) The fourth stage in group development, when the group is fully functional.

personality (4) The sum total of ways in which an individual reacts and interacts with others.

personality traits (4) Enduring characteristics that describe an individual's behaviour.

personality–job fit theory (4) Identifies six personality types and proposes that the fit between personality type and occupational environment determines satisfaction and turnover.

physical ability (2) The capacity to do tasks demanding stamina, dexterity, strength and similar characteristics.

piece-rate pay plans (7) Workers are paid a fixed sum for each unit of production completed.

planned change (18) Change activities that are intentional and goal-oriented.

planning (1) A process that includes defining goals, establishing strategy, and developing plans to coordinate activities.

political behaviour (13) Activities that are not required as part of one's formal role in the organisation, but that influence, or attempt to influence, the distribution of advantages and disadvantages within the organisation.

political science (1) The study of the behaviour of individuals and groups within a political environment.

position power (11) Influence derived from one's formal structural position in the organisation; includes power to hire, fire, discipline, promote and give salary increases.

power (13) A capacity that A has to influence the behaviour of B so that B acts in accordance with A's wishes.

power distance (3) A national culture attribute describing the extent to which a society accepts that power in institutions and organisations is distributed unequally.

power tactics (13) Ways in which individuals translate power bases into specific actions.

pre-arrival stage (16) The period of learning in the socialisation process that occurs before a new employee joins the organisation.

problem (5) A discrepancy between some current state of affairs and some desired state.

problem-solving teams (9) Groups of from five to 12 employees from the same department who meet for a few hours each week to discuss ways of improving quality, efficiency and the work environment.

procedural justice (6) Perceived fairness of the process used to determine the distribution of rewards.

process conflict (14) Conflict over how work gets done.

process consultation (18) A consultant assists a client to understand process events with which they must deal and identify processes that need improvement.

process reengineering (1) Reconsidering how work would be done and an organisation structured if it were starting over.

production-oriented leader (11) One who emphasises technical or task aspects of the job.

productivity (1) A performance measure that includes effectiveness and efficiency.

profit-sharing plans (7) Organisation-wide programs that distribute compensation based on some established formula designed around a company's profitability.

projection (5) Attributing one's own characteristics to other people.

psychological contract (8) An unwritten agreement that sets out what management expects from the employee, and vice versa.

psychology (1) The science that seeks to measure, explain and sometimes change the behaviour of humans and other animals.

punctuated-equilibrium model (8) Temporary groups go through transitions between inertia and activity.

quality circle (7) A work group of employees who meet regularly to discuss their quality problems, investigate causes, recommend solutions and take corrective actions.

quality management (QM) (1) The constant attainment of customer

satisfaction through the continuous improvement of all organisational processes.

quality of life (3) A national culture attribute that emphasises relationships and concern for others.

quantity of life (3) A national culture attribute describing the extent to which societal values are characterised by assertiveness and materialism.

rational (5) Making consistent, value-maximising choices within specified constraints.

rational decision-making model (5) A decision-making model that describes how individuals should behave in order to maximise some outcome.

reference groups (8) Important groups to which individuals belong or hope to belong and with whose norms individuals are likely to conform.

referent power (13) Influence based on possession by an individual of desirable resources or personal traits.

refreezing (18) Stabilising a change intervention by balancing driving and restraining forces.

reinforcement theory (6) Behaviour is a function of its consequences.

relationship conflict (14) Conflict based on interpersonal relationships.

representative heuristic (5) Assessing the likelihood of an occurrence by drawing analogies seeing identical situations in which they don't exist.

representative participation (7) Workers participate in organisational decision making through a small group of representative employees.

requisite task attributes theory (6) Identifies six characteristics of job complexity and the influence of the degree of job complexity on performance, satisfaction and absenteeism.

restraining forces (18) Forces that hinder movement from the existing equilibrium.

reward power (13) Compliance achieved based on the ability to distribute rewards that others view as valuable.

rituals (16) Repetitive sequences of activities that express and reinforce the key values of the organisation, which goals are most important, and which people are important and which are expendable.

role conflict (8) A situation in which an individual is confronted by divergent role expectations.

role expectations (8) How others believe a person should act in a given situation.

role identity (8) Certain attitudes and behaviours consistent with a role.

role perception (8) An individual's view of how he or she is supposed to act in a given situation.

role(s) (8) A set of expected behaviour patterns attributed to someone occupying a given position in a social unit.

selective perception (5) People selectively interpret what they see on the basis of their interests, background, experience and attitudes.

self-actualisation (6) The drive to become what one is capable of becoming.

self-efficacy (6) The individual's belief that he or she is capable of performing a task.

self-esteem (4) Individuals' degree of liking or disliking themselves.

self-fulfilling prophecy (5) A situation in which one person inaccurately perceives a second person and the resulting expectations cause the second person to behave in ways consistent with the original perception.

self-leadership (12) A set of processes through which individuals control their own behaviour.

self-managed work teams (9) Groups of from ten to 15 people who take on responsibilities of their former supervisors.

self-management (2) Learning techniques that allow individuals to manage their own behaviour so that less external management control is necessary.

self-monitoring (4) A personality trait that measures an individual's ability to adjust his or her behaviour to external, situational factors.

self-perception theory (3) Attitudes are used after the fact to make sense out of an action that has already occurred.

self-serving bias (5) The tendency for individuals to attribute their own successes to internal factors while putting the blame for failures on external factors.

sensitivity training (18) Training groups that seek to change behaviour through unstructured group interaction.

sexual harassment (13) Unwelcome advances, requests for sexual favours, and other verbal or physical conduct of a sexual nature.

shaping behaviour (2) Systematically reinforcing each successive step that moves an individual closer to the desired response.

share ownership (7) Company-established benefit plans in which employees acquire shares in the company as part of their benefits.

Shintoism (16) Mixture of ancestor worship, medical practices, shamanism and worship of nature.

short-term orientation (3) A national culture attribute that emphasises the past and present, respect for tradition and fulfilling social obligation.

simple structure (15) A structure characterised by a low degree of departmentalisation, wide spans of control, authority centralised in a single person and little formalisation.

single-loop learning (18) Errors are corrected using past routines and present policies.

situational leadership theory (SLT) (11) A contingency theory that focuses on followers' readiness.

skill-based pay plans (7) Pay levels are based on how many skills employees have or how many jobs they can do.

social facilitation effect (8) The tendency for performance to improve or decline in response to the presence of others.

social information processing (SIP) model (6) Employees adopt attitudes and behaviours in response to the social cues provided by others with whom they have contact.

social loafing (8) The tendency for individuals to expend less effort when working collectively than when working individually.

social psychology (1) An area within psychology that blends concepts from psychology and sociology and that focuses on the influence of people on one another.

socialisation (16) The process that adapts employees to the organisation's culture.

social-learning theory (2) People can learn through observation and direct experience.

sociology (1) The study of people in relation to their fellow human beings.

span of control (15) The number of subordinates a manager can efficiently and effectively direct.

status (8) A socially defined position or rank given to groups or group members by others.

stereotyping (5) Judging someone on the basis of one's perception of the group to which that person belongs.

storming stage (8) The second stage in group development, characterised by intragroup conflict.

stress (18) A dynamic condition in which an individual is confronted with an opportunity, constraint or demand related to what they desire and for which the outcome is perceived to be both uncertain and important.

strong culture (16) Culture in which the core values are intensely held and widely shared.

subcultures (16) Minicultures within an organisation, typically defined by department designations and geographical separation.

survey feedback (18) The use of questionnaires to identify discrepancies among member perceptions; discussion follows and remedies are suggested.

synergy (8) An action of two or more substances that results in an effect that is different from the individual summation of the substances.

systematic study (1) Looking at relationships, attempting to attribute causes and effects, and drawing conclusions based on scientific evidence.

Taoism (16) Philosophy of life based on ethical behaviour and the role of nature.

task conflict (14) Conflicts over content and goals of the work.

task group (8) Those working together to complete a job task.

task structure (11) The degree to which the job assignments are procedurised.

team building (18) High interaction among team members to increase trust and openness.

team structure (15) The use of teams as the central device to coordinate work activities.

technical skills (1) The ability to apply specialised knowledge or expertise.

technology (15) How an organisation transfers its inputs into outputs.

terminal values (3) Desirable end-states of existence; the goals that a person would like to achieve during his or her lifetime.

Theory X (6) The assumption that employees dislike work, are lazy, dislike responsibility and must be coerced to perform.

Theory Y (6) The assumption that employees like work, are creative, seek responsibility and can exercise self-direction.

three-component model of creativity (5) Proposition that individual creativity requires expertise, creative-thinking skills and intrinsic task motivation.

trade union (17) An organisation, made up of employees, that acts collectively to protect and promote employee interests.

traditional view of conflict (14) The belief that all conflict is harmful and must be avoided.

trait theories of leadership (11) Theories that consider personal qualities and characteristics that differentiate leaders from non-leaders.

transactional leaders (12) Leaders who guide or motivate their followers in the direction of established goals by clarifying role and task requirements.

transformational leaders (12) Leaders who inspire followers to transcend their own self-interests and who are capable of having a profound and extraordinary effect on followers.

trust (12) A positive expectation that another won't act opportunistically.

turnover (1) The voluntary and involuntary permanent withdrawal from an organisation.

two-factor theory (6) Intrinsic factors are related to job satisfaction, while extrinsic factors are associated with dissatisfaction.

Type A personality (4) Aggressive involvement in a chronic, incessant struggle to achieve more and more in less and less time and, if necessary, against the opposing efforts of other things or other people.

uncertainty avoidance (3) A national culture attribute describing the extent to which a society feels threatened by uncertain and ambiguous situations and tries to avoid them.

unfreezing (18) Change efforts to overcome the pressures of both individual resistance and group conformity.

unity of command (15) A subordinate should have only one superior to whom they are directly responsible.

utilitarianism (5) Decisions are made to provide the greatest good for the greatest number.

value system (3) A hierarchy based on a ranking of an individual's values in terms of their intensity.

values (3) Basic convictions that a specific mode of conduct or end-state of existence is personally or socially preferable to an opposite or converse mode of conduct or end-state of existence.

variable-interval schedule (2) Rewards are initiated after a fixed or constant number of responses.

variable-pay programs (7) A portion of an employee's pay is based on some individual and/or organisational measure of performance.

variable-ratio schedule (2) The reward varies relative to the behaviour of the individual.

virtual organisation (15) A small, core organisation that outsources major business functions.

virtual teams (9) Teams that use computer technology to tie together physically dispersed members in order to achieve a common goal.

visionary leadership (12) The ability to create and articulate a realistic, credible, attractive vision of the future for an organisation or organisational unit that grows out of and improves upon the present.

voice (3) Dissatisfaction expressed through active and constructive attempts to improve conditions.

wellness programs (18) Organisationally supported programs that focus on the employee's total physical and mental condition.

whistle blowers (5) Individuals who report unethical practices by their employer to outsiders.

work group (9) A group that interacts primarily to share information and to make decisions to help each group member perform within his or her area of responsibility (*see also* **group(s)**).

work sampling (17) Creating a miniature replica of a job to evaluate the performance abilities of job candidates.

work specialisation (15) The degree to which tasks in the organisation are subdivided into separate jobs.

work team (9) A group whose individual efforts result in a performance that is greater than the sum of the individual inputs.

workforce diversity (1) The concept that organisations are becoming more heterogeneous in terms of gender, race, ethnicity and inclusion of other diverse groups.

workplace spirituality (16) The recognition that people have an inner life that nourishes and is nourished by meaningful work that takes place in the context of community.

works councils (7) Groups of nominated or elected employees who must be consulted when management makes decisions involving personnel.

Zen (16) A derivative of Buddhism, involving self-contemplation and meditation to find enlightenment.

Index

Page references followed by *tab* indicate tables; those followed by *fig* indicate figures

abilities, 44–46
ability-job fit, 46
abortion, 367
absenteeism, 24–25
    effect of age, 40–41
    effect of gender, 42–43
    effect of job satisfaction, 85–86
    effect of paid sick leave, 55
Accenture, 605–606
accommodating, 433
accountability, 479
achievement need, 171–172, 189
achievement need theory, 170–172, 217
acquisitions and mergers, 505–506
action research, 576–578
Adams, J. Stacy, 182
adjourning stage, 244
administrative theory, 612
affect, 112
affective component, of attitudes, 76
affiliation, need for, 171–172
age
    effect on absenteeism, 40–41
    effect on creativity, 142
    effect on job performance, 40–41, 49
    effect on job satisfaction, 40–41
    effect on job turnover, 40–41
    effect on productivity, 40–41
    see also older workers
aggregate quantitative reviews, 626
agreeableness, 103
Airbus, 386
aircraft crashes, 326
airline industry, 577
Alderfer, Clayton, 170
Alfresco Design, 284
Allport, Gordon, 100
Allstate's Business Insurance Group, 330
Amana Refrigeration, 294
Amazon.com, 21, 228, 568
American Express, 554
AMES Consulting, 321
AMP, 21, 543
anger-management classes, 120
animism, 502
Ansett Airlines, 14, 21
anthropology, 13
AOL, 340
AOL Time Warner, 228
appreciative inquiry, 581
arbitrators, 444
Asea Brown Boveri, 370

Ashley and Munro, 329
assertiveness, 74
assessment centres, 536
AT&T, 224, 506
attitude surveys, 80–82
attitudes, 76–82
    components, 76
    consistency among, 78–79
    effect on behaviour, 79–80
    techniques for changing, 82–83
    types, 77–78
    and workforce diversity, 82
attribution theory, 133–135, 380
Aung San Suu Kyi, 367
Austar, 21
Australia Post, 522
Australian Bureau of Statistics (ABS), 222
Australian Catholic University, 554–555
Australian Prudential Regulation Authority, 479
Australian Taxation Office, 471
authority, 469
availability heuristic, 147
Avis Australia, 82
avoiding, 433
Avon, 337, 369, 581

Babbage, Charles, 609–610
baby-boomers, 70–71, 72
bargaining, 439–440
Barnard, Chester, 612, 614
Barnevik, Percy, 370
BATNA, 441
Becca Cosmetics Development Ltd, 485
behavioural approach, to OB, 614–618
behavioural component, of attitudes, 76
behavioural research
    ethical aspects, 626–627
    evaluation, 622–623
    purpose, 620
    research design, 623–626
    terminology, 620–622
behavioural science theorists, 616–618
behavioural theories of leadership, 330–343
behaviourally anchored rating scales (BARS), 547
Bell, Geoff, 567
Bezos, Jeff, 568
B.F. Goodrich Co., 615
BHP, 212, 248–249
BHP Billiton, 16, 218, 341
biases, in decision-making, 145–148, 154
Big Five model, 103–105
Blake, R.R., 342
Blanchard, Ken, 346–347
BMW, 15
board representatives, 209
body language, 311–312, 325fig

Body Shop, 519, 524
Boeing, 247, 284, 294, 477, 480
Boeing Australia, 586
Borders, 227
Bosch Australia, 321
boundaryless organisation, 479–480
bounded rationality, 143–144
brainstorming, 265–266
Branson, Richard, 339, 340, 369, 506
British Telecom, 586
Buddhism, 502
Bunnings, 4, 29
bureaucracy, 472, 474–475, 612, 613
Burger King, 15

career development, 540–541
Carnegie, Dale, 616
case studies, 623
causality, 621
centralisation, 471–472
CEOs
    and employee motivation, 187
    and leadership relevance, 379–381
    pay packages, 218, 341
Cerner Corporation, 318–319
chain of command, 469–470, 475, 491
Chambers, John, 218
change
    barriers to, 504
    coping with, 21–22
    episodic *versus* continuous, 597–598
    forces for, 568–569
    individual resistance, 570–572
    organisational resistance, 572–573
    overcoming resistance, 573–574
    planned change, 569–570
    politics of, 574–575
    value-driven, 72
change agents, 570
change management, 597
    cultural differences, 587–588
    learning organisations in, 583–586
    stimulating organisational innovation, 582–583
channel richness, 317
channels, of communication, 318
charismatic leadership, 367–370
charismatic power, 396
Charles Schwab, 596
chief executives. *see* CEOs
child care, 42–43
Chitlow, Bill, 248–249
Chodos, Colin, 203
Christianity, 502
Chrysler Corp., 369, 506
Chung Ju Yang, 506
Cisco Systems, 218, 228, 488
classical conditioning, 47–48
Clayton Utz, 350
Clear Communication (NZ) Ltd, 472

Coal & Allied, 175
coalitions, 399–401
Coca-Cola, 218, 480
Coca-Cola Amatil (CCA), 217
coercion, 574
coercive power, 395
cognitive component, of attitudes, 76
cognitive dissonance, 78
cognitive-dissonance theory, 78–79
cognitive evaluation theory, 172–173
cognitive intelligence, 45
cognitive resource theory, 346
cohesiveness, 257–258
cohorts, 257
Coles Myer, 393
collaborating, 433
collectivism, 73–74
command groups, 242
commitment, 14, 77–78, 148, 524
communication
    barriers to effective, 319–322
    choice of channel, 318–319
    cross-cultural, 324–328
    direction, 309–310
    in emergencies, 307
    functions, 308
    gender barriers, 322–323
    interpersonal, 310–313
    managerial implications, 329
    on-line, 378–379
    organisational communication,
        313–318, 596
    political correctness in, 323–324
    silence as, 323
    work-action divergence, 313
communication apprehension, 321–322
communication process, 309
company chants, 513
Compaq, 506, 507
comparable worth, 220–221
competing, 432
competition, 569
compromising, 433
Computer Associates, 99
computer technology
    computer-aided communication,
        315–318, 378–379
    effect on organisational structure, 480,
        488–489
    and virtual teams, 283–284
conceptual skills, of managers, 8
conciliators, 444
conflict
    conflict-handling intentions, 432–433
    defined, 426
    as five-stage process, 428–438
    functional *versus* dysfunctional,
        427–428, 434–436, 447–448
    intensity continuum, 434fig
    management implications, 435tab

managerial implications, 446–447
    perceived *versus* actual, 431
    structural causes, 431
    theoretical approaches, 426–427
    types, 427–428
    in work teams, 291
conflict process, 428
conformity, 251–252
Confucianism, 502
Conoco, 542
conscientiousness, 103–104
consideration, 340
consultants, 445
consumer satisfaction, 86–87
contingency theories of leadership,
    343–351
contingency variables, 13, 27
contingent workers, 225
continuous reinforcement schedule,
    50–51
Contract and Management Services
    (CAMS), 480
contrast effects, 136
controlling, 5
cooptation, 574
Corbett, Roger, 339
core values, 500
corporate failures, 479
corporate value statements, 72
correlation coefficient, 621–622
cost-minimisation strategy, 482
CPH Investment Corporation, 224
creativity, 141–142
critical incidents, 547
cross-cultural communication, 324–328
cross-functional teams, 282–283, 477
Cuffe, Chris, 224
cultural intelligence, 45
cultures
    effect of religion on, 502–503
    see also national cultures;
        organisational culture
Customer Care Solutions (CCS), 203
customer-responsive culture, 497,
    515–518
customer satisfaction, 20, 215
customer service, 18–19

Daewoo, 15
Daft, Douglas, 218
Daimler-Benz, 506
DaimlerChrysler, 219, 363
Darcy Kennedy accountants, 330
deadlines, 150
decentralisation, 471–472
decision making
    biases and emotions in, 118, 145–148
    bounded rationality, 143–144
    cultural differences in, 149, 151
    escalation of commitment, 148

ethical choices in, 151–152
    by firefighters, 146
    by groups, 260–267
    improving creativity in, 141–142
    as incremental, 147
    individual styles, 148–149, 149fig
    intuition in, 143–144
    judgmental shortcuts, 147–148
    organisational constraints, 149–150
    in organisations, 143–151
    problem identification, 145
    rational model, 140–141
decision-making process, 140–151, 154
decisional roles, 7
decisions, defined, 139
    see also decision-making process
defensive behaviours, 409–410
Dell, Michael, 372
Dell Computer, 478
Deloitte Touche Tohmatsu, 290, 350,
    587
Delta Airlines, 227
Demetrius, David, 485
departmentalisation, 468–469
dependency, 394, 396–397
dependent variables, 23–26, 621
deterrence-based trust, 364
Deutsche Bank, 513
development-oriented leaders, 342
deviant workplace behaviour, 119,
    252–253
Dick Smith, 519
Diedre Moire Corporation, 491
discipline. *see* employee discipline
displayed emotions, 113–114
disseminator role, 5
distributive bargaining, 439
distributive justice, 184
disturbance-handler role, 5
diversity, in workplace, 15–16, 504–505
    advantages and disadvantages, 295tab
diversity training, 82, 554, 557
    and effective communication, 321
dominant culture, 499
Domino's, 21
Donnelly Corporation, 208
double-loop learning, 583
downsizing, 386
driving forces, 575
Drucker, Peter, 353
Du Pont, 596
due process, in performance evaluation,
    549–550
Dunlap, Al 'Chainsaw,' 386
Dunoon, Andrew, 211
Dunphey, Kirsty, 39

e-mail, 316–317
early retirement, 41
Eastman Kodak, 212

economic shocks, 569
Educational Testing Services, 219
effect of change in company ownership, 92
effectiveness, 24
  in work teams, 285–291
efficiency, 24
Electronic Data Systems, 522
electronic mail. *see* e-mail
electronic meeting, 266–267
Elizabeth Andrews catering, 211
Emery Air Freight, 53–55
emoticons, 317tab
emotional intelligence, 45, 118
  and leadership effectiveness, 372–374
emotional labour, 113
emotional stability, 103
emotions, 58, 112–121, 320
  cultural differences, 117
  defined, 112–113
  dimensions, 114–116
  external constraints, 116–117
  felt *versus* displayed, 113–114
  gender differences, 116
  lack of, 116
  OB implications, 117–119, 121
employee deviance, 119
employee discipline, 55–56
employee effort, 139
employee empowerment, 20–21, 519–520
employee engagement, 14
employee interviews, 533–535
employee involvement, 208, 211–212, 230, 237–238, 596
employee involvement programs, 207–212
employee layoffs, 386
employee-oriented leaders, 342
employee performance. *see* job performance
employee recognition programs, 194–195
employee satisfaction. *see* job satisfaction
employer branding, 207
employment interviews, 138, 155–156, 412, 533–535
employment security, 519
empowerment, 20–21, 519–520
encounter stage (of socialisation), 509
English language training, 321
Enron, 366, 377, 515
Enterprise rent-a-Car, 386
entrepreneur role, 5
environment
  defined, 483–484
  effect on organisational structure, 483–484
  effect on personality, 101
environmental uncertainty, 483–484

equal pay, 220–221
equity theory, 182–184, 191, 192
  and comparable worth, 220–221
  and skill-based pay, 217
ERG theory, 170, 189, 217
Ergon Energy, 400
Ericsson, 513
Ernst & Young, 477
escalation of commitment, 148
ethical aspects
  of behavioural research, 626–627
ethics, 22–23, 71–73
  of behaving politically, 412–413, 418
  in decision making, 151–152
  ethical dilemmas, 22–23, 418
  national differences, 153
  in organisational culture, 514–515
  training in, 539
eToys, 228
evolutionary psychology, 58–59
Executive Discovery, 260
executives. *see* CEOs
exit, 86
expectancy theory, 184–186, 188, 191, 192
  and flexible benefits, 219
  and variable-pay programs, 214
expert power, 395–396
externals, 105
extranet, 317
extroversion, 103
ExxonMobil, 15

family-friendly benefits, 220
Fastenal Co., 507
Fayol, Henri, 4, 612, 613
Fels, Alan, 425–426
felt conflict, 431
felt emotions, 113–114
Festinger, Leon, 76
Fiedler, Fred, 344, 346, 617
Fiedler contingency model, 344–346
field experiments, 625–626
field surveys, 623–624
figurehead role, 5
filtering, 319–320
firefighters
  decision making by, 146
five-factor model, of personality, 103–105
five-stage group development model, 243–244
fixed-interval reinforcement, 51
fixed-ratio reinforcement schedule, 52
flexible benefits, 217–220, 219
Flight Centre, 203
flow experience, 180–182
Follett, Mary Parker, 614
Forbes magazine, 55
forced comparisons, 542, 547

Ford, Henry II, 511
Ford, William Clay, Jr, 404
Ford Australia, 212
Ford Motor Company, 21, 284, 294–295, 404, 511, 542
Forgeard, Noel, 386
formal groups, 242
formal power, 394–395
formalisation, 473
forming stage, 243
Fox Television, 22
framing issues, 366–367
friendship groups, 242
Fuji Xerox, 4, 18, 29, 212
Fujitsu, 205
fun, as business strategy, 203
fundamental attribution error, 135
Fusion Design Consultants, 330
future orientation, 74
FutureKids, 474

gain sharing, 213, 215
Garcia, Joe, 346
Gates, Bill, 99, 377–378, 506
Gen-Xers, 71, 72–73
gender
  communication barriers, 322–323
  differences in negotiation, 442
  effect on emotions, 116
  effect on job performance, 41–42
  and pay inequities, 220–221
gender discrimination, 221
General Electric, 16, 207–208, 218, 355, 479–480, 542
General Motors, 15, 317, 369
General Motors-Holden, 15, 21, 150, 212, 522
Generation Nexters, 67
Gerstner, Louis, 473
Gilbertson, Brian, 218, 341
Global Leadership and Organisational Behavior Effectiveness. *see* GLOBE research program
globalisation, 15, 511
GLOBE research program, 73–75, 383
goal-setting, 596
goal-setting theory, 173–175, 191, 205
goals, in work teams, 290
Godfrey, Brett, 14
Goh Chok Tong, 370
Goodnight, Jim, 561
grapevine, 314–315
graphic rating scales, 547
Great Plains Software, 33
group decision making
  performance, 267tab, 269
  strengths and weaknesses, 261tab, 262–265, 270–271
  techniques, 265–268
group demography, 256

group-level variables, 27
group order ranking, 548
groups
    composition and cohesion, 256–258, 269
    conformity in, 262–265, 273
    contrasted with work teams, 280
    decision making in, 260–267
    defined, 242
    intergroup development, 580–581
    leadership, 248
    members' attributes, 247–248
    norms, 250–251, 269
    performance, 245–260, 269–270
    power through, 399–401
    processes within, 258
    reasons for joining, 243tab
    roles, 248–249, 269
    size, 255–256, 270
    social loafing in, 255–256
    stages of development, 242–245
    status differences in, 253–255, 269
    tasks performed in, 259
    turnover, 257, 269
    types, 242, 244
groupshift, 262, 265
groupthink, 262–265
Guiliani, Rudolph W., 361–362, 373
gun control, 367

Habitat International, 554
Hackman, J. Richard, 176, 617–618
halo effect, 136
Harley-Davidson, 522
Harvey, Gerry, 506
Harvey Norman, 506
Hawke, Bob, 367
Hawthorne studies, 85, 615–616
Heathcote, Andrew, 341
Heinz Foods, 18
Hemstritch, Jane, 605–606
heredity, 100–101
Hersey, Paul, 346–347
Herzberg, Frederick, 166–169, 187, 617
heuristics, 147–148
Hewlett-Packard, 212, 284, 477, 479, 506, 519
hierarchy of needs theory, 164–165
high-context cultures, 327
higher-order needs, 165
HIH Insurance Group, 21, 479
Hinduism, 502–503
historical precedents
    and decision-making, 150
Hofstede, Geert, 73, 76
Holland, John, 110
Honda, 15
Horgan, Jo, 337, 369
House, Robert, 338, 349
Howard, John, 131

Hubbard, Graham, 370
Hull, Kylie, 400
human relations movement, 615–616
human relations view, of conflict, 427
human resources management (HRM), 290, 532
human skills, of managers, 7
humane orientation, 75
hygiene factors, 168
hypotheses, 621
Hyundai, 506

Iacocca, Lee, 369
IBM, 212, 215, 224, 283, 473, 513, 554, 586
idea champions, 583
identification-based trust, 365
IDS Financial Services, 216
IKEA, 506
illegitimate political behaviour, 403
imitation strategy, 482
implicit models, of organisational structure, 487–488
impression management, 410–412
in-group collectivism, 75
independent variables, 26–27, 621
India, 212
individual behaviour
    internal or external causation, 133–135
individual differences theory, 109
individual-level variables, 26
individual ranking, 548
individualism, 73–74
individualistic cultures
    creating team players in, 291–292
    group-based jobs in, 270–271
industrial psychology, 615
informal groups, 242
information overload, 320
information power, 395
informational roles, of managers, 5–6
initiating structure, 340
innovation, 21–22
    definition, 582
    sources, 582–583
    strategy, 482
institutionalisation, 498
instrumental values, 69
integrative bargaining, 440
intellectual abilities, 44–45, 44tab
intentions, in conflict-handling, 432–433
interacting groups, 265
interactionist view, of conflict, 427
interest groups, 242
intergroup development, 580–581
intermittent reinforcement, 51
internals, 105
Internet, 316
    see also computer technology

interpersonal communication, 310–313
interpersonal conflict, 118
interpersonal roles, 5
interpersonal skills. see people skills
intonations, 312tab
intranet, 317
intuition, 9–10, 143–144
intuitive decision-making, 144–145
Iraq War, 131
Irwin, Steve, 104
Islam, 503

Japan
    decision-making style, 149, 151
    job satisfaction, 88
    use of suggestion systems, 207
    variable-pay programs, 215
job analysis, 533
job characteristics model (JCM), 177–179
job description, 533
job design, 222
job enlargement, 222–223
job enrichment, 223–224
job interviews. see employment interviews
job involvement, 77
job performance
    effect of age, 40–41
    effect of marital status, 43
    effect of organisational design, 485–486
    effect of personality, 104–105, 105–108, 121
    effect of seniority, 43
    emotional intelligence in, 118
    gender differences, 41–42
    and lack of obstacles, 186
job performance on, 551–552
job redesign, 221–224, 596
job rotation, 222
job satisfaction, 26, 77, 82–92, 167–168, 269–270
    effect of age, 40–41
    effect of gender, 42
    effect of job previews, 155–156
    effect of organisational design, 485–486
    effect of seniority, 43
    effect on absenteeism, 85–86
    effect on consumer satisfaction, 86–87
    effect on organisational citizenship behaviour, 87
    effect on performance, 84–86
    effect on productivity, 84–85
    effect on turnover, 86
    genetic influences, 90
    impact of unions, 551–552
    in Japan and Singapore, 88
    measuring, 83–84

job selection
  cultural differences, 553
  emotional intelligence as criterion, 118
  methods, 532–536, 558
job specification, 533
John Deere Machinery, 215
Johnson & Johnson, 29, 514, 554, 596
judging others. *see* perception, of others
Jung, Andrea, 337, 369
justice, 152, 184

Kamprad, Ingvar, 506
Kathleen Jordan, 477–478
Katies, 137
Kay, Ira, 218
Kay, Mary, 506
Keenihan, Stephen, 92
Keirlin, Robert A., 507
Kingsley, Hugh, 187
KJ Enterprising Solutions, 477–478
Knight, Julian, 112
knowledge-based trust, 364–365
knowledge management, 586–587
Kodak Australasia Pty Ltd, 477
Korea, 135
Kotter, John, 338
KPMG, 477
KPMG Singapore, 586
Krispy Kreme, 512

laboratory experiments, 624–625
'labour-cost-minimisation' strategy, 30
language
  in communication, 320–321
  and organisational culture, 513–514
  political correctness in, 323–324
  training, 321
  see also body language
Larkin, T.J., 72
Lawrence, P.R., 176
layoffs, 386, 577
laziness, 166
leader-member exchange (LMX) theory, 348–349
leader-member relations, 344
leader-participation theory, 350–351
leaders
  charismatic, 367–369
  mentoring role, 375–376
  selection of, 381–382
  shaping of meaning by, 365–372
  significance and relevance, 379–381
  training and development programs for, 352–353, 381–382
  transactional, 369–371
  transformational, 369–371, 384
  visionary, 365, 371–372
  see also leadership

leadership
  attribution theory, 380
  behavioural theories, 330–343
  contingency theories, 343–351
  contrasted with management, 338
  defined, 338
  dimensions, 340
  effect of experience, 347
  effectiveness, 347
  emotional intelligence and, 372–374
  ethical aspects, 377–378
  of groups, 248
  on-line, 378–379
  as perceived attribute, 380
  role, 5, 119
  self-leadership, 376–377
  situational aspects, 343–351
  trait theories, 338–339
  trust as basis, 362–365
  in work teams, 289, 374–375
  see also GLOBE research program; leaders
leadership grid, 342
leadership style, 344
  Christine Nixon, 235
  cultural differences, 383–384
  gender differences, 373
  Guiliani, Rudolph W., 361–362
  Jack Welch, 355
  Nasser, Jacques, 404
  Ricardo Semler, 230, 237–238
leading, 5
learning
  definition, 46–47
  implications for managers, 57
  versus ingrained traits, 58–59
  managerial applications, 50–56
  and older employees, 49
  single- and double-loop, 583
  theories, 47–49
  see also shaping behaviour
learning organisations, 583–586
least preferred co-worker (LPC) questionnaire, 344
Lee Kuan Yew, 339, 367, 370
legitimate political behaviour, 403
legitimate power, 395
LEGO Serious Play, 260
Levi Strauss, 318, 480
Levin, Gerald, 228
Lew, Solomon, 393
liaison role, 5
Lion Nathan, 207, 366
Locke, Edwin, 174
locus of control, 105
long- and short-term orientation, 73–74
low-context cultures, 327
lower-order needs, 165
loyalty, 71–73, 86, 224, 524

see also customer satisfaction
Lucent Technologies, 21
Luthans, Fred, 8

Machiavellianism, 106
male competitiveness, 59
management
  contrasted with leadership, 338
  functions and roles, 4–5, 5–7, 6tab
  skills and effectiveness, 7–8, 8–9
management by objectives (MBO), 204–205
managerial grid, 342
managers, 4
Mandela, Nelson, 339, 352–353
manipulation, 574
marital status
  effect on creativity, 142
  effect on job performance, 43
Marriott International, 554
Mary Kay Cosmetics, 506
Maslow, Abraham, 164, 616
material symbols, 513
maternity leave, 42–43, 219, 555
Matrix Builders and Project Managers, 330
matrix organisational structure, 475–476
May, Peter, 290, 587
Mayo, Elton, 616
McClelland, David, 617
McClelland's theory of needs, 170–172
McDonald, Jacquie, 279
McDonald's, 15, 116, 247, 366, 467, 472
McGregor, Douglas, 165–166, 616
Mecca Cosmetica, 337, 369
mechanistic model, 481
mediators, 444
mentors, 375–376
Mercedes, 15
Merck & Co., 224
metamorphosis stage (of socialisation), 509–510
Microsoft, 21, 67, 194–195, 377–378, 480, 506, 542
Milgram, Stanley, 624, 626–627
Milton, Nicholas, 367
MIM, 212
Minter Ellison, 350
Mintzberg, Henry, 5
Mitsubishi, 212
Mobil Oil Corporation, 477
models, 23
moderating variables, 621
money, as motivator, 163, 191–192
monitor role, 5
Monsanto, 227
moods, 112
moral leadership, 377–378
motivating potential score (MPS), 177–179

motivation
  of contingent workers, 225
  definition, 164
  of diversified workforce, 225–226
  effect of money, 191
  effect of performance evaluation,
    543–544
  and emotional commitment, 119
  of low-skilled service employees, 226
  of professionals, 224–225
  of workers in repetitive jobs, 226
  see also employee involvement
    programs; employee recognition
    programs; flexible benefits; job
    redesign; management by
    objectives; motivation theories; skill-
    based pay plans; variable-pay
    programs
motivation-hygiene theory, 166
motivation theories
  contemporary theories, 169–189
  culture-bound character, 189–190
  early theories, 164–169
  and employee involvement programs,
    211–212
  managerial implications, 191, 227
  and skill-based pay, 217
Motorola, 477, 480
Moulinex, 531
Mouton, J.S., 342
Mt Isa Mines, 329
multidisciplinary teams, 480
multiple intelligences, 45
Münsterberg, Hugo, 615
Murdoch, Rupert, 107, 372
Murray, David, 341
Myers-Briggs Type indicator (MBTI),
  103

Nasser, Jacques, 404
National Australia Bank, 20
National Cash Register Company, 506,
  614–615
national cultures
  analysing variations among, 73–76
  applicability of motivation theories,
    189–190
  and attribution theory, 135
  as communication barriers, 234–328
  effect on change management,
    587–588
  effect on decision-making styles, 149,
    151
  effect on emotional expression, 117
  effect on employee involvement
    programs, 212
  effect on employee recognition
    programs, 206–207
  effect on job selection practices, 553
  effect on leadership style, 383–384

effect on negotiating styles, 443–444
effect on performance evaluation, 553
effect on status, 254–255
effect on variable-pay plans, 214–215
ethical differences, 153
and goal-setting theories, 175
high- versus low-context cultures, 327
versus organisational culture, 501–502
and reactions to organisational
  politics, 409
relation to personality types, 108–109
National Rifle Association, 367
NCR, 506
NEC (Australia), 467
need for achievement, 171–172
need for affiliation, 171–172
need for power, 171–172
need theories, of motivation, 164–172,
  191
neglect, 86
negotiation, 438
  bargaining strategies, 438–439
  in change management, 574
  cultural differences, 443–444
  gender differences, 442
  personality traits in, 442
  role of third parties, 444–445
  steps in the process, 441–442
negotiator role, 5
Neill, John, 158
networking, 406
Nexters (workforce generation), 67, 71
Nike, 478, 512, 596
Nixon, Christine, 235–236
Nokia, 497
nominal group technique, 266
non-verbal communication, 311–312
Nordstrom, 512
norming stage, 243
norms, 249–250, 253
Northwestern Mutual, 386
Novell, 513
Nudie Fruit Juice Company, 163
Nutrimental Foods, 581

OB Mod, 54–55
objectives, 204
  see also management by objectives
Odland, Lynn, 587
office parties, 428
Officeworks, 4, 19, 29
Ohio State studies of leadership,
  340–341
older workers
  learning capability, 41
  trainability, 49
  workforce participation rate, 41
  see also age
Oldham, G.R., 176, 617–618
Ollila, Jorma, 497

Olympia, 21
on-line leadership, 378–379
OneTel, 21
Onsman, Harry, 370
Ontario Government, 221
open-book management, 329–330
openness to experience, 103
operant conditioning, 48–49
opportunity to perform, 186, 188
Optics 1 Inc., 330
Optus, 21, 522
Oracle, 228
oral communication, 310–311
organic model, 481
organisation systems-level variables, 27
organisational behaviour (OB)
  American-centred orientation, 76
  challenges and opportunities, 14–17
  contingency approach, 13, 618
  contributing disciplines, 10–13
  defined, 9
  as discipline, 12fig
  effects of personality, 105–108
  historical evolution, 609–619
  implications for managers, 14–23, 29
  model, 23–28, 28fig
organisational change
  action research approach, 576–578
  effect on employees, 187
  Lewin's three-step model, 575
  organisational development (OD)
    approach, 578–581
  stimulating organisational innovation,
    582–583
organisational citizenship behaviour
  (OCB), 25–26
  effect of job satisfaction, 87
  effect of personality, 104
organisational commitment, 77–78
organisational communication, 313–318
  see also communication
organisational culture
  ability to reshape, 521–522
  creating and sustaining, 506–511
  customer-responsive, 515–518
  defined, 499
  effect of globalisation, 511
  ethics in, 514–515
  formalisation as aspect, 501
  functions, 503–504
  as liability, 504–506
  versus national culture, 501–502
  spirituality as aspect, 518–520
  strong versus weak, 501
  subcultures within, 499–501
  ways employees learn about, 511–514
organisational development (OD),
  578–581
organisational politics
  contributing factors, 405–408

employee responses to, 408–409
as fact of life, 403–405
networking, 406
organisational structure
and accountability, 479
defined, 466
effect of size on, 482
effect of strategy on, 481–482
effect of technology on, 483
effect on employee behaviour,
485–486
implicit models, 487–488
key elements, 466–473
managerial implications, 487–488
mechanistic and organic models, 481
types and designs, 473–481
organisations
defined, 4
see also organisational behaviour (OB);
organisational change;
organisational citizenship behaviour
(OCB); organisational
communication; organisational
culture; organisational
development; organisational politics
organising, 4–5
Owen, Robert, 610

paid maternity leave, 42–43, 55
paid sick leave, 55
paired comparison, 548
Parsons, Richard, 340
participation, 208–209
participative management, 208–209, 212
path-goal theory, 349–350
Patterson, Neal L., 318
Pavlov, Ivan, 47
pay
effect on decision making, 149–150
money as motivator, 191–192
well *versus* sick pay, 55
see also flexible benefits; reward
systems; skill-based pay plans;
variable-pay programs
'people first' strategy, 29–30, 33
people skills, 20, 29–30
of managers, 4–5, 9
perceived conflict, 431
perception, 132
effect on individual decision-making,
139
effect on job performance, 154
factors influencing, 132–133
perception, of others, 133–139
applications in organisations, 137–139
attribution theory, 133–135
shortcuts, 135–137
performance. *see* job performance
performance evaluation, 138–139,
541–551, 558

adverse effects, 175
appropriate evaluators, 545–547
criteria, 544–545
cultural differences, 553
effect on decision making, 149
effect on motivation, 543–544
feedback, 550–551
methods, 547–550
purposes, 542–543
of teams, 551
use of forced rankings, 542
for work teams, 289
performance expectations, 138
performance orientation, 75
performance-simulation tests, 536
performing stage, 243
person perception. *see* perception, of
others
personal power, 395–396
personality
definition, 100
determinants, 100–101
effect of national culture, 108–109
effect on group performance,
247–248
effect on organisational behaviour,
105–108, 121
effect on team behaviour, 286–287
and job-fit, 110–111, 110tab
managerial implications, 121
and organisational fit, 111–112
traits and dimensions, 102–105
personality job-fit theory, 110
personality traits, 58–59, 102–105, 442
'personnel office,' 614–615
Pethick, Tim, 163
Pfizer, 227
physical abilities, 46–47, 46tab
piece-rate pay plans, 213
pilot error, 326
Pizza Hut, 215
planned change, 569–570
planning, 4–5
political behaviour, 402–403
in organisations, 402–410
political correctness, 323–324
political science, 13
politics
of change, 574–575
in organisations, 403–410
world politics, as change agent, 569
position power, 344
power
bases and types, 394–396
contrasted with leadership, 394
defined, 394
as function of dependency, 394,
396–397
in groups, 399–400
need for, 171–172

position power, 344
tactics, 398–399
in workplace, 401–402
Power Brewing Company, 216
power distance, 73–74
pre-arrival stage (of socialisation), 509
preconceived notions, 11
PricewaterhouseCoopers, 513
problem-solving teams, 281–282
problems, 139, 145
procedural justice, 184
process conflict, 427
process consultation, 579
process reengineering, 17
Procter & Gamble, 212, 480, 507
production-oriented leaders, 342
productivity, 24
effect of age, 40–41
effect of gender, 42
effect of job satisfaction, 84–85
effect of quality circles, 210
professional employees
leadership skills, 350
motivation, 224–225
profit-sharing plans, 213
projection, 137
psychology, 11
punctuated-equilibrium model, 144–245
Purkis Partners, 329
Pygmalion effect, 138

Qantas Airways, 20, 577
quality circles, 209–211, 212
quality management (QM), 17, 294–295
quality of life, 73
quantity of life, 73
Queensland Health, 467
Queensland Police Service, 477

Rasmussen, Robert, 260
rational decision-making model,
140–141, 141tab
rationality, myth of, 112
readiness, 347
redundancies, 577
Reebok, 478
referent power, 396
refreezing, 575
reinforcement
positive *versus* negative, 50
schedules, 50–53, 52–55, 52tab, 53fig
and stock market trading, 51
reinforcement theory, 179–180, 189,
191, 192
and employee recognition programs,
206
and skill-based pay, 217
relationship conflict, 427
relaxation techniques, 595
reliability, 622

religions, 502–503
representative heuristic, 147–148
representative participation, 209, 212
requisite task attributes theory, 176
research methods, 620–626
resource-allocator role, 5
restraining forces, 575
retirement age, 40, 41
Reuning, Stephen, 491
reward power, 395
reward systems
  for work teams, 289, 294
  see also flexible benefits; share-option
    plans; share-ownership plans; skill-
    based pay plans; variable-pay
    programs
rights, 152
Rio Tinto, 175
risk avoidance, 58
risk-taking, 107
rituals, 512–513
Roddick, Anita, 352–353
Rokeach Value Survey, 69–70
role conflict, 249–250
role expectations, 249
role identity, 249
role perception, 249
roles
  gender, 137
  in groups and teams, 248–249, 287
  managerial, 5–7, 119
Royal & SunAlliance, 20, 465
Royal Dutch/Shell, 284

sabbaticals, 596
Sall, John, 561
Sanyo, 508
SAS Institute Inc., 561
Sather, Christine, 478
satisficing choices, 144
Savage, Marg, 67
Scandinavian studies of leadership,
  342–343
Schrempp, Jurgen, 363
scientific management, 610–612
selection
  effect of organisational culture, 507
  of leaders, 381–382
  as team players, 293
selective perception, 135–136, 320
self-efficacy, 174
self-esteem, 106
self-fulfilling prophecies, 138
self-leadership, 376–377
self-managed work teams, 282, 300
self-management, 56
self-monitoring, 106–107
self-perception theory, 80
self-serving bias, 135
Semco, 230, 237–238

Semler, Ricardo, 230, 237–238
senior management teams, 292
seniority, 43
sensitivity training, 578
service jobs, 19, 226
sex-role stereotypes, 137
sexual harassment, 401–402, 418, 428
shaping behaviour, 50–55
share-option plans, 194, 214, 227–228
share-ownership plans, 211, 212, 214
Shintoism, 502
sick leave, paid, 55
Siebel, Tom, 339–340
Siebel Systems, 215, 339
Siemens, 586
silence, as communication, 323
Sim, Ron, 372
simple organisational structures,
  473–474
Singapore
  job satisfaction, 88
Singapore Airlines, 4
Singapore Police, 585
single-loop learning, 583
SingTel, 480
situational leadership theory (SLT),
  346–348
situations
  effect on employee behaviour, 122
  effect on personality, 101
Six Sigma production technique, 16–17
skill-based pay plans, 216–217
Skinner, B.F., 58, 617
small-group networks, 313–314
Smith, Adam, 609
Smith, Dick, 506
Smith, John, Jr, 369
Smith, Michelle, 3
social facilitation effect, 258
social information processing theory,
  179
social learning, 48
social learning theory, 48
social loafing, 255–256
  in work teams, 291
'social man' theory, 612
social psychology, 13
social support network, 595
social trends, 569
socialisation, 508–510
sociology, 12–13
Sommerville, Vivienne, 92
Sony Technologies Malaysia, 586
Southwest Airlines, 520
span of control, 470–471
special deals, for employees, 414–415
spirituality, 518–520
Springfield Remanufacturing, 81, 330
St George Bank, 207
Starbucks, 29, 227

State bank, 300
status, and norms, 253
status differences, 241
status equity, 254
stereotyping, 58, 137
Stewart, Thomas, 72
Stokes, Kerry, 352–353
storming stage, 243
strategic alliances, 480
stress
  consequences, 593–594
  defined, 589
  individual differences, 592–593
  management of, 595–596
  sources, 590–592
stressors, 590–592
Strong, James, 367, 370
strong culture, 501
structural theory, 612
substantive evidence, 11
success, dangers of, 505
suggestion systems, 207
Sun Microsystems, 542
survey feedback, 579
sustainable organisations, 18
Switkowski, Ziggy, 16
Sydney Markets, 567
Sydney Water, 82
synergy, 258
systematic study, 9–10

T-form organisation, 479
Taoism, 502
task conflict, 427
task groups, 242
task structure, 344
tasks, 259
Taylor, Andrew, 386
Taylor, Frederick W., 610
Taylor, Morry, 339–40
team building, 579–580
team structures, 476–477
teams. *see* work teams
technical skills, of managers, 7
technology
  defined, 483
  effect on organisational structure, 483,
    488–489
technology-based organisation, 479
Telstra, 16, 21, 479, 522
Telstra National Business Women's
  Award, 39
'temporariness,' coping with, 21
temporary employees, motivation of, 225
temporary groups, 244
terminal values, 69
Texas Instruments, 212, 374
Textor, 329
Thatcher, Margaret, 339
The Limited, 508

theory, 622
Theory X, 165–166, 616
Theory Y, 165–166, 616
Thomas, Ken, 181
three-component model of creativity, 141–142
360-degree evaluations, 546–547
time-management, 595
Titan International, 339
Toop & Loop, 512
total quality management, 17tab
Toyota, 21
trade unions, 551, 559
traditional view, of conflict, 427
training programs, 56
  benefits, 558
  and differences in learning styles, 540
  in ethics, 539
  of leaders, 381–382
  methods, 539
  of performance evaluators, 549
  for skills, 536–540
  as team players, 293–294
trait theories of leadership, 338–339
traits, personality, 102–105
  effect on employee behaviour, 58–59, 121–122
transactional leaders, 369–371
Transfield, 554
transformational leaders, 369–371, 384
transformational leadership, 369–371
Travolta, John, 20
trust, 362–365, 366, 519
  in work teams, 289
TRW Systems, 219
Turner, A.N., 176
turnover, 25
  effect of age, 40–41
  effect of gender, 42–43
  effect of job satisfaction, 86
two-factor theory, 166–169
Type A personality, 107–108
Type B personality, 108

uncertainty avoidance, 73–74
unfreezing, 575
Unilever Malaysia, 586
Unipart, 158
United Engineers (M) Bhd, 465
unity of command, 470
University of Michigan leadership studies, 341–342
US Air Force, 118
US Army, 586
utilitarianism, 152

validity, 622
'value-driven' change, 72
value systems, 68–69
values, 68–76
  across national cultures, 73–76
  core values, 500
  corporate value statements, 72
  ethical behaviour, 71–73
  generational differences, 70–71
  importance, 68
  types, 69–71
variable-interval reinforcement, 52
variable-pay programs, 212–215
variable-ratio reinforcement schedule, 52
variables, 621
VeriFone, 284
Verizon, 219
veterans (workforce generation), 70, 72
Victorian Police Force, 235
videoconferencing, 317
Virgin Blue, 4, 14, 21, 29, 203
Virgin Group, 369, 506
virtual organisations, 477–479, 489
virtual teams, 268, 283–284
vision, 371–372
visionary leadership, 365, 371–372
voice, 86
Volkswagen, 586
Volvo, 221
Vroom, Victor, 184, 350–351

Wachner, Linda, 343
Wal-Mart, 117, 227, 513
Wang, Charles B., 99
Warburton, Dick, 341
Warnaco, 343
Way, Nicholas, 341
Weber, Max, 612, 613
Welch, Jack, 218, 355, 370, 479
wellness programs, 596
Western Electric, 85, 615
Western Mining, 92
Westpac Banking Corporation, 219, 480
Whirlpool, 586
whistle blowers, 152
Whitlam, Gough, 369
Williams, Rebecca Morrice, 485
women
  Accenture's policies to promote, 606–606
  Business Women's Awards, 39
  childcare, 43
  communication barriers with men, 322–323
  emotional expression, 116
  employment rates, 16

job performance, 41–43
leadership style, 373
pay inequalities, 220–221
sereotyping of, 137
see also gender
Woolworths, 317, 339
work design, 222, 285
work groups, 280
  see also groups
work/life initiatives, 22, 524, 554–556, 561
work sampling, 536
work specialisation, 466–467
work teams, 280
  accountability in, 289
  composition, 286–288
  contrasted with work groups, 280
  creating team players, 291–294
  effective performance by, 285–291
  goals and common purposes, 284, 290
  leadership, 289, 290, 374–375
  management skills for, 279
  managerial implications, 297
  managing diversity, 295
  members flexibility, 288
  performance evaluation of, 551
  popularity of, 280
  reinvigoration, 296
  roles in, 287
  in senior management, 292
  size, 287
  skills needed, 286
  sports teams as models, 297–298
  structures, 476–477
  team building, 579–580
  types, 281–284
  use in quality management, 294–295
workplace diversity, 15–16, 504–505
  advantages and disadvantages, 295tab
  diversity training, 82
  and effective communication, 321
workplace spirituality, 518
works councils, 209
world politics, 569
written communication, 311
written tests, 535–536, 547

Xerox, 477, 480

Yahoo!, 437
Yetton, Phillip, 350–351
Young Business Woman of the Year, 39

Zen, 502
Zimbardo, Philip, 250
Zore, Edward, 386